轮机英语词汇

郑 高 主 编
李国诚 吴 旭 副主编
陈忠维 主 审

国防工业出版社
·北京·

内 容 简 介

本书内容囊括船舶主推进装置、船舶辅助机械、船舶电气与自动化、轮机工程管理、国际公约与法规以及业务写作等方面的常用专业词汇，考虑到船舶领域新技术、新设备、新业务的发展，适当增加了船舶电气与自动化、信息化、智能化等方面的专业词汇以及船舶结构与原理、船舶维修与检验、船舶消防、水下作业等方面的专业词汇，并归纳了常用专业词汇的同义词、近义词和反义词。

本书结构清晰、词汇量大、覆盖面广、实用性强，既可作为全国海员船员适任统考的参考书和地方院校或军队院校"轮机英语"课程的参考书，能帮助轮机工程等专业的学生顺利通过海船船员适任证书轮机英语考试和评估，也可作为船舶与海洋工程、船舶电气与电子、船舶机械制造、船舶修理等专业的师生，以及地方船舶轮机部门人员或军用舰艇机电部门官兵的参考工具书。

图书在版编目（CIP）数据

轮机英语词汇/郑高主编. —北京：国防工业出版社，2022.4
ISBN 978-7-118-12503-0

Ⅰ. ①轮… Ⅱ. ①郑… Ⅲ. ①轮机-英语-词汇 Ⅳ. ①U676.4

中国版本图书馆 CIP 数据核字（2022）第 079242 号

※

国防工业出版社 出版发行
（北京市海淀区紫竹院南路 23 号　邮政编码 100048）
三河市腾飞印务有限公司印刷
新华书店经售

*

开本 710×1000　1/16　印张 40½　字数 805 千字
2022 年 4 月第 1 版第 1 次印刷　印数 1—2000 册　定价 129.00 元

(本书如有印装错误，我社负责调换)

国防书店：(010)88540777　　书店传真：(010)88540776
发行业务：(010)88540717　　发行传真：(010)88540762

前　　言

建设海洋强国是全世界临海国的普遍共识，走向远洋深海是中国未来生存、发展的必由之路。2013年下半年，中国提出"一带一路"的合作倡议，旨在建立亚欧非大陆及附近海洋的互联互通，实现沿线各国的共同发展，中国海洋运输业由此快速进入世界海运竞争舞台的前列。为了维护国家的海洋权益，为高速的经济发展保驾护航，中国的军用舰艇也逐渐从近海浅海走向远海深海。与此同时，日新月异的新技术、不断应用的新设备以及不断增加的新业务，对船舶轮机部门人员或舰艇机电部门官兵的专业素养提出了更高的要求。在此背景下，编写一本高质量的《轮机英语词汇》工具书，符合《STCW公约马尼拉修正案》对海船船员所具备英语运用能力的具体要求，满足船舶轮机部门人员或舰艇机电部门官兵的日常工作需求，具有十分重要的意义。

本书的编写借鉴了各种船舶设备与技术的英文资料、历届国家海事局海员船员适任证书考试"轮机英语"科目题库以及《轮机英语》《轮机英语阅读与写作》《轮机英语听力与会话》等教材，并力求去芜存精。除基本专业词汇以外，收集了船舶领域新技术、新设备、新业务方面的专业词汇，归纳了常用专业词汇的同义词、近义词和反义词，词汇量大，覆盖面广，实用性强，特色鲜明。

本书主编为武警海警学院机电管理系郑高教授，副主编为武警海警学院机电管理系李国诚副教授、吴旭副教授，主审为武警海警学院机电管理系陈忠维教授，参编人员有武警海警学院机电管理系张磊讲师、王龙飞讲师、邱鹏讲师以及武警海警学院维权执法系孙盛智副教授。本书编写工作具体分配如下：A、R、U部分由李国诚编写，B、C、T、X、Y部分由郑高编写，D、F部分由吴旭编写，E、H、L、Q部分由张磊编写，G、S部分由王龙飞编写，I、J、K、M、W部分由邱鹏编写，N、O、P、V、Z部分由孙盛智编写。本书的总体结构设计、统稿及文字校对工作由郑高完成。

本书的编写得到了"十三五"军队"双重"建设项目、宁波市"军事装备学"重点学科建设项目的支持，在此表示衷心的感谢！

由于编者精力与水平有限，书中难免存在错误，敬请广大读者谅解。

郑高

本书使用的缩略语

a. = adjective　形容词
ad. = adverb　副词
art. = article　冠词
conj. = conjunction　连接词
n. = noun　名词
num. = numeral　数词
pl. = plural　复数形式，复数词
pref. = prefix　前缀
prep. = preposition　介词
pron. = pronoun　代词
v. = verb　动词
Ant. = antonym　反义词
Syn. = synonym　同义词或近义词

本书使用的符号

[ ]　用于国际音标
~　　用于替代单词，如：
　　　electrically [i'lektrikəli] *ad.* 电力地，有关电地
　　　~ charged 带电的，充电的
　　　ballast ['bæləst] *n.* 压舱物，压载，稳定因素，镇重物，沙囊；*v.* 提供压舱物
　　　~ Water Management Convention 压载水管理公约，压载水公约
　　　bode [bəud] *n.* 波特(Bode，人名)；*v.* 预兆，预言，预告
　　　~ plot 波特图
( )　① 用于词汇剖析，如：
　　　boiling ['bɔiliŋ] *v.* (boil 的 ing 形式) 煮沸，汽化，激动；*a.* 沸腾的，激昂的
　　　boxed [bɔkst] *v.* (box 的过去式和过去分词) 装盒，打耳光，拳击；*a.* 盒装的
　　　higher ['haiə] *a.* (high 的比较级) 更高的，较高的
　　　② 用于补充说明，如：
　　　knot [nɔt] *n.* 节(海里/小时，航速单位)
　　　effect [i'fekt] *n.* 结果，效果，作用，影响，(在视听方面给人留下的)印象；*v.* 招致，实现，达到(目的等)
　　　③ 表示不同的拼写法，如：
　　　timetable ['taimteib(ə)l] *n.* 时刻表，时间表，课程表
　　　④ 用于缩写或全称说明，如：
　　　decibel ['desibel] (dB) *n.* 分贝
　　　LPG (liquefied petroleum gas) 液化石油气
　　　⑤ 用于归并义项，以节省篇幅，如：
　　　endurance [in'djuərəns] *n.* 耐久(力)，持久(力)，忍耐(力)
　　　salination [ˌsæli'neiʃən] *n.* 盐化(作用)
　　　⑥ 表示可省略的词汇，如：
　　　oil (level) meter 油位计，量油尺，油位表
‖　　该符号后为同义词(近义词)、反义词或同类词，如：
　　　dangerous ['deindʒrəs] *a.* 危险的　‖ ***Syn.*** hazardous 危险的，冒险的；perilous 危险的，冒险的；unsafe 危险的
　　　continuous [kən'tinjuəs] *a.* 连续的，延伸的，一系列的　‖ ***Ant.*** discrete 不

连续的，离散的
rectangle ['rektæŋgl] *n.* 长方形，矩形 ‖ circle 圆，圆形；ellipse 椭圆，椭圆形；parallelogram 平行四边形；rhombus 菱形；square 正方形；trapezoid 梯形；triangle 三角形

, 　表示同种词性、不同词义间的间隔，如：
abandon [ə'bændən] *n.* 放任，放肆，放纵，委付；*v.* 抛弃，舍弃，离弃，放弃，放纵，放任，停止，使屈从

; 　① 表示不同词性间的间隔，如：
aback [ə'bæk] *a.* 静止的，无法运动的；*ad.* 向后地，后退
② 表示同类词间的间隔，如：
depth [depθ] *n.* 深度，深处，纵深，距离，强度，范围，力度，潜力，后备力量，详尽，细节，最深处，中央，深奥 ‖ height 高度；length 长度；width 宽度

= 　表示词汇的变体，如：
approx [ə'prɔks] *ad.* (=approximately) 近似地，大约，大概

- 　表示连字符，如：
A-frame　A形建筑物，金字塔形建筑物

目 录

A	1
B	46
C	79
D	148
E	190
F	220
G	261
H	275
I	301
J	335
K	338
L	340
M	365
N	400
O	411
P	430
Q	472
R	474
S	507
T	575
U	604
V	613
W	624
X	636
Y	637
Z	637
参考文献	639

A

a [ei] *n.* 一,第一,A 字母,A 字形,甲等,甲级; *a.* A 的,第一的; *prep.* 单一,每一,每; *art.* 每一,任一,某一,一副,有个

~ faired set of lines 经过光顺的一组型线

~ load of 大量的,许多的

~ mass of 大量的

~ series of 一连串的,一系列的,一套的

A (ampere) 安培

A-frame A 形建筑物,金字塔形建筑物

A-shaped A 形的

~ frame A 形架

AB (able bodied seaman) 一级水手,合格水手,熟练水手,二等水兵 ‖ *Syn*. able seaman 一级水手,合格水手,熟练水手,二等水兵

aback [ə'bæk] *a.* 静止的,无法运动的; *ad.* 向后地,后退

abaft [ə'bɑ:ft] *ad.* 在船尾,向船尾; *prep.* 从…向船尾,在…后面

abandon [ə'bændən] *n.* 放任,放肆,放纵,委付; *v.* 抛弃,舍弃,离弃,放弃,放纵,放任,停止,使屈从

~ anchor 弃锚

~ ship 弃船 ‖ *Syn*. abandon vessel 弃船

~ ship drill 弃船演习

~ ship signal 弃船信号

~ ship station 弃船部署

~ ship training 弃船训练

abandonment [ə'bændənmənt] *n.* 放弃

~ cost 遗弃成本,遗弃费用

abate [ə'beit] *v.* 减少,减轻,除去,缓和,失效,打折扣,被废除

abatement [ə'beitmənt] *n.* 减少,减弱,减少额,折扣,消除,废除

abbreviate [ə'bri:vieit] *v.* 缩写,缩短,简化,简写成,缩写为

abbreviation [ə,bri:vi'eiʃən] *n.* 缩写,缩写词

ABDC (after bottom dead center) 下止点后,下死点后

abeam [ə'bi:m] *ad.* 正横着,与船身(或飞机机身)成直角

ablation [æb'leiʃən] *n.* 烧蚀,熔蚀,消融,切除

able ['eibl] *a.* 能干的,能…的,有才能的,有天赋的,能够的

~ bodied seaman (AB) 一级水手,合格水手,熟练水手,二等水兵 ‖ *Syn*. able seaman 一级水手,合格水手,熟练水手,二等水兵

~ person 能人,有能力的人,有用的人才

abnormal [æb'nɔ:məl] *a.* 不正常的,反常的,异常的,变态的 ‖ *Ant*. normal 正常的,正规的,标准的

~ behavior 异常行为

~ condition 反常条件,非常状态,非正常状态

~ indication 异常指示

~ injection 异常喷射

~ operating condition 反常操作情况

~ phenomena 异常现象

~ risk 特殊风险,非常风险

~ situation 异常情况

~ sound 异声,异响,不正常声音

abnormality [,æbnɔ:'mæliti] *n.* 异常性,畸形,变态

abnormally [æb'nɔ:məli] *ad.* 反常地,不规

则地，格外地，例外

aboard [ə'bɔ:d] *ad.* 在船(飞机、车)上，上船(飞机、车)； *prep.* 在船(飞机、车)上，上船(飞机、车)

above [ə'bʌv] *a.* 上面的，上述的，上文的； *ad.* 在上面； *prep.* 过于，超出，在…上方

above-mentioned 上述的，上面提到的

abovedeck [ə'bəuvidek] *ad.* 在甲板上，照直，光明磊落地

abrasion [ə'breiʒən] *n.* 磨损，磨耗，擦掉处，磨损处

~ mark 摩擦痕迹，摩擦刻痕，抛光

~ resistance 耐磨，抵抗磨损，抗磨损

~ wear 磨耗，磨损，磨蚀

~ wheel 磨轮，砂轮

abrasive [ə'breisiv] *n.* 研磨剂，磨料； *a.* 造成磨蚀的，研磨的，粗糙的，恼人的

~ belt 砂布，砂带 ‖ *Syn.* abrasive cloth 砂布

~ blasting (磨料)喷砂法，喷砂，喷砂打磨

~ disk 金刚砂磨盘，磨盘，砂轮 ‖ *Syn.* abrasive wheel 磨轮，砂轮

~ dust 磨屑

~ erosion 磨蚀性侵蚀

~ grain 磨粒 ‖ *Syn.* abrasive particle 磨粒

~ grinding 研磨

~ hardness 研磨硬度，磨料硬度，磨蚀硬度

~ machining 磨削加工，强力磨削，研磨加工

~ nature 磨损性质

~ paper 砂纸

~ tool 研磨工具

~ wear 磨料磨损，磨蚀

abreast [ə'brest] *ad.* 并排地，并肩地，最新，赶得上

abroad [ə'brɔ:d] *n.* 异国； *ad.* 往国外，在海外，到处地，广泛地，差得远，心里没有谱

ABS (American Bureau of Shipping) 美国船级社

abscissa [æb'sisə] *n.* 横坐标

~ axis 横坐标轴，横轴

absolute ['æbsəlu:t] *n.* 绝对，绝对事物，独立； *a.* 完全的，绝对的，独立的，未混合的，无限制的，无条件的，确定的，不容置疑的

~ atmosphere 绝对大气压

~ difference 绝对差，绝对差别，绝对差分，绝对偏差

~ error 绝对误差

~ humidity 绝对湿度

~ number 绝对数

~ pressure 绝对压力

~ temperature 绝对温度

~ urgency 绝对紧急情况

~ value 绝对值

~ viscosity 绝对黏度

absolutely ['æbsəlu:tli] *ad.* 完全地，绝对地，独立地，确实地

absorb [əb'sɔ:b] *v.* 吸收，吸引，引人注意，吸入，同化，消减，缓冲，忍耐，忍受，承担费用

absorbent [əb'sɔ:bənt] *n.* 吸收剂； *a.* 能吸收的

~ carbon 碳吸收剂

~ filter 吸收性滤器，吸水滤纸

~ material 吸收性材料

~ product 吸收性产品

~ solution 吸收剂溶液

absorber [əb'sɔːbə] *n.* 减震器，吸收体，吸收者

absorbing [əb'sɔːbiŋ] *v.* (absorb 的 ing 形式) 吸收，吸引，吸入，同化，消减，缓冲，忍耐，忍受；*a.* 吸收的，吸引人的，非常有趣的

~ agent 吸收剂 ‖ *Syn.* absorption agent 吸收剂

~ board 吸收纸板，吸声板，隐身盖板

~ capacity 吸收能力，吸附力

~ coil 吸收线圈

~ gas 吸收气体

~ liquid 吸气液体

~ material 吸收材料

absorption [əb'sɔːpʃən] *n.* 吸收，并吞，兼并，合并，专心，专注

~ agent 吸收剂 ‖ *Syn.* absorbing agent 吸收剂

~ of moisture in the insulation 绝缘材料中的水分吸收

~ rate 吸收率

~ refrigeration 吸收式制冷

abut [ə'bʌt] *v.* 邻接，毗邻，紧靠着，紧挨着

~ on 邻接，紧靠

AC (alternating current) 交流，交流电，交流电流

~ ammeter 交流安培计

~ ammeter with clamp 钳型表

~ asynchronous motor 交流异步电机

~ asynchronous motor drive 交流异步电机驱动

~ circuit 交流电路

~ commutator motor 交流整流式电动机

~ contactor 交流接触器

~ converter 交流换流器，交流交换器

~ distribution 交流配电

~ distribution system 交流配电系统

~ electric drive 交流电气传动

~ electric propulsion apparatus 交流电力推进装置

~ electromotive force 交流电动势

~ exciter 交流励磁机

~ generator 交流发电机 ‖ *Syn.* alternator 交流发电机

~ input 交流输入

~ line 交流线路

~ motor 交流电动机，交流马达

~ power control 交流电力控制

~ power controller 交流电力控制器

~ power cord 交流电源线

~ power electronic switch 交流电力电子开关

~ power station 交流电站

~ power system 交流电力系统

~ rectifier 交流整流器

~ relay 交流继电器

~ servomotor 交流伺服电动机

~ signalling 交流传信

~ single-phase three-wire system with neutral earthed 中性点接地的交流单相三线系统，中性点接地的交流单相三线制

~ squirrel cage induction motor 交流鼠笼型感应电动机

~ supply 交流电源

~ tacho-generator 交流测速发电机

~ three-phase three-wire insulated system 交流三相三线绝缘系统

~ three-phase three-wire system 交流三相三线系统，交流三相三线制

~ three-phase three-wire system with

hull as neutral wire 以船体为中性线的交流三相三线系统，以船体为中性线的交流三相三线制

~ torque motor 交流扭矩电动机，交流陀螺修正电动机

~ transmission 交流输电

~ voltage 交流电压

~ voltage controller 交流电压控制器，交流调压电路

AC-AC (alternating current-alternating current) 交流交流，交交

~ frequency converter 交交变频器

AC-DC-AC (alternating current-direct current-alternating current) 交流直流交流，交直交

~ frequency converter 交直交变频器

accelerate [æk'seləreit] v. 加速，加快，增速，促进，催促，加紧

accelerated [ək'seləreitid] v. (accelerate 的过去式和过去分词) 加速，加快，增速，促进，催促，加紧；a. 加速的，加快的

~ aging 加速老化，人工老化 ‖ *Syn.* accelerating aging 加速老化

~ charging 加速充电

~ combustion 加速燃烧

~ corrosion 加速腐蚀

~ corrosion test 加速腐蚀试验

~ depreciation 加速折旧

~ draft 加速通风

~ erosion 加速侵蚀

~ motion 加速运动

~ oxidation 加速氧化

~ period 加速期

~ speed 加速度，加速速率 ‖ *Syn.* accelerated velocity 加速度，加速速率

~ voltage 加速电压 ‖ *Syn.* accelerating voltage 加速电压；acceleration voltage 加速电压

~ weathering 加速风化

accelerating [æk'seləreitiŋ] v. (accelerate 的 ing 形式) 加速，加快，增速，促进，催促，加紧；a. 加速的，促进的，催化的

~ aging 加速老化 ‖ *Syn.* accelerated aging 加速老化

~ chamber 加速箱

~ contactor 加速接触器

~ force 加速力

~ impact 加速撞击

~ nozzle 加速型喷管

~ operating mode management 加速操作模式管理

~ relay 加速继电器 ‖ *Syn.* acceleration relay 加速继电器

~ trend 加快态势

~ voltage 加速电压 ‖ *Syn.* accelerated voltage 加速电压；acceleration voltage 加速电压

acceleration [æk,selə'reiʃ(ə)n] n. 加速，加速度

~ limiter 加速限制器

~ performance 加速性能

~ relay 加速继电器 ‖ *Syn.* accelerating relay 加速继电器

~ test 加速度试验

~ time 加速时间

~ transducer 加速度传感器，加速度变送器

~ voltage 加速电压 ‖ *Syn.* accelerating voltage 加速电压；accelerated voltage 加速电压

acceleration-deceleration 加速减速,加减速
- ~ control 加减速控制
- ~ delay 加减速延误
- ~ trial 加减速试航

accelerator [æk'seləreitə] *n.* 加速器,加速者

accelerometer [æk,selə'rɔmitə] *n.* 加速计

accept [ək'sept] *v.* 接受,认可,同意,承认,承担,承兑

acceptable [ək'septəbl] *a.* 可接受的,合意的

acceptably [ək'septəbli] *ad.* 可接受地

acceptance [ək'septəns] *n.* 接受,承诺,容忍,赞同,相信
- ~ certificate 验收合格证,验收证明书,验收证书
- ~ check 验收检查 ‖ *Syn.* acceptance inspection 验收检验
- ~ criteria 验收标准,接受标准,验收准则 ‖ *Syn.* acceptance level 验收标准
- ~ gauging 验收规,验收测量
- ~ procedure 验收过程
- ~ report 验收报告
- ~ test 验收测试,接受测试,接受试验
- ~ tolerance 验收公差

access ['ækses] *n.* 通路,访问,入门;*v.* 存取,接近
- ~ cover 进口盖,舱口盖
- ~ door 通道门,入口门,检修门
- ~ equipment 访问设备,取设备
- ~ hatch 出入舱口,检查口
- ~ hatchway 进出舱口
- ~ hole 进入孔,存取孔,人孔,检查孔,检修孔 ‖ *Syn.* access opening 检修孔,入口
- ~ plug 检修孔塞
- ~ to the ship 上船通道

accessibility [,ækəsesi'biliti] *n.* 易接近,可到达

accessible [ək'sesəbl] *a.* 易接近的,可到达的,易受影响的,可理解的
- ~ area 可进入区域
- ~ compressor 易卸压缩机,半密闭压缩机,现场用压缩机
- ~ environment 可进入环境
- ~ position 可达位置
- ~ route 易达路线
- ~ surface 可及面

accessory [æk'sesəri] *n.* 附件,附加物,零件,同谋者;*a.* 附属的,补充的,副的,同谋的
- ~ apartment 附属房
- ~ device 辅助装置,附属装置 ‖ *Syn.* accessory equipment 辅助设备,附属设备
- ~ kit 附属品,附属工具
- ~ power supply 助电源
- ~ shoe 附件插座板

accident ['æksidənt] *n.* 意外事件,意外事故,机遇,偶然,偶有属性 ‖ *Syn.* casualty 事故,伤亡; chance failure 偶发故障,意外事故; contingency 意外事故,紧急情况,不测事件; incident 事件,突发事件; misfortune 不幸,灾难,灾祸; mishap 灾祸,厄运,倒霉事
- ~ analysis 事故分析
- ~ analysis report 事故分析报告
- ~ boat 救生艇
- ~ book 事故记录册
- ~ cause 事故原因
- ~ conditions 事故情况
- ~ control or prevention 事故控制或预防
- ~ cost 事故费用
- ~ free 无事故

~ frequency 事故频率

~ hazard 事故危险，意外风险

~ indication light 事故显示灯

~ investigation 事故调查

~ pattern 事故类型

~ prevention 事故防止，事故预防，安全措施 ‖ *Syn.* protective measures 保全措施，保护措施；safety measures 安全措施，安全规程

~ prevention program 事故预防计划

~ probability 事故概率

~ rate 事故率，失事率 ‖ *Syn.* possibility of trouble 事故率

~ recorder 失事记录器，黑盒子

~ report 事故报告

~ spot 事故地点，失事地点 ‖ *Syn.* accidental site 事故地点，失事地点

~ statistics 事故统计

~ voucher of tooling 工艺装备事故报告单

accidental [ˌæksi'dəntl] *n.* 非本质属性，次要方面；*a.* 意外的，非主要的，附属的

~ death 意外死亡

~ error 偶然性错误，偶然误差，随机误差

~ fire 失火

~ oil discharge 意外泄油

~ oil spill 突发性溢油

~ pollution 事故污染

~ rate analysis 事故率分析

~ report 事故报告

~ risk 事故危险性

~ severity 事故严重程度

~ shutdown 事故停机

~ site 事故地点，失事地点 ‖ *Syn.* accident spot 事故地点，失事地点

~ situation 偶然状况

~ spill 事故性溢漏

accidentally [ˌæksi'dənt(ə)li] *ad.* 意外地，偶然地

accommodate [ə'kɔmədeit] *v.* 供应，供给，提供，容纳，(使)适应，调节，调和，和解

accommodation [əˌkɔmə'deiʃən] *n.* 住处，膳宿，预定铺位，适应性调节，迁就融合

~ air-condition freon piping to be done air-tightness test 房舱空调氟利昂管系密性试验

~ air-condition freon piping to be done vacuum test 房舱空调氟利昂管系真空试验

~ deck 舱室甲板，住舱甲板，旅客甲板

~ heating 住舱供暖

~ ladder 舷梯

~ ladder with intermediate swivel platform 带有中间旋转平台的舷梯

~ lighting 住舱照明

~ space 起居舱室

~ to be done air-flow adjustment test 房舱风量调整试验

accompanied [ə'kʌmpənid] *v.* (accompany 的过去式和过去分词) 陪伴，共存，一同发生，附加，补充，伴奏；*a.* 伴随的，相伴的，陪伴的，伴奏的，共存的

~ baggage 随身行李

~ by 附有，偕同，伴随

accompany [ə'kʌmpəni] *v.* 陪伴，伴奏，共存，一同发生，附加，补充

accomplish [ə'kɔmpliʃ] *v.* 完成，达到，实现

accord [ə'kɔ:d] *n.* 一致，符合，调和，和解，妥协，协定；*v.* 一致，符合，给

予，授予，赠予，送给

according [əˈkɔːdiŋ] *ad.* 依照
~ to 根据，按照，依据
~ to schedule 按预定计划

accordingly [əˈkɔːdiŋli] *ad.* 因此，从而

account [əˈkaunt] *n.* 计算，账目，说明，估计，报告，理由，价值，地位，重要性；*v.* 说明，总计，认为，得分，记述
~ for 负责任，说明(原因、理由等)，导致，引起，构成(数量、比例等)

accountable [əˈkauntəbl] *a.* 应负责的，有责任的，可解释的

accredit [əˈcredit] *v.* 归结于，归因于，属于，鉴定合格，确认达标，授权，委托，委派，派出信任

accrue [əˈcruː] *v.* 自然增加，产生

accumulate [əˈkjuːmjuleit] *v.* 收集，堆集，积累，增长，增加

accumulated [əˈkjuːmjuˌleitid] *v.* (accumulate 的过去式和过去分词) 收集，堆集，积累，增长，增加；*a.* 积累的，堆积的
~ carbon 积碳
~ error 累积误差，积累误差
~ temperature 积温，积累的温度，累计温度

accumulation [əkjuːmjuˈleiʃ(ə)n] *n.* 聚集，积累，积聚物，堆积物
~ of frost 结霜
~ of frost test 结霜试验
~ zone 堆积区，淀积带

accumulator [əˈkjuːmjuleitə] *n.* 蓄电池，积聚者，储存器，累加器，加法器 ‖ *Syn.* battery 电池，电池组，蓄电池；cell 电池
~ battery 蓄电池组
~ cell 蓄电池
~ container 蓄电池容器
~ charger 电池充电器
~ drive 电池牵引，电池驱动
~ grid 蓄电池栅板
~ lamp 蓄电池灯
~ plate 蓄电池极板
~ separator 蓄电池隔板
~ switch 蓄电池开关
~ tester 蓄电池检验器
~ voltage 蓄电池电压

accumulator-powered 蓄电池供电的
~ hand lamp 蓄电池供电手提灯，蓄电池手提灯

accuracy [ˈækjurəsi] *n.* 精度，精确度，精确性，准确度，正确度 ‖ *Syn.* precision 精度，精确度，精确性，准确度，正确度
~ class 精度等级，精度级别，精确度等级 ‖ *Syn.* accuracy grade 精度等级，精度级别，准确度级别
~ of measurement 量测准确度，度量精度，测量精度，测定准确度
~ of measuring 计量准确度
~ rating 精度标称值
~ test 精度检验

accurate [ˈækjurit] *a.* 正确的，精确的，准确的 ‖ *Ant.* inaccurate 错误的，不准确的
~ adjustment 精调
~ calibration 精确校准
~ grinding 精密磨削
~ measurement 精确测量
~ model 准确模型
~ positioning 精确定位
~ record 精确记录
~ thread 精密螺纹

accurately [ˈækjərətli] *ad.* 正确地，精确

地，准确地
acetylene [ə'setili:n] n. 乙炔，电石气
　～ cylinder 乙炔罐，乙炔瓶
　～ generator 乙炔发生器
　～ welding 气焊，乙炔焊，乙炔焊接
achieve [ə'tʃi:v] v. 达到，完成，实现，获得
achievement [ə'tʃi:vmənt] n. 完成，达到，成绩，成就
acid ['æsid] n. 酸，迷幻药；a. 酸的，讽刺的，刻薄的
　～ attack 酸侵蚀
　～ cleaning 酸洗
　～ concentration 酸浓度
　～ content 酸含量
　～ corrosion 酸腐蚀
　～ degree 酸性程度
　～ proof 耐酸的，防酸的 ‖ Syn. acid resistant 耐酸的
　～ proof gloves 耐酸手套
　～ proof paint 耐酸涂料，耐酸油漆
　～ resistant lacquer 耐酸漆
　～ resistant paper 抗酸纸，耐酸纸
　～ solution 酸溶液
　～ strength 酸液浓度，酸强度
　～ value 酸值，酸价
acidic ['æsidik] a. 酸的，酸性的
　～ compound 酸性化合物
　～ corrosion 酸性腐蚀
　～ products 酸性产物
acidity [ə'siditi] n. 酸度，酸性，酸过多，胃酸过多
acknowledge [ək'nɔlidʒ] v. 承认，确认，确认有效，承认权威，答谢，致谢，鸣谢，告知收到，公证
　～ button 确认按钮
　～ receipt 确认收到，确认签收
　～ signal 确认信号，肯定信号，认可信号
acknowledgment [ək'nɔlidʒmənt] n. 承认，承认书，感谢
acme ['ækmi] n. 顶点，极致
acoustic [ə'ku:stik] a. 有关声音的，声学的，音响学的
　～ filter 声滤波器
　～ hood 隔声罩，隔音罩
　～ insulation 隔音
　～ treatment 声学处理，防噪处理
　～ treatment facilities 防噪设施
acquaint [ə'kweint] v. 使熟知，介绍，了解，认识，通知
acquire [ə'kwaiə] v. 获得，取得，搜索，探测，捕获，占有
acquisition [,ækwi'ziʃən] n. 获得，取得，搜索，探测，获得物，买进
acquisitive [ə'kwizitiv] a. 想获得的，有获得可能性的，可学到的
across [ə'krɔs] ad. 横过，交叉地，在对面；prep. 越过，交叉，在…的那边，在…对面
　～ from 对面，对门
　～ the line starting 直接启动，全压启动
　～ the line starting by hand 手动直接启动
acrylic [ə'krilik] a. 丙烯酸的
　～ resin 丙烯酸树脂
act [ækt] n. 动作，举动，法案，法令，节目，幕；v. 行动，见效，担当，表演，扮演，假装，表现
　～ accordingly 核办
　～ as 充当，作为，担任
　～ for 代理，代表，充当，起…作用
　～ of god 天灾，不可抗力
　～ of reception 验收证书
　～ on 对…起作用，按照…行事，作用

于 ‖ *Syn.* act upon 对…起作用
~ with 以…方式行事

acting ['æktiŋ] *v.* 行动，见效，担当，表演，扮演，假装，表现；*a.* 代理的，起作用的，演戏的
~ chief engineer 代理轮机长
~ compressor 作用压缩机
~ face 作用面，压力面，推进面，压力面，推进面

action ['ækʃən] *n.* 动作，作用，战斗，行动，举动，行为，情节
~ current 作用电流，动作电流
~ message 动作信息
~ of gravity 重力作用
~ of rust 锈蚀作用
~ potential 动作电位
~ turbine 冲击式水轮机

activate ['æktiveit] *v.* 刺激，使活动，使活泼，有活力，净化污水，建军，成军

activated ['æktiveitid] *v.* (activate 的过去式和过去分词) 刺激,使活动,使活泼,有活力,建军,成军,净化污水；*a.* 有活性的,有活力的
~ sludge 活性污泥
~ sludge process 活性污泥法

activation [,ækti'veiʃən] *n.* 活化，激活，活化作用

activator ['æktiveitə] *n.* 催化剂，触媒剂

active ['æktiv] *n.* 积极分子，主动语态；*a.* 积极的，能起作用的，现行的，主动的，活动的，活跃的，活性的
~ agent 活性剂，活化剂
~ attitude stabilization 主动姿态稳定
~ carbon 活性炭
~ component 有功部分，有效部分，活性组分，实数部分，作用分量

~ corrosion 活性腐蚀
~ duty 现役 ‖ *Syn.* active service 现役
~ element 活性元件，有源元件
~ fin stabilizer 主动减摇鳍
~ ingredient 活性成分，有效成分，活性配料
~ load 有效负载，有效载荷 ‖ *Syn.* PLoad 有效负载，有效载荷；payload 有效负载，有效载荷
~ loss 有功损耗
~ material 活性材料，活性物质
~ part 能动部分，主动部分
~ plate 活动板块，移动板块
~ power 有功功率，有效功率，平均功率
~ rudder 主动舵
~ substance 活性物质

activity [æk'tiviti] *n.* 活跃，行动，行为，活性，活度，活动性，放射性

actor ['æktə] *n.* 行动者，参与者，男演员

actual ['æktjuəl] *a.* 事实上的，实际的，真实的，现实的，现行的，目前的
~ bottom time 实际潜水时间
~ condition 实际情况，实际状况
~ cost 实际成本，实际费用
~ demand 实际需求
~ discharge capacity 实际排量
~ displacement 实际位移
~ element 实有元件
~ empirical quantity 实际经验的数量
~ error 实际误差
~ indicator card 实际示功图
~ life 实际寿命
~ measurement 实际测量，实物测量，实测
~ measurement signal 实际测量信号
~ need 实际需要

9

~ output 实际输出
~ power output 实际功率输出
~ practice 实际应用
~ result 实际结果
~ situation 实际情况
~ size 实际尺寸
~ speed 实际速度
~ state 实际状况
~ strength 实际强度
~ total loss 绝对全部损失，全部损失，实际全损
~ value 实际值，实际价值，现实价值

actuality [ˌæktjuˈæliti] *n.* 实在，真实，事实，现状

actualize [ˈæktjuəlaiz] *v.* 实现，实施，成为现实，真实描述

actually [ˈæktjuəli] *ad.* 实际上，事实上，竟然，居然，如今

actuate [ˈæktʃueit] *v.* 开动，驱使，激励

actuating [ˈæktʃuˌeitiŋ] *v.* (actuate 的 ing 形式) 开动，驱使，激励；*a.* 起动的，启动的
~ appliance 启动设备，驱动设备
~ cylinder 动力气缸，主动油缸，主动筒
~ mechanism 操作机构，传动机构，驱动机构，执行机构 ‖ *Syn.* actuator 传动装置，执行机构
~ motor 驱动电动机，伺服马达，伺服电动机
~ signal 启动信号，作用信号

actuator [ˈæktjueitə] *n.* 促动器，传动装置，执行机构,制动器，激励者 ‖ *Syn.* actuating mechanism 传动机构，驱动机构，执行机构

AD (analog-digital, analogue-digital) 模拟数字，模数

AD (analog-to-digital) 模拟对数字的，模数的
~ converter 模拟数字转换器，模数转换器，AD 转换器
~ conversion 模拟数字转换，模数转换，AD 转换

adapt [əˈdæpt] *v.* 改装，改编，(使)适应，(使)适合

adaptability [əˌdæptəˈbiliti] *n.* 适应性

adaptable [əˈdæptəbl] *a.* 能适应的，可修改的

adapter [əˈdæptə(r)] *n.* (=adaptor) 适配器，转接器，多头电源插座，改编者

adaptive [əˈdæptiv] *a.* 适应的
~ autopilot 自适应自动驾驶仪
~ control 自适应控制，自适控制，适应控制，适应性控制
~ control system 自适应控制系统，适应式控制系统
~ faculty 适应力，适应能力

adaptor [əˈdæptə(r)] *n.* (=adapter) 适配器，转接器，多头电源插座，改编者

add [æd] *v.* 增加，添加，加，加起来，做加法，计算总和，补充说
~ to 增添，增加到，补充说

add-and-subtract 加与减，增与减
~ relay 加减继电器，增减继电器，双位继电器

add-ons 附件，附加，附加软件

added [ˈædid] *v.* (add 的过去式和过去分词) 增加，添加，加，加起来，做加法，计算总和，补充说；*a.* 更多的，附加的，额外的
~ mass 附加质量
~ value 增值，附加值

addendum [əˈdendəm] *n.* 附录，补遗

addition [ə'diʃən] *n.* 加，加法，增加，增加物，附加
   ~ agent 添加剂，助剂，合金元素
   ~ certificate for offshore supply vessels 海上供应船舶附加证书，海上供应船舶增补证书
additional [ə'diʃənl] *a.* 另外的，附加的，额外的
   ~ charge 补充装料，附加费
   ~ condition 附加条件
   ~ constant 附加常数
   ~ cost 额外成本，额外费用，附加成本
   ~ drag 附加阻力
   ~ equipment 辅助设备，补充设备
   ~ error 附加误差
   ~ fee 附加费用
   ~ freeboard 附加干舷
   ~ insurance 附加保险，附加险，追加保险
   ~ load 附加负载
   ~ product 附加产品
   ~ protective security measure 附加防护性保安措施
   ~ rate 附加比率
   ~ repair list 附加修理单
   ~ requirement 附加要求
   ~ survey 附加检验
   ~ verification 附加验证
   ~ winding 附加绕组，辅助绕组
additionally [ə'diʃənəli] *ad.* 此外，加之，又
additive ['æditiv] *n.* 添加剂；*a.* 添加的，附加的，加法的；*ad.* 附加的，加成的，添加的
adequacy ['ædikwəsi] *n.* 适当，足够
adequate ['ædikwit] *a.* 适当的，足够的，充分的 ‖ *Syn*. enough 充足的，足够的；sufficient 足够的，充足的，充分的
adhere [əd'hiə] *v.* 粘附，胶着，依附，坚持，追随，遵守
adherence [əd'hiərəns] *n.* 黏着，附着，忠诚，坚信，坚持
   ~ to 遵守，坚持，恪守
adhesion [əd'hi:ʃən] *n.* 黏附，黏连，黏附，黏着，附着力，黏附力，拥护，同意
   ~ belt 黏着带
   ~ coefficient 黏着系数
   ~ failure 胶黏力破坏
   ~ layer 黏附层
   ~ of a coating 涂层黏附力
   ~ test 附着力试验，附着力测试，黏附试验
adhesive [əd'hi:siv] *n.* 黏合剂；*a.* 带黏性的，涂胶的，胶黏的，难忘的
   ~ bonding 附着黏合
   ~ capacity 黏附能力，胶黏度
   ~ coated foil 涂胶铜箔
   ~ face 黏附面
   ~ meter 胶黏计
   ~ power 附着力，黏合力
   ~ strength 黏合强度
adiabatic [ˌædiə'bætik] *a.* 绝热的，隔热的
   ~ change 绝热变化
   ~ cooling 绝热冷却
   ~ curing 绝热养护
   ~ engine 绝热引擎，绝热发动机
   ~ expansion 绝热膨胀
   ~ wall 绝热壁
adjacent [ə'dʒeisənt] *a.* 邻近的，靠近的，毗连的，接近的，贴近的
   ~ angle 邻角
   ~ line 邻接线路，邻线

~ plate 相邻极板

~ position 相邻位置，邻位

~ sea 近海，邻海

adjoin [ə'dʒɔin] v. 邻近，靠近，毗连，接近，贴近

adjust [ə'dʒʌst] v. 调整，调节，校正，校准，相互适应

adjustable [ə'dʒʌstəb(ə)l] a. 可调整的，可调节的

~ barrel 套筒

~ boring tool 可调镗刀

~ eccentric 可调整偏心轮

~ parameter 可调参量，可调参数

~ pitch 可调螺距，活螺距

~ quantity 可调量

~ resistance 可调电阻，可变阻抗

~ resistor 可调电阻器

~ ring 控制环

~ second stage 可调二级头

~ spanner 活络扳手，活动扳手，可扳手 ‖ *Syn*. adjustable wrench 活络扳手，活动扳手，可调扳手

~ speed motor 调速电动机，变速电动机 ‖ *Syn*. variable speed motor 调速电动机，变速电动机

~ tool 可调刀具

~ transformator 可调变压器

adjusted [ə'dʒʌstid] v. (adjust 的过去式和过去分词) 调整，调节，校正，校准，相互适应；a. 调整过的，调节过的，修正后的

~ elevation 平差高程

~ no decompression limit 修正后最大免减压时间

~ pressure casting 调压铸造

adjuster [ə'dʒʌstə(r)] n. 调节器，调停者

adjusting [ə'dʒʌstiŋ] n. 调节(作用)，校准，调整，调制；v. (adjust 的 ing 形式) 调整，调节，校正，校准，相互适应

~ block 调整垫块，调整轴承

~ bolt 调整螺栓

~ device 调整设备

~ knob 调节旋钮

~ lever 调整杆

~ mechanism 调整机构

~ nut 调整螺母

~ plate 调节板

~ range 调整范围

~ rheostat 调节变阻器

~ safety device for hydraulic system 液压系统安全装置调整

~ screw 调节螺钉，调节螺旋

~ shim 调整垫片

~ spring 调整弹簧

~ tap 调节柄

~ valve 调整阀，调节阀

~ washer 调整垫圈，调节垫圈

~ wedge 调整楔

adjustment [ə'dʒʌstmənt] n. 调整，调节，调节器

~ mechanism 调整机构，调准机构，调整装置

~ process 调整过程

~ range 调整幅度，调整范围，调节范围

~ table 校准表，调准表

admeasure [æd'meʒə] v. 分配，配给

admeasurement [æd'meʒəmənt] n. 分配，配给

administer [əd'ministə] v. 管理，给予，执行，实施，处理，看护，照料

administrate [əd'ministreit] v. 管理，执行，处理

administration [ədminis'treiʃən] *n.* 管理，经营，行政管理，政府，行政机关，行政部门

administrative [əd'ministrətiv] *a.* 管理的，行政的

administrator [əd'ministreitə] *n.* 管理人，行政官

admiralty ['ædmərəlti] *n.* 海事法，海事法庭，海军上将职位，舰队司令职位，英国海军部(Admiralty)
- ~ bronze 船用青铜，海军青铜
- ~ coefficient 海军系数
- ~ constant 海军常数(估算舰船主机功率的经验系数)
- ~ port 海军要塞

admissible [əd'misəbl] *a.* 可容许的，可接纳的
- ~ clearance 容许间隙
- ~ control 容许控制
- ~ deviation 容许偏差
- ~ error 容许误差
- ~ estimate 容许估计
- ~ wear 容许磨损

admission [əd'miʃən] *n.* 准许进入，加入，入场费，进入权，坦白，承认，招认

admit [əd'mit] *v.* 允许进入，容许，承认，许可，准许，接纳，容纳，通往

adopt [ə'dɔpt] *v.* 采用，采纳，采取，批准，选定，正式通过，收养

adoption [ə'dɔpʃən] *n.* 采用，采纳，采取，选定，正式通过

adrift [ə'drift] *a.* 漂泊的；*ad.* 漂浮着，随波逐流地

ADS (atmospheric diving suits) 大气式潜水衣

adsorb [æd'sɔ:b] *v.* 吸附，被吸附

adsorbent [æd'sɔ:bənt] *n.* 吸附剂；*a.* 吸附的

adsorption [æd'sɔ:pʃən] *n.* 吸附，吸附作用
- ~ capacity 吸附容量
- ~ film 吸附膜
- ~ precipitation 吸附沉淀
- ~ refrigeration 吸附制冷

advance [əd'va:ns] *n.* 前进，提升，预付款；*v.* 前进，提前，预付；*a.* 前面的，预先的，预付的
- ~ coefficient 进速系数
- ~ preparation 事前准备，预先准备
- ~ speed 前进速度 ‖ *Syn.* advance velocity 前进速度

advanced [əd'va:nst] *v.* (advance 的过去式和过去分词) 前进，提前，预付；*a.* 高级的，年老的，先进的
- ~ application 高级运用，高级应用
- ~ control 先进控制
- ~ diver 中级潜水员 ‖ openwater diver 初级潜水员；specialty diver 专项潜水员
- ~ ignition 提前点火
- ~ material 先进材料
- ~ technology 先进技术

advantage [əd'va:ntidʒ] *n.* 优势，长处，有利条件，利益，便利 ‖ *Ant.* disadvantage 不利，不利条件，缺点，劣势，短处

advantageous [ˌædvən'teidʒəs] *a.* 有利的，有益的

adverse ['ædvə:s] *a.* 不利的，敌对的，相反的
- ~ condition 不利条件
- ~ current 逆流
- ~ effect 副作用，不良效应，不利影响
- ~ factor 有害因素，不利因素
- ~ impact 负面影响，不良影响，不利影响
- ~ pressure 反压力

~ reaction 不良反应

~ weather 不利天气

aerate ['eiəreit] v. 使暴露于空气中，通气，充气，打气

aeration [ˌeiə'reiʃən] n. 曝气，通气，充气，打气 ‖ **Ant.** deaeration 脱气，排气，除气

~ blower 曝气鼓风机

~ compartment 曝气室

~ equipment 通气设备

~ intensity 曝气强度

~ tank 曝气柜

aerator ['eiəreitə(r)] n. 通风装置，通气设备，充气器 ‖ **Ant.** deaerator 脱气器

aero ['ɛərəu] a. 空气的，航空的，飞行的，飞机的

~ foam fire extinguisher system 空气泡沫灭火系统

aerobic [ˌeiə'rəubik] a. 依靠氧气的，与需氧菌有关的，增氧健身法的

~ bacteria 需氧细菌，需气细菌，需氧菌，好气细菌

~ digestion 需氧消化

~ organisms 好气微生物，好氧微生物

~ respiration 有氧呼吸，需氧呼吸，好气呼吸

~ treatment 需氧处理，好气处理

aerodynamic [ˌɛərəudai'næmik] a. 空气动力学的，气动的

~ bearing 气动轴承

~ brake 气动制动装置

~ control 气动控制

~ damping 气动阻尼

~ resistance 气动阻力

~ turbine 气动透平，气动涡轮

aerometer [ɛə'rɔmitə] n. 量气计，气体计

affiliate [ə'filieit] n. 成员，分支机构；v. 接纳，接受，加入，联合，隶属，紧密联合，紧密联系，追溯

afford [ə'fɔ:d] v. 提供，给予，获得，买得起，供应得起

affreightment [ə'freitmənt] n. 租船货运

afloat [ə'fləud] a. 飘浮的，在海上的，传播的；ad. 飘浮地，在海上，传播地

aft [a:ft] ad. 在船尾，近船尾，向船尾

~ bridge 船艉桥楼

~ closet 后部壁橱

~ deck 后甲板

~ draft 艉吃水，后吃水 ‖ **Syn.** aft draught 艉吃水，后吃水

~ end 尾部，后端

~ lamp 尾灯

~ part 后部，尾部 ‖ **Syn.** after part 后部，尾部

~ peak bulkhead 艉尖舱壁 ‖ **Syn.** after peak bulkhead 艉尖舱壁

~ peak tank 后尖舱，艉尖舱 ‖ **Syn.** after peak tank 后尖舱，艉尖舱

~ perpendicular 尾垂线 ‖ **Syn.** after perpendicular 艉垂线 ‖ **Ant.** forward perpendicular 艏垂线

~ sidelight 艉舷灯

~ spring 后倒缆

~ steering test 倒车操舵试验

~ superstructure 尾上层建筑

~ terminal 后端点

after ['a:ftə] a. 以后的；ad. 以后，后来；conj. 在…以后；prep. 在…之后，在后面，关于，追赶，依照

~ bottom dead center (ABDC) 下止点后，下死点后

~ burning 后期燃烧，后燃，二次燃烧，迟燃

~ cooler 后冷却器，二次冷却器

~ engine arrangement 艉机型布置

~ hours 正常工作时间之后

~ part 后部，尾部 ‖ *Syn*. aft part 后部，尾部

~ peak bulkhead 艉尖舱壁 ‖ *Syn*. aft peak bulkhead 艉尖舱壁

~ peak tank 后尖舱，艉尖舱 ‖ *Syn*. aft peak tank 后尖舱，艉尖舱

~ perpendicular 艉垂线 ‖ *Syn*. aft perpendicular 艉垂线 ‖ *Ant*. forward perpendicular 艏垂线

~ shoulder 后肩 ‖ *Ant*. forward shoulder 前肩

after-mast 后桅

~ head light 后桅灯 ‖ *Syn*. range light 后桅灯

afterbody ['a:ftə'bɔdə] *n*. (船、飞机、导弹等的)后体，尾部

aftercooler ['a:ftə,ku:lə(r)] *n*. 后冷却机，二次冷却器

aftermost ['a:ftəməustə] *a*. 靠船尾的，最后的，最后部的

against [ə'genst] *prep*. 相反，反对，逆着，靠着，倚着

~ the wind 顶风，逆风

AGC (automatic generation control) 发电机组功率输出自动控制，出力自动控制

age [eidʒ] *n*. 使用年限，年龄，成年，同时期的人，时代；*v*. 变老，成熟

agency ['eidʒənsi] *n*. 代理处，行销处，代理，中介

~ cost 代理成本，代理费用 ‖ *Syn*. agency fee 代理费，佣金，中介费

agent ['eidʒənt] *n*. 代理人，代理商，执法官，政府代表，作用者，作用物，媒介，中介，手段

aggregate ['ægrigeit] *n*. 合计，总计，集合体；*v*. 聚集，集合，合计；*a*. 合计的，集合的，聚合的

~ amount 总金额

~ capacity 合计容量，总功率，聚集容量

~ data 综合数据

~ demand 总需求，总体需求，需求总量

~ motion 组合运动

~ supply 总供给，总供给量

~ tonnage 总吨位，总吨数

aggregation [ægri'geiʃən] *n*. 集合，集合体，聚合

aging ['eidʒiŋ] *n*. 老化，成熟的过程；*v*. (age 的 ing 形式) 变老，成熟

~ rate 老化率

agitate ['ædʒiteit] *v*. 摇动，搅动，鼓动，煽动

agitation [ædʒi'teiʃən] *n*. 摇动，搅动，鼓动，煽动，激动，不安，焦虑

aground [ə'graund] *a*. 搁浅的，触礁的；*ad*. 搁浅地，触礁地，地面上

ahead [ə'hed] *a*. 在前的，向前的，提前的，领先的；*ad*. 在前，向前，提前，领先

~ cam 正车凸轮，前进凸轮

~ of 在…前面，在…之前

~ of schedule 提前，提早

~ of time 提前，提早

~ oil cylinder 正车油缸

~ revolution 正车转速

AI (artificial intelligence) 人工智能

aid [eid] *n*. 帮助，援助，帮助者，辅助设备，有帮助的事物；*v*. 资助，援助，帮助

aided ['eidid] *v*. (aid 的过去式和过去分词) 资助，援助，帮助；*a*. 辅助的，半自动的

~ design 辅助设计

aider ['eidmən] n. 救护兵

air [ɛə] n. 空气，样子，天空，空中，曲调；v. 晾干，使通风，宣扬，夸耀，显示

~ amount used 空气消耗量
~ attemperator 气冷式调温器
~ bleed system 抽气方式
~ blower 空气鼓风机，鼓风机，风机
~ blowout 喷气，空气灭弧
~ bottle (压缩)空气瓶
~ brake 气闸
~ buffer 空气缓冲器，空气减震器，空气阻尼器
~ chamber 气囊，浮囊，贮气罐，气压室，空气包，空气分配室
~ change 换气，通风换气
~ change rate 通风换气次数
~ charge 充气
~ circuit breaker 空气电路断路器
~ circulation 空气环流，空气循环
~ clamp 气压夹具
~ cleaner 空气过滤器
~ cleaning 空气净化
~ clearance 余隙空气
~ cock 气阀，气栓，排气旋塞，放气活塞
~ collector 空气收集器
~ compressor 空压机，空气压缩机，压气机
~ conditioner 空调，空调机，冷气机
~ conditioning 空调
~ conditioning system 空调系统
~ conditioning apparatus dew point 空调设备露点
~ consumption 空气消耗量

~ control valve 空气控制阀
~ cooled compressor 风冷式压缩机，气冷式压缩机 ‖ *Syn*. air flow cooled compressor 风冷式压缩机，气冷式压缩机
~ cooler 空气冷却器
~ cooler cleaning system 空气冷却器净化系统
~ cooling 空气冷却(法)
~ cooling chamber 空气冷却室
~ cooling fin 散热片，气冷片
~ cooling valve 气冷阀
~ current 气流
~ cushion 气垫
~ cushion craft 气垫船
~ cushion eject rod 气垫顶杆
~ cushion plate 气垫板
~ cushion vehicle 气垫船，气垫车
~ cylinder 空气气缸，气缸，储气筒
~ damper 节气门
~ defense 防空，空中防御，空防
~ depletion 空气耗尽，没空气
~ diffuse disk 空气扩散盘
~ diffuser 空气扩散器，散流器
~ diffuser vane 空气扩散器叶片
~ director 空气导流器
~ distribution system 空气分布系统
~ distributor 空气分配阀，空气分配器
~ diving 空气潜水
~ draft 通气，通风，抽风，吸风，气流
~ dryer 空气干燥器
~ drying chamber 空气干燥室
~ duct 风管，风道
~ eddy 气流所产生的漩涡
~ ejector 空气喷射器
~ ejector condenser 空气喷射器冷凝器

~ escape 泄气

~ exhaust 排气，抽气，排风

~ filter 空气过滤器

~ flow 气流，空气流量

~ flow meter 空气流量计

~ foam nozzle 空气泡沫喷嘴

~ fuel ratio 空燃比，气燃比

~ gap 空气间隙，气隙

~ gap flux 气隙磁通

~ gap flux distribution 气隙磁通分布

~ gap line 气隙磁化线

~ grill 空气格栅

~ hammer 气动锤，气锤 ‖ *Syn*. pneumatic hammer 气动锤，气锤

~ heater 空气预热器，空气加热器

~ horn 气喇叭

~ hydraulic cylinder 气水罐

~ inlet valve 进气阀，空气进口阀

~ intake 进气口，空气进气

~ intake casing 进气道外壳

~ intake filter 空气滤清器

~ intake filter-silencer 空气滤清器消声器

~ intake silencer 进气口消声器

~ intake strainer 进气口过滤器

~ leak 漏气 ‖ *Syn*. air leakage 漏气

~ leak test 空气渗漏试验，空气漏气试验

~ lock 气锁，气闸，气阀

~ main 空气总管

~ manifold 空气歧管，压缩空气系统分路阀箱

~ manifold relief valve 空气歧管安全阀

~ moisture 空气湿度，空气水分，空气含湿量

~ movement 空气流动

~ nozzle 喷气嘴，空气喷嘴

~ outlet 出风口，排气口

~ pilot valve 空气导向阀

~ pipe 空气管，通风管，排气管

~ pipe closing arrangement 空气管关闭装置，通风管关闭装置，排气管关闭装置

~ pipe with cover 带盖空气管，带盖通风管，带盖排气管

~ plug 气塞

~ plug gauge 气动塞规

~ pocket 气陷，气穴

~ pollution 空气污染，大气污染，环境空气污染

~ preheater 空气预热机，空气预热装置

~ pressure 气压 ‖ *Syn*. pneumatic pressure 气压

~ pressure gauge 气压计

~ pressure test 空气压力试验，气压试验

~ proof 密封，不透气

~ pulse gauge 脉冲式气动量仪

~ pump 气泵

~ purification 空气净化

~ quantity 风量

~ receiver 储风筒，储气器，储气室，贮气箱

~ register 空气挡板，空气调节器，配风器，调风器

~ regulator 风流调节装置，送风调节器，空气调节器

~ relay 气动继电器，气压继电器，气动替续器，气动转换，气压替续器

~ relay valve 空气中继阀

~ release cock 放气旋塞

~ reservoir 储气缸，储气器，贮气器，压缩空气贮罐

~ resistance 空气阻力，空气阻抗

~ resistance coefficient 空气阻力系数

17

~ revitalization unit fan 再生通风机
~ scour pipe 空气冲刷管
~ seal 气封，防气圈
~ separator 空气分离器，风选器，除气设备
~ siren 汽笛
~ snap gauge 气动外径量规
~ source 空气源，气源
~ spring 气垫
~ start lever 空气起动杆
~ start valve return spring 空气起动阀复位弹簧
~ starting valve 空气起动阀
~ stream 空气流，气流
~ supply 气源，空气供给
~ supply diving-hose 水面供气潜水
~ supply mask 气管呼吸器
~ switch 空气开关
~ tank 空气储罐，空气贮罐，贮气罐
~ tap 气嘴，空气栓，气旋塞
~ temperature 气温
~ temperature automatic fire alarm 测温式火警自动报警器 ‖ *Syn*. automatic thermal type fire alarm 测温式火警自动报警器；automatic thermo type fire alarm 测温式火警自动报警器
~ tight 气密的，密封的
~ tightness 气密性
~ tightness test and safety valve adjusting for air horn receiver on board 汽笛空气瓶装船后气密试验和安全阀的调整
~ tightness test and safety valve adjusting for control air receiver on board 控制空气瓶装船后气密试验和安全阀的调整
~ tightness test and safety valve adjusting for main air receiver on board 主空气瓶装船后气密试验和安全阀的调整
~ tightness test for auxiliary boiler (economize boiler) on board 辅锅炉(废气锅炉)装船后气密试验
~ to close 气关式
~ to open 气开式
~ trunk 通风总管
~ valve 空气阀，气阀，空气阀门
~ velocity 气流速度
~ vent 通风口，通气孔，排气口
~ vent and overflow pipe 通气与溢流管
~ vent cock 排气口活栓
~ vent screw 通气螺钉
~ venting arrangement 排气装置
~ vessel 空气罐
~ whistle 空气笛，气笛
~ winch 气动绞车，风动绞车
~ wrench 气动扳手
~ zero gas 零点气 ‖ *Syn*. zero grade gas 零点气

air-cooled 空气冷却的，气冷的
~ condenser 气冷式冷凝器
~ engine 气冷发动机

air-driven 气体驱动的，气动的 ‖ *Syn*. air-operated 气体驱动的，气动的
~ water pump 气动水泵

air-filled 充气的
~ chamber 充气室，充气筒

air-operated 气体驱动的，气动的 ‖ *Syn*. air-driven 气体驱动的，气动的
~ pump 压缩空气驱动泵
~ valve 气动阀

airborne ['ɛəbɔ:n] *a*. 空运的，机载的，飞行的，空气传播的，风媒的
~ contaminant 空气污染物
~ solid particles 空气中的固体颗粒

aircraft ['ɛəkra:ft] *n*. 飞行器，航行器
~ carrier 航空母舰

airless ['ɛəlis] *a*. 没有气的，没有风的，不通风的
~ bottle 真空瓶
~ spray 无气喷涂

airtight ['eətait] *a*. 密封的，气密的，无懈可击的
~ canister 密封罐
~ container 密封容器，气密容器

AIS (Automatic Identification System) 自动识别系统

aisle [ail] *n*. 走廊，过道

alarm ['ɔla:m] *n*. 警报器，警铃，警报，闹铃，惊慌；*v*. 恐吓，警告 ‖ ***Syn***. alarm apparatus 报警器；horn 喇叭，警报器
~ and protection system 报警保护系统
~ and safety device testing of main diesel generator 主柴油发电机报警和安全装置试验
~ testing and safety device testing of ME 主机报警和安全装置试验
~ annunciator 警报信号器
~ apparatus 报警器 ‖ ***Syn***. alarm 警报器，警铃；horn 喇叭，警报器
~ bell 警铃，警钟
~ circuit 报警电路
~ clock 闹钟
~ device 告警装置，警报装置，报警装置，报警信号设备
~ equipment 报警器
~ for oil-gas concentration 油气浓度报警器
~ free 无报警
~ horn 警报器，报警喇叭

~ lamp 信号灯，告警灯
~ logger 报警记录仪
~ message 报警信息
~ monitoring system 警报监测系统，报警监控系统，警报监视系统
~ of fire 火灾警报
~ pressure gauge 警报信号压力计
~ printer 警报打字机
~ signal 警报信号
~ switch 警报开关
~ system 警报系统
~ system testing of ME 主机警报系统试验
~ valve 警报阀
~ whistle 警笛

ALC (automatic load control) 自动负载控制，自动载荷控制

alcohol ['ælkəhɔl] *n*. 酒精，酒
~ thermometer 酒精温度表，酒精温度计

Aldis ['ɔ:ldis] *n*. 奥尔迪斯(人名)
~ lamp 奥尔迪斯手提信号灯(舰船、飞机上用摩尔斯电码发信号时用的灯)

alert [ə'lə:t] *n*. 警惕，警报；*a*. 提防的，警惕的

algae ['ældʒi:] *n*. 藻类，海藻

algaecide ['ældʒi:said] *n*. 除海藻的药

alidade ['ælideid] *n*. 照准仪

align ['əlain] *v*. 对准，校直，调准，校正，排列，结盟，成一条线

aligning ['əlainiŋ] *n*. 矫正，对准；*v*. (align 的 ing 形式) 对准，校直，调准，校正，排列，结盟，成一条线
~ intermediate shaft and propeller shaft after launching 下水后中间轴和螺旋桨轴校中
~ main engine's crankshaft and interm-

ediate shaft after launching 下水后主机曲轴和中间轴校中

alignment ['əlainmənt] n. 直线排列，校正，对准，调整，平面图，结盟，联合
~ accuracy 对准精度
~ chock 组装校准用垫楔
~ error 校正误差
~ feeler 对准测隙规
~ inspection of shaft generator and gear box 轴带发电机和齿轮箱的对中检查
~ of shafting 轴线对中
~ tolerance 定位公差，对准公差，组对公差

alkalescence [,ælkə'lesəns] n. 弱碱性，碱性

alkali ['ælkəlai] n. 碱；a. 碱性的
~ cleaning 碱洗
~ liquor 碱液
~ metal 碱金属
~ resisting cast iron 耐碱铸铁
~ resistivity 耐碱性
~ treatment 碱处理

alkali-proof 耐碱的，抗碱的
~ varnish 耐碱清漆

alkaline ['ælkəlain] a. 碱的，碱性的
~ battery 碱性电池 ‖ *Syn.* alkaline cell 碱性电池
~ cleaner 碱洗装置，碱性清洗剂
~ cleaning 碱清洗
~ condition 碱性条件
~ pump 碱液泵
~ reaction 碱性反应
~ reagent 碱性试剂
~ solution 碱性溶液
~ water 碱性水

alkyd ['ælkid] n. 醇酸树脂
~ plastics 醇酸塑料
~ resin 醇酸聚酯树脂，醇酸树脂

all [ɔ:l] n. 全部；a. 全部的，所有的，整个的；ad. 完全，都，非常；pron. 一切，全部
~ about 所有关于，全部关于，都关于
~ drilled hole 全部钻孔
~ over 全部完结，到处
~ round 周围，四处，各方面
~ round frame 加强肋骨
~ round light 环照灯

all-weather 全天候的，全天候场地
~ facility 全天候设施

Allen ['ælin] n. 艾伦(男子名)
~ key 内六角扳手 ‖ *Syn.* Allen wrench 内六角扳手

alleviate [ə'li:vieit] v. 减轻，缓和

alleyway ['æliwei] n. (船上的)通道，小巷，窄街

alligator ['æligeitə] n. 产于美洲的鳄鱼
~ grab 颚式夹钳

allocate ['æləukeit] v. 分配，配给，分派，分拨

allocation [,æləu'keiʃən] n. 分配，配给，拨款，拨款量
~ proportion 分派比例，分配比例

allot [ə'lɔt] v. (按份额)分配，分派

allotment [ə'lɔmənt] n. 分配，分派

allow [ə'lau] v. 允许，容许，准许，分配，承认，同意，认为，断定，考虑，顾及 ‖ *Syn.* permit 许可，允许，准许

allowable [ə'lauəbl] a. 允许的，正当的，可承认的
~ bearing stress 容许承压应力
~ clearance 允许间隙，容许间隙
~ deviation 容许偏差
~ error 容许误差

~ limit 容许限度，允许极限

~ load 容许负荷，容许荷载，容许载荷，许用载荷

~ pressure 容许压力

~ pressure difference 容许压差

~ strength 容许强度，许用强度

~ stress 容许应力

~ temperature 容许温度

~ value 容许值

~ variation 允许偏差

allowance [ə'lauəns] n. 津贴，补助，宽容，允许；v. 定量供应

~ for depreciation 折旧率，备抵折旧

~ for roughness 粗糙度裕度

~ list 船舶供应和配件清单

alloy [æ'lɔi] n. 合金；v. 使成合金，减低成色

~ cast iron 合金铸铁

~ casting 合金铸件，合金铸造

~ layer 合金层，表面波纹层

~ plating 镀合金

~ powder 合金粉末

~ steel 合金钢，合金钢材，合金钢质

~ wire 合金钢丝，合金线

aloft [ə'lɔft] ad. 在高处，在上

alongside [ə'lɔŋ'said] ad. 在旁；prep. 横靠

alter ['ɔ:ltə] v. 改变，变更，更改

alteration [,ɔ:ltə'riʃən] n. 改变，变更，更新改造

alternate [ɔ:l'tə:nit] n. 供替代的选择，代理人，候补者，代替者；v. 交替，轮流，改变；a. 交替的，轮流的，间隔的，预备的，取代的，供替换的

~ air source 备用气源

~ days 隔日

~ energy source 代用能源

~ fuel 代用燃料

~ route 迂回进路，替代径路，比较路线，变更进路

~ with 交替，轮流，相间

alternately [ɔ:l'tə:nitli] ad. 交替地，隔一个地

~ rolling 交叉轧制

alternating [ɔ:l'tə:nətiv] v. (alternate 的 ing 形式) 交替，轮流，改变；a. 交流的，交互的

~ current (AC) 交流，交流电，交流电流

~ current ammeter 交流安培计

~ current ammeter with clamp 钳型表

~ current asynchronous motor 交流异步电机

~ current asynchronous motor drive 交流异步电机驱动

~ current circuit 交流电路

~ current commutator motor 交流整流式电动机

~ current contactor 交流接触器

~ current converter 交流换流器，交流交换器

~ current distribution 交流配电

~ current distribution system 交流配电系统

~ current electric drive 交流电气传动

~ current electric propulsion apparatus 交流电力推进装置

~ current electromotive force 交流电动势

~ current exciter 交流励磁机

~ current generator 交流发电机 ‖ *Syn.* alternator 交流发电机

~ current input 交流输入

~ current line 交流线路

~ current motor 交流电机，交流电动

机，交流马达
~ current power control 交流电力控制
~ current power controller 交流电力控制器
~ current power cord 交流电电源线
~ current power electronic switch 交流电力电子开关
~ current power station 交流电站
~ current power system 交流电力系统
~ current pulse 交流脉冲
~ current rectifier 交流整流器
~ current relay 交流继电器
~ current resistance 交流阻抗
~ current servomotor 交流伺服电动机
~ current signalling 交流传信
~ current single-phase three-wire system with neutral earthed 中性点接地的交流单相三线系统，中性点接地的交流单相三线制
~ current squirrel cage induction motor 交流鼠笼型感应电动机
~ current supply 交流电源
~ current tacho-generator 交流测速发电机
~ current three-phase three-wire insulated system 交流三相三线绝缘系统
~ current three-phase three-wire system 交流三相三线系统，交流三相三线制
~ current three-phase three-wire system with hull as neutral wire 以船体为中性线的交流三相三线系统，以船体为中性线的交流三相三线制
~ current torque motor 交流扭矩电动机，交流陀螺修正电动机
~ current transmission 交流输电
~ current voltage controller 交流电压控制器，交流调压电路
~ current voltage 交流电压
~ current-alternating current (AC-AC) 交流交流，交交
~ current-alternating current frequency converter 交交变频器
~ current-direct current-alternating current (AC-DC-AC) 交流直流交流，交直交
~ current-direct current-alternating current frequency converter 交直交变频器
~ electromagnet 交流电磁铁
~ flux 交变通量
~ load 反复载荷，交替荷载
~ magnetic field 交变磁场
~ pattern 交替模式
~ pulse 交替脉冲
~ resistance 交变阻抗
~ stress 交变应力
~ voltage 交流电压

alternation [ˌɔːltəˈneiʃən] *n*. 交替，轮流，间隔

alternative [ɔːˈltəːnətiv] *n*. 二中择一，可供选择的办法或事物；*a*. 选择性的，二中择一的
~ fuel 代用燃料

alternatively [ɔːˈltəːnətivli] *ad*. 作为选择地，二者择一地

alternator [ˈɔːltə(ː)neitə] *n*. 交流发电机 ‖ *Syn*. alternating current generator (AC generator) 交流发电机

altitude [ˈæltitjuːd] *n*. 高度，高处，顶垂线，高线，高等，地平纬度

ALU (arithmetic logic unit) 算术逻辑单元，运算逻辑单元

aluminium [ˌæljuˈminjəm] (=aluminum) *n*.

铝；a. 铝的

~ backing 铝敷层

~ bronze 铝青铜

~ forging 铝锻造，铝铸造

~ sulphate 硫酸铝

aluminum [ə'lju:minəm] (=aluminium) n. 铝；a. 铝的

~ alloy 铝合金，铝合金材料

~ alloy casting 铝合金铸件，铝合金铸造

~ alloy structure 铝合金结构

~ anode 铝阳极

~ bronze bushing 铝青铜套

~ coil 铝线，线圈

~ coil transformer 铝线变压器

~ paint 铝涂料

~ powder 铝粉

~ rivet 铝铆钉

~ welding powder 铝焊粉

~ welding wire 铝焊丝

aluminum-tin 铝锡

~ alloy 铝锡合金

alunite ['æljunait] n. 明矾石

~ grease 明矾石润滑脂

alveolus [æl'viələs] n. 小孔，肺泡

AM (amplitude modulation) 调幅

ambiance ['æmbiəns] n. (=ambience) 周围环境，气氛，格调 ‖ **Syn**. ambient 周围环境；atmosphere 气氛；circumstances 环境；environment 环境，外界，周围；surroundings 环境

ambience ['æmbiəns] n. (=ambiance) 周围环境，气氛，格调 ‖ **Syn**. ambient 周围环境；atmosphere 气氛；circumstances 环境；environment 环境，外界，周围；surroundings 环境

ambient ['æmbiənt] n. 周围环境；a. 周围的，包围的 ‖ **Syn**. ambiance 周围环境，气氛；ambience 周围环境，气氛；atmosphere 气氛；circumstances 环境；environment 环境，外界，周围；surroundings 环境

~ air 环境空气，周围空气

~ air quality 环境空气质量

~ condition 环境条件，外界条件

~ gas 周围气体

~ humidity 环境湿度

~ interference 环境干扰

~ light 环境光，环境光线，周围光

~ lighting 环境照明

~ noise 环境噪声

~ pressure 环境压力

~ sound 环境声

~ temperature 环境温度

ambulance ['æmbjuləns] n. 战时流动医院，救护车

~ barge 医务驳船

~ boat 医务艇，救护艇 ‖ **Syn**. ambulance launch 医务艇，救护艇

amend [ə'mend] v. 修正，改进，改正，改好，纠正，改善，改革

amendment [ə'mendmənt] n. 改善，改正

~ notice 修订通知

~ procedure 修改程序，修正案表决程序

America [ə'merikə] n. 美国，美洲(包括北美和南美洲)

American [ə'merikən] n. 美国人，美洲人；a. 美国的，美洲的

~ Bureau of Shipping (ABS) 美国船级社

amidship [ə'midsʃip] *ad*. (=amidships) 在船中部，向船的中部

amidships [ə'midsʃips] *ad*. (=amidship) 在船中部，向船的中部
~ area ratio 船中剖面面积比
~ beam ratio 船中剖面宽度比
~ depth 船中部舷高
~ launcher 舰艇中部发射装置
~ structure 船中部结构

amidships-engined 中机型的，机舱在船中部的
~ ship 中机型船

amino ['æminəu] *a*. 氨基的
~ group powder 氨基干粉
~ group powder extinguishing agent 氨基干粉灭火剂

ammeter ['æmitə] *n*. 安培计，电流表
~ commutator switch 电流转换开关
~ selector 安培计选择器
~ switch 安培计开关

ammonia [æ'məunjə] *n*. 氨，氨水
~ condenser 氨冷凝器，氨气冷凝器
~ cooler 氨气冷却器
~ cylinder 氨瓶
~ gas 氨气
~ helmet 防氨面具
~ hydroxide 氢氧化氨
~ nitrate 硝酸铵
~ refrigeration system 氨制冷系统
~ storage cylinder 氨储存罐
~ vapour detection 氨蒸气检测

amortisseur [ə'mɔ:tisər] *n*. 阻尼器

amount [ə'maunt] *n*. 数量；*v*. 总计，等于
~ consumed 消耗量
~ of drift 偏航程
~ to 总计

amperage ['æmpɛəridʒ] *n*. 安培数

ampere ['æmpeə(r)] (A) *n*. 安培
~ turns 安培匝数，安匝

ampere-hour 安培小时，安时
~ capacity 安培小时容量，安时容量

amphibious [æm'fibiəs] *a*. 两栖的

ample ['æmpl] *a*. 充足的，丰富的

ampliate [æmpli'eit] *a*. 广大的，膨胀的

ampliator [æmpli'eitə] *n*. 放大器
~ winding 放大绕组

amplidyne ['æmpli,dain] *n*. 电机放大机

amplification [ˌæmplifi'keiʃən] *n*. 扩大，放大，放大率，放大过程的结果，扩充，引申 ‖ *Syn*. gain 增加，扩大率，倍率

amplifier ['æmplifaiə] *n*. 放大器，扩音器

amplify ['æmplifai] *v*. 放大，增强，增加，使变大，使强大，补充说明，引申，发挥，详述

amplifying ['æmplifai] *n*. 放大，增强，增加；*v*. (amplify 的 ing 形式) 放大，增强，增加，使变大，使强大，补充说明，引申，发挥，详述
~ element 放大环节

amplitude ['æmplitju:d] *n*. 振幅，幅度，广阔，丰富
~ distribution function 幅度分布函数
~ modulation (AM) 调幅
~ selector 振幅选择器

anaerobic [ˌæneiə'rəubik] *a*. 没有空气而能生活的，厌氧性的，厌氧的
~ bacteria 厌氧细菌
~ decomposition 无氧分解
~ digester 厌氧消化池
~ process 厌氧过程

analog [ə'næləg] (=analogue) *n*. 相似物，类似物，类似情况，模拟，对等的人；

a. 模拟数据的，模拟计算机的 ‖ digital 数字；数字式，数字的，数位的
　　～ circuit　模拟电路
　　～ equipment　模拟装置
　　～ recorder　模拟记录仪
　　～ regulator　模拟调节仪表
analog-digital (AD)　模拟数字，模数
　　～ converter　模拟数字转换器，模数转换器，AD 转换器
　　～ conversion　模拟数字转换，模数转换，AD 转换
analog-to-digital (AD)　模拟对数字的，模数的
　　～ converter　模拟数字转换器，模数转换器，AD 转换器
　　～ conversion　模拟数字转换，模数转换，AD 转换
analogous [ə'næləgəs] *a.* 类似的，相似的，可比拟的
analogue ['ænɔlɔg] (=analog) *n.* 相似物，类似物，类似情况，模拟，对等的人；*a.* 模拟数据的，模拟计算机的 ‖ digital 数字；数字式，数字的，数位的
analogue-digital (AD)　模拟数字，模数
　　～ converter　模拟数字转换器，模数转换器，AD 转换器
　　～ conversion　模拟数字转换，模数转换，AD 转换
analyse ['ænəlaiz] *v.* (=analyze) 分析，分解
　　～ mechanics　分析力学
analysis [ə'nælisis] *n.* 分析，分解
analytic [ˌænə'litik] *a.* (=analytical) 分析的，解析的
analytical [ˌænə'litikəl] *a.* (=analytic) 分析的，解析的
　　～ graph　分析图表，阐发图表，分析图

～ train　成套分析设备
analyze ['ænəlaiz] *v.* (=analyse) 分析，分解
anchor ['æŋkə] *n.* 锚，支撑点，系缚物，依靠，支柱，主持人；*v.* 抛锚，锚定，停泊，使稳固，使稳定，主持
　　～ arm　锚臂，锚杆
　　～ ball　锚泊球
　　～ bar　锚筋，锚着钢筋
　　～ beam　锚梁
　　～ bill　锚式擒纵叉爪
　　～ bolt　锚螺栓，锚栓，地脚螺栓
　　～ buoy　锚标，锚泊浮标，锚用浮标
　　～ cable　锚链，锚索，锚定索 ‖ ***Syn.*** anchor chain 锚链；anchor line 锚索，锚线，拉线；anchor rope 锚索；anchor wire 锚索，支持线
　　～ cable stopper　锚链制动器
　　～ capstan　起锚绞盘
　　～ chain wash nozzle　锚链洗净喷嘴
　　～ chock　锚座，锚架
　　～ crown　锚冠
　　～ device　锚固装置
　　～ dragging　走锚
　　～ fluke　锚爪
　　～ gate　锚柱门
　　～ gear　起锚设备
　　～ handling equipment　起抛锚设备 ‖ ***Syn.*** anchor handling machinery 起抛锚设备
　　～ impeller　锚式搅拌器
　　～ lamp　停泊灯，抛锚灯 ‖ ***Syn.*** anchor light 锚泊灯，停泊灯
　　～ link　锚链环
　　～ mouth　锚唇
　　～ pile　锚桩，锚杆
　　～ plate　锚板，锚固板，锚定板
　　～ pocket　锚穴，锚窝 ‖ ***Syn.*** anchor

recess 锚穴

~ pocket shutter 锚穴盖

~ pocket shutter gear 锚穴盖传动装置

~ point 锚点，锚固点，定位点

~ rod 地脚螺栓，基础螺栓

~ shackle 锚钩环，锚穿链扣，锚环

~ stock 锚柄

~ stopper 锚制动器

~ windlass 起锚机 ‖ *Syn*. windlass 起锚机

anchorage ['æŋkəridʒ] *n*. 锚地，泊地，抛锚，停泊，停泊费，固定的方式，加固的方式

~ berth 锚位

anchoring ['æŋkəriŋ] *n*. 系泊，抛锚，锚定；*v*. (anchor 的 ing 形式) 抛锚，锚定，停泊，使稳固，使稳定，主持

~ accessory 锚定件的加固钢筋，地脚钢筋

~ and weighting test of windlass on sea trial 锚机航行中抛起锚试验

~ equipment 锚泊设备

~ orders 抛起锚口令，锚令，锚泊口令

~ point 锚位，固定点

~ system 锚泊系统

anemometer [ˌæni'mɔmitə] *n*. 风速计，风力计

angle ['æŋgl] *n*. 角，角落，鱼钩，渔具；*v*. 谋取，猎取，追逐，钓鱼

~ adjustable spanner 弯头活络扳手，弯头活动扳手

~ bar 三角铁

~ brass grease lubricator 弯头铜滑脂杯

~ check valve 角止回阀

~ crane 斜座起重机

~ crowbar 弯头铁撬杆

~ flange 角铁凸缘

~ gauge 量角规

~ iron 角铁

~ of advance 提前角

~ of attack 攻角，迎角

~ of elevation 仰角

~ of intersection 相交角

~ of lag 移后角，落后角，滞后角

~ of tilt 倾斜角

~ of torque 扭转角

~ of view 视角

~ on 角度对准

~ pin 角度针，双角度针

~ plate 角板

~ scraper 带角度刮刀

~ stability 功角稳定

~ steel 角钢

~ valve 角阀，角通阀

angled ['æŋgld] *v*. (angle 的过去式和过去分词) 谋取，猎取，追逐，钓鱼；*a*. 成角的

~ deck 斜角甲板，斜向飞行甲板

angular ['æŋgjulə] *a*. 角的，有角的，用角测量的，用弧度测量的，生硬的，固执的，不让步的

~ acceleration 角加速度

~ contact ball bearing 向心推力球轴承，角接触球轴承

~ deviation 角度偏差，角偏差，角偏移

~ displacement 角位移，失调角

~ frequency 角频率

~ measurement 角度测量，角度观测

~ misalignment 角度错位，角度失准，管子接偏

~ position 角位，角位置，角坐标

~ rate 角速率

~ rotation 角旋转，角位移

~ speed 角速度 ‖ *Syn*. angular velocity 角速度

angularity [ˌæŋgju'læriti] *n*. 有角，角状，有角性，多角状态

anneal [ə'ni:l] *n*. 退火，焖火，锻炼，磨练；*v*. (使)退火，(使)加强，(使)坚强，(使)变硬

annealed [ə'ni:ld] *v*. (anneal 的过去式和过去分词) (使)退火，(使)加强，(使)坚强，(使)变硬；*a*. 退火的

~ copper foil 退火铜箔

annex [ə'neks] *n*. 附件；*v*. 并吞，附加

~ Ⅳ of MARPOL TREATY 73/78 MARPOL 73/78 公约附则Ⅳ

annexure [ə'nekʃə(r)] *n*. 附加物，附录

annual ['ænjuəl] *n*. 一年生植物，年刊，年鉴；*a*. 一年一次的，每年的，一年生的

~ inspection 年度检查，年检

~ repair schedule 年度修理计划

~ report 年度报告

~ survey 年度检验

annually ['ænjuəli] *ad*. 一年一次，每年

annular ['ænjulə] *a*. 环的，环形的，有环纹的

~ bearing 环形轴承

~ bit 环孔锥，环形钻

~ burner 环状燃烧器

~ clearance 环空间隙

~ core 环形铁芯

~ flow 环流，环形流

~ gap 环形间隙

~ gasket 环形垫片

~ gear 环形齿轮

~ nozzle 环形喷嘴

~ pad 环形盘

~ ring 环形圈

~ space 环形空隙，环形空间

annunciator [ə'nʌnʃieitə] *n*. 信号器，报警器，通告者

anode ['ænəud] *n*. 阳极，正极 ‖ *Syn*. positive pole 阳极，正极 ‖ *Ant*. cathode 阴极，负极；negative pole 阴极，负极

anodize ['ænəudaiz] *v*. 阳极电镀，作阳极化处理

anomaly [ə'nɔməli] *n*. 不规则，反常，异常，不按常规，异常的人，异常物，畸形

anti ['ænti] *n*. 反对者，反对论者；*a*. 反对的；*prep*. 对抗，反对

anti-accident 反事故的

~ measures 反事故措施

~ technical measures 反事故技术措施

anti-clockwise 反时针的，逆时钟方向的

~ direction 反时针方向

~ loop 反向环

~ moment 逆时针力矩

~ spin 反时钟旋转

anti-collision 防撞，避碰

~ light 避碰灯

anti-corrosion 防腐蚀，防腐，防锈

~ admixture 阻锈剂

~ cable 防腐电缆

~ materials 防腐材料，耐腐材料

~ mechanism 防腐机制，防腐机理

~ method 防腐方法

~ oil 防腐油

~ oil plug 防腐油塞

~ protection 防腐保护

~ system 防腐系统

~ treatment 防腐处理

~ zinc plate 防腐锌板
anti-corrosive 防腐蚀的，防腐的，防锈的，耐蚀的
　　~ agent 防腐剂，防蚀剂
　　~ coating 防腐涂层
　　~ measure 防腐措施
　　~ paint 防腐油漆
　　~ preparation 防腐制剂
　　~ primer 防锈底漆
　　~ seal 防腐密封
　　~ treatment 防腐处理，防蚀处理，防锈处理
anti-explosion 防爆，防爆作用
　　~ bulkhead stuffing box 舱壁防爆填料函
　　~ fuel 防爆燃料
　　~ machine 防爆电机
　　~ material 防爆材料
　　~ membrane 防爆膜
　　~ technology 防爆技术
　　~ watching window 防爆观察窗
anti-exposure 抗暴露
　　~ suit 抗暴露服，抗浸服，海上救生服
anti-foaming 防泡沫，防泡
　　~ additive 防泡沫添加剂
　　~ agent 防沫剂，防泡剂，消泡剂
　　~ property 抗泡性
anti-fog 防雾
　　~ spray 防雾喷剂
anti-fouling 防污，防垢
　　~ coating 防污涂料
　　~ composition 防污漆，防污剂
　　~ inhibitor 防垢剂
　　~ paint 防污漆
　　~ technology 防污技术
anti-friction 抗摩擦，抗磨
　　~ bearing 抗磨轴承
　　~ composition 抗磨剂，抗磨制品，减磨制品
　　~ grease 减磨润滑脂
　　~ metal 低摩擦金属
　　~ ring 抗磨圈
anti-oxidant 抗氧化剂
　　~ additive 抗氧化添加剂
　　~ anti-corrosion additive compound 抗氧化抗腐蚀添加剂
anti-phase 反相
　　~ current 反相电流
　　~ input 反相输入
　　~ synchronization 反相同步
　　~ wave 反相波
anti-pitching 减纵摇，抗纵倾
　　~ device 减纵摇装置
　　~ fins 减纵摇鳍
　　~ rudder 减纵摇舵
　　~ tank 减纵摇水舱
anti-pollution 抗污染的，防污染的，反污染的
　　~ ability 抗污染能力
　　~ check 防污染检验，防止污染检查
　　~ equipment 污染防治设备
　　~ measure 防污染措施
　　~ valve 防污染阀门
　　~ zone 防污染区
anti-roll 抗侧倾，抗摇晃，防滚
　　~ fins 减摇鳍
　　~ pump 减摇泵
anti-rolling 抗横摇，防滚动
　　~ bar 防倾杆
　　~ couple 抗摇力偶
　　~ device 减摇装置
　　~ effectiveness 减摇效果
　　~ fins 减摇鳍

~ rudder 减摇舵
~ system 减摇系统，减摇装置
~ system with two tanks 双水舱减摇系统
~ tank 减摇水舱
~ tank stabilization system 减摇水舱稳定系统，减摇水舱稳定装置 ‖ *Syn*. rolling tank stabilization system 水舱室减摇装置，水舱减摇装置

anti-rust 防锈
~ ability 防锈性
~ additive 防锈添加剂
~ cap 防锈帽
~ grease 防锈润滑脂
~ lacquer 防锈漆 ‖ *Syn*. anti-rust paint 防锈漆

anti-scale 防垢，阻垢
~ alloy 阻垢合金

anti-slip 防滑的
~ coating 防滑涂层
~ finish 防滑饰面
~ mat 防滑垫
~ panel 防滑镶板，防滑面板
~ performance 抗滑性能
~ stability 抗滑稳定性
~ tape 防滑贴

anti-smuggling 缉私
~ boat 缉私艇
~ codes 缉私法规
~ enforcement 缉私执法
~ information 缉私情报
~ institution 缉私体制
~ operation 缉私行动
~ patrol boat 缉私巡逻艇
~ system 缉私系统

anti-swing 防摇摆，防摇，消摆
~ bracing 防摇摆支柱
~ control 防摇摆控制
~ controller 防摇摆控制器
~ crane 防摇摆起重机
~ device 防摇摆装置

anti-wear 抗磨，防磨损
~ measure 抗磨措施
~ strength 抗磨强度
~ technology 抗磨技术

anticipate [æn'tisipeit] *v*. 预订，预见，预期，期望，过早使用，先人一着，占先

anticipated [æn'tisə,peitid] *v*. (anticipate 的过去式和过去分词) 预订，预见，预期，期望，过早使用，先人一着，占先；*a*. 预先的，预期的
~ loads encountered at sea 在波浪中遭遇到的预期载荷

antiskid ['æntiskid] *n*. 防滑装置
~ plate 防滑板

anvil ['ænvil] *n*. 铁砧，似铁砧物

aperture ['æpətjuə] *n*. 孔，穴，缝隙，光圈，孔径
~ angle 孔径角
~ atomizer 喷孔式喷油嘴
~ size 孔径尺寸

apex ['eipeks] *n*. 最高点，顶点，顶峰，尖端

APD (auxiliary propulsion drive) 辅助推进系统

apparatus [ˌæpə'reitəs] *n*. 器械，设备，装备，仪器，机构 ‖ *Syn*. appliance 用具，器具；arrangement 布置；assembly 组装部件；device 装置，设备；equipment 装备，设备，器材，装置；facility 设备，工具；furniture 设备，家具；gear 设备，装备；installation 设备，装置；machine 机器，机械，机

构；machinery 机器(总称)，机械；mechanism 机器,机械装置,机构；plant 设备；provision 装备,供应品；turnout 装备,设备；unit 装置,设备

apparent [ə'pærənt] *a*. 显然的，明显的，外观上的，貌似的
~ capacity 视在容量，表观容量，视在电容，表观电容
~ coordinates 视坐标
~ dip 视倾斜，视倾角
~ material 透明材料
~ pitch 视螺距，视在螺距
~ power 视在功率，表观功率
~ slip 视在滑距，视滑距，视滑流
~ slip ratio 视滑流比
~ viscosity 表观黏度

apparently [ə'pærəntli] *ad*. 显然地，明显地

appearance [ə'piərəns] *n*. 出现，露面，外貌，外观

append [ə'pend] *v*. 附加，添加，悬挂，设置数据文件的搜索路径

appendage [ə'pendidʒ] *n*. 附加物,附属肢体

appendix [ə'pendiks] *n*. 附录,附属,附属品,阑尾

appliance [ə'plaiəns] *n*. 器具,用具,装置,设备,器械 ‖ *Syn*. apparatus 器械,设备，仪器；arrangement 布置；assembly 组装部件；device 装置,设备；equipment 装备,设备,器材,装置；facility 设备,工具；furniture 设备,家具；gear 设备,装备；installation 设备,装置；machine 机器,机械,机构；machinery 机械(总称),机器；mechanism 机器,机械装置,机构；plant 设备；provision 装备,供应品；turnout 装备,设备；unit 装置,设备

applicability [ˌæplikə'biləti] *n*. 适用性,适应性

applicable ['æplikəbl] *a*. 可适用的，可应用的
~ coverage 适用范围
~ extinguishing agent 适用灭火剂
~ object 适用对象
~ value 适用值

applicant ['æplikənt] *n*. 申请者，请求者

application [ˌæpli'keiʃən] *n*. 请求，申请，申请表，应用，运用，施用，敷用，应用程序，应用软件 ‖ *Syn*. use 使用，利用，用途，效用；utility 效用，有用；utilization 利用
~ fee 申请费，报名费，申请费用
~ field 应用领域
~ for bunkering 加装燃油申请
~ form 申请表，申请表格，申请书
~ management 应用管理
~ range 应用范围

applicative ['æplikeitiv] *a*. 可适用的，合用的

applied [ə'plaid] *v*. (apply的过去式和过去分词) 申请，应用，适用，使用，运用，涉及，涂，敷，专心；*a*. 应用的，实用的
~ force 作用力，施加力，外加力
~ load 施加负荷，外加负载，外施载荷，使用负荷，外施载荷
~ materials 应用材料
~ pressure 外加电压，外加压力
~ range 应用范围
~ voltage 外施电压，外加电压
~ voltage test 外施电压试验

apply [ə'plai] *v*. 申请,应用,适用,使用,运用,涉及,涂,敷,专心

~ to 适用于，应用于，申请

appoint [ə'pɔint] v. 装设，布置，约定，指定，任命，委任，委派

appointment [ə'pɔintmənt] n. 固定设备，任命，委派，指派职位，约定，约会

apportion [ə'pɔ:ʃən] v. 分配，分摊

apportionment [ə'pɔ:ʃənmənt] n. 分配，分派，分摊

apposable [ə'pəuzəbl] a. 可并置的

appose [ə'pəuz] v. 并列，放…在对面

appraisal [ə'preizəl] n. 评价，估价，鉴定

apprentice [ə'prentis] n. 学徒；v. 当学徒

~ electrician 电工学徒

~ engineer 实习轮机员

~ fireman 实习生火工

~ officer 实习航海员，实习驾驶员

~ Seaman 三等兵

apprenticeship [ə'prentisʃip] n. 学徒的身份，学徒的年限，学徒期

approach [ə'prəutʃ] n. 接近，逼近，走进，方法，步骤，途径，通路；v. 接近，靠近，动手处理 ‖ *Syn*. means 手段，方法；method 方法，办法；way 路线，路途，方式

appropriate [ə'prəupriət] v. 占用，拨出；*a*. 适当的，恰当的，合适的

~ manner 适当方式

~ path 适当路径

~ procedure 适当程序

~ sequence 适当顺序

~ time 适当时间

appropriative [ə'prəuprieitiv] a. 专用的，可拨用的，充当的

approval [ə'pru:vəl] n. 赞成，赞许，承认，正式批准，官方批准

~ certificate 批准证书

~ date 批准日期

~ period 核准期限

~ procedure 批准程序，审核手续

~ request 申请批复

~ test 鉴定试验，验收试验

approve [ə'pru:v] v. 赞成，满意，批准，通过，同意，证实，证明

approx [ə'prɔks] ad. (=approximately) 近似地，大约，大概

approximate [ə'prɔksimeit] v. 近似，接近，接近，约计；a. 近似的，大约的

~ error 近似误差

~ number 近似数

~ reasoning 近似推理

~ value 近似值

~ weight 约计重量

approximately [əprɔksi'mətli] ad. (=approx) 近似地，大约，大概

approximation [ə,prɔksi'meiʃən] n. 近似值，接近，走近

appurtenance [ə'pə:tinəns] n. 器械，配件，设备，附件，附属物，从属权利

apron ['eiprən] n. 船坞平台，停机坪，堤坝平台，挡板，围裙

APU (auxiliary power unit) 辅助电源设备

aqua ['ækwə] n. 水，溶液，水剂，水绿色，浅绿色；a. 浅绿色的

aquatic [ə'kwætik] a. 水的，水上的，水生的，水栖的

~ adjustment 水中调整

~ life 水生生物 ‖ *Syn*. aquatic organism 水生生物

arbitrary ['ɑ:bitrəri] a. 任意的，武断的，专断的

~ constant 任意常数

~ moment 任意时刻，任意力矩

31

~ parameter 任意参数
~ sequence 任意序列
~ time 任意时刻
~ value 任意值

arbor ['a:bə] *n*. 柄轴,心轴,轮的转轴
~ collar 心轴轴环
~ flange (铣刀杆上的)盘式刀架,柄轴凸缘
~ support 柄轴支架,刀杆支架

arc [a:k] *n*. 弧,电弧,弧光,弓形,拱形物,拱;*v*. 形成拱状物,走弧线,循弧线行进
~ chute 电弧隔板,熄弧沟
~ cutting machine 电弧切割机
~ discharge 电弧放电,弧光放电
~ extinction contactor 消弧接触器
~ extinguishing chamber 灭弧室
~ extinguishing coil 灭弧线圈 ‖ *Syn*. arc quenching coil 消弧线圈; arc suppression coil 灭弧线圈,抑弧线圈
~ reignition 电弧重燃
~ voltage 弧电压,电弧电压
~ welding 弧焊
~ welding machine 弧焊机,电焊机,电弧焊机

arch [a:tʃ] *n*. 拱门,弓形结构,拱形;*v*. (使)弯成弓形;*a*. 主要的

architect ['a:kitekt] *n*. 设计师,计划者,建筑师

architecture ['a:kitektʃə] *n*. 部件的有序安排,结构,体系机构,建筑学,建筑术

arcing ['a:kiŋ] *n*. 电弧作用;*v*. (arc 的 ing 形式) 形成拱状物,走弧线,循弧线行进;*a*. 电弧的
~ back 回弧,逆弧
~ brush 跳火电刷

~ chamber 灭弧腔,消弧室,灭弧罩 ‖ *Syn*. arcing shield 灭弧罩
~ contact 电弧接点,辅助消弧触点,弧触头,灭弧触点
~ current 电弧电流
~ damage 弧伤害
~ device 电弧装置
~ distance 放电距离,弧距,火花间隙
~ earth 电弧接地 ‖ *Syn*. arcing ground 电弧接地
~ effect 弧光效应
~ fault 闪故障,闪络故障
~ flashover 弧络
~ gas 电弧气体
~ horn 角形避雷器,招弧角,消弧角保护放电间隙
~ over 电弧放电,电弧击穿,跳弧放电
~ period 飞弧时间
~ point 起弧点
~ process 电弧燃烧过程
~ ring 电弧环,屏蔽环,环形消弧器
~ time 电弧作用时间,发弧时间,飞弧时间,起弧时间,燃弧时间
~ tip 电弧接点,断弧触点,角弧触点
~ voltage 弧电压,跳火电压

arcover [a:'kʌvə(r)] *n*. 电弧放电,闪络,飞弧
~ voltage 弧络电压,电弧放电电压

Arctic ['a:ktik] *n*. 北极,北极圈;*a*. 北极的,北极区的
~ Ocean 北冰洋

area ['ɛəiə] *n*. 范围,区域,面积,地区,空地
~ controller 区域控制器
~ of free surface 自由液面区域
~ of responsibility 责任范围,责任区

~ of responsibility surrounding the ship 船舶周围的责任区

~ of safe operation 安全工作区

~ ratio of combustion chamber passage 燃烧室通道面积比

aerometer [,æri'ɔmitə] *n.* 液体比重计

argon ['a:gɔn] *n.* 氩

~ arc welding 氩弧焊

arise [ə'raiz] *v.* 起立，起来，上升，升起，出现，发生，形成，源自，起因于

arithmetic [ə'riθmətik] *n.* 算术，算法

~ logic unit (ALU) 算术逻辑单元，运算逻辑单元

arithmetical [,æriθ'metikəl] *a.* 算术的，算术上的

~ average 算术平均数

~ average method 算术平均法

~ unit 运算器

arm [a:m] *n.* 臂，臂状物，衣袖，海湾，武器，军种，军事行动，兵役，扶手，分部，权力，权威；*v.* 供给，提供，武装，备战，装备

armature ['a:mətjuə] *n.* 电枢，转子，衔铁，引铁，支架，爪，盔甲，牙齿

~ bar 电枢线棒，电枢导条

~ bearing 电枢轴承，电枢支座

~ bender 衔铁弯曲器

~ circuit 电枢电路

~ coil 电枢线圈，电枢绕组 ‖ *Syn.* armature winding 电枢线圈，电枢绕组

~ core 电枢铁芯，电枢芯

~ current 电枢电流

~ field 电枢磁场

~ leakage inductance 电枢漏磁电感

~ MMF wave 电枢磁动势波

~ paper 绝缘纸

~ reactance 电枢电抗

~ reaction 电枢反应

~ resistance 电枢电阻

~ resistance starting 电枢串电阻启动

~ rotor 电枢转子

~ shaft 电枢轴

~ spider 电枢辐，电枢辐式机架

~ spider pin 电枢十字架销

~ stop 衔铁档

~ stroke 衔铁行程

~ tester 电枢试验器，电枢测试装置

~ winding equalizer 电枢绕组均衡线，电枢绕组均压线

armed [a:md] *v.* (arm 的过去式和过去分词) 供给，提供，武装，备战，装备；*a.* 有扶手的，武装的，有防卫器官的

~ beam 加强梁

arrange [ə'reindʒ] *v.* 布置，安排，整理，排列，计划，准备，解决，协商，达成一致意见

arrangement [ə'reindʒmənt] *n.* 布置，安排，整理，排列，商议，协调，调解 ‖ *Syn.* apparatus 器械，设备，仪器；appliance 用具，器具；assembly 组装部件；device 装置，设备；equipment 装备，设备，器材，装置；facility 设备，工具；furniture 设备，家具；gear 设备，装备；installation 设备，装置；machine 机器，机械，机构；machinery 机械(总称)，机器；mechanism 机器，机械装置，机构；plant 设备；provision 装备，供应品；turnout 装备，设备；unit 装置，设备

~ diagram 布置图

~ of shafting 轴系布置

~ of wires 线路布置

~ plan 布置图

array [ə'rei] *n.* 排列，编队，军队，衣服，大批；*v.* 部署，穿着，排列

arrest [ə'rest] *n.* 制动装置，逮捕，拘留；*v.* 停止，阻止，逮捕，拘留，吸引，表现

arrester [ə'restə(r)] *n.* 制动器，防止装置，避雷器，捕拿者

~ brake 制动器

arresting [ə'restiŋ] *n.* 停止，阻止；*v.* (arrest 的 ing 形式) 停止，阻止，逮捕，拘留，吸引，表现；*a.* 引人注意的，可观的

~ device 制动装置，止动装置，止挡，卡子

~ gear 制动装置，稳定装置，停车装置

~ lever 止动杆

~ nut 止动螺母

arrival [ə'raivəl] *n.* 到来，到达，抵达，到达者，到达物

~ ballast 抵港压舱水，到港压载

~ book 到达登记簿

~ condition 抵港船况

arrive [ə'raiv] *v.* 到来，到达，抵达，发生，来临，成功，成名

arrow ['ærəu] *n.* 箭，箭头记号

~ head 箭头

~ line 箭头线

articulate [a:'tikjulit] *v.* 用关节相连，说话，明白表示，清楚表达；*a.* 有关节的，表达力强的，说话发音清晰的

articulated [a:'tikjulitid] *v.* (articulate 的过去式和过去分词) 用关节相连，说话，明白表示，清楚表达；*a.* 铰接的，枢接的，有关节的

~ arm 关节杆

~ beam 连接梁

~ conduit 分节管道

~ connecting rod 活节连杆，副连杆

~ coupling 铰链式联轴器

~ gear 链式减速齿轮

~ mechanism 铰链机构

~ pin 活节销

~ pipe 关节管，铰接管

~ steering 活节转向

~ support 活节支座

articulation [a:ˌtikju'leiʃən] *n.* 清晰度，接合，连接，连接方法，关节，表达，发音，说话

artificial [ˌa:ti'fiʃəl] *a.* 人造的，人工的，假的，非原产地的

~ draft 人工通风，人工通气 ‖ *Syn.* artificial ventilation 人工通风，人工通气

~ grounding device 人工接地装置

~ intelligence (AI) 人工智能

~ reef 人工礁，人工岛礁

~ respiration 人工呼吸

~ rubber 人造橡胶，合成橡胶

artificially [ˌa:ti'fiʃəli] *ad.* 人工地，人为地，不自然地

artisan [a:ti'zæn] *n.* 技工，工匠

as [æs] *ad.* 同样地，被看作，像；*prep.* 当作；*conj.* 与…一样，当…之时，像，因为

~ a function of 根据

~ a whole 作为一个整体，整体看来，总体上

~ built drawings 竣工图

~ follows 如下 ‖ *Syn.* as the following 如下

~ much 如此，实际和那个一样

~ much as 到…程度，差不多，实际上，虽然，即使

~ necessary 视为必要，如有必要，必要时
~ per sample 与样品相符
~ required 按要求，按需要
~ soon as possible 尽快，尽可能快地
~ soon as possible shipment 立即(迅速)装船
~ spare 作备件
~ well 也，一样，同样地
~ well as 以及，也，和…一样

asbestos [æz'bestɔs] *n.* 石棉
~ backing 石棉背垫
~ board 石棉板
~ cable 石棉电缆
~ cap 石棉帽
~ clay 石棉粉，石棉泥
~ cloth 石棉布
~ cord 石棉绳
~ fiber 石棉绒
~ gloves 石棉手套
~ insulation 石棉绝缘
~ lagging 石棉外套
~ overall 石棉工作服
~ packed cock 石棉衬套旋塞
~ packing 石棉垫料，石棉垫
~ paper 石棉纸
~ plate 石棉板
~ ring 石棉环
~ sheet 石棉片
~ shoes 石棉鞋
~ tape 石棉带，石棉扁带
~ thread 石棉线，石棉绳
~ wadding 石棉垫塞料

asbestos-insulated 石棉绝缘的
~ cable 石棉绝缘电缆
~ switchboard 石棉绝缘配电板

ascend [ə'send] *v.* 上升，攀登
ascent [ə'sent] *n.* 上升，提高，攀登，上坡路 ‖ *Ant.* descent 降下，降落
~ rate 上升速率，上浮速度
ascertain [ˌæsə'tein] *v.* 发现，查明，探知，确定
ash [æʃ] *n.* 灰，灰烬
~ content 灰含量
~ gun 吹灰枪，吹灰器
~ handling equipment 灰处理装置
~ removal 除灰
~ to be cleaned off 要清除的灰
ash-ejecting 冲灰
~ pump 冲灰泵
ashore [ə'ʃɔː] *ad.* 向岸地，靠岸边，在岸上，在陆地，到岸上
aside [ə'said] *ad.* 在旁边，到旁边
aspect ['æspect] *n.* 样子，外表，面貌，方面
~ ratio 展弦比，长宽比，纵横比，高宽比
asphalt ['æsfælt] *n.* 沥青
asphaltene [æs'fælten] *n.* 沥青质，沥青烯
~ content 沥青含量
asphyxiate [æs'fiksieit] *v.* (使)室息
asphyxiation [æsˌfiksi'eʃən] *n.* 室息
aspirate ['æspəreit] *v.* 吸气
aspiration [ˌæspə'reiʃən] *n.* 吸气，热望，渴望
ASS (Automatic Synchronized System) 自动同步系统，自动准同期装置
assemble [ə'sembl] *v.* 集合，装配，集会，集结，汇编 ‖ *Syn.* build in 安装，固定；fit 安装；fix 安装，(使)固定；fix assemblage 安装；install 安装；mount 安装；set up 装配，竖立，架起
~ product 组装产品

~ product components 组装产品构件

assembled [ə'sembld] *v.* (assemble 的过去式和过去分词) 集合，装配，集会，集结，汇编；*a.* 装配的，组合的，聚集的

~ camshaft 组合式凸轮轴

~ part 装配部件

~ propeller 组合螺旋桨

~ structure 装配式结构，组合结构

assembling [ə'sembliŋ] *n.* 装配，组合；*v.* (assemble 的 ing 形式) 集合，装配，集会，集结，汇编；*a.* 装配的，组合的

~ bolt 装配螺栓，组合螺栓

~ clearance 装配间隙

~ nut 装配螺母

assembly [ə'sembli] *n.* 组装部件，集合，装配，集会，集结，汇编 ‖ ***Syn.*** apparatus 器械，设备，仪器；appliance 用具，器具；arrangement 布置；device 装置，设备；equipment 装备，设备，器材，装置；facility 设备，工具；furniture 设备，家具；gear 设备，装备；installation 设备，装置；machine 机器，机械，机构；machinery 机械(总称)，机器；mechanism 机器，机械装置，机构；plant 设备；provision 装备，供应品；turnout 装备，设备；unit 装置，设备

~ area 装配场，装配区，集合空域

~ bolt 装配螺栓

~ chain tension adjuster 装配链条张紧调节装置

~ cost 组装成本

~ drawing 装配图，组装图，总成图

~ fixture 装配架

~ floor 装配平台，装配车间

~ joint 组合接头

~ line 装配线

~ order 装配订单

~ plan 组合施工图

~ shop 装配车间，组合工场，装配工场

~ station 组装台，装配站

assess [ə'ses] *v.* 评估，评定，估价，估计，估算

assessment [ə'sesmənt] *n.* 评估，评定，估价，估计，估算

assessor [ə'sesə] *n.* 技术顾问，评估人，估价人，估税人

assign [ə'sain] *v.* 分配，指派，赋值

assignment [ə'sainmənt] *n.* 分配，委派，任务，(课外)作业

assist [ə'sist] *n.* 帮助，机械辅助装置；*v.* 援助，帮助，支援，出席

~ in 协助，帮助

~ to 辅助，帮助

assistance [ə'sistəns] *n.* 协助，援助，补助，国家补助

assistant [ə'sistənt] *n.* 助手，助教；*a.* 辅助的，助理的

~ electrical engineer 助理电气工程师，电助

~ engineer 轮机助理，轮助，副工程师，助理工程师

~ manager 副经理

~ officer 驾助，人事助理

~ radio officer 助理报务员

~ chief steward 管事部副经理

assisted [ə'sistid] *v.* (assist 的过去式和过去分词) 援助，帮助，支援，出席；*a.* 辅助的

~ circulation boiler 辅助循环锅炉

~ draft 强制通风，辅助通风 ‖ ***Syn.*** assisted draught 辅助通风，人工通风

associate [ə'səuʃieit] *n.* 合作人，同事；*v.* 使联系，使联合，交往，结交；*a.* 副的

associated [ə'səuʃieitid] *v.* (associate 的过去式和过去分词) 使联系，使联合，交往，结交；*a.* 联合的，关联的
~ equipment 辅助设备，相关设备
~ reaction 联合反应

association [ə,səusi'eiʃən] *n.* 协会，联合，结交，联想

assort [ə'sɔt] *v.* 相称，相配，协调，提供，分类，归类
~ with 相称，协调

assorted [ə'sɔ:tid] *v.* (assort 的过去式和过去分词) 相称，相配，协调，提供，分类，归类；*a.* 多样混合的
~ brass 杂铜

assurance [ə'ʃuərəns] *n.* 确信，断言，保证，担保，发誓，肯定，人寿保险，保险
~ coefficient 安全系数，保险系数 ‖ *Syn.* assurance factor 安全系数；coefficient of safety 安全系数；safety coefficient 安全系数；safety factor 安全系数
~ company 保险公司
~ factor of output of electric power plant 电站输出功率安全系数

astatic [æ'stætik] *a.* 无定向的，不安定的
~ governor 无定向调节器，恒速调速器
~ regulator 无定位调节器
~ wattmeter 无定向瓦特计

astern [əs'tə:n] *ad.* 在船尾，向船尾
~ cam 倒车凸轮
~ direction 倒车方向
~ exhaust cam 倒车排气凸轮
~ firing 艉向发射
~ guardian valve 倒车保护阀
~ ignition cam 倒车点火凸轮
~ maneuvering valve 倒车操纵阀
~ nozzle 倒车喷嘴
~ oil cylinder 倒车油缸
~ output 倒车出力，倒车功率 ‖ *Syn.* astern power 倒车功率
~ revolution 倒车转速
~ stage 倒车级
~ turbine 倒车涡轮机，倒车透平

asymmetric [æsi'metrik] *a.* 不均匀的，不对称的 ‖ *Ant.* symmetric 相称性的，均衡的

asymptote ['æsimptəut] *n.* 渐近线

asymptotic [,æsimp'tɔtik] *a.* 渐近线的，渐近的
~ stability 渐近稳定性，渐近稳定度

asynchronism [ei'siŋkrənizəm] *n.* 不同时性，异步(性)

asynchronization [əsiŋkrənai'zeiʃən] *n.* 异步，非同步化 ‖ *Ant.* synchronization 同步，同一时刻

asynchronize [ei'siŋkrənaiz] *v.* (使)异步 ‖ *Ant.* synchronize (使)同步，(使)同时发生

asynchronous [ei'siŋkrənəs] *a.* 不同时的，异步的 ‖ *Ant.* synchronous 同时的，同步的
~ AC generator 异步交流发电机
~ machine 异步电机
~ modulation 异步调制
~ motor 异步电动机，感应电动机
~ reactance 异步电抗

at [æt] *prep.* 在，于，向，对准，在…方面
~ any rate 无论如何，不管怎样，至少
~ every step 每走一步，步步
~ least references 最少的引用
~ most references 最多的引用

37

~ the bottom of 在…的底部

~ the commencement of the watch 在值更开始时

~ the first sign 一有迹象

~ the forward end 在前端

~ the left 在左边

~ the loading terminal 在装货码头，在装料站

~ the peak of 在…高峰期

~ the rate of 按…之速度，按…比率

at-sea (在)海上

~ replenishment 海上补给

ATC (automatic timing corrector) 自动时间校正器

athwart [ə'θwɔ:t] *ad.* 横跨着,斜穿过,逆,相反；*prep.* 横过，反对，逆

athwartship [ə'θwɔ:tʃip] *a.* 横过船的

~ axis 横轴

~ bulkhead 横舱壁

~ bunker 横燃料舱

~ inclination 横倾

~ leg 横向支管

~ moment 横向力矩

~ plane 横剖面，横向面

~ signature 横向(物理场)特征

~ stability 横稳性

~ tank 横舱，横柜

Atlantic [ət'læntik] *n.* 大西洋；*a.* 大西洋的

~ Ocean 大西洋

atmosphere ['ætməsfiə] *n.* 大气，空气，气氛，大气压力 ‖ *Syn.* ambiance 周围环境，气氛；ambience 周围环境，气氛；ambient 周围环境；circumstances 环境；environment 环境，外界，周围；surroundings 环境

~ discharge pipe 大气放出管

atmospheric [,ætməs'ferik] *a.* 大气的，朦胧的，模糊的，有气氛的

~ corrosion 大气腐蚀

~ corrosion resistant steel 耐候钢

~ diving suits (ADS) 大气式潜水衣

~ drain tank 大气压式排泄柜

~ exhaust 大气排气

~ pollution 大气污染

~ pressure 大气压力，大气压

atoll [æ'tɔl] *n.* 环礁，环状珊瑚礁

~ reef 环礁，环状珊瑚礁

atomic [ə'tɔmik] *a.* 原子的，原子能的，微粒子的

~ absorption spectroscopy 原子吸收光谱，原子吸收光谱法，原子吸收光谱学

~ energy 原子能

~ hydrogen welding 原子氢焊

~ powered ship 原子动力船

~ propulsion 原子推进

atomization [,ætəmai'zeiʃən] *n.* 分离成原子，雾化

atomize ['ætəmaiz] *v.* 使分裂为原子，雾化

atomizer ['ætəmaizə] *n.* 雾化器，喷雾器

atop [ə'tɔp] *ad.* 在顶上；*prep.* 在…的顶上

ATS (automatic transform system) 自动切换系统，厂用电源快速切换系统

attach [ə'tætʃ] *v.* 缚上，系上，贴上，配属，隶属于

~ to 附加，附上，重视

attached [ə'tætʃt] *v.* (attach 的过去式和过去分词) 缚上，系上，贴上，配属，隶属于；*a.* 附上的，附着的，附加的

~ cable 固定电缆

~ bulwark 舷边连接墙

~ cavities 附着空泡

~ clause 附加条件

~ pump 辅助泵，附属泵 ‖ *Syn*. auxiliary pump 辅助泵；donkey pump 辅助泵；service pump 辅助泵

~ sheet 附页，附单，附寄

attachment [ə'tætʃmənt] *n*. 附件，附加装置，配属

attack [ə'tæk] *n*. 进攻，攻击，抨击，批评，疾病发作，侵袭；*v*. 攻击，抨击，动手处理

~ ship 攻击舰

~ transport 武装运输舰，登陆人员运输舰，攻击作战运输舰

attain [ə'tein] *v*. 达到，获得，得到

attainable [ə'teinəbl] *a*. 可到达的，可获得的，可得到的

attained [ə'teind] *v*. (attain 的过去式和过去分词) 达到，获得；*a*. 达到的

~ pose drift 实际位姿漂移

~ subdivision index 达到的分舱指数

attemperator [ə'tempəreitə] *n*. 保温器，保温装置

attend [ə'tend] *v*. 出席，参加，照顾，照看，护理，注意，专心，留意，伴随

attendance [ə'tendəns] *n*. 出席，出席人数，伺候，照料

attended [ə'tendid] *v*. (attend 的过去式和过去分词) 出席，参加，照看，照顾，护理，注意，专心，留意，伴随；*a*. 有人照看的，伴随的

~ machinery space 有人值班机舱

~ mode 连接方式

~ operation 连接操作，伴随操作

~ station 值班台

~ time 值班时间

attention [ə'tenʃən] *n*. 注意，关心，关注，注意力，(口令)立正

~ line 注意线

attenuate [ə'tenjueit] *v*. 衰减，削弱，减弱，稀释

attenuation [ə,tenju'eiʃən] *n*. 衰减，变薄，稀薄化，变细

~ factor 衰减因数，衰减因子，衰减常数，衰减系数

attenuator [ə'tenjueitə(r)] *n*. 衰减器

attorney [ə'tə:ni] *n*. 律师，代理人

attract [ə'trækt] *v*. 吸引，有吸引力，引起注意

attributable [ə'tribjutəbl] *a*. 可归于…的

attribute [ə'tribju(:)t] *n*. 属性，品质，特征，加于，归结于

audibility [,ɔ:di'biliti] *n*. 可听到，能听度

audible ['ɔ:dəbl] *a*. 听得见的

~ alarm 声音报警，音响报警，音响报警器

~ and visual alarms 声光报警，声音和视觉报警，声光报警(器)，声音和视觉报警(器)

~ sound 可听见的声音，可听声

audio ['ɔ:diəu] *n*. 声音回路，声音信号；*a*. 音频的，声频的，声音的

audio-output 音频输出

~ device 音频输出设备

audion ['ɔ:diən] *n*. 三极管 ‖ *Syn*. triode 三极管

auger ['ɔ:gə] *n*. 螺丝钻 ‖ *Syn*. gimlet 手钻，螺丝锥

augment [ɔ:g'ment] *n*. 增加，加大；*v*. 增加，增大，扩大，加强

~ ability 可扩充性

~ of resistance 阻力增加

augmentation [,ɔ:gmen'teiʃən] *n*. 增加，增

加率，增加物

auric ['ɔ:rik] *a*. 金的，含金的，似金的，正金的，三价金的

~ salt humidity controller 金属盐式湿度控制器

auto ['ɔ:təu] *n*. (=automobile) 汽车；*v*. 乘汽车

auto-alarm 自动报警,自动报警装置 ‖ *Syn*. automatic alarm 自动报警，自动报警装置

~ receiver 自动紧急受信机

auto-clean 自动清洗

~ strainer 自动清洗滤器

auto-ranging 自变换量程，自动变换范围

~ power supply 自动适应电压电源

auto-starting 自动启动，自启动

~ air compressor 自动启动空气压缩机

auto-stop 自动停止，自停止

~ mechanism 自动停止机构，自动停车机构

~ protection 自动停止保护，自动停车保护

~ system 自动停止系统，自动停车系统

auto-transformer 自耦变压器

~ starter 自耦变压器启动器

~ starting 自耦变压器启动

autogenous [ɔ:'tɔdʒinəs] *a*. 自生的

~ cutting 气割

~ electrification 自起电

~ welding 氧炔焊

autographic [,ɔ:təu'græfik] *a*. 亲笔写成的

~ chart 自记图表

~ pyrometer 自动记录高温计

~ recorder 自动记录表

~ recording thermometer 自动记录温度计

autoignition [,ɔ:tɔi'niʃən] *n*. 自动点火，自燃

~ point 自燃点

automate ['ɔ:təmeit] *v*. 使自动化，自动操作，通过自动化控制或操作

automated ['ɔ:təumeitid] *v*. (automate 的过去式和过去分词) 使自动化，自动操作，通过自动化控制或操作；*a*. 自动化的

~ contingency plan 自动应急方案，自动应急计划

~ machine 自动化机器，自动化机械

~ welding 自动焊接

automatic [,ɔ:tə'mætik] *n*. 自动装置，自动武器，半自动武器；*a*. 自动的，自动调节的，半自动的，无意识的，机械的

~ air (circuit) breaker 自动空气断路器

~ air release valve 自动排气阀

~ alarm 自动报警,自动报警装置 ‖ *Syn*. auto-alarm 自动报警，自动报警装置

~ alarm receiver 自动警报接收器

~ alarm system 自动报警系统

~ alarming test for fire detector 火警检测器自动报警试验

~ and hand operation change-over switch 自动手动转换开关

~ arc welding 自动电弧焊

~ back flushing filter 自动反冲洗滤器

~ balancing 自动平衡

~ balancing line 平衡自动线

~ brake 自动制动，超速制动

~ burette 自给滴定管

~ changeover 自动转向机构

~ circuit breaker 自动开关，自动断路器

~ close-up device of standby supply 备用电源自动关闭装置

~ combustion control 燃烧自动控制
~ combustion regulating system 燃烧自动调节系统
~ compensation 自动补偿
~ constant tension towing winch 自动恒张力拖缆机
~ control 自动控制
~ control sequence 自动控制序列
~ control system 自动控制系统
~ control system for marine electric power plant 船舶电站自动控制系统
~ control theory 自动控制理论
~ controller test for auxiliary boiler 辅锅炉自动控制装置试验
~ cut-out device 自动切断装置
~ deaerating valve 自动除气阀
~ defrost 自动除霜
~ detection 自动检测，自动探测
~ device 自动装置
~ diesel and generator control unit 柴油机与发电机自动控制装置
~ discharge 自动放电，自动卸料，自动排放
~ distributor of active power 有功功率自动分配器
~ distributor of reactive power 无功功率自动分配器
~ equipment 自动设备
~ expansion valve 自动膨胀阀
~ explosion suppression system 自动抑爆系统
~ feed 自动进刀，自动进给，自动给料
~ feed water regulating system 自动给水调节装置
~ feed water regulator 自动给水调节器

~ filter cleaning 滤器自动清洗
~ fire alarm system 自动火灾报警系统
~ fire detection system 自动火灾探测系统
~ fire extinguisher 自动灭火器
~ fire extinguishing alarm system 自动灭火报警系统
~ fire signal 自动火灾信号，自动火警信号
~ fire sprinkler 自动洒水灭火装置
~ frequency and load regulator 自动调频调载器
~ frequency regulator 自动调频器
~ fuel shut off 自动停止进入燃料
~ fuse 自动熔断，自动熔丝
~ generation control (AGC) 发电机组功率输出自动控制，出力自动控制
~ governing test of voltage and frequency for main generator (emergency generator) 主发电机(应急发电机)电压与频率自动调节试验
~ hydraulic capacity control device 自动液压能量控制装置
~ Identification System (AIS) 自动识别系统
~ inspection 自动检查
~ interlock 自动联锁
~ intrusion detection device 自动入侵检测装置
~ lathe 自动车床
~ load control (ALC) 自动负载控制，自动载荷控制
~ load limitation 自动减负载(装置)
~ load-release system 自动卸载系统
~ load-sharing device 自动分载装置
~ machine 自动机床，自动机械

~ main engine remoter control 主机自动远程控制，主机自动遥控
~ manual station 自动手动操作器
~ marine boiler control 船用锅炉自动控制
~ measurement 自动测量
~ mode 自动化模式，自动模式，自动方式
~ mooring winch 自动系泊绞车
~ oil discharge device 自动排油装置
~ oil outlet valve 自动出油阀
~ operation 自动操作，自动运算，按钮控制
~ oscillograph 自动示波器
~ parallel off 自动解列
~ parallel operation 自动并车运行
~ parallel operation system for generating set 发电机组自动并车运行系统
~ pilot 自动驾驶仪 ‖ *Syn*. autopilot 自动驾驶仪
~ positioning 自动定位
~ power generating system 自动发电系统
~ power regulator 功率自动调节器
~ protection 自动保护(装置)
~ protective system 自动保护系统，自动防护系统
~ pump control 自动泵控制
~ recording hygrometer 自动湿度计
~ regulation 自动调节，自动调整，自控
~ regulator 自动调整器，自动调节器
~ release gear 自动释放装置，自动解扣机构
~ remote control system 自动远程控制系统，自动遥控系统
~ replenishing valve 自动补给阀
~ safety cut-out device 自动安全切断装置
~ safety device 自动安全装置，自动保护装置
~ set-up 自动设置
~ shut-down device 自动停车装置
~ slow down 自动减速
~ smoke type fire alarm 感烟式火灾自动报警器
~ sprinkling fire-extinguishing system 自动喷水灭火系统
~ star-delta starter 自动星形-三角形启动器
~ starter for prime mover 原动机自动启动装置
~ starting 自动启动
~ starting device 自动启动装置
~ start-stop control 自动启停控制
~ station 自动电台
~ steering 自动转向
~ substation 自动变电所，自动变换站
~ supply test of emergency generator 应急发电机自动供电试验
~ switch 自动开关
~ switchgear for parallel operation 并车运行自动开关装置
~ switching 自动开关，自动转换
~ Synchronized System (ASS) 自动同步系统，自动准同期装置
~ synchronizing device 自动同步装置
~ synchronizing indicating device 自动同步指示装置
~ system 自动系统，自动装置
~ telephone 自动电话
~ tension mooring winch 自动张力绞缆机 ‖ manual tension mooring winch 手动张力绞缆机

~ test system 自动测试系统
~ testing 自动检测
~ thermo type fire alarm 测温式火警自动报警器 ‖ *Syn.* air temperature automatic fire alarm 测温式火警自动报警器; automatic thermal type fire alarm 测温式火警自动报警器
~ timing corrector (ATC) 自动时间校正器
~ towing winch 自动拖缆机
~ tracking 自动跟踪,自动跟踪仪
~ tracking aids 自动跟踪辅助设备
~ transform system (ATS) 自动切换系统,厂用电源快速切换系统
~ transmission 自动传输,自动传送,自动传动装置
~ unloading control 自动卸载控制
~ valve 自动阀
~ voltage regulation (AVR) 自动电压调节
~ voltage regulator (AVR) 自动电压调节器
~ water level control 水位自动控制
~ water regulating valve 自动水量调节阀
~ welding 自动焊接

automatically [ɔ:tə'mætikəli] *ad.* 自动地,机械地,无意识地
~ defrost 自动除霜

automation [ɔ:tə'meiʃən] *n.* 自动化,自动学,自动控制,自动操作,自动状态
~ equipment 自动化设备
~ instrument 自动化仪表
~ of electric systems 电力系统自动化

automaton [ɔ:'tɔmətən] *n.* 自动机器,机器人

automooring [ɔ:tə'mɔ:riŋ] *n.* 自动系泊,自动锚泊
~ system 自动系泊系统,自动锚泊系统

autonomous [ɔ:'tɔnəməs] *a.* 自治的
~ underwater vehicle (AUV) 自主式水下潜器,自主水下载具
~ working 独立工作

autopilot ['ɔ:təpailət] *n.* 自动驾驶仪,自动舵 ‖ *Syn.* automatic pilot 自动驾驶仪
~ navigator 自动驾驶领航仪

autothermic [ɔ:təu'θə:mik] *a.* 热自动补偿的
~ piston 防热变形活塞

autotimer ['ɔ:təutaimə] *n.* 自动定时器

AUV (autonomous underwater vehicle) 自主式水下潜器,自主水下载具

auxiliary [ɔ:g'ziljəri] *n.* 机帆船,辅助性船只,辅助者,助手,外国援军; *a.* 辅助的,补助的,从属的,后备的,备用的
~ air compressor 辅助空气压缩机,辅空压机
~ and emergency diesel control station 辅助与应急柴油控制站
~ appliance for lighting system 照明系统附具
~ ballast tank 辅助压载柜
~ blower 辅助风扇,辅助鼓风机
~ boiler 辅助锅炉,副锅炉 ‖ *Syn.* donkey boiler 辅助锅炉,副锅炉
~ boiler automatic control system 辅助锅炉自动控制系统
~ boiler room 辅锅炉舱
~ boiler suitable for burning oil residues 适于燃烧油渣的辅助锅炉
~ circuit 辅助电路
~ circulating pump 辅循环泵
~ compress 辅助压缩
~ condenser 辅机冷凝器,辅助冷凝器
~ condenser circulating pump 辅助冷

凝器循环泵

~ cruiser 辅助巡洋舰，改装巡洋舰

~ device 辅助设备 ‖ *Syn*. auxiliary equipment 辅助设备，备用设备，附属设备；auxiliary machine 辅助机，备用机器；auxiliary machinery 辅助机械

~ diesel engine 辅助柴油机

~ energy 辅能量

~ engine 辅助发动机，辅机，副机

~ engine log book 辅机日志

~ engine room 辅机舱

~ engine sailer 机帆船

~ exhaust 辅机排气

~ exhaust range 辅机排气系统

~ feed check valve 辅助给水止回阀

~ feed line 辅给水系统

~ feed pump 辅给水泵

~ field 辅助场，辅助磁场，辅助电场

~ function 辅助功能

~ generator 辅助发电机

~ gunboat 改装炮舰

~ heat 辅助热

~ hose rigs 辅助软管设备

~ machinery room 辅机舱

~ material 辅助材料，辅助原料，辅料

~ memory 辅助存储器 ‖ *Syn*. auxiliary storage 辅助存储器

~ motor 辅助电动机

~ oil pump 辅助油泵

~ operating lever 辅助操作杆

~ operation 辅助操作，辅助作业

~ power supply 辅助电源

~ power unit (APU) 辅助电源设备

~ propulsion drive (APD) 辅助推进系统

~ protection 辅助保护

~ pump 辅助泵 ‖ *Syn*. attached pump 辅助泵；donkey pump 辅助泵；service pump 辅助泵

~ relay 中间继电器，辅助继电器

~ relay for control supply 控制电源中间继电器

~ rudder 副舵

~ rudder head 副舵杆头

~ scavenge blower 辅助扫气机

~ service 附属服务设备，附属服务

~ shaft 副轴

~ ship 辅助舰，辅助船

~ spring 副簧

~ starting valve 辅助启动阀，副启动阀

~ steam 辅助蒸汽，辅蒸汽

~ steam stop valve 辅助截汽阀

~ steam pipe 辅助蒸汽管，辅蒸汽管，副气管，副出气管

~ steering gear 辅助舵机，辅助操舵装置

~ stop valve 辅助制动阀，辅助短流阀

~ switchboard 辅助配电盘，辅配电盘，副配电板 ‖ *Syn*. sub switchboard 副配电板

~ system 辅助系统

~ tank 辅助柜，辅助水槽，(潜艇)调整水舱

~ valve 辅助阀

~ vessel 辅助船舶

~ winding 辅助绕组

avail [ə'veil] *n*. 效用，利益；*v*. 有益，有利，有帮助，有用

availability [ə,veilə'biliti] *n*. 可用性，有效性，实用性

available [ə'veiləbl] *a*. 可用到的，可利用的，有用的，有空的，接受探访的

~ energy 可用能量

~ heat 有用热量，可用热量

average ['ævəridʒ] *n.* 平均，平均水平，平均数，海损；*v.* 平均为，均分，使平衡，达到平均水平，买进，卖出；*a.* 一般的，通常的，平均的
~ discharge voltage 平均放电电压
~ error 平均差，平均误差
~ power 平均功率
~ specific heat 平均比热
~ speed for heaving anchor 起锚平均速度
~ temperature 平均温度
~ value 平均值
~ voltage 平均电压

avoid [ə'vɔid] *v.* 避免，消除，远离，逃避，防止发生，使作废，逐出

avoidable [ə'vɔidəbl] *a.* 可避免的

avoidance [ə'vɔidəns] *n.* 避免，避开，离开，废除令

AVR (automatic voltage regulation) 自动电压调节

AVR (automatic voltage regulator) 自动电压调节器

awash [ə'wɔʃ] *a.* 与水面齐平的，被浪冲打的，随波逐流的，冲平的，洗刷的，充斥的，泛滥的；*ad.* 淹没地，覆盖地，被海水冲洗地

aweigh [ə'wei] *a.* 起锚的，刚离开水底的；*ad.* 离开海底

awl [ɔ:l] *n.* 锥子，尖钻
~ pricker 锥子

awning ['ɔ:niŋ] *n.* 遮阳篷，雨篷
~ boom 天篷梁，天遮杆
~ deck 遮盖甲板，遮阳甲板，天幕甲板，天帘甲板
~ deck vessel 遮盖甲板船，天幕甲板船，遮阳甲板船 ‖ *Syn*. awning decker 遮盖甲板船，天幕甲板船，遮阳甲板船
~ jackstay 天遮撑杆
~ pole 纵向天篷支柱
~ rafter 天遮主梁，天遮脊梁，天遮纵木 ‖ *Syn*. awning ridge 天遮主梁，天遮脊梁，天遮纵木
~ side stops 天遮边系索
~ spar 天遮横木
~ stanchion 天篷支柱
~ stops 天遮系索
~ stretcher 天遮撑

axe [æks] *n.* 斧, (经费的)大削减

axial ['æksiəl] *a.* 轴的，轴向的，成轴的，沿轴的，轴上的
~ advance 轴向进速
~ blade clearance 轮叶轴向间隙
~ blower 轴流鼓风机
~ clearance 轴向间隙，纵向间隙
~ compression 轴挤压，轴向压缩，轴压
~ compressor 轴向式压缩机，轴流压气机
~ deformation 轴向形变
~ direction 轴向
~ displacement 轴向位移
~ flow 轴向流动，轴流
~ flow compressor 轴流式压气机
~ (flow) fan 轴流风机，轴流式通风机，轴流式扇风机
~ (flow) pump 轴流泵 ‖ *Syn*. propeller pump 旋浆泵，轴流泵
~ flow turbine 轴流涡轮机
~ force 轴向力，轴线力
~ impermeability 纵向密封性
~ length 轴长，轴向长度
~ line 轴线
~ load 轴向负荷，轴向载荷，轴向负载
~ load bearing 轴向承载轴承
~ loading 轴向载荷

45

~ movement 轴向运动，轴向位移
~ oil 轴油
~ piston hydraulic motor 轴向柱塞液压马达
~ piston hydraulic pump 轴向柱塞液压泵
~ piston pump 轴向柱塞泵，轴向活塞泵 ‖ *Syn*. axial plunger pump 轴向柱塞泵，轴向活塞泵
~ pitch 轴向节距
~ play 轴隙，轴向间隙，轴向游
~ plunger 轴向柱塞，轴向活塞
~ plunger type oil motor 轴向柱塞式油马达
~ stern ramp 尾直跳板
~ strain 轴向应变
~ stress 轴向应力
~ symmetry 轴向对称
~ thrust 轴向推力
~ thrust bearing 轴向推力轴承，轴向止推轴承
~ velocity 轴向速度
~ velocity ratio 轴向速度比
~ vibration 轴向振动
~ vibration damper 轴向振动阻尼器，轴向减震器，轴向减震装置
~ vibration of shafting 轴系轴向振动，传动轴轴向振动

axially ['æksiəli] *ad*. 向轴的方向

axis ['æksis] *n*. 轴
  ~ guide 轴套
  ~ inclination 轴倾度
  ~ of oscillation 振荡轴，摆动轴
  ~ of weld 焊接线

axle ['æksl] *n*. 轮轴，车轴，轴端
  ~ box 轴箱 ‖ *Syn*. journal box 轴箱
  ~ load 轴载荷，轴负荷

azimuth ['æziməθ] *n*. 方位，方位角，射弹的侧位偏差
  ~ compass 方位罗经
  ~ mirror 方位镜
  ~ table 方位表
  ~ thruster 方位推进器
  ~ vane 方位标

B

Babbit ['bæbit] *n*. 巴比特(人名)
  ~ layer 巴氏合金层
  ~ metal 巴比特合金，巴比合金，巴氏合金

back [bæk] *n*. 背部，背面，后面，后部，脊骨，脊柱，反面；*v*. 后退，支持，背靠，加固，支持，后援，引证，证明，逆时针转向；*a*. 后面的，在后面，早过去的，过时的，向后的；*ad*. 向后地
~ and forth 来回地
~ connected 背后连接的
~ cover 后壳，后盖，后罩，封底
~ feed 反馈，回授
~ fire 反燃，反焰
~ flashover 反向闪络
~ flush 反向冲洗
~ flushing 反向冲洗
~ haul 空载传输，返航，回送
~ header 后汽鼓，后汽筒
~ into 倒航撞上，倒车撞上
~ of ring 活塞环内表面
~ plate 底板
~ pressure 背压
~ pressure circuit 背压回路
~ pressure regulator 背压调节器
~ pressure sensor 背压式传感

~ pressure trip 背压脱扣

~ pressure valve 背压阀

~ roll entry 背滚式入水

~ seal 倒密封，回密封，背密封

~ support ring 背撑环

~ to back 背靠背，背对背

~ up 备份，援助，支持点

~ weld 封底焊道

back-to-back 靠背的，紧接的

~ ring 背靠背密封圈

~ test 成对试验

backbone ['bækbəun] n. 脊椎，中枢，骨干，支柱，意志力，勇气，毅力，决心

backfire [bæk'faiə(r)] n. 逆火

backflow ['bækfləu] n. 逆流，流向来源

background ['bækgraund] n. 背景，后台，不显眼的位置，经历，素养，衬底，底子

~ contamination 本底污染

~ noise 本底噪声

backing ['bækiŋ] n. 后盾，认可，赞成，衬背，援助，支持者，赞助者；v. (back 的 ing 形式) 后退，支持，背靠，加固，支持，后援，引证，证明，逆时针转向

~ board 垫板，载模板

~ device 衬垫装置

~ off angle 后角

~ off cone clutch 反转离合器

~ off lathe 铲齿车床，铲工车床

~ pass 封底焊道

~ resistance 倒航阻力

~ ring 垫环

~ rudder ship 倒车舵船

~ run 封底焊

~ strip 背垫条，衬板，垫板，衬里

~ structure 垫衬结构

~ wind 逆转风

backlash ['bæklæʃ] n. 齿轮隙，游隙，后冲，反撞，反撞力，反斜线，后座，缠结，激烈反应

~ characteristic 间隙特性

backplane ['bækplein] n. 底板

backstay ['bækstei] n. 桅杆，后部支索撑物

backup ['bækʌp] n. 备份，文件备份，后援，支持，阻塞；v. 做备份；a. 候补的，支持性的

~ and recovery 备份与恢复 ‖ *Syn.* backup and restore 备份与恢复

~ battery 后援电池

~ copy 备份

~ device 备份装置

~ fuse 保险丝

~ protection 后备保护

~ relaying 后备继电保护

~ ring 背撑环，垫圈

~ roll 支承辊

backward ['bækwəd] a. 向后的，相反的，逆向的，返回的，落后的，不愿做的，不情愿的，羞涩的

~ roll entry 镰刀式入水

backwards ['bækwədz] ad. 向后地，倒逆地，相反地，回溯地，退步地

backwash ['bækwɔʃ] n. 浪涛，逆流，反响

bacterial [bæk'tiəriəl] a. 细菌的

~ colony 细菌菌落

~ corrosion 微生物腐蚀

bacterium [bæk'tiəriəm] n. (pl. bacteria) 细菌

baffle ['bæfl] n. 障板，阻板，隔板，折流板，隔音板；v. 困惑，阻碍，为难

~ filter 挡板过滤器

~ plate 挡板，隔板

~ ring 挡环，隔环

~ scrubber 挡板式洗涤器

~ separator 挡板式分离器

~ wall 分水墙

bag [bæg] *n.* 气囊，囊状物，袋子，猎获物，兴趣，技巧；*v.* 装入，(使)鼓胀，松散地垂挂，获得，捕获，得到占有权

~ accumulator 皮囊式蓄能器

~ dredge 海底挖泥机

~ house 堆袋室，袋滤捕尘室

~ type accumulator 皮囊式蓄能器

~ type strainer 布袋滤器，滤袋

baggage ['bægidʒ] *n.* 行李，行装，辎重

~ gage carriage 行李架 ‖ *Syn.* baggage gage holder 行李架

~ gage compartment 行李舱，行李间 ‖ *Syn.* baggage gage room 行李间

bagged [bægd] *v.* (bag 的过去式和过去分词) 装入，(使)鼓胀，松散地垂挂，获得，捕获，得到占有权；*a.* 松弛下垂的，袋装的，喝醉的

~ cargo 袋装货物

bake [beik] *n.* 烘烤；*v.* 烘焙，烤，烧硬

bakelite ['beikəlait] *n.* 酚醛塑料，人造树胶，胶木，电木

~ junction box 胶木接线盒

~ rod 胶木棒

~ toggle switch 胶木拨动开关

~ turning switch 胶木旋转开关

baking ['beikiŋ] *n.* 烘焙；*v.* (bake 的 ing 形式) 烘焙，烤，烧硬

~ finish 烘漆，烘烤涂料

balance ['bæləns] *n.* 秤，天平，平衡，收支差额，结余，余额，资产平稳表；*v.* 平衡，称，权衡，对比，结算

~ check 平衡检验，零位检查

~ connection 平衡连接

~ equation 平衡方程

~ gas 平衡气

~ of power 均势，势力均衡

~ oil hole 平衡油孔

~ ratio 平衡比

~ shaft 平衡轴

~ spring 游丝

~ state 平衡状态

~ tank 平衡油柜，平衡油罐，平衡储槽

~ test 平衡实验，平衡测试

~ valve 平衡阀

~ weight 平衡重，配重，平衡器

~ weight fitting bolt 平衡块紧配螺栓

balanced ['bælənst] *v.* (balance 的过去式和过去分词) 平衡，称，权衡，对比，结算；*a.* 平稳的，安定的，和谐的

~ beam relay 平衡杆式继电器

~ cable 平衡电缆，对称电缆

~ circuit 平衡回路

~ condition 平衡状态

~ connection 平衡连接

~ cylinder 平衡缸

~ diaphragm 平衡式隔膜，等压

~ force 平衡力

~ groove 平衡槽

~ impact modulator 平衡冲流型元件

~ line 补偿管路

~ linkage 平衡连锁

~ load 对称负载，对称荷载，平衡负载，均衡负载 ‖ *Syn.* balancing load 对称负载，对称荷载，平衡负载，均衡负载

~ piston 平衡活塞

~ piston type relief valve 平衡活塞式安全阀

~ pressure vane pump 平衡叶片泵 ‖ *Syn*. balanced vane pump 平衡叶片泵
~ ratio 平衡比
~ relay 平衡继电器
~ relay core 平衡继电器芯
~ relief valve 平衡安全阀
~ rotor vane pump 平衡转子式叶片泵
~ rudder 平衡舵
~ seal 平衡式密封
~ self-sealing coupling 平衡式自封接头
~ spring 平衡弹簧
~ system 平衡系统
~ type cylinder 平衡式缸
~ type mechanical seal 平衡式机械密封
~ valve 平衡阀
~ vane motor 平衡式叶片马达

balancing ['bælənsiŋ] *n*. 平衡，结算，调零装置；*v*. (balance 的 ing 形式) 平衡，称，权衡，对比，结算
~ capacitor 平衡电容器
~ capacity 平衡容量
~ equipment 平衡装备
~ load 对称负载，对称荷载，平衡负载，均衡负载 ‖ *Syn*. balanced load 对称负载，对称荷载，平衡负载，均衡负载
~ machine 平衡机
~ piston 平衡活塞
~ test of armature 电枢平衡试验
~ valve 平衡阀，等量分流阀

bale [beil] *n*. 大包，大捆，货物；*v*. 打包，捆包，包装，灾难，痛苦，悲哀
~ capacity 包装容量，包装容积
~ press 填料压机，打包机
~ specification 扎捆明细单
~ strapping 打捆，打包

~ weight 打包重量

ball [bɔːl] *n*. 球，球状物，子弹，炮弹，舞会，尽情地玩
~ bearing 滚珠轴承
~ bearing slewing rim 滚珠轴承定位边
~ cage 滚珠隔离圈，滚珠轴承罩
~ check valve 球式单向阀
~ element 动球式元件
~ float 浮球，球状浮体
~ head 球形头，飞球头
~ joint 球窝接合，球窝接头
~ mill 球磨
~ pein hammer 圆头铁锤
~ piston motor 球塞马达
~ piston pump 球塞泵
~ rolling 钢球轧制
~ screw 滚珠螺杆，滚珠丝杆，球头螺钉
~ sleeve 球面卡套
~ type device 动球式元件
~ type directional control valve 球式换向阀
~ valve 球阀

ballast ['bæləst] *n*. 压舱物，压载，稳定因素，镇重物，沙囊；*v*. 提供压舱物 ‖ *Ant*. deballast 排放压舱水
~ arrangement 压载布置
~ branch pipe 压载水支管 ‖ *Syn*. branch ballast line 压载水支管
~ coil 镇流线圈，负载线圈
~ condition 压载状态，压载船况
~ keel 压载龙骨
~ main 压载水总管 ‖ *Syn*. water ballast main 压载水总管
~ movement 压舱物移动
~ oily water separator 压载水油水分离器
~ pump 压载泵，镇定泵，平衡泵

~ resistance 镇流电阻，镇定电阻，平稳电阻

~ suction pipe 压载水吸入管

~ system 压载系统，镇流系统

~ tank 压载舱，压载箱，压载水舱

~ trial 压载试航

~ water 压载水，压舱水

~ water exchange at sea 海上压载水置换

~ water management (BWM) 压载水管理

~ Water Management Convention 压载水管理公约，压载水公约

~ water management guideline 压载水管理指南

~ Water Management System (BWMS) 压载水管理系统

~ water treatment plant 压载水处理装置

~ water treatment standard 压载水处理标准

Baltic ['bɔ:ltik] *a*. 波罗的海的，波罗的诸国的，波罗的语的

~ and International Maritime Council (BIMCO) 波罗的海国际海事协会

~ Sea 波罗的海

ban [ba:n] *n*. 禁令；*v*. 禁止，取缔

band [bænd] *n*. 带子，镶边，波段，队，乐队；*v*. 联合，结合

~ brake 带闸

~ gap 带隙，能隙

~ gap voltage reference 电压带隙基准

~ pass filter 带通滤波器

~ saw 带锯

~ saw blade 带锯条

~ sawing machine 带锯机

~ seal 密封包带

~ viscometer 带状黏度计

banjo ['bændʒəu] *n*. 班卓琴，五弦琴

~ union 鼓形管接头

bank [bæŋk] *n*. 银行，堤，岸，沙洲，浅滩，堆，层，储藏库；*v*. 存于银行，储蓄，倾斜转弯

~ tube 管束

bar [ba:(r)] *n*. 条，棒，横木，栅，障碍物，酒吧间；*v*. 禁止，阻挡，妨碍，关门；*prep*. 除…之外

~ chart 条形图，条线图 ‖ *Syn*. bar graph 条形图，条线图

~ code 条形码，条码，条形代码

~ code reader 条形码读出器

~ commutator 铜条整流子

~ davit 圆形吊艇柱，圆柱形吊柱

~ keel 方龙骨，矩形龙骨

~ magnet 磁棒，杆磁铁

bare [bɛə] *v*. 使赤裸，露出；*a*. 赤裸的，无遮蔽的，空的

~ board 空板，裸印制板

~ boat charter 无条件租船

~ cable 裸电缆，裸缆

~ conductor 裸线，裸导线，裸导体

~ contract 接触不良，不良接点，不附担保的契约

~ displacement 裸船排水量，裸排水量

~ engine 无辅助设备发动机，光机

~ live part 裸带电部分

~ metal 裸金属，裸露金属

~ minimum 最低限度，最小限度，最起码

barge [ba:dʒ] *n*. 驳船，游艇；*v*. 用船运输，蹒跚，闯入

~ carrier 载货驳船，载驳船

~ derrick 浮式转臂吊车，船式起重机

~ drilling 驳船钻井，浮船钻井

～ in 闯入，干涉，打断
～ into 闯入，与…相撞
～ mooring 囤船
～ pole 驳船撑竿
～ price 驳船价

barnacle ['ba:nəkl] n. 藤壶，难以摆脱的东西，难以摆脱的人

barograph ['bærəugra:f] n. 自动气压计

barometer [bə'rɔmitə] n. 气压计
～ mercury 水银气压表，水银气压计

barometric [bærəu'metrik] a. 大气压力的

barothermogragh [bærəuθə:məg'ra:f] n. 自动压力温度表

barred [ba:d] v. (bar 的过去式和过去分词) 禁止，阻挡，妨碍，关门；a. 隔绝的，被禁止的，有铁条的，有木栅的
～ code 受阻码
～ speed range 禁用转速范围

barrel ['bærəl] n. 桶，圆筒，活塞筒，滚筒，枪管；v. 装入桶内，高速行驶；a. 桶状的，像桶的
～ core 心形轴，筒状芯
～ face 圆筒面
～ plating 滚镀
～ shaft 筒轴
～ skirt 筒裙
～ tumbling 转鼓抛光，转鼓除边
～ type tappet 筒形挺杆

barrier ['bæriə] n. 障碍物，分开物，隔离物，栅栏，屏障，挡板，壁垒，关卡，界线，限制
～ reef 堡礁

barring ['ba:riŋ] v. (bar 的 ing 形式) 禁止，阻挡，妨碍，关门；prep. 除非，不包括，除…以外
～ gear 盘车装置，曲柄移位装置，曲轴变位传动装置
～ rod 盘车撬棒，支杆
～ torque 盘车力矩

barrow ['bærəu] n. 手推车

base [beis] n. 底部，基础，根据地，基地，本部，基数，出发点；v. 基于，以…作基础；a. 卑鄙的，低级的
～ area 底面积，根据地
～ circle (齿轮的)基圆
～ coordinate system 基座坐标系
～ course 基础课程，基本课程，基层
～ film surface 基膜面
～ line 基线，底线，基准线
～ load 基本载重，基本负载
～ material 基材，基础材料，基本材质
～ metal 基本金属
～ mounting 底座安装
～ oil 基油
～ on 基于，以…为依据
～ plane 基准平面，基面，底平面
～ plate 基座板，底板，基板
～ point 原点
～ quantity 基本量
～ ring 基区环，基座圈，底环，底座圈
～ speed of an adjustable-speed motor 调速电动机基本速度
～ station 基台，基站
～ stock 基本原料，基本组分，基本汽油，(油)基

basic ['beisik] n. 基本，要素，基础；a. 基本的，碱性的
～ circuit 基本回路
～ component 基础部件，基本成分
～ design 基本设计
～ function 基本功能
～ insulation level (BIL) 基本绝缘水平

~ material 碱性材料，基本材料
~ neutralization number 碱性中和值
~ number 底数，基数
~ symbol 基本符号
~ testing 分批试验法
~ type cylinder 基本型缸

basically ['beisikəli] *ad.* 基本上，主要地

basin ['beisn] *n.* 盆，盆地，水池
~ spring coupling 面盆弹簧掀式龙头
~ turning coupling 面盆旋式龙头

basis ['beisis] *n.* 基础，基本，根据，主要成分，主要要素，基本原则，基本原理
~ material 基体材料，基体资料，基体，基础材料

basket [ba:skit] *n.* 篮，一篮
~ drier 篮式干燥机
~ strainer 篮式粗滤器

batch [bætʃ] *n.* 一批，一炉，批处理
~ manufacturing 批量制造
~ number 批号，批次号码，分批编号
~ operation 配料作业，分配操作，分批操作，分批式操作
~ operation method 分批作业法
~ processing 分批处理，批处理
~ quantity 批量，一次的量
~ size 批尺寸

bateau [bæ'təu] *n.* 小舟

bath [ba:θ] *n.* 沐浴，浴室
~ curve 浴缸曲线
~ tub curve 浴盆曲线
~ shower 沐浴花洒

bathtub ['ba:θtʌb] *n.* 浴缸，澡盆
~ section combustion chamber 浴缸式燃烧室

batten ['bætn] *n.* 板条，木条，固定板条，船舱周框的压条；*v.* 用板条固定，用木板钉牢

battening ['bætniŋ] *n.* 压紧；*v.* (batten 的 ing 形式) 用板条固定，用木板钉牢
~ arrangement 压紧装置 ‖ *Syn.* battening device 压紧装置
~ bar 舱围压条
~ iron 封舱塞条，货舱口压条，压条
~ wedge 封舱木楔，封舱楔

battery ['bætəri] *n.* 电池，电池组，蓄电池，连续猛击，排炮，列炮，炮架，殴打 ‖ *Syn.* cell 电池；accumulator 蓄电池
~ capacity 蓄电池容量
~ charging 蓄电池充电
~ charging and discharging board 蓄电池充放电板 ‖ *Syn.* battery charging and discharging panel 蓄电池充放电板
~ charging room 蓄电池充电室
~ circuit 电池电流
~ hydrometer 蓄电池液体比重计
~ maintenance 蓄电池维护
~ panel 电池盘，电池屏
~ room 蓄电池室，蓄电池舱
~ room exhaust blower 蓄电池舱通风机
~ room ventilation 蓄电池舱通风
~ storage locker 电池储存柜
~ switchboard 蓄电池配电板
~ voltage 电池电压
~ voltage meter 电池电压表

battery-powered 电池供电的，电池驱动的，电池动力的
~ hand-lamp 干电池手提灯，蓄电池手提灯

battle ['bætl] *n.* 战役，战争；*v.* 作战，战斗，搏斗，斗争
~ ship 战舰

bay [bei] *n.* 海湾，隔间部分，隔室，分

隔舱，军舰等的医务室，壁凹，绝路，狗吠声；v. 使走投无路
~ plan 箱位图，预配图，集装箱船积载图

bayonet ['beiənit] n. (电)卡销，刺刀
~ base lamp holder 卡口灯座
~ base receptacle 卡口插座灯座
~ flange 卡口法兰
~ type quick release coupling 卡口式快速接头

BBDC (before bottom dead center) 下止点前，下死点前

BC Code (Code of Safe Practice for Solid Bulk Cargoes) 固体散货安全操作规则

BCD (binary coded decimal) 二-十进制代码，二进码十进数，BCD 代码

BCD (Buoyancy Control Device) 浮力调节装置 ‖ **Syn**. Buoyancy Control Jackets 浮力调节背心

BCS (burner control system) 燃烧器控制系统

BDC (bottom dead center) 下止点，下死点 ‖ **Syn**. lower dead center (LDC) 下止点，下死点

be [bi:] prep. 是，在，存在
~ based on 基于
~ covered by 被覆盖

beach [bi:tʃ] n. 海滩
~ bar 滩坝

beacon ['bi:kən] n. 灯塔，烟火；v. 照亮

beam [bi:m] n. 梁，横梁，桁条，(光线)束，柱，电波；v. 播送
~ bracket 横梁肘板
~ compass 长臂圆规，横杆圆规
~ deflection element 流束偏转型元件
~ of light 光束
~ structure 梁结构

bear [bɛə] n. 熊；v. 负担，忍受，带给，具有，挤，向

bearer ['bɛərə] n. 送信人，搬运者
~ service 运载服务，承载业务

bearing ['bɛəriŋ] n. 轴承，关系，方面，意义，方向，方位；v. (bear 的 ing 形式) 负担，忍受，带给，具有，挤，向
~ alignment 方位对准
~ bracket 轴承架，托座，支架
~ bush 轴瓦，轴承衬
~ bush lower half 轴瓦下半块
~ cage 轴承罩
~ cap 轴承盖
~ capacity 承载能力，轴承能力
~ clearance 轴承间隙，轴承游隙
~ fittings 轴承配件
~ flange 轴承法兰，轴承凸缘
~ force 承压力
~ housing 轴承壳，轴承壳体，轴承座
~ knock 轴承撞击
~ length 导向长度
~ liner 轴承衬，轴承瓦
~ load 轴承负载，轴承载荷
~ lubrication 轴承润滑
~ lubrication system 轴承润滑系统
~ metal 轴承合金，轴瓦合金
~ pad 轴承垫，乌金轴瓦
~ plate 承压盘，承重盘
~ processing equipment 轴承加工机
~ reaction 轴承反力，支座反力
~ ring 导向套
~ separator 轴承分离器
~ shell 轴瓦，轴承壳套
~ shell upper half 轴瓦上半块
~ sleeve 轴承座套
~ steel 轴承钢
~ structure 轴承结构，承载结构，承重

结构，支承结构

~ support 轴承支持，轴承支撑，轴承支架

~ wear 轴承磨损

Beaufort ['bəufət] n. 蒲福(① 姓氏；② 19世纪英国海军上将，定义了风力等级)

~ scale 蒲福风级

bed [bed] n. 床，基础，路基，河底，海底，一堆，一层；v. 安置，嵌入，使睡，上床，分层

~ type milling machine 床式铣床

~ plate 底板，座板

~ plate bearing 主轴承

~ plate girder 基座纵桁

~ plate transverse member 底座横隔板

before [bi'fɔ:] ad. 在前，以前；prep. 在…之前；conj. 在…之前，与其…宁可

~ bottom dead center (BBDC) 下止点前，下死点前

~ repair 修理前

~ test 试验前，考试前

~ upper dead center (BUDC) 上止点前，上死点前

behind [bi'haind] ad. 在后面；prep. 在…之后

~ schedule 落后于预定计划，晚点，误期，误点

bell [bel] n. 铃，钟

~ book 车钟簿

~ crank 直角形杠杆，双臂曲柄，曲拐

~ curve 钟形曲线

~ mouth 喇叭口，漏斗口，钟形口

bell-shaped 钟形的

~ curve 钟形曲线

~ format 钟形结构

~ nozzle 钟形喷嘴

~ pulse 钟形脉冲

~ rotor 钟形转子

~ valve 钟形阀

belleville ['belvil] n. 酸模(一种食用植物)

~ spring 盘形弹簧，碟形弹簧，贝氏弹簧

bellow ['beləu] n. 波纹管，轰鸣声，吼叫声

~ expansion joint 膨胀节波纹管

bellows ['beləuz] n. (bellow的复数) 波纹管，风箱，风箱状物，咆哮

~ boot 波纹管防护罩

~ combination 波纹管组件

~ gauge 波纹管压力计，膜盒式压力计 ‖ Syn. bellows manometer 波纹管压力计，膜盒式压力计

~ pressure gauge 波纹管压力表

~ pressure switch 波纹管压力继电器

~ pump 隔膜泵

~ sealing valve 波纹管密封阀

~ thermostat 波纹管节温器

~ type accumulator 波纹管式蓄能器

~ type cylinder 波纹管缸

~ type pressure gauge 波纹管式压力表

~ type pressure switch 波纹管压力继电器

~ valve 波纹管阀

below [bi'ləu] ad. 在下，在页底；prep. 在…下面

~ deck 甲板下，甲板下部

belt [belt] n. 带子，地带，传送带；v. 环绕，包围，系

~ conveyer 皮带输送机，带式运输机

~ drive 皮带传动，皮带驱动 ‖ Syn. belt transmission 皮带传动，皮带驱动

~ filter 带式过滤器

~ pulley 皮带盘，皮带轮

~ punch pliers 接合带冲钳

~ tensioner 皮带松紧调整器

bench [bentʃ] n. 船中的横坐板，工作台，陈列台，长椅子
~ comparator 比长仪，台式比测仪
~ top supply 工作台电源
~ vice 台虎钳，台用虎钳

benchmark [bentʃ'ma:k] n. 基准，基准点；v. 标准检查

bend [bend] n. 弯曲；v. 弯曲，专心于，屈服
~ axis type axial piston motor 弯轴式轴向柱塞马达 ‖ *Syn.* bend axis type axial plunger motor 弯轴式轴向柱塞马达
~ axis type axial piston pump 弯轴式轴向柱塞泵 ‖ *Syn.* bend axis type axial plunger pump 弯轴式轴向柱塞泵
~ axis type hydraulic motor 弯轴式液压马达
~ axis type piston pump 弯轴式柱塞泵
~ factor 抗弯系数
~ friction factor 弯曲摩擦系数
~ loss 弯头损力
~ radius 弯管半径

bender ['bendə] n. 弯曲物，弯腰者，屈服者

bending ['bendiŋ] n. 弯曲(度)，挠度；v. (bend 的 ing 形式) 弯曲，专心于，屈服
~ angle 挠曲角，弯曲角
~ block 折刀，弯型块
~ fatigue 挠曲疲劳，弯曲疲劳
~ force 弯曲力，弯力，弯辊力
~ joint 曲节
~ load 弯曲荷载
~ machine 弯曲机，折弯机，弯折机
~ moment 弯矩，弯曲力矩，弯曲矩
~ moment curve 弯矩曲线
~ radius 弯曲半径，曲半径，折弯半径
~ roll 弯曲辊
~ strength 抗弯强度，抗折强度，折弯强度
~ stress 弯曲应力，弯应力，挠曲应力，挠应力
~ vibration 弯曲振动

bent [bent] n. 倾向，爱好；v. (bend 的过去式和过去分词) 弯曲，专心于，屈服；a. 弯曲的
~ frame 排架，弯肋骨，烘弯肋骨
~ handle fixed-socket hexagonal spanner 弯柄固定套筒六角扳手
~ pipe 弯管，弯头
~ portion 弯曲部分
~ spanner 弯头扳手
~ tube 曲管
~ tube boiler 曲管锅炉

berth [bə:θ] n. 停泊处；v. (使)停泊
~ light 寝台灯，床头灯
~ term 泊位条款，停泊期

berthing [bə:θ] n. 停泊地，船边或隔间的钢板；v. (berth 的 ing 形式) (使)停泊
~ bollard 靠泊系船柱

best [best] n. 最佳状态，最好的东西，最佳作品；a. 最好的；ad. 最好地，最，极
~ mode 最佳方式，最佳模态
~ orientation 最有利方位
~ quality 最好质量

between [bi'twi:n] prep. (=tween) 在…之间，连接，由…协力合作
~ deck 中层甲板，甲板间
~ deck frame 甲板间肋骨
~ deck pillar 甲板间支柱

~ deck space 甲板空间，甲板间舱
~ deck stanchion 甲板间支柱
~ deck tonnage 甲板间容积
~ flywheel and generator 飞轮和发电机之间

bevel ['bevəl] n. 斜角，斜角规，倾斜，斜面；v. (使)成斜角
~ angle 斜角，坡口角度
~ gauge 测角器，量角器，斜角规，曲尺
~ gear 锥齿轮
~ gearing 锥齿轮装置
~ joint 斜削接头
~ protractor 量角规，斜量角规
~ pulley 锥轮
~ seat valve 斜座阀
~ valve 斜角阀，斜阀
~ welding 斜角焊

bevelled ['bevəld] v. (bevel 的过去式和过去分词) (使)成斜角；a. 斜切的，开坡口的，带坡口的，锥形的

bevelled-ege 边缘坡口
~ oil control ring 边缘坡口油环

beyond [bi'jɔnd] n. 远处；ad. 在远处；prep. 在(到)…较远的一边，超过，那一边
~ repair 无法修复，无法补救

bi-drum 双汽包，双鼓筒
~ boiler 双汽包锅炉，双鼓筒锅炉

bi-rotational 双向的，能反转的
~ pump 双旋转泵

biannual [bai'ænjuəl] a. 一年二次的

bias ['baiəs] n. 斜线，偏差，偏压，偏见，偏爱；v. 使存偏见
~ flow 偏流流量
~ pressure 偏压

biased ['baiəst] v. (bias 的过去式和过去分词) 使存偏见；a. 有偏的，结果偏倚的
~ valve 承载阀

bidirectional [,baidi'rekʃənəl] a. 双向的
~ element 双向滤芯
~ relief valve 双向溢流阀
~ triode thyristor 双向三极晶闸管

big [big] a. 大的，重要的；ad. 夸大地，顺利地
~ push 大力推进

bight [bait] n. 曲线

BIL (basic insulation level) 基本绝缘水平

bilateral [bai'lætərə] a. 双向的，两面的，双边的
~ circuit 双向电路
~ contract 双边合同，双边契约
~ control 双向控制
~ filter 双边滤波器
~ rotation 双向旋转
~ servomechanism 双向伺服阀机构
~ symmetry 两侧对称
~ transducer 双向传感器，双向变换器，双向换能器

bilge [bildʒ] n. 舱底，舭，船身靠内侧最低的部分，船底污水；v. 使船舭漏水，把舭部破开，突出，膨胀
~ alarm system 污水报警系统
~ and ballast system 舱底和压载系统
~ automatic discharging device 舱底水自动排出装置
~ block 舭墩
~ bracket 舭肘板
~ branch pipeline 舱底水分支管路
~ compartment 浸水舱
~ eductor 舱底水排泄器
~ ejector 舱底水喷射器

~ injection valve 舱底喷水阀，污水喷射阀

~ keel 舭龙骨

~ longitudinal 舭纵桁，舭纵骨

~ main 舱底水总管，疏水总管

~ mud box 舱底水过滤箱 ‖ *Syn*. bilge sludge box 舱底水过滤箱；rose box 舱底水过滤箱，眼板箱

~ pipe 舱底水管

~ piping 舱底水管系

~ plug 舭部放水塞，底边放水栓

~ pump 舱底污水泵，海水潜水泵

~ radius 底边半径，舱底半径

~ sounding pipe 污水测深管，舭部边舱水深探管

~ strainer 舱底水过滤器

~ strake 舭列板

~ suction 舱底水吸口，舱底吸水管

~ suction strum plate 舱底水吸口滤板，舱底吸水管滤板

~ suction valve 舱底水吸入阀

~ system 舱底水系统，污水系统

~ tank 污水舱，水柜

~ vortex 舭涡

~ water 舱底水，舱底污水，毫无价值的话

~ water separator 舱底水分离器

~ water system 舱底水系统

~ well (舱底)污水井

bill [bil] *n*. 账单，钞票，票据，清单，议案，法案，广告；*v*. 用海报宣传，列表，开账单

~ of loading 提货单，提单

BIMCO (Baltic and International Maritime Council) 波罗的海国际海事协会

bimetal [bai'metl] *n*. 双金属材料，双金属器件

~ plate 双金属板

~ relay 双金属继电器

~ strip 双金属条

~ tube 双金属管，复合管

bimetallic [ˌbaimi'tælik] *a*. 双金属的

~ joints 双金属接头

~ thermometer 双金属温度计，双金属温度表

~ strip 双金属条

bimotor ['baiˌməutə] *a*. 双发动机的

bin [bin] *n*. 箱柜，二进制文件的扩展名

binary ['bainəri] *a*. 二进位的，二元的

~ circuit 二进制电路

~ element 二进位单元，二进制单元，二进制码元，二进制元件，二进制元素，双态元件

~ refrigeration 二元制冷

~ system 二进记数制，二进位制，二进制，二进制系统

binary-to-decimal 二进制对十进制的，二进制十进制的，二-十进制的

~ conversion 二进制十进制转换，二-十进制转换

binary-to-hexadecimal 二进制对十六进制的，二进制十六进制的，二-十六进制的

~ conversion 二进制二十六进制转换，二-十六进制转换

bind [baind] *n*. 捆绑，困境，讨厌的事情；*v*. 绑，约束，装订，包扎，凝固，结合

binder ['baində] *n*. 装订工，包扎者，黏合剂，包扎工具，临时契约

binding ['baindiŋ] *n*. 装订，捆绑，黏合物；*v*. (bind 的 ing 形式) 绑，约束，装订，包扎，凝固，结合；*a*. 有约束力的，

捆绑的

biochemical [baiəu'kemikəl] a. 生物化学的
~ analysis 生物化学分析
~ degradation 生物化学降解
~ reaction 生物化学反应，生化反应

biodegradable [ˌbaiəudi'greidəbl] a. 生物所能分解的

biodegradation [ˌbaiəudigrei'deiʃən] n. 生物降解

biofilter [ˌbaiəu'filtə] n. 生物过滤器，细菌过滤器
~ method 生物过滤器法

biological [baiə'lɔdʒikəl] a. 生物学的
~ catalyst 生物催化剂
~ feedback system 生物反馈系统
~ sewage treatment plant 生物污水处理装置
~ treatment 生物处理

biphase [bai'feiz] a. 双相的

bipolar [bai'pəulə] a. 有两极的，双极的
~ electric motor 双极电动机
~ plate 双极板
~ winding 双极焊接

bistable [bai'steib(ə)l] a. 稳态的，双稳定的
~ device 双稳元件 ‖ *Syn*. bistable element 双稳元件
~ directional valve 双稳换向阀

bit [bait] n. 位，比特，小块，少量，片刻；v. 控制

bite [bait] n. 咬，咬伤，一口，刺痛，固定器，腐蚀；v. 咬，刺痛，握住，攥住，抓住，腐蚀，侵蚀
~ fitting 卡套式管接头

bitt [bit] n. 系缆柱，缆柱；v. 系于缆柱 ‖ *Syn*. bollard 系船柱，带缆桩，护柱

bitter ['bitə] a. 苦的，严酷的，痛苦的，怀恨的
~ end 索端，最后痛苦的结局

bitumen ['bitjumin] n. 沥青
~ anticorrosive paint 沥青防锈漆
~ emulsion 沥青乳浊液
~ product 沥青产品

bituminous [bi'tju:minəs] a. 含沥青的
~ paint 沥青漆

black [blæk] n. 黑色，黑颜料；v. (使)变黑，涂黑；a. 黑色的，弄脏了的，忧郁的
~ adhesive tape 黑胶带
~ anticorrosive paint 黑防锈漆
~ box testing approach 黑箱测试法
~ enamel paint 黑磁漆
~ gas pipe 对缝焊接管
~ heat resisting paint 黑色耐高温漆
~ insulating tape 黑色绝缘胶布
~ insulating varnish 黑色绝缘漆
~ oil 黑油，润滑重油，重油渣
~ pipe 黑铁管，非涂锌管
~ product 黑色石油产品
~ Sea 黑海
~ start-up 全断电启动
~ water 废水和污水，粪便污水

black-out 全船失电，灯火管制，遮光，暗场，停电，短暂昏厥
~ effect 关闭效应，遮蔽效应
~ lamp 灯火管制灯
~ voltage 熄灭电压，截止电压

bladder ['blædə] n. 皮囊，囊状物，膀胱
~ type accumulator 气囊式蓄能器，气胆式蓄压器，气泡储压器，隔水管球胆蓄能器

~ (type) hydropneumatic accumulator 囊式蓄能器

blade [bleid] *n.* 刀刃，刀片，扁平部分，桨叶，翼
- ~ angle 托刀口角度，刃口角，桨叶角
- ~ antenna 刀形天线
- ~ area 叶片面积
- ~ face 叶片面
- ~ outline 叶片轮廓
- ~ pitch control 叶片带距控制
- ~ profile 叶片轮廓，叶片剖面，叶型桨叶轮廓
- ~ root 叶根
- ~ section 叶切面，叶片截面
- ~ thickness 叶片厚度

blank [blæŋk] *n.* 空白，表格；*a.* 空白的，空着的，失色的，没有表情的
- ~ end 无杆端
- ~ flange 管口盖凸缘，闷头法兰，法兰盲板，盲凸缘，无孔凸缘，死法兰，盲法兰，无孔法兰盘
- ~ screen 黑屏

blast [bla:st] *n.* 一阵(风)，一股(气流)，爆炸，冲击波；*v.* 爆炸，毁灭，损害
- ~ blower 鼓风机
- ~ cleaning 喷抛清理

blasting ['bla:stiŋ] *n.* 爆破(作业)；*v.* (blast 的 ing 形式) 爆炸，毁灭，损害
- ~ protection facilities 防爆设施

bleed [bli:d] *v.* 渗出，渗透，流出，扩散，抽取，耗尽，褪色
- ~ air 放气，引气
- ~ choke 泄放扼流器
- ~ line 放气管
- ~ screw (放气用)带孔螺钉
- ~ throttle 放气节流器
- ~ valve 排出阀，放泄阀

bleed-off 旁通
- ~ circuit 旁通电路
- ~ control 旁通控制
- ~ flow 旁通流量
- ~ flow control 旁通流量控制
- ~ flow control valve 旁通流量控制阀
- ~ flow regulator 溢流节流阀
- ~ fluid 旁通流体
- ~ line 泄压管道
- ~ passage 抽气通道，抽气道
- ~ pipe 溢流管
- ~ pressure 释放压
- ~ system 旁通系统
- ~ water 排出水
- ~ water pipe 分流水管

bleeder ['bli:də] *n.* 分压器，泄水管，放血，易出血者
- ~ hole 放气孔
- ~ pipe 放水管，排出管，放气管
- ~ plug 放油塞，放泄塞，放气塞
- ~ port 泄气孔
- ~ valve 放液阀，放水阀

blend [blend] *n.* 混合，混合物；*v.* 混合，掺杂，结合，相配，配合，调合，调制，相称

blended ['blendid] *v.* (blend 的过去式和过去分词) 混合，掺杂，结合，相配，配合，调和，调制，相称；*a.* 混合的，掺杂的，调和的，调制的
- ~ fuel 调和燃料，混合燃料
- ~ fuel oil 调和燃油

blind [blaind] *v.* 使失明，缺乏眼光或判断力；*a.* 瞎的，盲目的
- ~ end 无杆端
- ~ end pressure 无杆端压力

~ flange 法兰盲板，盲板，盲法兰
~ plate 盲板
~ riveting 盲铆接
~ sector 盲区死角，荧光屏阴影区
~ via hole 盲导孔

blinker ['bliŋkə] n. 闪光警戒灯，眨眼睛者，警视者

blister ['blistə] n. 水泡

block ['blɔk] n. 木块，石块，块，阻塞物，障碍物，街区，印版，滑轮，阻滞，(一)批; v. 支撑，加强，保持，制造，铸造，塑造，妨碍，封锁，阻塞
~ assembly 分组装配作业
~ brazing 块钎焊，加热块钎焊
~ coefficient 方形系数，填充系数
~ diagonalization 块对角化
~ diagram 方框图
~ gauge 块规
~ off 阻挡，封堵
~ sealed gear motor 密封块式齿轮马达

blockage ['blɔkidʒ] n. 封锁，妨碍

blocked ['blɔkt] v. (block 的过去式和过去分词) 支撑，加强，保持，制造，铸造，塑造，妨碍，封锁，阻塞; a. 堵塞的，被封锁的
~ centre valve 中位封闭阀

blocking ['blɔkiŋ] n. 阻塞，阻断，封闭，组块; v. (block 的 ing 形式) 支撑，加强，保持，制造，铸造，塑造，妨碍，封锁，阻塞
~ agent 阻断剂，阻滞剂，阻滞药
~ effect (水槽、水池、航道等的)封闭效应，截面尺寸效应
~ filter 闭塞滤波器，阻挡滤光片，间歇滤波器
~ high 阻塞高压

~ pin 堵塞销
~ relay 闭锁继电器，连锁继电器
~ signal 闭塞信号，闭锁信号
~ valve for turning gear 盘车机联锁阀
~ voltage 闭锁电压

blow [bləu] n. 殴打，突然的打击; v. 风吹，吹气于，叫，喘气
~ lamp 喷灯
~ molding 吹塑，吹塑成型
~ off 放出，吹掉
~ off cock 吹除开关，吹扫旋塞，吹泄旋塞
~ off through valve 吹通阀门
~ off valve 急泄阀，排出阀
~ through valve 安全阀，吹除阀
~ with compressed air 用压缩空气吹扫

blow-out 爆裂，吹出，熄火
~ disk 断开碟，防爆膜

blowdown ['bləudaun] n. 排放，突然爆裂，吹除
~ of boiler 锅炉排污
~ pump 排除泵，排污泵
~ rate 排污率
~ system 排放系统，放空系统，泄料系统
~ turbine 冲击式涡轮
~ valve 排污阀，泄压阀，泄料阀

blower ['bləuə] n. 送风机，吹风机，吹制工
~ casing 鼓风机壳，压气机罩壳
~ fan 鼓风机
~ impeller 鼓风机叶轮，压气机叶轮
~ pump 增压泵
~ scavenging 扫气泵扫气
~ stator 风扇导流定子

blowing ['bləuiŋ] n. 吹风，排泄，鼓风; v. (blow 的 ing 形式) 风吹，吹气于，

叫，喘气
~ dust 高吹尘，吹尘
~ fan 吹风机，压风机
~ tube 排污管
~ ventilator 通风机

blowout ['bləu'aut] *n.* 熔断，烧断，爆裂，喷出
~ current 熔断电流，遮断电流
~ preventer 防喷器，防喷装置
~ valve 排出阀，排气管

blowpipe ['bləupaip] *n.* 吹风管

blowtorch ['bləutɔ:tʃ] *n.* 吹管，喷灯

blue [blu:] *n.* 蓝色；*a.* 蓝色的，忧郁的，沮丧的
~ asbestos 青石棉
~ book 蓝皮书
~ enamel paint 蓝色瓷漆
~ oil checking 蓝油检验
~ oil test 蓝油试验
~ Peter 开船旗
~ tooth 蓝牙

blueprint ['blu:print] *n.* 蓝图，设计图，计划；*v.* 制成蓝图，计划

BMCR (boiler maximum continuous rating) 锅炉最大连续出力，锅炉最大连续蒸发量

board [bɔ:d] *n.* 木板，木板，甲板，会议桌，部，膳食费用；*v.* 上(船、飞机等)，用板盖上，提供膳食

boarding ['bɔ:diŋ] *n.* 寄膳宿，木板；*v.* (board 的 ing 形式) 上(船、飞机等)，用板盖上，提供膳食；*a.* 供膳宿的，上轮船(或飞机)的
~ book 上船检查登记簿
~ card 登船牌，登机牌
~ clerk 轮船公司登船代表

~ deck 登艇甲板
~ time 登船时间，登机时间

boat [bəu] *n.* 小船，艇；*v.* 划船
~ chock 艇座
~ conformation 船式构型
~ davit 吊艇杆
~ deck 救生艇甲板
~ deck lamp 登艇灯 ‖ *Syn.* boat embarkation light 登艇灯；boat deck light 登艇灯
~ diving 船潜
~ drill 救生演习
~ fall 吊艇滑车索
~ fall reel 吊艇索滚筒
~ grip gear 固艇索具
~ guy 稳艇索，艇牵索，艇牵条
~ shoe 船用鞋，划船鞋
~ winch 吊艇机

boatage ['bəutidʒ] *n.* 小船运输，小船运费

boatswain ['bəutswein] *n.* 水手长 ‖ *Syn.* bosun 水手长；deck serang 水手长
~ mate 副水手长 ‖ *Syn.* deck cassab 副水手长；deck tindal 副水手长
~ room 水手长室
~ store 甲板部仓库，水手长仓库
~ tool 帆缆用具

bob [bɔb] *n.* 摆动，振动，振子锤，轻拍，轻敲，短发；*v.* 上下动，来回动，轻拍，剪短

bobbin ['bɔbin] *n.* 线轴，绕线筒
~ winder 络筒机，绕线器

bobstay ['bɔbstei] *n.* 斜桅支索

bode [bəud] *n.* 波特(Bode，人名)；*v.* 预兆，预言，预告
~ plot 波特图 ‖ *Syn.* Bode diagram 波特图

body ['bɔdi] *n.* 身体，肉体，人，尸体，主要部分，团体，大量；*v.* 赋以形体
  ~ plan 机身平面图，弹体平面图，正视图，横剖面型线图
  ~ waste 身体排泄物，体内垃圾
BOG (boil-off gas) 蒸发气体
  ~ combustion system 蒸发气体燃烧系统
boil [bɔil] *n.* 沸点，沸腾，翻滚的液体，疖子；*v.* 煮沸，汽化，激动
  ~ away 不断沸腾，汽化
  ~ dry 煮干，蒸发至干
  ~ gas recovery system 锅炉气回收系统
  ~ off 煮去，使脱胶，退浆
  ~ return system 锅炉回流系统
  ~ up 煮沸，烧开
boil-off 蒸发，汽化，汽化损耗
  ~ gas (BOG) 蒸发气体
  ~ gas combustion system 蒸发气体燃烧系统
boiled [bɔild] *v.* (boil 的过去式和过去分词) 煮沸，汽化，激动；*a.* 煮沸的，煮熟的
  ~ water 白开水，煮开过的水
boiler ['bɔilə] *n.* 锅炉，汽锅，煮器
  ~ automatic control system 锅炉自动控制系统
  ~ auxiliary steam system 锅炉辅助蒸汽系统
  ~ baffle plate 锅炉挡板
  ~ blow down 锅炉排污
  ~ blow down valve 锅炉排污阀
  ~ blower 锅炉鼓风机
  ~ body 锅炉体
  ~ brush 锅炉刷
  ~ burner pump 锅炉燃油泵
  ~ capacity 锅炉容量

  ~ casing 锅炉套，锅炉外壁，锅炉围壁
  ~ crown 锅炉顶
  ~ drum 锅炉汽包，锅炉锅筒
  ~ dry pipe 锅炉干汽管
  ~ duty 锅炉产汽量
  ~ efficiency 锅炉效率
  ~ feed capacity 锅炉给水量
  ~ feed check valve 锅炉给水止回阀
  ~ feed pipe 锅炉给水管
  ~ feed system 锅炉给水系统
  ~ feed (water) 锅炉给水
  ~ feed (water) compound pump 锅炉给水双缸泵
  ~ feed (water) pump 锅炉给水泵
  ~ firing equipment 锅炉点火设备
  ~ fittings 锅炉配件，锅炉附件
  ~ flue 锅炉烟道
  ~ forced circulation pump 锅炉强制循环泵
  ~ forced draft fan 锅炉送风机
  ~ fuel oil injection pump 锅炉燃油喷射泵
  ~ fuel oil pump 锅炉燃油泵
  ~ fuel oil system 锅炉燃油系统
  ~ furnace 锅炉炉膛，锅炉火箱
  ~ header 汽锅联管箱
  ~ heat efficiency 锅炉热效率
  ~ heating surface 锅炉受热面
  ~ ignition light oil pump 锅炉点火轻油泵
  ~ induced-draft fan 锅炉引风机
  ~ lagging 锅炉隔热套层，锅炉套箱，锅炉外套
  ~ lighting up 锅炉点火
  ~ main steam system 锅炉主蒸汽系统
  ~ maximum continuous rating (BMCR) 锅炉最大连续出力，锅炉最大连续蒸发量

~ mounting 锅炉装配附件
~ pressure 锅炉压力
~ rated evaporating capacity 锅炉额定蒸发量
~ room 锅炉间，锅炉房
~ saddle 锅炉托架，锅炉支座
~ safety valve 锅炉安全阀
~ scale 锅垢
~ seam 锅炉接缝
~ secondary air blower 锅炉二次风鼓风机
~ securing 锅炉固定
~ shell 锅炉壳体，锅炉包
~ space 锅炉舱
~ stay 锅炉牵条
~ stay tube 锅炉牵条管
~ steel 锅炉钢，锅炉用钢
~ stool 锅炉座
~ survey 锅炉检测
~ test 锅炉试验
~ tube 锅炉管
~ tube wire brush 锅炉管钢丝刷
~ uptake 锅炉烟箱
~ water 锅炉水
~ water blow-down pipe 锅炉排污管
~ water circulating system 锅炉水循环系统
~ water density 锅炉水密度
~ water hardness 锅炉水硬度
~ water level gauge 锅炉水位计
~ water level regulator 锅炉水位调节器
~ water treatment 锅炉水位处理
~ water wall 锅炉水冷壁

boiling ['bɔiliŋ] *v.* (boil 的 ing 形式) 煮沸，汽化，激动；*a.* 沸腾的，激昂的
~ evaporation 沸腾蒸发
~ hot 滚烫
~ point 沸点 ‖ ***Syn***. boiling temperature 沸腾温度，沸点温度，沸点
~ point elevation 沸点升高
~ range 沸点范围，沸程，沸腾范围
~ water 沸腾水，沸水
~ water tube 沸水管

bollard ['bɔləd] *n.* 系船柱，带缆桩，护柱 ‖ ***Syn***. bitt 系缆柱，缆柱
~ cleat 带缆羊角，钩头缆桩
~ head 系缆桩
~ light 护柱灯，短柱灯，安全岛指示灯
~ pull 系柱拉力

bolster ['bəulstə] *n.* 垫子；*v.* 支持，支撑，鼓励

bolt [bəult] *n.* 螺栓，螺钉，锁簧，枪栓，枪机，突发事件，门闩，闪电，跑掉；*v.* 栓住，锁，上门闩，囫囵吞下，逃跑，退出，脱党

bolted [bəultid] *v.* (bolt 的过去式和过去分词) 栓住，锁，上门闩，囫囵吞下，逃跑，退出，脱党；*a.* 用螺栓固定的
~ cap 螺栓压帽
~ connection 螺栓连接
~ joint 螺栓联轴节，螺栓接合
~ method 螺栓固定法
~ pump 螺栓连接泵

bond [bɔnd] *n.* 结合(物)，黏结剂，联结，捆绑物，合同，票据，保证金，契约；*v.* 结合，连接，搭接，胶接，粘接，耦合，焊合，焊接，压焊，把(货物)扣在海关监管仓库里

bonded ['bɔndid] *v.* (bond 的过去式和过去分词) 结合，连接，搭接，胶接，粘接，耦合，焊合，焊接，压焊，把(货物)扣在海关监管仓库里；*a.* 抵押的，

以债券作保证的，有担保的，存入保税仓库的

~ area 保税区，保税地域 ‖ *Syn*. bonded zone 保税区，保税地域

~ fabric 黏合织物

~ goods 保税货物

~ seal 骨架密封，组合垫圈

~ store 保税物料

~ warehouse 关栈，保税仓库，关栈仓库

~ washer 组合垫圈

bonding ['bɔndiŋ] *n*. 结合，连接，搭接，胶接，黏接，耦合，焊合，焊接，压焊；*v*. (bond 的 ing 形式) 结合，连接，搭接，胶接，粘接，耦合，焊合，焊接，压焊，把(货物)扣在海关监管仓库里

~ agent 黏合剂，结合剂，键合剂

~ equipment 焊线机

~ layer 黏合层

~ material 黏合材料

~ point 黏合点

~ sheet 黏结片

~ strength 结合强度，键强度

~ wire 焊线，等电位连接线

Bonjean [bɔn'dʒein] *n*. 邦金(人名)

~ curve 邦金曲线

bonnet ['bɔnit] *n*. 阀帽，烟囱帽，无边女帽，童帽

booklet ['buklit] *n*. 小册子

boom [bu:m] *n*. 吊杆，帆下桁，栏障，尾桁，繁荣，激增，隆隆声；*v*. 发隆隆声，兴隆，大肆宣传，快速发展

~ configuration 引导配置，启动设置

~ crane 吊杆起重机

~ cylinder 动臂缸

~ failure 启动失败，启动故障

~ hoist 旋臂起重机，臂式吊车，悬臂起重机

boost [bu:st] *n*. 推举力，增加；*v*. 增压，升压，增强，增加，提高，拔高，推进，引导

~ capacitor 升压电容

~ chopper 升压斩波电路

~ gauge 增压计，进气压力表

~ pressure 升压压力，补油压力

~ pressure circuit 增压回路

~ pressure ratio 增压比

~ up cylinder 增压缸

~ pump 升压泵，辅助泵

~ up cylinder 增压缸

booster ['bu:stə] *n*. 调压器，增压机，辅助放大器，起推动作用的辅助装置，热心的拥护者，后推的人，支持者，后援者

~ circuit 升压电路，增压回路

~ clamp circuit 增压夹紧回路

~ fan 辅助鼓风机，辅助扇风机，增压风机，增压鼓风机，加压风机，升压风机

~ pump 增压泵，升压泵，加压泵 ‖ *Syn*. boosting pump 增压泵，升压泵，加压泵

~ ram 增压柱塞

~ station 增压站，辅助电台，辅助中继电台，接力电台

~ unit 助推器组

~ valve 增压阀，辅助阀

boosting ['bu:stiŋ] *n*. 增压，升压，加大，加速，助推；*v*. (boost 的 ing 形式) 增压，升压，增强，增加，提高，拔高，推进，引导

~ pump 增压泵，升压泵，加压泵 ‖ *Syn*. booster pump 增压泵，升压泵，加压泵

~ voltage 升压电压

boot [buːt] *n*. 防护罩，新兵，长靴，皮靴，胶套靴，行李箱，益处，用处；*v*. 穿靴子，踢，解雇，引导

boracic [bə'ræsik] *a*. 硼的，含硼的
　~ acid 硼酸
　~ acid solution 硼酸溶液

borax ['bɔːræks] *n*. 硼砂

bore [bɔː] *n*. 孔，枪膛，令人讨厌的人，怒潮；*v*. 钻孔，使烦扰
　~ area 缸孔面积
　~ check 精密小测定器

bore-to-stroke 缸径对行程的，缸径行程的
　~ ratio 缸径行程比

borescope ['bɔːskəup] *n*. 管道镜，光学孔径仪

boric ['bɔːrik] *a*. 硼的
　~ acid 硼酸

boring ['bɔːriŋ] *n*. 钻孔；*v*. (bore 的 ing 形式) 钻孔，使烦扰；*a*. 令人厌烦的
　~ cutter 镗刀，镗刀
　~ head 镗床主头，镗刀盘，镗削头
　~ machine 镗床，镗孔机，钻孔机器

boss [bɔs] *n*. 轮毂，冲头，凸饰，管理者，老板，上司，控制因素；*v*. 指挥，管理，控制，指使

bosun ['bəusn] *n*. 水手长，商船甲板长 ‖ *Syn*. boatswain 水手长；deck serang 水手长

bottle ['bɔtl] *n*. 瓶子，烈酒；*v*. 用瓶装，抑制，克制
　~ neck 瓶颈部，瓶颈

bottom ['bɔtəm] *n*. 底，底部，尽头，末端；*v*. 装底，查明真相，测量深浅，到达底部，建立基础；*a*. 底部的
　~ blow-down 底部排污
　~ blow-down valve 底部排污阀 ‖ *Syn*.

bottom blow valve 底部排污阀
~ blow-off 底部吹泄
~ blow-off valve 底部吹泄阀
~ board 底板，垫板，载型板
~ composition 船底涂料，船底漆，船底混合漆
~ construction 船底结构
~ cover 底盖，后盖
~ dead center (BDC) 下死点，下止点 ‖ *Syn*. lower dead center (LDC) 下死点，下止点
~ end (连杆)大头
~ end bearing 连杆大头轴承
~ end cover 下端盖
~ end of stroke 行程的下死点
~ hole 底眼，底孔，下部孔
~ layer 底层
~ line 概要，账本底线
~ longitudinal 船底纵骨
~ part 底部，下模
~ plate 主夹板
~ plating 底板，船底板
~ plug 底塞，船底塞，下模塞
~ side girder 旁底桁
~ side tank 底边舱
~ slamming 底部砰击
~ structure 底部结构
~ surface 底面
~ tank 底舱
~ time 水下工作时间
~ transverse 底部横材，船底横材，船底横向构件
~ up 自底向上，自下而上，颠倒，倒置
~ up design 自底向上设计
~ up development 自底向上研制
~ valve 底阀

~ water level gauge 低位水位表

bottomry ['bɔtəmri] *n*. 船舶抵押契约(如船舶损失, 则债务取消), 冒险借贷

boundary ['baundəri] *n*. 边界, 分界线, 界限, 范围
~ condition 边界条件
~ friction 边界摩擦
~ layer 边界层
~ layer thickness 边界层厚度
~ line 边界线
~ lubrication 边界润滑
~ point 边界点
~ value 边界值
~ value analysis 边界值分析

bourdon ['buədn] *n*. 低音, 最低音的钟, 波尔登(Bourdon, 人名)
~ effect 波尔登效应
~ gauge 波尔登管式压力计, 波尔登气压计, 弹簧管压力计 ‖ *Syn*. Bourdon tube type pressure gauge 波尔登管式压力表, 弹簧管压力计
~ tube 波尔登管, 弹簧管
~ tube pressure switch 波尔登管压力开关, 波尔登管压力继电器, 弹簧管压力开关, 弹簧管压力继电器

bow [bau] *n*. 船头, 船艏, 前桨手, 弓, 弓形物, 彩虹, 眼镜框, 眼镜腿; *v*. 鞠躬, 弯腰
~ chain stopper 艏链链制动器
~ control house 船头控制室
~ door (登陆舰的)艏门
~ flare slamming 船头猛倾
~ light 船头灯, 艏灯
~ line 头缆, 颔线, 艏缆, 艏部纵剖线, 艏纵剖面线
~ loading system 艏装载系统

~ man 头桨手
~ of weave 弓纬
~ ramp 船头跳板, 艏门跳板
~ rudder 艏舵
~ saw 弓锯
~ thrust full to port side 船艏推进器全速向左
~ thrust full to starboard side 船艏推进器全速向右
~ thrust half to port side 船艏推进器半速向左
~ thrust half to starboard side 船艏推进器半速向右
~ thrust stop 首侧推停车
~ thruster 艏侧推器
~ visor 艏遮板
~ wave 船艏两侧的浪花

bowl [bəul] *n*. 滚筒, 滚子碗, 碗状物, 木球; *v*. 滚, 稳而快地行驶, 打倒, 撞击, 投球
~ cover 燃油泵盖, 杯盖
~ guard 滤杯护罩, 油杯护罩
~ mill 球磨机
~ periphery 碗周
~ wall 分离筒壁

bowsprit ['bəusprit] *n*. 船首斜桅

box [bɔks] *n*. 正方形, 长方形, 信号装置, 盒子, 箱, 包厢, 岗亭, 一拳; *v*. 装盒, 打耳光, 拳击
~ cooler 箱式冷却器
~ girder 箱形梁, 匣形梁
~ spanner 套筒扳手 ‖ *Syn*. box wrench 套筒扳手
~ up 装箱, 打包
~ up in good order 有序装箱, 有序打包

boxed [bɔkst] *v*. (box 的过去式和过去分

词) 装盒,打耳光,拳击; a. 盒装的

~ dimension 总尺寸,全尺寸,最大尺寸,外形尺寸,轮廓尺寸

~ rod 方形连杆

brace [breis] n. 支柱,带子,振作精神; v. 支住,支持,撑牢,振作,奋起 a. 曲柄的

bracket ['brækt] n. 支架,墙上凸出的托架,括弧; v. 装上托架,容纳在内,括在一起

~ bearing 托架轴承

~ floor 框架肋板,空心肋板,组合肋板

~ light 壁灯,托架灯

brackets ['brækits] n. (bracket 的复数) 舱口围板支架,支架,墙上凸出的托架,括弧; v. (bracket 的第三人称单数) 装上托架,容纳在内,括在一起

brad [bræd] n. 曲头钉

braid [breid] n. 编织物,辫子,穗带,辫带,高军衔的海军官员; v. 编织,编造,蜿蜒前进

braided ['breidid] v. (braid 的过去式和过去分词) 编织,编造,蜿蜒前进; a. 编织的,编造的

~ cable 编织电缆,编包电缆,编缆

~ conductor 编织导体

~ hose 有编织物填衬软管,编织软管

~ shield 编织屏蔽

brake [breik] n. 闸,制动,制动器,把手,制动液,制动工作; v. 制动减速,拉闸,金属压弯成形机

~ assembly 制动系统 ‖ *Syn*. brake system 制动系统,制动装置

~ band 制动器带,闸带

~ crank arm 制动曲柄,制动曲臂

~ circuit 制动器回路

~ circuit valve 制动器控制阀

~ gear 闸装置,制动器装置

~ handle 制动手柄

~ holding load 制动负荷,制动拉力 ‖ *Syn*. holding load 保持负载,制动载荷

~ hydraulic cylinder 制动液压缸

~ hydraulic pipe 制动液压管

~ lining 制动衬面

~ magnet 制动磁铁,阻尼磁铁

~ moment 制动力矩 ‖ *Syn*. brake torque 制动力矩

~ pedal 制动踏板,刹车踏板,制动器踏板

~ power 制动功率,制动电力,制动电源

~ resistor 制动电阻,制动电阻器

~ servo circuit 制动器伺服回路

~ specific fuel consumption 制动耗油率,制动燃油消耗率

~ valve 制动阀

braking [breikiŋ] n. 闸,刹车,刹车设置,制动系统; v. (brake 的 ing 形式) 制动减速,拉闸,金属压弯成形机

~ circuit 制动回路

~ valve 减速阀,制动阀

~ valve unit 制动阀组

branch [brɑ:ntʃ] n. 部门,枝,分枝,分部,分店,(学科)分科,支流,支脉; v. 出现分歧,扩大活动范围,扩大兴趣,扩大业务

~ ballast line 压载水支管 ‖ *Syn*. ballast branch pipe 压载水支管

~ box 分线箱,分线盒

~ circuit 分支电路,分流电路,支路

~ flow 支流

~ flow rate 支流流量

67

~ line 支线，分支线，断叉线
~ network 分支网络，分支机构图，分支机构网
~ out into 分成，拓展到，涉足
~ pipe 歧管，岔管，支管，套管
~ point 分支点
~ service switch 支路开关

brand [brænd] n. 商标，牌子，特殊类型，烙印；v. 铭刻，打烙印，铭记，诬蔑

brass [brɑ:s] n. 黄铜，黄铜制品，厚脸皮
~ alloy 黄铜合金
~ angle cock 黄铜角旋塞
~ ball valve 黄铜球阀
~ bearing 黄铜轴承
~ bolt with round head 圆头黄铜螺栓，圆头黄铜螺钉
~ bush 黄铜衬套，铜衬
~ casting 黄铜铸件
~ cock 铜旋塞
~ electrode 黄铜电焊条
~ fittings 黄铜配件
~ grease cup 黄铜滑脂杯
~ hose coupling 黄铜软管接头，黄铜软管连接器
~ plate 黄铜名牌，黄铜牌
~ plated 镀铜的，用铜板包裹的
~ plated steel wire 镀黄铜钢丝
~ ring 黄铜圈，成功的机会
~ screw with flat head 平头黄铜螺钉，平头黄铜螺丝
~ screw with round head 圆头黄铜螺钉，圆头黄铜螺丝
~ sheet 黄铜板
~ sounding rod 黄铜测深杆
~ thumb nut 黄铜蝶形螺母，黄铜翼形螺母
~ tube 黄铜管
~ water valve 黄铜水阀
~ welding powder 黄铜焊粉
~ welding wire 黄铜焊丝
~ wire 黄铜丝
~ wire brush 黄铜丝刷
~ wire gauze 黄铜丝布
~ wood screw with flat head 平头黄铜木螺钉，平头黄铜木螺丝
~ wood screw with round head 圆头黄铜木螺钉，圆头黄铜木螺丝

braze [breiz] v. 铜焊，用黄铜镀，用黄铜制造

brazed [breiz] v. (braze 的过去式和过去分词) 铜焊，用黄铜镀，用黄铜制造；a. 钎焊的，铜焊的
~ fitting 焊接式管接头

brazing ['breiziŋ] n. 铜焊(接)；v. (braze 的 ing 形式) 铜焊，用黄铜镀，用黄铜制造
~ alloy 钎焊合金，硬钎料，钎料
~ flux 钎焊剂
~ machine 钎焊机
~ rod 铜焊条

breach [bri:tʃ] n. 破裂，裂口，违背，破坏；v. 打破，突破

breadth [bredθ] n. 宽度，(布的)幅宽，(船)幅，宽容，开明
~ extreme 最大宽度
~ moulded (船体)型宽
~ on water line 水线面宽

break [breik] n. (船舶)间断面，(电流)断路，破坏，破裂，折断，裂缝，裂口，中断，休息，暂停，打断，开始，敞开，津贴，突变；v. 打破，分开，分离，拆散，折断，中断，停止，减少，

变小，削弱，刺穿，贯穿，渗进，超过，突变，破解，解决，泄露，透露，取消，无用，无效，故障，出现，显现，违犯

~ contact 常闭触点

~ down 分解，打破，破除

~ up 分散，(使)分裂，(使)瓦解

break-bulk 散装的

~ agent 卸货代理人

~ cargo 零碎装卸货物，零碎货，散件货物

~ carrier 杂货船 ‖ *Syn*. break-bulk ship 杂货船；break-bulk vessel 杂货船

~ container ship 杂货集装箱船

~ facility 拆货设备

~ liner 杂货班轮

~ transport 杂货运输

break-in 闯入，非法进入

~ oil 磨合油

~ period 试运转期，间断期

~ tool 破拆工具

breakage ['breikidʒ] *n*. 破坏，破损，破裂处，裂口，破损量，破损费

breakaway ['breikəwei] *n*. 分离，脱逃，改变；*a*. 已分离的，已脱离的，已独立的

~ force 起步阻力，脱离点

~ pressure 始动压力

breakdown ['breikdaun] *n*. 损坏，停止运动，故障，击穿，崩溃，分解，衰弱，细目分类

~ maintenance 事后维修，停工检修，故障维修

~ point 击穿点，破坏点，屈服点

~ strength 破坏强度，击穿强度

~ test 电击穿试验，击穿试验，破坏性试验，折断试验

~ time 停工时间，击穿时间，破坏时期

~ torque 停转力矩，极限转矩，崩溃转矩

~ voltage 击穿电压

breaker ['breikə] *n*. 断路器，开关，轧碎机，破碎机

~ camshaft 断路器凸轮轴

~ malfunction protection 断路器故障保护

breaking ['breikiŋ] *n*. 破坏，阻断，破裂，折断；*v*. (break 的 ing 形式) 打破，分开，分离，拆散，折断，中断，停止，减少，变小，削弱，刺穿，贯穿，渗进，超过，突变，破解，解决，泄露，透露，取消，无用，无效，故障，出现，显现，违犯

~ capacity 致断容量，断开容量，断路容量，分断能力

~ current 断路电流，开闸电流，分断电流

~ current of switch 开关切断电流

~ length 断裂长度

~ load 裂断负荷，破坏荷载，破坏载荷，断裂载荷

~ point 转换点，击穿点，断裂点

~ strength 破坏强度

~ test 致断试验，断裂试验，破坏试验

~ time 断路时间

breakout ['breikaut] *n*. 爆发，突围，越狱，脱逃

~ force 起动力

~ friction 始动摩擦

~ pressure 始动压力

~ torque 始动扭矩

~ point 中断点，分叉点

breakthrough ['breikˈθruː] *n*. 突破，重大成就，突围

breakwater ['breikwɔ:tə(r)] *n.* 挡浪板，挡水板，防浪堤

breast [brest] *n.* 胸部，乳房，胸怀，心窝，心情；*v.* 以胸对着，升高，攀登，对付
~ line 船中部横缆

breasthook ['bresthuk] *n.* 船艏肘板，船艉肘材，尖蹼板

breath [breθ] *n.* 呼吸，气息，气味，空气，微风，暂停，瞬间

breathe [bri:ð] *v.* 呼吸，发出，透气，通风，进气，吸收，注入，活着，显露

breather ['bri:ðə] *n.* 通气阀，通道，呼吸者，喘息者，剧烈的运动
~ cap 通气口盖
~ capacity 通气器容量
~ cock 呼吸旋塞，通气旋塞
~ hole 通气孔
~ pipe cap 通气管盖
~ roof 呼吸顶，浮顶
~ valve 呼吸阀，通气阀

breathing ['bri:ðiŋ] *n.* 呼吸，瞬间，微风；*v.* (breath 的 ing 形式) 呼吸，发出，透气，通风，进气，吸收，注入，活着，显露；*a.* 呼吸的，逼真的，短暂的休息
~ air compressor 呼吸空气压缩机
~ air cylinder 呼吸气瓶
~ apparatus 通气设备，氧气呼吸器，呼吸器
~ capacity 通气容量
~ phenomenon 喘气现象
~ pipe 通气管,进气管,呼吸管 ‖ *Syn.* breathing tube 呼吸管，氧气管，气管导管
~ system 呼吸系统
~ valve 呼吸阀
~ valve pressure 呼吸阀压力

breech [bri:tʃ] *n.* 马裤，臀部，炮尾，枪炮后膛

breeches ['bri:tʃiz] *n.* (breech 的复数) 马裤，裤子
~ buoy 裤形救生圈

bridge [bri:dʒ] *n.* 桥，桥楼，驾驶台，舰桥，舰楼，电桥，分流器，鼻梁，桥牌；*v.* 架桥，渡过 ‖ *Syn.* wheel house 车轮罩，驾驶室，操舵房
~ arm 桥臂，支路
~ circuit 桥接电路，桥式回路，桥形接线，桥路
~ connection 桥式接线，桥接
~ console stand 驾驶室集中操作台
~ control 驾驶室控制，驾驶台控制
~ control system 驾驶室控制系统，驾驶台控制系统
~ deck 船桥甲板
~ fault 桥接故障
~ fittings 桥式连接器
~ gauge 桥规，桥式量规
~ method 桥路法
~ orders 驾驶台命令
~ rectifier 桥式整流器
~ remote control 驾驶台遥控
~ remote control system 驾驶台遥控系统
~ visibility 驾驶台可见度,驾驶室可见度
~ wing 驾驶台侧翼
~ wing workstation 驾驶台侧翼工作站

bridge-to-bridge 驾驶台到驾驶台的，驾驶台间的
~ communication 驾驶台间通信

bridle ['braidl] *n.* 系船索，马勒，缰绳；*v.* 昂首，抑制，上笼头

brief [bri:f] *n.* 摘要，大纲；*v.* 作总结，下达简令；*a.* 简短的，短暂的
~ introduction 简介，简短介绍，简要导言
~ trial 简要试车，简短测试
~ trial on power ahead and astern 正倒车简要试车，正倒车简短测试

briefly ['bri:fli] *ad.* 暂时地，简要地

brig [brig] *n.* 双桅船，旅长

bright [brait] *a.* 明亮的，辉煌的，欢快的，聪明的
~ light 明亮光线，强光
~ stock 光亮油，重质高黏度润滑油料

brighten ['braitn] *v.* (使)变亮，(使)发光，(使)愉快

brightener ['braitnə] *n.* 增白剂，抛光剂，光亮剂

brine [brain] *a.* 盐水，海水，大洋水；*v.* 用浓盐水处理
~ circulating pump 盐水循环泵
~ cooler 盐水冷却器
~ cooling 盐水冷却
~ discharging pump 盐水排出泵，排盐泵
~ discharging regulating valve 排盐调节阀
~ drum 盐水筒
~ ejector 盐水抽除器
~ gauge 盐浮计，盐水比重计
~ heat loss 排盐热损失，卤热损失
~ heater 盐水加热器
~ hydrometer 海水比重计
~ intake 冻结管
~ pump 盐水泵，卤水泵
~ rate 排盐量
~ refrigeration system 盐水冷冻系统

~ strength 盐水浓度
~ tank 盐水箱
~ water dissolving tank 融盐水箱

bring [briŋ] *v.* 拿来，带来，产生，引起，提出，停下
~ into operation 投入运转，实施，使生效
~ out 生产，使显示，出版，说出

British ['britiʃ] *a.* 英国的，英国人的，大不列颠的
~ Ship Research Association (BSRA) 英国船舶研究协会
~ Thermal Unit (BTU) 英国热力单位

brittle ['britl] *a.* 易碎的，易破裂的，尖利的，冷淡的，脆弱的
~ coating 脆性涂层
~ cracking 脆性开裂
~ deformation 脆性变形
~ failure 脆性损毁，脆断，脆性破坏
~ fracture 脆性破裂，脆性断裂
~ material 脆性物料
~ metal 脆性金属，脆金属
~ strength 脆性强度

brittlement ['britlmənt] *n.* 脆性，脆度 ‖ *Syn.* brittleness 脆性，脆度，脆弱性

brittleness ['britlnis] *n.* 脆性，脆度，脆弱性 ‖ *Syn.* brittlement 脆性，脆度
~ material 脆性材料

broach [brəutʃ] *n.* 手钻，凿子；*v.* 钻孔，开口，凿孔，扩大，提出，宣告

broaching ['brəutʃiŋ] *n.* 拉削，推削，铰孔，扩孔；*v.* (broach 的 ing 形式) 钻孔，开口，凿孔，扩大，提出，宣告
~ machine 铰孔机，拉床

broad [brɔ:d] *n.* 宽阔部分；*a.* 宽的，阔的，广泛的，显著的，主要的，明朗

的，露骨的；*ad*. 宽阔地

broaden ['brɔ:dn] *v*. 放宽，变宽，扩大，加宽

broadside ['brɔ:dsaid] *n*. 舷侧，较宽的一面；*a*. 全面的；*ad*. 侧面地

broken ['brəukən] *v*. (break 的过去分词) 打破，分开，分离，拆散，折断，中断，停止，减少，变小，削弱，刺穿，贯穿，渗进，超过，突变，破解，解决，泄露，透露，取消，无用，无效，故障，出现，显现，违反；*a*. 破碎的，打碎的，已骨折的，虚线的，断续的，被打断的

~ line 折线

~ stowage 亏舱

brominate ['brəumineit] *v*. 用溴处理，用溴化物处理，使溴化

brominated ['brəumineitid] *v*. (brominate 的过去式和过去分词) 用溴处理，用溴化物处理，使溴化；*a*. 溴化的

~ epoxy resin 溴化环氧树脂

bronze [brɔnz] *n*. 青铜，铜锡合金，铜像；*a*. 青铜色的

~ bearing 青铜轴承

~ casting 青铜铸件

~ liner 青铜衬里

~ powder 青铜粉

~ ring 青铜环

brown [braun] *n*. 褐色；*v*. (使)成褐色，晒黑；*a*. 褐色的，棕色的

~ anticorrosive paint 棕色防锈漆

~ enamel paint 棕色瓷漆

brush [brʌʃ] *n*. 刷子，毛刷，小冲突，灌木丛，画笔；*v*. 刷，掸，拂

~ gear 刷式机构，电刷装置

~ holder 刷握，笔筒

~ holder insulating bushing 电刷柄绝缘衬套

~ holder pin 刷柄销

~ holder spring 刷握弹簧

~ holder stud 刷杆，刷握支柱

~ holder yoke 刷握架

~ inclination 电刷倾角

~ lifting device 举刷装置

~ rocker 移动刷架，电刷摇移器

~ socket 电刷架

brushes [brʌʃis] *n*. (brush 的复数) 刷子，毛刷，画笔；*v*. (brush 的第三人称单数) 刷，掸，拂

~ on slip rings 滑环上的电刷

brushless ['brʌʃlis] *a*. 无刷的

~ alternator 无刷交流发电机

~ DC motor 无刷直流电动机，无刷直流马达

~ excitation 无刷激磁，无刷励磁

~ generator 无刷发电机

~ high-speed alternator 无刷高速交流发电机

~ motor 无刷电动机，无刷马达

~ synchronous generator 无刷同步发电机

BSRA (British Ship Research Association) 英国船舶研究协会

BTU (British Thermal Unit) 英国热力单位

bubble ['bʌbl] *n*. 保护罩，泡沫，气泡，幻想的计划，投机，骗局；*v*. 起泡，潺潺地流

~ barrier 气泡屏障

~ point 发生气泡点

~ test 气泡试验

bubble-tight 气密的

~ shut-off 气密关闭

buck [bʌk] *n*. 元，锯木架；*v*. 冲冰航行，冲撞，突然一跃，晃动，颠簸，坚决反对；*a*. 最低级的

～ converter 降压变换器

bucking [bʌkiŋ] *v*. (buck 的 ing 形式) 冲冰航行，冲撞，突然一跃，晃动，颠簸，坚决反对；*a*. 消除的，补偿的，反向的

～ resistance 纵弯曲强度

bucking-out 消除，补偿

～ system 补偿系统，抵消系统

bucket ['bʌkit] *n*. 铲斗，水桶，吊桶；*v*. 倾泻，颠簸，装在桶里，急速运动

～ capacity 铲斗容量

～ chain 铲斗链，斗链，链斗提升机

～ chain dredge 链斗式挖泥船

～ cylinder 铲斗缸

～ dredge 斗式挖泥船，斗式挖泥机，链斗式挖泥船

buckle ['bʌkl] *n*. 带扣，搭扣，搭钩，弯曲，褶皱，鼓胀；*v*. 扣住，变弯曲，使皱，屈服，让步，崩溃

buckling ['bʌkliŋ] *n*. 屈曲，膨胀，扣住，褶皱，下垂，粗糙度；*v*. (buckle 的 ing 形式) 扣住，变弯曲，使皱，屈服，让步，崩溃

～ action 压曲应力

～ allowable 挫曲(侧溃)容许值

～ amplitudes 压曲幅度

～ analysis 抗皱折计算，压曲强度计算，纵向弯曲强度计算

～ breaking 压曲破坏

～ collapse 失稳破坏 ‖ *Syn*. buckling damage 屈曲破损；buckling failure 失稳破坏，失稳损坏，屈曲破坏

～ configuration 压曲图形，压屈形态

～ constant 曲率常数

～ creep 压曲蠕变

～ deformation 失稳变形，翘曲变形

～ factor 失稳因数

～ fold 弯曲褶皱

～ limit 扭曲极限

～ load 压曲临界荷载，临界纵向荷载

～ strength 纵弯曲强度，纵向弯曲强度，压曲强度

～ stress 压曲应力，纵向弯曲应力，抗弯应力，屈曲应力

BUDC (before upper dead center) 上止点前，上死点前

buddy ['bʌdi] *n*. 密友，伙伴

～ breathe 共气

～ system 两人同行制，伙伴系统

buffalo ['bʌfələu] *n*. 水陆两用坦克，水牛，美洲野牛

buffer ['bʌfə] *n*. 缓冲器，缓冲物，缓冲地带，缓冲区，缓冲液，缓冲剂，擦光轮；*v*. 缓冲

～ action 缓冲作用

～ area 缓冲区

～ capacity 缓冲量，消振量，缓冲能力，消振能力

～ circuit 缓冲电路，阻尼电路

～ rack 缓冲架

～ screw 缓冲螺钉

～ shaft 缓冲轴

～ solution 缓冲溶液，缓冲液

～ space 缓冲空间

～ spring 缓冲弹簧，阻尼弹簧

～ system 缓冲系统

～ tank 缓冲罐，缓冲水箱，备用水箱

～ zone 缓冲区

build [bild] *n*. 构造，体格，体形；*v*. 建

造，建筑，创立，增加，加强，奠定基础，扩大，扩展，发展，达到，监督 ‖ *Syn.* construct 建造，构造，创立；erect 建造，建立，开创；form 形成，构成，塑造；make 制造，构造；put up 建造

~ in 安装，固定 ‖ *Syn.* assemble 装配；fit 安装；fix 安装，(使)固定；fix assemblage 安装；install 安装；mount 安装；set up 装配，竖立，架起

~ into 使固定于，使成为…的一部分

~ of 用…建造

~ on 基于，建立于，寄希望于 ‖ *Syn.* build upon 基于，建立于，寄希望于；count on 依靠，指望；depend on 依赖，依靠，取决于；depend upon 依赖，依靠，取决于；lie on 依赖，取决于；reckon on 指望，依赖；rely on 依赖，依靠

~ up 建立，树立，构建，增进，增大，堵塞

~ up by stainless steel welding 通过不锈钢焊接建造

build-up 积聚，积累，堆起，增强，组成，宣传

~ welding 堆焊

builder ['bildə] *n.* 建筑者，施工人员，营造商，增洁剂

building ['bildiŋ] *n.* 建筑物，营造物；*v.* (build 的 ing 形式) 建造，建筑，创立，增加，加强，奠定基础，扩大，扩展，发展，达到，监督

~ block valve 集成阀，积木式阀

~ site 建设工地，建筑工地

built [bilt] *v.* (build 的过去式和过去分词) 建造，建筑，创立，增加，加强，奠定基础，扩大，扩展，发展，达到，监督；*a.* 有特定体格的

built-in 内装式的，内置的，固有的，嵌入的，建设在里面的

~ check valve 内装式单向阀

~ contaminant 内藏污染物

~ contaminant migration 内藏污染物迁移

~ test equipment 机内测试仪器

built-up 组合的，建筑物多的，高楼林立的

~ connection 组合连接

~ crankshaft 组合曲轴

~ frame 组合构架

~ manifold 集成块

~ member 组装件，装配部件，组合构件

~ plate section 组合型材

bulb [bʌlb] *n.* 球物，灯泡

~ bar 球缘扁材

~ plate 球头扁钢，球缘板材

~ socket 灯泡插座

bulbous ['bʌlbəs] *a.* 球根的，球根状的，球根长成的

~ bow 球状船首，球鼻船首

~ hull 球鼻首船体

buld ['bʌld] *n.* 电珠

~ barometer 球管气压计

~ edge 厚圆边，边子，卷边子

bulge [bʌldʒ] *n.* 凸出部分，海底变曲部，暴涨，突增，优势；*v.* 凸出，膨胀，鼓起

bulk [bʌlk] *n.* 大小，体积，大批，大多数，散装；*v.* 显得大，显得重要

~ cargo 散装货，散货

~ cargo ship 散货船

~ carrier 散装货轮

~ chemical cargo containment 散装化学品防泄漏系统

~ compressibility 体压缩率，体积压缩性

~ container 散货集装箱

~ container carrier 散装集装箱船

~ dangerous goods carrier 散装危险货船

~ density 体积密度，堆积密度

~ filtration 粗过滤，粗滤 ‖ *Ant*. fine filtration 细过滤，细滤

~ freight 散装货物

~ liquids and gases 散装液体与气体

~ material handling 散装材料处理

~ modulus 体积模量

~ modulus of elasticity 体积弹性模量，体积弹性系数

~ oil carrier 散装油船

~ strain 体积应变

bulkhead ['bʌlkhed] *n*. (船)舱壁，隔壁，防水壁，堵壁，堤岸

~ branch tee 隔板支管三通

~ connector 穿板式连接器，穿墙式连接器，舱壁连接器

~ deck 舱壁甲板

~ door 舱壁门

~ fitting 闷头配件，闷头接头，舱壁具

~ lamp 舱壁灯 ‖ *Syn*. bulkhead light 舱壁灯

~ penetration 舱壁穿透，舱壁刺穿

~ side tee 支管穿过隔壁的三通接头

~ stiffener 舱壁扶强材，舱壁防挠材

~ stuffing box 隔舱壁填料函

~ wharf 岸壁型码头，堤岸式码头

bull [bul] *n*. 公牛，雄性大动物，训令，法令；*v*. 推，强迫；*a*. 雄的，公的，强壮的，像牛一般大的，价格上涨的

~ gear 大齿轮

~ gear drive 大齿轮驱动

bulldog ['buldɔg] *n*. 隔热材料，左轮手枪，牛头犬，摔倒

~ grip 钢丝绳夹，钢丝索扣

bullet ['bulit] *n*. 子弹，枪弹，弹药(筒)，弹丸，锥体

~ pad 子弹形盘，子弹盘

bulwark ['bulwə(:)k] *n*. 舷墙，堡垒，壁垒，防御物，防波堤，挡浪板；*v*. 用堡垒防护，提供防御，提供保护

~ chock 舷墙导缆孔，舷墙缆孔

~ ladder 舷墙梯，舷梯

~ line 舷墙线

~ molding 舷墙缘材

~ plate 舷墙板 ‖ *Syn*. bulwark plating 舷墙板

~ stanchion 后支杆，后拉索

~ stay 舷墙支柱

bump [bʌmp] *n*. 撞击，肿块；*v*. 碰伤，撞破，颠簸

bumper ['bʌmpə] *n*. 缓冲器，减震器，保险杠

bumpless ['bʌmplis] *a*. 无波动的，无冲击的，无扰动的

~ transfer 无扰动转换，无扰动切换

bunch [bʌntʃ] *n*. 串，束；*v*. 捆成一束，集中

bunched [bʌntʃid] *v*. (bunch 的过去式和过去分词) 捆成一束，集中；*a*. 束状的，成束的，成串的

~ cables 束状电缆

~ flame retardant cables 束状阻燃电缆

bundle ['bʌndl] *n*. 捆绑，束，包，包袱，包裹，包裹物，大量，许多；*v*. 捆绑，

扎，包，匆忙撵走，赶快，赶紧

～ into 乱放进，胡塞进

bundled ['bʌndld] v. (bundle 的过去式和过去分词) 捆绑，扎，包，匆忙撵走，赶快，赶紧；a. 捆绑的，附带的

～ conductor 分裂导线

～ conductor electrode 多导体接地极

bunk [bʌŋk] n. (轮船，火车等)铺位

～ light 床头灯

bunker ['bʌŋkə] n. 燃料舱，船上的煤仓，碉堡，掩体；v. 在燃料仓中储存，在燃料仓中放置

～ access door 燃料舱检修门，燃料舱入孔门

～ delivery note 燃油交付单

～ delivery receipt 加燃料收据

～ fuel 船用燃料

～ manifold 加油总管

～ receipt 燃料接受证

～ Supplier 船舶燃料供应公司

bunkering ['bʌŋkəriŋ] n. 装燃料，燃料储存；v. (bunker 的 ing 形式) 在燃料仓中储存，在燃料仓中放置

～ barge 燃料驳船，燃料供应驳

～ operation 油料添加作业

～ plan 加油计划

～ procedure 加油程序

～ station 加油站

～ vessel 燃料供应船

buoy [bɔi] n. 浮标，浮筒，救生圈；v. 使浮起，支撑，鼓励

～ float 浮标体

～ handling crane 浮筒装卸起重机

～ layer 布标船，浮筒带缆工

～ mooring 浮标系泊，浮筒系泊

～ mooring line 浮标锚链，浮标系索

～ ring 救生圈

～ tender 浮标供应船

～ up 使浮起，支持，支撑，激励，使振作

buoyage ['bɔiidʒ] n. 浮标装置，浮标安置方法

buoyancy ['bɔiənsi] n. 浮性，浮力，轻快

～ balance 浮力平衡

～ compensator 浮力补偿器

～ Control Device (BCD) 浮力调节装置 ‖ *Syn*. Buoyancy Control Jackets 浮力调节背心

～ control tank 浮力控制舱

～ force 浮力

buoyant ['bɔiənt] a. 有浮力的，轻快的

～ ascent 浮力上升法

～ box 浮箱

～ force 浮力

～ handle 救生把手

～ oar 可浮桨

～ paddle 可浮手划桨

～ tank 浮柜

burden ['bə:dn] n. 负载，负载量，吨位，担子，负担，重任，责任，义务；v. 负担，装载，超载，重压，压抑

bureau [bjuə'rəu] n. 局，办公署，部，处，社所等商业机构，办公桌，衣柜

～ Veritas 法国船级社

burette [bjuə'ret] n. 滴管，量管

～ brush 滴定管刷

～ clamp 滴定管夹

～ stand 滴定管架

buried ['berid] v. (bury 的过去式和过去分词) 埋葬，掩埋，隐藏；a. 埋在地下的，掩埋的，隐藏的

~ blind via 埋盲孔

~ via hole 埋导孔

Burmeister ['bəmi:stə] *n*. 布尔迈斯特(人名)

~ & Wain engine B&W 型发动机

burn [bə:n] *n*. 烧伤，灼伤；*v*. 燃烧，烧，烧焦，点(灯)，使感觉烧热

~ out 烧坏，烧掉，烧尽

burnable ['bə:nəl] *a*. 燃烧的，可燃的，灼伤的

~ absorber 可燃吸收剂

~ characteristic 燃烧特性

~ refuse 可焚化垃圾，可燃垃圾 ‖ **Syn.** burnable trash 可焚化垃圾，可燃垃圾；burnable waste 可燃废弃物，可燃垃圾

burner ['bə:nə] *n*. 燃烧器，燃烧装置，燃烧炉，燃烧者，燃烧工

~ atomizer 燃烧器雾化器

~ control system (BCS) 燃烧器控制系统

~ control box 燃烧器控制箱

~ jet 燃烧器喷嘴

~ nozzle 燃烧器喷嘴 ‖ **Syn.** burner tip 燃烧器喷尖

burning ['bə:niŋ] *n*. 燃烧；*v*. (burn 的 ing 形式) 燃烧，烧，烧焦，点(灯)；*a*. 烧的，强烈的，热烈的，极严重的，紧急的

~ agent 燃烧剂

~ area 燃烧区，火区

~ in site 现场燃烧

burnish ['bə:niʃ] *v*. 磨光，擦亮(金属)

burr [bə:] *n*. 毛口，毛头，毛刺

~ removal 除毛刺

burst [bə:st] *n*. 突然破裂，爆发，脉冲；*v*. 爆裂，炸破，急于，爆发

~ pressure rating 额定爆裂压力

~ pressure test 爆裂压力试验，爆破压力试验

~ test pressure 破裂试验压力，爆裂试验压力

bursting ['bə:stiŋ] *n*. 爆裂，爆破；*v*. (burst 的 ing 形式) 爆裂，炸破，急于，爆发

~ cap 爆裂帽

~ cap protector 爆裂帽保护罩

~ disc 爆裂盘

~ disk 防爆膜

~ pressure 爆破压力

~ strength 崩裂强度，耐破度，爆破强度

~ test 破裂试验，爆破试验

burton ['bə:tn] *n*. 小型滑车装置

~ man 联杆作业吊货时的接钩手

~ pendant 重货吊绳

~ rig 联杆操作补给装置

~ system 联杆吊货法

bury ['beri] *v*. 埋葬，掩埋，隐藏

~ barge 埋管驳船

bus [bʌs] *n*. 公共汽车，汇流条，母线，总线，数据传送总线；*v*. 用公共汽车运输

~ bar 汇流排，汇流条，母线

~ bar disconnecting switch 母线隔离开关

~ change-over switch 汇流排换向开关

~ interface 总线接口

~ line 汇流线

~ sectionalizing breaker 母线分段断路器

~ system 总线系统，母线系统，汇流排系统

~ tie breaker 总线联络断路器

~ tie cabinet 母线联络柜
~ tie circuit breaker 母线联络断路器
~ tie panel 母线联络盘
~ transfer 总线传输，总线传送

bush [buʃ] *n.* (机械)衬套，矮树丛；*v.* 加衬套于，加轴套于；*a.* 低级的，二流的
~ bearing 滑动轴承
~ burning-out 轴瓦烧熔
~ mosaic cracking 轴瓦龟裂
~ scrape 轴瓦擦伤

bushing ['buʃiŋ] *n.* (机)轴衬，(电工)套管；*v.* (bush 的 ing 形式) 加衬套于，加轴套于
~ block 衬套
~ tap grounding wire 套管末屏接地线

butt [bʌt] *n.* 铰链，粗大的一端，靶垛，抵触，顶撞，毗连；*v.* 抵触，顶撞，冲撞，首尾相连
~ contact 对接触头，对接触点
~ end 头端，粗端，底部
~ flange 对接法兰
~ joint 对接，对接接头
~ strap 搭板，对接贴板，对接衬板
~ weld 碰焊，平式焊接，对头焊接
~ welding 对接焊
~ welding pipe fittings 对焊管件，对焊管配件

butterfly ['bʌtəflai] *n.* 蝴蝶，蝶泳
~ screw cap 蝶形螺帽
~ valve 蝶形阀

Butterworth ['bʌtəwə:θ] *n.* 巴特沃斯(人名，英格兰姓氏)
~ filter 巴特沃斯滤波器
~ heater 巴特沃斯加热器，洗舱水加热器 ‖ *Syn.* tank cleaning seawater heater 洗舱水加热器
~ pump 巴特沃斯泵，洗舱泵 ‖ *Syn.* tank cleaning pump 洗舱泵

buttock ['bʌtək] *n.* 船尾，屁股；*v.* 背摔
~ line 船体纵剖线
~ planking 尾部外板
~ plate 船尾包板
~ section 船尾，臀部

button ['bʌtn] *n.* 钮扣，按钮，按钮开关，金属球，玻璃球，扣形物，圆形小徽章；*v.* 扣住，扣紧
~ switch 按钮开关

button-actuated 按钮操纵的

buttress ['bʌtris] *n.* 扶壁，撑墙，支持物，肋状物；*v.* 支持，维持，支撑，扶住

butyl ['bju:tail] *n.* 丁基，丁基合成橡胶
~ rubber 丁基橡胶
~ rubber seal 丁基橡胶密封件

buzz [bʌz] *n.* 嗡嗡声；*v.* 逼近，嗡嗡作响

buzzer ['bʌzə] *n.* 蜂鸣器，信号手，嗡嗡作声的东西

BWM (ballast water management) 压载水管理
~ Convention 压载水管理公约，压载水公约

BWMS (Ballast Water Management System) 压载水管理系统

by [bai] *ad.* 通过，经过，附近；*prep.* 在附近，在旁边，经，由，依据，按照，通过，用
~ and large 总的说来，大体上
~ convention 按照惯例，按照约定，根据习俗
~ ferry 乘渡轮，摆渡，乘船
~ means of 用，依靠，凭借，借助

~ means of lead wire 用压铅丝
~ means of metal lock 用金属扣合法
~ trial and error 反复试验,不断摸索
~ which 藉此,由此,凭这个 ‖ *Syn.* whereby 藉此,由此,凭这个

bypass ['baipɑ:s] *n.* 旁路,支路,迂回管道,绕开,导管,小道;*v.* 设旁路,迂回,疏通,回避
~ circuit 旁通回路
~ damper 支路气门,旁通气门
~ filter 旁通过滤器
~ filtration 旁通过滤
~ flow 旁通流量
~ flow control 旁通流量控制
~ flow control valve 旁通流量控制阀 ‖ *Syn.* bypass flow regulator 旁通流量调节阀
~ hose 旁通水管
~ hydraulic filter 旁通液压过滤器
~ line 旁通管道,旁路线
~ pipe 旁通管
~ valve 旁通阀

byproduct ['bai,prɔdʌkt] *n.* 副产品

C

C-stage C 级,丙阶
~ resin 丙阶树脂,不溶酚醛树脂

cab [kæb] *n.* 驾驶室,司机室,出租马车,出租汽车,计程车

cabin ['kæbin] *n.* 船舱,舱室,客舱,舱位,小屋;*v.* 拘禁,幽禁
~ boat 盖舱快艇
~ boy 船舱男服务员,船上侍者,房间服务生 ‖ *Syn.* cabin steward 船舱服务员,客舱服务员

~ class 二等舱,特别二等舱(在一二等舱中间)
~ condense piping to be done free-flowing test 房舱凝水、落水管系畅通试验
~ fan 房舱风扇,舱室通风机 ‖ *Syn.* cabin wall ventilator 舱壁通风器,舱室通风筒
~ lamp 客舱灯
~ passenger 客舱旅客
~ size 舱室尺寸
~ steam piping system to be done airtightness test 房舱蒸汽管系密性试验
~ store 舱室用品储藏室
~ supply fan to be done function test 房舱风机效用试验
~ type temperature control 舱室温度控制
~ type temperature controller 舱室温度控制器
~ ventilator 舱室通风机

cabinet ['kæbinit] *n.* 密室,小房间,橱柜,政府内阁;*a.* 可展示的,可保存的,小巧的,内阁的

cable ['keibl] *n.* 电缆,缆,索,海底电报;*v.* 打(海底)电报
~ anchor 电缆锚
~ and wire for ship 船用电缆和电线
~ box 分线盒,电缆盒,电缆箱
~ bracket 电缆架
~ bundles 电缆束,束状电缆
~ buoy 电缆浮标,布缆浮筒,水底电缆浮标
~ bush 电缆套筒
~ clamp 电缆夹
~ clip 锚链夹,缆索夹,电缆夹,电缆挂钩

~ coaming 穿线环围，线孔线围
~ connection 电缆连接，缆索接头
~ diameter 钢绳直径
~ for power system of ship 船用电力电缆
~ for telecommunications in ship 船舶通信电缆
~ gland 电缆填料函，填料函，电缆密封套
~ holder 导链轮，电缆支架，缆索支架
~ insulation 电缆绝缘
~ joint 电缆接头
~ layer 敷缆船
~ laying 电缆敷设，放缆
~ length 链(海上测距单位)，电缆长度
~ lifter 起锚机，锚链轮
~ lifter brake 起锚机制动器，锚链轮制动器
~ link 锚链环
~ locker 锚链舱
~ lug 电缆接线头，缆端卸套，电缆终端衔套
~ machinery 电缆机
~ modem 电缆调制解调器，有线通
~ orientation 缆索取向
~ outlet box 电缆引线盒
~ port 测试孔，电缆端口
~ post 电缆柱
~ push button switch 电缆按钮开关
~ reliever 锚链解脱器，弃链器
~ run 电缆敷设路径，电缆线路，光缆主干
~ shield 电缆包皮，电缆护套，电缆的输入套管
~ ship 海底电缆敷设船
~ stopper 锚链制动器，钢缆制动器

~ tension indicator 钢绳张力指示器
~ transit 船用贯通件
~ tray 电缆槽
~ vessel 电缆船
~ winch 钢索绞车

cabotage ['kæbətidʒ] n. 沿海贸易权，沿海航行权，国内航空运输

CAD (computer-aided design) 计算机辅助设计

CAD (computer-aided drawing) 计算机辅助制图，计算机辅助绘图

cadet [kə'det] n. 见习生，军校学员，警校学员

CAE (computer-aided engineering) 计算机辅助工程

cage [keidʒ] n. 笼子，鸟笼，兽笼，牢房，战俘营；v. 关入笼中，放到笼里
~ motor 鼠笼式电动机，鼠笼式马达
~ rotor 鼠笼式转子

caisson ['keisən] n. 沉箱，弹药箱，弹药车

calamity [kə'læmiti] n. 灾难，不幸事件 ‖ **Syn**. disaster 灾难，天灾，灾祸
~ detection 灾难检测

calcium ['kælsiəm] n. 钙
~ bicarbonate 碳酸氢钙，重碳酸钙
~ chloride 氯化钙
~ chloride brine 氯化钙卤水
~ hydroxide 氢氧化钙
~ oxide 氧化钙，生石灰
~ pyrophosphate 焦磷酸钙
~ sulfate 硫酸钙

calculate ['kælkjuleit] v. 计算，考虑，计划，打算，以为，认为

calculated ['kælkjuleitid] v. (calculate 的过去式和过去分词) 计算，考虑，计划，

打算，以为，认为；*a*. 计算出的，有计划的，适当的，适合的

~ capacity 计算容量，计算排量

calculation [ˌkælkjuˈleiʃən] *n*. 计算，考虑，估计，深思熟虑

~ accuracy 计算精度

~ based on three-mode operation 三类负载计算法

~ procedure 计算步骤

calculator [ˈkælkjuleitə] *n*. 计算机，计算器

caliber [ˈkælibə(r)] *n*. 口径，才干，器量

calibrate [ˈkælibreit] *v*. 校准，校正，确定口径，使标准化

calibrating [ˈkæləˌbreitiŋ] *n*. 校准，校正；*v*. (calibrate 的 ing 形式) 校准，校正，确定口径，使标准化

~ gas 校正气，标准气体，量距气

~ rudder angle indicator 舵角指示器校准

~ spot 校准标记，校准点

calibration [ˌkæliˈbreiʃən] *n*. 标度，刻度，校准

~ accuracy 校准精度，校准精确度

~ curve 校准曲线，校正曲线，标定曲线

~ deviation 校准偏差

~ facility 校验装置，标定设备

~ procedure 校准程序

caliper [ˈkælipə] *n*. (=calliper) 两脚规，测圆器

~ gauge 测径规，内卡规，内量规

~ square 测径直角尺

call [kɔːl] *n*. 喊声，叫声，命令，号召，访问，叫牌，通话，必要；*v*. 呼叫，召集，称呼，认为，命名，打电话

~ bell 呼叫铃

~ button 呼叫按钮

calliper [ˈkælipə] *n*. (=caliper) 两脚规，测圆器

calorie [ˈkæləri] *n*. 卡路里

calorific [ˌkæləˈrifik] *a*. 生热的，热的

~ capacity 热容量，卡值

~ value 发热值，热值，热当量

calorifier [kəˈlɔriˌfaiə] *n*. 水加热器，热发生器

calorimeter [ˌkæləˈrimitə] *n*. 热量计

CAM (computer-aided manufacturing) 计算机辅助制造

cam [kæm] *n*. 凸轮

~ and piston type pump 凸轮活塞式泵

~ base circle 凸轮基圆

~ clearance 凸轮间隙

~ controller 凸轮控制器

~ crown 凸轮冠

~ follower 凸轮从动件，凸轮从动滚轮，凸轮跟随器，挺杆

~ lobe 凸轮凸角

~ mechanism 凸轮机构

~ nut 凸轮螺母

~ plate 凸轮盘，平板形凸轮

~ profile 凸轮轮廓

~ ring 凸轮环

~ shaft 凸轮轴

~ sleeve 凸轮联轴节，爪形联轮节，牙嵌离合器

~ surface 凸轮面

~ switch 凸轮操纵开关，凸轮开关

cam-controlled 凸轮控制的 ‖ ***Syn***. cam-operated 凸轮操纵的，凸轮控制的

~ automatic bypass valve 凸轮控制的自动旁通阀

cam-operated 凸轮操纵的，凸轮控制的 ‖ *Syn*. cam-controlled 凸轮控制的
~ controller 凸轮控制器
camber ['kæmbə] *n*. 拱形；*v*. 呈拱形
camel ['kæməl] *n*. (船打捞用的)浮筒，骆驼
camflex [kæm'fleks] *n*. 通用控制阀
~ valve 偏心旋转阀，凸轮挠曲阀
camshaft ['kæmʃɑ:ft] *n*. 凸轮轴
~ bearing 凸轮轴轴承
~ bearing journal 凸轮轴轴颈
~ bush 凸轮轴轴衬，凸轮轴轴瓦
~ cover 凸轮轴盖
~ drive 凸轮轴驱动，凸轮轴传动
~ drive gear cover 凸轮轴驱动齿轮盖
~ gear 凸轮轴齿轮
~ gear wheel 凸轮轴齿轮
~ lathe 凸轮轴车床
~ lubricating oil pump 凸轮轴滑油泵
~ lubricating oil system 凸轮轴滑油系统
~ sprocket 凸轮轴链轮
~ time gear 凸轮轴正时齿轮
~ transmission gear 凸轮轴传动装置
canal [kə'næl] *n*. 导管，管子，槽，运河，小道，沟渠；*v*. 疏导，开运河
cancel ['kænsəl] *n*. 注销，删除；*v*. 取消，删去，使无效，约分，约去，消去，削除，抵消，中和
~ button 取消按钮
cancellation [kænsə'leiʃən] *n*. 取消
canister ['kænistə] *n*. (防毒面具的)滤毒罐，小罐，筒
~ gas mask 过滤器式防毒面具
canoe [kə'nu:] *n*. 独木舟，轻舟；*v*. 乘坐木舟，划独木舟

canopy ['kænəpi] *n*. 天篷，遮篷，顶篷，顶盖，帆布篷，驾驶舱盖，座舱盖
cant [kænt] *n*. 斜面，角落；*v*. 倾斜
~ beam 斜梁
~ frame 斜肋骨，艉端斜肋骨
cantilever ['kæntili:və] *n*. 悬臂
~ beam 悬臂梁
canvas ['kænvəs] *n*. 帆布，一面船帆，一套船帆，帐篷，背景
~ gloves 帆布手套
~ hose 帆布软管，帆布水带
~ windlass 帆布绞盘，帆布绞车
~ windsail 帆布通风筒
cap [kæp] *n*. 帽子，军帽，瓶帽，笔帽；*v*. 戴帽子，盖在顶上
~ bolt 帽螺钉，紧固螺栓，倒角螺栓
~ mut 螺母，盖形螺母
~ screw 帽螺钉
capability [,keipə'biliti] *n*. 能力，性能，容量，接受力 ‖ *Syn*. capacitance (电)容量；capacity 容量，生产量；tankage (桶、槽)容量；volume 体积，容积
capable ['keipəbl] *a*. 有能力的，能干的，有可能的，可以的
capacitance [kə'pæsitəns] *n*. (电)容量，电容 ‖ *Syn*. capacity 容量，生产量；capability 性能，容量；tankage (桶、槽)容量；volume 体积，容积
~ effect 电容效应
~ in parallel 并联电容
~ in series-parallel 串并联电容
~ sensor 电容传感器 ‖ *Syn*. capacitive sensor 电容传感器
capacitator [kə'pæsiteitə] *n*. (=capacitor) 电容器
capacitive [kə'pæsitiv] *a*. 电容性的

~ bridge 电容电桥

~ bushing 电容式套管

~ circuit 电容电路，容性电路

~ displacement transducer 电容式位移传感器

~ load 电容性负载，容性负载

~ sensor 电容传感器 ‖ *Syn.* capacitance sensor 电容传感器

~ storage circuit 电容存储电路

~ voltage transformer (CVT) 电容式电压互感器

capacitor [kə'pæsitə] *n.* (=capacitator) 电容器

~ bank 电容器组

~ type smoke detector 电容式感烟探测器

capacity [kə'pæsiti] *n.* 容量，生产量，智能，才能，能力，接受力，地位 ‖ *Syn.* capability 性能，容量；capacitance (电)容量；tankage (桶、槽)容量；volume 体积，容积

~ charateristic curve 容量特性曲线

~ of tank 油柜容量，水柜容量

~ plan 舱容图，容量图

~ rating 额定功率，额定容量 ‖ *Syn.* nominal capacity 额定功率，标称功率，额定容量，标称容量；nominal output 额定功率，额定出力，额定输出，标称输出；nominal power 额定功率，额定容量，标称功率，标称容量；power rating 额定功率；rated capacity 额定功率，额定容量，设计效率；rated output 额定功率，额定输出量，额定出力；rated power 额定功率，设计功率，额定动力，不失真功率；rated power output 额定功率，额定动力输出；rated power capability 额定功率；standard horsepower 额定功率，标准马力；standard power 额定功率，标准功率

~ regulator 电容调节器，出力调节器

cape [keip] *n.* 海角，岬

capillary [kə'pilәri] *n.* 毛细管；*a.* 毛状的，毛细作用的

~ action 毛细管作用

~ condensation 毛管凝缩作用，毛细冷凝，毛细凝结

~ effect 毛细管效应

~ force 毛细管力，毛细力，毛管力

~ network 毛细管网

~ tube 毛细管

~ viscometer 毛细管黏度计

CAPP (computer-aided process planning) 计算机辅助工艺过程设计

capsize [kæp'saiz] *v.* (船)倾覆

capsizing [kæp'saiziŋ] *n.* 倾覆；*v.* (capsize 的 ing 形式) (船)倾覆

~ moment 倾覆力矩

capstan ['kæpstən] *n.* 绞盘，绞车，起锚机，卷扬机，主动轮

~ barrel 绞盘卷筒，绞盘筒，绞车筒 ‖ *Syn.* capstan drum 绞盘卷筒，绞车卷筒；winch barrel 绞盘卷筒，绞车卷筒；winch drum 绞盘卷筒，绞车卷筒

~ box 绞盘箱

~ engine 起锚机，卷扬机

~ spindle 绞盘轴

capsulate ['kæpsjuleit] *a.* 包入胶囊的，形成胶囊的

capsule ['kæpsju:l] *n.* 瓶帽，太空舱，胶囊，蒴果；*v.* 装进小盒，提供小盒，概括，总结；*a.* 概要的，高度概括的，

非常简略的，微小的，小巧的

~ pressure gauge 膜盒式压力表

captain ['kæptin] n. 队长，首领，船长，机长,(空军、海军)上校,(陆军)上尉； v. 指挥,统帅 ‖ *Syn*. master 船长； sea captain 船长； skipper 船长

~ cabin 船长室

~ day room 船长休息室

~ office 船长办公室

captain's 船长的

~ bed room 船长卧室

~ boy 船长服务生

capture ['kæptʃə] n. 记录，捕获，赢得，战利品； v. 俘获，捕获，赢得，夺取，夺取，引起注意，长久保存

captured ['kæptʃəd] v. (capture 的过去式和过去分词) 俘获，捕获，赢得，夺取，夺取，引起注意，长久保存； a. 捕获的，被俘的

captured-air-bubble 封闭气泡

~ vehicle 封闭气泡式气垫船，侧壁式气垫船

car [ka:] n. 汽车，小汽车，车辆，客车，车厢

~ and passenger ferry 汽车客运渡船

~ carrier 汽车运载船，载车船

~ deck 车辆甲板，汽车甲板

carbide ['ka:baid] n. 碳化物

carbon ['ka:bən] n. 碳，复写纸

~ brush 碳刷，碳电刷

~ copy 复写本，副本

~ deposit 积碳，碳沉积

~ dioxide (CO_2) 二氧化碳

~ dioxide container 二氧化碳容器

~ dioxide cylinder 二氧化碳气瓶，二氧化碳气罐

~ dioxide discharge rate 二氧化碳排放率

~ dioxide distribution piping 二氧化碳分配管系

~ dioxide extinguishing agent 二氧化碳灭火剂

~ dioxide fire extinguisher 二氧化碳灭火器

~ dioxide (fire) extinguishing system 二氧化碳灭火系统，二氧化碳消防系统

~ dioxide flooding system 二氧化碳涌灭系统

~ dioxide release alarm 二氧化碳释放报警 ‖ *Syn*. carbon dioxide releasing alarm 二氧化碳释放报警

~ dioxide release control 二氧化碳释放控制

~ dioxide room 二氧化碳室

~ dioxide warning alarm 二氧化碳警报

~ dioxide welding 二氧化碳焊接

~ emission 碳排放，碳排放量，二氧化碳排放

~ equivalent 碳当量

~ filament lamp 碳丝灯

~ monoxide 一氧化碳

~ monoxide canister 一氧化碳滤毒罐

~ neutral 碳中和

~ remove 除碳

~ residue 碳渣，残碳

~ resistor 碳电阻

~ ring 碳精环，碳环

~ tetrachloride 四氯化碳

carbonaceous [ka:bə'neiʃəs] a. 碳的，碳质的，含碳的

~ deposit 含碳沉积

carbonic [ka:'bɔnik] a. 碳的，由碳得到的

~ acid gas compressor 碳酸气体压缩机

carbonization [ˌka:bənai'zeiʃən] n. 碳化，干馏，碳化物

carbonize ['ka:bənaiz] v. 碳化，使成碳，使与碳化合

carbonizing ['ka:bənaiziŋ] n. 碳化；v. (carbonize 的 ing 形式) 碳化，使成碳，使与碳化合

~ of valve 阀门碳化

carburetor [ka:bə'retə(r)] n. 汽化器，化油器

~ engine 汽化器式发动机

carburize [ˌka:bjurai'zeiʃən] v. 渗碳 ‖ *Ant*. decarburize 脱碳，除碳

carburization [ˌka:bjurai'zeiʃən] n. 渗碳 ‖ *Ant*. decarburization 脱碳，除炭

carcinogen [ka:'sinədʒən] n. 致癌物质

CARD (computer-aided researching and developing) 计算机辅助研究开发

cardinal ['ka:dinəl] n. 基数；a. 首要的，主要的，基本的

~ buoy 方位浮标

~ measurement 基数测量

~ plane 基平面

~ rule 基本原则

cardiopulmonary [ˌka:diəu'pʌlmənəri] a. 心肺的，与心肺有关的

~ Resuscitation (CPR) 心肺复苏，心肺复苏术

cargo ['ka:gəu] n. 货物，船货

~ agent 货运代理

~ area 货物区，装货区域

~ batten 货舱壁护条，舱壁护条

~ berth 货物码头

~ block 吊货滑车

~ boom 吊货杆，起重臂，吊杆

~ capacity 载货容积，载物能力

~ carrying hold 货舱 ‖ *Syn*. cargo carrying tank 货舱

~ cluster 装货照明灯

~ compressor room (液化气船)货物压缩机室

~ container 货物集装箱

~ containment 货物围护

~ containment system 货物围护系统

~ contamination 货物污染

~ control room 货物控制室

~ crane 船货(码头)起重机

~ cubic 载货容积

~ cubic capacity 载货容量

~ damage 货损

~ deadweight 载货量

~ declaration 到港货物报关单

~ handling 货物装卸

~ handling gear 货物装卸设备，货物装卸装置 ‖ *Syn*. cargo handling equipment 货物装卸设备，货物装卸装置；cargo handling machinery 货物装卸设备，货物装卸装置

~ handling procedure 货物装卸程序

~ handling space 货物装卸处所

~ hatch 货舱口

~ hold 货舱

~ hold bilge 货舱舱底

~ hold dehumidification system 货舱除湿系统，货舱空气干燥系统

~ hold ventilation 货舱通风

~ hook 货钩，吊货钩

~ insurance 货物运输保险

~ lamp 货舱工作灯 ‖ *Syn*. cargo light 货舱工作灯

~ load operating mode management 货物装载操作模式管理

~ loading door 货舱装料门，货舱加料门

~ main 货油总管

~ manifest 舱单，货物舱单，货物清单，货舱清单

~ monitoring 液货监测

~ net 吊货网，网兜

~ oil 货油

~ oil deck pipeline 甲板货油管系

~ oil heating system 货油加热系统

~ oil hose 货油软管

~ oil loading system 货油装载系统

~ oil pump 货油泵

~ oil pump room 货油泵舱，货油泵间

~ oil pump room pipeline 货油泵舱管系

~ oil pump room ventilation 货油泵舱通风

~ oil pump turbine 货油泵透平

~ oil pumping system 货油装卸系统

~ oil stripping pump 货油清舱泵

~ oil suction 货油吸口

~ oil suction heating coil 货油吸口加热盘管

~ oil tank 货油舱

~ oil tank breathing system 货油舱透气系统 ‖ *Syn*. cargo oil tank venting system 货油舱透气系统

~ oil tank cleaning installations 货油舱洗舱设备

~ oil tank gas-free installations 货油舱油气驱除装置

~ oil tank gas pressure indicator 货油舱气压指示器

~ oil tank stripping system 货油舱清舱系统

~ oil transfer main pipe line 货油输送总管 ‖ *Syn*. main cargo oil line 货油总管，货油主管

~ oil unloading system 货油卸载系统

~ oil valve 货油阀

~ piping 液货管系

~ pressure control 液货压力控制

~ record book for ships carrying noxious liquid substances in bulk 散装有害液体货物记录簿

~ residues 货物残渣

~ sampling 货物取样

~ securing manual 货物系固手册

~ segregation 货物分隔，货物隔离

~ service space 货运服务空间

~ service space of tanker 油轮的货运服务空间

~ ship 货船，货轮，货运船

~ Ship Safety Construction Certificate (CSSCC) 货船构造安全证书

~ Ship Safety Equipment Certificate (CSSEC) 货船设备安全证书

~ Ship Safety Radio Certificate (CSSRC) 货船无线电安全证书

~ space 货舱 ‖ *Syn*. cargo tank 货舱

~ spotter 货物定位装置

~ stage 货物平台，装卸跳板

~ stowage plan 货物配载图

~ surveyor 商检员，商检师

~ sweat 货物结露，货物汗湿

~ tank access 货舱入口

~ tank ballasting 液货舱压载

~ tank deballasting 液货舱卸载

~ tank gas piping system 货油舱透气管系 ‖ *Syn*. cargo tank vapor piping system 货油舱透气管系

~ tank inerting 货舱惰化

~ tank level gauging 货舱液位测量

~ tank purging 货油舱除气

~ tank stripping 扫舱
~ tank venting 货舱通风
~ temperature control 货物温度控制
~ terminal 货运终点站
~ transfer method 货物驳运方法
~ transfer rate 转货率
~ transport 货物运输
~ transport unit 货物运输组件
~ transportation insurance 货物运输保险
~ ventilation 货物通风
~ vessel 载货船，货轮
~ winch 起货机
~ winch motor 起货机电动机
cargo-associated 货物相关的
~ waste 货物所生相关废弃物
carpenter ['ka:pintə] n. 木匠
carpenter's 木工的
~ saw 木工锯
~ saw blade 木工锯条
carpet ['ka:pit] n. 地毯
carrack ['kærək] n. (=galleon) 大帆船 (15～18 世纪初军舰商船两用的)
carrier ['kæriə] n. 航空母舰，载波(信号)，运送者，行李架，搬运器，邮递员，带菌者
~ foil 载体箔
~ ring 承环，垫圈
~ tape 载带
carry ['kæri] n. 进位，射程，运载；v. 携带，运送，支持，支撑，传送，意味，被携带，能达到
~ bag 厚纸袋
~ down 搬下，取下
~ on 继续开展，坚持，举止失常
~ out 完成，实现，贯彻，执行 ‖ *Syn*. execute 执行，实行，完成；implement 贯彻，实现，执行
~ over 继续，结转次页，延期
carrying ['kæriiŋ] v. (carry 的 ing 形式) 携带，运送，支持，支撑，传送，意味，被携带，能达到；a. 运送的，运输的
~ capacity 载客量，容纳量
carton ['ka:tən] n. 硬纸盒，纸板箱
cartridge ['ka:tridʒ] n. 弹药筒
~ filter 滤筒过滤器
~ fuse 熔丝管，管形熔热
~ valve 筒形插装式阀，插装阀
cascade [kæs'keid] n. 串联，级联，层叠，喷流
~ control 级联控制，串级控制，逐位控制
~ evaporation 串级蒸发
~ protection 分级保护
~ set 串级机组，级联式机组
~ system 串联系统，级联方式，级联系统
~ tank 阶式柜，阶式水箱
~ transformer 级联变压器，串联变压器
case [keis] n. 容器，事，病例，案例，情形，场合，讼案
casing ['keisiŋ] n. 金属套筒，外壳，包装，保护性的外套
~ head 套管头
~ pipe 套管，井壁管
~ string 套管柱
~ tube 套管
~ wall 汽缸壁，缸壁
~ wear ring 泵壳密封环
cassab [kə'sa:b] n. 亚洲籍商船水手
cast [ka:st] n. 投掷，铸件，脱落物，一瞥；v. 投，抛，投射，浇铸，计算
~ aluminum rotor 铸铝转子

~ anchor 抛锚

~ away 抛弃，丢开

~ bedplate 铸造式底座

~ bronze 铸造青铜，铸青铜

~ by 排除，放弃

~ inblock 整体铸造

~ iron 铸铁

~ iron chock 铸铁座，铸铁轴承座

~ iron housing 铸铁机架

~ iron pipe 铸铁管

~ iron ring 铸铁环

~ iron welding wire 铸铁焊条

~ product 铸件

~ resin 铸塑树脂

~ steel 铸钢

~ steel apron 铸钢铺板

~ steel chock 铸钢轴承座

~ steel housing 铸钢机架

~ steel product 铸钢产品

~ steel stem post 铸钢艏柱

castability [ka:stə'biliti] *n*. 铸造性，可铸性，铸造质量

casting ['ka:stiŋ] *n*. 铸件，铸造；*v*. (cast 的 ing 形式) 投，抛，投射，浇铸，计算

~ aluminium 铸铝

~ blank 铸坯

~ bronze 铸青铜

~ copper 铸铜

~ gray iron 铸灰口铁

~ iron 铸铁

~ steel 铸钢

castle ['ka:sl] *n*. 城堡，避难所

~ nut 槽形螺母，槽顶螺母，蝶形螺母

casual ['kæʒjuəl] *a*. 偶然的，不经意的，临时的，肤浅的，宽大的，允许的

~ clothing 休闲装，便服 ‖ *Syn*. casual wear 休闲装，便服

~ inspection 抽检，不定期检查

~ leave 事假，例假

casualty ['kæʒjuəlti] *n*. 事故，伤亡，伤亡人员 ‖ *Syn*. accident 意外事件，意外事故；chance failure 偶发故障，意外事故；contingency 意外事故，紧急情况，不测事件；incident 事件，突发事件；misfortune 不幸，灾难，灾祸；mishap 灾祸，厄运，倒霉事

catalog ['kætəlɔg] (=catalogue) *n*. 目录，目录册；*v*. 编目录

catalogue ['kætəlɔg] (=catalog) *n*. 目录，目录册；*v*. 编目录

catalyst ['kætəlist] *n*. 催化剂

catalytic [,kætə'litik] *a*. 催化剂的，接触反应的

~ combustion analyzer 催化燃烧分析仪

~ converter 催化转化器

~ fines 催化剂粉末

~ reaction 催化反应

catamaran [,kætəmə'ræn] *n*. 双体船，筏

~ driller 钻井船，钻探船

~ ferry 双体渡船

~ hull 双船体

~ terminal 双体船码头

~ trawler 双体拖网渔船

~ tug 双体拖船

catboat ['kætbəut] *n*. 独桅艇

catch [kætʃ] *n*. 捕捉，捕获物；*v*. 捕获，赶上(车、船等)，发觉，感染，抓住，燃着

~ all 打捞工具，选择全部，设立预设账号

~ fan 扇形防护网架

~ pit 集水沟，排水井，集水井，聚泥坑
~ plate 拨盘，导夹盘
categorization [ˌkætəgəraiˈzeiʃən] *n.* 分类
~ of noxious liquid substances 有毒液体物质的分类
categorize [ˈkætigəraiz] *v.* 加以类别，分类
category [ˈkætigəri] *n.* 种类，类别，范畴
catenary [kəˈti:nəri] *n.* 悬链线；*a.* 悬链线的
~ anchor leg mooring 悬链锚腿系泊
~ mooring 悬垂系泊
~ suspension 悬链
cater [ˈkeitə] *v.* 备办食物，满足，投合
~ to 迎合，满足 ‖ *Syn.* content 使满足；fill 满足；fulfil 满足；meet 满足，达到要求；satisfy 满足，使满意
catering [ˈkeitəriŋ] *n.* 公共饮食业，给养；*v.* (cater 的 ing 形式) 备办食物，满足，投合
~ equipment 餐饮设备
~ service 餐饮服务
cathodal [ˈkæθəudəl] *a.* 阴极的
cathode [ˈkæθəud] *n.* 阴极，负极 ‖ *Syn.* negative pole 阴极，负极 ‖ *Ant.* anode 阳极，正极；positive pole 阳极，正极
cathodic [kəˈθɔdik] *a.* 阴极的，负极的
~ current 阴极电流
~ electrolysis 阴极电解
~ method 阴极防锈法
~ protection 阴极保护
~ protector 阴极保护装置
cattle [ˈkætl] *n.* 牛，家养牲畜
~ ship 牲口船
catwalk [ˈkætwɔ:k] *n.* 狭小通道，桥上人行道
caulk [kɔ:k] *v.* 填…以防漏
caustic [ˈkɔ:stik] *a.* 腐蚀性的，刻薄的

~ corrosion 碱腐蚀，苛性腐蚀
~ cracking 碱裂，碱脆，苛性裂纹
~ embrittlement 碱脆
~ lime 苛性石灰，生石灰，氧化钙
~ potash 氢氧化钾
~ soda 氢氧化钠，烧碱，火碱，苛性钠
~ solution 苛性碱溶液
~ wash 碱洗，氢氧化钠洗
cavitary [ˈkævitəri] *a.* 腔的，空洞的
cavitate [ˈkæviteit] *v.* 成穴，空化
cavitation [ˌkæviˈteiʃən] *n.* 气穴现象，成穴
~ damage 空蚀
~ effect 空化效应，气蚀效应
~ erosion 气蚀，空隙腐蚀，液流气泡侵蚀
~ number 空化数
~ test 空化试验，空泡试验，空隙现象试验
~ tunnel 空化水筒
cavity [ˈkæviti] *n.* 洞，空穴，腔
cay [kei] *n.* 礁岩，珊瑚礁，沙洲
CB (circuit breaker) 电路断路器，断路器
CBT (clean ballast tank) 清洁压载舱
CCD (charge coupled-device) 电荷耦合器件
CCITB (China Commodity Inspection and Testing Bureau) 中国商品检验局，中国商检局
CCL (copper clad laminate) 覆铜薄层压板，敷铜箔叠层板
CCM (continuous conduction mode) 连续导电模式，连续导通模式
CCS (China Classification Society) 中国船级社
CCS (coordinated control system) 联动调整系统，协调控制系统

CD (compact disc) 光盘，光碟机，激光唱片

CD-R (compact disc-recordable) 可写光盘，可烧录光盘

CD-ROM (compact disc-read only memory) 只读光盘存储器，只读光盘

CD-RW (compact disc-rewritable) 可擦除光盘

CDGT (combined diesel and gas turbine) 柴燃联合动力装置，复合式柴燃气涡轮

CE (chief engineer) 轮机长，大管轮，老轨，总工程师

ceil [si:l] v. 装天花板，装船内格子板

ceiling ['si:liŋ] n. 隔板，舱室垫板，天花板，上限，最高限度，云幕高度；v. (ceil 的 ing 形式) 装天花板，装船内格子板

~ height 升限，室内净高，楼底高度，层高

~ lamp 吊灯，吸顶灯，天花灯 ‖ *Syn*. ceiling light 吊灯，吸顶灯，天花灯

~ panel 顶棚镶板

~ type induction unit 吊顶式诱导器

ceiling-mounted 置式的，吊顶式的，天花板的

~ lighting fitting 天棚灯

celestial [si'lestiəl] a. 天上的，天空的，天体的，极好的

~ navigation 天文导航

cell [sel] n. 电池，(电池、光电)元件，单元，单人房间 ‖ *Syn*. accumulator 蓄电池；battery 电池，电池组，蓄电池 ‖ *Syn*. constituent 成分，要素；component 成分，部分，元件，零件，要素，组分；element 要素，元素，成分，元件；ingredient 成分，因素；organ 元件；part 零件，部件

~ guide 格槽导引装置

~ level 单元级

~ phone 手机 ‖ *Syn*. cellular phone 手机

cellular ['seljulə] a. 细胞的，多洞的，蜂窝式的

~ phone 手机 ‖ *Syn*. cell phone 手机

~ radiator 蜂窝式散热器

Celsius ['selsjəs] a. 摄氏的

cement [si'ment] n. 水泥，接合剂；v. 接合，用水泥涂，巩固，粘牢

~ carrier 水泥运输船

cementing [si'mentiŋ] n. 胶接，溶接，黏合；v. (cement 的 ing 形式) 接合，用水泥涂，巩固，粘牢

~ agent 黏合剂，胶结料 ‖ *Syn*. cementing material 胶结料，黏合剂，胶合材料

censor ['sensə] n. 检查员；v. 检查，审查 ‖ *Syn*. check 检查，核对；examine 检查，调查；inspect 检查，视察；review 检查，检阅；rummage 搜出，检查

center ['sentə] n. 中心，中央，中心点，中锋；v. 集中，定中心，居中，有中心，置于中心；a. 中央的，位于正中的

~ distance 中心距

~ girder 中底桁，中桁材

~ keelson 中内龙骨

~ line 中心线，中线

~ of gravity 重心，重力中心

~ punch 冲子，定准器，中心冲

~ tap connection 中心抽头连接

~ valve 中心阀

~ well 中央井 ‖ *Syn*. moonpool 中央井

center-castle 船中部上层建筑

centerline ['sentəlain] n. 中心线

~ bulkhead 中纵舱壁

centigrade ['sentigreid] *a.* 分为百度的，百分度的，摄氏温度的

centimeter ['sentimi:tər] (cm) *n.* 厘米

central [sen'trə:l] *n.* 电话总机；*a.* 中心的，中央的，重要的，主要的，中枢的，走中间道路的

~ air condition system 中央空调系统‖ ***Syn.*** central air conditioning system 中央空调系统

~ air conditioner 中央空调机

~ axis 中心轴

~ buoyancy 中性浮力

~ control 中心控制，中央控制

~ control emergency push button 应急集中控制按钮

~ control room 中央控制室

~ control station 中央控制站

~ cooling system 中央冷却系统

~ cooling water system 中央冷却水系统

~ engine 中置发动机

~ excitation system 集中激磁系统，中心励磁式，中央励磁式

~ fire alarm control unit 集中火灾报警控制器

~ heating 中央供暖，中央暖气系，集中供暖

~ part 中心部分

~ place 中心地

~ point 中心点

~ Processing Unit (CPU) 中央处理器

~ pumping unit 中央泵设备，中央抽油机，中央水泵机组

~ region 中部，腹地

~ signal system 中央信号系统

~ station 中心电站，总电站，中央车站

~ system 中心制，中央处理系统，集中系统

central-located 位于中心的

~ connecting rod 中心曲柄连杆机构

centrality [sen'træliti] *n.* 中心，中央，向心性，集中性

centralize ['sentrəlaiz] *v.* 集聚，集中，集中于中心

centralized ['sentrəlaizd] *v.* (centralize 的过去式和过去分词) 集聚，集中，集中于中心；*a.* 集中的，中央集权的

~ control 集中控制

~ control station 集中控制站，集控站

~ inverter 集中式逆变器

~ lubrication 集中润滑

~ maintenance 集中维护，集中维修(保养)

~ monitor 集中监测器

~ monitoring 集中监控

~ monitoring system 集中监控系统

~ operation 集中操作

~ operation cargo oil pumping system 集中操纵货油装卸系统

~ priming system 集中注油系统，集中注水系统，集中饮水系统

centre ['sentə] *n.* 中心，中央，中心区；*v.* 集中

~ cargo tank 货油舱中心

~ girder 主龙筋龙骨立板

~ line 中线，中心线

~ line girder 中内龙骨

~ line of boiler 锅炉中轴线，锅炉中线

~ of buoyancy 浮力中心，浮心

~ of flotation 漂心

~ of gravity 重心

~ of lateral resistance 侧向阻力中心，

91

横向阻力中心

~ of towing pull 牵引拉力中心

~ tank 中间液舱

~ valve 中心阀

centremost ['sentəməust] *a.* 在最中心的

centrifugal [sen'trifjugəl] *a.* 离心的，离心力的

~ acceleration 离心加速度

~ compressor 离心式压缩机，离心压气机

~ dehydrator 离心脱水机

~ fan 离心风机，离心式风扇，离心式鼓风机

~ filtration 离心过滤

~ force 离心力

~ governor 离心调速器，离心调节器

~ oil separator 离心分油机 ‖ *Syn*. centrifugal separator 离心澄清机，离心分离机，离心分离器；centrifuge 离心分离机

~ pump 离心泵

~ refrigerating compressor 离心式制冷压缩机

~ seal 离心密封

~ separation 离心分离，离心分离法

~ settling 离心沉降

~ switch 离心开关

centrifugate [,sen'trifjugeit] *n.* 以离心力分出之物；*v.* 使离心，利用离心力分离

centrifuge ['sentrifju:dʒ] *n.* 离心分离机，分油机 ‖ *Syn*. centrifugal oil separator 离心分油机；centrifugal separator 离心澄清机，离心分离机，离心分离器 ‖ clarifier 分杂机，澄清器；purifier 分水机

~ pump 离心泵

centrifuger [sentri'fʌgər] *n.* 离心机

centripetal [sen'tripitl] *a.* 向心的，利用向心力的

centroid ['sentrɔid] *n.* 质心

CEO (chief executive officer) 首席执行官，行政总裁

ceramic [si'ræmik] *n.* 陶瓷，陶瓷制品，陶器；*a.* 陶瓷的，陶器的

~ bearing 陶瓷轴承

~ capacitor 陶瓷电容器

~ filter 陶瓷过滤器

~ insulator 陶瓷绝缘子，陶瓷绝缘器

~ resistor 陶瓷电阻(器)，陶管电阻(器)

~ sensor element 陶瓷传感器

~ substrate printed board 陶瓷印制板

certificate [sə'tifikit] *n.* 证书，证明书；*v.* 发证明书，以证书形式授权

~ of approval 批准证书

~ of competency 合格证书

~ of Fitness for the Carriage of Dangerous Chemicals in Bulk 散装运输危险化学品适装证书

~ of Fitness for the Carriage of Liquefied Gases in Bulk 散装运输液化气体适装证书

~ of quality 质量证书，品质证书，合格证

~ of registration 注册证书，登记证书，注册执照

~ of registry 船籍证明

~ of seaworthiness 适航证书

~ to be issued 待签发的证书

certificated [sə'tifikitid] *v.* (certificate 的过去式和过去分词) 发证明书，以证书形式授权；*a.* 具有证明文件的，立有证

据的，业经证明的

~ for masters, officers or ratings 船长、高级船员或船员等级证书

~ propeller 合格螺旋桨

certification [ˌsə:tifi'keiʃən] *n*. 证明，证明书，合格证

~ card 证明卡

certified ['sə:tifaid] *v*. (certify 的过去式和过去分词) 证明，证实，保证，确认，签名，宣称，授予合格证书；*a*. 被鉴定的，有保证的，持有证明书的，持有执照的

~ manifest 签证输入品货单，签证舱单

~ person 有资质人员，持证人员，合格人员

~ pipette 检定吸管，检定量管

certify ['sə: tifai] *v*. 证明，证实，保证，确认，签名，宣称，授予合格证书

cessation [sə'seiʃən] *n*. 休止，停止，中止

cetane ['si:tein] *n*. 十六烷，鲸蜡烷

~ index 十六烷指数

~ number 十六烷值 ‖ *Syn*. cetane value 十六烷值

~ rating 十六烷品级

CFC (chlorofluorocarbon) 氯氟化碳，氯氟烃

~ ploymer 含氯氟烃聚合物

chafe [tʃeif] *v*. 擦热，擦破，使恼火

chafing ['tʃeifiŋ] *n*. 皮肤发炎；*v*. (chafe 的 ing 形式) 擦热，擦破，使恼火

~ chain 防磨链，防磨链

~ check 擦损检查

~ fatigue 疲劳磨损

~ gear 防擦装置，防擦用具，保护网

~ iron 冲铁

~ mat 防擦席，防擦垫

~ plate 防擦板

~ resistance 耐磨性

~ rod 防擦条

chain [tʃein] *n*. 链条，镣铐，一连串，一系列；*v*. 用链条拴住

~ block 起重机，链动滑轮，链滑车

~ cable 锚链，链索

~ cable stopper 制链器

~ drive 链传动装置

~ drive casing 链驱动箱

~ drum 链鼓轮，链盘，链筒

~ lifter 链式升降机

~ lifter brake 链式升降机止动器

~ link 链环，链节

~ locker 锚链舱

~ of command 指挥链

~ pipe 锚链管 ‖ *Syn*. hawse pipe 锚链孔衬管，锚链筒；Spurling pipe 锚链筒，锚链管

~ pitch 链条节距，链距

~ printer 链式打印机

~ reaction 链式反应

~ saw 链锯

~ sling 链式吊索

~ sprocket 链轮

~ stopper 锚链制动器

~ stripper 分链器

~ swivel 锚链转环

~ system 连锁制

~ transfer 链转移，链传递

~ transmission 链传动

~ wheel 链轮

chained [tʃeind] *v*. (chain 的过去式和过去分词) 用链条拴住；*a*. 链式的，装链的，被链锁住的

~ aggregation 链式集结

chalk [tʃɔ:k] *n*. 粉笔，白垩；*v*. 用粉笔写，

和以白垩

~ test 粉末渗透探伤法，白垩试验

chamber ['tʃeimbə] *n*. 室，房间，封闭空间，密闭分隔间，(枪)膛，议院，会所，议事厅

chamfer ['tʃæmfə] *n*. 斜面,沟槽; *v*. 斜切，削角

~ machine 倒角机

chance [tʃɑ:ns] *n*. 机会，可能性，偶然性，运气，机缘，侥幸; *v*. 碰巧，偶然发生，冒险; *a*. 偶然的，恰巧的

~ failure 偶发故障，意外事故 ‖ *Syn*. accident 意外事件,意外事故; casualty 事故，伤亡; contingency 意外事故，紧急情况，不测事件; incident 事件，突发事件; misfortune 不幸，灾难，灾祸; mishap 灾祸，厄运，倒霉事

change [tʃeindʒ] *n*. 改变，变化，转变，找回的零钱，找头，辅币; *v*. 替换，变换，转换，变化，改变，改造，兑换

~ gear 变速齿轮

~ in the load 负荷变化

~ into 变为，使改变

~ map 变化图

~ of state 物态变化，状态变化

~ over 改变，对调位置

~ over test between shaft generator and diesel generator on sea trial 航行试验中轴带发电机与柴油发电机之间的换车试验

~ pole 变极

~ pole moter 变极电动机

~ route 修改工序，替换路由，改变路线

~ valve 换向阀，多向阀，活页阀，三通阀

change-over 转换，转变，改革

~ cock 换向转心阀

~ condition 转换条件

~ contact 转换触点

~ key 换向按钮

~ lever 转换杆

~ point 转换点，变换点

~ relay 切换继电器

~ selector 转换选择器

~ switch 转换开关，换向开关

~ switching 换接

~ valve 变换阀，转换阀

~ valve chest 变换阀室，转换阀室

changeable ['tʃeindʒəbl] *a*. 可改变的，易变的

~ cost 变动成本

changing ['tʃeindʒiŋ] *n*. 替换,变换,转换，变化，改变，改造，兑换; *v*. (change 的 ing 形式) 替换，变换，转换，变化，改变，改造，兑换

~ load 交变负载，交变荷重

~ room 更衣室

channel ['tʃænl] *n*. 海峡，水道，沟，路线; *v*. 引导，开导，信道，频道，形成河道 ‖ *Syn*. path 路线

~ bar 槽材，槽铁

~ capacity 通道容量，信道容量

chaos ['keiɔs] *n*. 混乱，混沌

chaotic [kei'ɔtik] *a*. 混乱的，无秩序的

character ['kæriktə] *n*. 特性，特征，性质，品质，字符，性格，人物; *v*. 写，刻，印，使具有特征

characteristic [,kæriktə'ristik] *n*. 特性，特征，对数的整数部分; *a*. 特有的，表示特性的，典型的，显著的

~ curve 特征曲线

~ curve at constant speed 定速特性曲线

~ equation 特征方程

~ function 特征函数

~ locus 特征轨迹

~ value 特性值

characterize ['kæriktəraiz] v. 辨别, 描绘, 刻画, 形容, 表现…的特色, 刻画的…性格

charge [tʃɑ:dʒ] n. 负荷, 电荷, 费用, 主管, 掌管, 充电, 充气, 充油, 装料; v. 装满, 控诉, 责令, 告诫, 指示, 加罪于, 冲锋, 收费 ‖ Ant. discharge 卸下, 卸货, 放出, 腾空

~ air 充气, 增压空气

~ air cooler 中冷器

~ air cooling system 充气冷却系统, 增压空气冷却系统

~ and discharge key 充放电电键

~ and discharge operation test for battery and charge equipment 蓄电池和充电装置的充放电试验

~ air receiver 增压空气容器

~ characteristic curve 充电特性曲线

~ efficiency 充电效率

~ pump 电荷泵, 充电泵

~ rate 充电率, 收费率

~ valve 充气阀, 加载阀, 加液阀

charge-discharge 充电放电, 充放电

~ cycling 充放电循环

~ process 充放电过程

~ rate 充放电率

charging ['tʃɑ:dʒiŋ] n. 装料, 炉料; v. (charge 的 ing 形式) 装满, 控诉, 责令, 告诫, 指示, 加罪于, 冲锋, 收费

~ and discharging 充放电

~ and discharging curve 充放电曲线

~ apparatus 装料设备, 进料装置

~ current 充电电流

~ device 充电装置

~ door 加料门

~ efficiency 充电效率, 充气效率, 灌注效率

~ generator 充电发电机

~ hole 装料口

~ hopper 装料漏斗, 装料斗

~ machine 装料机

~ panel 充电屏

~ rate 充电率, 进料量, 进料速度, 加料速度, 注入速率

~ resistor 充电电阻器

~ set 充电装置, 增压装置, 燃气发生器

~ stroke 进气冲程, 充气冲程

~ system 充电系统, 加料系统

~ test and safety valve and automatic device adjusting for main compressor (auxiliary compressor) 主(辅)空气压缩机的充气试验、安全阀和自动装置的调整

~ time 充电时间, 收费时间

~ valve 充气阀, 加载阀, 加液阀

~ voltage 充电电压

chart [tʃɑ:t] n. 海图, 图表; v. 制图

~ area 绘图区域

~ drawing set 绘图仪器

~ room 海图室

~ table 图表架, 海图桌

charter ['tʃɑ:tə] n. 规章; v. 租, 包(船、车等)

~ contracts 租船契约

~ freight 租船运费

~ party 租船契约, (船只的)租赁

~ transport 租船运输

charterer ['tʃɑ:tərə] n. 租者, 租船主

chartering ['tʃɑ:tərɪŋ] *n.* 租用；*v.* (charter 的 ing 形式) 租，包(船、车等)
~ agent 租船代理人
~ broker 租船经纪人
~ business 租船业务
~ department 租船部
~ manager 租船经理
~ order 租船委托书，租船单
~ trade 船舶租赁业

check [tʃek] *n.* 阻止，制止，控制，阻止物，支票，检讫的记号；*v.* 检查，制止，核对，寄存，托运，证明无误，核对无误，逐项相符 ‖ *Syn.* censor 检查，审查；examine 检查，调查；inspect 检查，视察；review 检查，检阅；rummage 搜出，检查
~ according to the instruction book 根据说明书检查
~ after assemblage 组装后检查
~ completely 完全检查
~ dive 第一潜
~ for alignment 检查对准
~ for leakage 检查泄漏
~ for surface contact area (metallic contact) between stern shaft and propeller hub tapers 检查螺旋桨轴与螺旋桨锥度接触面
~ gauge 校验仪表
~ plate 垫板，挡板，防松板，止动板
~ valve 止回阀，单向阀，逆止阀，止逆阀 ‖ *Syn.* inverted valve 止回阀，单向阀，逆止阀，止逆阀；non-return valve 止回阀，单向阀，逆止阀，止逆阀；one-way valve 止回阀，单向阀，逆止阀，止逆阀

checker ['tʃekə] *n.* 检验员，寄存者，管理员；*v.* 以方格标记，呈多样化

checkered ['tʃekəd] *v.* 以方格标记，呈多样化；*a.* 多变的，网纹的
~ plate 网纹钢板，网纹板

checking ['tʃekɪŋ] *n.* 校核，检验，校验，检查，核算，验算；*v.* (check 的 ing 形式) 检查，制止，核对，寄存，托运，证明无误，核对无误，逐项相符
~ liner of main engine 主机垫片检查
~ rudder after completing (finished) 舵叶完工后检查
~ structure integrity of superstructure (deckhouse) after closed 上层建筑合拢后结构完整性检查
~ the joint accuracy and structure integrity between No.8 and No.9 block after closed No.8 与 No.9 分段合拢后大接头装配精确性和结构完整性检查

checklist ['tʃeklɪst] *n.* 清单，名单

checkout ['tʃekaʊt] *n.* 检验，校验，结账

chemical ['kemɪkəl] *n.* 化学制品，化学药品；*a.* 化学的
~ addition system 化学添加系统
~ agent 化学制剂，化学药剂
~ agents dealing with oil spills 处理溢油的化学制剂
~ analysis 化学分析
~ burn 化学烧伤
~ cargo ship 化学品船
~ cleaning 化学清洗，化学脱垢
~ composition 化学组成，化学构成，化学成分
~ compound 化合物
~ corrosion 化学腐蚀
~ descaling 化学除垢，药剂除垢
~ dispersant 化学分散剂

~ dosing unit 化学加药装置
~ dosing valve 化学加药阀
~ energy 化学能
~ fiber 化学纤维，化工化纤，化纤
~ fire extinguisher 化学灭火器
~ foam 化学泡沫
~ foam extinguisher 化学泡沫灭火器
~ materials 化工材料
~ oxygen demand (COD) 化学需氧量
~ pollution 化学污染
~ pollution response 化学污染反应
~ precipitation 化学沉淀
~ process 化学方法，化学过程，化学加工，化工工艺
~ product 化工产品，化学制品
~ property 化学性质
~ propulsion 化学推进
~ reaction 化学反应
~ reaction fire extinguisher 化学反应灭火器
~ stability 化学稳定性
~ storage facility 化学品储存设施
~ structure 化学结构
~ synthesis 化学合成(法)
~ tanker 化学品船，化学品运输船
~ treatment 化学处理

chemical-based 基于化学(方法)的
~ treatment system 基于化学(方法)的处理系统

chemical-resistant 防化学腐蚀的
~ film 防化学腐蚀膜，化学膜

chest [tʃest] *n.* 箱，柜，密封室，胸腔，胸膛

chief ['tʃi:f] *n.* 首领，领袖，酋长，长官，主要部分，最有价值的部分；*a.* 主要的，首要的，首席的，主任的

~ accountant 首席会计师，主任会计，总会计师
~ cook 厨师长，主厨，大厨，第一厨师
~ engineer (CE) 轮机长，大管轮，老轨，总工程师
~ engineer's office 轮机长办公室，总工程师办公室
~ executive officer (CEO) 首席执行官，行政总裁
~ financial officer 财务总监，首席财务官，财务长
~ mate 大副 ‖ *Syn.* chief officer 大副；first mate (海军)大副
~ of staff 参谋长，幕僚长，司令
~ officer's office 大副办公室
~ operating officer 首席运营官，首席经营官，首席运营干事
~ purser 主乘务长
~ radio officer 报务主任
~ representative 首席代表
~ steward 客运主任，管事部经理，事务长，总管事，大管事
~ tallyman 理货员

chill [tʃil] *n.* 寒意，寒战，寒心；*v.* 使冷，变冷，冷藏；*a.* 寒冷的，扫兴的

chilled [tʃild] *v.* (chill 的过去式和过去分词) 使冷，变冷，冷藏；*a.* 冷冻的，已冷的，冷硬了的
~ cargo 冷藏货，冷货
~ water circulation 冷却水循环

chiller ['tʃilə] *n.* 冷却器

CHIMBUSCO (China Marine Bunker Supply Company) 中国船舶燃料有限责任公司

chimney ['tʃimni] *n.* 烟囱，灯罩

China ['tʃainə] *n.* 中国，瓷器，瓷料

~ Classification Society (CCS) 中国船级社

~ COSCO Shipping Group (COSCO Shipping) 中国远洋海运集团,中国远洋海运集团有限公司

~ Daily 中国日报

~ Marine Bunker Supply Company (CHIMBUSCO) 中国船舶燃料有限责任公司

~ Maritime Arbitration Commission (CMAC) 中国海事仲裁委员会

~ MSA (Maritime Safety Administration of PRC) 中国海事局

~ National Chartering Corporation (CNCC) 中国租船公司

~ Ocean Shipping Agency (COSA) 中国外轮代理公司

~ Ocean Shipping Company Chartering Department (COSCHARD) 中国远洋运输总公司租船部

~ Ocean Shipping Group Company (COSCO) 中国远洋运输集团公司,中远集团

~ Ocean Shipping Supply Corporation (COSSC) 中国外轮供应公司

~ Ocean Shipping Tally Company (COSTC) 中国外轮理货公司

chip [tʃip] *n.* 芯片,集成电路,集成电路片,碎片,缺口,筹码;*v.* 削成碎片,凿碎,削下,碎裂

~ board 硬纸板,粗纸板,纸板

~ resistor 片式电阻,片电阻

~ transistor 片状晶体管

chipping ['tʃipiŋ] *n.* 碎屑,破片;*v.* (chip 的 ing 形式) 削成碎片,凿碎,削下,碎裂

~ edger 双削齐边锯

~ hammer 錾平锤,空鹤镐头,修整锤,敲渣锤,凿锤,气錾

chisel ['tʃizl] *n.* 凿子;*v.* 砍凿

chlorinate ['klɔ:rineit] *v.* 使氯发生作用,用氯消毒,用氯处理

chlorinator ['klɔ:rineitə] *n.* 氯化器

chlorinated ['klɔ:rineitid] *v.* (chlorinate 的过去式和过去分词) 使氯发生作用,用氯消毒,用氯处理;*a.* 加氯消过毒的,氯化的,绿色的

~ hydrocarbon 氯代烃

~ rubber 氯化橡胶

chlorination [ˌklɔ:ri'neiʃən] *n.* 氯化,用氯处理

~ compartment 氯化室

chlorine ['klɔ:ri:n] *n.* 氯

~ corrosion 氯腐蚀

~ contact tank 氯接触池

~ disinfectant 氯消毒剂

chlorofluorocarbon [ˌklɔ:rəu'fluərəuka:bən] (CFC) *n.* 氯氟化碳,氯氟烃

chock [tʃɔk] *n.* 导缆钳,塞块,楔,木楔,垫木,楔形物;*v.* 系泊,用塞块塞住,用塞块固定,用楔子垫,收放定盘上;*ad.* 满满地,尽可能彻底地,尽可能接近地

~ block 挡块,垫木

~ bolt 防松螺栓

choke [tʃəuk] *n.* 窒息,阻气门,堵塞物,细颈部;*v.* 阻止,堵塞,阻塞,阻碍,窒息,哽住,使呼吸困难 ‖ *Syn.* restrictor 节气门,限流器,闸门板

~ back 忍住,抵制

~ off 抑制,劝阻

~ up 阻塞,塞满,哽咽,噎住

chop [tʃɔp] *n.* 砍,排骨,官印,商标,

碎浪，碎浪区；v. 剁碎，砍，(风浪)突变

chopper ['tʃɔpə] n. 断路器，斩光器，直升机，菜刀，斧头；v. 用直升机
~ circuit 斩波电路
~ drive circuit 斩波驱动电路
~ trigger circuit 斩波触发电路

chopper-stabilized 斩波稳定的
~ amplifier 斩波稳定放大器
~ current 斩波稳定电流
~ DC amplifier 斩波稳定直流放大器

christen ['krisn] v. 命名，洗礼

christening ['krisəniŋ] n. 洗礼仪式；v. (christen 的 ing 形式) 命名，洗礼
~ ceremony 船舶命名礼，船舶命名仪式

chromatographic [ˌkrəumætə'græfik] a. 色析法的，层离法的
~ analysis 色谱层分析，色层分析

chromatography [ˌkrəumə'tɔgrəfi] n. 色谱法，套色版

chrome [krəum] n. 铬，铬合金

chrome-molybdenum 铬钼
~ alloy steel 铬钼合金钢
~ steel valve 铬钼钢阀门

chrome-plated 镀铬的 ‖ Syn. chromium-plated 镀铬的
~ cam 镀铬凸轮
~ contraption 镀铬的玩意
~ hinge 镀铬铰链
~ iron tube 镀铬铁管
~ liner 镀铬缸套
~ part 镀铬零件，镀铬件
~ piston ring 镀铬活塞环
~ resin 镀铬树脂

chromium ['krəumjəm] n. 铬

chromium-plated 镀铬的 ‖ Syn. chrome-plated 镀铬的
~ blade 镀铬叶片
~ brass 镀铬黄铜
~ coating 镀铬层
~ part 镀铬零件，镀铬件
~ roller 镀铬辊筒，镀铬滚筒
~ tube 镀铬管

chuck [tʃʌk] n. 轧头，夹盘，卡盘，解雇；v. 抛掷，驱逐，丢弃，用卡盘夹住

chute [ʃu:t] n. 斜道，瀑布

cigarette [sigə'ret] n. 香烟，纸烟
~ end 烟蒂 ‖ Syn. cigarette end 烟蒂

CIM (computer-integrated manufacturing) 计算机集成制造

CIMS (Computer-integrated Manufacturing System) 计算机集成制造系统

cinerator ['sinireitə] n. 焚烧炉

cipher ['saifə] n. 密码

circle ['sə:kl] n. 圆，圆形，圆周，圆形物，环状物，圆形区，圆形空间，行政区，领域，范围，派系，循环；v. 包围，环绕，盘旋 ‖ ellipse 椭圆形；rectangle 矩形；square 正方形；trapezoid 梯形；triangle 三角形；rhombus 菱形；parallelogram 平行四边形

circlip ['sə:klip] n. 簧环，弹性挡圈

circuit ['sə:kit] n. 电路，线路，电子零件，电子器材，连接结构，一圈，圆圈，环形线，周线，迂回路线，联盟，协会，周游，巡回
~ board 电路板，印刷电路
~ branch 支路
~ breaker (CB) 电路断路器，断路器
~ component 电路元件，电路部件
~ design 电路设计

~ diagram 电路图，电路框图

~ impedance 电路阻抗

~ measurement technology 电路测试技术

~ parameter 电路参数

~ simulation 电路仿真

~ switching 线路交换，线路转接

circuitry ['sə:kitri] n. 电路，线路

circular ['sə:kjulə] n. 函件，通知；a. 圆的，成圆形的，环形铁路，间接的，迂回的

~ motion 圆周运动，圆运动

~ saw 圆锯 ‖ *Syn*. buzzsaw 圆锯

~ saw blade 圆锯锯条

circulate ['sə:kjuleit] v. (使)流通，(使)运行，(使)循环，(使)传播

circulating ['sə:kjuleitiŋ] n. 流通，运行，循环，传播；v. (circulate 的 ing 形式) (使)流通，(使)运行，(使)循环，(使)传播

~ hot water 循环热水

~ lube oil tank 循环滑油柜

~ oil 循环油

~ period 循环周期

~ pump 循 环 泵 ‖ *Syn*. circulation pump 循环泵

~ tank 循环柜

~ valve 循 环 阀 ‖ *Syn*. circulation valve 循环阀

~ water 循环水，活水

~ water ejector 循环水喷射器

~ water outlet valve 循环水出口阀

~ water piping 循环水管系

~ water pump 循环水泵

~ water ratio 循环水倍率

circulation [,sə:kju'leiʃən] n. 循环，流动，流通，散布，散发，分配，发行量

~ cooling 循环冷却

~ pump 循环泵 ‖ *Syn*. circulating pump 循环泵

~ theory 循环理论

~ valve 循 环 阀 ‖ *Syn*. circulating valve 循环阀

circulatory [sə:kju'leitəri] a. 循环的，循环系统的

circumference [sə'kʌmfərəns] n. 圆周，周围

circumstance ['sə:kəmstəns] n. 情形，情况，详情，境遇，事实，细节，特定事件，官方礼节，仪式，环境(circumstances) ‖ *Syn*. ambiance 周围环境，气氛；ambience 周围环境，气氛；ambient 周围环境；atmosphere 气氛；environment 环境，外界，周围；surroundings 环境

circumvent [,sə:kəm'vent] v. 围绕，包围

civil ['sivl] a. 全民的，市民的，公民的，国民的，民间的，民事的，根据民法的，文职的，有礼貌的

~ liability 民事责任

~ Liability Convention (CLC) 民事责任公约

~ servant 文职人员，文职公务员

~ service 文职，行政事务

claim [kleim] n. 要求，要求权，主张；v. 要求，认领，声称，主张，需要

claimer [k'leimə] n. 申请者，要求者

clamp [klæmp] n. 夹子，夹具，夹钳；v. 夹住，夹紧 ‖ *Syn*. vice 老虎钳，钳住；vise 老虎钳，钳住

~ circuit 箝位电路

~ coupling 纵向夹紧联轴器

~ meter 钳形表

~ plate 夹板

~ screw 制动螺旋

clamping ['klæmpiŋ] *n.* 箝位，钳位；*v.* (clamp 的 ing 形式) 夹住，夹紧

~ action 箝位作用，钳位作用

~ device 夹紧设备，夹钳设备

~ lever 紧固柄，夹紧手柄

~ nut 夹紧螺母

~ plate 夹板，压板，夹持板

~ ring 夹紧环，压圈，夹圈，锁环

~ sleeve 夹紧连接轴套，夹紧套

~ slot 夹钳槽，螺栓连接槽

~ surface 夹紧面，固定面

~ system 夹紧系统，夹紧方式

~ voltage 钳位电压，箝制电压，箝位电压，限制电压

~ washer 夹紧垫圈

clarificant ['klærifikənt] *n.* 澄清剂，净化剂

clarification [ˌklærifi'keiʃən] *n.* 澄清，净化

~ compartment 澄清室

~ tank 澄清柜

clarifier ['klærəfaiə] *n.* 分杂机，澄清器 ‖ centrifuge 离心分离机，分油机；purifier 分水机

~ disc 澄清盘，澄清池

clarify ['klærifai] *v.* 澄清，阐明

clasp [kla:sp] *n.* 扣子，钩，紧握，抱住；*v.* 扣紧，紧握，搂抱，密切合作

class [kla:s] *n.* 班级，阶级，社会等级，种类，(一节)课；*v.* 分类，分等级

~ A fire A 类火灾，A 类火

~ B fire B 类火灾，B 类火

~ C fire B 类火灾，B 类火

~ cabin 三等舱

~ D fire D 类火灾，D 类火

~ diagram 类图

~ hierarchy 类层次，类层次结构，阶级等级

~ selector 分类器

~ survey （船舶）入级检验 ‖ *Syn.* classification survey (船舶)入级检验

classic ['klæsik] *n.* 杰作，名著；*a.* 第一流的

classification [ˌklæsifi'keiʃən] *n.* 分类，分级，类别，等级

~ Certificate 入级证书

~ Certificate for Hull 船体入级证书

~ criteria 分类标准

~ drawing 分类绘图

~ process 分类过程

~ rule 分类规则

~ society 船级社

~ survey （船舶)入级检验 ‖ *Syn.* class survey (船舶)入级检验

~ surveyor 船级社验船师

~ unload protection 分级卸载保护

classifier ['klæsifaiə] *n.* 分类者，分类器

classify ['klæsifai] *v.* 分类，分等，归类，列为机密

clause [klɔ:z] *n.* 子句，条款

claw [klɔ:] *n.* 爪，脚爪，爪形器具；*v.* 抓，挖，撕

CLC (Civil Liability Convention) 民事责任公约

clean [kli:n] *v.* 打扫，使干净，清扫；*a.* 清洁的，干净的，清白的

~ air 新鲜空气，纯洁空气

~ away thoroughly 彻底清除，彻底弄干净

~ ballast pump 清洁压载水泵 ‖ *Syn.* permanent water ballast pump 清洁压载水泵

~ ballast tank (CBT) 清洁压载舱

~ ballast tank operation manual 清洁压载舱操作手册

~ break 无火花断路

~ energy 清洁能源

~ oil outlet 干净油出口

~ out 清理,清理干净,清除

~ surface 洁净表面

~ water 干净水

~ with chemical compound 用化合物清洗

~ with sada solution 用苏打溶液清洗

clean-out 清除,扫荡

~ hole 清扫口

~ valve 清洗排放闸

cleaner ['kli:nə] n. 清洁器,清洁工人

~ technology 清洁工艺,无废工艺,少废工艺

cleaning ['kli:niŋ] n. 清洁,清洗; v. (clean 的 ing 形式) 打扫,使干净,清扫

~ agent 清洁剂,清洁剂

~ door 清除门,清扫门,修炉口

~ equipment 清理设备

~ fluid 清洗液

~ interval 清洁间隔

~ solution 澄清液,清洁液,清洗液

cleanly ['kli:nli] a. 干净的,洁净的,喜清洁的; ad. 干净地,清洁地,清白地

cleanness ['kli:nnis] n. 清洁,洁白

cleanse [klenz] v. 纯净,使清洁,清洗,净化,去掉恶习

cleanser ['klenzə(r)] n. 清洁剂,使清洁的东西,擦亮粉

~ powder 清洁剂粉末,去污粉

cleansing ['klenziŋ] n. 清洁,使清洁的人或物; v. (cleanse 的 ing 形式) 纯净,使清洁,清洗,净化,去掉恶习; a. 有去污作用的

~ fluid 清洁液

clear [kliə] v. 扫除,清除,晴,跳过,净得; a. 清楚的,清晰的,清澈的,光亮的,空旷的,有条理的; ad. 清楚地,完全地

~ canister 净化滤毒器

~ ground 明显依据

~ opening 净孔,净空,净宽,有效截面

~ view screen 清晰荧光屏,旋转视窗,回旋窗,雨雪清除器

~ water 清水,净水

~ width 净宽,内径

clearance ['kliərəns] n. 净空,余隙,空隙,间隙,清除,清洁,清扫,清理过的空间,清除区域,结关,准许通行,证明书

~ angle 后角,间隙角

~ gauge 量隙规,测厚规,塞尺

~ of goods 报关,货物结关

~ rate 清除率

~ to be measured by means of lead wire 用压铅丝测量间隙

~ volume 余隙容积

~ volume scavenging 余隙容积扫气

~ width 缝隙宽度,间隙宽度

cleat [kli:t] n. 楔子,防滑木,防滑钉,夹板,加强角片,耐磨钉,羊角,系索耳; v. 用楔子支持,用楔子收紧,用楔子加固

client ['klaiənt] n. 委托人,顾客,客户

climax ['klaimæks] n. 顶点,最高点,巅峰,鼎盛,高潮

clinometer [klai'nɔmitə] *n*. 测角器，倾斜仪

clip [klip] *n*. 夹子，回形针，子弹夹；*v*. 夹住，剪短，修剪

clipper ['klipə] *n*. 大剪刀，快速帆船，修剪者，指甲刀

~ bow 飞剪型船艏 ‖ *Syn*. clipper stem 飞剪型船艏；Atlantic bow 大西洋舰艏，飞剪型船艏

~ circuit 限幅电路，削波电路

cloak [kləuk] *n*. 覆盖物，掩护物，斗篷，大氅；*v*. 掩盖，掩饰，覆盖

clock [klɔk] *n*. 时钟，计时器，秒表，仪表，时钟脉冲，计程器；*v*. 计时，记录时速，打卡

~ expression of transformer wiring group 变压器接线组别的时钟表示法

clockwise ['klɔkwaiz] *a*. 顺时针的，顺时针方向的；*ad*. 顺时针地，顺时针方向地

~ direction 顺时针方向

~ propeller 右旋螺旋桨

~ rotation 顺时针旋转

clog [klɔg] *n*. 障碍，木底鞋；*v*. 障碍，阻塞

close [kləuz] *n*. 结束；*v*. 关，关闭，结束，停止，(使)靠近，会合，包围；*a*. 近的，紧密的，精密的，齐根的，封闭的，亲密的，闷气的；*ad*. 接近，紧密地

~ down 关闭，停业

~ position relay 合闸位置继电器

~ quarters 近距离

~ up 靠近，愈合，关闭，封闭

close-coupled 紧耦合的，强耦合的，短背的

~ nozzle 紧耦合喷嘴

~ pump 紧耦合泵

~ rudder 并联舵

close-in 接近中心的，近战的

~ fueling rig 燃油补给索具

close-up 特写

~ survey 近观检验

closed [kləuzd] *v*. (close 的过去式和过去分词) 关，关闭，结束，停止，(使)靠近，会合，包围；*a*. 有边界的，封闭的，关闭的，限定的，堵住的，保密的，秘密的，闭合曲线的，闭合曲面的，闭合区间的

~ architecture 封闭式体系结构，封闭架构

~ area 闭区，禁区

~ chock 闭式导缆孔，闭式导缆器

~ circuit 闭合电路，闭合回路，封闭电路

~ circuit television 闭路电视

~ circuit voltage 闭路电压

~ circulation 闭式循环，封闭循环，闭锁循环

~ cooling system 闭式冷却系统

~ cooling water system 闭式冷却水系统

~ crosshead 封闭十字头

~ cycle 闭合循环

~ end 闭端

~ flash point 闭杯闪点

~ form 封闭形式，闭合形式，闭环形式

~ gauging device 闭式计量装置

~ interval 闭区间

~ loop 闭环 ‖ open loop 开环

~ loop circuit 闭环电路

~ loop control 闭环控制

~ loop control system 闭环控制系统

~ loop pole 闭环极点

~ loop system 闭环系统

~ loop transfer function 闭环传函

~ loop voltage gain 闭环电压增益

~ oil system of the variable delivery pump 变量泵闭式系统

~ position 闭合位置，停止位置

~ ring 闭环

~ Ro-Ro cargo space 封闭式滚装货舱

~ root 闭根

~ sanitary system 封闭式粪便水系统，封闭式卫生系统 ‖ **Syn**. enclosed sanitary system 封闭式粪便水系统，封闭式卫生系统

~ spray chamber 封闭喷射室

~ structure 闭合构造，闭合结构

~ switch 闭合开关

~ system 封闭系统，闭合体系，闭路系统，闭式系统

closing ['kləuziŋ] *n*. 关闭，终止，结算；*v*. (close 的 ing 形式) 关，关闭，结束，停止，(使)靠近，会合，包围；*a*. 结束的

~ magnet 合闸磁铁

~ motor 密闭电动机

~ operation 闭合操作

~ plate 封闭板

~ relay 闭合继电器

~ surge current 合闸冲击电流

~ valve 隔离阀，节制阀，隔断阀，停汽阀

closure ['kləuʒə] *n*. 关闭，闭合，封闭物，结束，结尾；*v*. 使终止，结束

clothes [kləuðz] *n*. 衣服，被褥，各种衣服

~ locker 衣橱

cloud [klaud] *n*. 污点，云，烟云，天空；*v*. 玷污，以云遮蔽，使黯然，阴沉

~ point 浊点，混浊点，云点

clutch [klʌtʃ] *n*. 离合器；*v*. 抓住，攫住

~ band 带式离合器

~ beakhead 离合器搭爪

~ gear handle 离合器齿轮手柄

clutter ['klʌtə] *n*. 混乱，杂乱，喧闹；*v*. 乱糟糟地堆满

cm (centimeter) 厘米

CMAC (China Maritime Arbitration Commission) 中国海事仲裁委员会

CMOS (complementary metal-oxide semiconductor) 互补金属氧化物半导体

CNC (computer numerical control) 计算机数字控制，计算机数控

~ bending press 计算机数控压弯机

~ boring machine 计算机数控镗床，计算机数控镗孔机

~ drilling machine 计算机数控钻床，计算机数控钻孔机

~ EDM wire-cutting machine 计算机数控线切割机床

~ electric discharge machine 计算机数控电腐蚀机，计算机数控电火花加工机床

~ engraving machine 计算机数控雕刻机

~ grinding machine 计算机数控磨床

~ lathe 计算机数控车床

~ machine tool fittings 计算机数控机床配件

~ milling machine 计算机数控铣床

~ shearing machine 数控剪板机

~ tooling 数控工具

~ wire-cutting machine 数控线切割机

CNCC (China National Chartering Corporation) 中国租船公司

CO_2 (carbon dioxide) 二氧化碳
~ container 二氧化碳容器
~ cylinder 二氧化碳气瓶，二氧化碳气罐
~ discharge rate 二氧化碳排放率
~ distribution piping 二氧化碳分配管系
~ extinguishing agent 二氧化碳灭火剂
~ extinguishing system 二氧化碳灭火系统，二氧化碳消防系统
~ fire extinguisher 二氧化碳灭火器
~ fire extinguishing system 二氧化碳灭火系统，二氧化碳消防系统
~ flooding system 二氧化碳涌灭系统
~ release alarm 二氧化碳释放报警 ‖ *Syn*. CO_2 releasing alarm 二氧化碳释放报警
~ release control 二氧化碳释放控制
~ room 二氧化碳室
~ warning alarm 二氧化碳警报
~ welding 二氧化碳焊接

coagulate [kəuˈægjuleit] *v*. 凝结，使合成一体；*a*. 凝结的

coagulation [kəuˌægjuˈleiʃən] *n*. 凝结，凝结物

coal [kəul] *n*. 煤；*v*. 加煤
~ bunker 煤仓
~ burning boiler 燃煤锅炉
~ carrier 运煤船
~ tar 煤焦油
~ tar epoxy resin 环氧沥青树脂
~ tar pitch 煤焦沥青，硬煤沥青

coalesce [ˌkəuəˈles] *v*. 接合，愈合，结合，合并

coalescence [ˌkəuəˈlesns] *n*. 合并，接合，联合

coalescer [kəuəˈlesə] *n*. (燃油水分)凝聚过滤器

coaming [ˈkəumiŋ] *n*. 舱口栏板，边材
~ bar 围板角钢，围板用钢条
~ stay 围板撑柱，牛腿
~ stiffener 围板扶强材，缘围加强肋

coarse [kɔːs] *a*. 粗糙的，粗鄙的，低质量的，不细致的
~ abrasive 粗研磨剂
~ filter 粗滤器
~ filtering 粗滤
~ grinding 粗磨
~ knife file 粗刀锉
~ separating compartment 粗分离室
~ strainer 粗滤器
~ synchronizing method 粗同步法
~ thread tap 粗螺纹丝锥

coarse-fine 粗糙精细，粗精
~ action 粗精调节作用
~ control 粗精控制

coast [kəust] *n*. 海岸，滑坡；*v*. 沿海岸而行
~ dredging 沿海疏浚
~ guard 海岸警卫队，海岸巡逻队队员，海岸警卫队队员
~ guard vessel 海警船，缉私船
~ line 海岸线

coastal [ˈkəustl] *a*. 海岸的，沿海的
~ area 沿海区,海岸区,滨海区 ‖ *Syn*. coastal region 沿海区，滨海区，海岸产区
~ cargo ship 沿海货船
~ city 沿海城市，海滨城市，沿岸城市
~ navigation 沿岸航行
~ passenger-cargo ship 沿海客货船
~ plain 滨海平原，沿岸平原

~ state 沿海国家

~ waters 沿海水域，近海

coastdown ['kəustdaun] n. 减，减退，下降

coaster ['kəustə] n. 近海贸易货船

coastline ['kəustlain] n. 海岸线，海岸地形，海岸轮廓

coastwise ['kəustwaiz] a. 近海的，沿岸的；ad. 沿着海岸，沿岸

coat [kəut] n. 层，涂层，外套，皮毛，表皮；v. 涂上，包上

coated ['kəutid] v. (coat 的过去式和过去分词) 涂上，包上；a. 涂上一层的

~ abrasive 砂布，砂纸，砂带，涂敷磨料

~ electrode 涂层电极

~ fiber 涂层光纤，涂覆光纤

~ rod 涂料焊条，涂药焊条

COAX (coaxial cable) 同轴电缆 ‖ *Syn.* coaxial line 同轴电缆

coaxial [kəu'æksəl] a. 同轴的，共轴的

~ cable (COAX) 同轴电缆 ‖ *Syn.* coaxial line 同轴电缆

~ circuit 同轴电路

~ connector 同轴电缆连接器，同轴连接器，同轴线接插件

~ cord 同轴软线

Cochram [kɔk'ræm] n. 考克兰(人名)

~ boiler 考克兰锅炉

cock [kɔk] n. 龙头，公鸡，头目；v. 使耸立，使竖起，堆成锥形，翘起

COD (chemical oxygen demand) 化学需氧量

code [kəud] n. 代码，代号，密码，编码；v. 编码

~ for the Construction and Equipment of Mobile Offshore Drilling Units (MODU Code) 移动式近海钻井装置建造和设备规范

~ of Safe Practice for Solid Bulk Cargoes (BC Code) 固体散货安全操作规则

coefficient [kəui'fiʃənt] n. 系数

~ matrix 系数矩阵

~ of advance 进速系数，进程系数

~ of contraction 收缩系数

~ of cubic expansion 体积膨胀系数

~ of elasticity 弹性系数

~ of excess air 空气过剩系数

~ of friction 摩擦系数

~ of intensification 强化系数

~ of linear expansion 直线膨胀系数，线胀系数

~ of refrigerating performance 制冷性能系数

~ of safety 安全系数 ‖ *Syn.* assurance coefficient 安全系数，保险系数；assurance factor 安全系数；safety coefficient 安全系数；safety factor 安全系数

~ of thermal conductivity 导热系数

~ of thermal expansion 热膨胀系数

cofferdam ['kɔfədæm] n. 围堰

~ height 围堰高度

~ tank 隔离舱

cog [kɔg] n. 嵌齿，小船；v. 上齿轮，欺骗

coherence [kəu'hiərəns] n. 一致

cohesion [kəu'hi:ʒən] n. 结合，凝聚，内聚力

cohesive [kəu'hi:siv] a. 黏着的

~ force 内聚力，黏结力，粘合力

~ property 黏结性

~ strength 内聚力

coil [kɔil] n. 螺旋管，线圈，卷，圈，盘

卷，圈形物，扰动，骚扰；v. 盘绕，缠绕，卷，卷成一圈，绕成盘状

~ cooling 盘管冷却，旋管冷却，蛇管冷却

~ current 线圈电流

~ deck 盘管盖板

~ interpole 间极线圈

~ spring 螺旋形弹簧

~ spring loaded slotted oil control ring 螺旋弹簧加载双坡口油环

~ tube 盘管

~ tube boiler 盘管式锅炉

~ tube bracket 盘管托架

~ tube forced-circulation exhaust boiler 盘管式强制循环废气锅炉

~ tube with fins 带翅蛇形管

~ tube with ribs 带肋片蛇形管

~ winding 圈绕法

coincide [ˌkəuinˈsaid] v. 一致，符合，相同，完全相应，刚好重合，同时发生，同意

~ in phase with 与…同相

coincidence [kəuˈinsidəns] n. 一致，相合，同时发生的事，同时存在的事

~ circuit 符合电路

~ factor 一致性因数

~ rate 符合率，符合计数率

colatitude [kəuˈlætitjuːd] n. 余纬度

cold [kəuld] n. 寒冷，零下温度，伤风，感冒；a. 寒冷的，使人战栗的，冷淡的，不热情的，失去知觉的

~ bend 冷弯，冷弯曲

~ brittleness 冷脆性

~ chisel 冷錾，冷凿

~ crack 冷裂缝

~ engine start 发动机冷启动

~ forging 冷锻，锤锻，自由锻

~ forging press 冷锻压机

~ insulation resistance 冷态绝缘电阻

~ machining 冷加工，冷切削

~ resistivity 抗寒能力，抗冷性

~ room 冷藏间

~ site 冷站

~ starting 低温启动，冷启动

~ storage door 冷库门 ‖ *Syn*. insulated-door 隔热门，绝热门

~ store 冷藏库，冷库

~ test 冷试法，冷态试验，低温试验，不通电试验

~ treatment 冷处理

~ work 冷作

~ working 冷加工，冷作

collapse [kəˈlæps] n. 倒塌，崩溃，失败，虚脱；v. 倒塌，崩溃，瓦解，失败，病倒

collapsible [kəˈlæpsəb(ə)l] n. 衣领，颈饰，轴环；v. 扭住衣领，拿走；a. 可折叠的

~ container 可拆装集装箱，可折叠货柜

~ flattrhvack 折叠式板架集装箱

~ mast 可倒式桅杆

~ pot 捕鱼笼

collar [ˈkɔlə] n. 环管，轴环，衣领，项圈，轭，脖围，护肩；v. 逮捕，安装领圈

~ (thrust) bearing 环肩止推式滑动轴承，环式止推轴承，环形止推轴承，环形轴承

collect [kəˈlekt] v. 收集，聚集，集中，搜集

collecting [kəˈlektiŋ] v. (collect 的 ing 形式) 收集，聚集，集中，搜集；a. 收集的，汇集的

107

~ cover 收集罩，收集盖

~ pipe 集水管，收集管

collide [kə'laid] v. 碰撞，抵触

~ with 碰撞，抵触，冲突

collision [kə'liʒən] n. 碰撞，冲突

~ and grounding 碰撞和搁浅

~ avoidance 避碰，防撞 ‖ *Syn*. collision-prevention 避碰，防撞

~ avoidance procedure 避碰程序，防撞程序

~ bulkhead 防撞舱壁

~ damage 碰撞损伤

~ regulation 避碰规则

colophony ['kɔləfəni] n. 树脂，松香

~ soldering tin paste 松香焊锡膏

~ soldering tin wire 松香焊锡丝

color ['kʌlə] n. 颜色，色彩，脸色，风格，外貌；v. 涂颜色，变色，改变颜色，粉饰，脸红，歪曲

colorless ['kʌləlis] a. 无色的，无趣味的

~ liquid 无色液体

column ['kɔləm] n. 圆柱，柱状物，专栏，纵队

comb [kəum] n. 梳子，梳，鸡冠，蜂巢；v. 梳，搜索

~ type relay 梳状继电器

combine [kəm'bain] n. 联合企业；v. (使)联合，(使)结合

combination [ˌkɔmbi'neiʃən] n. 结合，联合，合并，化合，化合物

~ bearing 组合轴承

~ carrier 兼用船

~ electric propulsion apparatus 综合电力推进装置

~ key 组合键

~ pliers 组合钳，多用钳

~ starter 混合起动器，综合启动器

~ switch 复合开关，组合开关

~ type fire detector 复合式火灾探测器

~ valve 组合阀

~ wrench 组合扳手，多用扳手

combinational [ˌkɔmbi'neiʃənəl] a. 结合的，组合的，联合的 ‖ *Syn*. combinatorial 组合的

~ control system 组合控制系统

combinatorial [ˌkɔmbinə'tɔːriəl] a. 组合的 ‖ *Syn*. combinational 结合的，组合的，联合的

combine [kəm'bain] n. 联合企业；v. (使)联合，(使)结合

~ with 与…结合，合并，使联合

combined [kəm'baind] v. (combine 的过去式和过去分词) (使)联合，(使)结合；a. 结合的，联合的，组合的，相加的，化合的

~ action 共同作用，联合行动，复合作用

~ agent extinguishing system 混合灭火系统

~ carrier 兼用船

~ cast and rolled stem 混合型艏柱

~ cycle power plant 联合循环发电装置，联合循环发电厂

~ diesel and gas turbine (CDGT) 柴燃联合动力装置，复合式柴燃气涡轮

~ fault finding 综合故障发现，综合故障查找

~ filter 组合滤波器

~ fleet 联合舰队

~ frame system 混肋骨系统，混合骨架式

~ load 混合载重，综合载荷

~ mechanism 组合机构

~ merchant fleets 联合商船队

~ model 组合模型

~ non-return butterfly valve 复合止回式蝶阀

~ over-current and reverse power protection 过电流和逆功率联合保护(装置)

~ pressure and vacuum gauge 复合式真空压力表

~ shielding 连续屏蔽，综合防护，综合屏蔽

~ socket and switch 带开关插座，开关插座

~ system 复合系统，合流制

~ transport 联合运输

~ type valve 复合阀

~ water 化合水，结合水

~ with 联合，连接，化合，结合

combust [kəm'bʌst] v. 消耗，燃烧

combustibility [kəm,bʌstə'biliti] n. 燃烧性，可燃性

combustible [kəm'bʌstəbl] a. 易燃的，可燃的

~ gas 可燃气体

~ gas indicator 可燃气体指示仪

~ material 易燃材料

~ metal 可燃金属

combustion [kəm'bʌstʃən] n. 燃烧

~ ash 焚烧灰渣

~ chamber 燃烧室

~ chamber volume 燃烧室容积

~ efficiency 燃烧效率

~ engine 内燃机

~ gas 燃烧气体，炉气

~ head 燃烧室缸盖

~ knock 发动机爆震

~ noise 燃烧噪声

~ pressure 燃烧压力

~ process 燃烧过程

~ product 燃烧产物

~ pulse 燃烧脉冲

~ ratio 燃烧比

~ reaction 燃烧反应

~ reactivity 燃烧反应性

~ space 燃烧室

~ stroke 燃烧冲程

~ turbine 燃气轮机，燃气透平，燃气涡轮

~ value 热值，卡值

come [kʌm] v. 来，来临，进步，前进，到达，达到，出现，扩展，来自，出生，开始，有优先权

~ about 出现，发生，转向，改变航向

~ close 走近，接近

~ into force 生效，实施，开始实行 ‖ *Syn*. come into operation 生效，开始运转，开工

~ into use 投入使用

~ up 被提出，走近，发生，开始，上升，发芽

command [kə'ma:nd] n. 命令，掌握，司令部；v. 命令，指挥，克制，支配，博得，俯临

~ button 命令按钮

~ module 指挥舱，驾驶舱

~ pose 指令位姿

~ post 指挥所

~ set 指挥台

~ signal 指令信号，控制信号

~ system 命令系统

commander [kə'ma:ndə] n. 司令官，指挥官，海军中校，队长

~ in chief 总指挥，总司令，主帅

commence [kə'mens] v. 开始，着手，起动

commencement [kə'mensmənt] n. 开始，毕业典礼

commensurate [kə'menʃərit] a. 相称的，相当的

commerce ['kɔmə(:)s] n. 商业

commercial [kə'mə:ʃəl] a. 商业的，贸易的
~ diving 商业潜水
~ ship 商船 ‖ *Syn*. commercial vessel 商船

comminute ['kɔminju:t] v. 使成粉末，粉碎，分割

comminuter ['kɔminju:tə] n. 粉碎器，捣碎器

comminution [ˌkɔmi'nju:ʃnə] n. 粉碎

commissary ['kɔmisəri] n. 代表，物资供应所，委员
~ spaces 补给库舱室，粮食库

commission [kə'miʃən] n. 委任，委托，代办(权)，代理(权)，犯(罪)，佣金；v. 委任，任命，委托，委托制作，使服役

commissioner [kə'miʃənə] n. 委员，专员

commit [kə'mit] v. 犯(错误)，干(坏事)，把…交托给，提交，答应负责

commitment [kə'mitmənt] n. 委托事项，许诺，承担义务

committal [kə'mitl] n. 委托，承担义务，赞助

committee [kə'miti] n. 委员会

commodity [kə'mɔditi] n. 日用品

common ['kɔmən] n. 公有，普通，共通，平民；a. 共同的，公共的，公有的，普通的，庸俗的，伪劣的 ‖ *Syn*. commonplace 平凡的；general 一般的，普通的；ordinary 平常的，平凡的，普通的；pervasive 普遍的；popular 大众的，通俗的，普遍的；universal 普遍的，通用的；usual 平常的，通常的，惯例的；widespread 分布广泛的，普遍的
~ carrier 承运商，公用运输业者，公共承运人，运输业者
~ ground point 公共接地点
~ rail 共轨
~ rail system 共轨系统

commonplace ['kɔmənpleis] n. 平凡的事，平常话；a. 平凡的 ‖ *Syn*. common 公共的，普通的；general 一般的，普通的；ordinary 平常的，平凡的，普通的；pervasive 普遍的；popular 大众的，通俗的，普遍的；universal 普遍的，通用的；usual 平常的，通常的，惯例的；widespread 分布广泛的，普遍的

communicate [kə'mju:nikeit] v. 沟通，通信，相通，传达，感染
~ with 与…通信，沟通，通话

communication [kəˌmju:ni'keiʃən] n. 传达，信息，交通，通信
~ and alarm 通信和警报
~ channel 通信信道，通信电路
~ circuit 通信电路
~ equipment 通信设备
~ interface 通信接口
~ network architecture 通信网络体系结构
~ signal 联系信号
~ standard 通信标准
~ system 通信系统

commutate ['kɔmjuteit] v. 使方向转换，整流

commutating ['kɔmjuteitiŋ] *n.* 转换，整流；*v.* (commutate 的 ing 形式) 使方向转换，整流
~ capability 换向能力
~ circuit 换向电路，整流回路
~ factor 整流系数
~ flux 换向磁通
~ frequency 换接频率
~ machine 整流电机
~ voltage 换相电压
~ zone 换向区

commutation [ˌkɔmju(:)'teiʃən] *n.* 交换，代偿，整流
~ condition 换向状况

commutator ['kɔmjuteitə] *n.* 换向器，转接器
~ brush 换向器电刷
~ brush combination 换向器电刷总线
~ modulator 换向调制器
~ shell 换向谱筒
~ sleeve 整流子衬套
~ slotting file 整流子刮槽锉刀
~ stone 换向器研磨石
~ switch 换向开关，按序切换开关

commuter [kə'mju:tə] *n.* 通勤者，经常往返者

compact ['kɔmpækt] *n.* 契约，合同；*v.* 压紧，压实，塞满，结合；*a.* 紧凑的，紧密的，简洁的，密集的
~ disc (CD) 光盘，光碟机，激光唱片
~ disc-read only memory (CD-ROM) 只读光盘存储器，只读光盘
~ disc-recordable (CD-R) 可写光盘，可烧录光盘
~ disc-rewritable (CD-RW) 可擦除光盘

compactness [kəm'pæktnis] *n.* 紧密，简洁

companion [kəm'pænjən] *n.* 同伴，共事者
~ flange 配对法兰，成对法兰，结合法兰
~ heeling 伴随横倾
~ ladder 舱室扶梯，升降梯

company ['kʌmpəni] *n.* 公司，陪伴，（一）群，（一）队，（一）伙，连，连队

comparator ['kɔmpəreitə] *n.* 比较仪，精密度测量器
~ hysteresis 比较器迟滞
~ sensitivity 比较器灵敏度
~ with cover 有塞比色管

compare [kəm'pɛə] *n.* 比较；*v.* 比较，相比，比喻
~ with 与…相比较

comparing [kəm'pɛəriŋ] *n.* 比较；*v.* (compare 的 ing 形式) 比较，相比，比喻
~ check 比较检验
~ element 比较元件
~ rule 比例尺
~ unit 比较器，比较单元

comparison [kəm'pærisn] *n.* 比较，对照，比喻，比较关系

compart [kəm'pa:t] *v.* 分隔

compartment [kəm'pa:tmənt] *n.* 隔间，舱，间隔间，车厢

compartmental [ˌkɔmpa:t'mentəl] *a.* 分割为若干部分的，区划的

compartmentalization [kɔmpa:tmentəlai'zeiʃən] *n.* 区分，划分

compartmentation [kəmˌpa:tmen'teiʃən] *n.* 分隔，区分

compass ['kʌmpəs] n. 罗盘，指南针，圆规；v. 包围
    ~ adjustment 罗经校正
    ~ deck 罗经甲板
    ~ needle 罗盘针
    ~ repeater 分罗经
    ~ rose 罗盘，指南针
    ~ saw 截圆锯，斜形狭圆锯
compatibility [kəm,pæti'biliti] n. 兼容性
    ~ condition 兼容条件，协调条件
    ~ test 兼容性测试
compatible [kəm'pætəbl] a. 谐调的，一致的，兼容的 ‖ Syn. consistent 一致的，调和的，相容的 ‖ Ant. incompatible 性质相反的，矛盾的，不调和的
    ~ device 兼容设备
    ~ machine 兼容机
    ~ software 兼容软件
    ~ with 与…相配的，与…兼容的，与…和谐相处
compend ['kɔmpend] n. (=compendium) 手册概要，概略
compendium [kəm'pendiəm] n. (=compend) 手册概要，概略
compensate ['kɔmpənseit] v. 补偿，赔偿，抵消，弥补，报酬
compensating ['kɔmpenseitiŋ] n. 补偿，补助，修正；v. (compensate 的 ing 形式) 补偿，赔偿，抵消，弥补，报酬；a. 补偿的，平衡的
    ~ capacity 补偿容量
    ~ circuit 补偿电路
    ~ coil 补偿线圈
    ~ element 补偿元件
    ~ feedback 补偿反馈
    ~ feedforward 补偿前馈

    ~ field 补偿场
    ~ in HT side 高压侧补偿
    ~ in LT side 低压侧补偿
    ~ mechanism 补偿机制，补偿装置
    ~ needle valve 补偿针阀
    ~ network 补偿网络
    ~ resistance 补偿电阻
    ~ signals 补偿信号
    ~ starter 补偿式启动器
    ~ winding 补偿绕组
compensation [kɔmpen'seiʃən] n. 补偿，赔偿
    ~ water system 补偿供水系统
compensator ['kɔmpenseitə] n. 补偿者，补偿器
compensatory [kəm'pensətəri] a. 补偿性的
competence ['kɔmpətəns] n. 能力
competency ['kɔmpit(ə)nsi] n. 资格，能力，作证能力
competent ['kɔmpitənt] a. 有能力的，胜任的
    ~ authority 主管当局，主管部门
complement ['kɔmplimənt] n. 补足物，补语，余角；v. 补助，补足
complementary [kɔmplə'mentəri] a. 补充的，补足的
    ~ metal-oxide semiconductor (CMOS) 互补金属氧化物半导体
complete [kəm'pli:t] v. 完成，使完善，使齐全，使完整；a. 全部的，彻底的，完全的，完成的，熟练的
    ~ combustion 完全燃烧
    ~ delivery 完全交货，已交清，付清
    ~ equipment 成套设备，整套装置
    ~ failure 完全故障，完全失效

~ fusion 完全熔接，完全熔化物，助熔剂
~ information 完整信息，完全情报
~ inspection 全部检查
~ list 一览表，完整目录
~ plant 成套设备，成套工厂
~ set 整套，成套机组，完全集
~ set of equipment 成套设备
~ with 包括，连同

completely [kəm'pli:tli] *ad.* 十分，完全地
~ comply 完全相符

completeness [kəm'pli:tnis] *n.* 完全
~ delivery of accommodation (joiner work and interior decoration of accommodation) for master room (chief engineer room) 船长室(轮机长室)舱室完整性(木工和内部装饰)提交
~ of all cabin to be inspection 全船房舱完整性提交
~ of all locker to be inspection 全船储藏室完整性提交

completion [kəm'pli:ʃ(ə)n] *n.* 完成

complex ['kɔmpleks] *n.* 联合体；*a.* 复杂的，合成的，综合的
~ agent 络合剂
~ material 复合材料，合成材料
~ structure 复合结构，复杂结构，复结构，复数结构
~ type supercharging system 复式增压系统

complexity [kəm'pleksiti] *n.* 复杂，复杂性，复杂事物
~ analysis 复杂性分析，成分分析
~ factor 复杂因数

compliance [kəm'plaiəns] *n.* 柔量，灵活性，依从，顺从

complicate ['kɔmplikeit] *v.* (使)变复杂

complicated ['kɔmplikeitid] *v.* (complicate 的过去式和过去分词) (使)变复杂；*a.* 复杂的，难解的

complication [ˌkɔmpli'keiʃ(ə)n] *n.* 复杂，复杂化，(使复杂的)因素，并发症

component [kəm'pəunənt] *n.* 成分，部分，元件，零件，要素，组分；*a.* 组成的，合成的，构成的 ‖ *Syn.* cell (电池、光电)元件，单元；constituent 成分，要素；element 要素，元素，成分，元件；ingredient 成分，因素；organ 元件；part 零件，部件
~ hole 零件孔，元件孔
~ of force 分力
~ of a vector 向量分量
~ part 构件，组成部分
~ protection 分量保护
~ side 元件面

compose [kəm'pəuz] *v.* 组成，构成，(使)安定，调解，调整，妥当安排，写作，排字

composite ['kɔmpəzit] *n.* 合成物，复合材料；*a.* 合成的，复合的，混成的，可分解的，综合式的
~ bearing 多层轴瓦，复合轴承
~ boiler 复合锅炉
~ insulation 合成绝缘
~ insulator 合成绝缘子
~ laminate 复合层压板
~ material 复合材料
~ piston 组合活塞
~ structure 组合结构，复合机构，混合结构

composition [ˌkɔmpə'ziʃən] *n.* 组成,成分，

布局，合成物，混合物，写作，作文 ‖ *Ant*. decomposition 分解

compound ['kɔmpaund] *n*. 混合物，化合物；*v*. 混合，配合；*a*. 复合的
~ compressor 多级压缩机
~ configuration 混合式构型
~ excitation reactance 复励阻抗
~ excitation transformer 相复励变压器
~ gage 真空压力计
~ insulator 复合绝缘子
~ piston ring 组合式活塞环
~ pump 双缸泵

compound-wound 复激磁的，复励磁的，复绕的
~ generator 复励发电机
~ motor 复激电动机，复励电动机，复绕电动机

compounded [kɔm'paundid] *v*. (compound 的过去式和过去分词) 混合，配合；*a*. 复合的，混合的
~ impedance 复合阻抗

compress [kəm'pres] *n*. (外科)敷布；*v*. 压缩，浓缩

compressed [kəm'prest] *v*. (compress 的过去式和过去分词) 压缩，浓缩；*a*. 被压缩的，扁平的
~ air 压缩空气
~ air from air distributer 来自空气分配器的压缩空气
~ air hose 压气软管
~ air starting system 压缩空气起动系统
~ air system 压缩空气系统
~ natural gas 压缩天然气

compressibility [kəm,presi'biliti] *n*. 可压缩性

compression [kəm'preʃ(ə)n] *n*. 浓缩，压缩，压榨，压缩，密集
~ bar 压杆，不锈钢压紧扁钢
~ chamber 气压舱，加压室
~ curve 压缩曲线
~ deformation 压缩变形，相对收缩量
~ efficiency 压缩效率
~ ignition 压缩点火
~ ignition engine 压燃式发动机
~ molding 压缩模塑法
~ nut 压紧螺母
~ plate 压板
~ pressure 压缩压力
~ process 压缩过程，压缩法
~ ratio 压缩比
~ refrigerating plant 压缩制冷装置
~ refrigeration 压缩制冷
~ resistance 抗压性能
~ ring 压缩环，气环
~ set 压缩形变，压缩应变，压缩变定
~ shim 压缩垫片
~ spring 压缩弹簧
~ strength 抗压强度，压缩强度
~ stress 压应力，压缩应力
~ stroke 压缩行程
~ temperature 压缩温度
~ test 抗压试验，压力测试，耐压缩试验

compressive [kəm'presiv] *a*. 有压缩力的，能够压缩的
~ deformation 压缩变形，压缩形变
~ force 压缩力
~ load 压缩负载，压缩负荷
~ resistance 压应力，抗压力，抗压强度
~ strain 压缩应变，压缩变形
~ strength 抗压强度，压缩强度

~ stress 抗压应力，压应力

compressor [kəm'presə] *n*. 压缩物，压缩机
- ~ casing cover 压缩机罩盖
- ~ oil 压缩机油
- ~ plant 压缩机房，压缩机站
- ~ rotor 压缩机转子
- ~ set 压气机组，空气压缩机组
- ~ surge limit 压气机喘振极限
- ~ unit 压缩机组

comprise [kəm'praiz] *v*. 包含，包括，组成，构成

computation [,kɔmpju(:)'teiʃ(ə)n] *n*. 计算，估计

computational [,kɔmpju(:)'teiʃ(ə)n(ə)l] *a*. 计算的
- ~ fluid dynamics 计算流体动力学

compute [kəm'pju:t] *v*. 计算，估计，用计算机计算

computer [kəm'pju:tə] *n*. 计算机，电脑
- ~ analysis 计算机分析
- ~ based system 基于计算机的系统
- ~ competency 计算机能力
- ~ control 计算机控制
- ~ hardware 计算机硬件，电脑硬件，硬件
- ~ network 计算机网络
- ~ numerical control (CNC) 计算机数字控制，计算机数控
- ~ numerical control bending press 计算机数控压弯机
- ~ numerical control boring machine 计算机数控镗床，计算机数控镗孔机
- ~ numerical control drilling machine 计算机数控钻床，计算机数控钻孔机
- ~ numerical control EDM wire-cutting machine 计算机数控线切割机床
- ~ numerical control electric discharge machine 计算机数控电腐蚀机，计算机数控电火花加工机床
- ~ numerical control engraving machine 计算机数控雕刻机
- ~ numerical control grinding machine 计算机数控磨床
- ~ numerical control lathe 计算机数控车床
- ~ numerical control machine tool fittings 计算机数控机床配件
- ~ numerical control milling machine 计算机数控铣床
- ~ numerical control shearing machine 数控剪板机
- ~ numerical control tooling 数控工具
- ~ numerical control wire-cutting machine 数控线切割机
- ~ program 计算机程序
- ~ programming 计算机编程，计算机程序设计
- ~ software 计算机软件
- ~ technician 计算机技术人员

computer-aided 计算机辅助的 ‖ *Syn*. computer-assisted 计算机辅助的
- ~ design (CAD) 计算机辅助设计
- ~ drawing (CAD) 计算机辅助制图，计算机辅助绘图
- ~ engineering (CAE) 计算机辅助工程
- ~ manufacturing (CAM) 计算机辅助制造
- ~ process planning (CAPP) 计算机辅助工艺过程设计
- ~ researching and developing (CARD) 计算机辅助研究开发

computer-assisted 计算机辅助的 ‖ *Syn*. computer-aided 计算机辅助的
~ simulation 计算机辅助模拟
computer-based 基于计算机的
~ simulation 基于计算机的仿真，计算机模拟技术
computer-controlled 计算机控制的
~ cylinder lube system 计算机控制的油缸润滑系统
~ display 计算机控制显示器
~ starting air system 计算机控制起动空气系统
~ system 计算机控制系统
computer-integrated 计算机集成的
~ manufacturing (CIM) 计算机集成制造
~ Manufacturing System (CIMS) 计算机集成制造系统
computing [kəm'pju:tiŋ] *n*. 计算，处理；*v*. (compute 的 ing 形式) 计算，估计，用计算机计算
~ element 计算元件
con [kɔn] (=conn) *n*. 操舵台，掌舵，驾船，反对的理由，反对者，反对票，囚犯，肺病；*v*. 掌舵，指挥操舵，指挥(船的)航向，精读，学习，记住；*ad*. 不同意地，反对地
concave ['kɔn'keiv] *n*. 凹，凹面；*a*. 凹的，凹入的
~ head piston 凹顶活塞
concavity [kɔn'kæviti] *n*. 凹度
conceal [kən'si:l] *v*. 隐藏，隐蔽，隐瞒
concealed [kən'si:ld] *v*. (conceal 的过去式和过去分词) 隐藏，隐蔽，隐瞒；*a*. 隐藏的，隐蔽的，隐瞒的
~ hinge 内藏铰链，暗式链条

concentrate [kɔn'sentreit] *v*. 集中，浓缩
~ pump 泡沫原液泵
concentrated ['kɔnsentreitid] *v*. (concentrate 的过去式和过去分词) 集中，浓缩；*a*. 集中的，浓缩的
~ additive 浓缩添加剂
~ emulsion 浓缩乳剂
~ liquor 浓缩液
~ load 集中负荷，集中荷载
~ wave load 集中波浪载荷
concentration [ˌkɔnsen'treiʃən] *n*. 集中，集合，专心，浓缩，浓度
~ ratio 集中度，浓度比率
concentric [kɔn'sentrik] *a*. 同中心的
~ piston ring 同心活塞环
concentricity [ˌkɔnsen'trisəri] *n*. 同心，集中，集中性
concern [kən'sə:n] *n*. (利害)关系，关心，关注，关注，所关心的是；*v*. 关心，涉及，关系到
concerned [kən'sə:nd] *v*. (concern 的过去式和过去分词) 关心，涉及，关系到；*a*. 关心的，有关的
~ personnel 有关人员
concerning [kən'sə:niŋ] *n*. (concern 的 ing 形式) 关心，涉及，关系到；*prep*. 关于
conclude [kən'klu:d] *v*. 结束，终止，决定，推断，断定，缔结，议定，做出结论
conclusion [kən'klu:ʒən] *n*. 结束，缔结，结论
conclusive [kən'klu:siv] *a*. 确实的，最后的，决定性的
conclusively [kən'klu:sivli] *ad*. 最后地
concrete ['kɔŋkri:t] *n*. 混凝土，凝结物；*v*. 用混凝土修筑，浇混凝土，凝结，

硬化，固化；a. 具体的，凝固的，有形的，凝固的，真实的

concurrent [kən'kʌrənt] n. 同时发生的事件共同行动；a. 并发的，协作的，协调的，和谐的，一致的，聚集的

condensability [kəndensə'biliti] n. 可压缩性，可简约性

condensable [kən'densəbl] a. 可压缩的，可凝缩的 ‖ Ant. non-condensable 非凝性的，不凝性的

condensate [kɔn'denseit] n. 冷凝物，浓缩物

~ extraction pump 冷凝泵

~ line 冷凝线，冷凝水管路

~ outlet 冷凝液出口

~ pump 凝结水泵，冷凝泵

~ return pump 冷凝回水泵

~ seal 冷凝水密封

~ system 冷凝水系统

~ tank 冷凝槽

~ trap 凝汽筒，冷疑阱

~ undercooling 凝结水过冷

~ valve 凝结水阀

condensation [kɔnden'seiʃən] n. 浓缩，冷凝，凝固，聚合，浓缩物，浓缩液，摘要，经节缩的作品

~ reaction 缩合反应

condense [kɔn'dens] v. 浓缩，冷凝，凝固，聚合，精简，节略

condensed [kən'denst] v. (condense 的过去式和过去分词) 浓缩，冷凝，凝固，聚合，精简，节略；a. 浓缩的

~ liquid 凝析液，浓缩液

condenser [kən'densə] n. 冷凝器，凝结器，电容器，聚光器

~ circulating pump 冷凝器循环泵

~ inlet valve 冷凝器进口阀

~ outlet valve 冷凝器出液阀

~ pipe 冷凝管

~ tube 冷凝器管，凝结管

~ tube plate 冷凝器管板

condensing [kən'densiŋ] n. 浓缩，冷凝，凝固，聚合，精简，节略；v. (condense 的 ing 形式) 浓缩，冷凝，凝固，聚合，精简，节略

~ agent 冷凝剂，缩合剂

~ pressure 冷凝压力

~ steam turbine 凝汽透平，凝汽式汽轮机

~ temperature 冷凝温度，液化温度

~ turbine 冷凝式汽轮机，涡轮机

~ unit 冷凝装置，压缩冷凝机组

condition [kən'diʃən] n. 条件，情形，状态，环境，资格，前提，先决条件，健康，社会地位，事件本身；v. 作为条件，适应，使达到要求的情况，调节空气

~ alarm 工况报警

~ assessment scheme 条件评估方案

~ based maintenance 状态维修

~ monitor 状况监视器，工况监测器，设备监控模块

~ monitor of main engine 主机状况监视器，主机工况监测器

~ monitoring system 状态监测系统

~ of loading 负载情况

~ survey 情况调查

conditional [kən'diʃən(ə)l] a. 视…而定的，条件的，假定的，有条件的，由一定条件诱发的

~ stability 条件稳定

conditionally [kən'diʃənəli] ad. 有条件地

~ instability 条件不稳定性

117

conditioner [kən'diʃənə] *n.* 调节装置，调节者

conduct ['kɔndʌkt] *n.* 行为，操行，指导，管理；*v.* 指挥，引导，管理，为人，传导，充当导体

conductance [kən'dʌktəns] *n.* 电导，导率，电导系数

conducted ['kɔndʌktid] *v.* (conduct 的过去式和过去分词) 指挥，引导，管理，为人，传导，充当导体；*a.* 传导的，引导的

~ by 指挥

~ disturbance 传导干扰 ‖ *Syn*. conducted interference 传导干扰，馈电线感应干扰

~ heat 传导热

~ signal 传导信号

conduction [kən'dʌkʃən] *n.* 传导，导电，导热，输送，引流

~ and radiation 传导与辐射

~ angle 导通角，传导角

~ band 导带，传导带，导电带

~ of heat 热传导，导热性

~ system 传导系统

~ velocity 传导速度

conductive [kən'dʌktiv] *a.* 传导的，导电的，导热的，输送的

~ ceramic 导电陶瓷

~ contact 传导接头，导电触点

~ part 导电部分

~ pattern 导电图形，导电图

conductivity [ˌkɔndʌk'tiviti] *n.* 传导性，传导率

conductor [kən'dʌktə] *n.* 导体，避雷针，领导者，经理，售票员，列车长 ‖ *Ant*. insulator 绝缘体，绝热器

~ layer 导体层，导线层

~ load 导线荷载

~ size 导体尺寸

~ spacing 导线距离，导体间距

~ width 导线宽度

conduit ['kɔndit] *n.* 管道，导管，沟渠，泉水，喷泉

~ outlet 电线引出口

cone [kəun] *n.* 锥形物，圆锥体；*v.* 使成锥形

~ angle 锥角，圆锥角，锥体角度

~ belt 圆锥皮带，三角皮带

~ crusher 圆锥破碎机

~ gear 锥形齿轮

~ of silence 静锥区

conference ['kɔnfərəns] *n.* 会议，讨论会，协商会

~ room 会议室，会议厅

configuration [kənˌfigju'reiʃən] *n.* 构造，结构，布局，配置，外形，轮廓

configure [kən'figə] *v.* 配置，设定，使成形，使具一定形式

confine ['kɔnfain] *n.* 界限，边界，约束，范围，区间；*v.* 限制，使局限于，禁闭

confined [kən'faind] *v.* (confine 的过去式和过去分词) 限制，使局限于，禁闭；*a.* 被限制的，狭窄的

~ diving 限制水域潜水

~ space 密闭空间，有限空间

~ water 承压水，受压水

confirm [kən'fə:m] *v.* 确定，批准，使巩固，使有效

confirmation [ˌkɔnfə'meiʃən] *n.* 证实，确认，批准

conform [kən'fɔ:m] *v.* 符合，相似，适应环境，使一致，使遵守，使顺从；*a.* 一

致的，顺从的

conformance [kən'fɔ:məns] *n*. 顺应，一致

conformity [kən'fɔ:miti] *n*. 一致，符合，遵守

congeal [kən'dʒi:l] *v*. (使)冻结，(使)凝结

congest [kən'dʒest] *v*. (使)充满，(使)拥塞，(使)充血

congested [kən'dʒestid] *v*. (congest 的过去式和过去分词) (使)充满,(使)拥塞,(使)充血；*a*. 拥挤的，拥塞的

~ area 拥挤地区，人口稠密区

~ port 拥挤港口

~ waters 拥挤水域

congestion [kən'dʒestʃən] *n*. 充满，拥塞，充血

conic ['kɔnik] *n*. 圆锥部分，二次曲线；*a*. 圆锥的，圆锥形的

conical ['kɔnikəl] *a*. 圆锥的，圆锥形的

~ disc 锥形轮盘

~ double-screw 锥形双螺杆

~ gear 伞齿轮，锥形齿轮

~ plug 锥形塞，连接点

~ shell 锥壳，圆锥壳，锥形薄壳

~ slide valve 锥形滑阀

~ spring 锥形弹簧，圆锥螺旋弹簧

~ surface 锥形面

conjunction [kən'dʒʌŋkʃən] *n*. 连接，联合，关联，接连发生，时机，关头，连接词

conn [kɔn] (=con) *n*. 操舵台，掌舵，驾船，反对的理由，反对者，反对票，囚犯，肺病；*v*. 掌舵，指挥操舵，指挥(船的)航向，精读，学习，记住；*ad*. 不同意地，反对地

connect [kə'nekt] *v*. 连接，结合，联合，关联，联想，联络，插入插座，衔接，建立关系 ‖ *Ant*. disconnect 拆开，分离，断开

connecting [kə'nektiŋ] *n*. 连接，管接头，套管；*v*. (connect 的 ing 形式) 连接，结合，联合，关联，联想，联络，插入插座，衔接，建立关系

~ bar 连杆

~ bolt 连接螺栓

~ device 连接装置，连接设备

~ flange 连接法兰，连接凸缘

~ lever 连接棒，连接杆，连接杠杆

~ line 连接线，连线

~ link 可拆链环，连接环节

~ piece 连接件，中段

~ pin 连接销

~ pipe 连接管，导压管

~ plate 连接板，接合板，接线板

~ points 连接点

~ rod 连杆

~ rod bearing 连杆轴承

~ rod big end 连杆大头 ‖ *Syn*. connecting rod bottom end 连杆大头，连杆下端；connecting rod large end 连杆大头，连杆大端

~ rod bolt 连杆螺栓

~ rod bottom end bearing 连杆大头轴承，连杆下端轴承

~ rod cap 连杆盖

~ rod shank 连杆杆身，连杆体

~ rod small end 连杆小头，连杆小端

~ rod small end bearing 连杆小头轴承，连杆小端轴承

~ rod thrust 连杆方向的推力

~ rod top end 连杆上端

~ terminal 接线端子，连接终端，连接

触点
~ tube 导管，连接管
~ wire 连接线

connection [kə'nekʃən] n. (=connexion) 连接，关系，接线，线路，亲戚
~ block 接线板，接线条
~ bolt 连接螺栓
~ box 接线盒，连接盒，连接器
~ device 连接设备
~ panel 接线面板，连接屏
~ piece 连接片
~ plate 接线板
~ with 与…有关系

connectivity [kənek'tiviti] n. 连通性

connector [kə'nəktə(r)] n. 连接器，连接者，联系者

connexion [kə'nekʃən] n. (=connection) 连接，关系，接线，线路，亲戚

conning ['kɔniŋ] n. 掌舵，驾船；v. (con 的 ing 形式) 掌舵，指挥操舵，指挥(船的)航向，精读，学习，记住
~ arrangement 指挥驾驶装置
~ equipment 船舶控制设备
~ platform 驾驶指挥平台
~ position 指挥位置
~ station 舰艇操纵部位
~ tower 指挥塔，军舰司令塔

conquer ['kɔŋkə] v. 征服，战胜，占领，克服，破坏 ‖ *Syn*. defeat 击败，战胜，使失败；overcome 战胜，克服，胜过，征服；overwhelm 制服，控制，压倒，压服，击败；surmount 战胜，超越，克服

Conradson [kən'ræds(ə)n] n. 康拉特逊 (人名)
~ carbon apparatus 康拉特逊碳试验仪，康氏炭试验仪
~ carbon residue 康拉特逊残碳，康氏残炭
~ carbon residue test 康拉特逊残碳试验，康氏残碳试验
~ carbon value 康拉特逊残碳值，康氏残碳值

consecutive [kən'sekjutiv] a. 连续的，连贯的，结果的
~ reaction 连锁反应
~ starts 连续启动

consequence ['kɔnsikwəns] n. 结果，推理，推论，因果关系，重要的地位

consequent ['kɔnsikwənt] a. 作为结果的，随之发生的，必然的，合乎逻辑的

consequential [,kɔnsi'kwenʃəl] a. 结果的，相因而生的

consequently ['kɔnsikwəntli] ad. 从而，因此

conservation [,kɔnsə(:)'veiʃən] n. 守恒，保存，保持，节约
~ of mechanical energy 机械能守恒

conservative [kən'sə:vətiv] n. 保守派；a. 保守的，守旧的
~ system 保守系统

conserve [kən'sə:v] v. 守恒，保存，保藏，保持，节约

consider [kən'sidə] v. 考虑，照顾，认为，以为，评价，判断，尊重

considerable [kən'sidərəbl] a. 重要的，相当大的，相当多的，值得考虑的，相当可观的 ‖ *Syn*. critical 重要的；crucial 极其重要的；important 重要的，重大的；material 重要的

considerably [kən'sidərəbli] ad. 相当地

consign [kən'sain] v. 委托，托运

consignee [kənsai'ni:] *n.* 受托者，收件人，代销人

consigner [kən'sainə(r)] *n.* 发货人，委托人，交付人

consignment [kən'sainmənt] *n.* 交托，交货，发货，运送，托付物，寄存物
~ note 托运收据，托运单，寄销通知书

consist [kən'sist] *v.* 由…组成，在于，一致
~ of 由…组成

consistence [kən'sistəns] *n.* (=consistency) 连接，结合，坚固性，浓度，密度，一致性，连贯性

consistency [kən'sistənsi] *n.* (=consistence) 连接，结合，坚固性，浓度，密度，一致性，连贯性

consistent [kən'sistənt] *a.* 一致的，调和的，坚固的，相容的 ‖ *Syn.* compatible 谐调的，一致的，兼容的

consistently [kən'sistəntli] *ad.* 一贯地，一向，始终如一地

Consol ['kɔnsəl] *n.* 康索尔(多区无线电信标，电子方位仪)

console [kɔn'səul] *n.* 控制台；*v.* 安慰，慰藉

consonant ['kɔnsənənt] *a.* 协调一致的

constant ['kɔnstənt] *n.* 常数，恒量，不变的事物；*v.* 不变的，固定的，持续的，坚决的，时常发生的，连续不断的，忠心的，忠贞的
~ acceleration 等加速度
~ angular acceleration 等角加速度
~ clearance piston 恒定间隙活塞
~ current 恒定电流，恒电流，恒流
~ current charge 恒流充电
~ current source 恒定电流源，恒流电源
~ current system 恒流制
~ delivery pump 恒量泵，定量泵 ‖ *Syn.* constant displacement pump 恒量泵，定量泵
~ difference pressure-reducing valve 恒差减压阀，定差减压阀
~ difference valve 恒差阀，定差阀
~ exciter 恒定励磁器
~ flow 恒定流量，恒流量，恒流
~ flow regulation 恒流量调节，恒流调节
~ frequency 恒定频率，恒频
~ load 恒定负载，恒负载
~ output 恒定输出
~ output pump 恒功率泵
~ parameter 恒定参数
~ pitch propeller 固定螺距螺旋桨，定距桨
~ pressure 恒定压力，恒压，定压
~ pressure charging system 恒压增压系统
~ pressure combustion cycle 恒压燃烧循环
~ pressure cycle 恒压循环
~ pressure expansion valve 恒压膨胀阀
~ pressure reducing valve 恒压减压阀
~ pressure regulation 恒压调节
~ pressure supercharging 恒压增压
~ pressure system 恒压系统
~ pressure valve 恒压阀
~ rate 恒定速率，恒速率，恒速
~ ratio 恒定速比，定比
~ ratio pressure reducing valve 定比减压阀

~ ratio transmission 定比传动

~ ratio valve 定比阀

~ speed 恒速，匀速

~ speed governor 恒速调节器

~ speed motor 等速电动机，恒速电动机，定速电动机

~ state 定常态

~ supercharging system 恒定增压系统

~ temperature 恒温

~ temperature and humidity 恒温恒湿

~ temperature fire detector 定温火灾探测器 ‖ *Syn*. fixed temperature fire detector 定温火灾探测器

~ tension mooring winch 恒张力绞缆机

~ tension winch 恒张力绞车

~ term 常数项

~ value control 恒值控制

~ velocity 常速度，等速度，恒速

~ voltage 恒电压，恒压

~ voltage charge 恒压充电

~ voltage constant frequency (CVCF) 恒压恒频

~ voltage excited transformer 恒压励磁变压器

~ voltage reactor 恒压电抗器

~ voltage system 等电压系统，恒压制

~ volume 等容

~ volume cycle 等容循环

constantly ['kɔnstəntli] *ad*. 不变地，经常地，坚持不懈地

constituent [kən'stitjuənt] *n*. 成分，要素，委托人；*a*. 组成的，形成的，任命的，有选举权的，有宪法制定权的，有宪法修改权的 ‖ *Syn*. cell (电池、光电)元件，单元；component 成分，元件，要素，组分；element 要素，元素，成分，元件；ingredient 成分，因素；organ 元件；part 零件，部件

constitute ['kɔnstitju:t] *v*. 制定，建立，构成，组成，设立，创建，等同于，相等，任命，授权，指派

constrain [kən'strein] *v*. 强迫，抑制，限制，抑制，拘束

constraint [kən'streint] *n*. 约束，强制，限制，局促

~ condition 约束条件

constrict [kən'strikt] *v*. 压缩，收缩，紧缩

constriction [kən'strikʃən] *n*. 阻塞物，压缩，收缩，压抑

construct [kən'strʌkt] *n*. 构想，概念；*v*. 建造，构造，创立，作图 ‖ *Syn*. build 建造，建筑，创立；erect 建造，建立，开创；form 形成，构成，塑造；make 制造，构造；put up 建造

construction [kən'strʌkʃən] *n*. 构架，结构，建筑，建筑物，建造，建设，历程，解释，造句

~ cost 建造成本，工程费用，施工成本，施工费用

~ crane 建筑起重机，施工吊机，工程起重机

~ drawing 施工图，纸施工图

~ hall 建造车间

~ period 施工期

constructional [kən'strʌkʃənəl] *a*. 装配的，构造的，解释上的

constructive [kən'strʌktiv] *a*. 建设的，建设性的，积极的，有助益的，结构的，构造上的，指定的，推断的，解释的

~ total loss 准全损，推定全损

constructiveness [kən'strʌktivnis] *n*. 组织，构造

consumable [kən'sju:məbl] *n.* 消费品；*a.* 可消费的，会用尽的

consume [kən'sju:m] *v.* 消耗,消费,耗尽,毁灭,吃光,喝光,烧毁

consumed [kən'sju:md] *v.* (consume 的过去式和过去分词) 消耗，消费，耗尽，毁灭；*a.* 消费的，消耗的
- ~ cost 消费成本
- ~ material 消耗材料
- ~ oxygen 耗氧量
- ~ power 消耗功率
- ~ work 消耗功

consumer [kən'sju:mə] *n.* 消费者，用户，顾客，取食者
- ~ goods 生活消费品

consumption [kən'sʌmpʃən] *n.* 消费，肺病，耗尽，消耗性疾病

contact ['kɔntækt] *n.* 接触器,触点,接点,接触通电,接触,接触状态,相互联系,目视,关联,关系,熟人,隐形眼镜; *v.* (使)接触,联络,联系,与…来往；*a.* 接触的，由接触引起的，由接触传播的
- ~ angle 接触角，接触角度，交会角
- ~ damage 触损
- ~ DC converter 接触式直流变流器
- ~ person 接触者
- ~ point 接触点
- ~ resistance 接触电阻,接点电阻,(电刷和换向器间)瞬变电阻
- ~ stabilization process 接触稳定工艺
- ~ stress 接触面应力
- ~ surface 接触面

contactless ['kɔntæktlis] *a.* 无触点的，不接触的，遥控的
- ~ charging 非接触充电
- ~ control 无触点控制
- ~ controller 接触器控制器
- ~ element 无触点元件
- ~ gauge 非接触型测量仪
- ~ relay 无触点继电器
- ~ smart card 非接触式智能卡，非接触式智慧卡，无接触式智能卡

contactor ['kɔntæktə] *n.* 电流接触器
- ~ control system 接触器控制系统
- ~ controller 接触器控制器

contain [kən'tein] *v.* 包含，容纳，容忍，自制，牵制，可被除尽

container [kən'teinə] *n.* 箱，罐，容器，集装箱，货柜 ‖ *Syn.* vessel 容器
- ~ block 集装箱组
- ~ cargo 集装箱货物
- ~ carrier 集装箱运输船
- ~ crane 集装箱起重机
- ~ lashing equipment 集装箱绑扎件
- ~ liner 集装箱运输船
- ~ load 集装箱载荷
- ~ port 货柜港口
- ~ ship 货柜船，集装箱运货船
- ~ socket 集装箱承座
- ~ space 集装箱舱位
- ~ stowage on deck 甲板上集装箱配载
- ~ terminal 集装箱码头,集装箱装卸区
- ~ terminals limited 集装箱码头有限公司
- ~ transport 集装箱运输
- ~ yard 集装箱堆场

containerise [kən'teinəraiz] *v.* (=containerize) 用集装箱装，使(工业或运输管理)集装箱化

containerizable [kən'teinəraizəbl] *a.* 可集装箱化的
- ~ cargo flow 可集装箱化的货流

containerize [kən'teinəraiz] v. (=containerise) 用集装箱装,使(工业或运输管理)集装箱化

containerized [kən'teinəraizd] v. (containerize 的过去式和过去分词) 用集装箱装; a. 集装箱装运的,货柜装运的
~ cargo 集装箱运货物

containerization [kən,teinərai'zeiʃən] n. 货柜运输,货柜装货

containership [kən'teinəʃip] n. 货柜船

containment [kən'teinmənt] n. 容纳,遏制,遏制政策,防泄漏系统

contaminate [kən'tæmineit] v. 弄脏,污染,玷污,损害,毒害腐蚀; a. 污染的 ‖ *Syn.* pollute 弄脏,污染,玷污,亵渎

contaminated [kən'tæmineitid] v. (contaminate 的过去式和过去分词) 弄脏,污染,玷污,毒害,腐蚀; a. 被污染的
~ water 污染水

contaminating [kən'tæmineitiŋ] n. (contaminate 的 ing 形式) 弄脏,污染,玷污,毒害,腐蚀; v. 弄脏,污染,玷污,毒害,腐蚀
~ impurities 污染杂质
~ material 污染物质
~ metal 杂质金属

contamination [kən,tæmi'neiʃən] n. 弄脏,污染,玷污,毒害,污染物 ‖ *Syn.* pollution 弄脏,污染,污秽物
~ device 污染装置
~ index 污染指数

content [kən'tent] n. 内容,满足,(书等的)目录,容量; v. 使满足,使满意; a. 满足的,满意的,愿意的,心甘情愿的 ‖ *Syn.* cater to 迎合,满足; fill 满足; fulfil 满足; meet 满足,达到要求; satisfy 满足,使满意

contention [kən'tenʃən] n. 争夺,争论,争辩,论点 ‖ *Syn.* issue 论点; moot point 争论未决的问题,论点; point in question 论点

contiguous [kən'tigjuəs] a. 接触的,邻近的,毗连的,共同的

continent ['kɔntinənt] n. 大陆,陆地; a. 自制的,克制的,节欲的,贞洁的,禁欲的

continental [,kɔnti'nentl] n. 欧洲人,大陆人,侨居在外的美国人,(美国独立战争中发行的)大陆币; a. 大陆的,大陆性的,欧洲大陆的,(独立战争时)美洲殖民地的

contingency [kən'tindʒənsi] n. 意外事故,紧急情况,不测事件,可能性,偶然,偶然性,意外开支 ‖ *Syn.* accident 意外事件,意外事故; casualty 事故,伤亡; chance failure 偶发故障,意外事故; incident 事件,突发事件; misfortune 不幸,灾难,灾祸; mishap 灾祸,厄运,倒霉事

contingent [kən'tindʒənt] n. 偶然的事情,分遣队,小分队,代表团; a. 可能发生的,偶然的,暂时的,附带的
~ survey 临时检验

continual [kən'tinjuəl] a. 不间断的,不停的,多次重复的,频繁的

continually [kən'tinjuəli] ad. 持续地,频繁地,不停地,屡屡地,一再地

continuance [kən'tinjuəns] n. 持续,继续,停留

continuation [kən,tinju'eiʃən] n. 继续,续集,延长,延长物,扩建物,附加部

分，续刊，增刊，续篇

continue [kən'tinju:] *v*. 延期，持续，坚持，延伸，逗留，维持原状，使延伸，使持续，继续说

continuity [ˌkɔnti'nju:iti] *n*. 连续性，连贯性，继续，串联，衔接，分镜头电影剧本，(影视)剪辑

continuous [kən'tinjuəs] *a*. 连续的，延伸的，一系列的 ‖ **Ant**. discrete 不连续的，离散的

~ beam 连续梁

~ bulwark 连续舷墙

~ caster 连铸机

~ casting 连铸，连续浇铸，连桶连铸，全连铸

~ conduction mode (CCM) 连续导电模式，连续导通模式

~ control 连续控制

~ control system 连续控制系统

~ data 连续数据，连续资料

~ deck 连续甲板

~ duty 连续工作，连续运行，连续使用，连续负荷

~ duty system 长期工作制

~ feeding 连续补料，连续进料，连续供给

~ flow 连续流

~ improvement 持续改进，持续改善，持续进步，连续改进，不断改进

~ load 连续载荷，均匀分布的载荷

~ manner 连续方式

~ measurement 连续测量

~ operation 连续运算，连续工作

~ operation ability of the power supply 电源持续工作能力

~ output 连续出量，持续输出

~ power 连续功率

~ process 连续过程，连续法，连续制造程序，流水作业

~ production 连续生产，流水生产

~ rating 固定负载状态

~ running 连续运转

~ running test 连续运转试验

~ sampling 连续采样

~ service output 持续运行功率

~ servo 连续作用的随动系统，连续作用的跟踪系统

~ sludging centrifuge 污油连续分离器

~ survey 循环检验

~ survey of machinery 持续的机器检测

~ symmetry 连续对称性

~ synopsis record 连续概要记录，连续概要纪录

~ system 连续系统，连续制

~ variable 连续变量

~ watch 连续监视

~ wave 连续波

~ weld 连续焊缝

continuous-speech 连续语音

~ recognition system 连续语音识别系统

continuously [kən'tinjuəsli] *ad*. 不断地，连续地，连续不断地

~ invariable 恒定的，持续不变的，始终如一的

~ manned central control station 持续编配有负责船员的中央控制站

~ scanning 连续扫描

~ turn 连动

~ variable control 无级变速控制，连续可变控制

contour ['kɔntuə] n. 外形, 轮廓, 等高线, 周线, 海岸线, 恒值线; v. 画轮廓, 画等高线; a. 显示轮廓的, 与轮廓相合的, 沿着地势的
~ dimension 外形尺寸
~ grinding 仿形磨削, 成形磨削
~ light of floating dock 浮坞坞形灯
~ line 轮廓线, 等高线, 恒值线
~ milling 成形铣削, 外形铣削, 等高走刀曲面仿形法

contract ['kɔntrækt] n. 合同, 契约, 协议, 婚约; v. 签合同, 订约, 缩小, 使缩短, 感染
~ design 合同设计
~ in length and expand in diameter 长度收缩, 直径延长
~ life 合同有效期限
~ Regarding an Interim Supplement to Tanker Liability for Oil Pollution (CRISTAL) 油轮油污责任暂行补充约定
~ to build 承建

contracting ['kɔntræktiŋ] v. (contract 的 ing 形式) 签合同, 订约, 缩小, 缩短, 感染; a. 收缩的, 缩成的, 缩小的
~ carrier 契约承运人
~ Government 缔约国政府, 缔约政府
~ party 缔约方, 立约者, 订约方

contraction [kən'trækʃən] n. 收缩, 缩减, 缩略, 略体, 缩写, (开支等)缩减, (分娩时)子宫收缩
~ crack (收)缩裂(纹)
~ distortion 收缩变形
~ ratio 收缩比
~ stress 收缩应力

contractor [kən'træktə] n. 订约人, 承包人, 收缩物

contraption [kən'træpʃən] n. 奇妙的装置, 精巧的设计, 新发明

contrarotate [ˌkɔntrə'rəuteit] v. 逆时针旋转

contrarotating [ˌkɔntrə'rəuteitiŋ] n. 对转螺旋桨, 反转; v. (contrarotate 的 ing 形式) 反向旋转; a. 反转的
~ propeller 对旋螺旋桨

contrarotation [ˌkɔntrə'rəuteiʃən] n. 反向转动, 反旋, 反转

contrary ['kɔntrəri] n. 反面, 对立或相反的事物, 对立方, 反对命题; a. 相反的, 违反的, 反对的, 对立的, 顽固的, 任性的; ad. 相反地, 矛盾地

contrast ['kɔntræst] n. 对比, 对照, 差异, 对照物, 对立面, 反差; v. 对比, 形成对照, 使对照, 使对比

contribute [kən'tribju:t] v. 贡献出, 捐赠(款项), 投稿(给杂志等), 出力
~ to 有助于, 促成, 捐献, 投稿

contrive [kən'traiv] v. 策划, 设计, 发明, 创造, 设法做到, 计划, 谋划

control [kən'trəul] n. 控制, 支配, 管理, 调节, 抑制, 控制器, 调节装置; v. 控制, 操纵, 管理, 限制, 支配 ‖ *Syn*. govern 控制, 操纵, 调节, 支配, 管理; regulate 控制, 调节, 校准, 管制
~ ability 控制能力, 操纵性
~ accuracy 控制精度, 控制精确度, 控制准确度
~ action 控制动作, 控制行动, 控制作用
~ air 控制空气, 气动系统的工作空气
~ air inlet 控制空气进气口
~ board 仪器板, 控制台, 操纵台

~ box 操纵台，控制箱，操作箱
~ bus 控制总线
~ button 控制按钮，操纵按钮
~ cab 调度台，驾驶室，控制室
~ cabin 操纵室，操纵间，中央操纵站，驼峰站
~ cabinet 操纵室，操纵楼，操纵箱
~ circuit 控制电路
~ component 控制元件
~ console 控制台
~ device for reversing 换向控制装置，倒车控制装置
~ device for starting 启动控制装置
~ element 控制元件，控制棒
~ equipment 控制设备
~ function 控制操作，控制功能
~ gear 控制装置，控制机构，操纵装置，自动调整仪
~ lever 操纵杆，控制杆
~ lever for adjusting oil 调油控制杆
~ loop 控制回路，操纵系统，驾驶系统
~ measure 控制措施
~ mechanism 操纵机构
~ method 控制方式，检查法
~ mode 调节状态，控制方式
~ of 支配
~ of discharge of oil 排油控制
~ over 控制
~ panel 控制面板
~ performance 控制性能
~ plant 控制装置
~ platform 操纵台，控制平台
~ procedure 控制过程，控制程序
~ processor 控制处理机
~ push button 控制按钮

~ rack 控制板，控制台，操纵台，操纵板
~ range 控制范围
~ relay 控制继电器，监测继电器
~ rod 控制棒，操纵杆，驾驶杆
~ room 控制室，调整室，配电室，仪表室
~ room management system (CRMS) 控制室管理系统
~ room manoeuvring console 控制室操纵控制台
~ room manoeuvring panel 控制室操纵屏
~ selector 控制选择器
~ sleeve (柴油机油泵的)油量调节套
~ spindle 分配轴，凸轮轴
~ stand 控制台
~ station 控制站，控制点
~ station change-over switch 控制站换向开关
~ strategy 控制策略
~ switch 控制开关
~ switchboard 控制开关板
~ switchgroup 控制组合开关，控制开关组
~ synchro 同步发送机，控制同步机
~ system 控制系统
~ system synthesis 控制系统综合
~ theory 控制理论，控制原理
~ time horizon 控制时程
~ timer 控制定时器，时间传感器，时间控制继电器
~ transformer 控制变压器
~ transformer rotor 自动同步机转子，控制变压器转子
~ unit 控制部件，控制器

~ valve 控制阀，调节阀

~ variable 控制变量

~ voltage 控制电压，操作电压

~ winding 控制绕组，控制线匝

~ with line selection 选线控制

controllability [kəntrəulə'biliti] *n*. 可控性，可操纵性，可监督性，可控制性

controllable [kən'trəuləbl] *a*. 可管理的，可操纵的，可控制的

~ factor 控制因子，控制因素

~ gate 可控门

~ passive tank stabilization system 可控被动水舱式减摇装置

~ phase compensation compound excited system 可控相位补偿复励系统

~ pitch 可调螺距，活螺距 ‖ *Syn*. variable pitch 可变螺距，可变节距

~ pitch propeller (CPP) 可调螺距螺旋桨，可变螺距螺旋桨，调距螺旋桨，变距螺旋桨，调距桨，变距桨 ‖ *Syn*. variable pitch propeller (VPP) 可调螺距螺旋桨，可变螺距螺旋桨，调距螺旋桨，变距螺旋桨，调距桨，变距桨

~ pitch propeller transmission 调距桨传动，可调螺距螺旋桨传动装置

~ pitch thruster 可调螺距推进器

~ reactor 可控反应堆

~ self-excited constant voltage device 可控自励恒压装置

~ silicon 可控硅 ‖ *Syn*. controlled silicon 可控硅

~ synthesis 可控合成

controlled [kən'trəuld] *v*. (control 的过去式和过去分词) 控制，管理，限制，克制；*a*. 受约束的，克制的

~ area 控制区，监管区

~ condition 受控条件，控制条件，调节条件，一定条件，恒定条件

~ cooling 控制冷却，强制冷却

~ environment 受控环境，可控环境

~ function 控制函数

~ member 控制对象 ‖ *Syn*. controlled object 受控对象；controlled plant 受控设备，被控对象

~ parameter 受控参数

~ rectifier 可控整流器

~ silicon 可控硅 ‖ *Syn*. controllable silicon 可控硅

~ tank stabilizer 主动式减摇水舱

~ value 控制值，受控值

~ variable 控制量，可控变量，可调量，调节量

controller [kən'trəulə] *n*. 控制器，控制者，审计员 ‖ *Syn*. governor 调节器，管理者，主管人员；regulator 调整器，标准仪，调整者，校准者

~ output 控制器输出

controlling [kɔnt'rəuliŋ] *n*. 管理，控制，限制，克制；*v*. (control 的 ing 形式) 管理，控制，限制，克制

~ angle 控制角，节制角，转角控制

~ device 控制设备，调节装置

~ element 施控元件

~ factor 控制因子，控制因素

~ instrument 控制仪表

~ machine 控制机

~ magnet 控制磁铁

~ means 调节装置，控制设备，控制方法

~ torque 控制转矩，控制力矩，(仪表)稳定力矩

~ unit 控制环节，调节单元

~ valve 控制阀，控制开关，调节阀

convect [kən'vekt] v. 使热空气对流，借对流传热

convection [kən'vekʃən] n. 传送，对流，运流

convective [kən'vektiv] a. 传送性的，对流的

~ flow 对流流体，对流

~ heat exchange 对流换热，对流热交换

~ heat transfer 对流热传递

convenience [kən'vi:njəns] n. 便利，方便，有益，有用，方便的用具、机械、安排，厕所

convenient [kən'vi:njənt] a. 方便的，适当的，近便的，实用的

conveniently [kən'vi:njəntli] ad. 方便地，便利地，合宜地，随手，顺便，信手

convention [kən'venʃən] n. 会议，协定，全体与会者，国际公约，惯例，习俗，规矩

~ and certificate 公约和证书

~ on the Prevention of Marine Pollution by Dumping of Wastes and Other Matter (London Dumping Convention, LDC) 防止倾倒废物及其他物质污染海洋的公约，伦敦倾废公约

conventional [kən'venʃənl] a. 传统的，常规的，平常的，依照惯例的，约定的

~ system 常规系统

convergence [kən'və:dʒəns] n. 会聚，收敛，集合，相交，辐合

conversation [ˌkɔnvə'seiʃən] n. 交谈，会话，交往，交际，会谈，(人与计算机的)人机对话

converse [kən'və:s] n. 逆向，谈话，会谈，相反的事物，逆命题；v. 交谈，谈话，对话，会话，认识；a. 相反的，逆的，颠倒的

conversely ['kɔnvə:sli] ad. 反过来，反之，相反地，颠倒地，倒地

conversion [kən'və:ʃən] n. 变换，转变，改装物，财产转换，兑换，换位(法)

~ factor 转换因子，换算因数，转换因数，变换因数

convert [kən'və:t] n. 皈依者，改变宗教信仰者；v. (使)转变，使皈依，兑换，换算，侵占，经过转变，被改变，(橄榄球)触地得分后得附加分

~ to (使)改信，皈依(另一宗教)，(使)转而变为…

converter [kən'və:tə(r)] n. 变换器，换流器，变压器，变频器，炼钢炉，吹风转炉，使转变的人，使改变信仰的人

~ circuit 变换器电路，变频器电路，变频电路

~ conversion loss 转换器转换损耗

~ technique 变换法，变换技术

converting [kən'və:tiŋ] n. 吹(炉冶)炼，转炉炼钢；v. (convert 的 ing 形式) 转变，转化，皈依，改变(信仰)

~ transformer 换流变压器

~ valve 转换阀

convertor [kən'və:tə(r)] n. 变流器，变换器，转换器，转炉

convex ['kɔnveks] a. 凸形的，凸的，凸面的，凸状

~ bank 凸岸

~ body 凸体

~ head piston 冠状活塞，凸头活塞 ‖ **Syn.** crown head piston 冠状活塞，凸头活塞

129

~ hull 凸包，凸形外壳

~ lens 凸透镜，凸镜，凸球镜片，火镜

~ mirror 凸镜，凸面镜

~ surface 凸面，背弧面

convexity [kɔn'veksiti] *n*. 凸状，凸面

convey [kən'vei] *v*. 传递，运送，输送，转让(财产等)，表达，通知，通报，传达

conveyance [kən'veiəns] *n*. 运送，传送，运输，财产让与，转让证书，表达，运输工具，交通工具

conveyer [kən'veiə] *n*. (=conveyor) 运送装置者，让与人，运煤机

~ belt 输送带，传送带

conveyor [kən'veiə] *n*. (=conveyer) 运送装置者，让与人，运煤机

convolution [ˌkɔnvə'lju:ʃn] *n*. 回旋，盘旋，卷绕

convoy ['kɔnvɔi] *n*. 护送，护航队，被护送者；*v*. 护航，护送

cook [kuk] *n*. 厨师，厨子；*v*. 烹调，做菜，煮，密谋，编造，篡改，伪造

cooker ['kukə] *n*. 锅，炊具，炉灶，造谣者

cooking ['kukiŋ] *n*. 烹饪术，如火如荼地进行，热火朝天，在干什么；*v*. (cook 的 ing 形式) 烹调，做菜，煮，密谋，编造，篡改，伪造；*a*. 烹调用的

~ utensil 烹饪用具

cool [ku:l] *n*. 凉气，凉快的地方，凉爽，凉爽的空气；*v*. (使)变凉，(使)冷却，(使)冷静，平息；*a*. 凉爽的，冷静的，一流的，孤傲冷漠的

~ down 变凉，平静下来

coolant ['ku:lənt] *n*. 冷冻剂，冷却液，散热剂

~ clarifier 冷却液过滤器

~ cleaner 冷却液净化器

~ flow 冷却液流量，冷却剂流

~ fluid 冷却液，冷却剂流

~ pump 冷却液泵，冷却剂泵 ‖ *Syn*. cooling medium pump 冷却介质泵，冷却液泵

~ recovery system 密闭式冷却系统

~ system 冷却系统

~ temperature 冷却液温度

~ temperature gauge 冷却液温度表，冷却液温度计

cooler ['ku:lə] *n*. 冷却装置，冷却器，冷库，冷藏器，冰箱，冷饮，监狱；*a*. (cool 的比较级) 比…冷，比…冷静，比…凉爽，比…冷漠 ‖ *Ant*. heater 加热器，发热器

~ inlet 冷却器入口，冷却器进口

cooling ['ku:liŋ] *n*. 冷却；*v*. (cool 的 ing 形式) 冷却，变凉，冷静；*a*. 冷却的，凉的，凉爽的

~ agent 冷却剂

~ air 冷却空气

~ and dehumidifying 冷却和除湿

~ and humidifying 冷却和加湿

~ capacity 冷却能力

~ chamber 冷却室

~ coil 冷却旋管，冷却盘管，冷却线圈

~ device 冷却设备

~ effect 冷却效应，冷却效果，冷却作用

~ end 冷却部，冷却端

~ fan 冷却风扇

~ jacket 冷却套管

~ liquid 冷却液

~ load 冷负荷，冷却负荷，冷却载荷

~ loop 冷却回路，冷却闭合系统

~ medium 冷却介质，冷媒

~ medium pump 冷却介质泵，冷却液泵 ‖ *Syn*. coolant pump 冷却液泵，冷却剂泵

~ method 冷却法

~ pipe 冷却管

~ plant 冷却装置，冷却设备，冷藏库

~ process 冷却过程

~ rate 冷却速率，冷却率，降温速度，散热速率

~ seawater inlet valve 冷却海水进口阀

~ seawater outlet valve 冷却海水出口阀

~ seawater regulating valve 冷却海水调节阀，冷却海水控制阀

~ shock descaling 冷却振动除垢，冷冲除垢

~ spray descaling 冷却喷淋除垢，冷淋除垢

~ surface 冷却面

~ system 冷却系统

~ time 冷却时间

~ wall 冷却壁

~ water (CW) 冷却水

~ water inlet 冷却水进口

~ water outlet 冷却水出口

~ water piping for air compressor 空压机冷却水管

~ water piping for cylinder liner 气缸套冷却水管

~ water piping for fuel injector 燃油喷射器的冷却水管

~ water piping for shafting 轴系冷却水管

~ water piping for turbocharger 涡轮增压器冷却水管

~ water pressure 冷却水压力，冷却水压

~ water pump 冷却水泵

~ water pump outlet 冷却水泵出口

~ water ratio 冷却水比率

~ water system 冷却水系统

~ water treatment 冷却水处理

~ worm 冷却蛇管

cooperate [kəu'ɔpəreit] *v*. 合作，协作，配合，顺从，协助

~ with 与…合作，与…合力，与…协力，与…协同

cooperation [kəu,ɔpə'reiʃən] *n*. 合作，协作，配合，协助

cooperative [kəu'ɔpərətiv] *n*. 联合体，合作社，合作商店；*a*. 合作的，协助的，共同的

cooperativity [kəu,ɔpərə'tivəti] *n*. 协同(性)，协调(性)

coordinate [kəu'ɔ:dinit] *n*. 坐标，配套服装，同等者，同等物；*v*. 调节，使协调，使调和，协同，成为同等，被归入同一类别；*a*. 同等的，同格的，同位的，并列的，坐标的

coordinated [kəu'ɔ:dinitid] *v*. (coordinate 的过去式和过去分词) 调节，协调，调和，协同，成为同等；*a*. 协调的，调节的，配合的

~ control system (CCS) 联动调整系统，协调控制系统

~ Universal Time (UTC) 协调世界时，世界统一时间，世界标准时间，国际协调时间

coordination [kəu,ɔ:di'neiʃən] *n*. 协调，调和，和谐 ‖ *Ant*. discoordination 不协调，不调和，不和谐

131

coordinator [kəu'ɔ:dineitə] n. 协调者，同等的人(或物)
~ surface search (CSS) 海面搜救协调员，海面搜寻协调船

cope [kəup] n. 斗篷状覆盖物，墙帽，长袍；v. 笼罩，给…盖墙压顶，对抗，对付，成功地应付

copolymer [kəu'pɔlimə] n. 共聚物，共多聚体

copper ['kɔpə] n. 铜，铜币，紫铜色，警察；v. 镀铜于；a. 铜制的
~ alloy 铜合金
~ bush 铜套，铜轴套，铜衬套
~ cable 铜质电缆
~ clad laminate (CCL) 覆铜薄层压板，敷铜箔叠层板
~ claded surface 镀铜表面
~ coil transformer 铜芯变压器
~ forging 铜锻造
~ lead alloy 铜铅合金
~ loss 铜耗，铜损
~ nickel alloy 铜镍合金
~ pipeline 铜管
~ plated 镀铜的
~ rivet 铜铆钉，紫铜铆钉
~ sheet 铜片，铜皮，薄铜板
~ split pin 紫铜开口销
~ tube 铜管
~ welding wire 铜焊条，铜焊丝
~ wire 铜线，铜丝

coracle ['kɔrəkl] n. (用防水材料制成的小渔船)小圆舟

cord [kɔ:d] n. (细)绳，束缚；v. 用绳子捆绑，堆积(柴薪)

cordage ['kɔ:didʒ] n. 绳索，薪炭材的堆积数

cordless ['kɔ:dlis] a. (电话或电动工具)不用电线与电源相连的，无电线的，无塞绳式的
~ mouse 无线鼠标 ‖ *Syn*. wireless mouse 无线鼠标

core [kɔ:] n. 中心，核心，精髓，果心，果核，地核，磁心；v. 去(果)核，提取岩芯(样品)
~ material 型芯材料
~ saturation 铁芯饱和，磁芯饱和
~ wire 芯线，焊芯

corner ['kɔ:nə] n. 角落,(街道)拐角处,(遥远的)地区，偏僻处，困境，绝路，垄断，专卖权；v. 迫至一隅，垄断，使陷入绝境，把…难住，相交成角，囤积；a. 位于角落的，位于街角的
~ angle joint 角榫
~ joint 角接，角接接头
~ frequency 转角频率，拐点频率
~ joint 弯管接头，角接接头
~ radius 圆角半径，拐角半径，刀尖圆弧半径

Cornish ['kɔ:niʃ] n. (1800年前)康沃尔人说的凯尔特语，考尼什(雏)鸡；a. (英国)康沃尔郡的，康沃尔人的
~ mainland 康沃尔大陆

corona [kə'rəunə] n. 冠状物，王冠，光环

corp [,kɔ:p] n. (=corporation) 公司

corporate ['kɔ:pərit] a. 社团的，法人的，共同的，全体的

corporation [,kɔ:pə'reiʃən] n. 社团，法人，公司，企业，有限公司，自治机关，大肚皮

corrasion [kə'reiʒən] n. 侵蚀

correct [kə'rekt] v. 改正，纠正，告诫，惩戒；a. 正确的，合适的，符合公认准则的，得体的

correcting [kə'rektiŋ] v. (correct 的 ing 形式) 改正，纠正，告诫，惩戒；a. 正确的
- ~ circuit 校正电路
- ~ coefficient 校正系数
- ~ collar 校正轴环
- ~ condition 校正条件
- ~ device 校正装置
- ~ element 校正元件
- ~ function 校正函数
- ~ mechanism 校准机构

correction [kə'rekʃən] n. 校正，修改，改正，纠正，惩罚，有待改正，被改正的东西
- ~ factor 校正系数，校正因数，改正系数，改正因素
- ~ time 校正时间，恢复时间 ‖ *Syn*. recovery time 恢复时间

corrective [kə'rektiv] n. 矫正物，改善法，中和物，补救药；a. 纠正的，矫正的，惩治的
- ~ action 调整作用，校正动作
- ~ gauge 校正规

correctly [kə'rektli] ad. 恰当地，正确地，得体地，实事求是地

correlation [ˌkɔri'leiʃən] n. 相关(性)，相互关系

correspond [ˌkɔri'spɔnd] v. 符合，协调，通信，相当，相应

correspondence [ˌkɔri'spɔndəns] n. 对应，一致，符合，通信，信件，通感
- ~ address 通信地址 ‖ *Syn*. corresponding address 通信地址，联络地址

corresponding [ˌkɔri'spɔndiŋ] v. (correspond 的 ing 形式) 符合，协调，通信，相当，相应；a. 相当的，对应的，通信的，符合的，一致的
- ~ address 通信地址，联络地址 ‖ *Syn*. correspondence address 通信地址
- ~ author 通信作者，联系人
- ~ period 同期
- ~ proportion 相应部分，对应比例
- ~ to 相当于，与…相一致
- ~ speed 相应速度，对应速率
- ~ standard 相应标准

correspondingly [ˌkɔri'spɔndiŋli] ad. 相对地，比照地

corridor ['kɔridɔ:] n. 走廊，通道，走廊(一国领土通过他国境内的狭长地带)，覆道

corrode [kə'rəud] v. 腐蚀，削弱，侵蚀

corrosion [kə'rəuʒən] n. 腐蚀，侵蚀，锈蚀，受腐蚀的部位，衰败，腐蚀状态
- ~ allowance 腐蚀余度
- ~ control 腐蚀防止法，腐蚀控制
- ~ cracking 腐蚀断裂，腐裂
- ~ extent 腐蚀程度
- ~ fatigue 腐蚀疲劳
- ~ inhibitor 阻蚀剂，腐蚀抑制剂
- ~ margin 腐蚀裕量，腐蚀余裕，腐蚀限度
- ~ mechanism 腐蚀机理
- ~ prevention 防腐蚀，防蚀
- ~ prevention system 防腐蚀系统
- ~ preventive agent 防腐蚀剂
- ~ products 腐蚀产物
- ~ protection 腐蚀防护，防腐
- ~ rate 腐蚀速率
- ~ resistance 耐蚀性，耐腐蚀性，抗腐蚀性
- ~ resistant material 耐腐蚀材料
- ~ test 腐蚀试验
- ~ wear 腐蚀磨损

corrosional [kə'rəuʒənl] *a.* 因侵蚀而造成的

corrosive [kə'rəusiv] *n.* 腐蚀物，腐蚀剂；*a.* 腐蚀的，蚀坏的，腐蚀性的
~ action 腐蚀作用
~ environment 腐蚀环境，腐蚀介质
~ wear 腐蚀磨损

corrosivity [kərəu'siviti] *n.* 腐蚀性

corrugate ['kɔrugeit] *v.* 弄皱，起皱，(使)成波状

corrugated ['kɔrəgeitid] *v.* (corrugate 的过去式和过去分词) 弄皱,起皱,起波纹；*a.* 波纹的，波纹状的，缩成皱纹的，波纹面的
~ bulkhead 波形隔板
~ waveguide 皱波导管，波纹波导管(软波导)

corrupt [kə'rʌpt] *v.* 使腐败，使堕落，使腐烂，腐化，堕落，腐烂；*a.* 堕落的，道德败坏的，腐败的，腐烂的，错误百出的，混浊的，误用的

corruption [kə'rʌpʃən] *n.* 腐败，贿赂，堕落，变体

corsair ['kɔsɛə] *n.* 海盗，海盗船

COSA (China Ocean Shipping Agency) 中国外轮代理公司

COSCHARD (China Ocean Shipping Company Chartering Department) 中国远洋运输公司租船部

COSCO (China Ocean Shipping Group Company) 中国远洋运输集团公司，中远集团

COSCO Shipping (China COSCO Shipping Group) 中国远洋海运集团，中国远洋海运集团有限公司

cosine ['kəusain] *n.* 余弦

COSSC (China Ocean Shipping Supply Corporation) 中国外轮供应公司

cost [kɔst] *n.* 价钱，代价，花费，费用，牺牲，诉讼费(用复数)；*v.* 付出代价，估价，使丧失，使付出努力，价钱为，花费
~ control 成本控制

costal ['kɔstl] *a.* 肋的，前腺脉的

costate ['kɔsteit] *a.* 有肋骨的，肋骨的，主脉的，共态的

COSTC (China Ocean Shipping Tally Company) 中国外轮理货公司

costly ['kɔstli] *a.* 昂贵的，贵重的，代价高的

cotter ['kɔtə] *n.* 制销，锁销，扁销，开尾销
~ pin 开口销

cotton ['kɔtn] *n.* 棉，棉线，棉织物，(其他植物所生的绒毛状的)棉状物；*v.* 喜欢，赞成，开始理解
~ cloth 棉布，纯棉布料，棉织布
~ gloves 棉纱手套
~ textile 棉纺织品

count [kaunt] *n.* 总数，数数，罪状，论点，注意，伯爵；*v.* 数，计算，计算在内，认为，视为，看作，有价值，有用
~ as 算作，算为，计数
~ by 间隔数
~ down 倒计数，倒计时
~ on 依靠，依赖，对…有信心，预期 ‖ *Syn*. rely on 依靠，依赖；depend on 依靠，依赖，取决于
~ rate 计算速度，计数率

counter ['kauntə] *n.* 计算器，计数器，计算者，柜台，筹码，对立面，舣突出体，外倾舣端；*v.* 反击，还击，反向

移动，对着干，反驳，回答；a. 相反的，对立的；ad. 反方向地，相反地，对立地

~ bore 埋头孔，沉孔

~ clockwise 逆时针，逆时针方向

~ coil 补偿线圈

~ current 反向电流，逆流

~ current protection 逆流保护

~ EMF 反电动势，反电势

~ flow 逆流

~ flow action 逆流作用

~ force 反作用力

~ measure 对策，防范措施

~ relay 记数继电器

~ shaft 副传动轴，天轴，对轴，分配轴，凸轮轴，中间轴，侧轴

~ weight 平衡重

counteract [ˌkauntəˈrækt] v. 抵消，中和，阻碍

counteractive [ˈkauntəˈræktiv] n. 反对，反作用，抵抗；a. 反对的，反作用的，抵抗的

counterbalance [ˌkauntəˈbæləns] n. 平衡量，平衡力，势均力敌；v. 使平均，使平衡，弥补

~ shaft 自平衡轴

~ spring casing 平衡簧套

~ valve 背压阀，反平衡阀

countercheck [ˈkauntətʃæk] n. 阻挡，对抗方法，妨碍；v. 制止，防止，复查 ‖ Syn. forestall 预防，阻止，阻碍；guard 防止，保卫，警惕，警卫；prevent 预防，防止，制止，阻碍，阻止，阻挠

counterclockwise [ˌkauntəˈklɔkwaiz] a. 逆时针方向的，自右向左的；ad. 逆时针方向地，自右向左地

counterpart [ˈkauntəpɑ:t] n. 配对物，相对物，副本，极相似的人或物

countersink [ˈkauntəsiŋk] n. 埋头孔，暗钉眼；v. 钻孔装埋，打埋头孔

countersunk [ˈkauntəsʌŋk] v. (countersink 的过去式和过去分词) 钻孔装埋，打埋头孔；a. 埋头的

~ bolt 埋头螺栓

~ collar 埋头轴环

~ flat head screw 埋头平顶螺钉

~ raised head screw 埋头凸顶螺钉

~ rivet 埋头铆钉

~ riveting 埋头铆接

~ screw 埋头螺钉，埋头螺丝

~ seat (连接零件的)沉头座

~ washer 埋头垫圈

counterweight [ˈkauntəweit] n. 平衡物，秤锤，平衡力

~ tensioning device 平衡重张力装置

countless [kauntlis] a. 数不胜数，无数的，多得数不清的

couple [ˈkʌpl] n. 对，双，配偶，夫妻，连接物，几个，两三个；v. 联合，结合，连接，成双，结婚 ‖ Ant. decouple 分离，拆开，解耦，去耦

~ lever 耦合杆

~ of forces 力偶

~ transformer 耦合变压器

~ up 把…耦联起来

coupler [ˈkʌplə] n. 耦合器，联结器，联结者，配合者

coupling [ˈkʌpliŋ] n. 联结，耦合，管箍，(火车的)车钩；v. (couple 的 ing 形式) 连接

~ bolt 联结螺栓，联结器螺栓，接合螺栓

135

~ coefficient 耦合系数

~ condenser 耦合电容器

~ constant 耦合常数，耦合恒量

~ device 联结装置

~ effect 耦合效应

~ flange 联结翼板

~ guard 联轴器罩，联轴罩

~ half 半个法兰接头

~ loss 连接损耗，耦合损耗

~ mechanism 耦合器，联结机构

~ nut 联结螺母

~ pin 联结销

~ reaction 偶联反应，耦联反应，氧化偶联

~ resistance 耦合电阻

course [kɔ:s] *n.* 过程，经过，进程，方针，路线，水道，行动方向，跑道，系列，顺序，大横帆，课程，一道菜；*v.* 追猎，急行，运行，流动，行经，横渡，滑动，掠过 ‖ **Syn.** procedure 程序，工序，过程，进程，步骤；process 过程，程序，步骤

~ changing 航向变换

~ changing ability 变向能力，变向能力，改向性

~ changing quality 转艏性

~ converter 航路变换器

~ director 航向指示器

~ keeping 航向保持

~ keeping ability 航向保持能力

~ keeping stability 航向保持稳定性

~ manoeuvrability 航向机动性

~ recorder 航向记录器

~ sector 航道区

~ sector width 航道扇区宽度

~ selector 航向选择器

cove [kəuv] *n.* 山凹，小湾，小峡谷，狭长开阔地，穹窿，拱，家伙，男人；*v.* (使)内凹，(使)成拱形

cover ['kʌvə] *n.* 封面，掩护，覆盖物，避难所，借口；*v.* 覆盖，铺，掩饰，保护，掩护，包括，包含，适用，涂，代替

~ layer 覆盖层

~ plate (电机)活动盖板，盖片，盖板，(荧光屏前面)防护玻璃

~ with asbestos wrapping 用石棉包住

coverage ['kʌvəridʒ] *n.* 覆盖，范围，规模，保险项目，(新闻)报道，优势度

covered ['kʌvəd] *v.* (cover 的过去式和过去分词) 覆盖，铺，掩饰，保护，掩护，包括，包含，适用，涂，代替；*a.* 大量的，有遮盖物的，有顶的

~ area 覆盖区域

~ building dock 有遮蔽的造船坞，有雨棚的造船坞

~ dock 遮蔽式造船坞

~ electrode 包覆焊条，涂剂焊条，药皮电焊条，带焊皮焊条

~ with 覆盖，被覆盖

coverless ['kʌvəlis] *a.* 无覆盖的，无罩的

~ container ship 敞舱式集装箱船，无舱盖集装箱船

~ transformer 无罩变压器

COW (crude oil washing) 原油清洗

cowl [kaul] *n.* 蒙头斗篷，连有头巾的修道士服，(烟囱顶上的)通风帽

~ cover 风斗罩

~ flap 整流罩鱼鳞片，整流罩通风片

~ grille 通风格栅

~ head ventilator 喇叭式风斗

~ panel 围板，前罩板，前围通风蓖板

coxswain ['kɔkswein] *n*. 艇长，舵手

CPP (controllable pitch propeller) 可调螺距螺旋桨，可变螺距螺旋桨，调距螺旋桨，变距螺旋桨，调距桨，变距桨 ‖ *Syn*. VPP (variable pitch propeller) 可调螺距螺旋桨，可变螺距螺旋桨，调距螺旋桨，变距螺旋桨，调距桨，变距桨

~ transmission 调距桨传动，可调螺距螺旋桨传动装置

CPR (Cardiopulmonary Resuscitation) 心肺复苏

CPU (Central Processing Unit) 中央处理器

crab [kræb] *n*. 蟹，蟹肉，阴虱，脾气乖戾的人，沙果，沙果树；*v*. (使)偏航，发脾气，发牢骚，抱怨，破坏，捕蟹

crabber ['kræbə] *n*. 捕蟹者，捕蟹小船，专爱挑剔的人

crack [kræk] *n*. 裂缝，试图，尝试，缝隙，重击，笑话，玩笑，闲谈，碎裂声，爆裂声；*v*. 破裂，开瓶，打开，断裂，折断，失去控制，衰退，说(笑话)；*a*. 训练有素的，技艺高超的，优秀的，一流的

~ arrester 阻裂装置，止裂器

~ control 防裂

~ detection 探伤，裂纹检查

~ extension 裂纹扩张

~ formation 龟裂形成

~ growth 裂纹扩展，龟裂增长

~ length 裂纹长度，裂缝长度，裂隙长度

~ propagation 裂纹扩展

~ resistance 抗龟裂性

~ tip 裂纹尖端，裂纹端

~ width 裂缝宽度，裂缝宽度

cradle ['kreidl] *n*. 支船架，叉簧，摇篮，发源地，发祥地；*v*. 抚育，紧抱，把…搁在支架上，把…放在摇篮内

craft [krɑ:ft] *n*. 船，筏，飞行器，手艺，诡计；*v*. 手工制作，精巧地制作

craftsman ['krɑ:ftsmən] *n*. 工匠，手艺精巧的人，艺术家

craftsmanship ['krɑ:ftsmənʃip] *n*. 技术，技能，技艺

cramp [kræmp] *n*. 夹子，扣钉，痛性痉挛，抽筋，绞痛；*v*. 使痉挛，使抽筋，以铁箍扣紧，限制，束缚；*a*. 难懂的，难认的，受拘束的，狭窄的

crane [krein] *n*. 吊车，起重机，克令吊

~ beam 吊车梁，起重机梁，行车梁

~ boom 起重机起重臂

~ cable 起重机索，吊索

~ column 吊车柱，起重机柱

~ girder 吊车梁，起重机行车大梁

~ hook 起重机吊钩

~ jib 起重机吊杆

~ operator 起重机操作员

~ pedestal 起重机座

~ pillar 起重机(旋转)支柱，起重机(旋转)枢轴

~ radius 起重机起吊半径，起重机伸臂活动半径，起重机伸距

~ rigger 起重机指挥者，起重机吊运工，起重机指挥者，起重工

~ rope 起重机钢丝绳

~ ship 起重船，浮吊，水上起重机 ‖ *Syn*. crane vessel 起重船

~ wire 起重钢丝

crank [kræŋk] *n*. 曲柄，曲轴，奇想；*v*. 装

曲柄，转动曲柄；*a*. 奇异的，古怪的，易怒的，脾气暴躁的

~ and fly wheel pump 曲柄和飞轮泵

~ angle 曲柄角

~ arm 曲柄臂，曲臂，曲轴臂

~ arrangement 曲柄装置

~ chamber 曲柄箱，曲轴箱

~ gear 曲柄传动装置，曲轴齿轮

~ journal bearing 曲轴颈轴承

~ mechanism 曲柄机构

~ out 制成

~ pin 曲柄销，拐肘销

~ pin bearing 曲柄销轴承

~ pulley 曲轴皮带轮

~ shaft 曲轴

~ shaft journal 曲轴颈，曲轴枢

~ throw 曲柄行程

~ up 用曲柄开动，加快，做好准备

~ web 曲柄臂，曲臂

~ web deflection 臂距差

crank-rocker 曲柄摇杆，曲柄摇臂

~ mechanism 曲柄摇杆机构

crankcase ['kræŋkkeis] *n*. 曲轴箱，曲柄箱

~ assembly 曲轴箱总成

~ bleed pipe 曲轴箱通风管

~ bolt 曲轴箱螺栓

~ breather 曲轴箱通气管

~ capacity 曲轴箱容量

~ catalyst 曲轴箱(内油的氧化)催化剂

~ compression 曲轴箱压缩，在曲轴箱(腔)内升高压力

~ door 曲轴箱道门

~ emission 曲柄箱排放物

~ explosion 曲轴箱爆炸，曲柄箱爆燃

~ explosion proof door 曲轴箱防爆门

~ facing 曲轴箱凸缘

~ guard 曲轴箱护罩

~ guard mounting arrangement 曲轴箱护罩安装布置

~ heater 曲轴箱加热器

~ inspection door 曲轴箱检修门

~ inspection hole cover 曲轴箱检查孔盖

~ lubrication 曲轴箱润滑(油)

~ manhole 曲轴箱人孔

~ oil 曲轴箱润滑油

~ oil mist detection 曲轴箱油雾检测

~ relief valve 曲轴箱安全阀

~ scavenging 曲轴箱扫气

~ vent piping system 曲轴箱通气管道系统

~ venting 曲轴箱通风

~ volume 曲轴箱容积

crankpin ['kræŋkpin] *n*. 曲柄针，曲柄销

~ bearing 曲柄销承，连杆轴承

~ bearing shell 曲柄销轴承

~ bolt 曲柄销螺栓

~ brass 曲柄销黄铜衬，曲柄销铜衬套

~ bush 曲柄销衬套

~ diameter 曲柄销直径

~ grease 曲柄销滑脂

~ seat 曲柄销座

~ sliding block mechanism 曲柄销滑块机构

crankshaft ['kræŋkʃɑːft] *n*. 曲轴，机轴

~ adapter 曲轴转接器，曲轴适配器

~ bearing 曲轴轴承

~ compartment 曲轴室

~ connection rod type oil motor 曲轴连杆式油马达

~ counterweight 曲轴衡重，曲轴平衡重块，曲轴平衡重

~ coupling bolt 曲轴联轴节螺栓
~ coupling flange 曲轴联轴节法兰
~ deflection 曲轴臂距差，曲轴挠曲，曲轴拐挡
~ deflection dial gauge 曲轴臂距差千分表，曲轴挠度量规，曲轴拐挡表
~ deflection measurement 曲轴臂距差测量，曲轴挠度测量，曲轴拐挡测量
~ deflection to be measured before and after repair 修理前后所需测量的拐挡差(曲轴臂距差) ‖ *Syn*. crankshaft deflection to be taken before and after repair 修理前后所需测量的拐挡差(曲轴臂距差)
~ fatigue fracture 曲轴疲劳断裂
~ flywheel 曲轴飞轮
~ housing 曲轴箱
~ installation 曲轴安装
~ journal 曲轴轴颈
~ lathe 曲轴车床
~ pin 曲轴曲柄销
~ slippage 曲轴滑移
~ surface 曲轴表面

crash [kræʃ] *n*. 碰撞，坠落，坠毁，严重意外，失败，垮台，倒闭，大跌，崩溃，撞击声，爆裂声；*v*. 碰撞，坠落，坠毁，破产，垮台，闯入，冲进，住宿，躺下睡觉；*a*. 紧急的，应急的，全力以赴的，速成的
~ gate 机舱急救门
~ maneuver 应急操纵
~ maneuvering 特急操纵
~ pad 防震垫，缓冲垫，座舱口软垫圈
~ recovery 崩溃恢复
~ reversal 紧急倒车
~ stop 全速急停车

crate [kreit] *n*. 装货箱，机箱，板条箱，柳条箱

creak [kri:k] *n*. 吱吱响声；*v*. 吱吱作响

cream [kri:m] *n*. 乳霜，精英，精华部分，奶油色，乳脂，奶油；*v*. 起泡沫，撇去乳皮，提取或去除精华，搅成糊状(或奶油状)混合物，彻底打败，狠揍
~ enamel paint 奶黄色瓷漆

crease [kri:s] *n*. 折痕，皱褶，折缝，皱纹；*v*. 折，弄皱，使有皱褶，表面被子弹擦伤或击伤

creek [kri:k] *n*. 小港，小湾，小河，小溪

creep [kri:p] *n*. 爬行，蠕动，蠕变，惊恐，战栗，毛骨悚然，卑鄙小人，谄媚者；*v*. 爬，蹑手蹑脚，蔓延，徐行，缓慢地行进
~ distance 爬电距离，爬距 ‖ *Syn*. creepage distance 爬电距离，爬距
~ fatigue 蠕变疲劳
~ fluidity 蠕变怜性，塑流，蠕变流动性
~ speed 蠕变速度，慢行速率，爬坡速率，最低航速

creepage ['kri:pidʒ] *n*. 蠕变，蠕动，漏电
~ distance 爬电距离，爬距 ‖ *Syn*. creep distance 爬电距离，爬距
~ distance of insulation 绝缘漏电距离
~ protector 漏电保护器
~ pump 蠕动泵
~ spark 漏电火花
~ switch 漏电开关

crest [krest] *n*. 最高点，顶点，顶部，顶峰，浪头，纹章，饰章，鸟冠，盔上的装饰(如羽毛)；*v*. 形成峰,到达绝顶，到达顶部，加上顶饰

~ of wave 波峰

crevice ['krevis] n. (尤指岩石的)裂缝，缺口
~ corrosion 缝隙腐蚀，裂隙腐蚀，接触腐蚀

crew [kru:] n. 全体船员，全体乘务员，同事们，一群，一帮；v. 当船员，当机务人员，一起工作，集体操作
~ list 船员名册
~ member 船员，乘务员
~ negligence 船员疏忽

crew's 船员的
~ chamber 船员舱，士兵舱，水手舱 ‖ Syn. crew's quarters 船员舱，士兵舱，水手舱
~ mess 船员餐厅，船员食堂

crewman ['kru:mən] n. 海员，机组乘务员

CRISTAL (Contract Regarding an Interim Supplement to Tanker Liability for Oil Pollution) 油轮油污责任暂行补充约定

criteria [krai'tiəriə] n. (criterion 的复数) 标准，条件

criterion [krai'tiəriə] n. (pl. criteria) 标准，准据，规范 ‖ Syn. measure 标准，量度标准，尺度；norm 规范，标准，准则；standard 标准，规格；touchstone 标准，检验标准，检验手段
~ function 准则函数，判别函数

critical ['kritikəl] a. 评论的，鉴定的，批评的，重要的，有判断力的，危急的，临界的 ‖ Syn. considerable 重要的；crucial 极其重要的；important 重要的，重大的；material 重要的
~ accident alarm 临界事故报警器
~ adjustment 临界调整
~ altitude 临界高度，最大工作高度，最大射高
~ angle 临界角
~ breakdown voltage 临界击穿电压
~ clearing time 临界切除时间
~ compression ratio 临界压缩比
~ condition 临界条件，临界状态，临界情况，危笃状态
~ damping 临界阻尼
~ equipment 关键设备
~ factor 临界因子，临界因素
~ issue 关键问题，重要的问题
~ level 临界水平，临界高度
~ load 临界载荷，临界负荷
~ margin 临界增益
~ moment 关键时刻，临界力矩，临界时限
~ part 主要机件，要害部位
~ point 临界点，紧要关头
~ pressure 临界压力
~ resistance 临界电阻
~ rudder angle 临界舵角
~ speed 临界速率，临界转速
~ speed of shafting 轴系临界转速
~ stability 临界稳定性
~ state 临界状态
~ temperature 临界温度
~ value 临界值
~ velocity 临界速度
~ voltage 临界电压

CRMS (control room management system) 控制室管理系统

cross [krɔs] n. 十字头，十字架，十字管，十字形饰物，杂交品种，审判，痛苦，磨难，挫折；v. 使交叉，越过，横过，勾划，错，反对，杂交；a. 交叉的，相反的，乖戾的

~ beam 横梁

~ check 相互校验，反复核对，交互核对

~ cut saw 横割锯，横锯

~ deck 舱口间甲板，横跨甲板

~ dimensions 横断面尺寸

~ feed motor 交叉馈电式电动机

~ flow 交叉流动，横向流动

~ girder 横梁

~ head 十字头

~ head driver 十字头螺丝刀，十字头起子

~ head bearing 十字头轴承

~ head engine 十字头式柴油机

~ joint 十字接头，四通

~ linking 交联，交叉接合

~ over 横渡，横过，越过，穿过

~ pin 十字头销，插销

~ scavenge 横流扫气

~ scavenging 横流扫气

~ screw 左右交叉螺纹

~ section 横截面，横断面，横剖面，横切面

~ section area 横截面面积，横切面面积

~ shaft 横轴

~ tube boiler 横管锅炉

~ valve 十字阀，三通阀

cross-channel 横越海峡的，交叉流道，交叉通道

~ automobile ferry 横越海峡车客渡轮

cross-linked 交联的

~ polyethylene (XLPE) 交联聚乙烯

~ polyethylene cable 交联聚乙烯电缆

cross-sectional 横截面的，横断面的，代表性的

~ area 横截面面积，横断面面积

crosscut ['krɔskʌt] n. 捷径，横切，横穿，横越，横切过程；v. 横切，横穿，横越，剪接；a. 横切的，用来横切的

crossflow ['krɔsfləu] n. 交叉流动，横向流动

~ scavenging type engine 横流扫气式发动机

crosshead ['krɔshed] n. 十字头，丁字头，子题，小标题

~ bearing 十字头轴承

~ bearing bush 十字头轴承衬

~ bearing shell 十字头轴瓦

~ body 十字头体

~ bush 十字头轴衬

~ end 十字头端

~ engine 十字头柴油机

~ guide 十字头导承

~ guide bar 十字头导杆

~ guide plate 十字头导板 ‖ Syn. crosshead guide rail 十字头导板；crosshead guide way 十字头导板

~ liner 十字头衬瓦

~ link 十字头连杆

~ nut 十字头螺母

~ pin 十字头销

~ pin bearing 十字头销轴承

~ retainer 十字头护圈

~ rivet 十字头铆钉

~ shoe 十字头滑块 ‖ Syn. crosshead slipper 十字头滑块

~ type diesel 十字头式柴油机

~ type piston 十字头式活塞

crosswise [krɔswaiz] ad. 斜地，成十字状地，交叉地

crow [krəu] n. 撬棍，铁挺，乌鸦，似乌

鸦的鸟，雄鸡的啼声；v. 公鸡啼鸣，报晓，欢呼，吹嘘

crowbar ['krəuba:(r)] n. 撬棍，铁橇，起货钩；v. 用撬棍把…撬开

crowfoot ['krəu,fut] n. 天篷吊索，毛茛等的俗称

crown [kraun] n. 王冠，花冠，顶；v. 加冕，顶上有，表彰，使圆满完成
- ~ block 定滑轮
- ~ circle 锥齿轮冠圆，外端齿顶圆
- ~ head piston 冠状活塞，凸头活塞 ‖ *Syn*. convex head piston 冠状活塞，凸头活塞

crucial ['kru:ʃəl] a. 决定性的，关键性的，极其重要的，极其显要的，十字形的 ‖ *Syn*. critical 重要的；considerable 重要的；important 重要的，重大的；material 重要的

cruciform ['kru:sifɔ:m] a. 十字形的
- ~ beam 十字梁
- ~ bracing 框架横梁，十字撑
- ~ construction 十字形构造
- ~ core 十字形铁心
- ~ jet 十字孔形喷丝头
- ~ joint 十字接头

crude [kru:d] n. 原油，天然的物质；a. 天然的，未加工的，粗糙的，拙劣的，粗鲁的
- ~ carrier 运油船，运油轮 ‖ *Syn*. crude oil carrier 原油运输船，原油油船；crude oil tanker 原油船，原油轮
- ~ oil 原油
- ~ oil washer 原油清洗机
- ~ oil washing (COW) 原油洗舱
- ~ washing system 原油洗舱系统

cruise [kru:z] n. 巡游，巡逻，巡航，漫游；v. 巡游，巡逻，巡航，漫游
- ~ control 巡航控制
- ~ facilities 游船设施
- ~ liner 旅游船，旅游班轮
- ~ ship 游轮，游船，大型游轮

cruiser ['kru:zə] n. 巡洋舰，摩托艇，(配备生活设施的)游艇
- ~ stern 巡洋舰型艉

cruising [kru:ziŋ] v. (cruise 的 ing 形式) 巡游，巡逻，巡航，漫游；a. 巡航的
- ~ condition 巡航条件
- ~ distance 续航距离
- ~ ground 航行区
- ~ power 巡航功率
- ~ propulsion motor 巡航推进电动机
- ~ radius 巡航半径
- ~ range 巡航范围，巡航距离
- ~ speed 巡航速度，巡航航速

crush [krʌʃ] v. 压碎，碾碎，压服，压垮，粉碎，(使)变形

crusher ['krʌʃə] n. 粉碎机，轧碎机，压碎的东西，镇服人的事实，打击 ‖ *Syn*. grinder 研磨机，粉碎机；macerater 粉碎机，切碎机；pulverizer 粉碎机；shredder 切菜器，撕碎机

crushability [krʌʃə'biliti] n. 可破碎性，压碎，压不皱

crutch [krʌtʃ] n. 支持物，支撑物，拐杖，精神上的寄托，帮助，胯部；v. 支撑，支持

cryogenic [,kraiəu'dʒenik] a. 低温学的
- ~ compressor 低温压缩机
- ~ device 低温装置，低温设备
- ~ distillation 低温蒸馏
- ~ equipment 低温设备
- ~ glove 低温防护手套

~ liquid 低温液体

~ refrigerator 低温制冷器，低温冰箱

~ system 低温系统

~ valve 低温阀门

CSC (International Convention for Safe Containers) 国际集装箱安全公约

CSS (coordinator surface search) 海面搜救协调员，海面搜寻协调船

CSSCC (Cargo Ship Safety Construction Certificate) 货船构造安全证书

CSSEC (Cargo Ship Safety Equipment Certificate) 货船设备安全证书

CSSRC (Cargo Ship Safety Radio Certificate) 货船无线电安全证书

CSTI (current source type inverter) 电流源型逆变器

CT (current transfer) 电流传输，电流转移

CT (current transformer) 电流互感器

cube [kju:b] n. 立方形，立方体，立方，三次幂，小房间；v. 求立方，测体积，形成立方体，切成方块

cubic ['kju:bik] n. 三次曲线，三次表达式，三次曲线，三次方程；a. 立方体的，立方的，三次幂的

~ feet 立方英尺

~ metre 立方米

cubicle ['kju:bikl] n. 小卧室，小隔间

culinary ['kʌlinəri] a. 厨房的，烹调用的，厨房用的

cumulative ['kju:mjuələtiv] a. 累积的，渐增的，追加的，加重的

~ action 聚能作用

~ compound excitation 积复励

~ utility 总效用，累积效用

~ volume 累积体积，总体积

~ compound 积复励，积复绕

~ compound winding 积复激绕组

cumulatively ['kju:mjulətivli] ad. 累积地

~ compounded motor 积复励电动机

cup [kʌp] n. 杯子，酒杯，奖杯；v. 使成杯状，拔火罐

~ and ball jointing 球窝关节

~ and ball viscometer 球窝黏度计，杯球式黏度计

~ grease 润滑脂，稠黏润滑油

~ grinding wheel 环形砂轮

cuprous ['kju:prəs] a. 亚铜的，一价铜的

~ alloy 亚铜合金

~ oxide 氧化亚铜，一氧化二铜

cure [kjuə] n. 治愈，痊愈，疗法，药物，措施，对策，加工处理；v. 治愈，治疗，去除，整治，消除，加工处理，保存

curing ['kjuəriŋ] n. 食物加工法；v. (cure 的 ing 形式) 治愈，治疗，去除，整治，消除，加工处理，保存

~ agent 固化剂，硬化剂

~ temperature 固化温度

~ time 硬化时间，固化时间

current ['kʌrənt] n. 涌流，趋势，电流，水流，气流；a. 当前的，通用的，流通的，现在的，草写的，最近的

~ by phase 每相电流

~ carrying capacity 载流能力，最大允许电流

~ density 电流密度，扩散流密度，弥漫流密度

~ element 电流元件

~ force 水流力

~ indicating lamp 电流指示灯

~ intensity 电流强度

~ limit relay 限流继电器，限摆电器
~ limiter 限流器
~ loop 电流环路，电流闭环，电流环
~ loss 电流损耗，电流损失
~ meter 测流计，流速计
~ operational parameter 当前运行参数
~ probe 电流探针
~ production 流水作业，流水生产
~ rating 额定电流 ‖ *Syn*. nominal current 标称电流，额定电流；rated current 额定电流；rating current 额定电流，电流额定值
~ ratio 流动比率
~ relay 电流继电器
~ relay coil 电流继电器线圈
~ repair 小修，日常修理，现场修理
~ reversible chopper 电流可逆斩波电路
~ reversing key 电流换向开关，电流换向键
~ ripple 电流纹波
~ settings 当前设置
~ situation 现状，目前形势，现况 ‖ *Syn*. current status 现状，当前状态，目前状况，应用现状
~ source type inverter (CSTI) 电流源型逆变器
~ carrying capability 承载电流能力
~ carrying capacity of a single laid cable 单层敷设电缆的载流能力
~ carrying capacity of group laid cables 成组敷设电缆的载流能力
~ carrying conductor 载流导体
~ carrying part 载流部分
~ carrying plate 导电板，载流薄板
~ transfer (CT) 电流传输，电流转移

~ transfer ratio 电流传输比，电流转移比
~ transfers 转让，让与
~ transformer (CT) 电流互感器

curvature ['kə:vətʃə] *n*. 曲率，弯曲，曲度，弯曲部分
~ radius 曲率半径

curve [kə:v] *n*. 曲线，弯曲，曲线球，曲线图表，骗人把戏，欺骗；*v*. 弯，使弯曲，成曲形，转弯
~ fitting 曲线求律法，曲线拟合
~ of buoyancy 浮力曲线
~ of center of buoyancy 浮心曲线
~ of center of gravity of water plane 漂心曲线
~ of flotation 浮心曲线
~ of loads 负载曲线，载重曲线
~ of longitudinal centers of buoyancy 浮心纵向坐标曲线
~ of longitudinal centers of floatation 漂心纵向坐标曲线
~ of metacenter 稳心曲线
~ of resistance 阻力曲线
~ of sectional area 截面积曲线
~ of stability 稳性曲线，稳度曲线
~ of the blade 桨叶曲度
~ of transverse metacentre 横稳心曲线
~ of waterplane area 水线面面积曲线
~ of volumes of total displacements 总排水体积曲线

curves ['kə:vz] *n*. (curve 的复数) 曲线，弯曲，曲线球，曲线图表；*v*. (curve 的第三人称单数) 弯，使弯曲，成曲形，转弯
~ of form 船形曲线

curvilinear [kə:vi'liniə(r)] *a*. 曲线的，由曲线而成的

cushion ['kuʃən] *n.* 垫子，软垫，衬垫，缓冲；*v.* 保护，缓和，减轻，压制，隐忍，加衬垫，缓和冲击，减缓后果，以垫子覆盖

~ of air 气垫

custom ['kʌstəm] *n.* 习惯，风俗，海关，定期服劳役，缴纳租税，自定义，关税，老主顾，主顾，光顾，捧场；*v.* 定制，承接定做的活；*a.* 定做的，定制的

customs ['kʌstəmz] *n.* (custom 的复数)进口税，海关；*v.* (custom 的第三人称单数)，定制，承接定做的活

~ boarding officer 登轮关员，海关上船检验人员

~ charges 报关费

~ checking 海关检查，关验，海关查验

~ classification procedures 结关手续

~ clearance 结关，海关放行

~ duty 关税

~ examination 验关

~ fees 海关规费

~ formality 海关手续

~ manifest 报关单

~ officer 海关官员

~ paper 海关证件

~ patrol craft 海关巡逻艇

cut [kʌt] *n.* 切削，削减，删节，伤口，切口；*v.* 切割，切削，相交，剪，截，刺穿，刺痛，删节，开辟

~ away 去掉，切，切成，迅速离开

~ away view 剖视图

~ back 修剪，削减，急忙返回，倒叙

~ off 切断，中断，使死亡，剥夺继承权

cut-off 截止，定点，取舍点，界限

~ current 截止电流

~ frequency 截止频率，截频，断电频率

~ key 切断电键

~ level 截止电平

~ lever 截止杆，截断杆，追随杆，反馈杆

~ machine 切割机，切断机

~ relay 断路继电器

~ slide valve 断流滑阀

~ switch 断路开关，切断开关，断流开关，断路接触器

~ time 截止时间，(船舶)截货时间

~ tool 切断刀具，切断刀

~ valve 截止阀，关闭阀，断流阀，断流闸

~ voltage 截止电压

cut-out (自动断电)保险装置，断流器，切断，切出的洞，图案，花样

~ case 熔线盒，熔丝盒

~ cylinder test 停缸试验

~ device 切断装置，停油装置，安全开关

~ fuse 断流熔线

~ gear 断流装置，停气装置

~ plug 断流栓，断流塞

~ point 切断点，截止点

~ position 停油位置

~ relay 断流继电器，断路继电器，断流器

~ relay armature spring 断流继电器电转子弹簧

~ relay shunt coil 断流继电器并联线圈

~ relay contact bracket 断流继电器触点托架

~ servomotor 断油伺服马达

~ servomotor with slide valve 带滑阀的断油伺服马达

~ spring 分开弹簧

~ switch 断路开关，断路器

cutter ['kʌtə] n. 独桅纵帆船，小艇，小型武装快艇，轻便雪橇，刀具，切割机

~ blade (铣)刀片

~ head 刀头，刀盘，铣头，刀架

~ shaft 刀轴，滚刀轴，切碎装置轴

~ suction dredge 绞吸式挖泥机

~ suction dredger 绞吸式挖泥船

cutting ['kʌtiŋ] n. 切断，剪辑，切断，开凿，切下，道路，通道，剪报；v. (cut 的 ing 形式) 切割，切削，相交，剪，截，刺穿，刺痛，删节；a. 锋利的，刺骨的，尖锐的，严寒的，挖苦的，尖刻的，严厉的

~ blade 切削片，切割刀片，遮光叶片

~ block 錾锉砧，冲模，冲头

~ blowpipe 割炬，截割吹管，喷割器

~ depth 切削深度，开挖深度

~ edge 刃口，刀刃，剪刃，切削刃

~ force 切削力

~ gauge 切削规

~ head 刻纹头，机械录音头

~ mechanics 切割机械

~ pliers 钢丝钳，克丝钳，剪钳，手钳，扁嘴钳

~ speed 切削速度，切割速度

~ table 切桌，剪辑桌

~ tool 切削刀具，割削工具

~ torch 割炬，切割吹管

CVCF (constant voltage constant frequency) 恒压恒频

CVT (capacitive voltage transformer) 电容式电压互感器

CW (cooling water) 冷却水

cycle ['saikl] n. 周期，循环，自行车，时代，一段时间，周而复始，整套，(电学)周波；v. (使)循环，(使)轮转，骑自行车

~ by cycle 逐周期

~ by cycle current limit 逐周期电流限制

~ duration 循环时间

~ efficiency 循环效率

~ skipping 跳周

cyclic ['saiklik] a. (=cyclical) 周期的，循环的，轮转的

~ loading 周期载荷

~ remote control 循环遥控

cyclical ['siklik(ə)l] a. (=cyclic) 周期的，循环的，轮转的

cycloconverter [ˌsaikləukən'vəːtə] n. 周波变换器，循环换流器，双向离子变频器

cycloidal [sai'klɔidəl] a. 摆线的，圆形的

~ gear 摆线齿轮

~ gear pump 摆线齿轮泵

~ pump 摆旋泵

cyclone ['saikləun] n. 旋风，飓风，暴风，龙卷风，气旋

~ separator 旋风分离器，旋风除尘器

~ steam separator 旋风汽水分离器

cylinder ['silində] n. 圆筒，圆柱体，汽缸，柱面

~ air starting valve 气缸空气起动阀

~ block 气缸柱，气缸座，气缸体

~ block fins 缸体散热片

~ block frame 气缸体机架

~ blow-by 气缸漏气，气缸窜气

~ body 气缸体，缸体
~ bore 气缸内径，缸径，气缸内孔
~ brush 气缸刷
~ capacity 气缸容量，气缸总容积
~ clearance 气缸余隙
~ clearance space 气缸余隙空间
~ clearance volume 气缸余隙容积
~ control unit 气缸控制单元
~ cooling jacket 气缸冷却水套
~ cover 气缸盖，气缸头罩，气缸体罩
~ cover nut 气缸盖螺母
~ cover stud 气缸盖螺柱
~ cover water space 气缸盖冷却水空间
~ cowling 圆柱形通风帽，圆柱形风斗
~ diameter 气缸直径
~ frame 气缸座
~ head 气缸盖
~ head fins 缸盖散热片
~ head gasket 气缸盖垫片，气缸头垫片
~ head joint 气缸盖衬垫
~ head ring gasket 气缸盖密封环
~ in V formation V 形气缸
~ in W formation W 形气缸
~ jacket 气缸套，气缸罩
~ knocking 敲缸
~ liner 气缸套
~ lubricating oil system 气缸润油系统
~ lubricator 气缸注油器
~ luffing crane 缸体变幅起重机
~ number 缸数，柱面数
~ oil squirt 气缸注油器
~ oil transfer pump 气缸输油泵
~ output 单缸输出功率，气缸功率
~ packing ring 缸套密封环
~ pressure 气缸压力
~ scavenging system 气缸扫气系统
~ scraping 气缸刮削，拉缸
~ seal 气缸密封
~ sleeve 气缸套
~ spacer 气缸体隔片
~ starting valve 气缸起动阀
~ sticking 发动机咬缸，咬缸，轴颈擦伤
~ stock 气缸油
~ valve 气缸阀
~ volume 气缸容积，缸容
~ wall 气缸壁
cylindrical [si'lindrik(ə)l] a. 圆筒的，圆柱体的，圆筒状的，气缸(或滚筒)的，坐标系的
~ bearing 筒状轴承，筒形轴承
~ boiler 筒状锅炉，筒形锅炉，圆筒式锅炉
~ cam 凸轮轴，圆柱形凸轮
~ cavity 筒形腔，圆柱形谐振腔
~ coefficient 圆柱系数
~ coordinate 柱面坐标，圆柱坐标
~ gear 圆柱齿轮
~ gearing 圆柱齿轮传动
~ grinding 圆筒面研磨，外圆磨削
~ grinding wheel 筒形砂轮
~ interface 圆柱界面，柱状交界面
~ pin 筒形销
~ roller 圆柱形托辊，(输送机)圆筒形滚柱
~ roller bearing 圆柱滚子轴承，圆筒形滚柱轴承
~ rotor 鼓形转子
~ shell 柱形壳，筒壳
~ surface 柱面，圆柱体
~ surfaced bearing 弧形支座
~ turning 外圆车削

~ worm 圆柱蜗杆，柱形蜗杆

D

D [di:] ① (=derivative) *n*. 导数，微商，衍生物，派生物，导出物，派生词；*a*. 衍生的，导出的，拷贝的，无创意的 ② (=differentiation) *n*. 微分，区别，分化，变异

~ action 微分作用

~ control 微分控制，微分调节

~ control mode 微分控制方式，微分调节方式

~ control output 微分控制输出，微分调节输出

~ controller 微分控制器，微分调节器 ‖ *Syn*. D regulator 微分控制器，微分调节器

~ element 微分环节，微分元件，导数元件

~ feedback 微分反馈，导数反馈

~ mode 微分模式，导数模式

D-adjustable D 型调整的

~ buckle D 型调整扣环

DA (digital-analog, digital-analogue) 数字模拟(的)，数模(的)

DA (digital-to-analog) 数字对模拟的，数模的

~ conversion 数模转换

~ converter 数模转换器

daily ['deili] *n*. 日报，(不寄宿的)仆人，白天做家务的女佣；*a*. 每日的，日常的，一日的，每日一次的，每个工作日的；*ad*. 每日地，逐日地，日复一日地

~ load curve 日负荷曲线

~ maintenance 日常保养

~ necessities 日用品，生活必需品

~ report 日报单

~ routine 日常工作，日常例行，每日常规

~ service tank 日用油柜，日用水柜

~ sheet 日报表

~ tank 日用柜

~ use 日常使用，每日使用

~ variation 每日变动

dam [dæm] *n*. 障碍，水坝；*v*. 控制，筑坝

~ ring 阻水环

damage ['dæmidʒ] *n*. 损坏，损毁，损失，损害，伤害，赔偿金；*v*. 损害，损毁，招致损害 ‖ *Syn*. spoilage 损坏；worsement 损坏，破坏

~ accident 损坏事故

~ containment 损害抑制，损害控制

~ control 损害控制

~ control booklet 海损控制手册，破损控制手册

~ control plan 海损控制示意图，破损控制示意图

~ control team 损管组，损管队

~ repair 损伤修理，损坏修理

~ report 损坏报告书

~ stability 破舱稳性，破损稳度

~ stability calculation 破舱稳性计算

~ stability requirement 破舱稳性要求

~ survey 损坏调查，损失调查

~ threshold 损坏阈

damp [dæmp] *n*. 潮湿，消沉，失望，抑制，控制，有毒气体；*v*. 使潮湿，阻尼，使衰减，使沮丧，控制，抑止；*a*. 潮湿的，沮丧的，灰心的

~ air 潮湿空气，湿空气

~ check 防潮层

~ down 减少，减弱，润湿，降低，衰减，封火，使沮丧，使扫兴

~ heat test 湿热试验

~ winding 阻尼绕组

damp-proof 防潮的，防湿的，防水的

~ insulation 防湿绝缘

~ machine 防潮电机

~ packing 防潮包装

~ wire 防潮电线

damped [dæmpt] v. (damp 的过去式和过去分词) 抑制，控制；a. 阻尼的，衰减的，被窒息的

~ alternating current 减幅交流，阻尼交流

~ oscillation 阻尼振荡，阻尼振动，减幅振荡

dampen ['dæmpən] v. 使潮湿，变得潮湿，使沮丧，使扫兴，消除，抑制，压抑，隔音，防音

damper ['dæmpə] n. 抑制因素，挡板，调节风门，节气闸，断音装置，阻尼器，避震器，使人扫兴的人(事)；a. (damp 的比较级) 比…潮湿，比…沮丧，比…灰心

~ control 阻尼器控制，挡板控制，风门控制装置

~ hole 阻尼孔

~ winding 阻尼绕组，阻尼线圈

damping ['dæmpiŋ] n. 阻尼，衰减，减幅；v. (damp 的 ing 形式) 使潮湿，使衰减，使沮丧，控制，抑止

~ characteristic 阻尼特性

~ coefficient 阻尼系数，衰减系数

~ contactor 阻尼接触器

~ device 阻尼装置，减振装置

~ effect 阻尼效应，减振效果，衰减效应

~ force 阻尼力

~ mechanism 阻尼机构，减振机构

~ ring 阻尼环

~ spring 阻尼弹簧，减振弹簧，缓冲弹簧

~ vibration 阻尼振动

~ viscosity 阻尼黏性

dampness ['dæmpnəs] n. 湿度，湿气，潮湿

danger ['deindʒə] n. 危险，危害，危险物，威胁 ‖ *Syn*. hazard 冒险，危险，冒险的事；jeopardy 危险；peril 危险，危险物；risk 危险，风险，冒险

~ area 危险区域

~ arrow (用于高电压等场所中的)危险箭头

~ coefficient 危险系数

~ index 火险指数，火险指标，危险指数

~ limit value 危险极限值

~ money 危险工作津贴，危险工作的额外报酬

~ point 危险点，危险地点

~ protecting function 保险功能，危险保护功能

~ signal 危险信号，险阻号志，危险标志

dangerous ['deindʒrəs] a. 危险的 ‖ *Syn*. hazardous 危险的，冒险的；perilous 危险的，冒险的；unsafe 危险的

~ accident 险性事故，隐性事故，危险事故

~ area 危险区，危险路段，危险区域

~ cargo 危险货物，危险品

~ case 险情，危险的情况

~ device 危险装置

~ duty 危险任务

~ factor 危险因素

~ goods 危险物品

~ goods manifest 危险货物舱单

~ situation 危境，险境

~ source 危险源，危源，风险源

~ substance 危险物质

~ waters 危险水域

DAS (data acquisition system) 数据采集系统

dash [dæʃ] n. 少量(掺加物)，冲撞，破折号，锐气，精力，干劲；v. 猛掷，冲撞，泼溅，使猛撞，掺和，使破灭，使沮丧，匆忙完成

~ pot 缓冲筒，减振器，阻尼延迟器

data ['deitə] n. (datum 的复数) 资料，数据，材料，从科学实验中提取的价值

~ acquisition 数据采集

~ acquisition system (DAS) 数据采集系统

~ analysis 数据分析，资料分析

~ base 数据库，储存的资料，资料库

~ bus 数据总线

~ collection 数据收集，数据汇集，资料收集

~ display equipment 数据显示设备

~ fitting 数据拟合

~ handling 数据处理，信息处理

~ handling and logging 数据处理和记录

~ logger 数据自动测定，数据列表，记录装置，数据记录器

~ logging 数据资料记录

~ logging equipment 动力装置参数自记仪，数据巡回检测装置

~ logging recorder 数据记录器

~ logging system 参数自动记录系统

~ logging tool 数据记录工具

~ management 数据管理，资料管理

~ output 数据输出

~ preprocessing 数据预处理

~ processing 数据处理，资料处理

~ processing unit (DPU) 数据处理装置

~ processor 数据处理机，数据处理部件，数据处理程序

~ recorder 数据记录器

~ recording equipment 数据记录装置

~ security 数据安全

~ transmission device 数据传输装置

database ['deitəbeis] n. 数据库，资料库，信息库

date [deit] n. 日期，日子，(历史上某一)年代，时期，约会；v. 约会，定日期，注明…的日期，过时，显示或设置系统日期

~ logger 日期记录器

datum ['deitəm] n. (pl. data) 数据，资料，论据

~ speed 标称速度，基准速度

daughter ['dɔ:tə] n. 女儿，女继承人，关系像女儿的人，女儿似的人，继承元素；a. 女儿的，如女儿的，关系如女儿的

~ board 子板，子插件板

davit ['dævit] n. 吊柱，吊艇柱，吊艇架

~ arm 吊艇架臂

~ bearing 吊艇杆承座，吊艇柱座承

~ head 吊艇柱弯头，吊杆头，吊艇架弯头

~ span wire 吊缆

~ tackle 吊艇架绞辘，吊艇杆滑车，吊艇绞辘

davit-launched 吊放的，吊放式的

~ lifeboat 吊放救生艇

~ raft 吊放救生艇

day [dei] *n.* 天，白天，日子，白昼，黎明，工作日，节日，重要日子，机会；*a.* 白天的，日间的，逐日的

~ tank 日用油柜

daylight ['deilait] *n.* 日光，白昼，清早，黎明，理解，智慧，公开

~ lamp 日光灯

~ lamp starter 日光灯启动器

~ signal lamp 白天信号灯

~ signaling light 白昼信号灯

dB (decibel) 分贝

DblClmnTrans (double column transformer) 双绕组变压器 ‖ *Syn.* two-circuit transformer 双回路变压器；two-winding transformer 双绕组变压器，双线圈变压器

DC (direct current) 直流，直流电，直流电流

~ ammeter 直流电流表，直流安培表，直流安培计

~ circuit 直流电路

~ contactor 直流接触器

~ control 直流控制

~ distribution system 直流配电系统

~ dynamo 直流发电机 ‖ *Syn.* DC generator 直流发电机

~ electric propulsion apparatus 直流电力推进装置

~ electrical source 直流电源

~ exciter 直流励磁机

~ generator-motor set drive 直流发电机电机动组驱动

~ machine 直流电机

~ motor 直流电动机，直流马达

~ power station 直流电站

~ resistance 直流电阻

~ single wire system 直流单线制

~ switchboard 直流配电盘

~ three-wire insulated system 直流三线绝缘系统

~ two-wire insulated system 直流两线绝缘系统

~ voltage 直流电压

DC-AC-DC (direct current-alternating current-direct current) 直流交流直流，直交直

~ converter 直流交流直流变换器，直交直变换器

DC-DC (direct current-direct current) 直流直流，直直

~ converter 直流直流变换器，直直变换器

DCS (distributed control system) 分布式控制系统，分散式控制系统

DDC (direct digital control) 直接数字控制

DDPS (distributed data processing system) 分布式数据处理系统

dead [ded] *n.* 死者，最高阶段，最强阶段；*a.* 死的，疲倦的，消失的，无感觉的，呆板的，不流动的，闲置的，废弃了的，冷却的，熄灭的，失灵的，直接的，确切的，突然的；*ad.* 完全地，绝对地，突然地

~ angle 死角

~ astern 后退，正后方

~ axle 静轴，不转轴，从动轴

~ band 无控制作用区，(参数值的)死区

~ center 死点，静点，死顶点

~ contact 空触点

~ cover 风暴盖

~ earth 完全接地

~ flat 船中平行体

~ front 空正面，正面不带电的部件，死面

~ front switch 安全开关

~ front switchgear 表面不带电式配电设备，表面不带电式开关设备

~ front switchboard 表面不带电式配电板

~ front type panel 正面不带电式控制板

~ part 不带电部分

~ rack travel 齿条行程死区

~ reckoning 航位推测法

~ rise 底部升高量

~ ship condition 废船状态，瘫船状态

~ slow ahead 微速前进

~ slow astern 微速后退

~ time 最后期限，死时间(色谱分析)，静寂时间

~ water 死水，船舷侧旋涡

~ weight 静负载，固定负载

~ zone 死区，盲区，静区，无信号区

deadlight ['dedlait] *n.* 舷窗盖，中墙板

deadline ['dedlain] *n.* 最后期限，截止期限，死线，原稿截止时间

deadman ['dedmæn] *n.* 木桩或水泥桩，临时支撑物，拔杆，叉杆

~ alarm 紧急报警器

~ switch 安全操作开关，死人开关

~ feature 无人保护装置

deadweight [,ded'weit] *n.* 自重，载重量，重负

~ anchor 自重锚

~ capacity (总)载重吨位

~ cargo 重货，垫舱货

~ check 载重检查

~ gauge 静重仪

~ scale 载重量标尺

~ ship 载重船

~ tonnage (总)载重吨位

deaerate [di:'eiəreit] *v.* 使除去空气，从(液体)中除去气泡

deaerating [di'eiəreitiŋ] *n.* 除氧，除气；*v.* (deaerate 的 ing 形式) 除去空气，除去气泡

~ agent 去泡剂，脱气剂，除氧剂

~ chamber 除气室，除氧室

~ element 除氧元件

~ plant 除氧装置

~ system 除气系统

~ tank 脱气槽，除气槽

~ tower 除氧塔

~ trap 除气留水阀

deaeration [di'eiə'reiʃən] *n.* 脱气(法)，排气(法)，除气(法)，脱泡(作用)

deaerator [di:'eiə'reitə] *n.* 脱气器

deal [di:l] *n.* 交易，密约，待遇，分量，买卖；*v.* 处理，应付，做生意，分配，分给，给予，发牌

~ with 应付，安排，处理，涉及，做生意 ‖ *Syn.* dispose of 处理，安排，解决；handle 处理；manage 处理，应付；manipulate (巧妙地)处理，应付；treat with 处理，应付

deballast [di'bæləst] *v.* 排放压舱水 ‖ *Ant.* ballast 提供压舱物

debris ['debri:] *n.* 碎片，残骸，残渣，破片，垃圾

debur [di'bə:] *v.* 修边，清理毛刺

deburring [di'bə:riŋ] *n.* 修边，除去毛刺；*v.* (debur 的 ing 形式) 修边，除去毛刺

~ punch 压毛边冲子

decarburization [di:,ka:bjuərai'zeiʃən] *n.* 脱碳，除碳 ‖ *Ant.* carburization 渗碳

decarburize [di:'ka:bjuəraiz] *v.* 脱碳，除碳 ‖ *Ant.* carburize 渗碳

decay [di'kei] *n.* 腐朽，腐烂，衰减，衰退；*v.* 腐朽，腐烂，衰减，衰退
~ coefficient 衰减系数，衰变系数

decca ['dekə] *n.* 台卡导航系统

decelerate [di:'seləreit] *v.* (使)减速

decelerating [di:'seləreitiŋ] *v.* (decelerate 的 ing 形式) (使)减速；*a.* 使减速的
~ curve 减速曲线
~ device 减速装置
~ ducted propeller 减速型导管螺旋桨，减速导管推进器
~ machine 减速机
~ manoeuvre 减速操纵
~ monitor 减速器监测仪
~ motor 减速电机
~ nozzle 减速导流管

deceleration [di:selə'reiʃən] *n.* 减速

decenter ['di:səntə] *v.* 去中心性，使离心，使脱离中心地位，偏心

decentralize [,di:'sentrəlaiz] *v.* (=decentralise) 疏散，分散，密度分散，权力分散，人口疏散，地方分权 ‖ *Ant.* centralize (使)集聚, (使)集中

decentralise [,di:'sentrəlaiz] *v.* (=decentralize) 疏散，分散，密度分散，权力分散，人口疏散，地方分权 ‖ *Ant.* centralize (使)集聚, (使)集中

decibel ['desibel] (dB) *n.* 分贝

decibelmeter [,desi'bel,mi:tə] *n.* 分贝计，电平表

decimal ['desiməl] *n.* 小数；*a.* 十进的，小数的，以十为基础的，十进制

deck [dek] *n.* 甲板，舰板，覆盖物，一副(纸牌)；*v.* 装饰，修饰，打扮，装甲板
~ and sanitary water overboard discharge hole 甲板和卫生水舷外排水孔
~ and sanitary water piping system 甲板和卫生水管系
~ beam 甲板梁
~ boy 甲板员，舱面水手，舱面工
~ cabin 甲板舱室
~ cassab 副水手长 ‖ *Syn.* boatswain mate 副水手长；deck tindal 副水手长
~ covering 甲板敷料
~ covering compositions 甲板敷料的成分
~ crane 甲板起重机
~ crew 舱面人员
~ draining valve 甲板排水阀 ‖ *Syn.* deck water discharge valve 甲板排水阀
~ edge 甲板缘，甲板边，池缘
~ equipment 甲板装备
~ fastenings 甲板紧固件
~ fittings 舱面属具，甲板装置
~ flange 甲板法兰，甲板唇口，甲板边缘
~ flushing piping system to be done air-tightness test 甲板冲洗管系密性试验
~ gang (码头工人上船装卸货的)舱面工班
~ girder 甲板纵桁
~ girder angle 甲板纵桁角材
~ hand 甲板水手，舱面人员
~ hand uncertified (DHU) 见习水手，无证书的甲板人员
~ hatchway 甲板舱口
~ house 甲板室，舱面室
~ ladder 甲板间扶梯

~ lighting system 甲板照明系统

~ line at side 甲板边线

~ log book 航海日志

~ longitudinal 甲板纵骨

~ machinery 甲板机械，舱面机械

~ office 甲板部，舱面办公室

~ officer 船舶驾驶员，舱面甲级船员，驾驶部门高级船员

~ operated isolating valve 甲板操纵隔离阀

~ plan 甲板图，甲板布置图

~ plate 甲板板，波纹钢板，瓦垅钢板，盖板，台面板

~ plating 甲板钢板，钢甲板

~ scupper 甲板排水孔

~ scupper pipe 甲板排水管 ‖ *Syn*. deck water discharge pipe 甲板排水管

~ securing fitting 甲板绑扎固定用具

~ serang 水手长 ‖ *Syn*. boatswain 水手长；bosun 水手长

~ sill 顶棚纵向梁

~ sprinkler system 甲板洒水系统

~ store 甲板部门储藏室

~ strake 甲板列板，甲板铺板

~ stringer 甲板边板

~ structure 甲板结构，舱面建筑，上承结构，舱面结构

~ tank 甲板水柜，舱面水柜

~ transverse 强横梁，甲板横材

~ wash pump 甲板冲洗泵 ‖ *Syn*. deck flushing pump 甲板冲洗泵

~ washing piping system 甲板冲洗系统

~ water seal 甲板水封

deckhouse ['dekhaus] *n*. 舱面船室

declaration [ˌdeklə'reiʃən] *n*. 宣言，宣布，布告，宣言书，布告，申报

~ form 申报单

declare [di'klɛə] *v*. 断言，宣称，宣布，宣告，声明，揭示，表明，显示，(向海关)中报进口应纳税之货物

declared [di'klɛəd] *v*. (declare 的过去式和过去分词) 断言，宣称，宣布，宣告，声明，揭示，表明，显示；*a*. 公告的，公然的

~ working condition 额定工况

declination [ˌdekli'neiʃən] *n*. 磁偏角，偏差，衰退，倾斜，下倾，赤纬，磁偏角，婉拒，谢绝

decompose [ˌdi:kəm'pəuz] *v*. 分解，(使)腐烂 ‖ *Ant*. compose 组成

~ into 分解为

decomposite [ˌdi:'kɔmpəzit] *n*. 再混合物；*a*. 再混合的，与混合物混合的

decomposition [ˌdi:kɔmpə'ziʃən] *n*. 分解，降解，腐烂 ‖ *Ant*. composition 组成，构成

~ voltage 分解电压

decompression [ˌdi:kəm'preʃən] *n*. 减压，解压

~ chamber 减压室，减压舱

~ sickness 潜水减压病

~ time 减压时间，降压时间

decorate ['dekəreit] *v*. 装饰，布置，授勋给

decoration [ˌdekə'reiʃən] *n*. 装饰，装潢，装饰，勋章，奖章，装饰的程序、方法或艺术，装饰品

decouple [di:'kʌpl] *v*. 解耦，去耦，减低震波，分离，拆开 ‖ *Ant*. couple 联合，连接，结合

decoupling [di:'kʌpliŋ] *n*. 解耦(装置)，去耦(装置)；*v*. (decouple 的 ing 形式) 解耦，去耦，减低震波，分离，拆开

~ circuit 解耦电路，去耦电路

decrease [di'kri:s] *n.* 减少，减少量，减小；*v.* 减少，减小

decrement ['dekrimənt] *n.* 减量，消耗，缩减

deduct [di'dʌkt] *v.* 演绎，扣除，减去

deductible [di'dʌktəbl] *a.* 可扣除的

deduction [di'dʌkʃən] *n.* 减除，扣除，减除额，推论，演绎

deenergize ['di:nədʒaiz] *v.* 断电，断路，去激励 ‖ *Ant.* energize 激励，激发，使带电流，使通电，给予…电压，供给能量

deenergized ['di:nədʒaizd] *v.* (deenergize 的过去式和过去分词) 断电，断路，去激励；*a.* 不带电的，无电压的，切断电流的，去激励的，去能的

~ contact 静合接点，释放接点，后接点，失磁接点

~ period 释放周期，(继电器的)释放期间

~ position 去激励位置

~ state 去激励状态

~ tap changer 断电分接开关

deep [di:p] *n.* 深渊，深处；*a.* 深的，深远的，深奥的，重大的，深刻的，强烈的，痛切的，深厚的；*ad.* 深入地，迟

~ diving 深潜

~ draught vessel light 吃水限制船灯

~ floor 加强肋板，深肋板

~ groove ball bearing 深沟球轴承

~ hole drill 深孔钻头

~ ocean 深海，深海的

~ pipe laying 深管铺设

~ sea anchor gear 深水起放锚装置，深水起锚装置

~ sea anchor winch 深水抛锚绞车

~ tank 深水舱

~ V hull 深 V 型船体

deep-sea 深海的，远洋的

~ manned submersible 深海载人潜水器

~ motor 深海电动机

~ submersible 深海潜水器，深海潜水艇

~ tug 海洋拖船

deepen ['di:pən] *v.* 变深，加深，低沉，加浓

deepest [di:pist] *a.* (deep 的最高级) 最深的

~ subdivision load line 最深舱区划分载重线，最深分舱载重线

deexcitation [ˌdi:eksi'teiʃən] *n.* 去激励，去激(发)，退激(发) ‖ *Ant.* excitation 刺激，激励，激发，励磁

default [di'fɔ:lt] *n.* 默认(值)，缺省(值)，不履行责任，缺席，食言；*v.* 疏怠职责，不履行责任，不履行契约，缺席，拖欠，默认

defeat [di'fi:t] *n.* 击败，战胜，失败；*v.* 击败，战胜，使失败，挫折 ‖ *Syn.* conquer 征服，战胜，占领，克服；overcome 战胜，克服，胜过，征服；overwhelm 制服，控制，压倒，压服，击败；surmount 战胜，超越，克服

defect [di'fekt] *n.* 瑕疵，毛病，欠缺，缺点，过失；*v.* 叛逃，背叛，变节，脱党

defection [di'fekʃən] *n.* 缺点，背信，背叛，变节

defective [di'fektiv] *n.* 有缺陷的人，不完全变化动词；*a.* 有错误的，有缺陷的，有瑕疵的，变化不全的，智力低于正常的

~ casting 有缺陷铸件

~ circuit 有缺陷的电路

~ goods 不合格品，次品，残品

~ hardware 硬件保护

~ index 废品率

~ tightness 不够紧密性

~ weld 有缺陷焊缝

defence [di'fens] *n.* (=defense) 护卫措施，防御设施，防御体系，防卫物，捍卫，保卫，防卫，国防部

defend [di'fend] *v.* 防护，辩护，防卫，作…的辩护律师 ‖ **Syn**. protect 保护

~ against 防御，保卫

defense [di'fens] *n.* (=defence) 护卫措施，防御设施，防御体系，防卫物，捍卫，保卫，防卫，国防部

deficiency [di'fiʃənsi] *n.* 缺乏，缺点，缺陷，缺少，不足，不足额

~ and non-conformity 缺陷与不符合项，缺陷与不符合内容

deficient [di'fiʃənt] *a.* 不足的，缺乏的，有缺陷的，不完善的，不充分的

define [di'fain] *v.* 解释，下定义，阐述，阐释，详细说明，定范围，立界限

definite ['definit] *a.* 明确的，一定的，确切的，肯定的，有把握的

~ sequence 定顺序，固定次序

definitely ['definitli] *ad.* 明确地，确切地，干脆地，一定地，肯定地

definition [ˌdefi'niʃən] *n.* 定义，解说，精确度，清晰度

definitive [di'finitiv] *a.* 最后的，确定的，权威性的

deflagrate ['defləgreit] *v.* (使)突然燃烧，(使)爆燃

deflate [di'fleit] *v.* 放气，紧缩，瘪下来，使泄气

deflect [di'flekt] *v.* 使歪斜，使弯曲，使转向，偏转，偏离，偏斜

deflection [di'flekʃən] *n.* 偏斜，偏移，偏转，歪曲，偏斜度，偏角

deflector [di'flektə] *n.* 变流装置，偏针仪

deform [di'fɔ:m] *v.* 毁形，使变形，使残废，使变丑 ‖ **Ant**. form 形成，构成，塑造

deformation [ˌdi:fɔ:'meiʃən] *n.* 变形，畸形，扭曲变形，词的变形

deforming [di'fɔ:miŋ] *v.* (deform 的 ing 形式) 毁形，使变形，使残废，使变丑；*a.* 使变形的，致畸形的

~ force 变形力

defrost [di(:)'frɔst] *v.* 除霜，解冻，化冻，除冰，使(冰的食物)融化 ‖ **Ant**. frost 结霜，被冰霜覆盖

~ receiver 融霜贮液器

~ valve 除霜阀

degasser [di:'gæsə] *n.* 脱气装置，除气器，除气剂

degauss [di:'gaus] *v.* 消磁，去磁，退磁，删除信息，消除(船)四周磁场以防御磁雷

~ coils 消磁线圈

~ push button switch 消磁按钮开关

degaussing ['di:'gausiŋ] *n.* 消磁，去磁，退磁；*v.* (degauss 的 ing 形式) 消磁，去磁，退磁

~ cable 消磁电缆

~ facility 消磁设备

~ generator 消磁发电机

~ noise 消磁噪声

~ ring 消磁环

~ station 消磁站

~ vessel 消磁船

degradation [ˌdegrə'deiʃən] n. 降级，降格，退化，降解，恶化

degradative ['degrədeitiv] a. 使下降的，趋向下降的，趋向降解的

degrade [di'greid] v. (使)降级，(使)堕落，(使)退化，侵蚀，侮辱，羞辱 ‖ *Ant*. grade 评分，评级

degrease [ˌdi:'gri:z] v. 脱脂，除油污 ‖ *Ant*. grease 涂上油脂，用油润滑

degreaser [di:'gri:zə] n. 去(油)污剂，脱脂剂

degree [di'gri:] n. 度数，度，程度，轻重，学位，地位，身份，次数
　~ celsius 摄氏度
　~ of accuracy 精度，准确度
　~ of automation 自动化程度
　~ of compensation 补偿度，偿度
　~ of conformity 符合度
　~ of deviation 偏差度
　~ of distortion 畸变度，失真度
　~ of fuel atomization 燃料雾化度
　~ of safety 安全程度，安全系数
　~ of sensitivity 敏感度，灵敏度
　~ of vacuum 真空度

degrees [di'gri:z] n. (degree 的复数) 度数，度，程度，轻重，学位，地位，身份，次数
　~ of freedom 自由度

dehumidification ['di:hju(:)ˌmidifi'keiʃən] n. 除去湿气，除湿，空气减湿 ‖ *Ant*. humidification 潮湿

dehumidifier [ˌdi:hju(:)'midifaiə] n. 减湿器 ‖ *Ant*. humidifier 增湿器，湿润器

dehumidify [ˌdi:hju:'midifai] v. 除湿，使干燥 ‖ *Ant*. humidify 弄湿，使潮湿

dehydrate [di:'haidreit] v. (使)脱水，(使)无水，去水 ‖ *Ant*. hydrate 使水合

dehydrater [di:'haidreitə] n. (=dehydrator) 除水器，脱水器，脱水剂

dehydration [ˌdi:hai'dreiʃən] n. 脱水，失水，干燥，极度口渴 ‖ *Ant*. hydration 水化，水合(作用)

dehydrator [di:'haidreitə] n. (=dehydrater) 除水器，脱水器，脱水剂
　~ cartridge 干燥器

delay [di'lei] n. 耽搁，延迟，拖延，延期，迟滞; v. 耽搁，延迟，拖延，延期，迟滞
　~ action 延迟作用，缓办，拖拖拉拉
　~ action fuse 延时熔断器
　~ circuit 延迟电路
　~ element 延迟元件
　~ payment 延付，延期付款，延期支付
　~ period 延迟时间
　~ protection 延时保护
　~ thermal overcurrent relay 延时热过载继电器，延时热过电流继电器
　~ time 延迟时间，滞后时间，缓发时间

delayed [di'leid] v. (delay 的过去式和过去分词) 耽搁，延迟，拖延，延期，迟滞; a. 延时的，定时的
　~ transformation 延迟变换

deleterious [ˌdeli'tiəriəs] a. 有害的，有毒的

delete [di'li:t] v. 删除

deletion [di'li:ʃən] n. 删除，删除部分，被删除的字句、章节

delicate ['delikit] a. 精巧的，精致的，灵敏的，精密的，病弱的，脆弱的，微妙的，棘手的

deliver [di'livə] v. 递送，陈述，释放，发

表，交付，引渡，瞄准，给予(打击)
~ capacity 输送能力
~ over 交出，移交
~ the goods 送货，履行诺言
~ to 转交，交付，传达
~ up 交出，移交

deliverable [di'livərəbl] a. 可交付的，可交付使用的

delivered [di'livəd] v. (deliver 的过去式和过去分词) 递送，陈述，释放，发表，交付，引渡，瞄准，给予；a. 在…交货的，包括运费在内的
~ alongside 交到船边
~ alongside the vessel 船边交货
~ horsepower 输出马力，输出功率

delivery [di'livəri] n. 递送，交付，分娩，交货，发送，传输，引渡，财产等的正式移交
~ date 交货日期
~ head 水头，压力差
~ outlet 输出口
~ schedule 交货时间表
~ valve 导出阀，排气阀，出油阀

delta ['deltə] n. (河流的)三角洲，德耳塔(希腊字母的第四个字)
~ arrangement 三角接法
~ connection 三角形接线，三角形连接，Δ接法 ‖ star connection 星形接线，星形连接，Y 接法
~ formation 三角队形
~ modulation δ 调制，增量调制

demagnetization [di:mægnitai'zeiʃən] n. 退磁，消磁，去磁 ‖ Ant. magnetization 磁化

demagnetize [di:'mægnitaiz] v. 退磁，消磁，去磁

demagnetizing [di:mægnitai'ziŋ] n. 去磁，退磁，消磁；v. (demagnetize 的 ing 形式) 去磁，退磁，消磁
~ action 消磁作用，去磁作用
~ ampere turns 去磁安匝，退磁安匝
~ band 去磁线匝
~ breaker 去磁开关
~ effect 去磁作用
~ ship 消磁船
~ state 去磁状态
~ winding 消磁绕组，去磁绕组

demarcate ['di:ma:keit] v. 划分，区分，区别，定界线，定范围

demarcation [,di:ma:'keiʃən] n. 划分，区分，区别

demersal [di'mə:səl] a. 在底部的，居于水底的
~ trawling 底层拖网

demist [di:'mist] v. 除雾 ‖ Ant. mist 喷洒，被雾蒙上

demister [di:'mistə] n. 去雾器，除雾器

demodulate [di:'mɔdju:leit] v. 解调，使检波 ‖ Ant. modulate 调制，调节

demodulation ['di:,mɔdju:'leiʃən] n. 解调制，解调，反调制，检波 ‖ Ant. modulation 调制，调节

demodulator [di:'mɔdjuleitə] n. 解调器，检波器 ‖ Ant. modulator 调制器

demonstrate ['demənstreit] v. 论证，证明，证实，显示，展示，演示，说明

demonstration [,demən'streiʃən] n. 示范，证明，表露
~ site 示范点，演示地
~ test 示范试验

demulsibility [di:mʌlsi'biliti] n. 抗乳化性，反乳化率

demulsification [di'mʌlsifi'keiʃən] n. 反乳化作用，破乳化
~ number 抗乳化度，反乳化值

demulsify [di'mʌlsifai] v. 反乳化

demultiplexer [di'mʌltipleksə] n. 信号分离器，多路输出选择器 ‖ *Ant.* multiplexer 多路(复用)器

demurrage [di'mʌridʒ] n. (车、船等)停留过久，滞留，逾期费

denial [di'naiəl] n. 否认，否定，谢绝，拒绝
~ measure 禁止措施

dense [dens] a. 密集的，稠密的，浓密的，浓厚的，不透光的，愚钝的，笨的
~ packing 致密堆积，致密填积
~ parts 密致零件

densimeter [den'simitə] n. 比重计，密度计

density ['densiti] n. 密度，浓度，比重，致密度，愚钝，迟钝
~ function 密度函数

dent [dent] n. 凹，凹痕，(齿轮的)齿，弱点；v. 使凹下，凹进，削弱

deoil [di'ɔil] v. 去油，去油，脱脂

deoiled [di'ɔild] v. (deoil 的过去式和过去分词) 去油，去油，脱脂；a. 去油的，去油的，脱脂的
~ water 脱油水

deoiler [di'ɔilə] n. 油水分离器，脱油装置

deoxidation [di:,ɔksi'deiʃən] n. (=deoxidization) 去氧，还原

deoxidization [di:,ɔksidai'zeiʃən] n. (=deoxidation) 去氧，还原

depart [di'pa:t] v. 离开，离职，启程，出发，去世，脱轨，不按照；a. 过去的，逝世的

department [di'pa:tmənt] n. 部，局，处，科，部门，系，学部

departure [di'pa:tʃə] n. 离开，出发，违背，启程
~ ballast 出港压舱水
~ ballast tank 出港压载舱
~ date 出发日期
~ from 违反，违背

depend [di'pend] v. 依赖，依靠，信赖，决定于
~ on 依赖，依靠，取决于 ‖ *Syn.* build on 基于，建立于,寄希望于; build upon 基于，建立于,寄希望于; count on 依靠，指望; depend upon 依赖，依靠，取决于; lie on 依赖，取决于; reckon on 指望，依赖; rely on 依赖，依靠

dependability [di,pendə'biləti] n. 可靠性，可信任性

dependent [di'pendənt] n. 受抚养人，受赡养者，依赖他人者，扈从，侍从；a. 依赖的，依靠的，取决于，有瘾的
~ variable 因变量，应变数，它变数，因变数

deplete [di'pli:t] v. 耗尽，用尽，用光，使枯竭，消灭，减液，放血

depletion [di'pli:ʃən] n. 消耗，用尽，耗减

deploy [di'plɔi] v. 配置，施展，有效地利用，散开，展开，战斗部署

depose [di'pəuz] v. 放下，沉淀，宣誓作证，罢免，免职，废黜(君主等)

deposit [di'pɔzit] n. 堆积物，沉淀物，存款，押金，保证金，存放物；v. 存放，堆积，储蓄，寄存，放置，安置，付保证金

depositary [di'pɔzitəri] n. 保管人，受托人，受托公司，存放处，储藏所，仓库

deposition [ˌdepə'ziʃən] n. 沉积作用，沉积物，革职，废王位，免职
~ soldering 堆积焊合，沉积焊合

depress [di'pres] v. 压下，压低，使沮丧，使消沉，使不活泼，使萧条

depression [di'preʃən] n. 沮丧，消沉，低气压，低压，下陷处，坑，衰弱，减缓

depressurize [ˌdi:'preʃəraiz] v. 使减压，使降压

depth [depθ] n. 深度，深处，纵深，距离，强度，范围，力度，潜力，后备力量，详尽，细节，最深处，中央，深奥 ‖ height 高度；length 长度；width 宽度
~ gauge 深度计，水尺
~ micrometer 深度测微计，深度千分尺
~ moulded 型深，甲板边板
~ of discharge 放电深度
~ of fusion 熔透深度，熔化深度，熔深，焊透深度

depurate ['depjureit] v. (使)清洁，(使)净化

deputy ['depjuti] n. 代表，代理人，副手，副职

derate [di:'reit] v. 减免

derating [di:'ratiŋ] n. 降低定额值，降级；v. (derate 的 ing 形式) 减免
~ power 减额功率

derivative [di'rivətiv] (D) n. 导数，微商，衍生物，派生物，导出物，派生词；a. 衍生的，导出的，拷贝的，无创意的
~ action 微分作用
~ control 微分控制，微分调节
~ control mode 微分控制方式，微分调节方式
~ control output 微分控制输出，微分调节输出
~ controller 微分控制器，微分调节器 ‖ Syn. derivative regulator 微分控制器，微分调节器
~ element 微分环节，微分元件，导数元件
~ feedback 微分反馈，导数反馈
~ mode 微分模式，导数模式

derrick ['derik] n. 起重机，(油井的)井架
~ boom 吊杆，起重杆，起货吊杆
~ rig 吊杆装置

derust [di:'rʌst] v. 除锈 ‖ Ant. rust 生锈
~ by chipping 削屑除锈

desalinate [di:'sælineit] v. (=desalinize) 脱盐，除去盐分，淡化海水 ‖ Ant. salinate 盐化

desalination [di:ˌsæli'neiʃən] n. (=desalination) 淡化,减少盐分,脱盐作用 ‖ Ant. salination 盐化

desalinization [diˌsælənai'zeiʃən] n. (=desalination) 减少盐分，脱盐作用 ‖ Ant. salinization 盐化

desalt [di:'sɔ:lt] v. 脱盐,除去盐分 ‖ Ant. salt 加盐

desander [di:'sændə] n. 泥浆除砂器

descale [di:'skeil] v. 除鳞，除垢，除锈 ‖ Ant. scale 盖着锈，盖着污垢，覆以鳞状物，生水垢

descaling [di:'skeiliŋ] n. 除鳞，除垢，除锈；v. (descale 的 ing 形式) 除鳞，除垢，除锈
~ compound 除鳞化合物
~ powder 除垢粉

descend [di'send] v. 降临，下来，下降，

下斜，遗传，突击，突然造访

descent [di'sent] *n*. 降下，降落，世系，血统，侵袭 ‖ *Ant*. ascent 上升，攀登

desiccant ['desikənt] *n*. 干燥剂；*a*. 使干燥的，去湿的

desiccation [ˌdesi'keiʃən] *n*. 干燥，使失水

design [di'zain] *n*. 设计，图案，花样，企图，图谋，构思，纲要；*v*. 设计，计划，谋划，构思

~ depth 设计深度

~ drawing 设计图

~ fabricate 设计构造

~ feature 结构特点，设计特点，设计数据，设计形体

~ formula 设计公式

~ load 设计荷载，设计负荷

~ margin 设计余量，设计裕度

~ paper 图纸

~ phase 设计阶段

~ pressure 设计压力

~ rule checking 计划规则查验

~ temperature 设计温度

~ variable 设计变量

designate ['dezigneit] *v*. 指派，任命，指明，指出，表明，定名，意味

designated ['dezigneitid] *v*. (designate 的过去式和过去分词) 指派，任命，指明，指出，表明，命名，定名；*a*. 指定的，派定的

~ person (DP) 指定人士，指定人员，指认人士

~ person ashore (DPA) 岸上指定人员，岸基制定人员

~ value 指定值，标志值

designation [ˌdezig'neiʃən] *n*. 指示，指定，选派，名称

~ plate 铭牌，标示板

~ punch 标志孔

designed [di'zaind] *v*. (design 的过去式和过去分词) 设计，计划，谋划，构思；*a*. 有计划的，原意的

~ capacity 设计能力

designer [di'zainə] *n*. 设计师，设计者，构思者，阴谋家，制图师

desirable [di'zaiərəbl] *n*. 引人注意者；*a*. 令人想要的，值得要的，合意的，悦人心意的 ‖ *Ant*. undesirable 不合需要的，不受欢迎的，令人不快的，不良的

desire [di'zaiə] *n*. 愿望，心愿，要求，欲望，性欲；*v*. 要求，期望，希望，请求

desired [di'zaiəd] *v*. (desire 的过去式和过去分词) 要求，期望，希望，请求；*a*. 渴望的，想得到的

~ value 期望值

desk [desk] *n*. 书桌，办公桌，服务台，部门，讲道台

~ lamp 台灯，桌灯

desktop ['desktɔp] *n*. 桌面，台式电脑

~ system unit 台式电脑系统单元

desludge [di:'slʌdʒ] *v*. 清除泥渣，清除油泥

despatch [di'spætʃ] (=dispatch) *n*. 派遣，调遣，发送；*v*. 派遣，调遣，发送

despite [dis'pait] *n*. 侮辱，憎恨，怨恨，轻蔑的拒绝或不承认；*prep*. 不管，尽管，不论

destination [ˌdesti'neiʃən] *n*. 目的，目标，目的地，终点，指定，预定

~ file 目标文件，结果文件

destroy [dis'trɔi] *v*. 杀死，破坏，摧毁，毁坏，消灭，歼灭，使失败

destroyer [dis'trɔiə] *n.* 驱逐舰，破坏者，扑灭者，驱逐者，起破坏作用的事物

destruct [dis'trʌkt] *n.* 故意或有计划的破坏；*v.* 破坏；*a.* 破坏的

destruction [di'strʌkʃən] *n.* 摧毁，破坏，毁灭，毁灭原因，破坏手段

destructive [dis'trʌktiv] *a.* 破坏性的,毁灭性的，有害的

destructor [dis'trʌktə] *n.* 垃圾焚毁炉，破坏者，爆炸装置

desuperheat [di:ˌsjupə'hi:t] *v.* 减温，降温

desuperheated [di:ˌsjupə'hi:tid] *v.* (desuperheat 的过去式和过去分词) 减温，降温；*a.* 减温的，降温的

~ steam 减温蒸汽

desuperheater [di:ˌsjupə'hi:tə] *n.* (过热蒸气的)减温器

detach [di'tætʃ] *v.* 派遣，分开，分离，拆开，分派，使超然

detachable [di'tætʃəbl] *a.* 可分开的，可拆开的，可拆卸的，可摘下的

~ shackle 散合式连接卸扣

~ type fire detector 可拆式火灾探测器

~ valveseat 可拆下的阀座

detachment [di'tætʃmənt] *n.* 分开，拆开，特遣部队，超然，分离，分遣队

detail ['di:teil] *n.* 局部，细节，详情，细目，琐碎，分遣，选派，被选派的人员，指定的任务；*v.* 详述，细说，仔细汇报，选派

~ design 施工设计，详图设计

~ drawing 细部图

~ part 详细零件，细部构造

~ plan 详细图，零件图，施工图

detailed ['di:teild] *v.* (detail 的过去式和过去分词) 详细说明；*a.* 详细的，精细的，复杂的，详尽的

~ drawing 明细图，细节图，详图

~ estimate 详细概算

~ inspection 详细检查

~ schedule 明细进度表，进度计划明细表

detain [di'tein] *v.* 耽搁，留住，阻住，拘留，扣留

detainment [di'teinmənt] *n.* 挽留，延误

detect [di'tekt] *v.* 察觉，发现，发觉，侦查，探测，检定，检波

~ for leakage 渗漏检测

detectable [di'tektəbl] *a.* 可发觉的，可看穿的

detecting [di'tektiŋ] *n.* 察觉，发现，发觉，侦查，探测，检定，检波；*v.* (detect 的 ing 形式) 察觉，发现，发觉，侦查，探测，检定，检波

~ element 检测元件，检波元件，指示元件

~ instrument 检测仪器，探测仪器

detection [di'tekʃən] *n.* 察觉，发觉，侦查，探测，发现

~ pressure 探测压力

~ probability 检测概率

detective [di'tektiv] *n.* 侦探；*a.* 适于探测的，用于探测的，侦探的

detector [di'tektə] *n.* 发现者，侦察器，探测器，检波器，检电器

~ for fire alarm system 火灾报警系统探测器，火灾报警探测器

~ lamp 检漏灯

detergency [di'tə:dʒənsi] *n.* 去垢性，去垢力，洗净(作用)

detergent [di'tə:dʒənt] *n.* 洗涤剂，去垢剂

deteriorate [di'tiəriəreit] *v.* (使)恶化，削

弱，瓦解，衰退

deterioration [di,tiəriə'reiʃən] *n*. 恶化，退化，变坏，堕落

~ factor (DF) 劣化系数

determinable [di'tə:minəbl] *a*. 可决定的

determinate [di'tə:minit] *a*. 限定的，有限的，确定的，最终的

determination [di,tə:mi'neiʃən] *n*. 定值，定势，定义，限定，决心，决定，果断，断言，确定，查明，测定，计算

determine [di'tə:min] *v*. 解决，决定，判定，判决，确定，测定，定向，成为…的原因，控制，使下定决心，终止

detonate ['detəuneit] *v*. (使)爆炸，(使)爆裂，起爆，触发，引爆，发爆炸声

detonation [,detəu'neiʃən] *n*. 爆炸，爆炸声，爆裂

detriment ['detrimənt] *n*. 损害，损害物，伤害

detrimental [,detri'mentl] *a*. 有害的，不利的，引起损害的

develop [di'veləp] *v*. 发展，发达，发扬，进步，生长，发育，逐步显示，逐步展开，洗印，显影

developed [di'veləpt] *v*. (develop 的过去式和过去分词) 发展，发达，发扬，进步，生长，发育；*a*. 先进的，发达的，成熟的

~ area 展开面积

deviate ['di:vieit] *n*. 不正常者，不正常的人；*v*. 背离，偏离，脱离，越轨，违背，误入歧途，使脱离常轨

deviation [,di:vi'eiʃən] *n*. 背离，偏离，脱离，越轨，违背，偏移，离差，罗盘偏差，偏航

~ alarm 偏差报警

~ amplitude 偏差幅度

device [di'vais] *n*. 装置，设备，方法，策略，手段 ‖ ***Syn***. apparatus 器械，设备，仪器；appliance 用具，器具；arrangement 布置；assembly 组装部件；equipment 装备，设备，器材，装置；facility 设备，工具；furniture 设备，家具；gear 设备，装备；installation 设备，装置；machine 机器，机械，机构；machinery 机械(总称)，机器；mechanism 机器，机械装置，机构；plant 设备；provision 装备，供应品；turnout 装备，设备；unit 装置，设备

~ commutation 器件换相

~ complexity （集成电路中)线路元件数，装置的复杂性

~ for power absorption 功率吸收装置

devil ['devl] *n*. 扯碎机，魔鬼，恶棍，家伙，淘气鬼，冒失鬼，难事，极坏，惩罚；*v*. 扯碎，困扰，纠缠

devil's 魔鬼的

~ claw 锚链掣，掣链钩

devoid [di'vɔid] *a*. 全无的，缺乏的

dew [dju:] *n*. 露，露水般的东西，清新；*v*. 被露水弄湿

~ point 露点

dewater [di:'wɔ:tə] *v*. 去水，脱水，排水

DF (deterioration factor) 劣化系数

DFD (data flow diagram) 数据图

DGNSS (Differential Global Navigation Satellite System) 差分全球导航卫星系统

DGPS (Differential Global Positioning System) 差分全球定位系统

DHU (deck hand uncertified) 见习水手，无证书的甲板人员

diagnose ['daiəgnəuz] v. 诊断，做出诊断，判断

diagnosis [,daiəg'nəusis] n. 诊断，诊断结论，判断，结论，特征简述

diagonal [dai'ægənl] n. 斜线，斜行物，对角线，对顶线；a. 对角线的，斜的，斜线的，斜纹的
~ cutting nippers 斜嘴钳
~ line 对角线
~ stiffener 斜置加强筋

diagonally [dai'ægənəli] ad. 对角线地，斜线地

diagram ['daiəgræm] n. 图表，示意图，图解，线图；v. 图解，用图解法表示
~ of light arrangement 照明布置图
~ of light system 照明系统图
~ stage 图解阶段

diagrammatic [,daiəgrə'mætik] a. 图表的，概略的
~ sketch 示意图

diagrammatically [,daiəgrə'mætikli] ad. 用图解法地，概略地

diagrammatize [,daiə'græmətaiz] v. 作成图表，图解

dial ['daiəl] n. 表盘，钟(表)面，拨号盘，转盘，日晷，标度盘，调谐度盘，调谐钮；v. 拨，打电话，向某地通话
~ gauge 千分表，度盘式指示器，指示表 ‖ *Syn.* dial indicator 千分表，度盘式指示器，指示表
~ snap gauge 千分表卡规，卡规
~ speed indicator 拨号盘速度指示器
~ tone 拨号音

diameter [dai'æmitə] n. 直径，直径长，厚度或宽度 ‖ radius 半径，半径范围，活动半径

~ expanded conductor 扩径导线
~ factor 直径因子
~ ratio 直径比，内外径比，直径螺距比

diametrically [,daiə'metrikəli] ad. 作为直径地，直接地

diaphragm ['daiəfræm] n. 横膈膜，控光装置，照相机镜头上的光圈，(电话等)振动膜
~ control valve 膜片控制阀
~ gauge 薄膜式压力计
~ governor 膜片调节器，膜片调速器
~ gland 隔板汽封，隔板轴封，隔板汽封装置
~ gland ring 隔板轴封环
~ pressure gauge 膜片式压力表
~ regulating valve 膜片调节阀
~ type compressor 膜式压缩机
~ valve 膜板阀，隔膜阀，针阀，给水调整阀

die [dai] n. 钢型，硬模，骰子；v. 死亡，死于，熄灭，凋零，枯萎，渴望，盼望
~ cast 压铸件
~ casting 拉模铸造
~ casting machine (钢模的)压铸机，模铸机
~ cutter 压力裁断刀，冲刀

dielectric [,daii'lektrik] n. 电介质，绝缘体；a. 电介质的，绝缘的，隔电的，非传导性的
~ paper 隔电纸，绝缘纸

diesel ['di:zəl] n. 柴油机
~ batteries propulsion apparatus 柴油机蓄电池电力推进装置
~ boat 柴油机船

~ compressor 柴油压缩机

~ compressor aggregate 柴油压缩机组

~ cycle 柴油机循环，柴油循环机，狄塞尔循环

~ engine 柴油机

~ engine generator 柴油发电机

~ engine lubricating oil 柴油机润滑油

~ engine reversing gear 柴油发动机回动装置

~ fuel 柴油机燃料

~ generating set 柴油发电机组

~ generator 柴油发电机

~ generator governor sensitivity test 柴油发电机调速特性试验

~ generator room 柴油发电机舱

~ generator voltage characteristic test 柴油发电机电压特性试验

~ index 柴油指数

~ knock 柴油机爆震

~ oil 柴油

~ oil separator 柴油分离器

~ oil tank 柴油油舱

~ power plant 柴油发电站，柴油机动力装置

~ pump 柴油泵

~ smoke measuring instrument 柴油机排烟测定仪器

diesel-driven 柴油机驱动的

~ generator 柴油驱动发电机

diesel-electric 以柴油发动机发电的

~ propulsion 柴油电力推进

~ propulsion apparatus 柴油电力推进装置

diestock ['daistɔk] n. 螺丝攻

differ ['difə] v. 不同，相异，不同意，意见相左，争吵

difference ['difrəns] n. 差异，不同，相异，差别，分歧，争论，差额，差分，效果，改变，区别，分别；v. 辨别，区分；a. 微分的，差动的

~ equations 差分表示式

~ module 差模，增量模

different ['difrənt] a. 不同的，与众不同的，不平常的，个别的，各式各样的，多样的，单独的

differential [ˌdifə'renʃəl] n. 微分，差动齿轮，工资级差，变量无限小的增量；a. 差别的，差别的，特意的，微分的，差动的

~ block 差动滑车

~ coefficient 导函数，导数

~ control 微分控制，差动控制

~ current quick break protection 差动电流速断保护

~ curve 微分曲线

~ cylinder 差动油缸

~ fire detector 差温火灾探测器 ‖ *Syn.* rate-of-rise detector 差温(火灾)探测器

~ frequency meter 差示频率计,差频表

~ gear 差动齿轮，差动轮，差动装置，差速齿轮，分速轮

~ Global Navigation Satellite System (DGNSS) 差分全球导航卫星系统

~ Global Positioning System (DGPS) 差分全球定位系统

~ limit switch 差动限位开关

~ limit switch overflow valve 差动限位开关溢流阀

~ limit switch piston 差动限位开关活塞

~ limit switch positioning system 差动限位开关定位系统

~ limit switch pressure 差动限位开关压力

~ limit switch pressure alarm 差动限位开关压力报警(器)

~ limit switch pressure gauge 差动限位开关压力表

~ limit switch protection 差动限位开关保护

~ limit switch regulator 差动限位开关调节器，差动限位开关控制器

~ limit switch relay 差动限位开关继电器

~ limit switch voltage meter 差动限位开关电压表

~ motion piston 差动活塞 ‖ *Syn*. differential piston 差动活塞

~ oil cylinder 差动油缸

~ pressure 压差，差动压力，压力降，压力落差

~ pressure controller 差压控制器，差压调节器

~ pressure level meter 差压液位计

~ pressure transmitter 差压变送器

~ protection 差动保护(装置)

~ relay 差动继电器

~ thermocouple 差分热电偶，差动热电偶，差示热电偶

~ transformer displacement transducer 差动变压器式位移传感器

differentially [ˌdifəˈrenʃəli] *ad*. 差别地，区别地

~ compounded exciter 差复激励磁机

differentiation [ˌdifəˌrenʃiˈeiʃən] (D) *n*. 微分，区别，分化，变异

~ action 微分作用

~ control 微分控制，微分调节

~ control mode 微分控制方式，微分调节方式

~ control output 微分控制输出，微分调节输出

~ controller 微分控制器，微分调节器 ‖ *Syn*. differentiation regulator 微分控制器，微分调节器

~ element 微分环节，微分元件，导数元件

~ feedback 微分反馈，导数反馈

~ mode 微分模式，导数模式

~ regulator 微分控制器，微分调节器 ‖ *Syn*. differentiation controller 微分控制器，微分调节器

differentiator [ˌdifəˈrenʃiˌeitə] *n*. 微分器，区分者

diffuse [diˈfju:s] *v*. 散播，传播，漫射，扩散，散布，广布，(使)慢慢混合，减弱；*a*. 四散的，散开的，啰嗦的，冗长的，累赘的

diffuser [diˈfju:zə(r)] *n*. (=diffusor) 扩散器，散布者，扩散体，扩散道

~ pump 扩散泵，导轮式泵

diffusivity [difjuˈsiviti] *n*. 扩散性，扩散能力，扩散率

diffusor [diˈfju:zə(r)] *n*. (=diffuser) 扩散器，散布者，扩散体，扩散道

digest [daiˈdʒest] *n*. 文摘，摘要，汇集，要略，纲要；*v*. 消化，吸收，整理，领悟，玩味，领会，融会贯通，忍受

digestion [diˈdʒestʃən] *n*. 细菌分解，消化，领悟，消化能力，(精神上的)同化吸收，融会贯通

digit [ˈdidʒit] *n*. 数字，位，手指，足趾，一指宽

digital [ˈdidʒitl] *n*. 数字，数字式，手指，

(钢琴等的)琴键；*a*. 数字的，数据的，手指的，指状的

~ camera 数码照相机

~ circuit 计算电路，数字线路

~ converter 数字转换器

~ electrical technique 数字电子技术

~ Enhanced Cordless Telecommunications (DECT) 数字增强无线通信，数位增强无线电话系统

~ filter 数字滤波器，数位滤波器

~ micrometer 数字测微计

~ modems 数字调制解调器

~ note book 数字笔记本

~ processing 数字处理，数字加工

~ selective calling 数字选择呼叫

~ sensing device 数字式传感器

~ signal 数字信号

~ signal processing 数字信号处理

~ speed sensor 数字速度传感器

~ subscriber line 数字用户线路，数位用户线路，数码用户线路

~ versatile disc 数字多功能光盘

~ video camera 数字视频相机，数字摄像机，数码摄像机

~ video disk (DVD) 数字式视频光盘

~ video disk-random access memory (DVD-RAM) 数字式随机存取视频光盘

~ video disk-read only memory (DVD-ROM) 数字式只读视频光盘

~ video disk-recordable (DVD-R) 数字式可写视频光盘,数字式可烧录视频光盘

digital-analog (DA) 数字模拟(的)，数模(的)

~ conversion 数字模拟转换，数模转换，DA 转换

~ converter 数字模拟转换器，数模转换器，DA 转换器

digital-analogue (DA) 数字模拟(的)，数模(的)

~ conversion 数字模拟转换，数模转换，DA 转换

~ converter 数字模拟转换器，数模转换器，DA 转换器

digital-to-analog (DA) 数字对模拟的，数模的

~ conversion 数字模拟转换，数模转换，DA 转换

~ converter 数字模拟转换器，数模转换器，DA 转换器

digitization [,didʒitai'zeiʃən] *n*. 数字化

digitize ['didʒitaiz] *v*. 将资料数字化

digitizer ['didʒitaizə] *n*. 数字转换器

dilatation [,dailə'teiʃən] *n*. 膨胀，(中空器官或空洞)扩张，扩张过程，膨胀过程

dilatator [dai'leitætə] *n*. 扩张器

diluent ['diljuənt] *n*. 稀释液，稀释药；*a*. 冲淡的，稀释的

dilute [dai'lj u:t] *v*. 冲淡，变淡，变弱，稀释；*a*. 稀释的，冲淡的，淡的，弱的

dilution [dai'lju:ʃən] *n*. 稀释，稀释法，冲淡物

dimension [di'menʃən] *n*. 尺寸(面积、容积、大小、长、宽、厚、高度)，尺度，维(数)，度(数)，次元，量纲，方面，因素；*v*. 使形成所需尺寸，标出所需尺寸

dimensional [di'menʃənəl] *a*. 空间的，维的，尺寸的，量纲的，因次的

~ accuracy 尺寸精度

~ sketch 尺寸简图

dimensioned [di'menʃən] v. (dimension 的过去式和过去分词) 使形成所需尺寸, 标出所需尺寸; a. 切成特定尺寸的, 注明尺寸的

~ drawing 尺寸图, 尺寸详图

~ hole 准尺寸孔

dimensionless [di'menʃənlis] a. 无量纲的, 无因次的

diminish [di'miniʃ] v. 缩小, 减少, 减损, 变小, 减少, 逐渐变细

diminishing [di'miniʃiŋ] v. (diminish 的 ing 形式) 缩小, 减少, 减损, 变小, 减少, 逐渐变细; a. 逐渐缩小的

~ coil 降压线圈

dinghy ['diŋi] n. 救生艇, 小舢板, 无篷小船, 小艇

dine [dain] v. 吃饭, 进餐

dining ['dainiŋ] n. 进餐; v. (dine 的 ing 形式) 吃饭, 进餐, 设宴款待, 请客

~ room 饭厅, 餐厅

diode ['daiəud] n. 二极管

dioxide [dai'ɔksaid] n. 二氧化物

dip [dip] n. 下沉, 下降, 倾斜, 浸渍, 蘸湿; v. 浸, 下降, 下沉, 倾斜, 舀, 掏, 伸入

~ angle 倾角, 俯角

~ in 浸泡

~ with insulating paint 涂绝缘漆

dipper ['dipə] n. 浸渍者, 汲取的人, 浸染工, 显影液容器, 北斗七星

~ dredger 单斗挖掘船, 勺式挖泥船

dipstick ['dipstik] n. 量油计

direct [di'rekt] a. 径直的, 直接的, 直系的, 直率的, 由西向东运行的, 顺行的, 正变形的, 顽强的, 绝对的; v. 指引, 指示, 指挥, 指导, 命令, 导演; ad. 直接地, 笔直地, 不弯曲地 ‖ **Ant**. indirect 间接的, 迂回的

~ access 直接存取, 随机存取

~ acting overflow valve 直接作用溢流阀

~ acting reducing valve 直接作用减压阀

~ acting regulator 直接作用调整器

~ acting relief valve 直接作用安全阀

~ acting steam pump 蒸汽直动活塞泵, 蒸汽直接作用泵

~ acting valve 直接作用阀

~ air-flow valve 直接气流阀, 直流阀

~ axis 直轴

~ axis transient time constant 直轴瞬变时间常数

~ bearing 导向轴承

~ bilge pump suction 直通舱底泵吸管

~ connection 直接联结

~ control 直接控制

~ control sequence valve 直接顺序阀

~ coordination 直接协调

~ current (DC) 直流, 直流电, 直流电流

~ current ammeter 直流电流表, 直流安培表, 直流安培计

~ current circuit 直流电路

~ current contactor 直流接触器

~ current control 直流控制

~ current distribution system 直流配电系统

~ current dynamo 直流发电机 ‖ **Syn**. direct current generator 直流发电机

~ current electric propulsion apparatus 直流电力推进装置

~ current electrical source 直流电源
~ current exciter 直流励磁机
~ current generator-motor set drive 直流发电机电机动组驱动
~ current machine 直流电机
~ current motor 直流电动机，直流马达
~ current power station 直流电站
~ current resistance 直流电阻
~ current single wire system 直流单线制
~ current switchboard 直流配电盘
~ current three-wire insulated system 直流三线绝缘系统
~ current two-wire insulated system 直流两线绝缘系统
~ current voltage 直流电压
~ current-alternating current-direct current (DC-AC-DC) 直流交流直流，直交直
~ current-alternating current-direct current converter 直流交流直流变换器，直交直变换器
~ current-direct current (DC-DC) 直流直流，直直
~ current-direct current converter 直流直流变换器，直直变换器
~ digital control (DDC) 直接数字控制
~ digital system 直接数字系统
~ drive 直接传动，直接驱动
~ evaporating air cooler 直接蒸发式空气冷却器
~ excitation 直接励磁
~ expansion air cooler 直接蒸发式空气冷却器
~ expansion system 直接膨胀系统
~ filling line 直接装注油管 ‖ *Syn*.

direct loading pipe line 直接装注油管
~ hydraulic control 直接液压控制
~ injection 直接射油，直接喷油，直接注入
~ injection engine 直接喷射式发动机，直喷发动机
~ input 直接输入
~ load 直接荷载
~ machine control 直接机械控制
~ method 直接法
~ proportion 正比例，正比
~ repair 直接修复
~ replacement 直接置换
~ reversible 可直接逆转的
~ reversing diesel engine 可直接逆转柴油机
~ transmission 直接传动，直接传送，正透射
~ valve gear 直接式气门驱动机构
~ water injection 直接注水
~ winding 直接绕组
direct-cooled 直接冷却的
~ piston 直接冷却式活塞
direct-coupled 直接连接的，直接耦合的
~ generator 直连励磁机，直连式发电机
direct-on 直接的
~ starting 直接启动
~ starter 直接启动器
direct-on-line 直接在线的，直接的
~ indicator light 直接式信号灯
~ starter 直接在线启动器
~ starting 直接启动，全压启动
direction [di'rekʃən] *n*. 方向，指导，趋势，指示，用法，说明(书)，收件人地址

~ control valve 方向控制阀

~ finder 探向器，方位仪

~ control handle 方向操纵手柄

~ indicating device 示向器

~ of the feed motion 进给方向，进刀方向

~ of main movement 主运动方向

~ of rotation 旋转方向

~ protection 方向保护

~ safety interlock 方向安全联锁装置

directional [di'rekʃənəl] *a.* 定向的，方向的

~ control valve 方向控制阀，定向控制阀

directivity [direk'tiviti] *n.* 方向性，指向性

directly [di'rektli] *ad.* 直接地，不久，立即，正好地，恰好地，坦率地；*conj.* 一…就

director [di'rektə] *n.* 控制器，指挥仪主任，主管，导演，(机关)首长，(团体)理事，(公司)董事

directory [di'rektəri] *n.* 说明，指南，人名地址录，通讯录，号码簿，目录，董事会

dirt [də:t] *n.* 泥土，污垢，污泥，下流想法，恶意中伤的话

~ trap 集尘器，收泥器，集渣器

disable [dis'eibl] *v.* 使无能力，使残废，使伤残，使无资格，使不中用

disabled [dis'eibld] *v.* (disable 的过去式和过去分词) 使无能力，使残废，使伤残，使无效；*a.* 有残障的，有残疾的，有缺陷的

~ ship 破损船，损坏船，废船

disablement [dis'eiblmənt] *n.* 无力化，无能力

disadvantage [,disəd'va:ntidʒ] *n.* 不利，不利条件，缺点，劣势，短处，损失 ‖ *Ant.* advantage 优势，有利条件，利益

disaggregation [dis,ægri'geiʃən] *n.* 解集，解离，崩溃，解体 ‖ *Ant.* aggregation 集合，集合体，聚合

disagree [,disə'gri:] *v.* 不同意，不适宜，不一致，不适合，不符 ‖ *Ant.* agree 同意，赞成，与…一致，承认，适合

disagreement [disə'gri:mənt] *n.* 不一致，分歧，意见不合，异议，争论，不适合 ‖ *Ant.* 同意，一致，协定，协议

disallow ['disə'lau] *v.* 驳回，不准，不许可，不接受，拒绝 ‖ *Ant.* allow 允许，承认，接受

disallowance [disə'lauəns] *n.* 驳回，不准，不许可，不接受，拒绝 ‖ *Ant.* allowance 宽容，允许

disappear [,disə'piə] *v.* 不见，消失，不复存在，灭绝 ‖ *Ant.* appear 出现，公开露面

disappearance [,disə'piərəns] *n.* 失踪，消失，不见，消散，出走，一去不返 ‖ *Ant.* appearance 出现，露面

disassemble [,disə'sembl] *v.* 解开，分解 ‖ *Ant.* assemble 集合，聚集，装配

disaster [di'za:stə] *n.* 灾难，彻底的失败，不幸，祸患 ‖ *Syn.* calamity 灾难，不幸事件

disastrous [di'za:strəs] *a.* 灾难性的，损失惨重的，极坏的，悲惨的

disc [disk] (=disk) *n.* 磁盘，磁碟片，圆板，圆盘，圆盘状物；*v.* 把…录成唱片，使成圆盘状，用圆盘耕地

~ brake 盘式制动器

~ grinder 圆盘磨光机

discharge [dis'tʃɑ:dʒ] *n.* 卸下, 发射, 开火, 流出, 放出, 排出, 排放量, 排放物, 履行义务, 执行命令, 遵守规定, 尽职, 解雇, 放电, 排电, 退伍令, 撤销令, 流脓; *v.* 卸下, 卸货, 放出, 腾空, 清偿, 撤销, 履行义务, 执行命令, 遵守规定, 解雇, 开(炮), 放(枪), 射(箭), 流注, 流出, 放电 ‖ *Ant.* charge 装料, 装满

~ below the waterline 在水线以下排放
~ bowl 排出筒, 导流壳
~ character curve 放电特性曲线
~ characteristic curve 放电特性曲线, 流量特性曲线
~ criterion 排放标准
~ current recorder 放电电流记录仪
~ cycle 排出循环, 排气循环, 排渣周期, 放电循环
~ filter 排放过滤器
~ funnel for sludge 排污漏斗
~ gap 放电隙
~ gas 废气
~ head 输送压头
~ hose 泄水软管
~ nozzle 排放喷嘴
~ of cargo residue 货物残渣排放, 货物残余排放
~ of volatile organic compounds from the cargo area 货物区挥发性有机化合物的排放
~ outlet 排放口, 排水出口
~ pipe 排出管, 放出管, 散热管
~ pressure 排放压力, 排出压力, 泄放压力
~ rate 放电率, 排放率, 卸货率
~ valve 排气阀, 排出阀, 卸料阀
~ voltage 放电电压
~ wave 放电波

discharger [dis'tʃɑ:dʒə] *n.* 卸货人, 履行者, 开释人

discharging [dis'tʃɑ:dʒiŋ] *n.* 卸料; *v.* (discharge 的 ing 形式) 下(客), 卸船, 免除(自己的义务、负担等), 执行; *a.* 卸载的, 放电的

~ rate 卸货率, 放电率

discipline ['disiplin] *n.* 训练, 调教, 锻炼, 纪律, 规律, 学科, 风纪, 秩序, 自制, 教规, 戒律; *v.* 训练, 调教, 锻炼, 惩罚, 处罚, 规定, 使有纪律, 使有条理

disclaim [dis'kleim] *v.* 放弃, 弃权, 拒绝, 否认 ‖ *Ant.* claim 要求, 认领, 声称, 主张, 需要

disclaimer [dis'kleimə(r)] *n.* 放弃, 拒绝, 放弃者, 不承诺, 否认书, 放弃声明 ‖ *Ant.* claimer 要求者, 申请者

disclose [dis'kləuz] *v.* 公开, 揭露, 使显露, 使暴露 ‖ *Ant.* close 关, 关闭, 包围

disclosure [dis'kləuʒə] *n.* 公开, 泄露, 揭露, 开诚布公的话, 被公开的事情, 被披露的秘闻 ‖ *Ant.* closure 关闭

discoloration [disˌkʌləreiʃən] *n.* 变色, 污点 ‖ *Ant.* coloration 染色, 着色

discomfort [dis'kʌmfət] *n.* 不适, 不便之处 ‖ *Ant.* comfort 安慰, 舒适

disconnect [dis'kənekt] *v.* 拆开, 分离, 断开, 切断(电源), 脱离(关系), 断绝(关系) ‖ *Ant.* connect 连接, 联合, 关联

disconnecting [dis'kənektiŋ] *n.* 拆开, 解脱, 分离; *v.* (disconnect 的 ing 形式) 拆开, 分离, 断开, 切断(电源), 脱离(关

系),断绝(关系) ‖ *Ant*. connecting 连接
~ switch 断路开关,阻断开关,隔离开关 ‖ *Syn*. disconnector 隔离开关,切断器
~ reverser 隔离反向器

disconnection [ˌdiskəˈnekʃən] *n*. 断开,分离,切断 ‖ *Ant*. connection 连接

disconnector [diskəˈnektə] *n*. 隔离开关,切断器 ‖ *Syn*. disconnecting switch 断路开关,阻断开关,隔离开关 ‖ *Ant*. connector 连接器

discontinuance [ˌdiskənˈtinjuəns] *n*. 停止,废止,中止 ‖ *Ant*. continuance 持续,继续

discontinue [ˌdiskənˈtinju(ː)] *v*. 停止,废止,放弃 ‖ *Ant*. continue 继续,连续

discontinuity [ˈdisˌkɔntiˈnju(ː)iti] *n*. 断绝,不连续,中断 ‖ *Ant*. continuity 连续(性),连贯(性)

discontinuous [ˈdiskənˈtinjuəs] *a*. 非连续,不连续的,间断的,中断的 ‖ *Ant*. continuous 连续的,持续的
~ conduction mode 断续导电模式
~ discharge 断续放电

discoordination [diskəuɔːdiˈneiʃnəl] *n*. 不协调,不同等 ‖ *Ant*. coordination 协调,同等

discover [diˈskʌvə] *v*. 发现,碰见,撞见,获得知识

discoverable [disˈkʌvərəbl] *a*. 发现的,显露的

discovery [disˈkʌvəri] *n*. 发现,发明的东西,发觉,(剧情的)发展,被发现的事物,显示证据

discrepancy [disˈkrepənsi] *n*. 相差,差异,矛盾

discrete [disˈkriːt] *a*. 不连续的,离散的,分离的,分立的,不相关联的 ‖ *Ant*. continuous 连续的,持续的
~ event dynamic system 离散事件动态系统
~ signal 离散信号
~ steps 不连续的阶段,分立的阶段
~ system 离散系统
~ variable 离散变量,不连续变量

discrete-speech 离散语音,不连续语音
~ recognition system 离散语音识别系统

discretion [disˈkreʃən] *n*. 谨慎,周详,决定能力,明智,判断力,决定力,辨别力,自行决定的自由

discriminant [disˈkriminənt] *n*. 判别式
~ function 判别函数

disembark [ˈdisimˈbaːk] *v*. 上岸,登岸,(人)下船,使上岸,从船上卸货 ‖ *Ant*. embark 上船,装于船上,登上

disembarkation [ˈdisembaːˈkeiʃən] *n*. 起岸,登陆 ‖ *Ant*. embarkation 乘船,上船

disengage [ˈdisinˈgeidʒ] *v*. 脱离,解脱,解放,解开,释放,自由,撤离 ‖ *Ant*. engage 接合,啮合

dish [diʃ] *n*. 盘,碟,盘状物,凹形,凹面,凹陷,凹度,反射器,碟形卫星天线,盘装菜; *v*. 挖空,使成凹陷,呈现,给予,提出,装盘

dished [diʃt] *v*. (dish 的过去式和过去分词) 挖空,使成凹陷,呈现,给予,提出,装盘; *a*. 中凹的

disinfect [ˌdisinˈfekt] *v*. 消毒,除去(感染) ‖ *Ant*. infect 传染,感染

disinfectant [disinˈfekt(ə)nt] *n*. 消毒剂,杀菌剂 ‖ *Syn*. disinfection agent 消毒剂,杀菌剂 ‖ *Ant*. infectant 污染物,

传染物

disinfection [ˌdisin'fekʃən] *n.* 消毒，灭菌 ‖ *Ant.* infection 传染，传染病，感染

~ agent 消毒剂 ‖ *Syn.* disinfectant 消毒剂，杀菌剂

disinfector [ˌdisin'fektə] *n.* 消毒器具，消毒者，消毒剂 ‖ *Ant.* infector 传播者，传染者

disintegration [disˌinti'greiʃən] *n.* 瓦解，蜕变，崩溃，分解，分裂，裂变，碎裂，粉碎 ‖ *Ant.* integration 综合

disk [disk] (=disc) *n.* 磁盘，磁碟片，圆板，圆盘，圆盘状物；*v.* 把…录成唱片，使成圆盘状

~ cam 圆盘凸轮

~ centrifuge 碟式离心机

~ clutch 圆盘离合器

~ drive 磁盘驱动器，盘式离心机

~ type centrifuge 磁盘驱动器，盘式离心机

~ winding 圆盘式绕组

~ valve 圆盘阀，片状阀，平板阀

diskette [dis'ket] *n.* 磁盘，磁碟 ‖ *Syn.* magnetic disk 磁盘

dislocation [ˌdislə'keiʃən] *n.* 位错，混乱，紊乱，脱位，脱臼 ‖ *Ant.* location 位置，场所，特定区域

dislodge [dis'lɔdʒ] *v.* 移动，驱离，移走，离开 ‖ *Ant.* lodge 容纳，存放

dismantle [dis'mæntl] *v.* 拆卸，拆开，废除，取消

dismiss [dis'mis] *v.* 解散，下课，开除，免职，解职，拒绝接受，不承认，抛弃，让…离开，驳回，不受理

dismissal [dis'misəl] *n.* 解雇，免职，撤退，不予考虑，解职令，驳回

dismount [dis'maunt] *v.* 拆开，卸下，下车，下马，下自行车，从支撑物、底板、底座取下 ‖ *Ant.* mount 爬上，装上，乘马

dismountable [ˌdis'mauntəbl] *a.* 可拆卸的

disorder [dis'ɔ:də] *n.* 杂乱，混乱，无秩序状态；*v.* 扰乱，使失调，使紊乱 ‖ *Ant.* order 秩序，正常状态，整理

disparity [dis'pærəti] *n.* 不同，不等，不一致

dispatch [di'spætʃ] (=despatch) *n.* 派遣，调遣，发送；*v.* 派遣，调遣，发送

dispatcher [dis'pætʃə] *n.* 调度，发报机，收发

dispensary [dis'pensəri] *n.* 诊疗所，药房，防治站

dispense [dis'pens] *v.* 分配，分给，实施，施行，免除，豁免，配药，特许，豁免

dispersal [dis'pə:səl] *n.* 散布，分散，消散，驱散，疏散

disperse [dis'pə:s] *v.* (使)分散，驱散，疏散，传播，散播，传布，使(光)色散，消失

dispersion [dis'pə:ʃən] *n.* 散布，驱散，传播，散射，离差，差量

displace [dis'pleis] *v.* 移动，移走，替换，取代，排水，撤职

displacement [dis'pleismənt] *n.* 取代，替代，置换，免职，停职，排水量，置换

~ coefficient 排水量系数，位移系数

~ collision 位移碰撞

~ compressor 容积式压缩机

~ current 位移电流

~ curve 排水量曲线，排量曲线，驱替特征曲线

~ factor 位移因数，置换因数

~ length ratio 排水量船长比

~ mark 吃水标志，吃水标尺

~ pump 往复式泵，活塞泵，柱塞泵

~ vessel 排水型船

~ vibration amplitude transducer 位移振幅传感器

~ water 排水

display [dis'plei] *n.* 展现，展示，显露，表演，展览，陈列，陈列品，展览品；*v.* 陈列，展览，显示，夸示，炫耀，展开，伸展，表现

disposable [dis'pəuzəbl] *n.* 使用后随即抛掉的东西，一次性物品；*a.* 一次性的，可自由支配的，可任意处理的，免洗的，税后的，可用的

~ filter 一次性过滤器

disposal [dis'pəuzəl] *n.* 处理，处置，布置，安排，配置，支配，除掉，清除，销毁，使用，利用，控制

~ load 活动载荷，废物载重

~ of garbage 垃圾处置，垃圾处理

dispose [dis'pəuz] *v.* 处理，处置，部署，安排，除去，使愿意

~ of 处理，安排，解决，转让，卖掉，吃光，除掉 ‖ *Syn.* deal with 应付，安排，处理；handle 处理；manage 处理，应付；manipulate (巧妙地)处理，应付；treat with 处理，应付

disposition [dispə'ziʃən] *n.* 意向，倾向，排列，布置，配置，处理，最终的决定，赠予，出售，转让，支配权，处置权，处置的自由，管理，控制

disproportionate [,disprə'pɔ:ʃnit] *a.* 不成比例的，不相称的，不均衡的，打破平衡的

disprove [dis'pru:v] *v.* 反驳，驳斥，证明…为误 ‖ *Ant.* prove 证明，证实，检验

disregard [,disri'ga:d] *n.* 漠视，忽视，不尊重；*v.* 忽视，不理，漠视，不顾

disrupt [dis'rʌpt] *v.* 干扰，扰乱，打断，妨碍，使中断，使分裂，使瓦解，使陷于混乱，破坏

disruptive [dis'rʌptiv] *a.* 破坏的，使破裂的，分裂性的，制造混乱的

~ strength 击穿强度

dissatisfy ['dis'sætisfai] *v.* 使不满意，使不满足，使失望 ‖ *Ant.* satisfy 满足，使满意

dissemination [di,semi'neiʃən] *n.* 分发，传播

dissipate ['disipeit] *v.* 驱散，消散，浪费，挥霍，耗尽，消耗，用完

dissipation [,disi'peiʃən] *n.* 消散，分散，挥霍，损耗，浪费，放荡，狂饮 ‖ *Syn.* loss 损失，浪费，损耗；wastage 损耗；wear 磨损

dissipative ['disipeitiv] *a.* 消耗的，浪费的，放荡的

~ structure 耗散结构

dissociate [di'səuʃieit] *v.* 分离，游离，脱离，分裂，中止联系，分开

dissociation [di,səusi'eiʃən] *n.* 离解，分离，电解，脱离关系，离异，解体

dissolve [di'zɔlv] *n.* 叠化画面；*v.* 溶解，液化，崩溃，解散，解除，结束，衰减，衰退，消失，不能自己，失控，被感动

dissolved [di'zɔlvd] *v.* (dissolve 的过去式和过去分词) 溶解，液化，崩溃，解散，

解除，结束，衰减，衰退，消失，失控；*a.* 溶化的，溶解的

~ oxygen 溶解氧

distance ['distəns] *n.* 距离，远离，间隔，间距，一长段时间，远方，远景，遥远，经过，路程，宽阔的区域，分歧，不和，不同意，冷淡，不友好；*v.* 使远离，使疏远，把…远远甩在后面，与…保持距离，使显得遥远

~ disc 定距盘

~ level indicator 距离指示器

~ links 定距链节

~ piece 隔离段，定距块

~ protection 远距离保护(装置)

~ ring 定距环

distant ['distənt] *a.* 远离的，远隔的，遥远的，冷漠的，冷淡的，略同的，不太清晰的

distill [dis'til] *v.* 蒸馏，滴下，提取，精炼，浓缩，渗出，吸取精华

distillate ['distileit] *n.* 精华，蒸馏物，蒸馏液，馏出物，馏出液，馏分油

~ cooler 蒸馏冷却器

~ oil 馏出油

~ pump 蒸馏水泵

distillation [ˌdisti'leiʃən] *n.* 精馏，蒸馏，净化，蒸馏法，精华，蒸馏物

~ method 蒸馏法

~ plant 蒸馏装置

~ products jet pump 蒸气喷射真空泵

~ range 馏程，蒸馏区间，沸腾范围

distilled [dis'tild] *v.* (distill 的过去式和过去分词) 蒸馏，从…提取精华；*a.* 由蒸馏得来的

~ product 馏出物，蒸馏产品

~ water 蒸馏水

distiller [dis'tilə] *n.* 蒸馏器，蒸馏者

distinct [dis'tiŋkt] *a.* 明显的，清楚的，卓越的，不寻常的，独特的，有区别的，确切的

distinction [dis'tiŋkʃən] *n.* 区别，差别，级别，特性，声望，显赫

distinctive [dis'tiŋktiv] *a.* 独特的，有特色的，与众不同的，区别的，鉴别性的，特异

~ mark 区别标记，甄别符号，甄别标志

~ product 特殊产品

~ number 船舶编号，船舶呼号

distinctly [dis'tiŋktli] *ad.* 清楚地，显然地

distinguish [dis'tiŋgwiʃ] *v.* 区分，辨别，分清，辨别是非，识别，引人注目，有别于，使杰出，使著名

distort [dis'tɔ:t] *v.* 扭曲，变形，曲解

distortion [dis'tɔ:ʃən] *n.* 弄歪，扭曲，歪曲，误报

~ power 畸变功率，失真功率

~ shift 畸变位移

distract [dis'trækt] *v.* 分散，转移，使分心，使混乱，使困惑

distress [dis'tres] *n.* 不幸，危难，危急，忧伤，忧虑，恶化，损坏，悲痛，穷困；*v.* 使悲痛，使穷困，使忧伤，仿造，抑制，扣押(财物)

~ alert 遇险报警

~ call 遇险呼叫，遇难求救信号

~ flag 遇险信号旗

~ frequency 呼救信号频率，遇险频率

~ gun 遇险信号炮

~ message 遇险(呼救)信号，遇险(呼救)电报

~ signals 遇险信号，船舶失事信号

distribute [dis'tribju(:)t] v. 分发，分配，散布，分布，分类，分区

distributed [dis'tribju:tid] v. (distribute 的过去式和过去分词) 分发，分配，散布，分布，分类，分区；a. 分布式的

~ computing 分布式计算(技术)

~ constant 分布常数

~ control system (DCS) 分布式控制系统，分散式控制系统

~ data processing system (DDPS) 分布式数据处理系统

~ function 分布式功能

~ load 分布荷载

~ parameter system 分布参数系统

~ processing 分布处理，分散式处理

~ processing unit (DPU) 分布式处理单元

~ real-time system (DRTS) 分布式实时系统

distributing [dis'tribju:tiŋ] v. (distribute 的 ing 形式) 分发，分配，散布，分布，分类，分区；a. 分配的，散布的

~ board 配电板，配电盘

~ cam 分配凸轮

~ insulator 配线绝缘子

~ manifold 分配集管，分配管汇，分配歧管

~ pillar 配电箱

~ plate 分配板

~ ring 配气环，分配环

~ valve board 分配阀板

distribution [,distri'bju:ʃən] n. 分配，分发，配给物，区分，分类，发送，发行，销售，分布状态，法院对无遗嘱死亡者财产的分配

~ automation system 配电自动化系统

~ block 接线板

~ board 配电盘，配电屏 ‖ *Syn*. distribution panel 配电盘，分配盘，分配板；switchboard 配电盘，接线总机

~ box 配电箱 ‖ *Syn*. distribution cabinet 配电箱

~ circuit 配电线路

~ fuse 布线熔丝

~ link 分布路线，分配链路

~ network 配电网

~ station 配电站

~ system 配电系统，分配制

~ transformer 配电变压器

distributor [dis'tribjutə] n. 分电盘，配电器，分发者，分配者，销售者，批发商，发行人，散布者

~ lever 分配器杆

~ ring 布油环

district ['distrikt] n. 区域，行政区，地方，管区，行政区，众议院选区；v. 把…分区

~ feed system 分区供电系统

~ voltage regulation 区域调压

disturb [dis'tə:b] v. 骚动，动乱，打扰，干扰，骚乱，搅动

disturbance [dis'tə:bəns] n. 困扰，打扰，骚乱，变乱，烦闷，心神不安，骚动的原因，局部运动

~ compensation 扰动补偿

~ current 干扰电流，串音电流

~ variable 扰动变量，扰动量

~ variable compensation 干扰量补偿

disuse ['dis'ju:s] n. 不用，废弃，不被使用；v. 废止，停止使用

dive [daiv] n. 潜水，跳水，下潜，俯冲；

v. 潜水，跳水，下潜，俯冲
~ computer 潜水计算机表
~ light 潜水手电筒
~ master 潜水长，潜水教练
~ note or slate 水下记录板
~ planning 潜水计划
~ profile 潜水方案
~ site 潜水地点，潜水点 ‖ *Syn*. dive spot 潜水地点，潜水点
~ skin 水母衣

diver ['daivə] *n.* 潜水员，蛙人，跳水者，潜鸟

diverse [dai'və:s] *a.* 不同的，多种多样的，变化多的，形形色色的

diversion [dai'və:ʃən] *n.* 转移，转换，牵制，解闷，娱乐

diversity [dai'və:siti] *n.* 差异，多样化，多样性，分歧
~ factor 差异因数，不等率

divert [di'və:t] *v.* 转移，转向，消遣，娱乐，使高兴
~ from 转移

diverter [dai'və:tə] *n.* 分流器，析流器，分流调节器，分流电阻，转向器，(推力)换向器

diverting [dai'və:tiŋ] *v.* (divert 的 ing 形式) 转移，转向，娱乐，消遣；*a.* 有趣的，令人快乐的
~ valve 分流阀，换向阀

divide [di'vaid] *n.* 除法，分配，分开，分水岭，分界线；*v.* 分，划分，分开，使分裂，隔开，表决

divided [di'vaidid] *v.* (divide 的过去式和过去分词) 分，划分，分开，分裂，隔开，表决；*a.* 分开的，分离的，分割的，分裂的

~ combustion chamber 分离式燃烧室
~ crankcase 分离式曲柄箱

divider [di'vaidə] *n.* 分配器，分割者，间隔物，圆规
~ ratio (分压器)分压比

dividing [di'vaidiŋ] *v.* (divide 的 ing 形式) 划分，分，分离，(使)产生分歧；*a.* 区分的，划分的
~ line 分界线，界限
~ walls 隔离壁，分隔墙，间壁
~ worm wheel 分度蜗轮

dividual [di'vidjuəl] *a.* 分开的，分享的，可分割的

dividually [di'vidʒuəli] *ad.* 分开地，分享地，可分割地

diving ['daiviŋ] *n.* 跳水，潜水；*v.* (dive 的 ing 形式) 下潜
~ boat 潜水工作船
~ boots 潜水靴，珊瑚鞋
~ buddy 潜伴
~ computer 潜水电脑
~ equipment 潜水装备，潜水装具 ‖ *Syn*. diving gear 潜水装备，潜水装置
~ knife 潜水刀
~ log 潜水日志
~ support vessel 潜水支援船，潜水给养船
~ system safety certificate 潜水系统安全证书
~ timepiece 潜水表
~ tower 跳台

divisibility [di,vizi'biliti] *n.* 可分割，整除性，可除尽

division [di'viʒən] *n.* 分开，分割，区分，除法，公司，(军事)师，分配，分界线

~ bulkhead 分舱壁，分离舱壁

~ method 除法，分割法

~ of labour 劳动分工

~ of work 分工

divisional [di'viʒənəl] *a.* 分割的，分开的，分区的，分部的，除法的，师的

do [dəu] *n.* 要求，规定；*v.* 做，干，学习，研究，进行，完成，解答，整理，算出，引起，行过

~ repairs 修理

~ with 处理，需要，读完，与…相处

~ without 没有…也行，将就，用不着

~ work 工作，做功，做工作

DOC (Document of Compliance) 符合证明，符合文件

dock [dɔk] *n.* 码头，船坞，被告席，尾巴的骨肉部分；*v.* 靠码头，引入坞，入船坞，剪短

~ basin 船坞

~ floor (干)坞底，浮坞甲板

~ in 进坞

~ landing account 码头卸货账单

~ master 船坞长

~ repair 坞修

~ tests 码头试验，系泊试验，系岸试车

docker ['dɔkə] *n.* 码头工人，港口工人，剪截工

docket ['dɔkit] *n.* 摘要，记事表，诉讼事件表；*v.* 附加摘要

docking ['dɔkiŋ] *n.* 入坞；*v.* (dock 的 ing 形式) 靠码头，引入坞，入船坞，剪短；*a.* 入坞的

~ area 泊船区

~ block (船坞)龙骨墩

~ bridge 船尾桥楼，艉望台，尾桥台

~ capacity 船坞容量

~ plan 进坞图

~ plug 船底塞

~ schedule 进坞计划

~ station 系泊部位

dockside ['dɔksaid] *n.* 码头前沿，码头邻区，坞边；*a.* (在)码头前沿的，(在)码头邻区的，(在)坞边的

dockyard ['dɔkja:d] *n.* 造船所，修船所

document ['dɔkjumənt] *n.* 公文，文件，文档，档案，文献，证件，证据，物证；*v.* 记录，证明，为…提供证明，用文件证明，评述

~ file 文档文件

~ of Compliance (DOC) 符合证明，符合文件

~ of compliance with the special requirements for ships carrying dangerous goods 船舶载运危险货物特殊要求的符合文件

~ of contract 订约书

~ processing 文件处理，文献加工

documentation [ˌdɔkjumen'teiʃən] *n.* 文件证据的提供，证明文件，材料整理，文件管理，文件编制

dog [dɔg] *n.* 轧头，夹架，狗，犬，类似犬的动物，蹩脚货，小人，坏蛋；*v.* 跟踪，尾随，握住

~ clutch 爪形离合器

dollar ['dɔlə] *n.* 元，美元，一元纸币，一元硬币

dolphin ['dɔlfin] *n.* 海豚，(码头的)系船柱

~ puff 海豚呼吸法

domain [dəu'mein] *n.* 领土，领地，(活动、学问等的)范围，领域，定义域，域，磁场

dome [dəum] *n.* 圆屋顶,像圆屋顶一样的东西,圆顶体育场; *v.* 加穹顶状物于,使成穹顶状

~ head piston 圆顶活塞,凸顶活塞

~ joint 内盖铰链

domestic [də'mestik] *n.* 佣人,女仆; *a.* 国内的,家庭的,家的,驯养的,与人共处的,热心家务的

~ garbage 生活垃圾,家庭垃圾 ‖ *Syn.* domestic waste 生活垃圾,家庭垃圾

~ load 生活用电量,民用负荷

~ service 国内航线

~ sewage 生活污水,家庭污水

~ water 生活用水

~ water system 生活用水系统

dominance ['dɔminəns] *n.* 优势,统治,支配,优性

dominant ['dɔminənt] *a.* 占优势的,统治的,支配的,显性的,高耸的

~ pole 主导极点,主极点

~ zero 主导零点,主零点

dominion [də'minjən] *n.* 支配,控制,主权,领土,统治权

donkey ['dɔŋki] *n.* 驴,毛驴,笨蛋,傻瓜,顽固者

~ boiler 辅助锅炉 ‖ *Syn.* auxiliary boiler 辅助锅炉,副锅炉

~ crane 辅助起重机,起重力不大的蒸气起重机

~ engine 辅助发动,机轻便发动机

~ feed water pump 备用给水泵,辅助给水泵

~ pump 辅助泵 ‖ *Syn.* attached pump 辅助泵; auxiliary pump 辅助泵; service pump 辅助泵

donkeyman ['dɔŋkimən] *n.* 辅机管理工,辅机操作工

door [dɔ:] *n.* 门,户,出入口,一家,一户,通道

~ switch 门开关

doorway ['dɔ:wei] *n.* 门口,门道

dope [dəup] *n.* 黏稠物,浓液,涂料,涂布油,麻醉药物,笨蛋,内幕,消息; *v.* 上涂料,服麻醉品

Doppler ['dɔplə] *a.* 多普勒的(多普勒,1803—1853,奥地利物理学家、数学家、天文学家)

~ log 多普勒计程仪

~ navigation 多普勒导航

dot [dɔt] *n.* 点,圆点,小点,小数点,乘号,少量; *v.* 点缀,标记,加点,打点,以小圆点标出于,散布于

dotted ['dɔtid] *v.* (dot 的过去式和过去分词) 点缀,标记,加点,打点 *a.* 有点的,星罗棋布的

~ line 虚线,点线

~ line marker 点线时标,虚线时标

double ['dʌbl] *n.* 两倍,双精度型 *v.* (使)加倍,快步走,加倍努力; *a.* 双重的,两倍的

~ bevel butt weld K 形坡口对接焊缝

~ bevelled oil control ring 双坡口油环

~ bollard 双柱系缆桩

~ bottom 双层底,双底,夹底

~ bottom fuel tank 双层底燃料舱

~ bottom structure 双层底结构

~ bottom tank 双层底舱

~ busbar 双母线

~ cam 双凸轮

~ cam reversing device 双凸轮换向装置

~ canoe 双体船

~ chain 双链，双路

~ chain oil pressure self-locking valve 双路油压自锁阀 ‖ *Syn*. double circuit oil pressure self-closing valve 双路油压自锁阀

~ chain pulley 双链滑轮

~ check valve 双向止回阀 ‖ *Syn*. double non-return vale 双向止回阀

~ chock 双楔块

~ circuit 双电路，双回路，双路

~ circuit jack 双电路插孔

~ circuit line 双回路线路

~ circuit supply 双回路电源

~ circuit system 双回路系统

~ column 双柱，双绕组

~ column transformer (DblClmnTrans) 双绕组变压器 ‖ *Syn*. two-circuit transformer 双回路变压器；two-winding transformer 双绕组变压器，双线圈变压器

~ cone 双锥

~ cone shape 双锥形状

~ configuration 双重化配置，双重配量，双重化

~ connection 双路连接，二重接法

~ connection plane switch 双联开关

~ core 双芯

~ core cable 双芯电缆

~ core plastic wire 双芯塑料线

~ current 双电流，双流

~ current generator 双电流发电机，交直流发电机

~ current simplex circuit 双流式单电路，双流制单工电路

~ deck 双层甲板

~ delta connection 双三角形接法，双三角形接线

~ drum 双筒，双鼓

~ drum boiler 双锅筒锅炉

~ drum winch 双卷筒绞车，双卷筒卷扬机 ‖ *Syn*. double purchase winch 双卷筒绞车，双卷筒卷扬机

~ end 双端，双头，双接头 ‖ *Syn*. double head 双端，双头

~ end ring wrench 双头套头扳手

~ end screw 双头螺钉 ‖ *Syn*. double head screw 双头螺钉

~ full astern 再退三

~ hook 双钩

~ hull 双层船体，双层船壳，双壳体

~ hull tanker 双壳油船

~ injection 双喷射

~ insulation 双重绝缘

~ integral 二重积分，重积分

~ lead cable 双芯铅包电缆

~ pipe 套管，双管

~ pipe condenser 双管冷凝器

~ plate 双夹板

~ pole 双极

~ pole breaker 双极断路器

~ pole connector 双极连接器

~ pole contactor 双极接触器

~ pole cut-out 双极断流器

~ pole dynamo 双极发电机，两极电机

~ pole fuse 双极熔断器

~ pole relay 双极继电器，双组触点式继电器

~ pole socket 双极插座

~ pole switch 双刀开关，双极开关

~ purchase 双卷筒

~ replacement 双重取代，互换

~ ring full astern 双车后退三

~ row 双列，双排

~ row ball bearing 双列滚珠轴承，双列球轴承
~ screw 双螺旋，双螺杆
~ screw bolt 双头螺栓
~ screw pump 双螺杆泵
~ screw vessel 双螺旋桨船
~ screw washer 双螺杆垫圈，双螺旋洗矿机
~ seat 双座
~ seat stop valve 双阀座截止阀
~ skin 双层，双层皮
~ skin construction 双层壳结构
~ skin panel 双层面板
~ skin ship 双壳船
~ speed 双倍速，双速
~ speed governor 双制式调速器
~ speed motor 双速电动机
~ speed provision 倍速装置
~ stage 双级
~ stage compression refrigerating system 双级压缩制冷系统
~ stage compressor 双级压缩机
~ stage pump 双级泵
~ suction centrifugal pump 双吸式离心泵
~ thread 双头螺纹，双线螺纹
~ thread worm 双头蜗杆
~ umbrella 双伞
~ umbrella insulator 双伞形绝缘子
~ U-weld 双 U 形坡口焊
~ volute casing 双蜗形体
~ wire 双线
~ wire gauge 双层线规
double-acting 双重作用的，双作用的，双动的
　~ capstan 双动手摇绞盘
~ double piston-rod oil cylinder 双作用双活塞杆油缸
~ oil cylinder 双作用式油缸，双作用油缸
~ pump 双动泵，双效用泵，双作用泵
~ single piston-rod oil cylinder 双作用单活塞杆油缸
~ steam cylinder 双向作用的蒸汽汽缸
~ vane pump 双作用叶片泵，双效用叶片泵
double-ended 双端的，两端引出式的，艏艉同形的
　~ ferry 艏艉同形渡船
　~ spanner 双头扳手
　~ vessel 两头船
doubler ['dʌblə] n. 加倍装置，大碗
dowel ['dauəl] n. 销子，木钉，暗榫，合板钉；v. 用暗销接合，为…装暗榫
　~ pin 合销，合钉，接合销，开槽销，定缝销钉
down [daun] n. 软毛，绒毛，开阔的高地；a. 向下的；ad. 向下，在下面，下去，降下；prep. 往下，沿着
　~ corner 溢流管
　~ flooding angle 进水角，开始浸水角
　~ halyard 降帆索，落帆索
　~ shore current 沿岸流
　~ stroke 下行冲程，下行行程
downcast ['daunkɑ:st] a. 朝下的，向下的，气馁的，悲哀的，忧郁的，沮丧的 ‖ *Ant.* upturned 朝上的
　~ ventilator 下向通风筒，吸气通风筒
downcome ['daunkʌm] n. 下降，衰落

downcomer ['daunˌkʌmə(r)] n. 下水管，下导管

downflow ['daunfləu] n. 向下流，向下流之物

downhand ['daunhænd] n. 俯焊，平焊；a. 俯焊的，平焊的

downhaul ['daunhɔ:l] n. 收帆索，落帆索

downstream ['daunstri:m] a. 顺流而下的，在下游方向的；ad. 在下游地，顺流地

downtake ['daunteik] n. 下导气管，下降管，下气道

~ pipe 下导管，降液管

downward ['daunwəd] a. 向下的，往下的，降下的；ad. 向下地，往下地，降下地

downwards ['daunwədz] ad. 向下，往下，自古以来，从早期

DP (designated person) 指定人士，指定人员，指认人士

DPA (designated person ashore) 岸上指定人员，岸基制定人员

DPU (data processing unit) 数据处理装置

DPU (distributed processing unit) 分布式处理单元

draft [dra:ft] (=draught) n. 吃水深度，草稿，草案，草图，汇票，选派，吸入量，强大需求，负荷物，拖拽，调节气流的装置，(小股) 气流；v. 起草，制定，拟稿，绘样，征募，作草图

~ mark 吃水标志，吃水标尺，吃水标

drag [dræg] n. 拖拉，拖，拖累；v. 拖拉，拖曳，缓慢而吃力地行进，拖累

~ boat 挖泥船

~ force 拖曳力，阻力

~ torque 拖曳转矩，阻力矩

dragger ['drægə] n. 小型拖网渔船

dragging ['drægiŋ] v. (drag 的 ing 形式) 拖拉，拖曳，缓慢而吃力地行进，拖累；a. 拖曳用的，拖延的

~ motor 拖曳电动机

~ of anchor 走锚

drain [drein] n. 排水，下水道，排水管，排水道，损耗，消耗，消耗的东西，v. 排水，流干，排掉，弄干，变干，喝光，耗尽，使流出

~ cock 排气阀，排气旋塞，放水旋塞，放水龙头

~ connection 排液口，排水管接头

~ current 漏极电流，漏电流

~ petcock 放残小旋塞，放残小龙头

~ pipe 排水管，泄水管

~ plug 排水塞，排出螺塞，放油螺塞

~ tank 泄放柜

~ valve 放残阀，泄水阀

drainage ['dreinidʒ] n. 排水，排泄，排水装置，排水区域，排出物，消耗

~ hole 放泄孔，排泄孔，疏水孔

~ outlet 排水出口，出水口

~ piping 排水管路，排泄管路

~ pump 疏水泵，排泄泵

~ rate 滤水速度，排水速度，排水比率

draining ['dreiniŋ] n. 排水，泄水，排泄；v. (drain 的 ing 形式) 排水，流干，排掉，弄干，变干，喝光，耗尽，使流出

~ bilge 污水排泄

~ pipe 排水管

~ pump 排水泵

~ solenoid valve 泄流电磁阀

~ valve 泄水阀

draught [dra:ft] (=draft) n. 吃水深度，草稿，草案，草图，汇票，选派，吸入量，强大需求，负荷物，拖拽，调节气流的装置，(小股) 气流; v. 起草，制定，拟稿，绘样，征募，作草图

~ door 通风门

~ fan 通气风扇，引风机，通风机

~ marks 吃水标，吃水线 ‖ *Syn.* plimsoll line 载重线标志，载重吃水线，载货吃水线; plimsoll mark 吃水标，吃水线

~ pressure 压缩力，轧制力，轧制压力

~ regulator 牵引力调节器，通风器

draw [drɔ:] n. 拖曳，平局，和局; v. 拉，曳，牵，画，绘制，拖曳，汲取，领取，提取，引起，吸引，向…移动，挨近

~ away 拉走，退走

~ off 撤退，排除

~ out 抽出，拉长，使说出实情，拟订，跑到别人前面并拉开距离

draw-out 抽出的，抽取的

~ type HT switchgear 抽出式高压开关设备

drawable ['drɔ:əbl] a. 可曳的，可拉的

~ LT distribution panel 可拉伸的低压配电板

drawback ['drɔ:ˌbæk] n. 缺点，障碍，退还的关税，退税

drawer [drɔ:ə] n. 抽屉，画家，制图员，衬裤、内裤(drawers)

~ type switch cabinet 抽屉式开关柜，抽屉式配电箱

drawing ['drɔ:iŋ] n. 绘画，制图，图画，图样; v. (draw 的 ing 形式) 拉，曳，牵，画，绘制，拖曳，汲取，领取，提取，引起，吸引，向…移动，挨近

~ board 画板，制图板

~ compass 制图圆规，绘图圆规

~ machine 拉拔机，拉制机，引上机，抽丝机

~ mechanism 卸料装置，出料装置

~ paper 画纸，绘图纸

~ tool 拉制工具

drawknife ['drɔ:naif] n. (两端有柄的) 刮刀

drawn [drɔ:n] v. (draw 的过去分词) 拉，绘画，拖，拔出; a. 疲惫的，憔悴的，绷紧的，扭歪的，平局的，不分胜负的

dredge [dredʒ] n. 挖泥船，挖掘机，疏浚机，捞网; v. 挖掘，疏浚，挖出，捞取，撒

~ pump 疏浚泵，排污泵，泥泵

~ sample 海泥取样

dredged [dredʒd] v. (dredge 的过去式和过去分词) 挖掘，疏浚，挖出，捞取，撒; a. 疏浚的

~ area 挖浚区，疏浚区

~ berth 疏浚的泊位，疏浚过的锚泊地，挖成的泊位，疏浚后船席

~ channel 疏浚航道

~ oil 疏浚海泥

~ spoil 疏浚泥沙，疏浚废渣

dredger ['dredʒə] n. 挖泥机，挖泥船，捞网，撒粉器

dredging ['dredʒiŋ] n. 挖泥，捕捞; v. (dredge 的 ing 形式) 挖掘，疏浚，挖出，捞取，撒

~ engineering 疏浚工程

~ equipment 清淤设备，挖泥设备

~ method 挖泥方法

183

~ of anchor 拖锚，走锚

~ pump 挖泥泵，泥浆泵

~ vessel 疏浚船

dress [dres] *n.* 衣服，军服，礼服，连衣裙，装饰；*v.* 穿衣，加工，处理，整备，制作，使排列整齐，整队，装好，在(船)上挂旗

~ up 修整，打扮，装饰，穿上盛装

drib [drib] *n.* 点滴，一滴，滴，少量；*v.* 点滴地落下

drier ['draiə] *n.* 干燥器，干燥工，吹风机，甩干机；*a.* (dry 的比较级) 比…干燥

drift [drift] *n.* 漂移，偏移，趋势，动向，大意，放任自流，吹积物，冲积物，漂砾，主旨，意见，意向；*v.* 漂浮，漂荡，漂流，漂泊，流动，随意移动，浮现，吹积，堆积

~ along 随波逐流，任其自然

~ dive 漂流潜，放流潜水，放流

~ diving 放流潜水，漂流潜水

~ fishing boat 流网渔船，漂流渔船

~ velocity 漂移速度

drifter ['driftə] *n.* 漂流物，流浪者，漂网渔船

drill [dril] *n.* 军事训练，操练，(反复)练习，钻孔机，钻子，播种机，条播机；*v.* 训练，操练，钻孔，条播

~ bit 钻头

~ collar 钻铤

~ machine 钻床，钻机，半自动立式钻床

~ master 训练者，教官，教练

~ out 钻出

~ pad 钻垫

~ pipe 钻管，钻探管，钻杆

~ ship 钻井船，练习舰

~ string 钻柱

~ tap 钻孔攻丝复合刀具

drilled [drild] *v.* (drill 的过去式和过去分词) 训练，操练，钻孔，条播；*a.* 钻过孔的

~ anchor 预钻孔锚

~ passage 钻孔通道，钻道

driller ['drilə] *n.* 钻孔者，钻孔机

drilling ['driliŋ] *n.* 演练；*v.* (drill 的 ing 形式) 训练，操练，钻孔，条播

~ barge 钻探船 ‖ *Syn.* drilling vessel 钻探船；drilling ship 钻探船

~ equipment 钻机，钻孔设备

~ rig 钻机，钻探设备

~ tool 钻孔刀具，镗孔刀具

drink [driŋk] *n.* 饮料，酒，酗酒，一口(或一些)饮料；*v.* 喝，饮，喝酒，吸水，举杯庆贺

drinking ['driŋkiŋ] *n.* 喝饮料，喝酒；*v.* (drink 的 ing 形式) 喝，饮，喝酒，吸水，举杯庆贺

~ water 饮用水 ‖ *Syn.* potable water 饮用水

~ water boiler 饮用水锅炉，开水锅炉，茶炉

~ water ozone disinfector 饮用水臭氧消毒器

~ water pump 饮用水泵

~ water standard 饮用水标准

~ water system 饮用水系统

drip [drip] *n.* 水滴，滴落，滴水声，静脉滴注，无聊的人；*v.* 滴落，滴下，漏下，渗出，溢出，洋溢着，充满

~ cooler 水淋冷却器，点滴式冷却器

~ feed 滴油器，点滴注，油滴注

~ pan 油滴盘，盛液盘

~ tank 收油桶，集漏油箱，滴液箱
~ tray 滴油盘
~ valve 集液排放阀，滴水阀，排水阀
drip-proof 不透水的，防滴漏的，防滴式的
~ motor 防滴式电动机
drive [draiv] *n*. 驾车，驱动器，快车道，推进力，驱使，动力，干劲，击球；*v*. 开车，驾驶，驱赶，推动，发动，猛击，飞跑
~ away 赶走，开走
~ axis 驱动轴，主动轴
~ circuit 激励电路，驱动电路
~ current 驱动电流，激励电流
~ control 驱动控制
~ controller 驱动控制器
~ end bearing 主动端轴承，驱动端轴承
~ file 驱动文件
~ gear 传动齿轮，主动齿轮，驱动齿轮，传动机构
~ mechanism 驱动机构，传动装置
~ motor 驱动马达，传动马达，驱动电动机
~ on 可以开上去的
~ out 驱赶，开车外出
~ shaft 驱动轴，主动轴
~ shaft coupling 传动轴联轴节
~ system 传动系统
~ up 抬高，迫使…上升
~ wheel 驱动轮，主动轮
~ wire 激励线圈
~ worm and wheel 蜗轮蜗杆传动
driveability [,draivə'biləti] *n*. 驾驶性能，操纵性能，操纵灵活性
driven ['drivn] *v*. (drive 的过去分词) 驾驶，驱赶，推动，发动；*a*. 受到驱策的，发愤图强的，受…影响的，由…造成的
~ gear 被动齿轮，从动齿轮
~ shaft 被动轴，从动轴
~ system 传动系统，驱动系统
~ torus 从动环
~ wheel 被动轮，从动轮
driver ['draivə] *n*. 起子，主动轮，传动器，驱动器，驱动程序，司机，驾驶员
~ amplifier 激励放大器，功率放大器
driving ['draiviŋ] *n*. 操纵，驱赶，推动，驾驶；*v*. (drive 的 ing 形式) 开车，驾驶，驱赶，推动，发动，猛击，飞跑；*a*. 推进的，强劲的，精力旺盛的
~ circuit 激励电路
~ device 传动装置
~ direction 主动机械运动方向
~ force 驱动力，传动力，主动力
~ gear 驱动装置，驱动机构，传动装置，传动机构，传动齿轮，主动齿轮
~ gear box 传动齿轮箱，驱动齿轮箱，主动齿轮箱
~ mechanism 转仪装置
~ mode 驱动模态
~ moment 旋转力矩，转动力矩，传动力矩，驱动力矩
~ motor 主动电动机，驱动电动机
~ nut 传动螺母，主动螺帽
~ shaft 主动轴
~ shaft coupling 动轴耦合器
~ shaft system 传动轴系
~ sheave 主动槽轮
~ system 驱动系统
~ wheel 驱动轮，主动轮

droop [dru:p] *n.* 下垂，消沉；*v.* 低垂，下垂，凋萎，衰萎，萎靡，衰弱
～ characteristic 下垂特性，下降特性
～ correction 固定偏差校正，下垂度校正
～ rate 下降率

drop [drɔp] *n.* 落下，下降，滴，滴剂，点滴，微量，下跌；*v.* 滴下，落下，变弱，下降，使跌倒，使结束，不再讨论，停止交往
～ anchor 抛锚
～ leaf 活动翻板
～ off 离开，散去，逐渐减少，死去
～ out 不参与，离去，放弃
～ point 落点，滴点，下降点
～ speed 坠落速度，点滴速度

drop-proof 防滴的
～ type motor 防滴水式电动机

drop-shaped 水滴状的，水滴形的
～ bulbous bow 水滴形球艏
～ finned tube 水滴状翅片管
～ lamp 水滴形灯

droplet ['drɔplit] *n.* 小滴，微滴，小水珠
～ size 液滴大小，粒径，雾滴直径，滴尺寸，液滴尺寸

dropout ['drɔpaut] *n.* 遗失信息，辍学者，退学者，流失生
～ fuse 跳开式熔断器
～ voltage 回动电压，压差，跌落电压

dropwise ['drɔp,wais] *ad.* 逐滴地，一滴滴地
～ condensation 珠状凝结

DRTS (distributed real-time system) 分布式实时系统

drum [drʌm] *n.* 鼓，鼓声，鼓状物，鼓形圆桶，鼓膜，鼓室；*v.* 击鼓，打鼓，拍翅，鼓翅，大力争取，反复讲，鼓吹，轰走，开除 ‖ *Syn*. barrel 桶，桶状物
～ armature 鼓形电枢
～ boiler 汽包锅炉，锅筒锅炉
～ controller 磁鼓控制器，鼓形控制器
～ end head 汽包封头
～ filter 鼓式滤器
～ level 汽包水位，鼓筒水位
～ level indicator 汽包水位指示器
～ load 卷筒额定拉力

dry [drai] *v.* (使)干燥，(使)变干；*a.* 干的，干燥的，口渴的，固态的，无水的，缺水的，朴素的，枯燥无味的，冷嘲的，禁酒的
～ acid descaler 粒状酸性清洁剂
～ and wet thermometer 干湿球温度计
～ battery 干电池
～ bulb temperature 干球温度
～ bulk cargo 干散货
～ cargo ship 干货船
～ cargo space 干货舱
～ chemical 化学品，不含水化学品，干粉灭火剂
～ chemical fire extinguisher 干粉灭火器 ‖ *Syn*. dry powder extinguisher 干粉灭火器；powder fire extinguisher 干粉灭火器
～ chemical powder 化学干粉
～ chemical powder fire-extinguishing system 干粉灭火系统
～ container 干货集装箱
～ cylinder liner 干式缸套
～ dock 干船坞
～ docking 进干船坞
～ docking repairs 进坞修理

~ evaporator 干式蒸发机
~ film thickness 干膜厚度
~ friction 干摩擦，静摩擦，库伦摩擦
~ grinding 干磨削
~ ice 干冰
~ liner 干缸套
~ powder 干粉料，干粉
~ powder foam fire system 干粉泡沫灭火系统
~ saturated gas 干饱和气体
~ sprinkler system 干式喷水灭火系统
~ suit 干式潜水服，干式防寒衣
~ sump lubrication 干油底壳润滑
~ transformer 干式变压器
~ type bushing 干式套管
~ type evaporator 干式蒸发器
~ type transformer 干式变压器，干性变压器，空气冷却式变压器

dry-charged 干荷电的
~ battery 干蓄电池，免维护蓄电池

dryness ['drainis] *n.* 干燥度，干，干燥，干性

dual ['dju(:)əl] *n.* 双数，双数格；*a.* 双的，双数的，双重的，一分为二的，双重性格的
~ cable 双线电缆，双电缆制
~ circuit 对偶电路
~ duct air-conditioning system 双通道空调系统
~ fuel engine 双燃料发动机
~ function 双功能，双重职能
~ functional 双功能的
~ modulation telemetering system 双重调制遥测系统
~ overhead camshaft engine 双顶置凸轮轴发动机

~ purpose nozzle 两用喷嘴
~ system 双机系统，双重系统，双系统
~ valve 双联阀，复式阀，双气门
~ voltage 双电压
~ voltage motor 双电压电动机

duality [dju(:)'æləti] *n.* 二元性

duct [dʌkt] *n.* 管，输送管，排泄管；*v.* 通过管道输送
~ keel 导管骨，箱形龙骨，隧道式龙骨
~ pilot 控制回路

ducted [dʌktid] *v.* (duct 的过去式和过去分词) 用管道输送；*a.* 管道中的
~ blade 涵道桨叶
~ propeller 导管推进器，导管螺旋桨

ductile ['dʌktail] *a.* 易延展的，易教导的，柔软的，有韧性的，顺从的，易受影响的
~ cast iron 球墨铸铁
~ fracture 形变断裂，塑性破坏，塑性断口
~ iron 延性铁，球墨铸件
~ material 塑性物质，延性材料，延展性材料
~ metal 韧性金属

ductility [dʌk'tiliti] *n.* 韧性，塑性，展延性，柔软性，顺从，展性

due [dju:] *n.* 应得之物，权力，应付款；*a.* 到期的，预期的，应付的，应得的；*ad.* 正(置于方位词前)
~ date 到期日，期头，支付日
~ to 由于，因为，欠债，欠账，应给予，应归于

duel ['dju(:)əl] *n.* 决斗，争斗，争辩，双方抗争；*v.* 反对，决斗

duly ['dju:li] *ad.* 及时，按时，适当地，

充分地

dumb [dʌm] *a.* 哑的，无说话能力的，不说话的，无声音的

~ lighter 驳船

~ panel 哑面板，无声面板

dump [dʌmp] *n.* 堆存处，无秩序地累积；*v.* 转储，转出，倾销，倾泻，倾倒，倾卸，摆脱，扔弃，突然跌倒或落下，推卸责任

~ chute 投料口，排油斜管

~ energy 剩余能量，剩余电量

~ valve 倾泄阀，安全阀

dumping ['dʌmpiŋ] *n.* 倾销，倾泻，倾倒，倾卸；*v.* (dump 的 ing 形式) 转储，转出，倾销，倾泻，倾倒，倾卸，摆脱，扔弃，突然跌倒或落下，推卸责任

~ of wastes 废弃物倾倒

duplex ['dju:pleks] *n.* 联式房屋，两家合住房屋；*a.* 双工的，双向的，双重的，双倍的，复式的，双方的

~ compressor 双动压气机

~ filter 双重过滤器，双联过滤器

~ filter unit 双联滤器组

~ oil filter 双联油滤器

~ pump 双缸泵，双筒泵，联式泵

~ strainer 双联滤器，复式滤器

~ winding 串并联绕组，双绕组，复式绕组

duplicate ['dju:plikeit] *n.* 副本，复制品；*v.* 复写，复制，使加倍，使成双；*a.* 复制的，副的，两重的，两倍的，完全相同

~ supply 双路供电，重复供应 ‖ *Syn.* two-circuit feeding 双路供电

durability [,djuərə'biliti] *n.* 耐久性，经久，持久性

~ test against oil-vapour 耐油雾试验

durable ['djuərəbl] *n.* 耐用品，耐耗品，耐久品；*a.* 持久的，耐用的，耐久的，持久的，稳定的，长期的

durably ['djuərəbli] *ad.* 经久地，坚牢地

duration [djuə'reiʃən] *n.* 持续，持久，为期，持续时间，期间

~ of a voltage change 电压变化持续时间

~ of certificate 证书期限

~ of charging 充电时间，加注时间

during ['djuəriŋ] *prep.* 在…的时候，在…期间，当…之时

~ standby period 备航待机期间

~ the course of 在…期间

dust [dʌst] *n.* 灰尘，尘土，尘埃，无价值的东西，混乱，搅乱，暴乱；*v.* 除去灰尘，撒粉末于，擦粉状物

~ catcher 除尘器，吸尘器

~ emission 粉尘排放

~ extraction 除尘

~ extractor 集尘器

~ filter 滤尘器

~ fog 尘雾

~ particle 尘粒，微尘

~ removal 除尘

~ seal 防尘密封条，尘封

dusty ['dʌsti] *a.* 满是灰尘的，积满灰尘的，粉末状的，含糊的

duty ['dju:ti] *n.* 义务，责任，职责，职务，税

~ engineer 值班工程师，值班轮机师

~ exemption 关税豁免，免税

~ of engine 发动机功能

~ mess 值班船员餐厅

~ pump 工作泵，执勤泵 ‖ **Syn**. service pump 值勤泵
~ ratio 负荷比，占空率，能率比
~ room 值班室
~ schedule 值班安排表

DVD (digital video disk) 数字式视频光盘

DVD-R (digital video disk-recordable) 数字式可写视频光盘，数字式可烧录视频光盘

DVD-RAM (digital video disk-random access memory) 数字式随机存取视频光盘

DVD-ROM (digital video disk-read only memory) 数字式只读视频光盘

dynamic [dai'næmik] (=dynamical) *n*. 动力，动态，对抗性态势；*a*. 动态的，动力的，动力学的，不断变化的，充满变数的，充满活力的，精力充沛的 ‖ **Ant**. static 静态的，静止的，呆板的
~ accuracy 动态精度
~ balancing 动态平衡
~ braking 动力制动，动态制动
~ braking contactor 电机制动接触器
~ characteristic 动态特性，负载特性（曲线）
~ characteristic curve 动态特性曲线
~ characteristic curve of voltage regulation 动态调压特性曲线
~ check 动态检查，动态检验，动态校验
~ control 动力控制，动态控制
~ deviation 动态偏差
~ equilibrium 动力平衡，动态平衡
~ error 动态误差
~ error coefficient 动态误差系数

~ exactness 动态吻合性
~ evaluation 动态评价
~ factor 动力因数
~ fuel injection 动态燃油喷射
~ head 动压头，动水头
~ load 动载荷，动荷载，动力荷载
~ model 动力模型，动力学模型，动态模型
~ performance 动态特性，动态性能
~ performance analysis 动态性能分析，动态特性分析，动力性能分析
~ performance specification 动态性能指标
~ positioning 动态定位
~ positioning system 动态定位系统
~ pressure 动压力
~ range 动态范围
~ response 动态响应，动态特性
~ specification 动态指标，动态性能
~ stability 动态稳定性，动力稳定度
~ stability condition 动态稳定条件
~ state 动态
~ state operation 动态运行
~ steady 动态稳定
~ supported craft 动力支撑型船
~ system 动力系统
~ system response 动态系统频率特性，动态系统的反应
~ viscosity 动态黏度

dynamical [dai'næmikəl] (=dynamic) *n*. 动力，动态，对抗性态势；*a*. 动态的，动力的，动力学的，不断变化的，充满变数的，充满活力的，精力充沛的 ‖ **Ant**. static 静态的，静止的，呆板的
~ lever 动力杠杆

~ stability 动态稳定性，动态稳性
~ equilibrium 动态平衡
~ system 动力系统

dynamically [dai'næmikəli] ad. 动态地，充满活力地，不断变化地
~ balanced impeller 动力平衡叶轮
~ balanced rotor 动态平衡转子
~ supporting craft 机动支援艇
~ supported craft construction and equipment certificate 机动支援艇建造和设备证书

dynamics [dai'næmiks] n. (dynamic 的复数) 动力学，动态学，动态，社会力量

dynamo ['dainəmou] n. 发电机，精力充沛的人 ‖ **Syn**. electrical machine 发电机；generating machinery 发电机；generator 发电机
~ bracket 发电机托架
~ cut-off indicator lamp 发电机停止充电指示灯
~ oil 电机油

dynamometer [,dainə'mɔmitə] n. 测力计，功率计，动力计
~ test 测功器试验
~ wattmeter 功率计式瓦特计

dysfunction [dis'fʌŋkʃən] n. 机能不良，功能紊乱，官能障碍 ‖ **Syn**. failure 失灵，故障；fault 故障；out of order 次序颠倒，不整齐，状态不好；trouble 故障

E

eagle ['i:gl] n. 鹰，鹰状标志
~ nose pliers 鹰嘴钳，鹰鼻钳

ear [iə] n. 耳朵，耳状物，倾听，听觉，听力，耳把，把手，穗；v. 抽穗，听见
~ air space 耳腔
~ equalized 耳平衡
~ handle 耳柄

eardrum ['iədrʌm] n. 中耳，鼓膜，耳膜

earlier ['ə:liə] a. 早期的，初期的；ad. 早期地，初期地
~ ignition 点火提前，发火提前
~ stage 前期

early ['ə:li] a. 早期的，早的，早日的，(果实等)早熟的；ad. 早，提早，在初期，先前
~ deceleration 早期减速
~ warning 预警
~ warning of fault 故障预警

earmuff ['iəmʌf] n. 耳套，防寒耳罩

earphone ['iəfəun] n. 头戴受话器，耳机

earpiece ['iəpi:s] n. 听筒
~ plug 耳塞

earth [ə:θ] n. 地球，陆地，泥土，洞穴，地球上的人类，尘世，接地；v. 把…接地，埋入土中，把…赶入洞内，躲入洞内 ‖ **Syn**. ground 地面，土地，把…接地
~ clamp 接地夹子，接地端子
~ connection 接地线，接地
~ current 接地电流，大地电流
~ detector 接地检测器，漏电检查器
~ fault 接地故障
~ fault protection 接地保护
~ lamp 接地灯
~ resistance 接地电阻 ‖ **Syn**. earthing resistance 接地电阻
~ wire 地线，接地线 ‖ **Syn**. ground wire 地线，接地线

earthed [ə:θt] v. (earth 的过去式和过去分词) 接地，埋入土中；a. 接地的，通地的

~ neutral 接地中点，接地中线

earthing ['ə:θiŋ] *n.* 接地；*v.* (earth 的 ing 形式) 把…接地，埋入土中，把…赶入洞内，躲入洞内 ‖ *Syn.* grounding 接地

~ bus 接地母线

~ cable 接地电缆，接地线

~ conductor 地线，接地导体，接地导线

~ device 接地装置

~ inductor 接地电抗器

~ lug 接地线耳，接地片

~ of casing 外壳接地

~ resistance 接地电阻 ‖ *Syn.* earth resistance 接地电阻

~ switch 接地转换开关

~ system 接地系统

ease [i:z] *n.* 安逸，安心，不费力，悠闲；*v.* 使悠闲，使安心，减轻，放松，减弱，灵活地移动

easing ['i:ziŋ] *n.* 松开，放松；*v.* (ease 的 ing 形式) 使悠闲，使安心，减轻，放松，减弱，灵活地移动

~ gear 卸货装置，减压装置

east [i:st] *n.* 东方，东风，东部地区，东方国家；*a.* 东方的，向东的，从东方来的；*ad.* 向东方，在东方

eastern ['i:stən] *a.* 东方的，东部的

eastward ['i:stwəd] *a.* 向东方的，朝东的；*ad.* 向东

ebullition [ˌebə'liʃən] *n.* 沸腾，冒泡，迸发，(感情等的)爆发

eccentric [ik'sentrik] *n.* 偏心轮，古怪的人；*a.* 偏离轨道的，离心的，不同圆心的，偏轴的，古怪的，异常的，偏执的

~ arm 偏心臂

~ cam 偏心凸轮

~ gear 偏心轮(装置)

~ load 偏心负载

~ piston ring 偏心活塞环

~ pivot 偏心支点

~ radius 偏心半径

~ ring 偏心环

~ rod 偏心棒，偏心杆

~ shaft 偏心轴

~ sleeve 偏心套筒

~ throw 偏心距

~ wheel 偏心轮

eccentrically [ik'sentrikli] *ad.* 离开中心地，反常地

eccentricity [eksen'trisiti] *n.* 偏心，离心率，古怪

ECDIS (Electronic Chart Display and Information System) 电子海图显示与信息系统

ecological [ˌe:kə'lɔdʒikəl] *a.* 生态的，生态学的

~ balance 生态平衡

~ environment 生态环境

~ system 生态系统

economic [ˌi:kə'nɔmik] *a.* 经济的，经济学的，产供销的，合算的，有经济效益的

~ effectiveness 经济效率

~ speed 经济速度，经济航速

economical [ˌi:kə'nɔmikəl] *a.* 经济的，节约的，合算的

~ efficiency 经济效果，经济效率

~ operation 经济运行

~ operation of power systems 电力系统经济运行

~ power 经济功率

~ speed 经济航速，经济车速

~ use of water 节约用水，经济用水

economically [ˌiːkəˈnɔmikəli] ad. 在经济上，经济地，节约地，节省地

economiser [i(ː)ˈkɔnəmaizə] n. (=economizer) 省油器，节热器，节约装置，节约者

economization [i(ː)ˌkɔnəmaiˈzeiʃən] n. 节约，节省，节俭的东西

economize [i(ː)ˈkɔnəmaiz] v. 节省，减少开支，有效地利用

~ boiler 废气锅炉

economizer [i(ː)ˈkɔnəmaizə] n. (=economiser) 省油器，节热器，节约装置，节约者

economy [i(ː)ˈkɔnəmi] n. 经济，节约，节约措施，经济实惠，系统，机体，经济制度的状况

~ load 经济负载

ecosystem [iːkəˈsistəm] n. 生态系统

eddy [ˈedi] n. (水、烟等的)漩涡，涡流；v. 起漩涡，旋转

~ current 涡流，电涡流

~ current loss 涡流损耗

~ current sensor 电涡流传感器

~ current testing 涡流探伤，涡流检测

~ current thickness meter 涡流厚度计，涡流测厚仪

~ flow 涡流，旋流，紊流

~ resistance 涡旋阻力，涡流阻力

~ size 涡旋尺度

edge [edʒ] n. 刀口，利刃，锋，优势，边缘，优势，尖锐；v. 使锋利，挤进，镶边，开刃，缓缓移动，侧着移动

~ corrosion 边缘腐蚀

~ detection 边缘检测

~ preparation (焊接)接边加工，边缘整理

edged [edʒd] v. (edge 的过去式和过去分词) 挤进，镶边，开刃；a. 有边的，加边的，有刃的，微醉的

~ tool 有刃的工具，利器

edger [ˈedʒə] n. 轧边机

EDH (efficient deck hand) 二级水手

Edison [ˈedisn] n. 爱迪生(1847—1931，美国发明家、物理学家)

~ screw 螺口插座，螺口灯座，爱迪生螺旋灯头 ‖ *Syn*. Edison socket 螺口插座，螺口灯座，爱迪生螺旋灯头

EDM (electric discharge machining, electrical discharge machining) 电火花加工

educt [ˈiːdʌkt] n. 离析物

eductor [iːˈdʌktə] n. 喷射器，排泄器

effect [iˈfekt] n. 结果，效果，作用，影响，(在视听方面给人流下的)印象；v. 招致，实现，达到(目的等)

~ of inertia 惯性作用

effective [iˈfektiv] n. 现役兵额，战斗力，有生力量；a. 有效的，被实施的，给人深刻印象，实在的，实际的，有战斗力的，备战的，有生力量的

~ compression ratio 有效压缩比

~ current 有效电流，有功电流

~ delivery stroke 有效供油行程

~ head 有效压头，净压头，有效水头

~ horsepower (EHP) 有效马力

~ humidity 有效湿度

~ length 有效长度，计算长度

~ lubrication 有效润滑

~ measure 有效措施

~ output 有效输出(功率)

~ power 有效动力，有效功率

~ pressure 有效压力

~ radius 有效半径

~ range 有效范围

~ recombination velocity 有效复合速度

~ stroke 有效冲程

~ temperature 有效温度，实感温度，感触温度

~ thermal efficiency 有效热效率

~ value 有效值，实际值 ‖ *Syn*. virtual value 有效值

effectively [i'fektivli] *ad.* 有效地，有力地，实际上，事实上

effectiveness [i'fektivnis] *n.* 效力，有效性，效益，效用，有效，有力

effectuate [i'fektjueit] *v.* 实行，完成

efficacy ['efikəsi] *n.* 功效，效力，效验，生产率 ‖ *Syn*. efficiency 功效，效率，功率，效能，实力，能力，性能

efficiency [i'fiʃənsi] *n.* 功效，效率，功率，效能，实力，能力，性能 ‖ *Syn*. efficacy 功效，效力，效验，生产率

~ for charge-discharge 充放电效率

~ rating 效率评价，效率评估

~ rudder 效率舵

efficient [i'fiʃənt] *a.* 有效率的，高效的，生效的，能干的，收效大的

~ deck hand (EDH) 二级水手

~ deformation 有效形变

~ estimator 有效估计量

efficiently [i'fiʃəntli] *ad.* 有效率地，有效地

effluent ['efluənt] *n.* 流出物，排水道，污水，排水渠；*a.* 发出的，流出的

EHP (effective horsepower) 有效马力

EID (electrically initiated devices) 电启动设备

eject [i'dʒekt] *n.* 推断的事物；*v.* 逐出，撵出，驱逐，喷射

ejection [i'dʒekʃən] *n.* 射出，喷出，排出物，抛出，出坯

~ process 排渣过程

ejector [i'dʒektə(r)] *n.* 驱逐者，放出器，排出器，抽气泵，剔出器，发射器

~ nozzle 喷口，喷嘴

~ pin 出坯杆，起模杆，推出机杆，推顶杆

~ priming 喷射器，启动泵

~ pump 喷射泵

~ valve 顶出阀，推卸器阀

~ water air pump 喷水空气泵

elaborate [i'læbərət] *v.* 精心制作，详细阐述，详细描述；*a.* 精心制作的，详细阐述的，精细的

~ on 详细说明

elastic [i'læstik] *n.* 弹性织物，松紧带，橡皮圈；*a.* 柔韧的，有弹力的，可伸缩的，灵活的

~ bearing 弹性轴承

~ collision 弹性碰撞

~ coupling 弹性联轴器，弹性联轴节

~ coupling rubber bush 弹性联轴器橡皮衬套

~ deformation 弹性变形

~ element 弹性元件

~ force 弹力

~ limit 弹性极限，弹性权限，弹性限度

~ support 弹性支座

elasticity [ilæs'tisiti] *n.* 弹性，弹力，灵活性，伸缩性

elastohydrodynamic [i'læstəuˌhaidrəudai'næmik] *a.* 流体弹性动力(学)的

~ lubrication 弹流润滑

elastomer [i'læstəmə(r)] *n*. 弹性体，人造橡胶

elbow ['elbəu] *n*. 弯头，扶手，肘形管，弯管，弯曲处，肘部，肘关节；*v*. 用肘推挤，转弯

electric [i'lektrik] *n*. 电动机器，电器，电动车辆；*a*. 电动的，电的，用电的，带电的，发电的，导电的，令人激动的 ‖ *Syn*. electrical 电的，有关电的 ‖ hydraulic 水力的，水压的；pneumatic 气动的，风力的

~ actuator 电力传动装置，电动执行机构

~ anchor capstan 电动起锚绞盘

~ anemometer 电测风速仪

~ apparatus 电气设备，电气装置

~ appliance 电器，耗电器具

~ arc 电弧

~ arc resistance 电弧电阻材料，耐弧材料

~ arc welding helmet 电焊面具

~ attachments 电气附件

~ bench grinder 台式电动砂轮机

~ breakdown 电击穿 ‖ *Syn*. electric puncture 电击穿；electrical breakdown 电击穿

~ brush 电刷

~ cable 电缆

~ capstan 电力绞盘

~ cargo winch 电动起货机

~ circuit 电路

~ command device 主令电器

~ conductance level meter 电导式液位计

~ conduction 导电

~ conduction phenomenon 导电现象

~ conductivity 电导率，导电性

~ conductor 电导体

~ control 电气控制，电控制

~ control injection 电气控制喷射，电控喷射

~ control panel 电气控制面板，电控面板

~ control system 电气控制系统，电控系统

~ cooking appliance 电炊具

~ current 电流

~ defrost 电热融霜

~ defrost timer 电热融霜定时器

~ desk crane 电动回转式起货机

~ discharge machining (EDM) 电火花加工 ‖ *Syn*. electrical discharge machining (EDM) 电火花加工

~ drill 电钻 ‖ *Syn*. power drill 机械钻，动力钻机，电钻

~ drive 电力传动，电力拖动

~ drive control gear 电气传动控制设备

~ drive system 电力驱动系统

~ energy 电能

~ equipment 电气设备

~ field 电场

~ freshwater heater 淡水电加热器

~ fuel oil heater 燃油电加热器

~ generator 发电机

~ heater 电加热器，电暖气

~ heating 电热，电力供热，电热供暖

~ heating device 电热器

~ heating element 电热元件

~ heating unit 电热设备，电热单元

~ hydraulic converter 电液转换器

~ immersion heater 浸没式电热器

~ impulse 电脉冲 ‖ *Syn*. electric pulse 电脉冲；electrical impulse 电脉冲；

electrical pulse 电脉冲
~ installation 电气设备
~ insulation 电气绝缘
~ insulation tape 电气绝缘胶带
~ lubrication oil heater 电润滑油加热器
~ magnet 电磁铁
~ melting 电热熔炼，电熔
~ motor 电动机
~ motor ship 电动船
~ network 电网络，电力网，电网，网络
~ null 零电压
~ pneumatic converter 电气转换器
~ pneumatic valve 电空阀
~ podded propulsor 电动吊舱推进器
~ pole 电杆，电极
~ potential 电势
~ power 电力，电功率
~ power 380V/50A to be supplied 需供应的 380V/50A 的电力
~ power distribution system 配电系统，配电方式
~ power system 电力系统
~ power system of ship 船舶电力系统
~ power tool 电力工具，电动工具
~ power transmission 电力输送，输电
~ propeller shaft revolution transmitter 尾轴转速发送器
~ propulsion 电力推进，电推进
~ propulsion apparatus 电力推进装置
~ propulsion ship 电力推进船舶
~ propulsion system 电力推进系统
~ pyrometer 电测高温计
~ quantity 电量
~ refrigerator 电冰箱
~ rudder angle indicator 电动舵角指示器

~ rudder angle transmitter 电动舵角发送器
~ saw 电锯
~ saw blade 电锯片
~ seawater heater 海水电加热器
~ shielding 电屏蔽
~ shock 电震，电击
~ siren 电警报器，电警笛
~ soldering iron 电烙铁
~ soldering pliers 电焊钳 ‖ *Syn.* electric welding pliers 电焊钳
~ source 电源 ‖ *Syn.* electrical source 电源；power source 电源；power supply 电源；mains 电源
~ space heater 电暖器 ‖ *Syn.* electric space heating appliance 电暖器
~ spark 电火花
~ spark igniter 电火花点火器
~ spark machining 放电加工
~ steering control system 电力操舵系统
~ steering engine 电动舵机 ‖ *Syn.* electric steering gear 电动舵机
~ stepper motor 电动步进电机
~ stove 电炉
~ stove wire 电炉丝
~ switch 电开关，电钮
~ system 电力系统，电气系统
~ teakettle 电茶壶 ‖ *Syn.* electric teapot 电茶壶
~ technical standard 电气技术标准
~ tester 测电仪
~ testing instrument 电力试验仪器
~ timer 电子计时器，电定时器
~ towing winch 电动拖缆机
~ voltage 电压
~ welding machine 电焊机

~ welding mask 电焊面具
~ windlass 电动起锚机
~ wire 布线
~ wire plan 布线图
electrical [i'lektrik(ə)l] *a*. 电的，用电的，有关电的 ‖ *Syn*. electric 电的，用电的
~ anchor capstan 电动起锚绞盘
~ apparatus 电器，电气设备 ‖ *Syn*. electrical appliance 电器，电气设备
~ apparatus mechanism 电器机构
~ breakdown 电击穿 ‖ *Syn*. electric breakdown 电击穿；electric puncture 电击穿
~ cleaner 电器清洁剂
~ conduction 电导，电传导
~ conductivity 导电性，电导率
~ connection 电连接
~ connector 插塞，插座，接线盒
~ control 电气控制，电控制，电动调节
~ control system 电气控制系统
~ design 电气设计
~ device 电气设备，电气元件，电气装置，电气装备
~ discharge machining (EDM) 电火花加工 ‖ *Syn*. electric discharge machining (EDM) 电火花加工
~ drive and control 电力传动与控制
~ energy 电能，电力
~ engineer 电机员，电气工程师
~ engineering 电气工程
~ equipment 电气设备，电力设备，电器
~ field 电场
~ fire alarm sounder 电动火灾警报器

~ fittings 电气配件
~ flowmeter 电磁流量计
~ generator 发电机
~ generator set 发电机组
~ goniometer 电测角计
~ impulse 电脉冲 ‖ *Syn*. electric impulse 电脉冲；electric pulse 电脉冲；electrical pulse 电脉冲
~ inductance 电感
~ insulation 电绝缘 ‖ *Syn*. electrical isolation 电绝缘
~ interference 电干扰
~ interlocking 电气连锁
~ leakage 漏电，跑电
~ leakage tester 漏电测量计
~ load 电力负荷，电力负载
~ log book 电气日志
~ machine 发电机 ‖ *Syn*. dynamo 发电机；generating machinery 发电机；generator 发电机
~ machinery 电机，电力机械
~ material 电气材料
~ measurement 电气测量
~ outlet 电源插座，电插座
~ plant of a ship 船舶电站
~ potential energy 电位能，电能
~ potential difference 电位差
~ power 电功率
~ power engineering 电力工程
~ power system 电力系统
~ resistance 电阻
~ resistivity 电阻率
~ response time 电气响应时间
~ shock 电击
~ source 电源 ‖ *Syn*. electric source 电源；power source 电源；power supply

电源；mains 电源
~ system 电气系统
~ terms 电气术语
~ test bench 电工试验台
~ towage control system 电力拖动控制系统
~ windlass 电动锚机
~ wire 电线
~ zero 电零位
electrically [i'lektrikəli] ad. 电力地，有关电地
~ charged 带电的，充电的
~ charged body 带电体
~ connected 电气连接的
~ control 电气控制，电控
~ driven 电驱动的，电动的 ‖ *Syn.* electrically operated 电动操作的，电动的；electrically powered 电力驱动的，电动的
~ driven auxiliary blower 电动辅助风机
~ driven auxiliary servo actuator 电动辅助伺服执行机构
~ excited 电激励的，电励磁的
~ excited synchronous motor 电励磁同步电机
~ initiated 电启动的
~ initiated devices (EID) 电启动设备
~ isolated 电隔离的
~ isolated semiconductor device 电隔离半导体器件
~ neutral 电中性的
~ operated valve 电动阀
~ powered equipment 电动设备
~ welded 电焊接的
~ welded construction 电焊接结构
electrician [ilek'triʃ(ə)n] *n.* 电工，电气技师，电学家
~ certificate 电工证，电工操作证
~ engineer 电机员，电气工程师
~ knife 电工刀
electricity [ilek'trisiti] *n.* 电，电流，电学，触电感
~ transmission 输电
electricize [i'lektri‚saiz] *v.* 充电，使带电
electrification [ilektrifi'keiʃ(ə)n] *n.* 充电，电气化，电化
electro [i'lektrəu] *n.* 电镀物品，电版
~ servo 电伺服(机构)
~ servo control 电伺服控制
electrochemical [i‚lektrəu'kemikəl] *a.* 电化，电气化学的
~ attack 电化学腐蚀
~ cell 电化电池
~ corrosion 电化学腐蚀
~ deterioration 电化学腐蚀
electrode [i'lektrəud] *n.* 电极
~ susceptance 电极电纳
~ welding machine 电焊机
~ wire 焊条钢丝
electrodialysis [i‚lektrəudai'ælisis] *n.* 电渗析
~ method 电渗析法
electrogas [elektrəu'gæz] *n.* 电气
~ dynamics 电气体动力学
~ welding 电气焊
electrohydraulic [elektrəuhaid'rɔ:lik] *a.* 电动液压的，电液的
~ changeover valve 电液转换阀
~ controller 电液控制器
~ converter 电液转换器
~ direction control valve 电液方向控制阀

~ servo 电液伺服

~ servovalve 电液伺服阀

~ steering gear 电液舵机

~ valve 电液阀

~ winch 电动液压绞车，电动液压起货机

~ windlass 电动液压锚机

electrolysis [ilek'trɔlisis] *n*. 电解，电蚀除毛 ‖ *Syn*. electrolyte 电解

electrolyte [i'lektrəulait] *n*. 电解，电解液，电解质 ‖ *Syn*. electrolysis 电解

electrolytic [iˌlektrəu'litik] *a*. 电解的，由电解产生的

~ action 电解作用

~ analysis 电解分析

~ anti-fouling protection system 电解防污染保护系统

~ descaling 电解除锈，电解除垢，电解除氧化皮，电解脱膜

~ dissociation constant 电离常数

~ grinding 电解磨削

~ solution 电解质溶液，电解液

electromagnet [ilektrəu'mægnit] *n*. 电磁体，电磁铁

electromagnetic [ilektrəu'mægnitik] *a*. 电磁的

~ brake 电磁制动器，电磁闸

~ changeover valve 电磁转换阀

~ compatibility (EMC) 电磁兼容性

~ control 电磁控制

~ disturbance 电磁扰动，电磁干扰 ‖ *Syn*. electromagnetic interference (EMI) 电磁干扰

~ energy 电磁能量，电磁能

~ environment 电磁环境

~ field 电磁场

~ field intensity 电磁场强度

~ flow transducer 电磁流量传感器，电磁流速传感器

~ generator 电磁式发电机

~ induction 电磁感应

~ irradiation 电磁照射，电磁辐射，电磁放射

~ log 电磁船速仪

~ noise 电磁噪声

~ pollution 电磁污染

~ pulse (EMP) 电磁脉冲

~ pulse jamming 电磁脉冲干扰

~ screening 电磁屏蔽 ‖ *Syn*. electromagnetic shielding 电磁屏蔽

~ shielding chamber 电磁屏蔽室

~ ship propulsion apparatus 磁流体船舶推进装置

~ slide valve 电磁滑阀

~ starter 电磁启动器

~ susceptibility 电磁敏感性

~ torque 电磁转矩

~ transient process 电磁瞬态过程

~ valve 电磁阀

~ variable-speed motor 电磁调速电动机

~ wave 电磁波

electromechanical [iˌlektrəumi'kænikəl] *a*. 电动机械的，机电的，电机的

~ transmission 机电传动

electromotive [ilektrəu'məutiv] *a*. 电动的，电动势的，电测的

~ field 电动势场

~ force (EMF) 电动势

~ intensity 电场强度

~ power 电动力

~ relay 电动式继电器

~ unit 电动势单位

electromotor [i,lektrəu'məutə(r)] *n.* 电动机，电气马达

electron [i'lektrɔn] *n.* 电子

electronic [ilek'trɔnik] *a.* 电子的，电传导的，电子学的，电子仪器的 ‖ *Syn.* electronical 电子的

　　~ automatic tuning 电子自动调谐

　　~ ballast 电子镇流器，电子式镇流器

　　~ Chart Display and Information System (ECDIS) 电子海图显示与信息系统

　　~ circuit 电子线路，电子电路

　　~ commutator 电子转向器

　　~ component 电子元件

　　~ computer 电子计算机，电脑

　　~ control 电子控制

　　~ control and monitoring 电子控制与监控

　　~ cylinder lubricator 电子气缸注油器，电控气缸注油器

　　~ device 电子设施，电子仪表 ‖ *Syn.* electronic equipment 电子设备

　　~ document 电子文件

　　~ governor 电子调速器

　　~ industry 电子工业

　　~ jamming (人为)电子干扰

　　~ machine system 电子机械系统

　　~ mail 电子邮件

　　~ modular system for automatic control 电子模块自动控制系统

　　~ navigational aids 电子助航设备

　　~ navigational chart 电子海图

　　~ position fixing system (EPFS) 电子定位系统

　　~ position indicator 电子位置指示器

　　~ product 电子产品

~ regulator 电子稳压器，电子调节器

~ remote control system for main engine 电子式主机遥控系统

~ simulation 电子仿真，电子模拟

~ simulation device 电子模拟装置

~ switch 电子开关

~ system engineering 电子系统工程

~ tracking aid 电子跟踪援助，电子跟踪辅助装置

~ welding 电子焊接

electronical [ilek'trɔnikəl] *a.* 电子的 ‖ *Syn.* electronic 电子的

electronically [i,lek'trɔnikəli] *ad.* 电子地

　　~ controlled camless engine 电控无凸轮发动机

electronics [ilek'trɔniks] *n.* 电子学，电子工业，电子装置和组件

　　~ engineer 电子设备工程师，电子工程师

electropneumatic [elektrɔpnju:'mætik] *a.* 电动气动的

　　~ actuator 电动气动执行器，电动气动执行机构

　　~ braking connector 电动气动制动联结器

　　~ contactor 电动气动接触器

　　~ control 电动气动控制

　　~ remote control system for main engine 主机电动气动遥控系统

　　~ switch 电动气动开关

　　~ system 电动气动系统

　　~ transducer 电气转换器

　　~ valve 电动气动阀

electrostatic [i'lektrəu'stætik] *a.* 静电式的，静电的，静电学的

　　~ discharge (ESD) 静电放电

~ discharge rating 防静电放电等级

~ effect 静电效应

~ field 静电场

~ force 静电力

~ generator 静电发电机,静电振荡器

~ induction 静电感应

~ interaction 静电相互作用

~ interference 静电干扰

~ painting 静电喷涂

~ potential 静电势,静电位

~ precipitator 静电除尘器,电集尘器

~ screening 静电屏蔽 ‖ *Syn*. electrostatic shielding 静电屏蔽

~ separator 静电分离器,静电选矿机

~ spraying 静电喷漆,静电喷涂

~ voltmeter 静电电压表,静电伏特计

electrotechnics [i'lektrəu'tekniks] *n*. 电工学

~ principle of circuits 电路电工学原理

element ['elimənt] *n*. 要素,元素,成分,元件,自然环境 ‖ *Syn*. cell (电池、光电)元件,单元; component 成分,部分,元件,零件,要素,组分; constituent 成分,要素; ingredient 成分,因素; organ 元件; part 零件,部件

elemental [ˌeli'mentl] *n*. (古希腊)四元素的精灵,基本原理; *a*. 基本的,主要的,自然力的,元素的,强大的,可怕的

elementary [ˌeli'mentəri] *a*. 初等的,基本的,初级的,元素的

elevate ['eliveit] *v*. 提高,提升,举起,鼓舞

elevated ['eliveitid] *v*. (elevate 的过去式和过去分词) 提高,抬起,振奋,提拔; *a*. 提高的,高尚的,严肃的,欢欣的,微醉的

~ tank 高位水箱,高位槽,高位罐,压力罐 ‖ *Syn*. head tank 高位水箱,压力槽,压力罐,压头箱

~ temperature 高温,升高温度,提高温度

elevation [ˌeli'veiʃən] *n*. 高处,高地,高度,海拔,(枪炮的)仰角,射角,升级,上进,向上,高尚,正视图,立视图

~ drawing 前视图,正视图

elevator ['eliveitə] *n*. 电梯,升降机,升降舵

ELF (extremely low frequency) 极低频

eliminate [i'limineit] *v*. 淘汰,排除,消除,除掉,干掉

elimination [iˌlimi'neiʃən] *n*. 淘汰,排除,除去,根除

eliminator [i'limineitə] *n*. 消除者,消除器

ellipse [i'lips] *n*. 椭圆,椭圆形 ‖ circle 圆,圆形; parallelogram 平行四边形; rectangle 矩形; rhombus 菱形; square 正方形; trapezoid 梯形; triangle 三角形

ellipsoid [i'lipsɔid] *n*. 椭球,椭圆体,椭圆面

elliptic [i'liptik] *a*. (=elliptical) 椭圆形的,省略的

elliptical [i'liptikəl] *a*. (=elliptic) 椭圆形的,省略的

~ stern 椭圆艉

elliptically [i'liptikəli] *ad*. 椭圆形地,省略地

ellipticity [ˌelip'tisiti] *n*. 椭圆率,长短轴比,不圆度

elongation [ˌiːlɔŋ'geiʃən] *n*. 延长,延长线,延伸率,距(角)

~ rate 伸长率

~ test 延伸率试验，延伸试验，拉伸试验

~ thickness 延伸厚度

else [els] *a.* 别的，其他的；*ad.* 其他，否则，另外

elsewhere ['els'hwɛə] *ad.* 在别处

elucidate [i'lju:sideit] *v.* 阐明，解释

embankment [im'bæŋkmənt] *n.* 路堤，筑堤

embark [im'ba:k] *v.* 上船，上飞机，着手，从事，装于船上，登上

embarkation [,emba:'keiʃən] *n.* 登船，装载，从事，上飞机

~ card 登船卡，登机证，入境卡，签证

~ deck 登艇甲板，乘载甲板

~ facility 登乘设施，登船设施

~ ladder 登乘梯

~ notice 登乘通知，乘船通知，登船通知书

~ officer 登记员，登轮官员

~ order 登乘命令，登船命令

~ position 登乘位置

~ station 登乘地点

embed [im'bed] *v.* 使插入，使嵌入，深留，嵌入，包埋

embedded [im'bedid] *v.* (embed 的过去式和过去分词) 使插入，使嵌入，深留，嵌入，包埋；*a.* 植入的，深入的，内含的

~ computer 嵌入式计算机

~ pipe 埋藏管道，埋入式管道

~ software 嵌入式软件

~ temperature detector 嵌入式测温计，埋入式温度计，埋置式温度探测器

embody [im'bɔdi] *v.* 表现，象征，包含，收录，使具体化，组编

embolism ['embəlizəm] *n.* 栓塞，栓子，加闰日

embrittle [em'britl] *v.* 使变脆

embrittlement [em'britlmənt] *n.* 脆化，变脆，脆变，发脆

EMC (electromagnetic compatibility) 电磁兼容性

emerge [i'mə:dʒ] *v.* 出现，浮现，形成，暴露，摆脱

emergence [i'mə:dʒəns] *n.* 出现，发生，暴露，突出体，瓢胞

emergency [i'mə:dʒənsi] *n.* 紧急情况，突然事件，非常时刻，紧急事件；*a.* 紧急的，应急的

~ aid 紧急援助

~ air compressor 应急空气压缩机

~ alarm bell 紧急报警铃，紧急警铃

~ astern 紧急倒车

~ batteries 应急电池

~ bilge drainage 应急舱底水泄水系统

~ blige suction 应急舱底水吸口

~ blige suction valve 应急舱底水吸入阀

~ blower 应急鼓风机

~ brake 紧急刹车，紧急制动，紧急闸

~ button 应急按钮，备用按钮

~ call 紧急呼叫

~ commutator switch 应急转换开关

~ condition 事故状态，紧急情况

~ control console 应急控制台

~ dewatering system 应急排水系统

~ diesel generating set 应急柴油发电机组

~ electric equipment 应急电气设备

~ equipment 应急设备

~ escape breathing apparatus 紧急逃生

呼吸器

~ escape ladder 应急逃生梯

~ evacuation 紧急疏散

~ exit 紧急出口

~ exhaust valve 应急排气阀

~ fire pump 应急消防泵

~ fresh water tank 应急淡水柜

~ full ahead 紧急全速前进

~ full astern 紧急全速倒车

~ generating set 备用发电机组，应急发电机组

~ generator 应急发电机

~ generator circuit 应急发电机电路

~ hand control device 应急手动操纵装置

~ instruction 紧急指令，紧急指示

~ light set 应急照明电机

~ lighting 应急照明，紧急照明，事故照明，安全照明

~ lighting batteries 应急照明蓄电池组

~ lighting distribution box 应急照明配电箱，事故照明配电箱

~ lighting fitting 应急照明配件

~ lighting system 应急照明系统

~ manoeuving 应急操纵

~ manoeuving test of steering gear 舵机应急操舵试验

~ measure 紧急措施，应急措施

~ opening and closing test for cargo hatch cover 货舱舱口盖应急启闭试验

~ operation 紧急运转，应急操作

~ overflow 紧急溢流，事故溢流

~ panel (事故)备用配电盘

~ phone 紧急电话

~ position-indicating radio beacon (EPIRB) 应急无线电示位标

~ power 紧急备用动力

~ power source 应急电源，应急动力源 ‖ *Syn*. emergency power supply 应急电源，应急动力源

~ power station 应急电站

~ preparedness 应急准备

~ pressure increasing valve 紧急增压阀

~ procedure 应急操作步骤

~ propulsion motor 应急推进电动机

~ propulsion system 应急推进系统

~ pulse 呼救脉冲，呼救信号

~ relief 紧急救援，事故放水口

~ repair 应急修理

~ response 应急响应，紧急响应，应急反应

~ schedule 紧急措施，应急措施

~ service 应急供电，应急无线电通信业务

~ shutdown mechanism 紧急停车装置

~ shutdown system 紧急停车系统，应急切断系统

~ signal 紧急信号 ‖ *Syn*. urgency signal 紧急信号; urgent signal 紧急信号

~ situation 紧急情况

~ source 应急电源

~ starting 应急启动

~ steering gear 应急操舵装置

~ stop 紧急停车

~ stop button 急停按钮

~ stopping pushbutton 紧急停止按钮

~ switch 紧急开关，应急开关

~ switchboard 应急配电盘

~ towing arrangement 应急拖带装置 ‖ *Syn*. emergency towing equipment 应急拖带设备

~ trip mechanism 应急跳闸机构

~ trip system (ETS) 紧急跳闸系统，危急跳闸系统

~ trip valve 危急遮断阀，紧急止流阀，主汽门

~ valve 应急阀，安全阀

~ work 急救工作，应急工程

emergent [i'mə:dʒənt] *a.* 紧急的，浮现的，突然出现的，自然发生的

emery ['eməri] *n.* 金刚砂，刚玉粉

~ cloth 砂布，金刚砂布

~ paper 砂纸 ‖ *Syn.* sandpaper 砂纸

~ wheel 金刚砂旋转磨石，砂轮

EMF (electromotive force) 电动势

EMI (electromagnetic interference) 电磁干扰 ‖ *Syn.* electromagnetic disturbance 电磁干扰

emission [i'miʃən] *n.* 排放，辐射，排放物，散发物(尤指气体)，(书刊)发行，发布(通知)

~ concentration limit 排放浓度极限

~ control 排放控制

~ control equipment 排放控制设备

~ controlled mode 排放控制模式

~ limit 排放限度

~ performance 排放性能，排放特性

~ standard 排放标准，发射标准

emit [i'mit] *v.* 发出，放射，吐露，散发，发表，发行

emitter [i'mitə] *n.* 发射器

EMP (electromagnetic pulse) 电磁脉冲

emphasis ['emfəsis] *n.* 强调，着重，(轮廓、图形等的)鲜明，突出，重读

emphasize ['emfəsaiz] *v.* 强调，着重，加强语气，使突出

emphysema [ˌemfi'si:mə] *n.* 气肿，肺气肿

empire ['empaiə] *n.* 帝国，帝国领土，帝权，君权，最高统治权，大企业组织；*a.* 新古典风格的

~ tape 绝缘带

~ tube 绝缘套管

empirical [em'pirikəl] *a.* 经验主义的，凭经验的，以观察或实验为依据的

~ data 经验数据，经验公式

~ distribution 经验分布

~ equation 经验方程，经验公式

~ formula 经验式，实验式

~ value 经验值，实验数值

employ [im'plɔi] *n.* 使用，雇佣；*v.* 使用，采用，雇用，使忙于，使从事于

employee [im'plɔii] *n.* 雇工，雇员，职工

employment [im'plɔimənt] *n.* 雇用，使用，利用，工作，职业

~ agreement 就业协议

~ agreement for seafarers 海员雇佣协议，海员就业协议

empower [im'pauə] *v.* 授权，准许，使能够，使控制局势

empty ['empti] *v.* 倒空，腾空，解除，减轻，使失去；*a.* 空的，空洞的，空无意义的，虚的，无知的，徒劳的，缺乏的，贫乏的

~ container 空箱，空集装箱

EMS (energy management system) 能源管理系统

emulsible [i'mʌlsəbl] *a.* (=emulsifiable) 可乳化的，成为乳状的

emulsifiable [i'mʌlsifaiəbl] *a.* (=emulsible) 可乳化的，成为乳状的

emulsification [iˌmʌlsifi'keiʃən] *n.* 乳化，乳化作用

emulsify [i'mʌlsifai] *v.* 使乳化

emulsion [i'mʌlʃən] *n.* 乳状液,感光乳剂，

203

乳剂，乳胶漆

~ oil 乳化油

~ paint 乳化漆

emulsive [i'mʌlsiv] a. 乳剂质的，会流出乳状液的，可榨出油来的

enamel [i'næməl] n. 搪瓷，珐琅，指甲油；v. 上珐琅，涂瓷漆

enamelled [i'næməld] v. (enamel 的过去式和过去分词) 上珐琅，涂瓷漆；a. 珐琅的，搪瓷的，瓷漆的

~ wire 漆包线

encapsulate [in'kæpsjuleit] v. 形成囊状物，压缩，封装，概述

encircle [in'sə:kl] v. 环绕，围绕，包围，绕…行一周 ‖ *Syn*. enclose 围绕

enclose [in'kləuz] v. 放入封套，装入，围住，圈起，围绕 ‖ *Syn*. encircle 环绕，围绕，包围

enclosed [in'kləuzd] v. (enclose 的过去式和过去分词) 装入，围住，圈起，围绕；a. 封闭的，被附上的，(用墙等)围住的，与外界隔绝的

~ bridge 遮蔽式驾驶台

~ deckhouse 封闭式舱面船室，封闭式甲板室

~ fabrication shop 封闭式装配车间，封闭式制造车间

~ fuse 封闭式保险丝，管形熔断片

~ impeller 封闭式叶轮，闭式叶轮

~ lifeboat 封闭式救生艇

~ motor 封闭型电动机

~ sanitary system 闭式卫生水系统 ‖ *Syn*. closed sanitary system 闭式卫生水系统

~ self-ventilated type motor 封闭式自通风电动机

~ separate-ventilation 封闭式外通风

~ slot 封闭槽，封口槽，闭端槽

~ space 封闭空间，围蔽处所

~ water 封闭水域，闭合水区，孤立水区

enclosure [in'kləuʒə] n. 围绕物，附件，圈占，围绕，圈占地

encode [in'kəud] v. 编码，译成电码，译成密码 ‖ *Ant*. decode 解码

encoder [in'kəudə] n. 译码器，编码器 ‖ *Ant*. decoder 解码器

encounter [in'kauntə] n. 遭遇，遭遇战；v. 遭遇，遇到，相遇，邂逅

encourage [in'kʌridʒ] v. 促进，支持，鼓励，鼓舞，鼓动

encrypt [in'kript] v. 加密，将…译成密码

encryption [in'kripʃn] n. 加密，编密码

encumbrance [in'kʌmbrəns] n. 累赘，负担，阻碍，妨碍，妨害物

end [end] n. 端，结果，终止，最后部分；v. 结束，终止

~ bracket 尾架，尾轴承架

~ cap 节流阀端盖(三通阀)，弹簧盒盖

~ chock 端面挡块

~ chock bolt 端楔形螺栓

~ clearance 端隙

~ coaming 端围板，端缘围，缘围端板

~ cover 端盖，头盖

~ device 终端设备

~ instrument 终端设备，终端装置，传感器，敏感元件

~ journal bearing 端经向轴承，端枢轴承

~ launching 纵向下水

~ link 尾环

~ open link 末端链环
~ plate 端板，端面板，终板
~ point 终点，端点
~ point control 端点控制
~ point sensitivity 端点灵敏度
~ point voltage 端点电压
~ ring 锁紧环，端环
~ shackle 末端卸扣
~ user 最终用户
end-of-charge 充电终止，充电完成
~ voltage 充电终止电压
endanger [in'deindʒə] v. 危及
endorse [in'dɔ:s] v. 背书，认可，签署，赞同，在背面签名
endorsement [in'dɔ:smənt] n. 背书，认可，担保
endurance [in'djuərəns] n. 耐久(力)，持久(力)，忍耐(力)
endurant [in'djuərənt] a. 能忍耐的，耐劳的
endure [in'djuə] v. 度过，忍受，忍耐，容忍，持续，持续，持久，支持
energise ['enədʒaiz] v. (=energize) 激励，激发，加强，使带电流，使通电，给予电压，供给能量，使活跃，给予精力，用力，活动
energize ['enədʒaiz] v. (=energise) 激励，激发，加强，使带电流，使通电，给予电压，供给能量，使活跃，给予精力，用力，活动
energizing ['enədʒaiziŋ] n. 通电，激励，激发；v. (energize 的 ing 形式) 激励，激发，加强，使带电流，使通电，给予电压，供给能量，使活跃，给予精力，用力，活动
~ agent 催化剂，强化剂

~ circuit 励磁电路，激励电路
~ circuit relay 激励电路继电器
~ coil 励磁线圈
~ current 激励电流
~ impulse 激励脉冲
~ loop 激磁回路
~ lug 驱动用凸铁
~ spring 上紧弹簧
energy ['enədʒi] n. 精力，活力，能量，精神
~ capacity of battery 电池能量
~ chamber 气缸余隙容积，空气室
~ conservation 节能，能源节约，能量守恒
~ converter 能量转换器
~ efficient 能源效率
~ loss 能量损失，能量损耗
~ management system (EMS) 能源管理系统
~ of rotation 转动能，旋转能，自转动能
~ saving 能源节省，节能
~ saving device 节能装置
~ storage 能量储备，蓄能
~ storage capacitor 储能电容器
~ storing spring operating mechanism 储能弹簧工作机构
enforce [in'fɔ:s] v. 强迫，执行，坚持，加强
enforcement [in'fɔ:smənt] n. 强制，实施，执行
engage [in'geidʒ] v. 使忙碌，雇佣，预定，(使)从事，使参加，答应，交战，接合，啮合
~ on 开始(某种职业)
~ relay 接通继电器

engagement [in'geidʒmənt] *n.* 接合，约会，婚约，诺言，交战，雇佣

engine ['endʒin] *n.* 发动机，引擎，工具，机械装置，机车；*v.* 给…安装发动机

~ aft 艉机型船

~ and boiler room ventilation 发动机和锅炉房通风

~ and propeller characteristics 发动机和螺旋桨特性

~ bedplate 发动机底座板

~ block 发动机机体，发动机组

~ block heater 发动机缸体加热器

~ block stiffening rib 发动机缸体加强肋

~ bonnet 引擎罩，柴油机罩

~ cadet 轮机见习生，机舱学徒

~ capacity 发动机容量

~ camshaft 柴油机凸轮轴

~ casing 机舱围壁

~ component 引擎组件，发动机零部件，发动机部件

~ control room 机舱集控室

~ control system 发动机控制系统

~ coolant 发动机冷却液

~ cylinder 发动机汽缸

~ department 轮机部门

~ detail 发动机详图

~ displacement 发动机排量

~ frame 发动机机架

~ room hatchway 机舱口

~ health monitoring 发动机安全检查，发动机健康监测

~ hood 发动机罩

~ governor 发动机调速器

~ jacket cooling water 柴油机缸套冷却水

~ log book 机舱日志，轮机日志

~ manoeuvring stand 发动机操纵台

~ stability margin 发动机稳定性裕度

~ monitoring system 发动机监控系统

~ office 轮机部

~ oil 发动机机油，机油，引擎机油

~ orders 车令

~ telegraph order indicator 车钟指示器，车令指示器

~ output 发动机输出功率

~ parts 机件

~ performance 发动机性能

~ power 发动机功率

~ rating 发动机额定功率

~ room 机舱 ‖ *Syn*. machinery room 机舱；machinery space 机舱

~ room alarm system 机舱报警系统

~ room annunciator 机舱传令钟

~ room arrangement 机舱布置

~ room automation 机舱自动化

~ room auxiliary machine 机舱辅助机械，机舱辅机

~ room bilge 机舱舱底水

~ room bilge system 机舱舱底水系统

~ room emergency bilge suction valve 机舱应急舱底水吸入阀

~ room emergency bilge drainage valve 机舱应急舱底水排放阀

~ room fan 机舱通风机

~ room floor 机舱地板，机舱铺板

~ room frame 机舱肋骨

~ room hatch end beam 机舱口端梁

~ room ladder 机舱舷梯

~ room lighting system 机舱照明系统

~ room log book 机舱日志，轮机日志

~ room monitor alarm system 机舱监

测报警系统

~ room orders 机舱车钟指令，车令

~ room register 机舱登记簿

~ room simulator 机舱模拟器

~ room telegraph auto-shut-down device 机舱车钟自动停止装置

~ seating 发动机机座

~ scuffing 发动机拉缸

~ speed 发动机转速，引擎转速

~ speed recorder 发动机转速表

~ stopping 发动机停车

~ telegraph 机舱传令钟，车钟

~ telegraph alarm 车钟报警

~ telegraph logger 主机传令记录器

~ trials 发动机试验

engine-driven 发动机驱动的

~ compressor 发动机驱动的压缩机

~ cooling 发动机驱动制冷

~ generator 发动机驱动的发电机

~ high-pressure servo system 发动机驱动的高压伺服系统

~ pump 发动机驱动泵

~ supercharging 机械增压

engineer [ˌendʒi'niə] n. 工程师，技师，火车司机，轮机员，工兵；v. 建造，设计，策划，精明处理

~ in charge 主管工程师

~ in charge of the watch 负责值班的轮机员

~ in chief 总工程师

~ into 设计成为，制造成为

engineering [ˌendʒi'niəriŋ] n. 工程，工程学，工程技术，设计；v. (engineer 的 ing 形式) 建造，设计，策划，精明处理

~ accident 工程事故

~ drawing 工程图样，工程制图

~ qualitative accident 工程质量事故

~ ship 工程船

~ watch 机房值班人员

engrave [in'greiv] v. (使)铭记，雕刻，镌刻，深印于(心上)，印刷

engraving [in'greiviŋ] n. 雕刻，雕刻术，雕刻品；v. (engrave 的 ing 形式) 在…上雕刻，给…深刻的印象

~ machine 雕刻机，刻模机，带有缩放仪的平面仿形铣床

enhance [in'ha:ns] v. 加强，提高，增加 ‖ *Syn*. heighten 提高，升高；improve 提高，增进；increase 增加，加大；lift 升高，提高；raise 升起，提高；hoist 升起，吊起；upgrade 升级，提升

enhanced [in'ha:nst] v. (enhance 的过去式和过去分词) 加强，提高，增加；a. 增强的，提高的，放大的

~ survey programme (ESP) 加强检验计划

~ survey report file 加强检验报告文件

enlarge [in'la:dʒ] v. 扩大，放大，扩展，扩充，拉长说，详述

enlarged [in'la:dʒd] v. (enlarge 的过去式和过去分词) 扩大，放大，扩展，扩充，拉长说，详述；a. 放大的，增大的，扩展的

~ end 扩大端

~ link 加大环，加大链环

~ scale 放大比例尺，放大尺

~ view 放大图

enough [i'nʌf] n. 充足，足够，很多；a. 足够的，充足的，只够做…的；ad. 足够地，充足地；int. 够了！ ‖ *Syn*. adequate

207

适当的，足够的；sufficient 足够的，充足的，充分的

enquire [in'kwaiə] v. (=inquire) 询问，调查，问候，打听

enroute [a:n'ru:t] n. 在途中 a. 航路，在航，在途中，取道；ad. 在途中

~ to 在去…途中 ‖ **Syn**. enroute for 在去…途中

~ marker beacon 航线指点标

ensign ['ensain] n. 旗，船旗，国旗，海军少尉，(表示职别等的)徽章

~ staff 船尾旗杆

enter ['entə] n. 输入，回车进入；v. 进去，进入，登场，参加，开始，登记

~ into force 生效，实行

~ the water 入水

~ up 登记

enthalpy [en'θælpi] n. 焓，热函，热含量

entire [in'taiə] a. 整个的，全部的，全体的，囫囵的

entirely [in'taiəli] ad. 完全地，完整地，全部地，彻底地

entitlement [in'taitlmənt] n. 权利，授权，应得权益，命名，被定名

entity ['entiti] n. 实体，实际存在物，本质

entrain [in'trein] v. 乘火车，拖，拽，产生，流体带走，使空气以气泡状存在于混凝土中

entrained [in'treind] v. (entrain 的过去式和过去分词) 乘火车，拖，拽，产生，流体带走，使空气以气泡状存在于混凝土中；a. 裹入的，夹带的，带走的

~ air 裹入气，夹带空气

~ droplet 夹带液滴，夹带盐水

~ fluid 曳出流体

~ oil 带走的油

~ steam 残留蒸气

entrance [in'tra:ns] n. 进入，入口，进口，进入方法，进入方式，入场权；v. 使出神，使入迷，使喜悦，使狂喜

entry ['entri] n. 进入，入场，入口处，门口，登记，记录，条目，报关手续，侵占，侵入

~ instruction 进入指令，输入指令

~ point 入口点，进入点

enumerate [i,nju:mə'reit] v. 列举，枚举，数

enumeration [i,nju:mə'reiʃən] n. 计数，列举，细目，详表，点查

envelop [in'veləp] n. 包裹，封，包围，信封；v. 包围，包住，笼罩，遮盖

environment [in'vairənmənt] n. 环境，外界，周围，围绕，工作平台，(运行)环境 ‖ **Syn**. ambiance 周围环境，气氛；ambience 周围环境，气氛；ambient 周围环境；atmosphere 气氛；circumstances 环境；surroundings 环境

~ control 环境控制，环境管制，环境调控

~ protection 环境保护

~ variable 环境变数，环境变量

environmental [in,vairən'mentl] n. 环境论；a. 周围的，环境的，由个人环境产生的，环境艺术的

~ capacity 环境容量

~ condition 环境条件，环境状况

~ control 环境控制

~ load 环境荷载，环境载荷

~ monitoring 环境监测，环境监控

~ pollution 环境污染

~ protection 环境保护

~ Protection Agency (EPA) 环境保护署

~ protection policy 环保政策
~ Quality Program (EQP) 环境质量计划
~ testing 环境试验

environmentally [in,vaiərən'mentəli] ad. 有关环境方面地
~ sound technology 合乎环境要求的工艺

EPA (Environmental Protection Agency) 环境保护署

EPFS (Electronic Position Fixing System) 电子定位系统

EPIRB (emergency position-indicating radio beacon) 应急无线电示位标

epoch ['i:pɔk] n. 时期，纪元，世，新时代
~ angle 初相角

epoxy [i'pɔksi] n. 环氧基树脂; v. 用环氧树脂胶合; a. 环氧的
~ resin filled transformer 环氧浇注变压器
~ value 环氧值

eq-height 等高的
~ sleeves 等高套筒 ‖ Syn. eq-height spool 等高套筒

EQP (Environmental Quality Program) 环境质量计划

equal ['i:kwəl] n. 同样的人，相等的数量，能与之比拟的东西；v. 相等，相平，等于，比得上，使相等，同样看待；a. 相等的，平等的，平稳的，势均力敌的，胜任的
~ and opposite in direction 大小相等，方向相反
~ probability 等概率

equaliser ['i:kwəlaizə] n. (=equalizer) 平衡装置，均衡器，补偿器，凶器

equalize ['i:kwəlaiz] v. 补偿，使相等，使均衡，打成平局

equalizer ['i:kwəlaizər] n. (=equaliser) 平衡装置，均衡器，补偿器，凶器

equalizing ['i:kwəlaiziŋ] n. 平衡，补偿，调整; v. (equalize 的 ing 形式) (使)相等
~ anchor 均衡锚
~ bus-bar 均压母线
~ charge 均衡充电
~ circuit 均衡电路
~ components 平衡元件，补偿元件
~ phase 均等相
~ regulation 均功调节
~ ring 均衡环，均压环

equally ['i:kwəli] ad. 平均，相等地，平等地，公正地

equate [i'kweit] v. 等同，使相等，相当于

equation [i'kweiʒn] n. 方程式，等式，相等，反应式
~ of state of gas 气体状态方程

equidistant [,i:kwi'distənt] a. 距离相等的，等距的

equilibria [i:kwi'libriə] n. (equilibrium 的复数) 均衡，均势，平衡，均势，(心情、感情等)平静

equilibrium [,i:kwi'libriəm] n. (pl. equilibria) 平衡，均势，平静
~ constant 平衡常数，平衡恒量
~ growth 均衡增长
~ point 平衡点

equip [i'kwip] v. 装备，配备，使具备，使有准备

equipment [i'kwipmənt] n. 设备，装备，

器材，配件，(工作必需的)知识，素养 ‖ *Syn*. apparatus 器械，设备，仪器；appliance 用具，器具；arrangement 布置；assembly 组装部件；device 装置，设备；facility 设备，工具；furniture 设备，家具；gear 设备，装备；installation 设备,装置；machine 机器，机械，机构；machinery 机械(总称)，机器；mechanism 机器，机械装置，机构；plant 设备；provision 装备，供应品；turnout 装备，设备；unit 装置，设备

~ for collision avoidance 避碰装置

~ maintenance 设备维修保养

~ management 装备管理

~ number 设备号

~ replacement 设备更新

equivalent [i'kwivələnt] *n*. 等价物，相等物；*a*. 等价的，相等的，同意义的

~ circuit 等效电路

~ inertia 当量惯量

~ series resistance (ESR) 等效串联电阻

~ T-circuit 等效 T 型电路

erasable [i'reisəbl] *a*. 可消除的，可抹去的，使被忘却的

~ optical disk 可擦光盘

erase [i'reiz] *v*. 抹去，擦掉，消磁，杀死

erasure [i'reiʒə] *n*. 擦掉,删去,删掉的词，消音，抹音

erect [i'rekt] *v*. 建造，建立，开创，举起，(使)竖立,(使)直立，勃起；*a*. 直立的，竖立的，笔直的，垂直的，僵硬的 ‖ *Syn*. build 建造，建筑，创立；construct 建造，构造，创立；form 形成，构成，塑造；make 制造，构造；put up 建造

erection [i'rekʃən] *n*. 直立，竖起，建立，建造，建筑物，勃起

erector [i'rektə] *n*. 安装工，建设者

erode [i'rəud] *v*. 侵蚀，腐蚀，使变化，受腐蚀，逐渐消蚀掉

erose [i'rəus] *a*. 不规则形状的，不整齐牙齿状的，啮蚀状的，凹凸齿状的

erosion [i'rəuʒən] *n*. 腐蚀，侵蚀

~ corrosion 侵蚀腐蚀

~ hole 冲蚀坑

~ resistance 抗腐蚀性

erosive [i'rəusiv] *a*. 侵蚀性的，腐蚀性的

erratic [i'rætik] *n*. 古怪的人，漂泊无定的人；*a*. 无确定路线的，不稳定的，无规律的，奇怪的，反复无常的，不规则的

erratically [i'rætikəli] *ad*. 不规律地，不定地

erroneous [i'rəunjəs] *a*. 错误的，不正确的

erroneously [i'rəunjəsli] *ad*. 错误地，不正确地

error ['erə] *n*. 错误，过失，误审，违法，误差

~ analysis 误差分析

~ control technique 误差控制技术

~ correction 纠错，数据纠正

~ correction ability 纠错能力

~ curve 误差曲线

~ detection 误差检测，检错

~ detector 错误检测器，误差检测器，检错器

~ function 误差函数

~ rate 误码率，出错率
~ regulation 误差调节
~ signal 误差信号
escape [is'keip] n. 逃，逃亡，溢出设备，出口，逃跑，野生；v. 逃脱，避开，溜走，逃避，避免，被忘掉
~ breathing apparatus 逃生呼吸设备
~ exit 安全出口，紧急出口
~ from 逃脱
~ hatch 逃生舱口，安全舱口
~ route 脱险通道，疏散路线
~ system 避难系统，逃生系统
~ trunk 潜水艇逃生舱，应急出口，救生口
~ valve 安全阀，放汽阀
escort [is'kɔ:t] n. 护航舰，护航机，护卫队，伴随者，护送者，护卫，护航，护送，陪同(人员)；v. 护卫，护航，护送，陪同
~ carrier 护航航空母舰
~ destroyer 护航驱逐舰
~ minesweeper 护航扫雷艇
~ ship 护航舰艇，护航船 ‖ *Syn*. escort vessel 护航舰艇，护航船
~ tug 护航用拖船
ESD (electrostatic discharge) 静电放电
~ rating 防静电放电等级
ESP (enhanced survey programme) 加强检验计划
especially [is'peʃəli] ad. 尤其地，主要地，格外地，显著地，异常地
ESR (equivalent series resistance) 等效串联电阻
essence ['esns] n. 基本，本质，实质，精华，精髓，香精
essential [i'senʃəl] n. 本质，实质，要素，要点；a. 本质的，实质的，基本的，提炼的，精华的
~ component 主要成分
~ condition 必备条件，主要条件
~ difference 本质区别
~ element 必需元素，主要元素
~ equipment 关键设备，重要设备
~ goods 必需品，主要货物
~ parameter 基本参数，本质参数
~ requirements 基本要求，基本规范
essentially [i'senʃəli] ad. 本质上地，根本上地，本来地
establish [is'tæbliʃ] v. 建立，设立，安置，制定，确定，使定居，使人民接受
establishment [is'tæbliʃmənt] n. 确立，制定，设施，公司，军事组织
estimate ['estimeit] n. 估计，预测，报价，预算书，评价，判断；v. 估计，估算，评估，评价，评论，估量，估价 ‖ *Syn*. forecast 预言，预测，预报；predict 预言，预测，预报
estimated ['estimitid] v. (estimate 的过去式和过去分词) 估计，估算，评估，评价，评论，估量，估价；a. 估计的，估算的，预计的
~ amount 预计金额
~ cost 预算造价，估计成本
~ price 估计价格
~ time 预定期间，预计时间
~ time of arrival (ETA) 预计到达时间
~ time of departure (ETD) 预计离港时间
estimation [esti'meiʃən] n. 估计，估算，预算，估量，评价，判断，尊重 ‖ *Syn*. forecasting 预言，预测，预报；prediction 预言，预测，预报

estuary ['estjuəri] *n.* 港湾，海湾，河口，江口

ETA (estimated time of arrival) 预计到达时间

etch [etʃ] *v.* 蚀刻，侵蚀，刻画，描述，铭记

ETD (estimated time of departure) 预计离港时间

ETS (emergency trip system) 紧急跳闸系统，危急跳闸系统

Europe ['juərəp] *n.* 欧洲

evacuate [i'vækjueit] *v.* 疏散，撤退，撤空，排空，抽空，腾出，搬出，使空，倒空

evacuator [i'vækjueitə] *n.* 撤退的人，排除用具

evacuation [i,vækju'eiʃən] *n.* 疏散，撤离，撤退，撤空，走开
- ~ from the ship 从船上撤离
- ~ method 疏散方法，撤离方法
- ~ of safety 安全疏散，安全撤离
- ~ policy 疏散策略，撤离策略
- ~ pump 真空泵
- ~ route 避难方向，疏散路线，撤离路线
- ~ signal 疏散信号
- ~ site 疏散点，紧急疏散地
- ~ time 疏散时间，撤离时间，排气时间

evade [i'veid] *v.* 规避，避开，逃脱，逃避，躲避，逃税

evaluate [i'væljueit] *v.* 评价，求…的值，对…评价，评价，估价

evaluation [i,vælju'eiʃən] *n.* 估价，赋值，估计价值，诊断
- ~ technique 评价技术，评价方法

Evan ['evən] *n.* 埃文(人名)
- ~ evaporation 埃文蒸发

evaporate [i'væpəreit] *v.* (使)脱水，(使)蒸发，(使)挥发，(使)沉淀，消失，发散气体

evaporating [i'væpəreitiŋ] *v.* (evaporate 的 ing 形式) (使)脱水，(使)蒸发，(使)挥发，(使)沉淀，消失，发散气体；*a.* 蒸发用的，蒸发作用的
- ~ coil 蒸发盘管，蒸发蛇管
- ~ pressure 蒸发压力
- ~ property 蒸发特性
- ~ surface 蒸发表面，蒸发面
- ~ technology 蒸发技术
- ~ temperature 蒸发温度
- ~ tube 蒸发管

evaporation [i,væpə'reiʃən] *n.* 蒸发，蒸发作用
- ~ capacity 蒸发量，蒸发(容)量，蒸发能力
- ~ chamber 蒸发室
- ~ coefficient 蒸发系数
- ~ fog 蒸发雾
- ~ heat 蒸发热
- ~ rate 蒸发率，蒸发速度，蒸发速率

evaporative [i'væpərətiv] *a.* 成为蒸气的，蒸发的
- ~ condenser 蒸发式冷凝器
- ~ cooler 蒸发冷却器

evaporator [i'væpəreitə] *n.* 蒸发器，脱水器
- ~ capacity 蒸发器容量
- ~ coil 蒸发器盘管
- ~ coil over-feed 蒸发器盘管流量过大，蒸发器旋管流量过大，蒸发器蛇形管流量过大

~ core 蒸发器芯

~ pressure regulator 蒸发器自动调压器，蒸发器自动调压器压力调节器

~ tube bank 蒸发管束

~ water treatment 蒸发器水处理

~ with handle 带柄蒸发器

~ superheat 蒸发器过热

even ['i:vn] *n.* 偶数，偶校验；*v.* 使平坦，使相等，变平，相等；*a.* 平的，平滑的，偶数的，一致的，平静的，恰好的，平均的，连贯的；*ad.* 甚至…也，连…都，即使，恰好，正当

~ ballast pump 均匀压载泵

~ distribution 均匀分布

~ if 哪怕，虽然，即使，纵然，即若

~ keel 等吃水，平吃水，平载

~ length code 均匀电码

~ number 偶数 ‖ odd number 奇数

~ out 变平，(使)平稳，(使)均衡

~ pressure 均匀压力，均压

~ so 虽然如此，即使如此

~ up 使相等，拉平，结算账目，清算

evenly ['i:vnli] *ad.* 均匀地，平均地，平坦地

event [i'vent] *n.* 事件，事变，结果，活动，精力，竞赛

eventual [i'ventjuəl] *a.* 可能的，最后的，结局的，万一的，终于的

eventually [i'ventjuəli] *ad.* 终究，终于，最后

ever ['evə] *ad.* 曾经，永远，不断地，在任何时候，究竟

~ so 极其，非常

every ['evri] *a.* 每一的，每个的，全部的，每隔…的

~ single day 每一天

evidence ['evidəns] *n.* 明显，显著，明白，迹象，根据，证据，证词，证物；*v.* 表明，证实，证明

evident ['evidənt] *a.* 明显的，明白的

evolute ['i:vəlu:t] *n.* 渐屈线

evolution [,i:və'lu:ʃən] *n.* 进展，发展，演变，进化

evolve [i'vɔlv] *v.* (使)发展，(使)进展，(使)进化

ex [eks] *n.* 前妻，前夫；*prep.* 不包括，无权得到

~ post facto 事后地，追溯地

~ post facto analysis 事后分析

exact [ig'zækt] *v.* 要求，急需，苛求，迫使，强求；*a.* 精确的，准确的，原样的，精密的，严格的

exactly [ig'zæktli] *ad.* 恰恰地，确切地，正确地，精确地，完全地

exactness [ig'zæktnis] *n.* 正确，精确

examination [ig,zæmi'neiʃən] *n.* 考试，检查，细查，询问，审问

examine [ig'zæmin] *v.* 检查，调查，考试，研究，分析，诊察，审问，讯问 ‖ ***Syn.*** censor 检查，审查；check 检查，核对；inspect 检查，视察；review 检查，检阅；rummage 搜出，检查

exceed [ik'si:d] *v.* 超过，超越，胜过，突出，领先，越过…的界限

excellence ['eksələns] *n.* 优点，优秀，卓越，美德

excellent ['eksələnt] *a.* 优秀的，卓越的，杰出的，太好了

~ quality 优等品质

excess [ik'ses] *n.* 超过，超额量，多余量，放肆；*a.* 超重的，过量的，额外的

213

~ air 过量空气

~ air coefficient 过量空气系数

~ air ratio 过量空气系数

~ heat 余热

~ load 超负荷，过负载，超荷载，逾量荷载

~ pore pressure 超孔隙压力

~ temperature 超温，过温度

~ voltage 过电压

excessive [ik'sesiv] *a.* 过多的，过分的，过度的，极度的

~ clearance 过量余隙

~ consumption 过度消耗，超前消费

~ demand 过剩需求，过量需求，需求过旺

~ feed water temperature 给水温度过高

~ pressure 超量压力，超压

~ speed 超速

~ viscosity 过大的黏度

~ wear 过度磨损

excessively [ik'sesivli] *ad.* 过分地，过度地，极度地

exchange [iks'tʃeindʒ] *n.* 交换，调换，兑换，交流，交易；*v.* 交换，调换，兑换，交流，交易，互换，代换，退还，汇票，汇率

exchange-compression 换气压缩

~ stroke 换气压缩行程

exchanger [iks'tʃeindʒə] *n.* 交换器，交换机，交换剂，换热器，放热器，散热器

excitation [,eksai'teiʃən] *n.* 激发，激动，励磁，(由刺激引起的器官、组织等)应激反应

~ circuit 激磁电路，激励电路，励磁电路，触发电路

~ current 激磁电流，励磁电流

~ generator 激磁发电机，励磁发电机

~ power 激磁功率，励磁功率

~ regulation 励磁调节，励磁控制

~ regulator 激磁调节器，激磁控制器，励磁调节器，励磁控制器

~ system 激磁系统，励磁系统

~ voltage 激励电压，励磁电压

~ winding 激磁绕组，励磁绕组

excite [ik'sait] *v.* 激发，刺激，(使)兴奋，(使)紧张不安

exciter [ik'saitə] *n.* 励磁器，主控振荡器，刺激者，激励者，刺激物，兴奋剂

~ bulb 激励灯

~ lamp 激励灯

~ winding 激励器绕组

~ field winding insulation 励磁器磁场绕组绝缘

exciting [ik'saitiŋ] *v.* (excite 的 ing 形式)刺激；*a.* 使人兴奋的，令人激动的

~ current 激励电流，励磁电流

~ field 激磁场，励磁场

~ force 激振力，激发力

~ force moment 励磁力矩

~ voltage 激磁电压，励磁电压

~ winding 励磁绕组，激励线圈

exclusive [iks'klu:siv] *n.* 专有权，独家新闻，专有物，独家经营的产品；*a.* 排外的，孤高的，唯我独尊的，独占的，专有的，唯一的，完整的，高级的

excrement ['ekskrimənt] *n.* 屎，排泄物，粪便

excrete [eks'kri:t] *v.* 排泄，分泌，排出

excursion [iks'kə:ʃən] *n.* 偏移，漂移，行程，远足，游览，短程旅行，远足队，离题

execute ['eksikju:t] *v.* 执行，实行，完成，处死，制成，生效 ‖ ***Syn***. carry out 完成，执行；implement 贯彻，执行

execution [ˌeksi'kju:ʃən] *n.* 实行，完成，执行，死刑，制作，破坏效果，杀伤力

executive [ig'zekjətiv] *n.* 执行者，管理人员，经理，主管人员，行政部门；*a.* 实行的，执行的，行政的

~ circuit 执行电路

~ element 执行元件

exempt [ig'zempt] *v.* 免除，豁免；*a.* 被免除的，被豁免的

~ from 被豁免，被免除

exemption [ig'zempʃən] *n.* 解除，免除，免税

~ certificate 免除证书

~ condition 豁免条件

~ right 豁免权利

~ status 豁免地位

exert [ig'zə:t] *v.* 努力，竭尽全力，施加(压力等)，发挥

exhaust [ig'zɔ:st] *n.* 排气，废气，排气装置；*v.* 排出，排气，耗尽，使精疲力尽，彻底探讨；*a.* 用不完的，不会枯竭的

~ air 排气，废气

~ boiler 废气锅炉，废热锅炉

~ branch 排气支管

~ cam 排气凸轮

~ cam box 排气凸轮箱

~ duct 排风管

~ emission 废气排放

~ fan 排气风扇，抽风机

~ fume 排烟，废气

~ gas 废气

~ gas boiler 排气锅炉，废气锅炉

~ gas emission 尾气排放

~ gas line 废气管线

~ gas outlet 废气出口

~ gas receiver 排气汇集器

~ gas recirculation 废气再循环

~ gas regulating valve 排气调节阀

~ gas silencer 废气消音器

~ gas system 排气系统

~ gas treatment by catalyst 废气经催化剂处理

~ gas turbocharger 废气涡轮增压器

~ heat 废热

~ hole 排气孔

~ hood 排风罩

~ manifold 排气集管，排气音管，排气歧管

~ mission 废气排放，尾气排放

~ muffler 排气消声器 ‖ ***Syn***. exhaust silencer 排气消声器

~ noise 排气噪声

~ nozzle 排气喷管，喷口

~ opening 排气口

~ outlet 排气口，排风口

~ pipe 排气管

~ port 排气口，排出孔

~ pressure 排出压力

~ purifier 废气净化器

~ side 排气侧

~ smoke 排烟

~ smoke density 排烟浓度

~ stack 排气烟囱，废气烟囱，排气烟囱

~ steam 排出蒸汽(排汽)，废蒸汽

~ stroke 排气冲程，排气行程

~ system 排气系统

215

~ temperature 排气温度
~ turbine 废气涡轮
~ turbine generating set 废气涡轮发电机组
~ turbo compound system 废气涡轮复合系统
~ turbocharger 废气涡轮增压器
~ turbocharging 废气涡轮增压
~ valve 排气阀，排气门
~ valve cage 排气阀组件
~ valve guide 排气阀导管
~ valve lifter 排气阀挺杆
~ valve pin 排气阀销
~ valve regulation 排气阀调整
~ valve spindle 排气阀轴
~ valve spring 排气阀弹簧
~ valve tappet 排气阀挺杆
~ valve cap 排气阀盖
~ ventilation 排气通风，抽出式通风
~ whistle 排气笛

exhauster [ig'zɔːstə] *n.* 排气机，抽风机，进气通风机，排气装置
~ governor 真空泵调压器

exist [ig'zist] *v.* 存在，生存，生活，继续存在

existing [ig'zistiŋ] *v.* (exist 的 ing 形式) 存在，生存，生活，继续存在；*a.* 现存的，现有的
~ ship 现有船舶
~ state 现状

exit ['eksit] *n.* 出口，太平门，退场，去世；*v.* 退出，脱离，去世
~ direction sign 出口方向标志
~ point 出口点
~ sign 出口标志
~ the water 上岸

expand [iks'pænd] *v.* 张开，发展，展开，使膨胀，详述，扩张

expanded [iks'pændid] *v.* (expand 的过去式和过去分词) 张开，发展，展开，膨胀，详述，扩张；*a.* 膨胀的，扩大的，扩张的，延伸的，展开的，张开的
~ blade area 延伸的叶片面积
~ bracket 延伸肘板

expansion [iks'pænʃən] *n.* 扩张，扩大，扩张物，膨胀物，辽阔，浩瀚
~ agent 膨胀剂
~ card 扩充插件板，扩充插件卡
~ joint 伸缩接头，伸缩节，补偿节，膨胀节，膨胀缝，补偿器
~ pipe 伸缩管
~ plug 臌胀塞
~ rate 膨胀率，扩充率
~ ratio 扩张度，膨胀比，膨胀比率
~ stroke 膨胀冲程
~ tank 膨胀水箱，膨胀水柜
~ tank atmospheric ventilation 膨胀水柜通风
~ trunk (油船)膨胀深井
~ valve 膨胀阀，安全阀
~ valve regulator 膨胀阀调节器，膨胀阀控制器

expansion-exchange 膨胀换气
~ stroke 膨胀换气冲程

expect [iks'pekt] *v.* 期望，预料，要求，认为，期待，预期，怀胎

expected [iks'pektid] *v.* (expect 的过去式和过去分词) 期望，预料，要求，认为，期待；*a.* (用作定语)预期要发生的，期待中的
~ characteristics 期望特性
~ life 预期寿命，预期耐用年限，预估寿命

expel [iks'pel] v. 驱逐，开除，排出，发射

expense [iks'pens] n. 费用，代价，损失，开支，费钱之物；v. 向…收取费用，把…作为开支勾销

expensive [iks'pensiv] a. 昂贵的，花钱多的，豪华的 ‖ *Ant*. cheap 便宜的

experience [iks'piəriəns] n. 经验，体验，经历，阅历；v. 经验，体验，经历，阅历

experienced [iks'piəriənst] v. (experience 的过去式和过去分词) 经验，体验，经历，阅历；a. 有阅历的，有见识的，老练的，熟练的，有经验的，有丰富经验的

~ operator 有经验的操作者，熟练工

experiment [iks'perimənt] n. 尝试，实验，试验；v. 尝试，做实验，进行试验

experimental [iks,peri'mentl] a. 实验的，根据实验的，试验性的

~ data 实验数据，经验数据

~ precision 试验精度，实验精度

experimentally [iksperi'mentəli] ad. 实验(性)地，实际上，实践证明，通过实验，用实验方法

expert ['ekspə:t] n. 专家，行家，能手，(特等)射手；v. 当专家，在…中当行家；a. 熟练的，内行的，老练的

expertise [,ekspə:'ti:z] n. 专门技能，专门知识，专门知识，专家鉴定

expiration [,ekspaiə'reiʃən] n. 满期，呼出，呼气，终止

~ date 截止日期，产品有效期

expire [iks'paiə] v. 期满，终止，呼气，断气，届满

expiry [iks'paiəri] n. 满期，呼气，终了，终结

explode [iks'pləud] v. 爆发，爆炸，发怒，激增，迅速扩大，推翻，驳倒

exploded [ik'spləudid] v. (explode 的过去式和过去分词) 爆发，爆炸，发怒，激增，迅速扩大，推翻，驳倒；a. 爆炸了的，分解的，被破除的

~ drawing 爆炸图，零件分散图，爆炸图

explore [iks'plɔ:] v. 探索，探究，钻研，研究，考察，仔细查看，勘查，探测，勘探，探查(伤处等)

~ diving 体验潜水

explosibility [iks,pləuzə'biləti] n. 可爆性，可爆炸，容易爆炸

explosion [iks'pləuʒən] n. 爆发，爆炸，炸裂，扩张，激增，(感情，尤指愤怒的)突然爆发

~ chamber 灭弧箱，燃烧室

~ detector 爆炸探测器

~ protection 防爆(装置)

~ protection system 防爆系统

~ stroke 膨胀冲程，爆发冲程

~ suppressant 抑爆剂

~ suppression 隔爆，爆炸抑制

explosion-proof 防爆的，隔爆的

~ equipment 防爆设备 ‖ *Syn*. flame-proof equipment 防爆设备

~ fan 防爆风机

~ lamp 防爆灯 ‖ *Syn*. explosion-proof light 防爆灯

~ lighting fitting 防爆照明配件

~ lighting switch 防爆照明开关

~ motor 防爆马达，防爆电动机

explosive [iks'pləusiv] n. 爆炸物，炸药，爆破音；a. 爆炸的，易爆炸的，突增的，暴躁的

~ accident 爆炸事故

~ gas 易爆气，爆炸气，爆炸性气体

~ material 易爆材料

~ mixture 爆炸混合物

explosively [iks'pləusivli] ad. 爆发地，引起爆炸地

exponent [eks'pəunənt] n. 解释者，说明者，代表者，拥护者，示范者，倡导者，典型，指数；a. 说明的，讲解的，阐述的，说明的

exponential [,ekspəu'nenʃəl] n. 指数，倡导者，演奏者，例子，指数；a. 指数的，幂数的

~ lag 指数滞后

export ['ekspɔ:t] n. 出口货，输出，出口，出口商品；v. 输出，出口

~ packing 出口包装

exporter [iks'pɔ:tə] n. 出口商，输出者，输出国

expose [iks'pəuz] v. 揭露，揭发，使暴露，使遭受，使曝光

exposed [iks'pəuzd] v. (expose 的过去式和过去分词) 暴露，揭露，揭发；a. 暴露的，暴露于风雨中的，无掩蔽的

~ area 外露面积，气流浸润面积

exposure [iks'pəuʒə] n. 暴露，揭露，曝光，揭发，揭露，位向，方向，陈列

~ hazard 暴露危险

expulsion [iks'pʌlʃən] n. 驱逐，开除，排出，喷出

~ gap 冲出式熔丝保护放电器

~ of arc 弧的吹熄

expunge [eks'pʌndʒ] v. 除去，删去，擦掉，消除

extend [iks'tend] v. 扩充，延伸，伸展，扩大，使疏开，给予，提供，演化出的全文，对(地产等)估价

extended [iks'tendid] v. (extend 的过去式和过去分词) 延长，伸展，延伸，扩大，给予，提供；a. 延伸的，延长的，伸展的，扩大的

~ aeration process (废水处理的)充分曝气过程

extension [iks'tenʃən] n. 伸展，扩大，延长，延期，牵引，电话分机，扩展名；a. 外延的，客观现实的

~ alarm 延伸报警

~ cord 延长线，延长电线，延展线

~ line 延长线，分机线

~ set 增设装置，(电话)分机

~ spring 牵引簧，拉伸弹簧

~ telephone 电话分机

extensive [iks'tensiv] a. 广阔的，广大的，范围广泛的，广延的，外延的

~ repair 大修理，大修

extensively [iks'tensivli] ad. 广大地，广泛地

extent [iks'tent] n. 广度，宽度，长度，范围，程度，区域，扣押，临时所有权令

~ of damage 受损程度，受损失程度

exterior [eks'tiəriə] n. 外部，外面，表面，外形，外观，外貌，外景，户外布景；a. 外部的，外在的，表面的，外交的，外用的 ‖ Syn. external 外部的，外用的，外国的，表面的；outer 外部的，外面的，远离中心的 ‖ Ant. interior 内部的，国内的，内陆的，本质的；internal 内部的，内在的，国内的，内政的

external [eks'tə:nl] n. 外部，外面，外观，外部情况；a. 外面的，外部的，表面

上的，外用的，外国的 ‖ **Syn**. exterior 外部的，外在的，表面的，外交的，外用的；outer 外部的，外面的，远离中心的 ‖ **Ant**. interior 内部的，国内的，内陆的，本质的；internal 内部的，内在的，国内的，内政的

~ armature circuit 电枢外电路
~ bus 外部总线
~ characteristic 外(部)特性(曲线)，动态特性
~ characteristic curve 外特性曲线
~ circuit 外电路
~ combustion engine 外燃机
~ diameter 外径
~ dimensions 外形尺寸
~ disturbance 外界干扰
~ force 外力
~ gear 外齿轮
~ grinding 外圆磨削
~ insulation 外绝缘
~ magnetic field 外部磁场
~ malfunction 外部故障
~ pump gear 外部泵齿轮
~ ramp switch 外部接线端钮开关
~ relief valve 外部安全阀
~ signal 外部信号
~ work 外功

externally [iks'tə:nəli] *ad*. 在(或从)外部，在(或从)外面，外表上

extinguish [iks'tiŋgwiʃ] *v*. 熄灭，消灭，压制，使黯然失色，偿清

extinguisher [iks'tiŋgwiʃə(r)] *n*. 灭火器，熄灭者 ‖ **Syn**. FIREX 灭火器；fire annihilator 灭火器；fire apparatus 灭火器；fire extinguisher 灭火器；flame arrester 火焰清除器

~ voltage 灭火器电压

extinguishing [iks'tiŋgwiʃiŋ] *n*. 熄灭，消灭；*v*. (extinguish 的 ing 形式) 熄灭，消灭，压制，使黯然失色，偿清

~ action 灭火作用
~ agent 灭火剂 ‖ **Syn**. fire extinguishing agent 灭火剂；fire extinguishing medium 灭火介质；fire fighting agent 灭火剂；fire proofing agent 阻燃剂，防燃剂；fire retardancy 阻燃剂；fire retarding agent 防火剂，阻燃剂，耐火剂；fire suppressant 灭火剂；flame retardant 阻燃剂，阻燃物，灭火剂

extinguishment [iks'tiŋgwiʃmənt] *n*. 消灭，绝灭

extra ['ekstrə] *n*. 额外的人(或物)，(报纸)号外，上等产品，(电影)临时演员；*a*. 额外的，不包括在价目内的，特大的，特佳的；*ad*. 特别，非常，另外

~ allowance 特别津贴
~ appliance 额外设备

extract [iks'trækt] *n*. 精，汁，榨出物，摘录，选粹；*v*. 拔出，榨取，开方，求根，摘录，析取，吸取

extraction [iks'trækʃən] *n*. 抽出，取出，提取，萃取法，抽出物，摘要，血统，开方(法)

~ agent 提炼剂，萃取剂
~ pipe 抽气管
~ solvent 萃取溶剂
~ steam 抽汽
~ turbine 抽汽式汽轮机，抽汽式涡轮机

extraordinary [iks'trɔ:dnri] *a*. 非常的，特别的，非凡的，特派的

~ repairs 特别修缮费

extrapolate [eks'træpəleit] v. 推算，推断，外推

extrapolation [ˌekstrəpəu'leiʃən] n. 推断，外推(法)

extreme [ik'stri:m] n. 极端，困境，极限值，在两末端的事物(extremes)；a. 极端的，过激的，极限的，非常的，末端的，(政治上)激进的

~ breadth 最大宽度

~ draught 最大吃水

~ elevation 最大仰角，最大高度

~ environment 极限环境

~ length 最大长度

~ manoeuvre 极限操纵

~ point 极值点，满点，端点

~ position 极限位置

~ pressure 极端压力，极限压力，特压

~ temperature 极端温度，极限温度

~ value 极端值，极值

extremely [iks'tri:mli] ad. 极端地，非常，很

~ low frequency (ELF) 极低频

extremity [iks'tremiti] n. 末端，极端，极度，穷困，绝境，临死，非常手段，手足

eye [ai] n. 眼睛，视力，眼状物，风纪扣扣眼；v. 定睛地看，注视，审视，细看，打眼

~ bolt 环眼螺栓，有眼螺栓，螺丝圈

~ plate 眼板，吊环板

~ protector 护目镜

~ bolt rivet 有眼螺栓铆钉

~ of impeller 叶轮中心

~ nut 吊环螺母

~ brows 眉毛，(喷燃器的)眉状结焦，滴水，窗眉，(屋顶)波形老虎窗

F

fabric ['fæbrik] n. 织品，织物，布，结构，建筑物，构造

fabricate ['fæbrikeit] v. 制造，生产，加工，捏造，伪造，虚构，装配

~ and install according to the existing one 根据现有产品进行生产和安装

~ block 预制分段，组合体，组合船段

fabricated ['fæbrikeitid] v. (fabricate 的过去式和过去分词) 制造，加工，编造，伪造，建造；a. 编造的，捏造的，装配式的

~ bedplate 焊接式底座，结构式底座

~ bow 钢板焊接船首

~ ship 分段装配船

~ steel 结构钢

fabrication [ˌfæbri'keiʃən] n. 制作，构成，伪造物，装配工

~ cost 造价

~ facility 加工设施，建造设施

~ plant 加工厂，加工设备

~ procedure 制造工序，加工工艺，制造流程

~ processing 工艺处理

~ shop 制造工厂，加工工厂

face [feis] n. 脸，表面，面子，面容，外观，威信；v. 面对，面向，朝向，承认，抹盖

~ guard 护脸，护面罩

~ mask 面罩

~ off machine 使机器的表面平滑

~ piece 面具，面印模罩，面罩

~ pitch 面螺距

~ plate 划线平台，划线平板

~ seal 端面密封

~ shield 面罩

facet ['fæsit] *n.* (多面体的)面，(宝石等的)刻面，小平面，方面，琢面；*v.* 在…上刻画

facilitate [fə'siliteit] *v.* 使容易，使便利，推动，帮助，促进

facility [fə'siliti] *n.* 容易，简易，灵巧，熟练，便利，敏捷，设备，工具 ‖ ***Syn.*** apparatus 器械，设备，仪器；appliance 用具，器具；arrangement 布置；assembly 组装部件；device 装置，设备；equipment 装备，设备，器材，装置；furniture 设备，家具；gear 设备，装备；installation 设备，装置；machine 机器，机械，机构；machinery 机械(总称)，机器；mechanism 机器，机械装置，机构；plant 设备；provision 装备，供应品；turnout 装备，设备；unit 装置，设备

facing ['feisiŋ] *n.* 饰面，覆盖(如墙壁的)表面的覆饰，(衣服的)贴边；*v.* (face 的 ing 形式) 面对，面向，朝向，承认，抹盖

~ finish (法兰)面加工

~ head 回转刀架

facsimile [fæk'simili] *n.* 摹写，传真

fact [fækt] *n.* 实际，事实，实情，真相，证据，犯罪行为

facto ['fæktəu] *n.* 事实上，实际上

factor ['fæktə] *n.* 因素，要素，因数，系数，代理人；*v.* 把…作为因素计入，代理经营，把…分解成，做代理商

~ in 包括，把…计算在内

~ of safety 安全系数 ‖ ***Syn.*** assurance factor 安全系数；coefficient of safety 安全系数；safety coefficient 安全系数；safety factor 安全系数

FACTS (flexible AC transmission system) 柔性交流输电系统

Fahrenheit ['færənhait] *n.* 华氏温度计，华氏温标；*a.* 华氏温度计的，华氏的

fail [feil] *n.* 不及格；*v.* 不及格，使失望，忘记，舍弃，失败，破产，缺乏，衰退

~ safe 故障安全，失效保护，差错防止

~ to start and shutdown 无法启动和关闭

fail-safe 故障安全的，有安全保障的

~ system 故障安全系统

failure ['feiljə] *n.* 失灵，故障，失败，失败者，缺乏，破产，疏忽，不及格 ‖ ***Syn.*** dysfunction 机能不良，功能紊乱，官能障碍；fault 故障；out of order 次序颠倒，不整齐，状态不好；trouble 故障

~ button 故障按钮

~ diagnosis 故障诊断，失效诊断

~ mode and effect analysis 故障模式和影响分析

~ of insulation 绝缘失效

~ monitoring 故障监控

~ rate 故障率，失效率，失误率

failure-safe 故障安全

~ device 故障安全装置，故障自动排除装置

fair [fɛə] *n.* 展览会，市集，美人，美好的事物；*v.* 转晴；*a.* 美丽的，女性的，(肤色)白皙的，(头发)金黄的，干净的，公平的，(天气)晴朗的；*ad.* 公平地，公正地，直接地，清楚地

fairlead ['fɛəli:d] *n.* (=fairleader) 导缆孔，导缆器

fairleader ['fɛəli:də] n. (=fairlead) 导缆孔，导缆器

fairway ['fɛə,wei] n. 航路，水上跑道，(高尔夫球场上的)平坦球道

~ buoy 航标

~ speed 航路速度，航道航速

fall [fɔ:l] n. 秋天，落下，瀑布，减少；v. 跌倒，落下，减少，沦陷

~ out 争吵，结果，解散，掉队

falling ['fɔ:liŋ] n. 下降，坠落，落下，陷落；v. (fall 的 ing 形式) 降低，来临，成为，降落；a. 落下的，下降的

~ film evaporator 降膜式蒸发器

false [fɔ:ls] a. 错误的，虚伪的，假的，无信义的，伪造的，人工的，不老实的；ad. 欺诈地

~ action 假动作

~ alarm 假警报

~ alarm of fire 误报火警

~ alarm rate 虚警率，误报警率，报警失误率

~ touching 误碰

~ tripping 误跳，误脱扣

fan [fæn] n. 扇子，风扇，迷，粉丝，扇形物，扬谷机；v. 扇动，吹拂，扬去，成扇形

~ belt 风扇皮带

~ blade 风机叶片

~ hub 风机轮毂

~ motor 风扇电动机，风扇马达，风扇电机

~ pulley 风机皮带轮

~ shaft bearing 风机轴轴承

~ speed regulator switch 风扇变速开关

fan-cooled 风冷的

~ machine 风冷机械

~ motor 风冷马达，风冷电动机

~ radiator 风冷散热器

~ type induction motor 风冷式感应电动机

fast [fa:st] n. 斋戒，绝食；a. 快速的，迅速的，紧的，稳固的；ad. 迅速地，紧紧地，彻底地

~ acting fuse 快速熔断器

~ acting proportional control valve 快速作用比例控制阀，快动比例控制阀

~ acting valve 快速作用阀，快动阀

~ algorithm 快速算法

~ charging 快速充电，急速充气

~ ferry 快船，快速渡船

~ moving object 快速移动的物体，快速移动目标

~ rescue boat (FRB) 快速救助艇 ‖ *Syn*. fast rescue craft (FRC) 快速救助艇

~ response 快速反应，速动，快响应

~ thermocouple 小惯性热电偶，快速热电偶

fasten ['fa:sn] v. 使固定，扣紧，抓住，扎牢，强加于，集中于，集中注意力

fastener ['fa:snə] n. 紧固件，钮扣，使系牢之物

fastness ['fa:stnis] n. 牢固，固定，要塞，堡垒

fathom ['fæðəm] n. 英寻；v. 测量深度，看穿，理解真意，推测，领会，进行探索

fathometer [fə'ðɔmitə] n. 回声探测仪

fatigue [fə'ti:g] n. 疲劳，疲乏，劳务杂役，(士兵穿的)工作服；v. (使)疲劳，(使)疲乏

~ crack 疲劳裂缝

~ damage 疲劳损坏
~ effect 疲劳效应
~ failure 疲劳衰坏，疲劳破坏
~ life 疲劳负荷寿命，疲劳寿命
~ life cycle 疲劳循环次数
~ limit 疲乏强度，疲劳极限，疲劳限度
~ loading 疲劳负荷，疲劳加载
~ loss 疲劳损耗
~ phenomenon 疲劳现象
~ rupture 疲劳破断，疲劳破坏
~ strength 疲乏强度，疲劳强度
~ threshold 疲劳阈值
~ wear 疲劳磨损

fault [fɔ:lt] *n*. 缺点，缺陷，过错，责任，故障；*v*. 挑剔，找缺点，批评，做错，出错，产生断层，找错误，挑剔，变动从而产生断层 ‖ *Syn*. dysfunction 机能不良，功能紊乱，官能障碍；failure 失灵，故障；out of order 次序颠倒，不整齐，状态不好；trouble 故障
~ alarm display 故障报警显示
~ block 断块，故障闭塞，断裂地块
~ clearing time 故障清除时间，故障切除时间
~ correcting 故障修复
~ current 故障电流，事故电流
~ detection 探伤，故障检验
~ diagnosis 故障诊断
~ location 故障定位，故障位置
~ oscilloscope 故障录波器
~ prevention measure 故障预防措施
~ protection 异常保护，故障保护，故障防护
~ rate 故障率

~ tolerance 容错(性)
~ tolerant function 容错功能
~ tree analysis 故障树分析

faulty ['fɔ:lti] *a*. 错误的，有错误的，有过失的，有缺点的，不完美的
~ timing 故障定时

fax [fæks] *n*. 传真；*v*. 传真，传真传输
~ machine 传真机

FC (filtering capacitor) 滤波电容器
FCS (fieldbus control system) 现场总线控制系统

feasible ['fi:zəbl] *a*. 可行的，可用的，可实行的，可能的

feasibility [,fi:zə'biləti] *n*. 可行性，可能性，现实性
~ analysis 可行性分析
~ assessment 可行性评估，可行性估计
~ report 可行性报告
~ study 可行性研究

feather ['feðə] *n*. 桨叶的水平运动，羽毛，翎毛，状态，心情，种类；*v*. 使桨与水面平行，装羽毛，长羽毛
~ length 毛圈长

feathering ['feðəriŋ] *n*. 顺桨，羽毛箭，丛毛；*v*. (feather 的 ing 形式) 使(桨)与水面平行，装羽毛，长羽毛
~ blade 顺流变距桨叶

feature ['fi:tʃə] *n*. 特征，特点，容貌，面貌，(期刊的)特辑，故事片；*v*. 是…的特色，特写，放映，使有特色，描写…的特征，以…为号召物，起主要作用
~ detection 特征检测
~ extraction 特征抽取

feed [fi:d] *n*. 饲料，施肥，喂送；*v*. 喂养，满足(欲望等)，提供，供…作食物，吃，以…为食，流入，注入，进入(如油流

入机器），馈送电视节目

~ back 反作用，反馈

~ back loop 反馈环，反馈回路，反馈机制

~ check valve 给水止回阀

~ forward 前馈，正向输送

~ movement 进给(刀)运动

~ piping 供水管道

~ pitch 输送孔距，同步孔距

~ pump 进给泵，给水泵

~ rate 进给速率，进料速率，馈送率

~ ratio 馈电比，进给比，进料效率

~ treatment 给水处理

~ valve 进给阀，喂阀，给气阀，进水阀

~ water 给水

~ water check valve 给水止回阀

~ water filter tank 给水过滤舱，给水过滤箱

~ water flow 给水流量

~ water heater 给水加热器

~ water pump 给水泵

~ water ratio 给水率

~ water regulating valve 给水调节阀，给水控制阀

~ water stop valve 给水截止阀

~ water treatment 给水处理

~ water valve 给水阀

~ with 加上(油、煤等)

feedback ['fi:dbæk] n. 反馈，反应，回授

~ circuit 反馈电路

~ compensation 反馈补偿

~ component 反馈元件

~ control 反馈控制

~ loop 反馈回路，反馈环

~ path 反馈通道

~ rod 反馈杆

~ signal 反馈信号

~ switch 反馈开关

~ system 反馈方式，反馈系统

~ unit 反馈装置，反馈单元

~ variable 反馈变量

feeder ['fi:də] n. 进料器，馈电线，支流，饲养员，奶瓶

~ box 分线箱

~ bus bar 馈电线，馈路母线

~ cable 馈电电缆

~ circuit 馈路，供电路线，馈电线路

~ clamp 馈电接线柱，馈线夹

~ clip 馈线夹

~ drive link 进刀传动杆

~ main 馈电干线

~ panel 馈电线控制板

~ switchboard 馈电配电板

feedforward [,fi:d'fɔ:wəd] n. 前馈

~ path 前馈通道

feedstock ['fi:dstɔk] n. 进料,给料(指供送入机器或加工厂的原料)

feel [fi:l] n. 感觉，触摸；v. 觉得，感觉，认为，摸索，触摸，试探

feeler ['fi:lə] n. 触角，试探，试探者，厚薄规

~ gauge 塞尺，厚薄规，测隙规，千分垫

~ pin 触针，测头

feet [fi:t] n. 脚步，脚，底部，英尺(1 英尺=12 英寸或 30.48 厘米)

~ first entry 脚先入水

felt [felt] n. 毛毡；v. (feel 的过去式和过去分词) 觉得，感觉，认为，摸索，触摸，试探

felted ['feltid] a. 黏结起来的，用毡覆盖的

~ paper 毡纸

female ['fi:meil] *n.* 女人，雌性动物，雌性植物，雌株；*a.* 女性的，雌性的，能结果实的，电气设备，阴的 ‖ *Ant.* male 男人，男性，雄性，男性的，雄性的，阳刚的，阳的，凸的

~ connector 阴连接器，雌性接口，内孔连接器

~ coupling 阴螺纹接头

~ joint (管端的)套筒接合，插承接合

~ screw 阴螺旋，螺母，螺帽，内螺纹

~ thread nipple 阴螺纹接管

~ union 管子内接头，活接头扣圈，内螺纹联管节

femoral ['femərəl] *n.* 股动脉；*a.* 股骨的，大腿骨的，大腿的

fence [fens] *n.* 围墙，栅栏，篱笆，防护物，剑术；*v.* 防护，练习剑术，搪塞，围以栅栏，跳过栅栏

fend [fend] *v.* 谋生，防御，保护，供养，闪避，挡开，照料，供养，力争，努力

fender ['fendə] *n.* 防卫物，挡泥板，火炉围栏

ferric ['ferik] *a.* 铁的，三价铁的，含铁的，(正)铁的

ferromagnetic [,ferəumæg'netik] *a.* 铁磁的，铁磁体的

ferrosilicon [,ferəu'silikən] *n.* 铁矽(合金)

ferrous ['ferəs] *a.* 铁的，含铁的，亚铁的 ‖ *Ant.* nonferrous 不含铁的，非铁的

ferry ['feri] *n.* 渡船，渡口，摆渡，用船渡运；*v.* 航海，渡运，(乘渡船)渡过(河等)，摆渡

~ boat 渡船，渡轮

~ building 渡轮大厦

~ concourse 渡轮码头广场

~ service 轮渡服务

~ terminal 渡轮码头，渡船码头

FET (field effect transistor) 场效应晶体管，场效晶体管

fetch [fetʃ] *n.* 浪区，取得，诡计，计谋；*v.* 转航，绕道，接来，取来，带来，售得，引出，吸引，到达，抵达，演绎出

FFC (flexible flat cable) 挠性扁平电缆

FGW (fresh water generator) 海水淡化装置，造水机

fiber ['faibə] *n.* 光纤，纤维，纤维物质，(织物的)质地，基础力量

~ optics cable 光导纤维电缆

fiberglass ['faibəgla:s] *n.* 玻璃纤维，玻璃丝

fibre ['faibə] *n.* 纤维，构造，纤维制品

fibrid ['faibrid] *n.* 纤维质，纤条体

fid [fid] *n.* (一)块，(一)堆，(支撑中桅的)方形木杠(铁杠),(拼接用的)锥形木钉，木栓，桅栓

field [fi:ld] *n.* 领域，牧场，旷野，战场，运动场；*v.* 把暴晒于场上，使上场；*a.* 扫描场，田赛的，野生的

~ application 现场应用，野外使用，预涂涂装

~ application relay 供磁继电器，励磁继电器，场使用继电器

~ circuit 磁场电路

~ coil 激励线圈，励磁线圈

~ current 激励电流，励磁电流

~ distortion 场失真，磁场失真，磁通分布畸变

~ distribution 场分布

~ effect transistor (FET) 场效应晶体管，场效晶体管
~ exciter 场激励器
~ investigation 现场调查，现场试验
~ joint 安装接头
~ of vision 视野，视场
~ relay 磁场继电器，场继电器
~ resistor 场换向开关，磁场电阻器
~ strength 电场强度，磁场强度，场强
~ survey 实地调查，实地考察
~ test 现场试验，实地操作试验
~ winding 激磁绕组，磁场绕组

fieldbus [fi:ld'bʌs] *n*. 现场总线
~ control system (FCS) 现场总线控制系统

figure ['figə] *n*. 外形，轮廓，体形，图形，画像，数字，形状，身份；*v*. 描绘，表示，象征，演算，认为，出现，考虑，出名，塑造，扮演角色
~ of merit 品质因数，质量因数，佳度，灵敏值，工作值，性能系数，优良指数

file [fail] *n*. 文件，档案，文件夹，卷宗，锉刀；*v*. 把…归档，提出(申请等)，锉，琢磨，列队行进
~ brush 锉刷
~ compression 文件压缩
~ decompression 文件解压缩
~ off 排成一列纵队出发，归档
~ record 文件记录，文档记录
~ with handle 文件处理

fill [fil] *n*. 满足，饱，充分，填方；*v*. 装满，充满，注满，充满，填充，弥漫，供应，供给，满足 ‖ *Syn*. cater to 迎合，满足；content 使满意；fulfil 满足；meet 满足，达到要求；satisfy 满足，使满意
~ out 填写，使长大，变大
~ with 使充满，用…充满
~ with CO_2 gas 用二氧化碳气体充满

filler ['filə] *n*. 装填者，补白，装填物，活页纸，漏斗
~ metal 填充金属，焊料，焊丝
~ sheet 垫片

fillet ['filit] *n*. 头带，带子，带状物，平缘，肉片，鱼片；*v*. 用带缚或装饰，把(鱼、肉)切成片
~ weld size 角焊缝尺寸
~ weld connection 贴角焊连接

filling ['filiŋ] *n*. 填补物，饼馅，纬纱，填充，供应；*v*. (fill 的 ing 形式) 装满，充满，注满，填充，弥漫，供应，供给，满足
~ and sounding pipe 充装测深管
~ and sounding pipe connection 充装测深管接头
~ and sounding pipe valve 充装测深管阀门
~ line 充填管，灌装管 ‖ *Syn*. filling pipe 充填管，灌装管

film [film] *n*. 薄膜，膜层，胶卷，影片，薄雾，轻烟，电影；*v*. 覆薄膜，生薄膜，拍摄，拍成电影，变成朦胧
~ adhesive 胶膜，胶纸
~ strength 油膜强度
~ thickness (油)膜厚度

filter ['filtə] *n*. 滤波器，滤光器，滤色镜，过滤器；*v*. 过滤，透过，渗透，滤除，走漏，慢慢传开
~ aid 助滤剂，助滤器
~ cell 过滤器元件
~ element 滤芯，滤波(器)元件

~ material 过滤材料，反滤料
~ paper 滤纸
~ paper for oil 油滤纸
~ selector 滤波器选择器
~ sheet 滤板
~ silencer 过滤式消音器
~ system 过滤系统
~ type measuring apparatus 滤波器式测量装置
~ type respirator 过滤式呼吸器
~ type smokemeter 滤纸式烟度计
~ with back-flushing 反冲洗过滤器

filtering ['filtəriŋ] *n.* 过滤，滤除，滤清；*v.* (filter 的 ing 形式) 透过，(光或声)渗入，缓行，(交通指示灯处的交通)仅可左转行驶
　~ ability 过滤能力
　~ capacitor (FC) 滤波电容器
　~ centrifuge 过滤式离心机
　~ medium 过滤剂，过滤液

filtrate ['filtreit] *n.* 滤出液；*v.* 过滤，筛选

filtration [fil'treiʃən] *n.* 过滤，筛选，滤清，滤除
　~ efficiency 过滤效率
　~ method 过滤法
　~ process 过滤过程
　~ velocity 过滤速度

fin [fin] *n.* 鱼鳍，散热片，鳍状物，安定翼，直尾翼；*v.* 装上翅片，装上鳍片，游泳，猛烈地拍动鳍
　~ and tube core 管片式散热器芯
　~ angle feedback set 鳍角反馈装置
　~ housing and extending gear 减摇鳍收放装置
　~ indicator panel 减摇鳍位置指示器板

~ keel 鳍状龙骨，鳍龙骨
~ shaft 鳍轴
~ stabilizer 稳定鳍，减摇鳍
~ tilting gear 减摇鳍回转装置，倾转鳍机构
~ tilting machinery 水平舵转舵机构，减摇鳍传动机构

final ['fainl] *n.* 决赛，期末考试，当日报纸的末版；*a.* 最终的，决定性的，不可更改的
　~ act 最后决议
　~ assembly 总装(配)
　~ check 最后检查
　~ circuit 终接电路
　~ control element 末级控制元件，末控元件
　~ controlled condition 最终受控条件
　~ exit 最终安全出口
　~ filter 终滤器
　~ inspection 最后检查，最终检查
　~ shield grounding 末屏接地
　~ subcircuit 最后分路
　~ value 终值
　~ voltage 终止电压

finalize ['fainəlaiz] *v.* 完成，使结束，使落实，定案，把…最后定下来

find [faind] *n.* 发现物,被发现的人；*v.* 发现，找到，认为，觉得，感到，裁决，判定

finder ['faində] *n.* 发现者，探测器，测高仪，寻星镜

fine [fain] *n.* 罚；*v.* 罚款，澄清；*a.* 好的，优良的，细小的，精美的，健康的，晴朗的
　~ adjustment 精调,细调整,精密调整,微调

~ fast ship 纤细高速船

~ filter 细滤器 ‖ *Syn.* fine strainer 细滤器

~ filtering 细滤

~ filtration 细过滤，细滤 ‖ *Ant.* bulk filtration 粗过滤，粗滤

~ form 瘦长船型

~ grain 细粒，细晶粒，细晶 ‖ *Syn.* fine particle 细粒，微粒

~ grinding 细磨

~ mesh filter 精网滤器

~ separating compartment 细分离室

~ spray (水、油等)细雾

~ spray nozzle 细雾滴喷嘴

~ spray of fuel 细雾状燃油

~ thread tap 细螺纹丝锥

finely ['fainli] *ad.* 美好地，精细地，细微地

fineness ['fainnis] *n.* 精致，细微，纤细，优雅

finger ['fiŋgə] *n.* 手指，指状物，指针；*v.* 伸出，告发，用手指触摸，拨弄

fingerprint ['fiŋgəprint] *n.* 指纹，指印；*v.* 采指纹

finish ['finiʃ] *n.* 完成，结束，磨光，末道漆，完美；*v.* 完成，结束，终结，停止，终止，用完，毁掉，使完美

~ machining 精加工，完工切削

finished ['finiʃt] *v.* (finish 的过去式和过去分词) 完成，结束，终结，停止，终止，用完，毁掉；*a.* 完成了的，技术高超的，精湛的，完美的，精巧的

~ with engine (FWE) 停机，完车，用车完毕

finishing ['finiʃiŋ] *n.* 结尾，结束，完成，修整；*v.* (finish 的 ing 形式) 完成，结束，终结，停止，终止，用完，毁掉；*a.* 最后的，完工的，终点的

~ area 精整区域

~ bur 精修钻

~ coat 最后一道涂工，罩面，终饰层

~ file 磨光锉

~ gear 精整齿轮

~ light boat 精加工灯船

~ machine 精加工机床，精整机

~ paper 砂纸，研磨纸

~ tool 精加工刀具

~ work 精整工作

finite ['fainait] *n.* 有限性，有限的事物；*a.* 有限的，限定的，有穷的，有限的

~ region 有限区域

finned [find] *v.* (fin 的过去式和过去分词) 装上翅片，装上鳍片，游泳，猛烈地拍动鳍；*a.* 有鳍的，有鳍状物的

~ coil 有翅旋管，翅片盘管

~ cooler 肋形冷却器片式散热器

~ radiator 翅片式散热器，肋片式散热器

~ surface 肋化表面

~ surface evaporator 肋片式蒸发器

~ tube radiator 肋片管式散热器

fire ['faiə] *n.* 火，炉火，火灾，失火，闪光，炮火，热情，激情；*v.* 点燃，着火，烧火，烧制，使发光，加燃料，放枪，开枪，射击，激动，解雇

~ access 灭火口

~ accident 火灾事故

~ agent 消防部门

~ aisle 阻火通道

~ alarm 火警 ‖ *Syn.* fire bell 火警；fire call 火灾报警；fire warning 火警

~ alarm bell 火警铃

~ alarm box 火灾报警箱

~ alarm casing 火灾报警盒

~ alarm control and indicating equipment 火灾报警控制和显示设备

~ alarm control panel 火灾报警控制板

~ alarm control system 火灾报警控制系统

~ alarm control unit 火灾报警控制器

~ alarm detector of ion type 离子式火灾报警探测器

~ alarm detector of thermal type 消防感温式报警探测器

~ alarm device 火灾警报装置 ‖ *Syn*. fire alarm equipment 火灾警报装置

~ alarm evacuation signal 火警疏散信号

~ alarm indication device 火警显示装置

~ alarm remote indicating equipment 火警远程显示设备

~ alarm signal 火灾报警信号，火警信号

~ alarm signaling device 火灾报警信号装置，火灾信号发生装置

~ alarm sounder 火灾警报器

~ alarm sounding system 火警探测系统

~ alarm system 火灾报警系统

~ analysis 火情分析

~ and bilge pump 消防污水两用泵

~ and boat drill 火灾与救生演习

~ and explosion safety 防护和防爆安全

~ and explosive hazard 火灾和爆炸危险

~ annihilator 灭火器 ‖ *Syn*. fire extinguisher 灭火器 ‖ *Syn*. extinguisher 灭火器；FIREX 灭火器；fire apparatus 灭火器；flame arrester 火焰清除器

~ annihilator pipe 消防管

~ approach suit 隔热服 ‖ *Syn*. fire entry suit 隔火服；fire fighting clothing 消防战斗服；fire fighting suit 防火服；fire fighting turnout 消防战斗服；fire protection clothing 防火服；fire protection suit 防火服，防火衣；fire proximity suit 防火服，避火服；fire resistance coverall 耐火工作服；fire-resistant coverall 防火服；fire safety clothing 消防安全服；fire suit 消防服，救火服

~ area 避难区域

~ assembly 消防设施组件

~ attack line 灭火水带线

~ axe 消防斧

~ belt 防火带

~ blanket 灭火毯

~ boat 消防船 ‖ *Syn*. fire fighting boat 消防船；fire fighting ship 消防船；fire fighting vessel 消防船；fire float 消防艇；fire tender 消防船；fire vessel 消防船

~ branch 消防枪

~ break 防火间距

~ breakout 起火

~ breeding 自燃

~ bucket 消防桶

~ button 灭火按钮

~ cabinet 消火栓箱

~ cache 消防器材储藏处

~ casualty 火灾伤亡者

~ cause 起火原因

~ cause class 火灾类别

~ chamber 燃烧室
~ crack 加热裂缝，火裂(钢锭)，烧裂，烧成裂隙
~ clay insulating refractory 隔热耐火材料
~ clay plastic refractory 塑性耐火材料
~ coat 氧化皮，鳞皮
~ cock 消防栓
~ code 防火规范
~ combat station 消防岗位
~ command 消防指挥
~ command system 消防指挥系统
~ compartmentation 防火分隔
~ consumption 消防用水量
~ containment 遏制火灾
~ control equipment 消防器材，消防设备，火灾控制设备‖*Syn*. fire equipment 消防设备；fire extinction equipment 灭火设备；fire extinguishing apparatus 灭火装置，灭火设备；fire extinguishing appliance 灭火设备，消防设备，灭火器具；fire extinguishing equipment 灭火设备；fire extinguishing installation 灭火装置；fire extinguishing plant 灭火装置；fire fighting apparatus 消防设备；fire fighting appliance 消防用具；fire fighting device 消防设施；fire fighting equipment 消防设备；fire fighting unit 灭火装置，消防装置；fire gear 消防设备；fire installation 消防设施；fire protection device 防火装置；fire protection equipment 防火设备；fire service equipment 消防设备；fire service implement 消防器材
~ control operator 消防人员
~ control planning 灭火作战计划
~ crack 燃烧开裂，火裂，烧裂

~ crack mark 燃烧开裂迹印
~ crew 灭火作业组
~ curve 火灾曲线
~ cutoff 挡火物
~ cycle detector 循环式火灾探测器
~ cycle system 自动开关式喷水灭火系统
~ damage 火灾损失，火损
~ damp cap 焰晕
~ danger 火灾危险，火险‖*Syn*. fire peril 火灾危险
~ deaths 死亡人数
~ demand 消防需水量
~ department (pumper) connection 水泵结合器
~ detecting and extinguishing apparatus 火灾探测与灭火装置
~ detecting area 火灾探测区
~ detecting arrangement 火灾探测装置，探火装置‖*Syn*. fire detection apparatus 火灾探测设备；fire detection unit 火灾探测装置
~ detecting cabinet 火灾报警箱，火警警报箱
~ detecting system 火灾探测系统
~ detection 火灾探测，火灾侦测，探火，火焰检测
~ detection alarm system 火灾探测报警系统
~ detection system test switch 火警探测系统试验开关
~ detector 火警探测器，火灾探测器
~ detector element 火灾探测元件
~ detector switch 火警探测器开关
~ detector system 火警探测系统
~ determination 火灾判断

~ disaster 火灾
~ drill 消防训练，火灾避难训练
~ duration 燃烧持续时间
~ edge 火缘
~ effect 火灾影响
~ effect modeling 火灾影响模拟
~ effluent 火灾气流
~ emergency 火灾紧急情况
~ enclosure 火区密封
~ end 火端
~ endurance 耐火性 ‖ *Syn*. fire extinguishing performance 灭火性能；fire performance 耐火性能；fire resistance 耐火性，防火性能，阻燃性；fire resisting property 耐火性能；fire resistivity 耐燃法，耐火性；fireproofness 耐火性；flame resistivity 阻焰性，耐火性
~ endurance rating 耐火性等级，耐火等级 ‖ *Syn*. fire protection rating 耐火等级；fire rating 耐火等级，灭火级别，防火等级；fire resistance class 耐火等级；fire resistance rating 耐火等级
~ endurance test 耐火性测试
~ exercise 消防演习 ‖ *Syn*. fire extinguishing drill 灭火演习；fire fighting drill 消防演习
~ exit 安全出口
~ exit drill 消防疏散训练
~ exposure 暴露于火
~ exposure severity 暴露于火灾的严重程度
~ exposure test 暴露于火试验
~ exposure time 暴露于火的时间
~ extend 着火范围
~ extinction 灭火 ‖ *Syn*. fire extinguishing 灭火；fire fighting 消防，灭火；fire suppression 灭火，火灾扑灭
~ extinction by foam 泡沫灭火
~ extinguisher agent 灭火器用灭火剂
~ extinguisher bracket 灭火器架
~ extinguisher cabinet 灭火器箱
~ extinguisher dry chemical 灭火器干粉
~ extinguisher fluid 灭火器液
~ extinguisher handle 灭火器手柄
~ extinguisher switch 灭火器喷射开关
~ extinguisher symbol 灭火器符号
~ extinguisher system 灭火系统
~ extinguisher transfer switch 灭火器转换开关
~ extinguishing agent 灭火剂 ‖ *Syn*. extinguishing agent 灭火剂；fire extinguishing medium 灭火介质；fire fighting agent 灭火剂；fire proofing agent 阻燃剂，防燃剂；fire retardancy 阻燃剂；fire retarding agent 防燃剂，阻燃剂，耐火剂；fire suppressant 灭火剂；flame retardant 阻燃剂，阻燃物，灭火剂
~ extinguishing bottle 灭火瓶
~ extinguishing bullet 灭火弹
~ extinguishing cart 灭火手推车
~ extinguishing effectiveness 灭火效能
~ extinguishing foam 灭火泡沫 ‖ *Syn*. foam extinguishing agent 泡沫灭火剂
~ extinguishing gas 灭火气体
~ extinguishing pump 消防泵 ‖ *Syn*. fire pump 消防泵；fire service pump 消防泵，消防水泵；fireproofing pump 消防泵
~ extinguishing sand 灭火沙
~ extinguishing system 灭火系统

~ extinguishing test 灭火测试，灭火实验
~ extinguishing tube 灭火管
~ factor 火灾因素
~ failure 火灾事故
~ fatality 火灾死亡
~ fighter 消防员
~ fighter boots 消防靴
~ fighter gloves 消防手套
~ fighter helmet 消防头盔
~ fighting by equal pressure 均压灭火
~ fighting foam 泡沫灭火剂，灭火泡沫
~ fighting foam agent 泡沫灭火剂
~ fighting footwear 消防靴
~ fighting gun 消防水枪
~ fighting hose 消防水带，消防胶管 ‖ *Syn*. fire hose 灭火水带
~ fighting line 灭火水带线路
~ fighting method 灭火法
~ fighting safety 消防安全
~ fighting station 消防站，灭火站
~ fighting strategy 灭火战术
~ fighting supply 消防供水
~ fighting system 消防系统
~ fighting tactics 灭火战术
~ fighting technique 灭火技术，消防技术
~ fighting tug 消防拖船，消防拖轮 ‖ *Syn*. fire tug 消防拖船，消防拖轮
~ fighting window 消防窗口
~ fighting with fire extinguisher 用灭火器灭火
~ fighting with inert gas 用惰性气体灭火
~ floor 火灾层

~ foam 灭火泡沫
~ foam producing machine 灭火泡沫发生器
~ forcible entry tool 消防破拆工具
~ gas 可燃气体，易燃气体
~ gas detector 易燃气体探测器
~ gas explosion 易燃气体爆炸
~ goggles 消防护目镜
~ good 易燃物
~ ground 火场
~ ground TV system 火场电视系统
~ growth 火灾增长
~ growth model 火灾生长模型
~ gun 消防枪
~ hat 消防头盔
~ hazard 火灾
~ (hazard) classification 火险分类，火灾分类
~ head 火头
~ heat 火热
~ hole 火孔
~ hook 消防钩，火钩
~ hose cabinet 消防水带箱
~ hose coupling 消防水带接头
~ hose fitting 消防水带配件
~ hose nozzle 消防水龙带喷嘴
~ hose rack 消防水带架
~ hose reel 消防软管卷盘，消防水带卷盘
~ hydrant 消防栓，消防龙头，灭火龙头 ‖ *Syn*. hydrant 消防栓，消防龙头
~ ignition 着火
~ ignition energy 引燃能量
~ ignition sequence 着火顺序
~ ignition to external heat 外因火灾
~ indicating panel 火灾显示面板

~ inhibitor 火焰抑制剂
~ injury 烧伤
~ inspection 防火检查
~ insulation 耐火绝缘
~ insurance 火灾保险，火险
~ isolation 火区隔离
~ knockdown 控火
~ lagging 防火绝缘层，防火覆盖层
~ lamp 火警指示灯
~ life 火灾延续时间
~ lighter 点火剂，引火物
~ load 火灾荷载，火灾负荷，燃烧负荷
~ load density 火灾负荷密度
~ loss 火灾损失
~ loss insurance 火灾损失保险
~ loss statistics 火灾损失统计
~ main pipe 消防总管 ‖ *Syn*. fire service main 消防总管
~ main system 主消防系统
~ main with fire valve 带消火阀的消防总管
~ management 消防管理
~ management plan 消防管理计划
~ margin 火缘
~ mask 消防面具
~ model 火灾模型
~ nozzle 消火水枪
~ origin 起火源
~ out 开除，解雇
~ parameter 火灾参数
~ path (firepath) 火灾蔓延通道
~ personnel 消防人员
~ plan 消防设备布置图
~ planning 消防规划
~ play 火烫，玩火

~ plug 消防栓
~ pocket 隐蔽火点
~ point 燃点
~ point theory 着火点理论
~ precaution measure 防火措施
~ presuppression 灭火预备工作
~ preventing 预防火灾，防火的，防火，防火的，预防火灾，防火的
~ prevention 防火，消防 ‖ *Syn*. fire protection 防火，消防；fire safety 防火，消防；prevention of fire 防火
~ prevention code 防火规范
~ prevention district 防火区
~ prevention division 防火区域，防火区划
~ prevention pipe 消防水管
~ prevention principle 防火原则
~ prevention supervisor 防火负责人
~ prevention system 防火系统
~ proofing 防火，耐火装置，耐火材料
~ propagation 火焰传播，火灾蔓延
~ protection criteria 消防标准
~ protection flap 防火挡板
~ protection layer 防火层
~ protection measure 消防措施，防火措施
~ protection rule 消防规范
~ protection safety sign 消防安全标志
~ protection switch 防火开关
~ protection system 防火系统
~ protection water tank 消防水箱
~ protection water 消防用水
~ pump station 消防泵站
~ pump with drive 带发动机的消防泵
~ rated partition 耐火隔板
~ reel 水带卷筒

~ regulation 火力调节器
~ rescue equipment 消防救援设备
~ resistance classification 耐火性分类
~ resistance cloth 耐火布
~ resistance grading 耐火性分级
~ resistance period 耐火时间
~ resistance property 耐火特性
~ resistance steel door 钢质防火门
~ resisting bulkhead 抗火舱壁，耐火舱壁
~ resisting cable 耐火电缆
~ resisting construction 耐火构造
~ resisting damper 防火阀
~ resisting division 防火分隔
~ resisting material 耐火材料
~ resisting quality 耐火质量
~ retarding bulkhead 阻燃舱壁
~ retarding chemical 化学阻燃剂
~ retarding division 阻燃分隔，防火区间
~ retarding treatment 阻燃处理
~ risk 起火原因
~ room 锅炉舱，锅炉房，火室
~ runner 消防安全检查员
~ safety certificate 消防安全合格证书
~ safety measures 消防安全措施
~ safety rules 防火规范
~ safety shutter 防火安全板
~ safety system 防火安全系统
~ sand box 灭火砂箱，灭火沙箱
~ scale 耐火氧化皮
~ scar 火疤，火迹
~ scenario investigation procedure 火情调查程序
~ scene 火灾场景
~ science 消防科学，火灾科学，防火学
~ sealing 封闭火区
~ security measure 防火安全措施
~ separation 防火分隔
~ service belt 消防带
~ service connection 消防泵接水口
~ service inventory 消防用品
~ service meter 消防水表
~ service training 消防训练
~ severity 火灾烈度，火灾猛烈度
~ shaft 消防竖井，垂直火路
~ signal 火警信号
~ size class 火灾等级
~ smoke 火灾烟雾
~ smoke detection 烟火探测
~ smothering 窒息灭火
~ smothering blanket 灭火毯
~ smothering gas 窒息灭火气体
~ smothering gear 窒息灭火装置
~ smothering steam 窒息灭火用蒸汽
~ smothering system 窒息灭火系统
~ source 火源
~ spread 火蔓延
~ sprinkling system 喷淋灭火系统
~ stability 耐火稳定性
~ stage 火灾阶段
~ standpipe 消防竖管
~ station 消防站
~ stink 烟火气味
~ stop product 阻火产品
~ stopping 防火墙
~ storage 消防储水
~ strategy 灭火策略，灭火战略
~ stream 消防射流
~ suction hose 消防吸水管
~ supply 消防给水

~ suppression bottle 灭火瓶，灭火罐
~ suppressor 阻火器
~ symbol 消防标志
~ technology 消防技术
~ testing 耐火试验
~ trace 火灾控制线，火灾痕迹
~ training 消防训练
~ triangle 火三角
~ tube 烟管，火管
~ tube boiler 火管锅炉
~ under control 基本上得到控制的火灾
~ up 点燃，点火，发动(机器)，(使)突然生气
~ valve 灭火阀，消防阀
~ vent 事故排烟口
~ warning light 火警灯，着火警告灯
~ warning light test button 火警信号灯检查按钮
~ warning sensor 火警信号传感器
~ warning system 火警信号系统
~ warp 火警曳缆，火警备缆，火警电缆
~ waste 烧损
~ water 消防用水
~ water line 消防供水管线，消防供水线
~ water supply 消防给水
~ water supply duration 消防供水持续时间
~ whirl 火旋风
~ wind 火灾风
~ window 防火窗
~ wire 火线，带电线，有电线
~ wire port 火线端口
~ wound 火伤

~ zoning 防火分区

FIREX 灭火器 ‖ *Syn*. extinguisher 灭火器；fire annihilator 灭火器；fire apparatus 灭火器；fire extinguisher 灭火器；flame arrester 火焰清除器

fire-prone 有火灾危险的，容易发生火灾的

fire-protective 防火保护的
~ lining 防火衬层
~ paint 防火漆
~ property 防火性能

fire-resistant 耐火的，防火的 ‖ *Syn*. fireproof 耐火的,防火的; fire-resistive 耐火的,防火的; fire-retardant 防火的,阻火的
~ blanket 防火毯
~ cable 耐火电缆
~ cloth 防火布
~ construction 耐火构造
~ coverall 防火服 ‖ *Syn*. fire approach suit 隔热服；fire entry suit 隔火服；fire fighting clothing 消防战斗服；fire fighting suit 防火服；fire fighting turnout 消防战斗服；fire protection clothing 防火服；fire protection suit 防火服，防火衣；fire proximity suit 防火服，避火服；fire resistance coverall 耐火工作服；fire safety clothing 消防安全服；fire suit 消防服，救火服
~ material 耐火材料，防火材料
~ oil 抗燃油
~ paint 耐火油漆
~ property 耐火特性
~ shield 耐火屏蔽，耐火隔板
~ wire 耐火导线，耐火绝缘导线

fire-resistive 耐火的，防火的 ‖ **Syn**. fireproof 耐火的，防火的；fire-resistant 耐火的，防火的；fire-retardant 防火的，阻火的
  ~ construction 防火结构
  ~ material 防火材料

fire-retardant 防火的，阻火的 ‖ **Syn**. fireproof 耐火的，防火的；fire-resistant 耐火的，防火的；fire-resistive 耐火的，防火的
  ~ chemical 阻火剂
  ~ coating 滞火涂层，防火涂料
  ~ fiber 阻燃纤维
  ~ flame arrester 耐烧型阻火器
  ~ glass 防火玻璃
  ~ material 阻燃材料
  ~ mechanism 阻燃机理
  ~ paint 耐火涂料
  ~ polyester resin 耐火聚酯树脂，阻燃聚酯树脂
  ~ rating 耐火等级测定

fire-suppressant 抑制火的，灭火的
  ~ gas 灭火气体

fire-watch 防火检查

firebox ['faiəbɔks] *n*. 燃烧室，锅炉炉膛火室，火室

fireman ['faiəmən] *n*. 救火队员，消防队员

fireman's 消防员的
  ~ axe 消防斧
  ~ boots 消防员靴
  ~ gloves 消防员手套
  ~ outfit 消防员装备
  ~ uniform 消防员制服

fireplug ['faiəplʌg] *n*. 灭火塞，消防塞，消防栓

fireproof ['faiəpru:f] *v*. 使防火，使耐火；*a*. 耐火的，防火的 ‖ **Syn**. fire-resistant 耐火的，防火的；fire-resistive 耐火的，防火的；fire-retardant 防火的，阻火的
  ~ agent 阻燃剂，防燃剂
  ~ bay (装有防火隔板的)防火舱
  ~ bulkhead 防火舱壁，防火墙，耐火隔壁
  ~ cable 耐火电缆，防火电缆
  ~ casing 耐火衬套
  ~ casting 耐火铸件
  ~ cloth 防火布
  ~ coating 耐火涂料
  ~ covering 防火套
  ~ door 防火门
  ~ fiber 耐火纤维，不燃纤维
  ~ frame 防爆机座
  ~ insulation 防火绝缘
  ~ line 耐火绳
  ~ lining 耐火盖层
  ~ machine 防爆式电机
  ~ mat 防火垫
  ~ material 耐火材料，防火材料
  ~ structure 耐火结构
  ~ suit 防火服
  ~ tank 防火油箱

fireproofing ['faiə,pru:fiŋ] *n*. 防火，耐火；*v*. (fireproof 的 ing 形式) 使防火，使耐火
  ~ chemical 防火化学品
  ~ installation 防火设施
  ~ of cable 电缆的防火
  ~ protection 消防措施
  ~ pump 消防泵 ‖ **Syn**. fire extinguishing pump 消防泵；fire pump 消防泵；fire service pump 消防泵，消防水泵

fireproofness ['faiəpru:fnis] *n*. 耐火性 ‖ *Syn*. fire endurance 耐火性；fire extinguishing performance 灭火性能；fire performance 耐火性能；fire resistance 耐火性，防火性能，阻燃性；fire resisting property 耐火性能；fire resistivity 耐燃法，耐火性；flame resistivity 阻焰性，耐火性

firer ['faiərə] *n*. 发火器，放火者，烧火工人，开炮者

firewire ['faiəwaiə] *n*. 火线，带电线，有电线

~ control unit 火灾报警缆线控制装置

~ electrical cable 缆式火灾探测器

~ sensing element 缆式火灾探测器敏感元件

firing ['faiəriŋ] *n*. 开火，生火，烘烤；*v*. (fire 的 ing 形式) 点燃，着火，烧火，烧制，使发光，加燃料，放枪，开枪，射击，激动，解雇

~ behavior 燃烧行为

~ button 引爆按钮

~ cable 引火线

~ crack 烧裂

~ level 燃烧面

~ order (内燃机气缸)点火次序

~ point 起燃点

~ range 着火范围，引火点范围

~ shield 隔热板

~ speed (内燃机)发火速度

~ technique 点火技术

~ temperature 点火温度

~ time 燃烧时间

~ time test 燃烧速度试验

~ unit 燃烧装置

~ up 点火升温

~ zone 燃烧区，高温带

firm [fə:m] *n*. 公司，商号；*v*. 使牢固，使坚定，变稳固，变坚实；*a*. 坚定的，牢固的，严格的，结实的；*ad*. 稳固地，坚定地

firmware ['fə:m,wɛə] *n*. 固件，韧件(软件硬件相结合)

firmer ['fə:mə] *a*. 坚硬的，坚固的

firmly ['fə:mli] *ad*. 坚定地，坚决地，坚固地，稳固地

first [fə:st] *n*. 第一，最初，头等，一号，高音部；*a*. 第一流的，最初的，最早的，基本的，概要的，高音的；*ad*. 首次，最早，最初，宁愿，优先；*num*. 第一

~ aid 急救

~ aid box 急救箱，急救盒，急救药箱

~ aid equipment 急救装备

~ aid injury 急救创伤

~ aid kit 急救包

~ aid technique 急救技术

~ aid treatment 急救措施

~ aider 急救员

~ arrival first attack 初期灭火

~ floor 第一层

~ generation 第一代

~ in 第一个入场，最先到达火场的人员和设备

~ mate (海军)大副 ‖ *Syn*. chief officer 大副；chief mate 大副

~ order 一阶，第一级，初指令

~ order feedback system 一阶反馈系统

~ order linear system 一阶线性系统

~ phase (=phase 1) 第 1 阶段(即阴燃阶段)

~ responder 第一急救者

~ response district 责任区
~ stage 第一阶段，最初阶段
~ step 第一步，初步，首先
first-class 最好的，第一流的，头等舱，优秀的
~ load 一类负荷
first-degree 最低级的，最轻度的，第一度的
~ burn 一级烧伤，一度烧伤
first-in 第一的，先进的，快速输入的
firstly ['fə:stli] ad. 第一，首先
fish [fiʃ] n. 鱼，鱼类；v. 钓鱼，捕鱼，用钩捞取，搜寻
~ attraction light 诱鱼灯
~ buying boat 收鱼船
~ catch 渔获量
~ conveyor belt 鱼传送带
~ eye 鱼眼，鱼眼状裂纹，白点焊接
~ finding equipment 鱼群探测装备，捕鱼设备
~ hold 鱼舱
~ hold refrigerating plant 鱼舱冷藏装备
~ hook 钓鱼钩
~ pump 鱼泵
fisher ['fiʃə] n. 渔船，渔夫，食鱼动物，捞取者
fisherman ['fiʃəmən] n. 渔夫，渔民
fishery ['fiʃəri] n. 渔场，渔业，水产业，水产公司，捕鱼权，养鱼术
~ administration vessel 渔政船，渔业巡视船
~ Board 渔业部，渔业委员会
~ management 渔业管理
~ patrol vessel 渔政执法船
~ research vessel 渔业调查船

fishing ['fiʃiŋ] n. 钓鱼，捕鱼；v. (fish 的 ing 形式) 钓鱼，捕鱼，用钩捞取，搜寻
~ dredger 钓鱼式挖泥船，捕鱼挖泥船
~ net 渔网
~ pole 钓竿，竿钓，钓鱼竿
~ population 渔民
~ port 渔港
fissile ['fisail] a. 易分裂的，易裂的，分裂性的，可分裂的，裂变的
fission ['fiʃən] n. 裂开，分裂，分体，裂变；v. 裂变
fist [fist] n. 拳头，手，抓住，抓牢，笔迹，掌握，指标参见号；v. 拳打，握成拳，紧握
fit [fit] n. 适合，合身，发作，痉挛；v. 安装,(使)适应,(使)合格,(使)合身,(使)符合；a. 健康的，合适的，恰当的，准备好的 ‖ *Syn.* assemble 装配；build in 安装，固定；fix 安装,(使)固定；fix assemblage 安装；install 安装，mount 安装；set up 装配，竖立，架起
~ out 装配，配备，供给必需品
fitness ['fitnəs] n. 健康，适当，适合，合情理
~ for duty 适于当值
fitted ['fitid] v. (fit 的过去式和过去分词) 安装,(使)适应,(使)合格,(使)合身,(使)符合；a. 合适的，定做的，合身的
~ bearing 配合轴承
~ bolt 定位螺栓，配合螺栓
~ capacity 装配容量
~ key 导向键，装配键
~ power 配套动力

~ screw 定位螺钉

~ value 配适值，拟合值

fitter ['fitə] *n*. 装配工，钳工，质检员；*a*. 胜任的，适当的

fitting ['fitiŋ] *n*. 装修，试穿，试衣，设备，器材，装置；*v*. (fit 的 ing 形式) 安装，(使)适应，(使)合格，(使)合身，(使)符合；*a*. 适合的，适宜的，适当的，相称的

~ and tightness testing of propeller shaft before launching 下水前艉轴密性装置的安装与密性试验

~ and tightness testing of propeller shaft after sea trial 航行试验后艉轴密性装置的安装与密性试验

~ instruction 装配说明，安装说明

~ of propeller 螺旋桨安装

~ surface 安装面，配合面

~ up 组对，装配，初组装

fitting-out 装修，装置，舾装，装配船只

~ pier 舾装码头

~ dock 舾装船坞，舾装码头

~ shop 舣装车间，舾装车间

~ region 舾装区域

~ crane 舾装起重机

five [faiv] *n*. 五，五个，五美元钞票；*a*. 五的，五个的；*num*. 五，五个

~ piston radial slow speed high torque motor 五活塞径向低速大扭矩电动机

fix [fiks] *n*. 困境，方位，受操纵的事，应急措施；*v*. 安装，(使)固定，装置，修理，准备，凝视，整理，牢记，决定，选定，确定‖ *Syn*. assemble 装配；build in 安装，固定；fit 安装；

fix assemblage 安装；install 安装；mount 安装；set up 装配，竖立，架起

~ a date 确定日期，约期

~ attention on 集中注意力于

~ on 确定，固定，使集中于

~ one's eyes on 盯住

~ position 定位，实测船位

~ up 修理，解决，改进，做好安排，商妥

fixable ['fiksəbl] *a*. 可固定的，可确定的，可安装的，可装置的

fixed [fikst] *v*. (fix 的过去式和过去分词) 固定，修理，准备，使牢固，固着，变硬，安定；*a*. 固定的，确定的，准备好的，固执的，不易发挥的

~ bollard 固定系船柱

~ capacity motor 固定容量电动机，定容电动机

~ contact 静触点，固定触点，固定接点

~ cost 固定成本

~ deck foam system 固定式甲板泡沫系统

~ disk 固定硬盘

~ dry-powder fire-extinguishing system 固定式干粉灭火系统

~ extinguishing system 固定式灭火系统‖ *Syn*. fixed fire fighting system 固定式灭火系统

~ film 固定膜

~ fire detection and alarm system 固定式火灾探测与报警系统

~ fire extinguisher 固定式灭火器

~ fire extinguishing system 固定式灭火系统

~ fire fighting equipment 固定式消防设备

~ fire pump 固定式消防泵

~ gas detection system 固定气体探测系统

~ gas fire-extinguishing system 固定式气体灭火系统

~ installation 固定设备,固定装置

~ jib 固定臂

~ LT distribution panel 固定低压配电盘

~ displacement 固定排量

~ displacement oil motor 固定排量油马达

~ displacement pump 固定排量泵,定量容积泵,定量泵

~ parts 固定部件

~ pitch 固定螺距,固定桨距,固定字宽

~ pitch propeller (FPP) 固定螺距螺旋桨,定距桨 ‖ *Syn*. fixed pitch screw 固定螺距螺旋桨,定距桨

~ pitch spacing 固定间距

~ platform 跳台,固定式平台

~ point 定点,固定点

~ pressure water-spraying fire-extinguishing system 固定压力喷水灭火系统

~ pressure water-spraying system 定压喷水灭火系统

~ resistance 固定电阻,不可变电阻

~ sequence manipulator 固定顺序机械手

~ set point control 定值控制

~ structure 固定式结构

~ target 固定目标,固定靶

~ temperature 固定温度,恒定温度

定温度

~ temperature fire detector 定温火灾探测器,恒温火灾探测器 ‖ *Syn*. constant temperature fire detector 定温火灾探测器,恒温火灾探测器

~ value 固定值,不变值

~ vane 固定叶片,定叶

~ vane sealing strip 定叶密封条

fixing ['fiksiŋ] *n*. 固定,稳固,设备,安装,修理; *v*. (fix 的 ing 形式) 固定,修理,准备,使牢固,固着,变硬,安定

~ bolt 固螺栓

~ device 固定装置

~ pin 定位销

~ ring 固定圈

~ screw 定位螺钉

fixture ['fikstʃə] *n*. 固定装置,定期放款,定期存款,固定在某位置的人或物,(定期定点举行的)体育活动

flag [flæg] *n*. 旗,旗帜,信号旗; *v*. 标示,疲乏,变弱,热情衰减

~ administration 船旗国政府,船旗国主管机关

~ of convenience 方便旗(指商船为逃避税收而向别国注册并挂该国旗帜)

~ semaphore 旗语

~ signals 信号旗

~ State 船旗国

~ State Control (FSC) 船旗国监督,船旗国管理

~ State Implementation (FSI) 船旗国履约

~ State Performance Self Assessment Form 船旗国表现自我评估表

flagstaff ['flægstɑ:f] *n*. 旗杆

flame [fleim] *n*. 火焰,热情,激情,爱人,

情人，激动；v. 燃烧，发出火焰，激起，激怒，面红，闪光

~ arrester 火焰清除器 ‖ Syn. extinguisher 灭火器；FIREX 灭火器；fire annihilator 灭火器；fire apparatus 灭火器；fire extinguisher 灭火器

~ detector 火焰检测器，火焰探测器

~ failure control device 火焰中断控制器

~ resistivity 阻焰性，耐火性 ‖ Syn. fire endurance 耐火性；fire extinguishing performance 灭火性能；fire performance 耐火性能；fire resistance 耐火性，防火性能，阻燃性；fire resisting property 耐火性能；fire resistivity 耐燃法，耐火性；fireproofness 耐火性

~ retardant 阻燃剂，阻燃物，灭火剂 ‖ Syn. extinguishing agent 灭火剂；fire extinguishing agent 灭火剂；fire extinguishing medium 灭火介质；fire fighting agent 灭火剂；fire proofing agent 阻燃剂，防燃剂；fire retardancy 阻燃剂；fire retarding agent 防火剂，阻燃剂，耐火剂；fire suppressant 灭火剂

~ tip 焰舌

~ trap 火焰防止筒，火焰防止罩，防陷器，隔陷器

flame-proof 防火的，防爆的

~ cable 防火电缆

~ casing 隔爆外壳

~ equipment 防爆设备 ‖ Syn. explosion-proof equipment 防爆设备

flammability [ˌflæməˈbiləti] n. 易燃性，可燃性

~ analysis 易燃性分析

~ classification 易燃性分级

~ hazard 易燃性危险

~ index 可燃性指数

~ limit 可燃性极限，自燃极限

~ range 可燃性范围

~ test 可燃性试验

flammable [ˈflæməbl] a. 易燃的，可燃的

~ fluid 易燃液体

~ fume 易燃烟气

~ gas 可燃气体

~ limit 可燃极限

~ mixture 可燃混合物

~ range 可燃范围

~ solution 可燃溶液

~ substance 可燃物质

flange [flʌndʒ] n. 边缘，轮缘，凸缘，法兰；v. 装凸缘，装法兰

~ bearing 带法兰盘轴承

~ bolt 法兰螺栓，凸缘螺栓

~ bracing 纵向联杆

~ companion 传动轴凸缘

~ connector 凸缘连接器

~ coupling 凸缘联轴节

~ facing 法兰面，法立接触面，法兰密封面

~ width 法兰宽度，凸缘宽度，轮级宽度

~ wrench 凸缘扳手

~ yoke 凸缘叉

flanged [flændʒd] v. (flange 的过去式和过去分词) 装凸缘，装法兰；a. 带凸缘的，用法兰连接的，折边的

~ coupling 法定连接，法兰联轴节，凸缘联轴器

flank [flæŋk] n. 侧翼，侧面，侧腹，侧边；v. 位于侧面，侧面相接，侧面有，

守侧面，攻击侧面；ad. 在左右两边

flanking ['flæŋkiŋ] n. 下齿面加工，侧面攻击；v. (flank 的 ing 形式) 位于侧面，侧面相接，侧面有，守侧面，攻击侧面；a. 侧翼的

~ rudder 倒车舵

flap [flæp] n. 扁平物，襟翼，拍打，拍打声，不安，恐慌；v. 拍动，拍打，神经紧张，飘动，鼓翼而飞，垂下，扔，拉下帽边

~ gate 翻板闸门，铰链式闸门，阀式闸门

~ switch 拍动式开关

~ type rudder 襟翼舵

~ valve 片状阀，瓣阀

flapper ['flæpə] n. 挡板，(打苍蝇等的)拍子，蝇拍

flare [fleə] n. 闪光，闪耀；v. 闪光，突然烧起来，(使)闪耀，(使)张开，突然发怒，爆发，反射

~ gun 信号枪 ‖ *Syn.* flare pistol 信号枪

flash [flæʃ] n. 闪光，闪现，一瞬间；v. 闪光，闪现，反射，使迅速传遍；a. 闪光的，火速的

~ chamber 闪蒸室，闪发室

~ distilling unit 闪发蒸馏装置

~ evaporation 快速蒸发，闪急蒸发，闪蒸

~ evaporator 闪蒸器

~ gas 闪发气体，闪蒸气体

~ light 闪光灯

~ mold 溢料模具，溢出式铸塑模

~ point 闪点

~ point apparatus 闪点测定仪

flasher ['flæʃə] n. 使灯光忽明忽灭的装置，发出闪光之物

flashing ['flæʃiŋ] n. 闪光，闪烁，防水板，遮雨板；v. (flash 的 ing 形式) 闪光，闪现，反射，使迅速传遍

~ beacon 交通指示柱，闪光标灯

~ device 闪光装置，闪光设施

~ light 闪光灯，闪烁灯

~ light for huge vessel 大船标志灯

~ light for vessel carrying dangerous cargo 危险货船标志灯

~ signal light 闪光信号灯

~ temperature 闪点，闪蒸温度，发火温度，引火温度

~ vest 发光背心

flashlight ['flæʃlait] n. 手电筒，闪光灯

flashover ['flæʃ,əuvə] n. 闪络，跳火

flask [fla:sk] n. 瓶，长颈瓶，细颈瓶，烧瓶，小水瓶

flat [flæt] n. 平地，公寓，平面；v. 逐渐变平，以降调唱(或奏)；a. 平的，单调的，不景气的，干脆的，平坦的，扁平的，浅的

~ bar 扁条，条钢，扁钢条

~ bottom 平底

~ bulb-socket with Edison cap 螺口平头灯

~ chisel 平凿，扁凿

~ coarse file 粗齿扁锉，粗扁锉

~ cold-rolled bar 冷轧扁钢

~ cold-rolled sheet 冷轧薄板

~ head piston 平顶活塞

~ keel 平底，平板龙骨

~ nose pliers 平口钳，平头钳，扁嘴钳

~ pliers 平嘴镊，平钳，平口钳

~ scraper 平面刮刀

~ screw driver 平头螺丝刀

~ smooth file 细扁锉

~ steel 扁钢，平钢，平板钢

~ welding position 平焊位置

fleet [fli:t] *n*. 舰队，船队，港湾，小河；*v*. 消磨，疾驰，飞逝，掠过；*a*. 快速的，敏捷的，浅的，转瞬即逝的

~ Air Arm (FAA) 英国皇家海军航空兵

~ angle 走角，偏离角，偏角，绳索偏角

~ command 舰队指挥官

fleets [fli:ts] *n*. (fleet 的复数) 车队，舰队，捕鱼船队，(同一机构或统一调度的)机群

~ of vessels 船队，舰队

flex [fleks] *n*. 电线，松紧带；*v*. 弯曲(四肢)，伸缩，折曲

flexibility [ˌfleksə'biliti] *n*. 适应性，柔度，柔韧性，机动性，灵活性，弹性，伸缩性，可塑度

~ and hosing test for small water tight hatch cover (water tight door and window) 水密小舱口盖(水密门、窗)启闭灵活性检查和冲水试验

flexible ['fleksəbl] *a*. 柔韧性，易曲的，灵活的，柔软的，能变形的，可通融的

~ AC transmission system (FACTS) 柔性交流输电系统

~ connection 软连接，活动连接，柔性联轴节

~ coupling 挠性联轴器，柔性联轴器，柔性耦合

~ disk 软(磁)盘，柔性碟

~ flat cable (FFC) 挠性扁平电缆

~ hose 柔软管，挠性软管

~ pipe 软管，挠性管

~ wire 软线，花线

flexural ['flekʃərəl] *a*. 曲折的，弯曲的

~ capacity 受弯承载能力

~ member 挠曲杆件

~ rigidity 抗挠刚度

~ strength 挠曲强度

~ stress 弯曲应力，抗弯应力，挠曲应力

~ vibrations 弯曲振动

~ vibrations of shafting 轴系弯曲振动

flight [flait] *n*. 飞行，逃走，飞跃，飞机的航程，班机，追逐，楼梯的一段，射程；*v*. 成群飞行，迁徙，射击(飞禽)，使惊飞

~ deck 飞行甲板

~ schedule 航行时刻表

float [fləut] *n*. 漂流物，浮舟，漂浮，浮萍，彩车；*v*. 浮动，飘浮，散播，摇摆，动摇，容纳，淹没，发行，实行，用水注满

~ chamber 浮箱，浮标，浮子室

~ charge voltage 浮充电压

~ charging 浮充电

~ circuit 浮筒线路

~ off (搁浅的船)浮起

~ regulation valve 浮球调节阀,浮子调节阀

~ rod 浮标

~ switch 浮控开关

~ valve 浮阀

floatability [ˌfləutə'biləti] *n*. 浮动性，可漂浮性

floatation [fləu'teiʃən] *n*. (=flotation) 漂浮，(股票的)首次发行，浮选，浮性，浮力

floated ['fləutid] *v*. (float 的过去式和过去分词) 浮动，飘浮，散播，摇摆，动摇，

容纳，淹没，发行，实行，用水注满；a. 浮动的
~ cable 浮水电缆

floater ['fləutə] n. 漂浮物，浮子，漂浮者，游民，临时工，筹资开办人

floating ['fləutiŋ] n. 漂浮物，浮板，花车；v. (float 的 ing 形式) 浮动，飘浮，散播，摇摆，动摇，容纳，淹没，发行，实行，用水注满；a. 漂浮的，浮动的，移动的，流动的，可变的，不固定的
~ crane 水上浮式起重机，浮吊
~ dock 浮动船坞，浮船坞
~ dock centreline light 浮船坞中心线灯，浮坞中心线灯
~ dock marker light 浮船坞距离标志灯，浮坞标志灯
~ ferry terminal 浮动渡轮码头
~ floor 浮动地板，浮动底板，浮隔地板
~ floor of main deck 主甲板浮动地板
~ goods 过境货物，转口货物
~ ice 浮冰，流冰，漂冰
~ installation 浮动装置
~ installation vessel 浮动安装船
~ lever 游动杠杆
~ lever feedback mechanism 浮动杆反馈机构
~ oil 浮油，漂油
~ oil layer sampler 浮油层取样器
~ power station 浮动发电厂，浮动发电站
~ production storage and offload facility (FPSO) 浮式生产储油轮，浮式生产储存卸货装置
~ production system 浮动式采油系统
~ production vessel 浮动式采油船
~ structure 浮动式结构

~ type automatic oil return valve 浮动式自动回油阀
~ valve 浮阀
~ velocity 漂浮速度

floc [flɔk] n. 絮状物，棉丛
~ point 絮凝点
~ settling 絮凝沉降，絮凝沉淀

flocculant ['flɔkjulənt] n. 凝聚剂
~ aid 凝聚助剂，絮凝助剂

flocculate ['flɔkjuleit] v. 絮凝，絮结

flocculation [flɔkju'leiʃən] n. 絮凝，絮结产物
~ agent 凝聚剂，絮凝剂
~ sedimentation 絮凝沉淀
~ value 絮凝值，凝结值

floccule ['flɔkju:l] n. 絮状物，絮凝粒

flocculent ['flɔkjulənt] a. 絮凝的，羊毛状的，丛毛状的，柔毛状的

flood [flʌd] n. 洪水，水灾，(因雨)涨潮，水；v. 淹没，使泛滥，注满，充满，被水淹，溢出，涌进，喷出，涌出
~ control door 防洪门
~ light 泛光，投光灯

floodable [flʌdəbl] a. 可浸的，可浸水的
~ length (船)可浸长度
~ length curve 可浸长度曲线，可进长度曲线
~ pore 可注入的孔隙

flooded [flʌdid] v. (flood 的过去式和过去分词) 淹没，使泛滥，注满，充满，被水淹，溢出，涌进，喷出，涌出；a. 被水淹的
~ evaporator 满液式蒸发器，泛滥式蒸发器
~ tank 浸水舱

flooding [flʌdiŋ] n. 泛滥，灌溉，溢流，

变色，产后出血；v.(flood 的 ing 形式)淹没，使泛滥，注满，充满，被水淹，溢出，涌进，喷出，涌出

~ angle 泛水角，进水角
~ curve 可浸长度曲线
~ rate 溢流速度
~ valve 溢流阀

floodlight ['flʌdlait] n. 泛光灯，照明灯，探照灯；v. 泛光照明，用泛光灯照亮

floor [flɔ:] n. (房间，走廊等的)地面，地板，基底，(室内的)场地，层，海底，议员席；v. 在…上铺(地板)，击倒，难倒

~ tube 炉底水管

flotation [fləu'teiʃən] n. (=floatation) 漂浮，(股票的)首次发行，浮选，浮性，浮力

flotsam ['flɔtsəm] n. 废料，浮货，零碎物，流离失所者

flow [fləu] n. 流程，流动，(河水)泛滥，洋溢；v. 流动，涌流，川流不息，飘扬，溢过，淹没

~ chart 流程图，作业图，生产过程图解 ‖ **Syn**. flow diagram 流程图，作业图，生产过程图解
~ control 流量控制
~ control meter 流量控制表
~ control valve 流量控制阀，流量调节阀
~ field 流场
~ indicator 流量指示器
~ mark 波纹，流线谱
~ meter 流量计，流量表
~ of momentum 动量流
~ pattern 流型，流线谱，活动模
~ rate 流量，流率
~ regulator 流量调节器，调节速阀
~ resistance 流阻，抗流变
~ sensor 流量传感器，流速传感器 ‖ **Syn**. flow transducer 流量传感器，流速传感器
~ transmitter 流量变送器，流量传送仪
~ velocity 流速

flowing ['fləuiŋ] v. (flow 的 ing 形式) 流动，涌流，川流不息，飘扬，溢过，淹没；a. 流动的，如流的，平滑的，(文章等)流畅的，通顺的

~ proportion 流相比例

flowmeter ['fləumi:tə] n. 流量计

flowrate ['fləureit] n. 流速，流量

~ sensor 流速传感器，流量传感器

fluctuate ['flʌktjueit] v. (使)涨落，(使)上下，(使)动摇，(使)波动，(使)起伏

fluctuation [,flʌktju'eiʃən] n. 波动，涨落，起伏，脉动，动摇不定，踌躇，彷徨变异

~ of power 功率波动

flue [flu:] n. 烟洞，烟道，暖气管，蓬松的东西，渔网

~ blower 烟灰吹除器，吹灰机
~ boiler 焰管锅炉，炉胆式锅炉，燃烧管锅炉
~ dust 烟道尘，烟道灰，烟灰
~ gas 烟道气，废气
~ gas analysis 烟道气分析，废气分析
~ gas system 烟气填充防火系统，烟气系统
~ pass 烟道
~ pipe 烟道排气管，烟筒

fluence [fluəns] n. (神秘的)影响

fluid ['flu:id] n. 液体，流体，流动性，流

度；*a.* 流动的，不固定的，可改变的，可另派用场的，流畅的

~ bearing 液压轴承

~ clutch 液压离合器，液压驱动泵，液压联轴节

~ coupling 液力联轴节

~ drive mechanism 液压传动机构

~ dynamics 流体动力学

~ film 液体薄膜，润滑油膜

~ friction 流体摩擦

~ mechanics 水力学，液体力学

~ viscosity 流体的黏滞性，流体黏度

fluidization [flu:idai'zeiʃən] *n.* 液化，流化，流体化

fluidize ['flu:ədaiz] *v.* 使液化，流(态)化

fluke [flu:k] *n.* 锚爪，意外的挫折，侥幸，倒霉；*v.* 侥幸成功，意外受挫

fluorescent [ˌfluə'resənt] *a.* 荧光的，发荧光的，(颜色、材料等)强烈反光的，发亮的

~ lamp 荧光灯(管)，日光灯(管)

~ scale 荧光刻度盘

fluoro ['flu:ə] *n.* 氟代

fluoro-protein 氟蛋白

~ foamite 氟蛋白泡沫灭火液

flush [flʌʃ] *n.* 奔流，晕红，激动，萌芽，活力旺盛，发烧，惊鸟；*v.* (脸)发红，奔涌，充沛，惊飞，淹没，冲洗，使脸红，使齐平，使惊飞，使激动；*a.* 挥霍的，直接的，丰足的，泛滥的；*ad.* 齐平地，直接地

~ air intake 平直进气口

~ between hatch cover 平舱口

~ bolt 平头插销，平头螺栓

~ conductor 齐平导线

~ deck 平甲板

~ decker 平甲板船

~ deck vessel 平甲板型船

~ from (从隐蔽处)驱逐出去

~ hatch cover 平式舱口盖

~ head 埋头(螺钉头)

~ manhole 齐平人孔

~ mounting 嵌入装置，埋入装置

~ printed board 齐平印制板

~ switch 嵌入式开关，埋入式开关，埋装开关

~ type fluorescent lighting fitting 嵌入式荧光灯

~ with sea water 用海水冲洗

flush-mounted 平镶的，齐装的，暗装的

~ 2-pole receptacle 齐装式两极插座

~ single-pole toggle switch 暗装单极板钮开关

flush-through 溢流浇注

~ connection 冲洗接头

flushing ['flʌʃiŋ] *n.* 脸红；*v.* (flush 的 ing 形式) (脸)发红，奔涌，充沛，惊飞，淹没，冲洗，使脸红，使齐平，使惊飞，使激动；*a.* 使人脸红的

~ fuel oil system of ME 主机燃油管路投油清洗系统

~ lubrication oil of stern tube 艉轴管滑油管路投油清洗系统

~ lubrication oil system of ME 主机滑油管路投油清洗

~ of piping system for mooring winch 绞缆机管路系统的投油清洗

~ of piping system for steering gear 舵机管路系统的投油清洗

~ of piping system for windlass 锚机管路系统的投油清洗

~ procedure 清洗规程

~ pump 清洗用泵，冲洗泵

~ tank 冲洗水柜

~ valve 冲洗阀

~ water 冲厕用水，冲洗水

flute [flu:t] *n*. 长笛，笛状物，凹槽；*v*. 吹笛，发出笛声，刻出凹槽

flux [flʌks] *n*. 涨潮，变迁，流量，通量；*v*. 熔化，流出，使熔融，用焊剂处理

~ density 通量密度，辐射流密度，流量密度

~ leakage 磁漏

~ linkage 磁通匝连数，磁链

fly [flai] *n*. 飞行，苍蝇，两翼昆虫；*v*. 飞翔，飘扬，溃逃，飞越，使飘扬，逃脱；*a*. 机敏的，敏捷的

flyback ['flaibæk] *n*. 回扫，回描

flying ['flaiiŋ] *n*. 飞行，飞花，驾驶飞机；*v*. (fly 的 ing 形式) 飞翔，飘扬，溃逃，飞越，使飘扬，逃脱；*a*. 飞行的，会飞的，迅速的

~ jib 艏三角帆，飞帆，船首三角帆

~ saw 飞锯，随动锯机

flywheel ['flaiwi:l] *n*. 调速轮

~ cover 飞轮壳

FM (frequency modulation) 频率调制，调频

foam [fəum] *n*. 泡沫，泡沫材料，泡沫状物，泡沫橡皮，泡沫塑料；*v*. 起泡沫，冒汗水，吐白沫，使起泡沫，使成泡沫状物

~ concentrate 泡沫浓缩液，泡沫原液

~ extinguisher 泡沫灭火器 ‖ *Syn*. foam fire extinguisher 泡沫灭火器

~ extinguishing agent 泡沫灭火剂

~ extinguishing system 泡沫灭火系统 ‖ *Syn*. foam fire extinguishing system 泡沫灭火系统

~ generator 泡沫发生器 ‖ *Syn*. foam making apparatus 泡沫发生装置

~ making 泡沫发生，泡沫生成，泡沫制造

~ monitor 泡沫炮

~ solution 泡沫溶液

~ solution supply rate 泡沫溶液供给率

~ system 泡沫系统

~ type fire extinguisher 泡沫灭火器，泡沫灭火机

foamite ['fəumait] *n*. 泡沫灭火剂，灭火药沫

FOB (free on board) 离岸价格，船上交货价，离岸价就船交货价格船上交货

focal ['fəukəl] *a*. 焦点的，有焦点的，集中在点上的

focus ['fəukəs] *n*. (兴趣活动等的)中心，焦点，焦距，病灶，震源；*v*. 聚焦，注视，使集中在焦点上，定焦点，调焦，集中

~ on 集中于

fog [fɔg] *n*. 雾，烟雾，尘雾，迷惑，苔藓；*v*. 被雾笼罩，变模糊，使困惑，以雾笼罩

~ lamp 雾灯

~ lubrication 油雾润滑(作用)

~ spar 雾标

foil [fɔil] *n*. 箔，金属薄片，叶形片，烘托，衬托；*v*. 衬托，阻止，挡开，挫败，贴箔于

~ removal surface 去铜箔面

fold [fəuld] *n*. 折，折痕，羊栏，信徒；*v*. 折叠，包，合拢，抱住，笼罩，调入，交叠，折叠起来，彻底失败

folding ['fəuldiŋ] v. (fold 的 ing 形式) 折叠，包，合拢，抱住，笼罩，调入，交叠，折叠起来，彻底失败；a. 可折叠的

~ batch cover 折叠式舱口盖

~ fin stabilizer 折叠式减摇鳍

~ hatch cover 折叠式舱口盖

~ retractable fin stabilizer 折叠收放式减摇鳍

follow ['fɔləu] n. 跟随，追随；v. 跟随，追随，沿…而行，理解，遵循，从事，追求，注视，接着

follow-up 后续工作，继续的，增补的

~ control 随动控制，从动操纵，跟随控制，跟踪调节，跟踪控制

~ control system 随动控制系统

~ gear 随动装置

~ steering 随动操舵

~ system 随动系统

~ system of the mechanical lever feedback type 机械杠杆反馈式随动系统，应急手动操纵装置

~ system with electro-feed-back 电反馈随动系统

following ['fɔləuiŋ] n. 跟随，崇拜者，拥护者，部下，党羽，下列，如下，下列各项；v. (follow 的 ing 形式) 跟随，追随，沿…而行，理解，遵循，从事，追求，注视，接着；a. 后面的，其次的，下列的，顺风的；prep. 随后，在…之后

~ edge (螺旋桨)随边

~ error 跟踪误差

~ ship 后续船

food [fu:d] n. 粮食，食物，食品，材料，资料，养料，精神食粮

~ waste 食物垃圾，食物残渣，餐厨垃圾，厨余，食品废弃物

foodstuff ['fu:dstʌf] n. 粮食，食物，食品

~ refrigerated storage 食品冷藏

foot [fut] n. 足，底部，英尺，步调，步兵，末尾；v. 走在…上，支付，换底，结算，步行，跳舞，总计

~ pedal 脚踏开关

~ switch 脚踏开关，脚踏电门

~ valve 脚踩阀，底阀

footage ['futidʒ] n. 英尺长度，以尺计算长度，连续镜头

footwear ['futweə(r)] n. 鞋类

forecastle ['fəuksl] n. 前甲板，船头的船楼，前甲板下面的水手舱

~ deck 艏楼甲板，船首楼甲板

force [fɔ:s] n. 力，力量，武力，军队，魄力，精力，势力，暴力，影响力，队，组，人员；v. 促使，推动，强迫，强加，用力打开

~ balance 力平衡

~ cell 测力传感器，测力计

~ feedback 力反馈

~ majeure 不可抗力

~ of gravity 重力

forced [fɔ:st] v. (force 的过去式和过去分词) 促使，推动，强迫，强加，用力打开；a. 被迫的，强迫的，用力的，不自然的

~ air cooling 强迫空气冷却

~ circulating boiler 压力循环锅炉

~ circulating pump 强力循环泵，强制循环泵

~ circulation 强制循环，压力环流

~ circulation boiler 压力循环锅炉

~ circulation evaporation 强制循环蒸发
~ commutation 强制换向
~ convection 强制对流
~ draft 强制通风，压力通风 ‖ *Syn*. forced draught 强制通风，压力通风
~ draft control 送风调节
~ draft fan 压力通风风扇，压力送风机，强制通风风扇，鼓风机
~ draft system 压力通风系统
~ draught aerator 压力通气式曝气器
~ draught air pressure 强制通风气压
~ draught condenser 强制通风冷凝器
~ draught fan 压力抽风机，鼓风式风扇，送风机
~ excitation 强制励磁，强迫激励，强励
~ exhaust 强制排气
~ feed 强制进料，加压进料
~ feed lubrication 强制供油润滑(作用)，加压供油润滑(作用)
~ feed water circulation system 强制循环式化冷系统，封闭式液冷系统
~ induction 压力感应
~ lubricating system 压力润滑系统
~ lubrication 压力润滑，强制润滑，加压润滑
~ lubrication pump 压力润滑泵
~ march 强行军
~ oil circulation air cooling 强制油循环吹风冷却
~ oil circulation directed cooling 强迫油循环导向冷却
~ oil circulation water cooling 强迫油循环水冷
~ oil cooling 强迫油冷却
~ oscillation 受迫振荡

ford [fɔːd] *n*. 浅滩，*v*. 涉过，徒涉

fore [fɔr] *n*. 前部，船头；*a*. 以前的，在前部的；*ad*. 在前面，在船头；*prep*. 在前
~ body 前体(自船中到船首)，船身前半部
~ cabin 前部船舱(通常是二等舱)
~ end 前端，前端部分
~ masthead 前桅
~ masthead light 前桅灯
~ peak (tank) 艏尖舱，前尖舱
~ perpendicular 船首垂线，艏垂线，前垂线
~ pump 预抽真空泵，前置泵
~ shoulder 艏水线肩部，前肩，艏突肩
~ side 操作侧，操作面

fore-and-aft 纵向的，从船首到船尾的，前后的，船形的，前后有尖的
~ line 艏艉线，首尾线

forearm [fɔːrˈɑːm] *n*. 前臂；*v*. 准备，准备战斗，预先武装

forebody [ˈfɔːˌbɒdɪ] *n*. 船体前部，船体前半部，弹体前部

forecast [ˈfɔːkɑːst] *n*. 预言，预测，预报，预想；*v*. 预言，预测，预报，预想 ‖ *Syn*. estimate 估计，估算，估量；predict 预言，预测，预报

forecasting [ˈfɔːkɑːstɪŋ] *n*. 预言，预测，预报，预想；*v*. (forecast 的 ing 形式) 预言，预测，预报，预想 ‖ *Syn*. estimation 估计，估算，估量；prediction 预言，预测，预报

forecastle [ˈfəʊks(ə)l] *n*. 前甲板，船头的船楼，前甲板下面的水手舱
~ deck 艏楼甲板
~ head 船头甲板

~ port 船首楼左边

~ rail 艏楼栏杆，船首楼栏杆，首楼栏杆

~ space 艏楼舱，首楼舱

~ structure 首楼结构

forecastleman ['fɔ:kslemæn] *n.* 在前甲板值勤的水手，值勤水手

foreign ['fɔrin] *a.* 外国的，外交的，异质的，不相关的

~ matter 杂质

~ particle 杂质粒子，固体杂质

forelock ['fɔ:lɔk] *n.* 额发，额毛，栓；*v.* 以栓、楔固定，销住

foreman ['fɔ:mən] *n.* 领班，工头，陪审团主席

foremast ['fɔ:ma:st] *n.* 前桅

foremost ['fɔ:məust] *a.* 最重要的，最先的，最初的；*ad.* 首先，居于首位地

forepart ['fɔ:pɔ:t] *n.* 前段，最初，早期，最前部

forepeak ['fɔ:pi:k] *n.* 船首舱

~ bulkhead 艏尖舱壁 ‖ *Syn.* forepeak bulkhemarketing cmorningpaign 艏尖舱壁；forepeak cheaphemarketing 艏尖舱壁

~ pump 艏尖舱泵

~ tank 船头存水舱，艏尖舱

~ tank waterlogged 艏尖舱进水

~ water tank 艏尖水舱

forerake ['fɔ:reik] *n.* 前斜倾度

foresail ['fɔ:seil] *n.* 前桅的大帆

foreshore ['fɔ:ʃɔ:] *n.* 海滩，前滩

forest ['fɔrist] *n.* 森林，林木；*v.* 植树于，森林的，住在森林中的

~ product carrier 木材运输船

forestall [fɔ:'stɔ:l] *v.* 预防，阻止，阻碍，行动，占先一步，囤积居奇，垄断 ‖ *Syn.* countercheck 制止，防止；guard 防止，保卫，警惕，警卫；prevent 预防，防止，制止，阻碍，阻止，阻挠

forge [fɔ:dʒ] *n.* 熔炉，锻铁炉，铁工厂；*v.* 锻造，铸造，伪造，稳步前进

forgeability [,fɔ:dʒə'biləti] *n.* 可锻性

forged [fɔ:dʒd] *v.* (forge 的过去式和过去分词) 锻造，铸造，伪造，稳步前进；*a.* 锻的，伪造的

~ brass 锻造黄铜

~ carbon steel 锻压碳钢

~ flange 锻制法兰，锻接盘

~ joint 锻接合

~ roll 锻造辊

~ steel piston rod 锻钢活塞杆

~ steel stem 锻钢艏柱

~ tee 锻制三通

~ valve 铸造阀

~ weld 锻接焊缝，锻压焊缝

forging ['fɔ:dʒiŋ] *n.* 锻造，锻件，伪造；*v.* (forge 的 ing 形式) 锻造，铸造，伪造，稳步前进

~ die 锻模

~ press 锻压机

~ property 锻造性质

fork [fɔ:k] *n.* 叉，餐叉，耙；*v.* 叉起，分叉，分歧

~ connection 叉头连接，叉状连接

~ and blade connecting rod 叉形中间连杆，叉形连杆

forklift ['fɔ:klift] *n.* 铲车，堆高机，叉式升降机；*v.* 用铲车搬运

~ track 铲车，叉式举升车辆

form [fɔ:m] *n.* 形式，形状，形态，外形，方式，表格；*v.* 形成，构成，组成，

排列，组织，产生，塑造‖ ***Syn.*** build 建造，建筑，创立；construct 建造，构造，创立；erect 建造，建立，开创；make 制造，构造；put up 建造‖ ***Ant.*** deform 毁形，使变形

~ block 成型块

~ resistance 形状阻力，船形阻力，形阻力

form-wound 模绕

~ coil 模绕线圈

~ stator 成型绕组定子

formal ['fɔ:məl] *n.* 正式的社交活动，晚礼服；*a.* 形式的，正式的，拘谨的，有条理的，整齐匀称的

~ Safety Assessment (FSA) 综合安全评估

formaldehyde [fɔ:'mældi,haid] *n.* 甲醛，蚁醛

format ['fɔ:mæt] *n.* 格式，形式，版式，开本；*v.* 格式化，规定⋯的格式，设计版式

formation [fɔ:'meiʃən] *n.* 形成，构成，结构，编队，队形，排列

formation-keeping 航迹，队形保持

~ light 航迹灯，队形保持灯

former ['fɔ:mə] *n.* 模型，样板，形成者，创造者；*a.* 从前的，前者的，前任的

formula ['fɔ:mjulə] *n.* 公式，规则，准则，配方

formulate ['fɔ:mjuleit] *v.* 规划，用公式表示，阐明，明确地表达

formulation [,fɔ:mju'leiʃən] *n.* 构想，规划，公式化，阐明，简洁陈述

forth [fɔ:θ] *ad.* 向前，向外，自⋯以后

forward ['fɔ:wəd] *n.* 前锋；*v.* 促进，转寄，运送；*a.* 前部的，前面的，向前的，

早的，迅速的，反传统的；*ad.* 向前地，向将来，至将来，在将来

~ bow spring 前艏缆

~ channel 正向通道‖ ***Syn.*** forward path 正向通路

~ converter 正向变换器

~ draft mark 船艏水尺

~ draught 艏吃水

~ perpendicular 艏垂线‖ ***Ant.*** aft perpendicular 尾垂线；after perpendicular 艉垂线

~ reasoning 前向推理

~ shaft seal 前轴密封件

~ shoulder 前肩‖ ***Ant.*** after shoulder 后肩

~ stern tube sealing oil tank 艉管前密封滑油柜

~ stern tube sealing oil pump 艉管前密封滑油泵

~ transfer function 正向传递函数

~ voltage drop 正向电压降

~ wind key 速进键

forwarder ['fɔ:wədə] *n.* 运送者，促进者，运输业者，转运公司

forwards ['fɔ:wədz] *ad.* (=forward) 向前方，继续向前

fossil ['fɔsl] *n.* 化石，僵化的事物；*a.* 化石的，陈腐的，守旧的

~ fuel 矿物燃料，化石燃料

foul [faul] *n.* 犯规，缠绕；*v.* 弄脏，淤塞，缠住，缠结，犯规，妨害，腐烂；*a.* 犯规的，邪恶的，污秽的，淤塞的；*ad.* 违反规则地，不正当地

~ air 污浊空气

~ of anchor 缠锚，锚纠缠

~ of propeller 缠螺旋桨

~ water 污水，危险水域

~ weather 恶劣的气候，坏天气

fouling ['fauliŋ] n. 污染，污垢；v. (foul 的 ing 形式) 弄脏，淤塞，缠住，缠结，犯规，妨害，腐烂

~ air turbine 烟气轮机

~ resistance 污垢热阻

found [faund] v. (find 的过去式和过去分词) 发现，找到，认为，觉得，感到，裁决，判定；a. 找到的，找回的，拾得的，拣到的，自然形态的，天然的，不另加费供应的，装备齐全的

~ on 基于，使有根据 ‖ *Syn*. found upon 基于，使有根据

foundation [faun'deiʃən] n. 基础，根据，根本，创立，建立，地基，基金会

~ bolt 地脚螺栓，基础螺栓

~ plate 底座，基础板

foundry ['faundri] n. 铸造，翻砂，铸造厂

~ casting 翻砂铸造

~ equipment 铸造设备

four [fɔ:] n. 四，四个；a. 四的，四个的

~ years from the date of issue 自发行之日起 4 年

four-cycle 四冲程循环的

~ marine diesel engine 四冲程船用柴油机

four-dimensional 四维的，四次元的

four-ram 四柱塞的

~ steering gear 四柱塞操舵装置

four-stroke 四冲程的

~ cycle 四冲程循环

~ engine 四冲程发动机，四冲程引擎

~ marine diesel engine 四冲程船用柴油机

four-way 四面皆通的，由四人参加的

~ directional control valve 四通换向阀

~ valve 四通阀

fourfold ['fɔ:fold] a. 四倍的，四重的，四垒的；ad. 四倍，四重

Fourier ['furiei] n. 傅里叶(① 姓氏；② 1768-1830，法国数学家、物理学家)

~ expansion 傅里叶展开

~ transformation 傅里叶变换

fourth [fɔ:θ] n. 第四，月的第四日，四分之一；a. 第四的，第四个的，四分之一的

~ engineer 三管轮，四轨，四车

FPP (fixed pitch propeller) 固定螺距螺旋桨，定距桨 ‖ *Syn*. fixed pitch screw 固定螺距螺旋桨，定距桨

FPSO (floating production storage and offload facility) 浮式生产储油轮，浮式生产储存卸货装置

fract ['frækt] n. (=fraction) 部分，少许，片断，分数

fractal ['fræktəl] n. 不规则碎片形

fraction ['frækʃən] n. 分数，部分，小部分，片断，稍微

fracture ['fræktʃə] n. 破裂，断裂，骨折；v. (使)破裂，折断

fragile ['frædʒail] a. 脆的，易碎的

fragility [frə'dʒiliti] n. 脆弱，易碎性，虚弱

fragment ['frægmənt] n. 碎片，片段或不完整部分；v. 使成碎片，破碎或裂开

fragmentation [ˌfrægmen'teiʃən] n. 破碎，分裂，存储残片

fraise [freiz] n. 障碍物，爪棱钻

frame [freim] n. 框架，结构，画面；v. 设

计，建造，陷害，使适合，有成功希望；a. 有木架的，有构架的
~ arc lamp 弧光灯
~ box 销售滤光片包装盒，构箱
~ cap 隔框缘条
~ construction 框架结构
~ in 进入，框以…
~ of reference 参照系，坐标，参照标准
~ saw 框锯
~ space 肋距
~ spacing 肋骨间距
~ structure 框架结构
~ type automation air circuit 框架式自动空气循环
~ work 框架，结构
fray [frei] n. 磨损处，争论，打架；v. 使磨损，变得令人紧张、急躁
FRB (fast rescue boat) 快速救助艇 ‖ Syn. FRC (fast rescue craft) 快速救助艇
free [fri:] v. 使自由，解放，释放；a. 免费的，自由的，不受约束的，游离的；ad. 自由地，免费
~ acceleration method 自由加速法
~ access 自由存取，自由入口
~ air capacity 排气量 ‖ Syn. free air delivery 排气量
~ control 自由控制
~ diving 闭气潜水，自由潜水
~ end bearing 活动支承，自由支承
~ energy 自由能
~ exhaust 自由排气
~ expansion 自由膨胀
~ flow 自由流动，自由流向
~ flow valve 易流阀
~ from 使摆脱，免于，解除
~ from crack 无裂纹
~ height 自由高度，净空高度
~ moisture 游离水分，自由湿气
~ of 无…的，摆脱…的，在…外面
~ on board (FOB) 离岸价格，船上交货价，离岸价就船交货价格船上交货
~ oscillation 自由振荡，自由振动 ‖ Syn. free vibration 自激振动，自由振动
~ piston compressor 自由活塞式压缩机
~ port 自由港，无税港
~ radius 自由半径
~ rotating pointer 自由旋转指针
~ rotation 自由转动
~ running 自由航行，空转
~ running resistance 自由航行阻力
~ surface 自由表面，自由面
~ surface effect 自由液面效应
~ up 释放，腾出，解除
free-fall 自由下落，自由下降，自由下跌
~ acceleration 自由落体加速度
~ lifeboat 自由落水救生艇
~ time 自由下落时间
freeboard ['fri:bɔ:d] n. 干舷，出水高度，吃水线以上的船身，离地间隙，自由空间
~ computation 干舷计算
~ deck 干舷甲板
~ deck line 干舷甲板线
~ depth 平船高度
~ depth ratio 干舷型深比
~ mark 干舷标志
~ port 舷墙排水口
~ ratio 干舷比

freeing ['fri:iŋ] n. 解除 v. (free 的 ing 形式) 使自由, 解放, 释放, 免除; a. 任意的; ad. 免费地
  ~ arrangement 排水装置
  ~ installation 货油舱清除气油装置
  ~ line 逸气管路
  ~ port 放水闸, 排水口, 甲板排水孔
  ~ vegetable 冷冻蔬菜

freewheel [,fri:'wi:l] n. 自由轮, 飞轮; v. 靠惯性滑行, 随心所欲
  ~ diode 续流二极管

freeze [fri:z] n. 冻结, 凝固; v. (使)冻住, (使)结冰, 僵硬
  ~ plug 防冻塞, 冰冻保护塞

freezer ['fri:zə] n. 冷冻装置, 冰箱, 冷机, 冷藏库, 制冷工
  ~ defroster 冷冻机除霜器
  ~ vessel 冷藏船

freezing ['fri:ziŋ] n. (freeze 的 ing 形式) (使)冻住, (使)结冰, 僵硬; a. 冰冻的, 严寒的, 冷冻用的
  ~ chamber 冻结室, 冷冻室 ‖ *Syn.* freezing room 冻结室, 冷冻室
  ~ pipe 冻结管, 解冻管
  ~ point 凝固点, 凝固温度
  ~ temperature 冻结温度, 冻结点, 冰点, 凝固温度

freight [freit] n. 货运, 运费, 船货; v. 运送, 装货, 使充满
  ~ rate 运价, 运费率
  ~ carrying 货物运输, 货物承载, 货物载运
  ~ carrying capacity 货物运输能力, 货物承载能力, 货物载运容量
  ~ charge 货运费

freighter ['freitə] n. 货船, 承运人

freon ['fri:ɔn] n. 氟里昂, 二氯二氟代甲烷
  ~ cylinder 氟里昂瓶

frequency ['fri:kwənsi] n. 频率, 频繁
  ~ band 频带, 频段
  ~ characteristic 频率特性
  ~ component 频率成分
  ~ control 频率控制
  ~ conversion 频率变换
  ~ converter 变频器
  ~ division 分频, 频率划分
  ~ domain 频域, 频率范围
  ~ fluctuation 频率波动
  ~ indicator 频率指示器, 频率计, 频率指示计
  ~ meter 频率计
  ~ modulation (FM) 频率调制, 调频
  ~ offset 频率偏移, 频率偏置
  ~ range 频率范围
  ~ regulation 频率调整
  ~ response 频率响应
  ~ setting range 频率整定范围
  ~ spectrum 频谱, 频率谱
  ~ stability factor 频率稳定率
  ~ variation 频率变化

frequent ['fri:kwənt] v. 常到, 常去, 时常出入于; a. 频繁的, 时常发生的

frequently ['fri:kwəntli] ad. 频繁地, 经常地, 时常, 屡次
  ~ starting and stopping 频繁启动和停止

fresh [freʃ] n. 开始, 新生, 泛滥; a. 新鲜的, 清新的, 淡水的, 无经验的; ad. 刚刚, 才, 最新地
  ~ air 新鲜空气
  ~ cooling water inlet 冷却淡水入口

~ cooling water outlet 冷却淡水出口
~ food 新鲜食品
~ water 淡水
~ water circulating pump 淡水循环泵
~ water cooler 淡水冷却器
~ water cooling pump 淡水冷却泵
~ water cooling system 淡水冷却系统
~ water discharging valve 淡水排放阀
~ water filling main 淡水注入总管 ‖ *Syn*. fresh water inlet manifold 淡水注入总管
~ water flow meter 淡水流量计
~ water generator (FGW) 海水淡化装置，造水机
~ water loadline 淡水载重线
~ water pump 淡水泵
~ water system 淡水系统
~ water tank 淡水舱，淡水柜

fret [fret] *v*. (使)磨损，(使)腐蚀，(使)烦恼，(使)焦急

fretsaw ['fretsɔ:] *n*. 线锯，圆锯

fretting [fretiŋ] *n*. 微振磨损,侵蚀；*v*. (fret 的 ing 形式) (使)磨损，(使)腐蚀，(使)烦恼，(使)焦急
~ corrosion 摩擦磨蚀，接触腐蚀

friable ['fraiəbl] *a*. 易碎的，脆弱的

friction ['frikʃən] *n*. 摩擦，摩擦力
~ band brake 摩擦闸箍
~ bearing 滑动轴承
~ block 摩擦闸瓦，摩擦片
~ brake 摩擦刹车，摩擦制动器
~ brake handle 摩擦闸摇柄，摩擦闸摇把，摩擦制动手柄
~ clutch 摩擦离合器
~ coefficient 摩擦系数
~ damping 摩擦阻尼

~ force 摩擦力
~ horsepower 摩擦马力，摩擦功率
~ loss 摩擦损失
~ moment 摩擦力矩
~ velocity 摩擦速度

frictional ['frikʃənəl] *a*. 摩擦的, 由摩擦而生的
~ force 摩擦力
~ resistance 摩擦阻力

frigate ['frigit] *n*. 护卫舰，三帆快速战舰

fringe [frindʒ] *n*. 边缘，穗，刘海；*v*. 成为边缘，加缘饰；*a*. 边缘的，额外的，附加的

fringing ['frindʒiŋ] *n*. 边缘现象，散射现象,边缘通量；*v*. (fringe 的 ing 形式) 成为边缘，加缘饰
~ reef 裙礁，裾礁，岸礁，边礁

from [frɔm] *prep*. 来自，从，由于，今后
~ the point of view 从…的观点看
~ top to bottom 彻底，完全

front [frʌnt] *n*. 前面，开头，前线，阵线，态度,外表；*v*. 面对，朝向，对付 ‖ *Ant*. rear 后面，背后，后方，后面的，背面的，后方的
~ cover 前盖，封面
~ end processor 前端处理器,前端处理机
~ engine 前置发动机，前置引擎
~ feed 前馈
~ header 前管集箱，前管头箱
~ panel 面板
~ resistance 前沿阻力
~ roll entry 前倾式入水
~ side 正视图，正面，前侧
~ sight 前准星
~ stern tube 前艉轴管

~ view 前视图，正视图，正面图

~ water chamber 前水室

~ water space 前储水空间

frontier ['frʌntjə] *n.* 前沿，边界，国境；*a.* 边界的，开拓的

~ defence guard 边防警卫

~ defence inspection station 边防检查站

~ defence inspector 边防检查员

~ defence officer 边防官员

frost [frɔst] *n.* 霜，冰冻，严寒，冷淡；*v.* 结霜，受冻，冻坏

froth [frɔθ] *n.* 泡沫，泡，口沫；*v.* 发泡，吐白沫，起泡沫，使生泡沫

Froude [fru:d] *n.* 弗鲁德(姓氏)

~ number 弗鲁德数

~ wake value 弗鲁德伴流值

frozen ['frəuzn] *v.* (freeze 的过去分词) 结冰，凝固，变得刻板；*a.* 冻结的，冷冰的，冷酷的

~ cargo 冷冻货物，冷冻货，冰冻货

~ injury 冻伤，冻害

fruit [fru:t] *n.* 水果，产物；*v.* 结果

~ carrier 水果船，水果运输船，青果船

frustum ['frʌstəm] *n.* 截头锥体，平截头体

FSA (Formal Safety Assessment) 综合安全评估

FSC (Flag State Control) 船旗国监督，船旗国管理

FSI (Flag State Implementation) 船旗国履约

FSS (fuel safety system) 燃料安全系统

FSSS (furnace safeguard supervisory system) 炉膛安全监控系统

fuel [fjuəl] *n.* 燃料，燃烧剂，刺激因素；*v.* 供以燃料，加燃料，得到燃料

~ alcohol 燃料酒精，动力酒精

~ atomizer 燃油雾化器，燃料喷雾器，燃料雾化器

~ booster module 燃料增压模块

~ booster pump 燃油升压泵，燃油增压泵，燃料升压泵

~ cam 燃油凸轮

~ cell 燃料电池

~ charging valve 进油阀

~ circuit 燃料回路

~ consumption 耗油量

~ consumption rate 燃油消耗率，耗油率，燃料消耗率

~ delivery valve 输油阀，燃油供给阀

~ detergency 燃料净化性

~ economy 燃油经济性，耗热率

~ economy mode 燃油经济模式

~ efficiency 燃油效率，燃料效率

~ equivalence ratio 燃料当量比

~ evaporator 燃料蒸发器

~ flow 燃料流量，燃油流

~ flow meter 燃料流量计，燃油流量表

~ gas 可燃气体，燃料气体

~ gross calorific value 燃油高热值 ‖ *Syn*. fuel high calorific value 燃油高热值；fuel high heating value 燃油高热值

~ hand pump 燃油手泵

~ head 油面高度

~ heating system 燃油加热系统

~ hose 燃油软管

~ ignition quality 燃料自燃性

~ injection 燃油喷射，燃料喷射

~ injection pump 燃料油喷射泵

~ injection rate 喷油速率

~ injection system 燃油喷射系统

256

~ injection valve 燃油喷射阀
~ injection valve cooling pump 燃料喷射阀冷却泵，喷油器冷却泵，喷油嘴冷却泵
~ injection valve tester 燃料喷射阀测试仪
~ injector 燃料喷射器
~ injector cooling pump 喷油器冷却泵
~ injector cooling water pump 喷油器冷却水泵
~ injector holder 喷油器托架，喷油器夹持器
~ injector housing 喷油器壳体
~ injector sleeve 燃油喷射器套筒
~ injector valve 燃油喷射器阀
~ inlet hole 燃料进气孔
~ inlet port 进油口
~ level gauge 油位表，燃油存量表，燃油位调节
~ lever setting 燃油比率操纵杆调定
~ line 燃料管线
~ low calorific value 燃油低热值 ‖ *Syn.* fuel low heating value 燃油低热值；fuel net calorific value 燃油低热值
~ oil 燃料油，燃油，重油
~ oil additive 燃料油添加剂
~ oil automation viscometer 自动化燃油黏度计
~ oil barge 石油驳船，油驳船
~ oil carrier 燃油船
~ oil delivery pump 燃油压送泵
~ oil filling main 燃油充油总管 ‖ *Syn.* fuel oil manifold 燃油注入总管
~ oil filter 燃油过滤器，燃料油过滤器，燃油滤器
~ oil flow 燃油流量

~ oil heater 燃油加热器
~ oil injection system 燃油喷射系统
~ oil pump 燃油泵
~ oil service pump 常用燃油泵，燃料油泵，日用燃油泵
~ oil shift pump 燃油输送泵 ‖ *Syn.* fuel oil transfer pump 燃油输送泵
~ oil strainer 燃油过滤器，燃油滤清器
~ oil supply system 燃油供给系统，燃油系统，燃油供油系统
~ oil system 燃油系统
~ oil tank 燃油舱
~ oil treatment 燃油处理，燃料油处理剂
~ oil treatment system 燃油处理系统
~ penetration 燃料渗透
~ pressure regulating valve 燃油压力调节阀
~ priming pump 手压泵，起动注油泵，燃油充油泵
~ pump 燃油泵
~ pump index 油门刻度
~ pump plunger 燃油泵柱塞，油泵柱塞，燃料泵柱塞
~ pump rack 燃料泵架
~ rack 燃料架，油门齿条，燃料元件架
~ rack position 燃油齿条位置，燃油(喷油泵)齿条位置
~ rate 燃料比，燃料消耗率
~ ratio 燃料比
~ regulation linkage 燃料调节连杆
~ return hole 回油孔
~ return manifold 回油管，回油总管
~ return port 回油口
~ safety system (FSS) 燃料安全系统

~ separator 燃油分离器，燃油分别器，燃油分离装置
~ ship 燃料供应船，加油船，燃料油船
~ spray angle 燃油喷射角
~ spray nozzle 燃料喷嘴，燃油喷口
~ storage facilities 燃料储存设施
~ supply 供油，燃料供给
~ supply line 供油管路，供油管，燃料供给管路
~ supply vessel 燃料供应船舶
~ surcharge 燃油附加费，燃油费，燃油特别附加费
~ system 燃油系统
~ tank 燃料箱，燃油舱
~ transfer operation 燃料转输操作
~ transfer pump 燃油输送泵
~ treatment 可燃物处理
~ water emulsification 燃油水乳化
~ valve 燃油阀
~ valve cooler 喷油器冷却器
~ valve cooling 喷油器冷却
~ valve dribbling 喷油器滴漏，燃油阀滴漏
~ valve spindle 燃油阀轴

fuel-air 燃料空气，燃空
~ ratio 燃料空气比，燃空比

fulcrum ['fʌlkrəm] *n*. 支点，杠杆的支点，叶附属物

fulfill [ful'fil] *v*. 实现，实行，执行，满足 ‖ ***Syn***. cater to 迎合，满足；content 使满足；fill 满足；fulfil 满足；meet 满足，达到要求；satisfy 满足，使满意

fulfillment [ful'filmənt] *n*. 实现，实行，执行，满足

full [ful] *n*. 全部，完整，最大数量，完整数量，极点，鼎盛；*v*. 把衣服缝得宽大；*a*. 充满的，完全的，丰富的，具深度和强度的，大量的，许多的，宽松的，多褶的，完美的，详尽的，丰满的，有资格的，被认可的；*ad*. 完全地，充分地，正确地，直接地

~ ahead 前进三，全速正车
~ astern 后退三，全速倒车
~ automatic processing 全自动处理
~ bore 贯眼，全径
~ bridge converter 全桥变换器
~ bridge rectifier 全桥式整流器，全桥整流电路
~ container 整装货柜，整集装箱，整箱
~ container load 集装箱整箱货物
~ container ship 集装箱专用船
~ floating piston pin 全浮式活塞销
‖ semi-floating piston pin 半浮式活塞销
~ flow filter 全流式滤清器，满流过滤器
~ form 完全形式，肥线型，肥船型
~ length 全长，标准长度
~ liability 完全责任
~ load 满载，全负荷
~ load method 全负荷法
~ load torque 满载转矩
~ load weight 满载重量，总载重量
~ name 全名，全称
~ out 最快地
~ output current 最大输出电流
~ scale 全尺寸，原大的，完全的，全刻度的，满量程
~ scale seakeeping trials 实船适航性试验
~ scale trial result 全尺寸试验结果
~ scale trials 全面试验

~ scan 满扫描，全扫描试验
~ scantling 全尺寸
~ score 满分
~ set 全套，全组
~ speed 全速
~ time 专职，全部时间
~ wave rectifier 全波整流器
fuller [fulə] n. 套柄铁锤，漂洗工
fully ['fuli] ad. 充分地，完全地，足足，至少
~ automatic 全自动的
~ enclosed 全封闭的
~ enclosed transformer 全封闭变压器
~ integrated 全集成的
~ loaded 满载的
~ refrigerated type gas carrier 全制冷型气体运输船
fume [fju:m] n. 烟，气体，愤怒，烦恼；v. 熏，冒烟，发怒，愤怒地说
~ extraction 烟雾回收，烟雾提取
~ extractor 排烟装置
~ hood 通风橱，烟橱
function ['fʌŋkʃən] n. 官能，功能，作用，职责，典礼，仪式；v. 运行，活动，行使职责，起作用 ‖ Ant. malfunction 故障，失灵，功能障碍
~ test 功能测试，功能试验
~ test and adjust error for log on sea trial 航行试验中计程仪效用试验及误差调整
~ test and automatic controller test for ballast pump 压载泵效用试验和自动控制装置试验
~ test and calibration self-heterodyne curve for direction finder on sea trial 航行试验中测向仪效用试验及自差曲线校正

~ test automatic pilot 自动舵效用试验
~ test for economizer 废气锅炉效用试验
~ test for weather facsimile receiver 气象传真机效用试验
~ test of bilge oily water separator (sewage treatment plant, fresh water generator, incinerator) 舱底水油水分离器(污水处理装置、淡水制造装置、焚烧炉)效用试验
~ test of echo sounder 测深仪效用试验
~ test of engineer calling device 轮机员呼叫装置效用试验
~ test of fog horn 雾笛效用试验
~ test of radar on sea trial (mooring test) 航行试验(系泊试验)中雷达效用试验
~ test of radio console on sea trial 航行试验中组装报务台效用试验
~ test of remote control system of main engine 主机遥控系统性能试验
~ test of ultra-short wave radio telephone 超短波对讲机
functional ['fʌŋkʃənl] a. 功能的，职责的，函数的，实用的
~ component 功能组成部分，功能部件
~ decomposition 功能分解
~ similarity 功能相似，函数相似
~ software 功能软件
functionality [ˌfʌŋkʃə'næliti] n. 功能性，泛函性
fundament ['fʌndəmənt] n. 基础，臀部，肛门
fundamental [ˌfʌndə'mentl] n. 基本原理，基本原则；a. 基础的，基本的，根本的
~ component 基本成分，基波分量，基础分量

~ factor 基本因素，基波系数

~ fuel lower calorific value 基准燃油低热值

~ function 基本功能，特征函数，基本函数

~ law 基本法，基本定律

~ parameters of electric power system of a ship 船舶电力系统基本参数

~ plane 基面

~ principle 基本原则

~ unit 基本单位

fundamentals [ˌfʌndə'mentl] *n.* (fundamental 的复数) 基本面，基本原理

~ for Electrical Towage 电力拖动基础

~ of Circuit Measurement Technology 电路测试技术基础

fungus ['fʌŋgəs] *n.* 霉菌，真菌，菌类

funnel ['fʌnəl] *n.* 漏斗，漏斗状物，通风井，烟囱；*v.* (使)成漏斗状，经过漏斗，通过烟筒或通道

~ flue 烟道

~ mark 烟囱标记

~ mouth 漏斗状口

furnace ['fə:nis] *n.* 火炉，熔炉

~ door 炉门

~ explosion 炉膛爆炸，炉膛爆燃

~ flue 火管，焰管，炉子烟道

~ gas 炉气，炉内气体

~ lining 炉衬

~ safeguard supervisory system (FSSS) (锅炉)炉膛安全监控系统

~ temperature 炉温，燃烧炉温度

~ tube 炉管

~ uptake 锅炉烟囱

~ wall 炉壁

furnish ['fə:niʃ] *v.* 供应，提供，装备，布置

furniture ['fə:nitʃə] *n.* 设备，家具，储藏物 ‖ ***Syn***. apparatus 器械，设备，仪器；appliance 用具，器具；arrangement 布置；assembly 组装部件；device 装置，设备；equipment 装备，设备，器材，装置；facility 设备，工具；gear 设备，装备；installation 设备，装置；machine 机器，机械，机构；machinery 机械(总称)，机器；mechanism 机器，机械装置，机构；plant 设备；provision 装备，供应品；turnout 装备，设备；unit 装置，设备

further ['fə:ðə] *v.* 促进，助长，增进；*a.* 更远的，深一层；*ad.* 进一步地，更远地

~ development 进一步的发展

~ protective security measure 进一步的防护安全措施

furthermore [fə:rðə'mɔ:(r)] *ad.* 此外，而且，加之

fuse [fju:z] *n.* 保险丝，熔线，导火线，雷管；*v.* (使)融合，(使)熔化

~ breaker 熔丝断路器

~ cap 熔丝帽，保险丝铜帽，火雷管

~ carrier 熔线握，熔断器载具

~ cartridge 熔线盒

~ case 熔丝盒，保险丝箱

~ current 熔丝电流

~ cutout 保险器，熔丝断路器

~ element 熔线元件

~ equipment 熔丝装置，保险丝设备

~ holder 熔丝支持器，熔丝架，保险丝支架

~ protection 熔断保护

~ socket 熔丝管座

~ strip 片状熔丝

~ tester 熔丝测量器

~ together 熔合

~ wire 熔丝，保险丝

fusible ['fju:zəbl] *a.* 易熔的，可熔的

~ alloy 易熔合金，低熔合金

~ interlining 粘合衬，粘补，热熔衬

~ plug 易熔塞，保险丝插塞

~ plug boss 易熔塞座

~ resistor 可熔电阻，熔阻丝

fusion ['fju:ʒən] *n.* 融合，熔化，熔解，熔接，融合物，核聚变

fuzzy ['fʌzi] *a.* 模糊的，失真的，有绒毛的

FWE (finished with engine) 停机，完车，用车完毕

G

gabbard ['gæbəd] *n.* 苏格兰昔时的帆船，平底河船

gaff [gæf] *n.* 帆船上缘的斜桁，鱼叉；*v.* 用鱼叉捉，用鱼钩拖上来，欺骗，赌博

~ foresail 前桅主帆

~ halyard 斜桁吊索

gage [geidʒ] *n.* 计量器，挑战，抵押品；*v.* 以…为担保，以…为赌注

gain [gein] *n.* 增加，扩大率，倍率，增益，利润，收获；*v.* 增加，增长，获利，获得，增加，赚到，开腰槽于 ‖ *Syn*. amplification 扩大，放大，放大率

~ constant 增益常数，放大系数

~ crossover 增益窜度，放大临界点

~ crossover frequency 增益交越频率，增益交叉频率，增益窜度频率

galleon ['gæliən] *n.* (=carrack) 大帆船(15至18世纪初军舰商船两用的)

gallery ['gæləri] *n.* 船尾瞭望台，走廊，地道，阳台，眺望台，图库，旁听席；*v.* 修建走廊，挖地道

galley ['gæli] *n.* 狭长船，大型划船，船上厨房，军舰

~ and laundry equipment to be done function 厨房、洗衣间设备交验

~ boy 厨房服务生 ‖ *Syn*. galley steward 厨房服务生

~ CO_2 piping to be done air-tightness test 厨房 CO_2 管系密性试验

~ equipment 厨房设备

~ exhaust duct 厨房排风管道

~ machine 厨房设备

gallon ['gælən] *n.* 加仑(容量单位)

~ oil can 加仑油壶

gallonage ['gælənidʒ] *n.* 加仑数，加仑量

galvanic [gæl'vænik] *a.* 电流的，使人震惊的，触电似的

~ corrosion 接触腐蚀，原电池腐蚀，电化学腐蚀

galvanize ['gælvənaiz] *v.* 镀锌，通电，刺激

galvanized ['gælvənaizd] *v.* (galvanize 的过去式和过去分词) 镀锌，通电，刺激；*a.* 镀锌的，电镀的

~ iron sheet 镀锌铁皮，白铁皮

~ iron wire 镀锌铁丝，铅丝

~ pipe 镀锌管

~ stranded wire 镀锌钢绞线

~ steel wire 镀锌钢丝

~ steel wire fencing 镀锌钢栅网

galvanometer [ˌgælvə'nɔmitə] *n.* 检流计，电流计

gang [gæŋ] *n.* 群，团体，一伙，一组，一套；*v.* 使成群结队，结伙伤害或恐吓某人，成群结队

~ plank 跳板

~ saw 直锯

gangway ['gæŋwei] *n.* 舷梯，跳板，进出通路，座间过道；*int.* 让路！躲开！

~ bridge 通路船桥，步桥舷门跳板

~ chain 栏链

~ diaphragm 通道折棚

~ duties 舷梯值班

~ light 舷道灯

~ man 舷梯值班人员

~ net 舷梯安全网

~ port 舷门，梯口门

~ rail 梯口栏杆

~ screen 舷梯帆布条

~ tackle 舷梯绞辘

gantry ['gæntri] *n.* (*pl.* gantries) 桶架，构台，起重机架

~ beam 龙门架梁

~ type hatch cover crane 龙门式舱口盖起重机

gap [gæp] *n.* 缺口，裂口，间隙，缝隙，差距，隔阂；*v.* 使形成缺口，裂开

garbage ['gɔ:bidʒ] *n.* 垃圾，废物

~ boat 垃圾艇，垃圾船

~ can 垃圾桶，垃圾箱

~ chute 垃圾卸槽

~ disposal 垃圾处理

~ disposal log 垃圾处理日志

~ grinder 垃圾磨碎机

~ lighter 垃圾驳船，垃圾驳

~ management plan 垃圾管理计划

~ Record Book 垃圾记录簿

garboard ['ga:bɔ:d] *n.* 龙骨翼板

gas [gæs] *n.* 气体，气体燃料，瓦斯，汽油，毒气，窒息；*v.* 加油，放出气体，空谈 ‖ liquid 液体，流体；solid 固体

~ alarm 气体信号装置，瓦斯报警器，毒气警报

~ anchor 气锚

~ bearing 气体轴承

~ boiler 燃气锅炉，煤气锅炉

~ bottle 气瓶

~ brazing 火焰钎焊,气体火焰硬钎焊,火焰铜焊

~ buildup 气体积聚

~ bulb thermometer 充气式温度计

~ burette 气体量管，气体滴定管

~ cap 气顶，气冠，油箱门

~ cap injection 气顶注气

~ carrier 液化气船，气体运输船

~ carrier code 气体载运船章程

~ carrier standards 液化气船标准

~ carrier types 液化气船类型

~ cartridge fire extinguisher 贮气瓶式灭火器

~ charging 充气

~ charging valve 充气阀(蓄能器)

~ chromatography 气相色谱分析

~ compressor 气体压缩机

~ condensate 凝析油，气体凝析物

~ cutting 气割，氧炔切割

~ cylinder 集气筒，高压气瓶

~ dangerous space 气体危险处所

~ dehydrator 气体脱水器

~ detection 气体检测

~ detection system 气体探测系统

~ detector 气体检测器，气体探测器，瓦斯检查器，检气管

~ discharge lamp 气体放电灯

~ engine 内燃机，气体发动机

~ engine driven 燃气发动机驱动的

~ exchange 气体交换，换气

~ fire detector 气体火灾探测器
~ flow 气流
~ free 不含气的
~ free certificate (油舱)气体检验证书
~ freeing 脱气
~ freeing outlet 气体释放出口, 除气口
~ fuel 气体燃料
~ heater 气体加热器, 燃气热水器
~ heating 气体加热, 燃气供热, 煤气供暖
~ indicator 煤气指示器
~ injection 注气, 煤气喷射
~ inlet casing 进气箱,进气机匣 ‖ *Syn*. gas inlet chamber 进气箱
~ inlet housing 涡轮进气壳
~ leak 漏气, (底火)漏火
~ mask 防毒面具, 毒气面具
~ oil 柴油
~ outlet 气体出口
~ phase 气相, 气态
~ pliers 气管钳
~ pocket 气孔, 气泡, 气窝
~ pressure 气压, 气体压力, 煤气压力
~ pressure alarm device 降压告警器
~ processing equipment 气体发生设备
~ relay 闸流管
~ scrubber 气体洗涤器
~ safe space 气体安全舱
~ seal 气封
~ seal separation 气封分离
~ tanker 气槽船
~ tap 管螺纹丝锥, 管用丝锥
~ tight connection 气密连接
~ tightness 不透气性, 气密性
~ turbine 燃气轮机, 燃气涡轮
~ turbine generator set 燃气轮机发电机组
~ turbine power plant 燃气轮机发电设备, 燃气轮动力装置, 燃气轮机发电厂
~ turbine ship 燃气轮机船
~ type 燃气类型
~ up 加油
~ warning system 气体报警装置
~ welding blowpipe 气焊吹管
~ welding outfit 气焊机 ‖ *Syn*. gas welding machine 气焊机
gas-insulated 气体绝缘的
~ substation (GIS) 气体绝缘变电站
~ switchgear (GIS) 气体绝缘封闭组合电器
~ transformer (GIT) 气体绝缘变压器
gaseous ['gæsiəs] *a*. 气态的, 气体的, 无实质的
~ insulation 气体绝缘
gasification [ˌgæsifi'keiʃən] *n*. 气化
gasket ['gæskit] *n*. 垫圈, 衬垫, 束帆索
~ paper 垫片纸
~ seal 密封垫片, 固定密封
~ opening 密封垫开口
gasoline ['gæsəli:n] *n*. 汽油
~ engine 汽油机, 汽油发动机
~ oxidation 汽油氧化
gasometer [gæ'sɔmitə] *n*. 气量计, 储气器
gastight ['gæs'tait] *a*. 耐气构造的, 不漏气的
~ block 气闭头
~ bulkhead 气密舱壁
~ door 供应气密门
~ lighting 气密照明
~ machine 密封式电机
~ ring 气密环
~ sleeve 气密喉套

~ syringe 气密注射器

~ test 气密试验

~ thread 气密螺纹

gasway ['gæswei] *n.* 气体管道

gate [geit] *n.* 大门，出入口，门道；*v.* 装大门

~ turn-off thyristor (GTO) 门极可关断晶闸管

~ valve 闸门阀，闸式阀

gateway ['geitwei] *n.* 门，网关，方法，通道，途径

gather ['gæðə] *n.* 聚集，衣褶，收获量；*v.* 集合，(使)聚集，渐增，搜集，推断

gauge [gedʒ] *n.* 标准尺，规格，量规，量表，评估，相对位置，口径，直径，厚度；*v.* 测量，估计，判断，定规格，采用，切割

~ by means of micrometer 用千分尺测量

~ glass 玻璃液面计，水位玻璃管

~ plate 样本，样板，轨距板

~ pressure 表压，计示压力

gauging ['geidʒiŋ] *n.* 测定，测量，计量；*v.* (gauge 的 ing 形式) 测量，估计，判断，定规格，采用，切割

~ device 计量装置

~ disc 测径板

~ engineer 测量工程师，测试工程师，检具工程师

~ system 度量系统，计量系统

~ table 计量表

~ tank 计量桶，计量储槽

~ water 定量水

gear [giə] *n.* 齿轮，传动装置，设备，装备，工具，船上的索具，海员的个人财物；*v.* 开动，调整，调和，接上，(使)适合，装备，以齿轮装配，换挡 ‖ **Syn**. apparatus 器械，设备，仪器；appliance 用具，器具；arrangement 布置；assembly 组装部件；device 装置，设备；equipment 装备，设备，器材，装置；facility 设备，工具；furniture 设备，家具；installation 设备，装置；machine 机器，机械，机构；machinery 机械(总称)，机器；mechanism 机器，机械装置，机构；plant 设备；provision 装备，供应品；turnout 装备，设备；unit 装置，设备

~ assembly 齿轮传动装置，减速器

~ bag 潜水装备袋

~ bank 齿轮组

~ blank 齿轮坯料，齿轮毛坯

~ box 齿轮箱，传动箱

~ casing 齿轮箱，变速箱

~ coupling 齿轮联轴器，齿轮联轴节

~ cover 齿轮罩

~ cutting machine 切齿机，齿轮加工机床

~ drive 齿轮传动

~ grease 齿轮润滑脂

~ grinding 齿轮磨削

~ machining 齿轮加工

~ oil 齿轮油

~ pump 齿轮泵

~ quadrant steering gear 齿扇转舵装置

~ rack 齿条，齿轮齿条

~ ratio 齿轮齿数比

~ reducer 减速器，齿轮减速箱，齿轮减速装置

~ reduction ratio 齿轮减速比

~ shaft 齿轮轴

~ shaping 刨齿

~ teeth 齿轮齿，轮齿
~ to 使适合
~ train 齿轮系，传动机构，齿轮传动链
~ transmission 齿轮传动
~ tumbler 齿轮换向器，转向轮
~ type oil motor 齿轮式油马达
~ up 为…准备好
~ wheel 齿轮
~ with 适合，一致

gearbox ['giəbɔks] *n.* 变速箱，齿轮箱
~ casing 变速箱体，齿轮箱体

gearless ['giəlis] *a.* 无齿轮的，无传动装置的

GEF (Global Environment Facility) 全球环境基金会

gel [dʒel] *n.* 凝胶，胶冻，凝胶体；*v.* 胶凝，胶化，形成胶体，成形

gelling ['dʒeliŋ] *n.* 胶凝(作用)，凝胶化(作用)；*v.* (gel 的 ing 形式) 胶凝，胶化，形成胶体，成形
~ agent 胶凝剂
~ fluid 液凝胶
~ property 胶凝性能
~ power 胶凝力

general ['dʒenərəl] *n.* 普通，将军，概要，常规；*a.* 一般的，普通的，普遍的，流行的，综合的，概括的，全面的，全面的，大体的，最高的 ‖ **Syn.** common 公共的，普通的；commonplace 平凡的；ordinary 平常的，平凡的，普通的；pervasive 普遍的；popular 通俗的，普遍的，普及的，平民的；universal 普遍的，通用的；usual 平常的，通常的，惯例的；widespread 分布广泛的，普遍的

~ alarm 总报警，通用报警，全船报警装置
~ alarm bell 常规警铃，通用警铃
~ arrangement 总布置
~ arrangement plan 总布置图
~ average 共同海损
~ average act 共同海损法
~ cargo 一般货物，杂货，普通货物
~ cargo carrier 普通货轮，杂货船 ‖ **Syn.** general cargo ship 普通货轮，杂货船
~ corrosion 一般腐蚀，全面腐蚀
~ design 总设计，通用设计
~ distribution box 总配电箱
~ emergency alarm 通用紧急警报
~ fire alarm control unit 通用火灾报警控制器
~ inspection of lifesaving appliance 救生设备到位检查
~ installation details 普通的安装细节
~ level 一般水平，总水平
~ lighting 一般照明，全面照明
~ machining center 普通加工中心
~ maintenance 一般养护
~ plan 总体规划，总图
~ power outlet (GPO) 通用电源插座
~ pump 工频泵，一般泵
~ purpose 万能，通用
~ purpose function 通用函数，任意函数
~ repair 大修
~ requirements 一般要求，总要求，常规要求
~ rule 通则，一般规则
~ service pump 通用泵
~ test problem 一般试验问题
~ trend 一般趋势

generality [ˌdʒenəˈræliti] n. 一般性,通则,概论,一般原则,大多数,大部分

generally [ˈdʒenərəli] ad. 通常,普遍地,一般地

generate [ˈdʒenəˌreit] v. 产生,发生,形成,创造,造成

generating [ˈdʒenəˌreitiŋ] n. 产生,发生;v. (generate 的 ing 形式) 产生,发生,形成,创造,造成; a. 产生的,生成的

~ capacity 发电量,发电容量
~ circle (齿轮的)基圆
~ cost 发电成本
~ equipment 发电设备
~ line 发生线,母线,动线
~ machinery 发电机 ‖ Syn. dynamo 发电机; electrical machine 发电机; generator 发电机
~ plant 发电站,发电厂,发电设备 ‖ Syn. generating station 发电站
~ radius 创成半径
~ set 发电机组,发电装置
~ system 发电系统
~ tube (蒸汽锅炉的)热水管,拱砖管
~ unit 发电机组

generation [ˌdʒenəˈreiʃən] n. 产生,一代,一代人

generator [ˈdʒenəreitə] n. 发电机,发生器,生产者 ‖ Syn. dynamo 发电机; electrical machine 发电机; generating machinery 发电机

~ black emergency maneuver 发电机跳电应急操纵
~ body 发电机壳
~ bus bar 发电机母线
~ cap 发电机盖
~ charge indicator 发电机充电指示灯
~ circuit 发电机电路
~ commutation 发电机整流,发电机换向
~ control panel 发电机控制面板
~ coupling 发电机轴节
~ cutout 发电机断流器
~ excitation 发电机励磁
~ excitation circuit 发电机励磁回路
~ excitation panel 发电机励磁面板
~ excitation system 发电机励磁系统
~ exciter 发电机励磁机
~ frame 发电机机座
~ main brush 发电机主电刷
~ regulator 发电机调压器
~ set 发电机组
~ terminal 发电机线接头
~ tripping 发电机跳闸
~ voltage controller 发电机电压控制器,发电机电压调节器
~ voltage 发电机电压
~ yoke 发电机构架

generatrix [ˈdʒenəreitriks] n. 母线,母面,母点

genset [ˈdʒenset] n. 发电机组

~ running hour meter 机组运行小时表

gentleman [ˈdʒentlmən] n. 阁下,先生,有身份的人,绅士,男厕所,男盥洗室

gentlemen [ˈdʒentlmen] n. (gentleman 的复数) 阁下,先生,有身份的人,绅士,男厕所,男盥洗室

gentlemen's 男人的,男的

~ room 男厕所,男盥洗室

geography [dʒiˈɔgrəfi] n. 地理学,地理

geomagnetic [ˌdʒiːəumægˈnetik] a. 地磁的

geometric [dʒiə'metrik] *a.* (=geometrical) 几何的，几何学的
~ similarity 几何相似
~ solid 几何体

geometrical [dʒiə'metrikəl] *a.* (=geometric) 几何的，几何学的
~ position 几何位置

geometrically [dʒiə'metrikəli] *ad.* 几何学上，用几何学，按几何级数
~ similar form 几何相似形式

geometry [dʒi'ɔmitri] *n.* 几何学，几何结构
~ constraint 几何约束
~ correction 几何校正

geotechnical [dʒi:əu'teknikəl] *a.* 岩土工程技术的
~ ship 岩土工程船

get [get] *n.* 生殖，幼兽；*v.* 获得，收获，使得，到达，成为，变成，变得，受到，抓住，染上
~ a fix on (通过雷达等电子仪器)定出位置

giant ['dʒaiənt] *n.* 巨人，伟人，能力高强的人，巨大动物；*a.* 巨大的，庞大的
~ transistor 大功率晶体管

gig [gig] *n.* 赛艇，快艇，轻快的划艇，单列座小舢板，旋转物体

gigahertz ['gigəhə:ts] *n.* 千兆赫

gimlet ['gimlit] *n.* 手钻，螺丝锥 ‖ *Syn.* auger 螺丝钻

gin [dʒin] *n.* 起重机，打桩机，机械装置，陷阱；*v.* 轧

gird [gə:d] *v.* 束缚，佩带，拉紧，准备，装备，供应

girder ['gə:də] *n.* 大梁，纵梁，钢桁支架

~ of foundation 基座纵桁
~ pass 钢梁孔型
~ strop 梁磨刀皮带
~ truss 梁构桁架，桁架梁

GIS (gas insulated substation) 气体绝缘变电站

GIS (gas insulated switchgear) 气体绝缘封闭组合电器

GIT (gas insulated transformer) 气体绝缘变压器

give [giv] *n.* 弹性，弯曲，可弯性，伸展性；*v.* 给，授予，供给，献出，让步，引起，发表，捐助
~ full play to 充分发挥
~ two coats of A/C paint 给两层 A/C 油漆

given ['givn] *n.* 假设；*v.* (give 的过去分词) 给，授予，供给，献出，让步，引起，发表，捐助；*a.* 赠予的，沉溺的，特定的，假设的

gland [glænd] *n.* 腺，密封管，密封套，密封装置
~ bolt 压盖螺栓
~ box 填料函，填料箱，填料盒
~ box for piston rod 活塞杆填料函
~ bush 压盖，衬片，密封垫，密封装置，气封套
~ cover 密封压盖，填料盖，密封套
~ expansion joint 伸缩接合
~ packing 压盖填料，填料密封，填料压盖
~ plunger 压盖柱塞

glandless ['glændlis] *a.* 无垫料的，无密封垫的
~ circulating pump 无填料函循环泵
~ lining 压盖衬层

267

~ metering pump 无轴封计量泵

~ motor pump 全密封泵

~ pump 无压盖泵

glandular ['glændjulə] *a.* 腺的，腺状的

glass [gla:s] *n.* 玻璃，玻璃制品，玻璃杯，镜子，眼镜，望远镜，气压计，晴雨表；*v.* 成玻璃状，装玻璃于，反映

~ bottle 玻璃瓶

~ crushing unit 玻璃粉碎装置

~ cutter 玻璃刀

~ fabric 玻璃纤维布，玻璃纤维织物，玻璃织物

~ faceplate 玻璃面板

~ fiber 玻璃纤维

~ flake composite 玻璃片组合件

~ funnel 玻璃漏斗

~ gauge 玻璃管规

~ fuse 玻璃熔丝

~ insulator 玻璃绝缘子

~ mat 玻璃垫

~ pressure tube 玻璃压力管

~ stick 玻璃棒

~ tube 玻璃管

~ tube cutter 玻璃管切割机

~ water (level) gauge 玻璃水位计

~ cover 玻璃罩

~ cover measuring cylinder 玻璃罩量筒

glass-reinforced 玻璃增强的

~ pipe 玻璃增强管

~ plastic 玻璃钢，玻璃纤维增强塑料

~ thermoplastic molding 玻璃(纤维)增强热塑模制品

glasses ['glæsiz] *n.* (glass 的复数) 眼镜，玻璃，双筒望远镜

global ['gləubəl] *a.* 全球的，总体的，球形的

~ Ballast Water Management Programme (GloBallast) 全球压载水管理项目

~ Environment Facility (GEF) 全球环境基金会

~ Maritime Distress and Safety System (GMDSS) 全球海上遇险安全系统

~ Navigation Satellite System (GNSS) 全球导航卫星系统

~ Positioning System (GPS) 全球定位系统

~ System for Mobile Communication (GSM) 全球移动通信系统

~ warming 全球变暖

GloBallast (Global Ballast Water Management Programme) 全球压载水管理项目

globe [gləub] *n.* 地球，地球仪，球体，世界

~ buoy 球形浮标

~ lamp 球形灯

~ valve 球心阀

globoid ['gləubɔid] *n.* 球状体；*a.* 球状的，略成球状的

~ worm gear 球形蜗轮蜗杆

globular ['glɔbjulə] *a.* 球状的，全世界的，全球的

globule ['glɔbju:l] *n.* 水珠，小球，药丸，血球

glow [gləu] *n.* 白热，炽热，激情，热烈；*v.* 发光，发热

~ lamp 辉光灯，辉光放电管

~ plug 电热塞

~ radius 发光半径

glue [glu:] *n.* 胶，各种胶合物

~ solution 胶液，液体胶

glycerine ['glisəri:n] *n.* 丙三醇，甘油

glycol ['glaikɔl] *n.* 乙二醇，甘醇，二羟基醇

GMDSS (Global Maritime Distress and Safety System) 全球海上遇险安全系统

GNSS (Global Navigation Satellite System) 全球导航卫星系统

go [gəu] *n.* 去，进行；*v.* 离去，走，进行，变成，趋于，达到，求助于，诉诸，忍受

~ off duty 下班

~ on with 继续，进行，暂时使用

~ over 仔细检查，复习，重温，转变，润色

~ through 参加，经受，仔细检查，通过

~ with 伴随，与…相配，和交朋友

~ without 没有…也行

goggle ['gɔgl] *n.* 护目镜，防风镜，防水镜，瞪视；*v.* 瞪眼看，(使)眼珠转动；*a.* 瞪眼的，睁眼的

goggles ['gɔglz] *n.* (goggle 的复数) 风镜，护目镜，瞪视；*v.* (goggle 的第三人称单数) 瞪眼看，(使)眼珠转动 ‖ *Syn.* protective glasses 护目镜，防护眼镜；safety glasses 护目镜，防护眼镜

gold [gəuld] *n.* 金，黄金，金色，金币

~ bump 金隆起焊盘，金凸墥

~ enamel paint 黄色瓷漆

~ plated 镀金

golden ['gəuldən] *a.* 金色的，黄金般的，珍贵的，金制的

~ yellow flame 金黄色的火焰

gong [gɔŋ] *n.* 锣，钟状物，奖章

goniometer [ˌgəuni'ɔmitə] *n.* 测角器，角度计

good [gud] *n.* 好，好事，慷慨的行为，好处，利益；*a.* 好的，优良的，愉快的，虔诚的

~ performance 良好性能

~ quality 质量好

gooseneck ['gu:snek] *n.* 雁颈，鹅颈管，曲如鹅颈之物

~ bracket 鹅颈座，吊杆座

~ clamp 弯脖压板

~ crane 鹅颈式起重机

~ faucet 鹅颈形龙头

~ light 鹅颈式光

~ machine 鹅颈式压铸机

~ post lamp 鹅颈式柱灯

~ vent 鹅颈形通风管

~ ventilator 鹅颈式通风管 ‖ *Syn.* swanneck ventilator 鹅颈通风管

gouge [gaudʒ] *v.* 用半圆凿子挖，欺骗

govern ['gʌvən] *v.* 控制，操纵，调节，支配，统治，管理 ‖ *Syn.* control 控制，操纵，支配，调节，管理；regulate 控制，调节，校准，管制

governing ['gʌvəniŋ] *n.* 控制，治理，管理，操纵，调整，调节；*v.* (govern 的 ing 形式) 控制，操纵，调节，支配，统治，管理

~ equation 控制方程

~ error 控制误差，调节误差，主要误差

~ factor 控制因素，决定因素，支配因素

~ law 管辖法律，管辖法，准据法

~ performance test 调速性能试验

~ principle 指导原则

~ system 调节系统

~ time 调速时间

269

government ['gʌvənmənt] n. 政府，内阁，政治，政体
~ official 政府官员
governmental [ˌgʌvən'mentl] a. 政府的，政治的，统治上的
~ authorities 政府当局
governor ['gʌvənə] n. 调节器，管理者，主管人员，地方长官 ‖ **Syn**. controller 控制器，控制者；regulator 调整器，标准仪，调整者，校准者
　~ booster 调速器升压器，调速助力器
　~ bushing 调节器衬套
　~ control characteristic 调速器调速特性，调速器控制特性
　~ deflection 调速器偏转，调速范围
　~ flyweight 调速器离心重块
　~ overspeed switch 限速器超速开关
　~ pipe insulating joint 调压器绝缘连接管
　~ pressure 调速器压力
　~ pressure oil 调速器高压油
　~ switch 调速器开关
GPO (general power outlet) 通用电源插座
GPS (Global Positioning System) 全球定位系统
grab [græb] v. 抢夺，夺取，攫取，霸占，深深吸引
　~ crane 抓斗起重机
　~ discharge 抓斗卸货
　~ dredge 抓斗挖掘船，抓斗挖泥船，抓斗式挖泥机
　~ dredger 抓斗式挖泥机
　~ handle 握柄，抓具
　~ hook 抓钩，起重钩
　~ line 牵索，救生握索
　~ rope 系索

~ pole 扶手柱
grade [greid] n. 年级，等级，级别，成绩，阶段；v. 评分，评级，分等级
~ down 成比例降低，降级
~ of tolerance 公差等级
graded ['greidid] v. (grade 的过去式和过去分词) 评分，评级，分等级；a. 分等级的，按年级分的
~ approach 分级法，评分法
~ compensation 分级补偿
~ crushing 分级压碎，分段破碎
gradient ['greidiənt] n. 梯度，坡度，倾斜度；a. 倾斜的
gradual ['grædjuəl] a. 逐渐的，平缓的
gradually ['grædjuəli] ad. 逐步地，渐渐地
graduation [ˌgrædju'eiʃən] n. 刻度，分度，分等级，毕业，毕业典礼
grain [grein] n. 谷物，谷类，谷粒，细粒，颗粒，粮食，纹理，粗糙面；v. 形成颗粒，漆成木纹状
~ capacity 散货舱容，谷类货物装载容量
~ carrier 脱出物输送带，谷粒输送带
~ cubic 散装谷类货物舱容，散装舱容
~ density 颗粒密度
~ hatch 谷物舱口，谷物出口
grained [greind] v. (grain 的过去式和过去分词) 形成颗粒，漆成木纹状；a. 有颗粒的，有木纹的，除去毛的，漆成木纹的，粗糙的
~ cast iron 粒状铸铁
gram [græm] n. 克
granular ['grænjulə] a. 颗粒的，粒状的，由小粒而成的
graph [gra:f] n. 图表，曲线图
graphic ['græfik] a. (=graphical) 形象的，

图表的，图解的，绘画似的
~ display 图解显示，图形显示(器)
~ search 图形搜索
~ statement 图形决算表

graphical ['græfikəl] *a.* (=graphic) 形象的，图表的，图解的，绘画似的
~ form 图形形式
~ formula 图解式，构造式

graphite ['græfait] *n.* 石墨
~ coating 石墨涂层
~ electrode 石墨电极
~ grease 石墨(润滑)脂
~ powder 石墨粉

graphitization [,græfitai'zeiʃən] *n.* 石墨化

grate [greit] *n.* 筛滤栅，壁炉，炉，炉格栅；*v.* 装格栅，摩擦，磨碎

gravel ['grævəl] *n.* 碎石，砂砾；*v.* 使船搁浅在沙滩上，用碎石铺，使困惑

gravimetric [,grævə'metrik] *a.* 重量的，重量分析的
~ analysis 重量分析，重量分析法

graving ['greiviŋ] *n.* 船底的清洗和涂油
~ dry dock 干船坞

gravitation [,grævi'teiʃən] *n.* 地心吸力，引力作用
~ tank 重力罐，供料罐，供料储槽

gravitational [,grævi'teiʃənl] *a.* 重力的，引力的

gravity ['græviti] *n.* 重力，地心引力，严重性，重大后果，庄严
~ casting 重力浇注
~ center 重心
~ circulation water cooling system 重力循环水冷系统
~ davit 重力吊柱
~ disc 重力环，重力圆盘

~ drain system 重力排水系统，自流排水系统
~ drainage 重力排水，重力泄油，自流排水
~ feed 重力自流进料
~ force 重力
~ separation 重力分离
~ tank 重力柜，自动送料槽，自流式燃料供给箱

gray [grei] *a.* 灰色的，苍白的，灰白头发的，阴郁的
~ cast iron 灰口铸铁，灰铸铁

grease [gri:s] *n.* 油脂，贿赂；*v.* 涂脂于，贿赂
~ bearing 润滑轴承
~ gun 注油枪，滑脂枪
~ interceptor 截油井，除油器，隔油器
~ lubricant 润滑脂
~ lubricated 油脂润滑的
~ lubricated bearing 油脂润滑轴承
~ lubricator 滑脂灌注器，滑脂润滑器
~ packing 润滑填料，油封
~ separation 润滑脂分油
~ trap (GT) 润滑脂分离器，油脂捕集器

greaser ['gri:sə] *n.* 加油器，润滑工

greatly ['greitli] *ad.* 大大地，非常

green [gri:n] *n.* 绿色蔬菜，绿色颜料，植物；*a.* 绿色的，未成熟的，新鲜的，精力旺盛的，无经验的，青春的
~ enamel paint 绿色搪瓷
~ PC 绿色电脑，绿色计算机

greenhouse ['gri:nhaus] *n.* 温室，花房，周围有玻璃的座舱
~ effect 温室效应
~ gas 温室气体

~ gas emission 温室气体排放

grey [grei] *n.* 灰色；*a.* 灰色的，灰白的；*v.* 使变成灰色，使变老，变成灰色，老化

 ~ cast iron 灰口铸铁

 ~ fabric 坯布

 ~ iron 灰铸铁，灰生铁

 ~ water 灰水

grid [grid] *n.* 格子，栅格，地图上的坐标方格

gridiron ['grid,aiən] *n.* 船架，烤架

grille [gril] *n.* 格子，格子窗，铁格子

grim [grim] *a.* 冷酷的，残忍的，严厉的，阴冷的，可怕的，讨厌的

 ~ vane wheel 自由旋转桨后导叶轮，格林姆轮

grind [graind] *n.* 碾，磨，苦活儿，研细的程度；*v.* 磨(碎)，碾(碎)，压迫，折磨

 ~ down 碾碎

 ~ in 磨合，磨成

 ~ in site 现场研磨

 ~ out 机械地做出，用功做出

 ~ to bare metal 研磨出白，磨光金属

 ~ to the seat 与阀座磨合

 ~ up 碾成粉，磨碎，磨细

 ~ with lapping compound 用研磨剂研磨

grinder ['graində] *n.* 研磨机，粉碎机，研磨者，磨刀匠，白齿，用功学生 ‖ *Syn.* crusher 粉碎机，轧碎机；macerater 粉碎机，切碎机；pulverizer 粉碎机；shredder 切菜器，撕碎机

 ~ bench 磨床工作台

 ~ carrier 磨床座架

grinding ['graindiŋ] *v.* (grind 的 ing 形式) 磨(碎)，碾(碎)，压迫，折磨；*a.* 磨的，摩擦的，碾的

 ~ machine 磨床，砂轮机，研磨机 ‖ *Syn.* grinding mill 磨碎机，破碎机，研磨机，辊轧机

 ~ paste 磨削用冷却剂

 ~ tool 磨削工具

 ~ wheel 砂轮

 ~ wheel dresser 砂轮修整器，砂轮整形器

 ~ wheel drive motor 砂轮电机

grip [grip] *n.* 把手，握力，掌握，紧握，控制，抓牢，理解，能力，胜任；*v.* 握紧，抓牢，吸引，引起

gripping ['graipiŋ] *v.* (grip 的 ing 形式) 握紧，抓牢，吸引，引起；*a.* 引起人注意的，吸引人的

 ~ pliers 夹管钳

grit [grit] *n.* 细沙，沙砾，勇气，刚毅，坚韧；*v.* 轧，研磨，发出轧轧声，以沙砾覆盖，撒沙砾，咬紧牙关

gritty ['griti] *a.* 多沙的，含沙的，勇敢的，坚毅的，坚定的

groin [grɔin] *n.* 交叉拱，穹窿交接线，腹股沟，堤坝，折流坝；*v.* 使成穹窿形，建堤坝

groove [gru:v] *n.* 沟，槽，常规，确定的规范，理想状况；*v.* 刻沟，刻槽，投合，契合，过得快活

 ~ punch 压毛边冲子；压线冲子

gross [grəus] *n.* 总额；*v.* 总共收入；*a.* 总的，粗俗的，显而易见的，恶劣的

 ~ amount 总额，总量，毛额

 ~ calorific value 总热值

 ~ error 严重错误，过失误差

 ~ expenses 开支总额，总开支，总费用

 ~ horse power 总马力

~ negligence 重大过失，严重过失，显著的疏忽

~ power 总功率

~ ton 总吨

~ tonnage 总吨位

~ tons 总吨数

~ weight 毛重

grossly ['grəusli] *ad*. 非常，极其，很

ground [graund] *n*. 地面，土地，底，海底，战场，场所，范围，根据，理由，渣滓，沉淀物；*v*. ① (使)搁浅，着陆，接地，放在地上，限制，打基础，具有基础 ② (grind 的过去式) 磨(碎)，碾(碎)，压迫，折磨；*a*. 土地的，地面上的 ‖ *Syn*. earth 接地

~/air communication equipment 地面/空中通信设备

~ anchor 地锚

~ clearance 地面清除，离地距离

~ connection 接地

~ connector 地面电源插头，接地接头，接地器，搭铁片

~ detecting lamp 接地检测灯

~ detector 接地检验器

~ fault 接地故障

~ plane 水平投影，地平面

~ point 地面点

~ reference point 接地参考点

~ standing pot type circuit breaker 接地立罐式断路器

~ switch 接地开关

~ test 地面试验

~ wire 接地线，地线，避雷线 ‖ *Syn*. earth wire 地线，接地线

ground-based 陆基的，地基的

~ equipment 路基设备，地基设备

grounding ['graundiŋ] *n*. 接地，基础，底色；*v*. (ground 的 ing 形式) 放在地上，(使)搁浅，着陆，接地，限制，打基础，具有基础 ‖ *Syn*. earthing 接地

~ device 接地装置

~ electrode 接地极

~ screw 接地螺钉

~ system 接地系统

~ transformer 接地变压器

~ wire 接地线

group [gru:p] *n*. 组，团体，群，批，空军大队；*v*. 使成群，集合

~ alarm 成组告警，群警报，基群警报

~ by 分组依据，通过…来分组

~ by group 分批地，分组地

~ starter panel 组合启动屏

~ technology (GT) 成组技术，组合工艺学

growth [grəuθ] *n*. 生长，增长

~ rate 增长率，生长速度

groyne [grɔin] *n*. 防波堤；*v*. 筑造防波堤

GSM (Global System for Mobile Communication) 全球移动通信系统

GT (group technology) 成组技术，组合工艺学

GT (grease trap) 润滑脂分离器，油脂捕集器

GTO (gate turn-off thyristor) 门极可关断晶闸管

guarantee [ˌgærən'ti:] *n*. 保证，担保，保证人，保证书，抵押品；*v*. 保证，担保

~ agreement 担保协议，担保协定

~ claims 保证索赔

~ deposit 押金，存出保证金

~ letter 保函，保证书，担保书

~ load 额定安全负载，额定安全重量

~ period 保证期，保险期，保修期

guaranteed [ˌgærən'ti:] v. (guarantee 的过去式和过去分词) 保证，担保；a. 有保证的，有担保的

~ repair 保证维修，保修

guard [ga:d] n. 保卫，守护，防护装置，警卫，狱吏，护卫队；v. 保卫，守护，看守，警卫，防止，警惕，加防护装置，谨慎使用 ‖ Syn. safeguard 保护，防卫，安全装置，安全措施；protection 保护，保护装置 ‖ Syn. countercheck 制止，防止；forestall 预防，阻止，阻碍；prevent 预防，防止，制止，阻碍，阻止，阻挠

~ against 提防，预防

~ period 保护期

~ rail 护栏

~ relay 保持继电器

~ type surface-mounted 3-phase 4-pole receptacle 防护式表面安装三相四极插座

~ type switch 保护型开关

~ wire 安全线

gudgeon ['gʌdʒən] n. 枢轴，舵枢，易骗的人

~ bearing 耳轴承

~ bolt 舵枢螺栓

~ journal 轴颈

~ pin 活塞销，耳轴销，轴头销

~ pin bearing 活塞销轴承，耳轴销轴承

guidance ['gaidəns] n. 导航，指导，引导，领导，导航系统

~ system 导航系统，制导系统

~ tape 导向带

guide [gaid] n. 导游，向导，指导者，指南；v. 指导，支配，管理，带领，操纵

~ bar 导向杆，导杆，导向板，横梁

~ block 导块，导丝器，导丝板，导(向)滑车

~ book 指导书，指南，入门书，参考手册

~ bush for tie rod 贯穿螺栓导套

~ line 准则，指标，方针，指导路线

~ pad (深孔钻的)导向块

~ pile 导桩，定位桩

~ pin 滑槽销，定位销，导销

~ plate 导板

~ ring 导环，导料环，导向环

~ rod 导杆

~ roller 导向轮，导轮，导辊，导向滚轮

~ rope 导绳，调节绳

~ shoe 导块

~ sleeve 导套，导向轴套

~ vane 导(流叶)片，导向叶片

~ way 导轨，导向体，导向槽

~ wheel blade 导轮叶

guided ['gaidid] v. (guide 的过去式和过去分词) 指导，支配，管理，带领，操纵；a. 有向导的，有指导的，制导的

~ missile cruiser 导弹巡洋舰

guideway ['gaidwei] n. 导轨，导沟，导槽

gulf [gʌlf] n. 海湾，漩涡，分歧，隔阂，裂口；v. 吞没，卷进

~ Area 海湾区域，海湾地区

~ of Aden 亚丁湾

gun [gʌn] n. 炮，枪，手枪，油门，喷射器；v. 开枪，射击，加大油门，打猎

~ type burner 枪式油燃器

~ type soot blower 枪式吹灰机

gunmetal ['gʌnmetl] *n*. 炮铜，青铜，炮铜色
~ fittings 青铜配件
gunny ['gʌni] *n*. 粗黄麻布，麻布袋
gunwale ['gʌnl] *n*. 船舷上缘，舷边
~ (angle) bar 舷边角钢，舷边角材，甲板边角材
~ rounded thick strake 舷边圆弧厚板
gurdy ['gə:di] *n*. 卷绳车
gustiness ['gʌstinis] *n*. 狂风，阵风
gutter ['gʌtə] *n*. 排水沟，天沟，水槽，檐槽，装订线，贫民窟；*v*. 开沟于，装檐槽于
~ bar 排水沟角钢，槽条
guy [gai] *n*. (天线、帐篷等的)牵索，家伙，伙计，各位，一群人；*v*. 牵拉，固定，开玩笑，取笑，逃走
~ line 牵绳，绷索
~ ring 集索圈
gymbal [d'ʒimbl] *n*. 常平架
gypsum ['dʒipsəm] *n*. 石膏
~ powder 石膏粉
gypsyhead ['dʒipsihed] *n*. 绞缆筒 ‖ **Syn**. warping head 绞缆筒，卷缆筒，带缆卷筒；warping drum 绞缆筒，卷缆筒，卷索筒，卷绳筒；warping end 绞缆筒，摩擦鼓轮，绞车副卷筒
gyration [‚dʒaiə'reiʃən] *n*. 回转，旋转，回旋
gyro ['dʒaiərəu] *n*. 陀螺仪，回转仪
~ compass 陀螺罗经，陀螺罗盘，回转罗盘，陀螺仪，电罗经
~ drift rate 陀螺漂移率
~ dynamics 陀螺动力学
~ repeater 陀螺复示器，电罗经复示器，子罗经

gyropilot ['dʒaiərəupailət] *n*. 自动操纵装置
~ steering indicator 自动操舵操纵台
gyroscope ['dʒaiərəskəup] *n*. 陀螺仪，回旋装置，回转仪，纵舵调整器
gyroscopic [‚dʒaiərəs'kɔpik] *a*. 回转仪的
~ stabilizer 陀螺稳定器
gyrostat ['dʒaiərəustæt] *n*. 陀螺仪，回转仪

H

H-type H 形的
~ cable H 形电缆
habitability [‚hæbitə'biləti] *n*. 适居性，可居住性，可居住
habitable ['hæbitəbəl] *a*. 适于居住的
habitat ['hæbitæt] *n*. 生活环境，产地，栖息地，居留地，自生地，聚集处
hack [hæk] *n*. 砍痕，劈砍工具，出租；*v*. 砍，削减，删除，处理
~ saw 弓锯
~ saw blade 弓形锯片
~ saw frame 弓形锯架
~ sawing machine 弓锯机
hair [hɛə] *n*. 头发，毛发，绒毛，毛状物
~ line crack 发纹裂纹
half [ha:f] *n*. 半，一半，半品脱，半场；*a*. 一半的，半个的；*ad*. 一半，部分地
~ ahead 前进二，半速正车，半速前进 ‖ **Syn**. half speed ahead 前进二，半速正车，半速前进
~ ahead both 双进二，双车前进二
~ ahead both engines 双进二
~ ahead port 左车前进二，左进二
~ ahead starboard 右车前进二，右进二

275

~ astern 后退二，半速倒车，半速后退 ‖ *Syn*. half speed astern 后退二，半速倒车，半速后退

~ astern both 双车后退二

~ astern both engines 双退二

~ astern port 左车后退二，左退二

~ astern starboard 右车后退二，右退二

~ beam 半横梁，半宽，半梁

~ bearing 半轴承

~ block model 半边船模

~ breadth 半宽，中轴距离

~ breadth plan 半宽水线图，半宽线图，半宽图

~ bridge converter 半桥变换器

~ brass 半边黄铜轴衬

~ buckler 开口锚链孔盖，锚链孔盖

~ built-up crank shaft 半组合式曲轴

~ cardinals (罗经)隅点

~ cargo condition 半载状态

~ cell 半电池

~ chest 半箱

~ circle protractor 半圆分度器

~ coil 半节线圈

~ coil spacing 半节线圈间距，半圈间距，半加感节距

~ convergency 转换角

~ cooling time 半冷却时间

~ coupling 半边联轴节，半边联轴器

~ crown seizing 半冠形合扎

~ cut off 半切断

~ cycle 半周

~ davit 收锚杆

~ deck 半甲板，后部甲板，平台甲板

~ decked boat 半甲板艇

~ decker 半甲板船，半甲板艇

~ depth girder 半高桁材

~ diamond plate 半菱形板

~ ebb 半落期

~ elliptic spring 半椭圆形弹簧，弓形弹簧

~ flood 半涨潮

~ floor 半肋板

~ gantry crane 单脚高架起重机

~ hard steel 半硬钢

~ height 半高

~ height container 半高集装箱

~ hitch 半结

~ hitch and timber hitch 圆材结加半结

~ keystone ring 半梯形环，单面梯形活塞气环

~ life 半衰期

~ line 半直线

~ load 半负荷

~ mast 半旗，下半旗 ‖ *Syn*. half mast the ensign 下半旗；half staff 下半旗

~ model 半边船模

~ moon 半月形

~ nut 对开螺母

~ pay 半价

~ period average value 半周期平均值

~ pilotage 半引航费，半引水费

~ point 半方位

~ poop 半高艉楼，低艉楼，短船艉楼

~ port 半舵

~ power point 半功率点

~ revolution 半转

~ ring 半环

~ round 半圆条，半圆，半圆形的

~ round bar 半圆钢，半圆钢条，半圆杆

~ round bar steel 半圆棒钢

~ round chisel 半圆凿

~ round coarse file 半圆粗锉

~ round compasses 半圆规

~ round edge 圆弧棱边

~ round file 半圆锉

~ round head nail 半圆头钉

~ round head screw 半圆头螺钉

~ round iron 半圆铁

~ round middle file 半圆中锉

~ round molding 半圆缘材

~ round oil stone 半圆油石

~ round pliers 半圆钳

~ round reamer 半圆铰刀

~ round scraper 半圆刮刀

~ round smooth file 半圆细锉

~ rounded flat plate 半圆扁钢

~ rounds 半圆钢

~ sectional view 半剖面图

~ shadow 半影

~ sheave 桅头

~ siding ratio 龙骨水平半宽比

~ size 缩小一半

~ smooth file 中齿锉

~ solid floor 空心肋板

~ spaced ordinate 中间纵坐标

~ speed 半速

~ sunken ship 半沉船

~ tank 未满的水柜

~ thread 半螺纹

~ tide 半潮

~ tide basin 半潮港池 ‖ *Syn*. half tide dock 半潮港池

~ tide level 平均潮面，平均潮面

~ tide rock 半潮干出礁石,半潮干出礁

~ time 半期

~ time survey 中间检验

~ top 半桅合板，半顶

~ turn 半转，半匝

~ turn ahead 进车抵制后退

~ turn astern 倒车抵制前进

~ turn coil winding 半圈绕组

~ watt 半瓦

half-finished 半加工的

~ material 半成品 ‖ *Syn*. half finished product 半成品

half-formed 半成型的

~ winding 半成型绕组

half-V 半 V 型，半 V 形

~ weld 半 V 焊缝，半 V 形焊

halfway ['ha:f'wei] *a*. 中途的，部分的，不彻底的；*ad*. 在中途，到一半，在中间，大致上

halide ['hælaid] *n*. 卤化物，卤素；*a*. 卤化物的，卤素的

~ lamp 卤化物检漏灯，检卤漏灯，卤化物灯，卤素灯

~ torch 检卤漏灯，卤素管

hall [hɔ:l] *n*. 会堂，礼堂，大厅，走廊，门厅

Hall [hɔ:l] *n*. 霍尔(① 姓氏；② 1855-1938，美国物理学家)

~ angle 霍尔角

~ current 霍尔电流

~ displacement transducer 霍尔式位移传感器

~ effect 霍尔效应，内液增阻效应

~ effect compass 霍尔效应罗盘

~ effect element 霍尔效应元件

~ effect relay 霍尔效应继电器

~ effect transducer 霍尔效应传感器

Hall's 霍尔的

~ anchor 山字锚，霍尔锚

halliard ['hæljəd] *n*. 升降索，升降绳，旗绳

～ bend 扬帆结

haloalkane [hə'ləulkæn] *n.* 卤代烷

　～ extinguishing agent 卤代烷灭火剂

　～ extinguishing system 卤代烷灭火系统

　～ fire extinguisher 卤代烷灭火器

　～ suppressant 卤代烷抑制剂

halogen ['hælədʒən] *n.* 卤素

　～ compound fire extinguishing installation 卤化物灭火装置

　～ compound fire extinguishing system 卤化物灭火系统

　～ lamp 卤素灯 ‖ *Syn*. halogen light 卤素灯

halogenate ['hælədʒəneit] *v.* 卤化

halogenated ['hælədʒəneitid] *v.* (halogenate 的过去式和过去分词) 卤化；*a.* 卤化的

　～ fire extinguishing agent 氟溴烷烃灭火剂

　～ hydrocarbon 卤代烃

　～ hydrocarbon extinguisher 卤代烃灭火器

　～ hydrocarbon fire extinguishing system 卤代烃灭火系统

　～ hydrocarbon system 卤代烃系统

halon ['heilɔn] *n.* 卤代烷(灭火剂)

　～ fire extinguisher 哈龙灭火器，卤代烷灭火器

　～ system 哈龙系统，卤代烷系统

halt [hɔ:lt] *n.* 暂停，停止，中止，小火车站；*v.* 阻止，(使)停止，(使)立定，(使)中断，犹豫，有缺点

　～ instruction 停机指令

halyard ['hæljəd] *n.* 旗绳，帆绳，(旗帆等的)升降索

hammer ['hæmə] *n.* 链球，铁锤，榔头，木槌，音槌；*v.* 锤打，猛踢，猛击，反复敲打，连续，击败，轻易打败

　～ handle 锤柄，链球把手

hamper ['hæmpə] *n.* 船上必需的但是累赘的设备；*v.* 妨碍，阻碍，牵制

hand [hænd] *n.* 手，掌管，协助，支配，插手，指针，雇员，手艺；*v.* 传递，交给，搀扶，支持

　～ anchor capstan 人力起锚绞盘，手动起锚绞盘

　～ by-pass valve 手动旁通阀

　～ cable 软电缆

　～ capacity control valve 手动容量控制阀

　～ change-over valve 手动换向阀

　～ cleaning 除锈，人工清除，人工清洗

　～ cleaning centrifuge 人工去污油分离器

　～ control 手控，手工控制，手动操纵，人工操纵，人工控制

　～ control mechanism 手动操动机构

　～ control wheel 手动操纵轮

　～ crank 起动摇把，手动曲柄，手摇起动柄

　～ cut-off valve 手动截止阀

　～ drill 手钻

　～ electric drill 手提式电钻

　～ expansion valve 手动膨胀阀

　～ face shield 手持护目罩，(焊工的)面罩

　～ file 手锉，平锉，平板方锉；手夹

　～ flare 手持火焰信号

　～ grip 手柄，把手

　～ lamp 手提灯 ‖ *Syn*. portable lamp 手提灯

　～ lever 手柄

~ operating 手动操作，手工操作，徒手操作
~ operating device 手动操作装置
~ over the ship 移交船，交船
~ over to 移交给，上缴
~ press 手动泵，手压泵，手动压机，手动冲床
~ pump 手泵，手摇泵，手压泵，手力唧筒 ‖ *Syn*. manual pump 手动泵
~ rail 扶手，栏杆
~ rail bolt 扶手螺栓
~ regulating throttle 手动调节节流阀
~ saw 手锯
~ shears 手剪
~ starting 手启动
~ steering 手操舵，人力操舵
~ stop valve 手动截止阀，手动关闭阀
~ tight 用手上紧的
~ tiller 手操舵柄
~ tool 手工工具
~ wheel 手轮
~ wheel for main starting valve 主起动阀用手轮
~ wheel for starting valve 起动阀用手轮
~ wheel handle 手轮柄
~ windlass 手摇卷扬机，手动起锚机
hand-cleaned 人工清除的，人工清洗的
~ rack 人工清除格栅
hand-operated 手动操作的，人工操作的
~ by-pass valve 手动旁通阀
~ device 手动装置
~ sprayer 手动喷雾机
~ valve 手动阀
handbook ['hænd,buk] *n*. 手册，指南，便览
handgrip ['hændgrip] *n*. 手柄，有力的握手

handicap ['hændikæp] *n*. 障碍，阻碍，障碍赛跑；*v*. 妨碍，使不利，阻碍
handle ['hændl] *n*. 柄，把手，把柄，句柄，口实，手感；*v*. 处理，管理，支配，代表，操纵，操作，触摸，运用，买卖，搬运 ‖ *Syn*. deal with 应付，安排，处理；dispose of 处理，安排，解决；manage 处理，应付；manipulate (巧妙地) 处理，应付；treat with 处理，应付 ‖ *Ant*. mishandle 胡乱操纵，胡乱操作，错误处理
handler ['hændlə] *n*. 处理者，管理者，驯化者，处理机，拳击教练
handling ['hændliŋ] *n*. 处理，触摸，费用，操纵；*v*. (handle 的 ing 形式) 处理，管理，支配，代表，操纵，操作，触摸，运用，买卖，搬运；*a*. 操作的
~ capacity 处理容量，处理能力，吞吐量
~ characteristic 操纵特性，加工工艺，加工性能
~ requirement 处理要求
handover ['hændəuvə] *n*. 交接，移交
handwheel ['hændwi:l] *n*. 手轮，驾驶盘
handwrite ['hændrait] *v*. 用手写，亲手写
handwriting ['hændraitiŋ] *n*. 笔迹，书写体，书法，笔势；*v*. (handwrite 的 ing 形式) 用手写，亲手写
~ signature 亲笔签字，手写签名，手写签批
handy ['hændi] *a*. 手边的，就近的，便利的，敏捷的，容易取得的
hang [hæŋ] *n*. 悬挂的方式，暂停，中止；*v*. 悬挂，悬垂，垂下，附着，装饰，踌躇，(使)悬而未决
hanger ['hæŋə] *n*. 衣架，挂钩，悬挂工具，

弹簧吊架，饰带

~ shaft 吊轴

~ winch 顶索定位绞车

hanging ['hæŋiŋ] *n*. 悬挂，帘子，幔帐，绞死，绞刑；*v*. (hang 的 ing 形式) 悬挂，悬垂，垂下，附着，装饰，踌躇，(使)悬而未决

~ bracket 吊架

harbor ['ha:bə] (=harbour) *n*. 海港，港口，避难所，躲藏处；*v*. 隐匿，窝藏，包庇，心怀，怀有

~ (Administration) Bureau 港务(管理)局

~ boat 港口船

~ boom 港口拦障

~ dues 入港税，港务费

~ entrance 海港入口

~ generating set 停泊发电机组

~ installation 港口设施，港口设备

~ launch 港作船

~ Master 港务局长，港口主任(负责指定船舶泊位等工作)

~ Officer 港务监督员

~ pilot 领港员

~ pump 停港泵，停泊泵 ‖ *Syn*. port duty pump 港口作业泵

~ supervision office 港务监督办公室

~ traffic 海港货物进出港数量

~ tug 港口拖船

harbour ['hɔ:bə] (=harbor) *n*. 海港，港口，避难所，躲藏处；*v*. 隐匿，窝藏，包庇，心怀，怀有

hard [ha:d] *a*. 硬的，坚固的，困难的，艰苦的，猛烈的，确实的；*ad*. 努力地，辛苦地，坚硬地，牢固地，接近地，猛烈地，完全地，完整的

~ alloy 硬质合金

~ alloy tip for lathe tool 车刀硬质合金尖

~ alloy welding 硬质合金焊接

~ chine 尖舭

~ chromium 硬铬镀层

~ coating 硬涂层

~ disk 硬盘

~ grained 硬粒的，粗粒状的

~ ground 硬接地，硬底

~ hat 安全帽

~ switching 硬开关

~ tack (航海用的)压缩饼干

~ ware 硬件，硬设备

hard-over 尽量靠一边，满舵，信号过强

~ angle 最大转舵角，满舵角

~ position 最大转舵位置，满舵位置

~ rudder stopper 舵叶舵角限位器

~ stop 制舵器，转舵限制器

harden ['ha:dn] *v*. (使)变硬,(使)坚强,(使)冷酷，涨价

hardenability [ˌha:dənə'biliti] *n*. 可硬性，淬透性，可淬性，可硬化性

hardness ['ha:dnis] *n*. 硬，硬度，艰难，难度，困难，冷酷

~ of the paint dry film 油漆干膜的硬度

hardware ['hɔ:dwɛə] *n*. 五金器具,计算机硬件,(电子仪器的)部件，武器装备

~ component 硬件组件

~ connections 硬件连接

~ fitting 五金配件

harm [hɔ:m] *n*. 危害，伤害，损害；*v*. 危害，伤害，损害

harmful ['hɔ:mful] *a*. 不良的，不利的，有害的，伤害的

~ cargo 有害货物

~ substance 有害物质
~ substances carried by ships 船舶携带的有害物质

harmless ['ha:mlis] *a.* 无害的，无恶意的，无损失的，免于法律责任的

harmonic [ha:'mɔnik] *n.* 谐波，和声，谐函数，调和函数；*a.* 谐波的，谐和的，和声的，融洽的

harmonious [ha:'məunjəs] *a.* 协调的，和谐的，融洽的，音调优美的，悦耳的
~ hand and air brake 协调的手制动与空气制动

harmony ['ha:məni] *n.* 和谐，协调，融洽，一致，和声

harsh [hɔʃ] *a.* 刺耳的，残酷的，粗糙的，严厉的，严格的
~ environment 恶劣环境

hatch [hætʃ] *n.* 入口，舱口，舱口盖，船只水密舱，水闸门，开口，画阴影时用的细线，孵化；*v.* 策划，图谋，秘密设计，秘密制造，画阴影，孵，孵出
~ beam 舱口横梁
~ beam socket 舱口梁插口
~ board 舱口板，舱口盖
~ coaming 舱口围板
~ cover 舱口盖，舱盖，装货口盖
~ cover (handling) winch 舱口盖绞车
~ cover rack 舱口盖板隔架
~ cover seal 舱口盖密封
~ cover support pad 舱口盖支撑垫
~ coverless container ship 无舱盖集装箱船
~ crane 舱口起重机
~ end beam 舱口端梁
~ sealing 封锁舱口

~ side cantilever beam 舱口悬臂梁
~ side girder 舱口纵桁，舱口边桁，舱口侧纵梁
~ socket 活动梁座，舱口梁座
~ way 舱口，舱出入路
~ wedge 封舱楔
~ rail 舱口栏杆

hatchway ['hætʃwei] *n.* 舱口，地板，天花板出入口，天窗
~ beam 舱口梁
~ coaming 舱口围板
~ corner 舱口拐角
~ corner radius 舱口拐角半径
~ enclosure 舱口围封，井道围封
~ rest 舱口盖支座

haul [hɔl] *n.* 拖，拉，捕获物，努力得到的结果，一网捕获的鱼量，拖运距离；*v.* 拖，拉，拖运，改变方向，改变主意
~ in 拉进

hauling ['hɔliŋ] *n.* 拖运，搬运；*v.* (haul 的 ing 形式) 拖，拉，拖运，改变方向，改变主意
~ capacity 牵引能量，牵引力
~ load 牵引负荷
~ machine 拖运机，牵引机

have [hæv] *n.* 富人，有钱人；*v.* 拥有，具有，包含，占有，获得，收到，得到，接受，收纳，发挥，从事，必须，经受，遭受，经历，经验
~ an effect on 对…有影响

haven ['heivn] *n.* 港口，锚泊地，避难所，安全地方；*v.* 把(船)开进港，提供避难场所，掩护

hawse [hɔ:z] *n.* 锚链孔，停泊时船首与锚间的水平距离
~ hole 锚链孔

~ pipe 锚链孔衬管，锚链筒 ‖ *Syn*. chain pipe 锚链管；Spurling pipe 锚链筒，锚链管

hawser ['hɔ:zə] *n*. 大缆，曳船索，系船索

hazard ['hæzəd] *n*. 冒险，危险，冒险的事；*v*. 冒险，使遭危险，赌运气 ‖ *Syn*. danger 危险，危害，危险物，威胁；jeopardy 危险；peril 危险，危险物；risk 危险，风险，冒险

hazardous ['hæzədəs] *a*. 危险的，冒险的，碰运气的 ‖ *Syn*. dangerous 危险的；perilous 危险的，冒险的；unsafe 危险的

~ area 危险区域

~ cargo 危险货物，危险品

~ cargo residues 危险货物残留物

~ degree 危险度

~ element 有害元素

~ industry 危险行业

~ insurance 危险物品保险

~ items 危险物品

~ situation 危险情况

~ substance 有害物质

~ wastes 有害废物

~ zone 危险区域，危险地带

HCFC (hydro-chlorofluoro-carbon) 氢氯氟烃

HDTV (high definition television) 高清晰度电视

head [hed] *n*. 头部，头脑，上端，顶点，首脑，首长；*v*. 朝向，前进，出发，用头顶；*a*. 头的，在前头的，首要的，在顶端的

~ crash 磁头划碰，磁头碰撞

~ first entry 头先入水

~ flowmeter 压头式流量计，压力流量表

~ line 首缆，头缆，新闻提要，大字标题

~ lining 顶板，内顶板

~ loss 压头损失，水头抑损

~ of water 水头

~ off 阻止，拦截

~ ring 顶圈

~ ring for cylinder liner 缸套顶圈

~ rod 第一连接杆，尖端杆，(辙尖)头杆

~ stock 床头箱，机头，机头座，轮轴头架

~ tank 高位水箱，压力槽，压力罐，压头箱 ‖ *Syn*. elevated tank 高位水箱，高位槽，高位罐，压力罐

header ['hedə] *n*. 标题，报头，首领，队长，页眉

~ pipe 总管

~ tank 集水箱，总箱，(散热器的)上水箱，油枕，集水箱，集水槽，扩油器

headfirst ['hed'fəst] *ad*. 头向前地，不顾前后地

~ long entry 镰刀式入水

heading ['hediŋ] *n*. 标题，题名，信头，航向；*v*. (head 的 ing 形式) 朝向，前进，出发，用头顶

~ control 航向控制，方向控制

~ indicator lamp 航向指示灯

~ joint 顶头接，端接(合)

headland ['hedlənd] *n*. 岬，向水中突出的陆地

headroom ['hedru:m] *n*. 净空，头上空间，(拱梁等下面的)净空高度

headway ['hedwei] *n*. 进展，前进，净空高度，航行速度，前进速度，间隔时间

heal [hi:l] v. 修缮，复原，治愈，医治，结束

heap [hi:p] n. 堆，堆积，大量，许多；v. 堆，堆起，堆积，完全填满，完全充溢
~ up 堆起来，积累

heart [ha:t] n. 心，心脏，感情，要点，胸部；v. 鼓励，激励，结心
~ cam 心形凸轮

heat [hit] n. 热，热度，热烈，高潮，压力；v. 加热，发热，激昂，发怒
~ absorption capacity 吸热量
~ absorption intensity 吸热强度
~ absorptivity 吸热性
~ aluminum 热铝
~ aluminum paint 热铝漆
~ balance 热量平衡，热平衡
~ balance calculation 热平衡计算
~ capacity 热容量
~ conduction 热传导
~ conductivity 热导率
~ conductivity coefficient 导热系数
~ convection 热对流
~ dam 热堤，热阻
~ deformation 热变形
~ detector 热量探测器
~ dissipation 散热
~ distribution 热量分布
~ energy 热能
~ exchange 热交换
~ exchanger 热交换器
~ expansion 热膨胀
~ fatigue cracking 热疲劳裂纹
~ fatigue resistant 耐热疲劳的，抗热疲劳的
~ fire detector 感温火灾探测器 ‖ *Syn*. thermal detector 热探测器，热检测器

~ flow 热流
~ flow meter 热流计
~ humidity ratio 热湿比
~ insulating layer 隔热层
~ insulating material 绝热材料
~ insulation 保温，绝热，热绝缘，保冷
~ leakage 热漏
~ load 热负荷
~ loss 热损失，热损耗
~ loss due to chemically incomplete combustion 化学不完全燃烧引起的热损失
~ loss due to exhaust gas 排烟热损失
~ loss due to mechanically incomplete combustion 机械不完全燃烧引起的热损失
~ loss due to radition 辐射热损失
~ loss through vented vapour 排(蒸)汽热损失
~ of condensation 凝结热
~ of compression 压缩热
~ of evaporation 蒸发热
~ pipe 热导管，热管，导热管
~ preserving furnace 保温炉
~ protective clothing 隔热服
~ pump 热泵
~ pump air conditioner 热泵空调
~ quantity 热量
~ radiation 热辐射
~ release rate in furnace 炉内放热率
~ resistance 热阻，抗热性，热强性，耐热度
~ resisting 耐热
~ resisting alumimm alloy 耐热铝合金
~ resisting aluminum paint 耐热铝漆，

耐热银灰漆
- ~ resisting composite 耐热复合材料
- ~ resisting fabric 耐热织物，耐热布
- ~ resisting glass 耐热玻璃
- ~ resisting grease 耐热滑脂
- ~ resisting paint 耐热涂料
- ~ resisting rubber 耐热橡胶
- ~ resisting steel 耐热钢
- ~ resisting wire 耐热导线
- ~ shield 隔热屏
- ~ sink 散热片，吸热设备，冷源，(半导体的)热沉
- ~ stability 热稳定性
- ~ storage capacity 蓄热容量
- ~ tracing 伴热
- ~ transfer 传热，换热，热传递
- ~ transfer capacity 传热性能
- ~ transfer coefficient 传热系数
- ~ transfer rate 传热速率
- ~ treatment 热处理

heat-proof 耐热的，抗热的，隔热的 ‖ *Syn*. heat-resistant 耐热的，抗热的
- ~ aging 耐热老化
- ~ glass 耐热玻璃
- ~ mat 防火垫
- ~ material 耐热材料
- ~ mechanism 耐热机理
- ~ quality 耐热性，保热性
- ~ sheath 耐热护套
- ~ tubing 耐热油管

heat-resistant 耐热的，抗热的 ‖ *Syn*. heat-proof 耐热的，抗热的，隔热的
- ~ cable 耐热电缆
- ~ gloves 隔热手套
- ~ performance 耐热性能
- ~ quality 耐热品质

heated ['hi:tid] *v*. (heat 的过去式和过去分词) 加热，发热，激昂，发怒；*a*. 热的，激昂的，兴奋的
- ~ cargo 加热货物
- ~ filter 热过滤器
- ~ flame ionization detector 加热式氢火焰离子化检测器

heater ['hi:tə] *n*. 加热器，发热器，手枪 ‖ *Ant*. cooler 冷却装置，冷却器

heating ['hi:tiŋ] *n*. 供热，供暖，供暖系统；*v*. (heat 的 ing 形式) 加热，发热，激昂，发怒
- ~ appliance 加热器具
- ~ area 供热面积
- ~ cable 加热电缆
- ~ circulating valve 加热循环阀
- ~ coil 加热盘管
- ~ effect 热效应，发热量
- ~ efficiency 加热效率
- ~ element 加热元件
- ~ equipment 加热设备
- ~ freshwater inlet valve 热淡水进口阀
- ~ freshwater regulating valve 加热淡水调节阀
- ~ furnace 加热炉
- ~ medium 加热介质
- ~ pipe 加热管
- ~ power 加热功率
- ~ steam 加热蒸气
- ~ surface 受热面，加热表面，蓄热面积，放热面
- ~ surface area 受热面积
- ~ system 供暖系统
- ~ treatment furnace 加热炉
- ~ water ratio 加热水倍率

~ water treatment 热水处理

~ working medium 加热工作介质

~, ventilation and air conditioning (HVAC) 加热、通风及空调，采暖、通风及空调

heave [hi:v] *n*. 投掷，拉，拖，窒息，呕吐；*v*. 举起，升起，拉起，卷起，拖拉，投，掷扔，抛，移动，发出

~ to 将帆船顶风停船，将引擎动力船向风停位

~ up depth 起锚深度

~ velocity 升沉速度

heavily ['hevili] *ad*. 在很大程度上，沉重地，大量地，缓慢又高声地

heaving ['hi:viŋ] *n*. 举起，拿起，扔去；*v*. (heave 的 ing 形式) 举起，升起，拉起，卷起，拖拉，投，掷扔，抛，移动，发出

~ line 引缆索，抛缆，引缆，引缆绳

heavy ['hi:vi] *n*. 重物，庄重的角色；*a*. 重的，沉重的，大量的，浓密的，激烈的，重型的；*ad*. 密集地，大量地，笨重地

~ and lengthy cargo carrier 重大件货运输船，重大件运输船

~ body 高黏(稠)度

~ boiler oil 锅炉用重油

~ cargo 重件，特重货物

~ component (精馏的)较重组分，高沸点组分

~ crude 重质石油

~ diesel oil 重柴油

~ duty cleaner 强效清洁剂

~ duty flooring 重型地板

~ fuel 重质燃料

~ fuel oil (HFO) 重燃油

~ lift vessel 重型起重船

~ load 重载

~ load transportation system 重载运输系统

~ losses 重大损失

~ lubricating oil 重润滑油，稠润滑油，厚黏度润滑油

~ machinery 重型机械

~ maintenance 大修(理)

~ oil 重油

~ phase 重相

~ plate 厚钢板

~ pressure 高压，高压力

~ running of the fixed pitch propeller 螺旋桨的重载运行

~ toll 重大损失，严重损害

~ weather damage 恶劣天气损害

~ weather navigation operating mode management 恶劣天气导航运行模式管理

heel [hi:l] *n*. 桅脚，桅根，龙骨后端，倾侧，倾侧度，脚后跟，踵，跟部，踵状物；*v*. (使)倾斜，做鞋跟，尾随

~ piece 轭铁，动片，跟片，背接角材

heeling ['hi:liŋ] *n*. 倾斜；*v*. (heel 的 ing 形式) (使)倾斜，做鞋跟，尾随

~ angle 横倾角，侧倾角

~ corrector 倾斜校正器

~ deviation 倾斜自差

~ moment 倾斜力矩

~ pump 横倾平衡泵 ‖ *Syn*. list pump 横倾平衡泵 ‖ trim (ming) pump 纵倾平衡泵

~ resistance 横倾阻力

~ response 倾斜响应

~ rudder 横倾舵

~ tank (破冰船两侧的)倾侧水舱

height [hait] *n.* 高，高度，身高，海拔，高地，绝顶，顶点 ‖ depth 深度; width 宽度; length 长度

~ gauge 高度计，高度规，高度尺，高度游标卡尺，测高计

~ of capillary rise 毛细上升高度，毛细提升高度

~ of gravitational centre 重心高

heighten ['haitn] *v.* 增加，增强，升高，加高，加深 ‖ ***Syn***. enhance 提高，增加; hoist 升起，吊起; improve 提高，增进; increase 增加，加大; lift 升高，提高; raise 升起，提高; upgrade 升级，提升

Hele-Shaw 海尔-萧，海尔萧

~ pump 海尔-萧型径向柱塞泵,海尔萧泵

helical ['helikəl] *a.* 螺旋状的，螺旋线的

~ blade 螺旋叶片

~ duct intake 螺旋进气道进气

~ gear 斜齿轮

~ gear pump 斜齿齿轮泵

~ groove 螺旋槽

~ spur gear 斜齿圆柱齿轮

~ type hydraulic steering gear 螺旋式液压操舵装置

~ wheel 螺旋轮

helicoidal [heli'kɔidl] *n.* 螺旋面，螺圈

helicopter ['helikɔptə] *n.* 直升机; *v.* 用直升机载送，乘直升机前往

~ deck 直升机甲板

~ deck surface flood light 直升机甲板照明灯

~ landing area 直升机着陆区

~ pick-up area 直升机搭载区

helideck ['heli‚dek] *n.* 直升机甲板

heliox ['hi:liɔks] *n.* 氦氧混合气(含氦 98%、氧 2%，供潜水员在深水中维持呼吸用)

helium ['hi:ljəm] *n.* 氦(化学元素，符号为 He)

~ gas compressor 氦压缩机

~ refrigerator 氦冷冻机

helix ['hi:liks] *n.* 螺旋结构

helm [helm] *n.* 舵，舵柄，舵轮，枢纽，舵手，领导人; *v.* 掌舵，控制，给戴头盔，戴上头盔

~ order 舵令

~ wheel 舵轮

helmet ['helmit] *n.* 头盔，钢盔，盔形物，盔状物; *v.* 提供头盔，佩戴头盔

helmsman ['helmzmən] *n.* 舵手，舵工

helmsman's 舵手的

~ workstation 舵手工作站

hemisphere ['hemisfiə] *n.* 半球，地球的半球，大脑半球

hemispherical [‚hemi'sferikl] *a.* 半球的，半球状的

~ combustion chamber 半球形燃烧室

her [hə:] *pron.* 她的，她

~ Majesty's British Ship 英国皇家海军舰艇

~ Majesty's Ship (HMS) 女王陛下的舰艇，英国军舰

hereby ['hiə'bai] *ad.* 因此，据此

herefrom [hiə'frɔm] *ad.* 从此，由此

hereinafter ['hiərin'a:ftə] *ad.* 以下，在下文

hereof [‚hiər'ɔv] *ad.* 于此，关于此点

hereto [‚hiətu:] *ad.* 到此为止，关于这个

hereunder [hiə'ʌndə] *ad.* 在此之下，在下文

hereunto [‚hiərʌn'tu:] *ad.* 到此为止，迄今

herewith [hiə'wið] *ad.* 同此，因此

hermetic [hə:'metik] *a.* 密封的，不透气

的，与外界隔绝，不受外界影响的
~ bonding 密接
~ cabin 气密室，密封室，密封舱
~ case 密封壳
~ centrifuge 密封离心机
~ closure 密封
~ compressor 密闭式压缩机
~ deck valve 密封甲板阀
~ device 密封装置
~ drive 密封传动
~ lighting switch 密封照明开关
~ machine 密封式电机
~ motor 密封式电动机
~ packet type switch 气密式组合开关
~ refrigerating compressor unit 全封闭式制冷压缩机组
~ seal 密封，气密封口
~ sealing technique 密封技术
~ terminal 密封端子
~ terminal assembly 密封端子组件
~ window 密封窗

hermetically [həː'metikəli] ad. 密封地，炼金术地
~ sealed refrigerating compressor unit 全封闭冷冻压缩机组

herringbone ['heriŋbəun] n. 鲱鱼鱼骨，交叉缝式，人字形；v. (使)成箭尾形；a. 箭尾形的

Hertz ['həːts] (Hz) n. 赫，赫兹① 姓氏；② 1857-1894，德国物理学家；③ 频率单位：周/秒）

heterogeneous [ˌhetərəu'dʒiːniəs] a. 各种各样的，成分混杂的

hex [heks] n. 十六进制

hexadecimal [heksə'desim(ə)l] n. 十六进制；a. 十六进制的

hexagon ['heksəgən] n. 六角形，六边形
~ bar 六角钢条，六角钢
~ bar key 六角杆键
~ file 六角锉
~ head bolt 六角头螺栓
~ head wrench 六角头扳手
~ nipple 六角螺纹接头，六角螺母外螺纹接头
~ nut 六角螺母，六角螺帽
~ screw 六角螺钉
~ socket screw 内六角螺栓

hexagonal [hek'sæɡənəl] a. 六边的，六角形的
~ asbestos jointing 六角石棉垫圈
~ brass bolt 六角黄铜螺栓
~ brass nut 铜六角螺母
~ brass rod 六角黄铜棒
~ brass screw 铜六角螺钉
~ closed double head spanner 六角环形双头扳手
~ closed single head spanner 六角环形单头扳手
~ head bolt 六角头螺栓
~ head screw 六角头螺丝，六角螺钉
~ iron bolt 六角铁螺栓
~ iron screw 六角铁螺丝，六角铁螺钉
~ nut 六角螺母
~ rod 六角钢条
~ screw 六角螺钉
~ screw die 六角螺丝板牙
~ socket head plug 内六角螺塞
~ socket screw 六角凹头螺钉
~ spanner 六角扳手 ‖ *Syn*. hexagonal wrench 六角扳手
~ surface 六角平面

HFO (heavy fuel oil) 重燃油

hidden ['hidn] v. (hide 的过去分词) 隐藏，躲藏；a. 隐藏的
　~ danger 隐患 ‖ Syn. incipient fault 潜在故障，隐患
hierarchical [ˌhaiə'ra:kikəl] a. 分层的，等级体系的
　~ and district voltage regulation 分层次级和地区电压调整
　~ chart 层次结构图
　~ control 分级控制，阶层控制
　~ design 分层设计
　~ organization 等级结构，分层结构，层次组织
　~ planning 分级规划，递阶规划
　~ structure 分级结构，层级结构
hierarchy ['haiəra:ki] n. 层级，层次，等级制度
high [hai] n. 高度，高处；a. 高的，高原的，高等的，高音的，傲慢的，高尚的，昂贵的，严重的；ad. 高度地，奢侈地，高价地
　~ accuracy 高准确度，高精度
　~ and low pressure controller 高低压控制器
　~ and low pressure relay 高低压继电器
　~ bay lighting fitting 深照型灯具
　~ beam 远光灯
　~ boiling 高沸点
　~ capacity 大容量
　~ coolant temperature shutdowns 高水温故障停机
　~ current 高强度电流
　~ definition television (HDTV) 高清晰度电视
　~ degree 高度，高地位
　~ density 高密度，密度高
　~ density fuel oil 高密度燃油
　~ efficiency 高效率
　~ energy 高能量，高能
　~ energy battery 高能电池(组)
　~ energy igniter 高能点火器
　~ expansion air foam extinguishing system 高倍数空气泡沫灭火系统
　~ expansion foam 高膨胀泡沫
　~ expansion foam fire extinguishing system in machinery space 机舱高倍数泡沫灭火系统
　~ flash point cargo 高闪点货物
　~ frequency 高频率，频繁出现
　~ gain 高增益
　~ grade 高等级，高品位
　~ heat-proof 耐高热的
　~ heat resistant 高热稳定性，高耐热
　~ heating value 高热值
　~ humidity 高湿度
　~ inlet valve 自动高压进口阀
　~ level 高层，高电平
　~ level alarm 高位报警器
　~ level radioactive waste 高放射性废物，高放射性废料
　~ lift rocker arm 高升程摇臂
　~ output 高输出，高产量
　~ performance 高性能，高效能
　~ power 高功率，大功率
　~ power fuse 大功率熔丝
　~ precision 高精度
　~ pressure (HP) 高压，高气压
　~ pressure asbestos 高压石棉
　~ pressure asbestos sheet 高压石棉板
　~ pressure cleaner 高压清洁器
　~ pressure combustion chamber 高压燃烧室

~ pressure compressor 高压压缩机，高压压气机

~ pressure contact port 高压出气孔

~ pressure cut-out switch 高压切断开关

~ pressure draft 高压气流

~ pressure fuel delivery pipe 高压燃油输送管

~ pressure fuel pipe 高压油管，高压燃油管

~ pressure gas 高压气体

~ pressure grease gun 高压滑脂枪

~ pressure hose 高压软管

~ pressure insulating tape 高压绝缘胶布

~ pressure mercury fluorescent lighting fitting 高压汞荧光照明装置

~ pressure mercury vapor lamp 高压汞气灯，高压水银灯

~ pressure mercury vapor lighting fitting 高压汞蒸汽照明装置

~ pressure pump 高压泵，高压输液泵

~ pressure safety cut-out 高压安全切断器

~ pressure steam 高压蒸汽

~ pressure steam packing 高压蒸汽填料

~ pressure tube 高压管

~ pressure water jet 高压喷水器，高压水枪

~ pressure water jet flow 高压水射流

~ quality 高品质

~ rate 高速率，高效率

~ reliability 高可靠性，高可靠度

~ resistance 高电阻，高阻抗

~ resistance voltmeter 高阻伏计

~ resolution 高分辨，高分辨率

~ salinity alarm 高盐度报警

~ sea suction 高位海水吸口，高位海水门

~ side 高边，高压侧

~ speed 高速，全速

~ speed craft (HSC) 高速船

~ Speed Craft Safety Certificate 高速船安全证书

~ speed diesel engine 高速柴油机，高速引擎

~ speed drilling machine 高速钻床

~ speed low torque motor 高速低转矩电动机，高速低扭矩马达

~ speed monohull ferry 高速单体渡船

~ speed passenger catamaran 高速双体客船

~ speed turning tool 高速车刀

~ speed underway replenishment 高速航行补给

~ technology 高科技

~ temperature (HT) 高温

~ temperature corrosion 高温腐蚀

~ temperature test 高温试验，高温测试

~ tensile steel 高强度钢，高强钢

~ tension (HT) 高电压，高压 ‖ *Syn*. high voltage (HV) 高电压，高压

~ tension circuit 高压电路

~ tension circuit breaker 高压断路器

~ tension contactor 高压接触器

~ tension distribution cabinet 高压配电箱

~ tension electrostatic capacitor cabinet 高压静电电容器柜

~ tension equipment 高压设备

~ tension fuse 高压保险丝

~ tension isolator 高压隔离器

~ tension load switch 高压负荷开关

~ tension switchgear 高压开关设备

~ tension transformer 高压变压器

~ tension vacuum contactor 高压真空接触器

~ tide 高潮，满潮，高潮时间

~ torque low speed motor 高扭矩低速电动机

~ velocity 高速度，高速

~ velocity induction air conditioning system 高速诱导空气调节系统，高速诱导空调系统

~ viscosity fuel 高黏度燃油

~ viscosity fuel oil 高黏度燃油

~ viscosity index 高黏度指数

~ voltage alternating current (HVAC) 高压交流电

~ voltage cable for ship 船用高压电缆

~ voltage cutout 高压断路器，高压断流器

~ voltage DC transmission (HVDC) 高压直流输电

~ voltage disconnecting switch 高压隔离开关

~ voltage engineering 高电压工程

~ voltage generating station 高压电站

~ voltage IC 高压集成电路

~ voltage load break switch 高压负载断路开关

~ voltage power system 高压电源系统，高压电力系统

~ voltage relay 高压继电器

~ voltage switchgear 高压开关

~ voltage technology 高电压技术

~ voltage test 高电压试验

~ voltage testing technology 高压测试技术，高压实验技能

~ voltage testing transformer 高压试验变压器

high-limited 高限制的，高限的

~ value 高限值

higher ['haiə] a. (high 的比较级) 更高的，较高的

~ calorific value 高热值，高发热值，高发热量

~ strength material 高强度材料

highest ['haiist] a. (high 的最高级) 最高的

~ current 最大电流

~ efficiency 最高效率，最高的收效

~ gas pressure 最高爆发压力

~ priority 最高优先权

~ standard 最高标准

~ working water level 最高工作水位

highly ['haili] ad. 高度地，非常，非常赞许地

~ flexible cable 高柔性电缆

~ sensitive 高灵敏度的

~ skewed propeller 高歪斜螺桨，大侧斜螺旋桨

~ toxic 剧毒的，高毒性的

hind [haind] a. (=hinder) 后边的，后面的

hinder ['hində] v. 阻碍，阻碍，耽搁，打扰；a. (=hind) 后边的，后面的

hinge [hindʒ] n. 铰链，折叶，枢纽，枢要，中枢，关键，转折点；v. 装铰链，依…而转移

~ arm 铰接臂

~ armature 枢轴衔铁

~ bolt 铰接螺栓

~ bracket 铰链托架

~ joint 铰链接合，铰式接缝，铰接，活节连接

~ line 铰合线，枢纽线，蝶铰线

~ lug 铰链耳子

~ on 靠…转动，以…为转移

~ pin 铰链销，折页轴，销轴

~ pin bracket 折页销插

~ sleeve 铰链套筒

~ tooth 铰合齿，蝶铰齿

hinged [hindʒd] v. (hinge 的过去式和过去分词) 装铰链，依…而转移；a. 有铰链的，铰链式的

~ armature relay 旋转衔铁式继电器

~ connecting rod 铰接曲柄边杆机构

~ pipe vice 铰链式管子台虎钳

~ stern door 艉部吊门

~ support 铰接支点，铰接支承

~ type connecting rod 铰链式连杆

hint [hint] n. 提示，暗示，线索；v. 暗示，示意

HIP (hot isostatic pressure) 热等静压

histogram ['histəugræm] n. 直方图，柱状图

HMS (Her Majesty's Ship) 女王陛下的舰艇，英国军舰

hobby ['hɔbi] n. 嗜好，业余爱好

~ room 娱乐室

hogshead ['hɔgzhed] n. 大桶，液量单位

hoist ['hɔistiŋ] n. 提升，起重，起重机，旗宽，信号旗；v. 升起，提起，吊起，扯起

~ unit 起重装置，起升装置

~ universal joint 起重机万向节

hoisting ['hɔistiŋ] n. 起重，提升；v. (hoist 的 ing 形式) 升起，提起，吊起，扯起

~ beam 吊梁，起重梁，吊钩梁

~ block 起重滑车

~ capacity 提升能力

~ crane 起重机，升降起重机

~ device 起重装置

~ eye 吊眼

~ lever 提升杠杆

~ limit switch 过卷开关

~ machine 起重机，升降机，卷扬机

~ machinery 起重机械

~ main contactor 上升主接触器

~ motor 起重马达，起重电动机

~ ring 吊环

~ rope 起重绳

~ speed 提升速度，吊货速度

~ stopper 起吊止挡

~ tackle 起重滑车

~ test of engine room crane 机舱行车吊重试验

~ time 动臂举升时间，提升时间

~ winch 绞车，绞盘

~ winch motor 起重绞车电动机，起升电动机

~ wire 起重钢索

hold [həuld] n. 控制，保留，把握，把持力，柄，监禁，掌握，货舱；v. 握着，拿着，保存，保持，支持，占据，持有，拥有，有效

~ space 货舱舱容，保持空间

~ space of gas carrier 气体运输船货舱舱容

holder ['həuldə] n. 固定器，支持物，持有人，所有人

holding ['həuldiŋ] n. 举办，支持；v. (hold 的 ing 形式) 握着，拿着，保存，保持，支持，占据，持有，拥有，有效

~ circuit 吸持电路

~ coil 吸持线圈,自保线圈,保持线圈,支助线圈

~ down bolt 地脚螺栓,轴承紧固螺栓,锚杆

~ element 保持元件,自保元件

~ load 保持负载,制动载荷 ‖ **Syn**. brake holding load 制动负荷,制动拉力

~ magnet 吸持磁体,保持磁铁

~ power 握力,抓力

~ relay 吸持继电器

~ screw 紧定螺钉,紧固螺丝

~ tank 接受器,选集器,存储器,收集器

~ time 保持时间,占用时间,保留时间

hole [həul] *n*. 洞,孔,突破口; *v*. 凿洞,穿孔,进洞

~ cutting snips 铁皮剪

~ diameter 孔直径,刃口直径

~ location 孔位

~ pattern 穿孔图案

~ saw 孔锯

hollow ['hɔləu] *n*. 洞,山谷,窟窿; *a*. 空的,中空的,凹的,空腹的,虚伪的

~ axle 空心轴,管轴

~ conductor 空心导线,空心导体

~ punch 冲孔机,冲孔器,空心冲头

~ rod 空心抽油杆,空心钻杆

~ roll 卷筒接头,空心辊

~ screw 空心螺钉

~ shaft 管轴,空心轴

~ spindle 空心(主)轴

homeostasis [ˌhəumiəu'steisis] *n*. 动态静止,动态平衡,内稳态,体内平衡

homeostatic [ˌhəumiəu'stætik] *a*. 自我平衡的,原状稳定的

homogeneous [ˌhɔməu'dʒi:njəs] *a*. 均匀的,均一的,齐次的,同种的,同类的,同质的

~ cylinder 均质柱状体

homogenization [ˌhəumədʒənai'zeiʃən] *n*. 均化,均化作用

hone [həun] *n*. 磨刀石,想念,抱怨; *v*. 用磨刀石磨

~ and polish 镗磨光滑

honing ['həuniŋ] *n*. 珩磨,搪磨; *v*. (hone 的 ing 形式) 用磨刀石磨

~ machine 珩床,搪磨床,珩磨机,磨孔机,磨气缸机

hood [hud] *n*. 车篷,引擎罩,排风罩,强盗,枪手,头巾,覆盖,兜帽; *v*. 加罩,覆盖

~ baffle 挡烟罩

~ bracket 罩架

~ poop 鲸背型船尾楼

hook [huk] *n*. 挂钩,吊钩; *v*. 钩住,沉迷,上瘾

~ wrench 钩形扳手

hoop [hu:p] *n*. 箍,铁环,戒指,篮; *v*. 加箍于,环绕

hopper ['hɔpə] *n*. 料斗,漏斗,储料器,单足跳者

~ barge 泥舱船

horizon [hə'raizn] *n*. 地平线,视野,眼界,范围

horizontal [ˌhɔri'zɔntl] *a*. 地平线的,水平的

~ acceleration 水平加速度

~ accelerometer 水平加速度表

~ axis 水平轴,横轴

~ band saw 卧式带锯

~ boiler 卧式锅炉

~ component 水平分量，水平分力，水平部分

~ cylinder 卧式气缸

~ decomposition 横向分解

~ definition 水平清晰度

~ direction 水平方向，水平偏转

~ displacement 水平位移

~ distance 水平距离，平距

~ distribution 水平分布，平面分布

~ engine 卧式发动机

~ fish finder 水平鱼探仪

~ flow 水平流

~ flow pipe reactor 平流管式反应器

~ flue 横(式)气道

~ force 水平力，横向力

~ girder 水平梁，水平桁

~ lathe 卧式车床

~ laying 水平敷设，水平瞄准

~ line 水平线，横线

~ load 水平载荷，水平负载

~ machining center 卧式加工中心

~ milling machine 卧式铣床

~ pipe 水平管，横管

~ plane 水平面，地平，水平舵

~ portal 横向用户

~ position 水平位置

~ pump 卧式泵

~ return tubular boiler 卧式回火管锅炉

~ shell and tube evaporator 卧式壳管蒸发器

~ stiffener 水平扶强材，横向防挠材

~ stress 水平应力

~ strut 水平支杆，横梁

~ surface 水平面

~ traffic 水平装卸法，水平交通

~ transfer 横向转移

~ triple-pass fire-tube boiler 卧式三回程火管锅炉

~ welding position 横向焊接位置

~ windlass 卧式锚机

~ wipe 水平消除

horizontal-fixed 水平固定的，横向固定的

~ position 水平固定位置，固定横向焊位置

horizontal-rotated 水平旋转的

~ position 水平旋转位置

horn [hɔ:n] n. 角质，角，触角，角状物，号角，警报器，喇叭，(喇叭形)天线；v. 不请自来，闯入 ‖ **Syn**. alarm 警报器，警铃，警报；alarm apparatus 报警器

horsepower ['hɔ:s,pauə] n. 马力

horsepower-hour 马力时

horsepower-weight 马力重量

~ factor 马力重量系数

horseshoe ['hɔ:sʃu:] n. 马蹄铁，U形物；v. 装蹄铁于

~ magnet 马蹄形磁铁

hose [həuz] n. 软管，水龙带；v. 用软管浇水

~ clamp 软管夹，软管卡

~ connection 软管连接，软管接头

~ end 软管端头

~ end fitting 软管接头

~ expansion 管体膨胀

~ handling crane 软管起升吊机

~ hawser 软管吊绳，软管缆

~ nipple 软管螺纹接套

~ protector 软管防护套

~ rapid adapter 快速接头

293

~ reel assembly 软管绞盘装置

~ testing 射水试验，冲水试验，软管实验

~ thread 软管螺纹

hose-proof 防水的

~ motor 防水式电动机

hosepipe ['həuzpaip] n. 橡胶软管，水龙软管

host [həust] n. 主机，主人，主持人，军队，一大群，许多；v. 主持，做东，当主人招待

~ computer 主机

hot [hɔt] a. 热的，热情的，辣的，激动的，紧迫的，节奏强的；ad. 热，热切地，紧迫地

~ air duct 热风管道，热空气导管

~ air pipe 热空气管

~ and cold water pipe lines 冷热水管路

~ bending 热弯，热弯曲

~ brine defrost 热盐水融霜，热盐水除霜

~ bulb engine 热球式发动机，火球式发动机，烧球式引擎

~ cargo 热货

~ crack 热裂，过热裂缝

~ fix 热修复

~ fixture soldering technique 热夹具焊接技术

~ gas defrost 热气融霜

~ gas purification 热气净化

~ insulation resistance 热态绝缘电阻

~ isostatic pressure (HIP) 热等静压

~ melting 热熔

~ press 热压机

~ site 热站

~ size 热定径，热模精压，热校正

~ soak loss 热浸损失

~ space 高温区，高温带

~ starting 热态启动，热起动

~ water circulating pipe lines 热水循环管路

~ water circulating pump 热水循环泵

~ water heating system 热水供热系统

~ water regulating pump 热水循环泵

~ water regulating valve 水温调整阀

~ water return pipe lines 热水循环回流管

~ water stop valve 热水止阀

~ water tank 热水箱，热水槽

~ wet strength 高温湿强度

~ work 热作业，热加工，高温加工

houseboat ['hausbəut] n. 游艇，居住船，船屋

hover ['hɔvə] n. 徘徊，盘旋；v. 犹豫，盘旋，翱翔，徘徊

~ fan 升力风扇 ‖ Syn. lift fan 升力风扇

hovercraft ['hɔvəkra:ft] n. 气垫船

howsoever [,hausəu'evə] ad. 无论如何，不管怎样

HP (high pressure) 高压，高气压

~ asbestos 高压石棉

~ asbestos sheet 高压石棉板

~ cleaner 高压清洁器

~ combustion chamber 高压燃烧室

~ compressor 高压压缩机，高压压气机

~ contact port 高压出气孔

~ cut-out switch 高压切断开关

~ draft 高压气流

~ fuel delivery pipe 高压燃油输送管

~ fuel pipe 高压油管，高压燃油管

~ gas 高压气体
~ grease gun 高压滑脂枪
~ hose 高压软管
~ insulating tape 高压绝缘胶布
~ mercury fluorescent lighting fitting 高压汞荧光照明装置
~ mercury vapor lamp 高压汞气灯，高压水银灯
~ mercury vapor lighting fitting 高压汞蒸汽照明装置
~ pump 高压泵，高压输液泵
~ safety cut-out 高压安全切断器
~ steam 高压蒸汽
~ steam packing 高压蒸汽填料
~ tube 高压管
~ water jet 高压喷水器，高压水枪
~ water jet flow 高压水射流

HSC (high speed craft) 高速船
~ Safety Certificate 高速船安全证书

HT (high temperature) 高温
~ corrosion 高温腐蚀
~ test 高温试验，高温测试

HT (high tension) 高电压，高压 ‖ *Syn*.
HV (high voltage) 高电压，高压
~ circuit 高压电路
~ circuit breaker 高压断路器
~ contactor 高压接触器
~ distribution cabinet 高压配电箱
~ equipment 高压设备
~ fuse 高压保险丝
~ isolator 高压隔离器
~ load switch 高压负荷开关
~ switchgear 高压开关设备
~ transformer 高压变压器
~ vacuum contactor 高压真空接触器

hub [hʌb] *n*. 中心，毂，网络集线器，网络中心，木片

huge [hju:dʒ] *a*. 巨大的，庞大的，无限的

hulk [hʌlk] *n*. 废船，笨重的船，船体；*v*. 庞然大物般出现，笨拙地挪动，赫然显现

hull [hʌl] *n*. 船体，外壳
~ appendages 船舶附体
~ castings 船体铸件
~ construction 船体结构
~ efficiency 船身效率
~ fittings 舱面属具，船体属具
~ forgings 船体锻件
~ form 船型，船体线型
~ girder 主船体桁，船桁体，相当桁
~ girder strength 船体梁强度
~ girder stress 船体梁应力
~ insurance 船身保险
~ resistance characteristic 船体阻力特性
~ roughness 船体粗糙度
~ scantling 船体结构尺寸，船体构件尺寸
~ specification 船体说明书
~ steel 船体钢
~ stress 船体应力
~ stress monitoring system 船体应力监测系统
~ structure 船体结构

human ['hju:mən] *n*. 人，人类；*a*. 人的，人类的，人性的，有同情心的
~ control 人工控制

human-computer 人机 ‖ *Syn*. human-machine 人机；man-machine 人机
~ combination 人机联作校正
~ cooperative 人机结合

~ dialogue 人机对话

~ interaction 人机交互

~ interface 人机界面

human-machine 人机 ‖ *Syn*. human-computer 人机；man-machine 人机

humidification [hju:ˌmidifi'keiʃən] *n*. 加湿，潮湿

humidity [hju:'miditi] *n*. 湿度，湿气

~ controller 湿度调节器

~ correction factor 湿度修正系数

~ sensor 湿度传感器

hunt [hʌnt] *n*. 狩猎，搜寻；*v*. 打猎，追逐，搜索，搜寻

hunting ['hʌntiŋ] *n*. 打猎，追逐，搜索；*v*. (hunt 的 ing 形式) 打猎，追逐，搜索，搜寻

~ gear 从动装置，随动装置，跟踪装置

~ motor 从动电动机

HV (high voltage) 高电压，高压 ‖ *Syn*. HT (high tension) 高电压，高压

~ cable for ship 船用高压电缆

~ cutout 高压断路器，高压断流器

~ disconnecting switch 高压隔离开关

~ engineering 高电压工程

~ generating station 高压电站

~ IC 高压集成电路

~ load break switch 高压负载断路开关

~ power system 高压电源系统，高压电力系统

~ relay 高压继电器

~ switchgear 高压开关

~ technology 高电压技术

~ test 高电压试验

~ testing technology 高压测试技术，高压试验技能

~ testing transformer 高压试验变压器

HVAC (heating, ventilation and air conditioning) 加热、通风及空调，采暖、通风及空调

HVAC (high voltage alternating current) 高压交流电

HVDC (high voltage DC transmission) 高压直流输电

hybrid ['haibrid] *n*. 杂种，混血儿，混合物；*a*. 混合的，杂种的

~ circuit 混合电路

hydrant ['haidrənt] *n*. 消防栓，消防龙头 ‖ *Syn*. fire hydrant 消防栓，消防龙头

~ valve 消防龙头阀

hydrate ['haidreit] *n*. 水合物，氢氧化物；*v*. 与水化合 ‖ *Ant*. dehydrate (使)脱水

hydration [hai'dreiʃən] *n*. 水合，水合作用 ‖ *Ant*. dehydration 脱水

hydraulic [hai'drɔ:lik] *a*. 液压的，水力的，水压的 ‖ electric 电动的；pneumatic 气动的，风力的

~ accumulator 液压蓄能器

~ actuating mechanism 液压驱动机构 ‖ *Syn*. hydraulic actuator 液压执行器，液动装置

~ amplifier 液压放大器

~ anchor capstan 液压起锚装置

~ anchor windlass 液压起锚绞盘

~ blocking device 液压锁闭设施

~ booster 液压助力器，液力增压器

~ booster steering 液力助力转向(机构)

~ boring machine 液压镗床

~ brake 液压制动

~ breaker 液压制动器

~ buffer 液压缓冲器

~ capstan 液压绞盘，水力绞盘
~ cargo winch 液压起货机
~ chain tensioner 液压链张紧器
~ change-over valve 液动换向阀
~ circuit 液压回路
~ clutch 液压离合器
~ component 液压元件 ‖ *Syn*. hydraulic element 液压元件
~ connector 液压连接器
~ control 液压控制
~ control device for hatch covers 舱口盖液压控制装置
~ control lathe 液压控制车床
~ control mechanism 液压操纵机构
~ control non-return valve 液压控制止回阀
~ control pump 液压控制泵
~ control system 液压操纵系统
~ control valve 液压控制阀
~ controller 液压调节器
~ coupling 液压联轴节，水力联轴器，液压离合器，液力管接头 ‖ *Syn*. hydrocoupling 水压联轴器，液压联轴器
~ crane 液压起重机
~ cylinder 液压缸，液压油缸
~ device 液压装置
~ diagram 液压原理图
~ direction control valve 液压方向控制阀
~ dredge 吸扬式挖泥船
~ drift net capstan 液压流网绞盘
~ drilling 液压钻孔
~ drive 液压传动
~ efficiency 液压效率
~ efficiency servo-gear 液压伺服机构

~ efficiency towing winch 液压拖缆机
~ elevator 液压升降机
~ energy 液压能
~ equipment 液压设备
~ fender 液压防碰设备
~ filter 液压滤器
~ fluid 液压油，液压流体，液压液体 ‖ *Syn*. hydraulic liquid 液压油；hydraulic oil 液压油
~ fluid contamination 液压油污染
~ fracturing 水力压裂
~ gate 液压闸门
~ gear 液压传动装置
~ governor 液压调节器
~ hatch cover 液压舱口盖
~ hinge 液压铰链
~ hose 液压软管
~ interlocking 液压联锁
~ jack 液压千斤顶，液压起重器，液压油缸
~ joint 液压连接
~ lift 液压升降
~ lifter 液压升降机
~ lifting cylinder 液压提升油缸
~ lock 液压锁紧，液压卡紧，液压封闭
~ longline gurdy 液压延绳钓机
~ loss 水力损失，液体损失
~ luffing 液压变幅
~ machine 液压机，水压机
~ mechanism 液压机构
~ metal prop 液压金属支柱
~ motor 液压马达
~ oil contamination 液压油污染
~ oil cylinder 液压油缸
~ oil reservoir 液压油贮存器
~ oil storage tank 液压油储存柜

~ oil tank 液压油箱
~ operating mechanism 液压操动机构
~ operation 液压操作
~ piston 液压活塞
~ planer 液压刨床
~ plate bender 液压弯板机
~ power 水力，水能，液体力
~ power cylinder 液压缸
~ power tool 液压工具
~ power unit 液压动力组
~ power pack for pitch control 螺距控制液压动力组件
~ press 液压冲床，液压机，液压器，水压机
~ pressure 液压，水压
~ pressure indicator 水压计，水压表，液压表 ‖ *Syn*. hydraulic pressure gauge 水压计，水压表，液压表
~ pressure manifold 液压歧管
~ pressure test 液压试验
~ pressure treatment 液压处理
~ primer 液压起动机
~ profile 水力纵剖面
~ prop 液压支柱
~ propulsion 液压驱动
~ propulsion motor 液压驱动马达
~ protector 液压保护装置
~ pump 液压泵
~ pumping unit 液压泵装置
~ purse seine winch 液压围网起网机，液压围网绞车
~ push rod 液压推杆
~ ram 液压油缸，液压顶
~ ram tensioner 液压缸张力器
~ release gear 液压释放装置
~ resistance 水阻力

~ riveter 液压铆钉枪，液压铆接机，水力铆接机，水压铆机 ‖ *Syn*. hydraulic riveting machine 液压铆钉枪，液压铆接机，水力铆接机，水压铆机
~ rotary cylinder 液压回转缸
~ rotary transmission 水动力传动，液力传动
~ safety valve 液压安全阀
~ screw press 液压螺旋压力机，液压螺旋锤
~ selector 液压选择阀
~ servo-actuator 液压伺服执行机构
~ servomechanism 液压伺服机构
~ servomotor 液压伺服马达
~ servovalve 液压伺服阀
~ set 液压设备
~ shaft flange 液压轴法兰
~ shaper 液压牛头刨
~ shield 液压防护装置
~ slide valve 液压滑阀
~ stability 液压稳定性
~ stacker 液压堆垛机
~ steering 液压舵
~ steering control system 液压操舵系统
~ steering engine 液压舵机 ‖ *Syn*. hydraulic steering gear 液压舵机
~ steering telemotor 液压遥控操舵器
~ step motor 液压步进马达
~ stepless speed change 液压无级变速
~ supply system 液压供应系统
~ support 液压支架
~ swivel head 液压旋转水龙头
~ system 液压系统
~ system and equipment 液压系统和设备

~ tappet 液压挺杆
~ technique 液压技术
~ telecontrol 液压电力控制器
~ telemetry 液压遥测技术
~ telemotor 液压传动装置
~ tensioner 液压紧线器
~ test 液压测试
~ test for LO pipe for stern tube 艉管滑油管液压试验
~ tightening tool 液压压紧工具
~ tool 液压工具
~ torque converter 液压扭矩变换器
~ transmission 液压传动
~ transmission gear 液压传动装置
~ transmission system 液力传动系统
~ transmitter 液压传动器
~ trawl winch 液压拖网绞车
~ tube 液压管
~ tuner 液压调谐器
~ turbine 水轮机，水力透平
~ winch 液压绞车，带液压马达的绞车
~ windlass 液压起锚机，液压绞盘

hydraulic-mechanical 液压机械的
~ drive 液压机械传动

hydraulically [hai'drɔ:likəli] *ad.* 液压地，水力地，水压地
~ actuated 液压传动的，液压驱动的 ‖ *Syn*. hydraulically driven 液压传动的，液压驱动的；hydraulically powered 液压传动的，液压驱动的
~ actuated brake 液压制动器，液力制动器
~ actuated exhaust valve mechanism 液压式排气阀传动机构
~ controlled 液压控制的
~ controlled valve 液压控制阀

~ driven progressive cavity pump 液压驱动螺杆泵
~ driven pump 液压传动泵
~ driven transverse propeller 液压传动横向推进器
~ driving 液压驱动，液压传动
~ driving arrangement 液压驱动装置，液压传动装置
~ expanded 液压扩张的，液压胀接的
~ expanded joint 液压胀接接头
~ impact 液压冲击
~ intensified common-rail injection system 增压式共轨喷油系统
~ operated 液压操纵的
~ operated cargo valve 液压操纵货油阀，液力操作液货阀
~ operated clutch 液力操纵离合器
~ operated isolating valve 液压操纵隔离阀
~ operated oil valve 液压油阀
~ operated valve 液压操作阀
~ powered side thruster 液压传动侧推进器
~ powered winch 液力传动绞车

hydro ['haidrəu] *n.* 水电，水力发电，站水疗院；*a.* 水电的
~ air 液压气压联动(装置)
~ skimmer 气垫船，腾空船

hydro-chlorofluoro-carbon (HCFC) 氢氯氟烃

hydroblas ['haidrə,bla:st] *n.* 水力清理，水力清砂

hydrocarbon ['haidrəu'ka:bən] *n.* 碳氢化合物，烃
~ extraction 烃类抽提
~ gas 烃气，碳氢化合物气体

hydrochloride [ˌhaidrəu'klɔ:raid] n. 氢氯化物
~ acid 盐酸
hydrocoupling [ˌhaidrə'kʌpliŋ] n. 水压联轴器,液压联轴器 液压联轴器 ‖ *Syn.* hydraulic coupling 液压联轴节,水力联轴器,液压离合器,液力管接头
hydrocyanic ['haidrəusai'ænik] a. 氰氢的
hydrocyclone [haidrə'saikləun] n. 水力旋流器,涡流除尘器,旋液分离器
hydrodynamic ['haidrəudai'næmik] a. 水力的,流体动力学的
~ lubrication 液体动力润滑,液动润滑
hydrodynamics ['haidrəudai'næmiks] n. 流体力学,水动力学,流体动力学
hydrofoil ['haidrəfɔil] n. 水翼,水翼船
~ craft 水翼艇,水翼船
~ destroyer 水翼驱逐舰
hydroform ['haidrəfɔ:m] v. 液压成形
hydrographic [haidrə'græfik] a. 与水道测量有关的,与水文地理有关的
~ survey vessel 水文勘探船
hydrojet ['haidrədʒet] n. 水力喷射,液力喷射,喷液
~ boat 水力喷射艇
hydrolant ['haidrəulənt] n. (美国海军航路局发出的)大西洋航行危险警报
hydrometer [hai'drɔmitə] n. 液体比重计,浮秤
hydrophilic [ˌhaidrəu'filik] a. 亲水的,吸水的
hydrophore ['haidrəfɔ:] n. 采水样器,测不同海深的温度计
~ plant 采水样装置
hydropneumatic [ˌhaidrəunju:'mætik] a. 液压气动的,水气并动的

~ component 液压气动元件
~ cushion 液压气垫
~ device 液压气动设备
~ punch 液压气动打孔机
~ spring 带液压枕垫的板簧
~ test 液压气动测试,气水压力试验
hydropneumatics [ˌhaidrəunju:'mætiks] n. 液压气动学
hydropress ['haidrəpres] n. 液压机,水压平板机 ‖ *Syn.* hydrostatic press 液压机,水压机
hydroskimmer ['haidrəu'skimə] n. 滑行艇,漂水船,水翼船,水面掠行艇
hydrostatic [ˌhaidrəu'stætik] a. 静水力学的,流体静力学的
~ bearing 静压轴承
~ drive 静液压驱动
~ driver 静液压驱动器
~ forging 液压锻造
~ head 静压头
~ joint 承压接口,静水压接头
~ lubrication 静压润滑
~ power transmission 液压动力传动
~ press 液压机,水压机 ‖ *Syn.* hydropress 液压机,水压平板机
~ pressure 液体静压力,液静压
~ pressure apparatus 液静压设备
~ pressure system 液静压系统
~ release unit 静水压力释放器
~ sensor 静压传感器
~ sink 静流容器
~ test 水压试验,静水压试验,流体静压试验
~ transmission 液压静力传输,流体静力传动(装置),静液压传动装置,液压传动(装置)

hydrostatically [ˌhaidrəu'stætikli] *a.* 静水力学地，流体静力学地
~ balanced loading 静水平衡装载
hydrous ['haidrəs] *a.* 含水的，水合的
hydroxide [hai'drɔksaid] *n.* 氢氧化物，羟化物
hygrometer [hai'grɔmitə] *n.* 湿度计
hygroscopic [ˌhaigrəu'skɔpik] *a.* 易湿的，吸湿的
~ agent 吸湿剂
~ matter 吸湿性物质
~ medium 吸湿介质
~ water content 平衡湿量
hyper ['haipə] *n.* 宣传人员；*a.* 亢奋的，高度紧张的
hyper-voltage 过电压
~ of power systems 电力系统过电压
hyperbaric [ˌhaipə:'bærik] *a.* 施压力以供氧气的，高比重的
hyperventilate [ˌhaipə'ventileit] *v.* (使)强力呼吸，换气过度
hyperventilation [ˌhaipə(:)venti'leiʃən] *n.* 换气过度，强力呼吸
hypocapnia [ˌhaipəu'kæpniə] *n.* 低碳酸血(症)
hypothermia [ˌhaipəu'θə:miə] *n.* 体温过低
hypothesis [hai'pɔθisis] *n.* 假设
hypoxaemia [ˌhaipɔk'si:miə] *n.* 低氧血，血氧过少
hypoxia [hai'pɔksiə] *n.* 低氧，组织缺氧，氧不足
hysteresis [ˌhistə'ri:sis] *n.* 滞后作用，磁滞现象
~ error 磁滞误差，滞环误差，滞后误差
Hz (Hertz) 赫兹，赫

I

I [ai] ① (=integral) *n.* 积分，完整，部分；*a.* 积分的，完整的，整体的，构成整体所需要的 ② (=integration) *n.* 积分，集成，综合
~ action 积分作用
~ control 积分控制，积分调节
~ control mode 积分控制方式，积分调节方式
~ control output 积分控制输出，积分调节输出
~ controller 积分控制器，积分调节器 ‖ *Syn*. I regulator 积分控制器，积分调节器
~ element 积分环节，积分元件
~ mode 积分模式
I-drive 智能驾驶控制系统，网络硬盘驱动器
I-engine I 型发动机
I-shaped 工字形的
~ longitudinal girders 工字形纵梁，工字形纵桁
IACS (International Association of Classification Society) 国际船级社协会
IAFS (International Anti-Fouling System) 国际防污系统
~ Certificate 国际防污系统证书
IAPP (International Air Pollution Prevention) 国际大气污染防治
~ Certificate 国际大气污染防治证书
IBC (iron binding capacity) 铁结合能力
IBC Code (International Code for the Construction and Equipment of Ships

Carrying Dangerous Chemicals in Bulk) 国际散装运输危险化学品船舶构造与设备规则

IBS (Integrated Bridge System) 组合船桥系统，综合驾驶室系统，综合驾驶台系统

IBTS (Integrated Bilge Water Treatment System) 舱底水综合处理系统

IC (integrated circuit) 集成电路

ice [ais] *n*. 冰，冰淇淋，冰冻食品；*v*. 结冰，冰冻，冰镇
　～ beam　抗冰梁
　～ belt　浮冰带，冰带区
　～ chest　冰柜，冰箱，冷藏箱，冰库
　～ class　冰级
　～ class notation　冰级标志
　～ coating　结冰，敷冰
　～ diving　冰水潜水，冰潜
　～ doubling　破冰加强板
　～ load　冰负荷
　～ navigation　冰区航行
　～ pressure　冰压力
　～ resistant　抗冰
　～ resistant unit　抗冰装置
　～ strengthening　抗冰加强
　～ strengthened class　冰强度等级
　～ strip　窄冰带
　～ stringer　冰带舷侧纵桁

ice-covered　冰封的，冰雪覆盖的
　～ region　冰雪覆盖的地区

iceberg ['aisbəg] *n*. 冰山，显露部分，冷冰冰的人

icebreaker ['aisbreikə(r)] *n*. 碎冰船，破冰设备
　～ bow　破冰船弓

Iceland ['aislənd] *n*. 冰岛(欧洲岛名，在大西洋北部，近北极圈)

ICLL (International Convention on Load Lines) 国际载重线公约

ICMS (Integrated Control and Monitoring System) 综合监测控制系统，综合监控系统

ID (identification) 证明，身份证明，辨认，鉴定，识别，认同，有关联

ID (identity) 身份，同一性，一致，特性，恒等式
　～ card　身份证

ID (inside diameter) 内径，内直径，内部直径

idea [ai'diə] *n*. 想法，念头，意见，主意，思想，观念，概念

ideal [ai'diəl] *n*. 理想，典范，典型，目标，高尚的、有价值的原则或目标；*a*. 理想的，完美的，想象的，不切实际的
　～ cycle　理想循环，热力循环
　～ final value　理想终值
　～ Gas Law　理想气体定律
　～ propeller efficiency　理想螺旋桨效率
　～ source　理想电源
　～ value　理想值

identical [ai'dentikəl] *a*. 同一的，同样的，可互换的，完全相等的，完全相似的

identifiability [ai'denti,faiə'biləti] *n*. 可辨认性，可识别性，可鉴别性

identifiable [ai'dentifaiəbl] *a*. 可辨认的，可认明的，可以确认的

identification [ai,dentifi'keiʃən] (ID) *n*. 证明，身份证明，辨认，鉴定，识别，认同，有关联
　～ card　身份证 ‖ *Syn*. identity card　身份证
　～ checking system　识别检查系统

~ code 标识码

~ document 识别文件，鉴定文件，查验文件

identifier [ai'dentifaiə] *n.* 检验人，鉴定人，标识符，认同者

identify [ai'dentifai] *v.* 识别，鉴别，确定，确认，验明，融入，认为等同，成为一体

identity [ai'dentiti] *n.* 身份，同一性，一致，特性，恒等式

~ card 身份证 ‖ ***Syn.*** identification card 身份证

idle ['aidl] *v.* (使)空转，(使)不运转，(使)闲散，怠速转动，浪费，虚度，不做事；*a.* 空闲的，闲置的，懒惰的，停顿的，无用的，无价值的，无因的，无由的

~ run-normal run selector switch 怠速快速运行选择键，停机运行启动选择键

~ ship 等泊船，闲置船

~ speed emission limits 怠速排放限值

~ wheel 惰轮，空转轮

idling ['aidliŋ] *n.* 空转，闲置，慢速，虚度；*v.* (idle 的 ing 形式) (使)空转，(使)不运转，(使)闲散，怠速转动，浪费，虚度，不做事

~ speed 空转速度，空转转速

IEC (International Electrotechnical Commission) 国际电工委员会

IEE (Institution of Electrical Engineers) 国际电气工程师学会

IEEE (Institute of Electrical and Electronic Engineers) 电气和电子工程师协会

IFO (intermediate fuel oil) 中间燃油

IGBT (insulated gate bipolar transistor) 绝缘栅双极型晶体管

IGC (International Gas Carrier) 国际气体载运船

~ Code 国际气体载运船章程

IGC Code (International Code for the Construction and Equipment of Ships Carrying Liquefied Gases in Bulk) 国际散装运输液化气船舶构造和设备规范

IGCT (integrated gate commutated thyristor) 集成门极换流晶闸管

ignitability [ig,naitə'biləti] *n.* 可燃性，可点燃性

ignite [ig'nait] *v.* 点火，点燃，使燃烧，使发火，使激动，使灼热

igniter [ig'naitə] *n.* 点火器，触发器；引燃装置，引爆装置

~ electrode 点火电极

~ fuse 点火引线，点火引信

ignition [ig'niʃən] *n.* 着火，燃烧，点火，点燃，发火装置，点火器，点火开关

~ adance 点火提前

~ delay 着火滞后(期)，滞燃期

~ delay period 着火滞后期

~ device 点火装置

~ flame 点火火焰

~ governing 点火调节

~ inhibition for fire prevention 阻化防火

~ lag 着火落后

~ nozzle 点火喷油嘴

~ of burner 燃烧器点火

~ order 着火顺序，发火次序

~ point 燃点

~ quality 着火性，发火性能

~ switch 点火开关

~ tester 燃点测试器

~ temperature 着火温度，发火温度，着火点，燃烧温度

~ timing 点火定时，点火正时

~ transformer 点火变压器

~ tube 烧灼管，发火管

~ voltage 点火电压

ignore [ig'nɔ:] v. 忽视，不顾，驳回诉讼

IGS (inert gas system) 惰性气体系统

IHP (indicated horsepower) 指示马力

IISSC (Interim International Ship Security Certificate) 国际临时船舶保安证书

ILLC (International Load Line Certificate) 国际载重线证书

ILLC (International Load Line Convention) 国际载重线公约

illegibility [iledʒə'biliti] n. 不清不楚，不可辨认，模糊

ILLR (International Load Line Regulations) 国际载重线规则

illuminate [i'lju:mineit] v. 照明，照亮，阐明，说明，使灿烂，以灯火装饰

illumination [i,lju:mi'neiʃən] n. 照明，光亮源，照度，阐明，启发，灯彩，装饰

illustrate ['iləstreit] v. 举例说明，图解，加插图于，阐明

illustration [,iləs'treiʃən] n. 说明，例证，例子，图表，插图，图解

ILO (International Labor Organization) 国际劳工组织

image ['imidʒ] n. 图像，映像，典型，肖像，偶像，形象化比喻；v. 想象，反映，象征

~ capturing device 图像采集装置，图像获取装备

~ recognition 图像识别

imaginable [i'mædʒinəbl] a. 可能的，可想象的

imaginary [i'mædʒinəri] n. 虚数；a. 假想的，想象的，虚构的，虚数的

~ axis 虚数轴，虚(数)轴

~ part 虚数部分，虚部

imbalance [im'bæləns] n. 不平衡，不均衡，失调 ‖ *Syn*. unbalance 失衡，失去平衡，紊乱

IMCO (Intergovernmental Maritime Consultative Organization) 政府间海事协商组织

IMDG (International Maritime Dangerous Goods) 国际海上危险货物

~ Code 国际海上危险货物运输规则

IMEP (indicated mean effective pressure) 指示平均有效压力

immediate [i'mi:djət] a. 直接的，紧接的，紧靠的，立即的，知觉的

~ entrance 直接入口

~ error 暂误

immediately [i'mi:djətli] ad. 立即，马上，直接地，紧接地；conj. 马上，直接地

immerse [i'mə:s] v. 浸没，浸入，沉浸于，沉溺于，陷入

~ with insulating paint 用绝缘漆浸渍

immersed [i'mə:st] v. (immerse 的过去式和过去分词) 浸没，浸入，沉浸于，沉溺于，陷入；a. 浸入的，沉入的，沉思的

~ area 浸没区

imminence ['iminəns] n. 急迫，危急，迫近的危险，迫近的祸患

imminent ['iminənt] a. 迫在眉睫的，即将发生的，迫切的，危急的，逼近的

immiscible [i'misəbl] a. 不能混合的，不

融合的 ‖ *Ant*. miscible 易混合的，易融合的

immobilization [i,məubilai'zeiʃən] *n*. 固定，使停止流通

immobilize [i'məubilaiz] *v*. 使不动，使固定，固定不动

IMO (International Maritime Organization) 国际海事组织

~ Assembly 国际海事组织大会

~ Class 国际海事组织类号

~ Council 国际海事组织理事会

~ MEPC 国际海事组织海上环境保护委员会

~ MSC 国际海事组织海上安全委员会

~ Resolution 国际海事组织决议

~ TCC 国际海事组织技术合作委员会

impact ['impækt] *n*. 碰撞，冲击，冲突，影响，影响力，效果；*v*. 挤入，撞击，压紧，发生影响

~ closing test 冲击合闸试验

~ coefficient 冲击系数

~ damper 缓冲器，减震器

~ driver 冲击式驱动器，冲击起子

~ ductility 冲击韧性

~ force 冲击力

~ load 冲击负载

~ relay 冲击继电器

~ resilience 抗冲(击)性

~ test 冲击试验，碰撞试验，撞击试验

~ testing machine 冲击试验机

~ wrench 拧紧扳手，套筒扳手，机动扳手，冲头

impair [im'pɛə] *v*. 损害，削弱，削减，减少

impedance [im'pi:dəns] *n*. 阻抗 ‖ *Syn*. resistance 阻抗 ‖ reactance 电抗

~ test of all windings 所有绕组的阻抗试验

impede [im'pi:d] *v*. 阻碍，妨碍，阻挡，阻止，拖延

impel [im'pel] *v*. 推动，推进，激励，驱使，逼迫

impeller [im'pelə] *n*. 推动器，叶轮，推进者

~ blade 叶轮片，动叶片

~ diameter 叶轮直径

~ eye (离心压气机的)叶轮入口

~ hub 叶轮轮毂

~ inducer 导流叶轮，导风叶轮

~ neck 叶轮颈

~ output 叶轮排出量

~ pump 叶轮泵

~ speed 叶轮转速

~ wearing ring 叶轮抗磨环

~ wheel (径流式)叶轮

imperfect [im'pə:fikt] *n*. 未完成体，处理品，瑕疵品；*a*. 有缺点的，未完成的，减弱的

imperfection [,impə'fekʃən] *n*. 不完整性，非理想性，不完美，缺点，瑕疵

imperial [im'piəriəl] *n*. 纸张尺寸(23×23英寸)，特大号，特级品；*a*. 帝国的，皇帝的，皇家的，庄严的，特级的，英制的(度量衡)

~ unit 英制单位

impervious [im'pə:vjəs] *a*. 密封的，不让进入，不会受到损伤的，不受影响的

impinge [im'pindʒ] *v*. 撞击，冲击，打击，侵害，侵入

impingement [im'pindʒmənt] *n*. 侵犯，冲击

~ attack 冲击腐蚀，冲击侵蚀，滴蚀

305

~ soldering 冲击焊合

implement ['implimənt] n. 工具，器械，器具，装备，家具，服装，手段，媒介；v. 使生效，执行，实施，实现，履行，贯彻，提供工具 ‖ *Syn*. administer 执行；carry out 完成，实现，贯彻，执行；execute 执行，实行，完成，使生效；perform 履行，执行，完成

implementation [ˌimplimen'teiʃən] n. 执行，实施，实现，履行，贯彻

~ of IMO Conventions and Codes 国际海事组织公约和法规的实施

implication [ˌimpli'keiʃən] n. 牵连，涉及，推论，含意，暗指，暗示

implosion [im'pləuʒən] n. 向内破裂，向内爆炸，内爆，内爆拆除

import [im'pɔ:t] n. 进口货(imports)，进口，输入，意思，重要性；v. 输入，进口，含…的意思，有关系，重要，引入，有重要性

important [im'pɔ:tənt] a. 重要的，重大的，有权威的，有势力的，有地位的 ‖ *Syn*. considerable 重要的；critical 重要的；crucial 极其重要的；material 重要的

importation [ˌimpɔ:'teiʃən] n. 进口，输入，进口货，输入物

importer [im'pɔ:tə(r)] n. 进口商，进口者

impregnate ['impregneit] v. 灌注，注入，使饱和，使怀孕；a. 充满的，怀孕的

~ process 浸渍工艺，浸胶工艺

~ with insulation paint 浸渍绝缘漆

impress [im'pres] n. 印象，印记；v. 印，盖印，留下印象

impressed [im'prest] v. (impress 的过去式和过去分词) 印，盖印，留下印象；a. 印象深刻的，了不起的

~ current 外加电流

~ electromotive force 外加电动势

impression [im'preʃən] n. 印象，感想，意念，概念，盖印，印记，印痕，压痕，印刷品

improper [im'prɔpə] a. 不合适的，不适宜的，非正常的，不正确的，不正派的，不合礼仪的，不道德的

~ packing 包装不良

improve [im'pru:v] v. 提高，增进，改善，改进，改良 ‖ *Syn*. enhance 加强，提高，增加；heighten 提高，升高；hoist 升起，吊起；increase 增加，加大；lift 升高，提高；raise 升起，提高；upgrade 升级，提升

improvement [im'pru:vmənt] n. 改进，改善，改良，改进措施，改进处，改善处

improver [im'pru:və] n. 改进者，提高的人，改良物

impulse ['impʌls] n. 凭冲动行事，突如其来的念头，脉冲，冲动，搏动；v. 推动；a. 冲动的

~ current 冲击电流

~ flashover 脉冲闪络

~ pressure charging system 脉冲压力充电系统

~ response 脉冲响应

~ voltage 冲击电压

impure [im'pjuə] a. 不纯洁的，掺杂的，掺假的，脏的 ‖ *Ant*. pure 纯的，纯粹的，纯净的

impurity [im'pjuəriti] n. 污点，污染，掺杂，不纯，不道德，罪恶，混杂物，粗劣品 ‖ *Ant*. purity 纯净，纯洁，纯度

impute [im'pju:t] v. 归因于，归罪于，归咎于

in [in] n. 执政者，入口；a. 在里面的，执政的；ad. 进入，朝里，在家，已到达，已来临；prep. 在…之内(上)，在…期间，从事于，符合，穿着

~ a fix 处境困难，进退两难

~ a given period of time 在特定的时间周期

~ a good hour 在适当的时候，在幸运的时刻

~ accordance with 按照，依照，与…一致

~ addition to 除了

~ advance 预先

~ an attempt to 企图，试图，力图，为了

~ attendance 负责，值班

~ ballast 只装底货，只装压舱物

~ bulk 散装，大批

~ case of 万一

~ case of emergency 万一发生紧急情况

~ charge of 负责，经管，照顾

~ chief 主要地，尤其

~ comb in ation with 与…结合

~ common use 常用，通用，常用的

~ common with 和…一样

~ compliance with 依从，顺从

~ conformity with 和…相适应，和…一致，遵照

~ consultation with 商议，磋商

~ contact with 与…接触，联系

~ contemplation 计划中的，沉思，冥想

~ contrast 相反，大不相同

~ contrast to 与…对比，和…形成对照

~ distress 遇险，在危难中

~ dock 在船坞里，在码头

~ duplicate 一式两份

~ emergency 在紧急情况下，在危急关头

~ error 错误地

~ excess of 超过

~ fact 事实上

~ gear 处于正常工作情况，挂上离合器的

~ good order 有条不紊，整齐，情况正常

~ good working conditions 在良好工作条件下

~ good working order 运转良好

~ large part 在很大程度上

~ no way 决不

~ normal order 按正常顺序

~ normal practice 在正常实践中，在平时练习中

~ nothing flat 马上，立刻

~ operation 运转着，生效

~ order 整齐，状况良好，适宜

~ order to 为了

~ ordinary (待修的船只等)闲搁着的，常任的

~ parallel 并行，平行，并联

~ phase 同相

~ place 到位，就位，已确定，在场，未移动

~ port 在港

~ position 就位，在原位，在适当的位置

~ practical terms 实际上

~ practice 在实践中，实际上，熟练

~ principle 原则上，基本上，大体上
~ proper order 按适当顺序
~ proportion 相称
~ quadruplicate 一式四份地
~ quantity 大量
~ quintuplicate 一式五份地
~ relation to 关于，涉及，与…相比
~ respect of 关于
~ response 作为回应
~ response to 响应，适应
~ rotation 轮流地，交替地，依次地
~ rough weather 在恶劣天气下
~ round figures 以整数表示
~ running condition 在运转情况下，运转正常
~ series 串联
~ service 作帮工，在军中服役，在使用中
~ situ 在原位置，在原处
~ situ burning 原位焚烧，海上溢油现场燃烧
~ so far as 至于，就…
~ step 同步，齐步，合拍，步调一致
~ terms of 依据，按照，在…方面，以…措词
~ the case of 至于，在…的情况下
~ the control of 在…控制下
~ the event of 如果…发生
~ the extreme 非常，极度，极端
~ the field of 在…方面，在…领域
~ the manned condition 在有人驾驶条件下
~ the ocean 在海洋中，在海洋里
~ the order 按顺序
~ the ordinary course of events 在一般情况下，通常

~ the same measure 同一程度地，同样地
~ the way of 关于…方面
~ triplicate 一式三份地
~ trouble 在困难中，在监禁中，处于不幸中
~ turn 依次，轮流
~ unmanned condition 无人值守时，在无人驾驶条件下
~ use 在使用中
~ view of 鉴于，考虑到，由于
~ the way of 关于…方面
~ width 宽度方向上
in-line 同轴的，嵌入的，内嵌的
~ engine 直列式发动机，直列式内燃机，直立引擎
in-plane 结构平面内，面内
~ load 面内载荷
~ stress 平面应力
in-service 在职的，在职期间进行的，不脱产的
in-water 在水下
~ survey 水下检验
inaccessible [,inæk'sesəbl] a. 难达到的，难接近的，难见到的
inaccurate [in'ækjurit] a. 不准确的，错误的
~ calibration 不准确校准
inadequacy [in'ædikwəsi] n. 不适当，不充分，不完全，不十分
inadequate [in'ædikwit] a. 不充分的，不适当的
inadmissible [,inəd'misəbl] a. 不许可的，难承认的
inadvertence [,inəd'və:təns] n. 不注意，怠慢，疏忽

inadvertent [ˌinəd'vɜːtənt] a. 疏忽的,不注意的,无意中做的

inapplicable [in'æplikəbl] a. 不适用的,不相干的

inappropriate [ˌinə'prəupriit] a. 不适当的,不相称的

inasmuch [ˌinəz'mʌtʃ] ad. 因…之故,由于

inattentive [ˌinə'tentiv] a. 疏忽的,怠慢的,不注意的

inboard ['inbɔːd] a. 内侧的,舷内的；ad. 在船内,向内
~ cabin 内侧舱室
~ cargo 舱内货
~ derrick 舱口吊杆
~ end 固定端
~ end chain 船内端锚链节
~ profile (船)纵剖面

inbound ['inbaund] n. 入站；a. 内地的,归航的,入境的,归本国的
~ vessel 进口船,入站船 ‖ outbound vessel 出口船,出站船

incandescent [ˌinkæn'desnt] a. 辉耀的,炽热的,发白热光的
~ floodlight 白炽泛光灯
~ lamp 白炽灯 ‖ *Syn*. incandescent light 白炽灯

incapacitate [ˌinkə'pæsiteit] v. 使无能力,使不能,使不适于

incase [in'keis] v. 装进箱,包

inch [intʃ] n. 英寸,计量单位,气压测量单位,少量；v. 慢慢移动,渐进
~ bearing 英制轴承
~ screw tap 英制螺纹丝锥
~ (screw) thread 英制螺纹
~ screw thread range 英制螺纹范围

~ thread bolt 英制螺纹螺栓
~ thread parameter 英制螺纹参数
~ trim moment 每英寸倾斜力矩,每英寸纵倾力矩

inching ['intʃiŋ] n. 点动,微调尺寸,寸动,缓动；v. (inch 的 ing 形式) 慢慢移动,渐进
~ capability 寸动能力,微速性能
~ speed 爬行速度

incidence ['insidəns] n. 发生频率,入射,影响范围,落下的方式

incident ['insidənt] n. 事件,突发事件,事变,插曲；a. 入射的,附带的,易发生的,伴随而来的 ‖ *Syn*. accident 意外事件,意外事故；casualty 事故,伤亡；chance failure 偶发故障,意外事故；contingency 意外事故,紧急情况,不测事件；misfortune 不幸,灾难,灾祸；mishap 灾祸,厄运,倒霉事
~ angle 入射角

incidental [ˌinsi'dentl] n. 伴随事件,偶然事件,杂项；a. 附带的,伴随的,非主要的,偶然的,容易发生的

incidentally [ˌinsi'dentəli] ad. 顺便地,偶然地,附带地,顺便提及

incinerate [in'sinəreit] v. 焚化,烧成灰

incineration [inˌsinə'reiʃən] n. 焚化,烧成灰
~ furnace 焚烧炉,煅烧炉

incinerator [in'sinəreitə] n. 焚烧炉,焚尸炉,焚烧装置

incipient [in'sipiənt] a. 初期的,初始的,起初的,发端的
~ fault 潜在故障,隐患 ‖ *Syn*. hidden danger 隐患

inclination [ˌinkli'neiʃən] n. 倾斜，弯曲，倾度，倾向，爱好
~ angle 倾斜角，倾角
~ test 倾斜试验

incline [in'klain] n. 倾斜，斜坡，斜面；v. (使)倾斜，(使)倾向于

inclined [in'klaind] v. (incline 的过去式和过去分词) (使)倾斜,(使)倾向于；a. 倾向…的
~ engine 斜置式发动机
~ overhead valve 倾斜气门
~ tube 斜管
~ walks 斜坡走道

inclining [in'klainiŋ] n. 倾向，爱好；v. (incline 的 ing 形式) (使)倾斜，(使)倾向于
~ error 倾斜误差
~ experiment 倾斜试验
~ experiment force 倾斜试验力
~ experiment moment 倾斜实验力矩

include [in'klu:d] v. 包含，包括，含有，放入，算进去

included [in'klu:did] v. (include 的过去式和过去分词) 包含，包括，含有，放入，算进去；a. 包括的，内藏的
~ accessories 随附配件
~ angle (焊接)坡口角度

inclusion [in'klu:ʒən] n. 包含，内含物

inclusive [in'klu:siv] a. 包括的，包含的

incombustible [ˌinkəm'bʌstəbl] n. 不燃性物质；a. 不燃性的，不能燃烧的
~ fabric 不燃性织物，不燃纺织品，不燃织物
~ gas 非可燃气体，非可燃气
~ material 不燃物料，非燃性材料
~ matter 不燃物
~ paper 不燃纸，耐火纸
~ refuse 不可燃垃圾
~ substance 不可燃物
~ sulfur 不燃硫
~ wastes 不燃性垃圾

income ['inkʌm] n. 收入，收益，进款，所得

incoming ['inˌkʌmiŋ] n. 进入，到来，收入(incomings)，收益(incomings)；a. 引入的，进来的，到来的，即将就任的
~ degree 进入角度
~ gas 进气
~ generator 准备并车的发电机，待并发电机
~ high tide 涨潮
~ line 引入线，输入线，进线 ‖ Ant. outgoing line 引出线，输出线，出线
~ line panel 进线屏
~ machine 待并机
~ machine frequency 待并机频率
~ panel 进线配电盘

incompatibility ['inkəmˌpætə'biliti] n. 不相容，不两立，不协调，不一致

incompatible [ˌinkəm'pætəbl] a. 性质相反的，矛盾的，不调和的 ‖ Ant. compatible 谐调的，一致的，兼容的

incomplete ['inkəm'pli:t] a. 不完全的，不完善的，不完备的
~ combustion 不完全燃烧
~ penetration 未焊透，未钎透

inconsistency [ˌinkən'sistənsi] n. 矛盾，不一致，易变

inconsistent [ˌinkən'sistənt] a. 不一致的，不协调的，矛盾的

incorporate [in'kɔ:pəreit] v. 包含，吸收，体现，合并

incorporation [inˌkɔːpəˈreiʃən] *n.* 公司，合并，编入，团体组织

incorrect [ˌinkəˈrekt] *a.* 错误的，不正确的，不适当的，不真实的

~ timing 不正确定时

incorrectly [ˌinkəˈrektli] *ad.* 错误地，不适当地

increase [inˈkriːs] *n.* 增加，增大，增长，增加率；*v.* 增加，增大，增长，复制，繁殖 ‖ ***Syn.*** enhance 加强，提高，增加；heighten 提高，升高；hoist 升起，吊起；improve 提高，增进；lift 升高，提高；raise 升起，提高；upgrade 升级，提升

increased [inˈkriːst] *v.* (increase 的过去分词) 增加，增大，增长，复制，繁殖；*a.* 增加的，增强的

~ safety equipment 增安型设备

~ safety type fluorescent ceiling light 增安荧光篷顶灯

increasing [inˈkriːsiŋ] *v.* (increase 的 ing 形式) 增加，加大；*a.* 越来越多的，渐增的

~ oscillation 增幅振荡

increasingly [inˈkriːsiŋli] *ad.* 越来越多地，渐增地，日益，愈加

increment [ˈinkrimənt] *n.* 增量，增加，累加，增额，盈余

~ of measurement 测量增量

incremental [inkriˈmentəl] *a.* 增加的，增值的

~ plasticity 增量塑性

incumbent [inˈkʌmbənt] *n.* 在职者，现任者，领圣俸者；*a.* 现任的，依靠的，负有职责的

incur [inˈkə:] *v.* 获得，得到，招致，引发，蒙受

indefinite [inˈdefinət] *a.* 不确定的，无限的，模糊的

indefinitely [inˈdefinətli] *ad.* 不确定地，无限期地，模糊地，不明确地

indemnification [inˌdemnifiˈkeiʃən] *n.* 保护，保障，补偿，补偿物

indemnify [inˈdemnifai] *v.* 补偿，保护，保障，赔偿，使免于受罚

indentation [ˌindenˈteiʃən] *n.* 压痕，刻痕，凹陷，缩排，缺口，呈锯齿状

independence [ˌindiˈpendəns] *n.* 独立性，自立性，自主

independent [indiˈpendənt] *n.* 独立自主者，中立派，无党派者；*a.* 独立的，单独的，无党派的，不受约束的

~ exciter 独立激励器

~ excitation 独立励磁，他励

~ pole operation 分相操作

~ tank 独立舱柜

~ variable 自变量，自变数

independently [indiˈpendəntli] *ad.* 独立地，自立地

indeterminate [ˌindiˈtəːminit] *a.* 不确定的，模糊的，含混的

index [ˈindeks] *n.* 索引，指数，指标，指针；*v.* 指出，编入索引中，做索引

~ gauge 指示计，指示表，分度规

Indian [ˈindjən] *n.* 印度人，印第安人，印第安语

~ Ocean 印度洋

indicate [ˈindikeit] *v.* 指出，显示，象征，预示，需要，简要说明

indicated [ˈindiˌkeitid] *v.* (indicate 的过去分词) 指出，显示，象征，预示，需要，简要说明；*a.* 表明的，指示的

~ efficiency 指示效率

~ horsepower (IHP) 指示马力

~ mean effective pressure (IMEP) 指示平均有效压力

~ power (IP) 指示功率

~ specific energy consumption 指示油耗率

~ thermal efficiency 指示热效率

indicating ['indikeitiŋ] *n*. 表明，指示；*v*. (indicate 的 ing 形式) 表明，指示，要求

~ lamp 指示灯

indication [,indi'keiʃən] *n*. 指示，指出，迹象，象征

~ deflection 指示偏转

indicator ['indikeitə] *n*. 指标，标志，迹象，指示器，指示剂，指示符，压力计

~ bulb 指示灯泡

~ card 指示卡

~ cock 指示器旋塞，示功器旋塞

~ diagram 示功图，指示图

~ paper 试纸(浸有指示剂的纸)

~ valve 指示阀，带指示器的阀

indirect [,indi'rekt] *a*. 间接的，不直截了当的，闪烁其词的，不坦率的 ‖ *Ant.* direct 直接的，直截了当的，坦率的

~ air cooler 间接空气冷却器，间接空冷器

~ cooled piston 间接冷却活塞

~ cooling 间接冷却

~ cooling air cooler 间接冷却空冷器

~ current control 间接电流控制

~ DC-DC converter 直接电流变换电路

~ expansion system 间接膨胀系统

~ fire suppression 间接灭火

~ gauging device 间接计量装置

~ injection engine 间接喷射发动机

~ refrigeration 间接制冷

~ transmission 间接喷射发动机

~ valve gear 间接气门机构

indirectly [,ində'rektli] *ad*. 间接地，迂回地，婉转地，不坦率地

indispensable [,indis'pensəbl] *n*. 不可缺少的人或物；*a*. 不可缺少的，绝对必要的，责无旁贷的，不可避开的

indistinct [,indis'tiŋkt] *n*. 不清楚，模糊；*a*. 不清楚的，模糊的；*ad*. 不清楚地，模糊地

individual [,indi'vidjuəl] *n*. 个人，个体；*a*. 个人的，个别的，独特的

~ air conditioning system 单体空调系统

~ branch circuit 单支路

~ model 个体模型

~ unit air conditioning system 单体空调系统

individually [indi'vidjuəli] *ad*. 分别地，各个地，各自地，独特地

indivisible [,indi'vizəbl] *a*. 不能分割的，除不尽的

indoor ['indɔ:] *a*. 室内的，户内的 ‖ *Ant.* outdoor 户外的，室外的，野外的，露天的；out-of-door 户外的，室外的，露天的

induce [in'dju:s] *v*. 劝诱，促使，导致，引起，感应

induced [in'dju:st] *v*. (induce 的过去式和过去分词) 劝诱，促使，导致，引起，感应；*a*. 感应的

~ current 感应电流，诱导电流

~ draft 进气通风，诱导通风

~ resistance 诱导阻力

~ velocity 诱导速度，感生速度，扰动速度

inducement [in'dju:smənt] *n.* 诱导,诱因,动机,刺激物

inducer [in'dju:sə] *n.* 导流片,导流轮,诱导物,引诱者

induct [in'dʌkt] *v.* 感应,征召入伍,使正式就任,使入门

inductance [in'dʌktəns] *n.* 感应系数,感应,自感应,感应器,电感线圈 ‖ *Syn.* inductor 感应器

~ sensor 电感传感器,电感测微仪 ‖ *Syn.* inductive pick-off 电感传感器,感应式检出器; inductosyn 感应式传感器

induction [in'dʌkʃən] *n.* 感应,归纳法,感应现象,入门培训

~ AC generator 感应式交流发电机

~ coil 感应线圈,感应圈,电感线圈

~ generator 感应发电机,异步发电机,感应电机

~ machine 感应电机,感应式机械

~ motor 感应电动机,异步电机,异步电动机

inductive [in'dʌktiv] *a.* 归纳的,感应的,诱导的

~ circuit 电感电路,有感电路,电感性电路

~ component 感性分量,电感性分量,无功分量

~ force transducer 电感式力传感器,电感式位移传感器

~ load 电感负载,电感负荷,感性负载

~ modeling method 电感负载,电感负荷,感性负载

~ pick-off 电感传感器,感应式检出器 ‖ *Syn.* inductance sensor 电感传感器,电感测微仪; inductosyn 感应式传感器

~ pickup apparatus 感应式接收装置

inductivity [,indʌk'tiviti] *n.* 感应率,电容率,诱导性

inductor [in'dʌktə] *n.* 感应器,授职者,圣职授予的人 ‖ *Syn.* inductance 感应器

~ generator 感应发电机,感应体发电机

inductosyn [in'dʌktəsin] *n.* 感应式传感器 ‖ *Syn.* inductance sensor 电感传感器,电感测微仪; inductive pick-off 电感传感器,感应式检出器

industrial [in'dʌstriəl] *n.* 工业工人,工业股票; *a.* 工业的,产业的,实业的,从事工业的

~ accident 劳动事故,工伤事故

industrialize [in'dʌstriəlaiz] *v.* 使工业化

industrialized [in'dʌstriəlaizd] *v.* (industrialize 的过去式和过去分词) 使工业化; *a.* 工业化的

~ diving 工业化潜水

industry ['indəstri] *n.* 工业,产业,行业,勤奋

~ standard 行业标准,产业标准,工业标准

~ Standard Architecture (ISA) 工业标准结构

ineffective [,ini'fektiv] *a.* 无效的,失效的,不起作用的

ineffectively [,ini'fektivli] *ad.* 无效地,无能地,无用地

inefficiency [,ini'fiʃənsi] *n.* 效率低,无效率,无能

inefficient [,ini'fiʃənt] *a.* 效率低的,效率差的,不能胜任的,无能的

inelastic [ˌiniˈlæstik] a. 无弹性的
~ collision 非弹性碰撞
inert [iˈnə:t] a. 惰性的，呆滞的，迟缓的，无效的
~ atmosphere 惰性气氛，惰性气体，惰性环境
~ conductor 惰性导体
~ gas 惰性气体，惰气
~ gas blower 惰性气体鼓风机
~ gas cutting 惰性气体切割
~ gas explosion proof system 惰性气体防爆系统 ‖ Syn. inert gas explosion prevention system 惰性气体防爆系统
~ gas fire fighting 惰性气体灭火
~ gas fire fighting system 惰性气体灭火系统
~ gas generator 惰性气体发生器，惰气产生器
~ gas smothering system 惰性气体窒息灭火系统，惰性气体灭火系统
~ gas system (IGS) 惰性气体系统
~ gas welding 惰性气体焊接
inertia [iˈnə:ʃə] n. 惯性，惯量，惰性，迟钝，不活动
~ force 惯性力，加速阻力
inertial [iˈnə:ʃəl] a. 惯性的，不活泼的
~ coordinates 惯性坐标
~ coordinate system 惯性坐标系
~ wheel 惯性轮
inevitable [inˈevitəbl] a. 必然的，不可避免的
inevitably [inˈevitəbli] ad. 不可避免地，必然地
INF (irradiated nuclear fuel) 辐照核燃料
infeed [ˈinfi:d] n. 横切，横进给
inferior [inˈfiəriə] a. 下等的，下级的，差的，次的，自卑的，劣等的
infiltrate [inˈfiltreit] n. 渗透物；v. 渗透，潜入，混入，接收
infiltration [ˌinfilˈtreiʃən] n. 渗透，渗入，渗透物 ‖ Syn. osmosis 渗透，渗透作用，渗透性；permeation 渗入，透过
infirmary [inˈfə:məri] n. 医务室，医院，养老院
inflammable [inˈflæməbl] a. 易燃的，易怒的
~ compound 易燃剂
~ dissolvent 易燃溶剂
~ gas 易燃气体，可燃气体
~ liquid 易燃液体，可燃液体
inflammation [ˌinfləˈmeiʃən] n. 燃烧，发火，炎症，发炎
inflatable [inˈfleitəbl] n. 充气艇，可充气物品；a. 可膨胀的，可吹气的，充气式的
~ appliance 气胀式设备，充气设备
~ bag 气囊
~ boat 充气船，充气艇
~ closure 充气型密封
~ embarkation platform 充气登乘滑梯
~ dam 充气水闸，充气坝
~ dinghy 充气橡皮艇，充气船，充气筏
~ fender 膨胀式碰垫
~ life belt 气胀式救生带
~ lifeboat 气胀式救生艇，充气式救生艇
~ liferaft 气胀式救生筏，充气救生筏
~ slide 充气滑梯
~ structure 充气结构
inflate [inˈfleit] v. (使)膨胀，(使)充气
inflated [inˈfleitid] v. (inflate 的过去式和过去分词) (使)膨胀，(使)充气；a. 膨胀的，夸张的，通货膨胀的

~ appliance 充气式设备

~ tube 充气展开管

inflation [in'fleiʃən] *n*. 膨胀，暴涨，通货膨胀，夸张，自命不凡

inflator [in'fleitə(r)] *n*. 充气者，打气筒，增压泵

~ button 充气钮

inflow ['infləu] *n*. 流入，流入物

influence ['influəns] *n*. 影响，势力，感化，有影响的人或事

info ['infəu] *n*. 信息，情报

inform [in'fɔ:m] *v*. 通知，告诉，获悉，告知

information [,infə'meiʃən] *n*. 通知，报告，消息，信息，情报，知识，见闻，资料，起诉

~ acquisition 信息采集，信息获取

~ processing 信息处理，情报整理

~ receiver 信息接收者，信息接收方

~ technology (IT) 信息技术

infrared [,infrə'red] *n*. 红外线；*a*. 红外线的

~ fire alarm 红外火警警报器

~ flame detector 红外线烟火探测器，红外火焰探测器

~ gas analyzer 红外气体分析仪

~ heat alarm 红外热警报器，红外高温警报器

~ spectroscopy 红外光谱学，红外线分光镜

ingot ['iŋgət] *n*. 锭铁，工业纯铁

~ steel 锭钢

ingredient [in'gri:diənt] *n*. 原料，要素，成分，因素，组成部分 ‖ *Syn*. cell (电池、光电)元件，单元；component 成分，部分，元件，零件，要素，组分；

constituent 成分，要素；element 要素，元素，成分，元件；organ 元件；part 零件，部件

ingress ['ingres] *n*. 进入，入口，准许进入，入境

inhalation [,inhə'leiʃən] *n*. 吸入

inhale [in'heil] *v*. 吸入，吸气，猛吃猛喝

inhaul ['in,hɔ:l] *n*. 卷帆索，引索 ‖ outhaul 驶帆索

~ whip 内牵索

inherent [in'hiərənt] *a*. 固有的，内在的，与生俱来的，遗传的

~ characteristic 固有特性

~ defect 固有缺陷

~ law 内在规律，固有法

~ moisture 固有水分，固有湿度

~ quality 固有性质

~ regulation 固有变动率，自行调节，内不等率

~ reliability 固有可靠性

~ resistance 固有阻力，固有电阻

~ stability 固有稳定性

~ stress 预应力

~ vice 固有缺陷，内在缺陷

~ viscosity 固有黏度，特性黏度，比浓对数黏度

inherently [in'hiərəntli] *ad*. 内在地，固有地，天性地

inhibit [in'hibit] *v*. 抑制，禁止，约束

inhibition [,inhi'biʃən] *n*. 抑制，压抑，禁止

inhibitor [in'hibitə(r)] *n*. 抑制剂，抗化剂，抑制者

inhibitory [in'hibitəri] *a*. 禁止的，抑制的

inhomogenous ['inhəmədʒinəs] *a*. 不均一的，多相的，杂拼的，异成分的，非齐次的

~ field 不均匀场

initial [i'niʃəl] n. 词首大写字母；a. 最初的，词首的，初始的

~ charging 初次充电

~ condition 初始条件，起始条件，原始条件

~ condition response 初始条件响应

~ course 启程航路，始航向，初始航向

~ creep 初始蠕变

~ data 原始数据，起始数据，初始数据

~ deviation 起始偏差

~ integrity failure 初始整体性破坏

~ phase 初相位，初相

~ stability at small angle of inclination 小倾角时的初稳定性

~ stress 初应力，初始应力，预应力

~ survey 初步检测

~ tension 初始张力，初张力

~ value 初始值，初值，原始价值，基础资料

~ verification 首次鉴定

~ viscosity 初始黏度，初黏度

initialization [iˌniʃəlai'zeiʃən] n. 初始化，设定初值，赋初值

initialize [i'niʃəlaiz] v. 初始化

initially [i'niʃəli] ad. 最初，首先，开头

initiate [i'niʃieit] n. 新加入者，被传授知识的人；v. 开始，发动，发起，传授，接纳

initiative [i'niʃiətiv] n. 主动，主动权，首创精神；a. 开始的，起初的，初步的

initiator [i'niʃieitə] n. 发起人，创始者，教导者，启动程序，引爆器

inject [in'dʒekt] v. 注入，注射，置于，插话

injection [in'dʒekʃən] n. 喷射，注射，注射剂，充血，射入轨道

~ advance 喷射提前，喷油提前，供油提前

~ advance angle 喷油提前角，喷射提前角，供油提前角

~ amplifier 注入式放大器

~ angle 喷射角

~ characteristic 喷油特性，喷射特性

~ circuit (信号)注入电路

~ hole 注入孔，注入钻孔

~ lag 喷射迟缓，喷射滞后

~ molding machine 注射模塑机，注模机，注压机

~ nozzle 射出喷嘴，喷油嘴，喷嘴

~ of flame 火焰喷射

~ oil pressure 喷油压力

~ pipe 喷射管，注射管，气化总管

~ piston 注射柱塞

~ pressure 注射压力，喷射压力，射出压力

~ pump 喷射泵，压注泵

~ rate 注射速率，射出率，注入量

~ scheme 喷射图，喷射方法

~ system 注射系统，喷油系统

~ technology 注入工艺

~ timing 喷油定时，喷油正时，喷射正时

~ valve 喷射阀

~ water 喷射水，注射水

~ well 注入井

injector [in'dʒektə] n. 注射器，注射者，注水器

injure ['indʒə] v. 伤害，损害

ink [iŋk] n. 墨水，墨汁，油墨；v. 涂墨水，附加签名

ink-jet 喷墨，喷墨式

~ printer 喷墨印刷机，墨水喷射打印

机，墨水喷射式印刷机

inland ['inlənd] n. 内地, 内陆; a. 内陆的, 国内的; ad. 在内地, 向内地
~ navigation 内河航行
~ waterways vessel 内河船

inlet ['inlet] n. 入口, 进口, 小港, 插入物, 水湾
~ cam 进气凸轮
~ distributing header 进口分配联箱 ‖ **Ant**. outlet distributing header 出口分配联箱
~ eye (离心压气机)进气孔
~ grid 进风栅
~ guide blade 进口导叶
~ manifold 进气总管, 入口集合管, 进气歧管
~ nipple 进口螺纹接套
~ stroke 吸入冲程, 进气冲程
~ tube 进水管, 进油管, 入口管
~ valve 进汽阀, 进给阀, 吸油阀, 吸入阀 ‖ **Syn**. intake valve 进气阀; suction valve 吸入阀

INMARSAT (International Maritime Satellite Organization) 国际海事卫星组织

innage ['inidʒ] n. (货柜交货后留下的)剩余货物, (飞行结束后的)剩余油料

inner ['inə] n. 内部; a. 内部的, 内心的, 精神的, 秘密的
~ bottom plating 内底板
~ bottom construction plan 内底结构图
~ bottom longitudinal 内底纵骨, 内底纵材
~ bow door 船首内侧门
~ case of stern tube 艉轴套内壳, 尾轴管衬套
~ casing 内(汽)缸

~ cylinder 内圆筒
~ gear 内齿轮, 内齿
~ gearing 内啮合, 内齿轮传动
~ guiding post 内导柱
~ heating surface 内加热面
~ hexagon screw 内六角螺钉
~ hexagon spanner 内六角扳手
~ loop 内循环, 内环路, 局部回路 ‖ **Syn**. minor loop 副回路, 小回路, 局部回路
~ ring 内环, 内圈, 轴承内轮
~ ring spacer 内隔圈
~ rotor (齿轮泵的)内齿轮, 内转子
~ surface 内表面
~ surface inspection 内表面检查
~ valve spring 气门内弹簧

innermost ['inəməust] a. 最里面的, 最深处的, 内心的, 秘密的

innocuous [i'nɔkjuəs] a. 无害的, 无毒的, 无伤大雅的, 不得罪人的
~ effluent 无害废水, 无害排出物
~ gas 无害气体
~ substance 无害物质

innovate ['inəuveit] v. 创新, 改革, 革新

innovation [,inəu'veiʃən] n. 创新, 革新, 新方法, 新技术

inoperative [in'ɔpərətiv] a. 不起作用的, 无效力的

inordinate [in'ɔ:dinit] a. 不规则的, 过度的, 过分的, 无节制的, 紊乱的

inorganic [,inɔ:'gænik] a. 无机的, 无生物的

input ['input] n. 输入, 输入物, 输入电路, 能量, 功, 电流, 电能, 电力, 输入资料, 输入端, 信息; v. 输入
~ circuit 输入电路, 输入回路

~ impedance 输入阻抗
~ information 输入信息
~ power 输入功率
~ resistance 输入电阻，入端电阻
~ sensitivity 输入灵敏度
~ shaft 输入轴，主动轴
~ signal 输入信号
~ stage 输入级
~ terminal 输入端
~ unit 输入单元，输入装置
~ value 输入值
~ variable 输入变量，输入变数
~ voltage 输入电压，工作电压
~ wave form 输入波形

input-output (IO) 输入输出，投入产出
~ channel 输入输出通道
~ device 输入输出设备

inquire [in'kwaiə] v. 查究，询问，问明，询价

inquiry [in'kwaiəri] n. 探究，调查，质询

inrush ['inrʌʃ] n. 涌入，侵入，流入
~ current 涌流，浪涌电流，突入电流，瞬间起峰电流

inscription [in'skripʃən] n. 铭文，题词，刻印

insecurely [ˌinsi'kjuəli] ad. 不安全地，不可靠地

insensitive [in'sensitiv] a. 感觉迟钝的，对…没有感觉的

insert [in'sə:t] n. 插入物，管芯，镶块；v. 插入，嵌入
~ bearing 外球面轴承，嵌入式轴承
~ plate 插入板，嵌入板
~ pyrometer 插入式高温计
~ with good contact 接触良好的插入

insertion [in'sə:ʃən] n. 插入，嵌入，插入物

~ loss 插入损失，介入损失

inshore ['in'ʃɔ:] a. 近海岸的，沿海岸的

inside [in'said] n. 里面，内侧，内容，内幕，内脏；a. 里面的，内部的，内幕的，内侧的；ad. 在内地，在内部地，在内侧地；prep. 少于，在…之内
~ area malfunction 内部区域故障
~ axle box 内轴箱
~ cabin 内侧舱室
~ calipers 内卡钳，内卡尺，内卡规
~ diameter (ID) 内径，内直径，内部直径
~ gearing pump 内齿轮泵
~ micrometer 内径测微计，内径千分尺
~ micrometer with rod 带杆内径千分表

inside-hexagonal 内六角的
~ spanner 内六角扳手

insofar [ˌinsəu'fa:] ad. 在…的范围，在…情况下

insolubility [inˌsɔlju'biliti] n. 不溶性，解决不了，不可解

insoluble [in'sɔljubl] a. 不能解决的，不能溶解的，难以解释的
~ floc 不溶性絮凝物

inspect [in'spekt] v. 检查，视察，检阅，审查 ‖ *Syn*. censor 检查，审查；check 检查，核对；examine 检查，调查；review 检查，检阅；rummage 搜出，检查
~ for leakage 渗漏检查

inspecting [in'spektiŋ] v. (inspect 的 ing 形式) 检查，视察，检阅，审查；a. 检查的
~ alignment of stock, rudder blade and pintle 舵杆、舵叶、舵销连接后中心线检查

~ anchor throwing away appliance 弃锚装置检查
~ centerline positioning for shaft system and rudder system before boring 轴、舵系镗孔前中心线定位检查
~ fitting accuracy of draught mark (loadline mark) 吃水标志(载重线标志)安装后精确性检查
~ fitting accuracy of hatch coaming on berth 货舱口围板船上安装精度检查
~ integrity and flexibility of rudder appliance 舵装置完整性与轻便性检查
~ integrity of steering gear 操舵装置完整性检查
~ welding seam of hatch coaming after welding 货舱口围板焊接后焊缝检查
~ zero (datum) position of rudder blade 舵叶0位检查

inspection [in'spekʃən] n. 视察，调查，检查，审查
~ air pressure test (with water head) for No1. ballast water tank (No. 15 block) No.1 压载水舱(No.15 分段)气压试验(压头试验)检查
~ air outlet grilles of superstructure after fitting 上层建筑通风门门片安装后检查
~ alignment of stock, rudder blade and pintle 舵杆、舵叶、舵销连接后中心线检查
~ arrangement correctness of aluminium anodes 防蚀板布置正确性检查
~ certificate 检查证明
~ cover 检查盖，观测盖板，人孔盖
~ dimension of loadline after marking out 载重线标志划线后尺度检查
~ distance between draught marks and keel plate after marking out 划线后吃水标尺至平板龙骨之间的距离检查
~ door 检查门，检查孔
~ earthing 检修接地
~ equipment 检验设备，检测设备 ‖ *Syn*. inspection instrument 检查仪器
~ examination 查验
~ glass for oil level 油位观察镜
~ hole lamp 视孔灯
~ hosing test for upper deck 上甲板冲水试验检查
~ installation and water tight for log's underwater parts on berth 计程仪水下部分船台安装和水密性检查
~ installation and water tight transducer of echo sounder on berth 测深仪的换能器船台安装和水密性检查
~ installation correctness of ship's name plate (funnel mark) 船名牌(烟囱标志)安装正确性检查
~ installation for antenna of radio console and measuring its insulation resistance 组装报务台天线安装检查和绝缘测量
~ installation for loop antenna of direction finder on berth 测向仪环状天线船台安装检查
~ insulation installation for master room, chief engineer room (electrical engineer room) before panel 船长室、轮机长室(电机员室)敷板前检查隔热安装
~ integrity of mooring winch 绞缆机完整性检查
~ machining dimension of propeller shaft (intermcdiate shaft or counter shaft) 螺旋浆轴(中间轴)机加工尺寸检查

~ machining dimension of rudder pintle 舵销机加工尺寸检查

~ machining dimension of rudder stock 舵杆机加工尺寸检查

~ main cable installation for wheel house before paneling decoration 敷板前驾驶室主干电缆安装检查

~ opening 检查孔，检查口

~ procedure 检验程序，检验方法，商检程序

~ push-up load for fore and aft stern tube bushes 艉轴管前、后衬套压入检查

~ record 检验记录，检查记录

~ report 检查报告，检验报告

~ rudder carrier after assembly 上舵承组装后检查

~ structure integrity after completing the superstructure 上层建筑完后结构完整性检查

~ structure integrity and welding seam on completing No.56 block 56分段完工后结构完整性和焊缝检查

~ water-tightness doors and windows of superstructure after fitting 上层建筑水密门窗安装后检查

~ welding seam and dimension of cargo hatch cover 货舱舱口盖焊缝和尺度检查

~ wet fitting the propeller 螺旋桨压入检查

~ the structure and loading test of the lifeboat (rescue boat) davit 救生(助)艇吊架结构和压重试验

inspector [in'spektə] *n.* 检查员，巡视员，视察员

inspectorate [in'spektərit] *n.* 检查员、视察员、巡视员等的总称

instability [,instə'biliti] *n.* 不稳定(性)，缺乏稳定性，基础薄弱，变化无常

instable [in'steibl] *a.* 不稳定的，不牢固的

install [in'stɔ:l] *v.* 安装，装设，装置，安置，安顿，任命，使就职 ‖ **Syn**. assemble 装配；build in 安装，固定；fit 安装；fix 安装，(使)固定；fix assemblage 安装；mount 安装；set up 装配，竖立，架起

~ driver 安装驱动程序

~ in position 安装到位

~ panel 安装面板

installation [,instə'leiʃən] *n.* 安装，装设，设备，装置，就职 ‖ **Syn**. apparatus 器械，设备，仪器；appliance 用具，器具；arrangement 布置；assembly 组装部件；device 装置，设备；equipment 装备，设备，器材，装置；facility 设备，工具；furniture 设备，家具；gear 设备，装备；machine 机器，机械，机构；machinery 机械(总称)，机器；mechanism 机器，机械装置，机构；plant 设备；provision 装备，供应品；turnout 装备，设备；unit 装置，设备

~ and alignment inspection of windlass 锚机安装与校中检查

~ inspection of main diesel generator 主柴油发电机组安装检查

~ of life-saving equipment 救生设备安装

installed [ins'tɔ:ld] *v.* (install 的过去式和过去分词) 安装，装设，装置，安置，安顿，任命，使就职；*a.* 安装的，设置的，就任的，就职的

~ capacity 装置容量，装机容量，设备容量

~ power 装机功率，设备功率

instance ['instəns] n. 实例，建议，要求，情况，场合，程序，步骤；v. 引证，举例，例示

instant ['instənt] n. 瞬间，立即，片刻，顷刻，速食食品；a. 立即的，即时的，直接的，紧迫的，刻不容缓的，速溶的，方便的

~ messaging 即时通信，即时消息，即时信息

~ stability criteria 即时稳定性标准

instantaneous [ˌinstən'teinjəs] a. 瞬间的，即时的，即刻的

~ amplitude 瞬时振幅，瞬态振幅

~ combustion 瞬时燃烧

~ electric power 瞬时电功率

~ electromagnetic overcurrent relay 瞬时电磁式过电流继电器

~ magnetic trip 瞬时磁力跳闸

~ mechanical power 瞬时机械功率

~ overload relay 瞬时过载继电器

~ overvoltage 瞬时过电压，瞬间过电压

~ phase 瞬时相位

~ rate of diacharge 瞬时排放率

~ relay 瞬时继电器，瞬动继电器

~ safety gear 瞬时式安全钳装置，瞬时式安全钳

~ state 瞬时状态，瞬间状态

~ transmission 瞬时传动

~ transmission ratio 瞬时传动比

~ trip 瞬时切断，瞬间跳闸

~ value 瞬时值 ‖ actual value 实际值

~ velocity 瞬时速度，瞬间速度

~ voltage 瞬时电压，瞬间电压

instantaneously [ˌinstən'teinjəsli] ad. 即刻，突如其来地

~ changing 瞬跳

instantly ['instəntli] a. 立即地，即刻地

instead [in'sted] ad. 代替，改为，抵作，更换

~ of 代替，而不是

instinctive [in'stiŋktiv] a. 本能的，直觉的，天生的

institute ['institju:t] n. 学会，学院，协会；v. 创立，开始，制定，开始(调查)，提起(诉讼)

~ of Electrical and Electronic Engineers (IEEE) 电气和电子工程师协会

~ of Marine Engines (IME) 船用发动机研究所

institution [ˌinsti'tju:ʃən] n. 制度，协会，建立，公共机构，习俗

~ of Electrical Engineers (IEE) 国际电气工程师学会

instruct [in'strʌkt] v. 指导，通知，命令，指示，教授

instruction [in'strʌkʃən] n. 指令，命令，指示，教导，用法说明 ‖ *Syn.* specification 说明书

~ book 说明书

~ for on-board maintenance 船上保养说明，机上维修说明

~ for use 使用说明书

~ list 指令表

~ manual 安装手册，操作工序说明书，工艺规范

~ plate 使用说明牌，指示板

instructional [in'strʌkʃənəl] a. 教学的，指导的，教育的

instructor [in'strʌktə] n. 指导书，指导者，教员，教师，讲师

~ trainer 教练训练员，教练培训官

instrument ['instrəmənt] n. 仪器，工具，乐器，手段，器械
~ air 仪表气源
~ console 仪表盘
~ container 仪器箱
~ constant 仪器常数，仪表常数
~ identification 仪器标记，仪器识别，仪表鉴定
~ panel 仪表板
~ transducer 测量互感器
~ transformer 仪表变压器

instrumentation [ˌinstrumen'teiʃən] n. 手段，工具，使用仪器，检测仪表，测量仪器，测试设备，仪表制，仪表化

insufficiency [ˌinsə'fiʃənsi] n. 不足，不充分，机能不全，不适当

insufficient [ˌinsə'fiʃənt] n. 不足，缺乏；a. 不足的，不充足的，不胜任的，缺乏能力的

insufficiently [ˌinsə'fiʃəntli] ad. 不够地，不能胜任地

insulate ['insjuleit] v. 隔离,(使)孤立,(使)绝缘,(使)隔热

insulated ['insjuleitid] v. (insulate 的过去式和过去分词) 隔离，(使)孤立，(使)绝缘，(使)隔热；a. 绝缘的，隔热的
~ body 绝缘体
~ clip 绝缘夹线板
~ combination pliers 绝缘钢丝钳，绝缘鲤鱼钳，绝缘剪钳
~ conductor 绝缘导线
~ container 绝缘集装箱，保温货柜，绝热集装箱
~ cooling 隔热缓冷，隔热冷却
~ container 绝缘容器，保温容器，隔热容器

~ core 绝缘线蕊
~ door 隔热门，绝热门 ‖ *Syn*. cold storage door 冷库门
~ gate bipolar transistor (IGBT) 绝缘栅双极型晶体管
~ hatch cover 隔热舱口盖，隔热舱盖，冷藏舱口盖
~ hook 绝缘钩
~ plier 绝缘钳，胶柄钳
~ rubber glove 绝缘橡胶手套，绝缘胶手套
~ section 绝缘区段
~ sleeve 绝缘套管
~ tongs 绝缘钳子
~ wire 绝缘线

insulating ['insəleitiŋ] v. (insulate 的 ing 形式) 隔离，(使)孤立，(使)绝缘，(使)隔热；a. 绝缘的，隔热的
~ board 绝缘板
~ flange 绝缘法兰
~ glass 中空玻璃
~ layer 绝缘层
~ material 绝缘材料，隔热材料，绝缘物
~ oil 绝缘油，变压器油
~ paint 绝缘漆，绝缘涂料
~ paper 绝缘纸，电缆纸，绝热纸，线圈绝缘纸
~ property 绝缘性能
~ refractory 隔热耐火材料
~ resistance 绝缘电阻 ‖ *Syn*. insulation resistance 绝缘电阻
~ strength 绝缘强度
~ tape 绝缘胶带
~ tube 绝缘管，保温管
~ varnish 绝缘清漆

insulation [,insju'leiʃən] *n*. 绝缘,隔离,孤立,绝热,绝缘体,绝缘材料
~ aging 绝缘老化,绝缘老化的,绝缘劣化
~ board 保温板,隔热板,隔音板
~ breakdown 绝缘击穿
~ class 绝缘等级,绝缘种类
~ coating 绝缘涂层
~ coordination 绝缘配合
~ covering 绝缘套
~ film 绝缘薄膜,绝缘膜
~ layer 绝缘层
~ material 绝缘材料
~ monitoring device 绝缘监测装置
~ of A-deck (including A60 insulation) A 甲板绝缘(包括 A60 绝缘)
~ of cargo space 货舱隔热
~ of CO_2 room CO_2 室绝缘
~ of emergency generator room 应急发电机室绝缘
~ of escape in engine room 机舱逃生口绝缘
~ of hot surface 热表面绝缘
~ of main deck 主甲板绝缘
~ of wheel house 驾驶室绝缘
~ paper 绝缘纸,隔电纸
~ resistance 绝缘电阻 ‖ *Syn*. insulating resistance 绝缘电阻
~ resistance test 绝缘电阻试验,绝缘电阻测试
~ sheet 绝缘片
~ spacer 绝缘垫片,绝缘隔离片
~ test instrument 绝缘(电阻)测试仪器
~ thickness 绝缘厚度
~ varnish 绝缘漆
~ wall 绝缘壁,绝缘层

~ washer 绝缘垫圈,绝缘垫
insulator ['insjuleitə] *n*. 绝缘体,绝热器,绝缘装置 ‖ *Ant*. conductor 导体
insurable [in'ʃuərəbl] *a*. 可保险的,适合保险的
insurance [in'ʃuərəns] *n*. 保险,保险单,保险业,保险费
~ conditions 保险条件
~ expense 保险费
~ for adult 成人保险
~ interest 保险权益
insure [in'ʃuə] *v*. 确保,保证,投保
insurer [in'ʃuərə] *n*. 保险公司,承保人
intact [in'tækt] *a*. 完整的,未经触动的,原封不动的,未受损伤的
~ stability 完整稳性(即非破损时的稳定性),车辆稳定性
~ stability booklet 完整稳性手册
intake ['inteik] *n*. 摄取量,通风口,引入口,引入的量
~ adance angle 进气提前角,进气持续角,进气提早角
~ adit 供风通道,供风口
~ camshaft 进气凸轮轴
~ casing 进气口外室,进气室
~ duration angle 进气持续角,进气连续角
~ fan 进气风扇
~ lag angle 进气迟后角,进气滞后角
~ manifold 进气歧管,进气总管
~ port 进气道,进气口,进气门孔
~ pressure 进气压力,吸入压力
~ pressure difference 进气压差
~ process 进气过程
~ screen 进口滤网,进口拦网
~ silencer 消音器,消声器

~ stroke 进气冲程，吸入冲程

~ swirl 进气涡流

~ system 吸入系统，进气系统

~ turbulence 进气紊流

~ valve 进气阀 ‖ *Syn*. inlet valve 进给阀，吸入阀；suction valve 吸入阀

integral ['intigrəl] (I) *n*. 积分，部分，完整；*a*. 积分的，完整的，整体的，构成整体所必需的

~ action 积分作用

~ control 积分控制，积分调节

~ control mode 积分控制方式，积分调节方式

~ control output 积分控制输出，积分调节输出

~ controller 积分控制器，积分调节器 ‖ *Syn*. integral regulator 积分控制器，积分调节器

~ element 积分环节，积分元件

~ equation 积分方程

~ method 积分法

~ mode 积分模式

~ multiple 整倍数

~ of absolute value of error criterion 绝对误差积分准则

~ of squared error criterion 平方误差积分准则

~ part 积分部分，整数部分，主要的部分

~ representation 整数表示，积分表示

~ solution 整数解

~ structure 整体结构

~ tank 整体油箱，整体油舱，整体油柜

~ time 积分时间

~ transform 积分变换，积分转换

~ transmission package 整体式传动装置，综合传输装置

~ value 整数值

integrally ['intigrəli] *ad*. 完整地，整体地，固有地

integrate ['intigreit] *v*. 合并，联合，整合，结合，使成整体，求积分

~ with 使与…结合

integrated ['intigreitid] *v*. (integrate 的过去式和过去分词) 合并，联合，整合，结合，使成整体，求积分；*a*. 综合的，完整的，互相协调的

~ automation 全盘自动化，综合自动化，整体自动化

~ Bilge Water Treatment System (IBTS) 舱底水综合处理系统

~ Bridge System (IBS) 组合船桥系统，综合驾驶室系统，综合驾驶台系统

~ circuit (IC) 集成电路

~ Control and Monitoring System (ICMS) 综合监测控制系统，综合监控系统

~ design 综合设计

~ full electric propulsion 综合全电力推进

~ gate commutated thyristor (IGCT) 集成门极换流晶闸管

~ package 集成组件，集成块

~ reclosing mode 综合重合闸方式

~ system 集成系统，综合制度，综合体系

~ voltage regulator 集成电压调节器，集成稳压电路，集成稳压器

integrating ['intigreitiŋ] *n*. 集成化，综合化；*v*. (integrate 的 ing 形式) 合并，联合，整合，结合，使成整体，求积分

integration [,inti'greiʃən] (I) *n*. 积分，集

成，综合

~ action 积分作用

~ control 积分控制，积分调节

~ control mode 积分控制方式，积分调节方式

~ control output 积分控制输出，积分调节输出

~ controller 积分控制器，积分调节器 ‖ *Syn*. integration regulator 积分控制器，积分调节器

~ element 积分环节，积分元件

~ mode 积分模式

integrator ['intigreitə] *n*. 积分器，积分电路，综合者，合成者

integrity [in'tegriti] *n*. 正直，诚实，完整，完全，完整性

intelligence [in'telidʒəns] *n*. 智力，情报工作，情报机关，理解力，才智，智慧，天分

intelligent [in'telidʒənt] *a*. 智能的，聪明的，有才智的，理解力强的

~ diesel engine 智能化柴油机

~ equipment 智能设备，智能装备

~ instrument 智能仪器

~ power module (IPM) 智能功率模块

~ terminal 智能终端，智能型终端设备

intend [in'tend] *v*. 打算，计划，想要，意指

intendant [in'tendənt] *n*. 监督官，管理者

intended [in'tendid] *v*. (intend 的过去式和过去分词) 打算，计划，想要，意指；*a*. 故意的，有意的，已经订婚的

~ voyage 预定航次

intense [in'tens] *a*. 强烈的，紧张的，非常的，热情的

intensely [in'tensli] *ad*. 强烈地，紧张地，热情地

intensification [in,tensifi'keiʃən] *n*. 强化，加剧，激烈化，增强明暗度

intensity [in'tensiti] *n*. 强烈，剧烈，强度，亮度

intensive [in'tensiv] *n*. 加强器；*a*. 加强的，集中的，透彻的，加强语气的

intensively [in'tensivli] *ad*. 集中地，强烈地

intent [in'tent] *n*. 意图，目的，含义，意向，故意；*a*. 专心的，急切的，坚决的

intention [in'tenʃən] *n*. 意图，目的，意向，愈合

intentional [in'tenʃənəl] *a*. 故意的，蓄意的，策划的

intentionally [in'tenʃənəli] *ad*. 故意地，有意地

inter [in'tə:] *v*. 埋葬，葬，埋

~ alia 尤其，特别是，除了其他事物之外

~ cooler 中间冷却器，中冷器

~ locking 联锁法

inter-stage 级间的

~ compensation 级间补偿

~ stator blade 中间级定子叶片

~ temperature 级间温度

~ water seal 级间水密封

interact [,intə'rækt] *v*. 互相影响，互相作用

interacted [,intə'ræktid] *v*. (interact 的过去式和过去分词) 互相影响，互相作用；*a*. 互相作用的

~ system 互联系统，关联系统

interacting [,intə'ræktiŋ] *n*. 互相作用，互相影响；*v*. (interact 的 ing 形式) 互相影响，互相作用

~ goal 相互关联目标

interaction [,intər'ækʃən] *n*. 相互作用，交

互作用，互相影响

interactive [ˌintər'æktiv] *a.* 交互式的，相互作用的

~ drawing design 交互式制图设计

intercardinal ['intə'ka:dinəl] *n.* 罗盘上的(方位)点间的点；*a.* 位于两主要点之间的

intercept [ˌintə'sept] *n.* 拦截，截击，截距，截获的情报；*v.* 拦截，截断，窃听，中途阻止

interception [ˌintə(:)'sepʃən] *n.* 拦截，截住，截断，截取，中途夺取，侦听，窃听

interchange [ˌintə'tʃeindʒ] *n.* 互换，立体交叉道；*v.* 互换，交换，相互交换

~ method 互换法，替换法

interchangeability [ˌintə(:)ˌtʃeindʒə'biliti] *n.* 可交换性，可交替性

interchangeable [intə'tʃeindʒəb(ə)l] *a.* 可互换的，可交换的，可交替的

~ part 互换部件，互换零件，通用件

interconnect [ˌintə(:)kə'nekt] *v.* 使互相连接，互相联系

interconnection [ˌintə(:)kə'nekʃən] *n.* 互连，互相联络

~ line 互连线

~ switch 联络开关

intercooler [ˌintə(:)'ku:lə] *n.* 中间冷却器，中冷器，冷热气自动调节机

intercostal [ˌintə(:)'kɔstl] *n.* 肋间部分；*a.* 肋间的，肋材间的，间断的，叶脉间的

interface ['intə(:)ˌfeis] *n.* 接触面，界面，接口，接合点，接合部位，边缘区域；*v.* (通过界面)连接，(通过接口)接合，作为界面，成为界面，顺利地相互作用与合作

~ card 接口卡，介面卡

~ circuit 接口电路

~ detector 界面探测器

~ distortion 界面失真，界面畸变

~ module 接口模块

interfacial [ˌintə'feiʃəl] *a.* 界面的

interfere [ˌintə'fiə] *v.* 干扰，干涉，干预，妨碍，打扰，冲突，介入

~ with 妨碍，乱动，干涉，干扰

interference [ˌintə'fiərəns] *n.* 干扰，干涉，妨碍，阻挠，冲突

~ fit 干涉配合

interfering [ˌintə'fiəriŋ] *v.* (interfere 的 ing 形式) 干扰，干涉，干预，妨碍，打扰，冲突，介入；*a.* 干扰的，干涉的，多管闲事的

~ element 阻挠元素，干扰元素

~ energy 干扰能量

~ process 干扰过程

~ resource 干扰源 ‖ *Syn.* interfering source 干扰源

intergovernmental [ˌintəɡʌvən'mentəl] *a.* 政府间的

~ Maritime Consultative Organization (IMCO) 政府间海事协商组织

interim ['intərim] *n.* 过渡时期，中间时期，过渡期间，暂定；*a.* 临时的，暂时的，中间的，间歇的

~ International Ship Security Certificate (IISSC) 国际临时船舶保安证书

~ storage 暂时储藏，临时储藏

~ verification 临时验证

interior [in'tiəriə] *n.* 内部，本质，内陆，内政，室内布景；*a.* 内部的，国内的，内陆的，本质的，心灵的，精神的 ‖ *Syn* internal 内部的，内在的，国

内的，内政的 ‖ *Ant.* exterior 外部的，外在的，表面的，外交的，外用的；external 外部的，外用的，外国的，表面的；outer 外部的，外面的，远离中心的

~ extent 内延

interlock [ˌintə'lɔk] *n.* 连锁装置；*v.* 互锁，连锁，连串

~ circuit 联锁电路，联锁回路

~ device 联锁装置

~ pin 联锁销

~ plug 安全插件

~ protection 联锁保护

~ protection of parallel operation 供电联锁保护

~ protection of shore power connection 岸电联锁保护

~ relay 联锁继电器

~ switch 联锁开关

~ time 联锁时间

interlocking [ˌintə(:)'lɔkiŋ] *v.* (interlock 的ing 形式) 互锁，连锁；*a.* 连锁的

~ block 连锁砌块，连锁块

~ device 联锁装置

~ electromagnet 联锁电磁铁

~ pore 连通孔

~ relay 联锁继电器

~ reliability test 联锁可靠性试验，联锁测试

~ segment 联锁块

~ switch 联锁触点，联锁开关，联锁转辙器

intermediary [ˌintə'mi:diəri] *n.* 中间人，仲裁者，调解者，媒介物；*a.* 中间的，媒介的，中途的

intermediate [ˌintə'mi:djət] *n.* 中间人，中间产物，媒介物；*v.* 调解，干涉；*a.* 中间的，中级的

~ bearing 中间轴承

~ body 中间体，中介机构

~ bottom 中间底部

~ buffer 中间缓冲器

~ casing 技术套管，中间套管

~ clarifier 中间澄清器，中间澄清池

~ frequency 中频

~ frequency contactor 中频接触器

~ frequency generating set 中频发电机组

~ frequency generating station 中频电站

~ frequency generating station at intermediate voltage 中频中压电站

~ frequency generator 中频发电机

~ frequency power system 中频电力系统

~ frequency power system at intermediate voltage 中压中频电力系统

~ fuel oil (IFO) 中间燃油

~ gear 中间齿轮

~ gear bracket 中间齿轮托架

~ layer 中间过渡层

~ phase 中间相

~ pipe 消声器连接管

~ point 中间点

~ pressure 中压，中间压力，次高压

~ pressure compressor 中压压缩机，中压压缩器，中压压气机

~ product 中间体，中间产物，半制品，半成品，部分乘积

~ relay 中间继电器

~ ring 中间环

~ shaft 中间轴

327

~ shaft bearing 中间轴轴承
~ shafting 中间轴
~ speed 中等速度，中速，第二速，第二档 ‖ *Syn*. medium speed 中等速度，中速，平均速度；moderate speed 中等速度，中速，平均速度
~ stage 中间阶段，中间级，中间期
~ state 中间状态，居间态
~ stern tube 中尾轴管，中舯轴管
~ survey 中间检验
~ tap 中间丝锥，中间抽头
~ value 中间值，介值
~ verification 中期核查，期间核查
~ voltage 中压 ‖ *Syn*. medium voltage (MV) 中压；middle voltage 中压
~ voltage generating station 中压电站
~ water 中层水，过渡带水，中间水域
~ wheel 中间齿轮，过桥齿轮，介轮
~ wheel gear 带中间齿轮的减速装置
~ zone 中间区，过渡带，二次燃烧区

intermittent [ˌintə(ː)'mitənt] *a*. 间歇的，断断续续的
~ control 间歇控制，断续控制
~ current 间歇电流，断续电流
~ duty 间歇工作方式，间歇负载
~ duty system 间歇运行制
~ earth 断续接地
~ light 脉动光，间歇灯光
~ light source 断续光源
~ load 间歇负载
~ loading 间歇加载
~ lubrication 间歇式润滑
~ mode 间歇模式
~ motion 间歇运动
~ operation 间歇式操作，间歇运行
~ oscillation 间歇振荡，断续振荡

~ service 间歇工作，断续使用
~ weld 间断焊缝

intermittently [intə'mitəntli] *ad*. 间歇地

intermodal [ˌintə(ː)'məudl] *a*. 联合运输的，用于综合运输的
~ container 联运集装箱
~ transport 协调联运

internal [in'təːnl] *a*. 内部的，内在的，国内的，内政的 ‖ *Syn* interior 内部的，国内的，内陆的，本质的，心灵的，精神的 ‖ *Ant*. exterior 外部的，外在的，表面的，外交的，外用的；external 外部的，外用的，外国的，表面的；outer 外部的，外面的，远离中心的
~ bevel bottom 内下坡口
~ bevel top 内上坡口
~ casing 套管内部
~ casing corrosion 套管内部腐蚀
~ cause 内因
~ circulation 内循环
~ combusiton engine 内燃机
~ combustion engine power plant 内燃机动力装置
~ communication distribution box 内部通信配电箱
~ communication system 内部通信系统
~ control 内部控制，内控
~ crankshaft passage 曲轴内部通道
~ disturbance 内部干扰，内干扰，内扰
~ energy 内能
~ equalizer 内部均压装置，内平衡管
~ feed pipe 内给水管
~ force 内力
~ grinding 内表面研磨，内圆磨削
~ grinding attachment 内磨附件
~ hard disk 内置硬盘

~ insulation 内绝缘

~ insulation tank 内部隔热式液舱

~ phone 内部电话

~ pipe 内管

~ ramp 内跳板，内坡道

~ recirculation 内部再循环，内循环

~ resistance 内部阻力，内阻

~ tank insulation 舱内绝缘

~ transfer 内部转移，内部转岗

~ verification 内部验证，内部检定

~ vibration 内振动

~ volute vibration 内部蜗壳振动

~ water 内水，内部水，内陆水

~ water circulation 内部水循环，内河循环

internally [in'tənəli] *ad.* 在内，在中心

international [ˌintə(ː)'næʃənəl] *n.* 国际性组织，国际比赛；*a.* 国际的，世界的，超越国界的

~ Air Pollution Prevention Certificate (IAPP Certificate) 国际大气污染防治证书

~ Anti-Fouling System Certificate (IAFS Certificate) 国际防污系统证书

~ Association of Classification Society (IACS) 国际船级社协会

~ Code for the Construction and Equipment of Ships Carrying Dangerous Chemicals in Bulk (IBC Code) 国际散装运输危险化学品船舶构造与设备规则

~ Code for the Construction and Equipment of Ships Carrying Liquefied Gases in Bulk (IGC Code) 国际散装运输液化气船舶构造和设备规范

~ Convention for Safe Containers (CSC) 国际集装箱安全公约

~ Convention for the Prevention of Pollution from Ships (MARPOL) 国际防止船舶造成污染公约，MARPOL 防污公约

~ Convention for the Safety of Life at Sea (SOLAS Convention) 国际海上人命安全公约，SOLAS 公约

~ Convention on Load Lines (ICLL) 国际载重线公约

~ Convention on Standards of Training, Certification and Watchkeeping for Seafarers, 1978 (STCW Convention, 1978) 1978 年海员培训、发证和值班标准国际公约，1978 年 STCW 公约

~ Convention on Tonnage Measurement of Ships, 1969 (TONNAGE, 1969) 1969 年国际船舶吨位丈量公约

~ Electrotechnical Commission (IEC) 国际电工委员会

~ Gas Carrier Code (IGC Code) 国际气体载运船章程

~ Labor Organization (ILO) 国际劳工组织

~ Life saving Appliance Code (LSA Code) 国际救生设备规则

~ Load Line Certificate (ILLC) 国际载重线证书

~ Load Line Convention (ILLC) 国际载重线公约

~ Load Line Regulations (ILLR) 国际载重线规则

~ Management Code for the Safe Operation of Ships and for Pollution Prevention (ISM Code) 国际船舶安全营运和防止污染管理规则，ISM 规则

~ Maritime Dangerous Goods Code

(IMDG Code) 国际海上危险货物运输规则

~ Maritime Organization (IMO) 国际海事组织

~ Maritime Organization Assembly 国际海事组织大会

~ Maritime Organization Class 国际海事组织类号

~ Maritime Organization Council 国际海事组织理事会

~ Maritime Organization Marine Environment Protection Committee 国际海事组织海上环境保护委员会

~ Maritime Organization Maritime Safety Committee 国际海事组织海上安全委员会

~ Maritime Organization Resolution 国际海事组织决议

~ Maritime Organization Technical Cooperation Committee 国际海事组织技术合作委员会

~ Maritime Satellite Organization (INMARSAT) 国际海事卫星组织

~ Mobile Satellite Organization (IMSO) 国际移动卫星组织

~ Oil Pollution Prevention Certificate (IOPP Certificate) 国际防止油污证书，IOPP 证书

~ Organization for Standardization (ISO) 国际标准化组织

~ Safety Management (ISM) 国际安全管理

~ Safety Management Code 国际安全管理规则，ISM 规则

~ Sewage Pollution Prevention Certificate (ISPP Certificate) 国际防止生活污水污染证书，ISPP 证书

~ Ship and Port Facility Security Code (ISPS Code) 国际船舶和港口设施保安规则，ISPS 规则

~ shore connection 国际通岸接头

~ signal flags 国际信号旗

~ Telecommunication Union (ITU) 国际电信联盟

~ Tonnage Certificate (ITC) 国际吨位证书

~ Towing Tank Conference (ITTC) 国际船模试验水池会议，国际拖曳水池会议

internationally [ˌintə'næʃənəli] ad. 国际性地

internet ['intənet] n. 因特网，国际互联网络，网际网

~ telephone 因特网电话

~ terminal 互联网终端，网络终端，互联网末端

internetwork [intə'netwə:k] n. 互联网络

interoperability ['intərˌɔpərə'bilət] n. 互用性，协同工作的能力

interpolation [inˌtə:pəu'leiʃən] n. 插入，篡改，填写，插值

interpole ['intə(:)pəul] n. 极间极，附加极，辅助整流极，换向极

~ coil 附加线圈，极间极线圈，整流极线圈

~ flux 整流极磁通

~ generator 辅极发电机，带中间极的发电机

~ machine 有整流磁极的电机

~ motor 有整流极的电动机

~ shoe 辅助磁极极靴，整流磁极极靴

~ space 极间空隙

~ winding 匝极绕组

interpret [in'tə:prit] v. 解释，阐明，说明，评注，口译，翻译

interpretation [in,tə:pri'teiʃən] n. 解释，阐明，说明，评注，口译，演出

interpretive [in'tə:pritiv] a. 解释的，作为说明的

interrupt [,intə'rʌpt] n. 中断信号；v. 打断，中断，妨碍，插嘴

interrupting [,intə'rʌptiŋ] v. (interrupt 的 ing 形式) 打断，中断，妨碍，插嘴；a. 中断的，断续的
~ capacity 断开容量，断路容量
~ pulse 断续脉冲

interruption [,intə'rʌpʃən] n. 中断，打断，干扰，中断之事

intersect [,intə'sekt] v. 横断，横切，贯穿，相交，交叉

intersection [,intə(:)'sekʃən] n. 交集，交叉点，交叉，十字路口

interstitial [,intə(:)'stiʃəl] a. 空隙的，裂缝的，形成空隙的
~ hole 中间孔，间隙孔

interturn [,intə'tə:n] a. 匝间的

interval ['intəvəl] n. 间隔，时间间隔，间距，幕间休息

intervene [,intə'vi:n] v. 干预，干涉，调停，插入，介入，介于其间

intervention [,intə(:)'venʃən] n. 干涉，干预，调解，介入，插入

intestine [in'testin] n. 肠；a. 内部的，国内的

intranet [intrə'net] n. 内联网

intricacy ['intrikəsi] n. 复杂，错综，难懂，错综复杂的事物

intricate ['intrikit] a. 错综复杂的，难理解的，复杂的

intrinsic [in'trinsik] a. 本征的，固有的，内在的，本质的，体内的，先天性的
~ viscosity 特性黏度，本征黏度，固有黏度

intrinsical [in'trinsikəl] a. 本质的，固有的

intrinsically [in'trinzikli] ad. 本质地，从本质上(讲)，固有地
~ safe 本质安全，本安
~ safe equipment 本质安全型设备，本安型设备
~ safe type electrical apparatus 本质安全型电气设备，本安型电气设备

introduce [,intrə'dju:s] v. 介绍，引荐，推荐，传入，引进，提出，带领，纳入，放入

introduction [,intrə'dʌkʃən] n. 介绍，传入，初步，导言，绪论，入门
~ valve 注射阀，进样阀

intrude [in'tru:d] v. 闯入，打扰，侵入，侵扰，打扰，把观点强加于他人

intrusion [in'tru:ʒən] n. 闯入,打扰,干扰,干涉
~ alarm 入侵报警

invalid [in'vælid] n. 病人，病号，残废者，伤病军人；v. 使病弱，使伤残；a. 有病的，残废的，无效的 ‖ *Ant.* valid 有效的，有根据的，正当的，正确的
~ sequence 无效顺序，不合理顺序

invalidate [in'vælideit] v. 使作废，使无效，使无束缚力 ‖ *Ant.* validate 使有效，使生效

invalidation [in,væli'deiʃən] n. 无效，失效 ‖ *Ant.* validation 生效，有效

invalidity [,invə'lidəti] n. 无效力

invar [in'va:] n. 不胀钢

~ strut piston 镶殷钢活塞

invariable [in'vɛəriəbl] n. 不变,恒定,不变量; a. 恒定的,不变的,始终如一的,不可更改的

invariant [in'vɛəriənt] n. 不变式,不变量; a. 无变化的,不变的
~ equilibrium 无变度平衡,不变(更)平衡

invent [in'vent] v. 发明,创造,虚构

inventory ['invəntri] n. 存货,存货清单,详细目录,财产清册,总量
~ control 存货控制
~ cost 存货成本

inverse ['in'və:s] n. 反面,相反,倒转,反数,倒数,负数; v. 使倒转,使颠倒; a. 相反的,倒置的,反转的,倒转的,倒数的
~ current 反向电流,逆电流
~ Laplace transform 逆拉普拉斯变换
~ matrix 逆矩阵,反矩阵
~ Nyquist diagram 逆奈奎斯特图
~ ratio 反比例
~ time thermal over current trip 反时限热过电流脱扣
~ transform 逆变换,反转换

inversely [,in'və:sli] ad. 相反地,倒转地

inversion [in'və:ʃən] n. 倒置,反向,倒转

invert [in'və:t] n. 颠倒的事物,倒置物,倒悬者; v. 使颠倒,使倒置,使转化; a. 转化的

inverted [in'və:tid] v. (invert 的过去式和过去分词) 使颠倒,使倒置,使转化; a. 反向的,倒转的,倒置的
~ amplifier 倒相器,逆相放大器,栅极接地放大器
~ valve 止回阀,单向阀,逆止阀,止逆阀 ‖ **Syn**. check valve 止回阀,单向阀,逆止阀,止逆阀; non-return valve 止回阀,单向阀,逆止阀,止逆阀; one-way valve 止回阀,单向阀,逆止阀,止逆阀

inverted-L 倒 L 形
~ antenna 倒 L 形天线

inverter [in'və:tə] n. 变换器,倒换器,逆变器,换流器,电流换向器
~ station 换流站
~ transformator 倒相变压器

invisible [in'vizəbl] n. 看不见的人,隐者; a. 无形的,看不见的,不显眼的,视力外的,暗藏的

invoice ['invɔis] n. 发票,货物,发货单; v. 开发票,记清单

involute ['invəlu:t] n. 渐开线,切展线; v. 恢复原状,消失; a. 纷乱的,复杂的,难解的,错综的,边缘内卷的,内旋的
~ gear 渐开线齿轮

involve [in'vɔlv] v. 包含,含有,涉及,卷入,伴随,连同,密切关联,牵连,笼罩,包围,裹住,影响,使陷于,潜心于
~ with 涉及,卷入,牵扯

involvement [in'vɔlvmənt] n. 包含,连累,牵连,混乱

inward ['inwəd] n. 内部,内脏,密友; a. 向内的,内部的,内心的,亲密的,熟悉的; ad. 向内,在内
~ flange 内边缘,内向折边
~ flow turbine 向心式透平,心流涡轮,内流涡轮

inwards ['inwədz] ad. 向内地,向内部地

IO (input-output) 输入输出,投入产出

~ channel 输入输出通道
~ device 输入输出设备
iodine ['aiədi:n] *n.* 碘，碘酒
ion ['aiən] *n.* 离子
~ smoke detector 离子感烟探测器
ionic [ai'ɔnik] *a.* 离子的，电价的
ionizable ['aiənaizəbl] *a.* 可电离的，电离的
ionization [,aiənai'zeiʃən] *n.* 离子化，电离
ionize ['aiənaiz] *v.* 电离，(使)离子化
IOPP (International Oil Pollution Prevention) 国际防止油污染
~ Certificate 国际防止油污证书，IOPP证书
IP (indicated power) 指示功率
IPM (intelligent power module) 智能功率模块
iron ['aiən] *n.* 铁，铁制工具，熨斗，坚强，强壮，刚强，烙铁，镣铐；*v.* 烫平，压去，装上铁器，包以铁器，用铁装备；*a.* 铁的，残酷的，刚强的，强健的
~ alloy 铁合金
~ bacterium 铁细菌
~ binding capacity (IBC) 铁结合能力
~ body valve 铁体阀
~ canvas nail 铁帆布钉
~ carbide 碳化铁，渗碳体
~ cement 铁质胶合剂
~ clad switch 铁壳开关 ‖ *Syn.* iron cover switch 铁壳开关；metal clad switch 铁壳开关
~ clad switch gear 铁壳开关装置
~ core 铁芯
~ core inductor 铁心感应线圈
~ cringle 索圈，索眼
~ curved plane 铁弯刨
~ drum 铁桶
~ dust 铁粉，铁屑
~ flat nut 平头铁螺母
~ grease cup 铁滑脂杯，铁油杯
~ grey 铁灰色
~ loss 铁损失，磁心损耗
~ nail 铁钉
~ pipe 铁管
~ plane 铁刨
~ plug 铁插头，熨斗插头
~ pole piece 磁极片
~ round washer 铁圆垫圈
~ screw with flat head 平头铁螺钉
~ screw with round head 圆头铁螺钉
~ screw with square head 方头铁螺钉
~ sheet shears 铁皮剪刀
~ shield 铁屏蔽
~ split pin 铁开尾销
~ square nut 方头铁螺母
~ square washer 铁方垫圈
~ stain 铁斑
~ thumb nut 铁蝶型螺母
~ tin funnel 白铁漏斗
~ tin oil springe 白铁注油器
~ wood screw with flat head 铁平头木螺钉
~ wood screw with round head 铁圆头木螺钉
ironclad [aiən'klæd] *n.* 装甲舰；*a.* 装甲的，打不破的，坚固的，刻板的，固定不变的
ironsmith ['aiənsmiθ] *n.* 铁匠，锻工
irradiate [i'reidieit] *v.* 照耀，照射，发光，启发，阐明,辐射 ‖ *Syn.* radiate 放射，辐射，发光

irradiated [i'reidieitid] v. (irradiate 的过去式和过去分词) 照耀，照射，发光，启发，阐明，辐射；a. 受辐照的，被辐射的，照亮的
~ area 受辐照面积
~ nuclear fuel (INF) 辐照核燃料

irradiation [iˌreidi'eiʃən] n. 照射，发光，放射

irregular [i'regjulə] n. 非正规军军人，不合格品，次品；a. 不规则的，违规的，异常的，无规律的，不法的，不稳定的，不平坦的，不整齐的

irregularity [iˌregju'læriti] n. 不规则，不整齐，不合常规，不规则性，无规律，不规则的事物 ‖ Ant. regularity 规律性，规则性，整齐，匀称

irregularly [i'regjələli] ad. 不规则地，不整齐地

irrelevant [i'relivənt] a. 不相干的，不切题的

irrespective [ˌiris'pektiv] a. 不顾的，不考虑的，无关的
~ of 不论，不顾，不管

irretrievably [iri'tri:vəbli] ad. 不能挽回地，不能补救地

irreversible [ˌiri'və:səbl] a. 不可逆的，不能撤回的，不能取消的，不能倒转的
~ process 不可逆过程，单向磁化过程

irrevocably [i'revəkəbli] ad. 不能取消地，不能撤回地

irritant ['iritənt] n. 刺激物，刺激剂；a. 刺激的，刺激性的

irritate ['iriteit] v. 刺激，激怒，使急躁，使兴奋

irritating ['iriˌteitiŋ] v. (irritate 的 ing 形式) 刺激，激怒，使急躁，使兴奋；a. 刺激的，气人的，使愤怒的
~ gas 刺激性毒气，刺激性气体

ISA (Industry Standard Architecture) 工业标准结构

island ['ailənd] n. 岛，岛屿，飞行甲板上层建筑，安全岛，岛状物，孤立体；v. 孤立，隔离，使成岛状

isle [ail] n. 岛，小岛；v. 使成为岛屿，住在岛屿上 ‖ Syn. islet 小岛

islet ['ailit] n. 小岛 ‖ Syn. isle 小岛

ISM (International Safety Management) 国际安全管理
~ Code 国际安全管理规则，ISM 规则

ISM Code (International Management Code for the Safe Operation of Ships and for Pollution Prevention) 国际船舶安全营运和防止污染管理规则，ISM 规则

ISO (International Organization for Standardization) 国际标准化组织

isobar ['aisəubɑ:] n. 等压线，同重核，同重元素

isobaric [ˌaisəu'bærik] n. 等压线；a. 同重元素的，表示等压的

isobath ['aisəuˌbɑ:θ] n. 等深线，等水深线

isochronous [ai'sɔkrənəs] a. 等时的，等步的

isogonal [ai'sɔgənl] a. (=isogonic) 等偏角的

isogonic [ˌaisəu'gɔnik] a. (=isogonal) 等偏角的

isolate ['aisəleit] n. 隔离种群；v. (使)隔离，(使)孤立，(使)绝缘，(使)离析；a. 隔离的，孤立的，独自的，单独的

isolated ['aisəleitid] v. (isolate 的过去式和过去分词) (使)隔离，(使)孤立，(使)

绝缘，(使)离析；*a.* 隔离的，孤立的，单独的，绝缘的
- ~ imperfection 孤立缺陷
- ~ measurement 隔离测量
- ~ value 孤值

isolating ['aisəleitiŋ] *v.* (isolate 的 ing 形式) 使隔离，使绝缘；*a.* 孤立的，绝缘的
- ~ arrangement 隔离装置
- ~ switch 隔离开关，切断开关，断路器
- ~ valve 隔离阀

isolation [,aisəu'leiʃən] *n.* 隔绝，孤立，隔离，绝缘，离析
- ~ pad 隔离盘，隔离垫
- ~ parameters 隔离参数
- ~ valve 隔离阀

isolator ['aisəleitə] *n.* 隔离器，隔音装置，绝缘体，隔离的人

isometric [,aisəu'metrik] *n.* 等距线；*a.* 等角投影的，等量的，等体积的，等容量的，等尺寸的
- ~ diagram 轴测图
- ~ embedding 等距嵌入

isophase ['aisəfeiz] *n.* 等相线

isothermal [,aisəu'θə:məl] *n.* 恒温线，等温线；*a.* 恒温的，等温的，等温线的
- ~ expansion 等温膨胀

ISPP (International Sewage Pollution Prevention) 国际防止生活污水污染
- ~ Certificate 国际防止生活污水污染证书，ISPP 证书

ISPS Code (International Ship and Port Facility Security Code) 国际船舶和港口设施保安规则，ISPS 规则

issue ['isju:] *n.* 论点，问题，出版，发行，(报刊等)期、号，结果，流出；*v.* 发行，发布，出版，发给，(使)流出，放出，造成，辩护，传下 ‖ ***Syn.*** contention 论点；moot point 争论未决的问题，论点；point in question 论点
- ~ of certificate 证书的颁发
- ~ of fact 事实上的争论点

IT (information technology) 信息技术

ITC (International Tonnage Certificate) 国际吨位证书

item ['aitəm] *n.* 条款，项目，短文，细节，一些信息，一则，一条；*v.* 计算；*ad.* 同样，也是

iteration [,itə'reiʃən] *n.* 迭代，迭代法，反复，重复

itinerary [ai'tinərəri] *n.* 旅程，路线，旅行指南，游记，旅行日程；*a.* 路线的，旅行的，巡回的，巡游的

ITTC (International Towing Tank Conference) 国际船模试验水池会议，国际拖曳水池会议

J

jack [dʒæk] *n.* 插孔，插座，起重器，千斤顶，(舰船上悬挂的)国旗，男人，杰克(Jack，男子名，也特指各种男性工人)；*v.* 抬起，提醒，增加，放弃，提高；*a.* 雄的
- ~ bolt 定位螺栓，起升螺栓，调整螺栓
- ~ ladder (船)软梯，索梯
- ~ plane 粗刨
- ~ up 顶起，托起

jacket ['dʒækit] *n.* (锅炉、水管等的)套，封套，绝缘护套，护封，文件套，公文夹，磁盘套子，外皮，短上衣，夹克，书籍的封面套纸；*v.* 加外套，装封套

~ cooling 水套冷却
~ cooling water pump 气缸套冷却水泵
~ cooling water system 气缸套冷却水系统
~ pump 增压泵
~ space 水套空间
~ water 水套冷却水，水套水
~ water cooler 气缸套冷却水冷却器，汽缸套水冷却器
~ water pump 气缸套冷却水泵
~ water tank 气缸套冷却水柜

jackstaff ['dʒækstɑ:f] *n*. 舰首旗杆，船首旗杆

Jacob ['dʒeikəb] *n*. 雅各(圣经人物以撒之次子)，雅各布(男子名)

Jacob's 雅各的，雅各布的
~ ladder 扶手绳，软梯，绳梯

jam [dʒæm] *n*. 拥挤，堵塞，困境，果酱；*v*. (使)塞满，(使)堵塞，拥挤，混杂，压碎，轧住，挤进

Japanese [dʒæpə'ni:z] *n*. 日本人，日语，日文；*a*. 日本的，日本人的，日语的
~ 10-mode test cycle 日本十工况法
~ 4-mode test cycle 日本四工况法

jar [dʒɑ:] *n*. 震动，刺耳声，震惊，争吵，罐，广口瓶；*v*. 震惊，冲突，发刺耳声，不一致，震动，刺激

jaw [dʒɔ:] *n*. 颚，颌，下巴，叉钳，钳夹，狭窄的入口；*v*. 闲谈，教训，唠叨
~ brake 爪闸
~ clutch 颚式离合器牙，嵌式离合器，爪盘联轴节
~ coupling 爪形联轴节

jeopardy ['dʒepədi] *n*. 危险 ‖ **Syn**. danger 危险，危害，危险物，威胁；

hazard 冒险，危险，冒险的事；peril 危险，危险物；risk 危险，风险，冒险

jerk [dʒə:k] *n*. 急推，猛拉，反射，性情古怪的人，肌肉抽搐，牛肉干；*v*. 痉挛，急拉，猛拉，颠簸地行进
~ pump 脉动泵，高压燃油喷射泵

jerky ['dʒə:ki] *n*. 牛肉干；*a*. 停停动动的，急拉的，急动的，抽筋的，不平稳的，傻的，愚蠢的
~ motion 蠕动

jet [dʒet] *n*. 喷射，喷嘴，喷气式飞机，黑玉；*v*. 射出，乘喷气式飞机；*a*. 墨黑的
~ gas turbine 喷气式燃气轮机
~ nozzle 喷嘴，尾喷口，喷射管
~ propulsion 喷气推进
~ propulsive efficiency 喷射推进效率
~ pump 喷射泵，射流泵
~ pump system 喷射泵系统
~ reaction 射流反应

jetsam ['dʒetsəm] *n*. 漂流到海岸的货物，投弃货物，船舶遇险时投弃的货物

jettison ['dʒetisn] *n*. 投弃，投弃货物，被抛弃的东西；*v*. 投弃(船舶遇难时投弃货物以减轻负载)，抛弃，丢弃，扔掉
~ of cargo 抛弃货物

jetty ['dʒeti] *n*. 码头，防波堤；*a*. 乌黑发亮的，黑色的，煤玉似的

jib [dʒib] *n*. 船首三角帆，起重机臂，挺杆；*v*. 踌躇不前，停止不动，移转
~ radius indicator 悬臂伸距指示器
~ sheave (起重机的)挺杆滑车
~ rest 起重臂支架
~ stopper 旋臂止动器

jigger ['dʒigə] *n*. 盘车，小帆船，补助帆，

小滑车，计量杯，小玩意

~ mast 后桅，小船船尾用于张小帆的短桅

job [dʒɔb] n. 工作，零活，职位，事情；v. 做零工，打杂，假公济私，代客买卖，批发，承包，欺骗

job-lot 分批数量，整批杂货

~ control 批量控制

job-sharing 轮班制

join [dʒɔin] n. 连接，结合，接合点；v. 参加，结合，加入，连接

joined [dʒɔind] n. 连接，接合点；v. (join 的过去式和过去分词) 加入，参加，连接

~ mark 连码，联合标记

joiner ['dʒɔinə] n. 接合者，工匠

~ arrangement 接合装置

joint [dʒɔint] n. 关节，接缝，接合处，接合点；v. 连接，接合，使有接头，贴合；a. 共同的，联合的，连接的，合办的

~ clearance 接合间隙

~ flange 连接法兰，接合凸缘

~ inspection party 联检小组

~ inspection procedure 联合检查手续

~ ring 垫圈，接合密封环

jolt [dʒəult] n. 颠簸，摇晃，震惊，令人震惊的事；v. (使)颠簸，(使)摇动，摇撼，震惊，诧异，重击，击入，激起，唤起

journal ['dʒə:nl] n. 航海日志，日志，日记，轴颈，期刊，报纸，杂志，分类账

~ bearing 径向滑动轴承，径向轴承，轴颈轴承

~ box 轴颈箱，轴箱 ‖ *Syn*. axle box

轴箱

~ bush 轴颈衬套

~ collar 轴颈环

journey ['dʒə:ni] n. 旅行，旅程，历程，过程；v. 旅行，出游

joystick ['dʒɔi,stik] n. 操纵杆，控制杆

judge [dʒʌdʒ] n. 法官，裁判员，鉴定人；v. 断定，判断，认为，审理，鉴定，判决

judgement ['dʒʌdʒmənt] n. 判断，判断力，意见，看法，评价，审判，判决

jumbo ['dʒʌmbəu] n. 庞然大物，大型喷气式飞机，巨人，巨物；a. 巨大的，特大的

jump [dʒʌmp] n. 跳跃，上涨，惊跳；v. (使)跳跃，跃过，突升，暴涨

jumping ['dʒʌmpiŋ] v. (jump 的 ing 形式) (使)跳跃，跃过，突升，暴涨；a. 跳跃的

~ cushion 救生垫

~ dial 跳字钟表盘，日历盘

junction ['dʒʌŋkʃən] n. 连接，接合，交叉点，汇合处

~ box 接线盒，分线箱

junior ['dʒu:njə] n. 年少者，晚辈，地位较低者，大学三年级学生；a. 年少的；后进的，下级的，初级的

~ electrician 初级电工

~ engineer 初级工程师，工程员

~ officer 初级干事，低级官员，下级军官

junk [dʒʌŋk] n. 舢板，垃圾，废物

jurisdiction [,dʒuəris'dikʃən] n. 权限，权力，管辖区域，司法权，审判权，管辖权

just [dʒʌst] a. 公正的，合理的，正直的，

正义的，正确的，应得的，有充分根据的；ad. 只是，仅仅，刚才，刚刚，正好，恰好，不过
~ so 正是如此

K

kayak ['kaiæk] n. 皮船，爱斯基摩小艇
keel [ki:l] n. 龙骨，船，运煤平底船，龙骨脊；v. 装龙骨，(使)倾覆，使变凉
　~ line 龙骨线，艉艇线
　~ molding 龙骨线脚
　~ strake 龙骨板，平板龙骨
　~ support 龙骨支撑
keelblock ['ki:lblɔk] n. 龙骨墩
keelson ['kelsn] n. 内龙骨，底材
keep [ki:p] n. 保持，保养，生计，监狱，要塞；v. 保持，保存，遵守，经营，看守，拘留，维持，记，继续不断
　~ abreast of 保持与…并列
　~ an eye on 照看，留意，密切注视
　~ away 防范
　~ away from 远离，回避
　~ healthy 保持健康
　~ in 隐瞒，隐藏，抑制，继续燃烧
　~ in mind 记住
　~ in touch with 与…保持联系
　~ moving 继续运动，保持前进，不断移动
　~ on 继续，穿着…不脱
　~ out 使在外
　~ out of 置身于外
　~ pace with 并驾齐驱，保持同步
　~ the ship on even keel 保持船身平稳，保持船平稳运行
　~ the weather 占上风
　~ track 保持跟踪，注意动向，保持追踪
　~ track of 记录，掌握线索，保持联系，了解动态
　~ track with 记录，了解动态，密切注视
　~ up 保持，继续，不低落，不落后
　~ up with 跟上
　~ working 继续工作，永不停顿
keeper ['ki:pə] n. 监护人，饲养员，看守人，管理人
keg [keg] n. 小桶
kelp [kelp] n. 海藻，巨藻，海草灰
　~ diving 海藻潜水
Kelvin ['kelvin] n. 绝对温标，开氏温标，开(绝对温度单位)，开尔文(1824-1907 英国物理学家)
　~ connection 开尔文连接
Kenter ['kentər] n. 肯特尔(人名)
　~ shackle 双半式连接卸扣，双半式连接链环
kernel ['kə:nl] n. 核心，要点，精髓，内核，仁，麦粒，谷粒
kerosene ['kerəsi:n] n. 煤油，火油
kettle ['ketl] n. 壶，罐，釜，鼓
key [ki:] n. 钥匙，关键，解答，答案，密码本，索引，键，基调，调子，对译本，(开钟表、发条的)栓，楔，要害；v. 锁上，插上栓，提供线索，调节音调；a. 关键的，有重大意义的
　~ board 键盘
　~ component 基础组分，标准物质，关键组分
　~ factor 关键因素，关键因子，关键要素
　~ feeder 键式传送装置

~ file 关键文件
~ lamp 同步指示灯，钥匙灯
~ lock switch 键锁开关
~ machine 主导机械，关键性机械
~ operation 关键操作
~ out 切断，断开
~ ship board operation 船上关键操作
~ signal 键控信号

keyed [ki:d] v. (key 的过去式和过去分词)锁上，插上栓，提供线索，调节音调；a. 键控的，有键的，定在某调的
~ fitting 有键连接，有键安装
~ insertion 键控插入
~ propeller 键接螺旋桨，有键螺旋桨

keyless ['ki:lis] a. 无键的，以转柄上发条的
~ fitting 无键连接，无键安装
~ propeller 无键螺旋桨
~ propeller fitting 无键螺旋桨安装

keystone ['ki:stəun] n. 重点，要旨，基本原理，拱心石，楔石

keyway ['ki:ˌwei] n. 扁形钥孔，键槽，键沟

keyword ['ki:wəd] n. 密码,暗号,关键字，重要词，参考词

kick [kik] n. 反冲，后座力，踢；v. 踢，反冲，反弹，抱怨

kidney ['kidni] n. 肾脏，腰子，个性，性格

kidney-shaped 肾形的

Kiel [ki:l] n. 基尔(德意志联邦共和国北部港市)
~ canal lamp 基尔运河灯

kilo ['ki:ləu] n. 千

kilocalorie ['kiləkæləri] n. 大卡(热量单位)

kilogram ['kiləgræm] (kg) n. 千克，公斤

kilovolt ['kiləuvəult] n. 千伏特
~ amper 千伏特安培
~ meter 千伏特计

kilowatt ['kiləuwɔt] (kW) n. 千瓦(功率单位)
~ hour 千瓦(特)小时
~ meter 千瓦计

kindle ['kindl] v. 点燃，(使)着火，引起，照亮，煽动，激起，发亮

kinematic [ˌkaini'mætik] a. 运动学上的，运动学的
~ system 运动系统
~ train 传动系统
~ viscosity 动黏滞率，动黏度

kinetic [kai'netik] a. 运动的,动力(学)的，活跃的
~ analysis 动力学分析
~ energy 动能
~ force 动能力
~ head 动力水头，动水头，流速水头，速度头
~ heating 动力加热
~ stability 动力学稳定性
~ stress 动力应力
~ tank 活动油箱，移动式油箱，动力柜

kit [kit] n. 成套工具，全套元件，用具包，工具箱，成套用具，装备

kitchen ['kitʃin] n. 厨房，厨师，炊具，炊事人员

klaxon [klæksn] n. 高音喇叭，高音气笛，电喇叭

knee [ni:] n. 膝，膝盖，膝部，膝状物；v. 用膝盖碰，用膝撞击
~ plate 连接板，三角板，肘板

knife [naif] n. 刀，匕首，餐刀；v. 用刀切割，划过

~ blade 刀框，刀片滑块，滑动刀架

~ fuse knife blade with bakelite cover and porcelain base switch 带有胶木盖和瓷底座开关的保险丝刀片

~ smooth file 细刀锉

~ spotlight 切割器的照明灯

~ switch 闸刀开关

knight [nait] *n.* 骑士，武士，爵士；*v.* 授以爵位

~ engine 套阀发动机

knob [nɔb] *n.* 球形捏手，节，瘤，旋钮，球形突出物，小块；*v.* 鼓起，使有球形突出物

knock [nɔk] *n.* 敲，敲打，敲击，碰撞，敲击声，爆震声；*v.* 敲，敲打，敲击，击打，(使)碰撞，灌输，发出爆震或相撞的声音

knockdown ['nɔk'daun] *n.* 船的破损，易拆卸的东西，价格的压低；*a.* 极低的，猛的，可拆开的

knot [nɔt] *n.* 节(海里/小时，航速单位)，测速绳结，一海里距离，结，节瘤，疙瘩，花结，结合，群，复杂问题；*v.* 打结

knurl [nə:l] *n.* 球形突出物，隆起，瘤，硬节，压花，滚花；*v.* 滚花

knurled ['nə:ld] *v.* (knurl 的过去式和过去分词) 滚花；*a.* 有凸边的，有节的

~ nut 滚花螺帽，滚花螺母

~ piston 滚花修复活塞，滚花活塞

~ roll 网纹轧辊，槽纹轧辊

knurling ['nə:liŋ] *n.* 滚花，压花纹；*v.* (knurl 的 ing 形式) 滚花

~ tool 滚花刀具，压花刀具，滚花刀

krypton ['kriptɔn] *n.* 氪

~ lamp 氪灯

L

L-combustion L 形燃烧

~ chamber L 形燃烧室，楔形燃烧室

L-engine L 形发动机

label ['leibl] *n.* 标签，签条，商标，标志；*v.* 贴标签于，指…为，分类，标注

labor ['leibə] (=labour) *n.* 劳动，努力，工作，劳工，分娩，阵痛；*v.* 颠簸摇晃，工作，劳动，努力争取，苦干，详细分析，麻烦；*a.* 劳动的，工党的

~ insurance 劳动保险

~ protect and safety devices 劳动保护与安全装置

~ protection 劳动保护

~ protection science 劳动保护学

laboratory ['læbərətəri] *n.* (=lab.) 实验室，实验课，研究室

labour ['leibə(r)] (=labor) *n.* 劳动，努力，工作，劳工，分娩，阵痛；*v.* 颠簸摇晃，工作，劳动，努力争取，苦干，详细分析，麻烦；*a.* 劳动的，工党的

labyrinth ['læbərinθ] *n.* 迷宫，错综复杂，难解的事件

~ air seal 迷宫式气封

~ bearing 迷宫轴承，曲径式密封轴承

~ gland 迷宫式压盖，迷宫密封装置

~ gland housing (迷宫)气封体

~ oil seal 迷宫式油封

~ packing 迷宫式密封，气封

~ ring 迷宫环，气封环，曲折密封圈，阻气环

~ seal 迷宫式密封

lack [læk] *n.* 缺乏，不足，没有，缺少的

东西；v. 缺乏，缺少，没有，需要，需要的东西
~ of breathing 呼吸不足

lacquer ['lækə] n. 漆器，漆，天然漆；v. 涂漆于，使…表面或外观光滑

ladder ['lædə] n. 梯子，阶梯，梯状物，途径；v. 装设梯子
~ diagram 梯形图
~ gangway 梯形舷梯

lade [leid] v. 装载，装船，舀出

laden ['leidn] v. (lade 的过去分词) 装载，装船，舀出；a. 满载的，负载的，受压迫的
~ tanker 满载油船
~ vessel 载货船
~ voyage 装运航次
~ with 载满，充满烦恼

lag [læg] n. 落后，迟延，防护套，桶板，囚犯；v. 滞后，落后，缓缓而行，加防冻保暖层，加上外套；a. 最后的

lagan ['lægən] n. (商船失事时)系浮标投海的货物

lagging ['lægiŋ] n. 绝缘层材料；v. (lag 的 ing 形式) 滞后，落后，缓缓而行，加防冻保暖层，加上外套

lagoon [lə'gun] n. 泻湖，礁湖

laid [leid] v. (lay 的过去式和过去分词) 放置，铺设，提出，平息，布置，打赌，产卵；a. 松弛的，从容不迫的

laid-up 卧病在床的
~ tonnage 停泊吨位

laminar ['læminə(r)] a. 层流的，薄片状的，薄层的，层状的，板状的，流线的
~ flow 层流

laminate ['læmineit] n. 薄片制品，层压制件；v. 碾压，锤打，分成薄片，用薄片覆盖
~ bearing 层压轴承，层压胶木轴承
~ molding 积层成型

laminated ['læmineitid] v. (laminate 的过去式和过去分词) 碾压，锤打，分成薄片，用薄片覆盖；a. 薄板状的，薄片状的，层积的，层压的
~ core 叠片铁芯

lamination [,læmi'neiʃən] n. 层积，叠层结构，叠片结构，层状体

lamp [læmp] n. 灯，照射器；v. 照亮，发亮
~ globe 圆灯罩
~ holder 灯座

LAN (local area network) 局域网

land [lænd] n. 陆地，国家，国土，地带，地产，田产；v. (使)靠岸，(使)登陆，(使)登岸，(使)到达，(使)使上岸
~ hemisphere 陆半球
~ lockwater 内陆水域

lander ['lændə] n. 着陆器，出铁槽，斜槽，司罐工人

landfall ['lændfɔ:l] n. 着陆，远航后初见陆地，到达陆地

landing ['lændiŋ] n. 登陆，着陆，码头，楼梯平台，降落；v. (land 的 ing 形式) (使)靠岸，(使)登陆，(使)登岸，(使)到达，(使)上岸
~ craft 登陆艇
~ ship 登陆舰

landless ['lændlis] a. 无陆地的，无地产的，无主地的

landmark ['lændma:k] n. 陆标，地标，界标，里程碑，纪念碑，地界标，划时代的事；a. 有重大意义的，有重大影响的

341

landward ['lændwəd] *a*. 近陆的，向陆的；*ad*. 向陆地

landwards ['lændwədz] *ad*. 向陆地

lane [lein] *n*. 小巷，狭窄的通道，航线，车道

langoustier [la:ŋgus'tɛə] *n*. 龙虾艇

lantern ['læntən] *n*. 信号，天窗，灯笼，提灯，幻灯

lanyard ['lænjəd] *n*. 系索

lap [læp] *n*. 大腿前部，膝盖，舔声，溅泼声，重叠的部分，(跑道的)一圈，范围，衣兜，下摆；*v*. (使)重叠，围住，包围，轻拍，拍打，泼溅，舔

lapin ['læpin] *n*. 兔子，兔皮毛

~ joint 搭接，叠接

~ plate 搭接板

Laplace [la:'pla:s] *n*. 拉普拉斯(1749-1827，法国天文学家、数学家)

~ transform 拉普拉斯变换

lapping ['læpiŋ] *n*. 搭接，搭叠，重叠；*v*. (lap 的 ing 形式) (使)重叠，围住，包围，轻拍，拍打，泼溅，舔

~ machine 缠绕机，卷板机，精研机，搪磨工具，走合工具

lapse [læps] *n*. 失误，下降，流逝，丧失，过失；*v*. 失检，背离，堕入，流逝，失效，下降

large [la:dʒ] *n*. 大；*a*. 大的，巨大的，宽大的，夸大的；*ad*. 顺风地，大大地，夸大地

~ air volume 风量大

~ bore diesel engine 大缸径柴油机

~ capacity 大容量

~ crude oil carrier (LCC) 大型油轮，大型油船

~ diameter 大直径

~ diameter cylinder 大直径圆筒

~ diameter member 大直径构件

~ diameter wire 大号线

~ fire control 大火控制

~ grade 大型的，尺寸大的，大规格的

~ quantity 大量，大数量

~ scale integrated circuit (LSIC) 大规模集成电路

~ scale system 大系统

~ sea water circulated cooler 大型海水循环冷却器

~ tanker 大型油船，大型油轮

~ vice 大虎钳，锻用虎钳

largely ['la:dʒli] *ad*. 主要地，大部分，大量地，很大程度上

largeness ['la:dʒnəs] *n*. 巨大，广大，大量，广博

laser ['leizə] *n*. 激光

~ beam 激光束

~ beam cutting 激光束切割

~ beam flying 激光束扫描

~ cutter 激光切割机

~ cutting 激光切割

~ cutting machine 激光切割机

~ engraving machine 激光雕刻机

~ printer 激光打印机

lash [læʃ] *n*. 鞭子，鞭打，睫毛，讽刺；*v*. 鞭打，摆动，扎捆，冲击，煽动，讽刺，猛击，急速甩动

LASH (lighter aboard ship) 载驳轮船，载驳货船

lashing ['læʃiŋ] *n*. 鞭打，痛斥，大量，许多；*v*. (lash 的 ing 形式) 鞭打，摆动，扎捆，冲击，煽动，讽刺，猛击，急速甩动

~ bars 绑扎杆

~ belt 绑扎带

~ equipment 绑扎设备

~ eye 地铃，固定孔

~ point 十字底座，系固点

~ ring (钢绳断线自动停车装置的)触线圈，系绳环

~ wire 拉金，拉筋，束缚线

last [la:st] *n*. 最后，末尾，临终；*v*. 持续，支持，维持；*a*. 最后的，临终的，末尾的，最近的，结论性的；*ad*. 最后，后来

~ step 最后一档，上一步

lastly ['la:stli] *ad*. 最后，终于

latch [lætʃ] *n*. 门闩，插销，撞锁，弹簧锁；*v*. 锁住，闭锁

late [leit] *a*. 晚的，迟的，已故的，最近的；*ad*. 晚，迟，最近，在晚期

lately ['leitli] *ad*. 近来，最近，不久前

latent ['leitənt] *n*. 隐约的指印；*a*. 潜在的，潜伏的，隐藏的

~ defect 潜在事故，潜在缺陷，隐蔽故障

~ heat 潜伏热

~ heat of condensation 凝结潜热

~ heat of fusion 熔化潜热

~ heat of vaporization 汽化潜热

later ['leitə] *a*. 更迟的，更后的；*ad*. 后来，稍后，随后

lateral ['lætərəl] *n*. 侧部，支线，边音；*v*. 横向穿越；*a*. 侧面的，横向的，横的

~ area exposed to wind 受风侧面积

~ attitude 倾斜姿态，坡度

~ axis 横向轴线，横轴，水平轴

~ bending 横向弯曲，侧弯，侧向弯曲

~ flange 横向法兰

~ flexibility 横向柔度

~ force 侧向力，侧力

~ instability 横向不稳定性

~ load 横向载荷，横向负荷

~ manoeuvrability 横向操纵性

~ plane area 横向平面区域，横向平面面积

~ plate 侧板

~ resistance 横向阻力，侧向阻力

~ response 侧向干扰运动,侧向运动频率特性

~ section 横截面

~ transfer 横向迁移

~ vibration 横向振动，侧向振动

~ view 侧面图，侧面图

latex ['leiteks] *n*. 乳胶，橡胶，乳液，乳汁

lathe [leið] *n*. 车床，机床；*v*. 用车床加工

~ bench 车床工作台

~ carriage 车床托板，车床刀架

~ tool 车刀

latitude ['lætitju:d] *n*. 纬度，界限，范围，地区，活动范围

latitudinal [ˌlæti'tju:dinl] *a*. 纬度的，纬度方向的

latter ['lætə] *a*. 后者的，近来的，后面的，较后的

lattice ['lætis] *n*. 晶格，格子，点阵，栅格，格构，格架；*v*. 使成格子状

launch [lɔ:ntʃ] *n*. 下水，汽艇，发射，发行，投放市场；*v*. (使)下水，投掷，发射，开办，发动，发起，开始，起飞，投入

~ and recovery system 下水与收回系统

~ azimuth 发射方位(角)

~ date 下水日期

launcher ['lɔ:ntʃə] n. 发射器，发射台，发射者，运载火箭

launching ['lɔ:ntʃiŋ] n. 发射，下水；v. (launch 的 ing 形式) (使)下水，投掷，发射，开办，发动，发起，开始，起飞，投入

~ appliance or arrangement 下水装置或布置

~ bowsing tackle 下水收系滑轮，下水收拉滑轮

~ ceremony 下水仪式，下水典礼

~ gear 放艇装置，下水装置

~ of caisson 沉箱下水

~ ramp length 下水滑轨长度

~ release system 下水施放系统

~ station 下水平台，下水站，发射站

~ time 下水时间，发射时间

~ ways 下水滑道

laundry ['lɔ:ndri] n. 洗衣房，洗衣店，要洗的衣服，洗熨，洗好的衣服

laundryman ['lɔ:ndrimən] n. 洗衣工 ‖ washman 男洗衣工

lavatory ['lævə,təri] n. 厕所，抽水马桶，洗脸盆，浴室

law [lɔ:] n. 法律，诉讼，法学，法治，司法界，规律，规则，惯例；v. 起诉，控告

~ of electromagnetic induction 电磁感应定律(法拉第定律)

~ of gravity 万有引力定律

~ of the PRC on the Prevention and Control of Environmental Pollution by Solid Waste 中华人民共和国固体废物污染环境防治法

lawful ['lɔ:fəl] a. 合法的，法定的，法律许可的，受自然规律支配的

lawfully ['lɔfəli] ad. 合法地，守法地

lay [lei] n. 位置，层面，形势，短叙事诗；v. ① 放置，铺设，产(卵)，提出，平息，布置 ② (lie 的过去式) 展现，展开，位于，平放，摆放，存在，内含，处于…状态，延伸，躺，说谎；a. 世俗的，外行的，没有经验的

~ back 使向后，放回，送回

~ days 装卸货日数，停泊日数，出港迟延日数

~ down 放下，放弃

~ off 解雇，停止工作，休息，划出

~ open 摊开，揭露

~ out 布置，安排，摆开，展示，投资

~ to 把…归(功、罪)于，努力干，打

~ up dry 干法敷层，干敷层

~ up wet 湿法保存

lay-up 休息，停止，暂时停用，修船

laycan ['leikən] n. 受载期限，销约期

layday ['leidei] n. 装卸天数，停泊天数

layer ['leiə] n. 层，层次，阶层，深度；v. 形成层次，分成层次

~ structure 层状结构，层状组织，层状构造

~ thickness 层厚度

layout ['lei,aut] n. 规划，设计，编排，版面，配线，企划，设计图案，布局图，版面设计

~ adjustment 布局调整

~ board (模样)设计板，伸图板，放样板

~ efficiency 布局效率

~ for drilling 钻孔划线

~ file 布局文件

~ of the ship 船舶布置

laytime ['leitaim] n. 装卸时间，装卸期间

LBP (length between perpendiculars) 两

柱间长，垂线间距

LCC (large crude oil carrier) 大型油轮，大型油船

LCD (liquid crystal display) 液晶显示(器)
  ~ monitor 液晶监视器
  ~ screen 液晶屏幕

LCP (local control panel) 现场控制盘，局部控制盘，就地控制屏

LDC (line drop compensation) 线路电压降补偿

LDC (line drop compensator) 线路电压降补偿器

LDC (London Dumping Convention, Convention on the Prevention of Marine Pollution by Dumping of Wastes and Other Matter) 防止倾倒废物及其他物质污染海洋的公约，伦敦倾废公约

LDC (lower dead center) 下止点，下死点 ‖ *Syn*. BDC (bottom dead center) 下止点，下死点

leach [li:tʃ] *n*. 过滤，过滤器，过滤剂；*v*. 过滤，滤去，溶解，萃取

lead [li:d] *n*. 领导，领先，导线，铅，(自船上测海水深度的)铅锤，石墨，铅笔芯；*v*. 领导，引导，致使，通向，导致，用水砣测深
  ~ accumulator 铅蓄电池
  ~ acid battery 铅酸蓄电池
  ~ air compressor (两台空压机运行时的)领机
  ~ alkali metal alloy 铅碱金属合金
  ~ frame 引线框，(双列直插式)焊接框架，铅框架
  ~ free 无铅的
  ~ powder primer 铅粉底漆
  ~ prediction 提前量预测
  ~ rail 导轨，合拢轨
  ~ rod 铅棒，铅条
  ~ sheet 铅片
  ~ tube 铅管
  ~ wire 铅丝，导线，引线，引出线
  ~ wire compensator 导线(影响)补偿器

leading ['li:diŋ] *n*. 领导，铅框，行距；*v*. (lead 的 ing 形式) 领导，引导，致使，通向，导致，用水砣测深；*a*. 领导的，指导的，第一位的，最主要的，主要的
  ~ block 导滑车，导向滑车，导块
  ~ edge 翼或螺旋桨之前缘，最先着风之帆缘
  ~ phase operation 进相运行
  ~ pile 导桩，定位桩
  ~ power factor 超前功率因数

leaf [li:f] *n*. 页，一张，叶子
  ~ blade 叶片
  ~ clarifier 叶片澄清器
  ~ switch 叶片开关

leak [li:k] *n*. 漏洞，漏出，漏出物，泄漏，撒尿；*v*. 漏，泄漏，使渗漏
  ~ detection 检漏，密闭性检查
  ~ detection lamp 泄漏检测灯
  ~ drainage 渗漏排水
  ~ finding 检漏
  ~ test 泄漏测试，泄漏试验，泄漏检测
  ~ tester 检漏器

leak-off 漏气，漏水
  ~ connection 引漏接头
  ~ pipe 引漏管线，泄流管
  ~ pressure 裂开压力
  ~ steam 漏泄的蒸汽
  ~ valve 放泄阀

leak-proof 防漏的，密封的

~ cover 防漏罩

~ device 防漏装置

~ fit 气密配合

~ function 防滴漏功能

~ fuel tank 防漏的燃油柜,防漏的燃料储器

~ quality 密封性

~ tank 密闭容器

~ treatment 防渗治理

leakage ['li:kidʒ] *n.* 漏,泄漏,渗漏,渗漏物,漏出量

~ current 泄漏电流

~ flux 漏通量

~ loss 漏泄损失,漏失,漏气损失,漏电损失

~ protection switch 漏电保护开关

~ relay 漏电继电器,接地继电器

leaky ['li:ki] *a.* 漏的,有漏洞的

lean [li:n] *n.* 倾斜,倾斜度,倚靠,倾向; *v.* 倚靠,倾斜,依赖,倾向,偏向,使倾斜; *a.* 贫乏的,歉收的,瘦的

~ point 倾斜点,倾点

leather ['leðə] *n.* 皮革,皮革制品; *v.* 用皮革包盖,鞭打,抽打; *a.* 皮的,皮革制的

~ cloak 仿皮革

~ gloves 皮手套

~ jacket 皮夹克

~ measuring tape 皮卷尺

~ tool bag 皮工具袋

leaves [li:vz] *n.* (leaf 的复数) 页,张,叶子

~ thickness gauge 分叶测厚仪,分叶厚度规

LED (light emitting diode) 发光二极管

ledge [ledʒ] *n.* 暗礁,壁架,架状突出物,矿层

lee [li:] *n.* 庇荫,保护,庇护所,背风处; *a.* 避风的,背风的,下风的,保护的

~ side 下风舷

leeward ['li:wəd] *n.* 背风面,下风面,下风; *a.* 顺风的,下风的,在下风方向的; *ad.* 向下风

~ side 背风侧,背风面

~ tidal current 顺风潮流

leeway ['li:wei] *n.* 风压差,偏航,风压角,可允许的误差,退路,落后,回旋余地

left [left] *n.* 左,左边,左派; *v.* (leave 的过去式和过去分词) 离开,动身,剩下,遗忘,遗弃,委托,出发,动身; *a.* 左边的,左倾的,左侧的,左派的,左翼的; *ad.* 在左面

~ alone 不干涉,不管,放开

~ arrow 左箭头键

~ and right 左右

~ bank 左岸

~ border 左侧边框

~ fork 叉车,铲车

~ hand 左手,左侧

~ hand engine 左旋发动机

~ hand rotation 左旋

~ hand rule 左手定则

~ hand side 左手边

~ hand threed 左螺纹

~ hand thread tap 左旋螺纹丝锥

~ over 剩余,留下,遗留

~ side 左侧

~ side spin 左侧旋

~ turn 左旋

left-handed 左手的,左旋的,笨拙的

~ propeller 左旋螺旋桨,左旋进桨

leftward ['leftwəd] *a.* 在左方的，在左侧的；*ad.* 在左方，在左侧
~ heeling 左倾
legal ['li:gəl] *a.* 法律的，合法的，法定的，依照法律的
~ basis 法律根据，法律依据
~ counsel 法律顾问
~ man 法人
~ obligation 法律义务
~ protection 法律保护
~ provision 法律条文，法律规定
~ rights 法定权利
~ valuation 法定评价
legally ['li:gəli] *ad.* 合法地，法律上
legend ['ledʒənd] *n.* 传奇，说明，图例，铭文
~ of symbols 常用符号表
legibility [,ledʒə'biləti] *n.* 易读性，易辨认，易理解
legible ['ledʒəbl] *a.* 清晰的，易读的，易辨认的
legislate ['ledʒis,leit] *v.* 立法，制定法律，通过立法
legislation [,ledʒis'leiʃən] *n.* 立法，法律的制定，法律的通过
LEL (lower explosive limit) 爆炸下限
length [leŋθ] *n.* 长度，长，时间长短，音长 ‖ depth 深度；height 高度；width 宽度
~ between perpendiculars (LBP) 两柱间长，垂线间距
~ curve 长曲线
~ cutting 纵切
~ of service 服务年限
~ of wave 波长
~ on waterline 吃水线长

~ overall (LOA) 总长，全长
~ wise direction 纵向
lengthen ['leŋθən] *v.* (使)延长，(使)变长，加长
lengthways ['leŋθweiz] (=lengthwise) *a.* 纵长的，纵向的；*ad.* 纵长地，纵向地
lengthwise ['leŋθwaiz] (=lengthways) *a.* 纵长的，纵向的；*ad.* 纵长地，纵向地
lessen ['lesn] *v.* 使小，变小，减少，减轻
letter ['letə] *n.* 信，字母，文字，证书，文学，学问，字面意义；*v.* 用字母标明，刻字，题字，写印刷体字母
~ of intent 意向书，合同草约
levee ['levi] *n.* 防洪堤，大堤，码头；*v.* 筑防洪堤于
level ['lev(ə)l] *n.* 水平，水平面，水准，标准，级别；*v.* 使水平，使同等，夷平，瞄准，对准，变平，拉平；*a.* 同高的，平坦的，齐平的，水平的
~ controller 液面控制器，电平控制器
~ shift 电平转换
~ gauge 水准仪，水准器，液面计，水位计
~ gauging system 液位测量系统
~ guidance force 水平导向力
~ indicating device 液位指示装置 ‖ *Syn.* level indicator 液位指示器
~ luffing 水平变幅
~ measurement 液位测量，水平测量
~ probe 液位探头
~ switch 电平开关，箱位电平转换
~ transmitter 液面传感器，液位变送器，液位传感器，物位变送器
~ trier 水准检定器
leveler ['levələ] *n.* 水平测量员，轧平机，平等主义者

leveling ['levəliŋ] *n.* 水平测量，水准测量，平整；均匀化；*v.* (level 的 ing 形式) 使水平，使同等，夷平，瞄准，对准，变平，拉平
~ block 水平校正块
~ bulb 水准球管

lever ['li:və] *n.* 杆，杠杆，控制杆；*v.* 用杠杆撬动，抬起
~ for luffing and slewing 变幅和回转杠杆

LF (low frequency) 低频率，低频
~ filter 低频滤波器

LFL (lower flammable limit) 可燃下限

liability [,laiə'biliti] *n.* 责任，义务，倾向，可能性，不利因素，债务

liable ['laiəbl] *a.* 有责任的，有义务的，易于…的，有…倾向的，负有责任的，很有可能的
~ to accident 易于发生事故

liberate ['libəreit] *v.* 解放，释放，释出

licence ['laisəns] *n.* 许可证，执照，特许；*v.* 许可，特许，认可，发给执照

lid [lid] *n.* 盖子，眼睑，限制；*v.* 盖盖子

lie [lai] *n.* 谎言，状态，位置，栖息处，隐藏处；*v.* 展现，展开，位于，平放，摆放，存在，内含，处于…状态，延伸，躺，说谎
~ on 依赖，取决于 ‖ ***Syn***. build on 基于，建立于，寄希望于；build upon 基于，建立于，寄希望于；count on 依靠，指望；depend on 依赖，依靠，取决于；depend upon 依赖，依靠，取决于；reckon on 指望，依赖；rely on 依赖，依靠

life [laif] *n.* 寿命，生命，一生，生命力，生活，传记
~ buoy 救生圈，救生衣
~ cycle 生活周期
~ equipment 救生设备
~ jacket 救生衣 ‖ ***Syn***. life vest 救生衣；floatation jacket 救生衣
~ jacket light 救生衣灯
~ line 救生索，(潜水员的)信号绳，升降索，重要的交通线(通讯联络线)，命脉
~ line throwing appliance 救生抛绳设备
~ net 救生网
~ pack 救生袋
~ preserver 救生用具
~ saving 救生
~ saving apparatus 救生设备 ‖ ***Syn***. life saving appliance (LSA) 救生设备；life saving arrangement 救生设备
~ Saving Certificate (LSC) 拯溺证书
~ saving channel 救生通道
~ saving device 救生器材
~ saving reel 救生绳圈
~ saving signals 救生信号
~ saving station 救生站
~ saving surgery 救生手术
~ slide 救生滑梯
~ sliding pole 救生滑杆
~ support system 生命保障系统
~ throwing appliance 救生抛投器

lifebelt ['laifbelt] *n.* 救生圈，救生带
lifeboat ['laifbəut] *n.* 救生艇
~ accident 救生艇事故
~ deck 救生艇甲板
~ drill 救生艇训练
~ equipment 救生艇装备
~ station 救生艇站，救生站

~ stern 救生艇艉,尖形艇艉
~ (rescue boat) to be done lowering and hoisting test 救生(助)艇收放试验
~ winch 救生艇绞车

lifeboatman ['laif,bəutmən] *n.* 救生艇人员

liferaft ['laifræft] *n.* 救生筏

lifesaver ['laifseivə] *n.* 救生者,水难救生员,济急的人

lift [lift] *n.* 电梯,举起,起重机,搭车; *v.* 升高,提升,升起,举起,抬起,空运,鼓舞,消散,耸立 ‖ *Syn.* enhance 加强,提高,增加; heighten 提高,升高; hoist 升起,吊起; increase 增加,加大; improve 提高,增进; raise 升起,提高; upgrade 升级,提升
~ fan 升力风扇 ‖ *Syn.* hover fan 升力风扇
~ off 起飞,升空,发射
~ offset 提升偏移
~ out 举起,提升
~ trunk 升降机通道

lift-away 升空,起吊
~ hatch cover 起吊舱口盖

lift-on-lift-off (Lo-Lo) 运输装在货柜中之货物的,货柜运输的,吊上吊下的
~ barge carrier 吊装式载驳船
~ container ship 吊装式全集装箱船
~ vessel 吊上吊下船,细胞式货柜船

lifter ['liftə] *n.* 升降机,举起的人,举重运动员,小偷
~ guide pin 浮升导料销
~ pin 升降销
~ roller 挺杆滚轮

lifting ['liftiŋ] *n.* 举起,起重,提高,上升; *v.* (lift 的 ing 形式) 升高,提升,升起,举起,抬起,空运,鼓舞,消散,耸立
~ appliance 升降设备,提升装置
~ bag 提升袋
~ beam (安装机座用的)起重横梁,起重天平
~ chain 起重链,吊链,起重链条,起升链
~ eye 吊耳,吊眼
~ force 起重力,提升力
~ frame 吊运架
~ gearing 提升机构,起落机构
~ height 上升高度
~ jack 千斤顶,举重机,起重器
~ time 上升时间

light [lait] *n.* 光,光线,光源,灯,信号灯,指引,打火机,领悟,浅色,天窗,黎明,破晓,信息,说明,眼光,角度,视力,榜样,典范; *v.* 点燃,照亮,点着,变亮; *a.* 轻的,浅色的,明亮的,轻松的,容易的,清淡的; *ad.* 轻地,清楚地,轻便地
~ bulb 电灯泡
~ color 灯光颜色,灯色
~ component 轻质组分,轻组分
~ concentration 低浓度
~ displacement 空载排水量
~ draught 轻载吃水,空船吃水 ‖ *Syn.* light load draft 空载吃水
~ drilling boom 轻型钻臂
~ emitting 发光
~ emitting area 发光面积
~ emitting diode (LED) 发光二极管
~ load 空载,轻载
~ load period 轻载期间,轻负荷期间
~ obscuration 不透光度
~ obscuration smoke detection 减光型

349

感烟火灾探测

~ oil 轻油

~ oil distillate 轻油馏分

~ ship 空载船

~ ship condition 空载状态

~ source 光源

~ switch 照明开关

~ triggered thyristor (LTT) 光控晶闸管，光触发晶闸管

~ up 点燃

~ weight 空船重量

~ weight diving 轻潜水

lighten ['laitn] v. 减轻，变轻，(使)轻松，(使)发亮，闪光，打闪，闪电

lightening ['laitniŋ] n. 发光；v. (lighten 的 ing 形式) 减轻，变轻，(使)轻松，(使)发亮，闪光，打闪，闪电

~ hole 发光孔，减重孔，点火孔

lighter ['laitə] n. 驳船，打火机，点火者；v. 驳运

~ aboard ship (LASH) 载驳轮船，载驳货船

lighterage ['laitəridʒ] n. 驳运费，驳运

lightest ['laitst] (light 的最高级) a. 最轻的，最浅的；ad. 最轻地，最清楚地

~ seagoing condition 最低开航条件

lighthouse ['laithaus] n. 灯塔

lighting ['laitiŋ] n. 照明，照明设备，舞台灯光，点火；v. (light 的 ing 形式) 点燃，照亮，点着，变亮

~ distribution box 照明配电箱

~ feeder panel 照明馈电线控制板

~ fitting 装灯配件，照明配件

~ fixture and signal 照明器材和信号

~ load 照明负载，电光负载

~ network 照明网络

~ protective earthing 照明保护接地

~ pylon 照明塔

~ transformer 照明变压器

~ tube 荧光管，灯管

~ voltage 照明电压

lightly ['laitli] ad. 轻轻地，轻松地，容易地，不费力地

lightning ['laitniŋ] n. 闪电；v. 打闪，释放光火花；a. 闪电似的，闪电的，极快的

~ arrester 避雷器 ‖ **Syn**. lightning protector 避雷器

~ arresting 防雷措施

~ impulse insulation 闪电脉冲绝缘

~ proof 防雷的

~ proof transformer 避雷变压器

~ protection 避雷(装置)，防雷法

~ protection grounding 防雷接地

~ protection grounding code 防雷接地规范

~ rod 避雷针

~ shielding 雷电屏蔽，避雷，防雷

~ shielding design 避雷设计，防雷设计

~ stroke 雷击

lightship ['laitʃip] n. 灯塔船，灯标船，灯船

lightweight ['laitweit] n. 轻量级，轻量级选手，无足轻重的人；a. 重量轻的，平均重量以下的，不重的，不重要的，没有影响力的

lignum ['lignəm] n. 木材

~ vitae 愈疮木

~ vitae bearing 层压胶木轴承

like [laik] n. 同样的人(或物)，喜好，爱好；v. 喜欢，希望，愿意；a. 同样的，相似的；ad. 可能；prep. 像，如同

~ so 同样的，相似的
likelihood ['laiklihud] n. 可能性，可能
likely ['laikli] a. 很可能的，合适的，可靠的，有希望的；ad. 很可能；或许
likewise ['laik,waiz] ad. 同样地，照样地，又，也
limb [lim] n. 肢，臂，分支，枝干，典型物，(四分仪等的)分度弧或圆圈；v. 肢解
limber ['limbə] n. (拖炮车的)前车；v. 使柔软，变得柔软；a. 可塑的，柔软的，有弹性的
  ~ hole 排污水孔
lime [laim] n. 石灰，酸橙，绿黄色；v. 撒石灰于
limit ['limit] n. 限制，限度，界线，极限值，界点；v. 限制，限定，规定，指定
  ~ cycle 极限环，极限周值
  ~ gauge 极限量规，限制量计
  ~ load 极限载荷
  ~ position 极限位置
  ~ pressure protection 限压保护
  ~ range 极限范围
  ~ value 极限值，边界值，极值
  ~ switch 限位开关，极限开关
limited ['limitid] n. 高级快车；v. (limit 的过去式和过去分词) 限制,限定,规定,指定；a. 有限的，有限制的，狭窄的，缺乏创见的
  ~ capacity 有限容量
  ~ characteristic 限制特性
  ~ quantity 限量，有限数量
  ~ range 有限范围
  ~ visibility diving 低能见度潜水
limiter ['limitə] n. 限制器，限幅器，限制物，限制者

limiting ['limitiŋ] v. (limit 的 ing 形式) 限制，限定，规定，指定；a. 限制的，加以限定的
  ~ current 极限电流，限制电流
  ~ draft mark 极限吃水标志
  ~ drawing ratio 极限拉延比，极限拉延程度
  ~ margin 限幅边际
  ~ pin 限制销
linchpin ['lintʃpin] n. 关键，关键人物，关键事物，制轮，制轮楔
line [lain] n. 路线，航线，排，索，绳；v. 排成一行，排队，顺…排列，划线于，使有线条，使起皱纹
  ~ conductor 导线
  ~ contactor 线路接触器
  ~ diagram 单线图，线路图
  ~ drop compensation (LDC) 线路电压降补偿
  ~ drop compensator (LDC) 线路电压降补偿器
  ~ fishing boat 钓鱼船，钓船
  ~ fittings 线路配件
  ~ input 线路输入，行输入
  ~ loss 线路损耗
  ~ regulation 线路调整率
  ~ shaft 动力轴，主传动轴，总轴，中间轴，总轴系
  ~ sharting 直接启动
  ~ sheet 限额表
  ~ side 线路侧，线路端
  ~ throwing gun 抛绳枪
  ~ type fire detector 线型火灾探测器
  ~ type heat detector 线型感温探测器
  ~ type smoke detector 线型感烟探测器
  ~ voltage 线电压

line-of-sight 视线，视距
~ communication 视距通信
~ contact 视线接触
~ coverage 视距范围

line-to-neutral 线与中性点间的，线到中性点间的

linear ['liniə] *a*. 线的，线条的，直线的，线性的，长度的，用线条勾画出外形的 ‖ ***Ant***. nonlinear 非直线的，非线性的
~ angle encoder 线性角编码器
~ circuit 线性电路，线性网络
~ combination 线性组合
~ commutation 直线性换向
~ eccentricity 偏心律，偏心距
~ equation 线性方程
~ filter 线性滤波器
~ map 线性映射，线性变换
~ motion 直线运动
~ motion valve 直行程阀
~ range 线性范围
~ reciprocating motion 直线往复运动

linearity [ˌlini'æriti] *n*. 线性，线性度，直线性 ‖ ***Ant***. nonlinearity 非线性
~ error 线性误差

linearization [ˌliniərai'zeiʃən] *n*. 线性化，直线化

linearize ['liniəˌraiz] *v*. 使线性化，使具有线状

linearly ['liniəli] *ad*. 成直线地，线性地，在线上地

liner ['lainə] *n*. 班轮，班机，衬垫，画线者
~ conference 班轮公会
~ service 班轮业务，班轮运输
~ trade 班轮运输

~ wear rate 缸套磨损率

lines [lainz] *n*. (line 的复数) 路线，航线，排，索，绳
~ plan (船)型线图

link [liŋk] *n*. 连杆，环，环节，链环，纽带，连接，连结物，链接，关联，关系；*v*. 连接，联结，联合，结合，挽着
~ line equipment 联络中继设备
~ span 连接架
~ speed 线速度(链传动)

linkage ['liŋkidʒ] *n*. 连接，结合，联结，联动装置，碰撞，匝链，关联原则

liquefiable ['likwifaiəbl] *a*. 液化的，可溶解的

liquefied ['likwifaid] *v*. (liquefy 的过去式和过去分词) (使)溶解，(使)液化；*a*. 液化的
~ gas carrier 液化气船，液化气运输船
~ propane gas tanker 液化丙烷运输船
~ natural gas (LNG) 液化天然气
~ natural gas carrier 液化天然气船 ‖ ***Syn***. liquefied natural gas tanker 液化天然气船
~ natural gas containment system 液化天然气密封系统
~ petroleum gas (LPG) 液化石油气
~ petroleum gas carrier 液化石油气船 ‖ ***Syn***. liquefied petroleum gas tanker 液化石油气船

liquefier ['likwiˌfaiə] *n*. 液化器，液化器操作工

liquefy ['likwifai] *v*. (使)溶解，(使)液化

liquid ['likwid] *n*. 液体，流体，流音；*a*. 液体的，清澈的，明亮的，流动的，易变的

~ abrasion cleaning 喷湿砂清洗
~ alkaline cleaner 碱性液态清洁剂
~ bulk cargo carrier 液体散货船
~ cargo 液体货物
~ cargo pump 液货泵
~ cargo ship 液货船 ‖ *Syn*. liquid cargo tanker 液货船
~ cargo space 液体货舱
~ chemical tanker 液体化学品船,液体化学品运输船
~ chemical wastes 液体化学废料,液态化学废料
~ column 液柱
~ column gauge 液柱压力计
~ cooling equipment 液体冷却设备,液体冷却装备
~ crystal 液晶
~ crystal display (LCD) 液晶显示(器)
~ crystal display monitor 液晶监视器
~ crystal display screen 液晶屏幕
~ distributor 布液管,液体分配头
~ fuel 液体燃料,液态燃料
~ hammer 液击,液锤
~ head 液压头
~ impact 液击
~ in glass thermometer 液体温度计,玻璃充液温度计
~ in metal thermometer 金属管充液温度计
~ indicator 液位计,液面计
~ level 液面,液位
~ level control 液面控制,液位控制,液位调节
~ level indicator 液面仪,液位计
~ level relay 液位继电器
~ level sensor 液面传感器

~ limit 液限,流限
~ limit curve 液体界限,液态极限曲线
~ lubricant 液体润滑剂,流体润滑剂
~ noxious substance 液体有毒物质,液体有害物质
~ phase 液相
~ phase chromatography 液相色谱(法)
~ pump 液泵
~ pump recirculation 液泵供液
~ quantity meter 液体流量计
~ receiver 贮液器
~ refrigerant flooding back 制冷剂回液
~ seal 液封
~ separator 液体分离器
~ state 液态
~ suction heat exchanger 液体吸气换热器
~ thermometer 液体温度计,液体温度表,液温计
~ transfer operations 液体驳送操作
~ trap 集液器,疏液器,液体分离器,液阱
~ vacuum gauge 液位真空表
~ viscometer 液体黏度计

liquor ['likə] *n*. 液体,酒精饮料,烧酒,汁,溶液; *v*. 浸水,喝酒

list [list] *n*. 目录,名单,列表,序列,数据清单,明细表,条纹; *v*. 列出,列于表上,记入名单内,装布条
~ pump 横倾平衡泵 ‖ *Syn*. heeling pump 横倾平衡泵 ‖ trim (ming) pump 纵倾平衡泵
~ range 数据区域

liter ['li:tə] *n*. 升,公升

lithium ['liθiəm] *n*. 锂
~ bromide water absorption refrigerating

plant 溴化锂吸收式制冷装置
　　~ bronze 锂青铜
litmus ['litməs] *n*. 石蕊
live [liv] *v*. 活着，生活，居住，过着，度过，经历，实行，留在记忆中；*a*. 带电的，充电的，天然的，活的，热门的，生动的，精力充沛的，实况转播的，点燃的；*ad*. 以实况地
　　~ cable test cap 电缆在加压测试时用的终端接头
　　~ line 带电线路，活线
　　~ line measurement 带电测量
　　~ part 有压部分，有电部件，有电零件，常电部分
　　~ circuit breaker 带电断路器
livestock ['laivstɔk] *n*. 牲畜，家畜
　　~ carrier 牲畜运输船，牲畜运输车
living ['liviŋ] *n*. 生活，生计，生存空间，居住面积；*v*. (live 的 ing 形式) 活着，生活，居住，过着，度过，经历，实行，留在记忆中；*a*. 活的，起作用的，逼真的，现存的
　　~ accommodation ventilation 居住舱通风
　　~ allowance 生活津贴
　　~ aquatic resources 水生生物资源
　　~ and utility spaces 居住与公用舱室
　　~ conditions 生活条件，居住状况
　　~ resources 生活资源，生物资源
　　~ room 客厅，起居室
Lloyd [lɔid] *n*. 劳埃德(男子名)
Lloyd's 劳埃德的
　　~ Register of Shipping (LR) 英国劳埃德船级社，英国劳氏船级社
　　~ Rules 劳埃德规范
LNG (liquefied natural gas) 液化天然气

　　~ carrier 液化天然气船 ‖ *Syn*. LNG tanker 液化天然气船
　　~ containment system 液化天然气密封系统
LO (lube oil, lubricating oil, lubrication oil) 润滑油，滑油
　　~ batch purification 润滑油定期净化
　　~ by pass purification 滑油连续净化
　　~ circulation 润滑油环流
　　~ consumption 润滑油消耗(量)
　　~ container 润滑油容器
　　~ cooler 润滑油冷却器
　　~ dilution 润滑油稀释，机油稀释
　　~ distillation 润滑油蒸馏
　　~ drain tank 润滑油泄油柜，润滑油循环柜
　　~ drainage tank 润滑油放残柜，污滑油柜
　　~ evaporation loss 润滑油蒸发损失
　　~ filling main 润滑油注入总管
　　~ filter 润滑油过滤器
　　~ header 机油集流管
　　~ manifold 润滑油总管
　　~ preheater 润滑油预热器
　　~ pressure 润滑油压力
　　~ pump 滑油泵，机油泵
　　~ separator 机油分离器，润滑剂分离器
　　~ shifting pump 润滑油输送泵 ‖ *Syn*. LO transfer pump 润滑油输送泵
　　~ sludge 润滑油淤渣
　　~ starting pump 起动机油泵
　　~ strainer 润滑油滤器
　　~ sump 润滑油油槽，滑油池，滑油集油池
　　~ tank 润滑油柜
Lo-Lo (lift-on-lift-off) 运输装在货柜中

之货物的，货柜运输的，吊上吊下
~ barge carrier 吊装式载驳船
~ container ship 吊装式全集装箱船
~ vessel 吊上吊下船，细胞式货柜船
LOA (length overall) 总长，全长
load [ləud] *n*. 负荷，重担，装载量，工作量，负载，加载；*v*. 装载，装填，装货，装弹药，装料，使担负
~ absorption 承载能力
~ and performance test for main generator (emergency generator) 主发电机(应急发电机)负荷及特性试验
~ balancing 负载平衡
~ bearing 承载，承重
~ bearing capacity 负荷能力，载重能力
~ bearing face 承压面
~ calculation table 负荷计算表
~ capacitance 负载电容
~ capacity 负载能力，载重能力
~ cell 测压元件
~ characteristic 负荷特性，负载特性，负载特性曲线
~ characteristic test 负荷特性试验
~ circulation 循环负荷
~ commutation 负载换流，负载换相
~ compensating 载荷补偿，负载力补偿
~ conditions 负荷状态，负荷条件
~ control unit 负荷控制装置
~ control valve 负载控制阀
~ current 负载电流
~ cutting off 负载切断
~ cycle 负荷循环
~ distribution 载荷分布，负载分配
~ distribution indicator 货油分布指示器
~ disturbance 负荷扰动，负载扰动

~ duration factor 负载持续率
~ governor 负荷调节器，负荷控制器
~ indicator 负荷指示器
~ limit setting 负载限制设置
~ limitation 负荷极限，载荷极限
~ line (船舶的)载重线
~ line mark 载重线标志，满载吃水标线
~ loss 负载损耗
~ on top (LOT) 装于上部法，顶装法
~ rate 单位载荷，荷载率
~ rating 额定负载，额定负荷 ‖ *Syn*. nominal load 标称负载，标称负荷，额定负载，额定负荷；rated load 额定负载，额定负荷
~ ratio adjuster 有载电压调整装置
~ regulation 负载调整率，负载调节
~ segment 输入段，装入段
~ sharing 均分负载，负载分配
~ speed 负荷速度，负荷转速
~ spread 荷载分布
~ switch 负载开关
~ test 负载测试，负荷试验，负载试验
~ test for shaft generator and its function test on sea trial 轴带发电机负荷试验和航行时效用试验
~ test to be carried out 要进行的负载测试
~ transfer 负荷转移
~ trial to be carried out 要进行的负载试验
~ up 装载货物
~ waterplane 载重水线面
~ with 装载某物
load-down 降负荷
~ program 减负荷程序，减载程序，减载方案

load-shedding 用电限制，电力平均分配
load-up 加载，加负荷
~ program 加载程序，加载方案
loaded ['ləudid] v. (load 的过去式和过去分词) 装载，装填，装货，装弹药，装料，使担负；a. 负重的，装满东西(或人)的，装填子弹的，摆满食品的，富有的，有含意的，意味深长的，陶醉的
~ draught 满载吃水，重载吃水，满负载时的下沉量
~ filter 反滤层
loader ['ləudə] n. 装货人，装卸工，装货设备，装卸机，装弹机
loading ['ləudiŋ] n. 装载，装填；v. (load 的 ing 形式) 装载，装填，装货，装弹药，装料，使担负
~ and unloading 装卸工作
~ arm 装卸臂，装载装备
~ back 负载反馈法
~ capacity 载荷能力，负荷容量，充填容量，萃取容量，离子交换容量，吸附容量
~ certificate 装货证明书，装载证书，加载证书
~ chamber 加料室
~ computer 装载计算机
~ condition 荷载条件，负载条件，装载情况
~ crane 装料吊车
~ device 装料器，装载装置，装载设备
~ dock 码头，装货码头
~ instrument 配载仪，装载仪
~ lever 装载杠杆
~ machine 装料机，带载机组
~ manual 装载手册

~ performance 负荷特性，承载性能，受力性能
~ rate 承载率
~ resistor 负荷电阻，镇流电阻
~ sheet 装料板
~ sharing characteristics 加载共享特征
~ system 载带系统，装载设备，加感制
~ test 荷载试验，载重试验，带负荷试验
~ test of accommodation ladder (pilot ladder) 舷梯(引水员梯)压重试验
~ time 装填持续时间，装载时间
lobe ['ləub] n. 圆形突出部，圆裂片，叶
~ rotary pump 凸叶转子泵
local ['ləukəl] n. 局部，当地居民，地方分支，本地新闻，慢车；a. 局部的，地方的，当地的，乡土的 ‖ Ant. remote 远方的，远程的
~ application extinguishing system 局部应用灭火系统
~ area network (LAN) 局域网
~ control 机旁控制，就地控制，本机控制，局部控制
~ control panel (LCP) 现场控制盘，局部控制盘，就地控制屏
~ control terminal 局部控制终端
~ equilibrium 局部平衡
~ lighting fitting 局部灯，局部照明灯
~ lighting transformer 局部照明变压器
~ operating conditions 局部工作情况，就地工作条件
~ ring 局部环
~ run-stop-remote starting selector switch 本地运行停机远程启动选择器开关
~ settings 机旁设置，本地设置 ‖ Ant.

remote settings 远程设置
~ stress 局部应力
~ variation 局部变动
locality [ləu'kæliti] *n.* 所在，位置，地点
localize ['ləukəlaiz] *v.* 局限，(使)局部化，(使)地方化，停留在一地方
localized ['ləukəlaizd] *v.* (localize 的过去式和过去分词) 局限,(使)局部化,(使)地方化，停留在一地方；*a.* 局部的，地区的，小范围的
~ corrosion 局部腐蚀
locally ['ləukəli] *ad.* 在地方上，在本地，局部地
locate ['ləukeit] *v.* 查找地点，找出，定位，(使)位于，确定，设置，住下来
located ['ləukeitid] *v.* (locate 的过去式和过去分词) 查找地点，定位，(使)位于，确定，找出，设置，住下来；*a.* 处于，位于，坐落的
~ block 定位块
~ pin 定位销
location [ləu'keiʃən] *n.* 定位，地点，位置，场所，特定区域，外景拍摄场地
~ accuracy 定位精度，定位准确度
~ button 现场点选择按钮
locator [ləu'keitə] *n.* 定位器，探测器
loch [lɔk] *n.* (狭长的)海湾，湖
lock [lɔk] *n.* 锁，水闸，船闸，枪机；*v.* 锁上，锁住，关好，固定，追踪，锁定，握住，纠缠，装上水闸，穿过水道的水闸，拘禁
~ nut 锁紧螺帽，锁紧螺母，防松螺母
~ nut bearing 锁紧螺帽座
lockage ['lɔkidʒ] *n.* 通过船闸，船闸系统，水闸通行税，水闸的构筑，水位高度
locked [lɔkt] *v.* (lock 的过去式和过去分词) 锁上，锁住，关好，固定，追踪，锁定，握住，纠缠，装上水闸，穿过水道的水闸，拘禁；*a.* 锁定的，上锁的，不灵活的，下定决心
~ nut 夹紧螺母
~ rotor 止转转子，锁定转子
~ rotor torque 制动转子力矩，静态力矩
locker ['lɔkə] *n.* 上锁的人，有锁的橱柜，冷藏间，锁扣装置，有锁的存物柜
locking ['lɔkiŋ] *n.* 锁闭，锁紧；*v.* (lock 的 ing 形式) 锁上，锁住，关好，固定，追踪，锁定，握住，纠缠，装上水闸，穿过水道的水闸，拘禁
~ bar 锁闭杆，锁簧杆，锁条，锁尺
~ coil 保持线圈
~ nut 锁紧螺帽
~ pawl 制动爪
~ pin 锁定销
~ plate 防松板，锁片，防松板，锁紧木片
~ pliers 大力钳
~ ring 锁紧环
~ segment 锁闭片
~ spring 锁紧弹簧，锁簧
~ time 锁定时间，锁闭时间
~ tooth 锁闭齿
~ washer 锁紧垫圈，防松垫圈
~ wire 锁线，锁紧用钢丝
lockout ['lɔkaut] *n.* 停工，闭厂
locksmith ['lɔksmiθ] *n.* 钳工，修锁工，锁匠
locus ['ləukəs] *n.* 轨迹，地点，所在地
loft [lɔft] *n.* 阁楼；顶楼；*v.* 展示(船的外壳等)详细尺寸的图纸，储藏于，推入

高弧线，高高地升到空中

~ floor 放样台，打样台

log [lɔg] *n.* 航行日志，航海记录，飞行日志，日志，测程器，原木；*v.* 记入航行日志，记录，行进，度过，积累，伐木，锯成段 ‖ *Syn*. logbook 航海日志，航空日志，飞行日志

~ apparatus 计程仪

~ book 航海日志，记录簿，值班日记

~ carrier 运木船

~ in 登录，输入指令开始 ‖ *Syn*. log on 登录，输入指令开始

~ off 注销，输入指令结束 ‖ *Syn*. log out 注销，输入指令结束

~ raft 木排，木筏

~ record 航海日志记录

logarithm ['lɔgəriθm] *n.* 对数

logarithmic [ˌlɔgə'riθmik] *a.* 对数的

~ decrement 对数衰减，对数减量

logbook ['lɔgbuk] *n.* 航海日志，航空日志，飞行日志 ‖ *Syn*. log 航行日志，航海记录，飞行日志

logging ['lɔgiŋ] *n.* 记录，伐木工作，伐木搬运业；*v.* (log 的 ing 形式) 记入航行日志，记录，行进，度过，积累，伐木，锯成段

~ data 存入数据

logic ['lɔdʒik] *n.* 逻辑，逻辑学，逻辑性

~ algebra 逻辑代数

~ board 逻辑插件，逻辑板

~ circuit 逻辑电路

~ component 逻辑元件，逻辑构件，逻辑组件

~ control 逻辑控制

~ design 逻辑设计

~ design automation 逻辑设计自动化

~ diagram 逻辑图，逻辑框图

~ operation 逻辑运算

~ order 逻辑指令

~ simulation 逻辑仿真，逻辑模拟

~ unit 逻辑单元，逻辑运算器，逻辑装置，逻辑部件

logical ['lɔdʒikəl] *a.* 逻辑的，逻辑上的，逻辑学的，合乎逻辑的

~ operation 逻辑操作，逻辑运算

~ valve 逻辑阀

long [lɔŋ] *n.* 长时间，长音节，长尺寸，长裤；*v.* 渴望，热望；*a.* 长的，长期的，做多头的，高的；*ad.* 长期地，始终

~ focus 长焦距

~ forecastle 长艏楼，长首楼

~ glass 航海望远镜，长性玻璃

~ handle wire brush 长柄钢丝刷

~ nose pliers 尖嘴钳

~ nozzle oil can 长嘴油壶

~ range 远程，长期，长远

~ range ship 远程船舶，长航程船

~ residue 常压渣油

~ round nose combination pliers 胶柄尖嘴钳

~ rubber boots 长筒胶靴

~ stroke 长冲程

~ stroke cylinder 长行程汽缸

~ stroke diesel engine 长冲程柴油机

~ stroke engine 长冲程发动机

~ stroke piston 长行程活塞

~ stroke pump 长冲程泵

~ stroke pumping unit 长冲程抽油机

~ stroke steam engine 长冲程蒸汽机

~ term charter 长期租船

~ term drift 长期漂移

~ time delay 长延时

longitude ['lɔndʒitju:d] n. 经度，经线

longitudinal [ˌlɔndʒi'tju:dinl] a. 纵向的，纵长的，纵的，经度的，纵观的 ‖ *Ant.* transverse 横向的，横断的

~ bending 纵向弯曲

~ coefficient 棱形系数，纵向系数 ‖ *Syn.* prismatic coefficient 棱形系数，棱柱系数

~ differential protection 纵联差动保护(装置)

~ equilibrium coefficient 纵向平衡系数

~ force 纵向力

~ frame 纵向构架

~ frame system 纵肋系统，纵骨架式

~ framed ship 纵向构架船

~ framing 纵向肋架，纵骨架式

~ hull girder strength 纵向船体梁强度

~ insulation 纵向绝缘

~ joint 纵结合，纵接头，纵焊缝，纵向接缝

~ section 纵剖面，纵断面

~ section plan 纵剖面图

~ separation 前后距离，纵向间隔

~ sequence 纵向焊接顺序

~ strength 纵向强度

~ vibration 纵向振动

~ vibration damper 轴向减振器，纵向减振器

longitudinally [ˌlɔndʒi'tju:dinəli] ad. 纵向地，纵长地，纵地，纵观地

~ framed system 纵骨架式结构

longline ['lɔŋlain] n. 多钩长线

longshore ['lɔŋʃɔ:(r)] a. 沿岸的，在海岸工作的

longshoreman ['lɔ:ŋʃɔ:mən] n. 港口工人，码头装卸工人

loop [lu:p] n. 环，回路，回线，循环，线圈，绳圈，弯曲部分，翻圈飞行；v. 使成环，以圈结，以环连结，打环，翻筋斗

~ current 回路电流

~ distribution system 环路配电系统

~ flow scavenging type engine 回流扫气式发动机

~ scavenge 回流扫气

~ scavenged cylinder 回流换气汽缸

~ scavenging 回流扫气，回流换气法

~ system 环形制，环形系统

~ table 转环台

loose [lu:s] n. 放纵，放任，发射，解放；v. 开船，释放，开枪，开火，变松；a. 宽松的，不精确的，不牢固的，散漫的，自由的；ad. 松散地

~ change gear 可互换变速齿轮，常啮齿轮

~ gear 可卸零部件

~ goods 散粒货物，零星货物

loosen ['lu:sn] v. 解开，放松，松开

loran ['lɔ:rən] n. 远距离无线电导航系统

lose [lu:z] v. 遗失，浪费，错过，输掉，丧失，使失去，使迷路，使沉溺于，受损失，失败

loss [lɔs] n. 损耗，损失，遗失，失败，输，浪费，错过，伤亡，降低 ‖ *Syn.* dissipation 损耗，浪费；wastage 损耗；wear 磨损

~ of load 负载损耗，失载，失荷，甩负荷

~ of moisture 水分损失，(冷藏)干耗(量)

~ of synchronization 失去同步

~ of time 立刻，马上

loss-free 无损耗的，无损失的，无损的，免损的 ‖ *Syn*. lossless 无损耗的，无损的 ‖ *Ant*. lossy 有损耗的，致损耗的
~ line 无损耗传输线，无损耗线
~ power 免损电源

lossless ['lɒsləs] *a*. 无损耗的，无损的 ‖ *Syn*. loss-free 无损耗的，无损的，免损的 ‖ *Ant*. lossy 有损耗的，致损耗的

lossy ['lɒsi] *a*. 有损耗的，致损耗的 ‖ *Ant*. loss-free 无损耗的，无损的，免损的；lossless 无损耗的，无损的

lost [lɒst] *v*. (lose 的过去式和过去分词) 遗失，浪费，错过，输，丧失，使失去，使迷路，使沉溺于，受损失，失败；*a*. 失去的，丧失的，错过的，迷惑的，不为人知的

lot [lɒt] *n*. 签，抽签，一堆，许多，命运，份额；*v*. 划分，抽签，抓阄
~ numbe 批号

LOT (load on top) 装于上部法，顶装法

lotus ['ləutəs] *n*. 莲属，荷花，莲花，睡莲
~ position 莲花坐

loud [laud] *a*. 大声的，高声的，不断的，喧吵的；*ad*. 大声地，高声地，响亮地
~ speaker 扩音器，扬声器，喇叭
~ speaking telephone 扬声电话机

lough [lɒk] *n*. 湖，海湾，入海口

lounge [laundʒ] *n*. 休闲室，闲逛，长沙发；*v*. 闲逛，懒洋洋地躺，虚度光阴

louver ['lu:və(r)] *n*. 百叶窗，天窗，散热孔

low [ləu] *n*. 低，低价，低点，牛叫声；*v*. 牛叫；*a*. 低的，浅的，卑贱的，粗俗的，消沉的；*ad*. 低下地，谦卑地，低声地，低价地

~ alloy steel 低合金钢
~ battery voltage 电池电压过低
~ boiling point 低沸点
~ carbon 低碳
~ carbon alloy 低碳合金
~ concentration 低浓度
~ concentration gas alarm 低浓度可燃气报警
~ consumed 低消耗的
~ cost 低成本
~ density 低密度
~ energy 低能量，低能
~ expansion 低膨胀
~ expansion foam 低倍数泡沫，低倍泡沫
~ expansion foam fire extinguishing system in machinery space 机舱低倍泡沫灭火系统
~ flammability 不易燃性
~ flash point cargo 低闪点货物
~ frequency (LF) 低频率，低频
~ frequency filter 低频滤波器
~ grade 低级的，低质量的
~ in 缺乏的，低的
~ incidence 小冲角，小攻角，小迎角
~ level alarm 低限报警器，低位报警器
~ loss transformer 低损耗变压器
~ loss power transformer 低损耗电力变压器
~ lubricating oil pressure trip device 低滑油压力脱扣装置
~ noise 低噪声，低噪音
~ oil pressure shutdowns 低油压故障停机
~ pass filter 低通滤波器 ‖ *Syn*. lowpass 低通滤波器

~ permeability 低渗透性，低渗透率
~ permeability alloy 低导磁率合金
~ power 低功率，小功率
~ power consumption 低功耗，低电耗
~ pressure (LP) 低气压，低压
~ pressure bearing oil temperature 低压轴承油温度
~ pressure bulb 低压灯泡
~ pressure compressor 低压压气机，低压压缩器
~ pressure contact port 低压出气孔
~ pressure cutout 低压断流器
~ pressure cutout switch 低压断路开关
~ pressure exhaust pipe 低压废气管
~ pressure gauge 低压计，低压压力表
~ pressure hose 低压软管
~ pressure lubricating system 低压润滑系统
~ pressure receiver 低压贮液筒，低压贮液器
~ pressure safety cutout 低压安全切断器
~ pressure steam generator 低压蒸气产生器，低压蒸气发生器
~ pressure steam generator feed (water) pump 低压蒸气发生器给水泵
~ pressure tube 低压管
~ quality 低劣质量
~ resistance 低阻力，低电阻
~ resistance alloy 低电阻合金，低变形抗力合金
~ speed 低速，慢速
~ speed diesel engine 低速柴油机，低速柴油发动机
~ speed high torque oil motor 低速高扭矩油马达
~ temperature (LT) 低温

~ temperature corrosion 低温腐蚀
~ tension (LT) 低电压，低压 ‖ **Syn.** low voltage (LV) 低电压，低压
~ tide 低潮，低落期
~ viscosity 低黏度
~ voltage distribution board 低压配电盘
~ voltage fuse link 低压保险丝
~ voltage lamp 低压灯
~ voltage locking 低压锁定
~ voltage protection 低电压保护(装置)，欠压保护
~ voltage relay 低压继电器
~ voltage release circuit 低电压释放电路
~ water level alarm 低水位警报器
~ water level cut-off device 低水位保险装置
~ water pressure trip 低水压脱扣

lower ['ləuə] *n*. 威胁，阴沉，或生气的样子，不祥之兆；*v*. 降低，跌落，减弱，放下，降下，减弱，贬低，变少，缩小；*a*. (low 的比较级) 较低的，下级的，下等的，下游的

~ berth 下铺 ‖ **Syn.** lower bunk 下铺
~ bound 下界
~ boundary 下边界
~ cable 下索
~ calorific value 低发热量，低热量值
~ dead center (LDC) 下止点，下死点 ‖ **Syn.** bottom dead center (BDC) 下止点，下死点
~ deck 下甲板
~ explosive limit (LEL) 爆炸下限
~ flammable limit (LFL) 可燃下限
~ header 下水室，下水箱
~ layer 底层
~ limit 下限

~ sail 降帆

~ sliding plate 下滑块板

~ surface 下表面,底面

~ tank 下水箱,车底水箱

~ tween deck 下二层舱

~ water cut-out 低水断流器

lowering ['ləuəriŋ] v. (lower 的 ing 形式) 降低,跌落,减弱,放下,降下,减弱,贬低,变少,缩小;a. 低劣的,昏暗的,减少体力的

~ and hoisting test for life boat 救生艇收放试验

~ and hoisting test of accommodation ladder (pilot ladder) 舷梯(引水员梯)和绞车收放试验

~ main contactor 下降主接触器

~ test and tension test of anchor 锚投掷试验和拉力试验

lowest ['ləuist] ad. (low 的最高级) 最低的,最底下的,最小的

~ continuous speed with load 最低稳定工作转速

~ critical value 最小临界值

~ working water level 最低工作水位

lowpass ['ləupa:s] n. 低通滤波器 ‖ *Syn.* low pass filter 低通滤波器

LP (low pressure) 低气压,低压

~ bearing oil temperature 低压轴承油温度

~ bulb 低压灯泡

~ compressor 低压压气机,低压压缩器

~ contact port 低压出气孔

~ cutout 低压断流器

~ cutout switch 低压断路开关

~ exhaust pipe 低压废气管

~ gauge 低压计,低压压力表

~ hose 低压软管

~ lubricating system 低压润滑系统

~ receiver 低压贮液筒,低压贮液器

~ safety cutout 低压安全切断器

~ steam generator 低压蒸气产生器,低压蒸汽发生器

~ steam generator feed (water) pump 低压蒸汽发生器给水泵

~ tube 低压管

LPG (liquefied petroleum gas) 液化石油气

~ carrier 液化石油气船 ‖ *Syn.* LPG tanker 液化石油气船

LR (Lloyd's Register of Shipping) 英国劳埃德船级社,英国劳氏船级社

LSA (life saving appliance) 救生设备 ‖ *Syn.* life saving apparatus 救生设备;life saving arrangement 救生设备

~ Code (International Life saving Appliance Code) 国际救生设备规则

LSIC (large scale integrated circuit) 大规模集成电路

LT (low temperature) 低温

~ corrosion 低温腐蚀

LT (low tension) 低电压,低压 ‖ *Syn.* low voltage (LV) 低电压,低压

LTT (light triggered thyristor) 光控晶闸管,光触发晶闸管

lubber ['lʌbə] n. 不熟练的海员,笨人;a. 粗笨的,笨拙的

~ line 航向标线,罗盘准线,基准线,准线

lube [lu:b] n. (=lubrication) 润滑,润滑油,润滑剂

~ oil (LO) 润滑油,滑油 ‖ *Syn.* lube 润滑油,润滑剂;lubricant 滑润剂

lubricating oil (LO) 润滑油，滑油；
lubrication oil (LO) 润滑油，滑油
~ oil batch purification 润滑油定期净化
~ oil by pass purification 滑油连续净化
~ oil circulation 润滑油环流
~ oil consumption 润滑油消耗(量)
~ oil container 润滑油容器
~ oil cooler 润滑油冷却器
~ oil dilution 润滑油稀释，机油稀释
~ oil distillation 润滑油蒸馏
~ oil drain tank 润滑油泄油柜，润滑油循环柜
~ oil drainage tank 润滑油放残柜，污滑油柜
~ oil evaporation loss 润滑油蒸发损失
~ oil filling main 润滑油注入总管
~ oil filter 润滑油过滤器
~ oil header 机油集流管
~ oil manifold 润滑油总管
~ oil preheater 润滑油预热器
~ oil pressure 润滑油压力
~ oil pump 滑油泵，机油泵
~ oil separator 机油分离器，润滑剂分离器
~ oil shifting pump 润滑油输送泵 ‖ *Syn*. lube oil transfer pump 润滑油输送泵
~ oil sludge 润滑油淤渣
~ oil starting pump 起动机油泵
~ oil strainer 润滑油滤器
~ oil sump 润滑油油槽，滑油池，滑油集油池
~ oil tank 润滑油柜

lubricant ['lu:brikənt] *n.* 润滑剂，润滑油，能减少摩擦的东西，调解人；*a.* 润滑的 ‖ *Syn*. lube 润滑油，润滑剂；lube oil (LO) 润滑油，滑油；lubricating oil (LO) 润滑油，滑油；lubrication oil (LO) 润滑油，滑油
~ separator 机油分离器，润滑剂分离器

lubricate ['lu:brikeit] *v.* 润滑，加润滑油，加润滑剂

lubricating ['lu:brikeitiŋ] *v.* (lubricate 的 ing 形式) 润滑，加润滑油，加润滑剂；*a.* 润滑的
~ film 润滑油膜
~ nipple 润滑喷嘴，润滑油枪
~ oil (LO) 润滑油，滑油 ‖ *Syn*. lube 润滑油，润滑剂；lube oil (LO) 润滑油，滑油；lubricant 润滑剂；lubrication oil (LO) 润滑油，滑油
~ oil batch purification 润滑油定期净化
~ oil by pass purification 滑油连续净化
~ oil circulation 润滑油环流
~ oil consumption 润滑油消耗(量)
~ oil container 润滑油容器
~ oil cooler 润滑油冷却器
~ oil dilution 润滑油稀释，机油稀释
~ oil distillation 润滑油蒸馏
~ oil drain tank 润滑油泄油柜，润滑油循环柜
~ oil drainage tank 润滑油放残柜，污滑油柜
~ oil evaporation loss 润滑油蒸发损失
~ oil filling main 润滑油注入总管
~ oil filter 润滑油过滤器
~ oil header 机油集流管
~ oil manifold 润滑油总管
~ oil preheater 润滑油预热器
~ oil pressure 润滑油压力
~ oil pump 滑油泵，机油泵

~ oil separator 机油分离器，润滑剂分离器

~ oil shifting pump 润滑油输送泵 ‖ *Syn*. lubricating oil transfer pump 润滑油输送泵

~ oil sludge 润滑油淤渣

~ oil starting pump 起动机油泵

~ oil strainer 润滑油滤器

~ oil sump 润滑油油槽，滑油池，滑油集油池

~ oil tank 润滑油柜

~ stud 注油塞

~ system 润滑系统

~ value 润滑值

lubrication [ˌluːbriˈkeiʃən] *n*. (=lube) 润滑，润滑油，润滑剂

~ oil (LO) 润滑油，滑油 ‖ *Syn*. lube 润滑油,润滑剂; lube oil (LO) 润滑油,滑油; lubricant 润润剂; lubricating oil (LO) 润滑油，滑油

~ oil batch purification 润滑油定期净化

~ oil by pass purification 滑油连续净化

~ oil circulation 润滑油环流

~ oil consumption 润滑油消耗(量)

~ oil container 润滑油容器

~ oil cooler 润滑油冷却器

~ oil dilution 润滑油稀释，机油稀释

~ oil distillation 润滑油蒸馏

~ oil drain tank 润滑油泄油柜，润滑油循环柜

~ oil drainage tank 润滑油放残柜，污滑油柜

~ oil evaporation loss 润滑油蒸发损失

~ oil filling main 润滑油注入总管

~ oil filter 润滑油过滤器

~ oil header 机油集流管

~ oil manifold 润滑油总管

~ oil preheater 润滑油预热器

~ oil pressure 润滑油压力

~ oil pump 滑油泵，机油泵

~ oil separator 机油分离器，润滑剂分离器

~ oil shifting pump 润滑油输送泵 ‖ *Syn*. lubrication oil transfer pump 润滑油输送泵

~ oil sludge 润滑油淤渣

~ oil starting pump 起动机油泵

~ oil strainer 润滑油滤器

~ oil sump 润滑油油槽，滑油池，滑油集油池

~ oil tank 润滑油柜

~ system 润滑系统，润滑系，润滑方式

lubricator [ˈljuːbrikeitə] *n*. 润滑器，润滑物，注油器，加油者

luff [lʌf] *n*. 抢风行驶，纵帆前缘; *v*. 转舵，抢风行船，抢风驶帆，无风张帆，升降

~ angle 上下摆动角

~ line 帆前缘索

~ tackle 纵帆滑车，三倍复滑车

~ rope 桅前缘索

~ to 转向迎风

~ up 船侧受风而行

luffing [ˈlʌfiŋ] *n*. 俯仰运动，上下摆动，起重机臂的转动; *v*. (luff 的 ing 形式) 转舵，抢风行船，抢风驶帆，无风张帆，升降

~ and slewing type crane 能变幅及旋转的起重机

~ arm type davit 倒臂型艇架

~ boom 升降起重臂

~ cableway mast 倾斜式缆道桅杆

~ crane 动臂起重机，俯仰式起重机，水平起重机，旋臂起重机

~ davit 俯仰式吊艇杆，俯仰式吊艇柱

~ derrick 俯仰式吊杆，俯仰式吊货杆

~ device or hoist device 俯仰装置

~ gear 摆动装置吊杆，倾角调节器，吊杆倾角调节装置

~ jib crane 俯仰摇臂式起重机，俯仰旋臂起重机

~ mechanism 变幅机构

~ motor 吊杆俯仰电动机

~ winch motor 俯仰式起重机电动机

~ speed 全程变幅时间，变幅速度

~ test 变幅试验

~ winch 俯仰式起重机，变幅绞车

~ winch motor 俯仰式起重机电动机

lug [lʌg] n. 支托，接线片，耳状物；v. 拖拉

~ down method 加载减速法

~ flange 耳形凸缘

luggage ['lʌgidʒ] n. 行李，皮箱

~ room 行李间，行李舱

~ shelf 行李搁架

lumber ['lʌmbə] n. 木材，废物，无用的杂物，隆隆声；v. 砍伐，乱堆，笨重地行进

~ cargo ship 木材船

~ carrier 木材运输船

~ freeboard 载木干舷

lung [lʌŋ] n. 呼吸器，肺，肺脏

lux [lʌks] n. 勒克斯(照明单位)

LV (low voltage) 低电压，低压 ‖ *Syn*. LT (low tension) 低电压，低压

~ distribution board 低压配电盘

~ fuse link 低压保险丝

~ lamp 低压灯

~ locking 低压锁定

~ protection 低电压保护(装置)，欠压保护

~ relay 低压继电器

~ release circuit 低电压释放电路

lynchpin ['lintʃpin] n. 关键

M

macerate ['mæsəreit] v. 软化分离，浸软，浸化

macerater [mæsə'reitə:] n. 粉碎机，切碎机，浸渍者，纸浆制造机 ‖ *Syn*. crusher 粉碎机，轧碎机；grinder 研磨机，粉碎机；pulverizer 粉碎机；shredder 切菜器，撕碎机

~ pump 粉碎泵

machine [mə'ʃi:n] n. 机械，机器，机构，机动车辆，机械般工作的人，领导集团，核心组织；v. 机器制造，机器加工，车床加工 ‖ *Syn*. apparatus 器械，设备，仪器；appliance 用具，器具；arrangement 布置；assembly 组装部件；device 装置，设备；equipment 装备，设备，器材，装置；facility 设备，工具；furniture 设备，家具；gear 设备，装备；installation 设备，装置；machinery 机械(总称)，机器；mechanism 机器，机械装置，机构；plant 设备；provision 装备，供应品；turnout 装备，设备；unit 装置，设备

~ center 机械中心，加工中心

~ control system 机械控制系统

~ drawing 机械制图，工程画，机械图纸

~ frame 机架，曳引机架，机框

~ to definite size 车至规定尺寸
~ to order 车至订货要求，车至所需要求
~ to round 加工成圆形，车成圆形
~ tool 机床
~ welding 机械焊接
~ welding torch 机械焊接吹管
~ with double air-circuit contra-flow cooling 双空气回路逆流冷却机

machine-turned 车削的

machinery [mə'ʃi:nəri] n. 机器(总称)，机械，系统，方法，工具，机关，团体，机构，组织 ‖ *Syn*. apparatus 器械，设备，仪器；appliance 用具，器具；arrangement 布置；assembly 组装部件；device 装置，设备；equipment 装备，设备，器材，装置；facility 设备，工具；furniture 设备，家具；gear 设备，装备；installation 装置；mechanism 机器，机械装置，机构；machine 机器，机械，机构；plant 设备；provision 装备，供应品；turnout 装备，设备；unit 装置，设备
~ arrangement 机舱设备布置，机舱布置，机械布置
~ control room (MCR) 机械控制室，设备控制室
~ equipment 机械设备，机器设备
~ installation repair 机械安装修理
~ overhaul 机械大修
~ parts 机械部件，机械零件
~ room 机舱 ‖ *Syn*. engine room 机舱；machinery space 机舱
~ space of category A A类机舱
~ space opening 机舱开口
~ space operation 机舱操作
~ space ventilation 机舱通风
~ specification 机械设备说明书

machining [mə'ʃi:niŋ] n. 制造，加工；v. (machine 的 ing 形式) 机器制造，机器加工，车床加工
~ accuracy 加工精度
~ allowance 机械加工余量
~ center 加工中心
~ conditions 加工条件，切削条件
~ symbol 机械加工符号

made [meid] v. (make 的过去式和过去分词) 制造，安排，使成为，认为，产生，获得，进行，构成，开始，前进，增大；a. 已制成的，人工制造的，成功的，虚构的
~ to order 定制的

magazine [,mægə'zi:n] n. 杂志，期刊，军火库，弹药库，弹仓，胶卷盒

magenta [mə'dʒentə] n. 红紫色，品红色，洋红色；a. 紫红色的，品红色的，洋红色的

magnaflux ['mægnəfluks] n. 磁粉探伤，寻求金属表面和内表面缺陷的磁性方法
~ testing 磁力探伤法，磁力线检验

magnesium [mæg'ni:zjəm] n. 镁
~ alloy 镁合金

magnet ['mægnit] n. 磁铁，磁体，磁石
~ gantry crane 电磁门式起重机
~ steel 磁钢，磁性钢
~ wire 磁线，线圈线

magnetic [mæg'netik] a. 地磁的，有磁性的，有吸引力的
~ circle 磁圈
~ circuit 磁路
~ compass 磁罗盘，磁罗经

~ compass pilot 磁罗经自动操舵装置，磁罗经自动驾驶仪
~ contactor 磁接触器
~ control mechanism 磁驱动机构
~ disk 磁盘，磁碟 ‖ *Syn*. diskette 磁盘，磁碟
~ double coil 双铁芯线圈
~ field 磁场
~ field coil 磁场线圈
~ field treatment 磁场处理，磁处理
~ flux 磁通量
~ flux density 磁通量密度，磁通密度
~ force 磁力
~ inclination 磁倾角，磁倾
~ induction 磁感应
~ induction intensity 磁感应强度
~ inductivity 导磁率，磁感应率
~ interference 磁场干扰
~ intensity 磁化强度
~ material 磁性材料
~ motive force (MMF) 磁通势，磁动势 ‖ *Syn*. magnetomotive force (MMF) 磁通势，磁动势
~ needle 磁针
~ particle 磁粉，磁性粒子，磁性颗粒 ‖ *Syn*. magnetic powder 磁粉
~ particle test 磁粉试验，磁粉探伤
~ pole 磁极
~ refrigeration 磁制冷
~ refrigerator 磁制冷机
~ resistance 磁阻
~ shielding 磁屏蔽
~ starter 磁力启动器
~ starter combination 磁力启动器组合
~ steel 磁钢
~ susceptibility 磁化率
~ switch 磁开关
~ tape 磁带
~ tool 磁性工具，磁化刀具
~ torque 磁矩，磁转矩
~ trip 电磁脱扣器

magnetism ['mægnitizəm] *n*. 磁，磁性，磁力，磁学，吸引力

magnetize ['mægnitaiz] *v*. (使)磁化，受磁，吸引，诱惑，影响

magnetizing ['mægnitaiz] *n*. 磁化；*v*. (magnetize 的 ing 形式)(使)磁化，受磁，吸引，诱惑，影响
~ current 起磁电流，磁化电流
~ exciter 励磁器
~ current 磁化电流
~ solenoid 磁化螺线管
~ velocity 磁化速度

magneto [mæg'ni:təu] *n*. 磁发电机
~ alternator 永磁式交流发电机
~ hydrodynamic propulsion apparatus 磁流体动力推进装置
~ ohmmeter 永磁电阻表，摇表

magneto-electric 磁电的
~ generator 磁电发电机，永磁发电机

magnetoelastic [mæg'ni:təui'læstik] *a*. 磁致弹性的，磁弹性的
~ weighing cell 磁弹性式称重传感器

magnetomotive [mægni:təu'məutiv] *a*. 磁势的
~ force (MMF) 磁通势，磁动势 ‖ *Syn*. magnetic motive force (MMF) 磁通势，磁动势

magnetoresistive [mæg,ni:təuri'zistiv] *a*. 磁阻的
~ compass 磁罗盘
~ effect 磁阻效应

magnetron ['mægnitrɔn] *n.* 磁电管

magnify ['mægnifai] *v.* 放大，扩大，赞美，夸大，夸张

magnifying ['mægnifaiiŋ] *v.* (magnify 的 ing 形式) 放大，扩大，赞美，夸大，夸张；*a.* 放大的

~ glass 放大镜，放大器

magnitude ['mægnitju:d] *n.* 大小，数量，巨大，广大，量级

~ frequency characteristic 幅度频率特性，幅频特性

~ margin 幅值裕度

~ of a voltage fluctuation 电压波动量

~ phase characteristic 幅度相位特性，幅相特性

~ portion 尾数部分

~ scale factor 幅值比例尺，幅度比例尺

~ versus phase plot 幅相曲线，幅相图

maiden ['meidn] *n.* 少女，处女；*a.* 未婚的，纯洁的，处女的，无经验的

~ voyage 初航，首航，处女航

mail [meil] *n.* 邮件，邮政，盔甲；*v.* 邮寄，投邮

~ liner 邮船，邮轮 ‖ *Syn.* mail ship 邮船，邮轮

mailing ['meiliŋ] *n.* 邮寄，邮件，农场租金；*v.* (mail 的 ing 形式) 邮寄，投邮

~ list 邮寄名单，发送文件清单

main [mein] *n.* 和主桅有关的，在主桅附近的，主要管道，主要部分，体力，力量，大陆，要点，主群组，干线；*v.* 主要的，重要的，全力的

~ and transfer busbar 单母线带旁路

~ bearing 主轴承

~ bearing cap 主轴承盖

~ bearing holding down bolt 主轴承撑杆螺栓 ‖ *Syn.* main bearing stay bolt 主轴承撑杆螺栓

~ bearing knock 主轴承敲击声(由于间隙过大而引起)

~ bearing of underslung type 倒挂式主轴承

~ bearing shell 主轴瓦

~ bearing stud 主轴承柱螺栓

~ board 主体，机身，主要部分

~ body 主体，主要部分，主船体，机身

~ boiler 主锅炉

~ bus bar 主母线

~ cable 主缆，主干电缆

~ cargo oil line 货油总管，货油主管 ‖ *Syn.* cargo oil transfer main pipe line 货油输送总管

~ circuit 主电路，主回路，主磁路

~ circuit breaker 主断路器，干线用断路器

~ combustion chamber 主燃烧室

~ component 主要成分 ‖ *Syn.* main constituent 主要成分

~ condenser circulating pump 主冷凝器循环泵

~ connecting rod 主连杆

~ content 主要内容

~ control room 主控制室

~ deck 主甲板，正甲板

~ drive 主传动，主传动装置

~ drive gear 主(传)动齿轮

~ electric power source 主电源,总电源

~ electric power supply fuse 总电源保险丝

~ engine (ME) 主机，主发动机

~ engine driven alternator 主机驱动的

交流发电机
~ engine fault emergency maneuver 主机故障应急操纵
~ engine lubricating oil system 主机润滑油系统
~ engine remote control panel 主机遥控屏，主机远程控制屏
~ engine telegraph 主车钟，主机传令钟
~ engine turbo-blower 主机涡轮鼓风机
~ exciter 主励磁机
~ feature 主要特征，主要特点
~ feed pump 主给水泵
~ feeder cable 主馈电电缆
~ fleet 主力舰队
~ force 主力，主力军
~ frame 主肋骨，主体，主框架，主机
~ generating set 主发电机组
~ generating station 主发电站
~ generator 主发电机
~ idea 主要意思，主要思想，主要理念，主旨
~ impeller 主推叶轮
~ inlet control valve 主调节阀，主进气控制阀
~ insulation 主绝缘
~ journal 主轴颈
~ magnetic field 主磁场
~ magnetic pole 主磁极
~ manifold 主歧管
~ memory 主存，主存储器
~ motion 主运动 ‖ *Syn*. main movement 主运动
~ muffler 主消声器
~ oil pump 主油泵
~ part 主要部分，主件
~ power circuit 主电路

~ power supply 主电源
~ procedure 主过程
~ program 主程序
~ propelling shafting 主推进轴系
~ propulsion motor 主推进电动机
~ propulsion motor switchboard 主推进电动机控制板
~ propulsion plant 主推进装置
~ propulsion power 主推进动力(装置)
~ protection 主保护(装置)
~ pump 主泵
~ purpose 主要目的
~ reason 主要原因
~ route distribution system 主要路线分布系统
~ routine 主程序
~ shaft 主轴，总轴
~ shaft driven feed pump 轴带给水泵，由主机减速齿轮轴系驱动的给水泵
~ shaft lube oil 主轴润滑油
~ shafting 主轴，主轴系
~ source of electrical power 主电源
~ starting valve 主起动阀
~ steam distributing header 主蒸汽分配联箱
~ steam range 蒸汽总管
~ steam stop valve 主蒸汽阀，主汽门
~ steam valve 主蒸汽阀
~ steering gear 主操舵装置
~ steering position 主操舵位置
~ stop valve 主停气阀
~ structure 主结构
~ switch 总开关，主开关
~ switchboard 总开关板，总控制板，主配电板，总交换台(电话)
~ valve 主阀，主阀盘

~ vertical zones 主垂直防火区
main-engine-driven 主机驱动的
　~ pump 主机驱动泵
mainframe ['meinfreim] *n.* 主机，大型机
mainly ['meinli] *a.* 大体上，大部分地，主要地，基本上
mainmast ['meinmɑ:st] *n.* 主桅
mains [meinz] *n.* (main 的复数) 电源，干线，输电干线 ‖ ***Syn.*** electric source 电源；electrical source 电源；power source 电源；power supply 电源
　~ input 电源输入(功率)
　~ unit 供电整流器
　~ voltage 电源电压
mainsail ['meinseil] *n.* 主帆，主桅帆
mainstay ['meinstei] *n.* 支柱，中流砥柱，主要依靠，主桅支索
maintain [men'tein] *v.* 维持，继续，维修，主张，供养
maintenance ['meintinəns] *n.* 维护，维修，保持，养护，生计，生活费用，非法干涉
　~ access 维修入口，维修通道
　~ and repair 保养与修理
　~ chemicals 保养化学剂
　~ control report (MCR) 维修管理报告
　~ man 维修员，维护员
　~ management 维修管理
　~ manual 维护手册，维修手册，保养手册
　~ margin 维修范围
　~ mode 维护模式
　~ of a reasonable speed 保持合理速度
　~ of class 保持船级
　~ room 保全室，维修室
　~ schedule 维修计划，保养安排，维护计划，维修图表
　~ service 维修业务，技术维护
　~ test 维护检测，维护试验
　~ time 维护时间，维修时间
　~ tracking 维护跟踪
　~ work 维修工作
major ['meidʒə] *n.* 成年人，专业，主修科目，主修课，少校；*v.* 主修；*a.* 主要的，重要的，卓越的，显著的，多的，大的，成年的，主修的，专攻的，大调的
　~ accident 重大事故，主要事故 ‖ ***Syn.*** major breakdown 大事故，重大阻断；major failure 严重失效，主要故障；serious accident 严重事故，重大事故，严重意外
　~ axis 长轴，主轴
　~ component 主要部件，主要元件
　~ diameter 大直径，外径，螺纹大径
　~ element 主要元素
　~ equipment 主要设备
　~ face 主面
　~ factor 主要因素
　~ failure of tanker 油轮的主要故障
　~ function 主要功能，强函数
　~ in 主修，专攻
　~ loop 主回路，大回路
　~ part 主要部分，重要部件，大部分，主要零件
　~ product 主要产品
　~ profile 主要剖面
　~ repair 大修
　~ ship 大型船舶
　~ subject 专业，主科
majority [mə'dʒɔriti] *n.* 多数,大半,成年,法定年龄

make [meik] *n.* 制造，构造，生产量，性格，形状，样式；*v.* 制造，构造，安排，使成为，认为，产生，获得，进行，构成，开始，前进，增大 ‖ *Syn.* build 建造，建筑，创立；construct 建造，构造，创立；erect 建造，建立，开创；form 形成，构成，塑造；put up 建造

~ a declaration to 做声明

~ and supply 制造和供应

~ clear 解释

~ dead 断开，切断

~ for 向前进，有助于，走向，有利于，倾向于，导致

~ headway 取得进展

~ it 好转，达到预定目标，及时抵达，走完路程

~ mistake 犯错

~ out 书写，填写，拼凑，进展，说明，设法应付，理解，辨认出，了解

~ repairs 修理

~ sense 有意义

~ smooth 弄平滑，除去障碍

~ smooth in way of fracture 平顺断裂部位

~ the scene 参与，露面

~ tight 密封，紧固，上紧

~ time 进行，抽空

~ up 弥补，补足，拼凑，虚构，缝制，整理，包装，和解，编辑，化妆

~ up valve 补给阀

~ use of 使用，利用

~ water 小便，漏水

makeup ['meikʌp] *n.* 补充，虚构，组成，结构，补考，体格，天性，化妆品

male [meil] *n.* 男子，雄性；*a.* 男的，雄的，男性，阳刚的，阳的，凸的 ‖ *Ant.* female 女性，女人，雌兽，女性的，女子的，妇女的，雌的，凹的，柔弱的

~ and female face 阴阳面，凸凹面

~ connector 阳螺纹接头，插头

~ contact 刀口触片，插头，插塞，插塞接点，闸刀

malfunction [mæl'fʌŋkʃən] *n.* 失灵，故障，功能障碍；*v.* 失灵，发生故障 ‖ *Ant.* function 功能，作用，运行，行使职责，起作用

~ log 故障日志

~ probability 误动作概率

man [mæn] *n.* 男人，人类，人，丈夫，雇工；*v.* 配备人手，操纵，就位，使振奋

~ hours 工作小时，工时

~ overboard (MOB) 落水人员，人员落水，人员落海

~ overboard boat 应急救生艇

~ overboard maneuver 救落水人员操纵

~ overboard prevention and recovery 人员落水的预防和救护，防止人员落水和重新登艇

~ overboard rescue boat 人员落水救生艇

~ overboard retrieval equipment 人员落水回收设备

~ overboard signal 人员落水信号

man-machine 人机 ‖ *Syn.* human-computer 人机；human-machine 人机

~ communication system 人机通信系统

~ conversation 人机对话

~ coordination 人机协调

~ interface 人机接口

man-made 人造的，人工的，人为的，合成的

~ interference 人为干扰

man-of-war 军舰，僧帽水母

MAN (德国)曼集团

~ engine 曼型柴油机

manpower ['mænpauə] n. 人力

manage ['mænidʒ] v. 处理，应付，管理，控制，操纵，维持，运用，设法，搞成，达成 ‖ *Syn*. deal with 应付，安排，处理；dispose of 处理，安排，解决；handle 处理；manipulate (巧妙地)处理，应付；treat with 处理，应付

management ['mænidʒmənt] n. 经营，管理，处理，操纵，驾驶，手段，管理人员，经营才能

~ function 管理功能，管理职能，管理机能

~ Information System (MIS) 管理信息系统

~ level 管理水平

~ measure 管理措施，管理办法

~ of fuels and lubricants 燃料与润滑油管理

~ review 管理评论，管理评审，管理审查

manager ['mænidʒə] n. 经理，管理人员，管理器，经营人，经纪人

mandate ['mændeit] n. (书面)命令，训令，要求，授权，托管地，代理契约，委任托管权；v. 托管，批准，授权

mandatory ['mændətəri] n. 受托者；a. 强制的，命令的，托管的，受委托的

~ insurance 强制保险

~ maximum requirements 强制性最高要求

~ minimum requirements 强制性最低要求

~ particulars 必须填报的细节

~ plan 指令性计划，强制性计划，指导性计划

~ provision 约束性条款

~ rule 强制性规则

maneuver [mə'nu:və] (=manoeuvre) n. 调遣，调动，部署，操纵，策略；v. 调动，演习，操纵，用策略，用计

maneuverability [mə,nu:vərə'biliti] n. 可操作性，机动性

maneuvering [mə'nu:vəriŋ] n. 调遣，调动，部署，操纵；v. (maneuver 的 ing 形式) 调动，演习，操纵，用策略，用计

~ apparatus 控制设备

~ capability 操纵能力，机动能力

~ condition 机动条件，机动工作状态

~ handle 操纵手柄 ‖ *Syn*. maneuvering lever 操纵手柄

~ handwheel 操纵手轮，倒正车手轮

~ light 操纵灯，操纵信号灯

~ motion of ship 船舶操纵运动

~ pattern 机动模式，操纵模式

~ platform 操纵台，指挥平台

~ ship 运转船

~ speed 机动速率

manganese [,mæŋgə'ni:z] n. 锰

~ bronze 锰青铜

manhole ['mæn,həul] n. 人孔，进人孔，检修孔，探孔，入孔

~ door 人孔门

manifest ['mænifest] n. 载货单，旅客名单；v. 显示，表明，证明，使显现；a. 明白的，明显的

manifestation [ˌmænifes'teiʃən] *n*. 表示,显示,表现

manifold ['mænifəuld] *n*. 多样性,复印件,多支管,歧管,总管; *v*. 复写,复印,增多,增加,使多样化; *a*. 十足的,多种的,繁多的,多方面的,同时操作的

manifolder ['mænifəuldə] *n*. 复写机,复印机

Manila [mə'nilə] *n*. 马尼拉(菲律宾首都)
~ Amendments to STCW Convention STCW 公约马尼拉修正案

manipulate [mə'nipjuleit] *v*. (熟练地)操作,使用,操纵,巧妙地处理,应付,利用,假造 ‖ *Syn*. deal with 应付,安排,处理; dispose of 处理,安排,解决; handle 处理; manage 处理,应付; treat with 处理,应付

manipulated [mə'nipjuleitid] *v*. (manipulate 的过去式和过去分词) (熟练地)操作,使用,操纵,巧妙地处理,利用,应付,假造; *a*. 被操作的,被操纵的
~ range 操纵范围
~ variable 操纵量

manipulation [mə,nipju'leiʃən] *n*. 处理,操作,(被)操纵

manipulator [mə'nipjuleitə] *n*. 操作者,操纵者,操纵器

manner ['mænə] *n*. 方式,方法,做法,态度,样子,举止,礼貌,规矩,风俗,习惯,惯例,生活方式

manoeuvrability [mənu:vrə'biliti] *n*. 机动性,可操纵性,适航性,灵活性
~ coefficient 操纵性系数
~ criteria 操纵性衡准

~ of the ship 船舶机动性
~ prediction 操纵性预报
~ standard 操纵性标准

manoeuvrable [mə'nu:vrəbl] *a*. 可调动的,可移动的,机动的,操纵灵活的,可演习的

manoeuvre [mə'nu:və] (=maneuvre) *n*. 调遣,调动,部署,操纵,策略; *v*. 调动,演习,操纵,用策略,用计
~ for man overboard 救助落水人员操纵

manoeuvring [mə'nu:vəriŋ] *n*. 调遣,调动,部署,操纵; *v*. (manoeuvre 的 ing 形式) 调动,演习,操纵,用策略,用计
~ console 操纵控制台
~ gear 操纵装置
~ information 操纵资料,操纵信息
~ parameter 操纵参数
~ safety 操纵安全
~ speed 操纵速度
~ stand 操纵站
~ standard 操纵标准
~ test 操纵试验 ‖ *Syn*. manoeuvring trial 操纵试验
~ time 操纵时间,机动时间
~ valve 操纵阀,调节阀

manometer [mə'nɔmitə] *n*. 压力计
~ pressure gauge 压力表
~ tube 压力管

manpower ['mænpauə] *n*. 人力,劳动力,人数,人手

manrope ['mænrəup] *n*. 舷梯扶索,扶手绳,安全索

mantle ['mæntl] *n*. 覆盖物,幕,披风,斗篷; *v*. 覆盖,披风

373

manual ['mænjuəl] *n.* 手册，指南，键盘，示范；*a.* 手的，手动的，手工的，体力的，手册的，实际占有的

~ arc welding 手工电弧焊，手工弧焊

~ auger 手摇钻机

~ control 人工控制，手控

~ control lever 操纵手柄

~ cutting 手工切割，人工裁切

~ data input 手动数据输入

~ defrost 手动除霜

~ degaussing 人工消磁

~ fire alarm call point 手动火灾报警按钮

~ fire alarm sounder 手动火灾警报器

~ frequency regulator 手动频率调节器

~ gas cutting 手工气割

~ install 手动安装

~ labor 体力劳动，体力活

~ mode 手控式，人工式

~ operating mechanism 手动操作机构

~ operation 手工操作，人工操作，人工控制

~ override system 人工越控装置

~ pump 手动泵 ‖ *Syn.* hand pump 手泵，手摇泵，手压泵，手力唧筒

~ recovery 手工恢复

~ regulation 手调，手控

~ starter 手动起动器

~ starter switch 手控起动开关

~ starting 手动起动

~ station 手动操作器

~ steering force 手操纵力，手动转向力

~ steering workstation 人工操舵室

~ system 手动系统，手工系统

~ tension mooring winch 手动张力绞缆机 ‖ automatic tension mooring winch 自动张力绞缆机

~ testing 人工测试

~ transmission 人力操纵传动

~ valve 手控阀

~ voltage regulator 手动电压调节器

~ welding 手工焊接

~ welding process 焊接工艺手册

~ work 体力劳动，手工作业

~ workers 体力劳动者

manually ['mænjuəli] *ad.* 用手地，手工地

~ controlled 人工控制的，手控的

~ operated 用手操作的，手动的

~ operated air compressor 手动空气压缩机

~ resettable fire detector 手动复位火灾探测器

manufacture [ˌmænjuˈfæktʃə] *n.* 制造，制造业，制成品，产品；*v.* 制造，加工，生产，捏造，虚构

manufacturer [ˌmænjuˈfæktʃərə] *n.* 制造商，制造厂，厂主，厂商

manufacturing [ˌmænjuˈfæktʃəriŋ] *n.* 制造业；*v.* (manufacture 的 ing 形式) 制造，加工，生产，捏造，虚构；*a.* 制造业的，制造的

~ Automation Protocol (MAP) 制造自动化协议

~ burden 制造费用

~ inspection 制造检验

~ process 制造过程，制造工艺

~ production 工业生产

map [mæp] *n.* 地图，示意图，天体图，对应关系，人脸；*v.* 绘制地图，绘制形态图，勘查，详细规划

~ out 计划

MAP (Manufacturing Automation Protocol)

制造自动化协议

mar [ma:] n. 污点，瑕疵，障碍，损伤，毁损；v. 毁坏，损坏，弄坏，弄糟，糟蹋，玷污

march [ma:tʃ] n. 行进，前进，行军，游行示威，进行曲；v. (使)行进，(使)前进，(使)行军，(使)进展，游行示威

margin ['ma:dʒin] n. 页边的空白，边缘，边界，极限，利润，差数，差额，富余；v. 加边于，界定，加旁注于

～ line 边缘线

～ of error 误差幅度

～ plate 缘板

marginal ['ma:dʒinəl] a. 边的，边缘的，毗连的，临界的，最低限度的，不重要的，少量的，边际效用的，旁注的

～ efficiency 边际效率

marina [mə'ri:nə] n. 码头，小艇船坞，小船停靠区，散步道

marine [mə'ri:n] n. 舰队，水兵，海军部，海运业；a. 海的，海产的，航海的，船舶的，海运的，海事的，海军陆战队的

～ abrasion 海蚀

～ accident 海上事故

～ accumulate battery 船用蓄电池 ‖ *Syn.* marine storage battery 船用蓄电池

～ air conditioning 船舶空调

～ auxiliary machinery 船舶辅机

～ batteries 船用蓄电池组

～ biological sewage treatment plant 海洋生物污水处理设备，海洋生物污水处理厂

～ boiler 船用锅炉

～ centrifugal separator 船用离心分离机

～ compressor 船用压缩机

～ coupling 船用联轴器

～ desalination plant 船用脱盐设备，船用海水淡化设备，船用海水淡化厂

～ diesel 船用发动机，船用柴油机

～ diesel engine 船用柴油机

～ diesel oil (MDO) 船用柴油

～ distiller 船用蒸馏器

～ ecology 海洋生态，海洋生态学

～ ecology protection 海洋生态保护

～ ecosystem 海洋生态系统

～ electric cooking range 船用电灶

～ electric power system 船舶电力系统

～ electrical apparatus 船舶电气设备 ‖ *Syn.* marine electrical equipment 船舶电气设备

～ electrical system and automation 船舶电气系统及自动化

～ emergency batteries 船用应急蓄电池组

～ engine 船用发动机，船用柴油机

～ engine room 船舶机舱

～ engineer 轮机工程师

～ engineering 轮机工程，海洋工程

～ Engineering Major 轮机工程专业，海洋工程专业

～ environment 海洋环境

～ Environment Division (MED) 海洋环境保护司

～ environment preservation 海洋环境保护

～ Environment Protection Committee (MEPC) 海洋环境保护委员会

～ environmental impact assessment 海洋环境影响评估

～ environmental monitoring 海洋环境监测

~ Environmental Protection Law of the People's Republic of China 中华人民共和国海洋环境保护法
~ environment quality 海洋环境质量
~ environmental quality assessment 海洋环境质量评估
~ environmental quality standards 海洋环境质量标准
~ evacuation system 海上撤离系统
~ evaporator 船用蒸馏器
~ fuel oil (MFO) 船用燃料油
~ fuel saving 船舶燃料节约
~ galvanometer 船用检流计
~ gas oil (MGO) 船用轻柴油
~ gas turbine 船用燃气涡轮
~ gear box 船用齿轮箱
~ guidance 海面导航
~ Industrial Organization (MIO) 海洋工业组织
~ inspector 海事检查员
~ installation 船舶装置
~ insurance 海上保险
~ kitchens waste disposal shredder 船用厨房垃圾粉碎机
~ lives 水产，海产
~ light 航海标志灯，航路标志灯
~ machinery insurance claim 船舶机械设备保险索赔
~ mammal 海洋哺乳动物
~ natural reserve 海洋自然保护区
~ navigation 航海导航
~ noise 海洋噪声
~ nuclear power plant 船舶核动力装置
~ organism 海洋生物
~ organism corrosion 海洋生物腐蚀（作用）

~ ozonizer 船用臭氧发生器
~ perils 海上危险，海上风险，海难
~ plant 海生植物
~ pollutant 海洋污染物
~ pollution 海洋污染
~ pollution from land based discharge 陆地排放引起的海洋污染
~ pollution from maritime transportation 海洋运输引起的海洋污染
~ pollution hazard 海洋污染危害
~ pollution monitoring 海洋污染监测
~ pollution prevention 海洋污染防治
~ power plant 船舶动力装置
~ power plant economy 船舶动力装置经济性
~ power plant maintainability 船舶动力装置可维护性
~ power plant maneuverability 船舶动力装置可操纵性，船舶动力装置机动性
~ power plant service reliability 船舶动力装置可靠性
~ product 海产，航海用具，水产品
~ propeller 船用螺旋桨
~ propulsion shafting 船舶推进轴系
~ pump 船用泵 ‖ *Syn*. ship's pump 船用泵
~ railway 船排
~ refrigerating plant 船舶制冷装置 ‖ *Syn*. marine refrigeration plant 船舶制冷装置
~ refrigeration 船舶制冷
~ resources 海洋资源
~ Safety Administration of PRC (China MSA) 中华人民共和国海事局
~ safety valve 船用安全阀

~ searchlight 船用探照灯
~ sediment 海底沉积物
~ shafting 船用轴系
~ starting batteries 船用启动蓄电池
~ steam boiler 船用蒸汽锅炉
~ steam engine 船舶蒸汽机
~ steam turbine 船用蒸汽轮机
~ store 船具，船具店
~ system 船舶系统 ‖ **Syn**. ship system 船舶系统
~ terminal 海运油库，航海站，水运枢纽
~ traffic 水上运输，水运
~ traffic engineering 水运工程
~ transformer 船用变压器
~ transport 海上运输，海运
~ transportation 海上运输，海运
~ type fan 船用式风机
~ type impeller 船用式叶轮
~ type lamp 船用式灯具

mariner ['mærinə] *n*. 海员，水手

marital ['mæritl] *a*. 婚姻的，夫妻(间)的
~ leave 婚假

maritime ['mæritaim] *a*. 海的，海上的，海事的，海运的，海船的，航运的，海员的
~ Agreement Regarding Oil Pollution of Liability (MARPOL) 有关油污责任的海运协定
~ arbitration commission 海事仲裁委员会
~ climate 海洋气候，海洋性气候
~ commerce 海上贸易
~ commission 海事委员会
~ court 海事法庭
~ Environment Protection Committee (MEPC) 海洋环境保护委员会
~ industry 航运业，海事工业
~ inquiry 海事调查
~ insurance 海洋运输保险
~ law 海商法
~ lien 海上留置权
~ organization 海事组织，海运机构
~ patrol aircraft 海上巡逻机
~ right 海洋权
~ Safety Committee (MSC) 海上安全委员会，海事安全委员会
~ Safety Division (MSD) 海事安全司

mark [ma:k] *n*. 标志，分数，痕迹，记号；*v*. 做标记于，做记号，打分数，标志
~ disk of speed adjusting 速度调整标度盘
~ down 记下，削减价目，标低价格
~ sensing 标记检测

marker ['ma:kə] *n*. 标兵，标识，标记，记号笔，记分员，纪念碑，里程碑

marking ['ma:kiŋ] *n*. 记号，做记号，记分，斑纹；*v*. (mark 的 ing 形式) 做标记于，做记号，打分数，标志
~ gauge 量规

marline ['ma:lin] *n*. 双股细缆

marlinespike ['ma:linspaik] *n*. 穿索针，解索针

MARPOL (International Convention for the Prevention of Pollution from Ships) 国际防止船舶造成污染公约，MARPOL 防污公约

MARPOL (Maritime Agreement Regarding Oil Pollution of Liability) 有关油污责任的海运协定

marshal ['ma:ʃəl] *n*. 元帅，典礼官，执行官，司仪官；*v*. 整顿，配置，汇集，

排列，集合

MARVS (maximum allowable relief valve setting of a cargo tank) 货舱最大允许安全阀设置

mashroom ['mʌʃru:m] n. 蘑菇，伞菌；v. 迅速增长，迅速发展，迅速蔓延，呈蘑菇状升起

~ valve 菌形阀 ‖ **Syn.** poppet valve 菌形阀，提升阀

mask [ma:sk] n. 罩，防护罩，氧气罩，防毒面具，面罩，面具，伪装，掩饰，掩体，掩蔽物，遮光板，电路模板，面部特写；v. 带上，隐瞒，掩盖，遮盖，遮蔽，掩护，中断反应，使模糊，化装，戴面具

~ clearing 面镜排水，面罩排水

~ strap 面罩带，面镜带

masked [ma:skid] v. (mask 的过去式和过去分词) 带上，隐瞒，掩盖，遮盖，遮蔽，掩护，中断反应，使模糊，化装，戴面具；a. 隐蔽的，潜伏的，戴面具的，化妆的

~ valve intake 导流屏式气门进气

~ wheel 带罩棘轮

mass [mæs] n. 团，块，堆，集结，集合，质量，体积，大量，主体，主要部分，大多数，群众；v. 使集合，聚集，集结，集中；a. 大规模的，集中的，完整的，全部的，完全的，群众的，以大众为对象的

~ dismissal 大量解雇

~ fire 大火团，大火，密集射击

~ lamination panel 预制内层覆箔板

~ load 惯性力，惯性负载

~ per liter 质量/升

mast [ma:st] n. 桅，桅杆，柱，旗杆，天线竿；v. 装桅杆于

~ clutch 桅座

~ crane 桅杆(式)起重机

~ head 桅顶

~ head light 桅杆灯

~ house 桅室

~ lamp 桅灯

master ['ma:stə] n. 船长，硕士，主人，雇主，(男)教师，熟练技工，师傅，大师；v. 征服，控制，精通；a. 主要的，主人的，熟练的，高明的 ‖ **Syn.** captain 船长；sea captain 船长；skipper 船长

~ card 主卡片

~ computer 主计算机，主电脑

~ control 总控制

~ control routine (MCR) 主控程序

~ control valve 主控制阀

~ controller 主控制器

~ cylinder 主缸，控制缸

~ cylinder body 主汽缸体

~ drawing 样图，发令图

~ electrician 高级电工

~ equation 主方程

~ gyro compass 电罗经主仪

~ key 万能钥匙

~ plan 总平面图，总体规划，总规则

~ plate 靠模板，样板，测平板

~ program 主程序

~ schedule 主要图表，综合图表，设计任务书，主要作业表

~ scuba diver 名仕潜水员

~ selector 主调节器，主选波器，主选择器

~ station 主控台，主站，主台

~ switch 总开关，主开关

~ valve 总阀，主阀

master's 船长的

 ~ responsibility and authority 船长的责任和权力

masthead ['ma:sthed] *n.* 桅顶，报头；*v.* 升至桅顶

 ~ lamp 桅顶灯

mat [mæt] *n.* 席子，垫子，防爆毯，擦鞋垫，踏脚垫，消光面，消光器，丛，团，簇；*v.* 遮盖，保护，缠结，铺席子

 ~ glass 毛玻璃，磨砂玻璃

match [mætʃ] *n.* 火柴，比赛，竞赛，匹配；*v.* 相配，相称，比赛，相比，匹配 ‖ *Ant.* mismatch 错配，失谐，使配错，使配合不当

matching ['mætʃiŋ] *n.* 匹配；*v.* (match 的 ing 形式) 相配，相称，比赛，相比，匹配；*a.* 相同的，相配的

 ~ criterion 匹配准则

 ~ surface 配合面

mate [meit] *n.* 大副，下士，配偶，对手，助手，伙伴，同事；*v.* 使配对，使一致，结伴，紧密配合

material [mə'tiəriəl] *n.* 原料，物资，材料，素材，布料，用具，设备，适当人选；*a.* 物质的，肉体的，具体的，重要的，必要的，实质性的 ‖ *Syn.* considerable 重要的；critical 重要的；crucial 极其重要的；important 重要的，重大的

 ~ consumption 原料耗用，物质消费

 ~ factor 材料因素

 ~ handling 物料输送，原材料处理

 ~ handling equipment 材料装卸设备

 ~ list (ML) 材料清单，物料清单，物料表

 ~ property of the commodity 商品的物质属性

 ~ resources 物质资源，物力

 ~ safety circuit 本质安全电路

 ~ shortage 材料缺乏

 ~ strength 材料强度，物料强度

materially [mə'tiəriəli] *ad.* 本质上，物质上，极大的，相当的

mate [meit] *n.* 同学，朋友，伴侣，助手；*v.* 连接，使配对，使紧密配合，交配

mating ['meitiŋ] *n.* 配套，交配，杂交；*v.* (mate 的 ing 形式) 连接，使配对，使紧密配合，交配

 ~ surface 配合面，啮合面

matrix ['metriks] *n.* 矩阵，矩阵元素，模型，压模，基质

matt [mæt] *n.* 无光泽颜色，哑光漆，无光泽涂层，衬底，镶边；*v.* 使无光；*a.* 无光泽的，不光滑的

 ~ finishing 涂无光漆，面漆磨褪(光泽)

matte [mæt] *n.* 锍，冰铜；*a.* 不光滑的

 ~ side 磨砂边

 ~ smelting 锍冶炼，冰铜冶炼

matter ['mætə] *n.* 问题，事件，物质，内容，实质，原因，文件，素材；*v.* 有关系，要紧

max [mæks] *n.* 最大限度；*v.* 竭尽全力，达到最高点；*ad.* 最大，至多

 ~ current and voltage 最大电流和电压 ‖ *Ant.* min current and voltage 最小电流和电压

 ~ depth 最大深度，最大强度

maximize ['mæksmaiz] *v.* 取最大值，最大化，最佳化，极为重视

maximum ['mæksiməm] *n.* 最大量，最大限度，极大；*a.* 最高的，最多的，最

大极限的

~ ahead service speed 最大前进航速

~ allowable bottom time 最大滞底时间

~ allowable relief valve setting of a cargo tank (MARVS) 货舱最大允许安全阀设置

~ allowable working pressure 最大容许工作压力,最大允许工作压力

~ astern speed 最大倒车航速

~ breadth 最大宽度

~ charging current 最大充电电流

~ charging voltage 最大充电电压

~ clearance 最大间隙

~ combustion pressure 最高燃烧压力

~ continuous rating (MCR) 最大持续出力,最大连续出力

~ cylinder volume 最大气缸容积

~ delivery 最高排出压力

~ demand indicator 最大需量指示器

~ depth 最大深度

~ evaporative capacity 最高蒸发量

~ explosion pressure gauge 最高爆发压力表

~ explosive pressure 最高爆发压力

~ extent 最大程度,最大范围

~ height 最大高度

~ height of lift 最大起升高度

~ likelihood estimation 最大似然估计

~ limit 最高限度

~ load 最大负载,最大载荷,最大载重量

~ moment 最大力矩

~ noload governed speed 受控最高空载转速

~ operation mode 最大运行方式

~ output 最大产量,最大输出功率

~ overshoot 最大过调量

~ pressure 最大压力

~ pressure gauge 最大压力表

~ principle 极大值原理

~ quantity 最高量,最大量,最大限

~ rated conductor temperature 导线最大额定温度

~ sensitive angle 最大灵敏角

~ speed 最大速度,最高速度,最大转速,全速

~ speed governor gear 最高转速调速装置

~ stress 最大应力

~ stress limit 最大应力极限

~ torque 最大转矩

~ value 最大值,极大值

~ wear of bore 钻孔最大磨损

~ work 最大功

~ working oil pressure 最高工作油压力

~ working pressure 最大工作压力,最大使用压力,最高工作压力

MB (model base) 模型库

MCC (motor control center) 电机控制中心

MCCB (molded case circuit breaker, moulded case circuit breaker) 塑壳断路器

MCR (machinery control room) 机械控制室,设备控制室

MCR (maintenance control report) 维修管理报告

MCR (master control routine) 主控程序

MCR (maximum continuous rating) 最大持续出力,最大连续出力

MCR (micro carbon residue) 微量残余碳,微残碳

MCR (modular circuit reliability) 模块化电路可靠性
MCS (modulating control system) 调制控制系统
MDO (marine diesel oil) 船用柴油
ME (main engine) 主机，主发动机
~ driven alternator 主机驱动的交流发电机
~ fault emergency maneuver 主机故障应急操纵
~ lubricating oil system 主机润滑油系统
~ remote control panel 主机遥控屏，主机远程控制屏
~ telegraph 主车钟，主机传令钟
~ turbo-blower 主机涡轮鼓风机
meal [mi:l] n. 餐，饭，进餐，一餐，一顿饭，膳食，粗粉；v. 进餐
~ allowance 伙食补贴
mean [mi:n] n. 平均数，中间，平均值，中等，方法，手段；v. 意味，象征，想要，图谋，企图，造成，预定，用意，有意义；a. 低劣的，普通的，简陋的，平均的，惭愧的，不舒服的
~ draught 平均吃水
~ effective pressure (MEP) 平均有效压力
~ free path 平均自由程
~ indicated pressure (MIP) 平均指示压力
~ nautical mile 平均海里(6079.91英尺)
~ of escape 逃逸平均值
~ of observation 观测值的平均
~ piston speed 平均活塞速度
~ place 平均位置
~ pressure meter 平均压力计
~ square 均方
~ square error 均方误差，均方差
~ square error criterion 均方误差准则
~ square error norm 均方误差范数
~ time between failures (MTBF) 平均故障间隔时间，平均失效间隔时间，平均故障间隔期
~ time between overhauls (MTBO) 平均检修间隔时间，平均大修间隔时间
~ time to failure (MTTF) 平均故障时间
~ time between removals (MTTR) 平均拆换间隔时间
~ time to repair (MTTR) 平均维修时间，平均修复间隔时间
~ value (MV) 平均数，平均值
~ variation (MV) 平均偏差
~ velocity 平均速度
meaningful ['miniŋful] a. 有意思的，有意图的，有目的的，有意图的
~ manner 有意义的方式
meaningless ['mi:niŋlis] a. 无谓的，无意义的，无价值的
means [mi:nz] n. (mean 的复数) 手段，方法，收入，财富；v. (mean 的第三人称单数) 意味，想要，预定，用意，有意义 ‖ *Syn*. approach 方法,途径,通路；method 方法,办法；way 路线,路途,方式
~ of evacuation 疏散设施
~ of rescue 救援手段
meantime ['mi:n'taim] n. 其时，其间；ad. 同时，其间
measurand ['meʒərənd] n. 被测变量,被测物理量 ‖ *Syn*. measured variable 测定变量
measure ['meʒə] n. 尺寸，量度器，量度

标准，方法，测量，措施；v. 测量，估量，分派，权衡，调节 ‖ *Syn*. criterion 标准，准据，规范；norm 规范，标准，准则；standard 标准，规格；touchstone 标准，检验标准，检验手段

~ by means of ultrasonic instrument 利用超声波设备测量

~ of control 控制措施，管理措施

~ with caliper 用游标卡尺测量

measured ['meʒəd] v. (measure 的过去式和过去分词) 测量，估量，分派，权衡，调节；a. 测量的，标准的，整齐的，有规则的

~ data 测量数据，测定数据，实验数据

~ feedback 测定反馈，实测反馈(信号)

~ element 被测要素

~ value 测定值，测量值

~ variable 测定变量 ‖ *Syn*. measurand 被测变量，被测物理量

measurement ['meʒəmənt] n. 测量(法)，度量，尺寸，量度制

~ accuracy 量测精度

~ and weight list 容积重量表

~ freight 按体积计算的运费

~ error 测量误差，量度误差

~ instrument 测量仪表，测量仪器

~ of cylinder liner and piston ring 气缸套和活塞环测量

~ of electromagnetic interference 电磁干扰测量

~ panel 测量面板，计量屏

~ pattern 测量模式

~ process 测量过程

~ range 测量范围，量程，计量范围

~ results 测量结果，测试结果

~ signal 测量信号

~ space 测量空间

~ strategy 测量策略

~ technique 测量技术，检测技术，计量技术

~ to be taken with bridge gauge 用桥规测量

~ uncertainty 测量不确定度，量测不确定度

~ units 度量单位

measuring ['meʒəriŋ] n. 测量，衡量；v. (measure 的 ing 形式) 测量，估量，分派，权衡，调节；a. 测量用的

~ accuracy 测量精度，测量准确度

~ apparatus 计量仪器，定量装置，定量给料器

~ bottle 量瓶，测试瓶

~ circuit 测量电路，测验电路

~ clearance between propeller shaft & bearing 螺旋桨轴与轴承间隙测量

~ clearance of rudder jumping stopper 舵止跳块的间隙测量

~ coil 测量线圈，测试线圈

~ cup 量杯

~ cylinder 量筒

~ data 测量资料，测量数据，测试数据

~ deflection of crank shaft of main diesel generator before running test (after sea trial) 主柴油发电机动车前(系泊试验后)曲轴甩档测量

~ deflection of crank shaft of ME before starting up (after sea trial) 主机动车前(航行试验后)曲轴甩档测量

~ device 测量装置，测量仪表

~ dial 测量度盘

~ diameter of fore and aft stern tube

bearing and bushes 艉轴管前、后轴承与衬套直径测量
~ dimension of shaft coupling bolts and reamer hole 轴系连接螺栓和孔尺寸测量
~ element 测量元件，测定元件，计量元件
~ equipment 测量设备，测量装置
~ head 测量头
~ hull's main dimensions: length overall (LOA), length between perpendiculars (LPP), breath molded (B mld), depth molded and deflection before launching 下水前测量船体主尺度：总长、两柱间长、型宽、型深、基线挠度
~ installation clearance of rudder bearing 舵轴承安装间隙测量
~ instrument 测量仪表，测量仪器
~ insulation resistance and reliability test protection device for main switchboard (emergency switchboard) 总配电板(应急配电板)绝缘电阻测量和保护装置可靠性试验
~ line 测量线，测绳，测线
~ means 量度工具，测量装置，测量器
~ method 测量方法，测定方法，测量法
~ needle 量针
~ point 测量点，测定点，测点
~ range 测定范围，测量范围，量程
~ result 测量结果，测定结果
~ scale 量尺，量表
~ screw 测微螺丝，微动螺丝
~ system 测量系统，测定系统，计量系统
~ tool 测量工具，量具

~ transducer 测量传感器，测量变换器
~ unit 测量装置，测量单元，计量单位
~ vector 度量向量
meat [mit] n. 肉，肉类，要旨，实质，内容
~ ship 肉类装运船，肉类船
MEC (most economic control) 最经济控制
mechanic [mi'kænik] n. 技工，机修工，制造工
mechanical [mi'kænikl] a. 机械的，机械制的，机械似的，呆板的，无意识的，手工操作的
~ adhesion 机械黏附
~ adjustment 机械调整
~ aeration 机械通风，机械曝气
~ aeration basin 机械曝气池
~ and electrical products 机电产品
~ and electrical technology 机电技术
~ attack 机械腐蚀
~ automation 机械自动化
~ brake 机械制动器，机力闸
~ brake cylinder 机械制动油缸
~ breakdown 机械故障
~ characteristic 机械特性
~ cleaning 机械清洗，机械清洁，机械清理
~ cutting 机械切削
~ descaling 机械除鳞，机械除垢，机械除锈
~ drawing 机械制图，机械图样，设备图纸
~ dredge 铲斗式挖泥船，机械疏浚
~ durability 机械耐久性，机械寿命
~ efficiency 机械效率，力学效率
~ element 机械元件

~ energy 机械能，力学能
~ equipment 机械设备，机电设备，机械装备
~ equivalent 功当量
~ equivalent of heat 热功当量，机械热当量
~ erosion 机械浸蚀，机械腐蚀
~ foam extinguisher 机械泡沫灭火机
~ force 机械力
~ force feed lubrication 机械压力润滑，高压下自动润滑
~ governor 机械式调速机，机械调速器，机械式调节器
~ impurities 机械杂质
~ linkage 机械连接
~ load 机械负荷，机械负载，机械载荷
~ load factor 机械负载系数
~ loader 装载机，机械装货器
~ loading 机械装载，机械加料，机械负荷
~ locker relay 机械闭锁继电器
~ loss 机械损失，机械损耗
~ lubricator 机械润滑器，机械加油器，机械注油器，机械式压油机
~ motion 机械运动，力学运动
~ mouse 机械鼠标
~ movement 机械运动，机械运动牵引
~ part 机械构件，机械部件，机械零件
~ passivity 机械钝性
~ hoist 机械吊机
~ pilot hoist 引航员机械升降器
~ pipe 机械缩孔
~ polishing 机械抛光
~ power lift 机械式自动起落机构
~ property 机械性能，力学性质

~ purchase 机械滑车
~ rectifier 机械整流器
~ reliability 机械可靠性
~ seal 机械密封，机械轴封
~ sediment 机械沉积物
~ smoke control 机械控烟
~ steering control system 机械操舵系统
~ strength 机械强度
~ stress 机械应力
~ supercharging 机械增压
~ supercharging diesel engine 机械增压柴油机
~ term 机械术语
~ testing 机械试验
~ variation 机械变化
~ ventilation 机械通气，机械通风
~ work 机械功，机械作业
mechanical-electrical 机械电气的，机电的
~ integration 机电一体化
mechanical-hydraulic 机械液压的
~ governor 机械液压调速器
mechanically [mi'kænikəli] ad. 机械地，呆板地
~ actuated valve mechanism 机械式气阀传动机构，机械制动阀机构
~ capped steel 机械封顶钢
~ operated cargo oil valve 机械操纵货油阀
mechanism ['mekənizəm] n. 机器，机械装置，机械系统，机构，机制，办法，途径，过程，手法，技巧 ‖ *Syn.* apparatus 器械，设备，仪器；appliance 用具，器具；arrangement 布置；assembly 组装部件；device 装置，设备；equipment 装备，设备，器材，装置；facility 设备，工具；furniture 设

备，家具；gear 设备，装备；installation 设备，装置；machine 机器，机械，机构；machinery 机械(总称)，机器；plant 设备；provision 装备，供应品；turnout 装备，设备；unit 装置，设备

~ model 机理模型

~ of action 作用机理

mechanize ['mekənaiz] v. (使)机械化，以机械制造

mechanized ['mekənaizd] v. (mechanize 的过去式和过去分词) (使)机械化，以机械制造；a. 机械的，呆板的

~ gas cutting 机械气割

MED (Marine Environment Division) 海洋环境保护司

media ['mi:diə] n. (medium 的复数) 媒介，媒质，介质，媒介物，传导体，途径，溶剂，中间层

medical ['medikəl] n. 医生，体格检查；a. 医学的，药的，内科的

~ insurance premiums 医疗保险费

Mediterranean [ˌmeditə'reinjən] n. 地中海；a. 地中海的，地中海民族的

~ Sea 地中海

medium ['midiəm] n. (pl. media) 媒介，媒质，介质，媒介物，传导体，途径，溶剂，中等，中间；a. 中间的，中等的，半生熟的

~ corrosion test 介质腐蚀试验

~ pressure 中等压力，中压，介质压力

~ pressure lubricating system 中压润滑系统

~ pressure molding 中压模塑法

~ speed 中等速度，中速，平均速度 ‖ *Syn*. intermediate speed 中等速度，中速；moderate speed 中等速度，

中速，平均速度

~ speed diesel engine 中速柴油机

~ speed engine 中速引擎，中速柴油机，中速机

~ voltage (MV) 中压 ‖ *Syn*. intermediate voltage 中压；middle voltage 中压

~ voltage network 中压供电网，中压(电力)系统

meet [mi:t] n. 会，集会；v. 遇见，相遇，迎接，赴约，会面，相识，对付，接触；a. 适宜的，合适的 ‖ *Syn*. cater to 迎合，满足；content 使满足；fill 满足；fulfil 满足；satisfy 满足，使满意

~ an emergency 应变，应急，应付紧急情况

~ the requirement of 满足…的要求

megaphone ['megəfəun] n. 扩音器，喇叭筒；v. 用喇叭筒讲，广泛宣传

megger ['megə] n. 高阻表

~ meter 兆欧表，高阻表

~ test 绝缘测试，兆欧表测试

megohm ['megəum] n. 兆欧姆

~ meter 兆欧计，高阻计，摇表

melamine ['meləmi(:)n] n. 三聚氰胺

~ formaldehyde resin 三聚氰胺甲醛树脂

~ plastic 蜜胺塑料，三聚氰胺塑料

melt [melt] n. 熔化，熔化物，融化量，融化过程；v. (使)融化，(使)熔化，(使)软化，(使)感动

~ current 熔体电流

~ down 熔化

~ viscosity 熔融黏度

melting ['meltiŋ] v. (melt 的 ing 形式) (使)融化，(使)熔化，(使)软化，(使)感动；a. 熔化的，融化的，溶解的，混合的

385

~ furnace 熔窑，熔化炉，熔炼炉

~ fusion 熔融

~ interface 熔化分界面

~ loss 熔炼损耗

~ point 熔点

membrane ['membrein] *n*. 膜，薄膜，隔膜，羊皮纸

~ switch 薄膜开关，薄膜按键开关，膜片开关

~ tank 薄膜贮罐，膜式舱柜，薄膜液舱

~ tension 膜片张力，膜片硬度

~ tube wall 膜管壁

~ type cargo containment system 货物密封系统

~ water wall 膜式水冷壁

memo ['meməu] *n*. 备忘录，便笺，便函

memorandum [ˌmemə'rændəm] *n*. 备忘录，买卖契约书，便笺，便函

mend [mend] *n*. 改进，改良，补丁，修理部分，好转；*v*. 修改，改进，加快，修理，修补，好转，改善，改正

mention ['menʃən] *n*. 提及，说起；*v*. 提到，谈到，提及，论及，说起

menu ['menju:] *n*. 菜单，饭菜

~ bar 菜单栏，功能列表

MEP (mean effective pressure) 平均有效压力

MEPC (Maritime Environment Protection Committee) 海洋环境保护委员会

merchandise ['mə:tʃəndaiz] *n*. 商品，货物；*v*. 买卖，推销，经商

merchant ['mə:tʃənt] *n*. 商人，店主，批发商，贸易商；*a*. 商业的，商人的

~ ship 商船

~ Shipbuilding Return 商船建造统计表

~ shipper 出口商，商货托运人

merchantability [ˌmə:tʃəntə'biləti] *n*. 适销性，可销性

~ specification 商品材规格

mercury ['mə:kjuri] *n*. 汞，水银，温度，水星

~ battery 水银电池，汞电池

~ contact-type fixed temperature detector 水银接触式定温探测器

~ filled thermometer 水银温度计

~ lamp 汞灯，水银灯

mercury-in-glass 水银玻璃

~ thermometer 玻璃水银温度计，水银温度计

meridian [mə'ridiən] *n*. 子午线，经线，顶点，正午，全盛时期；*a*. 子午线的，正午的，顶点的，全盛时期的

merit ['merit] *n*. 优点，价值，功绩；功过；*v*. 有益于，值得，应得，应受报答

~ rating 成绩评定，优点评定

mesh [meʃ] *n*. 网孔，网丝，网眼，圈套，陷阱，啮合；*v*. 以网捕捉，落网，啮合，编织

mess [mes] *n*. 混乱，食堂，伙食团，困境，脏乱的东西；*v*. 弄乱，弄脏，毁坏，使就餐，把事情弄糟

~ boy 餐厅服务生,餐室侍应生 ‖ *Syn*. mess steward 餐厅服务生,餐室侍应生

~ hall 食堂 ‖ *Syn*. mess room 餐厅，餐室，食堂

~ tin 饭盒

messgirl ['mesgə:l] *n*. 女服务生

messman ['mesmən] *n*. (海军)食堂值勤兵，餐厅服务生

messroom ['mesru:m] *n*. (海军基地或军舰)

食堂

metacenter ['metəˌsentə(r)] *n.* 外心点,定倾中心

metacentric [ˌmetə'sentrik] *a.* 稳心的,定倾中心的
- ~ arm 稳性力臂
- ~ diagram 稳心曲线图
- ~ height 稳心高度,定倾中心高度
- ~ involute 稳心轨迹曲线
- ~ radius 稳心半径
- ~ stability 初稳性,静稳性

metal ['metl] *n.* 金属,金属制品,合金,熔化铸铁,玻璃熔液,基本特征,本性
- ~ alloy 金属合金
- ~ base printed board 金属基印制板
- ~ brightener 金属去污剂
- ~ casing 金属壳,金属包皮
- ~ chock 金属支架,金属楔子
- ~ container 金属集装箱,金属容器
- ~ core printed board 金属芯印制板
- ~ cutting 金属切削
- ~ fabrication 金属预制件
- ~ finishing 金属表面精整
- ~ framework 金属框架
- ~ inert-gas (MIG) 金属惰性气体
- ~ inert-gas welding 金属惰性气体电弧焊
- ~ insert 金属嵌件
- ~ oxide arrestor (MOA) 金属氧化物避雷器
- ~ plate path 金属板电镀槽
- ~ polish 金属抛光剂,金属擦亮剂
- ~ polish paste 金属亮光膏,擦铜膏
- ~ worker 金属工
- ~ working shop 金工车间
- ~ clad 金属包裹,金属包层,金属铠装
- ~ clad plate 金属铠装板
- ~ clad bade material 覆金属箔基材
- ~ clad switch 铁壳开关 ‖ **Syn**. iron clad switch 铁壳开关; iron cover switch 铁壳开关

metallic [mi'tælik] *a.* 金属的,金属性的,含金属的
- ~ bellows type expansion joint 金属波纹管式膨胀接头
- ~ bellows gauge 金属膜盒压力计
- ~ cable 钢丝索
- ~ element 金属元素
- ~ enamel 金属搪瓷
- ~ lifeboat 金属救生艇
- ~ lubricant 金属润滑剂
- ~ materials 金属材料
- ~ materials and products 金属材料和产品
- ~ paper 金属箔纸
- ~ pickup 金属粘接
- ~ reflector 金属反射器,金属反射罩
- ~ seal 金属密封
- ~ sheath 金属套管,金属包皮

metallize ['metəlaiz] *v.* 用金属处理,使金属化

metallurgical [ˌmetə'lə:dʒikəl] *a.* 冶金的,冶金学的
- ~ structure 金相组织,冶金结构
- ~ technology 金属工艺学

metalworking ['metəlˌwə:kiŋ] *n.* 金属加工术,金属制造,金属工

metatarsal [ˌmetə'ta:səl] *n.* 跖骨; *a.* 跖骨的
- ~ guard 脚面罩

meter ['mi:tə] (=metre) *n.* 米,公尺,计,

表，仪表，节拍，拍子；v. 定量供应，用计，仪表计量

~ liquid column (MLC) 米液柱(泵的压头单位)

~ multiplier 测量仪表扩程器

~ panel 仪表盘，仪表板，仪表面板

meterage ['mi:təridʒ] n. 测量，计量费

metering ['mi:təriŋ] n. 测量(法)，测定，计量，配量；v. (meter 的 ing 形式) 定量供应，用计，仪表计量

~ pump 计量泵，计量泵，定量泵

methane ['meθein] n. 甲烷，沼气

~ tanker 甲烷运输船

method ['meθəd] n. 方法，办法，条理，秩序，规律，程序，技巧 ‖ **Syn.** approach 方法,途径,通路；means 手段，方法；way 路线，路途，方式

~ of disposal of oil residues 油渣处理方法

~ of fabrication 制造方法

methyl ['meθil] n. 甲基，木精

~ chloride 氯甲烷(制冷剂)

methylase ['meθilez] n. 甲基化酶

metre ['mi:tə] (=meter) n. 米，公尺，计，表，仪表，节拍，拍子；v. 定量供应，用计，仪表计量

metric ['metrik] n. 度量，度量标准；a. 公制的，米制的，公尺的，距离的

~ screw thread 公制螺纹

~ thread bolt 公制螺纹螺栓

~ ton 公吨

~ unit 米制单位，公制单位

mezzanine ['mezəni:n] n. 中层楼，夹楼，包厢

~ deck 夹层甲板

MFN (Most Favored Nation) 最惠国

~ Treatment 最惠国待遇

MFO (marine fuel oil) 船用燃料油

MGO (marine gas oil) 船用轻柴油

mica ['maikə] n. 云母

micro ['maikrəu] n. 微型计算机，微处理器，微波炉；a. 极小的，基本的，微小的

~ ammeter 微安计

~ analysis 微量分析，个体分析

~ carbon residue (MCR) 微量残余碳，微残碳

~ electro hydraulic control system 微型电液控制系统

~ floc 微絮状物

~ mist 微粉

microammeter [,maikrəu'æmitə(r)] n. 微安培计，微安计

microbial [mai'krəubiəl] a. 微生物的，由细菌引起的

microchip ['maikrəutʃip] n. 微型集成电路片，微芯片

microcomputer ['maikrəukəmpju:tə(r)] n. 微型电子计算机，微型计算机，微电脑

~ based 基于微机的

~ based protection 微机保护

~ type relaying 微机型继电保护

microcontroller [maikrəukənt'rəulər] n. 微控制器

micrometer [mai'krɔmitə(r)] n. 千分尺,测微计

~ calipers 千分卡尺

~ depth gauge 深度千分尺，深度卡规

micron ['maikrɔn] n. 微米(百万分之一米)

microohmmeter [mik'rəu'əummi:tə] n. 微欧计

microphone ['maikrəfəun] *n.* 扩音器，麦克风

microprocessor [maikrəu'prəusesə(r)] *n.* 微处理器

microswitch ['maikrəu,switʃ] *n.* 微动开关，微型开关

middle ['midl] *n.* 中间，中央，内部，腰部；*v.* 放在中间，对折；*a.* 中间的，中部的，中级的，中等的

~ flat file 中扁锉

~ half-round file 中半圆锉

~ knife file 中刀锉

~ line plane 中线面

~ round file 中圆锉

~ square file 中方锉

~ standing pillar 中间立柱

~ triangular file 中三角锉

~ voltage 中压 ‖ **Syn**. intermediate voltage 中压；medium voltage (MV) 中压

mid-frequency 中心频率，中频

~ band 中频段

midlatitude ['midlætitju:d] *n.* 中间纬度

midlength ['midleŋθ] *n.* 船中

midnight ['mid,nait] *n.* 午夜，子夜，半夜12点钟；*a.* 子夜的，午夜的，半夜的，漆黑的

midship ['mid,ʃip] *n.* 船体中央部，船中；*a.* 船体中央的

~ draft mark 船中吃水标志

~ frame 中部肋骨，舯肋骨

~ plane 船中剖面

~ section 船中断面图，舯横剖面

~ section coefficient 舯剖面系数

~ section modulus 舯剖面模数

~ shaft bearing 中间轴轴承

midships ['midʃips] *ad.* 在船中央部

midstream ['mid'stri:m] *n.* 中流，中游，河流正中

MIG (metal inert-gas) 金属惰性气体

~ welding 金属惰性气体电弧焊

migration [mai'greiʃən] *n.* 移动，徙动，迁徙，回游，迁移，移居，移民，移民群，移栖群，成群的候鸟

~ channel 运移通道

mil [mil] *n.* 千分之一寸，密耳(量金属直径和薄板的单位)

mild [maild] *n.* 淡味啤酒；*a.* 可锻的，温和的，温柔的，淡味的，轻微的，适度的，不含有害物质的

~ steel 软钢，低碳钢

mildew ['mildu] *n.* 霉，霉菌，霉病，变色，褪色；*v.* 生霉，(使)发霉

~ proof 防霉

mile [mail] *n.* 英里，较大的距离

Milford ['milfəd] *n.* 米尔福德(男子名，姓氏)

~ Haven 米尔福德港

milk [milk] *n.* 乳状物，牛奶；*v.* 榨取，挤奶

mill [mil] *n.* 压榨机，磨粉机，工厂，制造厂；*v.* 碾，磨，磨细，搅拌，(使)乱转，打

miller ['milə] *n.* 铣床，铣工，碾磨工

milliammeter [,mili'æmi:tə] *n.* 毫安表

millibar ['miliba:r] *n.* 毫巴

millimeter ['milimi:tə(r)] *n.* 毫米

milling ['miliŋ] *n.* 碾，磨，制粉，轧齿边；*v.* (mill 的 ing 形式) 碾，磨，磨细，搅拌，乱转，打

~ cutter 铣刀

~ head 铣刀头

389

~ machine 铣床

million ['miljən] *n*. 百万元，无数(millions)，大众(millions)；*num*. 百万；*a*. 百万的，无数的

millivoltmeter ['mili,vəult'mi:tə] *n*. 毫伏计

millscale ['milskeil] *n*. 轧制铁鳞(热轧钢锭表面的氧化皮)

mimic ['mimik] *n*. 仿制品，效颦者，模仿者，小丑；*v*. 模仿，摹拟；*a*. 模仿的，模拟的，假装的，拟态的
  ~ diagram 站场模型图
  ~ panel 模拟盘

MIMO (multi-input multi-output) 多输入多输出的
  ~ system 多输入多输出系统

mine [main] *n*. 地雷，水雷，矿，矿藏，矿山，矿井，源泉，宝库；*v*. 开采，采掘，开矿，布雷，破坏，*pron*. 我的
  ~ hunter 猎雷舰艇，猎雷舰
  ~ sweeper 扫雷舰，扫雷器

mineral ['minərəl] *n*. 矿物，矿石，元素，有机衍生物，无机元素，无机物；*a*. 矿物的
  ~ cleaner 矿物油清洁剂
  ~ insulation 矿物绝缘
  ~ oil 矿物油

minesweeper ['main,swi:pə] *n*. 扫雷舰，军船扫雷艇

minesweeping ['main,swi:piŋ] *n*. 扫雷
  ~ cable 扫雷电缆，排雷电缆

miniature ['miniətʃə] *n*. 缩小的模型，缩图，缩影；*a*. 微型的，缩小的
  ~ circuit breaker 微型断路器，小型断路器，小型电路断路器
  ~ fuse 微型熔断器，小型熔断器

~ lamp 指示灯，小型灯
~ pole relay 微极继电器
~ switch 微型开关，小型开关

miniaturization [,minətʃərai'zeiʃən] *n*. 小型化，微型化

miniaturize ['miniətʃəraiz] *v*. 使小型化，使微型化

minibulker [mini'bʌlkə] *n*. 小型散货船

minicomputer ['minikəm,pju:tə] *n*. 微型计算机，小型机

minimal ['miniməl] *a*. 最小的，极少的，最小限度的

minimization ['minimai,zeiʃən] *n*. 最小限度，最低额，轻视

minimize ['minimaiz] *v*. 使减到最少，使缩到最小，成极小，求最小值，最小化

minimum ['miniməm] *n*. 最小值，最低限度，最小化，最小量；*a*. 最小的，最低的
~ breaking load 最小断裂载荷
~ capacity 最小容量
~ charge 最低费用，起码收费
~ comfortable condition of habitability 最低舒适性的居住条件
~ cost 最小代价
~ distance 最短距离
~ error 最小误差
~ load 最低负荷
~ oil circuit breaker 少油断路器
~ phase system 最小相位系统，最小相位系
~ phase shift system 最小相移系统
~ rate 起码运费，最低比率
~ requirements 最低要求
~ safe manning certificate 最低安全配员证书 ‖ *Syn*. minimum safe manning

document 最低安全配员证书

~ size 最小尺寸

~ standard 最低标准

~ starting pressure 最低启动压力

~ steady speed test 最低稳定转速试验

~ steady test 最低稳定性试验

~ temperature 最低温度

~ value 最小值

~ variance estimation 最小方差估计

~ damage 最小损失，最小伤害

ministerial [minis'tiəriəl] *a.* 代理的，工具性的，部的，部长的，内阁的，行政的

ministry ['ministri] *n.* (政府的)部门，部办公楼，服务，工具

~ of Transport of the PRC 中华人民共和国交通运输部

minor ['mainə] *n.* 副修科目，未成年人；*v.* 辅修；*a.* 较小的，次要的，二流的，未成年的

~ axis 短轴，短径，弱轴

~ damage 较小损伤，轻微损害

~ diameter 小径

~ failure 轻微故障，一般故障，次要故障

~ failure of tanker 油轮轻微故障

~ imperfections 轻微缺陷，小缺陷

~ in 辅修

~ loop 副回路，小回路，局部回路 ‖ *Syn.* inner loop 内循环，内环路，局部回路

~ repair 小修理

minus ['mainəs] *n.* 负数；*a.* 减的，负的；*prep.* 减去

minute [mai'nju:t] *n.* 分，分钟，片刻，一瞬间，备忘录，笔记；*v.* 记录，摘录，测定时间；*a.* 微小的，详细的，仔细而准确的

MIO (Marine Industrial Organization) 海洋工业组织

MIP (mean indicated pressure) 平均指示压力

mirror ['mirə] *n.* 镜子，典范；*v.* 反射，反映

~ axis 对称轴

~ control 镜像控制

~ finish 镜面磨光，镜面抛光

~ lamp 镜面型灯，镜灯 ‖ *Syn.* mirror light 镜面型灯，镜灯

MIS (Management Information System) 管理信息系统

misalign ['misəlain] *n.* 不重合，位移；*v.* 偏移，未对准，不同心

misalignment ['misəlainmənt] *n.* 不重合，未对准

~ value 偏中值

miscellaneous [misi'leinjəs] *a.* 混杂的，各种各样的，多方面的，多才多艺的

~ item 杂项

miscibility [ˌmisi'biliti] *n.* 可混合性

miscible ['misibl] *a.* 相溶的，易混合的 ‖ *Ant.* immiscible 互不相溶的

misfortune [mis'fɔ:tʃən] *n.* 不幸，灾难，灾 ‖ *Syn.* accident 意外事件，意外事故；casualty 事故，伤亡；chance failure 偶发故障，意外事故；contingency 意外事故，紧急情况，不测事件；incident 事件，突发事件；mishap 灾祸，厄运，倒霉事

mishandle ['mis'hændl] *v.* 胡乱操纵，胡乱操作，错误处理，虐待 ‖ *Ant.* handle 操纵，操作，处理

391

mishap ['mishæp] *n*. 灾祸，厄运，倒霉事 ‖ *Syn*. accident 意外事件，意外事故；casualty 事故，伤亡；chance failure 偶发故障，意外事故；contingency 意外事故，紧急情况，不测事件；incident 事件，突发事件；misfortune 不幸，灾难，灾祸

mismatch ['mis'mætʃ] *n*. 错配，失配，不重合，不协调，失谐；*v*. (使)配错，(使)配合不当 ‖ *Ant*. match 相配，匹配

mismatched [mis'mætʃid] *v*. (mismatch 的过去式和过去分词) (使)配错，(使)配合不当；*a*. 配错的，不匹配的，不势均力敌的

~ impedance 失配阻抗

MISO (multi-input single-output) 多输入单输出的

~ system 多输入单输出系统

mist [mist] *n*. 薄雾，细雨，迷糊，朦胧，模糊；*v*. 被雾蒙上，喷洒

~ blower 喷雾器 ‖ *Syn*. mist sprayer 喷雾器

~ detector 雾检测器

~ droplet 雾滴，霭滴

~ spray 喷雾

miter ['maitə] *n*. 角规，斜槽规，斜接，斜接面；*v*. 使斜接，斜拼接

mitigate ['mitigeit] *v*. 减轻，使缓和，使减轻，使平息

mix [miks] *n*. 混合；*v*. (使)混合，混淆

mixed [mikst] *v*. (mix 的过去式与过去分词) (使)混合，混淆；*a*. 混合的

~ cycle 混合循环

~ divider (阻容)混合分压器

~ excitation 混合励磁

~ feed distribution system 混合给水分配系统

~ flow 混合流，混流

~ frame system 混合骨架式

~ gas insulation 混合气体绝缘

~ stowage 混装

mixer ['miksə] *n*. 混合者，搅拌器，混频器

mixing ['miksiŋ] *n*. 混合，混合物，良莠不齐，混频；*v*. (mix 的 ing 形式) (使)混合，混淆

~ bunker 混合仓

mixture ['mikstʃə] *n*. 混合，混合物，混合剂

~ ratio 混合比例，混合比

mizzen ['mizn] *n*. 后桅

~ mast 后桅

ML (material list) 材料清单，物料清单，物料表

MLC (meter liquid column) 米液柱(泵的压头单位)

MMF (magnetic motive force, magnetomotive force) 磁通势，磁动势

MOA (metal oxide arrestor) 金属氧化物避雷器

MOB (man overboard) 落水人员，人员落水，人员落海

~ boat 应急救生艇

~ maneuver 救落水人员操纵

~ prevention and recovery 人员落水的预防和救护，防止人员落水和重新登艇

~ rescue boat 人员落水救生艇

~ retrieval equipment 人员落水回收设备

~ signal 人员落水信号

mobile ['məubail] *n*. 运动物体；*a*. 机动

的，可移动的，行动自如的，易变的，流动性的
~ communication 移动通信
~ deck lifter 活动甲板升降机
~ fire extinguisher 移动式灭火器
~ offshore drilling unit (MODU) 移动式海上钻井平台，移动式海上钻井装置
~ production unit 移动式生产装置
~ pump 轻便泵，可移式泵 ‖ *Syn.* portable pump 轻便泵，可移式泵

mobility [məu'biliti] *n.* 活动性，灵活性，迁移率，机动性

modal ['məudl] *a.* 样式的，形态上的，模式的，情态的，语气的

mode [məud] *n.* 方式，模式，样式

model ['mɔdl] *n.* 样式，型，模范，典型，模型，原型，模特；*v.* 模仿，模拟，做成模型；*a.* 典型的，模范的
~ base (MB) 模型库
~ fidelity 模型逼真度
~ reference adaptive control system 模型参考适应控制系统
~ test 模型试验
~ testing tank 船模试验池
~ verification 模型验证

moderate ['mɔdərit] *v.* 缓和；*a.* 有节制的，稳健的，温和的，适度的
~ discharge 中等排量
~ speed 中等速度，中速，平均速度 ‖ *Syn.* intermediate speed 中等速度，中速；medium speed 中等速度，中速，平均速度

moderately ['mɔdərətli] *ad.* 适度地，普通地，温和度，不过度地

modern ['mɔdən] *n.* 现代人，有思想的人；*a.* 现代的，近代的，新式的，当代风格的

modernize ['mɔdə(:)naiz] *v.* 使现代化，使适应现代需要

modification [ˌmɔdifi'keiʃən] *n.* 修改，更改，修正，变更，改良，缓和

modified ['mɔdifaid] *v.* (modify 的过去式和过去分词) 改变，更改，修改，减轻，减缓；*a.* 改良的，改进的，修正的
~ variable 修改变量

modifier ['mɔdifaiə] *n.* 调节器，修正的人，改造者

modify ['mɔdifai] *v.* 改变，更改，修改，减轻，减缓

MODU (mobile offshore drilling unit) 移动式海上钻井平台，移动式海上钻井装置
~ Code (Code for the Construction and Equipment of Mobile Offshore Drilling Units) 移动式海上钻井装置建造和设备规范

modular ['mɔdjulə] *a.* 模块化的，模的，有标准组件的
~ circuit 模块化电路，模块电路
~ circuit reliability (MCR) 模块化电路可靠性
~ circuit design 模块化电路设计，模件电路设计

modularization [ˌmɔdjulərai'zeiʃən] *n.* 模块化

modularize ['mɔdjuləraiz] *v.* 模块化

modulate ['mɔdjuleit] *v.* 调节，调制，调整 ‖ *Ant.* demodulate 解调，检波

modulating ['mɔdjuleitiŋ] *v.* (modulate 的 ing 形式) 调节，调制，调整；*a.* 调制的

~ action 调制作用

modulation [ˌmɔdju'leiʃən] n. 调制，调节，调谐 ‖ Ant. demodulation 解调，检波

modulator ['mɔdjuleitə] n. 调制器，调节器

module ['mɔdju:l] n. 模块，组件，模数，指令舱

modulus ['mɔdjuləs] n. 系数，模数

moist [mɔist] n. 潮湿；a. 潮湿的，微湿的，多雨的

moisture ['mɔistʃə] n. 水分，湿气，潮湿，降雨量
 ~ capacity 湿度
 ~ control 湿度控制
 ~ ejector 除湿器，去湿器 ‖ Syn. moisture eliminator 除湿器，去湿器
 ~ proof 防潮 ‖ Syn. moisture protection 防潮；moisture resistant 防潮
 ~ resistivity 耐潮性
 ~ separator 水气分离器，去湿器
 ~ trap 气水分离器，脱湿器

mold [məuld] (=mould) n. 模子，模式，类型，铸型；v. 浇铸，塑造

molded ['məuldid] v. (mold 的过去式和过去分词) 浇铸，塑造；a. 模塑的
 ~ breadth 型宽
 ~ case circuit breaker (MCCB) 塑壳断路器
 ~ circuit board 模塑电路板
 ~ depth 型深

mole [məul] n. 莫尔式管道测弯仪(Mole)，摩尔，防波堤，筑有防波堤的海港

molten ['məultən] v. (melt 的过去式和过去分词) (使)熔化，(使)融化，(使)软化，(使)感动；a. 熔化的，铸造的，炽热的
 ~ iron 铁水，熔铁

moment ['məumənt] n. 片刻，瞬间；a. 片刻的，瞬间的，力矩的
 ~ compensator 力矩补偿器
 ~ of force 力矩
 ~ of inertia 惯性矩，转动惯量
 ~ of statical stability 静稳性力矩
 ~ of torsion 扭转力矩，扭矩，转矩

momentarily ['məuməntərili] ad. 顷刻之间，马上，立刻

momentary ['məuməntəri] a. 瞬间的，短暂的，刹那间的，随时会发生的
 ~ contact 瞬时接触
 ~ contact start button 瞬时接触启动按钮
 ~ voltage 瞬时电压

momentum [məu'mentəm] n. 动量，要素

Monel [məu'nel] n. 蒙乃尔
 ~ metal 蒙乃尔铜镍合金

monitor ['mɔnitə(r)] n. 监控器，监测仪，显示器，班长；v. 监测，监视，监听，监督，控制，追踪，记录

monitoring ['mɔnitəriŋ] n. 监测，监视，监听，监督，控制，追踪，记录；v. (monitor 的 ing 形式) 监测，监视，监听，监督，控制，追踪，记录
 ~ and controlling system 监控系统
 ~ and measuring with line selection 选线检测
 ~ data 监测数据
 ~ desk of main engine operation 主机运行监控台
 ~ device 监视装置，监视仪表，监控装置，监控仪表 ‖ Syn. monitoring equipment 监视装置，监视仪表，监控装置,监控仪表；monitoring instrument 监视装置，监视仪表，监控装置，监控仪表

~ of ship security 船舶安全监控

~ panel 监视屏，监控板

~ point 监控点

~ program 监督程序

~ screen of screw working condition 螺杆工作状态监测屏

~ station 监测站，监控台

~ system 监视系统，监控系统

~ unit 监控器

monkey ['mʌŋki] *n.* 猴，猿，淘气鬼；*v.* 胡闹，捣蛋

~ island 罗经平台

mono ['mɔnəu] *n.* 单声道唱片；*a.* 单声道的；*pref.* 一，单一

~ screw pump 单螺杆泵

mono-wall 整体式水冷壁

monobloc ['mɔnə,blɔk] *a.* 整体的，单块的，单层的

~ forging 整体锻造，整锻

~ forging crankshaft 整体锻造曲轴，整锻曲轴

monomer ['mɔnəmə] *n.* 单体

monorail ['mɔnəureil] *n.* 单轨索道，单轨铁路

~ provision crane 单轨式起重机，单轨式吊车

monosulfide [,mɔnə'sʌlfaid] *n.* 一硫化物

monotonic [mɔnəu'tɔnik] *a.* 单调的，无变化的

~ function 单调函数

monoxide [mə'nɔksaid] *n.* 一氧化物

month [mʌnθ] *n.* 月，月份，一个月的时间

monthly ['mʌnθli] *n.* 季刊；*a.* 每月的；*ad.* 每月一次

Mooney ['mu:ni] *n.* 穆尼(姓氏)

~ viscosity 穆尼黏度

moonpool [mu:n'pu:l] *n.* 中央井 ‖ *Syn.* center well 中央井

moor [muə] *n.* 沼地，荒野；*v.* 停泊，抛锚

mooring ['muəriŋ] *n.* 停泊处，系船具，下锚；*v.* (moor 的 ing 形式) 停泊，抛锚

~ anchor 系泊锚，固定锚

~ arrangement 系泊设备 ‖ *Syn.* mooring equipment 系泊设备

~ buoy 系泊浮筒

~ capstan 系泊绞盘

~ chock 导缆器，导缆钩

~ cleat 系缆耳

~ deck 系泊甲板

~ dolphin 靠船墩，系船柱

~ drum 绞缆筒

~ fittings 系泊属具，系泊设备

~ line 系泊缆，系船缆，系缆

~ machinery 系泊机械

~ operating mode management 系泊工况管理

~ outfit 系泊全套设备

~ pattern 系泊缆布置方式，系泊方式

~ ring 系船环，系泊环

~ shackle 系船接环

~ speed 系缆速度

~ system 系泊系统

~ test 系泊试验

~ test of mooring winch 绞缆机系泊试验

~ test (sea trial) of ME and inspection attached pumps and piping system 主机系泊(航行)试验并检查其附属泵与管路

~ test of steering gear 舵机系泊试验

~ test of windlass 锚机系泊试验

~ trial 系泊试车，系泊试验

~ winch 系泊绞车，绞缆机

~ winch brake design capacity 系泊绞车制动设计容量，绞缆机制动设计容量

~ winch drive 系泊绞车驱动，绞缆机驱动

~ winch foundation 系泊绞车基部，绞缆机基部

moot [mu:t] *n.* 大会，审议会；*v.* 提出…供讨论；*a.* 未决议的，无实际意义的

~ point 争论未决的问题，论点 ‖ ***Syn.*** contention 论点；issue 论点；point in question 论点

more [mɔ:(r)] *n.* 更多；*a.* 更多的，附加的，额外的；*ad.* 更，更多，更加，超过，多，大大高于；*num.* 更多

~ detailed inspection 更详细的检查

~ favorable treatment 更优惠的待遇

~ so 尤其如此

moreover [mɔ:'rəuvə] *ad.* 而且，此外

morse [mɔ:s] *n.* 海象，莫尔斯电码(Morse)，莫氏电码

~ lamp 莫氏信号灯

~ light bulb 莫氏信号灯泡

~ signal light 莫氏信号灯

~ taper gauge 莫氏锥度规

mortal ['mɔ:tl] *n.* 凡人，人类；*a.* 极端的，非常大的，非常长的，致命的，必死的，人类的，临终的

~ danger 致命危险

mosaic [mɔ'zeiik] *n.* 镶嵌图案；*a.* 嵌花式的

most [məust] *n.* 大多数，大部分；*a.* 最大的，最多的，多数的，大部分的；*ad.* 最，最多，很，十分，最，最大的，其中大多数，极其

~ economic control (MEC) 最经济控制

~ Favored Nation (MFN) 最惠国

~ Favored Nation Exemptions 最惠国豁免

~ Favored Nation Treatment 最惠国待遇

mostly ['məustli] *ad.* 大部分，多半，主要地，基本上，通常

mother ['mʌðə] *n.* 母亲，妈妈，母性，根本，源泉，巨大的事物；*a.* 母亲的，本源的，本国的

~ board 母板

motion ['məuʃən] *n.* 运动，动作；*v.* 运动

motionless ['məuʃ(ə)nlis] *a.* 静止的，不动的

motive ['məutiv] *n.* 动机，目的；*a.* 运动的，发动的，积极的

motor ['məutə] *n.* 汽车，马达，电动机，发动机；*a.* 原动的，有引擎的

~ bedplate 电动机机座

~ control 电动机控制器

~ control center (MCC) 电机控制中心

~ drive 电动机拖动，电机驱动

~ driver 电机驱动器

~ enclosure 电机壳

~ oil 润滑油

~ operating mechanism for air circuit-breaker 空气断路器电机操作机构

~ sailer 机帆船

~ ship (MS) 摩托船，内燃机船 ‖ ***Syn.*** motor vessel (MV) 摩托船，内燃机船

~ siren 电动警笛

~ speed 电动机转速

~ starting current 电机启动电流

~ system 电机系统

~ yacht 动力游艇

motor-driven 电动机驱动的，电动机拖动的，电动的

~ feed pump 电动给水泵

~ operating mechanism 电动操动机构

~ pump 电动泵

motor-generator 电动机发电机

~ set 电动机发电机组

~ system 电动机发电机系统

motorization [,məutərai'zeiʃən] n. 动力化，摩托化

motorize ['məutəraiz] v. 使机动化，使摩托化

motorman ['məutəmən] n. 司机，电动机操作者，机工

motorship ['məutəʃip] n. 内燃机船，柴油机船

mould [məuld] (=mold) n. 模型，霉；v. 铸造，发霉

~ growth test 长霉试验

~ loft (船厂)型线放样间

~ proof 防霉的

moulded ['məuldid] v. (mould 的过去式和过去分词) 铸造，发霉；a. 模具的，模制的

~ breadth 型宽

~ breadth extreme 模塑宽度极值

~ case circuit breaker (MCCB) 塑壳断路器

~ depth 型深

~ draught 型吃水

~ line 型线

moulding ['məuldiŋ] n. 模制件，铸造物，模制，浇铸；v. (mould 的 ing 形式) 铸造，发霉

~ plane 型刨

mount [maunt] n. 装配，乘用马，衬纸，山；v. 安装，爬上，增长，设置，安放，乘马，制作标本，上演 ‖ **Syn**. assemble 装配；build in 安装，固定；fit 安装；fix 安装，(使)固定；fix assemblage 安装；install 安装；set up 装配，竖立，架起

mounting ['mauntiŋ] n. 装备，底托，衬托纸，登上，乘骑

~ bedplate 装配架

~ bracket 安装托架

~ hole 安装孔

mouse [maus] n. 鼠标，老鼠；v. 搜寻

mouth [mauθ] n. 口，出入口，传闻

~ piece 管头

~ ring 防磨衬套垫环

movable ['mu:vəbl] n. 可移动物体；a. 变动的，活动的，不固定的，可移动的，动产的

~ carriage 活动滑架

~ lighting 活动照明

~ plate 活动板

~ vane 活动叶片

move [mu:v] n. 移动，迁居，步骤；v. 移动，离开，运行，迁移，搬家，感动，鼓动

movement ['mu:vmənt] n. 运动，活动，动作，运转

mover ['mu:və] n. 原动力，行动者，搬运家具的人，鼓吹者

moving ['mu:viŋ] v. (move 的 ing 形式) 移动，离开，运行，迁移，搬家，感动，鼓动；a. 感人的，可移动的，搬家的，搬运的

~ armature loud speaker 动电枢扬声器

~ blade shutter 动片快门
~ contact 动触点
~ part 运动机件
~ plate 移动模板
~ vane 活动轮叶
~ weight stabilizer 移动重量式减摇装置
MS (motor ship) 摩托船，内燃机船 ‖ **Syn**. MV (motor vessel) 摩托船，内燃机船
MSC (Maritime Safety Committee) 海上安全委员会，海事安全委员会
MSD (Maritime Safety Division) 海事安全司
MTBF (mean time between failures) 平均故障间隔时间，平均失效间隔时间，平均故障间隔期
MTBO (mean time between overhauls) 平均检修间隔时间，平均大修间隔时间
MTTF (mean time to failure) 平均故障时间
MTTR (mean time between removals) 平均拆换间隔时间
MTTR (mean time to repair) 平均维修时间，平均修复间隔时间
muck [mʌk] *n.* 污物，污泥，废石，湿粪，秽物；*v.* 弄脏，搞坏，捣乱
mud [mʌd] *n.* 泥，没价值的东西，污物，诽谤的话；*v.* 抹泥
~ ball 泥球
~ box 澄泥箱
~ charge header 泥浆充填集箱
~ collector 集泥器
~ hole 排垢孔
~ pump 抽泥泵，污水泵
~ system 泥浆冲洗法

~ treatment 泥浆处理
multi ['mʌlti] *n.* 多，多种，多个
multi-effect 多向作用的，多效的
~ evaporator 多效蒸发器
multi-buoy 多浮标的，多浮筒的
~ mooring 多浮标系泊，多浮筒系泊
multi-channel 多频道的，多信道的，多通道的，多波道的，多路的
~ television 多频道电视机
multi-input 多输入的
~ multi-output (MIMO) 多输入多输出的
~ multi-output system 多输入多输出系统
~ single-output (MISO) 多输入单输出的
~ single-output system 多输入单输出系统
~ switch 多输入开关
multi-ship 多种船型的，多船的
~ program 多种船型建造规划
multi-throw 多拐的
~ crank shaft 多拐曲柄
multi-valve 多气门的，多阀门的，多阀的
~ engine 多气门发动机
multicoil ['mʌltikɔil] *a.* (电器装置等)有数道线圈的
multicore ['mʌltikɔ:] *a.* 多芯的
~ cable 多芯电缆
multicriteria [mʌlti'kraitiəriə] *n.* 多目标，多指标，多准则
multicycle ['mʌltisaikl] *a.* 多循环的,多周期的
~ controlled by half-cycle 按半周进行的多周期控制

multifuel [mʌlti'fju:əl] *a.* 多种燃料的
~ engine 多燃料发动机

multifunction [,mʌlti'fʌŋkʃən] *n.* 多功能
~ control valve 多功能控制阀

multifunctional [,mʌlti'fʌŋkʃənl] *a.* 多功能的
~ device 多功能设备

multihull ['mʌltihʌl] *a.* 多船体的，多船体船的
~ vessel 多体船

multilayer ['mʌlti,leiə] *n.* 多层

multilevel [,mʌlti'levəl] *n.* 多级，多层次
~ computer control system 计算机多级控制系统
~ hierarchical structure 多级递阶结构
~ processing 多级处理
~ security proof 多级安全证明

multiloop ['mʌltilu:p] *a.* 多回路的
~ control 多回路控制
~ control system 多回路控制系统

multimeter ['mʌltimi:tə] *n.* 万用表

multimodal [mʌlti'mɔdl] *a.* 多模式的，多种方式的

multiobjective [mʌlti:əub'dʒektiv] *n.* 多目标

multiphase ['mʌltifeiz] *n.* 多相

multiple ['mʌltipl] *n.* 倍数；*v.* 成倍增加；*a.* 多重的，多路的
~ acting 多重作用
~ cylinder engine 多汽缸发动机
~ disc brake 多片盘式制动器
~ effect evaporation 多效蒸发
~ evaporator 多次蒸发器
~ feed system 多路供电式
~ integral 多重积分
~ loop fire alarm control unit 多路火灾报警控制器
~ phase ejector 多相喷射泵
~ standard 多重标准
~ stage flash evaporation 多次闪蒸，多级闪发
~ technologies and combined systems 多种技术及组合系统

multiplex ['mʌltipleks] *v.* 多路传输，多路通信；*a.* 多元的，多重的，复合的，多路传输的

multiplexer ['mʌlti,pleksə] *n.* 多路复用器，多路转换器 ‖ ***Ant.*** demultiplexer (多路)信号分离器，多路输出选择器

multiplicity [,mʌlti'plisiti] *n.* 多样性

multiplier ['mʌltiplaiə] *n.* 增加者，繁殖者，乘数，增效器，乘法器

multiply ['mʌltiplai] *v.* 繁殖，乘，增加

multipoint ['mʌltipɔint] *a.* 多点的，多位置的
~ change-over switch 多点转换开关

multipulse [mʌlti'pʌls] *a.* 多脉冲的
~ pressure charing system 多脉冲增压系统

multipurpose ['mʌlti'pə:pəs] *a.* 多用途的，多目标的
~ anchor winch 多用途起锚机
~ bulk container carrier 多用途散货集装箱运输船
~ cargo ship 多用途货船
~ dry cargo vessel 多用途干货船
~ fishing boat 多用途渔船
~ ship 多用途船
~ towing ship 多用途拖船
~ transformer 多用途变压器
~ wrench 多用途扳手

multirange ['mʌlti'reindʒ] *a.* 多量程的，多

刻度的

~ current transformer for measurement 多量程电流互感器

multispeed ['mʌltispi:d] *a.* 多速的

~ motor 多速电动机

multispindle ['mʌltispindl] *n.* 多轴；*a.* 多轴的

~ drilling machine 多轴钻床

multistage ['mʌltisteidʒ] *a.* 多级的

~ centrifugal pump 多级离心泵

~ compressor 多级压缩机

~ flash evaporation 多级闪蒸

~ pump 多级泵

multistate ['mʌltisteit] *a.* 多态的，多国的，各州的

~ input 多状态输入

~ output 多状态输出

multiway ['mʌlti,wei] *n.* 多路，多向，多位(加工)形式；*a.* 多路的，多向的，复合的

muriatic [,mjuəri'ætik] *a.* 盐酸化的

~ aci 盐酸

mushroom ['mʌʃrum] *n.* 蘑菇，暴发户；*v.* 迅速生长，迅速增加，采蘑菇；*a.* 蘑菇形的，迅速生长的

~ outlet closing and opening by hand to be inspected 菌形风帽手动启闭试验

~ ventilator 蘑菇形通风筒

muster ['mʌstə] *n.* 集合，阅，样品，清单，一群；*v.* 集合，召集，征召，鼓起，集聚

~ list 集合表

~ point 集合点

~ station 紧急集合点

mutual ['mju:tʃuəl] *a.* 相互的，共有的

~ conductance 互导

~ effect 相互影响

~ exclusion 互相排斥

~ flux 互磁通，互感磁通

~ inductance 互感(系数)

~ induction 互感应

~ inductor 相互推动者

~ reactance 互电感

~ repulsion 互相排斥

~ security 共同安全

~ solubility 互溶度

~ supervision 互相监督

mutually ['mju:tʃuəli] *ad.* 互相地，互助

~ exclusive attribute 互斥属性

MV (mean value) 平均数，平均值

MV (mean variation) 平均偏差

MV (medium voltage) 中压 ‖ *Syn.* intermediate voltage 中压；middle voltage 中压

~ network 中压供电网，中压(电力)系统

MV (motor vessel) 摩托船，内燃机船 ‖ *Syn.* motor ship (MS) 摩托船，内燃机船

N

nadir ['neidiə] *n.* 最低点，最底点

nail [neil] *n.* 指甲，钉，钉子；*v.* 钉，钉牢

~ hammer 钉锤

~ puller 拔钉器

naked ['neikid] *a.* 裸体的，无遮盖的，无装饰的，无保护的，无证据的，未证实的

~ flame 明火

name [neim] *n.* 名字，名称，姓名，名誉；

v. 命名，提名，叫出，指定；*a.* 姓名的，据以取名的

namely ['neimli] *ad.* 即，也就是，换句话说

nameplate ['neimpleit] *n.* 铭牌，名牌，标示牌
- ~ lamp 铭牌灯
- ~ rating 铭牌额定值
- ~ value 铭牌价值

nano ['nænəu] *n.* 纳米技术，毫微技术

nanometer ['neinə,mi:tə] *n.* 纳米，毫微米，十亿分之一公尺

naphtha ['næfθə] *n.* 轻油，石脑油，挥发油，粗汽油

narrow ['nærəu] *n.* 海峡，狭路，隘路，狭窄部分；*v.* (使)变窄，(使)缩小，限制，限定；*a.* 狭窄的，精密的，严密的，有限的，气量小的，勉强的，眼光短浅的

nation ['neiʃən] *n.* 国家，民族，国民，政府

national ['næʃənəl] *a.* 国家的，国民的，国有的，民族主义的
- ~ authorities 国家当局
- ~ fairway 国家航道
- ~ flag 国旗
- ~ standard 国家标准

natrium ['neitriəm] *n.* 钠

natrium-cooled 钠冷却的，钠冷的
- ~ valve 钠冷却气门，钠冷排气阀 ‖ *Syn.* sodium-filled valve 钠冷却气门，钠冷排气阀

natural ['nætʃərəl] *n.* 天赋；*a.* 自然的，自然界的，关于自然界的，天生的，天赋的，普通的，正常的，自然数的，简单自然的
- ~ circulation 自然循环
- ~ circulation boiler 自然循环锅炉
- ~ circulation of water 水的自然循环
- ~ circulation type cooling system 自然循环式冷却系统
- ~ commutation 自然换向
- ~ condition 自然条件
- ~ environment 自然环境
- ~ fiber rope 天然纤维绳
- ~ frequency 固有频率
- ~ gas 天然气
- ~ grounding device 自然接地装置
- ~ organic absorbent 天然有机吸收剂
- ~ power 自然功率
- ~ power factor 自然功率因数
- ~ resource 自然资源
- ~ smoke control 自然控烟
- ~ ventilation 自然通气

naturally ['nætʃərəli] *ad.* 自然地
- ~ aspirated 自然吸气的
- ~ aspirated engine 自然吸气发动机，无增压发动机

nature ['neitʃə] *n.* 性格，本性，性质，特性，天性，自然，自然界，大自然，自然状态，种类 ‖ *Syn.* performance 性能；property 性质，特性，属性

nautical ['nɔ:tikəl] *a.* 海上的，航海的，船舶的，海员的，水手的，海军的
- ~ assessor 航海顾问
- ~ characteristics 航海性能
- ~ chart 航海图，海图 ‖ *Syn.* nautical map 航海图，海图
- ~ mile 海里
- ~ planisphere 航海用平面图
- ~ scale 海图比例尺
- ~ sextant 航海六分仪

~ table 航海表

navaid ['næveid] *n.* 助航系统

 ~ class 助航舱

 ~ lighting 助航灯光

 ~ system 助航系统

 ~ wind-finding 导航测风

naval ['neivəl] *a.* 海军的，军舰的，船的

 ~ architect 造船工程师，造船技师

 ~ architecture 造船学

 ~ ship 舰艇，军船

navigability [ˌnævigə'biləti] *n.* 适航性，耐航性，可操纵性

navigable ['nævigəbl] *a.* 可航行的，可领航的，可通航的，可操纵的

 ~ canal 航行运河

 ~ condition 通航条件

 ~ depth 适航水深

 ~ period 通航期

 ~ route 通航航线

 ~ semicircle 可航半圆

 ~ span 适航跨距

 ~ speed 可航速率

 ~ water 可航行的水域

navigate ['nævigeit] *v.* 航行，航海，航空，驾驶，操纵，横渡，跨越，使通过，排除困难

navigation [ˌnævi'geiʃən] *n.* 航海，航空，导航，领航，航行

 ~ aids 助航设备，导航辅助设备，航行标志

 ~ and manoeuvring workstation 导航操纵台

 ~ area 航行区域

 ~ bar 导航栏

 ~ bridge 驾驶室

 ~ bridge visibility 驾驶台能见度

 ~ channel 通航水道

 ~ deck 驾驶甲板

 ~ equipment 导航设备

 ~ equipment distrubution 导航设备分配

 ~ lamp 航行灯 ‖ *Syn*. navigation light 航行灯；running light 航行灯

 ~ lock 船闸

 ~ mark 航标

 ~ radar 导航雷达

 ~ satellite 导航卫星

 ~ service vessel 导航服务船

navigational [ˌnævi'geiʃənl] *a.* 航行的，航海的

navigator ['nævi,geitə] *n.* 领航员，航海家，航行者，航海者，导航装置

navy ['neivi] *n.* 海军，船队，藏青色

naze [neiz] *n.* 山甲，海角

NC (numerical control) 数字控制

near [niə] *v.* 接近，走近；*a.* 亲近的，亲密的，近，左侧的，吝啬的；*ad.* 在近处，在附近，近，不远

near-universal 几乎全体的，准万向的

 ~ gear 准万向舵机

nearby ['niəbai] *a.* 附近的，邻近的；*ad.* 在近处，在附近

nearest ['niərist] *a.* 最近的

 ~ land 最近陆地

nearly ['niəli] *ad.* 几乎，差不多，密切地

nearness ['niənis] *n.* 靠近，接近，近，亲密，密切

necessary ['nesisəri] *n.* 必需品；*a.* 必要的，强制的，必然的

 ~ and not sufficient aspect 必要而非充分的条件

necessitate [ni'sesiteit] *v.* 成为必要，需要，强迫，迫使

necessity [ni'sesiti] *n.* 必要性，需要，必需品 ‖ *Syn.* requirement 需求，要求，必要条件，需要的东西

neck [nek] *n.* 海峡，颈，脖子，衣领，颈状物
~ ring 颈环，项圈，颈圈

needle ['ni:dl] *n.* 针，针状物
~ bearing 滚针轴承
~ tube 针管
~ valve 针阀

negative ['negətiv] *n.* 否定，负数，底片；*v.* 否定，拒绝；*a.* 否定的，消极的，负的，阴性的
~ attitude 消极态度
~ charge 负电荷 ‖ *Ant.* positive charge 正电荷
~ effect 负面影响
~ electrode 负电极
~ factor 消极因素
~ feedback 负反馈 ‖ *Ant.* positive feedback 正反馈
~ feedback control system 负反馈控制系统
~ grounded DC two-wire system 直流负极接地双线制
~ growth 负增长
~ influence 消极作用
~ ion 阴离子 ‖ *Ant.* positive ion 阳离子
~ number 负数 ‖ *Ant.* positive number 正数
~ phase 负相
~ phase sequence relay 负(相)序继电器
~ pole 阴极，负极 ‖ *Syn.* cathode 阴极，负极 ‖ *Ant.* anode 阳极，正极; positive pole 阳极，正极

~ pressure 负压，负压力
~ rake 负前角，负倾角
~ sequence 负序 ‖ *Ant.* positive sequence 正序 ‖ zero sequence 零序
~ sequence impedance 负序阻抗
~ suction head 真空吸入压头，负压头
~ supply 负电源
~ temperature 零下温度
~ terminal 负端
~ value 负值，消极因素

neglect [ni'glekt] *n.* 忽视，疏忽，漏做；*v.* 忽略，疏忽，遗漏，疏于照顾

neglectful [ni'glektful] *a.* 疏忽的，忽略的，不注意的

negligence ['neglidʒəns] *n.* 疏忽，粗心大意

negligent ['neglidʒənt] *a.* 疏忽的，粗心大意的
~ packing 包装马虎

neither ['ni:ðə] *a.* 两个都不；*ad.* 也不，一样不；*conj.* 均非，既不…也不；*pron.* 两个都不

net [net] *n.* 网，网状织物，球网，网罩；*v.* 用网捕，净赚，得到；*a.* 净余的，纯粹的
~ horsepower 有效功率
~ load curve 净载荷曲线
~ positive suction 净正吸力
~ positive suction height 净正吸力高度
~ power 有效功率
~ scantling 净偏差
~ tonnage 净吨位
~ horsepower 有效功率
~ positive suction head 净吸引，净压头

network ['netwə:k] *n.* 网络，网状物，广播网

~ communication 网络通信

~ connection 网络接线

~ fault 网络故障

~ interconnection 网络互连

~ of a ship 船舶网络

~ terminal 网络终端

neutralise ['nju:trəlaiz] v. (=neutralize) 使中立化，使无效，使中性，中和，抵消，压制

neutralize ['nju:trəlaiz] v. (=neutralise) 使中立化，使无效，使中性，中和，抵消，压制

neutral ['nju:trəl] n. 齿轮的空档，中立者，非彩色；a. 中立的，中性的，无确定性质的，不确定的

~ axis 中性轴

~ beam 中性束

~ current 中性线电流

~ detergent 中性洗涤剂

~ equilibrium 中性平衡

~ ground 中性点接地

~ grounding 中线接地，中性接地

~ line 中性线 ‖ Syn. neutral wire 中性线

~ plane 中和面 ‖ Syn. neutral surface 中性面

~ point 中和点，中性点

~ position 中立地位，中性位置，空档

~ zone action 中性区作用

neutrality [nju:'træliti] n. 中立，中立地位，中性

neutralization [,nju:trəlai'zeiʃən] n. 中立化，中立状态，中和

neutralize ['nju:trəlaiz] v. 中和，使中立化，使无效，宣布中立，抵消，压制

never ['nevə] ad. 从不，从来没有，一点也不，决不

nevertheless [,nevəðə'les] ad. 不过，仍然；conj. 不过，然而

new [nju:] a. 新的，初见的，更新的；ad. 新近

~ energy 新能源

newly ['nju:li] ad. 新近，最近，重新，以新的方式

~ made as per sample 按原样生产

~ mould with cast iron 新铸铁模具

nib [nib] n. 嘴，鹅管笔的尖端，钢笔尖；v. 装尖头，削尖，插入

~ strake 船首尾水道内列板

nichrome ['nikrəum] n. 镍铬铁合金，镍铬耐热合金

~ wire 镍铬线，镍铬合金线

Nichols ['nikəls] n. 尼科尔斯(人名、英格兰姓氏)

~ chart 尼科尔斯海图 ‖ Syn. Nichols diagram 尼科尔斯图

nickel ['nikl] n. 镍，镍币，(美国和加拿大的)五分镍币；v. 镀镍于

~ electro plate 电镍板

~ iron battery 镍铁电池

~ plate 镍镀层

nickel-cadmium 镉镍

~ battery 镍镉电池

nickel-plated 镀镍的

~ steel wire 镀镍钢丝

night [nait] n. (=nite) 晚上，夜，黑暗，死亡

~ dive 夜潜

~ diving 夜潜

~ patrol 巡更，夜间巡逻

nil [nil] n. 无，零，零分

nipple ['nipl] *n.* 螺纹接头，滑油嘴，水龙头，(枪炮的)火门，喷灯喷嘴，乳头，橡皮奶头

nite [nait] *n.* (=night) 晚上，夜，黑暗，死亡

nitrate ['naitreit] *n.* 硝酸盐，硝酸钾

nitric ['naitrik] *a.* 氮的，含氮的，硝石的
~ acid 硝酸

nitrite ['naitrait] *n.* 亚硝酸盐

nitrocellulose [naitrəu'seljuləus] *n.* 硝化纤维

nitrogen ['naitrədʒən] *n.* 氮，氮气
~ generation plant 制氮机，氮气发生器 ‖ ***Syn***. niteogen generator 制氮机，氮气发生器
~ oxides (NOx) 氮氧化物
~ oxides converter 氮氧化物转化器
~ oxides emission 氮氧化物排放
~ Oxides Technical Code 氮氧化物技术章程

nitroglycerin ['naitrəu'glisəri:n] *n.* 硝化甘油，炸药

no [nəu] *n.* 否定，投反对票者；*a.* 没有，不许，反对；*ad.* 不，并不，毫不
~ decompression 免减压
~ decompression limit 最大免减压时间
~ fuse breaker 无熔丝开关
~ fuse position 无保险丝位置
~ refill 不再充填，不再装满，不再灌满
~ response 无响应，没有响应
~ risk 无风险，不负风险

no-load 空载的，无载的，以资产净值出售的，不取佣金的
~ characteristic 无载特性，空载特性，无载特性曲线
~ current 空载电流
~ loss 空载损耗
~ operation 空载运行
~ speed 空车速度，空载速度，空转速度，空行程速度
~ test 空载试验，无负荷试验
~ voltage 空载电压

no-trouble 无故障的
~ trip 无故障跳闸

no-voltage 无电压的，零电压的

nocuous ['nɔkjuəs] *a.* 有害的，有毒的

nod [nɔd] *n.* 点头，同意，打瞌睡，粗心大意；*v.* 上下摆动，低垂，点头，过失

node [nəud] *n.* 网点，节点，结点

nodular ['nɔdjulə(r)] *a.* 小节的，小瘤的，小结的
~ cast iron 球墨铸铁

noise [nɔiz] *n.* 噪声，杂音，嘈杂声，喧闹声，干扰噪声，无用数据
~ clipper 静噪器，噪声限制器
~ insulation 隔音，噪声绝缘
~ level on board ship 船上的噪声水平
~ measurement 噪声测量

noisy ['nɔizi] *a.* 嘈杂的，聒噪的

nominal ['nɔ:minl] *a.* 名义上的，微不足道的，票面上的，名字的，列名的
~ bandwidth 标称带宽，额定带宽 ‖ ***Syn***. rated bandwidth 额定带宽
~ bore 公称管径
~ capacity 额定功率，标称功率，额定容量，标称容量，标称容积，额定容积 ‖ ***Syn***. capacity rating 额定功率，额定容量；nominal output 额定功率，额定出力，额定输出，标称输出；

nominal power 额定功率，额定容量，标称功率，标称容量；power rating 额定功率；rated capacity 额定功率，额定容量，设计效率；rated output 额定功率，额定输出量，额定出力；rated power 额定功率，设计功率，额定动力，不失真功率；rated power capability 额定功率；rated power output 额定功率，额定动力输出；standard horsepower 额定功率，标准马力；standard power 额定功率，标准功率

~ current 标称电流，额定电流 ‖ *Syn*. current rating 额定电流；rated current 额定电流；rating current 额定电流，电流额定值

~ data 标定数据，名目数据

~ diameter 公称直径，标称直径

~ dimension 公称尺寸，标称尺寸，毛尺寸 ‖ *Syn*. nominal size 标称尺寸，公称尺寸，毛尺寸

~ horsepower 标称马力，额定马力 ‖ *Syn*. rated horsepower 额定马力

~ load 标称负载，标称荷载，额定负载，额定荷载 ‖ *Syn*. load rating 额定负载，额定负荷；rated load 额定负载，额定负荷

~ load capacity 标称载重量，额定载重量 ‖ *Syn*. rated load capacity 额定载重量

~ power factor 标称功率因数，额定功率因数 ‖ *Syn*. rated power factor 额定功率因数

~ pressure 标称压力，额定压力 ‖ *Syn*. rated pressure 额定压力

~ revolution 额定转速 ‖ *Syn*. nominal speed 标称速度，标称转速，额定速度，额定转速；rated revolution 额定转速；rated speed 额定速度，额定转速

~ stress 公称应力

~ torque 标称转矩，额定转矩 ‖ *Syn*. rated torque 额定转矩；torque rating 额定转矩

~ voltage 标称电压，额定电压 ‖ *Syn*. rated voltage 额定电压；voltage rating 额定电压

nomogram ['nɔməgræm] *n*. 列线图，列线图装置

non [nuŋ] *ad*. 非，不

non-additive 无添加剂的

~ oil 无添加剂润滑油

non-adjustable 不可调校的，不可调的，固定式的

~ cam 不可调凸轮

~ control thermostat 不可调控制温控器，固定式控制温控器

~ master jet 不可调主喷嘴

~ restrictor 不可调节流器，不可调节流阀

~ stroke 非可调行程

~ wrench 固定扳手

non-all-phase 非全相，缺相 ‖ *Syn*. non-full-phase 非全相，缺相

~ cutoff 非全相切断，缺相切断

~ operation 非全相运行，缺相运行

non-burnable 不可燃烧的，不燃的

~ refuse 不可燃烧的垃圾

~ waste 不燃废物

non-circular 非圆形的，非圆的

~ pad 非圆形盘

non-clearance 无间隙的

~ tappet 无间隙挺杆 ‖ *Syn*. zero-rush tappet 无间隙挺杆

non-combustible 非燃烧体，非易燃的，不可燃的
~ cargo 非易燃货物
~ construction 非燃性构造
~ covering 不燃覆盖物，不燃的电缆包皮
~ fabric 非易燃织物
~ impurities 非易燃杂质
~ material 非易燃物质
~ refuse 非易燃垃圾
non-condensable 非凝性的，不凝性的 ‖ *Ant*. condensable 可凝性的
~ gas 非凝性气体
~ pipeline 非凝性气体管道
~ purger 非凝性净化机，非凝性气体排除器
~ vapor 不凝性蒸汽
non-conductive 非导电的
non-conformity 不一致，和规则等不适合
~ of quality 质量不符
non-conventional 非常规的，非传统的
non-cooperative 不合作的，非合作的，非协同的
non-coplanar 非共面的，不共面的
~ cylinder 非共面缸
non-destructive 无损的，非破坏性的
~ inspection 无损检测
~ install 非破坏性安装
~ test 无破坏试验
non-detachable 不可拆卸的，不可拆开的
~ type fire detector 不可拆卸式火灾探测器
non-essential 不重要的，非本质的
~ auxiliary 次要属件
~ concession 非主要条款
~ document 不必要文件

non-explosive 无爆炸性的，防爆的
non-fitted 非紧配的，不合身的
~ bolt 非紧配螺栓
non-flammable 不易燃的，非燃的
~ fibre 不燃纤维
~ fluid 不燃液体
~ gas 不燃性气体
~ material 不易燃材料
~ paint 不燃漆，耐火漆
~ refrigerant 不易燃制冷剂
non-full-phase 非全相，缺相 ‖ *Syn*. non-all-phase 非全相，缺相
~ operation 非全相运行 ‖ *Syn*. non-full-phase running 非全相运行
~ protection 非全相保护
~ state 非全相状态，缺相状态
non-hazardous 无危险的，无害的，无事故的
~ area 非危险区域
non-intensive 非集中的，非集约的
~ inspection 非集中检验
non-inverting 非反相的，同相的
~ connection 非反相连接，同相连接，同相接法
non-lubricated 非润滑的
~ compressor 无润滑压缩机 ‖ *Syn*. oil-free compressor 无油压缩机
non-metallic 非金属的
~ component 非金属件，非金属成分
~ gear 非金属齿轮
~ hose 非金属软管
~ materials and products 非金属材料及制品
~ pipe 非金属管道
~ seal 非金属密封
~ sheath 非金属护套

~ sheathed wire 非金属铠装线
non-moving 不动的，定点的
　～ lifting 定点起吊
Non-Parties 非缔约国
non-poisonous 无毒的
　～ compressed gas 无毒压缩气体
　～ material 无毒材料
　～ stabilizer 无毒稳定剂
non-positive 负的，负值的，非正的
　～ compressor 非容积式压缩机
　～ displacement 非正排量式
non-reply 无应答的
　～ call 无应答呼叫
non-resettable 不可复位的
　～ fire detector 不可复位火灾探测器
non-retractable 不可伸缩的，不可收放的
　～ fin stabilizer 不可收放式减摇鳍，非收放型减摇鳍装置
non-return 单向的，止回的，不返回的
　～ flap 逆止门，止回瓣
　～ seal 反逆流油封
　～ suction 止回吸入口
　～ suction valve 止回吸入阀
　～ valve 止回阀，单向阀，逆止阀，止逆阀 ‖ *Syn*. check valve 止回阀，单向阀，逆止阀，止逆阀；inverted valve 止回阀，单向阀，逆止阀，止逆阀；one-way valve 止回阀，单向阀，逆止阀，止逆阀
non-reversible 不可逆的，不可倒置的，不能反转的
　～ deformation 不可逆形变，永久形变
　～ electric drive 不可逆电驱动
non-self-priming 非自吸的，非自充满的
　～ pump 非自吸泵，非自引液泵
non-slip 防滑的，不滑的

～ lining 防滑里
～ material 防滑材料，止滑材料
～ treatment 防滑处理
non-sparking 无火花的
　～ metal 无火花金属
　～ motor 无火花电机
　～ tool 无火花工具
non-split 非分裂式的，合并式的
　～ type mooring drum 非分裂式绞缆筒，合并式绞缆筒
non-standard 非标准的，不标准的，不规范的
　～ control box 非标准控制箱
non-stationary 非平稳的，不稳定的，非平稳
non-toxic 无毒的
　～ process 无毒化工艺，无害化工艺
　～ substance 无毒物质
　～ waste 无毒废物
non-uniform 不均匀的，不统一的，不同的 ‖ *Ant*. uniform 统一的，一律的，一致的，均质的，相同的，始终如一的，均衡的
　～ field 不均匀场
　～ flow 不均匀流，非等速流，不等速流，变速流
　～ motion 非均匀运动，变速运动
　～ pitch 非等螺距
　～ pitch propeller 非等螺距螺旋桨
　～ placement 非均匀放置
　～ transmission 不均匀传输，非匀速传输，变速传输
non-uniformity 非一致(性)，不均匀(性)
　～ characteristics 非均匀性特性
　～ materials 非匀质类材料
　～ structure 非均匀结构

non-volatile 不挥发的，非易失的
~ contaminant 不挥发性污染物
~ oil 不挥发油
~ petroleum 非挥发性石油
~ residue 非挥发性残留，非挥发性残渣
~ solid 非挥发性固体

non-watertight 非水密的，漏水的，不防水的
~ box 非水密闭盒
~ bulkhead 非水密舱壁
~ diaphragm 非水密隔板
~ door 非水密门
~ pillar bulkhead 非水密支承舱壁
~ plug 非水密插头
~ snap switch 非水密瞬动开关
~ structure 非水密结构

non-work 非工作的
~ compensation in power systems & application 电力系统非功补偿及其应用

non-woven 无纺的
~ fabric 无纺布，非织物

noncoherent ['nɔnkəu'hiərənt] a. 非相干的，疏松的，松散的，不黏聚的，不附着的，无黏性的

none [nʌn] ad. 决不，毫不；pron. 一个也没有，毫无

nonequilibrium ['nɔnikwi'libriəm] n. 非平衡态，不平衡；a. 不平衡的
~ state 非平衡态

nonferrous [nɔn'ferəs] a. 不含铁的，非铁的
~ metal 有色金属，非铁金属

nonius ['nɔniəs] n. (计算尺等上的)游标

nonlinear [nɔn'liniə] a. 非线性的，非直线的，非一次的 ‖ *Ant*. linear 线性的，直线的，线的

nonlinearity [,nɔnlini'æriti] n. 非线性 ‖ *Ant*. linearity 线性，直线性

nor [nɔ:r] ad. 也不，也没有；conj. 也不，也不是

norm [nɔ:m] n. 规范，标准，准则，定额，向量长度，平均，模范 ‖ *Syn*. criterion 标准，准据，规范；measure 标准，量度标准，尺度；standard 标准，规格；touchstone 标准，检验标准，检验手段

normalization [,nɔ:məlai'zeiʃən] n. 正常化，标准化

normal ['nɔ:məl] n. 正规，常态，法线；a. 正常的，正规的，标准的
~ acceleration 法向加速度，垂直加速度
~ charging 正常充电，标准装药，正常装药，正常收费
~ clearance 正常间隙
~ condition 基准状态，标准状态，常规条件，正常情况
~ distribution 正态分布
~ form 标准型，正规形式，规格化形式
~ function 正态函数，正常函数
~ level 正常水平，正常能级，法线分类
~ load 正常负载
~ mode 正常模式，简正模式，自然振荡，固有状态
~ operating condition 正常工作状态，常规运作状况，正常操作条件，正常使用状态，正常使用条件
~ operation 正常运行，常规操作
~ operation mode 正常运行方式，正常操作模式
~ output service 正常输出服务
~ phenomenon 正常现象
~ pressure 正常压力，标准气压

409

~ running 正常运转，机组运行正常
~ service speed 正常使用转速
~ shift 正常移距
~ source 常用电源，正常电源
~ starting sequence 正常起动程序
~ state 正常状态
~ stress 正应力，法向应力
~ value 正常价值，标准值
~ vector 法向量，法向向量，法向矢量
~ wear 正常磨损

normality [nɔ:'mæliti] *n.* 常态，规定浓度

normalize ['nɔ:məlaiz] *v.* (使)正常化，(使)标准化，(使)规格化

normally ['nɔ:məli] *ad.* 正常地，通常地
~ closed 正常闭合的，常闭的
~ closed contact 常闭触点
~ closed valve 常闭阀
~ open 正常断开的，常开的
~ open contact 常开触点
~ open valve 常开阀

normative ['nɔ:mətiv] *a.* 标准的，规范的

north [nɔ:θ] *n.* 北方，北部，北；*a.* 北的，北方的；*ad.* 在北方，向北方
~ Pole 北极

northeastward [nɔ:θ'i:stwəd] *n.* 东北；*a.* 在东北方的；*ad.* 在东北

northern ['nɔ:ðən] *a.* 北方的，北部的

northward ['nɔ:θwəd] *a.* 向北的；*ad.* 向北方

northwest ['nɔ:θ'west] *n.* 西北部，西北，西北方向；*a.* 西北的

northwestern ['nɔ:θ'westən] *a.* 西北的，西北方的，来自西北的

nose [nəuz] *n.* 鼻子，(飞机、船等的)前端；*v.* 侦察出
~ of tool 刀尖

not-under-command (NUC) 不受指挥的，不能操纵的，失去控制的
~ light 失控信号灯

notably ['nəutəbli] *ad.* 尤其，显著地，特别地

notarial [nəu'tɛəriəl] *a.* 公证人的，公证的
~ survey 公证检验

notary ['nəutəri] *n.* 公证人，公证员

notation [nəu'teiʃən] *n.* 记号，符号，标记法

notch [nɔtʃ] *n.* 刻痕，凹口，槽口；*v.* 刻凹痕，用刻痕计算，开槽，切口，得分

notching ['nɔtʃiŋ] *n.* 槽口，凹痕，切口；*v.* (notch 的 ing 形式) 刻凹痕，用刻痕计算，开槽，切口，得分；*a.* 下凹的
~ press 冲缺口压力机，冲切机，冲槽机

note [nəut] *n.* 笔记，短信，(外交)照会，注解，注释，票据，纸币，音符；*v.* 注意，记录，笔记

notebook ['nəutbuk] *n.* 笔记本
~ computer 笔记本电脑
~ system unit 笔记本系统单元

nowadays ['nauədeiz] *ad.* 现在，当今，现今

NOx (nitrogen oxides) 氮氧化物
~ converter 氮氧化物转化器
~ emission 氮氧化物排放
~ Technical Code 氮氧化物技术章程

noxious ['nɔkʃəs] *a.* 有害的，有毒的
~ liquid substance 有毒液体物质
~ liquid substance carried in bulk 散装运输的有毒液体物质

nozzle ['nɔzl] *n.* 管嘴，喷嘴
~ angle 喷嘴角，喷口扩散角

~ cooling passage 喷嘴冷却通道
~ holder 喷油器壳
~ hole 喷嘴孔，喷孔
~ nut 喷嘴螺母，喷嘴螺帽
~ orifice 喷嘴孔口，喷口
~ pressure 喷嘴压力
~ ring 喷嘴环
NUC (not-under-command) 不受指挥的，不能操纵的，失去控制的
~ light 失控信号灯
nuclear ['nju:kliə] a. 原子核的，原子能的，核子的，核的，中心的
~ fission energy 核裂变能
~ fuel 核燃料
~ plant 核电站 ‖ *Syn*. nuclear power station 核电站
~ power 核能，核动力
~ propulsion 核动力推进
~ radiation 核辐射
~ radiation level meter 核辐射量计
~ radiation test 核辐射试验
~ submarine 核子动力潜艇，核潜艇
nuclear-powered 核动力的
~ vessel 核动力船
nude [nju:d] n. 裸体，裸体像；a. 裸体的，裸的，与生俱有的，无装饰的
~ packing 裸装
null [nʌl] n. 零，空，零信号；a. 无效力的，无效的，无价值的，等于零的
number ['nʌmbə] n. 数量，号码，数字，编号；v. 编号，共计，计入，计算，算入
~ of poles 极数
~ plate 号码牌，铭牌
numeral ['nju:mərəl] n. 数词，数字；a. 数字的，表示数字的

numerary ['nju:mərəri] a. 数目的
numeric [nju:'merik] n. 数，数字；a. 数字的，数值的
~ entry 数值输入，数字输入
numerical [nju:'merikəl] a. 数字的，用数字表示的，数值的
~ code 数码，数字码
~ control (NC) 数字控制
numerically [nu'merikəli] ad. 数字上，用数表示地
numerous ['nju:mərəs] a. 数不清的，众多的，许多的
nutrient ['nju:triənt] n. 营养物，养分；a. 营养的
nylon ['nailən] n. 尼龙
~ insulation tape 尼龙绝缘胶带
Nyquist ['naikwist] n. 奈奎斯特(1889—1976，美国物理学家)
~ diagram 奈奎斯特图
~ stability criterion 奈奎斯特稳定判据

O

oakum ['əukəm] n. 油麻丝,麻絮,填絮(用于填塞船缝)
oar [ɔ:] n. 桨，橹
obey [ə'bei] v. 服从，遵循，顺从
object ['ɔbdʒikt] n. 物体，目标，宾语，客体，对象；v. 反对，拒绝，抗议
~ function 目标函数，原函数 ‖ *Syn*. objective function 目标函数
~ of measurement 测量对象
objection [əb'dʒekʃən] n. 异议，缺陷，妨碍，反对，反对的话，反对的理由
objectionable [əb'dʒekʃənəbl] a. 令人不快的，令人反感的，讨厌的，引起反

对的

objective [əb'dʒektiv] n. 目标，目的；a. 目标的，客观的，实体的

~ function 目标函数 ‖ **Syn**. object function 目标函数，原函数

objectivity [,ɔbdʒek'tivəti] n. 客观性，客观现实

obligate ['ɔbligeit] v. 使负责任，使负义务，施以恩惠；a. 有责任的，有义务的，必要的

obligation [,ɔbli'geiʃən] n. 义务，责任，债务，证券，契约，恩惠

obligatory [ɔ'bligətəri] a. 义务的，必须的，应尽的，强制性的

oblique [ə'bli:k] a. 斜，倾斜的，间接的，不坦率的，无诚意的

~ bitts 斜式双柱系缆桩

oblong ['ɔblɔŋ] n. 长方形，椭圆形；a. 长方形的，椭圆的，矩形的，椭圆体的

~ pad 长方形焊盘

OBO (oil-bulk-ore) 石油散货矿砂

~ carrier 石油散货矿砂运输船

obscuration [,ɔbskjuə'reiʃən] n. 昏暗，暗淡，朦胧

~ smoke detector 减光型感烟探测器

obscure [əb'skjuə] v. 使暗，使不明显；a. 暗的，朦胧的，模糊的，晦涩的

observability [əb'zə:vəbiliti] n. 可观测性，可观察性，能观测性

observation [,ɔbzə:'veiʃən] n. 观察，观察力，评论，观察资料，观察报告

~ deck 瞭望甲板，观测甲板，观景台

observational [,ɔbzə'veiʃənəl] a. 观察的，观测的

~ data 观测资料，观测数据

observe [əb'zə:v] v. 观察，遵守，庆祝，评述

obsolete ['ɔbsəli:t] a. 废弃的，老式的，已过时的

~ document 作废文件

~ vessel 老式舰，废船

obstruct [əb'strʌkt] n. 阻碍物，障碍物；v. 阻碍，阻止，阻塞，堵塞

obstruction [əb'strʌkʃən] n. 障碍物，阻塞，妨碍

obtain [əb'tein] v. 获得，得到，流行，达到，成功

obtainable [əb'teinəb(ə)l:] a. 可获得的，可取得的，可到手的

obvious ['ɔbviəs] a. 明白的，明显的，显而易见的，显著的，挡路的

obviously ['ɔbviəsli] a. 明显地

occasion [ə'keiʒən] n. 场合，机会，时机

occasional [ə'keiʒənəl] a. 临时的，偶尔的，不经常的，特殊场合的

~ survey 临时检验，临时检查，不定期调查

occasionally [ə'keiʒnəli] ad. 偶尔，偶然，有时候

occlusion [ə'klu:ʒən] n. 咬合，堵塞，闭塞，闭塞物

occupational [,ɔkju'peiʃənəl] a. 职业的，工作的，占领的

occupy ['ɔkjupai] v. 占领，占用，占据，居住，忙于，填满

occur [ə'kə:] v. 发生，出现，存在，生存，闪现，想起，想到

occurrence [ə'kʌrəns] n. 发生，出现，遭遇，事件，发生的事情

ocean ['əuʃən] n. 海洋，洋，大海，许多，广阔

~ basin 洋盆，海洋盆地

~ bottom 洋底，海床

~ circulation 海洋环流，大洋环流

~ currents 海流，洋流

~ dredging 海洋疏浚

~ engineering 海洋工程

~ engineering vehicle 海洋工程船

~ environment 海洋环境

~ floor 大洋底，洋底，海底

~ freight 海运运费，海运费

~ liner 远洋邮轮，远洋班轮，远洋定期客轮

~ monitoring ship 海洋监测船

~ shipping 远洋运输，海运

~ transportation 远洋运输，海运

~ wave 海浪

~ weather ship (OWS) 海洋气象船，海洋测候船

ocean-going 远洋航行的，远洋的

~ engineer 远洋工程师

~ ship 远洋船

oceanic [ˌəuʃi'ænik] a. 远洋，海洋的，海洋产出的，生活于海洋的

oceanographic [ˌəuʃiənəu'græfik] a. 海洋学的，有关海洋学的

~ buoy 海上浮筒，海上浮标，海洋观测浮标，海洋浮标

~ chart 海洋图，海图，海洋作业图

~ research vessel 海洋调查船

octagon ['ɔktəgən] n. 八边形，八角形

~ hammer 八角锤

octagonal [ɔk'tægənl] a. 八边形的

~ steel bar 八角钢筋

~ steel rod 八角钢棒

octal ['ɔktl] a. 八进制的

octopus ['ɔktəpəs] n. 章鱼

~ alternate air source 章鱼式

OD (outside diameter) 外直径，外径，大端直径

odd [ɔd] a. 奇数的，单数的，单只的，不成对的，临时的，不固定的，残留的，残余的，剩余的，带零头的 ‖ **Syn**. remainder 残留的，残余的，剩余的；redundant 多余的，过剩的，累赘的，冗余的；remanent 残留的，残余的，剩余的；residual 残留的，残余的，剩余的；residuary 剩余的，残余的；superfluous 多余的，过剩的，过量的；surplus 过剩的，剩余的

~ number 奇数 ‖ even number 偶数

odor ['əudə] n. 气味，名声

odorless ['əudəlis] a. 没有气味的，无臭的

off [ɔ:f] a. 向海的，远的，空闲的，不精确的，不正确的，不工作的；ad. 离开，离去，分离，中断，完成，距离，被取消，在远方；prep. 从…离开，脱离

~ air 停播，消失

~ center loading 偏离中心的装载，偏心加载

~ limit 越界

~ state 关断状态，关闭状态

off-going 走开的，出发的，离去的

~ generator 待解列发电机

off-hire 停租，退租

~ survey 退租检验

off-limit 越限的，禁止的

~ alarm 越限报警

~ contacts 限位触点

off-line 离线；离线的，脱机的 ‖ **Ant**. on-line 在线；在线的，即时的

off-load 卸载，卸货，发泄，摆脱

~ sequence valve 卸载顺序阀

offer ['ɔfə] *n*. 出价,提议,意图; *v*. 提供,提议,出价,贡献,(使)出现,企图,演出

office ['ɔfis] *n*. 办公室,办事处,事务所,办公楼,问询处,重要官职,政府机关,部,公职,职责,帮助

  ~ equipment 办公用具,办公室设备

officer ['ɔfisə] *n*. 高级船员,高级职员,船长,军官,警官,公务员; *v*. 指挥

  ~ of the watch 舰上值班军官,值班驾驶员

officer's 高级船员的

  ~ mess 高级船员餐厅

official [ə'fiʃəl] *n*. 官员,公务员; *a*. 正式的,官方的,法定的,职务上的,公职的,公务的

  ~ business 公务

  ~ logbook 航海日志,船舶日志

  ~ number 船舶号数,官方号码,正式编号

  ~ number of ship 船舶正式编号

offset ['ɔ:fset] *n*. 偏移量,抵消,弥补,分支,平版印刷,胶印; *v*. 偏移,形成分支,抵消,补偿,弥补,用平版印刷

  ~ connecting rod 偏置连杆

  ~ land 偏置连接盘

  ~ table 型值表

offshore ['ɔ(:)ʃɔ:] *a*. 近海的,离岸的,海面上的,海外的,国外的

  ~ crane 海上起重机,海域起重机

  ~ drilling assembly 海上钻探装置

  ~ mobile units 海上移动式装置

  ~ structure 近海结构,海域结构物,离岸工程结构物

  ~ supply vessel 近海供应船

  ~ units 海上设施

ohm [əum] *n*. 欧姆(电阻单位)

  ~ gauge 电阻计,欧姆表 ‖ *Syn*. ohmmeter 欧姆计,欧姆表

ohmmeter ['əum,mi:tə] *n*. 欧姆计,欧姆表 ‖ *Syn*. ohm gauge 电阻计,欧姆表

oil [ɔil] *n*. 油,石油,油类,油状物; *v*. 加油,上油,涂油,行贿,给小费

  ~ absorbent 吸油剂

  ~ absorbing 吸油

  ~ air separator 油气分离器

  ~ barge 油驳,油驳船,油趸

  ~ bath 油槽,油池

  ~ boiler 燃油锅炉

  ~ boom 围油栏,防油栅,油栅

  ~ break fuse 油熔断器

  ~ break switch 油断路器,油开关

  ~ buffer 油压缓冲器,油压减振器

  ~ carrier 油船,油轮

  ~ catcher 油滴接头,集油器

  ~ channel 油槽,滑油槽,漏油槽

  ~ circuit breaker 油压断路器,油断路器

  ~ clearance 油膜间隙,油膜间隙,油隙

  ~ collecting agent 集油剂

  ~ collecting space 储油空间

  ~ collector 储油箱,集油器

  ~ consumption 耗油量

  ~ contamination 油污染

  ~ content meter 油分浓度计,油含量计

  ~ control ring 护油环,护油圈

  ~ cooler 油冷却器,油冷器

  ~ cup 油杯,润滑油杯

  ~ cushion 油垫

  ~ cylinder 油缸

  ~ defector ring 挡油环

~ disc 油盘
~ discharge 卸油，排油
~ discharge criteria 油类排放标准
~ discharge monitoring and control system 排油监控系统
~ dispersant 油分散剂，消油剂 ‖ *Syn*. oil dispersing agent 油分散剂，消油剂
~ distributing ring 分油环，布油环
~ distribution casing 配油盘 ‖ *Syn*. oil distribution disc 配油盘
~ distribution port 配油口
~ distribution shaft 配油轴
~ distribution sleeve 配油套
~ distributor 油量分配器，配油器
~ drain plug 放油塞
~ drainage 排油，放油
~ drainage port 排油口，放油口
~ droplet 油滴，油珠
~ emulsion 油乳剂，油品乳化液
~ filler 油料加入器，加油口
~ film 油膜
~ filter 滤油器
~ filtering equipment 滤油设备
~ filtering system 滤油系统
~ fired auxiliary boiler 辅助燃油锅炉
~ flow distribution valve 配油流阀
~ foaming 油泡沫
~ gallery 油沟，回油孔
~ gelling agent 凝油剂
~ gun 油枪，注油器
~ hammer 油击
~ heater 油加热器
~ hole 注油孔
~ in water emulsion 乳化油，水包油乳剂，水包油乳状液
~ in water monitor 油分浓度检测器

~ leakage 漏油
~ level alarm protection 油位报警保护
~ (level) gauge 油位计，量油尺，油位表 ‖ *Syn*. oil (level) meter 油位计，量油尺，油位表
~ like extreme pressure additive 油状极压添加剂
~ like substance 类油物质
~ line 输油管
~ lubricanting 油润滑
~ minimum circuit breaker 少油断路器
~ mist 油雾
~ mist detector 油雾探测器
~ mixture 混合油
~ motor 油马达，油电动机
~ motor control 油马达控制
~ orifice 油孔
~ outlet 出油口
~ pan 油底壳，油盘
~ pillow 吸油枕
~ pipe 油管
~ pollution 油类污染，油污染
~ Pollution Act (OPA) 油污法案
~ pollution bulletin 油污染公报
~ pollution control 油污染控制
~ pollution emergency plan 油污染应急计划
~ pollution emergency response and cooperation 油污染应急响应与合作
~ pollution for ship 船舶油污染
~ pollution prevention 防止油污染
~ preheater 燃油预热器
~ pressure 油压
~ pressure control 油压控制
~ pressure differential controller 油压差控制器

~ pressure gauge 油压计
~ pressure regulation valve 油压调节阀
~ pressure sensor 油压传感器
~ pump 油泵
~ quantity 油量
~ rag bin 油布箱
~ rags 油布
~ record book 油料记录簿，油类记录簿
~ recovery 油回收
~ recovery and sludge treatment system 油回收与污泥处理系统
~ removal 除油
~ renewal 油再生，油更新
~ residues 油类残留物，油渣
~ resisting rubber hose 耐油胶管
~ resisting rubber jointing 耐油橡胶垫
~ resistivity 耐油性
~ return device 回油装置
~ return pipe 油回流管，回油管
~ return regulation valve 回油调节阀
~ sample 油样
~ scraper 刮油器，刮油机，刮油刀
~ scraper ring 刮油圈，刮油环
~ seal 油封
~ separator 油分离器
~ skimmer 油撇取器，撇油器，油回收船
~ sludge and sediment to dug and removed 油泥沉淀物挖除
~ sludge tank 油泥罐
~ soluble 油溶性，油溶性的
~ sorbent 吸油剂，吸油材料
~ sorbent mat 吸油毡
~ sounding steel tape 量油钢皮尺
~ spill 溢油，漏油，浮油 ‖ *Syn*. oil

spillage 溢油
~ spill control 溢油控制
~ spill kit 油泄漏工具包
~ spill recovery equipment 溢油回收设备
~ spill treating agent 溢油处理剂
~ spillage in ocean 海洋溢油
~ stone 油石
~ storage tank 储油槽，储油箱，储油柜
~ strainer 滤油器，机油滤器，机油过滤器
~ suction pipe 吸油管
~ sump 油槽，油池，油沉淀池
~ tanker 油船，油轮，油罐车
~ tight 油封，不漏油
~ trap 集油器，集油池，隔油池
~ treatment 油处理
~ vapor 油蒸汽
~ viscosity 油黏度
~ water 油水
~ water disposal boat 油水处理船
~ water interface detector 油水界面检测器
~ water separator 油水分离器
~ way 油路，油道
oil-bulk-ore (OBO) 石油散货矿砂
~ carrier 石油散货矿砂运输船
oil-contaminated 油污染的
~ space 油污染空间
oil-cooled 油冷式的，油冷的
~ engine 油冷式发动机
oil-filled 油浸的，充油的
~ transformer 油浸式变压器，充油式变压器
oil-free 无油，不含油的
~ compressor 无油压缩机 ‖ *Syn*. non-

lubricated compressor 无润滑压缩机
oil-immersed 油浸没的，油浸的 ‖ *Syn*. oil-impregnated 油浸渍的，油浸的
~ rheostat 油浸变阻器
~ transformer 油浸变压器
oil-impregnated 油浸渍的，油浸的 ‖ *Syn*. oil-immersed 油浸没的，油浸的
~ paper 油浸渍纸
oil-proof 防油的，耐油的，不漏油的
~ sheath 防油套，耐油鞘
oil-recovery 浮油回收，油回收
~ vessel 浮油回收船
oil-rig 钻油架
~ cable 油井用电缆
oiler ['ɔilə] *n.* 加油工，油轮，运油船，油商，注油壶
oiliness ['ɔilinis] *n.* 油性，含油(性)，油质，油气，油腻
~ bearing 含油轴承
oilskin ['ɔilskin] *n.* 油布，防水布
oiltight ['ɔiltait] *a.* 不漏油的，油密的
~ cofferdam 油密围堰
oily ['ɔili] *a.* 油的，油腻的，油滑的，油质的
~ ballast water 含油压舱水
~ bilge separator 油污分离器
~ water separator 油水分离器
OLTC (on load tap changer) 有载调压分接开关，有载调压开关
omni ['ɔmni] *n.* 全部，总
omni-directional 全向的
~ pressure 全向压力
OMS (Outage Management System) 停电管理系统
on [ɔn] *ad.* 在上，向前，行动中，作用中；*prep.* 在…之上，依附于，临近，靠近，向，在…时候，关于，涉及
~ and Off Hire Surveys 船舶承租和解租公证
~ berth 在泊位上，在泊
~ board 在船(火车、飞机)上，上船(火车、飞机)
~ completion 完成后，完工时，完工
~ deck 置于甲板，在甲板上，准备就绪的，下一个将轮到的
~ high 在高处，在天空
~ line 在线的，联机的
~ load tap changer (OLTC) 有载调压分接开关，有载调压开关
~ passage 在运输途中，在航行中
~ patrol 在巡逻，巡逻中
~ schedule 按时，按照预定时间
~ the berth 在泊位上
~ the bow 在首舷方向，在船头前方左右45°范围内
~ the first try 第一次尝试
~ the left 在左边
~ the portside 在左舷，走向左舷
~ the scene 在场，出现，到场
~ the spot 立刻，当场，在危险中，处于负责地位
~ the starboard 在右舷，走向右舷
on-deck 在甲板上，准备就绪的
~ cargo 舱面货
~ container 甲板集装箱
~ girder 甲板上桁架，甲板上纵梁
~ operation 舱面作业
~ storage 甲板储存，平台储存
on-line 在线；在线的，即时的 ‖ *Ant*. off-line 离线；离线的，脱机的
~ monitoring 在线监测
on-load 带载的，有载的，负载的，带负

荷的
~ operation 带载操作，有载运行
~ regulating transformer 带负荷调压变压器，有载调压变压器
~ regulation 有载调节
~ speed 带负载转速，有载转速
~ test 有载试验，带负荷试验
~ voltage regulator 带负荷电压调整器
~ washing 带负荷清洗
on-off 开关，通断，开关的，通断的
~ action 通断作用
~ control 通断控制
~ controller 通断控制器，开关控制器
~ switch 通断开关，换向开关，双位开关
~ two position regulator 双位开关调整器
on-scene 现场，现场的
~ commander (OSC) 海难现场指挥员，现场指挥官，现场指挥
~ security survey 现场安全调查
onboard ['ɔn'bɔ:d] *a.* 机载的，舰载的，随车携带的
~ communication station 船上通信电台 ‖ *Syn.* ship communication station 船舶通信电台，船舶通信站
once [wʌns] *n.* 一次，一回；*a.* 曾经的，以前的；*ad.* 仅仅一次，一次，关系相隔一代的，从前，曾经；*conj.* 一旦，一…就，当…时
once-through 直流，直通
~ flash evaporator 直流闪发蒸发器
one [wʌn] *n.* 一，一个；*a.* 一方的，某一的，同样的，同一的，整体的；*num.* 一，一个；*pron.* 一个人，任何人，一方

~ thirds 三分之一
one-circuit 单回路的
one-piece 一体式的，整体式的
~ crankshaft 整体式曲轴
~ piston 整体式活塞
one-way 单向的，单程的，单行道的，单方面的
~ feed 单向馈电，单路馈电
~ pressure reducing valve 单向减压阀
~ sequence valve 单向顺序阀
~ throttle valve 单向节流阀
~ valve 止回阀，单向阀，逆止阀，止逆阀 ‖ *Syn.* check valve 止回阀，单向阀，逆止阀，止逆阀；inverted valve 止回阀，单向阀，逆止阀，止逆阀；non-return valve 止回阀，单向阀，逆止阀，止逆阀
onerous ['ɔnərəs] *a.* 繁重的，麻烦的，负有义务的，负有法律责任的
onset ['ɔnset] *n.* 开始，动手，攻击，袭击，发病
onshore ['ɔn'ʃɔ:] *a.* 海岸的，在岸上的，在近岸处的，朝着岸的；*ad.* 向着海岸，在陆上
onus ['əunəs] *n.* 责任，义务，负担，重担
ooze [u:z] *n.* 软泥；*v.* 渗出，泄漏，使液体缓缓流出，充分地表露或散发
OPA (Oil Pollution Act) 油污法案
opacimeter [,əupə'simitə] *n.* 乳浊度计，暗度计
opacity [əu'pæsiti] *n.* 不透明性，不透光，费解，难懂，模糊，黑暗，愚蠢
~ of exhaust gas 烟度计
opal ['əupəl] *n.* 蛋白石，猫眼石，乳色玻璃

~ bulb 乳白灯泡，乳白玻壳

opaque [əu'peik] *n*. 不透明物；*a*. 不透明的，无光泽的，不传导性的，不传热的，迟钝的

open ['əupən] *n*. 公开，户外，空旷；*v*. 开放，张开，打开，公开，展开，开始；*a*. 开着的，敞开的，无篷的，开阔的，营业着的，公开的，坦率的，未决定的

~ architecture 开放式体系结构

~ circuit 断路 ‖ *Ant*. short circuit 短路

~ circuit photo-voltage 开路光电压

~ combustion chamber 开式燃烧室

~ cooling system 开放式冷却系统

~ cooling water system 开放式冷却水系统

~ delta connection 开口三角形连接，开口三角联结

~ end 开口端

~ flame 明火

~ floor 组合肋板，构架肋板，开框肋板

~ hydraulic system 开式液压系统

~ loop 开环

~ loop control 开环控制

~ loop control system 开环控制系统

~ loop model 开环模型

~ loop pole 开环极点

~ loop system 开环系统

~ loop transfer function 开环传递函数，开环传函

~ mooring 八字锚泊

~ on 开放，通往

~ phase 断相，缺相，开相

~ phase protection 缺相保护装置

~ position 打开位置

~ road 开敞锚地，敞开的路

~ Ro-Ro cargo space 开式滚装处所

~ sea 公海

~ side container 侧开式集装箱

~ switch 开启式开关，扳动开关

~ system 开放系统

~ systems interconnection 开放系统互连

~ tank venting system 开放式储罐放空系统

~ top container 开顶集装箱

~ type motor 开敞式电动机

~ type panel 开敞式面板

~ up 打开，开发，开始，展示，揭露

~ up for inspection 开放检查

~ water diving 开放水域潜水

~ waters 外海，开阔水域

~ with 以…开始，始于

~ yacht 敞篷快艇

opener ['əupənə] *n*. 开启者，开始者，开启工具

opening ['əupniŋ] *n*. 开，开放，开始，口子，穴，通路，空缺，机会；*v*. (open 的 ing 形式) 开放，张开，打开，公开，展开，开始；*a*. 首次的，开始的，打开的，开幕的

~ and closing test for cargo hatch cover 货舱舱口盖启闭试验

~ pressure 开启压力

openwater ['əupən'wɔːtə] *n*. 开敞水面，开阔水面，无冰水面

~ diver 初级潜水员 ‖ advanced diver 中级潜水员；specialty diver 专项潜水员

operable ['ɔpərəbl] *a*. 可操作的，可行的，可动手术的，可开刀的

operate ['ɔpəreit] *n*. 作军事行动；*v*. 操

作，工作，控制，运转，管理，经营，开动，生效，起作用，影响，进行军事行动，进行海上活动，动手术，开刀
~ function 操作功能

operating ['ɔpəretiŋ] *v.* (operate 的 ing 形式) 操作，工作，控制，运转，管理，经营，开动，生效，起作用，影响，进行军事行动，进行海上活动，动手术，开刀；*a.* 操作的，营运的，运行的，工作的，手术的
~ area 操作区
~ characteristic 运行特性
~ condition 运行状态，运行条件，操作规范
~ cost 使用费用，生产费用，运转成本
~ cycle 工作循环，营业循环，经营周期
~ device 操作装置，控制设备
~ efficiency 工作效率，营业效率，经营效率
~ environment 操作环境
~ handle 操作手柄，操纵杆 ‖ **Syn.** operating lever 操纵杆，操作杆
~ instruction 使用说明书
~ irregularity 工作事故
~ log 工作记录，运行记录
~ manual 使用说明书
~ mechanism 操作机构，工作机构
~ method 操作方法
~ mode 操作模式，工作模式
~ mode selector valve 工况选择阀
~ overvoltage 操作过电压
~ parameter 操作参数，运行参数
~ performance 操作性能，营业实绩
~ power source 操作电源
~ pressure 操作压力，工作压力，控制压力

~ principle 工作原理，操作原理
~ procedure 操作程序，作业程序
~ range 工作范围，运行范围
~ rules 操作规程，运行规程
~ sequence 操作程序，操作顺序
~ slide disc 操作滑板
~ speed 运行速度，运转速度，工作速度
~ supply voltage 电源工作电压
~ system 操作系统
~ temperature 工作温度，操作温度，动作温度
~ time 工作时间，操作时间，作业时间
~ trouble 运行故障，操作故障，行车故障
~ value 动作值
~ voltage 工作电压，运行电压
~ water tank 工作水柜
~ width 操作宽度，工作宽度

operation [,ɔpə'reiʃən] *n.* 运转，操作，实施，作用，业务，工作，手术，军事行动
~ accident 操作事故
~ against rules 违章操作
~ amplifier 运算放大器
~ and maintenance 运行与维护
~ and maintenance of main engine 主机运行与维护
~ manual 操作指南，操作手册
~ mechanism 运行机制，工作机构
~ of electric systems 电力系统运行
~ panel 操作面板，操纵板
~ password 操作密码
~ system (OS) 操作系统
~ technique of electric systems 电力系统运行技术

~ test of emergency switching-off device for oil pump and ventilator (bilge pump) in engine room 机舱风、油(舱底泵)应急切断装置操作试验

~ test of remote control device for fire pump and emergency fire pump 消防泵、应急消防泵遥控装置操作试验

operational [ˌɔpəˈreiʃənl] *a.* 操作的，能使用的，胜任的，可用的，实行的，有效的，军事行动的，手术的，经营的

~ architecture 体系结构

~ command 操作指令，运算指令

~ description 操作说明

~ problem and remedies 操作问题与补救措施

~ procedure and arrangement 操作程序与安排

~ safety 操作安全性

~ test 运行试验，运转试验，操作测试

~ test for automatic fire alarm system 火灾自动报警系统运行试验

~ test for automatic sprinkler system 自动喷水灭火系统运行试验

~ test for inert gas system 惰性气体系统运行试验

~ test for water fire-extinguishing system 水灭火系统运行试验

operative [ˈɔpərətiv] *a.* 运转着的，实施中的，起作用的，最适合的，手术的

operator [ˈɔpəreitə] *n.* 操作员，经营者，算子，运算符，报务员，接线员，行家，手术员

opinion [əˈpinjən] *n.* 意见，主张，评价，鉴定，判定

opportunity [ˌɔpəˈtjuːniti] *n.* 机会，时机，良机，适当的时机

oppose [əˈpəuz] *v.* 抵制，反对，抗争，使对立，使对抗

opposed [əˈpəuzd] *v.* (oppose 的过去式和过去分词) 抵制，反对，抗争，对立，对抗；*a.* 相反的，反对的，敌对的

~ cylinder engine 对置气缸式发动机

~ piston engine 对置活塞式发动机

~ piston internal combustion engine 对置活塞式内燃机

~ pistons 对置活塞

opposite [ˈɔpəzit] *n.* 对立面，对立物，相反的人，相反的事物；*a.* 相对的，对面的，对立的，相反的，对等的，对应的

~ in phase 反相，相位相反

opposition [ˌɔpəˈziʃən] *n.* 障碍物，相反，反对，反抗，阻挠，敌对，反对派

opt [ɔpt] *v.* 选择，挑选，选取，决定做

optic [ˈɔptik] *n.* 眼睛,光学镜；*a.* 光学的,视觉的，眼的 ‖ *Syn.* optical 光学的，视觉的，眼的

~ fiber tachometer 光纤式转速表

optical [ˈɔptikəl] *a.* 光学的，视觉的，眼的 ‖ *Syn.* optic 光学的，视觉的，眼的

~ aligned check for shaft system after boring 轴系镗孔后光学校中检查

~ disk 光盘

~ fiber 光纤

~ fiber sensor 光纤传感器

~ flame fire detector 感光火灾探测器

~ mouse 光学鼠标

~ scanner 光电扫描仪，光扫描器

~ smokemeter 光学烟度计

optimal [ˈɔptiməl] *a.* 最佳的，最优的，最理想的，最适宜的，最令人满意的

~ allocation 最优配置
~ control 最优控制
~ design 优化设计
~ design of power system 电力系统优化设计
~ parameter setting 最优参数设置
~ performance 最优性能
~ planning of power source in a power systems 电力系统电源优化规划
~ position 最优位置
~ process 最优过程
~ solution 最优解
~ strategy 最优策略
~ technology of power systems 电力系统优化技术

optimality [,ɔpti'mæliti] *n.* 最优性，最佳性

optimise ['ɔptimaiz] *v.* (=optimize) 使最优化，使尽可能有效，充分利用

optimization [,ɔptimai'zeiʃən] *n.* 最佳化，最优化，优选法，优化组合
~ design 优化设计
~ technique 优化技术，最优化技术

optimize ['ɔptimaiz] *v.* (=optimise) 使最优化，使尽可能有效，充分利用

optimum ['ɔptiməm] *n.* 最佳效果，最适宜条件，最适度；*a.* 最适宜的
~ heating temperature 最佳加热温度
~ load sharing 最佳负荷分配
~ quantity of oil separation 最佳分离油量
~ speed 最佳转速，最佳速度

option ['ɔpʃən] *n.* 选项，选择权，买卖的特权

optional ['ɔpʃənəl] *a.* 可选择的，随意的

or [ɔ:] *conj.* 或，或者，还是，不然，否则，就是，或者说
~ else 否则，要不然
~ more 或…以上
~ otherwise 或相反
~ rather 确切地说，说得更准确些
~ so 大约，上下

orange ['ɔrindʒ] *n.* 柑橘，橙子，橙色；*a.* 橙色的

order ['ɔ:də] *n.* 次序，顺序，秩序，正常状态，会议规则，命令，订购，订单；*v.* 命令，订购，订制，整理 ‖ *Syn.* sequence 次序，顺序，序列
~ book 订货簿
~ line 订货线
~ number 订单号，订单编号
~ parameter 有序参数
~ quantity 订货量，订购量，订单数量

orderliness ['ɔ:dəlinis] *n.* 规律，整齐，整洁，秩序井然

orderly ['ɔ:dəli] *n.* 传令兵，勤务兵；*a.* 整齐的，有秩序的，整洁的；*ad.* 依次地，顺序地

ordinance ['ɔ:dinəns] *n.* 条例，法令，训令，布告，传统的风俗习惯

ordinarily [,ɔ:di'nərili] *ad.* 按说，平常地，通常地

ordinary ['ɔ:dinəri] *a.* 平常的，普通的，平凡的，一般的 ‖ *Syn.* common 公共的，普通的；commonplace 平凡的；general 一般的，普通的；pervasive 普遍的；popular 大众的，通俗的，普遍的；universal 普遍的，通用的；usual 平常的，通常的，惯例的；widespread 分布广泛的，普遍的
~ accident 一般事故
~ course 常规过程，正常贸易

~ goods 一般品，普通货物
~ quality 普通质量，常规品质
~ repairs 普通修理，一般修护
~ Seaman (OS) 普通海员，普通水手，二等水手，三等水兵，(美国)海岸警卫队成员
~ temperature 常温，室温

ordinate ['ɔ:dinit] n. 纵坐标，纵线

ore [ɔ:(r)] n. 矿，矿石，矿砂
~ carrier 矿砂船
~ hatchway 矿石舱口，装矿舱口

organ ['ɔ:gən] n. 元件，机构，器官，机关，机关报，嗓音 ‖ **Syn.** cell (电池、光电)元件，单元；component 成分，部分，元件，零件，要素，组分；constituent 成分，要素；element 要素，元素，成分，元件；ingredient 成分，因素；part 零件，部件

organic [ɔ:'gænik] a. 有机的，有组织的，系统的，建制的，器官的
~ acid 有机酸
~ content 有机物含量，有机质含量

organism ['ɔ:gənizəm] n. 有机体，生物体，微生物

organization [,ɔ:gənai'zeiʃən] n. 组织，机构，团体

organize ['ɔ:gənaiz] v. 组织，安排，规划，建立组织

orient ['ɔriənt] n. 东方，东方诸国；v. 标定方向，确定方向，(使)适应形势，(使)向东；a. 东方的，上升的，灿烂的

orientation [,ɔ(:)rien'teiʃən] n. 方向，方位，定位，倾向性，向东方

orifice ['ɔ:rifis] n. 孔，口，洞口
~ plate 孔板，挡板，节磷板，量孔板

origin ['ɔridʒin] n. 原点，起源，由来，起因，出身，血统

original [ə'ridʒənəl] n. 原物，原作；a. 原始的，最初的，独创的，新颖的
~ data 原始资料，源数据
~ setting 原始设置

originally [ə'ridʒənəli] ad. 原本，起初，原来

originate [ə'ridʒineit] v. 引起，创始，发生，发明，起源，发生

orlop ['ɔ:lɔp] n. 最下层甲板

orthogonal [ɔ:'θɔgənl] a. 直角的，矩形的，直交的，垂直的

OS (Ordinary Seaman) 普通海员，普通水手，二等水手，三等水兵，(美国)海岸警卫队成员

OS (operation system) 操作系统

OSC (on-scene commander) 海难现场指挥员，现场指挥官，现场指挥

oscillate ['ɔsileit] v. (使)振荡，(使)振动，(使)动摇，犹豫

oscillating [asə'leitiŋ] v. (oscillate 的 ing 形式) 振荡，摆动；a. 振荡的，犹豫的
~ circuit 振荡电路
~ current 振荡电流
~ oil cylinder 摆动油缸
~ period 振荡周期

oscillation [,ɔsi'leiʃən] n. 振动，波动
~ absorber 减振器，缓冲器

oscillator ['ɔsileitə] n. 振荡器，振子

oscilloscope [ɔ'siləskəup] n. 示波镜

osmosis [ɔz'məusis] n. 渗透，渗透作用，渗透性 ‖ **Syn.** infiltration 渗透，渗入，渗透物；permeation 渗入，透过

osmotic [ɔz'mɔtik] a. 渗透的，渗透性的

423

~ pressure 渗透压力

other ['ʌðə] *a.* 其他的，另外的，从前的，别的；*ad.* 另外地，不同地；*pron.* 其他的，他人，另外一个

~ accidents 其他事故

~ casting technologies 其他铸造工艺

~ equipment 其他设备，其他器材

~ forging parts 其他锻造件

~ than 除了，不同于

~ types of fishing ship 其他类型渔船

otherwise ['ʌðəwaiz] *a.* 另外的,其他方面的；*ad.* 否则，另外，不同地，别的方式

otto ['ɔtəu] *n.* 玫瑰油，奥托(Otto，男子名)

~ cycle 奥托循环，等定容循环

~ cycle engine 奥托循环发动机

ounce [auns] *n.* 盎司，少量

out [aut] *n.* 外面，外出，外观；*v.* 外出，暴露，赶出，击倒，使退场；*a.* 外面的，下台的，出局的；*ad.* 在外，出声地，显露出来地，明显地，从头至尾地；*prep.* 通过

~ drive stage 输出驱动级

~ going degree 入度

~ of commission 退役的，损坏的，不能使用的

~ of control 失去控制

~ of fix 已损坏的，(钟表等)不准，(身体)不舒服

~ of order 次序颠倒，不整齐，状态不好 ‖ *Syn.* dysfunction 机能不良，功能紊乱，官能障碍；failure 失灵，故障；fault 故障；trouble 故障

~ of phase 异相，异相地，不协调，不协调地

~ of place 不合适的，不相称的，不在适当的位置

~ of round 不圆，失圆

~ of step 不合拍，步调不一致

~ of sticky situation 脱离险境

~ of the ordinary 与众不同的，不平常的

~ strake 外列板

out-of-door 户外的，室外的，露天的 ‖ *Syn.* outdoor 户外的，室外的，露天的 ‖ *Ant.* indoor 室内的，户内的

out-of-phase 不同相的，异相位的

~ diagram 失相图，移位示功图

outage ['autidʒ] *n.* 减耗量，断供期，断供

~ gauging 油柜空高量油

~ Management System (OMS) 停电管理系统

outboard ['autbɔ:d] *n.* 舷外发动机，尾挂机船；*a.* 船外的，舷外的，装有舷外发动机的，外侧的，外端的

~ discharge valve 通海排出阀

~ motor 舷外发动机，舷外马达

~ profile 船舶侧视图

outbound ['autbaund] *a.* 开往外地的，开往外国的

~ vessel 出口船,出站船 ‖ *Ant.* inbound vessel 进口船，入站船

outbreak ['autbreik] *n.* 爆发，突然发生，发作

outcome ['autkʌm] *n.* 结果，结局，成果，出路

outdoor ['autdɔ:] *a.* 户外的，室外的，露天的 ‖ *Syn.* out-of-door 户外的，室外的，露天的 ‖ *Ant.* indoor 室内的，户内的

~ oil tank 室外油柜

outer ['autə] n. (射击)环外命中；a. 外面的，外部的，远离中心的 ‖ **Syn**. exterior 外部的，外在的，表面的，外交的，外用的；external 外部的，外用的，外国的，表面的 ‖ **Ant**. interior 内部的，国内的，内陆的，本质的；internal 内部的，内在的，国内的，内政的

~ balance pipe 外平衡管

~ bearing 外轴承

~ bottom 外底，外层底板，外层底

~ boundary 外边界

~ bush 外导套

~ diameter 外径

~ edge 外缘，外刃

~ gear 外齿轮

~ guiding post 外导柱

~ jib 外首帆

~ jib staysail 外吊臂眼圈

~ loop 外回路，外侧环路，外层循环

~ membrane 外膜

~ radial clearance 外径向间隙

~ ring 外圈，外环

~ rotor 外转子，外齿轮

~ valve spring 外阀弹簧，外气门弹簧

~ wall 外壁，外墙

outermost ['autəməust] a. 最外面的，离中心最远的

outfire [aut'faiə] v. 灭火

outfit ['autfit] n. 用具，配备，机构，全套装配；v. 装备，配备，供应，得到装备

outfitting ['autfitiŋ] n. 舾装，全套服装；v. (outfit 的 ing 形式) 装备，配备，供应，得到装备

~ department 舾装部

~ quay 舾装码头

outgo [aut'gəu] n. 支出，消耗；v. 赶上，超过，优于，走得远，走得快

outgoing ['autgəuiŋ] n. 流出，外出，开支；v. (outgo 的 ing 形式) 赶上，超过，优于，走得远，走得快；a. 往外去的，离去的，开朗的，外出的，即将离任的

~ gas 排出气体，出气

~ interface 输出接口，输出界面，发送接口

~ line 引出线，输出线，出线 ‖ **Ant**. incoming line 引入线，输入线，进线

~ low tide 退潮

~ panel 出线屏，馈电盘，输电板

outhaul ['autho:l] n. 驶帆索 ‖ inhaul 卷帆索，引索

~ whip 外牵索

~ winch 拉出绞机

outlay ['autlei] n. 费用，花费，支出，开销，费用额；v. 花费，花钱

outlet ['autlet] n. 出水口，出路，电源插座

~ box 出线箱，出线盒

~ connection 出口接头

~ diameter 出口直径，排出口直径，出水口径

~ distributing header 出口分配联箱 ‖ **Ant**. inlet distributing header 进口分配联箱

~ grid 出风栅

~ intermediate relay 出口中间继电器

~ line 输出线，出口管线

~ nozzle 出口喷嘴

~ opening 排出口，出油口

~ pipe 出口管，排水管，去水管，排气管

~ pressure 出口压力

~ temperature 出口温度

~ valve 出油阀，排出阀

~ velocity 出口速度

~ water 废水，排水

outline ['əutlain] n. 略图，外形，大纲，轮廓，要点，概要；v. 概述，略述

output ['autput] n. 输出，输出量，输出信号，产量，产品，作品；v. 输出

~ current 输出电流

~ data 输出数据

~ polarity 输出极性，输出端极性

~ port 输出端口，输出端，出油口

~ power 输出功率

~ shaft 输出轴

~ signal 输出信号

~ torque 输出转矩，输出力矩，输出扭矩

~ value 输出值，产值

~ variable 输出变量

~ voltage 输出电压

outreach [aut'ri:tʃ] n. 伸出，超出极限伸距；v. 到达顶端，超越，超过

outrigger ['autrigə] n. 舷外支架，突出的梁，突出的桁

outside [aut'said] n. 外面，外表，外界；a. 外面的，外部的，外表的，外界的，室外的；ad. 在外面，外表，出界；prep. 在…外

~ air 室外空气，户外空气

~ area fault 外区故障

~ calipers 外卡钳，外卡尺

~ diameter (OD) 外直径，外径，大端直径

~ gearing pump 外啮合齿轮泵

~ micrometer 外径千分尺，外径测微计，螺旋卡尺

outstand [aut'stænd] v. 忍耐，停留，突出，凸出，卓然独立

outstanding [aut'stændiŋ] n. 未偿贷款；v. (outstand 的 ing 形式) 忍耐，停留，突出，凸出，卓然独立；a. 突出的，杰出的，显著的，有待完成的，未解决的，未支付的

outstretch [aut'stretʃ] v. 伸出，伸展

outward ['autwəd] n. 外表，周围世界；a. 外面的，外表的，公开的，向外的，外出的；ad. 向外，在外，表面上

~ heeling 外倾

outwards ['autwədz] ad. 向外地，外表地

oval ['əuvəl] n. 椭圆，椭圆形；a. 椭圆形的，卵形的

~ man-hole jointing 椭圆人孔垫圈

~ piston 椭圆形活塞

~ wheel gear flowmeter 椭圆齿轮流量计

ovality [əu'væliti] n. 椭圆度，椭圆变形，椭圆形

oven ['ʌvən] n. 烤箱，烤炉，灶

over ['əu'və] n. 额外的东西；v. 越过，超过；a. 上面的；ad. 结束，越过，从头到尾；prep. 在…之上，越过

overage ['əuvəridʒ] n. 过剩，过多；a. 过老的

overall ['əuvəro:l] a. 全部的，全体的，全面的，一切在内的

~ design 总体设计，总设计

~ dimension 最大尺寸，轮廓尺寸，总尺寸

~ efficiency 总效率

~ performance 整体性能，总指标

~ stability 总稳定度，总稳定性

~ survey 全面调查

overboard ['əuvəbɔ:d] ad. 在船外，自船上

落下
~ discharge 舷外排放，舷外排水
~ discharge control 舷外排放控制
~ discharge outlet 舷外排出口，舷外排水口 ‖ *Syn*. overboard scupper 舷外排出孔，舷外排水口
~ discharge pipe 舷外排泄管
~ discharge valve 舷侧排水阀
~ valve 舷外阀

overcharge [əuvə'tʃa:dʒ] *n.* 超载，过重的负担，过度充电；*v.* 过量装填，过度充电，讨价过高
~ of refrigerant 制冷剂过充

overcome [,əuvə'kʌm] *v.* 战胜，克服，胜过，征服 ‖ *Syn*. conquer 征服，战胜，占领，克服；defeat 击败，战胜，使失败；overwhelm 制服，控制，压倒，压服，击败；surmount 战胜，超越，克服

overcurrent [,əuvə'kʌrənt] *n.* 过电流，过量电流，过载电流
~ impulse 过流脉冲
~ protection 过电流保护，过流保护，过载保护，过流保护装置
~ protector 过流保护器
~ reply 过流继电器
~ relay test 过流继电器测试，过流继电器实验
~ trip 过流跳闸(装置)，过流脱扣(器)

overdamp [əuvə'dæmp] *v.* 过阻尼，阻尼超过，强衰减

overdesign ['əuvədi,zain] *n.* 超安全标准的设计

overdischarge ['əuvə,dis'tʃa:dʒ] *n.* 过量放电，过放电，过量卸料，过卸料
~ protection point 蓄电池过放电保护点

~ recovery voltage 过放电恢复电压
~ voltage 过放电电压
~ voltage return 过放电返回电压

overdue ['əuvə'dju:] *a.* 逾期的，过期的，延误的，误点的，迟到的

overexcitation [əuvə,iksai'teiʃən] *n.* 过激励，超激磁

overfall [,əuvəfɔ:l] *n.* 溢流，湍流，瀑布

overfeed ['əuvə'fi:d] *v.* 给料过多，给吃得过多，吃得太多

overfill ['əuvə'fil] *v.* 装得太满，装得过满

overflow ['əuvə'fləu] *n.* 溢出，超值，泛滥，充满，洋溢，溢流口，溢流管；*v.* (使)泛滥，(使)溢出，(使)充溢
~ blowdown 溢流排污
~ control 溢流控制
~ control system 溢油控制系统
~ cutting machines for aluminium wheel 铝轮溢流切割机
~ main line 溢流总管 ‖ *Syn*. overflow main pipe 溢流总管
~ pipe 下导管，溢流管
~ plate 溢流板
~ tank 溢流罐，溢流柜
~ valve 溢流阀

overfrequency ['əuvə'frikwənsi] *n.* 超频率，过频率，超过额定频率
~ protection 过频保护，过频保护装置
~ relay 过频继电器

overhang ['əuvə'hæŋ] *n.* 突出船首(或船尾)，突出量，突出物，突出部分；*v.* 外悬，悬垂，突出，伸出，逼近，威胁，弥漫

overhaul [,əuvə'hɔ:l] *n.* 修理工作，全面检查，全面修订；*v.* 彻底检查，大修，拆修，放松绳索，松开滑轮，革新，

赶上，越过，超过

~ and repair 大小修

~ interval 大修周期，大修间隔期

~ period 检修周期

overhauling [,əuvə'hɔ:liŋ] *n.* 大修，拆修，卸修，翻修；*v.* (overhaul 的 ing 形式) 彻底检查，大修，拆修，放松绳索，松开滑轮，革新，赶上，越过，超过

~ main engine after sea trial 主机航行试验后的拆检

~ tool 检修工具

overhead ['əuvəhed] *n.* 顶部，高空，架空，天花板；*a.* 在头上的，高架的；*ad.* 在头顶上，在空中，在高处

~ camshaft engine 顶置凸轮轴发动机

~ environments 水面闭封潜水环境

~ valve 顶置阀，顶阀，顶置气门

overheat [,əuvə'hi:t] *v.* 使过热，变得过热，使过分激动，使发展过快

overheating [,əuvə'hi:tiŋ] *n.* 过热；*v.* (overheat 的 ing 形式) 使过热，变得过热，使过分激动，使发展过快

~ wear 过热磨损

overlap ['əuvə'læp] *n.* 重叠部分，覆盖物；*v.* 重叠，交叠，互搭

~ joint 搭接接头，重叠结合

overlapping ['əuvə'læpiŋ] *n.* 重叠部分，互搭量；*v.* (overlap 的 ing 形式) 重叠，交叠，互搭；*a.* 相互重叠的，相互搭接的

~ angle 重叠角，重合角

~ decomposition 交叠分解

overload ['əuvə'ləud] *n.* 超载，负荷过多；*v.* 使超载，超过负荷

~ capacity 过载容量，过载能力

~ circuit breaker 过载断路器

~ coil 过载线圈

~ fracture 过载断裂

~ operation 超负荷运行，过载运行

~ output 过载输出，过载功率

~ protection 过载保护

~ protector 过载保护器

~ rating 额定过载

~ relay 过载继电器

~ switch 过载开关

overpower [,əuvə'pauə] *v.* 压倒，制服，供给力量

~ protection 过功率保护

overpressure ['əuvə'preʃə] *n.* 过度重压，过压，超压力，过劳

overshoot ['əuvə'ʃu:t] *n.* 超调量，过振比；*v.* 打过头，飞过目标，射击越标

~ clipper 过冲限制器，过电压限制器

overside ['əuvəsaid] *a.* 从船边的，越舷的；*ad.* 越舷地

overspeed ['əuvə'spi:d] *n.* 超速；*v.* (使)超速运行；*a.* 超速的

~ contactor 超速接触器

~ governor 限速器，超速调节器，超速限制器

~ indicator 超速指示器

~ limiter 超速限制器

~ power 超速功率

~ preventer 限速器

~ protection 超速保护

~ protection device 超速保护装置

~ relay 超速继电器

~ shutdown 超速停车

~ trial 超速试验，超速试航

~ trip 超速跳闸，超速脱扣

oversquare ['əuvə'skwɛə] *a.* 超方的

~ engine 超方发动机(汽缸直径大于活

塞行程的发动机)

overtake ['əuvə'teik] *v.* 压倒, 追上, 赶上, 突然来袭

overtemperature ['əuvə'tempəˌritʃə] *n.* 超温, 过温, 过热

~ alarm of an electric machine 电机的超温报警

~ fuse 超温熔断器

~ protection 超温保护, 过热保护, 超温保护装置

overtime ['əuvətaim] *n.* 额外时间, 延长时间, 加班, 加班费; *v.* 使超时; *a.* 超时的, 加班的; *ad.* 加班地

overvoltage ['əuvə'vəultidʒ] *n.* 过电压, 超电压

~ circuit 过电压电路

~ condition 过电压状态

~ protection 过电压防护, 过压保护, 过电压保护装置

~ relay 过电压继电器

~ suppressor 过电压抑制器, 过压抑制器

overwear [ˌəuvəwɛə] *v.* 使过度疲乏, 使过度磨损

overwhelm ['əuvə'welm] *v.* 制服, 控制, 压倒, 压服, 击败, 受打击, 淹没, 覆没 ‖ *Syn.* conquer 征服, 战胜, 占领, 克服; defeat 击败, 战胜, 使失败; overcome 战胜, 克服, 胜过, 征服; surmount 战胜, 超越, 克服

owe [əu] *v.* 欠, 感激, 应给予, 应归功于

owing ['əuiŋ] *v.* (owe 的 ing 形式) 欠, 感激, 应给予, 应归功于; *a.* 欠着的, 应付的, 未付的, 归功于, 由于, 因为

~ to 归功于, 由于, 因为

owler ['aulə(r)] *n.* 走私船, 走私者

own [əun] *v.* 拥有, 承认, 自认; *a.* 自己的, 特有的, 嫡亲的, 同胞的

~ to 承认

owner ['əunə] *n.* 船东, 业主, 物主, 所有人

owner's 船东的, 业主的

~ cabin 船东舱室

~ emblem 船东标志

ownership ['əunəʃip] *n.* 所有权, 物主身份

OWS (ocean weather ship) 海洋气象船, 海洋测候船

oxidation [ˌɔksi'deiʃən] *n.* 氧化

~ by-products 氧化副产物

~ reaction 氧化反应

~ stability 氧化稳定性

oxide ['ɔksaid] *n.* 氧化物

oxides ['ɔksaidz] *n.* (oxide 的复数) 氧化物

~ of carbon 碳氧化物

oxidize ['ɔksidaiz] *v.* (使)氧化, (使)生锈

oxidizer ['ɔksidaizə(r)] *n.* 氧化剂 ‖ *Syn.* oxygenant 氧化剂; oxidizing agent 氧化剂

oxidizing ['ɔksidaiziŋ] *v.* (oxidize 的 ing 形式) (使)氧化, (使)生锈; *a.* 氧化的

~ agent 氧化剂 ‖ *Syn.* oxidizer 氧化剂; oxygenant 氧化剂

oxygen ['ɔksidʒən] *n.* 氧, 氧气

~ analyzer 氧气分析仪, 氧气分析器

~ breathing apparatus 氧气呼吸器

~ canister 氧气罐 ‖ *Syn.* oxygen cylinder 氧气瓶, 储氧筒

~ compressor 氧气压缩机, 氧压机

~ correction 氧校正

~ cutting 氧气切割

~ deficiency 缺氧
~ demand 需氧量
~ generating plant 氧气发生装置，制氧车间
~ indicator 氧气指示剂
~ mask 氧气面罩
~ scavenger 去氧剂，氧气清除剂
~ supply 供氧，氧源
oxygenant ['ɔksidʒinənt] n. 氧化剂 ‖ **Syn**. oxidizing agent 氧化剂；oxidizer 氧化剂
oxygenate ['ɔksidʒineit] v. 以氧处理，氧化
oxygenation [,ɔksidʒi'neiʃən] n. 以氧处理，氧化
ozonator [əuzəu'neitə] n. 臭氧发生器 ‖ **Syn**. ozone generator 臭氧发生器；ozonizer 臭氧发生器，臭氧管
ozone ['əuzəun] n. 臭氧，新鲜空气
~ depleting substances 消耗臭氧层物质
~ generator 臭氧发生器 ‖ **Syn**. ozonator 臭氧发生器；ozonizer 臭氧发生器，臭氧管
~ layer 臭氧层 ‖ **Syn**. ozonosphere 臭氧层
ozonize ['əuzənaiz] v. 以臭氧处理，使含臭氧
ozonizer ['əuzənaizə(r)] n. 臭氧发生器，臭氧管 ‖ **Syn**. ozonater 臭氧发生器；ozone generator 臭氧发生器
ozonosphere [əu'zəunəsfiə] n. 臭氧层 ‖ **Syn**. ozone layer 臭氧层

P

P [p:] ① (=proportion) n. 比率，比例，均衡，面积，部分；v. 使成比例，使均衡，分摊 ② (=proportional) n. 比例项，比例量；a. 比例的，成比例的，相称的，协调的，均衡的
~ action 比例作用
~ control 比例控制，比例调节
~ control mode 比例控制方式，比例调节方式
~ control output 比例控制输出，比例调节输出
~ controller 比例控制器，比例调节器 ‖ **Syn**. P regulator 比例控制器，比例调节器
~ element 比例环节，比例元件
~ mode 比例模式
PA (public address) 公用地址，扩音装置
~ system 扩声系统，有线广播系统，公用地址系统
pacific [pə'sifik] n. 太平洋(Pacific); a. 和平的，平静的
~ Ocean 太平洋
pack [pæk] n. 包裹，一群，一副，背包，包装，大块浮冰；v. 包装，捆扎，塞满，群集，压紧
package ['pækidʒ] n. 预装件，建议，提议，包裹，包装袋
~ cargo 包装货
packaged ['pækidʒd] a. 成套的
~ boiler 移动式锅炉，快装锅炉，组合锅炉
~ evaporator 组装式蒸发器
~ form 包装形式
~ power distribution equipment 成套配电设备
packed [pækt] v. (pack 的过去式和过去分词) 包装，捆扎，塞满，群集，压紧；

a. 充满的，塞满的

　　~ gland 离心水封

　　~ gland joint 填料函式连接

packet ['pækit] *n*. 班轮，定期邮船，小包，小捆

packing ['pækiŋ] *n*. 包装，填料，填充物；*v*. (pack 的 ing 形式) 包装，捆扎，塞满，群集，压紧

　　~ box 填料盒，填料函

　　~ gland 填料盖，填料函，填料函压盖，填密函盖，密封衬垫，密封套，密封压盖

　　~ gland for piston rod 活塞杆填料压盖

　　~ gland lock spring 填密函盖弹簧

　　~ knife 填料割刀

　　~ material 填充材料，填塞料，密封材料，衬料

　　~ media 填料

　　~ ring 密封圈，填料环，垫圈

　　~ screw 衬垫螺旋

packless ['pæklis] *a*. 无包装的，无填料的，无填充的

pad [pæd] *n*. 垫，衬垫，便笺簿；*v*. 加上衬垫

paddle ['pædl] *n*. 宽叶短桨，短桨，桨状物，明轮翼，划桨；*v*. 划桨，搅，拌，涉水

　　~ wheel vessel 明轮船

paddle-wheel-propelled 明轮推进的

padeye ['pædai] *n*. 垫板孔眼，吊点

pail [peil] *n*. 桶，提桶，一桶的量

paint [peint] *n*. 油漆，颜料，涂料；*v*. 油漆，画，绘，描绘

　　~ blistering 油漆起泡

　　~ cracking 油漆开裂

　　~ drier 漆干剂

　　~ with red lead 涂红丹漆

　　~ with two coats of antifouling paint 涂两层防污漆

paintbrush ['peintbrʌʃ] *n*. 漆刷，画刷，画笔

paintwork ['peintwə:k] *n*. 油漆工作，涂上的油漆

pair [pεə] *n*. 一副，一对，一双

pair-twisted 对绞线的

　　~ cable 对绞线电缆

　　~ telephone cable for ship 船用对绞式电话电缆

pallet ['pælit] *n*. 扁平工具，棘爪，托盘

palletize ['pæli‚taiz] *v*. 放在货盘上，码垛堆集，用货盘装运

palletized ['pæli‚taizd] *v*. (palletize 的过去式和过去分词) 放在货盘上，码垛堆集，用货盘装运；*a*. 托盘化的

　　~ cargo 托盘化货物

pamphlet ['pæmflit] *n*. 小册子

Panama [‚pænə'ma:] *n*. 巴拿马

　　~ Canal 巴拿马运河

　　~ Canal signaling light 巴拿马运河信号灯

　　~ container vessel 巴拿马集装箱船

pane [pein] *n*. 窗格，方框，窗玻璃，边，面

panel ['pænl] *n*. 面板，嵌板，仪表板

　　~ board 镶板，控制盘

pant [pænt] *n*. 气喘；*v*. 气喘

panting ['pæntiŋ] *v*. 脉动，波动，晃动，振动；*a*. 喘气的

　　~ beam 强胸横梁

　　~ stringer 抗拍击纵材，防挠纵梁

pantry ['pæntri] *n*. 餐具室，食品储存室

　　~ boy 餐配服务生 ‖ *Syn*. pantry steward 餐配服务生

parabola [pə'ræbələ] n. 抛物线

parachute ['pærəʃu:t] n. 降落伞，缓降物；v. 伞投，跳伞，伞降
~ distress rocket signal 降落伞遇险火箭信号
~ rockets 降落伞火箭

paraffin ['pærəfin] n. 石蜡

paragraph ['pærəgra:f] n. 段，节，段落
~ ship 分节船

parallax ['pærəlæks] n. 视差

parallel ['pærəlel] n. 平行线，平行面，类似，相似物；v. 相应，相比，平行；a. 平行的，相同的，类似的，并联的
~ circuit 并联电路，平行电路
~ computation 平行计算，并行运算
~ connection 并联接法，并联
~ data transmission 并行数据传输
~ excitation 并联励磁，并联激磁，并励，并激
~ flow air register 平流式调风器
~ in 并行输入，并网，并联输入
~ interface 并行接口
~ key 平行键，平键，平面键
~ misalignment 平行度偏差
~ operation 并车操作
~ operation at change over of generator 发电机换车并联运行
~ ports 并行端口，并口
~ rule 平行直尺
~ running 并联运行，平行运转，并行处理
~ running test for main generator 主发电机并联运行试验

parallel-connected 并联连接的，并联的
~ thermocouple 并联热电偶，并联温差电偶

paralleling ['pærəleliŋ] n. 并联，平行线，平行面，类似，相似物；v. (parallel 的 ing 形式) 相应，相比，平行
~ panel 并车屏
~ switch 并联开关

parallelogram [,pærə'leləgræm] 平行四边形 ‖ circle 圆，圆形；ellipse 椭圆，椭圆形；rectangle 矩形；rhombus 菱形；square 正方形；trapezoid 梯形；triangle 三角形

parameter [pə'ræmitə] n. 参数，参量，变量，要素，限制因素，特色，特征，母数
~ adjustment 参数调整，参数平差
~ non-uniform rate 参数不均匀率
~ setting 参数设定
~ value 参数值

parametric [,pærə'metrik] a. 参(变)数的，参(变)量的

paramount ['pærəmaunt] a. 最高的，至上的，最重要的

paratactic [,pærə'tæktik] a. 并列的

parcel ['pa:sl] n. 小包，包裹；v. 分，分配，区分，用油布盖或缠裹
~ tanker 多隔舱油船，散装化学品船

paring ['pɛəriŋ] n. 削下的皮，去皮
~ disc 配水盘
~ disc for operating water 工作水配水盘
~ disc pumping hole 配水盘泵出孔

parity ['pæriti] n. 奇偶，奇偶性，奇偶校验，平价，平等，相等，等值，势均力敌

parse [pa:z] n. 分列；v. 解析，分解，仔细检查，细致分析

part [pa:t] n. 部分，局部，零件，等分，

职责，义务，地区，领域，段落，器官，角色；v. 分配，分开，分离，拆移，断裂，分手；a. 部分的，局部的；ad. 部分地，不完全的，有几分 ‖ **Syn**. cell (电池、光电)元件，单元；component 成分，部分，元件，零件，要素，组分；constituent 成分，要素；element 要素，元素，成分，元件；ingredient 成分，因素；organ 元件

~ drawing 零件图，部分图

~ load 部分负荷，部分负载，部分载荷，低负荷，低负载，低载荷

~ load characteristic 部分负荷特性

~ load condition 部分负荷工况，低负荷工况

~ load operation 部分负荷运行，部分负荷运转，低负荷运行

~ load ratio 部分负荷率

~ number 零件号码，产品型号

~ throttle characteristic 部分节流特性

partial ['pa:ʃəl] n. 偏微商；a. 部分的，局部的，偏爱的，偏袒的

~ bulkhead 局部舱壁

~ container ship 部分集装箱船

~ differential 偏微分

~ discharge 局部放电，部分放电，部分履行

~ load line 部分载重线

partially ['pa:ʃəli] ad. 部分地，偏爱的

participation [pa:ˌtisi'peiʃən] n. 参加，分享

particle ['pa:tikl] n. 粒子，微粒，质点，点，极小量，小品词，语气

~ matter emissions 颗粒物质排放

particular [pə'tikjulə] n. 特色，细节，详细；a. 特殊的，特别的，独特的，详细的，精确的，挑剔的

~ average 单独海损(海上保险)

particulate [pə'tikjulit] n. 微粒，粒子；a. 微粒的

~ matter 微粒物质，悬浮微粒

partition [pa:'tiʃən] n. 分割，划分，瓜分，分开，隔离物；v. 区分，隔开，分割

~ bulkhead 分隔舱壁

~ wall 隔断(墙)，间隔墙

partner ['pa:tnə] n. 伙伴，合伙人，股东；v. 合伙，组成一对，做伙伴，当助手

parts [pa:ts] n. (part 的复数) 组装零件，部件

~ book 零件册，零件簿

~ drawing 零件图，分件图

~ list 配件清单，零件清单

~ per million (PPM) 百万分之，兆比率

~ per million carbon (PPMC) 百万分率碳

party ['pa:ti] n. 当事人，随行人员，聚会，党，政党，党派，同类

~ branch 党支部

~ branch secretary 党支部书记

pass [pa:s] n. 经过，关口，途径，护照，通行证，入场券，及格；v. 通过，经过，流通，审查，忽略，传递，变化，宣判，终止

passage ['pæsidʒ] n. 通过，经过，通道，通路，段，节

passageway ['pæsidʒwei] n. 通道，走廊，过道，出入口

passband ['pa:sbænd] n. 通频带，传输频带

passenger ['pæsindʒə] n. 乘客，旅客，行人

~ access door 乘客通道门

433

~ access facilities 旅客出入设施

~ cabin 客舱

~ capacity 载客量，客运量

~ cargo ship 客货船，客货轮

~ liner 定期客船，邮轮

~ seat 乘客座，旅客席

~ ship 客船，客轮，邮船，医务船，医院船

~ Ship Safety Certificate (PSSC) 客船安全证书

passimeter [pæ'simitə] *n.* 内径仪，内径指示规

passive ['pæsiv] *a.* 中性的，被动的，消极的，默许的

~ tank stabilization system 被动水舱式减摇装置

passport ['pɑ:spɔ:t] *n.* 护照，通行证

password ['pɑ:swə:d] *n.* 口令，密码

past [pɑ:st] *n.* 往事，过去，过时；*v.* (pass的过去分词) 通过，经过，流通，审查，忽略，传递，变化，宣判，终止；*a.* 过去的，结束的，前任的；*ad.* 超过地，晚于；*prep.* 越过，超过，远于，经过

~ voltage within power system 电力系统内部过电压

patch [pætʃ] *n.* 补丁，补片，碎片，斑点，眼罩，傻瓜；*v.* 修补，拼凑，掩饰，平息

~ up by welding 焊接修补

patent ['pætənt] *n.* 专利，专利权，执照；*v.* 获得专利，请准专利；*a.* 专利的，特许的，显著的，明白的，新奇的

path [pɑ:θ] *n.* 小路，小径，路线，通道，轨道 ‖ *Syn.* channel 路线

patrol [pə'trəul] *n.* 巡逻；*v.* 巡逻，巡查

~ boat 巡逻艇

~ inspection 巡回检查

~ on deck 甲板巡逻

~ ship 巡逻舰，巡逻船

pattern ['pætən] *n.* 模范，式样，模式，样品，格调，图案；*v.* 模仿，仿造，以图案装饰

~ interface 接口模式

pawl [pɔ:l] *n.* 棘爪，制转杆；*v.* 用制转杆使停转

~ coupling 爪形联轴器

pay [pei] *n.* 工资，薪水；*v.* 支付，给予，交纳，有利，值得，合算

~ for the damage 赔偿损坏

payload ['pei,ləud] *n.* 有效负载，有效载荷 ‖ *Syn.* active load 有效负载，有效载荷；PLoad 有效负载，有效载荷

PC (personal computer) 个人计算机，个人电脑

PCA (principal component analysis) 主成分分析

PCB (printed circuit board) 印制电路板 ‖ *Syn.* PWB (printed wiring board) 印制线路板

PCC (pure car carrier) 汽车运输船

PCI (Peripheral Component Interconnect) 外设部件互连(标准)

PD (proportion-differentiation) 比例微分

PD (proportional-derivative) 比例微分的

PD (proportional plus derivative) 比例加微分的，比例微分的

~ action 比例微分作用

~ control 比例微分控制，比例微分调节

~ controller 比例微分控制器，比例微

分调节器 ‖ *Syn*. PD regulator 比例微分控制器，比例微分调节器

PD (potential drop) 电压降，电位降，势能落差 ‖ *Syn*. voltage drop 电压降

PDA (personal digital assistant) 个人数码助理，个人数字助理，掌上电脑

PDC (Personal Digital Cellular) 个人数字蜂窝(通信)

PDP (post design processing) 设计后处理

PE (protective earth) 保护接地，安全接地，安全接地线

peak [pi:k] *n*. 山顶，顶点，帽舌，最高峰；*v*. 到达最高点，缩小，使竖起，消瘦；*a*. 最高的，最大值的
  ~ current 峰值电流，峰电流
  ~ load 峰值负荷
  ~ load regulation 峰值负荷调节
  ~ period 波峰周期，尖峰期
  ~ power 峰值功率
  ~ pressure 峰值压力，最大压力
  ~ pressure indicator 峰值压力指示器
  ~ time 高峰时间
  ~ value 峰值
  ~ voltage 峰值电压，峰压，最大电压
  ~ voltmeter 峰值电压表

pedestal ['pedistl] *n*. 底座，基架，基础，操纵台；*v*. 加座，搁在台上，支持

peen [pi:n] *n*. 锤顶，锤的尖头；*v*. 敲击，打平

peep [pi:p] *n*. 窥看，隐约看见；*v*. 窥视，偷看
  ~ hole 窥孔，观察孔

pein [pi:n] *n*. 锤的尖头；*v*. 敲击，打平

pelagic [pi'lædʒik] *a*. 远洋的，海面的，浮游的
  ~ trawler 大型远洋拖网渔船

pelorus [pi'lɔ:rəs] *n*. 罗经刻度盘，哑罗经

penetrate ['penitreit] *v*. 渗入，穿透，渗透，看穿，洞察，刺入，弥漫

penetrating ['penitreitiŋ] *v*. (penetrate 的 ing 形式) 渗入，穿透，渗透，看穿，洞察，刺入，弥漫；*a*. 敏锐的，有洞察力的，明察秋毫的，尖锐的
  ~ fluid 渗透液
  ~ oil 渗透润滑油

penetration [peni'treiʃən] *n*. 渗透，穿透，穿过，突破

people ['pi:pl] *n*. 人，人们，民族，人类，公民；*v*. 使住(满)人

people's 人民的
  ~ Republic of China (PRC) 中华人民共和国

per [pə] *prep*. 每，每一，由，经
  ~ capita 人均，每人，按人口计算
  ~ unit value 标幺值

per-unit 每单位
  ~ value 标幺值
  ~ value normalization 标幺值化，标幺化

perborate [pə'bɔ:reit] *n*. 过硼酸盐

percentage [pə'sentidʒ] *n*. 百分数，百分率，百分比
  ~ of air 气体分压
  ~ of current load 负载电流百分比
  ~ of oxygen 含氧百分比

percolation [ˌpə:kə'leiʃən] *n*. 过滤，浸透，渗滤，渗漏

perfect ['pə:fikt] *n*. 完成式；*v*. 使完美，修改，使熟练；*a*. 完美的，全然的，理想的，正确的，熟练的，精通的，

完成式的

~ cleanliness 彻底清洁

perfectly ['pə:fiktli] a. 极佳的，完美的；ad. 很，完全，完美地，理想地

perforate ['pə:fəreit] v. 打孔，打洞，穿孔，刺穿，在…上打眼；a. 被穿透的

perform [pə'fɔ:m] v. 做，操作，履行，执行，实行，完成任务，表演，演出

performance [pə'fɔ:məns] n. 履行，执行，成绩，性能，表演，演奏 ‖ **Syn.** property 性质，特性，属性；nature 本性，性质，特性

~ analysis 性能分析

~ characteristic 性能特征，工作特性

~ check 性能检查，性能检验

~ curve 性能曲线

~ evaluation 性能评估

~ index 性能指标

~ limitation 性能极限

~ specification 性能说明，性能规格

~ test 性能试验

peril ['peril] n. 危险，危险物；v. 冒险 ‖ **Syn.** danger 危险，危害，危险物，威胁；hazard 冒险，危险，冒险的事；jeopardy 危险；risk 危险，风险，冒险

perilous ['periləs] a. 危险的，冒险的 ‖ **Syn.** dangerous 危险的；hazardous 危险的，冒险的；unsafe 危险的

perimeter [pə'rimitə] n. 周长，周围，边界

period ['piəriəd] n. 时期，周期，学时，节，句点；a. 过去某段时期的

~ of flaming 火焰期

periodic [piəri'ɔdik] a. 周期的，定期的

~ current 周期电流，周期性流，周期潮流

~ damping 周期性阻尼

~ duty 周期工作制，周期运行，循环使用

~ function 周期函数

~ inspection 定期检查，定期检修

~ review 定期检查，按期盘点

~ survey 定期检验

~ wave 周期波

periodical [,piəri'ɔdikəl] n. 期刊，杂志；a. 周期的，定期的

~ blowdown 定期排污

~ hull survey 定期船体检验

~ monitoring 定期监测，定期预察

~ test 周期性检查，定期试验，周期检测，定期检测

periodically [,piəri'ɔdikəli] ad. 周期性地，定时性地

peripheral [pə'rifərəl] n. 外部设备；a. 外围的，周缘的，辅助的，非重要的

~ Component Interconnect (PCI) 外设部件互连(标准)

~ equipment 外部设备，外围设备

~ pump 旋涡泵，周边泵

~ speed 圆周速度，边缘速率，周速

periphery [pə'rifəri] n. 外围，边缘，边界，外表面

periscope ['periskəup] n. 潜望镜，展望镜

~ hole 潜望镜孔

perish ['periʃ] v. (使)麻木，(使)毁坏，死亡，腐烂，枯萎

perishable ['periʃəbl] a. 易腐烂的，易腐败的，易损耗的

permanent ['pə:mənənt] a. 永久的，持久的，永恒的

~ change 永久变形

~ connection 固定连接，永久接驳

~ current 持恒电流，恒定电流

~ hardness 永久硬度

~ magnet 永久磁铁，永磁体

~ magnet direct current motor 永磁直流电动机

~ magnet generator 永磁发电机

~ magnet synchronism motor 永磁同步电动机

~ set 永久变形，最后凝结，固定装置

~ storage area 固定存储区

~ water ballast pump 固定压舱水泵

permanently ['pə:mənəntli] *ad*. 永久地，长期不变地

permeability [ˌpə:miə'biliti] *n*. 渗透，渗透性，渗透度，渗透率，磁导率

~ of free space 真空磁导率

permeate ['pə:mieit] *v*. 弥漫，渗入，渗透，透过，充满

permeation [ˌpə:mi'eiʃən] *n*. 渗入，透过 ‖ ***Syn***. infiltration 渗透，渗入，渗透物；osmosis 渗透，渗透作用，渗透性

permissible [pə(:)'misəbl] *a*. 许可的，可允许的，可容许的，可承认的

~ discharge 允许排放

~ error 容许误差

~ length 许可长度，许可舱长

~ restriction 容许缩小量

~ rope length of drum 卷筒卷绳量

~ stack load 容许堆载

~ stress 容许应力，许用应力

~ temperature 容许温度

~ tolerance 容许公差，容许变量，容许剂量

~ value 容许值，允许值

permission [pə(:)'miʃən] *n*. 许可，允许，批准，正式认可

permit [pə(:)'mit] *n*. 通行证，许可证，执照；*v*. 许可，允许，准许 ‖ ***Syn***. allow 允许，承认

~ to Operate High Speed Craft 高速船营运许可证

permit-to-work 工作许可，允许开工

~ card 工作证许可证

~ system 工作许可证制度

perpendicular [ˌpə:pən'dikjulə] *n*. 垂线；*a*. 垂直的，正交的

persistence [pə'sistəns] *n*. 持续，坚持，坚持不懈

persistent [pə'sistənt] *a*. 持续的，持久的，持久稳固的

~ knocking 持续爆震

person ['pə:sn] *n*. 人，身体，容貌，人称

~ boarding the ship 登船人员

~ subject to control 受管制人士

personal ['pə:sənl] *a*. 私人的，个人的，亲自的，容貌的，身体的，人身的，针对个人的

~ casualty 人员伤亡

~ computer (PC) 个人计算机，个人电脑

~ digital assistant (PDA) 个人数码助理，个人数字助理，掌上电脑

~ Digital Cellular (PDC) 个人数字蜂窝(通信)

~ handy-phone system (PHS) 个人手持式电话系统

~ identification number (PIN) 个人身份号码

~ laser printer 个人激光打印机

~ protection clothing 个人防护服

~ protective equipment 个人防护装备，

437

个人防护用品

~ responsibility 个人责任，人事责任

~ safety 人身安全，个人安全

~ security 个人安全，人身担保

personnel [ˌpəːsə'nel] n. 全体员工，人员，员工，人事部，人事处

~ allocation 定编，人员配备

~ evacuation system 人员疏散系统

perspective [pə'spektiv] n. 透视画法，透视图，各部分的比例，远景，前途，观点，看法，观察，洞察力；a. 透视法的，透视的

~ drawing 透视图

pertain [pə(:)'tein] v. 适合，关于，附属

~ to 关于，从属于，适合

pertinent ['pəːtinənt] a. 有关的，相干的，恰当的，中肯的

pervasive [pə:'veisiv] a. 普遍的，普遍深入的，遍布的，弥漫性的，渗透性的 ‖ *Syn.* common 公共的，普通的；commonplace 平凡的；general 一般的，普通的；ordinary 平常的，平凡的，普通的；popular 大众的，通俗的，普遍的；universal 普遍的，通用的；usual 平常的，通常的，惯例的；widespread 分布广泛的，普遍的

pervious ['pəːviəs] a. 可被渗透的，可通行的

petcock ['petkɔk] n. 小活栓，小龙头

Petersen ['piːtəsən] n. 彼得森(人名)

~ coil 消弧线圈，消弧电抗线圈

petrochemical [ˌpetrəu'kemikəl] n. 石油化学产品，石化产品；a. 石油化学的，石化的

petrol ['petrəl] n. 汽油

petroleum [pi'trəuliəm] n. 石油

~ degrading microorganism 石油降解微生物

~ gas 石油气

~ jelly 凡士林，矿油

~ product 石油产品，石油产物，石油制品

petty ['peti] a. 小的，不重要的，小规模的，小型的，细微的，小气的，卑鄙的

PFSO (Port Facility Security Officer) 港口设施保安官员

PFSP (Port Facility Security Plan) 港口设施保安计划

PH (potential of hydrogen) 酸碱度

~ test 酸碱度测试

~ value 酸碱度值

phase [feiz] n. 相，相位，相角，阶段，状态，时期，方面，部分，态度；v. (使)定相，使同步，分阶段实行

~ 1 (=first phase) 第1阶段(即阴燃阶段)

~ 2 (=second phase) 第2阶段(即产生火焰阶段)

~ 3 (=third phase) 第3阶段(即危险阴燃阶段)

~ angle 相位角，相角

~ change 相变

~ comparator 相位比较器

~ converter 变相机，相位变换器

~ delay 相位延迟

~ diagram 相图

~ difference 相位差

~ displacement 相位移，相移 ‖ *Syn.* phase shift 相位移，相移

~ failure protection 断相保护，相故障保护

~ imbalance 相不平衡
~ in 逐步采用，分阶段引入
~ indicator 相位指示器，相位计
~ inverter 倒相器，反相器
~ lag 相位滞后
~ lead 相位超前
~ locked loop 锁相环路，锁相回路，锁相环
~ locking 锁相
~ locus 相轨迹
~ margin 相位裕量，相位裕度，相补角，相位容限
~ meter 相位表
~ node 开关节点
~ reversal 反相，倒相，相序逆转
~ separation 相位分离，相位差
~ sequence 相序
~ sequence indicator 相序指示器
~ transformation 相位变换，相变
~ transition 相变
~ voltage 相电压

phase-to-phase 相位到相位的，相位间的，相间的
  ~ arrester 相间避雷器
  ~ distance protection 相间距离保护
  ~ fault 相间故障
  ~ interaction 相间相互作用
  ~ short circuit fault 相间短路故障
  ~ spacing 相间距离
  ~ voltage 相间电压

phasing ['feiziŋ] v. (phase 的 ing 形式) (使)定相，使同步，分阶段实行；n. 定相，相位调整，变相
  ~ verification 相位检定

phenolic [fi'nɔlik] a. 酚的，石碳酸的
  ~ resin 酚醛树脂，酚树脂

phenolphthalein [ˌfinɔl'fθæli:n] n. 酚酞
phial ['faiəl] n. 小玻璃瓶，药瓶
  ~ type temperature controller 温包式温度控制器

phone [fəun] n. 电话，电话机；v. 打电话
phosgene ['fɔzdʒi:n] n. 光气，碳酰氯
  ~ gas 光气，碳酰氯

phosphate ['fɔsfeit] n. 磷酸盐
  ~ adjustment 磷酸调整剂
  ~ comparator 磷酸根比色管
  ~ powder 磷酸盐干粉

phosphor ['fɔsfə] n. 荧光体，磷，启明星 (Phosphor)
  ~ bronze 磷青铜
  ~ bronze sheet 磷青铜板
  ~ bronze wire 磷青铜线

photo ['fəutəu] n. 照片，相片
photoconductive [ˌfəutəukən'dʌktiv] a. 光电导的，光敏的
photoeffect [ˌfəutəui'fekt] n. 光电效应
photoelectric [ˌfəutəui'lektrik] a. 光电的，光电子照相装置的
  ~ cell 光电池，光电管
  ~ effect 光电效应
  ~ obscuration smoke detector 减光型光电感烟探测器
  ~ smoke detector 光电感烟探测器
  ~ smoke meter 光电烟尘计
  ~ switch 光电开关
  ~ tachometric transducer 光电转速传感器

photoelectricity [ˌfəutəuilek'trisiti] n. 光电，光电学，光电现象
photoelectromotive [ˌfəutəuiˌlektrə'məutiv] a. 光电动的
  ~ force 光电动势

photomultiplier [ˌfəutəu'mʌltiplaiə] n. 光电倍增器，光电倍增管

photosensitive [ˌfəutəu'sensitiv] a. 光敏的，感光的
~ diode 光敏二极管

phototransistor [ˌfəutəutræn'zistə] n. 光电晶体管，光敏晶体管，光敏三极管

phototube ['fəutəutju:b] n. 光电管，光电器

photovoltage [ˌfəutəuvəultidʒ] n. 光电压

photovoltaic [ˌfəutəuvɔl'teiik] a. 光电的，光生伏打的
~ cell 光伏电池，光电池，硒电池

photronic [fəu'trɔnik] a. 光电池的
~ cell 硒整流光电管

PHS (personal handy-phone system) 个人手持式电话系统

physical ['fizikəl] n. 身体检查；a. 物理的，身体的，自然(界)的，按自然法则的，物质的
~ change 物理变化
~ characteristic 物理特性
~ construction 机械结构
~ design 物理设计，结构设计，实体设计
~ electric power source 物理电源
~ property 物理性质，实物财产
~ quantity 物理量
~ response time of opacimeter 烟度计物理反应时间
~ security 物理安全，人身安全，实体安全

PI (proportion-integration) 比例积分

PI (proportional-integral) 比例积分的

PI (proportional plus integral) 比例加积分的，比例积分的

~ action 比例积分作用
~ control 比例积分控制，比例积分调节
~ controller 比例积分控制器，比例积分调节器 ‖ *Syn*. PI regulator 比例积分控制器，比例积分调节器

PIC (Protection and Indemnity Clubs) 保赔协会

picaroon [ˌpikə'ru:n] n. 海盗船，海盗；v. 做海盗

pick [pik] n. 精选，掘；v. 挑选，挑拣，挖，摘，掘，凿，拾取，挑剔

pick-off 传感器，敏感元件，自动脱模装置，拾取，摘下
~ gear 可互换齿轮，选速齿轮
~ unite 产品检测装置

pickup ['pikʌp] n. 加速能力，起动加速性能，乘客，货物，检波器，接收装置，转播装置，拾起，获得

pictorial [pik'tɔ:riəl] n. 画报，画刊；a. 绘画的，图示的
~ drawing 示意图，插图，立体图

PID (proportion-integration-differentiation) 比例积分微分

PID (proportional-integral-derivative) 比例积分微分的

PID (proportional plus integral plus derivative) 比例加积分加微分的，比例积分微分的
~ action 比例积分微分作用
~ control 比例积分微分控制，比例积分微分调节
~ controller 比例积分微分控制器，比例积分微分调节器 ‖ *Syn*. PID regulator 比例积分微分控制器，比例积分微分调节器

pier [piə] n. 桥墩，码头
　～ embarkation 送往邮轮码头

pierce [piəs] v. 刺破，刺穿，穿透，突破，深深感动

piezo [piəzəu] n. 压力

piezoeffect ['pi:zəuifekt] n. 压电效应

piezoelectric [pai,i:zəui'lektrik] a. 压电的
　～ ceramic 压电陶瓷
　～ force transducer 压电式力传感器
　～ pressure transducer 压电式压力传感器

piezoelectricity [pai,i:zəuilek'trisiti] n. 压电，压电现象

piezoid [pai'i:zɔid] n. (压电)石英片，石英晶片

piezomagnetic [pai,i:zəumæg'netik] a. 压磁的
　～ effect 压磁效应
　～ sensor 压磁传感器

piezoresistance [pai,i:zəuri'zistəns] n. 压电电阻

piezoresistive [pai,i:zəuri'zistiv] a. 压阻的，压阻现象的
　～ sensor 压阻式传感器

pig [pig] n. 生铁，生铁块，金属铸模，猪，猪肉，贪婪的人；v. 生小猪，贪婪地吃
　～ iron 生铁
　～ iron electrode 生铁焊条
　～ iron welding wire 生铁焊丝

piggy ['pigi] n. 小猪；a. 贪心的

piggy-back 背负式运输的，背驮式的
　～ anchor 加重锚

pile [pail] n. 电池组，反应堆，桩，堆，大堆，高大建筑，大量钱财；v. 堆起，堆积，堆于，积累，挤，堆叠，打桩于，用桩支撑
　～ driving barge 打桩船

pillar ['pilə] n. 柱，支柱，台柱，栋梁，顶梁柱
　～ bolt 支撑螺栓
　～ buoy 柱形浮筒，柱形浮标

pilot ['pailət] n. 引水员，引航员，飞行员；v. 引水，领航，驾驶
　～ access door 引航通路门
　～ air 先导气流
　～ boat 领航艇，引水船
　～ control valve 先导控制阀
　～ exciter 副励磁机
　～ hole 导孔，导向钻孔，定位孔
　～ ladder 引水梯，领航员梯，绳梯
　～ lamp 领航灯，信号灯，指示灯
　～ operated reducing valve 先导式液压阀，先导式减压阀
　～ operated relief valve 先导式溢流阀 ‖ *Syn*. pilot overflow valve 先导式溢流阀
　～ piston 导向活塞
　～ run 试运行，初步操作试验
　～ station 引航站，港口引水入室
　～ valve 操纵阀，导向阀
　～ vessel 领航船

pilotage ['pailətidʒ] n. 导航技术，引航，领港，引水，领航费

pin [pin] n. 钉，销，栓，大头针，别针，腿；v. 钉住，别住，阻止，扣牢，止住，牵制
　～ down 确定，使受约束，阻止，船首前倾
　～ finned tube 针翅管
　～ gauge 销规，针规
　～ gear 滚销齿轮

~ gear drive 销齿传动，销齿轮传动

~ jig 限位胎架

~ roll 小齿轮，销辊

PIN (personal identification number) 个人身份号码

pincers ['pinsəz] *n.* 钳子，螯

pinch [pintʃ] *n.* 收缩，紧急关头，匮乏，压力，捏，撮；*v.* 收缩，节省，掐，夹痛，修剪，勒索，使感缺乏，使萎缩，偷

~ bar 尖头长杆，撬杆，爪棍

pinhole ['pinhəul] *n.* 针孔，小孔

pinion ['pinjən] *n.* 小齿轮

~ and rack 齿轮齿条

pinnace ['pinis] *n.* 装载于舰上的中型艇

pinnacle ['pinəkl] *n.* 顶峰，顶点；*v.* 加尖塔，放在极高处

pintle ['pintl] *n.* 枢轴，柱销，扣针，舵栓，牵引挂钩

PIO (process input-output) 过程输入输出

PIP (project implementation plan) 项目实施计划

pipe [paip] *n.* 管子，导管，笛声；*v.* 以管输送，吹笛，尖叫，吹哨子

~ & tube making machine 制管机

~ bend 管肘，弯头，肘管弯头

~ bracket 管托

~ connection 管接头，管道连接

~ diameter 管径

~ expander 扩管器，胀管机

~ fittings 管件，管附件，管道配件，管配件

~ graphite 管状电极

~ in 用电讯设备传送，用管道输入

~ joint 管接头，管节，喉管连接处

~ laying barge 铺管驳船

~ laying system 铺管系统

~ laying vessel 铺管船，敷管船

~ line 管路，管道，管线，导管

~ network 管网，管道系统

~ nut 管螺母

~ pile 管桩，钢管桩

~ pliers 管钳 ‖ *Syn.* pipe tongs 管钳

~ spanner 管子扳手

~ string 管柱，一段管线，管道支线

~ system 管路系统

~ turnbuckle 套筒松紧螺旋扣

~ wall 管壁

~ wrench 管扳钳

pipeline [paip‚lain] *n.* 管道，管线，渠道，途径，传递途径；*v.* 用管道输送，安装管道

~ characteristic curve 管路特性曲线

~ fittings 管路配件

~ layer 管道船

~ refrigerating 冷供应管线

~ system 管线系统，流水线系统

pipette [pi'pet] *n.* 吸液管，吸量管，移液管

piping [‚paipiŋ] *n.* 管道系统，管道网，管道，管线，吹笛，笛声，尖声；*v.* (pipe 的 ing 形式) 以管输送，吹笛，尖叫，吹哨子；*a.* 吹笛的，尖音的，平静的，平和的；*ad.* 滚烫地

~ arrangement 管道布置，管路布置图

~ components 管道组件

~ drawing 管道图

~ system 管道系统

piston ['pistən] *n.* 活塞，活塞阀键

~ body 活塞体

~ boss 活塞销座

~ chamber 活塞顶内燃烧室，滑阀腔

~ clearance 活塞间隙
~ complete 活塞总成
~ compressor 活塞式压缩机
~ cooling 活塞冷却
~ cooling pipe 活塞冷却管
~ cooling pump 活塞冷却泵
~ cooling water piping 活塞冷却水管系
~ cooling water pump 活塞式冷却水泵
~ cooling water system 活塞冷却水系统
~ cooling water tank 活塞冷却水箱
~ crown 活塞顶，活塞头，活塞冠
~ crown impingement 活塞顶烧蚀
~ cup expander 活塞皮碗扩张器
~ displacement 活塞位移
~ gland 活塞压盖
~ gudgeon pin 活塞销
~ head 活塞头，活塞顶
~ head plate 活塞顶板
~ mark 活塞标记
~ pin 活塞销
~ pin bearing 活塞销轴承
~ pin boss 活塞销座
~ pin bushing 活塞销衬套
~ pump 活塞泵
~ ring 活塞环
~ ring axial clearance 活塞环轴向间隙
~ ring belt 活塞环带
~ ring diagonal cut 活塞环对角切削
~ ring end clearance 活塞环对口间隙
~ ring expander 活塞衬环
~ ring gap clearance 活塞环接口间隙
~ ring groove 活塞涨圈槽，活塞环槽
~ ring joint clearance 活塞环接口间隙
~ ring land 活塞环棱
~ ring side clearance 活塞环端面间隙

~ ring sticking 活塞环卡紧，活塞环结胶，活塞环黏着
~ rod 活塞杆
~ rod flange 活塞杆凸缘
~ rod nut 活塞杆螺母
~ rod stuffing box 活塞杆填密函
~ scraping 拉缸
~ seizure 抱缸
~ skirt 活塞裙
~ skirt expander 活塞裙扩大器
~ speed 活塞速度
~ stroke 活塞冲程
~ swept volume 活塞排量，气缸换气量，气缸工作容积，活塞移动容积
~ throttle 活塞式节流阀
~ underside 活塞下侧
~ underside pump 活塞下侧泵
~ underside pump scavenging 活塞下侧泵扫气
~ water cooler 活塞水冷却器
~ wrench 活塞扳手
piston-connecting-rod 活塞连杆
~ arrangement misalignment 活塞连杆装置失中

pitch [pitʃ] n. 螺距，节距，程度，斜度，投掷，定调，(船只)前后颠簸，倾斜，树脂，沥青；v. 偏航，投掷，向前倾跌，坠落，倾斜，定位于，树起，搭起，建立，扎营，用沥青涂
~ actuation system 俯仰驱动系统
~ and roll 纵摇和横摇
~ angle indicator 螺距角指示器
~ diameter 层心直径，(螺纹的)中径，(齿轮的)节径
~ factor 节距因数，节距系数
~ indicator 螺距指示器，俯仰指示器

~ interval 间距，音程

~ ratio 螺距比，节圆直径比

pit [pit] n. 凹陷，深坑，深渊，陷阱；v. 起凹点，凹陷，(使)凹下，(使)留疤痕

pitting ['pitiŋ] n. 点状腐蚀，斑蚀，小孔，烧熔边缘，软化；v. (pit 的 ing 形式) 起凹点，凹陷，(使)凹下，(使)留疤痕

~ corrosion 点状腐蚀，斑蚀

pivot ['pivət] n. 枢轴，支点，中心点，中枢，重点；v. 装枢轴于，绕…旋转，在枢轴上转动；a. 枢轴的

~ pin 中心承枢，中心销钉，枢轴销

pivotal ['pivətəl] a. 关键的，中枢的，枢轴的

pivoted ['pivətid] v. (pivot 的过去式与过去分词) 装枢轴于，绕…旋转，在枢轴上转动；a. 转动的，回转的，装在枢轴上的

~ bolt 尖轴栓，枢轴螺栓

~ compensator 摆式松紧架

~ lever 回转杆

~ nose 枢接头部

~ relay 枢轴继电器，支点继电器

~ window 旋转窗

pixel ['piksəl] n. 像素

place [pleis] n. 地方，地点，位置，职位，处境，住所，地位；v. 放置，寄予，任命，名次列前

~ of safety 安全区 ‖ *Syn*. safe area 安全区域，安全区；safe region 安全区域，安全区；safety zone 安全地带，安全区

placement ['pleismənt] n. 安置，放置，布置，布局，编班，工作安排

plain [plein] n. 无格式，平原，草原；a. 简单的，明白的，平常的，清晰的，普通的，朴素的；ad. 清楚地

~ bearing 滑动轴承，平面轴承，普通轴承，滑体轴承

~ sedimentation 自然沉淀

~ structure 平纹组织

~ tube 光管，光管束

~ washer 平垫圈，普通垫圈

~ water fire extinguisher 清水灭火器

plainly ['pleinli] ad. 平坦地，明白地，明显地，清楚地

plan [plæn] n. 计划，安排，方案，大纲，概要，策略，进度表，轮廓，设计图，平面图，说明图，详；v. 计划，定计划，设计，筹划，部署，画图示

~ view 平面图，俯视图，主视图

plane [plein] n. 飞机，平面，水平，程度，刨子；v. 滑翔，刨平，飞行；a. 平的，平面的

~ clamp 平面夹具

~ grinding 平面磨削

~ iron 刨铁

~ joint 滑动关节，平面关节

~ strain 平面应变，平面变形

planer ['pleinə] n. 刨床，刨机，刨工

planetary [,plænitri] a. 行星齿轮的，行星的，地球的，游荡的，飘忽不定的

~ cam 行星凸轮

~ differential 封闭差动轮系

~ gear 行星齿轮

~ gearing 行星齿轮传动装置

~ rolling 行星轧机，行星轧机

planform ['plænfɔ:m] n. 平面图，俯视图

planing ['pleiniŋ] n. 平刨；v. (plane 的 ing 形式) 滑翔，刨平，飞行；a. 滑行的，正交法的，刨的

~ boat 滑行艇,滑航艇 ‖ ***Syn***. planing hull 滑航式船体,滑航艇

~ machine 龙门刨床

plank [plæŋk] *n*. 厚木板,支架,政纲条款; *v*. 铺板

planned [plænd] *v*. (plan 的过去式和过去分词) 计划,设计,筹划,部署; *a*. 计划了的,根据计划的

~ budget 计划预算

~ maintenance system (PMS) 计划维修系统,计划保养系统

~ target 计划指标,计划目标,控制数字

plant [plɑ:nt] *n*. 工厂,车间,设备,植物,庄稼; *v*. 安置,种植,栽培,培养 ‖ ***Syn***. apparatus 器械,设备,仪器; appliance 用具,器具; arrangement 布置; assembly 组装部件; device 装置,设备; equipment 装备,设备,器材,装置; facility 设备,工具; furniture 设备,家具; gear 设备,装备; installation 设备,装置; machine 机器,机械,机构; machinery 机械(总称),机器; mechanism 机器,机械装置,机构; provision 装备,供应品; turnout 装备,设备; unit 装置,设备

~ level 机器设备层

~ renewal 设备更新

plasma ['plæzmə] *n*. 等离子体,等离子区,血浆,乳浆

~ arc cutting 等离子弧切割

~ propulsion 等离子体推进

plastic ['plæstik] *n*. 塑胶,可塑体,塑料制品; *a*. 塑胶的,塑造的,有可塑性的,造型的

~ bag 塑料袋

~ cable 塑料绝缘电缆

~ deformation 塑性变形,塑性应变 ‖ ***Syn***. plastic distortion 塑性变形

~ garbage bag 塑料垃圾袋

~ hammer 塑料锤

~ handle 塑料手柄

~ hinge 塑胶铰链,塑性铰

~ insulation 塑料绝缘体,塑料绝缘

~ pipe 塑料管,塑料管材

~ set square 塑料三角尺

~ steel 塑钢

~ T-square 塑料丁字尺

~ viscosity 塑性黏度

plasticity [plæs'tisiti] *n*. 可塑性,塑性

plasticize ['plæstisaiz] *v*. 使成可塑体

plasticizer ['plæstisaizə] *n*. 可塑剂

plate [pleit] *n*. 金属板,板块,图版,盘子; *v*. 镀(金、银等),电镀,装钢板

~ evaporator 平板式蒸发器

~ finish 原始光洁面

~ floor 实肋板,平板肋板

~ freezer 板式冷冻机

~ friction coefficient 板摩擦系数

~ heat exchanger 板式换热器,膜片式热交换器

~ keel 平板龙骨

~ rack 餐具架

~ type contact freezer 接触式平板冻结装置,接触式平板冻结机

~ type cooler 板式冷却器,平板式冷却器

~ type evaporator 板式蒸发器

~ type heat exchanger 板式换热器

plated ['pleitid] *v*. (plate 的过去式和过去分词) 镀(金、银等),电镀,装钢板; *a*. 镀金的,电镀的,装甲的

~ metal 电镀金属，镀金属
~ through hole (PTH) 镀通孔
~ wire 镀磁线，磁膜线

platform ['plætfɔ:m] *n.* 平台，钻井平台，月台，讲台，讲坛，政纲，宣言
~ deck 平台甲板
~ supply vessel 钻井平台供应船

play [plei] *n.* 游戏，比赛，运动，赌博，剧本；*v.* 行动，处置，运转，扮演，担任，玩，播放，进行比赛
~ a role 起作用
~ adjustment 隙缝调整
~ an important role in 在…起重要作用
~ button 工作按钮

PLC (programmable logic controller) 可编程逻辑控制器

plenty ['plenti] *n.* 充裕，富裕，大量，充足，繁荣；*a.* 丰富的，充足的，充分的

plenum ['pli:nəm] *n.* 充实，充满，全体会议，高压

plexiglass ['pleksigla:s] *n.* 树脂玻璃

plier ['plaiə(r)] *n.* 钳子，镊子

plimsoll ['plimsəl] *n.* 橡皮底帆布鞋，普利姆索尔(Plimsoll，1824-1898，英国船运改革者)
~ line 载重线标志，载重吃水线，载货吃水线 ‖ **Syn**. draught mark**s** 吃水标，吃水线；plimsoll mark 吃水标，吃水线

PLoad 有效负载，有效载荷 ‖ **Syn**. active load 有效负载，有效载荷；payload 有效负载，有效载荷

plot [plɔt] *n.* 小块土地，图，地区图，秘密计划，情节，结构；*v.* 划分，绘图，制图，密谋，策划

plug [plʌg] *n.* 塞子，插头，插销；*v.* 堵，塞，插上，插栓
~ and play 即插即用
~ and socket 插塞和插座，插头插座，接插件
~ braking 反相序制动
~ cock 塞嘴，旋塞，油塞
~ fuse 插塞式熔丝，插入式保险丝
~ head bulb 卡口灯泡
~ in 插入，插上插头
~ into 把插头插入
~ socket 塞孔，插座
~ up 堵住，塞住
~ valve 旋塞阀
~ weld 塞焊焊缝
~ welding 塞焊
~ wire 插线

plug-in 插件程序，插件式的，插入式的
~ board 插件
~ fuse 插入式保险丝

plumb [plʌm] *n.* 铅锤，铅弹；*v.* 垂直，使垂直，探测，用铅增加重量；*a.* 垂直的
~ line 铅垂线
~ rule 锤规，垂直准测规

plummer ['plʌmə] *n.* 轴台，垫块，承载台
~ block 止推轴承，中间轴承

plunge [plʌndʒ] *n.* 跳进，投入；*v.* 投入，跳进，陷入，用力插入

plunger ['plʌndʒə] *n.* 柱塞，活塞，潜水者
~ barrel 柱塞套
~ cross pin 柱塞十字头销，柱塞横销
~ guide 柱塞导承，柱塞套

~ guide bush 柱塞套筒
~ lead 柱塞导套，柱塞套筒
~ load 柱塞负荷
~ pump 柱塞泵
~ ring 柱塞环
~ rod 柱塞杆
~ spring 柱塞弹簧
~ type fuel injection pump 柱塞式喷油泵
~ type oil motor 柱塞式油马达

plural ['pluərəl] *n.* 复数，复数形式；*a.* 复数的

plus [plʌs] *n.* 正号，加号，正数，有利的情况或因素；*a.* 加的，正的，附加的，额外的，正极的，略大的，超过标准的，受欢迎的；*prep.* 加，加上

plywood ['plaiwud] *n.* 胶合板，夹板，层压木板

PM (preventative maintenance) 预防性维修，防护检修

PMS (planned maintenance system) 计划维修系统，计划保养系统

pneuma ['nju:mə] *n.* 元气，精神，灵魂
~ lock 气动夹紧

pneumacator [,nju:'mækətə] *n.* 气动发送器

pneumatic [nju(:)'mætik] *n.* 气胎；*a.* 装满空气的，有气胎的，气动的，风力的，灵魂的 ‖ hydraulic 水力的，水压的；electric 电的，电动的
~ actuator 气动执行机构，气压传动装置
~ amplifier 气动放大器
~ circuit 气动回路
~ control 气动控制
~ control system 气动控制系统

~ control valve 气动控制阀
~ controller 气动控制器
~ cylinder 气压缸
~ dredge 气动挖掘
~ dredge pump 气动挖泥泵
~ drive 气动驱动，气动传动，气力传动
~ film flap valve 气动薄膜瓣阀
~ gauging 气动测量
~ hair humidity controller 毛发式气动湿度控制器
~ hammer 气动锤，气锤 ‖ *Syn.* air hammer 气动锤，气锤
~ hydraulic clamp 气动液压夹具
~ motor 风动马达，气动机
~ operating mechanism 气动操作机构 ‖ *Syn.* pneumatic operator 气动操作机构
~ plant 气动装置
~ press 气动压力机
~ pressure 气压 ‖ *Syn.* air pressure 气压
~ regulator 气动调节器
~ remote control system for main diesel engine 柴油主机气动遥控系统
~ servo 气动伺服装置
~ signal 气动信号
~ steering gear 气动操舵装置
~ structure 充气结构
~ system 气动系统
~ tool 气动工具
~ tube 气动导管

pneumatical [nju:'mætikəl] *a.* 气动的，充气的，灵魂的，精神的

pneumatically [nju:'mætikəli] *ad.* 由空气作用地，气动地

447

pocket ['pɔkit] *n.* 衣袋，口袋，凹地，仓库；*v.* 装…在口袋里，忍受，容忍，隐藏，压抑，据为己有；*a.* 袖珍的，小型的

~ size ohmmeter 袖珍欧姆表

pod [pɔd] *n.* 吊舱，分离舱，壳，外壳，流线型的外壳，插座，纵沟，豆荚

podded ['pɔdid] *a.* 吊舱式的，有荚的，富裕的

~ propulsor 吊舱式推进器

point [pɔint] *n.* 点，尖端，分数，要点；*v.* 弄尖，指向，指出，表明，瞄准，加标点于

~ in question 论点 ‖ *Syn.* contention 论点；issue 论点；moot point 争论未决的问题，论点

~ of contact 接触点，切点

~ of view 观点

~ out 指出

~ plane gap 针板间隙

pointer [,pɔintə] *n.* 指针，指示器

pointing ['pɔintiŋ] *n.* 弄尖，磨尖，指示，指点，勾缝，填缝材料；*v.* (point 的 ing 形式) 弄尖，指向，指出，表明，瞄准，加标点于

~ stick 指点杆，指示棍，指点杆，触控点

poison ['pɔizn] *n.* 毒药，毒害，败坏道德之事；*v.* 毒害，败坏，放毒，下毒

poisonous ['pɔiznəs] *a.* 有毒的

poke [pəuk] *n.* 刺，戳，拨；*v.* 刺，戳，拨开，伸出

polar ['pəulə] *n.* 极线，极面；*a.* 两极的，极地的，南辕北辙的，南极的，极性的，北极的，(北极星似的)指引的

~ angle 极角

~ axis 极轴

~ region 极地，近极区域

polar-exploration 极地考察

~ craft 极地考察船

polarity [pəu'læriti] *n.* 极性，极，正负极，对立，极端

~ effect 极性效应，极化效应

~ indicator 极性指示器

~ protection 极性保护

~ switch 极性开关

~ test 极性试验，极性测试

polarization [,pəulərai'zeiʃən] *n.* 极化，产生极性，偏振，分化

polarize ['pəuləraiz] *v.* 使极化，使偏振，使两极分化

pole [pəul] *n.* 极点，极，磁极，电极，顶点，棒，柱，杆；*v.* 用竿支撑，用棒推

~ assignment 极点配置

~ coil 磁极线圈

~ plate 极板

pole-zero 零点极点，零极点

~ cancellation 零极点相消

police [pə'li:s] *n.* 警察，警察队，警察机关，公安部门；*v.* 管辖，维持治安；*a.* 警察的，有关警察的

~ patrol 公安巡逻艇

polish ['pɔliʃ] *n.* 擦亮，磨光，擦亮剂，上光剂，光泽，精良；*v.* 磨光，擦亮，发亮，润色，推敲

~ to mirror finish 抛光至镜面度

political [pə'litikəl] *a.* 政治的，行政上的

~ commissar 政委

pollutant [pə'lu:tənt] *n.* 污染物

~ emission 污染发散物

~ recovery 污染物回收

pollute [pə'lu:t] v. 弄脏，污染，玷污，腐败，败坏，亵渎 ‖ **Syn**. contaminate 弄脏，污染，玷污

pollution [pə'lu:ʃən] n. 弄脏，污染，败坏，污秽物 ‖ **Syn**. contamination 弄脏，污染，玷污，污染物

~ abatement 减轻污染

~ and accident control ship 污染与事故控制船

~ by garbage from ship 船舶垃圾污染

~ by sewage from ship 船舶污水污染

~ monitor 污染监测器

~ monitoring 污染监测

~ prevention 污染防治，防污染

~ prevention from ship 船舶污染防治，船舶防污染

~ source 污染源

POLY ['pɔli] n. (=polyethylene) 聚乙烯

polyconic [,pɔli:'kɔnik] a. 多圆锥的

polyelectrolyte [,pɔlii'lektrəu,lait] n. 聚电解质，聚合(高分子)电解质

polyester ['pɔliestə] n. 聚酯

~ resin 聚酯树脂

polyethylene [,pɔli'eθili:n] n. (=POLY) 聚乙烯

polyfunctional [,pɔli'fʌŋkʃənəl] a. 多官能的，多机能的，多重性的

~ epoxy resin 多官能环氧树脂

polyhedron [pɔli'hedrən] n. 多面体

polyimide [,pɔli'imaid] n. 聚酰亚胺

~ film 聚酰亚胺膜

~ resin 聚酰亚胺树脂

polymer ['pɔlimə] n. 聚合体，聚合物

polymeric [,pɔli'merik] a. 聚合的，聚合体的

polymerization [,pɔliməraɪ'zeiʃən] n. 聚合，聚合作用

polyphosphate [,pɔli'fɔsfeit] n. 多磷酸盐

polyurethane [,pɔli'juəriθein] n. 聚亚安酯

~ foam 聚氨酯类泡沫

polyvinyl [,pɔli'vainil] a. 乙烯聚合物的

~ chloride (PVC) 聚氯乙烯

~ chloride foamed plastic 聚氯乙烯泡沫塑料

~ chloride sheathed wire 聚氯乙烯护套线

pontoon [pɔn'tu:n] n. 平底船，(架设浮桥用的)浮舟，浮桥，浮筒，浮码头；v. 架浮桥于

~ catamaran 双体趸船

~ hatch cover 箱形舱盖

~ lifeboat 浮箱式救生艇，水密双层底救生艇

pony ['pəuni] n. 小型马；v. 付清；a. 小型的

~ bottle 小型气瓶

poop [pu:p] n. 船尾，船尾楼，真实的消息；v. 冲打(船尾)，使精疲力尽，疲乏

~ beam 尾梁

~ control 舵机间控制

~ deck 尾楼，尾楼甲板

~ front 尾楼前端

~ front bulkhead 尾楼前端舱壁

poor [puə] a. 贫穷的，贫乏的，不足的，可怜的，乏味的，卑鄙的，拙劣的，差的

~ atomization 不良雾化

~ combustion 不良燃烧

~ cooling 不良冷却

~ filtration 不良过滤

~ quality feed water 劣质给水，劣质水

poppet ['pɔpit] *n.* 提升阀

~ valve 菌形阀，提升阀 ‖ ***Syn***. mashroom valve 菌形阀

popular ['pɔpjulə] *a.* 流行的，大众的，通俗的，普遍的，普及的，平民的，便宜的 ‖ ***Syn***. common 公共的，普通的；commonplace 平凡的；general 一般的，普通的；ordinary 平常的，平凡的，普通的；pervasive 普遍的；universal 普遍的，通用的；usual 平常的，通常的，惯例的；widespread 分布广泛的，普遍的

porcelain ['pɔ:slin] *n.* 瓷，瓷器；*a.* 瓷制的，精美的，脆的

~ bushing 陶瓷套管

~ cleat 瓷夹板

~ column type SF₆ circuit breaker 瓷柱式 SF₆ 断路器

~ connector 瓷壳接线盒

~ insulator 瓷绝缘子

port [pɔ:t] *n.* 港口，舱门，左舷，避风港，端口，枪眼；*v.* 左转舵，转舵左，持(枪)

~ addition 港口附加费

~ area 码头区，港口区，喷口面积

~ Authority 港务局

~ beam 左舷，左舷横梁

~ bow 左舷船首，左舷船头

~ call 沿途到港停靠

~ city 港口城市

~ direction 端口方向

~ duty generating set 停泊发电机组

~ duty pump 港口作业泵 ‖ ***Syn***. harbor pump 停港泵，停泊泵

~ facilities 港湾设施，港口设备

~ Facility Security Officer (PFSO) 港口设施保安官员

~ Facility Security Plan (PFSP) 港口设施保安计划

~ number 端口号，通道数

~ of destination 目的港

~ of discharge 卸货港

~ of loading 装货港

~ of registry 船籍港

~ of shipment 装运港

~ office 港务局

~ quarter 左舷船尾，左舷后部

~ quarantine office 口岸检疫机关

~ selector 端口选择器

~ state 港口国

~ State Control (PSC) 港口国监督，港口国管理，港口国控制

~ State Control Officer (PSCO) 港口国控制官，港口国检查官

port-scavenged 气孔扫气式的

~ engine 气孔扫气式发动机

portable ['pɔ:təbl] *n.* 轻便易携物；*a.* 轻便的，手提式的，便携式的，耐用的，经用的

~ ammeter 便携式安培计

~ carbon dioxide fire extinguisher 便携式二氧化碳灭火器

~ compressor 便携式压缩机

~ device 便携设备 ‖ ***Syn***. portable equipment 便携设备

~ disinfector 轻便消毒器

~ drill 移动式钻床，便携式钻机，轻便钻床

~ electronics 便携式电子设备

~ extinguisher 手提灭火器

~ fan 可移式风机

~ fire extinguisher 手提式灭火器

~ fire (fighting) unit 便携式消防装置，

便携式灭火装置

~ fire pump with engine 手抬机动消防泵

~ floodlight 便携式泛光灯

~ foam applicator unit 轻便泡沫喷雾器

~ foam fire extinguisher 手提式泡沫灭火器

~ lamp 手提灯 ‖ *Syn*. hand lamp 手提灯

~ pendant lamp 便携式吊灯

~ pump 轻便泵，可移式泵 ‖ *Syn*. mobile pump 轻便泵，可移式泵

~ scanner 便携式扫描仪

~ set 便携设备

~ tool 便携工具

~ water pump 便携式水泵

portage ['pɔ:tidʒ] *n*. 水陆联运，搬运，运费；*v*. 水陆联运，(两水路间的)陆上联运路线

portal ['pɔ:təl] *n*. 入口，正门，大门

porthole ['pɔ:thəul] *n*. 舷窗，射击孔，炮眼

portion ['pɔ:ʃən] *n*. 一部分，一份；*v*. 划分，分配

portside ['pɔ:tsaid] *n*. 港口附近地区，码头区；*a*. 左舷的，码头边的，滨水区的，左边的，左派的，惯用左手的

~ lamp 左舷灯 ‖ *Syn*. portside light 左舷灯

~ oar 左舷桨

~ wharf 临港码头

position [pə'ziʃən] *n*. 位置，方位，职位，职业，职务，立场，姿势，姿态，形势，状态，状况，情势，见解，阵地；*v*. 安置，放置，确定位置，排列，设于，位于

~ angle 方位角，位置角

~ controller 位置控制器

~ desired 期望职位

~ error 位置误差

~ feedback 位置反馈

~ indicator 位置指示器

~ lamp 位置灯

~ loop 位置回路，位置环

~ measuring instrument 位置测量仪

~ mooring system 定位系泊系统

~ scale 位置刻度

~ switch 座席开关，座席按钮，行程开关

positional [pə'ziʃənl] *a*. 位置的，地位的

positioning [pə'ziʃəniŋ] *n*. 配置，布置，定位；*v*. (position 的 ing 形式) 安置，放置，确定位置，排列，设于，位于

~ accuracy 定位精度

~ motor 定位电动机，定位马达

positive ['pɔzətiv] *n*. 明确的要素，正值，正电，正片，正面，原级；*a*. 正的，(电)阳的，肯定的，实际的，积极的，绝对的，确实的，独断的，实证的，原级的

~ charge 正电荷 ‖ *Ant*. negative charge 负电荷

~ and negative 正负，正反，肯定和否定

~ and negative effects 正负作用

~ circulation cooling system 压力式水冷却系统

~ direction 正向，正方向

~ displacement pump 正排量泵，容积泵，排代泵

~ feedback 正反馈 ‖ *Ant*. negative feedback 负反馈

~ ion 阳离子 ‖ *Ant*. negative ion 阴离子

~ mold 全压式模具，阳模，不溢式压缩模

~ number 正数 ‖ *Ant*. negative number 负数

~ pole 阳极，正极 ‖ *Syn*. anode 阳极，正极 ‖ *Ant*. cathode 阴极，负极；negative pole 阴极，负极

~ response 正响应，肯定回应

~ righting moment 正扶正力矩

~ sequence 正序 ‖ *Ant*. negative sequence 负序 ‖ zero sequence 零序

~ sequence impedance 正序阻抗

~ terminal 正极端子，正端钮，正接线柱

positively ['pɔzətivli] *ad*. 明确地，断然地，肯定地

possess [pə'zes] *v*. 占有，拥有，持有，摆布，掌握，支配

possession [pə'zeʃən] *n*. 拥有，占有，所有，领土，领地，财产，支配，控制，自制，影响

possibility [ˌpɔsi'biliti] *n*. 可能，可能性，可能发生的事物

~ of trouble 事故率 ‖ *Syn*. accident rate 事故率，失事率

possible ['pɔsəbl] *a*. 可能的，不确定的，做得到的，行得通的，具潜力的，有发展的

possibly ['pɔsəbli] *ad*. 可能地，也许，或者

post [pəust] *n*. 岗位，职位，柱，邮件，邮政；*v*. 张贴，揭示，布置，邮递，快速旅行；*ad*. 加速地

~ allowance 岗位津贴

~ design processing (PDP) 设计后处理

post-accident 事故后的

~ condition 事故后状况

pot [pɔt] *n*. 罐，壶，锅，容器，巨款；*v*. 射杀，射击，贮藏在罐中

pot-shaped 筒形的

~ piston 筒形活塞

potable ['pəutəbl] *n*. 饮料；*a*. 可以喝的，适合饮用的

~ water 饮用水 ‖ *Syn*. drinking water 饮用水

~ (water) pump 饮水泵

~ water treatment 饮水处理

potassium [pə'tæsjəm] *n*. 钾

~ bicarbonate powder 碳酸氢钾干粉

~ bichromate 重铬酸钾

~ chromate 铬酸钾

~ cyanide 氰化钾

potential [pə'tenʃ(ə)l] *n*. 潜能，潜力，电压，势能，电势，电位；*a*. 潜在的，可能的，势的，位的，有能力的

~ danger 潜在危险，潜在威胁，事故隐患

~ distribution 电位分布

~ divider 分压器

~ drop (PD) 电压降，电位降，势能落差 ‖ *Syn*. voltage drop 电压降

~ energy 势能

~ of hydrogen (PH) 酸碱度

~ of hydrogen test 酸碱度测试

~ of hydrogen value 酸碱度值

~ security threat 潜在安全威胁

~ temperature 位温，温位

~ transformer (PT) 电压互感器，变压器，仪表变压器 ‖ *Syn*. voltage transformer 电压互感器，变压器

~ transformer cabinet 电压互感器柜
~ trouble measure 潜在故障预防措施
potentially [pə'tenʃəli] ad. 潜在地
potentiometer [pə,tenʃi'ɔmitə] n. 电位计，分压计，电势计，分压器
pound [paund] n. 磅，英镑，重击，拘留所；v. 连续重击，连续敲打，苦干
pounds [paundz] n. (pound 的复数) 磅，英镑
~ per square inch (PSI) 磅/平方英寸
pour [pɔ:] n. 倾泻；v. 涌出，灌注，倾泻，涌入，流，倾盆大雨
~ point 倾点，流点，流动点，浇注点
~ point depressant 降凝剂
powder ['paudə] n. 粉，粉末，火药，散剂，尘土；v. 搽粉于，撒粉，使成粉末，变成粉末，重击
~ blower 磁粉喷枪，喷粉机，喷粉器
~ extinguisher 粉末灭火器
~ extinguishing agent 干粉灭火剂
~ extinguishing system 干粉灭火系统
~ fire extinguisher 干粉灭火器 ‖ *Syn.* dry chemical fire extinguisher 干粉灭火器；dry powder extinguisher 干粉灭火器
~ fire monitor 干粉炮
~ suppressant 干粉抑爆剂
power ['pauə] n. 幂，功率，电力，动力，(透镜的)放大率，能力，体能，智能，力量，权力，势力，影响力；v. 使有力量，供以动力，激励
~ and lighting system 动力与照明系统
~ assist 动力辅助
~ button 电源按钮，电源开关
~ change-over box 电源切换箱
~ circuit 电源电路，电力网

~ consumption 能量功耗，功耗
~ converter 电源转换器，功率变流器
~ diagram 功率图
~ distribution 配电，功率分布
~ distribution box 电力配电箱，动力配电箱，配电柜 ‖ *Syn.* power distribution cabinet 电力配电箱，动力配电箱，配电柜
~ distribution equipment 配电装置
~ distribution system 配电系统
~ down 电源休眠，掉电，停电措施，电源中断
~ drill 机械钻，动力钻机，电钻 ‖ *Syn.* electric drill 电钻
~ efficiency 功率效率，出力效率
~ electronic circuit 电力电子电路
~ electronic device 电力电子器件
~ electronic equipment 电力电子设备
~ equipment 电力设备，发电设备，动力设备
~ factor 功率因数
~ factor of motor 电动机功率因数
~ feeder 馈电线，电力馈线
~ feeder panel 动力馈电屏
~ frequency 电力频率，工业频率
~ generation 发电
~ generation equipment 发电设备
~ generator 发电机
~ good 电源正常
~ grid 电网 ‖ *Syn.* power network 电网
~ ground 电源接地，电源地线
~ input 电源输入，功率输入
~ level 功率级，功率电平，功率位准
~ load 电力荷载，电力负荷
~ meter 瓦特计，功率计
~ of battery 电池功率

~ off 关机，停车，停电
~ operation 动力操作，带电操作，功率操作
~ outlet 电源输出口，电源插座
~ output 功率输出，电源输出
~ per cylinder 单缸功率
~ per liter 功率/升
~ performance 动力性能
~ plant 动力装置，发电厂
~ plug 电源插头，电力插头
~ pump 动力泵，电动泵
~ quantity 电量
~ rating 定额功率 ‖ *Syn*. capacity rating 额定功率，额定容量；nominal capacity 额定功率，标称功率，额定容量，标称容量；nominal output 额定功率，额定出力，额定输出，标称输出；nominal power 额定功率，额定容量，标称功率，标称容量；rated capacity 额定功率，额定容量，设计效率；rated output 额定功率，额定输出量，额定出力；rated power 额定功率，设计功率，额定动力，不失真功率；rated power output 额定功率，额定动力输出；rated power capability 额定功率；standard horsepower 额定功率，标准马力；standard power 额定功率，标准功率
~ reserve 动力储存，功率后备，能量储备
~ save mode 节电模式，节电方式
~ selector switch 功率选择器开关
~ shortage 电力短缺，电荒
~ source 电源，能源 ‖ *Syn*. electric source 电源；electrical source 电源；power supply 电源；mains 电源
~ source of a ship 船舶动力源

~ stability 功率稳定性
~ station 发电站，发电厂
~ stroke 动力冲程
~ supply box 电源箱
~ supply change-over device 电源转换装置
~ supply installations 供电设施
~ supply of a ship 船舶电源
~ supply system 供电系统
~ switch 电源开关
~ system 电网，电力系统，动力系统
~ system automation equipment 电力系统自动装置
~ system relay protection 电力系统继电保护
~ system reliability 电力系统可靠性
~ system shortcuts 电力系统短路
~ system stabilization (PSS) 电力系统稳定
~ system stabilizator (PSS) 电力系统稳定器
~ take-off (PTO) 动力输出装置
~ transfer 能量输送
~ transformation 变电
~ transformer 电力变压器，电源变压器
~ transmission 电力传输，输电
~ transmission system 电力传输系统，输电系统
~ unit 动力设备，供电装置
~ up 上电，加电
~ utilization 用电，电能的利用
~ utilizing device 用电设备
~ voltage 电源电压
power-driven 电动的，动力驱动的，机动的
~ vessel 机动船，动力船

powered ['pauəd] v. (power 的过去式和过去分词) 使有力量，供以动力，激励；a. 有动力装置的，用动力推动的，产生动力的

~ bakelite plate 粉质胶木板

powerful ['pauəful] a. 动力的，强大的，有力的，有效的，巨大的，强烈的

PPM (parts per million) 百万分之，兆比率

PPMC (parts per million carbon) 百万分率碳

practicable ['præktikəbl] a. 实用的，行得通的，切实可行的

practical ['præktikəl] a. 实际的，实践的，实用的，应用的，有实际经验的

~ guide 实用向导，实用手册

practically ['præktikəli] ad. 实际上，实践上，事实上，几乎，简直

practice ['præktis] n. 实行，实践，实际，惯例，习惯，练习，实习，专业，开业，业务，工作；v. 练习，习惯于，训练，从业，从事，执业

pratique ['præti:k] n. 入港许可，检疫入港许可证

PRC (People's Republic of China) 中华人民共和国

pre-dive 潜水前的

~ activity 潜水前活动

~ double check 潜水前仔细检查

~ procedures 潜水前工作程序，潜水前常规

~ training 潜水前训练

pre-exciting 预励的，预激的

~ switch 充磁开关，激磁开关

preadjust ['pri:ə'dʒʌst] v. 预调

preadjusted ['pri:ə'dʒʌstid] v. (preadjust 过去式和过去分词) 预调；a. 预调的

~ pressure 预调压力

precast ['pri:'ka:st] v. 预制，预浇铸；a. 预制的，预浇铸的

precaution [pri'kɔ:ʃən] n. 预防，警惕，防范，预防措施，预防方法

~ device 预警器

precautionary [pri'kɔ:ʃənəri] a. 预防的，警惕的，防范的

~ measure 预防措施，安全措施

precautions [pri'kɔ:ʃəns] n. (precaution 的复数) 预防措施，预防方法，注意事项

~ against fire 防火注意事项

precede [pri(:)'si:d] v. 在…之前发生，领先，先于

precedence ['presidəns] n. 优先，居先，优先权

precedent [pri'si:dənt] n. 先例，判例，惯例；a. 在前的

precept ['pri:sept] n. 规则，规矩，训令

precession [pri'seʃən] n. 先行，进动，运动，领先

prechamber [pri:'tʃæmbə] n. (柴油机) 预燃室

precipitate [pri'sipiteit] n. 沉淀物；v. 猛抛，促成，使陷入，使沉淀，猛地落下；a. 突如其来的，陡然下降的，贸然轻率的

precipitation [pri,sipi'teiʃən] n. 沉淀，沉淀作用，急躁，仓促，雨量

~ number 沉淀值

precipitator [pri'sipiteitə] n. 沉淀剂

precise [pri'sais] v. 精确；a. 精确的，准确的

precisely [pri'saisli] ad. 精确地，严谨地，

正好

precision [pri'siʒən] *n.* 精确，精度，精确度 ‖ *Syn.* accuracy 精确性，正确度，精确度
　　~ feeler 精密触头
preclude [pri'klu:d] *v.* 排除
precombustion [pri:kəm'bʌstʃən] *n.* 预燃
　　~ burner 预燃式燃烧器
　　~ chamber 预燃室，预燃烧室
　　~ device 预燃装置
　　~ diesel 燃室式柴油机
　　~ engine 预燃式发动机
　　~ reaction 预燃反应
precool [pri:'ku:l] *v.* 预冷却，预冷，预冻
precooling [pri:'ku:liŋ] *n.* 预冷却，预冷，预冻；*v.* (precool 的 ing 形式) 预冷却，预冷，预冻
precursor [pri(:)'kə:sə] *n.* 预兆，先兆，前辈，先锋
predeterminate ['pri:di'tə:minit] *a.* 预定的，先定的
predetermination ['pri:di,tə:mi'neiʃən] *n.* 预先决定，预先确定
predetermine ['pri:di'tə:min] *v.* 预先决定，预先确定
predetermined [,pri:di'tə:mind] *v.* (predetermine 的过去式和过去分词) 预先决定，预先确定；*a.* 预先决定的，预先确定的
　　~ tension 预紧力
　　~ value 预定值
predict [pri'dikt] *v.* 预言，预测，预报 ‖ *Syn.* estimate 估计，估算，估量；forecast 预言，预测，预报
prediction [pri'dikʃən] *n.* 预言，预测，预报 ‖ *Syn.* estimation 估计，估算，估量；forecasting 预言，预测，预报
predominant [pri'dɔminənt] *a.* 主要的，占优势的，卓越的，支配的，突出的，有影响的
　　~ axis 供设计优化坐标轴，主导轴
predominantly [pri'dɔminəntli] *ad.* 占主导地位地，显著地
predominate [pri'dɔmineit] *v.* 掌握，控制，支配，统治，成为主流，占优势
prefabrication [,pri:fæbri'keiʃən] *n.* 预先制造，配件预先制造，预制
prefer [pri'fə:] *v.* 更喜欢，宁愿，优先偿付，提出(控告)，推荐
preferable ['prefərəbəl] *a.* 更好的，更可取的，更优越的
preferably ['prefərəbli] *ad.* 更可取地，更适宜地
preference ['prefərəns] *n.* 偏爱，优先选择，优先权
preferential [,prefə'renʃəl] *a.* 优先的，先取的，特惠的
preheat ['pri:'hi:t] *v.* 预先加热，预热
preheater ['pri:'hi:tə] *n.* 预热器
preignition [,pri:ig'niʃən] *n.* (内燃机的)提前点火，自动点火，预燃
preimpregnate ['pri:im'pregneit] *n.* (混合成分)保混剂，预浸(渍)
preliminary [pri'liminəri] *n.* 开端，初步，初试，预赛，准备工作；*a.* 初步的，初级的，预备的
　　~ adjustment 初调，预调整
　　~ calculation 初步计算
　　~ damage stability calculations 初步损伤稳定性计算
　　~ design 初步设计
　　~ main equipment 一次主要设备

~ meeting 筹备会议，预备会议，预备会，筹备会

~ study 初步研究

~ treatment 预处理

preload ['pri:'ləud] n. 预加负载，预加负荷，预载；v. 预加负载，预加负荷，预载

preloaded [pri:'ləudid] v. (preload 的过去式和过去分词) 预加负载，预加负荷，预载；a. 预加载的，预安装的

~ bearing 预紧轴承，装配过紧的轴承

~ gear 预先组合装备

preparation [,prepə'reiʃən] n. 准备，预备

preparations [,prepə'reiʃənz] n. (preparation 的复数) 准备，预备

~ for standby 备车

preparatory [pri'pærətəri] a. 预备的，准备的，筹备的，预科的；ad. 正在预备，正在筹备

prepare [pri'pɛə] v. 准备，预备，着手做，办妥，装备

~ budget 编预算，编制预算

~ data 准备资料

~ for survey 准备调查，准备检验

~ to 准备

preparedness [pri'pɛədnis] n. 有准备，已准备

preplan ['pri:'plæn] v. 预先计划，预先打算

prerequisite ['pri:'rekwizit] n. 先决条件，前提；a. 必要的，首要必备的

prescribe [pris'kraib] v. 指定，规定，开处方

prescribed [pri'skraibd] v. (prescribe 的过去式和过去分词) 指定,规定,开处方；a. 指定的，规定的

~ limit 规定极限，给定极限，已知范围

~ period 规定期限，规定时限

~ range 规定范围

prescription [pri'skripʃən] n. 训令，指示，规定，命令，处方，药方

presedimentation [presedimən'teiʃən] n. 预沉淀

present ['prizent] n. 现在，瞄准，赠品，礼物；v. 提出，介绍，引见，赠送，上演，呈现，举枪瞄准；a. 现在的，出席的，当面的

~ value 现值

presentable [pri'zentəbl] a. 可提供的，像样的，拿得出的，体面的

presentation [,prezen'teiʃən] n. 显示，展示，介绍，陈述，表达，提出，赠送，提供

presently ['prezəntli] ad. 目前，不久

preservation [,prezə(:)'veiʃən] n. 保护，保存，保管，保持，维持，保留，防腐

preservative [pri'zə:vətiv] n. 保护剂,防腐剂；a. 有保护能力的

preserve [pri'zə:v] n. 禁区，防护物；v. 保护，保持，保存，保藏

preset ['pri:'set] v. 预先设置，事先调整

~ value 预置值，预设值

press [pres] n. 压，按，印刷，压力，拥挤，紧握，新闻；v. 压，按，受压，压榨，紧抱，拥挤，逼迫

~ button 按钮开关

~ into 使压成，按入，压入

pressing ['presiŋ] n. 压，压制；v. (press 的 ing 形式) 压，按，受压，压榨，紧抱，拥挤，逼迫；a. 紧迫的，紧急的，迫切的，真切的，坚持的

~ die 压模

~ lead wires 压铅丝

pressure ['preʃə(r)] *n.* 压力，压强，电压，压迫，强制，紧迫，压紧，压缩，困扰，印象，印记，挤，压，按，榨；*v.* 迫使，增压

~ accumulation test 蓄压试验

~ angle 压力角

~ chamber 压力室，压力舱

~ charging 增压

~ charging system 增压系统

~ coaming 阻力式舱口防水挡板

~ control 压力控制

~ control valve 压力控制阀

~ controlled unit 压力控制单元

~ controller 压力控制器

~ cylinder 增压缸，压力缸

~ difference 压力差，差压

~ differential controller 压差控制器

~ differential switch 压差开关

~ drop 压降

~ drop across the filter 过滤器压降

~ energy 压能

~ equalizing 压力均衡

~ feed 压力送料，压送

~ gauge 压力表

~ gauge with bakelite case 胶壳压力表

~ gauge with electric contact 电接点压力表

~ gauge with iron case 铁壳压力表

~ grease point 压力润滑点

~ head 压头，压力水头，压位差

~ hull 耐压壳体

~ intensity 压力强度，压强

~ limiting cut-off valve 限压切断阀

~ loss 压力损失

~ lubrication 压力润滑，加压润滑，强制润滑

~ measurement 压力测量

~ oil atomizer 压力喷油器

~ pipe 压水管

~ pulse 压力脉冲

~ rating 压力等级，压力定额

~ ratio regulator 压力比调节器

~ reducing manometer for oxygen 氧气减压计

~ reducing valve 减压阀，减压活门

~ regulating valve 调压阀

~ regulation 压力调节

~ regulator 调压器

~ relay 压力继电器

~ release 降压，放压，放气

~ release protection 卸压保护

~ relief system 除压系统，减压系统，压力安全系统，压力释放系统

~ relief valve 安全阀，卸压阀

~ ring 压力环

~ ring for stuffing box 填料函压力环

~ screw 压力螺钉，压紧螺钉

~ stop valve 压力截止阀

~ surge 压力波动，冲击压力

~ sustaining valve 恒压阀

~ swing adsorption (PSA) 变压吸附(法)

~ swing adsorption nitrogen generator 变压吸附制氮机

~ switch 压力开关，压力操纵开关，压力继电器

~ tank 压力箱，高压锅

~ test 试压，气压试验

~ test to check for leakage 检查渗漏的压力试验

~ transducer 压力传感器 ‖ *Syn*. pressure transmitter 压力传感器

~ type cooling 加压式冷却法

~ type gas carrier 压力式气体运输船

~ type mechanical oil atomizer 机械压力雾化喷油器

~ vessel 压力容器

~ water 压力水

~ water spraying system 压力喷水系统，压力水雾灭火系统

pressure-temperature 压力温度

~ conversion 压力温度转换

~ curve 压力温度曲线

~ rating 压力温度等级

~ relief device 压力温度安全器

pressure-vacuum (PV) 压力真空

~ release valve 压力真空释放阀，呼吸阀

~ valve 压力真空阀

pressure-volume 压力容积，压容

~ diagram 压力容积图，压容图

pressurize ['preʃəraiz] *v*. 施加压力，使耐压，增压，密封

pressurized ['preʃəraizd] *v*. (pressurize 的过去式和过去分词) 施加压力，使耐压，增压，密封；*a*. 加压的，受压的，增压的

~ equipment 加压设备

~ fuel 增压燃油

~ fuel oil system 增压燃油系统

~ hold system 压力稳固系统

~ kettle 压力容器

prestress ['pri:'stres] *v*. 预加应力

pretend [pri'tend] *v*. 装扮，假装；*a*. 仿制的，模仿的

pretension [pri'tenʃən] *n*. 假装，做作，要求，主张，借口，自负；*v*. 预张紧，预拉伸

pretensioned [pri'tenʃənd] *v*. (pretension 的过去式和过去分词) 预张紧，预拉伸；*a*. 预张紧的，预拉伸的

~ spring 预张紧弹簧

pretensioner [pri'tenʃənə] *n*. 紧固器，预紧器，安全带预紧装置

pretreat ['pri:'tri:t] *v*. 预先处理，预处理

prevail [pri'veil] *v*. 流行，盛行，获胜，成功

prevailing [pri'veiliŋ] *v*. (prevail 的 ing 形式) 流行，盛行，获胜，成功；*a*. 盛行的，普遍的，占优势的

~ circumstances 当时环境

~ value 一般数值

prevalent ['prevələnt] *a*. 流行的，普遍的

prevent [pri'vent] *v*. 预防，防止，制止，阻碍，阻止，阻挠 ‖ *Syn*. countercheck 制止，防止；forestall 预防，阻止，阻碍；guard 防止，保卫，警惕，警卫

~ from 阻止，制止，妨碍

preventative [pri'ventətiv] *a*. 预防性的

~ maintenance (PM) 预防性维修，防护检修

~ resistance 防止短路用的电阻

preventer [pri'ventə] *n*. 妨碍物

~ guy 制动控索，辅助拉索，辅助稳索

preventing [pri'ventiŋ] *n*. 预防，防止；*v*. (prevent 的 ing 形式) 预防，防止，制止，阻碍，阻止

~ freezing 防冻，防止结冰

prevention [pri'venʃən] *n*. 预防，防止，预防法，阻挠，阻碍，障碍

~ of accident 事故预防

~ of fire 防火 ‖ *Syn*. fire prevention

459

防火；fire protection 防火，消防；fire safety 防火，消防

preventive [pri'ventiv] *a.* 预防的，预防性的

~ action 预防措施 ‖ *Syn.* preventive measure 预防措施；preventive precaution 预防措施

~ maintenance 预防性维修，定期检修

previous ['pri:viəs] *a.* 以前的，先前的

previously ['pri:vju:sli] *ad.* 以前，事先

prewarming [pri:'wɔ:miŋ] *n.* 预加热，预加温，预热

~ bypass 预热旁路，预热旁通

prewarning [pri:'wɔ:niŋ] *n.* 预警

~ system 预警系统，预警机制

prewash [pri:'wɔʃ] *n.* 预先洗涤，预洗

~ procedure 预洗程序

prick [prik] *n.* 锥，刺，扎，刺痛；*v.* 戳，刺，扎，刺痛，竖起；*a.* 竖起的

prill ['pril] *n.* 金属小球；*v.* 使变颗粒状

primal ['praiməl] *a.* 原始的，最初的，第一的，最重要的，主要的

primarily ['praimərili] *ad.* 首先，起初，主要地，根本上

primary ['praiməri] *n.* 初级线圈，第一位，最好者，要素，恒星；*a.* 原线圈的，首要的，主要的，第一位的，最早的，初步的，初级的，原来的，根源的，基本的，立即的，直接的

~ air 一次空气

~ barriers 一级防护，一级屏障

~ battery 原电池(组)，一次电池(组)

~ bridge navigational equipment 主驾驶台导航设备

~ cell 原电池

~ circuit 原电路，初级电路

~ coolant 初冷却剂，一次冷却剂，一次载热剂

~ data 原始数据，原始资料

~ demand 基本需求，初级需求

~ distribution link 初级分布线路

~ distribution network 一次配电网络

~ distribution system 一次配电系统

~ equipment 主设备，一次设备

~ exploration 初探

~ member 主构件，主要构件

~ membrane 初级膜

~ network 一次电力网，一次网络

~ refrigerant 初级制冷剂

~ relaying 主继电保护

~ storage 主存储器

~ structure 一级结构，原始结构

~ valve 主阀，根部阀

~ voltage 初级电压，一次电压 ‖ *Syn.* transformer input voltage 初级电压，一次电压

~ winding 一次绕组，原绕组

prime [praim] *n.* 最初，精华，青春；*v.* 灌注，填装，预先准备好，让人吃(喝)足；*a.* 主要的，最初的，最好的，第一流的，根本的，素数的

~ motor 原动机 ‖ *Syn.* prime mover 原动机

~ mover automatic starter 原动机自动起动装置

primer ['praimə] *n.* 雷管，底火，导火线，底漆，初级读本

~ coating 涂底剂，涂底漆，初级涂烘

~ pump 启动泵

priming ['praimiŋ] *n.* 灌注，填装，装填物，雷管，起爆药，底漆；*v.* (prime 的 ing 形式) 灌注，填装，预先准备好，

让人吃(喝)足
~ arrangement 起动注水器
~ line 灌注管路
~ pump 引水泵
~ unit 起动装置
~ valve 起动阀

principal ['prinsəp(ə)l] n. 负责人, 首长, 校长, 本金; a. 主要的, 首要的
~ component analysis (PCA) 主成分分析
~ dimensions 主尺度, 主要尺寸

principally ['prinsipli] ad. 主要地

principle ['prinsəpl] n. 法则, 原则, 原理, 准则, 元素, 成分, 道义, 本能, 天性
~ dimensions 主尺度
~ of electrical system's relay protection 电气系统继电保护原理

principles ['prinsəplz] n. (principle 的复数) 法则, 原则, 原理
~ of electric circuits 电路原理

print [print] n. 版, 印刷物, 印迹, 印章, 印刷业, 照片; v. 打印, 印刷, 出版, 用印刷体写

printed [printid] v. (print 的过去式和过去分词) 打印, 印刷, 出版, 用印刷体写; a. 印刷的, 已印好的
~ circuit 印刷电路
~ circuit board (PCB) 印制电路板 ‖ ***Syn***. printed wiring board (PWB) 印制线路板

printer ['printə] n. 打印机, 印刷工

printing ['printiŋ] n. 印刷, 印刷术, 印花; v. (print 的 ing 形式) 打印, 印刷, 出版, 用印刷体写
~ finished signal 打印完成信号, 打印结束信号

prior ['praiə] n. 预先; a. 优先的, 在前的; ad. 在前, 居先
~ to 在…之前, 居先

priority [prai'ɔriti] n. 先前, 优先, 优先权

prism ['prizəm] n. 棱镜, 棱晶, 棱柱
~ file 棱柱挫

prismatic [priz'mætik] a. 棱柱形的, 用三棱镜的, 棱镜的
~ coefficient 棱形系数, 棱柱系数 ‖ ***Syn***. longitudinal coefficient 棱形系数, 纵向系数

privacy ['praivəsi] n. 隐私, 秘密
~ lock 保密锁, 隐私锁

private ['praivit] n. 士兵, 二等兵; a. 私人的, 私有的, 私营的, 秘密的, 隐蔽的, 非官方的
~ bathroom 私人浴室

privateer [ˌpraivə'tiə] n. (战时特准攻击敌方商船的)武装民船, 私掠船

probability [ˌprɔbə'biliti] n. 可能性, 或然性, 概率, 几率

probable ['prɔbəbl] a. 可能的, 大概的

probably ['prɔbəbli] ad. 大概, 或许

probe [prəub] n. 探头, 探针, 探测仪; v. 探查, 查明
~ refueling device 探头加油装置

problem ['prɔbləm] n. 问题, 难题, 困难; a. 难对付的, 难处理的, 社会问题的
~ location 问题定位, 问题地点

problematic [ˌprɔblə'mætik] a. (=problematical) 成问题的, 有疑问的, 未知的

problematical [ˌprɔblə'mætikl] a. (=problematic) 成问题的, 有疑问的, 未知的

procedural [prə'si:dʒərəl] a. 程序上的

procedure [prə'si:dʒə] n. 程序, 工序, 过程, 进程, 步骤 ‖ ***Syn***. course 过

程，经过，进程；process 过程，程序，步骤

~ for contingency response 应急反应程序

proceed [prə'si:d] v. 进行，继续下去，发生

process ['prə'ses] n. 过程，作用，方法，程序，步骤，进行，推移；v. 处理，加工 ‖ **Syn**. course 过程，经过，进程；procedure 程序，工序，过程，进程，步骤

~ control 过程控制

~ control system 过程控制系统

~ input-output (PIO) 过程输入输出

~ monitoring 过程监控

~ of self-excitation 自激过程，自励过程

processed [prə'sest] v. (process 的过去式和过去分词) 加工，处理；a. 加工过的，处理的

~ data 处理后的数据

processing [prəu'sesiŋ] n. 加工，处理，进程，步骤；v. (process 的 ing 形式) 加工，处理

~ capacity 处理能力，处理容量

~ equipment 加工设备

~ gain 处理增益，加工盈余

processor ['prəusesə] n. 处理器，处理机

procure [prə'kjuə] v. 取得，获得

procurement [prə'kjuəmənt] n. 获得，取得

produce [prə'dju:s] n. 产物，产品；v. 提出，出示，生产，制造，引起，招致，创作

product ['prɔdʌkt] n. 产品，产物，乘积

~ performance 产品性能

~ quality 产品质量

~ tanker 成品油船

production [prə'dʌkʃən] n. 生产，产品，作品，成果

~ cost 生产成本

~ equipment 生产设备

~ quantity 生产量

~ test 生产测试，产品检验

productivity [ˌprɔdʌk'tiviti] n. 生产率，生产力

profession [prə'feʃən] n. 职业，专业，表白，宣布

professional [prə'feʃnl] n. 专业人士，自由职业者；a. 专业的，职业的

professionalism [prə'feʃənəˌlizəm] n. 专业技巧，职业化，职业道德，职业特性

proficiency [prə'fiʃənsi] n. 熟练，精通，熟练程度

proficient [prə'fiʃənt] n. 专家，内行，精通；a. 熟练的，精通的

profile ['prəufail] n. 外形，轮廓，剖面，侧面

~ chart 轮廓图，剖析图，剖面图

profit ['prɔfit] n. 利润，益处，得益；v. 得益，利用，有益于

prognostic [prɔg'nɔstik] n. 预兆；a. 预兆的

program ['prəugræm] (=programme) n. 程序，纲要，计划，计划节目；v. 编程序，规划，拟计划，安排节目

~ command 程序指令

programmable ['prəugræməbl] a. 可设计的，可编程的

~ controller 可编程控制器

~ logic controller (PLC) 可编程逻辑控制器

~ terminal 可编程终端

programme ['prəugræm] (=program) n. 程序，纲要，计划，计划节目；v. 编程序，规划，拟计划，安排节目

programmed [prəu,græmd] v. (programme 的过去式和过去分词) 编程序，规划，拟计划，安排节目；a. 程序的，循序渐进式的

~ control 程序控制

programmer ['prəugræmə] n. 程序师，程序员，程序规划员

programming ['prəugræmiŋ] n. 程序设计，编程，节目编排；v. (programme 的 ing 形式) 编程序，规划，拟计划，安排节目

~ control language 编程控制语言

~ environment 程序设计条件，程序设计环境

~ technique 编程技术

progress ['prəugres] n. 前进，进步，发展；v. 前进，进步，发展，进行

progression [prə'greʃən] n. 进展，行进，级数，连续动作

progressive [prə'gresiv] n. 改革论者，进步论者；a. 前进的，累进的，进步的

~ drift 逐渐地漂移

~ flooding 递进进水，累进进水

~ fracture 扩展裂缝

~ scanning 顺序扫描，步进扫描，逐行扫描

~ wave 行波

progressively [prə'gresivli] ad. 逐步地，日益增多地

prohibit [prə'hibit] v. 禁止，阻止，妨碍，避免

prohibition [,prəuhi'biʃən] n. 禁令，禁止，阻止，妨碍，避免

project ['prɔdʒekt] n. 计划，方案，事业，企业，工程；v. 设计，计划，投射，放映，射出，发射，凸出

~ implementation plan (PIP) 项目实施计划

~ manage 项目管理

~ manager 项目经理，项目管理人

~ schedule 工程计划

projection [prə'dʒekʃən] n. 发射，投射，投影，设计，凸出物，规划，预测，估计

~ light 投射光

projector [prə'dʒektə] n. 投影仪，放映机

prolong [prə'lɔŋ] v. 延长，拉长，延期，拖延

prolonged [prə'lɔŋd] v. (prolong 的过去式和过去分词) 延长，拉长，延期，拖延；a. 延长的，拖延的

~ blast 长笛

promenade [,prɔmi'na:d] n. 散步，闲逛；v. 散步，漫步；a. 散步的，漫步的

~ deck 散步甲板

prominent ['prɔminənt] a. 著名的，显著的，卓越的，突出的

promote [prə'məut] v. 促进，推进，发扬，提升，提拔，晋升

promotion [prə'məuʃən] n. 促进，推进，发扬，提升，提拔，晋升

prone [prəun] a. 倾向于，易于，倾斜的，俯卧的；ad. 仰卧地

proof [pru:f] n. 证据，试验，考验，校样；v. 检验，校对，使不被穿透；a. 不能透入的，证明用的，防…的，有耐力的

~ test for fire extinguishing system 灭火系统的验收试验

propagate ['prɔpəgeit] v. 繁衍，增殖，扩散，传播，宣传

propagation [,prɔpə'geiʃən] n. 宣传，繁殖，传播，动植物

~ coefficient 繁殖系数，繁殖率

propane ['prəupein] n. 丙烷

propel [prə'pel] v. 推进，驱使，驱策

propellant [prə'pelənt] n. 推进物，发射火药；a. 推进的

propeller [prə'pelə] n. 推进器，螺旋推进器，推进者，推进物

~ blade 螺旋桨叶片

~ boss 轴毂

~ cavitation 螺旋桨旋转真空，螺旋桨空泡，螺旋桨气穴

~ characteristic 螺旋桨特性

~ design 螺旋桨设计

~ diameter 螺旋桨直径

~ effect 螺旋桨效应

~ fitting 螺旋桨配件

~ hub 螺旋桨桨毂

~ material 螺旋桨材料

~ nozzle 螺旋桨导流管，螺旋桨喷嘴

~ nut 螺旋桨螺母

~ pitch 螺旋桨螺距，浆距

~ post 螺旋桨柱，推进器柱

~ pump 旋桨泵，轴流泵 ‖ *Syn*. axial (flow) pump 轴流泵

~ racing 螺旋桨飞车

~ shaft 螺旋桨轴，螺旋轴，传动轴

~ shaft bearing 螺旋桨轴轴承

~ shaft bracket 艉轴架

~ shaft earthing equipment 螺旋桨轴接地装置

~ shaft lining 尾轴衬套

~ slipping rate 螺旋桨滑移率

~ statical equilibrium 螺旋桨静平衡

~ stern tunnel 螺旋桨轴隧

~ strut 人字架，尾轴架

~ surface finish 螺旋桨表面光洁度，螺旋桨表面抛光

~ thrust 螺旋桨推力

~ to be cleaned in site 螺旋桨现场清洗

~ to be polished in site 螺旋桨现场抛光

~ to be scraped in site 螺旋桨现场刮削

propelling [prə'peliŋ] v. (propel 的 ing 形式) 推进，驱使，驱策；a. 推进的

~ force 推进力

proper ['prɔpə] a. 适当的，正确的，固有的，特有的，正当的，严格意义上的，彻底的

~ alkalinity 适当的碱度

~ communication 适当的沟通，得体的交际

~ metering 合理计量

~ packing 合格包装

property ['prɔpəti] n. 性质，特性，属性，财产，所有物，所有权，道具 ‖ *Syn*. nature 本性，性质，特性；performance 性能

proportion [prə'pɔ:ʃən] (P) n. 比率，比例，均衡，面积，部分；v. 使成比例，使均衡，分摊

~ action 比例作用

~ control 比例控制，比例调节

~ control mode 比例控制方式，比例调节方式

~ control output 比例控制输出，比例调节输出

~ controller 比例控制器，比例调节器 ‖ *Syn*. proportion regulator 比例控制器，比例调节器

～element 比例环节，比例元件
～mode 比例模式
proportion-differentiation (PD) 比例微分
　～action 比例微分作用
　～control 比例微分控制，比例微分调节
　～controller 比例微分控制器，比例微分调节器 ‖ ***Syn***. proportion regulator 比例微分控制器，比例微分调节器
proportion-integration (PI) 比例积分
　～action 比例积分作用
　～control 比例积分控制，比例积分调节
　～controller 比例积分控制器，比例积分调节器 ‖ ***Syn***. proportion-integration regulator 比例积分控制器，比例积分调节器
proportion-integration-differentiation (PID) 比例积分微分
　～action 比例积分微分作用
　～control 比例积分微分控制，比例积分微分调节
　～controller 比例积分微分控制器，比例积分微分调节器 ‖ ***Syn***. proportion-integration-differentiation regulator 比例积分微分控制器，比例积分微分调节器
proportional [prə'pɔ:ʃənl] (P) *n*. 比例项，比例量；*a*. 比例的，成比例的，相称的，协调的，均衡的
　～action 比例作用
　～band 比例区，比例带，比例尺范围
　～control 比例控制，比例调节
　～control mode 比例控制方式，比例调节方式
　～control output 比例控制输出，比例调节输出
　～controller 比例控制器，比例调节器 ‖ ***Syn***. proportional regulator 比例控制器，比例调节器
　～dividers 比例分规，比例规
　～element 比例环节，比例元件
　～error 比例误差，相对误差
　～fairness 比例公平
　～intensification 比例加强
　～limit 比例极限，比例限界
　～mode 比例模式
　～operation apparatus 比例操作器
　～part 比例部分
　～plus derivative (PD) 比例加微分的，比例微分的
　～plus derivative action 比例微分作用
　～plus derivative control 比例微分控制，比例微分调节
　～plus derivative controller 比例微分控制器，比例微分调节器 ‖ ***Syn***. proportional plus derivative regulator 比例微分控制器，比例微分调节器
　～plus integral (PI) 比例加积分的，比例积分的
　～plus integral action 比例积分作用
　～plus integral control 比例积分控制，比例积分调节
　～plus integral controller 比例积分控制器，比例积分调节器 ‖ ***Syn***. proportional plus integral regulator 比例积分控制器，比例积分调节器
　～plus integral plus derivative (PID) 比例加积分加微分的，比例积分微分的
　～plus integral plus derivative action 比例积分微分作用
　～plus integral plus derivative control 比例积分微分控制，比例积分微分调节

~ plus integral plus derivative controller 比例积分微分控制器，比例积分微分调节器 ‖ *Syn*. proportional plus integral plus derivative regulator 比例积分微分控制器，比例积分微分调节器

~ sampling 比例抽样，比例采样

~ selection 比例选择

~ solenoid 比例电磁铁，比例电磁阀，比例螺线管

~ variation 比例变化

proportional-derivative (PD) 比例微分的

~ action 比例微分作用

~ control 比例微分控制，比例微分调节

~ controller 比例微分控制器，比例微分调节器 ‖ *Syn*. proportional-derivative regulator 比例微分控制器，比例微分调节器

proportional-integral (PI) 比例积分的

~ action 比例积分作用

~ control 比例积分控制，比例积分调节

~ controller 比例积分控制器，比例积分调节器 ‖ *Syn*. proportional-integral regulator 比例积分控制器，比例积分调节器

proportional-integral-derivative (PID) 比例积分微分的

~ action 比例积分微分作用

~ control 比例积分微分控制，比例积分微分调节

~ controller 比例积分微分控制器，比例积分微分调节器 ‖ *Syn*. proportional-integral-derivative regulator 比例积分微分控制器，比例积分微分调节器

proportionally [prə'pɔːʃənəli] *ad*. 按比例地，相配合地，适当地

proportionate [prə'pɔːʃnit] *v*. 成比例；*a*. 相称的，成比例的

proprietary [prə'praiətəri] (=proprietory) *n*. 所有权，所有者；*a*. 所有的，专有的，专利的，私人拥有的

proprietory [prəu'praiətəri] (=proprietary) *n*. 所有权，所有者；*a*. 所有的，专有的，专利的，私人拥有的

propulsion [prə'pʌlʃən] *n*. 推进，推进力

~ boiler 推进锅炉

~ characteristic 推进特性

~ characteristic test 推进特性试验

~ device 推进器

~ drive 行走部分传动装置，推进传动

~ equipment 推进设备 ‖ *Syn*. propulsion machinery 推进机械，推进装置；propulsion unit 推进装置

~ generator 推进发电机

~ motor 推进电动机

~ system 推进系统

propulsive [prəu'pʌlsiv] *a*. 推进的，有推进力的

~ characteristic 推进特性

~ coefficient 推进系数

~ efficiency 推进效率

~ fan 推进风机

~ force 推力

~ liquid 推进液

~ nozzle 推进喷嘴

~ output 推进功率

~ shaft 推进轴

~ thrust 推进器推力，推进推力

propulsor [prə'pʌlsə] *n*. 推进器，推进物，推进剂

protect [prə'tekt] *v.* 保护，保卫，防护，关税保护，投保 ‖ *Syn*. defend 保卫

protected [prə'tektid] *v.* (protect 的过去式和过去分词) 保护，保卫，防护，关税保护，投保；*a.* 受保护的
~ motor 防护式电动机

protecting [prə'tektiŋ] *n.* 保护，保卫，防护；*v.* (protect 的 ing 形式) 保护，保卫，防护，关税保护，投保
~ cap 防护罩，护帽 ‖ *Syn*. protecting cover 保护罩；protecting shield 保护罩；protective cover 防护罩，覆盖保护层；protective jacket 保护罩，保护套
~ cover for tie rod 拉杆保护罩

protection [prə'tekʃən] *n.* 保护，保护装置，保护者，保护动作，受到保护的状态，通行证，护照，保护贸易制，保护费 ‖ *Syn*. guard 保卫，守护，防护装置；safeguard 保护，防卫，安全装置，安全措施
~ against flooding 浸水防护
~ against single-phasing 单相保护
~ against noise 噪声保护
~ and Indemnity Clubs (PIC) 保赔协会
~ class 防护等级，保护级别，密封等级
~ device 保护设备，防护设备
~ factor of protective device 保护装置保护因数
~ feature 保护特性，保护机构
~ grade 防护等级
~ grounding 保护接地
~ principle of power system elements 电力系统元件保护原理
~ ratio 保护比
~ setting 保护整定
~ system 保护系统

protective [prə'tektiv] *a.* 保护的，防护的，给予保护的
~ agent 保护剂，防护剂
~ boots 防护靴
~ circuit 保护电路
~ clothing 防护服
~ coating 保护涂层，防护涂料
~ cover 防护罩，覆盖保护层 ‖ *Syn*. protecting cap 防护罩，护帽；protecting cover 保护罩；protective jacket 防护罩，保护套；protecting shield 保护罩
~ covering 保护敷层，防护涂层，保护层
~ covering for tie rod 拉杆防护罩
~ device 防护装置 ‖ *Syn*. protective equipment 防护设备，保护装置，设备，防护装置；protective gear 保护装置
~ earth (PE) 保护接地，安全接地，安全接地线
~ earthing 保护接地
~ effect 保护效应，防护作用
~ film 保护膜 ‖ *Syn*. protective membrane 保护膜；protective tape 保护膜，保护带
~ glasses 护目镜，防护眼镜 ‖ *Syn*. goggles 风镜，护目镜；safety glasses 护目镜，防护眼镜
~ guard 防护屏板
~ interlock 保安互锁装置
~ layer 保护层
~ measures 保全措施，保护措施 ‖ *Syn*. accident prevention 事故防止，事故预防，安全措施；safety measures 安

467

全措施，安全规程
~ relay 保护继电器
~ relaying 继电保护
~ ring 护圈
~ ring for cylinder liner 缸套护圈
~ screen 防护屏，保护遮板
~ system 保护系统，保护贸易制
~ vest 防护背心

protector [prə'tektə] *n*. 保护物，保护者，防护器，防御者

protein ['prəuti:n] *n*. 蛋白质；*a*. 蛋白质的
~ foam concentrate 蛋白泡沫液

prototype ['prəutətaip] *n*. 原型

protract ['prɔtrækt] *v*. 延长，拖延，测绘

protractor [prə'træktə] *n*. 量角器，分度规

provable ['pru:vəbl] *a*. 可证明的，可证实的，可查明的

prove [pru:v] *v*. 证明，证实，检验，验证，考验，原来(是)

provide [prə'vaid] *v*. 供应，供给，规定，准备，预防，采取预防措施，制订条件
~ against 规定禁止，预防
~ for 提供
~ oneself 自备
~ service 提供服务
~ starting torque 提供起动力矩
~ with 给…提供…

provider [prə'vaidə] *n*. 供给者，供应者，养家者

provision [prə'viʒən] *n*. 供应，补给物，装备，(一批)供应品，准备，预备，防备，规定，条款 ‖ *Syn*. apparatus 器械，设备，仪器；appliance 用具，器具；arrangement 布置；assembly 组装部件；device 装置，设备；equipment 装备，设备，器材，装置；facility 设备，工具；furniture 设备，家具；gear 设备，装备；installation 设备，装置；machine 机器，机械，机构；machinery 机械(总称)，机器；mechanism 机器，机械装置，机构；plant 设备；turnout 装备，设备；unit 装置，设备
~ crane 补给吊车

provisional [prə'viʒənl] *n*. 临时人员；*a*. 暂定的，临时的

provisionally [prə'viʒənəli] *ad*. 暂时地，临时地

proximate ['prɔksimit] *a*. 最近的，近邻的，紧接的，贴近的，直接的

proximately ['prɔksimeitli] *ad*. 近似地

proximity [prɔk'simiti] *n*. 接近，邻近，亲近

PSA (pressure swing adsorption) 变压吸附(法)
~ nitrogen generator 变压吸附制氮机

PSB (Public Security Bureau) 公安局

PSC (Port Sate Control) 港口国监督，港口国管理，港口国控制

PSCO (Port State Control Officer) 港口国控制官，港口国检查官

PSI (pounds per square inch) 磅/平方英寸

PSS (power system stabilizator) 电力系统稳定器

PSS (power system stabilization) 电力系统稳定

PSSC (Passenger Ship Safety Certificate) 客船安全证书

psychrometer [sai'krɔmitə] *n.* 干湿球湿度计，干湿计

psychrometric [saikrəu'metrik] *n.* 湿度计的
~ chart 湿度图

PT (potential transformer) 电压互感器，变压器，仪表变压器 ‖ **Syn.** voltage transformer 电压互感器，变压器
~ cabinet 电压互感器柜

PTH (plated through hole) 镀通孔

PTO (power take-off) 动力输出装置

public ['pʌblik] *n.* 公众，大众，(特定的)人群，公共场所；*a.* 公众的，公共的，公立的，公用的
~ address (PA) 公用地址，扩音装置
~ address system 扩声系统，有线广播系统，公用地址系统
~ official 公务人员，政府工作人员
~ room 公用舱室
~ Security Bureau (PSB) 公安局

pull [pul] *n.* 把手，拉，拖，拉力，牵引力，影响力；*v.* 摇桨，划船，以划桨推进，由…划动，拉，拖，拔，撕裂，扯裂
~ apart 撕开，扯断
~ back 拉回，撤回，拉为平手，反悔
~ down 摧毁，推翻，拉下来，使下跌
~ in 进站，吸入，提到警察局
~ into 拉入
~ on 穿，戴，继续拉
~ out 离开，撤离，拔出，渡过难关，恢复健康
~ out for inspection 拔出检查
~ out of 退出，拉出，取出
~ over 靠岸，开到路边，靠边停车
~ rod 拉杆，推杆
~ switch 拉线开关，拉线电门
~ the trigger 扣扳机
~ up 拔起，停下来，阻止

pull-in 拉入，牵入
~ torque 牵入转矩

pull-out 活页，撤出，可拉出的
~ manoeuvre 拉出操纵
~ manoeuvre test 拉出操纵试验
~ manoeuvre torque 拉出操纵力矩

pulley ['puli] *n.* 滑轮装置，滑轮，滑车
~ block 滑轮组

pulling ['puliŋ] *n.* 拉，拉力，牵引，拔，拖；*v.* (pull 的 ing 形式) 拉，牵引，拔，拖
~ force 拉力，牵引力，引力，牵力
~ lifeboat 划桨救生艇

pulmonary ['pʌlmənəri] *a.* 肺部的
~ alveolus 肺泡

pulsate ['pʌl'seit] *v.* 搏动，脉动，悸动，有规律地跳动

pulsating [pʌl'seitiŋ] *v.* (pulsate 的 ing 形式) 搏动，脉动，悸动，有节奏地跳动；*a.* 搏动的，脉冲的，脉动的，节奏强的，极为兴奋的
~ rate of revolution 转速波动率

pulsation [pʌl'seiʃən] *n.* 脉搏，悸动，震动，有节奏地跳动

pulse [pʌls] *n.* 脉搏，脉冲，脉动，律动，搏动，跳动，断续跳动
~ duration 脉冲持续时间
~ frequency 脉冲频率
~ frequency modulation control system 脉冲调频控制系统
~ generator 脉冲发生器
~ modulation 脉冲调制

~ pressure system 脉冲压力系统，脉压系统

~ supercharging system 脉冲增压系统

~ system supercharging 脉冲系统增压，脉冲增压

~ width 脉冲宽度，脉宽

~ width modulation (PWM) 脉宽调制

~ width modulation inverter 脉宽调制逆变器

pulverize ['pʌlvəraiz] v. 粉碎，研磨成粉

pulverizer ['pʌlvəraizə] n. 粉碎机 ‖ **Syn**. crusher 粉碎机，轧碎机；grinder 研磨机，粉碎机；macerater 粉碎机，切碎机；shredder 切菜器，撕碎机

pump [pʌmp] n. 泵，抽水机；v. 用泵抽，注入，抽水，汲取，输送，充能，启动泵

~ auto-change over device 泵自动切换设施

~ bed 泵床

~ body 泵体

~ capacity 泵容量，泵流量

~ casing 泵壳

~ chamber 泵室

~ characteristic curve 泵特性曲线

~ circulation cooling system 水泵循环冷却系统

~ cover 泵盖

~ cylinder 泵缸

~ discharge volute 泵出口蜗壳

~ dredge 泵式挖掘船，吸扬式挖泥船

~ dredger 泵吸挖泥船

~ frame 泵架

~ head 泵压头，泵扬程

~ housing 泵壳

~ liner 泵缸套

~ motor 泵电动机，泵马达

~ oil can 泵用油壶

~ priming 泵启动前注液

~ priming system 泵注液系统

~ room 泵房

~ room sea valve 泵舱通海阀

~ room sea suction valve 泵室海水吸入阀

~ room ventilator 油泵舱通风机

~ shaft 泵轴，泵转轴，油泵轴

~ stroke 泵冲程

pumpable ['pʌmpəbl] a. 可用泵抽吸的，可用泵抽送的

pumping ['pʌmpiŋ] n. 抽吸，脉动；v. (pump 的 ing 形式) 用抽水机抽水

~ rate 抽运率，泵送率

~ system 抽运系统，泵激系统，泵水系统

pumpman ['pʌmpmən] n. 泵工，泵管理员，唧筒工

punch [pʌntʃ] n. 冲压机，冲床，打孔机；v. 冲孔，打孔

puncture ['pʌŋktʃə] n. 刺痕，小孔；v. 刺，刺破

pure [pjuə] v. 提纯，精制，提纯，净化，精炼；a. 纯的，单纯的，纯净的，干净的，纯粹的，无垢的，完美的，抽象的 ‖ **Ant**. impure 不纯洁的，掺杂的，掺假的，脏的

~ car carrier (PCC) 汽车运输船

~ color 纯色

~ copper 纯铜

~ gold 纯金

~ iron 纯铁

~ metal 纯金属

~ oxygen 纯氧

~ resistance circuit 纯电阻电路

~ resistance load 纯电阻负载

~ water 净水，纯水，纯净水

~ white 纯白色

purely ['pjuəli] *ad.* 纯粹地，完全地，清白地，纯洁地

purge [pə:dʒ] *n.* 净化，清除，整肃，肃清；*v.* 净化，清除，整肃，肃清

~ button 二级头排水按钮

~ valve 放气阀

purging ['pə:dʒiŋ] *n.* 清洗，换气；*v.* (purge 的 ing 形式) 净化，清除，整肃，肃清

~ of cargo tanks with inert gas 用惰性气体清洗货舱

purification [,pjuərifi'keiʃən] *n.* 提纯，洗净

purifier ['pjuərifaiə] *n.* 分水机，清洁者，清洁器，精炼者 ‖ *Syn*. clarifier 分杂机，澄清器；centrifuge 离心分离机，分油机

~ room 净油机舱室，净化室

purifying ['pjuərifaiiŋ] *n.* 精制，提纯，净化，精炼；*v.* (purify 的 ing 形式) 提纯，精制，净化，精炼

~ rate 净化率

purity ['pjuəriti] *n.* 纯净，纯洁，纯度 ‖ *Ant*. impurity 杂质，混杂物，不洁，不纯

purse [pə:s] *n.* 钱包，财力，财源，奖金，捐款；*v.* 使皱起

~ seiner 围网渔船，围网船

purser ['pə:sə] *n.* (轮船、班机等)事务长，主计官

~ department 事务部，管事部

push [puʃ] *n.* 推，推动，奋发，干劲，进取心，攻击；*v.* 推，推动，推进，推行，增加，努力争取，逼迫

~ and pull button 推拉式电钮

~ back 向后推，推回

~ bar 推杆，推手，推门横条

~ boat 推船

~ button 按钮 ‖ *Syn*. push knob 按钮

~ button for sound release 声音释放按钮

~ button in field 现场按钮

~ button momentary contact switch 按钮式瞬时接触开关

~ button switch 按钮开关

~ button telephone set 按钮电话机

~ power 助推力

~ rod 推棒，顶杆，制动缸推杆

push-in 插入的，插入式的

~ fuse 插入式保险丝

push-pull 推挽式的，推挽的

~ converter 推挽变换器

~ power amplifier 推挽功率放大器

pushdown ['puʃdaun] *n.* 下推

pusher ['puʃə] *n.* 推进器，推杆，推动者，作家，文书

~ barge 推驳船，顶推驳船

put [pʌt] *n.* 掷，投击，笨蛋，怪人；*v.* 搁，放，摆，估计，安置，表达，陈述，迫使，移动，提出，赋予，出发，航行，驶进，击，发芽；*a.* 固定不动的

~ in 提出，提交，放入，种植，使就职

~ into 使进入，放进，投入

~ into operation 使生效，使运转，使开动

471

~ out 熄灭，伸出，出版，使不方便，打扰

~ up 建造，举起，抬起，进行，提供，表现出，提名，推举 ‖ *Syn*. build 建造，建筑，创立；construct 建造，构造，创立；erect 建造，建立，开创；form 形成，构成，塑造；make 制造，构造

putty ['pʌti] *n*. 油灰，灰泥；*v*. 用油灰接合

~ scraper 腻子刮刀，油灰刮刀

PV (pressure-vacuum) 压力真空

~ valve 压力真空阀

~ release valve 压力真空释放阀，呼吸阀

PVC (polyvinyl chloride) 聚氯乙烯

~ foamed plastic 聚氯乙烯泡沫塑料

~ sheathed wire 聚氯乙烯护套线

PWB (printed wiring board) 印制线路板 ‖ *Syn*. PCB (printed circuit board) 印制电路板

PWM (pulse width modulation) 脉宽调制

~ inverter 脉宽调制逆变器

pyramid ['pirəmid] *n*. 金字塔，角锥，棱锥；*v*. (使)成金字塔状，(使)渐增，(使)上涨

pyramidal [pi'ræmidl] *a*. 金字塔形的，锥体的

~ model 金字塔模型

pyrometer [ˌpaiə'rɔmitə] *n*. 高温计

pyrophoric [ˌpairəu'fɔrik] *a*. 自燃的，发火的，生火花的

Q

QC (quality control) 质量管理，质量控制

QLoad (reactive load) 无功负载，电抗负载

quadra ['kwɔdrə] *n*. 正方形的框架，浅浮雕周围的方框

quadrant ['kwɔdrənt] *n*. 象限，四分仪，九十度弧，四分之一圆，扇形体，信号区

~ block 扇形座

~ blocks 弧齿形吊艇滑车

~ davit 弧齿形吊艇柱

~ depression 俯角

~ elevation 仰角，高低角

~ gear 扇形齿轮

~ scale 扇形天平，扇形秤

~ steering gear 舵扇式转舵装置

quadrantal ['kwɔdrəntl] *a*. 象限的，四分仪的

quadripole ['kwɔdripəul] *n*. 四极

quadruplicate [kwɔ'dru:plikit] *n*. 四组中的一个，一式四份的文件；*a*. 四倍的

qualification [ˌkwɔlifi'keiʃən] *n*. 资格，条件，限制，限定，赋予资格

qualify ['kwɔlifai] *v*. 限制，限定，具有资格，证明合格，限制修饰

qualitative ['kwɔlitətiv] *a*. 定性的，定质的

~ measurement 定性测量，定性测定

quality ['kwɔliti] *n*. 质量，品质，性质，本质，特性，出众，才能；*a*. 优良的

~ and quantity 质量和数量

~ assurance 质量保证

~ certificate 质量证书

~ control (QC) 质量管理，质量控制

~ inspection 质量检查

~ management 质量管理

~ manual 质量手册

~ monitoring 质量监督

~ of life 生活质量，基本生活条件

~ of power supply 供电质量

~ rating 质量评价

~ standard 质量标准

quant [kwɔnt] *n.* 船桨

quantify ['kwɔntifai] *n.* 量化；*v.* 量度，确定数量

quantitative ['kwɔntitətiv] *a.* 测量的，数量的，定量的，量的，与数量有关的

~ data 定量数据

~ evaluation 定量评价

~ governing 量变调节

~ measurement 定量测量，定量测定

quantities ['kwɔntitiz] *n.* (quantity 的复数) 量，数量，若干，大量

~ of 大量的

quantitive ['kwɔntitiv] *a.* 数量的，定量的

quantity ['kwɔntiti] *n.* 量，数量，若干，大量

~ discharged 排放量

~ in 进货数量

~ of 数量

~ of flow 流量

~ of heat 热量

~ remaining in tank 舱内剩余量

~ shipped 装运数量

quantize ['kwɔntaiz] *v.* 使量子化，使量化

quantized ['kwɔntaizd] *v.* (quantize 的过去式和过去分词) 使量子化，使量化；*a.* 量子化的，量化的

~ error 量化误差

~ noise 量化噪声

~ signal 量化信号

quarantine ['kwɔrənti:n] *n.* 封锁，隔离，孤立，检疫，检疫期，检疫所；*v.* 封锁，隔离，孤立，检疫

~ boat 检疫船，检疫艇

~ doctor 检疫医生

~ officer 检疫官员，检疫员

quarter ['kwɔ:tə] *n.* 四分之一，方向，地区，方面，季，季度，一刻钟，象限，船侧后半部，住舱区，住处，寓所，军营

~ davit 尾舷吊艇柱

~ pillar 舱内侧梁柱

quartering ['kwɔ:təriŋ] *n.* 四等分，军营或其他住所之分配；*a.* 从斜后侧方向吹来的

~ sea 船尾浪，尾斜浪

quarterly ['kwɔ:təli] *n.* 季刊；*a.* 一年四次的，每季的；*ad.* 每季地

quartermaster ['kwɔ:təma:stə(r)] *n.* 舵手，舵工，军需官

quasi ['kweisai] *a.* 类似的，准的；*ad.* 半，准，类似

~ steady 准稳定的，准定常的

quasi-synchronization 自准同期，准同步 ‖ *Syn*. quasi-synchronizing 自准同期，准同步

~ device 自准同期装置，准同步装置

~ method 准同步法

quasi-synchronizing 自准同期，准同步 ‖ *Syn*. quasi-synchronization 自准同期，准同步

~ device 自准同期装置，准同步装置

quay [ki:] *n.* 码头

quayside ['ki:said] *n.* 码头周围，码头区

~ container crane 岸边集装箱起重机，码头区集装箱起重机

quench [kwentʃ] *v.* 结束，熄灭，淬火，平息

queue [kju:] *n.* 行列，长队，队列；*v.* 排队，排队等待

quick [kwik] *n.* 要点，本质，核心，感觉敏锐的部位，活人，生物；*a.* 急速的

~ acting charging 快速充电

~ acting fuse 快速熔断器，速动保险丝 ‖ ***Syn.*** quick action fuse 快速熔断器，速动保险丝

~ acting cleat 速动夹扣，快速夹板

~ acting operator 快速操纵器

~ acting switch 速动开关

~ action contact 速动触点

~ action valve 快动阀，速动阀

~ action vice 快动虎钳

~ closing emergency valve 应急速闭阀，应急快闭阀

~ closing hatchcover 速闭舱盖

~ closing lock 速闭装置

~ closing stop valve 速闭截止阀

~ closing valve 速闭阀，高速阀，急闭阀

~ freezing 速冻

~ release buckle 快卸扣

~ release cap 快卸口盖

~ release connector 快拆接头

~ release hook 快速解缆钩，快速脱缆钩

~ release pin 快卸销

~ release ratchet 快速释放棘轮

~ release ring 快卸环

~ release safety coupling 快速释放安全联轴节

~ response 快速响应，快速反应

~ set adhesive 速凝粘合剂

~ settling 快速沉淀

quiescent [kwai'esənt] *a.* 不动的，静止的，静态的

~ point 静点，静态工作点

quiet ['kwaiət] *n.* 安静，闲适；*v.* 平静下来，使平静，使安心，减轻；*a.* 静止的，宁静的，从容的

quintuplicate [kwin'tju:plikit] *a.* 五倍的

quoit [kwɔit] *n.* 金属环，铁环，绳圈；*v.* 掷（圈环）

quotation [kwəu'teiʃən] *n.* 报价单，价格，引用语，行情表

quote [kwəut] *n.* 引用语，语录；*v.* 报价，引述，引用，引证，提供，提出

R

rabbet ['ræbit] *n.* 槽口，榫头，槽口接缝处；*v.* 嵌接，榫接，开槽口于

~ plane 槽刨

race [reis] *n.* 急流，沟槽，竞争，种族，民族，种族特征，赛跑；*v.* 空转，全速运送，参加比赛，使比赛

raceabout ['reisə,baut] *n.* 竞赛用游艇

rack [ræk] *n.* 齿条，齿轨，支架，行李架，卧铺，床铺，破坏；*v.* 变形，倾斜，放在架上，在架上制作，变形，折磨，使痛苦，榨取，随风飘

rack-and-pinion 齿轮齿条

~ drive system 齿轮齿条驱动系统

racking ['rækiŋ] *n.* 倾斜，变形，船体扭转变形；*v.* (rack 的 ing 形式) 变形，倾斜，放在架上，在架上制作，变形，折磨，使痛苦，榨取，随风飘；*a.* 拷问的，痛苦的

~ door 倾斜门

racon ['reikən] *n.* 雷达信号台

radar ['reidə] *n.* 雷达，电波探测器

radial ['reidjəl] *n.* 光线，射线；*a.* 径向的，半径的，辐射状的，光线状的

~ acceleration 径向加速度

~ and axial clearance 径向和轴向间隙

～ clearance 径向间隙

～ dimension 径向尺寸

～ direction 径向

～ drill 摇臂钻床，旋臂钻床 ‖ *Syn*. radial drilling machine 摇臂钻床，旋臂钻床

～ engine 星形发动机

～ flow 径向流，辐流

～ flow pump 径流泵

～ force 径向力，辐射力

～ impermeability 径向密封性

～ load 径向载荷，径向负载

～ piston hydraulic motor 径向柱塞式液压马达

～ piston hydraulic pump 径向柱塞式液压泵

～ piston pump 径向活塞泵，径向柱塞泵

～ plane 径向平面

～ plunger pump 径向柱塞泵，径向活塞泵

～ plunger type oil motor 径向柱塞式油马达

～ pump 径向泵，径流泵

～ slot 沿径槽，径向槽

～ system 径向配电制，径向系统

～ thrust 径向压力，径向推力

～ turbine 辐流式涡轮机，径流式涡轮

～ velocity 径向速度

radially ['reidjəli] *ad*. 放射状地

radian ['reidjən] *n*. 弧度

radiance [ˌreidiəns] *n*. 光辉，闪烁，辐射率，深粉红色

radiant ['reidjənt] *n*. 光点，流星群的辐射点；*a*. 发光的，充满光的，辐射的，明亮的，容光焕发的

～ heating surface 辐射受热面

radiate ['reidieit] *v*. 发光，放射，辐射，传播，广播，流露；*a*. 有射线的，辐射状的 ‖ *Syn*. irradiate 照耀，照射，发光，辐射

radiating ['reidieitiŋ] *v*. (radiate 的 ing 形式) 发光，放射，辐射，传播，广播，流露；*a*. 散热的，辐射状的

～ fin 散热片

radiation [ˌreidi'eiʃən] *n*. 发散，发光，发热，辐射，放射，放射线，放射物

～ protection 辐射防护

～ shield 辐射屏蔽

radiator ['reidieitə] *n*. 散热器，水箱，冷却器，电暖炉，辐射体

～ coil tube 散热盘管

～ core 散热器芯子

radio ['reidiəu] *n*. 无线电通信，无线电接收装置，无线电广播设备；*v*. 用无线电发送讯息

～ beacon 无线电导航台

～ communication 无线电通信

～ communication station 无线电通信站

～ communication workstation 无线电通信工作站

～ distress signal 无线电求救信号

～ equipment 无线电设备 ‖ *Syn*. radio installation 无线电设备

～ navigation 无线电导航

～ officer 报务员 ‖ *Syn*. radio operator 报务员；radio personnel 报务员

～ room 无线电室，报房，广播室

～ telephone 无线电话

～ transmitter 无线电广播发射机

radioactive [ˌreidiəu'æktiv] *a*. 放射性的，有辐射能的

radioactivity [ˌreidiəuæk'tiviti] *n*. 放射

(性)，放射能，辐射能

radiogram ['reidiəugræm] n. 收音机，无线电报 ‖ **Syn**. radiotelegram 无线电报；radiotelegraphy 无线电报

radiotelegram ['reidiəu'teligræm] n. 无线电报 ‖ **Syn**. radiogram 无线电报；radiotelegraphy 无线电报

radiotelegraphy ['reidiəutə'legrəfi] n. 无线电报 ‖ **Syn**. radiogram 无线电报；radiotelegram 无线电报

radiotelephone ['reidiəu'telifəun] n. 无线电话；v. 打无线电话 ‖ **Syn**. radiotelephony 无线电话

radiotelephony ['reidiəutə'lefəni] n. 无线电话 ‖ **Syn**. radiotelephone 无线电话

radius ['reidjəs] n. 半径，范围，辐射光线，有效航程，范围，界限 ‖ diameter 直径
~ of gyration 回转半径
~ rod 半径杆，支杆，推杆

raft [ra:ft] n. 筏，救生艇，橡皮船，大量；v. 乘筏，筏运，制成筏
~ davit 吊筏架

rag [ræg] n. 抹布，破布，破旧衣服，碎屑，少量；v. 揶揄，戏弄，欺负

rail [reil] n. 横杆，围栏，扶手，铁轨；v. 将…围起来，铺铁轨，责骂，抱怨
~ ferry 火车轮渡

rain [rein] n. 雨，下雨，雨天，雨季；v. 下雨，使大量落下，大量地给
~ coat 雨衣
~ shelter 雨棚，避雨亭

raise [reiz] n. 上升，高地，提出；v. 升起，唤起，提高，使出现，解除，饲养，筹集，使复活 ‖ **Syn**. enhance 提高,增加；heighten 提高，升高；increase 增加，加大；improve 提高，增进；lift 升高，提高；upgrade 升级，提升；hoist 升起，吊起

raised [reizd] v. (raise 的过去式和过去分词) 升起，唤起，提高，出现，解除，饲养，筹集，复活；a. 凸起的，浮雕的，发酵的
~ floor 活地板，提升地板，升高肋板
~ forecastle 升高首楼甲板
~ manhole 升高人孔

rake [reik] n. 斜度，向船尾的倾斜，耙子，放荡者；v. (使)倾斜，搜索，掠过，用耙子耙
~ angle 倾角，刀面角，投弹角
~ face 倾斜面，前面

raked [reikt] v. (rake 的过去式和过去分词) (使)倾斜，搜索，掠过，用耙子耙；a. 倾斜的
~ bow 前倾式船首
~ joint 捋缝，带齿的接缝
~ stem 斜艏柱，斜船首

ram [ræm] n. 活塞，撞锤，撞击装置，船首金属撞角，冲压机，公羊；v. 猛击，撞，猛击，装填，填塞，灌输
~ type electrohydraulic steering gear 柱塞式电动液压舵机，柱塞式电动液压操舵装置
~ type hydraulic steering gear 柱塞式液压舵机，柱塞式液压操舵装置
~ type steering gear 柱塞式舵机，柱塞式操舵装置

ramp [ræmp] n. 土堤斜坡，斜道；v. 使有斜面，蔓延，狂跳乱撞，敲诈
~ cover 坡道盖
~ down 斜降，缓降，软停止
~ up 倾斜升温，产能提升，斜升

ramshorn ['ræmzhɔ:n] n. 扁卷螺，鹦鹉螺
~ hook 山字钩
random ['rændəm] n. 随意，任意，偶然的行动；a. 随机的，任意的，随便的，胡乱的 ‖ Syn. stochastic 随机的
~ disturbance 随机干扰
~ error 随机误差，偶然误差
~ failure 随机故障
~ quantity 随机量
~ sampling 随机抽样，随意采样
~ selection 随机选择，杂乱选择
~ signal 随机信号
~ variable 随机变数，随机变量，无规变量
~ variation 无规则变化，随机变化
randomly ['rændəmli] ad. 随便地，未加计划地
range [reindʒ] n. 范围，界限，阶级，等级，射程，行列，山脉；v. 解开锚缆，朝向，流向，搜寻，排列，整理，配置，归类于，确定射程，平行，延伸，漫游
~ indicator 区域指标，距离指示器
~ light 导航灯，航迹灯，后桅灯 ‖ Syn. after-mast head light 后桅灯
~ of stability 稳定范围，稳性范围，安定阶段
~ out 定位
~ selector 变速杆，量程选择器，波段开关
rank [ræŋk] n. 等级，横列，秩，阶级；v. 排列，列为，列队，归类于，把…分等；a. 繁茂的，恶臭的，讨厌的，下流的
rapid ['ræpid] n. 急流，高速交通工具，高速交通网；a. 快速的，迅速的，飞快的，险峻的
~ auto-reclosing 快速自动再接通，快速自动再合闸
~ cooling 快速冷却
~ response 快速反应
rapidly ['ræpidli] ad. 很快地
rasp [ra:sp] n. 粗锉，木锉，擦菜板；v. 以粗锉打磨，粗刮，锉磨
rat [ræt] n. 老鼠
~ guard 鼠挡，防鼠板
ratchet ['rætʃit] n. (防倒转的)棘齿；v. 安装棘轮于
ratcheting ['rætʃitiŋ] n. 棘轮(效应)，棘齿；v. (ratchet 的 ing 形式) 装棘轮于
~ mechanism 棘轮机构
rate [reit] n. 比率，速度，等级，价格，费用；v. 估价，认为，鉴定等级，被评价，责骂
~ constant 速率常数，速度常数
~ integrating gyro 速率积分陀螺
~ of discharge 倾卸速度，卸货率，排出速率，放电率
~ of false alarm 误报率
~ of injection 注入速率
~ measuring network 速率测量电路
~ of occurrence of voltage changes 电压变化发生速率
~ of regulating speed in stability 稳定调速率
~ of safe operation 安全运行率 ‖ Syn. safe operation rate 安全运行率
rate-of-rise 增长速度，上升率
~ detector 差温(火灾)探测器 ‖ Syn. differential fire detector 差温火灾探测器
rated ['reitid] v. (rate 的过去式和过去分词)

估价，认为，鉴定等级，被评价，责骂；*a.* 定价的，额定的

~ audio-frequency output power 额定音频输出功率

~ bandwidth 额定带宽 ‖ *Syn*. nominal bandwidth 标称带宽，额定带宽

~ breaking capacity 额定熔断能力，额定断电容量

~ capacity 额定功率，额定容量，设计效率 ‖ *Syn*. capacity rating 额定功率，额定容量；nominal capacity 额定功率，标称功率，额定容量，标称容量；nominal output 额定功率，额定出力，额定输出，标称输出；nominal power 额定功率，额定容量，标称功率，标称容量；power rating 额定功率；rated output 额定功率，额定输出量，额定出力；rated power 额定功率，设计功率，额定动力，不失真功率；rated power capability 额定功率；rated power output 额定功率，额定动力输出；standard horsepower 额定功率，标准马力；standard power 额定功率，标准功率

~ current 额定电流 ‖ *Syn*. current rating 额定电流；nominal current 标称电流，额定电流；rating current 额定电流，电流额定值

~ horsepower 额定马力 ‖ *Syn*. nominal horsepower 标称马力，额定马力

~ load 额定负载，额定负荷 ‖ *Syn*. load rating 额定负载，额定负荷；nominal load 标称负载，标称负荷，额定负载，额定负荷

~ load torque 额定负载转矩

~ load capacity 额定载重量 ‖ *Syn*.

nominal load capacity 标称载重量，额定载重量

~ making capacity 额定接通容量

~ operating range 额定工作范围，额定使用范围

~ power factor 额定功率因数 ‖ *Syn*. nominal power factor 标称功率因数，额定功率因数

~ pressure 额定压力 ‖ *Syn*. nominal pressure 标称压力，额定压力

~ pull of mooring winch 系泊绞车额定拉力

~ radio frequency output power 额定射频输出功率，额定无线电频率输出功率

~ revolution 额定转速 ‖ *Syn*. nominal revolution 额定转速；nominal speed 标称速度，标称转速，额定速度，额定转速；rated speed 额定速度，额定转速

~ speed of engine 发动机额定转速

~ stock torque 额定转舵扭矩

~ torque 额定转矩 ‖ *Syn*. nominal torque 标称转矩，额定转矩；torque rating 额定转矩

~ value 额定值 ‖ *Syn*. rating value 标准值，额定值

~ voltage 额定电压 ‖ *Syn*. nominal voltage 标称电压，额定电压；voltage rating 额定电压

rather ['rɑːðə] *ad.* 宁愿，宁可，更正确，更合适，有点，相当

~ than 而不是，宁可…也不愿

~ too 稍微，稍微…一点

ratification [ˌrætɪfɪ'keɪʃən] *n.* 正式批准，认可

ratify ['rætifai] v. 批准，认可
rating ['reitiŋ] n. 等级，评定，额定值，收视率；v. (rate 的 ing 形式) 估价，认为，鉴定等级，评价
~ agency 评级机构
~ current 额定电流，电流额定值 ‖ *Syn*. nominal current 标称电流，额定电流；current rating 额定电流；rated current 额定电流
~ of equipment 设备额定值
~ of the generator 发电机额定值
~ plate 铭牌
~ scale 量表，评定量表，等级量表，分等量表
~ system 评级系统，评分系统，配给制
~ value 标准值，额定值 ‖ *Syn*. rated value 额定值
ratio ['reiʃiəu] n. 比，比率，比例
~ control 比率控制，比例控制，比例调节
~ differential protection 比率差动保护
~ of winding 匝数比，线圈比，绕组比 ‖ *Syn*. turn ratio 匝数比，变比，匝比
ration ['ræʃən] n. 定量，配给量；v. 配给，分发，限量供应
rational ['ræʃənl] n. 有理数，合理的事物；a. 理性的，合理的，推理的
rationalization [ˌræʃənəlai'zeiʃən] n. 合理化
ratline ['rætlin] n. 横索的梯绳
raw [rɔ:] n. 原料，生肉，擦伤处，身上的痛处；v. 擦伤；a. 原质的，未加工的，生疏的，自然状态的，不掺水的，擦掉皮的，阴冷的，刺痛的，残酷的，不公平的，直率的

~ material 原材料，原料
~ or unprocessed data 原始数据或未处理数据
RC (resistance-capacitance) 电阻电容，阻容
RCC (Rescue Coordination Centre) 救援协调中心
RE (reliability evaluation) 可靠性评估
reach [ri:tʃ] n. 延伸，区域，河段，范围，联接杆，横风行驶；v. 到达，达到，延伸，伸出，影响，传开
reachability ['ritʃə'biliti] n. 可达性，能达到性
reachable ['ritʃəbl] a. 可达成的，可获得的
react [ri'ækt] v. 起反应，起作用，反抗，背离，起反作用
reactance [ri'æktəns] n. 电抗 ‖ impedance 阻抗；resistance 电阻，电阻器，阻抗
~ coil 电抗线圈
~ voltage 电抗电压
reaction [ri(:)'ækʃən] n. 反应，反作用力，反动，反动力，核反应，保守，习惯性行为
~ force 反作用力
~ mechanism 反应机理
~ motor 反应式电动机，反应式发动机
~ principle 反应原理，反作用原理，反酌原理
~ propulsion 反酌推进
~ rate 反应速率
~ system 反应系统
~ time 反应时间
~ turbine 反动式涡轮机，反力式涡轮，反动式汽轮机
reactive [ri(:)'æktiv] a. 反应的，起反作用的，反动的，电抗性的

~ chamber 反应室 ‖ *Syn*. reactive cell 反应室

~ characteristics 反应特性

~ component 电抗成分，虚数部分，无功部分

~ current 无功电流，电抗性电流

~ in respect to 相对…呈感性

~ load (QLoad) 无功负载，电抗负载

~ loss 无功损耗

~ power 无功功率

reactivity [ˌri(:)æk'tiviti] *n*. 反应性，反应，反动

~ hazard 反应性危险

reactor [ri(:)'æktə] *n*. 电抗器，反应器，核反应堆

~ interturn protection 电抗器匝间保护

~ room air compressor 反应堆舱空气压缩机

read [ri:d] *n*. 阅读，读书；*v*. 读，阅读，理解，学习；*a*. 有学问的

~ only memory (ROM) 只读存储器

readiness ['redinis] *n*. 准备就绪，愿意

readjust [ri:ə'dʒʌst] *v*. 重新整理，再调整

~ within the limit of 0.10 mm 在0.10毫米的范围内重新调整

readjustment [ri:ə'dʒʌstmənt] *n*. 重新整理，再调整

reaeration [riˌeiə'reiʃən] *n*. 再充气，再吹风

reagent [ri(:)'eidʒənt] *n*. 反应物，试剂，反应力

real ['ri:əl] *n*. 真实，实数；*a*. 真的，真实的，实质的，严重的，天然的，不动产的；*ad*. 非常地

~ engine diagnosis system 发动机实时诊断系统

~ time 实时，同时，即时

~ time application 实时应用

~ time clock 实时钟

~ time control 实时控制

~ time data processing 实时数据处理

~ time processor 实时处理器

~ time regulation 实时调节

~ time telemetry 实时遥测

~ time video 实时视频

realign [ˌriə'lain] *v*. 重新排列，再结盟

realise ['riəlaiz] *v*. 实现，了解，觉悟，明白

realistic [riə'listik] *a*. 现实的，逼真的

reality [ri(:)'æliti] *n*. 事实，现实，真实，本体，逼真

realizability [riəlaizəbi'liti] *n*. 可实现性，现实性

realization [ˌriəlai'zeiʃən] *n*. 实现，认识，领会，变卖

realize ['riəlaiz] *v*. 认识到，认知，体会，了解，实现，实行，获得

ream [ri:m] *n*. 大量，许多，令，大量的纸；*v*. 铰除，刮，扩展，榨取，欺骗

reamer ['ri:mə] *n*. 铰刀，铰床，钻孔器

~ bolt 铰刀螺栓，密配合螺栓

rear [riə] *n*. 后面，背后，后方，屁股；*v*. 举起，树立，高耸，暴跳，用后腿站起培养，饲养，栽种；*a*. 后面的，背面的，后方的 ‖ *Ant*. front 前面的

~ arch 后拱

~ axle 后轴

~ door 后门

~ end 后部，臀部

~ engine 后置发动机

~ header 后管箱，后方头

~ housing 后壳体

~ stern tube 后尾轴管

~ view 后视图

~ water wall tube 后水冷壁管

rearmost ['riəməust] *a.* 最后的

rearrangement [ˌriːəˈreindʒmənt] *n.* 重新整理

reason ['riːzn] *n.* 理由，原因，动机，理智，前提；*v.* 说服，劝说，推论，辩论，思考

reasonable ['riːznəbl] *a.* 合理的，公道的，适当的，讲道理的，有道理的，通情达理的

~ interval 合理区间

reasonably ['riːzənəbli] *ad.* 适度地，相当地

reassemble [ˌriːəˈsembl] *v.* 重新组装，重新装配，再聚集

~ test 再装配试验

~ with new packing 用新包装再装配

reassembly [riːəˈsembli] *n.* 重新组装，再会合，重装配

rebabbit [ˌriːˈbæbit] *n.* 重铸巴氏(轴承)合金

rebalance [riˈbæləns] *v.* 再平衡，使重新平衡，换位平衡

rebore ['riːˈbɔː] *v.* 重镗，镗大(内燃机汽缸)的孔径

rebreathe [riːˈbriːð] *v.* 再呼吸

recalibrate [riˈkælibreit] *v.* 重新校准，再校准

receipt [riˈsiːt] *n.* 收据，发票，收条，收到，收入，收益；*v.* 收到

receivable [riˈsiːvəbl] *a.* 可接收的

receive [riˈsiːv] *v.* 收到，接到，接收，遭到，受到，接待，接见

receiver [riˈsiːvə] *n.* 接收器，接受者，收信机

receiving [riˈsiːviŋ] *n.* 接受，接收，收货，收款；*v.* (receive 的 ing 形式) 收到，接到，接收，遭到，受到，接待，接见；*a.* 接收的，接受的

~ circuit 接收电路

~ end 接收端

~ note 收货单，验收单

~ point 受理点

~ space 收货区

~ unit 接收单元，接收部分

recent ['riːsnt] *a.* 新近的，近来的

recently ['riːsəntli] *ad.* 近日，最近

receptable [riˈseptəkl] *n.* 插座，容器，贮藏器

~ box for miscellaneous power supplies 多种电源插销箱

~ socket 接受孔插座

reception [riˈsepʃən] *n.* 接收，接待，招待会

~ facility 接收设施

recharge ['riːˈtʃɑːdʒ] *n.* 再充电，再装填，再袭击；*v.* 再充电，再装填，再控告，再袭击

~ current 充电电流

~ line 补给速度，补给率，回灌率

~ rate 补给率

rechargeable ['riːˈtʃɑːdʒəbl] *a.* 可再充电的

recheck ['riːˈtʃek] *v.* 复检，再核对，再核查

recipient [riˈsipiənt] *n.* 容器，接受者，容纳者；*a.* 容易接受的，感受性强的

reciprocal [riˈsiprəkəl] *n.* 倒数，互相关联的事物；*a.* 互惠的，倒数的，相互的，彼此相反的

reciprocate [riˈsiprəkeit] *v.* 往复，来回，互给，酬答，互换，报答

reciprocating [ri'siprəkeitiŋ] n. 往复摆动，往复式发动机；v. (reciprocate 的 ing 形式) 往复，来回，互给，酬答，互换，报答；a. 往复的，来回的，交替的，互换的，摆动的
~ air compressor 往复式空压机
~ compressor 往复式压缩机，活塞式压缩机
~ displacement pump 往复活塞泵
~ internal combustion engine 往复式内燃机
~ pump 往复泵，循环泵
~ refrigeration compressor 往复冷冻压缩机
~ type steering gear 往复式操舵装置

recircle [ri:'sə:kl] v. 再循环

recirculate [ri'sə:kjuleit] v. 再通行，再流通

recirculated [ri'sə:kjuleitid] v. (recirculate 的过去式和过去分词) 再循环，再流通；a. 再循环的，再流通的
~ air 再循环空气

recirculation [,ri:'sə:kju'leiʃən] n. 再通行，再流通
~ damp 再循环水气
~ flash evaporator 再循环闪发蒸发器
~ line 回输管路
~ pump 重复循环泵
~ rate 再循环速度
~ region 回流区
~ valve 再循环阀
~ water 循环水

reckon ['rekən] v. 认为，计算，数，总计，估计，猜想，料想，依赖
~ on 指望，依赖 ‖ *Syn.* build on 基于，建立于，寄希望于；build upon 基于，建立于，寄希望于；count on 依靠，指望；depend on 依赖，依靠，取决于；depend upon 依赖，依靠，取决于；lie on 依赖，取决于；rely on 依赖，依靠

reclaim [ri'kleim] v. 回收，取回，再生，利用，矫正，使悔改，要求归还，开拓

reclamation [rikleiˈmeiʃən] n. 回收，取回

reclose [ri:'kləuz] v. 重接通，重闭合，重合闸，重闭

reclosing [ri:k'ləuziŋ] n. 再投入，重合，重合闸，重接；v. (reclose 的 ing 形式) 重接通，重闭合，重合闸，重闭
~ fuse 重合熔断器
~ overvoltage 重合闸过电压

recoat ['ri:'kəut] v. 重新涂

recognize ['rekəgnaiz] v. 认可，承认，公认，赏识，具结

recognized ['rekəgnaizd] v. (recognize 的过去式和过去分词) 认可，承认，公认，赏识；a. 公认的，经过验证的
~ standard 认可标准，公认标准

recompression [,ri:kəm'preʃən] n. 再压缩
~ chamber 加压舱

recompute [,ri:kəm'pju:t] v. 再计算，验算

reconstitute ['ri:'kɔnstitju:t] v. 再组成，再构成，重新组成，重新设立

reconstruct ['ri:kən'strʌkt] v. 重建，改造，推想

reconstruction [,ri:kən'strʌkʃən] n. 重建，改造

record ['rekɔ:d] n. 履历，档案，报告，诉状，最高纪录，唱片；v. 记录，标明，录音；a. 创纪录的
~ book 纪录簿，记录册
~ drawing 记录绘图，施工记录图

recordable [ri'kɔ:dəbl] *a.* 可记录的，值得记录的

recorder [ri'kɔ:də] *n.* 录音机，录像机，记录员，记录器

recover [ri'kʌvə] *v.* 重新获得，恢复，复原，回收，痊愈，使改过，找回

recoverable [ri'kʌvərəbl] *a.* 可重获的

recovered [ri'kʌvəd] *v.* (recover 的过去式和过去分词) 重新获得，恢复，复原，回收，痊愈，使改过，找回；*a.* 恢复的，回收的

~ oil valve 回收油阀

recovery [ri'kʌvəri] *n.* 恢复，痊愈，防御

~ repair 修复

~ time 恢复时间 ‖ *Syn*. correction time 校正时间，恢复时间

~ vessel 回收船只

~ voltage 恢复电压

recreate ['ri:kri'eit] *v.* 重现，重建，再创造，(使)得到休养

recreation [rekri'eiʃ(ə)n] *n.* 消遣，娱乐

~ room 康乐室，娱乐室

rectangle ['rektæŋgl] *n.* 长方形，矩形 ‖ circle 圆，圆形；ellipse 椭圆，椭圆形；parallelogram 平行四边形；rhombus 菱形；square 正方形；trapezoid 梯形；triangle 三角形

rectangular [rek'tæŋgjulə] *a.* 矩形的，成直角的

rectification [ˌrektifi'keiʃən] *n.* 纠正，整顿，校正，精馏，整流

~ excitation 整流励磁

rectifier ['rektifaiə] *n.* 整流器，纠正者，整顿者，校正者

~ type protective relay 整流器式保护继电器

rectify ['rektifai] *v.* 改正，校正，调整，精馏

~ after welding 焊后矫正

~ deficiency before departure 开航前矫正缺陷

~ deficiency within 2 days 在 2 天内矫正缺陷

~ on the lathe 在车床上校正

recyclable [ri:'saikələbl] *n.* 可回收物；*a.* 可回收的，可循环再用的

recycle ['ri:'saikl] *n.* 再循环，再生，重复利用；*v.* 回收利用，使再循环，反复应用

red [red] *n.* 红色，红衣服，红颜料，赤字，亏空；*a.* 红色的，革命的

~ anticorrosive paint 紫红色防锈漆

~ enamel paint 红色瓷漆

~ fibre 红色纤维，红筋

~ jointing 红纸柏垫

~ lead 四氧化三铅，铅丹，红丹

~ lead oil 红丹油

~ lead powder 红丹粉

~ litmus paper 红石蕊试纸

~ obstruction lamp for aviation 红色障碍灯

~ oil 油酸，红油

~ Sea 红海

redeliver ['ri:di'livə] *v.* 再投递，再交付

redelivery [ri:di'livəri] *n.* 再装船

~ date 再装船日期

redissolve ['ri:di'zɔlv] *v.* 再溶解，再驱散

redistillation [ri:disti'leiʃən] *n.* 重蒸馏，再蒸馏

reduce [ri'dju:s] *v.* 减少，缩小，简化，还原，控制，征服，强迫，迫使，攻陷，毁坏，降级，冶炼，提炼，约分，变

为，化为

~ pollution 减少污染

reduced [ri'dju:st] *v.* (reduce 的过去式和过去分词) 减少，缩小，简化，还原，控制，征服，强迫，迫使，攻陷，毁坏，降级，冶炼，提炼，约分，变为，化为； *a.* 减少的，简化的

~ density 对比密度，约化密度

~ nipple 异径螺纹接套

~ parameter 换算变量，简约参数，简化参数

~ pipe bend 异径管弯头

~ pressure 对比压强，折算压力，换算压力

~ scale 缩尺，缩小比例尺

~ tee pipe coupling 异径 T 形管接管

~ viscosity 比浓黏度，折合黏度

~ voltage starter 降压启动器

~ voltage starting 降压启动

reducer [ri'dju:sə] *n.* 还原剂，减压器

reducing [ri'dju:siŋ] *n.* 减低，还原，减肥；*v.* (reduce 的 ing 形式) 减少，缩小，简化，还原，控制，征服，强迫，迫使，攻陷，毁坏，降级，冶炼，提炼，约分，变为，化为

~ agent 还原剂

~ bush 缩口轴衬

~ elbow 渐缩弯管，异径弯头，异径弯管接头，变径弯头

~ gear 减速齿轮，自动传动轮

~ nipple 变内径内螺纹接头，异径管接头

~ piece 缩小接管，缩小管接头

~ socket 缩径承窝，异径管节，异径套筒，异经管节

~ valve 减压阀

reduction [ri'dʌkʃən] *n.* 减少，缩小，降低，约简，缩影，缩图，缩版，变形，缩减量

~ agent 还原剂

~ drive 减速传动

~ gear 减速齿轮，自动传动轮

~ gear box 减速齿轮箱

~ ratio 减速比

redundancy [ri'dʌndənsi] *n.* 冗余，过多，过剩，超静定性，备份，裁员

redundant [ri'dʌndənt] *a.* 多余的，过剩的，累赘的，冗余的 ‖ *Syn.* odd 残留的，残余的，剩余的；remainder 残留的，残余的，剩余的；remanent 残留的，残余的，剩余的；residual 残留的，残余的，剩余的；residuary 剩余的，残余的；superfluous 多余的，过剩的，过量的；surplus 过剩的，剩余的

reecho [ri:'ekəu] *n.* 回响，回声；*v.* 使回响

~ depth sound 回声测深仪

reef [ri:f] *n.* 礁，收帆；*v.* 收帆，缩帆

reefer ['ri:fə] *n.* 冷藏车，冰箱，收帆的人，双排扣水手上衣

~ box 冷藏集装箱,冷冻集装箱 ‖ *Syn.* reefer container 冷藏集装箱，冷冻集装箱

~ engineer 冷藏员

~ space 冷藏货舱位

~ vessel 冷藏船，冷冻船

reel [ri:l] *n.* 卷轴，一盘，旋转；*v.* 卷于轴上，(使)旋转，摇晃，眩晕，骚乱，退缩

reestablish [,ri:i'stæbliʃ] *v.* 重建，使复原，使复位

reexpand [,ri:ik'spænd] *v.* 再扩展，再次膨胀

reface [ri'feis] *v.* 重修表面

refasten [ri'fɑ:sən] *v.* 再次固定,再次稳固

refer [ri'fə:] *v.* 提交,谈及,涉及,查阅,咨询,归诸于,指点把…提交,使求助于

~ to 涉及,指的是,提及,参考,适用于

reference ['refrəns] *n.* 提及,参考,参考书

~ cell 参比电池,参比池

~ circuit 基准电路

~ clock 基准时钟

~ frame 参考系,参考坐标系

~ input variable 参考输入变量,基准输入变量

~ line 参考线,基准线

~ manual 参考手册

~ point 参考点,控制点

~ value 参考值,标准值,参照值

~ voltage 参考电压,基准电压,基准势

refill ['ri:'fil] *n.* 替换物,再注满,新补充物;*v.* 再注满,再装满,再充填,补充

~ air 填充空气

~ mechanism 填充机制

~ opening 加油口

~ with Freon 氟里昂填充

refine [ri'fain] *v.* 提炼,提纯,净化,精炼,精制,改善

refined [ri'faind] *v.* (refine 的过去式和过去分词) 提炼,提纯,净化,精炼,精制,改善;*a.* 精制的,精炼的,优雅的,精确的

~ product 轻精炼产品,精制石油产品

refit ['ri:'fit] *n.* 改装,整修;*v.* 改装,整修

~ in order 按顺序改装

~ with new packing 用新包装重新包装

reflect [ri'flekt] *v.* 反射,反映,表现,反省,细想

reflection [ri'flekʃən] *n.* 反射,映象,倒影,反省,沉思,反映

reflector [ri'flektə(r)] *n.* 反射器,反射体,反射镜

~ lamp 反光灯,反射灯

reflex ['ri:fleks] *n.* 反射,反映,映象;*v.* 反折,反曲,反射;*a.* 弯折的,反射的,反省的,反作用的,优角的,本能的

refloat [ˌri:'fləut] *v.* (使)再浮起

refract [ri'frækt] *v.* (使)折射,测定折射度

refraction [ri'frækʃən] *n.* 折光,折射(程度),折射角

refractoriness [ri'fræktərinis] *n.* 耐火性,耐熔性,耐热度

refractory [ri'fræktəri] *n.* 耐火物质,耐火材料;*a.* 耐熔的

~ alloy 难熔合金

~ lining 耐火衬砌,耐火炉衬,耐火衬里

~ material 耐火材料

~ protection 防火装置,耐火防护设备

~ steel 热强钢,耐热钢

refrain [ri'frein] *n.* 重复,叠句;*v.* 抑制,克制,节制,避免,制止

refresh [ri'freʃ] *v.* 使恢复,使振作,更新

refrigerant [ri'fridʒərənt] *n.* 制冷剂;*a.* 制冷的

~ bottle 制冷剂瓶

~ pump 制冷剂泵

refrigerate [ri'fridʒəreit] *v.* 冷冻,冷藏,使冷却,使变冷,使清凉

refrigerated [ri'fridʒəreitid] *v.* (refrigerate 的过去式和过去分词) 冷冻，冷藏，使冷却，使变冷，使清凉；*a.* 冷冻的，冷却的

~ (cargo) hold 冷藏货舱，冷藏舱 ‖ ***Syn.*** refrigerated (cargo) space 冷藏货舱，冷藏间；refrigerated room 冷藏室，冷藏库；refrigerated storeroom 冷藏库；refrigerating chamber 冷藏室，冷藏库，冷冻库

~ cargo ship 冷藏货物运输船

~ centrifuge 冷冻离心机

~ container 冷藏集装箱，冷冻货柜

~ fish carrier 冷藏渔船

~ lorry 冷藏车

~ storage space 冷藏存储空间

~ stowage 冷冻货物积载

~ transport 冷藏运输

refrigerating [ri'fridʒəreitiŋ] *n.* 冷冻，冷藏；*v.* (refrigerate 的 ing 形式) 冷冻，冷藏，使冷却，使变冷，使清凉；*a.* 冷冻的，冷藏的

~ cabinet 冰柜

~ capacity 制冷量，冷冻能力，制冷能力

~ chamber 冷藏室，冷藏库，冷冻库 ‖ ***Syn.*** refrigerated (cargo) hold 冷藏货舱，冷藏舱；refrigerated (cargo) space 冷藏货舱，冷藏间；refrigerated room 冷藏室，冷藏库；refrigerated storeroom 冷藏库

~ container 冷藏集装箱，冷冻货柜

~ effect 产冷量，制冷能力

~ effect per brake horse power 单位轴马力制冷量

~ effect per unit volume 单位容积制冷量

~ medium 冷却介质

~ medium pump 冷煤泵

~ mode 制冷方式

~ plant 冷冻设备，制冷装置 ‖ ***Syn.*** refrigerating unit 制冷装置，冷冻机

~ system 制冷系统，冷却系统

~ ton 冷冻吨，制冷吨

refrigeration [ri,fridʒə'reiʃən] *n.* 冷藏，制冷，冷冻

~ and air conditioning 船舶制冷和空调

~ cabinet 制冷室，冷藏柜

~ compressor 制冷压缩机，冷冻机

~ cycle 制冷循环

~ engineer 制冷工程师

~ fluid 制冷液

~ machinery space 制冷机械空间，制冷机舱

~ oil 冷冻机油，冷冻油

~ system 制冷系统

~ unit 制冷机组

refrigerator [ri'fridʒəreitə] *n.* 电冰箱，冷藏库

~ defrost 冰箱除霜

~ oil 冷冻机油

~ to be done function test 冰箱效用试验

refuel [ri:'fjuəl] *v.* 加油，补给燃料

refurnish ['ri:'fə:niʃ] *v.* 再供给，重新装备

refurnishment ['ri:'fə:niʃmənt] *n.* 翻新

refuse [ri'fju:z] *n.* 垃圾，废物，废弃物；*v.* 拒绝，回绝

regeneration [ri,dʒenə'reiʃən] *n.* 恢复，再生，重建

regenerative [ri'dʒenərətiv] *a.* 再生的，更生的，恢复的

~ brake 再生制动器

~ braking 再生制动，反馈制动

~ pump 涡流泵，再生泵

~ switch 再生开关

region ['ri:dʒən] *n.* 区域，地方，地区，领域，层

~ filling 填充域

regional ['ri:dʒən(ə)l] *a.* 地区的，地方的，区域的，整个地区的

~ control 区域控制

~ task forces (RTFs) 区域工作队

register ['redʒistə] *n.* 记录，登记簿，登记，注册，寄存器；*v.* 记录，登记，注册，提示，挂号

~ book 船舶登记簿，船籍登记簿

~ of Shipping 船舶检验局，船舶登记局

~ of the People's Repulic of China 中华人民共和国船舶检验局

registered ['redʒistəd] *v.* (register 的过去式和过去分词) 记录，登记，注册，提示，挂号；*a.* 已注册的，已登记的，记名的

~ breadth 登记宽度

~ depth 登记深度

~ tonnage 注册吨位

Registo ['ridʒistəu] *n.* 雷吉斯托(人名)

~ Italiano Navade (RINA) 意大利船级社

registration [,redʒis'treiʃən] *n.* 挂号，登记，报到，注册

~ Bureau 登记局，挂号处

registry ['redʒistri] *n.* 船舶的国籍，记录，登记，登记处

regrind [ri:'graind] *v.* 再磨研，再压榨

regular ['regjulə] *n.* 正常体，正规军，正式队员；*a.* 等边的，合格的，定期的，经常的，规则的，有秩序的，整齐的，常备军的 ‖ *Ant.* irregular 不规则的，无规律的，异常的

~ inspection 定期检查

~ intervals 定期

~ polyhedron 正多面体

regularly ['regjuləli] *ad.* 定期地，有规律地，有规则地，整齐地，匀称地

regulate ['regjuleit] *v.* 控制，调节，校准，管制 ‖ *Syn.* control 控制，操纵，支配，调节，管理；govern 控制，操纵，调节，支配，管理

regulating ['regjuleitiŋ] *n.* 管制，控制，调节，校准；*v.* (regulate 的 ing 形式) 管制，控制，调节，校准

~ device 调节设备

~ knob of fuel pressure 燃油压力调节钮

~ lever for pump stroke 喷油泵行程调整杆

~ mechanism 调节机构，调速机构 ‖ *Syn.* regulating organ 调节机构，调速机构

~ range 调节范围，控制范围

~ ratio 调节比

~ relay 调节继电器

~ repair 定期修理

~ ring 调整环，蝶环

~ rod 调节杆

~ screw 调整螺钉，调整螺丝

~ system 调节系统，自动控制系统

~ unit 调节单元

~ valve 调节阀，溢流阀

~ winding 调压绕组

regulation [regju'leiʃən] *n.* 规则，规章，管理，控制，调节，校准

~ handle 调节手柄

~ lever for pump stroke 泵行程调节杆

regulations [regju'leiʃnz] *n.* (regulation 的复数) 规则，规章，管理，控制，调节，校准

~ for the Prevention of Air Pollution from Ships 船舶大气污染防治条例

regulator ['regjuleitə] *n.* 调整器，标准仪，调整者，校准者 ‖ *Syn.* controller 控制器，控制者；governor 调节器，管理者，主管人员

~ clearing 调节器排水

~ recovery 调节器复位

~ system 调节系统

regulatory ['regjulətəri] *a.* 管理的，监督的，调整的

reheat ['ri:'hi:t] *v.* 重新加热，再加热，再热

reheater ['ri:'hi:tə] *n.* 再热器，回热器

reheating [ri:'hi:tiŋ] *n.* 重新加热，再加热，再热；*v.* (reheat 的 ing 形式) 重新加热，再加热，再热

~ air conditioning system 再热式空调系统

~ coil 再加热盘管，再热器

reignition [rei'niʃən] *n.* 再点燃，二次点燃

reinforce [,ri:in'fɔ:s] *n.* 加强，加固物；*v.* 增加，加强，加固，补充，修补，增援

reinforced [ri:in'fɔ:st] *v.* (reinforce 的过去式和过去分词) 增加，加强，加固，补充，修补，增援；*a.* 增强的，加强的，强行的

~ excitation 强行励磁

~ insulation 加强绝缘

reinforcement [,ri:in'fɔ:smənt] *n.* 增援，加强，加固，援军

reinforcing [,ri:in'fɔ:siŋ] *n.* 增强，加强；*v.* (reinforce 的 ing 形式) 增加，加强，加固，补充，修补，增援

~ material 增强材料

reinsert [,ri:in'sə:t] *v.* 重新插入，再插入

reinspect [,ri:in'spekt] *v.* 复察，重新视察，再考察

reinspection [,ri:in'spekʃən] *n.* 复察，重新视察，再考察

reinstall [,ri:in'stɔ:l] *v.* 重新设置，重新安装

reinstate [,ri:in'steit] *v.* (使)恢复

reject [ri'dʒekt] *n.* 被拒之人，被弃之物，不合格品，落选者，不及格者；*v.* 拒绝，抵制，否决，驳回，丢弃，呕出

rejection [ri'dʒekʃən] *n.* 拒绝，被拒绝的事物，排异反应

relate [ri'leit] *v.* 叙述，讲，使联系

~ to 涉及，有关

relation [ri'leiʃən] *n.* 关系，联系，叙述，故事，亲戚

relational [ri'leiʃənəl] *a.* 相关的，有关的，亲属的

relationship [ri'leiʃənʃip] *n.* 关系，联系，关联

relative ['relətiv] *n.* 亲戚，关系词，相关物，亲缘植物；*a.* 相对的，相关的，比较而言的

~ accuracy 相对精度

~ density 相对密度

~ density of liquid 液体相对密度

~ height 相对高度

~ humidity 相对湿度

~ motion 相对运动 ‖ *Syn.* relative movement 相对运动

~ pressure 相对压力

~ rotative efficiency 螺旋桨效率比

~ speed 相对速度 ‖ *Syn.* relative velocity

相对速度

~ stability 相对稳定性

~ to 相对于，涉及

~ viscosity 相对黏度

relatively ['relətivli] ad. 相关地

~ permanent current 相对恒定电流

relativity [,relə'tiviti] n. 相关性，相对性，相对论

relay ['ri:lei] n. 继电器，接替；v. 分程传递，使接替，转播

~ characteristic 继电器特性

~ comparator 继电器比较器，继电器比较仪

~ contact 继电器触点，继电匹点

~ contactor 继电器接触器

~ contactor control 继电器接触点控制

~ for auto-operation 自动操作继电器

~ panel 继电器盘，继电铺，继电器屏

~ protection 继电保护 ‖ Syn. relaying protection 继电保护

relaying ['ri:leiŋ] n. 继电保护，继电器，转播，中继利用；v. (relay 的 ing 形式) 分程传递，使接替，转播

~ current transformator 继电器用变流器

~ protection 继电保护 ‖ Syn. relay protection 继电保护

release [ri'li:s] n. 释放，让渡，豁免，发行的书，释放证书，版本，发布；v. 释放，解放，放弃，让与，免除，发表

~ mechanism 释放机构，安全机构，分离机构，脱开机械装置

~ of parallel operation 并行操作释放

~ piston 释放活塞

~ unit 发布单元，释放装置

relevant ['relivənt] a. 有关的，相应的，中肯的，确切的

reliability [ri,laiə'biliti] n. 可靠性，可信赖

~ condition 可靠性条件

~ evaluation (RE) 可靠性评估

reliable [ri'laiəbl] a. 可靠的，可信赖的

~ data 可靠数据

~ operation 操作可靠

~ performance 性能可靠

~ quality 质量可靠

reliance [ri'laiəns] n. 信任，信心，依靠，依靠的人或物

relief [ri'li:f] n. 减轻，免除，救济，调剂，安慰，浮雕，地貌

~ angle 后角，离隙角

~ valve 安全阀，溢流阀，泄压阀，减压阀 ‖ Syn. relieve valve 安全阀；safety valve 安全阀

relieve [ri'li:v] v. 减轻，解除，援救，救济，换班

~ guard 换岗

~ valve 安全阀 ‖ Syn. relief valve 安全阀，溢流阀，泄压阀，减压阀；safety valve 安全阀

relieving [ri'li:viŋ] v. (relieve 的 ing 形式) 减轻，解除，援救，救济，换班；a. 救助的，救援的

~ engineer officer 接班轮机员

reliquefaction [ri'likwi'fækʃən] n. 再液化

~ disposal 再液化处理

~ installation 再液化装置 ‖ Syn. reliquefaction plant 再液化装置

~ installation on LNG ship LNG 船上的再液化装置

~ principle 再液化原理

~ system 再液化系统

relocation ['ri:ləu'keiʃən] n. 再定位，再布

置，变换布置

reluctance [ri'lʌktəns] *n*. 磁阻，不愿，勉强

～ motor 磁阻电动机，磁阻马达

reluctant [ri'lʌktənt] *a*. 不顾的，勉强的，难得到的，难处理的

rely [ri'lai] *v*. 依赖，依靠，信赖，信任，依赖于

～ on 依赖，依靠 ‖ *Syn*. build on 基于，建立于，寄希望于；build upon 基于，建立于，寄希望于；count on 依靠，指望；depend on 依赖，依靠，取决于；depend upon 依赖，依靠，取决于；lie on 依赖，取决于；reckon on 指望，依赖

remain [ri'mein] *n*. 剩余物，残骸，剩余，残存，保持，逗留

remainder [ri'meində] *n*. 残余，剩余物，其他的人，余数；*v*. 廉价出售；*a*. 残留的，残余的，剩余的，出售剩书的 ‖ *Syn*. odd 残留的，残余的，剩余的；redundant 多余的，过剩的，累赘的，冗余的；remanent 残留的，残余的，剩余的；residual 残留的，残余的，剩余的；residuary 剩余的，残余的；superfluous 多余的，过剩的，过量的；surplus 过剩的，剩余的

remanent ['remənənt] *a*. 残留的，残余的，剩余的 ‖ *Syn*. odd 残留的，残余的，剩余的；redundant 多余的，过剩的，累赘的，冗余的；remainder 残留的，残余的，剩余的；residual 残留的，残余的，剩余的；residuary 剩余的，残余的；superfluous 多余的，过剩的，过量的；surplus 过剩的，剩余的

remeasure [ri:'meʒə] *v*. 重新测量

remedial [ri'mi:djəl] *a*. 补救的，纠正的，治疗的

～ action 补救行动，矫正措施

～ management 补救管理

～ measure 补救措施

remedy ['remidi] *n*. 补救，赔偿，药物，治疗法；*v*. 矫正，修缮，修补，治疗，补救

remit [ri'mit] *n*. 提交，移交事项；*v*. 宽恕，赦免，免除，缓和，推迟，汇出，传送，使复职

remote [ri'məut] *a*. 遥控的，周边设备线路的，远程的，遥远的，偏僻的，细微的 ‖ *Ant*. local 局部的，当地的

～ automatic control 远程自动控制

～ communication 远距离通信，远程通信

～ control 远程控制，遥控

～ control abnormal alarm 遥控异常报警

～ control station 遥控站

～ control system 远程控制系统，遥控系统

～ load-reduction device 远程减负荷装置

～ manipulator 遥控操作器，远程控制器

～ measurement 远程测量，遥测

～ mode 远程模式

～ monitoring 远程监控

～ operating valve 远程操作阀

～ regulating 远程调节，遥调 ‖ *Syn*. remote regulation 远程调节，遥调

～ set point adjuster 远程设定点调整器

～ settings 远程设置 ‖ *Ant*. local settings 机旁设置，本地设置

～ starting and alarm test for steering gear motor 舵角电动机遥控启动和报警试验

~ tachometer 遥测转速表

~ terminal 远程终端

~ thermometer 遥测温度表

~ tripping of fuel supply valve 燃油供给阀的远程跳闸

~ tripping protection 远程跳闸保护

~ water level indicator 遥测水位表

remote-reading 远程读取

~ water lever indicator 远程读取水位指示器

remotely [ri'məutli] ad. 远程地，遥远地，偏僻地

~ operated vehicle (ROV) 遥控潜水器

~ resettable fire detector 遥控复位火灾探测器

removable [ri'mu:vəbl] a. 可移动的，抽取式的

~ ballast 可移压载

~ component 可拆部件

~ connector 可拆接头

~ shelf 活动搁板

~ tweendeck 可拆卸双层甲板

~ washer 可拆垫圈

removal [ri'mu:vəl] n. 拆卸，移动，除去，搬迁，免职，切除

remove [ri'mu:v] n. 移动，距离，班级，升级；v. 移动，开除，移交，迁移，搬家

remover [ri'mu:və] n. 搬运工，去除剂

rend [rend] v. 撕碎，分裂

render ['rendə] n. 交纳，粉刷，打底；v. 呈递，归还，着色，汇报，致使，放弃，实施，给予补偿

rendezvous ['rɔndivu:] n. 会面，约会，集合点，会面点；v. 在指定地点集合

~ and docking 交会和对接

renew [ri'nju:] v. (使)更新，(使)恢复，重申，补充，续借，复兴，重新开始

renewable [ri'nju(:)əbl] a. 可再生的，可更新的，可恢复的

~ energy 再生能源，可更新能源

renewal [ri'nju(:)əl] n. 更新，复兴，恢复，续借，重申，补充

~ and renovation of equipment 设备更新

~ survey 换证检验

~ verification 换证核验

renumber [ri:'nʌmbə] v. 重新编号

reorganization ['ri:,ɔ:gənai'zeiʃən] n. 改组，改编，整编，重新组织

repack [ri:'pæk] n. 重新打包，重新装箱

~ after fitting back 重新装配后重新打包

repaint [ri:'peint] n. 重漆，重画；v. 重漆，重画，重新绘制，恢复原来的色彩

repair [ri'pɛə] n. 修理，修补，前往，维修状态，修理工作；v. 修理，修补，补救，纠正，恢复

~ as required 按要求修理

~ charge 修理费

~ rate 返修率，修复率

~ room 修理室，修理分间

~ time 修理时间，修复时间

~ as new condition 按新情况修理

repairer [ri'pɛərə] n. 修理工人，修补者

repeat [ri'pi:t] n. 重复，反复；v. 重复，重做，复述，转述，复制，使再现，留有味道

repeatability [ri'pi:tə'biliti] n. 可重复性，反复性，再现性

~ error 重复性误差

repeated [ri'pi:tid] v. (repeat 的过去式和过去分词) 重复，重做，复述，转述，复制；a. 反复的，重复的，再三的

~ fire 复火

~ starting sequence 重复启动程序

repeatedly [ri'pi:tidli] *ad.* 反复地，再三地

repeater [ri'pi:tə] *n.* 转发器

repetition [ˌrepi'tiʃən] *n.* 重复，循环，复制品，副本

~ period 重复周期

~ rate 重复率

repetitive [ri'petitiv] *a.* 重复的，反复性的

~ diving 重复潜水

~ diving surface interval time 重复潜水间隔时间

replace [ri(:)'pleis] *v.* 取代，替换，代替，偿还，归还，退回，把…放回原处

~ with ship's spare 用船舶备件替换

replaceable [ri'pleisəbl] *a.* 可代替的

replacement [ri'pleismənt] *n.* 归还，复位，交换，代替者，补充兵员，置换，移位

replenish [ri'pleniʃ] *v.* 补充，重装，再装满，鼓舞

replenishing [ri'pleniʃiŋ] *n.* 补充，重装；*v.* (replenish 的 ing 形式) 补充，重装，再装满，鼓舞

~ ship 补给船，补给舰

replenishing-at-sea 海上补给，航行补给 ‖ *Syn.* replenishment at sea 海上补给，航行补给；underway replenishment 海上补给，航行补给

~ gear 海上补给装置 ‖ *Syn.* seagear 海上补给装置

replenishment [ri'pleniʃmənt] *n.* 补给，补充

~ at sea 海上补给 ‖ *Syn.* replenishing-at-sea 海上补给，航行补给；underway replenishment 海上补给，航行补给

report [ri'pɔ:t] *n.* 报告，传说，谣言，声誉，名声，爆炸声；*v.* 报道，汇报，报到，告发

~ of continuous machinery survey 连续机械检验报告

reporting [ri'pɔ:tiŋ] *n.* 报告，报道；*v.* (report 的 ing 形式) 报道，汇报，报到，告发；*a.* 报告的，报道的

~ point 报告点

reproduce [ˌri:prə'dju:s] *v.* 繁殖，再生，复制，使…在脑海中重现

reproducibility [riprəˌdju:sə'biliti] *n.* 重复能力，再现性

reproducible [ˌri:prə'dju:səbl] *a.* 可复写的，能繁殖的，可再生的

reproduction [ˌri:prə'dʌkʃən] *n.* 复制品，繁殖，生殖，再生产，再现

request [ri'kwest] *n.* 请求，要求，邀请；*v.* 请求，要求

~ bridge control 驾驶室请求遥控

require [ri'kwaiə] *v.* 需要，要求，命令

required [ri'kwaiəd] *v.* (require 的过去式和过去分词) 需要，要求，命令；*a.* 必须的，必修的

~ subdivision index 规定要求的分舱指数

requirement [ri'kwaiəmənt] *n.* 需求，要求，必要条件，需要的东西 ‖ *Syn.* necessity 必要性，需要，必需品

~ for lifesaving equipment 救生设备配置定额

requisite ['rekwizit] *n.* 必需品；*a.* 需要的，必不可少的，必备的

requisition [ˌrekwi'ziʃən] *n.* 正式请求，申请，需要，命令，征用，通知单；*v.* 征用，征发，要求

reroute [ri:'ru:t] *v.* 变更旅程

rescind [ri'sind] *v.* 撤销，废除，解约

rescue ['reskju:] *n.* 援救，营救；*v.* 援救，营救

~ action 救援行动，救助活动

~ basket 救生篮

~ beacon 求救信标

~ boat 救生艇

~ boat davit 救生艇吊艇架，救生艇吊艇柱

~ Coordination Centre (RCC) 救援协调中心

~ boat davit (life raft davit) to be done static (dynamic) loading test 救助艇架(救生筏吊架)静(动)负荷试验

~ equipment 救援设备

~ litter 救援担架

~ net 救生网

~ plan 救援计划，救助计划

~ scrambling net 救援爬网

~ sling 救援吊锁

~ team 救援小组

rescuer ['reskju:ə(r)] *n.* 救助者

research [ri'sə:tʃ] *n.* 调查，探索，研究，探求；*v.* 研究，探究，进行研究

~ and extension 研究与推广

~ field 研究领域

~ vessel 调查船，考察船，研究船

reseat [ri:'si:t] *v.* 重新安置，使再坐，使复位，换底座，装新座

reservation [ˌrezə'veiʃən] *n.* 保留，预订

reserve [ri'zə:v] *n.* 储备(物)，储藏量，预备队，保护区；*v.* 储备，保存，保留，预定，预约；*a.* 贮存的

~ battery 备用电池，储备电池

~ buoyancy 储备浮力

~ capacity 储备功率，备用容量，备用能力

~ power 备用功率

reset ['ri:set] *n.* 重置，重置之物；*v.* 重置，重排

~ button 重复启动按钮，回零按钮，清除按钮

~ contactor 复位接触器，复原接触器

resettable [ri:'seteibl] *a.* 可重调的，可复零的

~ fire detector 可复位火灾探测器

reship [ri:'ʃip] *v.* 重新安置，再装上船，再上船

residual [ri'zidjuəl] *n.* 剩余额；*a.* 残留的，残余的，剩余的 ‖ ***Syn***. odd 残留的，残余的，剩余的；redundant 多余的，过剩的，累赘的，冗余的；remainder 残留的，残余的，剩余的；remanent 残留的，残余的，剩余的；residuary 残余的，残余的；superfluous 多余的，过剩的，过量的；surplus 过剩的，剩余的

~ capacitance 剩余电容，残余电容

~ charge 剩余电荷

~ error rate 残留错误率，漏检故障率，漏检错误率，残留误差率

~ fuel 剩余燃料

~ fuel oil 残余燃料油

~ gas 残余气体，残气

~ heat 余热

~ nitrogen 残余氮

~ oil standard discharge connection 残油类标准排放接头

~ stability 残留稳定度

~ stress 残余应力

~ voltage 残留电压，剩余电压，残余

电压，零序电压
~ volume 肺余气量，余气量，剩余容积

residuary [ri'zidjuəri] a. 剩余的，残余的
~ resistance 剩余阻力
~ resistance coefficient 剩余阻力系数

residue ['rezidju:] n. 残余，渣滓，滤渣，残数，剩余物

resilience [ri'ziliəns] n. 弹力，复原力，恢复力，顺应力，弹回，轻快，愉快的心情

resilient [ri'ziliənt] a. 能复原的，有回弹力的，弹回的

resist [ri'zist] n. 抗蚀剂；v. 抵抗，挡开，抵制，反抗，阻止，忍住
~ oxidation 抗氧化

resistance [ri'zistəns] n. 阻力，电阻，电阻器，阻抗，反抗，抵抗，抵抗力，阻力‖ *Syn.* impedance 阻抗‖ reactance 电抗
~ braking 电阻制动
~ coefficient 电阻系数
~ load 电阻性负载，有功负载
~ thermometer 电阻温度计
~ thermometer sensor 热电阻

resistance-capacitance (RC) 电阻电容，阻容

resistant [ri'zistənt] a. 有抵抗力的，抵抗的
~ wire 电阻线，电阻丝

resister [ri'zistə] n. 电阻器，抵抗者，反抗者

resistive [ri'zistiv] a. 电阻的，抵抗的，有抵抗力的，有耐力的
~ characteristics 电阻特性
~ divider 电阻式分压器

resistivity [ˌri:zis'tiviti] n. 电阻率，电阻系数，抵抗力

resistor [ri'zistə] n. 电阻器，电阻
~ and capacitor protection 阻容保护
~ sensor 电阻式传感器

resistors [ri'zistəz] n. (resistor 的复数) 电阻器，电阻
~ in parallel 并联电阻器
~ in series 串联电阻器
~ in series-parallel 串并联电阻器

resolution [ˌrezə'lju:ʃən] n. 分辨率，辨析率，解析度，简化，解决，坚定，决心，决定，决议，分解，分解过程
~ capability 分辨能力，分解能力

resolve [ri'zɔlv] n. 决意，决定，决心；v. 决心，决定，(使)分解，溶解，解决

resonance ['rezənəns] n. 谐振，共振，共振子，共鸣，反响，回声，中介
~ frequency 共振频率，谐振频率，共鸣频率
~ test 共振试验

resonant ['rezənənt] a. 共振的，引起共鸣的
~ frequency 谐振频率，共振频率

resource [ri'sɔ:s] n. 资源，物力，财力，办法，智谋
~ allocation 资源分配

respect [ris'pekt] n. 关系，有关，注意，考虑，尊敬，敬重，尊重，敬意；v. 尊重，尊敬，不违背

respective [ris'pektiv] a. 各自的，分别的

respectively [ri'spektivli] ad. 各自地，各个地

respirable ['respiərəbl] a. 可呼吸的

respirate ['respəreit] v. 进行人工呼吸

respiration [ˌrespi'reiʃən] n. 呼吸，一次呼吸，呼吸作用

respirator ['respəreitə] *n.* 呼吸器，口罩，防毒面具

respiratory [ris'paiərətəri] *a.* 呼吸的
~ and eye protection 呼吸和眼睛保护

respire [ris'paiə] *v.* 呼吸

respond [ris'pɔnd] *v.* 回答，响应，作出反应，有反应，回报，回复
~ to 回应

responder [ri'spɔndə(r)] *n.* 应答器，回答者，响应器

responding [ri'spɔndiŋ] *n.* 反应，响应；*v.* (respond 的 ing 形式) 反应，响应；*a.* 反应的，响应的
~ value 响应值，动作值

response [ris'pɔns] *n.* 反应，回答，响应
~ characteristic 响应特性
~ curve 响应曲线
~ function 响应函数
~ speed 响应速度
~ system 反应系统
~ time 响应时间
~ time error 响应时间误差

responsibility [ris,pɔnsə'biliti] *n.* 责任，职责

responsible [ris'pɔnsəbl] *a.* 负责的，有责任的，可靠的，可依赖的

responsive [ris'pɔnsiv] *a.* 应答的，响应的，作出响应的

responsivity [ris'pɔnsiviti] *n.* 响应度，敏感度，响应率

rest [rest] *n.* 休息，静止，支持物，台，架，其余；*v.* (使)休息，(使)睡眠，静止，依靠，搁在，保持，取决于
~ room 休息室

restart [ri:'sta:t] *v.* 重新开始

restoration ['restə'reiʃən] *n.* 恢复，归还，复位，复职，赔偿，修补，重建，修复物

restore [ris'tɔ:] *v.* 复原，恢复，修复，归还，使回复，交还，重建

restoring [ris'tɔ:riŋ] *v.* (restore 的 ing 形式) 复原，恢复，修复，归还；*a.* 复原的，修复的，恢复的
~ component 复原构件
~ moment 复原力矩，恢复力矩

restrain [ris'trein] *v.* 制止，抑制

restraint [ris'treint] *n.* 拘束，抑制，制止，克制

restrict [ris'trikt] *v.* 限制，限定，约束

restricted [ris'triktid] *v.* (restrict 的过去式和过去分词) 限制，限定，约束；*a.* 有受限制的，有限的
~ area 禁区，限制区，限航区，专用区
~ gauging device 限制计量装置
~ maneuver light 操纵限制灯
~ visibility 能见度不良
~ water 限制水域

restriction [ris'trikʃən] *n.* 限制，约束

restrictor [ris'triktə] *n.* 节气门，限流器，闸门板 ‖ *Syn*. choke 阻气门

result [ri'zʌlt] *n.* 结果，成效，计算结果；*v.* 起因，由于，以…为结果，导致
~ from 起因于，由…造成
~ in 导致

resultant [ri'zʌltənt] *n.* 合矢量，合力，产物，结果；*a.* 组合的，合成的
~ force 合力
~ movement 合成运动
~ movement of cutting 合成切削运动
~ movement of feed 合成进给运动
~ stress 合成应力

resume [ri'zju:m] *n.* 简历，履历，摘要，

概略；v. 恢复，再用，再继续，重新开始，重新占用

resumption [ri'zʌmpʃən] n. 重获，取回，恢复，再开始，再继续

resuscitate [ri'sʌsiteit] v. (使)复苏，(使)复兴

resuscitation [ri,sʌsi'teiʃən] n. 苏醒，复兴，复生

retain [ri'tein] v. 保持，保留，雇用，记住

retainer [ri'teinə] n. 承盘，挡板，保持者，固定器

retaining [ri'teiniŋ] v. (retain 的 ing 形式)保持，保留，雇用，记住；a. 留住的，定位的，使固定的

~ board 垫板

~ ring 扣环，扣套，定位环

retard [ri'ta:d] n. 减速，放慢，阻滞；v. 延迟，使减速，阻止，妨碍，阻碍

retardance [ri'ta:dəns] n. 阻滞，阻止，迟缓

retardancy [ri'ta:dənsi] n. 阻滞性，阻止性

retardant [ri'ta:dənt] n. 延缓剂；a. 延缓的，使迟滞的

retardation [,rita:'deiʃən] n. 延迟，延迟程度，妨碍，障碍，留级

retarded [ri'ta:did] v. (retard 的过去式和过去分词) 延迟，减速，阻止，妨碍，阻碍；a. 延迟的，发展迟缓的，智力迟钝的

~ firing 延迟点火，推迟发射

retarding [ri'ta:diŋ] n. 智力迟钝者；v. (retard 的 ing 形式) 延迟，减速，阻止，妨碍，阻碍

~ torque 减速转矩，制动转矩

retention [ri'tenʃən] n. 保留，保持力

~ of oil on board 船上保留油量额

retest [ri:'test] n. 再测验，再测试，再考验；v. 再测验，再测试，再考验

~ after necessary repair 必要维修后的再测试

rethread [ri:'θred] n. 重新喂料，重新穿进

retighten [ri:'taitən] v. 重新固定，重新上紧，重新拉紧

~ by hydraulic pressure 用液压重新紧固

retract [ri'trækt] v. 缩回，缩进，收回，取消

retractable [ri'træktəbl:] a. 可收回的

~ fin stabilizer 伸缩式鳍板稳定器

retraction [ri'trækʃən] n. 缩回，收回，撤回，收缩力

retreat [ri'tri:t] n. 撤退，降旗号，军队的降旗仪式；v. 撤退，后退，缩回，逃避，向后倾斜

~ signals 撤退信号

retrieval [ri'tri:vəl] n. 取回，恢复，修补，重获，挽救，拯救

retrieve [ri'tri:v] n. 取回，找回，恢复；v. 重新得到，取回，恢复，纠正，营救，挽救，追忆，记起

retroreflective [,retrəuri'flektiv] a. 回射的，反向反射器的

~ material 逆向反光材料

return [ri'tə:n] n. 回来，返回，来回票，利润，回答；v. 返回，归还，回返，回报，报告，获得，回答；a. 返回的，回程的，报答的，反向的，重现的

~ air 回风，循环空气，回流空气

~ flow 回流，逆流回流，返回流量

~ flow oil atomizer 回流式喷油器

~ flow solenoid valve 回流电磁阀

~ pipe 回流管，回水管

~ spring 回位弹簧，复位弹簧

~ to normal 恢复正常

~ valve 回流阀

returnable [ri'tə:nəbl] *a.* 可返回的，可退回的，可归还

reuse ['ri:'ju:z] *n.* 重新使用；*v.* 再用，重新使用

revalue ['ri:'vælju:] *v.* 再评价，重新估价

reveal [ri'vi:l] *n.* (门、窗)框边，窗侧，门侧；*v.* 展现，显示，揭示，暴露，泄露，透露

revenue ['revinju:] *n.* 收益，税收，财政收入

~ cutter 缉私船

reverberate [ri'və:bəreit] *v.* 反响，弹回，挡回，驱回，击退

reverberation [ri,və:bə'reiʃən] *n.* 反响，回响，反射，反射物

reversal [ri'və:səl] *n.* 颠倒，反转，反向，逆转，撤销

~ protection 反向保护

reverse [ri'və:s] *n.* 相反，背面，反面，倒退；*v.* 颠倒，倒转；*a.* 相反的，倒转的，颠倒的

~ current protection 反向电流保护

~ current relay 反向电流继电器

~ current test 反向电流测试

~ frame 内底横骨

~ osmosis 反渗透

~ osmosis method 反渗透法

~ over current relay 反向过电流继电器，逆过载继电器

~ phase relay 反相继电器

~ phase current relay 反相电流继电器

~ polarity 反极性，反极性接法，反接

~ power 逆功率

~ power protection 逆功率保护

~ power relay 逆功率继电器

~ power relay trip test 逆功率脱扣试验

~ power test 逆功率测试

~ power trip 逆功率跳闸

~ rotation 反向旋转，反转

~ rotation solenoid 反转电磁线圈

~ starting sequence 反向启动程序，换向启动程序

~ voltage 反向电压

reversed [ri'və:st] *v.* (reverse 的过去式和过去分词) 翻转，倒转；*a.* 相反的，倒转的，颠倒的

~ polarity 反向极性

reversibility [ri,və:sə'biliti] *n.* 可逆性，可取消

reversible [ri'və:səbl] *a.* 可逆的，可逆性的，双面可用的

~ booster 可逆增压机

~ electric drive 可逆电气传动

~ engine 可反转发动机

~ liferaft 可翻转救生筏

~ motor 可逆电动机

~ pump 可逆泵，双向泵，双向旋转泵

reversing [ri'və:siŋ] *v.* (reverse 的 ing 形式) 翻转，倒转；*a.* 换向的，回动的

~ arrangement 换向装置

~ contactor 换向接触器

~ control lever 换向操纵杆，换向控制杆

~ coupling 换向联轴器

~ device 换向装置

~ gear 回动装置，换向齿轮

~ interlock 换向联锁

~ lever 回动杆，换向手柄

~ servomoter 换向伺服电动机，换向伺服马达

~ servomotor for camshaft 凸轮轴换向伺服电动机，凸轮轴换向伺服马达

~ stud switch 换向按钮开关

~ switch 换向开关

~ test 逆转试验

~ time 换向时间

~ valve 换向阀，回动阀，反向阀

revetment [ri'vetmənt] *n.* (防弹片的)障壁，护墙，挡土墙，铺面，堑壕

review [ri'vju:] *n.* 回顾，复习，评论，评估；*v.* 回顾，复习，检查，批评 ‖ *Syn.* censor 检查，审查；check 检查，核对；examine 检查，调查；inspect 检查，视察；rummage 搜出，检查

revise [ri'vaiz] *v.* 修订，校订，修正，修改

revision [ri'viʒən] *n.* 修订，修改，修正，修订本

revocation [ˌrevə'keiʃən] *n.* 废止，撤回

revoke [ri'vəuk] *v.* 废除，撤销，撤回，宣告无效

revolution [ˌrevə'lu:ʃən] *n.* 旋转，绕转，革命，变革

~ counter 旋转计数器，转速计，转速表 ‖ *Syn.* revolution indicator 转速计，转数指示器

~ speed transducer 转速传感器

revolutions [ˌrevə'lu:ʃəns] *n.* (revolution 的复数) 旋转，绕转

~ per minute (RPM) 每分钟转数

~ per second (RPS) 每秒转数

revolve [ri'vɔlv] *v.* (使)旋转，循环出现，考虑

rewind [ri:'waind] *n.* 重绕；*v.* 重绕

rewritable [ˌri:'raitəbl] *a.* 可重写的，可复写的，可修改的

rewrite [ri:'rait] *v.* 重写，改写，书面答复

rheostat ['ri:əˌstæt] *n.* 可变电阻器，变阻器

~ brush 变阻器电刷

rheostatic [ˌri:əs'tætik] *a.* 变阻器的，电阻的

~ starter 启动用变阻器

rhombus ['rɔmbəs] *n.* 菱形，斜方形 ‖ circle 圆，圆形；ellipse 椭圆，椭圆形；parallelogram 平行四边形；rectangle 矩形；square 正方形；trapezoid 梯形；triangle 三角形

rhumb [rʌm] *n.* 罗盘方位，罗盘方位单位

rib [rib] *n.* 肋骨，肋材，圆拱，凸纹

RIB (rigid inflatable boat) 刚性充气船，硬式充气艇

~ flange 肋骨凸缘，肋凸缘

ribbon ['ribən] *n.* 缎带，丝带，带，带状物，带子

~ punch 压筋冲子

~ type radiator 带式散热器

rid [rid] *v.* 使摆脱，解除，免除

ride [raid] *n.* 骑，乘，乘坐装置，交通工具；*v.* 航进，飘游，停泊，依托，依靠，依附，照旧进行，经过，运载，骑，乘

~ at anchor 抛锚停泊，抛锚停船

riding ['raidiŋ] *n.* 停泊，行政区，区，马术，骑术；*v.* (ride 的 ing 形式) 航进，飘游，停泊，依托，依靠，依附，照旧进行，经过，运载，骑，乘

~ lamp 锚灯，停泊灯

rifle ['raifl] *n.* 步枪，来复枪，来复线，膛线；*v.* 掠夺，抢夺，用步枪射击

rig [rig] *n.* 索具装备，钻探设备，钻探平台，钻塔；*v.* 配备，装配，装上索具

~ move 钻井船移位

rigging ['rigiŋ] *n.* 船上的全部设备，索

具，帆缆，支索，绳索，传动装置；
v. (rig 的 ing 形式) 配备，装配，装上
索具

~ screw 装配螺钉，松紧螺旋扣

right [rait] n. 正义，公正，正确，权利，右，右边，右派；v. 扶直，扶正，整理，整顿，纠正，补偿，修补，赔偿，弥补，恢复平衡；a. 正当的，正确的，对的，合适的，恰当的，正面的，垂直的，直角的，笔直的，健康的，健全的；ad. 正当地，正确地，一直地，直接地，完全地，彻底地，在右边

~ aft 右后方，正后方，在正船尾

~ angle 直角

~ angle one-way valve 直角单向阀

~ hand 右手，右侧

~ hand engine 右旋轴发动机

~ hand rotation 右旋

~ hand rule 右手定则

~ of way 通行权，公用道路

right-handed 右手的，惯用右手的，右旋的

~ propeller 右旋螺旋桨，右旋进桨

rightful ['raitful] a. 合法的，正当的，正直的，公正的

righting ['raitiŋ] n. 正义，公正，正确，权利，右，右边，右派；v. (right 的 ing 形式) 扶直，扶正，整理，整顿，纠正，补偿，修补，赔偿，弥补，恢复平衡

~ arm 扶正力臂，恢复力臂，稳性力臂

~ lever 复原力臂

~ moment 直力矩，(船)扶正力矩，复原力矩

rightly ['raitli] ad. 正确地，公正地，端正地，正当地，恰当地

rigid ['ridʒid] a. 僵硬的，严格的,刚性的，刚硬的

~ body 刚体，刚性体

~ frame 刚性构架，刚架

~ frame bridge 刚构桥，刚架桥，刚架式桥梁

~ inflatable boat (RIB) 刚性充气船，硬式充气艇

~ insulation 刚性绝缘

~ liferaft 刚性救生筏

~ side wall 刚性边壁

rigidity [ri'dʒiditi] n. 刚度，坚硬，僵化，刻板，严格

~ criterion 刚度准则

rigidly ['ridʒidli] ad. 严格地，严厉地，坚硬地，牢牢地

rigor ['rigə] n. 精确，严密，严格，严厉，苛刻，严酷

rigorous ['rigərəs] a. 严格的，严厉的，严酷的，严峻的

rim [rim] n. 边，轮缘，蓝框；v. 镶边，装边，沿边缘滚动，形成边状

RINA (Registo Italiano Navade) 意大利船级社

RINA (Royal Institution of Naval Architects) (英国)皇家造船工程师学会

ring [riŋ] n. 环，环形物，环状，铃声，声调，打电话，拳击场；v. 包围，套住，按铃，敲钟，成环形，响，鸣，回响

~ distribution system 环形配电网

~ for 按铃，摇铃，召唤某人

~ gate 环门，环形浇口，环形进模口

~ gauge 环规

~ off engine 主机定速

~ piston blower 环形活塞式鼓风机

~ ridge 环脊

~ rolling 环轧，环锻

~ system 环状系统，环系

~ the alarm 拉警报，敲警钟

~ the bell 鸣钟，按门铃

~ valve 环形阀，环状阀

~ zone 活塞环区

rinse [rins] *n.* 嗽洗，漂洗，漂清，冲洗；*v.* 冲洗，漂洗，漂净，漱口，刷

rip [rip] *n.* 粗齿锯，裂口，裂缝；*v.* 撕，剥，劈，锯，裂开，撕裂

~ dispersal area 激流区

ripple ['ripl] *n.* 涟漪，涟波，波纹；*v.* 起波纹

~ current 波纹电流，脉动电流，涟波电流

rise [raiz] *n.* 上升，增加，上涨，发生，出现，高地，小山；*v.* 升起，起身，高耸，增长，上升，复活，使飞起，发源，起义

~ of floor 底升，船底斜度，舭部升高，(舯)横斜高

~ time 上升时间，上沿时间，升压时间，升起时间，增长时间，生成时间

~ up 上升，起义，叛变

riser ['raizə] *n.* 起床者，起义者，叛乱者，楼梯的踏步竖板

~ tube 上升管，升液管

rising ['raiziŋ] *n.* 上升，起立，起义；*v.* (rise 的 ing 形式) 升起，起身，高耸，增长，上升；*a.* 上升的，上涨的，增加的，有前途的

~ edge 前沿，上升边

~ main 上行水管，上行电缆，直上干线

risk [risk] *n.* 危险，风险，冒险，被保险人或物；*v.* 冒…的危险 ‖ *Syn.* danger 危险，危害，危险物，威胁；hazard 冒险，危险，冒险的事；jeopardy 危险；peril 危险，危险物

river ['rivə] *n.* 河，江，溪，巨流

~ boat 内河船，江船，河船 ‖ *Syn.* river vessel 内河船舶

~ water quick settling unit 河水快速沉降装置

riverine ['rivəˌrain] *a.* 河的，河流的，河边的

~ warfare vessel 内河舰艇

rivet ['rivit] *n.* 铆钉，包头钉；*v.* 铆接，固定，凝神，吸引

riveted ['rivitid] *v.* (rivet 的过去式和过去分词) 铆接，固定，凝神，吸引；*a.* 用铆钉钉牢的，铆接的

~ boiler 铆接锅炉

~ joint 铆钉接合

riveter ['rivitə] *n.* 铆钉机 ‖ *Syn.* riveting machine 铆钉机

riveting ['rivitiŋ] *n.* 铆接(法)；*v.* (rivet 的 ing 形式) 铆接，固定，凝神，吸引；*a.* 使人目不转睛的，吸引人的，极迷人的

~ machine 铆钉机 ‖ *Syn.* riveter 铆钉机

RMS (root mean square) 均方根

~ input voltage 均方根输入电压

~ value 均方根值

~ voltage 均方根电压，电压有效值

Ro-Ro (roll-on-roll-off) 滚式装卸的，滚装的

~ cargo pace 滚装货舱

~ cargo handling gear 滚装货物装卸装置

~ container ship 滚装集装箱船

~ passenger ship 滚装客船

roadstead ['rəudsted] *n.* 锚地，停泊处，碇泊处

robot ['rəubɔt] *n.* 机器人，遥控设备，自动机械，机械般工作的人

robust [rə'bʌst] *a.* 坚定的，精力充沛的，粗野的
~ construction 坚固结构
~ control 鲁棒控制

robustness [rəu'bʌstnis] *n.* 鲁棒性，坚固性，健壮性

rock [rɔk] *n.* 岩石，暗礁，石头，摇动；*v.* 摇，摇动，摇摆，使动摇
~ bottom 最低点

rocker ['rɔkə] *n.* 摇杆，摇轴，摇椅，摇的人
~ arm 摇臂，摇杆
~ arm shaft 摇臂轴
~ shaft 摇杆轴

rocket ['rɔkit] *n.* 火箭，火箭发射器；*v.* 飞速上升，迅速上升，猛涨，用火箭运送
~ parachute flare 火箭降落伞焰火信号，火箭式降落伞照明弹

rod [rɔd] *n.* 活塞杆，杆，拉杆，平方杆，水准尺，避雷针，测量用的棒，惩罚，体罚，棍棒，手枪

role [rəul] *n.* 作用，角色，责任，功能，职位

roll [rəul] *n.* 卷，卷形物，摇晃，摆动，名单；*v.* 摇摆，摇晃，滚，绕，转动，辗，轧，卷起，卷拢
~ call 点名，名单，登记表
~ collar 辊脊，辊环
~ gap measuring instrument 轧辊间隙测量仪
~ out 铺开，滚出，推出

roll-off 滚下的

roll-on 滚上的
~ berth 滚装码头
~ unload 滚装卸载

roll-on-roll-off (Ro-Ro) 滚式装卸的，滚装的
~ cargo pace 滚装货舱
~ handling gear 滚装货物装卸装置
~ container ship 滚装集装箱船
~ passenger ship 滚装客船

rolled [rəuld] *v.* (roll 的过去式和过去分词) 摇摆，摇晃，滚，绕，转动，辗，轧，卷起，卷拢；*a.* 轧制的，滚制的，包金箔的
~ copper foil 压延铜箔
~ steel 轧钢，钢材
~ steel beam 辊压钢梁，轧制型钢梁

roller ['rəulə] *n.* 滚筒，辊子，滚压机
~ bearing 滚柱轴承
~ lifter 滚子式气门挺杆 ‖ *Syn.* roller tappet 滚轮挺杆，滚柱挺杆
~ pin 滚针，滚轮销
~ shaft 滚轮轴
~ track davit 滚柱导轨
~ type chock 滚柱式轴承座
~ type hatch cover 滚子式舱盖

rolling ['rəuliŋ] *n.* 旋转，翻滚，动摇；*v.* (roll 的 ing 形式) 摇摆，摇晃，滚，绕，转动，辗，轧，卷起，卷拢；*a.* 旋转的，转动的，摇摆的，起伏的
~ bearing 滚动轴承
~ blackout 轮流停电，轮番停电
~ cargo 滚装货物
~ damping coefficient 横摇阻尼系数
~ hatch cover 滚动舱盖
~ mill 轧机，轧钢机

~ moment 滚动力矩，横摇力矩，滚转力矩

~ resistance 滚动阻力，横摇阻力

~ tank stabilization system 水舱室减摇装置，水舱减摇装置 ‖ *Syn*. anti-rolling tank stabilization system 减摇水舱稳定系统，水舱室减摇装置

ROM (read only memory) 只读存储器

root [ru:t] *n*. 根，根部，根本，根源；*v*. (使)生根，(使)扎根，使立定不动，坚定不移，确立

~ locus 根轨迹

~ mean square (RMS) 均方根

~ mean square input voltage 均方根输入电压

~ mean square value 均方根值

~ mean square voltage 均方根电压，电压有效值

~ method 根方法

Roots [ru:ts] *n*. 罗茨(人名)

~ blower 罗茨鼓风机

~ blower pump 罗茨增压泵，机械增压泵

rope [rəup] *n*. 绳，索，绳索；*v*. 围起

~ guide 绳罐道，导绳器

~ socket 绳接头，索接头，绳帽，绳头扣紧座，钢丝绳绳头套，钢索连接眼环

rose [rəuz] *n*. 蔷薇属，玫瑰，玫瑰红；*v*. (rise 的过去式) 上升，增强，起立，高耸，使飞起，使浮上水面

~ box 舱底水过滤箱，眼板箱 ‖ *Syn*. bilge sludge box 舱底水过滤箱；bilge mud box 舱底水过滤箱

rosin ['rɔzin] *n*. 松香，树脂；*v*. 用松香

roster ['rəustə] *n*. 值勤人，名簿，花名册，逐项登记表

rota ['rəutə] *n*. 值班表，花名册，勤务轮值的一轮

rotameter ['rəutə,mi:tə] *n*. 旋转式流量计，转子流量计，曲线测长计

rotary ['rəutəri] *n*. 绕轴旋转的部件或装置，交通环岛，环形交叉；*a*. 旋转的，转动的

~ actuator 旋转引动器，摇动液压缸，旋转式激励器，旋转式致动装置

~ compressor 回转式压缩机

~ current 旋转潮流，旋转流

~ eccentric plug valve 偏心旋转阀

~ exhaust valve 回转式排气阀

~ frequency converter 变频机组

~ mechanical atomizing oil burner 旋转式燃烧器

~ motion 旋转运动，回转运动，转动

~ motion valve 角行程阀

~ oil burner 旋转式燃烧器

~ packing ring 动密封环

~ pump 旋转泵，回转泵，旋转式泵

~ screw propeller 回转式螺旋推进器

~ silica-gel dehumidifier 转动式硅胶吸湿装置

~ sliding-vane refrigerating compressor 转动滑叶冷冻压缩机

~ spool type 旋转阀芯

~ switch 旋转开关

~ table 转盘，回转台

~ transformer 旋转变压器

~ trochoidal engine 旋轮线转子发动机

~ valve 回转阀，旋转阀

~ vane 旋叶，回转片

~ vane pump 回转式滑片泵，转动叶片泵

~ vane sealing strip 转叶密封条

~ vane steering gear 转翼式操舵装置

~ vane type oil cylinder 转叶式油缸

~ vane type steering gear 转叶式舵机

rotatable ['rəuteitəbl] *a.* 可旋转的，可转动的

~ thruster 旋转推力器

rotate [rəu'teit] *v.* 旋转，循环，轮流，交替，轮作；*a.* 车轮状的

rotating [rəu'teitiŋ] *v.* (rotate 的 ing 形式) 旋转，循环，轮流，交替，轮作；*a.* 旋转的

~ blade 转动叶片，旋转叶片

~ commutator 旋转换向器，旋转整流子

~ disc type 转盘式

~ joint 旋转接头，旋转连接

~ magnetic field 旋转磁场

~ mechanical graphite seal 旋转机械石墨密封

~ piston 旋转式活塞

~ plate 旋转台

~ seal ring 旋转密封圈，旋转密封环

~ transformer 旋转变压器

rotation [rəu'teiʃən] *n.* 旋转，转动

~ angle 旋转角，旋转角度，回转角度

~ reversal test 换向试验

~ to the left 向左转动

rotational [rəu'teiʃənəl] *a.* 转动的，轮流的

~ frequency 转动频率，转数

~ motion 回转运动，转动运动

~ ring 旋转环

rotor ['rəutə] *n.* 旋翼，轮子，转子，回转轴，旋转体

~ blade 转动叶片

~ core 转子铁芯

~ plate 电容器动片，旋转板

~ resistance 转子电阻

~ shaft 转子轴，转轴

~ short-circuit 转子短路

~ turn short-circuit 转子匝间短路

~ winding 转子绕组，转子线圈

rotor-resistance 转子(串)电阻

~ starting 转子(串)电阻启动

rough [rʌf] *v.* 大体描述；*a.* 粗糙的，粗略的，大致的，粗野的，粗暴的，粗略叙述的；*ad.* 粗糙地

~ grained 粗颗粒

~ handling 粗率的处理(搬运，装运货物)

~ machining 粗加工

~ sea 大浪，狂浪，风大浪急的海面

roughly ['rʌfli] *ad.* 粗略地，大致上，大体上

round [raund] *n.* 圆，圆形物，一轮，巡回，轮唱；*v.* 弄圆，变圆，绕行，环行，拐弯，完成，围捕，四舍五入，进展；*a.* 圆的，球形的，大概的，十足的，完全的，率直的，肥胖的；*ad.* 围绕着，循环地，在周围，迂回地，朝反方向，挨个；*prep.* 围着，附近，绕过，在…周围

~ bar 圆钢，圆条，圆钢筋

~ boiler tube brush 圆管刷

~ brass rod 黄铜棒

~ brass washer 黄铜垫圈

~ brush 圆刷

~ copper rod 圆铜杆

~ copper wire 圆铜线

~ fuse 圆熔丝

~ man hole 圆形人孔

~ pad 圆垫

~ plug 圆插头

~ punch 圆冲子，圆形凸模

~ thread 圆螺丝板牙

~ smooth file 细圆锉

~ socket 圆插座

~ spring steel 圆弹簧钢

~ spring washer 弹簧圆垫圈

~ steel 圆钢

round-to-even 向偶数舍入

roundabout ['raundəbaut] n. 绕道,迂回路线,环形交通枢纽; a. 迂回的,转弯抹角的

rounded ['raundid] v. (round 的过去式和过去分词) 弄圆,变圆,绕行,环行,拐弯,完成,围捕,四舍五入,进展; a. 圆形的,全面的,丰满的

~ gunwale 修圆的舷边

~ sheer strake 圆弧舷板

rounding ['raundiŋ] n. 制圆,舍入,凑整; v. (round 的 ing 形式) 弄圆,变圆,绕行,环行,拐弯,完成,围捕,四舍五入,进展; a. 圆的,环绕的,凑整的

~ chamfer 倒角

~ error 化整误差,修整误差,舍入误差

~ number 约整数

roundness ['raundnis] n. 圆,圆满,完整,率直

route [ru:t] n. 航线,路,路线,途经,渠道; v. 规定路线,发送,安排顺序

router ['ru:tə] n. 路由器,刳刨机,刳刨工具,刳刨者

routh [ru:θ] n. 丰盛,丰富,大量,劳斯 (Routh, 人名)

~ approximation method 劳思近似判据,劳斯近似法

~ Criterion 劳斯判据,劳斯稳定判据

Routh-Hurwitz 劳斯-赫尔维茨

~ stability criterion 劳斯-赫尔维茨稳定性判据

routine [ru:'ti:n] n. 常规,例行公事,日常事务,程序; a. 常规的,例行的,习惯性的,平凡的

~ adjustment 定期调整,例行调整

~ maintenance 日常维修,例行维护,常规维护

routing ['ru:tiŋ] n. 行程安排,邮件路由; v. (route 的 ing 形式) 规定路线,发送,安排顺序

~ problem 路径问题,巡行问题,走线问题

ROV (remotely operated vehicle) 遥控潜水器

row [rəu] n. 排,行; v. 划船

rowboat ['rəubəut] n. 划艇,小舟

royal ['rɔiəl] a. 皇家的,王室的,第一流的,高贵的

~ Institution of Naval Architects (RINA) (英国)皇家造船工程师学会

RPM (revolutions per minute) 每分钟转数

RPS (revolutions per second) 每秒转数

RTFs (regional task forces) 区域工作队

rub [rʌb] v. 擦,摩擦

rubber ['rʌbə] n. 橡皮,橡胶,合成橡胶,胜局比赛,决胜局

~ ball 橡皮球

~ bearing 橡胶轴承

~ belt 橡皮带,胶带

~ boots 橡胶靴

~ cable 橡胶电缆

~ heat resisting cable 橡胶耐热电缆

~ hose clamp 橡胶管卡圈

~ hose for acetylene 乙炔胶管

~ hose for oxygen 氧气胶管
~ insulating tape 橡皮包带
~ insulation 橡皮缘绝，橡胶绝缘
~ mallet 橡皮锤
~ mask 橡胶面罩，黑胶面镜
~ packing 橡皮填料，橡胶垫圈，橡胶密封垫
~ plug 橡皮塞
~ ring 橡胶圈，橡胶环
~ sealing ring 橡皮密封圈
~ tile 树胶阶砖，橡胶板，橡皮瓦，橡皮地砖
~ water hose 橡胶水管
rubbing ['rʌbiŋ] *n.* 擦，拓本，拓印；*v.* (rub 的 ing 形式) 擦，摩擦
　~ plate 摩擦板，摩擦片
　~ surface 摩擦面
rudder ['rʌdə] *n.* 舵，船舵，方向舵，指导原则
　~ actuator 方向舵传动器
　~ angle 舵角
　~ angle indicator 舵角指示器
　~ angle receiver 舵角接收器
　~ angle transmitter 舵角发送器
　~ area 舵叶面积，舵面积
　~ bearing 舵承
　~ blade 舵叶，舵板
　~ carrier 舵承，舵托
　~ control rod 操舵杆
　~ controller 舵机控制器
　~ gudgeon 舵钮，舵枢，舵轴承
　~ horn 半悬舵承架，吊舵支架
　~ indicator 舵角指示器
　~ lever 舵杆 ‖ *Syn*. rudder stock 舵杆
　~ order 舵令
　~ order indicator 舵令指示器
~ pintle 舵栓，舵销
~ position 舵位
~ position indicator 舵位指示器，舵角指示器
~ post 舵柱
~ propeller 舵式车叶，导管螺旋桨舵
~ quadrant 舵扇
~ shaft 舵轴 ‖ *Syn*. rudder spindle 舵轴
~ stock diameter 舵杆直径
~ stock moment 舵杆扭矩 ‖ *Syn*. rudder stock torque 舵杆扭矩
~ tiller 舵柄
~ trunk 舵杆管，舵杆筒，舵杆箱道，舵杆围井
~ yoke 横舵柄
rule [ru:l] *n.* 规则，水线，惯例，统治，章程，准则，标准，控制，破折号；*v.* 规定，统治，支配，管辖，裁决，裁定
rule-of-thumb 经验法则，经验方法
　~ prediction technique 经验预测技术
rummage ['rʌmidʒ] *n.* 翻查，检查，零星杂物；*v.* 翻寻，搜出，检查 ‖ *Syn.* censor 检查，审查；check 检查，核对；examine 检查，调查；inspect 检查，视察；review 检查，检阅
run [rʌn] *n.* 运转，趋向，跑，赛跑，奔跑；*v.* (使)跑，奔，跑步，蔓延，进行，行驶，追究，管理，运行，开动，逃跑，竞选，参赛；*a.* 熔化的，融化的，浇铸的
~ button 启动按钮，运行按钮
~ down 撞倒，使变弱，停止，浏览，追溯

~in 试车，使不间断，跑进，顺便探访，拘留

~in full load 4 hours 满负荷运行 4 小时，满载运行 4 小时

~in half load 2 hours 半负荷运行 2 小时，半载运行 2 小时

~in over load 1 hour 超负荷运行 1 小时

run-in 试车，插入部分，平行式，口角

~ test 空车试验

run-up 将引擎加速使热以供试验，抬高，预备阶段，事件的前奏曲，助跑

running ['rʌniŋ] *n.* 奔跑，赛跑，转动，运转；*v.*(run 的 ing 形式) 跑，蔓延，进行，行驶，运行，开动；*a.* 奔跑的，赛跑的，流动的，不断的，连续的，连接的

~ direction 转向

~ direction interlock 转向联锁装置

~ direction safety interlock 运行方向安全联锁

~ Down Clause (船舶)碰撞条款

~ fire 狂燃火

~ light 航行灯 ‖ *Syn.* navigation lamp 航行灯；navigation light 航行灯

~ light control panel 航行灯控制面板

~ losses 运行损失，运行损耗

~ maintenance 经常维修，日常保养，巡回小修

~ position 运行位置

~ rigging 动索，活动吊索

~ test and hoisting test for 4t provision crane 4 吨食物吊运转试验和吊重试验

~ test and safety valve and safety device adjusting for emergency compressor 应急空气压缩机的运转试验、安全阀和安全装置的调整

~ test for emergency compressor 应急压缩机运行试验

~ test of emergency diesel generator 应急柴油发电机运转试验

~ test of machines in repair room 机修间设备运转试验

~ test of main diesel generator 主柴油发电机运转试验

~ test of motor for windless (steering gear) 锚机(舵机)电动机运转试验

~ test of shaft generator 轴带发电机运转试验

~ test of shaft generator and clutching test between ME and shaft generator 轴带发电机运转试验及主机与轴带发电机之间的离合器的效用试验

~ winding 运行绕组

running-in 磨合，试运转，试车

~ period 磨合期

runoff ['rʌnɔf] *n.* 径流，流走之物，决赛，决胜投票，附加赛

runway ['rʌnwei] *n.* 滑道，跑道，河床，飞机跑道，斜坡跑道

rupture ['rʌptʃə(r)] *n.* 破裂，决裂，敌对，割裂；*v.* 破裂，裂开，断绝，割裂

rush [rʌʃ] *n.* 突进，突击，匆忙，冲进，急流，急速行进，蜂拥；*v.* 催促，猛进，猛冲，冲，奔，闯，突袭，急速流动，急匆匆搬运，仓促行事；*a.* 急需的，紧急的

rushing ['rʌʃiŋ] *v.*(rush 的 ing 形式) 催促，猛进，猛冲，冲，奔，闯，突袭，急速流动，急匆匆搬运，仓促行事；*a.* 急流的，旺盛的

~ water 激流，急流

rust [rʌst] *n.* 铁锈，锈，衰退，赭色，深

褐色；v. 生锈，衰退，损害，变成红褐色

~ preventive 防锈剂

~ remover 除锈剂

rusty ['rʌsti] a. 生锈的，迟钝的，腐蚀了的，铁锈色的，生了锈的

S

sacrifice ['sækrifais] n. 牺牲，献祭，献身，祭品，供奉；v. 牺牲，献出，献祭，供奉

sacrificial [sækri'fiʃəl] a. 牺牲的，供奉的，献祭的

~ anode cathodic protection 牺牲阳极阴极保护

saddle ['sædl] n. 马鞍，鞍状物；v. 承受

~ hatchway 鞍型舱口，鞍形舱口

safe [seif] n. 保险箱，保险柜；a. 安全的，保险的，肯定的

~ area 安全区域，安全区 ‖ *Syn*. place of safety 安全区；safe region 安全区域，安全区；safety zone 安全地带，安全区

~ distance 安全距离

~ ground wire 安全地线

~ life 安全寿命

~ load 安全负载

~ management and operation 安全管理与运行

~ manning document 安全配员证书

~ net 安全网

~ operation 安全操作，安全运行

~ operation rate 安全运行率 ‖ *Syn*. rate of safe operation 安全运行率

~ prediction 安全预测

~ productivity 安全生产率

~ reliability 安全可靠性

~ second stage 备用二级头

~ speed 安全速度

~ state 安全状态

~ strategy 安全策略

~ working condition 安全操作状态

~ working load (SWL) 安全工作负荷

~ working practice 安全操作准则

~ working pressure 安全工作压力，容许工作压力

safeguard ['seif,ga:d] n. 保护，防卫，安全装置，安全措施，安全处理，保证条款；v. 维护，保护，捍卫，防护 ‖ *Syn*. guard 保卫，守护，防护装置；protection 保护，保护装置

safety ['seifti] n. 安全，保险，安全性，安全处所，安全设备，保险装置

~ alarm device 安全报警装置

~ allowance 安全津贴

~ analysis 安全性分析，安全分析

~ and environmental-protection policies 安全环保政策

~ and fire fighting on board 船舶安全与消防

~ and limit control 安全和极限控制

~ and limit protection 安全和极限保护

~ appliance 安全用具

~ block 安全钳体，保险块

~ cap 安全帽

~ certificate 安全证书

~ check 安全检查

~ code 安全规程，安全法则，安全码 ‖ *Syn*. safety procedures 安全程序；safety regulations 安全规程，安全守则；safety rules 安全规程，安全条例

~ coefficient 安全系数 ‖ *Syn*. assurance coefficient 安全系数，保险系数；assurance factor 安全系数；coefficient of safety 安全系数；safety factor 安全系数

~ colo(u)r 安全色

~ control 安全控制

~ control mark 安全控制标记

~ cut-out 安全断流器，保安器

~ destructor 安全自毁器

~ device 安全装置

~ device testing for emergency diesel generator 应急柴油发电机安全装置试验

~ earthing 保护接地

~ education 安全教育

~ equipment 安全设备

~ enclosed switch 密封式保险开关，金属盒开关

~ fairway 安全航道

~ glasses 护目镜，防护眼镜 ‖ *Syn*. goggles 风镜，护目镜；protective glasses 护目镜，防护眼镜

~ head 安全盖

~ in production 安全生产

~ inspection 安全检查

~ interlock 安全联锁装置

~ interlock for running direction 转向安全联锁装置

~ lamp 安全灯

~ lighting fitting 安全照明装置

~ load 安全荷载

~ load factor 安全荷载系数

~ man 安全人员

~ management audit 安全管理审计

~ Management Certificate (SMC) 安全管理证书

~ Management Manual (SMM) 安全管理手册

~ management objective 安全管理目标

~ Management System (SMS) 安全管理系统

~ margin 安全界限，安全裕度，安全系数 ‖ *Syn*. degree of safety 安全程度，安全系数

~ mark 安全标志

~ measures 安全措施，安全规程 ‖ *Syn*. accident prevention 事故防止，事故预防，安全措施；protective measures 保全措施，保护措施

~ net 安全网

~ of operation 操作安全

~ operating rules 安全操作规程

~ operation test 安全运行试验

~ performance 安全性能

~ plug 安全塞，安全插头

~ precaution 安全预防措施

~ problem 安全问题

~ program 安全计划

~ protection 安全防护

~ record 安全记录

~ and reliability 安全性与可靠性

~ science 安全科学

~ signal 安全信号

~ spring 安全弹簧

~ stop 安全停止器，安全停止，安全止挡

~ stop device 安全止动装置

~ system 安全系统

~ system engineering 安全系统工程

~ value 安全值

~ valve 安全阀 ‖ *Syn*. relief valve 安

全阀，溢流阀，泄压阀，减压阀；relieve valve 安全阀

~ valve adjusting and accumulating test for auxiliary boiler 辅锅炉安全阀检验及蓄压试验

~ valve operation test 安全阀调整试验，安全阀动作试验

~ voltage 安全电压

~ zone 安全地带，安全区 ‖ *Syn*. place of safety 安全区；safe area 安全区域，安全区；safe region 安全区域，安全区

safety-related 安全相关的

~ component 安全相关部件

~ interlock 安全联锁装置

~ software 安全相关软件

sag [sæg] *n*. 中垂，下垂，下垂度，下弯，下陷，随风漂流，物价下跌；*v*. 松弛，(使)下垂，漂流，下陷，(物价)下跌

sagging ['sægiŋ] *n*. 松弛，下垂，漂流，下陷，下跌；*v*. (sag 的 ing 形式) 松弛，下垂，漂流，下陷，下跌

~ of journal 轴颈下垂

sail [seil] *n*. 航行，帆，篷；*v*. 航行，启航，开船

sailboat ['seilbəut] *n*. 帆船

sailer ['seilə] *n*. 船，船只

sailing ['seiliŋ] *n*. 航海，启航，航海术，帆船运动；*v*. (sail 的 ing 形式) 航行，启航；*a*. 航行的

~ yacht 风帆游艇

sailor ['seilə] *n*. 海员，水手，海员，驾船人，不大会晕船的人

salient ['seiliənt] *n*. 凸角，突出部分；*a*. 易见的，显著的，突出的，跳跃的

~ pole 凸极

salination [ˌsæli'neiʃən] *n*. 盐化(作用) ‖ *Ant*. desalination 减少盐分，脱盐作用

saline ['seilain] *n*. 盐湖，盐泉，盐溶液；*a*. 含盐的，咸的，苦涩的，由碱金属(或含镁等盐类)组成的

salinity [sə'liniti] *n*. 盐分，盐度

~ indicator 测盐计

~ sensor 盐度传感器

salinometer [ˌsæli'nɔmitə] *n*. 盐量计，盐度计

~ valve 盐量计阀，盐度计阀

SALM (single anchor leg mooring) 单锚腿系泊

saloon [sə'lu:n] *n*. 货轮上的交谊厅，客轮上的大社交厅，大厅，酒吧，酒馆，轿车

~ boy 房间服务生 ‖ *Syn*. saloon steward 房间服务生

~ deck 客舱甲板

salt [sɔ:lt] *n*. 盐，食盐，风趣，刺激；*v*. 加盐于，用盐腌；*a*. 含盐的，咸的，风趣的，辛辣的

~ mist test 盐雾试验

~ water 盐水，咸水

~ water activated battery 盐水激活电池

salvage ['sælvidʒ] *n*. 海上救助，抢救，打捞，抢救财货，获救的财货，救难的奖金；*v*. 海上救助，抢救，打捞，营救

~ and rescue ship 打捞救助船

~ lifting vessel 打捞救生船,浮力打捞船

~ pump 救助泵

~ ship 打捞船

~ shop 修理工厂

~ vessel 救助打捞船

salvor ['sælvə] *n*. 打捞人员，救助人，救助船

sample ['sæmpl] *n*. 标本，样品，例子；*v*. 取样，采样，抽取…的样品，试验的一部分，尝试

~ cell 样品中心

~ connection 取样口

~ extraction smoke detection system 样品提取

~ feed pump 样品供给泵

~ hold device 采样保持器

~ mean 样本均值，采样均值

~ point 采样点

~ rate 采样率

~ set 样本集

~ space 样本空间

sampled ['sa:mpld] *v*. (sample 的过去式和过去分词) 取样，采样，抽样；*a*. 取样的，抽样的

~ data 采样数据，抽样数据，取样数据，样本数据

~ data control system 采样数据控制系统 ‖ *Syn*. sampling control system 采样控制系统

sampling ['sa:mpliŋ] *n*. 取样，采样，抽样；*v*. (sample 的 ing 形式) 取样，采样，抽样

~ cock 取样旋塞

~ connection 取样接口

~ control system 采样控制系统 ‖ *Syn*. sampled data control system 采样数据控制系统

~ error 采样误差，抽样误差

~ frequency 采样频率

~ interval 采样间隔

~ opacimeter 取样烟度计

~ oscilloscope 取样示波器，采样示波器

~ period 采样周期

~ piping 取样管路

~ probe 采样探头，取样探针

~ theorem 采样定理

samson ['sæmsən] *n*. 大力士

~ post 起重柱

SAN (strong acid number) 强酸值

sanction ['sæŋkʃən] *n*. 约束力，影响力，批准，同意，支持，制裁，认可；*v*. 批准，同意，容忍，支持，鼓励，认可

sand [sænd] *n*. 沙，沙子，沙滩，沙地；*v*. 撒沙子

sandblast ['sændbla:st] *n*. 喷沙，喷沙器；*v*. 喷沙

sandpaper ['sændpeipə] *n*. 砂纸；*v*. 打磨 ‖ *Syn*. emery paper 砂纸

sanitary ['sænitəri] *n*. 公共厕所；*a*. 卫生的，清洁的，清洁卫生的

~ discharge 卫生水管

~ ejector 卫生水喷射器

~ piping system sewage piping 卫生管道系统污水管道

~ pressure tank 卫生水压力柜

~ pump 卫生泵，卫生水泵，污水泵

~ system 卫生系统

~ tank 卫生水柜

~ treating arrangement 污水处理装置

sanitate ['sæniteit] *v*. 使合卫生，装设卫生设备

sanitation [sæni'teiʃən] *n*. 卫生，卫生设施

Sapporo [sə'pɔ:rəu] *n*. 札幌(日本北海道西部城市)

SAR (search and rescue) 搜索救援，搜救

SART (search and rescue transponder) 搜救(雷达)应答器

satellite ['sætəlait] *n.* 卫星，人造卫星，仆从，随从，附属国，卫星区
~ communication 卫星通信
~ gear 行星齿轮，行星轮
~ navigation 卫星导航 ‖ *Syn.* satellite-based navigation 星基导航，卫星导航

satellite-based 基于卫星的，星基的
~ communication 星基通信，卫星通信
~ navigation 星基导航，卫星导航 ‖ *Syn.* satellite navigation 卫星导航

satisfaction [ˌsætis'fækʃən] *n.* 满足，满意，补偿，确信，使人满意的原因或手段

satisfactorily [sætis'fæktərili] *ad.* 令人满意地，心安理得地，可靠地

satisfactory [ˌsætis'fæktəri] *a.* 令人满意的，符合要求的，赎罪的

satisfy ['sætisfai] *v.* 满足，使满意，确保，说服，使相信，清偿，补偿，消除，履行 ‖ *Syn.* cater to 迎合，满足；content 使满足；fill 满足；fulfil 满足；meet 满足，达到要求 ‖ *Ant.* dissatisfy 使不满意，使不满足，使失望

saturable ['sætʃərəbl] *a.* 可饱和的

saturate ['sætʃəreit] *v.* 浸湿，浸透，使饱和，使充满；*a.* 饱和的，浸透的

saturated ['sætʃəreitid] *v.* (saturate 的过去式和过去分词) 浸湿，浸透，饱和，充满；*a.* 饱和的，浸透的，深颜色的
~ reactor (SR) 饱和电抗器
~ steam 饱和水蒸气，饱和蒸汽 ‖ *Syn.* saturated vapour 饱和水蒸气，饱和蒸汽

saturation [ˌsætʃə'reiʃən] *n.* 饱和度，饱和（状态），浸润，浸透

~ characteristic 饱和特性
~ curve 饱和曲线
~ effect 饱和效应
~ pressure 饱和压力
~ temperature 饱和温度

save [seiv] *n.* 救援，救援；*v.* 解救，挽救，保存，保全，保留，节省，储蓄；*prep.* 除…之外
~ energy 节能

save-all 节约装置，罩衫

saw [sɔː] *n.* 锯；*v.* (see 的过去式) 锯，看见
~ blade 锯片，锯条
~ cut 锯痕
~ cutting 锯切，锯解，锯片割缝
~ dust 锯屑，木屑
~ off 锯断
~ setting 锉锯齿
~ tooth 锯齿，锯齿形

sawing ['sɔːiŋ] *n.* 锯，锯切，锯开；*v.* (saw 的 ing 形式) 锯，锯切，锯开
~ machine 机械锯床，电锯

SBN (strong base number) 强碱值

SBT (segregated ballast tank) 分隔压载舱，专用压载舱，隔离压载舱

SCADA (supervisory control and data acquisition) 监控与数据采集

scalar ['skeilə] *n.* 数量，标量；*a.* 标量的，梯状的，分等级的，数量的

scale [skeil] *n.* 刻度，衡量，比例，数值范围，比例尺，天平，等级；*v.* 测量，衡量，剥落，生水垢，依比例决定，攀登
~ formation 结垢
~ power 标度功率

scaling ['skeiliŋ] *n.* 缩放比例，鳞片排列；

511

v. (scale 的 ing 形式) 剥落，刮鳞，生水垢

~ factor 比例因数，换算系数，计数递减率，标度因子

~ hammer 除锈锤，敲水垢锤，锅锈锤

scan [skæn] n. 扫描；v. 扫描，细看，审视，浏览

scanner ['skænə] n. 扫描仪，扫描器

scantling ['skæntliŋ] n. 一点点，少量，小梁，建材尺寸

~ draft 结构吃水 ‖ *Syn*. scantling draught 结构吃水，强度吃水

~ length 结构长度

~ numeral 船材尺度定数，构件数

~ rules 船材尺度法则

scanty ['skænti] a. 不足的，缺乏的，稀疏的，俭省的

scar [ska:] n. 伤痕，疤痕；v. 结疤，使留下伤痕，创伤

scarcely ['skɛəsli] ad. 几乎不，简直不

scarcity ['skɛəsiti] n. 稀少，罕见，不足

scare [skɛə] n. 惊恐，恐慌，恐惧；v. 惊吓，受惊，威吓

scarp [ska:p] n. 峭壁，陡坡，悬崖，内斜坡；v. 使成陡坡

scatter ['skætə] v. 分散，散开，撒开，驱散

~ around 散乱放置，分散在

scavenge ['skævindʒ] v. 打扫，清除污物，从内燃机气缸排出废气，从废物中提取

~ air 扫气空气

~ air belt 扫气道

~ air cooler 扫气冷却器

~ (air) port 扫气口

~ (air) space 扫气空间

~ air system 扫气系统

~ box 扫气箱

~ box drain room 扫气箱放水室

~ manifold 扫气歧管

~ (trunk) fire 扫气箱着火

scavenging ['skævindʒiŋ] n. 净化，清除，除气法；v. (scavenge 的 ing 形式) 净化，清除，打扫，排除废气

~ air box 扫气箱 ‖ *Syn*. scavenging air chamber 扫气箱；scavenging air receiver 扫气箱

~ air duct 扫气道

~ air manifold 驱气歧管

~ air pipe 扫气管

~ air plate valve 扫气片状阀

~ air trunk 扫气总管

~ air valve 扫气阀，换气阀

~ arrangement 换气装置

~ blower 扫气鼓风机

~ box fire 扫气箱着火

~ efficiency 扫气效率

~ method 扫气法

~ period 换气过程

~ port 扫气口

~ port area 扫气口面积

~ pressure 扫气压力

~ pressure ratio 扫气压比

~ pump 驱气泵，扫气泵，换气泵

~ system 扫气系统，清除系统

~ temperature 扫气温度

~ valve 驱气阀，扫气阀

SCBA (self-contained breathing apparatus) 自给式呼吸器

scene [si:n] n. 现场，场面，情景，景色，发生地点，一场，布景，道具布置

~ of fire 火灾现场，火场

schedule ['ʃedju:l] n. 时刻表，进度表，清

单，日程计划，课程表，附录；v. 确定时间

~ control 进度控制，工程管理，预定输出控制

~ coordination 生产规程协调

~ drawing 工程图，工序图

~ reviews 施工生产进度审核

schematic [ski'mætik] n. 示意图；a. 图解的，图表的，梗概的，示意性的

~ diagram 原理图，示意图

schematically [ski:'mætikəli] ad. 计划性地，示意性地，按照图式地

scheme [ski:m] n. 安排，配置，计划，阴谋，方案，图解，摘要；v. 设计，计划，谋划，图谋，策划

schooner ['sku:nə] n. (有两个以上桅杆的)纵帆船，大酒杯

science ['saiəns] n. 科学，理科，学科，分科，技术，学问，知识

scientific [saiən'tifik] a. 科学的，有技术的

~ surveying ship 科学考察船

~ way 科学方法

scissor ['sizə] n. 剪刀；v. 剪，剪取，截取，删除，削减

SCM (single chip microcomputer) 单片微型计算机，单片机

scoop [sku:p] n. 铲斗，铲子；v. 掘，挖

~ cooling 自流冷却

~ cooling system 自流冷却系统

scope [skəup] n. 领域，范畴，范围，机会，余地，眼界，见识，锚缆长度，锚缆范围；v. 仔细研究

~ of supply 供货范围

score [skɔ:] n. 得分，分数，抓痕，二十，终点线，刻痕，账目，起跑线，乐谱；v. 评分，得分，获得，记下，记分，刻划，划线，评价，刻痕

Scotch [skɔtʃ] n. 苏格兰，苏格兰人，苏格兰语，刻痕；v. 镇压，粉碎，刻痕，使受伤 a. 苏格兰人的，苏格兰语的

~ boiler 苏格兰锅炉

scour ['skauə] n. 冲刷，擦，洗，洗涤剂，腹泻；v. 冲刷，擦，洗，擦亮，急速走遍，腹泻，急速穿行

~ coaming 挡泥堰墙

~ for 搜索

scow [skau] n. 平底驳船，平底船

SCR (silicon controlled rectifier) 可控硅，硅可控整流器

scrap [skræp] n. 小片，废料，残余物，打架，剪下来的图片、文章；v. 扔弃，敲碎，拆毁，互相殴打；a. 零碎的，废弃的

scrape [skreip] n. 擦，刮，擦痕，刮擦声，困境；v. 擦，擦掉，擦伤，刮掉，挖成，刮出刺耳声

~ and repaint 刮擦与重漆

~ off 刮掉，擦去

scraper ['skreipə] n. 刮刀，平土机，铲土机，刮的人

~ blade 刮刀，刮土铲

~ ring 刮油环

~ ring for stuffing box 填料函刮刀环，填料箱刮油环

scratch [skrætʃ] n. 乱写，刮擦声，抓痕，擦伤；v. 乱涂，勾抹掉，擦，刮，搔抓，挖出，发刮擦声；a. 打草稿用的，凑合的

~ off 刮掉，刮下，划掉，速写

screen [skri:n] n. 屏，银幕，筛子，掩蔽

513

物，屏风；v. 掩蔽，包庇，放映，拍摄，筛

~ bulkhead 轻舱壁

~ operation locking 屏操作锁定

~ protect film 屏幕保护膜

screw [skru:] n. 螺丝钉，螺旋，螺杆，螺孔，螺旋桨，吝啬鬼；v. 调节，旋，转动，加强，压榨，强迫，鼓舞

~ anchor 螺形地锚

~ aperture 螺桨拱

~ arbor 螺旋轴，螺杆

~ base lamp holder 螺口灯座

~ base receptable 螺口插座灯座

~ block 螺旋顶高器，千斤顶

~ bolt 螺栓

~ cap 螺帽

~ compressor 螺杆式压缩机

~ connection 螺纹接口，螺旋接头，螺钉连接，螺钉接头

~ down 用螺钉钉住，拧紧，使降低价格，束缚

~ driver 螺丝刀，螺钉起子，改锥

~ driver with iron handle 铁柄螺丝刀

~ driver with wooden handle 木柄螺丝刀

~ effect 螺丝效应

~ extractor 螺杆旋出器，起螺丝器

~ fuse 螺旋熔断器

~ gauge 螺纹规

~ gear 螺旋齿轮，斜齿齿轮

~ head 螺钉头，螺丝头

~ head bulb 螺口灯泡，螺丝头灯泡

~ home 拧到头，拧紧

~ hook (带)螺旋(的)钩，有钩螺旋

~ in 拧入，旋进

~ into 划桨时上体内倾

~ jack 螺旋千斤顶

~ joint 螺纹套管接头，螺管接头

~ luffing 螺杆变幅

~ mandrel 螺旋心轴，丝杆

~ pitch gauge 螺距规

~ plate 搓丝板，板牙，螺丝模

~ plug 螺旋塞，安全塞，螺旋接线柱

~ plug fuse 螺塞熔断器，螺旋式熔断器，旋入式保险丝，旋入式熔断器，旋塞式熔断器

~ propeller 螺旋桨

~ propeller ship 螺旋推进船

~ pump 螺杆泵，螺旋泵

~ receptacle 螺旋插座

~ rod 螺旋杆，丝杆

~ shaft 艉轴，尾轴，螺杆轴，螺丝杆，螺旋桨轴，螺旋轴，推进器轴

~ shaft tube 艉轴管，艉轴套

~ socket 螺旋口插座

~ steering gear 螺杆操舵装置，螺旋操舵装置

~ stem 螺杆中心轴

~ tap 螺丝攻

~ template 螺纹样板

~ thread micrometer 螺旋测微计，螺纹千分尺，螺旋千分尺

~ tip 蜗杆梢

~ type fuse 螺旋式熔断器

~ type refrigerating compressor 螺杆式制冷压缩机

screw-down 压下机构

~ non-return valve 截止止回阀，螺旋止回阀

scribe [skraib] n. 划线器，抄写员，作者；v. 用划线器划，担任抄写员

scriber ['skraibə] n. 划线器，描绘标记的用具

scrim [skrim] *n.* 网状织物，平纹棉麻织物

scroll [skrəul] *n.* 卷轴，卷形物，名册；*v.* (使)成卷形，卷起
~ saw 钢丝锯

scrub [skrʌb] *n.* 洗擦，擦净，擦洗者，灌木，丛林地，矮小的人(或动物)；*v.* 洗擦，擦净，擦洗，使(气体)净化；*a.* 次等的，矮小的，临时凑合的

scrubber ['skrʌbə] *n.* 洗涤器，洗刷者

SCS (sequence control system) 顺序控制系统

scuba ['sku:bə] *n.* 水肺，水中呼吸器，配套水下呼吸器
~ diving 水肺潜水，戴呼吸器潜水
~ driver 轻潜水员，水肺潜水员
~ equipment 重装
~ gloves 潜水手套
~ tank 水中呼吸氧气瓶，气瓶

scuff [skʌf] *n.* 磨损之处，拖着脚走；*v.* (使)磨损，践踏，以足擦地，拖足而行

sculler ['skʌlə] *n.* 摇桨，划船者，比赛用的小船

scullery ['skʌləri] *n.* 洗涤室，碗碟洗涤处

scullion ['skʌljən] *n.* 帮厨，小厨，卑鄙的人

scum [skʌm] *n.* 浮渣，浮垢，糟粕，泡沫，铁渣；*v.* 将浮渣去除掉，产生泡沫，被浮渣覆盖
~ dish (锅炉)表面排污盘，浮渣盘
~ hole 出渣口
~ valve 上部排污阀，上排污阀
~ washing 滤泥洗涤

scupper ['skʌpə] *n.* 甲板上的排水孔，排水口，出水口；*v.* 破坏，摧毁，故意沉船，破坏计划
~ board 挡水板

~ pipe (甲板)排水管
~ plug 排水口栓，排水孔栓，船用堵漏塞
~ shoot 舷侧排水孔
~ shutter 排水孔盖，排水孔的堵头

scuttle ['skʌtl] *n.* 舷窗，天窗，舱室小孔，煤桶，急速逃走；*v.* 急促地跑，急忙撤退，凿沉，毁坏

sea [si:] *n.* 海，海洋，海域，水域，大浪，大量，许多，似海的东西，广阔，无限，浩瀚
~ area 海域
~ articles 船装运货，舶来货
~ bottom 海底
~ captain 船长 ‖ *Syn.* captain 船长；master 船长；skipper 船长
~ chest 海箱，海底门，海底阀箱
~ chest discharge valve 海箱排放阀
~ clutter 海面杂乱回波，海面干扰
~ coal 海运煤
~ connection 通海连接头
~ connection valve 通海连接阀
~ cook 船上厨师
~ inlet value 海水吸入阀，进水阀
~ island 海岛
~ keeping performance 耐波性
~ margin 海上功率裕度
~ state 海面状况，海况
~ state monitoring system 海况监测系统
~ suction valve 通海阀 ‖ *Syn.* sea valve 海水阀，通海阀
~ term 航海用语，水手用语
~ train 海上运输队
~ trial 海上试验，海上试航，试航
~ trial condition 试航条件
~ trial for life boat 救生艇试航试验

~ trial program 试航方案

~ valve chest 通海阀箱，海阀箱

~ vessel 航海船只，海船

~ wall 海堤，防波堤

~ water 海水

~ water circulating pump 海水循环泵

~ water cooling pump 海水冷却泵

~ water cooling system 海水冷却系统

~ water desalination 海水淡化，海水脱盐

~ water desalination plant 海水脱盐装置，海水淡化装置 ‖ *Syn*. sea water desalting plant 海水脱盐装置，海水淡化装置

~ water evaporator 海水蒸发器

~ water heater 海水加热器

~ water inlet 海水入口

~ water outlet 海水出口

~ water pump 海水泵

~ water service system 海水系统

~ water strainer 海水过滤器

~ water system 海水系统

seafarer ['si:feərə] *n*. 海员，船员，航海家

seagoing ['si:gəuiŋ] *a*. 适于远航的，出海的，用于航海的，从事航海的

~ ability 适航性，航海性能

~ catamaran 双体海船

~ dredger 自航式挖泥船

~ freighter 远洋货轮

~ pipeline 海底油管

~ ship 远洋船，远洋航轮 ‖ *Syn*. seagoing vessel 海船

~ tanker 海洋油轮

~ tender 海洋供应船

~ tug 海洋拖轮，远洋拖轮

seal [si:l] *n*. 封铅，封条，印，图章，密封，海豹，海豹毛皮；*v*. 封，密封

~ cartridge 密封盒

~ coat 封闭层，封闭底漆

~ plate 密封板，密封片

~ ring 密封圈

~ test 密封试验

~ water 密封水

sealant ['si:lənt] *n*. 密封胶，密封剂

sealed [si:ld] *v*. (seal 的过去式和过去分词) 封，密封；*a*. 未知的，密封的

~ container 密闭集装箱，密封容器，气密封罐

~ cooling system 封闭式冷却系统，密封冷却系统

~ cowling 密封罩

~ housing of evaporative emission determination (SHED) 密闭室测定蒸发排放物法

sealing ['si:liŋ] *n*. 密封件，密封，封闭，猎捕海豹业；*v*. (seal 的 ing 形式) 封，密封

~ agent 封口剂，密封剂，密封涂料

~ arrangement 围护设备，密封装置

~ cover 密封盖

~ fins 密封翅片

~ flange 密封法兰，密封凸缘

~ lead 封口铅

~ medium 密封介质，密封用物质，焊接剂

~ pliers 封口钳，铅印钳，封印钳

~ ring 密封环，密封圈

~ ring bushing 密封环衬套

~ ring for stuffing boxe 填料箱密封环

~ strip 围堰带

~ surface 瓶口，封接面

seam [si:m] *n.* 接缝，线缝，缝合线，衔接口，伤疤，裂痕，皱纹，层；*v.* 缝合，接合，焊合，使留下伤痕，裂开，发生裂痕

~ welding 缝焊，线焊接，滚焊

~ width 卷边宽度，卷边高度

seaman ['si:mən] *n.* (*pl.* seamen) 海员，水手，水兵

seamanship ['si:mənʃip] *n.* 航海技术，船舶驾驶术，船艺

seamless ['si:mlis] *a.* 无缝合线的，无伤痕的

~ connection 无缝连接

~ mild steel 无缝低碳钢

~ pipe 无缝钢管 ‖ *Syn.* seamless steel pipe 无缝钢管

seaport ['si:pɔ:t] *n.* 海港，港口城市，港口都市

search [sə:tʃ] *n.* 搜查，调查，探求；*v.* 搜索，搜寻，探求，调查

~ and recovery 搜索与寻回

~ and rescue (SAR) 搜索救援，搜救

~ and rescue boat 搜索救援船只，搜救船只

~ and rescue transponder (SART) 搜救(雷达)应答器

~ around 查究

~ light 探照灯

~ the person 搜身

~ unit 搜索单元，搜索装置

~ warrant 搜索证

searching ['sə:tʃiŋ] *n.* 搜索，搜寻；*v.* (search 的 ing 形式) 搜查，找寻；*a.* 搜索的，彻底的，透彻的

~ party 搜索队

~ path 搜索路径

searchlight ['sə:tʃlait] *n.* 探照灯

seasick ['si:sik] *a.* 晕船的

seasickness ['si:ˌsiknis] *n.* 晕船

season ['si:zn] *n.* 季节，季，活动期；*v.* (使)适应，(使)适用，调味

seasonal ['si:zənl] *a.* 季节性的，周期性的，随季节变化的

~ variation 季节性变动，季节性波动

seat [si:t] *n.* 座，座位，底座，支座，所在地，场所，席位，票；*v.* 使就座，使就职，使…固定在位置上，装上

~ belt 座椅安全带

seawards ['si:wədz] *ad.* 向海地

seawater ['si:ˌwɔ:tə(r)] *n.* 海水

~ pump 海水泵

seaway ['si:wei] *n.* 海路，海上航道，船只在海上航行，波涛汹涌的海面

seaweed ['si:wi:d] *n.* 海草，海藻

seaworthiness ['si:wə:ðinis] *n.* 适于航海，适航性

seaworthy ['si:wə:ði] *a.* 适于航海的，经得起航海的

~ packing 海运包装，耐航包装

secant ['si:kənt] *n.* 割线，正割；*a.* 切的，割的，交叉的

second ['sekənd] *n.* 秒，片刻，瞬间，第二名，第二者，第二人，助手，次货，二等品；*v.* 支持，赞成；*a.* 第二的，交替的，另一个，又一个；*num.* 第二

~ class load 二级负荷

~ cook 二厨，第二厨师

~ electrician 电机员

~ energy 二次能量

~ engineer 大管轮，二车，二轨

~ mate 二副 ‖ *Syn.* second officer (舰艇)二副

517

~ motion shaft 第二运动轴
~ phase (=phase 2) 第2阶段(即产生火焰阶段)
~ precombustion 二次预燃
~ stage 第二级
~ steward 第二服务员

secondary ['sekəndəri] n. 副手，代理人，感应线圈，行星，卫星；a. 次要的，二级的，中级的，第二的，副的，劣等的，感应电流的，次级电流的
~ air 二次空气
~ air conditioning system 二次空调系统
~ arc current 二次电弧电流
~ armament 辅助兵器，副炮
~ barrier 二级屏蔽
~ battery 二次电池
~ circuit 次级回路，二次回路
~ coil 次级线圈，二级线圈
~ coolant 二次冷却剂
~ data 次级资料，二次资料
~ distribution link 次级分布线路
~ distribution network 次级分布网络，二级配电网络
~ distribution system 次级分布系统，二级配电系统
~ equipment 二次设备
~ explosion 二次爆炸
~ flow 二次流
~ injection 二次喷射
~ member 次要杆件
~ memory 辅助存储器
~ network 二次侧电力网，二次网络
~ processing 二次处理，二次加工
~ refining 二次精炼
~ refrigerant 二次制冷剂
~ storage device 二次存储设备

~ structure 次级结构，二次结构
~ treatment 二次处理
~ voltage 二次电压
~ winding 次级线圈，次级绕组，二级绕组，复卷绕组
~ wiring drawing 二次接线图

secondly ['sekəndli] ad. 其次，第二

section ['sekʃən] n. 部分，断片，部件，零件，段落，小队，分队，节，项，区域，地域，横断面，截面；v. 切开，切片，切割，画剖面
~ board 分配电板，区配电板
~ view 剖视，剖视图

sectional ['sekʃənəl] n. 组合式家具；a. 组装的，拼凑成的，搭配组合的，断面的，截面的，剖面的，局部的，地区的
~ loaded antenna 分段加载天线

sectionalize ['sekʃənəlaiz] v. 使具有地方性

sectionalized ['sekʃənəlaizd] v. (sectionalize 的过去式和过去分词) 使具有地方性；a. 分段的，分块的，划分的，分解的
~ double busbar with bypass 带旁路的分段双母线
~ machine manufacture 通用机械制造
~ panel 分区面板，分段屏
~ single busbar with bypass 带旁路的分段单母线

sector ['sektə] n. 部分，部门，地区，象限，扇区，扇形；v. 使分成部分，把…分成扇形

secure [si'kjuə] v. 保证，保障，保护，紧闭，确信；a. 安全的，可靠的，稳固的，紧闭的，保险的，放心的，无虑的

securely [si'kjuəli] ad. 牢固地，安全地

securing [si'kjuəriŋ] n. 固定；v. (secure 的 ing 形式) 保证，保障，保护，紧闭，确信；a. 固定的，固定住的，作为固定用的
~ key 定位销，定位键
~ ring 紧固环，锁紧环

security [si'kjuəriti] n. 安全，安全设施，保安措施，防卫措施，保护程度，警卫，保障，担保，保证
~ alerting system 安全警报系统
~ clearance 安全许可
~ design 安全设计
~ drill 安全演练
~ feature 安全特性
~ incident 安全事故
~ isolation 安全隔离
~ lamp 安全灯
~ level 安全级，保密级
~ log 安全日志
~ measure 安全措施
~ operation of the ship 船舶安全操作
~ patrol 安全巡逻
~ regulation 治安条例
~ strip 固定板条
~ threats 安全威胁
~ transformer 安全变压器

sediment ['sedimənt] n. 沉积，沉积物，沉淀物

sedimentation [ˌsedimen'teiʃən] n. 沉淀，沉降

seek [si:k] v. 寻找，探寻，追求，谋求

seeker ['si:kə] n. 搜索者，探求者，自导头，自导导弹

seepage ['si:pidʒ] n. 渗漏，渗液，渗流，渗漏量

segment ['segmənt] n. 段，段落，环节，片断，线段，弓形，扇形；v. 分割，切割，划分
~ block stopper for servomotor 伺服电机扇形凸块

segregate ['segrigeit] v. 隔离,分离,分开；a. 分开的，孤立的

segregated ['segrigeitid] v. (segregate 的过去式和过去分词) 隔离，分离，分开；a. 分开的，被隔离的
~ ballast water tank system 专用压载水舱系统
~ ballast tank (SBT) 分隔压载舱，专用压载舱，隔离压载舱

segregation [ˌsegri'geiʃən] n. 分离，隔离，种族隔离
~ of goods 货物分离

seine [sein] n. 围网；v. 用围网捕鱼

seiner ['seinə] n. 围网渔船，使用围网捕鱼的人 ‖ **Syn**. trawler 拖网渔船，拖网捕鱼者，拖网渔民

seize [si:z] v. 抓住，逮住，夺取，没收，查封

seizing ['si:ziŋ] n. 抓，夺，捆绑，扣押；v. (seize 的 ing 形式) 抓住，逮住，夺取，没收，查封
~ end 捆头
~ line 缠扎绳，缠扎用油麻细绳
~ load 启动负荷
~ mark 抱轴伤痕，卡挤伤痕，粘附伤痕
~ rope 扎用麻绳
~ strand 卷缠钢缆用的镀锌细钢丝绳
~ stuff 缠填材料

seizure ['si:ʒə] v. 抓，捉，没收，查封，夺取

select [si'lekt] *v.* 选择，挑选，选拔；*a.* 精选的

selecting [si'lektiŋ] *n.* 选择；*v.* (select 的 ing 形式) 选择，挑选，选拔

~ switch for types of operation 操作方式选择开关

selection [si'lekʃən] *n.* 选择，挑选，选集，精选品

selective [si'lektiv] *a.* 选择的，选择性的

~ control 选择性控制

~ corrosion 选择性腐蚀，局部腐蚀作用

~ release 选择性释放

~ tripping 选择断路，选择解扣

selectivity [silek'tiviti] *n.* 选择，选择性

selector [si'lektə] *n.* 选择者，选择器

~ channel 选择通道

~ switch 选线开关

~ valve 选择阀，选择活门

self [self] *n.* 自己，自我，本性，本质，本人，私心；*v.* 使近亲繁殖，自花受精；*a.* 同一的，纯净的，单一的

self-acting 自作用的，自力的

~ injector 自动喷射器，自控式喷油器

~ valve 自动阀

self-adjusting 自调节的，自调整的

~ seal 自紧密封

self-alignment 自动对准，自对准，自动定心

self-checking 自检验的，自校验的

~ function 自检验功能

~ system 自检验系统

self-cleaning 自清洗的，自洁的

~ centrifuge 自洁式离心机

~ filter 自洁式过滤器

~ separator 自洁式分离器

self-closing 自关闭的，自闭合的

~ valve 自闭阀，自锁阀

self-contained 成套的，设备齐全的，独立的，沉默寡言的

~ air conditioner 成套空调机组

~ air conditioning system 成套空调系统

~ breathing apparatus (SCBA) 自持呼吸器，自给式呼吸器

self-control 自我控制，自制，克制，自我克制

self-cooled 自冷却的，自冷的

~ transformator 自冷式变压器

self-detection 自检测，自诊断

self-diagnosis 自诊断

self-discharge 自放电，自卸载

self-discharging 自放电的，自卸载的

~ bulk carrier 自卸载散货船

self-excitation 自励，自激

~ process 自激过程

self-excited 自我刺激的，自激的，自励的

~ constant voltage AC generator 自励恒压交流发电机

~ oscillation 自激振荡，自励振荡

self-exciting 自励的，自激的

~ alternator 自励交流发电机

~ dynamo 自励发电机

~ winding 自激绕组

self-extinction 自消灭，自消失，自消

~ of arc 自消弧

self-extinguishing 自熄火，自动灭火，自熄性材料

~ arcing 自熄电弧

~ material 自动灭火材料，自熄材料

self-ignition 自发火，自燃

~ point 自燃点

self-induced 自感应的，自感的，自诱导的

～EMF 自感电动势
self-loading 自行载入，自动装卸
　～and unloading system 自动装卸系统
self-locking 自锁的
　～bracket 自锁托架
　～mechanism 自锁机构
　～valve 自锁阀
self-operated 自力式，自控式
　～flow controller 自力式流量控制器
　～thermostatic controller 自动调温器
self-positioning 自动定位的
　～system 自动定位系统
self-priming 自充满的，自吸的
　～centrifugal pump 自吸式离心泵
　～pump 自吸泵
self-propulsion 自力推进，自推进，自驱动
　～test 自推进试验
self-regulation 自动调节，自调节
self-regulating 自调节的，自控的
self-repair 自修复
self-righting 自纠正的，自扶正的
　～liferaft 自动扶正救生筏
self-stripping 自冲洗的，自清洗的
　～unit 自冲洗装置，自清洗装置
self-sustained 自我维持的，支持的
　～oscillation 自持振荡
self-sustaining 自立的，自谋生活的
　～gear 自动制动机构
　～ship 自备起重设备的集装箱船，有装卸设备的集装箱船 ‖ *Syn*. self-sustaining vessel 自有装卸机械的船舶
　～structure 自稳结构，自维持结构
self-synchronizing 自同步的
　～method 自同步方法
self-tapping 自攻的
　～screw 自攻螺丝，自攻螺钉，自攻钉

self-tensioning 自张紧的
　～winch 自调缆绞车
self-test 自检，自测试
self-tuning 自校正的，自调节的
　～control 自校正控制
self-ventilated 自通风，自通风式
　～type motor 自通风式电动机
selsyn ['selsin] *n*. 自动同步机
　～receiver 自整角接收机
　～train 自同步传动装置，自整角传动装置
　～transmitter 自整角发送机，自同步发送机
semaphore ['seməfɔ:] *n*. 旗语
semi ['semi] *n*. 半独立式住宅，半挂车；*pref*. 一半的，部分的，不完全的
semi-automatic 半自动的
　～welding 半自动焊接
semi-balanced 半平衡的
　～rudder 半平衡舵
semi-built-up 半组合的
　～crankshaft 半组合曲轴
semi-closed 半封闭的，半密闭的，半闭的 ‖ *Syn*. semi-enclosed 半封闭的；semi-hermetic 半封闭的
　～circuit rebreather 半密闭式循环呼吸器
　～control 半闭环控制
　～system 半封闭系统
semi-duplex 半双工
　～operation 半双工操作
semi-enclosed 半封闭的 ‖ *Syn*. semi-closed 半封闭的，半密闭的，半闭的；semi-hermetic 半封闭的
　～compressor 半封闭式压缩机
semi-floating 半浮动的，半浮的

521

~ piston pin 半浮式活塞销 ‖ full floating piston pin 全浮式活塞销

semi-hermetic 半封闭的 ‖ *Syn.* semi-closed 半封闭的，半密闭的，半闭的；semi-enclosed 半封闭的

~ refrigerating compressor unit 半封闭制冷压缩机机组

semi-membrane 半膜(动)

~ tank 半薄膜槽

semi-submerged 半潜的

~ drilling rig 半潜式钻机

~ propeller 半潜式螺旋桨

~ ship launching 平地造船法

~ ship 半潜式船

~ shipway 半潜式造船台

semiconductor ['semikən'dʌktə] *n.* 半导体

~ air conditioner 半导体空调

~ refrigerating plant 半导体制冷装置

~ refrigeration 半导体制冷

~ refrigerator 半导体制冷机

semicircle ['semisə:kl] *n.* 半圆，半圆形，半圆物，半圆形的周长

semidiameter ['semidai'æmitə] *n.* 半径

semipermanent [ˌsemi'pə:mənənt] *a.* 非永久的，暂时的

SENC (system electronic navigational chart) 系统电子航行海图

send [send] *v.* 送，寄，发送，推送，驱使，派遣，打发

sender ['sendə] *n.* 发报机，发射机，发送机，送话器

sending ['sendiŋ] *n.* 发送，派遣，发射；*v.* (send 的 ing 形式) 送，寄，发送，推送，驱使，派遣，打发

~ and receiving device 发送接收装置

senior ['si:njə] *n.* 年长者，上级，中学或大学的四年级学生；*a.* 年长的，资格较老的，地位较高的，高级的

~ officer 高级军官，高级职员

~ official 高级官员

sense [sens] *n.* 官能，感觉，直觉，判断力，见识，含义，意义，理性；*v.* 感到，理解，领会，认识，自动检测

~ line 感应线，读出线

~ resistor 感应电阻

~ response 读出响应，检测响应

sensibility [ˌsensi'biliti] *n.* 敏感性，灵敏度，感光性，感光度

sensible ['sensəbl] *a.* 有感觉的，可觉察的，明智的，有判断力的

sensing ['sensiŋ] *n.* 感觉；*v.* (sense 的 ing 形式) 感到，理解，领会，认识，自动检测

~ element 传感元件，敏感元件，灵敏元件

sensitive ['sensitiv] *a.* 敏感的，灵敏的，感觉的

sensitivity [ˌsensi'tiviti] *n.* 敏感，灵敏度，灵敏性

~ of smoke detector 烟雾探测器灵敏度

~ to heat 热敏度，热热灵敏度

~ to light 光敏度，感光灵敏度

~ to smoke 烟雾敏度，感烟雾灵敏度

sensor ['sensə] *n.* 传感器，灵敏元件

separable ['sepərəbl] *a.* 可分离的，可分的

separate ['sepəreit] *v.* 分开，切断，隔离，脱离，分散，分别，解除；*a.* 区别的，不同的，分开的，分离的，个别的，单独的

~ bilge pump 分离式舱底泵

~ blade 分离叶片，薄根叶片

~ piping system 分离管道系统

~ processor mode 分隔数据处理方式
~ tank 分离池
separated ['sepəreitid] v. (separate 的过去式和过去分词) 分开,切断,隔离,脱离,分散,分别,解除; a. 分开的,分离的,离开的,个别的,单独的
~ layer 分离层
~ time 分离时间
~ water 分离水
separately ['sepərətli] ad. 个别地,分离地
~ controllable 单独可控的
~ driven circuit 分激电路,他励电路 ‖ Syn. separately excited circuit 分激电路,他励电路
~ excited generator 分激发电机,他励发电机
~ ventilated type motor 外通风式电动机
separating ['sepəreitiŋ] v. (separate 的 ing 形式) 分开,切断,隔离,脱离,分散,分别,解除; a. 分开的,分离的,分裂的
~ disc 分离盘
~ filter 分离滤器
~ plate 隔板,分离板,分离盘
~ power 分离能力
separation [,sepə'reiʃən] n. 分离,分开,间隔,分隔区,空隙,解除,退伍
~ system module 分离系统模块
separator ['sepəreitə] n. 分离器,分离装置,离析器,脱脂器,隔离物
sequence ['si:kwəns] n. 顺序,数列,序列,类,相关联; v. 安排顺序,确定成分的顺序 ‖ Syn. order 次序,顺序,秩序,正常状态
~ control 顺序控制 ‖ Syn. sequential control 顺序控制

~ controller 顺序控制器
~ starting and automatic exchange of motors for auxiliary machine and pump 辅机和泵的电动机程序启动和自动转换
~ valve 顺序阀
sequential [si'kwenʃəl] a. 连续的,相续的,有继的,有顺序的,结果的
~ control 顺序控制 ‖ Syn. sequence control 顺序控制
~ control processing 顺序控制处理
~ control start 顺序控制起动
~ data set 顺序数据集
~ decomposition 顺序分解
sequentially [si'kwenʃəli] ad. 继续地,从而,按顺序地
serial ['siəriəl] a. 连续的,连载的,顺序排列的
~ number 序列号,序号,轴号
serial-parallel 串行并行的,串并行的
~ conversion 串并行转换
serializer ['siəriəlaizər] n. 串行(化)器
series ['siəri:z] n. 连续,系列,丛书,级数
~ compensation 串联补偿,级联补偿
~ condenser 串联电容器
~ connection 串联连接
~ excitation 串励
~ field 串激磁场
~ field coil 串联励磁线圈,串联磁场线圈
~ flow control valve 串联式流量调节阀
~ flow turbine 单轴(多缸)汽轮机,串流式透平
~ reactor 串联电抗器,串联电抗器,串联扼流圈
~ regulator 串联调节器

series-parallel 串联并联的，串并联的
　~ starting 串并联启动
　~ connection 串并联连接
　~ connection pump 串并联泵
series-wound 串联的，串绕的，串激的，串励的
　~ dynamo 串励发电机，串联磁电机
　~ generator 串励发电机
　~ motor 串励电动机
serious ['siəriəs] *a.* 严肃的，认真的，严重的
　~ accident 严重事故，重大事故，严重意外 ‖ *Syn*. major accident 重大事故，主要事故；major breakdown 大事故，重大阻断；major failure 严重失效，主要故障
　~ deficiency 严重缺陷
serrate ['serit] *a.* 锯齿状的
serve [sə:v] *v.* 服务，服役，供职，招待，侍候，供应，适合，当仆人
server ['sə:və] *n.* 服务器
　~ motor 伺服电机
service ['sə:vis] *n.* 服务，服务性工作，服役，仪式；*v.* 保养，维修；*a.* 服现役的，服务性的，耐用的，仆人的
　~ engineer 维护工程师
　~ lifetime 使用寿命，使用期
　~ load 操作负载，营运负载，工况负载
　~ manual 维修守则，使用细则
　~ pipe 给水管
　~ pump 辅助泵，值勤泵 ‖ *Syn*. attached pump 辅助泵；auxiliary pump 辅助泵；donkey pump 辅助泵 ‖ *Syn*. duty pump 值勤泵
servo ['sə:vəu] *n.* 伺服，伺服系统

~ actuator 伺服执行机构，伺服拖动装置
~ adjuster 伺服调节器，伺服调整器
~ amplifier 跟踪系统放大器，伺服放大器
~ authority 伺服传动装置工作范围
~ control 伺服控制
~ dynamics 伺服机构动力学
~ lever 伺服杆
~ lock detection 伺服锁定检测
~ mechanism 伺服机构
~ motor 伺服电动机
~ oil accumulator 伺服蓄油器，伺服油液蓄压器
~ oil cylinder 伺服油缸
~ parameter 随动系统参数，跟踪系统参数，伺服系统参数
~ piston 伺服活塞
~ platform 伺服平台
~ press 伺服压力机
~ principle 伺服原理
~ system 伺服系统
~ valve 伺服阀
SES (surface effect ship) 表面效应船
session ['seʃən] *n.* 开会，会议，会议期，学期，集体
set [set] *n.* 一套，一副，一批，装置，接收机，趋势，布景；*v.* 放，置，移动到，提出，树立，规定，调整；*a.* 固定的，规定的，坚决的，固执的，事先做好的
~ bolt 固定螺栓，防松螺栓
~ forth 阐明，宣布，提出，陈列，出发，把(会议等)提前，动身
~ out 出发，启程，开始，装饰，陈列，展示，测定，宣布，陈述

~ point 设定值，给定值，调整点，凝结点 ‖ *Syn*. set value 设定值，给定值，调整点，凝结点

~ screw 固定螺丝，定位螺丝

~ screw piston pin 固定螺钉式活塞销

~ speed 设定速度，给定速度

~ spring 离合杆簧

~ square 三角板

~ stud 定位销

~ up 装配，竖立，架起，升起，设立，创(纪录)，提出，开业 ‖ *Syn*. assemble 装配；build in 安装，固定；fit 安装；fix 安装，(使)固定；fix assemblage 安装；install 安装；mount 安装

~ value 设定值，给定值，调整点，凝结点 ‖ *Syn*. set point 设定值，给定值，调整点，凝结点

setting ['setiŋ] *n*. 安置，安装，(太阳)落山，框架，底座；*v*. (set 的 ing 形式) 放，置，移动到，提出，树立，规定，调整

~ knob 拨针钮，调整钮

~ mark 定位符号，定位线，定位分度线

~ point 设置点

~ position 装置位置，调整位置

~ pressure 设定压力

~ tank 沉降池

~ time 凝固时间，调整时间，定位时间

~ value 设定值，整定值

settle ['setl] *n*. 有背长凳；*v*. 安放，使定居，安排，解决，决定，整理，支付，使平静，下陷，沉淀，澄清

settlement ['setlmənt] *n*. 沉降，解决，和解，建立，结算，协议，转让，殖民，殖民地

settling ['setliŋ] *n*. 沉淀物；*v*. (settle 的 ing 形式) 安放，使定居，安排，解决，决定，整理，支付，使平静，下陷，沉淀，澄清

~ tank 沉淀池

~ time 设定时间，定位时间，调整时间，调定时间，稳定时间，间隔时间，凝固时间

sever ['sevə] *v*. 分离，分开，切断，切开，隔开

sewage ['sju(:)idʒ] *n*. 污水，污物，下水道；*v*. 用污水灌溉，装下水道于

~ holding tank 污水贮槽

~ inlet 污水进口

~ piping system 生活污水排泄系统，污水管路系统

~ pump 污水泵，排泄泵

~ sludge gas 污水污泥气体

~ standard discharge connection 污水标准排放接头

~ system 污水系统

~ tank 污水池，污水槽，化粪池

~ treatment 污水处理

~ treatment device 污水处理装置

~ treatment plant 污水处理装置，污水处理厂 ‖ *Syn*. sewage treatment unit 污水处理装置

~ treatment structure 污水处理结构

~ treatment system 污水处理系统

~ water 污水

sewer ['sjuə] *n*. 排水沟，下水道，缝具，缝纫者

sewerage ['sjuəridʒ] *n*. 排水设备，污水

sextant ['sekstənt] *n*. 六分仪，圆的六分之一

SF$_6$ (sulfur hexafluoride) 六氟化硫

~ circuit breaker 六氟化硫断路器

SFOC (specific fuel oil consumption) 燃油消耗率

shackle ['ʃækl] *n.* 妨碍，U 型钩套，桎梏，枷锁，手铐，脚镣，镣铐；*v.* 妨碍，束缚，桎梏，上镣铐

shade [ʃeid] *n.* 荫，阴暗，阴凉处，图案阴影，黑暗，颜色深浅，遮光物，帘；*v.* 渐变，遮蔽，使阴暗，使渐变，微减

shaded ['ʃeidid] *v.* (shade 的过去式和过去分词) 渐变，遮蔽，使阴暗，使渐变，微减；*a.* 遮蔽的，加深的，有阴影的，颜色较深的
~ pole 罩极，屏蔽极
~ pole relay 屏蔽磁极式继电器

shaft [ʃa:ft] *n.* 柄，轴，机械轴，箭杆，矛柄，一束光，光线，通道，竖井，坑道；*v.* 装柄，装轴
~ bearing 轴承
~ bearing replacer 轴承拆卸器
~ bossing 轴包套，轴包架
~ bracket 轴架
~ bushing 轴衬，轴瓦
~ collar 轴环，轴颈，凸缘，井筒锁口盘，井颈
~ coupling 联轴器
~ eccentricity 轴偏心度
~ generator 轴带发电机，轴传动发电机 ‖ *Syn*. shaft-driven generator 轴带发电机，轴驱发电机
~ horsepower 轴马力
~ journal 轴颈，轴枢
~ liner 轴衬，轴套
~ packing 轴封填料
~ passage 轴隧
~ power 轴功率

~ seal 轴封
~ seal ring 轴密封环
~ sleeve 轴套，密封衬套
~ speed transducer 轴转速传感器
~ tunnel 轴隧
~ turning gear 盘动装置

shaft-driven 轴驱动的，轴驱的，轴带的
~ injection 轴驱喷射
~ generator 轴带发电机，轴驱发电机 ‖ *Syn*. shaft generator 轴带发电机，轴传动发电机

shafting ['ʃa:ftiŋ] *n.* 轴系，制轴材料，欺骗，怠慢，拒绝；*v.* (shaft 的 ing 形式) 装柄，装轴
~ alignment 轴系校中
~ bearing 轴承
~ brake 轴系制动器
~ hanger 传动轴用吊架，轴系吊架
~ transmission efficiency 轴系传动效率

shake [ʃeik] *n.* 摇动，摇，颤抖，震动；*v.* 摇动，摇，颤抖，震动

shaker ['ʃeikə] *n.* 摇动者，搅拌机，混合器

shallow ['ʃæləu] *n.* 浅水处，浅滩，浅水域；*v.* 变浅，变浅薄；*a.* 浅的，浅薄的，微弱的
~ discharge 浅放电
~ end 浅端
~ layer 浅层
~ sea 浅海
~ water 浅水
~ water resistance 浅水阻力

shank [ʃæŋk] *n.* 锚柄，柄部，杆胫，腿骨

shape [ʃeip] n. 外形，形状，形态，体形，形式；v. 制作，定形，使成形，塑造，使符合

shaper ['ʃeipə] n. 牛头刨床，定型模套，整形器，造形者，塑造者

shear [ʃiə] n. 剪，修剪，剪切；v. 剪，折断，扭断
- ~ buckling 剪切屈曲，剪切失稳
- ~ curve 剪切曲线
- ~ diagram 剪力图
- ~ force 剪力
- ~ leg 起重臂，起重机挺杆，剪股
- ~ leg crane 剪臂起重机，动臂起重机，人字吊起重机，双腿式起重机
- ~ pin 安全销，剪切销
- ~ strength 切变强度

shearing ['ʃiəriŋ] n. 剪羊毛，剪取的羊毛；v. (shear 的 ing 形式) 剪，折断，扭断
- ~ force 剪力
- ~ machine 剪床，剪切机，剪板机，剪毛机
- ~ pin 剪切安全销，抗剪销
- ~ stress 剪切应力

sheath [ʃi:θ] n. 鞘，护套，外壳；v. 包，盖

sheave [ʃi:v] n. 滑车轮，槽轮；v. 捆，反桨划船

shed [ʃed] n. 分水岭，棚，小屋，工棚，货棚；v. 流出，发散，散发，脱落，脱皮，摆脱，流下

SHED (sealed housing of evaporative emission determination) 密闭室测定蒸发排放物法

sheer [ʃiə] n. 偏航，偏离方向，舷弧，单锚系泊的船位；v. 偏航，避开，躲避；a. 全然的，纯粹的，绝对的，彻底的，透明的，峻峭的；ad. 完全，全然，峻峭
- ~ aft 艉舷弧，船尾舷弧
- ~ drawing 剖面图
- ~ forward 艏舷弧
- ~ hulk 人字起重机船
- ~ plane 纵剖面
- ~ profile 舷弧侧面图，总剖线，纵剖图，型线图
- ~ strake 舷顶列板，舷缘列板，舷侧厚列板
- ~ stress 剪切应力

sheet [ʃi:t] n. (一)片，(一)张，薄片，板，帆脚索，被单，被褥；v. 展开风帆，铺盖，使成片；a. 片状的
- ~ iron 铁皮
- ~ metal forming machine 金属板成型机，板料成形机
- ~ metal relay house 金属薄板继电器室
- ~ metal part 钣金件
- ~ metal working machine 金属板材加工机
- ~ molding compound (玻璃钢)片状模塑料

shelf [ʃelf] n. 架子，搁板，搁板状物，暗礁，沙洲，浅滩
- ~ coil air cooling type freezer 鼓风搁架冻结装置，吹风搁架冻结装置

shell [ʃel] n. 贝壳，壳，外形，炮弹；v. 去壳，脱落，剥落，脱壳，炮轰，设定命令行解释器的位置
- ~ and tube condenser 管壳式冷凝器
- ~ and tube cooler 管壳式冷却器
- ~ and tube heat exchanger 管壳式换热器
- ~ condenser 壳式冷凝器
- ~ expansion plan 外板展开图
- ~ extractor 拔钉钩，拉子钩
- ~ plating 船壳板

~ temperature 壳体温度

~ vacuum 壳层真空

~ zone 壳状区

shelter ['ʃeltə] *n*. 掩蔽处，掩蔽，保护，庇护所，掩体；*v*. 庇护，保护，遮挡，躲避，隐匿，寻求保护

sheltered ['ʃeltəd] *v*. (shelter 的过去式和过去分词) 庇护，保护，遮挡，躲避，隐匿，寻求保护；*a*. 掩蔽的，隐蔽的，受保护的，受庇护的

~ waters 隐蔽水域

shield [ʃi:ld] *n*. 防护物，护罩，盾，盾状物；*v*. 保护，防护，遮蔽

~ arc welding 封闭电弧焊

~ cap 防护罩

~ earthing 屏蔽接地

shielding ['ʃi:ldiŋ] *v*. (shield 的 ing 形式) 保护，防护，遮蔽；*a*. 防护的，屏蔽的

~ angle 屏蔽角

~ can 隔离罩

~ cable 屏蔽电缆

shift [ʃift] *n*. 移动，轮班，移位，变化，办法，手段；*v*. 替换，转换，转移，移动，改变，移转，推卸，推托，变速

~ spanner 活动扳手，活络扳手，换挡扳手

~ the blame to other shoulders 推卸责任给别人

~ to 转向

~ transformation 推移变换，移位变换

shifting [ʃiftiŋ] *n*. 移位，转移，偏移，狡猾；*v*. (shift 的 ing 形式) 替换，转换，转移，移动，改变，移转，推卸，推托，变速

~ board 止移板，隔舱板

~ coil voltage regulator 移圈式调压器

~ fork 齿轮换挡叉，拨叉

~ lever 变速杆

~ lever boot 变速杆(保护)罩

~ ring 调整圈

~ spanner 活络扳手

shim [ʃim] *n*. 薄垫片；*v*. 用垫片填

ship [ʃip] *n*. 船，舰，海船，三桅船，全体船员，运气；*v*. 装船，乘船，使上船，航运，载运，雇佣船员，在船上工作，离开

~ board sewage 船上污水

~ bottom paint for steel ship 钢壳船底漆

~ breadth 船宽

~ breaker 包拆废船的人

~ breaking 废船拆卸业

~ broker 船舶经纪人，经营船舶买卖的代理人

~ chandler 船具商

~ communication station 船舶通信电台，船舶通信站 ‖ *Syn*. onboard communication station 船上通信电台

~ complement identification number 船舶补充识别号，船舶补充识别码

~ construction 舰艇建造，船舶建造

~ control center 船舶控制中心

~ depth 船深

~ direction finding station 船舶无线电定位台，舰船测向站

~ draft mark 船舶吃水标志

~ elevator 升船机，浮船式链斗升运机，浮动式搬运机

~ engine room 船舶机舱

~ engine room fire detection 船舶机舱火灾探测

~ fitter 船体装配工，造船装配工

~ flooding valve 沉船阀

~ form 船型，船体线型
~ hull 船体
~ hydrodynamics 船舶流体动力学
~ hydrodynamics laboratory 船舶水动力学研究室
~ identification number 船舶识别号，船舶识别码
~ jack 船舶起重器
~ main switchboard 船舶主配电盘
~ manoeuvrability 船舶操纵性
~ management 船舶管理
~ manoeuvring 船舶操纵
~ mechanical ventilation 船舶机械通风
~ motion 船舶运动
~ natural ventilation 船舶自然通风
~ registry 船舶登记
~ report 船舶报告
~ rules and regulations 船舶规章制度，船舶规范与规则
~ search manoeuvre 舰艇搜索机动
~ security alert system (SSAS) 船舶安全警报系统
~ security assessment (SSA) 船舶保安评估
~ security assessment report 船舶保安评估报告
~ security equipment 船舶保安设备
~ security inspection 船舶安全检查
~ security measure 船舶保安措施
~ security officer (SSO) 船舶保安员
~ security plan (SSP) 船舶保安计划
~ security record 船舶安全记录
~ security survey 船舶安全检验
~ speed 船速
~ stabilizer 船舶稳定器，船舶减摇装置 ‖ *Syn*. ship stabilizing gear 船舶稳定器，船舶减摇装置
~ station 船舶站
~ steel 造船钢
~ structure and arrangement 船舶结构与布置
~ survey 船舶检验
~ surveyor 船舶检验员，船舶检查员
~ system 船舶系统 ‖ *Syn*. marine system 船舶系统
~ tanks 油船
~ type 船型
~ ventilation 船舶通风
ship-to-ship 自船至船上的，船对船的，船际的
 ~ communication 船际通信
 ~ distress alerting 船际遇险警报
 ~ transfer operation 船际转移操作，船际传送操作
ship-to-shore 自船至岸上的，船对岸的，船岸的
 ~ communication 船岸通信
 ~ connection 船岸连接
 ~ distress alerting 船岸遇险警报
 ~ pipe line 船岸输油管
 ~ radio 船岸无线电
 ~ submarine line 舰对岸海底线路
ship's 船舶的
 ~ light control system 船舶灯光控制系统
 ~ power station 船舶电站
 ~ pump 船用泵 ‖ *Syn*. marine pump 船用泵
shipboard ['ʃipbɔːd] *n*. 舷侧，船侧，船帮，在船上的状态，船；*a*. 船上的
 ~ coaxial cable 船用同轴电缆
 ~ incineration 船上焚烧

~ incinerator 船用焚烧炉
~ interrogator 船只询问器
~ low smoke toxic-free cable 船用低烟无毒电缆
~ Marine Pollution Emergency Plan (SMPEP) 船上海洋污染应急计划
~ Oil Pollution Emergency Plan (SOPEP) 船舶油污应急计划
~ pair-twisted telephone cable 船用对绞式电话电缆
~ power cable 船用电力电缆
~ technical mannual 船舶技术手册,船舶技术规范,船舶技术条令
~ telecommunication cable 船用通信电缆

shipborne ['ʃipbɔ:n] *a.* 用船装运的,为船运设计的,船用的

shipbuilder ['ʃip,bildə(r)] *n.* 造船专家,造船工程师

shipbuilding ['ʃipbildiŋ] *n.* 造船
~ industry 造船工业
~ shapes 造船型材

shipmaster ['ʃip,ma:stə] *n.* 船长

shipment ['ʃipmənt] *n.* 装船,发货,运货,送货,发货量,载货量
~ date 装运期,装船日期

shipowner ['ʃipəunə] *n.* 船主,船东
shipowners' 船东的
~ Mutual Protection and Indemnity Association 船东互保与保赔协会

shipper ['ʃipə] *n.* 承运商,托运人,发货人

shipping ['ʃipiŋ] *n.* 海运,运送,航行,运输船只,船舶吨数,船只总数,船舶运输业,航运业;*v.* (ship 的 ing 形式) 装船,乘船,使上船,航运,载运,雇佣船员,在船上工作,离开

~ agency 航运公司,船舶代理
~ agent 运货代理商
~ container 集装箱,装运容器,货运包装
~ document 船务文件
~ schedule 船期表,送货排程
~ space 船位,舱位,装货场所,订舱

ships [ʃips] *n.* (ship 的复数) 船,舰,海船,三桅船,全体船员,运气;*v.* (ship 的第三人称单数) 装船,乘船,使上船,航运,载运,雇佣船员,在船上工作,离开
~ of non-parties 非缔约国船舶

shipway ['ʃipwei] *n.* 船架,造船台

shipwright ['ʃiprait] *n.* 造船工人,造船木匠

shipyard ['ʃipja:d] *n.* 造船厂,造船所,船坞

shiver ['ʃivə] *n.* 发抖,颤抖,碎块,破片;*v.* 颤抖,打碎,碎裂,(由于风的力量)颤动

shoal [ʃəul] *n.* 浅滩,沙洲,鱼群;*v.* (使)变浅,驶入(浅水等),(鱼等)群集;*a.* 水浅的

shock [ʃɔk] *n.* 震动,打击,冲突,休克,突击;*v.* 使震动,使休克,使受电击,震惊,震动,吓人;*a.* 蓬乱的,浓密的
~ absorber 减震器,缓冲器,阻尼器
~ absorption 缓冲,减震,消震
~ condition 激波条件
~ cord 减震绳
~ load 冲击荷重,振动荷载,突加荷载
~ loss 冲击损失,激波损失
~ test 冲击试验
~ test machine 冲击试验台

shoot [ʃu:t] *n.* 射击，发射，摄影，急流；*v.* 射击，投射，伸出，拍摄，用完，挥出，注射，使爆炸

~ a bolt 关上或打开插销

shoot-through 贯通，穿透

~ current 贯通电流，穿透电流

shop [ʃɔp] *n.* 商店，车间，工厂，办事处；*v.* 买东西，购货

~ primer 预涂底漆

~ test 车间试验，工厂试验

shore [ʃɔ:] *n.* 岸，海滨，支撑柱；*v.* 支撑，支持

~ connecting cable 岸边连接电缆 ‖ *Syn.* shore connection cable 岸边连接电缆

~ connection 通岸接头

~ connection box 岸电箱 ‖ *Syn.* shore power connection box 岸电箱

~ diving 岸潜

~ effect 海岸效应

~ power supply 岸电

~ reception facility 岸边接收设施 ‖ *Syn.* shore side reception facility 岸边接收设施

~ rights 停泊权

~ steam supply connection pipe 岸接供气管

~ tackle 岸吊

shore-to-ship 自岸至船上的，岸对船的，岸船的

~ communication 岸舰通信

~ distress alerting 岸舰遇险警报

shoreline [ˈʃɔ:lain] *n.* 海岸线

short [ʃɔ:t] *n.* 简略，短路，短裤；*a.* 短的，矮的，不足的，不够的，弱的，浅薄的，简短的；*ad.* 突然，缺乏，不足

~ break 短暂断开

~ circuit 短路 ‖ *Ant.* open circuit 断路

~ circuit capability 短路能力

~ circuit capacity 短路容量

~ circuit characteristic 短路特性

~ circuit current 短路电流

~ circuit current protection 短路电流保护

~ circuit impulse current 短路冲击电流

~ circuit point 短路点

~ circuit protection 短路保护

~ circuit reactance 短路电抗

~ circuit ring 短路环

~ circuit stability 短路稳定性

~ circuit torque 短路转矩

~ circuit voltage 短路电压

~ cycle 短周期

~ rubber boot 短胶靴

~ term 短期

~ term planning 短期规划

~ term reliability 短期可靠性

~ time 短时

~ time delay 短时延迟

~ time delay loading 短时延迟加载

~ time duty system 短时工作制，短时运行制

~ time Fourier transform 短时傅里叶变换

~ time horizon coordination 短时程协调

~ time test 短时试验

~ trouble 短路故障

shortage [ˈʃɔ:tidʒ] *n.* 短缺，不足，缺乏，匮乏

~ of fresh water 淡水短缺

~ of refrigerant 制冷剂短缺

~ of water 缺水

shortcut [ˈʃɔ:tkʌt] *n.* 捷径，近路

shorten ['ʃɔ:tn] v. (使)变短,缩短

shortfall ['ʃɔ:tfɔ:l] n. 亏空,缺少,不足之数,不足量

shortly ['ʃɔ:tli] ad. 立刻,即刻,不久,简略地,简言之

shot [ʃɔt] n. 开枪,射击,射程,射击手,一节链(一个锚链的长度),子弹,炮弹,企图,尝试,机会; v. ① 装弹丸,用铅丸加重于 ② (shoot 的过去式和过去分词) 射击,投射,伸出,拍摄,用完,挥出,注射,使爆炸; a. 两色交织的,闪色的,杂色的,摆脱…的,解脱了的,与…绝交的

shovel ['ʃʌvl] n. 铲子,铁锹,单斗挖掘机; v. 铲,铲除,挖清

shower ['ʃauə] n. 淋浴,淋浴器,大量涌溢,倾泻,(一)阵,(一)大批; v. 倾注,抛洒,洒落,大量地给予
~ nozzle 淋浴喷头,喷头

shred ['ʃred] n. 碎片,破布,少量剩余,最少量; v. 撕碎,切碎,撕毁

shredder ['ʃredə] n. 切菜器,撕碎机 ‖ *Syn*. crusher 粉碎机,轧碎机; grinder 研磨机,粉碎机; macerater 粉碎机,切碎机; pulverizer 粉碎机

shrink [ʃriŋk] n. 收缩,收缩量; v. 收缩,皱缩,(使)缩水,退缩,畏缩

shrinkage ['ʃriŋkidʒ] n. 收缩,皱缩,缩水
~ crack 收缩裂缝,收缩裂纹
~ fit 收缩配合
~ fracture 收缩裂缝
~ joint 收缩缝

shroud [ʃraud] n. 覆盖物,船的横桅索,护罩,裹尸布; v. 覆盖,遮蔽,隐藏,用裹尸布包

shrouded [ʃraud] v. (shroud 的过去式与过去分词) 覆盖,遮蔽,隐藏,用裹尸布包; a. 覆盖的
~ impeller 闭式叶轮
~ screw 带帽螺钉,导管螺旋桨

shudder ['ʃʌdə] n. 战栗,颤动,打颤; v. 震动,战栗,发抖,颤动

shunt [ʃʌnt] n. 分路,分流器,调轨,转轨; v. (使)分流,避开,移开,转向
~ capacitor 分路电容,并联电容,旁路电容
~ compensation 并联补偿
~ conductance 分流电导,旁路电导
~ displacement current 旁路位移电流
~ excitation 并激,分激,分路激励
~ field 并激磁场
~ trip 并联跳闸装置
~ wound 并联的,并激的,并励的
~ wound coil 并励线圈
~ wound dynamo 并激(发)电机
~ wound field coil 并联励磁线圈
~ wound generator 并励发电机
~ wound motor 并励电动机

shunted ['ʃʌntid] v. (shunt 的过去式和过去分词) (使)分流,避开,移开,转向; a. 分路的
~ interpole 分路中间磁极
~ interpole winding 分路中间磁极绕组,分路间极绕组
~ meter 有分流器的电流表

shut [ʃʌt] n. 关闭,焊缝; v. 关闭,闭上,合上,封闭,阻挡,停止运行

shut down 放下关下,(使)机器等关闭,停车

shut-off 终止,截止
~ nozzle 止流式喷嘴
~ valve 截止阀,断流阀,闸阀

shuttle ['ʃʌtl] *n.* 往返汽车(列车、飞机),航天飞机, 梭子, 穿梭; *v.* 穿梭往返

~ tanker 穿梭运输油轮

sickbay ['sikbei] *n.* 船上的医务室

SID (system identification number) 系统标识号

side [said] *n.* 边, 旁边, 侧面, 面, 一方, (一个)方面; *v.* 支持, 站在同一边, 同意; *a.* 旁边的, 侧面的, 副的, 枝节的

~ board 弦面板, 边材板

~ bunker 侧燃料舱, 侧舱, 边煤舱

~ clearance 旁隙

~ cover 边盖, 侧盖

~ cutter 侧铣刀, 侧刀

~ door 侧门, 边门

~ draught 侧吸

~ frame 侧梁, 侧面机架, 侧壁, 侧板

~ girder 边梁, 旁桁, 旁桁材

~ keelson 旁内龙骨

~ lamp 侧灯

~ launching 横向下水

~ layer 边铺料, 侧边料

~ lift frame 侧提升框架

~ light 侧光, 侧向照明, 间接说明

~ lining (集装箱)侧壁内衬板

~ loading system 侧装载系统

~ longitudinal 船侧纵骨

~ plate 侧板

~ play 侧面间隙, 侧隙, 轴端余隙, 轴向间隙

~ play mount 偏移量

~ scuttle 舷窗

~ shoot 舷侧排泥管

~ stringer 舷侧纵桁

~ thrust 侧向力

~ thruster 侧推器, 横向推力器

~ valve 侧阀

~ valve engine 侧置气门发动机, 旁阀发动机

~ vane 侧叶

~ view 侧视图, 侧景

~ water wall tube 侧水冷壁管

side-arm 侧臂

~ bridge 侧臂桥

~ electrode 侧臂电极

side-chock 侧楔垫, 侧垫块

~ bolt 侧楔垫螺栓

sideways ['saidweiz] *a.* 一旁的, 向侧面的; *ad.* 向一旁, 向侧面地, 斜地里

sidewise ['saidwaiz] *a.* 向一边的, 横斜的

sieve [siv] *n.* 滤网, 筛; *v.* 筛, 筛选, 过滤

sight [sait] *n.* 景象, 看见, 视力, 视野, 视域, 眼界, 瞄准器, 瞄准; *v.* 瞄准, 看见, 发现, 目视, 观察, 调准瞄准器, 瞄准

~ flow indicator 可视流量指示器

~ glass 视镜, 窥镜, 观察孔

~ hole 瞄准孔, 检查孔

signal ['signl] *n.* 信号, 信号灯, 讯号, 图像, 电波, 暗号, 预兆, 征象, 动机, 导因, 导火线; *v.* 发信号, 以信号告知; *a.* 信号的

~ amplifier 信号放大器

~ buoy cable 信号浮标电缆

~ converter 信号转换器

~ detection and estimation 信号检测与估计

~ flag 信号旗

~ flow diagram 信号流程图

~ generator 信号发生器

~ horn 信号喇叭
~ lamp 信号灯
~ line 信号线
~ output 信号输出
~ panel 信号板，信号盘
~ pistol 信号枪
~ reconstruction 信号重构
~ relay 信号继电器
~ rocket 烟火信号弹
~ transducer 信号传感器
~ tube 信号管

signal-to-noise 信号对噪声的，信噪的
~ ratio of strong signal 大信号信噪比

signaling ['signliŋ] n. 打信号，发信号；v. (signal 的 ing 形式) 发信号，以信号告知
~ light for air 空气信号灯
~ searchlight 信号探照灯

signatory ['signətəri] n. 签字人，签字者，签约国；a. 签署的，签约的

signature ['signitʃə] n. 签名，署名，信号

significance [sig'nifikəns] n. 意义，重要性，意思

significant [sig'nifikənt] a. 有意义的，重大的，重要的，相当数量的，意味深长的
~ digit 有效数字
~ oil spill incident at sea 海上重大溢油事故
~ part 有效部分

signify ['signifai] v. 表示，表明，象征，意味，要紧，有重要性，颇为重要

silane ['silein] n. 硅烷

silence ['sailəns] n. 沉默，无言，无表示，无声，沉静；v. 使安静，使沉默，压制

silencer ['sailənsə] n. 消声器，灭声器
~ element 消声器元件
~ mounting 消声器，防振器

silicate ['silikit] n. 硅酸盐

silicon ['silikən] n. 硅，硅元素
~ carbide 金刚砂
~ chip 硅片
~ controlled rectifier (SCR) 可控硅，硅可控整流器
~ controlled rectifier excitation device 可控硅励磁装置
~ dioxide 二氧化硅
~ rectifier 硅整流器

silicone ['silikəun] n. 硅树脂，硅酮
~ plastics 有机硅塑料
~ resin 有机硅树脂
~ resin coating 有机硅树脂涂料

sill [sil] n. 基石，门槛，窗台，岩床

silt [silt] n. 淤泥，残渣，煤粉，泥沙；v. (使)淤塞，充塞

silver ['silvə] n. 银，银色，银币，银制品；v. 镀银；a. 银的，银色的，银制的，银白色的
~ brazing 银焊
~ enamel paint 银瓷漆
~ fuse wire 银保险丝
~ insulating varnish 银绝缘漆
~ plating 镀银

silver-zinc 银锌
~ battery 银锌电池

silvery ['silvəri] a. 似银的，有银色光泽的，银铃一般的，清脆的

similar ['similə] a. 相似的，类似的，同样的

similarity [,simi'læriti] n. 类似，相像性，类似处

similarly ['siməli] *ad.* 类似地，相似地，同样地

SIMO (single-input multi-output) 单输入多输出的

~ system 单输入多输出系统

simplex ['simpleks] *n.* 单形体；*a.* 单纯的，单一的，单工的

~ pump 单缸泵

~ radio telephone 单工无线电话机

simplicity [sim'plisiti] *n.* 简单，简易，朴素，直率

simplify ['simplifai] *v.* 单一化，简单化

simplistic [sim'plistik] *a.* 过分简单化的，过分单纯化的

simply ['simpli] *ad.* 简单地，完全，简直，仅仅，只不过，朴素地，只是

simulant ['simjulənt] *a.* 拟态的，模拟的

simulate ['simjuleit] *v.* 模拟，模仿，假装，冒充

simulated ['simjuleitid] *v.* (simulate 的过去式和过去分词) 模拟，模仿，假装，冒充；*a.* 模仿的，模拟的，冒充的，仿造的，假装的

~ engine room 模拟机舱

~ experiment 模拟实验

~ interrupt 模拟中断

simulation [ˌsimju'leiʃən] *n.* 模仿，模拟，仿真，假装

~ analysis 仿真分析

~ block diagram 模拟框图

~ data 仿真数据

~ equipment 仿真设备

~ experiment 仿真实验

~ panel 模拟面板

~ procedure 仿真程序

~ test 模拟试验

~ velocity 模拟速度

simulator ['simjuleitə] *n.* 模拟器，模拟装置，假装者

simultaneity [ˌsiməltə'niəti] *n.* 同时性，同时发生，同时

~ factor 同时率，同时系数

simultaneous [ˌsiməl'teinjəs] *a.* 同时的，同时发生的，同时存在的

sine [sain] *n.* 正弦

~ wave 正弦波 ‖ *Syn.* sinusoidal wave 正弦波

~ wave distortion rate 正弦波失真率

single ['siŋgl] *n.* 一个，单打，单精度型；*v.* 选出；*a.* 单一的，单身的，单纯的，孤独的，专一的，个别的

~ anchor leg mooring (SALM) 单锚腿系泊

~ arm pivot davit 单臂枢轴吊艇架

~ bunk 单人床，单人铺位

~ cabin 单舱

~ cam reversing device 单凸轮换向装置

~ cantilever gantry crane 单悬臂龙门起重机

~ chip microcomputer (SCM) 单片微型计算机，单片机

~ component 单组分，单分量

~ connection plane switch 单连接平面开关

~ core cable 单芯电缆

~ duct 单导管

~ floodable compartment 单舱进水舱

~ line 单线

~ mode 单模

~ out 挑选

~ purchase winch 单卷筒绞车 ‖ *Syn.* single-drum winch 单卷筒绞车

535

~ room 单人房
~ shafting 单轴系
~ steady speed method 单稳态速度法
~ strainer 单滤器
~ throw crankshaft 单拐曲轴
~ type supercharging system 单式增压系统
~ unit 单一机组
single-acting 单作用式的，单动式的
  ~ oil cylinder 单作用油缸
  ~ plunger oil cylinder 单作用柱塞油缸
  ~ pump 单作用泵
  ~ radial plunger type oil motor 单作用径向柱塞式油马达
  ~ single-piston rod oil cylinder 单作用单活塞杆油缸
  ~ vane pump 单作用叶片泵
single-chamber 单腔的，单室的
  ~ capacity 单室容量
  ~ furnace 单室炉
  ~ model 单室模型
single-channel 单信道的，单通道的，单波道的，单路的
  ~ cordless telephone 单信道无绳电话
single-cylinder 单气缸的，单缸的
  ~ engine 单缸发动机
  ~ pump 单缸泵
  ~ test 单缸试验
single-drum 单卷筒的，单鼓筒的，单筒的
  ~ boiler 单鼓筒锅炉，单筒锅炉
  ~ mooring winch with warping head 带翘曲头的单卷筒系泊绞车
  ~ winch 单卷筒绞车 ‖ *Syn.* single purchase winch 单卷筒绞车
single-effect 单向作用的，单效的

~ evaporation 单效蒸发
~ evaporator 单效蒸发器
~ vacuum boiling evaporator 单效真空沸腾蒸发器
single-end 单端的，单头的
  ~ austable spanner 单端可调扳手
  ~ earthed 单端接地的
  ~ input 单端输入
  ~ ring wrench 单端环扳手
  ~ round handle wrench 单端圆柄扳手
  ~ windlass 单侧式起锚机
single-entry 单入口的
  ~ centrifugal pump 单入口离心泵
single-head 单头的
  ~ spanner 单头扳手
single-input 单输入的
  ~ controller 单输入控制器
  ~ multi-output (SIMO) 单输入多输出的
  ~ multi-output system 单输入多输出系统
  ~ single-output (SISO) 单输入单输出的
  ~ single-output system 单输入单输出系统
single-layer 单层的
  ~ coil tube 单层线圈管
  ~ lining 单层衬里
  ~ shell 单层壳体
  ~ structure 单层结构
single-loop 单循环的，单环路的，单环的
  ~ coil 单回路线圈
  ~ controller 单回路控制器
  ~ feedback 单回路反馈
  ~ fire alarm control unit 单回路火灾报警控制器

single-phase 单相的
~ asymmetrical control 单相不对称控制
~ circuit 单相电路
~ motor 单相电动机
~ purifier 单相净化器
~ short-circuit current 单相短路电流
~ symmetrical control 单相对称控制
~ transformer 单相变压器
~ two-wire insulated system 单相二线绝缘系统

single-point 单点的
~ mooring buoy 单点系泊浮标
~ mooring pipes 单点系泊管
~ mooring terminal 单点系泊码头
~ mooring unit 单点系泊装置
~ mooring 单点系泊

single-pole 单极的
~ cutout 单极断路器
~ double-throw switch 单刀双掷开关
~ earthing 单极接地
~ receiver 单极接收机

single-pulse 单脉冲的
~ laser 单脉冲激光器
~ loading 单脉冲加载

single-row 单排的
~ ball bearing 单列滚珠轴承
~ core 单排芯
~ engine 单列发动机
~ rivet 单行铆钉

single-screw 单螺旋的，单螺杆的，单车叶的
~ propeller 单螺旋桨
~ pump 单螺杆泵
~ ship 单螺旋桨船
~ steamer 单螺旋桨轮船

single-sided 单面的

~ printed board (SSB) 单面印制板

single-stage 单级的，单阶段的
~ compression refrigerating system 单级压缩制冷系统
~ compressor 单级压缩机
~ converter 单级变换器
~ cycle 单级循环
~ evaporator 单级蒸发器
~ flash evaporation 单级闪蒸
~ flash evaporator 单级闪蒸器
~ load 单级负荷
~ pump 单级泵
~ purifier 单级净化器
~ supercharging 单级增压
~ turbocharging 单级涡轮增压

single-step 单步的
~ glider 单断级滑行艇
~ run 单步运行

single-way 单通的，单路的，单向的
~ connection 单向连接
~ duct 单向管道
~ propagation 单向传播
~ rectifier 单向整流器

single-welded 单面焊接的
~ butt joint 单面焊接对接接头
~ lap joint 单面焊接搭接接头

singular ['siŋgjulə] n. 单数；a. 单一的，非凡的，异常的，持异议的

sink [siŋk] n. 水槽，水池，接收器；v. (使)下沉，沉下，淹没，下落，倾斜

sinkage ['siŋkidʒ] n. 下沉，沉陷

sinking ['siŋkiŋ] n. 沉没，下沉；v. (sink 的 ing 形式) (使)下沉，沉下，淹没，下落，倾斜
~ of the main shaft 主轴下沉
~ of the tail shaft 尾轴下沉

sinus ['sainəs] *n*. 弯曲处，凹陷处

sinusoid ['sainə,sɔid] *n*. 正弦波，正弦曲线

sinusoidal [,sainə'sɔidəl] *a*. 正弦的，正弦曲线的

~ current 正弦电流

~ density wave 正弦密度波

~ signal 正弦信号

~ time function 正弦时间函数

~ wave 正弦波 ‖ *Syn*. sine wave 正弦波

siphon ['saifən] *n*. 虹吸管

siren ['saiərin] *n*. 汽笛，警报器，空袭警报

SISO (single-input single-output) 单输入单输出的

~ system 单输入单输出系统

sister ['sistə] *n*. 姐妹，姐，女会员，修女，妹；*v*. 姐妹般对待

~ ship 姊妹船，同型船

site [sait] *n*. 地点，位置，场所，站点，网站，地皮；*v*. 定…的地点

situate ['sitjueit] *v*. 使位于，使处于

situation [,sitju'eiʃən] *n*. 位置，地点，情况，处境，形势，局面，职业，职务

situs ['saitəs] *n*. 位置，地点

six [siks] *num*. 六，六个，六个单位组成的东西

~ degrees of freedom 六自由度

six-way 六路的，六向的，六通的

~ valve 六通阀

size [saiz] *n*. 规模，大小，尺寸，尺码，大量，数量，能力，能耐，胶料，浆糊；*v*. 按大小排列，依尺寸制造，上胶；*a*. 一定大小的

~ factor 尺寸系数，比例系数

~ marking 尺寸标注

~ relationship 大小关系，尺寸关系

skeg [skeg] *n*. 龙骨的后部，导流尾鳍

skeleton ['skelitən] *n*. 骨架，骨骼，基干，纲要，万能钥匙

~ type 骨架式

sketch [sketʃ] *n*. 略图，草图，概略，梗概，草图，拟定；*v*. 绘略图，勾画，素描

~ drawing 简图，草图，略图

skew [skju:] *n*. 歪斜，扭曲；*v*. 走偏，斜进，斜视，使歪斜，曲解，歪曲；*a*. 斜的，歪的，不对称的

~ angle 斜拱角，相交角，斜交角，歪扭角

skid [skid] *n*. 船舷木，滑动垫木，滑材，刹车，制轮器；*v*. 打滑，滑行

skiff [skif] *n*. 小艇，小型帆船，摩托小快艇

skim [skim] *n*. 撇取，撇渣，表面的薄覆盖层；*v*. 撇去，从液体上移走，掠过，擦过，浏览，略读

skimmer ['skimə] *n*. 撇渣器，撇乳器，撇去浮物的器具

skin [skin] *n*. 皮，皮肤，兽皮，皮毛，外皮，外壳；*v*. 长皮，剥皮，削皮，擦破皮，使覆盖

~ diving 轻装潜水

~ friction 表面摩擦

~ friction coefficient 表面摩擦系数

skip [skip] *n*. 跳跃，跳，蹦跳；*v*. 跳，蹦，急速改变，跳读，遗漏，跳跃

skipper ['skipə] *n*. 船长，领导，教练员；*v*. 担任船长 ‖ *Syn*. captain 船长；master 船长；sea captain 船长

skylight ['skailait] *n*. 天窗

slack [slæk] *n*. 松弛，静止，淡季，闲散；*v*. (使)懈怠，(使)放松，(使)松弛，减

速，马虎从事；*a.* 松弛的，不流畅的，疏忽的，软弱的，漏水的，呆滞的，懒散的；*ad.* 马虎地，缓慢地
~ tank 半载舱，空罐
~ tide 平潮

slackage ['slækidʒ] *n.* (绳索的)可松弛量

slag [slæg] *n.* 炉渣，矿渣，火山岩渣；*v.* 起溶渣，成溶渣

slam [slæm] *n.* 砰，猛击，撞击，冲击；*v.* 砰地关上，砰地放下，猛力抨击，冲击

slant [slɑ:nt] *n.* 倾斜，斜线，斜面，倾向性，偏见；*v.* (使)倾斜，歪曲；*a.* 倾斜的
~ engine 倾斜式发动机
~ mill 斜轧式轧机

slave [sleiv] *n.* 从动装置，奴隶；*v.* 辛勤努力，作苦工
~ connecting rod 从动连杆
~ controller 从属控制器，从动调节器
~ system 从动系统，从系统

sleeve [sli:v] *n.* 套筒，套管，套子，袖子；*v.* 装套筒，装套子，装袖子
~ bearing 套筒轴承，滑动轴承
~ coupling 套筒联轴节
~ valve 套阀，圆柱滑阀，筒阀

slew [slu:] *n.* 许多，大量；*v.* 使旋转，使回旋

slewing ['slu:iŋ] *n.* 快速定向，快速瞄准；*v.* (slew 的 ing 形式) 使旋转，使回旋；*a.* 回转的
~ boom 吊车旋转杆
~ davit 回转吊艇架，回转吊柱
~ hydraulic motor 回转液压马达
~ motor 回转电动机
~ rim 回转底盘

~ table 回转台，转盘
~ winch 回转绞车，回转吊货杆绞车
~ winch motor 回转绞车马达，回转绞车电动机

slick [slik] *n.* 光滑之处，平滑水面，平滑器，修光工具，一层浮油；*v.* 使光滑，使光亮，打扮整洁；*a.* 光滑的，熟练的，聪明的，华而不实的，陈腐的，平凡的，老套的；*ad.* 熟练地，灵活地，聪明地

slide [slaid] *n.* 滑，滑动，幻灯片；*v.* (使)滑动，(使)滑行，潜行，滑倒，滑落，略过，回避
~ bar 滑杆
~ bar bracket 滑杆托
~ bearing 滑动轴承
~ block 滑块
~ caliper 游标卡尺 ‖ *Syn.* vernier caliper 游标卡尺
~ friction 滑动摩擦
~ out 滑出
~ over 回避，略过
~ rail 滑轨
~ regulator 滑动调节器
~ valve 滑阀

sliding ['slaidiŋ] *v.* (slide 的 ing 形式) (使)滑动，(使)滑行，潜行，滑倒，滑落，略过，回避；*a.* 滑行的，变化的
~ bearing 滑动轴承
~ block 滑块
~ block linkage 滑块链系
~ door 拉门，滑门
~ dowel block 滑动固定块
~ fit 滑动配合，滑配合，滑合座
~ plate 滑床台
~ rheostat 滑动变阻器，滑线变阻器

~ rod 滑杆

~ shoe 滑动式蹄，仿形滑脚，滑瓦

~ spool 滑阀芯

slime [slaim] *n*. 黏液，黏质物，黏泥，黏土，软泥；*v*. 涂，糊，变黏滑

slimy ['slaimi] *a*. 黏滑的，似黏液的，泥泞的

~ layer 黏稠层

sling [sliŋ] *n*. 投掷，钩悬带，吊索，投石器，弹弓；*v*. 吊起，悬挂，投掷

slip [slip] *n*. 跌倒，失足，事故；*v*. (使)滑动，滑过，滑倒，失足，减退，摆脱，闪开，塞入；*a*. 滑动的，活络的，有活结的

~ joint pliers 鲤鱼钳

~ joint shaft 滑动接合轴

~ ratio 转差率，滑率，滑移比率，滑差系数

~ ring 滑动环，集电环

~ type expansion joint 滑动式伸缩接头

~ up 跌倒，疏忽，遭到不幸

slipper ['slipə] *n*. 制轮器，拖鞋；*v*. 用拖鞋打

~ guide 滑块导板，滑导件，导滑槽

~ pad 滑块衬垫，滑块支座

~ piston 滑块活塞，滑履活塞

~ pump (径向柱塞泵的)滑履泵

~ ring 滑环

~ stern 斜形艉

~ skirt 滑履式活塞裙

~ skirt piston 滑裙活塞

slippery ['slipəri] *a*. 滑溜的，狡猾的，不可靠的

slipway ['slipwei] *n*. 滑台，船台，下水滑道

slog [slɔg] *n*. 拼命工作，长途跋涉；*v*. 猛击，步履艰难地行走，努力苦干

slogging ['slɔgiŋ] *n*. 苦工；*v*. (slog 的 ing 形式) 猛击，步履艰难地行走，努力苦干

~ ring wrench 梅花敲击扳手

sloop [slu:p] *n*. 单桅帆船

slop [slɔp] *n*. 污水，蒸馏物(slops)，残羹剩饭(slops)，人的排泄物(slops)；*v*. 溢出，溅溢

~ chute 污水斜槽，垃圾滑道

~ tank 污油罐

slope [sləup] *n*. 斜坡，斜率，倾斜，斜面；*v*. (使)倾斜，(使)顺斜，有斜度

~ angle 倾角

~ surface 坡面

~ switch 斜坡开关

sloping [sləup] *v*. (slope 的 ing 形式) (使)倾斜，(使)顺斜，有斜度；*a*. 倾斜的，有坡度的

~ top plate of bottom side tank 底边舱斜顶板，底侧油柜倾斜顶板

slot [slɔt] *n*. 缝，狭槽，位置，水沟，细长的孔，硬币投币口，狭通道，足迹；*v*. 开槽于，跟踪

~ weld 槽缝熔焊，槽塞焊，槽焊，长孔焊

slotted [slɔt] *v*. (slot的过去式和过去分词) 开槽于，跟踪；*a*. 槽形的，有开槽沟的，有槽的

~ adjustment plate 槽形调整板

~ commutator 有槽整流子

~ oil control ring 开槽护油环，开槽护油圈，开槽油环

~ pile 开槽桩

~ pin 开槽销

~ pin screw 开槽销螺钉

~ plug 有槽塞

~ screw 有槽螺钉

slotting [slɔt] *n.* 打孔，立刨，开槽；*v.* (slot 的 ing 形式) 开槽于，跟踪

~ machine 立式刨床，插床

slow [sləu] *v.* 放慢，变慢，减缓，阻碍，变萧条；*a.* 慢的，迟钝的，不活跃的，缓慢的；*ad.* 慢慢地，缓慢地

~ ahead 前进一，缓慢前行

~ and steady 稳扎稳打地

~ astern 后退一，慢速倒车

~ down 慢下来

~ flash light 慢闪光灯

~ speed diesel engine 低速柴油机

~ speed high torque motor 低速大扭矩电动机

~ speed indication 慢速显示，慢速指示

~ speed main propulsion disesl 低速主推进装置

~ speed two-stroke engine 低速二冲程发动机

sludge [slʌdʒ] *n.* 软泥，淤泥，矿泥，煤泥，沉淀物

~ discharge 排泥，排渣

~ oil 淤渣油

~ outlet 污泥排出口

~ pump 污泥泵

~ scraper 刮泥器

~ tank 污泥槽

~ valve 污泥阀

sluice [slu:s] *n.* 水闸，泄水；*v.* 开闸放水，流出，冲洗，奔泻

~ valve 水闸，闸式阀，闸门阀

small [smɔ:l] *n.* 狭窄部分，零星物品 (smalls)；*a.* 小的，少的，微小的，小规模的，次要的，稀释的；*ad.* 零星地，轻微地

~ bore 小口径，小截面

~ bore engine 小径气缸发动机

~ porcelain tube 小型瓷管

~ quantity 小量，少量

~ scale 小比例尺，小比例，小规模

~ waterplane area twin hull (SWATH) 小水线面双体船

SMC (Safety Management Certificate) 安全管理证书

SMC (surface mount component) 表面贴装元件，表面组装元件，表面安装元件

smear [smiə] *n.* 油迹，污点，涂片，釉，黏稠物，中伤；*v.* 涂上，抹掉，涂污，诽谤，抹去

SMM (Safety Management Manuel) 安全管理手册

smoke [sməuk] *n.* 烟，烟尘，烟幕；*v.* 冒烟，吸烟，抽烟

~ alarm 烟雾报警器

~ chamber 烟室，烟腔，熏烟室

~ column 烟柱

~ damper 烟气挡板，烟气调节风门

~ density factor 烟雾密度因数

~ detection system 烟雾探测系统

~ detector 烟雾探测器

~ exhauster 排烟器

~ evacuation 排烟

~ fire detector 感烟火灾探测器

~ flue 烟道

~ helmet 救火帽，防毒面具

~ limiting horsepower 排烟极限功率

~ mask 防烟面罩

~ opacimeter 烟度计

~ pipe fire alarm system 烟管式火警信号系统

~ room 吸烟室

~ test 烟气试验

~ tester 烟浓度检验计

~ tube 烟管

~ tube boiler 烟管式锅炉

smokemeter ['sməukˌmi:tə] n. 烟度计

smoky ['sməuki] a. 冒烟的，烟状的，充满烟的，烟熏味的

smolder ['sməuldə] n. 焖燃，焖烧，文火，冒烟；v. 焖烧，阴燃，冒烟，郁闷，愤恨

smoldering ['sməuldəriŋ] n. 焖烧，阴燃；v. (smolder 的 ing 形式) 焖烧，阴燃，冒烟，郁闷，愤恨

~ fire 阴燃火

smooth [smu:ð] n. 一块平地，平滑部分；v. 使光滑，变平滑，变平静，消除；a. 平滑的，平坦的，平稳的，无毛的，流畅的，圆滑的

~ off 使平滑，使平稳

smoothing ['smu:ðiŋ] n. 滤波；v. (smooth 的 ing 形式) 使光滑，变平滑，变平静，消除

~ reactor 平滑电抗器

~ resistor 平流电阻(器)

smoothly ['smu:ðli] ad. 顺利地，平稳地，平滑地，流畅地

SMPEP (Shipboard Marine Pollution Emergency Plan) 船上海洋污染应急计划

SMPS (switch mode power supply) 开关式电源供电

SMS (Safety Management System) 安全管理系统

smuggler ['smʌglə(r)] n. 走私船，走私者，走私犯

snag [snæg] n. 突出物，残桩，暗桩，尖齿，尖角，尖刺；v. 抓住，戳坏，清除暗桩

snap [snæp] n. 猛咬，突然折断，劈啪声；v. 猛地吸住，突然折断，使劈啪地响，猛咬；a. 突然的

~ gauge 外径规，卡规

~ ring 扣环，止动环，卡环

snap-in 咬接

~ connector 卡扣式连接器，卡入接头

snatch [snætʃ] n. 抢夺，攫取，一瞬间，短时，片刻，一点点；v. 抢夺，攫取，夺得

~ block 扣线滑轮，开口滑车

snip [snip] n. 剪，剪切声，片断，切口，小片，一点点，便宜货，零星；v. 削减，剪去，剪断

snipe [snaip] n. 香烟屁股,鹬,狙击；v. 猎鸟，狙击，诽谤

~ nose pliers 尖嘴钳

snorkel ['snɔ:kl] n. 水下呼吸管，水下通气管；v. 戴呼吸管潜泳

~ attachment 呼吸管固定扣，呼吸管附件

snorkeling ['snɔ:kliŋ] n. 潜水，潜浮；v. (snorkel 的 ing 形式) 戴呼吸管潜泳

~ equipment 轻装

~ vest 潜浮背心

snubber ['snʌbə] n. 缓冲器，斥责者，拒绝者

SO_2 (sulphur dioxide) 二氧化硫

soak [səuk] n. 湿透，浸透，浸泡，浸湿；v. 浸湿，浸泡，渗入，渗进，浸透，淋湿

soap [səup] n. 肥皂

~ powder 皂粉

~ solution 皂液

society [sə'saiəti] *n*. 社会，协会，伴随，陪伴，友伴，交际，社交界，上流社会

socket ['sɔkit] *n*. 插座，灯座，窝，穴，孔，牙槽；*v*. 装入插座，配插座

~ and turning switch 插座与转向开关

~ box 插座盒

~ head bolt 套筒螺栓

~ head screw 凹头螺钉，内六角头螺丝，窝头螺丝

~ screw key 凹头螺钉键

~ spanner 套筒扳手

~ wrench 管钳

soda ['səudə] *n*. 苏打，碳酸水

~ acid 苏打酸，酸碱

~ acid fire extinguisher 苏打酸灭火器，酸碱灭火器

~ acid fire extinguishing agent 苏打酸灭火剂，酸碱灭火剂

~ ash 碳酸钠，苏打灰，纯碱

sodium ['səudjəm] *n*. 钠(符号 Na)

~ bicarbonate 碳酸氢钠，小苏打

~ bicarbonate powder 碳酸氢钠粉，小苏打粉

~ carbonate 碳酸钠

~ chloride 氯化钠

~ content 钠含量

~ hydroxide 氢氧化钠

~ nitrate 硝酸钠

~ phosphate 磷酸钠

~ polyphosphate 多聚磷酸钠

~ potassium carbonate 碳酸钠钾

~ sulfite 亚硫酸钠

~ sulphate 硫酸钠，芒硝

sodium-filled 充钠的

~ valve 钠冷却气门，钠冷排气阀 ‖ ***Syn***. natrium-cooled valve 钠冷却气门，钠冷排气阀

soft [sɔft] *n*. 软件，柔软之物，柔软的部分；*a*. 软的，柔软的，温和的，柔和的，模糊的，无保护的，不含酒精的，纸币的

~ brush 软刷

~ iron 软铁

~ iron core 软铁芯

~ packing 软填料

soft-packed 软填料的

~ gland 软填料压盖

~ stuffing box 软填料填料箱

soften ['sɔ(:)fn] *v*. (使)变柔软，(使)变柔和，弄软

~ up 使软化，劝解，削弱

software ['sɔftwεə] *n*. 软件

soil [sɔil] *n*. 粪便，土壤，土地，国土，国家，温床，务农；*v*. 弄脏，污辱，变脏

~ pollution 土壤污染

solar ['səulə] *a*. 太阳的，日光的，利用太阳能的，根据太阳测定的

~ array pointing control 太阳帆板指向控制

~ battery 太阳能电池 ‖ ***Syn***. solar cell 太阳能电池

~ energy 太阳能

SOLAS Convention (International Convention for the Safety of Life at Sea) 国际海上人命安全公约，SOLAS 公约

solder ['sɔldə] *n*. 焊料，焊锡；*v*. (使)焊接，焊合

~ bump 焊料隆起焊盘，焊锡球，焊接凸点

543

~ club 焊条

~ side 焊接面

~ spray 焊料

solderability [ˌsɔldərə'biləti] *n.* 软焊性，可焊性 ‖ **Syn**. weldability 焊接性

soldered ['sɔldəd] *v.* (使)焊接，焊合；*a.* 焊接的，焊合的

~ connection 焊接头

~ joint 焊接接头，焊接接缝

soldering ['sɔldəriŋ] *n.* 软焊，锡焊，低温焊接，热焊接，软钎焊；*v.* (solder 的 ing 形式) (使)焊接，焊合

~ iron 烙铁

~ tin 焊锡

~ tin wire 焊锡丝

solenoid ['sɔulinɔid] *n.* 螺线管，筒形线圈

~ brake 螺线管制动器

~ directional control valve 电磁换向阀，电磁方向控制阀

~ driver 螺线管驱动器

~ operated three-way valve 电磁操作式三通阀，电磁式三通阀

~ valve 电磁阀

~ valve box 电磁阀盒

solid ['sɔlid] *n.* 固体，立体，立方体；*a.* 固体的，实心的，坚固的，结实的，立体的，可靠的，一致的，纯粹的

~ alkaline cleaner 固体碱性清洗剂

~ dielectric cable 固体介质电缆，实芯绝缘电缆

~ fuel 固体燃料

~ impurities 固体杂质

~ iron core 实铁心

~ particle 固体微粒，固体粒子

~ phase 固相

~ phase condensation 固相缩合

~ propeller 固体推进器

~ shaft 实心轴

~ shaft piston 实心轴活塞

~ silicon circuit 固态硅电路

~ skirt 整体活塞裙

~ skirt piston 导缘实心活塞

~ solubility 固溶性，固溶度

~ state 固态

~ state phase changes 固态相变

~ state storage 固态存储器

~ waste 固体废物

~ waste classification 固体废物分类

solidification [sɔˌlidifi'keiʃən] *n.* 凝固

~ value 凝固点，固化温度

solidify [sə'lidifai] *v.* (使)凝固，(使)团结，巩固

solidifying [sə'lidifaiiŋ] *n.* 凝固，固化；*v.* (solidify 的 ing 形式) (使)凝固，(使)团结，巩固

~ characteristic of oil 油料的固化特性

~ point 凝点

~ substance 固化物质

solubility [ˌsɔlju'biliti] *n.* 溶度，溶性，可解决性，可解释性，溶解性

soluble ['sɔljubl] *a.* 可溶的，可溶解的，可以解决的

solute ['sɔljuːt] *n.* 溶解物，溶质

solution [sə'ljuːʃən] *n.* 解答，解决办法，解决方案，溶解，溶液

solve [sɔlv] *v.* 解决，解答，解释，清偿

solvent ['sɔlvənt] *n.* 溶媒，溶剂，解决方法；*a.* 溶解的，有溶解力，有偿付能力的

~ emulsifier 溶剂乳化剂

~ emulsion cleaner 溶剂乳化清洗剂

sonar ['sɔunɑː] *n.* 声呐装置，声波定位仪

sonic ['sɔnik] a. 音波的，音速的，有关声波的

soot [sut] n. 油烟，煤烟，烟灰；v. 用煤烟弄脏

~ blower 烟灰吹除机，吹灰器

sooty ['suti] a. 煤烟熏黑的，乌黑的

SOPEP (Shipboard Oil Pollution Emergency Plan) 船舶油污应急计划

sophisticate [sə'fistikeit] n. 老于世故的人，见多识广的人；v. 篡改，曲解，使变得世故，掺合，弄复杂

sophisticated [sə'fistikeitid] a. 复杂的，高度发展的，精密复杂的，富有经验的，老练的，练达的

sorbent ['sɔ:bənt] n. 吸附剂

sorption ['sɔ:pʃən] n. 吸着，吸附作用

sound [saund] n. 声音，语音，噪音，吵闹，海峡，听力范围，探条；v. 使发出声音，回响，测深，测深，试探，听起来，宣告，听诊；a. 健全的，可靠的，合理的，有效彻底的，健康的；ad. 彻底地，充分地

~ insulation 隔音，声绝缘，隔音材料

~ signal 听觉信号，音响信号

sound-and-fire 声音与火，音火

~ proof 隔音防火

sounding ['saundiŋ] n. 探测液体的深度，试探；v. (sound 的 ing 形式) 使发出声音，回响，测深，测深，试探，听起来，宣告，听诊；a. 发声的，夸大的

~ lead 测深锤

~ pipe 测深管

~ pole 测深杆

~ rod 测深杆，探棒，探针，塞规

~ tape 测深尺

~ thermometer 深水温度计

source [sɔ:s] n. 来源，源头，水源，原始资料，发起者；v. 获得，资料来源，原料来源

south [sauθ] n. 南，南部；a. 南的，南方的；ad. 在南方，向南方

~ Pole 南极

southeastward [sauθ'i:stwəd] n. 东南；ad. 往东南

southern ['sʌðən] a. 南的，南部的，南方的

southward ['sauθwəd] a. 向南的；ad. 向南

southwards ['sauθwədz] ad. 往南地，向南地

southwest ['sauθ'west] n. 西南部，西南，西南方；a. 西南的，向西南方的；ad. 西南地，向西南方地

SOx (oxysulfide) 氧硫化物

~ emission 氧硫化物排放

~ control area 氧硫化物排放控制区域

space [speis] n. 空间，间隔，距离，空地，余地，一段时间；v. 留间隔，隔开

~ heater 小型供暖器

spacing ['speisiŋ] n. 间隔，跨距，疏密；v. (space 的 ing 形式) 留间隔，隔开

~ ring 隔离圈，隔环，限位环

~ sleeve 隔离套筒

~ table 限位工作台

spade [speid] n. 铁锹，铲子；v. 铲

~ rudder 铲形舵，吊舵，悬挂舵

~ tag 扁形软线接头

span [spæn] n. 跨绳，跨度，跨距，范围，间距，时距，一段时期，延伸体；v. 跨越，持续，延伸

spanner ['spænə] n. 扳手，活络扳手，扳子

spare [spɛə] n. 备用零件，备用品；v. 节约，节省，阻碍，分让，提供，不伤害，宽恕；a. 多余的，剩下的，少量的，贫乏的，备用的，高而瘦的人的
~ air adapter 备用小气瓶转换头
~ air tank 备用气瓶
~ battery 备用电池
~ cabin 备用舱室
~ capacity 备用容量
~ circuit 备用线路
~ inventory 备用库存
~ parts 备件
~ parts kit 备件箱
~ parts purchase requisition 备件采购申请
~ parts requisition 备件申请
~ parts store 备件库

spark [spa:k] n. 火花，火星，闪光，活力，电信技师，瞬间放电；v. 发动，触发，鼓舞，发火花
~ arrester 火花避雷器
~ blowout 火花熄灭装置
~ blowout coil 火花熄灭线圈
~ erosion 电火花腐蚀
~ inductor 火花感应线圈
~ plug 火花塞
~ regulation 火花调节器

sparse [spa:s] a. 稀疏的，稀少的

spate [speit] n. 大量，大批，洪水，暴涨，大雨，倾泻

spatially ['speiʃəli] ad. 空间地，存在于空间地

spatula ['spætjulə] n. 抹刀，压舌板

spear [spiə] n. 矛，枪，标枪；v. 用矛刺
~ gun 捕鱼枪

special ['speʃəl] n. 特派员，专车，专刊，特约稿；a. 特别的，特殊的，专门的，专用的
~ area 特别区域
~ equipment 特殊装置
~ function 特殊功能
~ heat-resistant steel 特种耐热钢
~ limit 特殊限制
~ marine reserve 海洋特别保护区
~ monitoring 特殊监测
~ purpose ship 特殊用途船舶，专用船
~ Purpose Ship Safety Certificate 特殊用途船舶安全证书
~ shape punch 特殊形状冲头
~ steel 特种钢
~ survey 特别检验
~ tool 专用工具

specialist ['speʃəlist] n. 专家，行家，专科医生，专门医生

speciality [ˌspeʃi'æliti] n. 特性，特质，专业，特殊性

specialization [ˌspeʃəlai'zeiʃən] n. 专门化，特别化，特化作用

specialize ['speʃəlaiz] v. 专攻，专门研究，专业化，限定范围，使专用于

specially ['speʃəli] ad. 特别地，专门地，特意地，格外地，临时地

specialty ['speʃəlti] n. 专业，专长，特点，特性，特质，特制，特制品，特产
~ diver 专项潜水员 ‖ advanced diver 中级潜水员；openwater diver 初级潜水员

species ['spi:ʃiz] n. 物种，种类，类型，式样，个体

specific [spi'sifik] n. 特性，细节，显著的性质，特效药；a. 比率的，详细而精确的，明确的，特殊的，特有的，特

定的，特效的

~ application 专门应用

~ body force 单位体力

~ capacity 比容量

~ combustion intensity 燃烧室热容强度，燃烧负荷率

~ consumption 单位消耗量，消耗率

~ fuel consumption 耗油率，燃料消耗率

~ fuel oil consumption (SFOC) 燃油消耗率

~ gravity 比重

~ heat 比热

~ heat consumption 单位热耗，热耗率，单位热量消耗

~ heat ratio 比热比，绝热指数

~ humidity 比湿度

~ impulse 比冲，比冲量，比推力

~ lubricating oil consumption 滑油消耗率，比润滑油消耗量

~ power consumption 单位耗电量，耗电率，比功率消耗，比功耗

~ rate 比速率

~ rate constant 比速率常数

~ speed 比速，比转数(离心泵或离心风机)，特定速率，额定转速

~ steam consumption 汽耗(率)

~ susceptance 电纳率

~ viscosity 比黏度，条件黏度，增比黏度

specifically [spi'sifikəli] ad. 特有地，特定地，明确地，按种别地，按特性地

specification [ˌspesifi'keiʃən] n. 详述，规格，说明书,规范 ‖ **Syn**. instruction 用法说明

~ for acceptance test of water-cooling tower 水冷塔验收试验规程

specificity [ˌspesi'fisiti] n. 特异性，种别性，种特性，特征

specified ['spesifaid] v. (specify 的过去式和过去分词) 指定，详述，提出条件，明确提出，载入说明书，列入清单；a. 指定的，规定的

~ account 专用账户，特种账单

~ period 规定限期，具体期限

~ project 按技术规范编制的计算，按技术规范编制的设计

specify ['spesifai] v. 指定，详述，提出条件，明确提出，载入说明书，列入清单

specimen ['spesimən] n. 范例，标本，样品，样本，待试验物

speck [spek] n. 斑点，污点，少量，一点点；v. 使有斑点，用斑点标记

spectra ['spektrə] n. (spectrum 的复数) 光，光谱，型谱，频谱，系列，范围，幅度

spectral ['spektrəl] a. 光谱的

spectrometer [spek'trɔmitə] n. 分光计，分光仪

spectroscopy [spek'trɔskəpi] n. 光谱学,波谱学，分光镜使用

spectrum ['spektrəm] n. (pl. spectra) 光，光谱，型谱，频谱，系列，范围，幅度

~ analyzer 频谱分析仪

speed [spi:d] n. 迅速，快速，速度，速率，平均速度，变速器，感光度，聚光率；v. 加快，超速，速飞，飞跑，促进，增加，加快，超速驾驶

~ adaptive coefficient 转速适应性系数

~ adjustable 速度可调的

~ adjusting lever 调速杆
~ adjusting rheostat 调速变阻器
~ adjustment 速度调节，调速
~ adjustment by series-parallel control 串并联调速
~ at maximum torque 最大转矩速度
~ belt 速带
~ changer 变速器，转速调节装置
~ control 速度控制，调速
~ control by rheostat variation 变阻器速度控制，变阻器调速
~ control switch 速度控制开关
~ control system 调速系统
~ droop 速度降低，降速
~ fluctuation 速度波动
~ fluctuation rate 速度波动率
~ gauge 速度计
~ gear 变速齿轮，高速齿轮
~ governor 调速器
~ increasing contactor 增速接触器
~ increasing relay 增速继电器
~ limit 速度限制
~ log 速度计程仪
~ margin 速度储备
~ monitoring system 速度监控系统
~ of advance 前进速度
~ of rotation 旋转速度
~ reduction ratio 减速比
~ reference 速度参考值
~ regulating characteristic 调速特性
~ regulating valve 调速阀
~ regulation 速度调节，调速
~ regulation by cascade control 级联控制调速，梯列控制调速
~ regulation by constant torque 恒转矩调速
~ regulation by frequency variation 变频调速
~ regulation by pole changing 变极调速
~ regulator 速度调节器
~ setting value 速度设定值
~ spanner 快速扳手
~ sprayer 高速喷雾机
~ up 加速
~ variation 速度变化
~ without load 空载速度
speed-torque 速度转矩
~ characteristic 速度转矩特性
~ curve 速度转矩曲线
speedometer [spi:'dɔmitə] n. 速度计，里程计
speedy ['spi:di] a. 快的，迅速的，敏捷的
sphere [sfiə] n. 球，球体，范围，领域，方面，圈子，半球；v. 形成球体，包围，围绕，置于球面内部
spherical ['sferikəl] a. 球形的，球面的，天体的
spider ['spaidə] n. 三脚架，蜘蛛
spill [spil] n. 溢出，溅出，摔下，木片，小塞子，溢出量；v. (使)溢出，使散落，洒，使流出，使摔下，倒出，涌流，充满
~ control gear 溢流控制装置
~ current 差电流，动作电流
~ valve 溢流阀
~ valve type fuel injection pump 溢流阀式喷油泵
spillage ['spilidʒ] n. 溢出，溢出量
spin [spin] n. 旋转，快速回旋，短途旅行；v. 快速旋转，回旋，奔驰，疾驰，抽制成丝线状

~ axis 自旋轴，旋转轴线

~ bath 沉降槽

spindle ['spindl] n. 锭子，纺锤，细长的人(或物)，轴，杆，心轴；v. 长得细长，装锭子于；a. 锭子似的，细长的

~ bore 主轴孔径

~ oil 锭子油

spine [spain] n. 中心，脊骨，书脊，地面隆起地带，刺

spiral ['spaiərəl] n. 螺线，螺旋，螺旋形物，连续的升降；v. 螺旋式移动，盘旋上升或下降，连续上升或下降；a. 螺线的，螺线似的，绕线轴的

~ bevel gear 螺旋伞齿轮，弧齿锥齿轮

~ casing 蜗壳

~ pipe 螺旋管，螺盘管，盘管

~ pointed tap 螺尖丝锥，枪式丝锥

~ tube 螺旋管

spirit [spirit] n. 精神，灵魂，幽灵，妖精，勇气，火力，活力，力量，锐气，精力，生气，本质，热情，情绪，基本条件；v. 诱拐，鼓励，鼓舞

~ level 水平仪，气泡水准仪

splash [splæʃ] n. 溅，飞溅，斑点，扩散图，少量；v. 溅，泼，溅湿，涉水前行

~ feed 飞溅润滑，喷射送料，喷射送料

~ lubrication 飞溅润滑

~ plate 挡水板

~ pocket 飞溅油箱

~ proof 防溅的，防水的

~ ring 润滑油环，润滑油圈，溅油环

splice [splais] n. 连接，结合处；v. 接合，粘接，胶接，绞接，捻接，叠接

spline [splain] n. 方栓，齿条，止转楔，花键；v. 用花键联接，开键槽

split [split] n. 裂开，裂口，裂痕，裂片，分歧，不和，香蕉船；v. 分裂，分开，划开，划分，劈开，分担，迅速离去，密告，泄密

~ collet 夹头，(气门)锁夹

~ conductor 多芯线，多股绝缘线

~ drum mooring winch 分筒式系泊绞车

~ mold 组合模，可拆模，拼合铸模，对开铸模

~ phase breaker malfunction protection 分相式断路器失灵保护

~ phase motor 分相电动机

~ pin 开口销

~ range 分割区域，分区，分割界限，分程

~ rang control 分程控制，分程调节

~ range positioned 分段定位器

~ ring 开口环，扣环

~ skirt piston 裙部开槽的活塞，导缘开缝活塞

~ mooring drum 分体式绞缆筒

~ up 分裂

~ windlass 分离式锚机

spoil [spɔil] n. 赃物，猎物，战利品；v. 扰乱，损坏，破坏，毁掉，搞糟，抢劫，剥夺，变质，变坏，宠坏，溺爱

spoilage ['spɔilidʒ] n. 损坏，损耗，腐败 ‖ Syn. damage 损坏，损毁，损失，损害；worsement 损坏，破坏

sponge ['spʌndʒ] n. 海绵，海绵体，海绵状物，棉球，纱布；v. 用海绵洗涤，用海绵擦拭，用海绵吸收，海绵般吸收

sponson ['spɔnsn] n. 舷侧突出部，突出炮座，水鳍

~ deck 伸出甲板，外伸甲板，舷伸甲板

spontaneous [spɔn'teinjəs] a. 自发的，自然的，天然产生的，无意识的
 ~ combustion 自燃
 ~ emission 自发发射
 ~ ignition 自发着火

spontaneously [spɔn'teinjəsli] ad. 自然地，自发地，本能地，不由自主地

spool [spu:l] n. 线轴，卷轴，卷盘，磁带轴，所绕的数量，有边筒子状物；v. 缠绕在线轴上，缠绕

spot [spɔt] n. 斑点，污点，位置，部位，地点，场所，现场，困境，聚光灯，少量，少许；v. 玷污，弄脏，放置，安置，配备，侦察，认出，辨认，发现
 ~ facing machining 孔加工
 ~ field investigation 现场调查
 ~ type 点式，点型
 ~ type fire detector 点式火灾探测器
 ~ type heat detector 点式热探测器
 ~ type smoke detector 点式感烟探测器

spotlight ['spɔtlait] n. 聚光灯，探照灯，公众的注意力；v. 聚光照明，集中

spray [sprei] n. 喷雾，飞沫，浪花，压力容器，喷雾器；v. 喷射，喷溅
 ~ bottle 喷雾瓶
 ~ can 喷壶，喷雾器
 ~ evaporative condenser 喷淋蒸发式冷凝器，喷洒蒸发式冷凝器
 ~ film 喷雾薄膜
 ~ film evaporator 喷雾薄膜蒸发器
 ~ shield 防溅板

sprayer ['spreiə] n. 喷雾，喷雾器

spraying ['spreiiŋ] n. 喷雾；v. (spray 的 ing 形式) 喷射，喷溅
 ~ extinguisher 喷雾灭火器

~ nozzle 喷雾嘴，雾化喷头
~ overlay 喷镀堆焊

spread [spred] n. 伸展，展开，传播，蔓延，宴会，桌布；v. 伸展，展开，铺，涂，敷，摆，传播，散布
 ~ sheet 总分析表

spreading ['sprediŋ] n. 散布，扩张，扩展，扩散；v. (spread 的 ing 形式) 伸展，展开，铺，涂，敷，摆，传播，散布
 ~ rate 扩张速率
 ~ resistance 扩展电阻，扩散电阻

spring [spriŋ] n. 弹簧，发条，弹性，弹力，根源，春天，跃起，泉；v. 跳，跃，跃出，使跳跃，使爆炸，触发
 ~ base 弹簧座
 ~ box 弹簧箱
 ~ cap 弹簧盖
 ~ carrier 弹簧托架
 ~ carrying block 板簧支座，簧架
 ~ clamp 弹簧夹
 ~ cleaner 弹簧清洁器
 ~ hinge 弹簧铰链
 ~ holder 弹簧盘
 ~ lay rope 麻与金属丝合股绳
 ~ line 斜系船缆，倒缆，拱脚线
 ~ lock washer 弹簧锁紧垫圈
 ~ out 跳出，冲出，突然冒出
 ~ plate 簧片
 ~ plunger 弹簧定位销，弹簧锁销
 ~ retainer 弹簧限位器
 ~ return 弹力恢复，自复
 ~ steel wire 弹簧钢丝
 ~ stirrer 弹簧箍，弹簧夹头
 ~ water stopper 弹簧止水夹
 ~ wedge plate 弹簧楔片

spring-loaded 弹簧支撑的，受弹簧力作

用的，弹簧加载的

~ cock 弹簧旋塞

~ contactor 弹簧接触器

~ gear 弹簧加载齿轮

~ regulator 弹簧加载调节器，弹簧承力调节器

~ valve 弹簧阀

spring-operated 弹簧驱动的，弹簧操作的

~ band brake 弹簧带式制动器，弹簧带式闸

~ fire damper 弹簧驱动防火阀

sprinkle ['spriŋkl] *n.* 小雨，少量，洒的动作；*v.* 洒，撒，点缀

sprinkler ['spriŋklə] *n.* 洒水器，喷洒器，洒水装置，洒水车

~ head 喷灌头，洒水装置的莲蓬头

~ system 自动洒水装置，自动喷水灭火系统

sprit [sprit] *n.* 斜撑帆杆，船篙

spur [spə:] *n.* 马刺，激励因素，刺激物，突出物，支柱，支墩；*v.* 鞭策，刺激，疾驰，驱策

~ gear 正齿轮 ‖ *Syn.* spur wheel 正齿轮

~ gear pump 正齿轮泵

~ gear transmission 正齿轮传动

Spurling ['spə:liŋ] *n.* 斯珀林(人名，英格兰姓氏)

~ line 驾驶轮卷筒连接索，桅前支索跨接导索

~ pipe 锚链筒，锚链管 ‖ *Syn.* chain pipe 锚链管；hawse pipe 锚链孔衬管，锚链筒

square [skwɛə] *n.* 正方形，广场，平方，直角尺；*v.* 使成方形，弄平，使直，一致，符合，自乘，结算；*a.* 正方形的，四方的，直角的，正直的，公平的，结清的，平方的，彻底的；*ad.* 成直角地，正直地，公平地，坚定地 ‖ circle 圆，圆形；ellipse 椭圆，椭圆形；parallelogram 平行四边形；rectangle 矩形；rhombus 菱形；trapezoid 梯形；triangle 三角形

~ brass nut 方形黄铜螺母

~ butt 方形握把

~ coarse file 粗方锉

~ coil 方形线圈

~ cut stern 方型艉，方艉

~ engine 等径程发动机，方形发动机

~ file 方锉

~ head bolt 方头螺栓

~ master 直角尺

~ matrix 方矩阵，矩形矩阵

~ nose shovel 方头锹

~ root 平方根

~ smooth file 细方锉

~ socket wrench 方套筒扳手

~ wave 方波

squeeze [skwi:z] *n.* 挤压，压榨，抱紧，拥挤人群，榨出量；*v.* 挤压，握紧，夹紧，压榨，挤入，塞入，设法腾出，设法找出

~ grip type release valve 压柄式放泄阀

~ head 压头，压板

squirrel [skwirəl] *n.* 松鼠；*v.* 贮藏，隐藏，储存

~ cage induction motor 鼠笼式感应电动机

~ cage motor 鼠笼式电动机

SR (saturated reactor) 饱和电抗器

SS (switching selector) 开关选择器

551

SSA (ship security assessment) 船舶保安评估

SSAS (ship security alert system) 船舶安全警报系统

SSB (single-sided printed board) 单面印制板

SSC (surface search coordinator) 海面搜救协调船，海面搜救协调员

SSO (ship security officer) 船舶保安员

SSP (ship security plan) 船舶保安计划

stability [stə'biliti] n. 稳定性，可信性，可靠性，稳固

~ limit 稳定极限，稳定边界

~ margin 稳性储备，稳定边际，稳定储备，稳定裕度

~ regulation 稳定性调节

stabilization [ˌsteibilai'zeiʃən] n. 稳定性，稳定化，安定面

~ control 稳定控制

~ efficiency 稳定效率

~ network 稳定网络

stabilize ['steibilaiz] v. 使稳定，使稳固，使不变，使平衡

stabilizer ['steibilaizə] n. 稳定器，安定装置，水平尾翼

~ control gear 减摇控制设备，稳定器控制装置

~ control room 减摇控制室

~ of power system 电力系统稳定器

~ system 稳定器系统

stabilizing ['steibəˌlaiziŋ] n. 稳定化处理；v. (stabilize 的 ing 形式) 使稳定，使稳固，使不变，使平衡

~ feature 稳定特征

~ feedback 稳定反馈，稳定回授

~ fin 稳定翅，稳定尾，舷侧可操纵鳍

~ transformer 稳压变压器，稳定变压器

~ treatment 稳定化处理(使合金结构或零件尺寸稳定)

stable ['steibl] a. 稳定的，不变的，永久的，耐久的，保持平衡的，自我修复的，稳定可靠的

~ element 稳定元件

~ equilibrium 稳定平衡

~ operation 稳定运行，稳定操作

stack [stæk] n. 堆，一堆，大量，堆栈，层积，烟囱，烟道，枪架；v. 堆叠，堆积，堆起来，覆盖住

~ up 加起来

stacked [stækt] v. (stack 的过去式和过去分词) 堆叠，堆积，堆起来，覆盖住；a. 入栈的，栈式的，妖艳的，身材婀娜多姿的

~ cell 参比室

~ content 虚积量，散堆量

staff [staːf] n. 棒，杖，杆，旗杆，支柱，全体职员，全体工作人员，参谋机构，五线谱；v. 供给人员，充当职员，任职于

stage [steidʒ] n. 发展进程，阶段，行程，时期，级，水位，舞台，戏剧，活动场所，驿站；v. 举行，发起，筹备，筹划，展现，扎营，上演

~ casing pump 多级套管泵

staged ['steidʒid] v. (stage 的过去式和过去分词) 举行，发起，筹备，筹划，展现，扎营，上演；a. 分阶段的，分段的，阶梯式的

~ evacuation 分阶段疏散

~ research 分段搜索

stagger ['stægə] n. 摇晃，蹒跚，交错，摇

摇摆摆，犹豫，间隔，错开时间，惊愕；*a*. 交错的

stagnate [stæg'neit] *v*. (使)淤塞,(使)停滞,(使)沉滞,(使)变萧条

stain [stein] *n*. 污点,色斑,瑕疵,着色剂；*v*. 玷污,弄脏,污染,染色
  ~ proofing 防锈处理
  ~ removal 去污(斑),除锈

stainless ['steinlis] *a*. 不锈的,不会脏的,无污点,纯洁的
  ~ steel 不锈钢
  ~ steel electrode 不锈钢焊条
  ~ steel liner 不锈钢衬里
  ~ steel pipe 不锈钢管
  ~ steel round bar 不锈钢圆棒
  ~ steel welding wire 不锈钢焊丝

stair [stɛə] *n*. 楼梯,(楼梯的)一级

staircase ['stɛəkeis] *n*. 楼梯,楼梯间 ‖ *Syn*. stairway 楼梯,阶梯

stairway ['stɛəwei] *n*. 楼梯,阶梯 ‖ *Syn*. staircase 楼梯

stake [steik] *n*. 平台的桩杆,树桩,股份,资金；*v*. 界定,界分,用桩支撑,用桩保护,用木桩系住,资助,投资

stall [stɔ:l] *n*. 小隔间,护套,熄火,失速,抛锚,货摊,畜栏,厩,出售摊；*v*. (使)停转,(使)停止,抛锚,熄火,失速,迟延

stamp [stæmp] *n*. 标志,印记,印花,印,邮票,图章,踩脚,顿足；*v*. 压印,冲压,踩(脚),顿(足)

stamped [stæmpt] *v*. (stamp 的过去式和过去分词) 压印,冲压,踩(脚),顿(足)；*a*. 铭刻的,顿足的,有邮戳的
  ~ punch 冲压冲头

stamping ['stæmpiŋ] *n*. 冲压,模锻；*v*. (stamp 的 ing 形式) 压印,冲压,踩(脚),顿(足)
  ~ part 冲压零件,冲压件,冲件
  ~ press 压印机,模压机,冲压机,压箔机,烫金机

stanchion ['stɑ:ntʃən] *n*. 立柱,支柱；*v*. 用支柱支撑

stand [stænd] *n*. 停止,抵抗的状态,立场,立足点,看台,架子,台；*v*. 站立,站起,(使)竖立,(使)位于,维持不变,保持稳定,保持特定的航向,持久,经受,测量,承担责任,容忍,益于
  ~ by engine 备车
  ~ generator 立式发电机
  ~ good 依然真实,仍然有效
  ~ pipe 立管,竖管,管柱
  ~ pump 立式泵

standard [,stændəd] *n*. 标准,规格；*a*. 标准的,合格的,普遍的,一般的,公认为优秀的 ‖ *Syn*. criterion 标准,准据,规范；measure 标准,量度标准,尺度；norm 规范,标准,准则；touchstone 标准,检验标准,检验手段
  ~ component 标准部件
  ~ discharge connection 标准排放接头
  ~ dome lighting fitting 标准穹顶照明配件
  ~ engine order 标准发动机指令
  ~ fire test 标准火灾试验
  ~ horsepower 额定功率,标准马力 ‖ *Syn*. capacity rating 额定功率,额定容量；nominal capacity 额定功率,标称功率,额定容量,标称容量；nominal output 额定功率,额定出力,额定输出,标称输出；nominal power 额定功

553

率，额定容量，标称功率，标称容量；power rating 额定功率；rated capacity 额定功率，额定容量，设计效率；rated output 额定功率，额定输出量，额定出力；rated power 额定功率，设计功率，额定动力，不失真功率；rated power capability 额定功率；rated power output 额定功率，额定动力输出
~ input signal 标准输入信号
~ input signal level 标准输入信号电平
~ loading conditions 标准载荷条件，标准加载条件
~ logic module 标准逻辑微型组件
~ measurement and display data 标准测量和显示数据
~ nozzle 标准喷嘴
~ of accuracy 准确度标准
~ power output 标准功率输出
~ shore connection 标准通岸接头
~ signal amplifier 标准信号放大器
~ toolbar 标准工具栏
~ tooth 标准轮齿

standardization [ˌstændədaiˈzeiʃən] n. 标准化，规范化

standardize [ˈstændədaiz] v. 使符合标准，使标准化

standardized [ˈstændəˌdaizd] v. (standardize 的过去式和过去分词) 使符合标准，使标准化；a. 标准的，定型的
~ format 标准化格式
~ part 标准化零件
~ level difference 标准(声)级差

standby [ˈstændbai] n. 备用品，替代品，可信赖的人，使船待命的信息；a. 机动的，备用的；ad. 应急的，备用地，待命地

~ air compressor 备用空压机
~ capacity 备用容量
~ condition 等待状态，准备状态，待用状态
~ engine 备用发动机
~ generating set 备用发电机组
~ generator 备用发电机
~ pump 备用泵
~ source 备用电源

standing [ˈstændiŋ] n. 站立，身份，名望，持续；v. (stand 的 ing 形式) 站，立，站起, (使)竖立，(使)位于，维持不变，保持稳定，保持特定的航向，持久，经受，测量，承担责任，容忍，益于；a. 直立的，停滞的，固定的，常备的，标准的，常设的
~ order 委托书，现行命令
~ rigging 固定索具，静索
~ water 死水

standpipe [ˈstændpaip] n. 竖管，管体式水塔

standpoint [ˈstændpɔint] n. 立场，观点

standstill [ˈstændstil] n. 停顿, 停止, 停滞, 静止状态

staple [ˈsteipl] n. 钉书钉，钉，主要产品，主要商品，原材料，主要成分，来源；v. 用钉书钉钉住，分类，分级；a. 主要的，常用的，大宗生产的

star [staː] n. 星，恒星，星形物，明星，名角；v. 主演，标星号，表现出众
~ connection 星形接线，星形连接，Y 接法 ‖ delta connection 三角形接线，三角形连接，△接法
~ network 星形网络

star-delta 星形三角形
~ connection 星形三角形连接

~ starter 星形三角形启动器

starboard ['sta:bəd] *n.* (船舶、飞机的)右舷，右侧；*v.* 向右转；*a.* 右舷的

~ bow 右舷船首，右舷前方，船首右舷方向

~ direction 右舷方向

~ lamp 右舷灯

~ quarter 右舷后方，右舷后部

~ side 右舷

start [sta:t] *n.* 动身，出发点，开始，优先地位，惊起，惊跳，赛跑的先跑权；*v.* 启动，发动，出发，启程，开始，着手，惊动，惊起

~ by 先做某事

~ failure alarm 启动故障报警

~ for 动身去

~ mode 启动模式

start-finish 启动结束

~ signal 启动结束信号

start-up 启动

starter ['sta:tə] *n.* 启动器

~ motor 启动电动机

starting ['sta:tiŋ] *n.* 出发，开始；*v.* (start 的 ing 形式) 启动，发动，出发，启程，开始，着手，惊动，惊起

~ air compressor 启动空气压缩机

~ air control pipe 启动空气控制管

~ air control valve 启动空气控制阀

~ air cut off 启动空气切断

~ air distributor 启动空气分配器

~ air inlet 启动空气入口

~ air manifold 启动空气总管

~ air pilot valve 启动空气控制阀

~ air pipe 启动空气管

~ air relief valve 启动空气阀

~ air reservoir 启动空气瓶

~ air stop valve 启动截止阀

~ air system 启动空气系统

~ air tank 启动空气箱

~ air valve 启动空气阀

~ button 启动按钮 ‖ *Syn*. starting pushbutton 启动按钮

~ cam 启动凸轮

~ control valve 启动控制阀

~ controller 启动控制器

~ current 启动电流

~ device 启动装置

~ handle 启动手柄

~ interlock 启动联锁

~ lever 启动杆

~ motor 启动电动机

~ performance 启动性能

~ resistor 启动电阻

~ servomotor 启动伺服电动机

~ speed 启动速度

~ time 启动时间

~ torque 启动转矩

~ value 初值，起始值

~ valve 启动阀

~ valve interlock device 启动阀连锁装置

state [steit] *n.* 情形，状态，地位，仪式，盛观，领土，国家，政府，州；*v.* 声明，陈述，规定，预定，指定；*a.* 国家的，国有的，国营的，州的，正式的，典礼用的

~ of alarm 报警状态

~ of emergency 紧急状态

stateroom ['steitru:m] *n.* 特等客舱，高级包厢，政府公寓

static ['stætik] *n.* 静电，静电噪声，随机噪声，干涉，阻碍；*a.* 静止的，静态

的，静力的，静电的，不变的
~ accuracy 静态精度
~ balancing 静态平衡 ‖ *Syn*. static equilibrium 静态平衡；statical balance 静态平衡
~ characteristic 静态特性
~ characteristic curve of voltage 电压静态特性曲线
~ compensation 静态补偿
~ controller 静态控制器
~ error 静态误差
~ friction 静摩擦力
~ loading 静载荷，静负荷
~ mixer 静态混合器，静止混合器
~ pressure 静压
~ pressure regulator 静压调节器
~ seal 静密封
~ state 静态
~ value 静态值
~ var compensator (SVC) 静态无功补偿装置
~ var system (SVS) 静态无功补偿系统
~ variable 静态变量

statical ['stætikəl] *a*. 静止的，静电的
~ balance 静态平衡 ‖ *Syn*. static balancing 静态平衡；static equilibrium 静态平衡
~ feature 静力特征
~ moment 静力矩

statically ['stætikli] *a*. 静止地，静态地

station ['steiʃən] *n*. 位置，岗位，地位，身份，局，站，所；*v*. 配置，安置，派驻，驻扎
~ accuracy 定点精确度

stationary ['steiʃ(ə)nəri] *n*. 固定物；*a*. 不动的，固定的，静止的，不变的

~ phase 静止期，稳定期，平稳期
~ ring 固定环
~ seal ring 固定密封环
~ vane 固定叶片

statistic [stə'tistik] *n*. 统计量，统计数据；*a*. 统计的，统计学的

statistical [stə'tistikəl] *a*. 统计的，统计学的

statistics [stə'tistiks] *n*. 统计学，统计表，统计，统计数字

stator ['steitə] *n*. 定子，固定片
~ blade 静叶片，定子叶片
~ coil 定子线圈
~ contactor 定子接触器
~ core 定子铁心
~ ring 定子环
~ winding 定子绕组

status ['steitəs] *n*. 地位，身份，情形，状况，状态

statutory ['stætjut(ə)ri] *a*. 法定的，法令的，依照法令的，可依法处罚的
~ certificate 法定证书
~ survey 法定检验

staunch [stɔ:ntʃ] *a*. 水密的，气密的，坚固的，坚定的，忠诚可靠的

stave [steiv] *n*. 狭板，梯级，棍棒；*v*. 击穿，弄破，避开，压扁，延缓，破碎

stay [stei] *n*. 支柱，逗留，延缓，中止；*v*. 暂住，坚持，止住，抑制，延缓，停下
~ bolt 拉杆螺栓，撑螺栓，长螺栓，拉杆，系杆，拉撑
~ bolt nut 拉杆螺栓螺母
~ tube 撑管，(锅炉的)拉管

stead [sted] *n*. 代替，用处，好处；*v*. 对…有利，对…有用

steadily ['stedili] *ad.* 稳定地，持续地，稳固地，有规则地

steady ['stedi] *v.* (使)稳定，(使)稳恒，(使)稳固；*a.* 稳定的，稳恒的，不变的，镇定的，沉着的，坚定的

~ direct current 稳恒直流电流

~ load 稳定负载

~ state 稳定状态，稳态

~ state analysis of power system 电力系统稳态分析

~ state condition 稳态条件

~ state deviation 稳态偏差

~ state error 稳态误差

~ state error coefficient 稳态误差系数

~ state frequency variation 稳态频率变化

~ state short circuit current 稳态短路电流

~ state speed governing rate 稳态调速率

~ state stability 定态稳定度，静态稳定度

~ state value 稳态值

~ state voltage variation 稳态电压变化

~ working condition 稳定工作状态

steam [sti:m] *n.* 蒸汽，水汽，蒸汽动力，雾，情绪，精力；*v.* 蒸发，冒蒸汽，蒸煮，汽动，成蒸汽上升，使愤怒，使兴奋

~ anchor capstan 蒸汽起锚绞盘

~ boiler 蒸汽锅炉

~ cargo winch 蒸汽绞车

~ chest 蒸汽室

~ cleaner 蒸汽清洁器

~ cock 蒸汽旋塞

~ coil 蒸汽盘管

~ condensate 蒸汽冷凝液

~ condenser 蒸汽冷凝器

~ condition 蒸汽状态，蒸汽参数

~ conduit 蒸汽管道

~ distributor 蒸汽分配器

~ ejector 蒸汽喷射器

~ ejector gas-freeing system 蒸汽喷射器油气抽除系统，蒸汽喷射器油气抽除装置

~ engine 蒸汽机

~ flow 汽流，蒸汽流量

~ flushing 蒸汽清洗，汽冲

~ generator 蒸汽发生器

~ heated evaporator 蒸汽加热蒸发器

~ heater 蒸汽加热器

~ heating coil 蒸汽加热盘管

~ heating pipe 蒸汽加热管

~ heating system 蒸汽供暖系统

~ hose 蒸汽软管，输送蒸汽用软管

~ injection 蒸汽喷射，蒸汽注入，射汽法

~ inlet 蒸汽入口

~ jet refrigeration 蒸汽喷射制冷

~ nozzle 蒸汽喷嘴

~ oil 燃油蒸汽

~ oil atomizer 蒸汽雾化喷油器

~ outlet 蒸汽出口

~ parameter 蒸汽参数

~ pocket 汽囊，汽袋

~ power plant 蒸汽动力装置

~ propulsion 蒸汽推进

~ pump 蒸汽泵

~ purifier 蒸汽净化器

~ raising (锅炉)生汽，气化蒸发，蒸汽蒸发

~ receiver 储汽器

~ separator 蒸汽分离器

~ ship 蒸汽船

~ smothering system 蒸汽灭火系统

~ steering gear 蒸汽操舵装置,蒸汽舵机

~ stop valve 蒸汽截止阀

steamer ['sti:mə] n. 汽船,蒸汽机,蒸汽锅 ‖ *Syn*. steamship 汽船

steaming ['sti:miŋ] v. (steam 的 ing 形式) 蒸发,冒蒸汽,蒸煮,汽动,成蒸汽上升,使愤怒,使兴奋; a. 冒热气的,热气腾腾地

~ header 蒸汽联箱,蒸汽集管

steamship ['sti:mʃip] n. 汽船,轮船 ‖ *Syn*. steamer 汽船

steel [sti:l] n. 钢,钢铁,钢制品,兵器,钢铁工业; v. 包钢,使坚硬; a. 钢的,钢制的,钢铁业的,坚强的

~ anchor 钢锚

~ belt 钢带

~ bottle 钢瓶 ‖ *Syn*. steel cylinder 钢瓶

~ bracket 钢支架

~ cage 钢笼

~ casting 铸钢件

~ container 钢制集装箱

~ deck 钢板层,钢甲板

~ drum 钢桶,铁桶

~ forging 钢锻件

~ frame 钢框架,钢架

~ measuring tape 钢卷尺

~ pack muffler 金属垫片式消声器

~ pile 钢桩

~ pipe 钢管

~ plate 钢板

~ plate pre-treatment shop 钢板预处理车间

~ ruler 钢尺

~ shell 钢壳

~ welding rod 钢焊条

steelwork ['sti:lwə:k] n. 钢铁架

steep [sti:p] n. 悬崖,峭壁,浸渍,浸渍液; v. 浸,泡,沉浸; a. 陡峭的,险峻的,急剧升降的,不合理的

steepness ['sti:pnis] n. 陡度,险峻,不合道理

steer [stiə] n. 一条建议; v. 驾驶,操纵,控制,掌舵,取道,前进

steerage ['stiəridʒ] n. 最低票价的舱位,士官的二等室,操纵,驾驶,掌舵,舵能,驾驶装置,统舱

~ way 舵效航速

steering ['stiəriŋ] n. 操纵,掌舵,指导; v. (steer 的 ing 形式) 驾驶,操纵,控制,掌舵,取道,前进

~ column 驾驶杆

~ control system 操舵系统

~ cylinder 操纵动作筒,转向助力油缸

~ engine 舵机 ‖ *Syn*. steering gear 操舵装置,舵机

~ engine room 舵机室 ‖ *Syn*. steering gear compartment 舵机室

~ equipment 转向装置

~ gear control system 舵机控制系统

~ gear flat 操舵装置平台

~ gear housing 转向器壳

~ gear hydraulic oil 舵机液压油

~ gear power unit 舵机动力设备

~ gear worm 转向蜗轮

~ hunting gear 舵机追随机构

~ nozzle 转向喷嘴

~ shaft 转向轴

~ system 转向系统

~ telemotor 操舵遥控传动装置

~ tie rod 转向系杆

steersman ['stiəzmæn] *n.* 舵手

stem [stem] *n.* 艏柱，晶体管管座，转柄，锁芯轴，茎，干；*v.* 阻止，遏制，滋生，起源于，装上柄

~ contour 艏柱型线

~ light 船艏灯，艏灯

~ overlap 气门重叠度

~ plug 心柱插头

step [step] *n.* 桅座，脚步，步幅，极短的距离，步调，步伐，步骤，措施，级别，踏脚板，梯级，台阶；*v.* 把桅杆放在桅座中，走，举步，移步，踏，步测

~ back 退后，后退，进入毫无意义的地位

~ by step 逐步地

~ by step control 逐步控制

~ change 阶跃变化，步进变化，阶段变化，单增量变化，级变

~ charging 正常充电

~ down 走下，逐步减低，辞职，下台

~ forward 向前走

~ function 阶梯函数

~ function response 阶梯函数响应

~ head 阶梯顶，阶梯头

~ head piston 阶梯顶活塞

~ in 介入，干涉，进入，作短时间的非正式访问

~ input 阶式信号输入，步进输入

~ into 步入

~ length 步长

~ motor 步进电动机，步进马达

~ on it 赶快，加把劲，加大油门

~ response 瞬态特性，过渡特性，阶跃响应

~ transformer 升降压变压器，分级变压器

~ transition 阶梯跃变，阶跃变化，阶跃过渡

step-by-step 按部就班的

~ control 步进控制

step-down 减缓的，下降的

~ transformer 降压变压器

step-up 把电压升高的，递升的

~ transformer 升压变压器

stepless ['stipləs] *a.* 平滑的，无极的，不分级的

~ friction transmission 无级摩擦式传动

~ speed regulation 无级调速

stepped [stept] *v.* (step 的过去式和过去分词) 走，举步，移步，踏，步测；*a.* 有阶梯的，梯形的

~ bulkhead 阶梯式舱壁，凹入舱壁

~ cam 分级凸轮

~ piston 阶梯活塞

~ refining 分段精炼，分级精炼，分级调质

stepper ['stepə] *n.* 快行者，跳舞者

~ motor 步进马达，步进电机 ‖ *Syn.* stepping motor 步进马达，步进电机

stepping ['stepiŋ] *n.* 步进，分级；*v.* (step 的 ing 形式) 走，举步，移步，踏，步测

~ motor 步进马达，步进电机 ‖ *Syn.* stepper motor 步进马达，步进电机

~ switch 步进开关，分级转换开关

sterilization [ˌsterilai'zeiʃən] *n.* 灭菌，杀菌，消毒，绝育

~ compartment 消毒舱

~ dose 杀菌剂量，消毒剂量

sterilize ['sterilaiz] *v.* 消毒，杀菌，使无菌，使不起作用

sterilizer ['sterilaizə] *n.* 消毒者，消毒器

sterilizing ['sterilaiziŋ] *n.* 灭菌，消毒；*v.* (sterilize 的 ing 形式) 消毒，杀菌，使无菌，使不起作用

~ agent 杀菌剂，灭菌剂

~ unit 消毒装置

~ value 杀菌值

stern [stə:n] *n.* 船尾，艉，尾部，末端；*a.* 严厉的，苛刻的

~ barrel 艉滚筒，艉筒

~ bearing 艉轴承

~ chase (紧跟着前船)尾追，追击

~ door 艉门

~ foremost 船尾朝前，倒退，笨拙地

~ frame 艉架

~ fueling rig 船尾加油索具

~ lamp 艉灯

~ line 艉线

~ ramp 尾滑道，艉跳板

~ shaft 艉轴

~ thrust stop 艉推力止动器

~ thruster 艉推进器

~ tube 艉轴管

~ tube bearing 艉轴管轴承

~ tube gland 艉轴管压盖

~ tube head tank 艉轴管重力油柜

~ tube lubricating oil 艉轴管润滑油

~ tube lubricating oil pump 艉轴管滑油泵

~ tube oil 艉轴管油

~ tube seal 艉轴管密封

~ tube sealing oil pump 艉轴管密封油泵

~ tube stuffing 艉轴管填料

~ tube stuffing box 艉轴管填料函

~ wave 艉波

stevedore ['sti:vidɔ:] *n.* 码头装卸工人，搬运工；*v.* 装(卸)货

steward ['stju:əd] *n.* 服务员，乘务员，干事，管家，理事；*v.* 当服务员，当乘务员

stewardess [stju:ə'des] *n.* 女服务员，女乘务员

STCW Convention, 1978 (International Convention on Standards of Training, Certification and Watchkeeping for Seafarers, 1978) 1978 年海员培训、发证和值班标准国际公约，1978 年 STCW 公约

stick [stik] *n.* 桅杆，操纵杆，黏性，集束炸弹，棍棒，手杖，棍枝，枝条，一件家具；*v.* 粘住，粘贴，刺，戳，钉住，阻延，推迟，坚持，固守

~ to 粘住，坚持，遵守，紧随，紧跟

sticky ['stiki] *a.* 黏的，黏性的，困难的，棘手的

stiff [stif] *a.* 硬的，僵直的，拘谨的，呆板的，艰难的，费劲的，僵硬的

~ buffer spring 刚性缓冲弹簧

stiffen ['stifn] *v.* 使硬，使僵硬，使生硬，使黏稠，变黏，变硬，变猛烈

stiffener ['stifnə] *n.* 加强筋，使变硬的东西

~ material 加强筋材料

stiffening ['stifniŋ] *n.* 硬化，变硬的材料；*v.* (stiffen 的 ing 形式) 使硬，使僵硬，使生硬，使黏稠，变黏，变硬，变猛烈

~ plate 加强板，补强板

~ rib 加强筋，加强肋

~ rib punch stinger 加强筋冲子

stiffness ['stifnis] n. 坚硬，硬度

still [stil] n. 平静，寂静，剧照，静止画面，静态图片，蒸馏器；a. 静止的，静寂的；ad. 还，仍，更，还要，尽管如此，依然

~ water bending moment 静水弯矩

stimulate ['stimjuleit] v. 刺激，激励，鼓舞，使兴奋，起促进作用，起刺激作用

stimulus ['stimjuləs] n. 促进因素，刺激物，刺激

stipulate ['stipjuleit] v. 规定，保证，约定，讲明，制定，明确要求

stipulation [,stipju'leiʃən] n. 规定，条文，约定，约束，条款说明，契约

stir [stə:] n. 搅动，轰动，骚乱，激动；v. 移动，摇动，激起，搅和，惹起，走动，传播，流行

Stirling ['stə:liŋ] n. 斯特林(苏格兰城市)

~ engine 斯特林发动机

stirrer ['stə:rə] n. 搅拌器，搅拌者，搅拌用勺子

stochastic [stəu'kæstik] a. 随机的 ‖ *Syn.* random 随机的，任意的，随便的，胡乱的

stock [stɔk] n. 库存，原料，股票，股份，托盘，树干，祖先，血统；v. 装把手，进货，备有，采购；a. 股票的，普通的，常备的，存货的，繁殖用的

~ allowance (机械)加工余量

~ consumption 备品消耗量

~ on hand 现存量

~ piston 备用活塞

stockless [s'tɔkles] a. 无柄的，无锚杆的

stokehold [s'təukhəuld] n. (汽船上的)锅炉舱，锅炉口

~ floor 锅炉舱地板，锅炉舱平台

~ skylight 锅炉舱天窗

stool [stu:l] n. 凳子，大便，厕所；v. 诱捕

stop [stɔp] n. 停止，逗留，障碍，填塞，车站；v. 停止，塞住，堵塞，阻止，击落，断绝，终止，难倒

~ bar 止动杆

~ button 停止按钮，制动按钮

~ engine port 左停车

~ engine starboard 右停车

~ lever 止动杆，制动杆，锁定杆，定位杆，挡杆

~ pin 止动销，防转销，拦钩销

~ plate 盲板，挡板

~ position 停止状态，停止位置

~ ring 止动环

~ rod 止动杆

~ screw 止动螺钉，防松螺钉

~ short 突然停止

~ starboard 右停车

~ still 完全停止

~ valve 停止阀，闭塞阀

~ watch 秒表

stoppage ['stɔpidʒ] n. 停止，中止，阻塞，阻滞，堵塞，扣留

stopper ['stɔpə] n. 塞子，制动器，阻塞物，制止者；v. 塞住

stopping ['stɔpiŋ] n. 停止，填塞物；v. (stop 的 ing 形式) 停止，塞住，堵塞，阻止，击落，断绝，终止，难倒

~ ability 停船性能，停止能力，制动能力

~ agent 阻化剂

~ tooth 限动齿

561

storage ['stɔ:ridʒ] *n.* 储存,储藏,储藏量,储藏处,仓库
  ~ battery 蓄电池
  ~ capacity 存储容量,蓄电池容量,储藏能力,积聚电容
  ~ element 存储元件
  ~ tank 储油罐
store [stɔ:] *n.* 商店,储存物,仓库,货栈,大量;*v.* 储藏,储备,存储,填充
  ~ carrier 供应运输船,补给运输船
  ~ keeper 物料管理员,仓库管理员,仓库保管员
  ~ room 储藏室
storm [stɔ:m] *n.* 暴风雨,暴风雪,骚乱,动荡,猛袭,巨响,喧哗;*v.* 猛攻,突袭,猛烈地吹,猛烈地刮,愤怒,狂怒;咆哮
  ~ valve 排水口止回阀,节气阀
  ~ warning 风暴警报
stove [stəuv] *n.* 炉,火炉,窑,干燥室,烘房;*v.* 用火炉烤
stow [stəu] *v.* 装,装载,安置,装填,储备,容纳,暂停
stowage ['stəuidʒ] *n.* 装载,仓库,储存处,存储物,堆装物
  ~ factor 积载因素
stowaway ['stəuə,wei] *n.* 偷乘船者,偷渡者
straight [streit] *n.* 直线,直线部分,直立部分,直路;*a.* 直的,直立的,平坦的,正确的,连续的,有次序的,整齐的,标准的,重要的,直率的,诚实的,正直的;*ad.* 成直线地,直地,直立地,直接地,整齐地,不停地
  ~ bevel gear 直齿伞(锥)齿轮
  ~ brass cock 铜直通旋塞

  ~ burr 直纹
  ~ circlip pliers 直卡簧手钳
  ~ comparator 直接比较器
  ~ one-way valve 直通单向阀
  ~ reciprocation 直线往复运动
  ~ toothed spur gear 直齿圆柱齿轮
  ~ tube 直管
  ~ tube boiler 直管锅炉
straight-through 直连,直通
  ~ cable 直通线
  ~ cock 直通旋塞
straighten ['streitn] *v.* (使)变直,(使)变平,(使)变整
straightening ['streitniŋ] *n.* 直线折旧法;*v.* (straighten 的 ing 形式) (使)变直,(使)变平,(使)变整
  ~ machine 矫正机,矫直机
strain [strein] *n.* 张力,应变,紧张,过度的疲劳;*v.* 过滤,滤去,扭伤,损伤,拉紧,扯紧,(使)紧张,尽力
  ~ gauge 应变仪,变形测量器
  ~ gauge load cell 应变式负荷传感器,应变式称重传感器
  ~ rate 应变速率,应变率
strainer ['streinə] *n.* 滤网,松紧扣,过滤器
straining ['streiniŋ] *n.* 变形,应变;*v.* (strain 的 ing 形式) 过滤,滤去,扭伤,损伤,拉紧,扯紧,(使)紧张,尽力
  ~ meter 应变仪,应变计
strait [streit] *n.* 海峡;*a.* 艰难的,苦恼的,窘迫的
strake [streik] *n.* 船底板,列板,轮箍,轮铁
strand [strænd] *n.* 线,绳,串,海滨,河岸;*v.* (使)搁浅,使落后,使陷于困境,弄断,搓

strap [stræp] *n.* 皮带，带子；*v.* 用带缚住，用带捆扎

stratification [ˌstrætifi'keiʃən] *n.* 分层，层理，成层，层化

stray [strei] *n.* 迷路，偏离，漂泊，漂泊游荡；*v.* 散开的，分离的，迷路的，离群的，偶遇的
~ loss 杂散损耗

stream [stri:m] *n.* 河流，小河，潮流，趋势，倾向，流出，一串，等级；*v.* 倾注，流动，流出，渗出，溢出，鱼贯而行，按能力等级分类，飘扬

streamline ['stri:mlain] *n.* 流线，流线型；*v.* 使成流线型，使现代化，组织，使简单化；*a.* 流线型的

streamlined ['stri:mlaind] *v.* (streamline 的过去式和过去分词) 使成流线型，使现代化，组织，使简单化；*a.* 流线型的，流线的，最新型的，改进的，精简的
~ casing 流线型套管

strength [streŋθ] *n.* 力，力量，力气，实力，兵力，浓度
~ bulkhead 强度隔板
~ character 强度性能
~ curve 强度曲线
~ deck 强度甲板
~ of a structure 结构强度
~ of attack 灭火强度

strengthen ['streŋθən] *v.* 加强，增强，变强

stress [stres] *n.* 应力，重压，逼迫，压力，重点，着重，强调，重音；*v.* 受到机械力压力，加压，着重，强调，重读
~ concentration 应力集中
~ concentration factor 应力集中系数
~ condition 应力状态
~ corrosion 应力腐蚀
~ corrosion cracking 应力腐蚀裂纹
~ field 应力场
~ monitoring system 应力监视系统
~ response 应激反应

stretch [stretʃ] *n.* 伸展，舒展，伸缩性，一段时间，一段路程；*v.* 伸展，延伸，伸开，张开，持续，变长，变宽，拉紧，张紧，持续；*a.* 可伸缩的，有弹性的
~ bending 拉弯

stretcher ['stretʃə] *n.* 担架，延伸器，撑具，撑架

strike [straik] *n.* 罢工，攻击；*v.* 打，击，攻击，敲响，罢工，打火，划火柴，找到，发现，朝某一方向前进，拉下(桅杆或帆)，降低(旗帜或帆)，放低(货物)进入货舱

string [striŋ] *n.* 线，细绳，一串，一组字符，一行；*v.* 成线形，排成一列，上弦，调弦

stringer ['striŋə] *n.* 纵梁，纵材，系梁，纵向加强索
~ angle 舷边角钢，舷边角材
~ flat 甲板边板

strip [strip] *n.* 条，带；*v.* 除去，剥去，剥夺，删除，清除，拆除，刮除，剥光，放置
~ seal 带状密封

stripe [straip] *n.* 条纹，斑纹，种类，军士军阶，臂章，肩章；*v.* 使带有条纹，鞭打，抽打

stripping ['stripiŋ] *n.* 抽锭，脱模，拆模，*v.* (strip 的 ing 形式) 除去，剥去，剥夺，删除，清除，拆除，刮除，放置

~ pipe 清舱管

~ pipe line 清舱管路

~ plate (漏)模板

~ pump 扫舱泵

stroke [strəuk] *n.* 冲程，尾桨手，尾桨手位置，击，敲，报时钟声，一击，一划，一笔，一次努力，打击；*v.* 作尾桨手，(为划桨手)设定节奏，指挥划桨，每分钟以特定的频率划船，划掉，轻抚，轻触，敲击，击球

~ coefficient 冲程系数

~ volume 每搏输出量，每搏量

stroke-bore 冲程缸径

~ ratio 冲程缸径比

strong [strɔŋ] *a.* 强，强壮的，坚固的，浓的，强烈的，强大的，强的，强硬的

~ acid number (SAN) 强酸值

~ base number (SBN) 强碱值

structural ['strʌktʃərəl] *a.* 构造的，结构的，建筑上的

~ adjustment 结构调整

~ bead 结构加强筋

~ component 构件，结构零件

~ failure 结构损坏，结构破坏，结构失效

~ features 构造细部，结构要点

~ frame 结构框架，构架

~ information 结构信息

~ inspection 结构检查

~ instability 结构不稳定性

~ member 结构构件，结构件

~ test 结构试验

~ testing 结构性测试

structure ['strʌktʃə] *n.* 结构，构造，建筑物，构造物，体系；*v.* 建筑，构成，组织，排列，安排

~ completeness of rescue boat davit to be inspected 救助艇架结构完整性交验

strum [strʌm] *n.* 轻弹，乱弹的声音；*v.* 乱弹，乱奏

~ box 舱底水滤盒，舱底水过滤箱

strut [strʌt] *n.* 支柱，撑木，压杆，趾高气扬的步态；*v.* 支撑，炫耀，肿胀，大摇大摆地走

stub [stʌb] *n.* 烟蒂，票根，存根，树桩，铅笔头；*v.* 踩熄；*a.* 短而秃的

~ out 踩熄，把弄灭

~ pipe 短管

~ pole 主梁

~ bolt 柱螺栓

stuff [stʌf] *n.* 材料，原料，资料，填充物；*v.* 塞满，填满，填充

stuffiness ['stʌfinəs] *n.* 不通风，不通气，闷热

stuffing [stʌf] *n.* 填塞料；*v.* (stuff 的 ing 形式) 塞满，填满，填充

~ box 填料函

~ box casing 填料函外壳

~ box cock 填料函旋塞，有填料开关

~ box drain oil cleaning system 填料函排油清洗系统，填料函排油清洗装置

~ box for piston rod 活塞杆填料函

~ box gland 填料函盖，填料函压盖

sturdy ['stə:di] *a.* 坚固的，耐用的，坚定的，强壮的，健全的

sub [sʌb] *n.* 代替者，潜水艇，低能者；*v.* 做替身

~ switchboard 副配电板 ‖ ***Syn.*** auxiliary switchboard 辅助配电盘，辅配电盘，副配电板

subassembly ['sʌbə'sembli] *n.* 部件，组件，分组合件

subcircuit ['sʌb'sə:kit] *n.* 支电路

subcool ['sʌb'ku:l] *v.* 使过冷，使低温冷却

subdivision [,sʌbdi'viʒən] *n.* 细分，再分，一部，分支，分部
~ index 分舱指数
~ load line 分舱载重线
~ load line mark 分舱载重线标记

subfeeder ['sʌbfi:dər] *n.* 分支配电线，副馈电线
~ cable 分支电缆，分支光缆

subject ['sʌbdʒikt] *n.* 题目，主题，科目，学科，研究领域，对象，理由，起因，主语；*v.* 遵照，服从，使遭受，使经历，制服，征服，使…隶属，提供，提出；*a.* 服从的，支配的，易于…的，倾向于…的，依…而定的

sublevel ['sʌb'levl] *n.* 支级，次级，亚级，次层，副准位

submarine ['sʌbməri:n] *n.* 潜水艇，潜艇；*v.* 用潜艇攻击，驾驶潜艇，滑入底下；*a.* 水下的，海底的，海面下的
~ batteries 潜艇蓄电池组
~ cable 海底电缆
~ chaser 猎潜艇
~ manoeuvrability 潜艇操纵性

submerge [səb'mə:dʒ] *v.* 浸没，淹没，潜水

submerged [səb'mə:dʒd] *v.* (submerge 的过去式和过去分词) 浸没，淹没，潜水；*a.* 在水中的，淹没的
~ bio-filter treatment system 淹没式生物滤池处理系统
~ burner 水下燃嘴，水下燃烧器，浸没燃烧器

~ cargo pump 潜油泵
~ lamp 潜灯
~ nozzle 浸入式水口
~ tube evaporator 浸没管式蒸发器

submersible [səb'mə:səbl] *n.* 潜水器，潜艇；*a.* 浸没式的，能沉入水中的，能潜水的
~ motor 潜水式电动机
~ platform 浸没式平台
~ pump 潜水泵
~ support vessel 潜水器工作母船
~ watertight cable 深水密封电缆

submersion [səb'mə:ʃən] *n.* 淹没
~ skimmer 浸没式撇油器，浸没式浮油回收装置
~ watch 潜水表

submit [səb'mit] *v.* (使)服从，(使)顺从，提交，呈送，建议，主张

subordinate [sə'bɔ:dinit] *n.* 部属，部下，下级；*v.* 使居下位，(使)服从，战胜；*a.* 次要的，从属的，隶属的，下级的

subscript ['sʌbskript] *n.* 下标，下角码；*a.* 下标的，写在下面的，印在下面的

subsection ['sʌb'sekʃən] *n.* 分部，分段，小部分，小单位，细分

subsequence ['sʌbsikwəns] *n.* 后果，后续，后继，随后

subsequent ['sʌbsikwənt] *a.* 随后的，后来的，作为结果而发生的

subsequently ['sʌbsikwəntli] *ad.* 其后，随后，后来

subsidiary [səb'sidjəri] *n.* 辅助物，子公司；*a.* 辅助的，补助的，次要的，附属的，补助金的
~ combustion chamber 辅助燃烧室

subsidy ['sʌbsidi] *n.* 补贴，津贴，助学金

substance ['sʌbstəns] n. 物质，材料，实质，内容，主旨

substandard [ˌsəb'stændəd] a. 不够标准的，在标准以下的，低等级标准

substantial [səb'stænʃəl] n. 本质，结实的东西；a. 坚固的，实质的，真实的，充实的，结实的，牢固的

substantially [səb'stænʃ(ə)li] ad. 主要地，重大地，实质上地，相当大地

substation ['sʌbsteiʃən] n. 分站，分所，变电站，变电所

~ in workshop 车间变电站

~ transformator 配电变压器

~ integrated automation 变电站综合自动化

substitute ['sʌbstitju:t] n. 代用品，代替者，替代品；v. 代替，替换，代用

substitution [ˌsʌbsti'tju:ʃən] n. 代替，置换，取代作用，代入法

substrate ['sʌbstreit] n. (=substratum) 基础，本源，底层，下层，感光底层，底土层

substratum ['sʌb'stra:təm] n. (=substrate) 基础，本源，底层，下层，感光底层，底土层

subsystem ['sʌbˌsistim] n. 子系统，分系统，次要系统

subtotal ['sʌbˌtəutl] n. 小计；v. 求部分和；a. 几乎全部的

subtract [səb'trækt] v. 减去，减，扣除

subtraction [səb'trækʃən] n. 减去，减少，减法，扣除

succeed [sək'si:d] v. 取得成功，继承，继任，继位

success [sək'ses] n. 成功，成就，胜利，发迹，兴旺

~ rate 成功率

successful [sək'sesful] a. 成功的，如愿以偿的

successfully [sək'sesfuli] ad. 成功地，顺利地

successive [sək'sesiv] a. 逐次的，连续的，相继的，接替的，继承的

~ cuts 连续切削

successor [sək'sesə] n. 后续事物，继承人，继任者

suck [sʌk] n. 吮吸，吸力，吸入物；v. 吮吸，吸取，吸入

suction ['sʌkʃən] n. 吸入，吸力，抽气，抽气机，抽水泵，吸引

~ back of a blade 桨叶抽吸叶背

~ chamber 吸入腔，吸入室

~ cleaner 吸尘器，吸式清扫机

~ dredger 吸扬式挖泥船，吸泥机，抽砂挖泥机

~ filter 吸滤器

~ head 吸入压头

~ lift 吸升高度，吸入升程

~ lift regulation 吸升调节

~ line 吸入管路，吸入管线，吸入管

~ line liquid accumulator 回气管集液器

~ main 吸入总管

~ nozzle 吸嘴，吸气管

~ pressure 吸入压力

~ pressure regulating valve 吸入压力调节阀

~ pressure regulator 吸入压力调节器

~ skimmer 吸入式撇油器，吸入式浮油回收装置

~ stop valve 吸入断流阀

~ strainer 吸入滤器

~ stroke 吸气冲程

~ trap 液体分离器，吸捕器

~ tube 吸入管

~ valve 吸入阀 ‖ *Syn*. inlet valve 进汽阀，进给阀，吸油阀，吸入阀；intake valve 进气阀

suffice [sə'fais] *v.* 足够，有能力，使满足

sufficiency [sə'fiʃənsi] *n.* 足量，充足，充裕，自满

sufficient [sə'fiʃənt] *a.* 足够的，充足的，充分的 ‖ *Syn*. adequate 适当的，足够的，差强人意的；enough 充足的，足够的

sufficiently [sə'fiʃəntli] *ad.* 十分地，充分地

suffocate ['sʌfəkeit] *v.* 使窒息，噎住，闷熄，被闷死，受阻

suffocation [,sʌfə'keiʃən] *n.* 窒息

suit [sju:t] *n.* 一套衣服，套装，套，组，副；*v.* 合适，适合，适宜于，相配，相一致，协调

suitability [,sju:tə'biləti] *n.* 合适，适当，相配，适宜性

suitable ['sju:təbl] *a.* 适当的，相配的

suitably ['sju:təbli] *ad.* 合适地，适宜地，相称地

suite [swi:t] *n.* (一批)随员，(一套)家具，套房，套，组

sulfide ['sʌlfaid] *n.* 硫化物

sulfite ['sʌlfait] *n.* 亚硫酸盐

sulfur ['sʌlfə] *n.* 硫磺，硫磺色；*v.* 用硫磺处理

~ hexafluoride (SF$_6$) 六氟化硫

~ hexafluoride circuit breaker 六氟化硫断路器

sulfuric [sʌl'fjuərik] *a.* 硫磺的，含多量硫磺的

~ acid 硫磺酸

sulphate ['sʌlfeit] *n.* 硫酸盐

sulphite ['sʌlfait] *n.* 亚硫酸盐

sulphur ['sʌlfə] *n.* 硫磺

~ content 硫含量

~ dioxide (SO$_2$) 二氧化硫

~ dioxide probe 二氧化硫探针

sulphuric [sʌl'fjuərik] *a.* 硫磺的，含多量硫磺的

~ acid 硫酸

~ acid solution 硫酸溶液

sulphurous ['sʌlfərəs] *a.* 硫磺的，含有硫磺的

~ acid 亚硫酸

sum [sʌm] *n.* 总数，总和，全部，总共，一笔(金额)，算术，计算；*v.* 归纳，总计，总结，概括

summation [sʌ'meiʃən] *n.* 总和，总结，合计

summer ['sʌmə] *n.* 夏，夏天；*v.* 避暑，过夏天；*a.* 夏季的

~ draft mark 夏季吃水标志

~ load water line 夏季载重水线

~ waterline 夏季水线

summit ['sʌmit] *n.* 顶点，高层会议，最高阶层；*a.* 最高级的，政府首脑的

sump [sʌmp] *n.* 污水坑，水坑，池，机油箱；*v.* 挖深

sundry ['sʌndri] *a.* 各式各样的

super ['sju:pə] *n.* 特级品，管理人，不重要的角色；*v.* 用冷纱布加固；*a.* 上等的，特大的，特级的，十分的，过分的，极好的；*ad.* 非常，过分地

~ cavitating propeller 超空化螺旋桨

supercargo ['sju:pə,ka:gəu] *n.* (商船上的)押运员，货物管理员

supercharge [ˌsjuːpəˈtʃɑːdʒ] v. 增加负荷，用增压器增压

supercharged [ˈsjuːpətʃɑːdʒd] v. (supercharge 的过去式和过去分词) 增加负荷，用增压器增压；a. 超动力的

~ engine 增压发动机

supercharger [ˈsjuːpətʃɑːdʒə] n. 增压器，增压机

~ impeller 增压器叶轮

supercharging [ˈsjuːpətʃɑːdʒiŋ] n. 增压(作用)；v. (supercharge 的 ing 形式) 增加负荷，用增压器增压

~ in parallel system 并联增压系统

~ in series-parallel system 串并联增压

~ in series system 串联增压系统

~ pressure 增压压力

~ system 增压系统

superconduct [ˌsjuːpəkənˈdʌkt] v. 显示超导(电)性，起超导(电)体作用，无电阻导电

superconducting [ˌsjuːpəkənˈdʌktiŋ] v. (superconduct 的 ing 形式) 显示超导(电)性，起超导(电)体作用，无电阻导电；a. 超导(电)的，无电阻率的，使用无电阻物质的

~ propulsion motor 超导推进电动机

superconductor [ˈsjuːpəkənˈdʌktə] n. 超导(电)体

~ electric propulsion plant 超导电力推进装置

supercool [ˌsjuːpəˈkuːl] v. 过度冷却

superfluous [sjuːˈpəːfluəs] a. 多余的，过剩的，过量的 ‖ *Syn*. odd 残留的，残余的，剩余的；redundant 多余的，过剩的，累赘的，冗余的；remainder 残留的，残余的，剩余的；remanent 残留的，残余的，剩余的；residual 残留的，残余的，剩余的；residuary 剩余的，残余的；surplus 过剩的，剩余的

superheat [ˌsjuːpəˈhiːt] n. 过热；v. 使过热

superheated [ˌsjuːpəˈhiːtid] v. (superheat 的过去式和过去分词) 使过热；a. 过热的

~ steam 过热蒸汽

~ temperature 过热温度

superheater [ˈsjuːpəhiːtə] n. 过热设备，过热器

superimpose [ˌsjuːpərimˈpəuz] v. 添加，双重

superintend [ˌsjuːpərinˈtend] v. 主管，指挥，管理，监督

superintendency [ˌsjuːprinˈtendənsi] n. 监督者的地位

superintendent [ˌsjuːpərinˈtendənt] n. 主管，负责人，指挥者，管理者

superior [sjuːˈpiəriə] n. 长者，高手，上级；a. 较高的，上级的，上好的，出众的，卓越的，高傲的

~ performance 卓越性能

superliner [ˌsjuːpəˈlainə] n. 超级班轮，超级邮船

supernatant [ˌsjuːpəˈneitənt] a. 浮在表面的

supernumerary [ˌsjuːpəˈnjuːmərəri] n. 定额以外的人，临时雇工

superposition [ˌsjuːpəpəˈziʃən] n. 叠加，重叠，重合，叠合

supersede [ˌsjuːpəˈsiːd] v. 代替，取代，紧接着到来，延期，推迟行动

superstructure [ˈsjuːpəˌstrʌktʃə] n. 上部结构，上层建筑，甲板上部结构

~ compressed air piping to be done

air-tightness test 上层建筑压缩空气管系密性试验

~ compressed control air piping to be done air-tightness test 上层建筑控制空气管系密性试验

~ deck 上层建筑甲板

~ drainage air piping to be done air-tightness test 上层建筑疏排水管系密性试验

~ fire fighting piping (including emergency fire fighting piping) to be done air-tightness test 上层建筑消防管系(包括应急消防管系)密性试验

~ life-saving and fire fighting equipment to be done inspection 上层建筑救生与消防设备交验

~ smoke detection piping to be done air-tightness test 上层建筑烟雾报警管系密性试验

~ water supply piping to be done air-tightness test 上层建筑供水管系密性试验

~ water-tightness doors and windows to be done hosing test 上层建筑水密门窗冲水试验

supervise ['sju:pəvaiz] v. 监督,管理,指导,负责

supervising ['sju:pəvaiziŋ] n. 监督,管理; v. (supervise 的 ing 形式) 监督,管理,指导,负责

~ device 监控装置

supervision [,sju:pə'viʒən] n. 监督,管理

~ and alarm system 监督报警系统

~ in advance 事前监督

supervisor ['sju:pəvaizə] n. 监督人,管理人,检查员,主管人,超级用户

supervisory [,sju:pə'vaizəri] a. 监督的,管理的

~ control and data acquisition (SCADA) 监控与数据采集

supplement ['sʌplimənt] n. 增补,补充,补充物,增刊,副刊; v. 增补,补充

supplemental [,sʌpli'mentl] a. 补足的,追加的

supplementary [,sʌpli'mentəri] n. 增补者,增补物; a. 补充的,额外的

~ charging 补充充电

supplied [sə'plaid] v. (supply 的过去式和过去分词) 补给,供给,提供,补充,代理; a. 提供的

supplied-air 供气

~ respirator 供气呼吸器

supplier [sə'plaiə] n. 供应者,补充者,厂商,供给者

supply [sə'plai] n. 供给物,供应品,粮食,补给,供给; v. 补给,供给,提供,补充,代理

~ chain 供应链

~ demand balance 供需平衡

~ network 供电网络

~ pump 补给泵

~ ship 补给船

~ voltage 电源电压

support [sə'pɔ:t] n. 支撑,支柱,支持,支援,维持,赡养,支持者; v. 支撑,扶持,支持,支援,拥护,维持,赡养,忍受

~ bracket 支托,支撑架,承托架,支撑肘板

~ centre 供应中心

~ level 支持水平,支持水准,维持点

~ lug 支承凸缘

~ plug 支撑插头

~ tube 支撑管

supported [sə'pɔːtid] v. (support 的过去式和过去分词) 支撑, 扶持, 支持, 支援, 拥护, 维持, 赡养, 忍受; a. 支持的, 支撑的

~ beam 支持梁, 支撑梁

~ bedplate 支撑底板

~ hole 支撑孔

supporter [sə'pɔːtə] n. 支持物, 支持者, 拥护者

supporting [sə'pɔːtiŋ] v. (support 的 ing 形式) 支撑, 扶持, 支持, 支援, 拥护, 维持, 赡养, 忍受; a. 支持的, 支撑的

~ block for location 定位支撑块

~ capacity 承载能力, 承重量

~ force 支撑力

~ pin 支承销

~ plane 支撑平面

suppress [sə'pres] v. 镇压, 压制, 止住, 忍住, 阻止, 查禁

suppression [sə'preʃən] n. 镇压, 压制, 止住, 忍住, 阻止

supra ['suːprə] ad. 在上, 在前

surcharge ['səːtʃaːdʒ] n. 超载, 追加罚款, 额外费; v. 使装载过多, 追加罚款

surf [səːf] n. 海浪, 拍岸碎浪; v. 冲浪, 在激浪上驾(船)

~ zone 碎浪带

surface ['səːfis] n. 表面, 外观, 外表, 面, 地面, 水面, 平面, 坐标点集合; v. 形成表面, 提供表面, 升到水面, 升到地面; a. 表面的, 外观的, 平地上的; 肤浅的

~ air cooler 表面空气冷却器

~ blow-down valve 表面排污阀, 表面吹扫阀

~ blowhole 表面气孔

~ blow-off valve 浮渣吹泄阀, 水面排沫阀

~ breakdown 表面击穿, 表面破坏

~ cleaning 表面清洗

~ crack 表面裂纹

~ creepage 表面漏电

~ effect ship (SES) 表面效应船

~ finish 表面加工, 表面抛光

~ finishing 表面精加工, 表面修整

~ friction 表面摩擦

~ gauge 平面规

~ imperfection 表面缺陷

~ integral 曲面积分, 球面积分, 面积分

~ manoeuvrability 水面操纵性

~ mount component (SMC) 表面贴装元件, 表面组装元件, 表面安装元件

~ nozzle 水面式喷口

~ preparation and coating 表面加工处理与喷涂

~ pressing 表面压力

~ search coordinator (SSC) 海面搜救协调船, 海面搜救协调员

~ tension 表面张力

~ time 表面时间

surface-mounted 表面安装的, 明装的

~ 2-pole receptacle 明装双极插座

~ single-phase 3-pole receptacle 明装单相三极插座

~ single-pole toggle switch 明装单极按钮开关

surface-to-surface 地对地的, 地地的, 面对面的, 面面的

~ contact model 面面接触模型，表面接触模型

surface-to-volume 表面积对体积的，表面积对容积的

 ~ ratio 表面积体积比，表面积容积比

 ~ ratio of combustion chamber 燃烧室表面容积比

surfactant [sə'fæktənt] n. 表面活性剂；a. 表面活性剂的

surge [sə:dʒ] n. 巨涌，汹涌，澎湃；v. 汹涌，澎湃，振荡，滑脱，放松

 ~ impedance 波阻抗，特性阻抗，浪涌阻抗

 ~ protector 浪涌电压保护器

 ~ tank 缓冲罐，稳压罐，气室，平衡罐，减震筒

surmount [sə'maunt] v. 战胜，超越，克服，在顶上 ‖ *Syn*. conquer 征服，战胜，占领，克服；defeat 击败，战胜，使失败；overcome 战胜，克服，胜过，征服；overwhelm 制服，控制，压倒，压服，击败

surpass [sə:'pa:s] v. 超过，优于，胜过

surplus ['sə:pləs] n. 剩余，过剩，盈余，剩余额；v. 转让，卖掉；a. 过剩的，剩余的 ‖ *Syn*. odd 残留的，残余的，剩余的；redundant 多余的，过剩的，累赘的，冗余的；remainder 残留的，残余的，剩余的；remanent 残留的，残余的，剩余的；residual 残留的，残余的，剩余的；residuary 剩余的，残余的；superfluous 多余的，过剩的，过量的

 ~ air 剩余空气

 ~ power 剩余电力，剩余功率

 ~ product 剩余产品

 ~ pressure 剩余压力

 ~ valve 溢流阀

surround [sə'raund] n. 边缘，四周，周围，环境；v. 包围，围绕

surrounding [sə'raundiŋ] n. 环境，围绕物；v. (surround 的 ing 形式) 包围，围绕；a. 周围的

surroundings [sə'raundiŋz] n. (surrounding 的复数) 环境，围绕物 ‖ *Syn*. ambiance 周围环境，气氛；ambience 周围环境，气氛；ambient 周围环境；atmosphere 气氛；circumstances 环境；environment 环境，外界，周围

surveillance [sə:'veiləns] n. 监视，监测，监督

 ~ boat 监测船

 ~ receiver 监测接收机

 ~ system 监测系统

survey ['sə:vei] n. 测量，调查，俯瞰，概观，纵览，视察；v. 调查，测量，勘定，审视，视察，俯瞰，通盘考虑，测量土地

 ~ feedback 调查反馈

 ~ of boiler 锅炉检验

 ~ procedure 调查程序

 ~ report 调查报告

 ~ report file 调查报告文件

 ~ report to be issued 待发布的调查报告

 ~ requirement 测量要求

surveying ['sə:veiiŋ] n. 测量；v. (survey 的 ing 形式) 调查，测量，勘定，审视，视察，俯瞰，通盘考虑，测量土地

 ~ vessel 测量船

surveyor [sə'veiə] n. 检查员，调查员，鉴定人

survivable [sə'vaivəbl] a. 可长存的，可存活的，可免于死亡的

survival [sə'vaivəl] n. 生存，幸存，残存，幸存者，残存物
- ~ craft 救生艇
- ~ craft station 救生艇站
- ~ float 求生浮力棒 ‖ *Syn*. survival buoy 求生浮力棒
- ~ kit 求生背包

susceptance [sə'septəns] n. 电纳

susceptibility [sə,septə'biliti] n. 磁化系数，易感性，感受性，感情

susceptible [sə'septəbl] n. 易得病的人；a. 易受影响的，易受感染的，可以接受的，允许的

suspend [sə'spend] v. 暂停，延缓，悬挂，吊

suspended [sə'spendid] v. (suspend 的过去式和过去分词) 暂停，延缓，悬挂，吊；a. 暂停的，缓期的，悬浮的
- ~ matter 悬浮物，浮游物
- ~ oil 悬浮油类
- ~ solid 悬浮固体
- ~ particle 悬浮颗粒

suspension [sə'spenʃən] n. 吊，悬浮，悬浮液，暂停，中止，悬而未决，延迟

sustain [sə'stein] v. 维持，持续，支撑，撑住，支持，供养

sustained [sə'steind] v. (sustain 的过去式和过去分词) 维持，持续，支撑，撑住，支持，供养；a. 持续不变的，相同的
- ~ deviation 持续偏差
- ~ discharge 持续放电
- ~ fault 持续故障
- ~ oscillation 持续振荡
- ~ overspeed 持续超转

- ~ overvoltage 持续过电压
- ~ short circuit current 持续短路电流

SVC (static var compensator) 静态无功补偿装置

SVS (static var system) 静态无功补偿系统

swage [sweidʒ] n. 型铁，铁模；v. 用型铁弄弯曲

swallow ['swɔləu] n. 通索孔，停泊钩，吞咽，喉；v. 吞咽，淹没，取消，忍受，轻信，压制，耗尽

swan [swɔn] n. 天鹅，天鹅座，杰出的诗人，杰出的歌手
- ~ socket 插入式插座

swanneck ['swɔnnek] n. 鹅颈
- ~ ventilator 鹅颈式通风管 ‖ *Syn*. gooseneck ventilator 鹅颈式通风管

swap [swɔp] n. 交换，交换物；v. 交换，易物交换
- ~ body tank 交换式罐箱

swash [swɔʃ] n. 泼水声，虚张声势，吓唬；v. 冲激，摇晃，冲洗，虚张声势
- ~ bulkhead 缓冲舱壁
- ~ plate 防波板，旋转斜盘

SWATH (small waterplane area twin hull) 小水线面双体船

sway [swei] n. 摇摆，挥动，支配，统治，控制，权力，影响；v. 摇摆，摇动，歪，倾斜，使转移，升起桅杆
- ~ test 横荡试验，摆动试验

swell [swel] n. 膨胀，凸出，隆起，连续起伏的波浪；v. 膨胀，肿胀，高涨，增大，增强，充满；a. 优秀的，精彩的

swept [swept] v. (sweep 的过去式和过去分词) 膨胀，肿胀，高涨，增大，增强，充满；a. 扫频的

~ volume 工作容积，体积排量，活塞排量

swing [swiŋ] n. 摇摆，摆动，摆程，振幅，环程，音律；v. 摇摆，摆动，悬摆，悬吊，回转，侧转，转弯，旋转，急旋转，抬高

~ check valve 旋启式止逆阀，摆动式止回阀

swirl [swə:l] n. 漩涡，涡状形；v. 使成漩涡，打漩，盘绕，头晕

~ chamber 涡流室

~ combustion chamber 旋流式燃烧室，涡流式燃烧室

~ rate 旋流比，进气涡流

~ tube 旋流管

~ vane 涡旋叶片

swirler ['swə:lə] n. 涡旋式喷嘴，离心式喷嘴

swirlmeter ['swə:lmitə] n. 旋涡计

switch [switʃ] n. 开关，转换，电闸，调换，调包，转换器，接线台；v. 转换，转变，改变，迅速转动，开启，摆动

~ amplifier 开关放大器

~ box 开关盒

~ cabinet 开关柜

~ control 开关控制

~ for control supply 控制电源开关

~ fuse 开关熔断器

~ gear 互换机，开关装置

~ in 转入

~ interlock socket 开关联锁插座

~ mode power supply (SMPS) 开关式电源供电

~ off 关掉，切断

~ on 接通

~ over 切换

~ range 开关范围

~ rating 开关额定值

~ station 交换站

~ step 切换阶段

~ timing error 开关定时误差

switching ['switʃiŋ] n. 开关，转换，交换，配电，配电系统，整流；v. (switch 的 ing 形式) 转换，转变，改变，迅速转动，开启，摆动

~ overvoltage 开关过电压

~ packets 交换信息包

~ point 开关点，转接点

~ position 切换位置

~ selector (SS) 开关选择器

~ station 交换站

~ time 切换时间

switchboard ['switʃ,bɔ:d] n. 配电盘，接线总机，控制板 ‖ *Syn*. distribution board 配电盘，配电屏；distribution panel 配电盘，分配盘，分配板

swivel ['swivl] n. 转体，转环，旋转轴承，旋转座架，旋转机枪；v. 使旋转，用转体安装、固定或支撑，转动

~ base parallel bench vice 旋转底座平行台虎钳

~ block 转动滑块，转环滑车，转枕

~ disturbance 旋转扰动

~ gun 回旋枪，回旋炮

~ shackle 旋转钩环

SWL (safe working load) 安全工作负荷

symbol ['simbəl] n. 符号，象征，标志，记号；v. 用符号代表

symmetric [si'metrik] a. 相称性的，均衡的

~ short circuit 对称短路

symmetrical [si'metrikəl] a. 对称的，匀称的

~ impeller 对称叶轮
~ limiting 对称限幅
~ voltage 对称电压

symmetrically [si'metrikəli] ad. 对称性地，对称地，平衡地

symptom ['simptəm] n. 症状，征兆

synchro ['siŋkrəu] a. 同步的
~ converter 同步变换器，同步转换器，同步换流器
~ data 自动同步机数据
~ indicator 同步指示器

synchrolock [siŋk'rəulɔk] n. 同步保持电路

synchrometer [siŋ'krɔmitə] n. 同步计，同步指示计，回旋共振质谱仪，射频质谱计

synchronism ['siŋkrə,nizəm] n. 同步性，同期性，声像同步

synchronization [,siŋkrənai'zeiʃən] n. 同步，同一时刻
~ of generators 发电机同步

synchronize ['siŋkrənaiz] v. 同步，整步，使同时发生

synchronizer ['siŋkrənaizə] n. 同步器，同步装置，同步闪光装置

synchronizing ['siŋkrənaiziŋ] v. (synchronize 的 ing 形式) 同步，整步，使同时发生；a. 同步的
~ channel 同步通道
~ device 同步装置
~ indication 同步指示
~ lamp 同步灯
~ reactor 同步电抗器
~ relay 同步继电器

synchronous ['siŋkrənəs] a. 同时的，同步的 ‖ *Ant.* asynchronous 不同时的，异步的
~ AC generator 同步交流发电机 ‖ *Syn.* synchronous alternator 同步交流发电机
~ belt 同步带
~ condenser 同步调相机
~ generator 同步发电机
~ impedance 同步阻抗
~ induction motor 同步感应电动机
~ motor 同步电动机
~ reactance 同步电抗
~ speed 同步速度

synchroprinter [,siŋkrəu'printə] n. 同步印刷器

synchroscope ['siŋkrə,skəup] n. 同步检定器

synonymous [si'nɔniməs] a. 同义词的，同义的，内涵相同的

synopses [si'na:psi:z] n. (synopsis 的复数) 大意，要略，纲要，大纲

synopsis [si'nɔpsis] n. (*pl.* synopses) 大意，要略，纲要，大纲

synoptic [si'nɔptik] a. 提纲的，概要的，天气的

syntheses ['sinθəsis] n. (synthesis 的复数) 综合，合成，综合体，合成物

synthesis ['sinθisis] n. (*pl.* syntheses) 综合，合成，综合体，合成物

synthesize ['sinθisaiz] v. 综合，合成

synthetic [sin'θetik] n. 合成物，合成纤维；a. 合成的，人造的，综合的
~ fibre 合成纤维
~ fiber rope 合成纤维绳
~ foam spraying fire-extinguishing system 合成泡沫喷雾灭火系统
~ oil 合成油

syphon ['saifən] *n.* 虹吸管，吸水管，弯管；*v.* 用虹吸管抽出

syringe ['sirindʒ] *n.* 注射器，注油器，洗涤器；*v.* 注射，冲洗，灌洗

system ['sistəm] *n.* 系统，体系，制度，体制，秩序，规律，方法
~ assessment 系统评价
~ call 系统调用，系统调入
~ capacity 系统容量
~ clock 系统时钟
~ component 系统组件
~ effectiveness 系统效能
~ electronic navigational chart (SENC) 系统电子航行海图
~ engineering 系统工程
~ expansion 系统扩展
~ fail 系统失效
~ function 系统功能
~ identification number (SID) 系统标识号
~ integrator 系统集成商，系统综合供应商
~ integrity 系统完整性
~ isomorphism 系统同构
~ language 系统语言
~ log 系统日志
~ performance index 系统性能指标
~ response 系统响应
~ software 系统软件

systematic [ˌsisti'mætik] *a.* 有系统的，系统化的，有条理的，规划的，有计划的
~ error 系统误差
~ error checking code 系统误差校验代码

T

T-beam T型梁，丁字梁
T-connection T型连接
T-joint T形接头，丁字接头，三通管接头
T-shape T形的，丁字形的
~ strainer T形滤网
T-square 丁字尺

tab [tæb] *n.* 制表，标号，TAB键，标签，制表符，小报，账单，短小突出部，调整片，补翼；*v.* 安装标签，饰以小垂片，认出

table ['teibl] *n.* 桌子，表格，目录，一览表，镶板，工作台，餐桌；*v.* 搁置，嵌合，制表；*a.* 桌子的，台子的
~ vice 台虎钳

tabular ['tæbjulə] *n.* 列表，排成表格式；*a.* 表格式的，制成表的，扁平的，平坦的

tachogenerator ['tækə'dʒenəreitə] *n.* 测速发电机，转速表传感器

tachometer [tæ'kɔmitə] *n.* 转速计，流速计

tack [tæk] *n.* 航向，行动方针，大头钉，粗缝，食物；*v.* 以大头针钉住，附加，抢风航行，作文字形移动
~ weld 临时点焊，间断焊，预焊

tackle ['tækl] *n.* 工具，复滑车，滑车，辘轳，用具，装备，扭倒；*v.* 固定，应付，处理，解决，抓住，捉住，扭住，扭倒

tactic ['tæktik] *n.* 策略，战略，手段；*a.* 按顺序的，排列的

tag [tæg] *n.* 标签，末端金属物，垂下物，附属物，名称，标记符，陈词滥调，

结束语；*v.* 加标签于，紧随，添饰，连接

~ of instrument 仪器标签

tail [teil] *n.* 尾部，尾巴，尾状物，后部，反面，踪迹，长队，限定继承权，辫子；*v.* 为…装尾，附于其后，尾随，跟踪，使搭牢，监视，使架住，嵌入，船尾搁浅；*a.* 尾部的，后面来的，后部的，在后面的，从后面而来的，限定继承的

~ gas 尾气，废气

~ pipe 尾管

~ resistance 尾阻力

~ rod 导杆，活塞尾杆，节制杆

~ shaft 尾轴

~ shaft bearing 尾轴轴承

~ shaft liner 尾轴衬板

~ shaft to be drawn out for inspection 尾轴抽出检查

~ stabilizer anchor 尾翼式锚

~ stock 尾架

take [teik] *n.* 镜头，看法，捕获量，收入额，场景；*v.* 拿，拿走，取，取得，获得，接受，没收，抓，握住，占领，感受，吸入，吸纳，结合，联合，安置

~ account of 考虑到

~ action 采取行动

~ care of 照顾

~ full advantage of 充分利用

~ in 吸收，接纳

~ into account 考虑

~ into consideration 考虑到

~ off 拿掉，取消，脱衣，起飞，减弱，离开，岔开，复制

~ out 拿出，取出，去掉，出发，取得，扣除，抵充，发泄

~ part in 参与

~ place 发生

~ steps 采取措施

~ up 拿起

talcum ['tælkəm] *n.* 滑石

~ powder 滑石粉

tally ['tæli] *n.* 记账，得分，标记牌，标签，符合，对应物，计数器；*v.* 点数，计算，记录，加标签于，(使)符合，吻合，记分

~ office 理货员办公室

tallyman ['tælimən] *n.* 以分期方式售货的商人，装卸货计数人

TAN (total acid number) 总酸值

tandem ['tændəm] *ad.* 一个跟着一个地，纵列地

tangency ['tændʒənsi] *n.* 接触，相切

tangent ['tændʒənt] *n.* 切线(面)，正切，直线区间；*a.* 接触的，切线的，相切的，离题的

tangential [tæn'dʒenʃ(ə)l] *a.* 切线的，正切的，略为触及的，附带的

~ acceleration 切向加速度

~ air admission 切向进气

~ duct intake 切向进气道进气

~ equation 切线方程

~ flow fan 切向流风机

~ force 切向力

~ grinding force 切向磨削力

~ viscous force 切向黏滞力

tangerine [ˌtændʒə'ri:n] *n.* 柑橘，橘红色，橘黄色

tangy ['tæŋi] *a.* 味道浓烈的，扑鼻的，有刺激性的

tank [tæŋk] *n.* 桶，箱，罐，槽，柜，储

水池，池塘，坦克，战车；v. 储于槽中，击败

~ barge 油罐驳船

~ bottom 油罐底部

~ cleaning 油罐清洗

~ cleaning installation 油罐清洗装置

~ cleaning machine 舱柜清洗机，油罐清洗机

~ cleaning pump 洗舱泵 ‖ **Syn**. Butterworth pump 巴特沃斯泵，洗舱泵

~ cleaning seawater heater 洗舱水加热器 ‖ **Syn**. Butterworth heater 巴特沃斯加热器，洗舱水加热器

~ cleaning system 油舱清洗系统

~ cleaning validation (TCV) 油舱清洗验证

~ coil 振荡电路线圈

~ container 罐状集装箱，液体集装箱

~ cover 箱盖，加油用盖

~ for oil residues 油渣罐

~ gauge 油罐液位计

~ jet cleaning machine 油箱喷气清洗机

~ overflow control system 油箱溢流控制系统

~ ship 油船

~ steaming-out piping system 蒸汽熏舱管系

~ stripping 油舱清底

~ table 油罐校正表

~ valve 油箱阀，油罐阀，柜阀

~ valve rod spring 放出阀阀杆弹簧

~ washing machine 洗舱机

~ washing water 洗舱水

tankage ['tæŋkidʒ] n. (桶、槽)容量，(桶、槽)租费 ‖ **Syn**. capability 性能，容量；capacitance (电)容量；capacity 容量，生产量；volume 体积，容积

tanker ['tæŋkə] n. 油轮，油罐车

~ container ship 集装箱油船

~ displacement 油船排水量

~ Owners Voluntary Agreement Concerning Liability For Oil Pollution (TOVALOP) 油轮船东关于油污责任的自愿协议

~ piping system 油船管路系统

tankerman ['tæŋkəmən] n. 油船船员

tannic ['tænik] a. 丹宁的，鞣质的

~ acid 丹宁酸，鞣酸

tap [tæp] n. 龙头，阀门，塞子，熄灯号 (taps)；v. 轻打，轻敲，敲打出，开发，分接，使流出，选择，攻螺纹于

~ bolt 螺基，(带头)螺栓

~ changer 抽头变换器，抽头转换开关

~ position 抽头位置，分接头位置

~ position indicator 抽头位置指示器，分接头位置指示器

~ rivet 螺旋式铆钉

~ spanner 螺丝攻扳手，攻丝扳手，丝锥扳手 ‖ **Syn**. tap wrench 螺丝攻扳手，攻丝扳手，丝锥扳手

tape [teip] n. 带子，卷尺，胶带，录音带，磁带；v. 用带子捆起来，录音

~ measure 卷尺

taper ['teipə] n. 锥形，锥度；v. 逐渐变细，变尖，逐渐减弱；a. 逐渐变小的

~ dowel pin 锥形定位销

~ face 锥面

~ faced washer 锥面垫圈

~ pin 锥形销

~ plug gauge 锥体塞规

~ roller bearing 圆锥滚子轴承

~ rolling 斜坡轧制

tapered ['teipəd] *v.* (taper 的过去式和过去分词) 逐渐变细，变尖，逐渐减弱；*a.* 锥形的，渐缩的

~ bore 圆锥形孔，锥形孔

~ casing string 复式套管柱，复合套管柱

~ face 锥面

~ increaser 锥形扩大器

~ joint 锥形接头

~ leaf spring 斜片簧

~ roller 圆锥辊，锥形滚筒

~ rope 变断面钢丝绳

tapped ['tæpid] *v.* (tap 的过去式和过去分词) 轻打，轻敲，敲打出，开发，分接，使流出，选择，攻螺纹于；*a.* 抽头的，有螺纹的，套了丝的，发接触音的

~ transformer 抽头式变压器

tapper ['tæpə] *n.* 开孔器，攻丝，轻敲者，电报键

tappet ['tæpit] *n.* 挺杆，凸子

~ assembly 挺杆总成，挺杆组件

~ block 支柱，支架

~ clearance 挺杆间隙

~ rod 挺杆，推杆，锁簧杆，锁条，锁尺

~ rotation 挺杆转位

~ screw 挺杆调整螺钉

tar [ta:] *n.* 焦油，沥青，柏油，尼古丁，水手，水兵，一种压缩文件的扩展名；*v.* 以焦油或沥青覆盖或涂抹

target ['ta:git] *n.* 目标，目的，对象，靶子，标板，小而圆的徽章；*v.* 瞄准，以…为目标

~ flow transmitter 目标流量变送器

tarpaulin [ta:'pɔ:lin] *n.* 防水帆布，防水油布，防水帆布罩

task [ta:sk] *n.* 作业，工作，任务，苦差事；*v.* 分派任务

~ cycle 任务周期，作业周期

~ data 任务数据

taut [tɔ:t] *a.* 紧张的，紧的，拉紧的，绷紧的，整洁的，整齐的

TBN (total base number) 总碱值

TCC (Technical Cooperation Committee) 技术合作委员会

TCT (thyristor controlled transformer) 晶闸管控制变压器

TCV (tank cleaning validation) 油舱清洗验证

TDC (top dead center) 上死点,上止点 ‖ *Syn*. upper dead center (UDC) 上死点,上止点

teakettle ['ti:,ketl] *n.* 茶壶，烧水壶

team [ti:m] *n.* 团队，队，组，工作组，一窝，一群；*v.* 协同工作，结成一队，合作

technic ['teknik] *n.*(=technique) 技术，技巧，技能，技艺，方法，手法

technical ['teknikəl] *a.* 技术的，技术上的，技巧方面的

~ Cooperation Committee (TCC) 技术合作委员会

~ data 技术数据

~ file 技术文档

~ measure 技术措施

~ paper 技术论文

~ personnel 技术人员

~ regulation 技术法规

~ requirement 技术要求

~ specification 技术规范

technician [tek'niʃ(ə)n] n. 技师，技术员，技巧纯熟的人

technique [tek'ni:k] n. (=technic) 技术，技巧，技能，技艺，方法，手法

technological [ˌteknə'lɔdʒikəl] a. 工艺学的，科技的

~ process 工艺流程

technology [tek'nɔlədʒi] n. 工艺，工艺学，科技，技术，工业技术

~ of electrical power generation 发电技术

~ of metals 金属工艺学

~ of waste disposal 废物处置技术

tee [ti:] n. 球座，字母T，T形物，三通；v. 置球于球座上；a. T形的，三通的

~ cock 三通旋塞

~ cock pipe coupling 三通管接头

~ cock valve 三通旋塞阀

~ connection 三通接头

telecommand [telikə'mɑ:nd] n. 遥控（指令）

telecommunication [ˌtelikəmju:ni'keiʃən] n. 电信，长途通信，无线电通信，电信学

telecontrol ['telikən'trəul] n. 遥控，远距离控制

~ equipment 遥控设备

~ system pulse generator 遥控系统脉冲发生器

telecontrolled [teli:kənt'rəuld] a. 遥控的，远距离控制的

~ substation 遥控（分）站

~ valve 遥控阀

telegram ['teligræm] n. 电报；v. 发电报

telegraph ['teligrɑ:f] n. 电报机，电报；v. 打电报，发电报，流露，暴露

~ communication 电话通信

telegraphy [ti'legrəfi] n. 电信技术，电报，电报学，电报机装置

telemanometer [telimə'nɔmitə] n. 遥测压力表

telemessage ['teli:məsidʒ] n. 电信通信

telemeter ['telimi:tə] n. 测距仪，测远计，遥测仪；v. 遥测，用遥测发射器传送

telemotor ['telimәutə] n. 液压传动操舵装置

~ steering gear 遥控液压操舵装置

telephone ['telifəun] n. 电话，电话机，话筒，受话器；v. 打电话

~ set 电话机

telephony [ti'lefəni] n. 电话通信，电话技术，电话学

teleprinter ['teliˌprintə] n. 电传打字机 ‖ Syn. teletype 电传打字机

telescope ['teliskəup] n. 望远镜；v. 缩短，叠缩，嵌入

telescopic [ˌteli'skɔpik] a. 远视的，伸缩的，望远镜的，眼力好的

~ davit 伸缩吊艇架

~ gauge 伸缩式量规，伸缩式仪表

~ jib 伸缩臂，伸缩吊臂

~ jib crane 伸缩臂架起重机

~ joint 伸缩接头，套管连接

~ oil cylinder 伸缩式油缸

~ pipe 伸缩管，套筒管，望远镜式管

teletype ['teliˌtaip] n. 电传打字机，电报交换机，打字电报通信；v. 用电传打字机拍发 ‖ Syn. teleprinter 电传打字机

telex ['teleks] n. 电报，电传收发机；v. 发电传

telltale ['telteil] n. 舵角指示器，指示器，

警告悬条标，迹象，告密者；a. 泄露底细的，泄露实情的

~ hole 指示孔，警报孔

telnet ['telnet] n. 远程登录

temperature ['tempritʃə(r)] n. 温度，气温，体温，发烧

　　~ adjustment 温度调节

　　~ alarm 过热报警器，过热信号

　　~ classification 温度分级

　　~ compensation 温度补偿

　　~ compensating circuit 温度补偿电路

　　~ control 温度控制

　　~ difference 温差

　　~ distribution 温度分布

　　~ drift 温度漂移

　　~ drop 温度降

　　~ equalizing 温度均衡

　　~ field 温度场

　　~ range 温度范围

　　~ recorder 温度记录仪

　　~ regulating device 温度调节装置

　　~ relay 温度继电器

　　~ rise 温升

　　~ rise test 温升试验

　　~ sensor 温度传感器 ‖ *Syn*. temperature transducer 温度传感器；temperature transmitter 温度传感器，温度变送器

　　~ switch 温度开关

　　~ variation 温度变化

temperature-time 温度时间

　　~ curve 温度时间曲线

template ['templeit] n. 模板，样板，型板

　　~ base 模板库

temporarily [tempə'rerili] ad. 暂时地，临时地

　　~ store 临时存储

temporary ['tempərəri] n. 临时工，临时雇员；a. 短暂的，临时的，暂时的

　　~ connection 临时连接

　　~ emergency lighting batteries 临时应急照明电池

　　~ emergency network 临时应急网络

　　~ emergency power source 临时应急电源

　　~ repair 临时修理

　　~ survey 临时调查

tenacity [tə'næsiti] n. 韧性，韧度，固执，坚持

tendency ['tendənsi] n. 倾向，趋势，可能性，脾性，修养，天才

　　~ prediction 趋势预测

tender ['tendə] n. 补给船，照管人，投标，标书，估价单，提出；v. 正式提出，投标，履行；a. 易倾斜的，温柔的，嫩的，纤弱的，疼痛的

tenon ['tenən] n. 榫，凸榫，榫舌；v. 接榫，造榫，开榫，榫接

tensile ['tensail] a. 拉力的，张力的，伸展的，可拉长的

　　~ strain 拉伸应变，抗拉应变

　　~ strength 抗张强度

　　~ stress 张应力，拉伸应力，拉应力

tensiometer [,tensi'ɔmitə] n. 张力计

tension ['tenʃən] n. 拉紧，压力，张力，牵力，电压，紧张，不安；v. 紧张，使紧张

　　~ force 张力

　　~ fracture 拉裂，拉断，伸长破裂

　　~ spring 拉伸弹簧，牵引簧，张力簧

tensioner ['teʃənə] n. 张紧轮(装置)

tensioning ['tenʃəniŋ] n. 张力调整，拉紧，张紧；v. (tension 的 ing 形式) 紧张，

使紧张

~ pulley 张紧带轮

~ wheel 张紧轮

tensive ['tensiv] *a*. 张力的，使人紧张的

tentative ['tentətiv] *n*. 尝试，假设，实验；*a*. 试验性的，试探的，尝试的，暂定的

terminal ['tə:minl] *n*. 终点站，终端，末端，端子，接线柱，接线端；*a*. 末端的，末期的，每期的，定期的，每学期的

~ block 接头排，接线盒，接线板，线夹

~ box 接线盒

~ heater 终端加热器

~ interface processor (TIP) 终端接口处理机

~ reheat air conditioning system 终端再热空调系统

~ subsystem 终端子系统

~ voltage 终端电压

~ voltage drop 终端电压降

terminate ['tə:mineit] *v*. 停止，结束，终止，解雇

termination [,tə:mi'neiʃən] *n*. 结束，结局

terminative ['tə:minətiv] *a*. 终结的，结束的，限定的，结尾的

terminology [,tə:mi'nɔlədʒi] *n*. 术语，专门名词

terrace ['terəs] *n*. 倾斜的平地，台地阳台，平台，平屋顶，梯田；*v*. 使形成阶梯形

terrain ['terein] *n*. 地带，地域，地势，地形

territorial [,teri'tɔ:riəl] *n*. 地方自卫队士兵；*a*. 领土的，区域的，地方的

territory ['teritəri] *n*. 领地，领土，版图，领域，范围

tertiary ['tə:ʃəri] *a*. 第三的，第三位的，第三世纪的

~ winding 三级绕组

terylene ['teri,li:n] *n*. 涤纶，的确良

test [test] *n*. 测验，试验，检验；*v*. 测验，检验，试验，检查，探测，勘测

~ automation 测试自动化

~ board 试验板，测试仪表板

~ by sighting 瞄准试验

~ cock 试验旋塞

~ cycle 试验循环

~ data 试验数据

~ equipment 试验装置

~ for leakage 泄露试验

~ for taking on a full load suddenly 突加负载试验

~ load 试验载荷，实验负荷

~ loop 测试回路

~ object 测试对象

~ panel 试验样板，检验样板

~ pen 测试笔

~ plug 测试插头，试验放泄塞

~ pressure 测试压力

~ probe 测试探针，测试探头

~ sample 试验样本，试样

~ to prove tightness 密封性试验

~ under running conditions 运行条件下的试验

tester ['testə] *n*. 测试员，试验装置，检测器，华盖

testify ['testifai] *v*. 作证，证明，证实，公开宣称，声明，宣布

testing ['testiŋ] *n*. 测试；*v*. (test 的 ing 形式) 测验，检验，试验，检查，探测，

勘测；*a.* 与试验有关的，试验的
  ~ bed trial 试验台试验
  ~ equipment 测试设备
  ~ fee 品质检验费
  ~ hammer 尖嘴锤，检验锤
  ~ voltage 测试电压

tetrachloride [ˌtetrə'klɔ:raid] *n.* 四氯化物

textbook ['tekstbuk] *n.* 教材，教科书，课本；*a.* 规范的，标准的

textile ['tekstail] *n.* 纺织业，纺织品；*a.* 纺织的

texture ['tekstʃə] *n.* 质地，纹理，肌理，结构

TFTM (thin film transistor monitor) 薄膜晶体管监控器

thence [ðens] *ad.* 从此，从那时起

theorem ['θiərəm] *n.* 定理，一般原理，公理，定律，法则
  ~ proving 定理证明

theoretical [ˌθiə'retikəl] *a.* 理论的，推想的，假设的
  ~ calculation 理论计算
  ~ model 理论模型

theoretically [ˌθiə'retikəli] *ad.* 理论地，理论上

theory ['θiəri] *n.* 理论，原理，意见，学说，推测

thereabout ['ðɛərəbaut] *ad.* 在那附近，左右，上下，大约

thereafter [ðɛə'ra:ftə] *ad.* 其后，在那之后

thereby [ðɛə'bai] *ad.* 因此，从而，在那方面，在那附近

therefor [ðɛə'fɔ:] *ad.* 为此，因此

therefore [ðɛəfɔ:] *ad.* 因此，所以

therefrom [ðɛə'frɔm] *ad.* 从那里，从此

thereof [ðɛər'ɔv] *ad.* 在其中，关于

thereto [ðɛə'tu:] *ad.* 另外，往那里，到那

thermal ['θə:məl] *n.* 上升的暖气流；*a.* 热的，热量的，热力的，温度的
  ~ breakdown 热分解
  ~ bulb 测温筒
  ~ conduction 热传导
  ~ conductivity 热导率
  ~ couple 热电偶
  ~ deformation 热变形
  ~ detector 热探测器，热检测器 ‖ *Syn.* heat fire detector 感温火灾探测器
  ~ effect 热效应
  ~ efficiency 热效率
  ~ energy 热能
  ~ expansion 热膨胀
  ~ expansion valve 热膨胀阀
  ~ fatigue 热疲劳
  ~ flame safeguard 火焰监测器
  ~ insulation 热绝缘，绝热
  ~ insulation layer 热绝缘层，绝热层
  ~ load 热应力，热负荷
  ~ oil heater 热油加热器，热油汀
  ~ oil heating system 导热油加热系统
  ~ overload 热过载
  ~ overload relay 热过载继电器
  ~ power 热动力，热功率
  ~ printer 热敏打印机
  ~ protective aid 保温用具，保温袋
  ~ relay 热继电器
  ~ shield 热屏蔽
  ~ slug 散热片
  ~ softening 热软化
  ~ stability 热稳定性
  ~ stress 热应力
  ~ time constant 热时间常数

~ treatment 热处理，热加工

~ unit 热量单位

~ valve 热动式调节阀

thermistor [θə'mistə] n. 热敏电阻，电热调节器

~ type fixed temperature detector 热敏电阻式恒温探测器

thermo ['θə:mə] n. 热，热电

~ current 热流

~ forming 热加工成型

~ overcurrent trip 热过电流脱扣器

thermocline ['θə:mə,klain] n. 温跃层，温度突变层(较热的水面区与冷的深冷水区之间的水层)

thermocouple ['θə:məu,kʌpl] n. 热电偶，温差电偶

~ meter 热电偶计

~ type fixed temperature detector 热电偶式定温探测器

thermodynamic [,θə:məudai'næmik] a. 热力学的，使用热动力的

~ cycle 热力循环

thermoelectric [,θə:məui'lektrik] a. 热电的

~ air conditioner 热电式空调器

~ alarm 热电报警器

~ couple 热电偶，温差电偶

~ effect 热电效应

~ refrigeration type air conditioner 热电制冷式空调器

thermoelectrode [θə:məui'lektrəud] n. 热电电极

thermograph ['θə:məgra:f] n. 温度记录器，热录像仪

thermometer [θə'mɔmitə(r)] n. 温度计，体温表

~ with brass case 铜壳温度计

thermoplastic [,θə:məu'plæstik] n. 热塑性塑料；a. 热塑性的

~ resin 热塑树脂

thermoregulator [,θə:məu'regjuleitə] n. 温度调节器，调温器

thermosensitive [,θə:məu'sensitiv] a. 热敏的

thermoset ['θə:məset] n. 热固树脂，热固塑料；a. 热固的

thermosetting [,θə:məu'setiŋ] a. 热固的，热硬化性的

~ resin 热固树脂

thermostability [θə:məstə'biliti] n. 耐高温，热稳定性，耐热性

thermostat ['θə:məstæt] n. 自动调温器，温度调节装置

~ bypass valve 恒温器旁通阀

~ housing 恒温器壳体

~ flexible bellows 恒温柔性波纹管

~ main valve 恒温器主阀

~ regulator 恒温调节器

thermostatic [,θə:mə'stætik] a. 恒温的，温度调节装置的

~ bypass valve 恒温旁通阀

~ expansion valve 恒温膨胀阀

~ valve 恒温阀

thermostatically [,θə:mə'stætikəli] ad. 恒温地，自动调节温度地

~ controlled furnace 恒温调节炉

thick [θik] n. 最厚的部分，最活跃的部分，最激烈的部分；a. 厚的，粗的，稠的，浓的，深厚的，充满的，显眼的；ad. 厚重地，密集地

~ film 厚膜

thicken ['θikən] v. (使)变厚,(使)变粗,(使)

变浓

thickness ['θiknis] n. 厚度，浓度，稠密，(一)层，混浊

~ meter 厚度计

thimble ['θimbl] n. 顶针，心环，嵌环，套管，支撑环

~ tube boiler 指型管式锅炉，套管锅炉

thin [θin] n. 细小部分；v. (使)变薄，(使)变细，(使)稀少，使淡；a. 薄的，细的，瘦的，稀少的，稀疏的，稀薄的，淡的，空洞的；ad. 稀疏地，微弱地，薄地

~ copper foil 薄铜箔

~ film 薄膜

~ film evaporation 薄膜蒸发

~ film hybrid circuit 薄膜混合电路

~ film hybrid integrated circuit 薄膜混合集成电路

~ film transistor monitor (TFTM) 薄膜晶体管监控器

~ wall 薄壁，薄层

~ wall carburized gear 薄齿渗碳齿轮

~ wall structure 薄壁结构

~ wall welded barrel 薄壁焊接筒体

third [θə:d] n. 第三个，第三档，三分之一；a. 第三的，三分之一的；ad. 第三，三分之一；num. 第三，三分之一

~ class load 三级负荷

~ engineer 二管轮，三车，三轨

~ mate 三副 ‖ *Syn*. third officer 三副

~ phase (=phase 3) 第3阶段(即危险阴燃阶段)

thirsty ['θə:sti] a. 耗油的，口渴的，渴望的，干旱的，缺水的

ThrClnTrans (three column transformer) 三芯柱变压器，三柱变压器，三绕组

变压器

thread [θred] n. 螺纹，螺丝，线，细丝，线索，思路；v. 穿过，小心地通过，蜿蜒前进，刻螺纹，装上，装入

~ cutting 螺纹切削

~ die 切丝板牙

~ grinder 螺丝(纹)磨床

~ processing 螺纹加工

~ seal tape 螺纹密封带

~ spindle 螺纹轴

~ tap 螺纹丝锥

~ pin 螺纹销

threaded ['θredid] v. (thread 的过去式和过去分词) 穿过,小心地通过,蜿蜒前进,刻螺纹，装上，装入；a. 有线状图案装饰的

~ rod 螺杆

three [θri:] n. 三，第三；a. 三的，三个的；num. 三，第三

three-axis 三轴的

~ attitude stabilization 三轴姿态稳定

~ control 三轴控制

~ drive 三轴驱动

~ integrative 三轴一体化的

~ measurement 三轴测量

three-column 三芯柱的，三柱的

~ centrifuge 三柱离心机，三足离心机

~ separator 三柱分离器

~ structure 三柱结构

~ transformer (ThrClnTrans) 三芯柱变压器，三柱变压器，三绕组变压器

three-element 三元素的，三元件的，三元的

~ servo system 三元件伺服系统

~ system 三元体系

three-phase 三相位的，三相的

~AC 三相交流电
~alternator 三相交流发电机
~bridge 三相桥
~cable 三相电缆
~circuit 三相电路
~current 三相电流
~fault 三相故障
~five-wire system 三相五线制
~four-wire system 三相四线制
~load 三相负载
~motor 三相电动机
~power 三相功率
~short circuit 三相短路
~short circuit current 三相短路电流
~slip ring induction motor 三相滑环感应电动机
~source 三相电源
~squirrel-cage induction motor 三相鼠笼式异步电动机
~synchronous motor 三相同步电机
~tertiary winding transformer 三相三绕组变压器
~three-wire system 三相三线制
~transformer 三相变压器

three-pole 三极的
~breaker 三极断路器
~circuit 三极电路
~HV circuit-breaker 三极高压断路器
~reactor 三极电抗器
~switch 三极开关
~transformer 三极变压器

three-position 三位的
~five-way valve 三位五通阀
~four-way directional control valve 三位四通换向阀

three-stage 三级的，三阶段的

~gear 三级齿轮
~network 三级网络

three-state 三状态的，三态的
~buffer 三态缓冲器
~component 三态分量
~controller 三态控制器

three-way 三通的，三路的，三向的
~fuse plug 三通熔断器插头
~fuse socket 三通保险丝插座
~plug with socket 带插座的三通插头
~switch 三通开关，三联开关
~valve 三通阀

three-winding 三绕组的，三线圈的
~transformer 三绕组变压器

three-wire 三线的
~installation 三线装置
~insulated neutral system 中点绝缘三线制
~line 三线线路
~meter 三线式电度表，三线式仪表，三线制电量计
~method 三线法
~principle 三线制，三线原理
~transformer 三线变压器
~trunk 三线中继线

threshold ['θreʃhəuld] *n.* 阈值，阈限，上限，下限，最低限度，门槛，门口，起点，开端
~level 阈值电平，门限电平，门槛值
~limit value (TLV) 容许最高浓度，阈限值

thrive [θraiv] *v.* 茁壮成长，兴旺，繁荣，兴盛，兴隆，长得健壮

throttle ['θrɔtl] *n.* 节流阀，节流杠，节流圈，风门，喉咙，气管；*v.* 节流，降速，调节，压制，扼杀，勒死

~ governing 节流调节

~ governor 节流调节器，节流调速器

~ loss 节流损耗

~ slot 节流缝隙，节流槽

~ spindle 节流阀轴

~ valve 节流阀

throttling ['θrɔtliŋ] *n.* 节流，节气；*v.* (throttle 的 ing 形式) 节流，降速，调节，压制，扼杀

~ action 节流作用，扼流作用

~ sleeve 节流短管

~ valve 节流阀

through [θru:] *a.* 直达的，对穿的，直通的，做完的，完成的，完毕的；*ad.* 穿过，通过，贯穿，从头到尾，自始至终，全程地，直达地，彻底，完全，情况好，取得成功；*prep.* 穿过，通过，从开始到结束，借着，经由，由于，因为

~ bolt 贯穿螺栓

~ crack 贯通裂缝，穿透性裂纹

~ current 直通电流

throughflow ['θru:fləu] *n.* 通流，直流

throughout [θru(:)'aut] *ad.* 到处，始终，全部，从头到尾；*prep.* 遍及，贯穿

throw [θrəu] *n.* 投，掷；*v.* 扔，抛，投掷，使苦恼，惊扰

~ overboard 抛弃

thrust [θrʌst] *n.* 推力，插，戳，刺，猛推；*v.* 力推，冲，插入，挤进，刺，戳，强加，延伸

~ bearing 止推轴承，推力轴承 ‖ **Syn.** thrust block 止推轴承，推力轴承

~ bearing seating 止推轴承座，推力轴承座 ‖ **Syn.** thrust block seat 止推座，止推轴承座，推力轴承座；thrust

bearing stand 止推轴承座，推力轴承座

~ bearing shoe 止推轴承瓦

~ bolt 夹紧螺栓

~ coefficient 推力系数

~ collar 止推环，止推套环，止推轴承定位环

~ component 推力分量

~ deduction coefficient 推力减额系数

~ horsepower 推进马力，牵引马力

~ pad 推力块，止推垫，止推轴承衬

~ performance 推进特性，推力特性

~ plate 止推板，推力板

~ ring 止推环

~ shaft 推力轴

~ vector control system 推力矢量控制系统

thruster ['θrʌstə] *n.* 推进器，向上钻营的人

thwart [θwɔ:t] *n.* 横座板；*v.* 挫败，阻挠，反对，阻碍，横过；*a.* 横放的，横着的，穿过的，固执的；*ad.* 横跨，穿过

thyristor [θai'ristə] *n.* 半导体闸流管，硅可控整流器

~ controlled transformer (TCT) 晶闸管控制变压器

~ converter 可控硅变流器，可控硅变频器

~ converter set 可控硅变流器组，可控硅变频器组

~ excited system 晶闸管励磁系统

~ inverter 可控硅换流器

~ speed control 晶闸管调速

tidal ['taidl] *n.* 潮汐的，有潮的，受潮水影响的，定时涨落的

~ current 潮流

~ volume 一次换气量，潮气量，潮气

容积，呼吸容量

~ wave 潮汐波，浪潮

tide [taid] n. 潮汐，潮流，涨潮，高潮，趋势，时机，时期，季节；v. 随潮水漂浮

~ currents 潮流，潮汐流

tie [tai] n. 带子，线，鞋带，不分胜负，关系，领带，领结，平局；v. 系，打结，扎，结合，约束，成平局，不分胜负

~ bolt 连接螺栓，系紧螺栓，枕木螺栓

~ chain 系紧链条

~ rod 尖端杆，尖轨连接杆，系杆，拉杆，连杆，支柱，转向横拉杆

~ up 停泊，绑好，缚牢，包扎，占用，阻碍，密切联系，合伙

tier [tiə] n. 列，行，排，层，等级；v. 层层排列

tight [tait] a. 不漏水的，不透气的，由压迫产生的，绷紧的，紧密的，困难的，吝啬的，严厉的；ad. 紧紧地，牢固地

tighten ['taitən] v. 收紧，变紧，绷紧，拉紧，加紧

tightening ['taitniŋ] n. 上紧，固定，紧密；v. (tighten 的 ing 形式) 收紧，变紧，绷紧，拉紧，加紧

tightly ['taitli] ad. 紧紧地，坚固地，牢固地

tightness ['taitnis] n. 密封性，坚固，紧密，紧致

~ test 密性试验

~ test (opening and closing test, emergency opening and closing test) for cargo hatch cover 货舱舱口盖密性试验(启闭试验、应急启闭试验)

tiller ['tilə] n. (小船的)舵柄，耕种者，农夫

tilt [tilt] n. 倾斜，歪斜，斜坡，坡度，偏向，顶篷；v. (使)倾斜，(使)翘起，倾向，用帐篷遮盖，攻击，斗争，抨击，争论

~ rating 额定倾斜值

tiltable ['tilteibl] a. 可倾斜的，倾动式的

tilting ['tiltiŋ] n. 倾卸台；v. (tilt 的 ing 形式) (使)倾斜，(使)翘起，倾向，用帐篷遮盖，攻击，斗争，抨击，争论；a. 倾斜，倾卸

~ angle 倾斜角，倾角

timber ['timbə] n. 船骨，木材，木料，素质，气质；v. 用木料支撑，用木料建造

~ carrier 运木船

time [taim] n. 时间，时候，时机，期限，次数，时期，比赛限时，节拍；v. 安排时间，记录时间，计时，定时；a. 时间的，计时的，定时的，定期的，分期的

~ constant 时间常数

~ consuming work 费时工作

~ delay 延时

~ delayed fuse 延时熔断器

~ domain 时域

~ extension 时间延长

~ frame 期限，时帧

~ interval 时间间隔

~ invariant system 时不变系统

~ lag 时滞

~ limit 时限

~ module 时间模块

~ normalization 时间归一化法

~ of rudder movement 转舵时间

~ phase 时间相位

~ relay 定时继电器，时间继电器
~ schedule 时间表
~ schedule controller 时序控制器，程序调节器，时间表控制器
~ varying parameter 时变参数
~ varying system 时变系统

timeliness ['taimlinəs] *n.* 适时，时效性

timely ['taimli] *a.* 及时地，适时地

timepiece ['taimpi:s] *n.* 时钟，座钟

timer ['taimə] *n.* 定时器，计时器，点火调节装置，跑表，时计

timetable ['taimteib(ə)l] *n.* 时刻表，时间表，课程表

timing ['taimiŋ] *n.* 适时，时间选择，定时，调速；*v.* (time 的 ing 形式) 安排时间，记录时间，计时，定时
~ circuit 定时电路
~ diagram 时序图，定时图，正时图
~ gear 定时齿轮，分配齿轮
~ mechanism 时序机制
~ motor 定时电动机
~ relationship 时序关系
~ relay 定时继电器
~ resistor 定时电阻器
~ simulation 时序仿真
~ valve 定时阀

tin [tin] *n.* 锡，马口铁，罐头盒；*v.* 镀锡，包锡，包白铁；*a.* 锡制的
~ bronze 锡青铜
~ snips 铁皮剪
~ soldering 锡焊

tinned [tind] *v.* (tin 的过去式和过去分词) 镀锡，包锡，包白铁；*a.* 镀锡的，包锡的，罐头的，罐装的
~ annealed copper wire 镀锡退火铜线

tiny ['taini] *a.* 极小的，微小的

~ bubble 微小气泡

tip [tip] *n.* 倾斜，顶，尖端，梢，轻击，末端，小费，提示，技巧，秘密消息；*v.* (使)倾斜, (使)翻倒，在顶端装附加物，暗示，轻击，泄露，给小费
~ clearance 齿顶间隙，顶部空隙，(螺杆螺纹的)外径间隙
~ easing 齿顶修边
~ of a blade 桨叶叶梢
~ radius 齿顶圆半径
~ vortex 翼梢旋涡

TIP (terminal interface processor) 终端接口处理机

tissue ['tisju:] *n.* 薄纱织品，薄纸，棉纸，组织

titanium [ti'teiniəm] *n.* 钛
~ alloy 钛合金
~ dioxide 二氧化钛
~ plate heat exchanger 钛材平板式换热器

titrate [tai'treit] *n.* 滴定法被测溶液；*v.* 用滴定法测量

titrimeter [tai'trimitə] *n.* 滴定计

TLV (threshold limit value) 容许最高浓度，阈限值

to [tu:] *prep.* 向，往，直到…为止，在…之前，比，对，到，达，给…
~ a great extent 在很大程度上，非常
~ some extent 在某种程度上, (多少)有一点
~ the extreme 极度地，非常地
~ the limit 达到极限，到顶点

toe [təu] *n.* 趾，脚趾，足尖，轴踵；*v.* 以趾踏触，用脚尖碰，用脚尖走，斜钉

toed [təud] *v.* (toe 的过去式和过去分词) 以趾踏触，用脚尖碰，用脚尖走，斜

钉；a. 有趾的，斜钉的，斜着钉进去的

toggle ['tɒgl] n. 绳针，套索钉，肘结机件，连接；v. 拴牢，切换，装上肘接，用肘接固定

~ key 切换键

~ lever 肘节杆

~ press 肘杆式冲床，肘杆式压力机

toilet ['tɔilit] n. 洗手间，盥洗室 ‖ *Syn*. wash room 卫生间，洗漱间，盥洗室；water closet (WC) 盥洗室，厕所

tolerance ['tɔlərəns] n. 公差，宽容，忍受，容忍，容许量；v. 给(机器部件等)规定公差

~ limit 容许极限，容限，公差极限

tolerant ['tɔlərənt] a. 宽容的，忍受的，有耐力的，能在困难条件下操作的

toluene ['tɔljui:n] n. 甲苯

ton [tʌn] n. 吨，大量，许多

tong [tɒŋ] n. 钳，煤钳；v. 用钳子钳起

tonnage ['tʌnidʒ] n. 载重吨位，登记吨位，排水量，容积吨，吨位，吨税，每吨货物的运输费，总吨数

~ deck 量吨甲板，吨位甲板

~ depth 量吨船深，量吨舱深，量吨深度

TONNAGE, 1969 (International Convention on Tonnage Measurement of Ships, 1969) 1969 年国际船舶吨位丈量公约

tool [tu:l] n. 工具，用具，刀具机床，切割器，关键，手段，压印机；v. 用工具加工，使用设备，压印，驾驶

~ steel 工具钢

toolbar ['tu:lba:] n. 工具栏，刀杆，镗杆

~ button 工具栏按钮

toolbox ['tu:lbɒks] n. 工具箱

tooling ['tu:liŋ] n. 用工具修整，加工；v. (tool 的 ing 形式) 用工具加工，使用设备，压印，驾驶

~ hole 工具孔，定位孔

tooth [tu:θ] n. 齿，牙，齿状部分，粗糙表面；v. 给…装齿，啮合，使成齿状

~ armature 刻槽电枢，齿形衔铁

~ trace 齿轨迹，齿间曲线

toothed [tu:θt] v. (tooth 的过去式和过去分词) 给…装齿，啮合，使成齿状；a. 有齿的，锯齿状的

~ gearing 齿轮传动

~ wheel 齿轮，齿缘轮

top [tɒp] n. 顶部，顶端，极点，顶蓬，陀螺，上部，盖子；v. 盖，戴，高耸，达到顶端，高过，胜过，超越，结束，完成；a. 最高的，顶上的，头等的

~ bracing 顶撑，顶拉条，上平联

~ cover 顶盖，上盖

~ dead center (TDC) 上死点，上止点 ‖ *Syn*. upper dead center (UDC) 上死点，上止点

~ deck 顶甲板

~ diameter 梢头，顶径

~ ventilator 顶部通风机

~ view 顶视图

top-down 自顶向下的，自上而下的，组织管理严密的

~ design 自顶向下的设计

~ testing 自上而下的测试

topgallant [tɒp'gælənt] n. 上桅，上桅帆；a. 上桅的，最高的，最佳的

~ mast 上桅

topmost ['tɒpməust] a. 最高的，顶端的

topping ['tɒpiŋ] n. 除顶部，构成顶部的东西；v. (top 的 ing 形式) 盖，戴，

589

高耸，达到顶端，高过，胜过，超越，结束，完成；*a.* 高耸的，杰出的，一流的

~ lift 千斤索，顶牵索，吊杆顶索，俯仰顶索

topple ['tɔpl] *v.* 倾倒，跌倒，使倾覆，使倒塌，推翻，翻倒

topside ['tɔpsaid] *n.* 干舷，最上面，最上层；*a.* 水线以上部分的；*ad.* 在甲板上，在首席

~ tank 顶边舱，顶边水舱，肩舱，上部油舱

torch [tɔ:tʃ] *n.* 手电筒，火把，火炬，照明物，喷枪，向导；*v.* 放火烧，纵火烧，使迅速燃烧

torque [tɔ:k] *n.* 扭矩，转矩，扭转力，变曲力；*v.* 使旋转，附加旋转力于

~ coefficient 力矩系数

~ converter 液力变矩器，转矩变换器

~ force 扭力

~ margin 转矩裕度

~ master 转矩传感器

~ motor 力矩马达，陀螺修正马达，罗盘矫正电动机

~ rating 额定转矩 ‖ *Syn.* nominal torque 标称转矩，额定转矩；rated torque 额定转矩

~ sensor 转矩传感器

~ spanner 转矩扳手，扭力扳手

torrential [tə'renʃəl] *a.* 似急流的，猛烈的，汹涌的；*ad.* 急流地

torsion ['tɔ:ʃən] *n.* 扭转，转矩，反扭倾向，反扭性

~ meter 扭力计，扭曲强度试验仪

~ stress 扭转应力

torsional ['tɔ:ʃənəl] *a.* 扭力的，扭转的

~ resonance 扭转共振

~ stress deformation 扭转应力变形

~ vibration 扭转振动，扭振

~ vibration damper 扭转振动阻尼器

~ vibration frequency 扭转振动频率

~ vibration of shafting 轴系扭振

total ['təutl] *n.* 总计，总数，全体数量；*v.* 合计，总数达，达到；*a.* 总的，全部的，整个的

~ acid number (TAN) 总酸值

~ base number (TBN) 总碱值

~ capacity 总容量

~ digital control system 全数字控制系统

~ efficiency 总效率

~ flooding 全面洪泛

~ flooding extinguishing system 全淹没灭火系统

~ flow 总流量，总消耗量

~ head 总扬程

~ heat 总热，变浓热

~ installation power 装机功率，安装功率

~ length 总长度

~ load 总负荷

~ moisture 总湿度

~ output 总产量

~ quality control (TQC) 全面质量管理

~ quantity discharged 排放总量

~ quantity of oil residues 油渣总量

~ variation 全变差，总变量

totally ['tɔt(ə)li] *ad.* 完全地，完整地，全体地，彻底地

~ enclosed 全封闭的

~ enclosed type induction motor 全封闭式电动机，防爆型电动机

~ enclosed type motor 全封闭式感应电动机，防爆型电动机

touch [tʌtʃ] *n.* 触，碰，轻触，接触，触觉，联系，缺点，格调；*v.* (使)接触，触摸，触及，达到，涉及，点缀，感动，接近，涉及，提到

~ screen 触摸屏，接触式屏幕

~ sensitive glove 超薄手套

~ up with anti-rust paint 涂上防锈漆

touch-tone 按键式的

touchstone ['tʌtʃstəun] *n.* 标准，检验标准，检验手段，试金石 ‖ *Syn.* criterion 标准，准据，规范；measure 标准，量度标准，尺度；norm 规范，标准，准则；standard 标准，规格

tough [tʌf] *n.* 恶棍；*a.* 强硬的，艰苦的，坚强的，坚韧的，强壮的，吃苦耐劳的，凶恶的，粗暴的；*v.* 忍受，坚持，耐；*ad.* 强硬地，顽强地

~ rubber sheathed cable 硬质橡胶铠装电缆

toughen ['tʌfn] *v.* (使)变坚韧，(使)变顽固，变困难，变凶暴

tour [tuə] *n.* 轮班，任职期，出差，参观，旅行，游历，旅游；*v.* 旅行，游历，巡回，漫游

tourist ['tuərist] *n.* 旅行者，观光客，旅游者

~ ship 旅游船

tourniquet ['tuəniket] *n.* 止血带，压脉器

TOVALOP (Tanker Owners Voluntary Agreement Concerning Liability For Oil Pollution) 油轮船东关于油污责任的自愿协议

tow [təu] *n.* 拖，曳，拉，牵引，拖缆，拖曳的某物，被拖曳的某物；*v.* 拖，曳，拉，牵引，拖行，被拖带

~ hook 拖钩

~ line 拖绳

towage ['təuidʒ] *n.* 拖，拉，曳，拖船费

towboat ['təubəut] *n.* 拖船，拖轮

towed [təud] *v.* (tow 的过去式和过去分词) 拖，曳，拉，牵引，拖行，被拖带；*a.* 被拖曳的

~ vessel 被拖船

towel ['tauəl] *n.* 纸巾，毛巾，手巾；*v.* 用毛巾擦

tower ['tauə] *n.* 塔，塔楼，高楼，塔状物，伟人；*v.* 屹立，高耸，高飞，胜过，超出

~ crane 塔吊，塔式起重机

~ pincers 核头钳

towing ['təuiŋ] *n.* 拖，拉，拽；*v.* (tow 的 ing 形式) 拖带，拖，拉，拽

~ davit 拖缆吊杆

~ dolly 小拖车

~ gear 拖曳装置

~ light 拖曳灯

~ operating mode management 牵引运行方式管理

~ speed 拖曳速度

~ tank 拖曳水池，船模试验水池

~ vessel 拖引船

~ winch 拖缆绞车，拖曳绞车

~ yoke 拖轭

towline ['təulain] *n.* 拖绳，拖链，拖索

toxic ['tɔksik] *a.* 毒的，中毒的，有毒的

~ product 有毒产品

~ residue 残毒

~ vapour detection equipment 有毒蒸汽检测设备

toxic-free 无毒的

~ cable 无毒电缆

toxicant ['tɔksikənt] n. 毒剂，毒药，有毒物

~ leaching rate 渗毒率

toxicity [tɔk'sisiti] n. 毒性，毒力

toxin ['tɔksin] n. 毒素，毒质

TQC (total quality control) 全面质量管理

trace [treis] n. 痕迹，踪迹，微量，极少量，迹线；v. 追踪，回溯，探索，描绘，映描，画轮廓

~ heating 伴随加热

traceable ['treisəbl] a. 可追踪的，起源于

tracer ['treisə] n. 追踪者，描图者，绘图工具

~ gas 探漏气体，探测气体

~ line 伴随管线

track [træk] n. 跟踪，航迹，途径，方针，路线，轨迹，车辙，足迹，路，磁轨；v. 循路而行，追踪，通过，用纤拉

tracking ['trækiŋ] n. 跟踪，按成绩分组；v. (track 的 ing 形式) 追踪，回溯，探索，描绘，映描，画轮廓

~ accuracy 跟踪精度

~ error 跟踪误差

traction ['trækʃən] n. 拖拉，牵引力，附着摩擦力

tractive ['træktiv] a. 牵引的，曳引的

~ force 牵引力

trade [treid] n. 贸易，商业，交易，生意，职业，行业，信风，顾客；v. 交易，买卖，经商，对换，购物，交换

trademark ['treidmɑ:k] n. 商标，特征，标记；v. 打上商标，注册商标

trader ['treidə] n. 商船，交易者，商人

traditional [trə'diʃn(ə)l] a. 传统的，惯例的，传说的，口传的

traditionally [trə'diʃənəli] ad. 传统上，传说上

traffic ['træfik] n. 交通，通行，运输，交通量，通信量，贸易，交易，交往；v. 作交换，通行，交易，买卖

~ boat 交通艇

trail [treil] n. 踪迹，痕迹，形迹；v. 跟踪，追踪，拉，拖，蔓延，没精打采地走

trailing ['treiliŋ] n. 泥浆彩饰；v. (trail 的 ing 形式) 跟踪，追踪，拉，拖，蔓延，没精打采地走；a. 拖尾的，曳尾的，被拖动的，蔓延的

~ idler 从动空转轮

~ suction hopper dredger 耙斗挖泥船

train [trein] n. 火车，行列，后果，顺序，长队，导火线，随行人员，一连串，系(一套连接的机械部件)；v. 训练，锻炼，培训，培养，瞄准，关注，拖拽，修整

~ ferry 火车轮渡

training ['treiniŋ] n. 训练，锻炼，培训，练习；v. (train 的 ing 形式) 训练，锻炼，培训，培养，瞄准，关注，拖拽，修整；a. 训练的

~ and drill 培训和演习

~ cruise 航行实习

~ cruiser 教练巡洋舰

~ schedule 训练计划

~ ship 训练船

trajectory ['trædʒiktəri] n. 弹道，轨道，轨线

trammel ['træməl] n. 拘束，阻碍物，束缚物，三层刺网，椭圆规，量规，调整机器部件用规；v. 拘束，阻碍，束缚，

妨碍

transceiver [træn'si:və] n. 无线电收发机，收发器

transcript ['trænskript] n. 抄本，副本，誊本，打字本

transducer [trænz'dju:sə] n. (=XDCR) 传感器，换能器，变换器，换流器，变频器

~ signal input 传感器信号输入

transductor [trænz'dʌktə(r)] n. 饱和电抗器

transfer [træns'fə:] n. 迁移，移动，传递，转移，调任，转账，过户，转让；v. 转移，调转，调任，传递，转让，改变

~ characteristic 传递特性

~ function 传递函数

~ function matrix 传递函数矩阵

~ press 多工位压力机

~ pump 传送泵，输送泵

~ switch 转换开关

~ time 转移时间

~ to 转移到

transferable [træns'fə:rəb(ə)l] a. 可转移的，可转换的，可传递的

transfigure [træns'figə] v. 使变形，美化，理想化

transform [træns'fɔ:m] n. 变换式，转换；v. 转换，改变，改造，使变形，转化，变换

transformation [ˌtrænsfə'meiʃən] n. 变化，转化，转换，改革

~ condition 转换条件

~ point 转换点

transformer [træns'fɔ:mə(r)] n. 变压器，促使变化的人(或物)，改革者

~ amplifier 变压器放大器

~ electromotive force 变压器电动势

~ factor 变压器系数

~ input voltage 初级电压，一次电压 ‖ *Syn*. primary voltage 初级电压，一次电压

~ main line system 变压器主线系统

~ matching 变压器匹配

~ oil 变压器油

~ platform 变压器平台

~ ratio 变压比

~ room 变压器室，变压器室，配电室

~ station 变电所，变电站 ‖ *Syn*. transformer substation 变电所，变电站

transient ['trænziənt] n. 瞬时现象，临时旅客；v. 短暂的，短期的，临时的，瞬时的，瞬变的

~ deviation 瞬态偏差

~ process 过渡过程

~ reactance 瞬态电抗

~ response 瞬态响应

~ short-circuit current 暂态短路电流

~ stability 暂态稳定

~ state 过渡状态，瞬态，非稳定状态

~ state analysis of power system 电力系统暂态分析

~ state component 暂态分量

~ state frequency variation 暂态频率变化

~ state travelling wave 瞬态行波

transistor [træn'zistə] n. 晶体管，晶体管收音机

transit ['trænzit] n. 经过，通行，搬运，运输，运输线，转变，中天，经纬仪；v. 横越，通过，经过，旋转

~ speed 运输速度

transition [træn'ziʃən] n. 转变，转换，跃迁，过渡，变调

~ diagram 转换图

transitional [træn'siʃənl] *a.* 变迁的，过渡期的，渐变的，转变的，转移的

transitivity [ˌtrænsi'tiviti] *n.* 传递性，转移性，及物性

transitory ['trænsitəri] *a.* 短暂的，暂时的，刹那间的

translate [træns'leit] *v.* 翻译，解释，转化，转变，调动

translation [træns'leiʃən] *n.* 翻译，译文，转化，调任，转换，平移

transmissible [trænz'misəbl] *a.* 可传送的，可遗传的

~ pressure gauge 传送式压力计

transmission [træns'miʃən] *n.* 播送，转播，发射，传送，传输，传动，传动装置

~ channel 传输信道，传输通路

~ gear 传动齿轮

~ line 传输线，波导线

~ line malfunction 输电线路故障

~ loss 传输损耗

~ medium 传输介质

~ path 传输路径

~ ratio 传动比

~ relay 传输继电器

~ security 传输安全性

~ shaft 传动轴

~ shafting 传动轴系

~ system 传动系统，传输系统，输电系统

~ trunking 传输集群

transmit [trænz'mit] *v.* 传输，转送，传达，传导，发射，遗传，传播，发射信号，发报

~ information 传输信息

transmit-receiver 收发讯机

transmittance [træns'mitns] *n.* 播送，发射，传动，透明度，透射作用

~ meter 能见度测量仪

transmitted [trænz'mitid] *v.* (transmit 的过去式和过去分词) 传输，转送，传达，传导，发射，遗传，传播，发射信号，发报；*a.* 传输的，传送的，传达的

~ beam 发射束

~ chain 传输链

~ intensity 射线强度，穿透强度

transmitter [trænz'mitə] *n.* 传送者，传达人，传导物，发报机，话筒，发射机，让渡者

~ panel 发射机面板

transom ['trænsəm] *n.* 气窗，横窗，横梁，结构中横向构件

~ stern 方艉

~ stern vessel 方艉船

~ window 气窗，顶窗

transparent [træns'pɛərənt] *a.* 透明的，显然的，明晰的

transpiration [ˌtrænspi'reiʃən] *n.* 出汗，散发，蒸发，蒸发物，蒸腾作用，流逸

transpire [træn'spaiə] *v.* (使)排出，(使)蒸发，发散，发生，得知，泄露

transponder [træns'pɔndə(r)] *n.* 发射机应答器，异频雷达收发机

transport ['trænspɔ:t] *n.* 传送器，运输，运输船，运输机，运输系统，激动；*v.* 传送，运输，运送，流放，放逐

~ machinery 运输机械

~ to 把⋯运输到

~ undertaking 运输事业

transportable [træn'spɔ:təbl] *n.* 便携式计算机，便携式电视机；*a.* 可运输的

~ fire extinguisher 移动式灭火器

transportation [ˌtrænspɔː'teiʃən] n. 运送，运输，输送，运输业，运输工具，流放

transposition [ˌtrænspəˈziʃən] n. 换位，转位，调换，变换，移项

transshipment ['trænsʃipmənt] n. 转运，转载

~ of cargo 货物转运

transverse ['trænzvəːs] a. 横向的，横断的，横穿的

~ bending 横向弯曲

~ bulkhead 横舱壁

~ bulkhead plating 横隔舱壁板

~ centre of gravity 横向重心，横重心

~ crack 横向断裂，横向裂缝，横裂

~ cross section 横剖面

~ force 横向力

~ frame system 横骨架式，横框架式结构，横肋系统

~ framing 横向构架

~ member (起重机的)吊杆，挺杆，横梁，横臂，横向撑

~ section 横切面

~ section area 横切面面积

~ stability 横向稳定性

~ stay 横撑条

~ strength 横向强度

~ vibration of shafting 轴系横向振动

transversely ['trænzvəːsli] ad. 横切地，横断地，横着

trap [træp] n. 活板门，汽水闸，圈套，陷阱，诡计，存水弯；v. 使受限制，诱设圈套，设陷阱，诱捕，诱骗，计捉，设陷，坑害

trapezoid ['træpizɔid] n. 梯形，不等边四边形 ‖ circle 圆，圆形；ellipse 椭圆，椭圆形；parallelogram 平行四边形；rectangle 矩形；rhombus 菱形；square 正方形； triangle 三角形

trash [træʃ] n. 垃圾，废物；v. 拆掉，废弃，破坏，拆毁，拆毁

trauma ['trɔːmə] n. 外伤，损伤

travel ['trævl] n. 移动，行进，旅行，旅程；v. 前进，行进，移动，运送，传送，旅行

~ distance 行进距离，流动距离，疏散距离

traveling ['trævliŋ] v. (travel 的 ing 形式) 前进，行进，移动，运送，传送，旅行；a. 活动的，移动的，旅行的，同行的

~ block 游动滑车

~ crane 行车，自走式起重机

traverse [trəˈv(ə)ːs] n. 横贯，横断，横木，通廊，障碍，否认，反驳；v. 横过，横断，穿过，经过，来回移动，旋转，反对，详细研究；a. 横断的，横的

trawl [trɔːl] n. 拖网；v. 搜索，搜罗，用拖网捕鱼

~ winch 拖网绞车

trawler ['trɔːlə] n. 拖网渔船，拖网捕鱼者，拖网渔民 ‖ Syn. seiner 围网渔船，使用围网捕鱼的人

tread [tred] n. 踏，步态，梯级，踏板，轮胎面，交尾，鞋底；v. 踏，行走，踩碎，践踏，交尾

treat [triːt] n. 宴请，请客，款待，招待；v. 处理，处置，交涉，谈判，协商，对待，看待，款待，表现，视为，论述，治疗

~ as 当作

~ by annealing 退火处理

~ by tempering 回火处理

~ of 论及，涉及

~ with 处理，应付 ‖ **Syn.** deal with 应付，安排，处理；dispose of 处理，安排，解决；handle 处理；manage 处理，应付；manipulate (巧妙地)处理，应付

treatability [tri:tə'biliti] *n.* 可处理性,能治疗性

treated [tri:tid] *v.* (treat 的过去式和过去分词) 处理，处置，交涉，谈判，协商，对待，看待，款待，表现，视为，论述，治疗；*a.* 已处理过的，加工过的，精制过的

~ oil 处理过的油

~ side 处理面

treatment ['tri:tmənt] *n.* 处理,对待,待遇,治疗,疗法

tremendous [tri'mendəs] *a.* 极大的，巨大的，惊人的，极好的

trend [trend] *n.* 趋势，趋向，倾向，走向，时尚；*v.* 伸向，倾向，通向

tri-folded 三折的

~ umbrella type insulator 三折伞型绝缘子

trial ['traiəl] *n.* 试验，检验，验证，考验，尝试，努力，磨难，磨炼，麻烦，预赛，审讯，审判；*a.* 试验的，试用的，临时的，审讯的

~ and error 试错法，反复试验

~ speed 试验速度，试车速度，试航速度

~ to be carried as follows 按以下方式进行试验

triangle ['traiæŋgl] *n.* 三角形；三人一组；三角铁；三角板 ‖ circle 圆，圆形；ellipse 椭圆,椭圆形；parallelogram 平行四边形；rectangle 矩形；rhombus 菱形；square 正方形；trapezoid 梯形

triangular [trai'æŋgjələ] *a.* 三角的，三角形的，有三角形底的，三方的

~ coarse file 三角粗锉

~ hollow scraper 三角形空心刮刀

~ scraper 三角刮刀

~ section girder 三角断面梁

~ smooth file 三角光滑锉

~ spring 三角簧

~ symbol 三角符号

~ thread 三角螺纹，V 形螺纹

tribasic [trai'beisik] *a.* 三盐基的，三元的

tribological [traibəu'lɔdʒikəl] *a.* 摩擦学的

tributyltin [tri'biti:ltin] *n.* 三丁基锡

trig [trig] *n.* 楔子，垫石，刹车装置；*v.* 使停止转动，支撑，撑起；*a.* 整洁的，漂亮的，良好的，坚实的

trigger ['trigə] *n.* 扳机，扳柄，启动装置，触发器，触发电器，引发其他事件的一件事；*v.* 引发，引起，触发，发射，使爆炸

~ circuit 触发电路

~ control 触发控制，扳机控制

~ electrode 触发电极

~ element 触发元件

trihedral [trai'hedrəl] *a.* 有三面的

~ rule 三棱尺

trim [trim] *n.* 装饰，修剪，整理，调整，废弃物，船的航行状态，船的平衡，船的吃水差，配平，整齐，整洁，准备就绪，身体状况良好；*v.* 装饰，修剪，整理，调整，调整以适应风向，保持平稳，准备船帆和帆桁以使扬帆航行，装稳，装备，配备，加工整理，

削减，击败；*a.* 整齐的，整洁的，线条简洁的，有条不紊的，修长的，苗条的

~ (ming) pump 纵倾平衡泵 ‖ heeling pump 横倾平衡泵；list pump 横倾平衡泵

~ by bow 艏倾，前倾，船艏纵倾

~ by stern 艉倾，后倾，船艉纵倾

~ by the head 船头平舱

~ pump 纵倾泵

~ pump sea stop valve 纵倾泵海水止回阀

trimaran ['traimə,ræn] *n.* 三个船体并列的游艇

trimmed [trimd] *v.* (trim 的过去式和过去分词) 装饰，修剪，整理，调整，调整以适应风向，保持平稳，准备船帆和帆桁以使扬帆航行，装稳，装备，配备，加工整理，削减，击败；*a.* 平衡的，纵倾的，整齐的，整洁的

~ band gap 修整带隙

trimmer ['trimə] *n.* 微调电容器，托梁，承接梁，修剪器，整修者

trimming ['trimiŋ] *n.* 修剪，整理，装饰品，配料，附属品；*v.* (trim 的 ing 形式) 装饰，修剪，整理，调整，调整以适应风向，保持平稳，准备船帆和帆桁以使扬帆航行，装稳，装备，配备，加工整理，削减，击败

~ moment 平衡力矩

~ punch 精整冲头，切边冲头

~ resistor 微调电阻器

trinity ['triniti] *n.* 三位一体，三合一

triode ['traiəud] *n.* 三极管，三极真空管 ‖ *Syn.* audion 三极管

trioxide [trai'ɔksaid] *n.* 三氧化物

trip [trip] *n.* 旅行，绊倒，摔倒，失足，往返，差错，支吾，旅程；*v.* 起锚，竖帆，解扣，脱扣，使跌倒，使犯错，使失败，挑剔，犯错

~ breaker 急停开关，跳闸断路器

~ cam 释放凸轮

~ circuit 解扣电路

~ coil 解扣线圈

~ device 解扣装置，脱扣装置

~ dog 自动爪，自动停车器，脱扣钩，跳挡，解扣

~ point 断路点，跳闸点，跳变点

~ setting 事故保护定值器

triple ['tripl] *n.* 三倍数，三倍量，三个一组；*v.* 成三倍，增至三倍；*a.* 三倍的，三次的，三部分的

~ integral 三重积分

~ modulation telemetering system 三重调制遥测系统

~ series 三重级数

~ valve 三通阀

triple-cable 三电缆的，三相的

~ plug 三相插头

triple-core 三芯的

~ cable 三芯电缆

triple-pole 三极的

~ contactor 三极接触器

~ reverser 三极反向器，三极反演机构

~ switch 三极开关

triple-screw 三螺杆的

~ pump 三螺杆泵

triplicate ['triplikit] *n.* 三分之一，三份中之一；*a.* 三倍的，三重的，三乘的

tripping ['tripiŋ] *n.* 绊跌，轻快的舞；*v.* (trip 的 ing 形式) 起锚，竖帆，解扣，脱扣，使跌倒，使犯错，使失败，挑

剔，犯错；*a*. 平稳地进行的，流畅的
~ bracket 防颠肘板
~ coil 脱扣线圈
~ device 解扣装置
~ force 启动力，解脱力，释放力

trivalent [trai'veilənt] *a*. 三价的

troller ['trəulə] *n*. 小钓船，拖钩渔船

trolley ['trɔli] *n*. 手推车，手摇车，台车，滚轮；*v*. 用手推车运
~ crane 悬挂式起重机，架空吊车
~ wheel 触轮，滑接轮，滚轮

trouble ['trʌbl] *n*. 故障，问题，烦恼，麻烦，纠纷，疾病；*v*. (使)烦恼，麻烦，打扰，费神，费心 ‖ **Syn**. dysfunction 机能不良，功能紊乱，官能障碍；failure 失灵，故障；fault 故障；out of order 次序颠倒，不整齐，状态不好
~ indicating lamp 故障指示灯
~ relay 故障继电器
~ shooter 故障检修员，解决麻烦问题的能手
~ spot 故障点，出故障处，动荡地区

trouble-free 无故障的，可靠的
~ life 无故障寿命

troubles ['trʌblz] *n*. (trouble 的复数) 故障，问题，烦恼，麻烦，纠纷，疾病；*v*. (trouble 的第三人称单数) (使)烦恼，麻烦，打扰，费神，费心
~ inside the sample space 区内故障

troubleshooting ['trʌblʃu:tiŋ] *n*. 发现并修理故障，解决纷争

troublesome ['trʌblsəm] *a*. 困难的，费事的，讨厌的，惹麻烦的

trough ['trɔ:f] *n*. 波谷，低潮，槽，水槽，低气压槽

trowel ['trauəl] *n*. 小铲，泥刀，抹刀；*v*. 用铲子铲，用泥铲涂

trumpet ['trʌmpit] *n*. 喇叭，小号，喇叭形状的东西，喇叭筒；*v*. 大声说出，发出回声，吹喇叭，吹小号，回声
~ type silencer 管式消音器

trunk [trʌŋk] *n*. 干线，树干，躯干，箱子，主干，象鼻；*a*. 树干的，躯干的，干线的，箱形的
~ piston 柱塞，筒状活塞
~ piston engine 筒状活塞发动机
~ system 干线系统

trunnion ['trʌnjən] *n*. 耳轴，炮耳

truss [trʌs] *n*. 一捆，一束，构架；*v*. 捆绑

trust [trʌst] *n*. 信任，信赖；*v*. 信任，信赖，盼望，希望，热望

trustworthy ['trʌst,wə:ði] *a*. 可靠的，可信的，信得过的

try [trai] *n*. 尝试，实验；*v*. 试，试图，努力，试验，磨难，考验，审问
~ again 再试一次
~ doing 试着做
~ for 争取，谋求，申请
~ hard 努力，苦干
~ one's best 尽全力
~ on 试穿，试验
~ out 试验，考验，提炼
~ to do 试着做

tsunami [tsju:'na:mi] *n*. 海啸

tube ['tju:b] *n*. 管，管子，电子管，真空管，显像管，内胎，电视，电视机，地铁；*v*. 提供管子，插入管道，装管，漂流
~ bending machine 弯管机
~ bundle (塑料)管束
~ condenser 管式冷凝器
~ plate 管板

tubular ['tju:bjulə] *a.* 管状的，管式的，管形的，有管的，由管组成的
　~ boiler 管式锅炉
　~ lamp 管状灯
　~ plug with socket 带插座的管状插头
　~ radiator 管状散热器
　~ rheostat 管状电阻
　~ shaft 管状轴

tug [tʌg] *n.* 拖船，绳索链条，拖，推力，竞争，斗争，苦干；*v.* 用拖船拖曳，用力拖，拖拉，吃力地搬运，竞争，比赛，苦干

tugboat ['tʌgbəut] *n.* 拖船，拖轮

tuggage ['tʌgidʒ] *n.* 拖带，拖带费

tulle [tju:l] *n.* 薄纱，尼龙纱

tumble ['tʌmbl] *n.* 跌倒，跌落，一片混乱，紊乱不堪；*v.* 翻倒，摔倒，涌出，下跌，倒塌，滚动，翻筋斗，仓皇地行动，弄乱，使摔倒，使滚翻
　~ home 舷缘内倾
　~ in 嵌入，镶上

tune [tju:n] *n.* 曲调，曲子，和谐，调谐，语调，心情；*v.* 调整，协调，调谐，使和谐，使一致

tungsten ['tʌŋstən] *n.* 钨
　~ alloy 钨合金
　~ bronze 钨青铜

tunnel ['tʌnl] *n.* 隧道，地道，烟道；*v.* 挖掘隧道，打通隧道，打开通道
　~ type air cooling freezer 隧道式空冷器
　~ wall effect 隧道壁效应

turbid ['tə:bid] *a.* 混浊的，混乱的，紊乱的，脏的，浓密的

turbidity [tə:'biditi] *n.* 混浊，混乱

turbine ['tə:bin] *n.* 涡轮，涡轮机，汽轮机，透平机
　~ blade 涡轮叶片
　~ driven feed pump 涡轮驱动给水泵
　~ driven pump 涡轮泵，汽轮机驱动泵
　~ dynamometer 涡轮功率计
　~ flowmeter 涡轮流量计
　~ generator 涡轮发电机 ‖ *Syn.* turbo-generator 涡轮发电机
　~ oil 透平油
　~ pump 涡轮泵，涡轮抽水机
　~ steamer 汽轮机轮船，汽轮机船，涡轮船
　~ steel 透平用钢，汽轮机用钢
　~ wheel impeller 涡轮叶轮

turbo ['tə:bəu] *n.* 涡轮(发动机)，增压涡轮
　~ blower 涡轮鼓风机，透平鼓风机

turboalternator [tə:'bəultənətə] *n.* 涡轮交流发电机

turbocharge ['tə:bəutʃa:dʒ] *v.* 用涡轮增压，装涡轮增压器

turbocharged ['tə:bəutʃa:dʒd] *v.* (turbocharge 的过去式和过去分词) 用涡轮增压，装涡轮增压器；*a.* 涡轮增压的
　~ engine 涡轮增压发动机
　~ lubricating oil pump 涡轮增压润滑油泵

turbocharger ['tə:bəu,tʃa:dʒə] *n.* 涡轮增压器
　~ casing 涡轮增压器壳体
　~ cleaner 涡轮增压器清洗器
　~ lubricating oil pump 涡轮增压器润滑油泵
　~ surge 涡轮增压器喘振

turbocharging ['tə:bəutʃa:dʒiŋ] *n.* 涡轮增压；*v.* (turbocharge 的 ing 形式) 用涡轮增压，装涡轮增压器

~ auxiliary blower 涡轮增压辅助鼓风机

~ emergency blower 增压系统应急鼓风机

turboelectric [,tə:bəui'lektrik] a. 涡轮机发电的，用涡轮发电机的

~ drive 涡轮电驱动

turbogenerator ['tə:bəu'dʒenəreitə] n. 涡轮发电机 ‖ *Syn*. turbine generator 涡轮发电机

turbulence ['tə:bjuləns] n. 紊乱，湍流，狂暴，动荡，骚动，骚乱

~ combustion chamber 湍流式燃烧室，涡流式燃烧室

~ damping 湍流阻尼

turbulent ['tə:bjulənt] a. 狂暴的，动荡的，骚乱的，暴乱的

~ flow air register 旋流式调风机，旋流调风器

turn [tə:n] n. 转动，旋转，转变方向，轮流，时机，倾向，(一)回；v. (使)转动，(使)变质，(使)变为，翻转，扭转，超过，车(成)

~ around 转身，回转，转向

~ away 不准入内，走开，转过脸，解雇，避免，防止

~ back 往回走，使停止往前，翻回到，重新提到，折转，挡住

~ down 减小，关小，拒绝

~ in 上交

~ into 变成

~ left 左转

~ off 关掉

~ on 打开

~ out 打扫，驱逐，使外倾，生产，翻出，制造，关掉，起床

~ over 打翻，营业额达到，周转，移交给，反复考虑，翻身，折腾，翻阅

~ right 右转

~ slot 转动翼缝，转弯开缝

~ to 转向，变成，求助于，致力于，开始行动

~ up 调大，翻起，出现

turn-to-turn 匝对匝的，匝间的

~ capacitance 匝间电容

~ short circuit 匝间短路

turnable ['tə:neibl] a. 可转的，可回转的

~ blade 可转动叶片

~ conveyor belt 可转式运输带

~ shrouded screw 转动导管螺旋桨

turnbuckle ['tə:n,bʌkl] n. 螺丝扣，套筒螺母

turning ['tə:niŋ] n. 旋转，转向，转弯处，车削；v. (turn 的 ing 形式) (使)转动,(使)变质，(使)变为，翻转，扭转，超过，车(成)

~ ability 车削性能

~ gear 盘车装置，旋转装置，回转装置

~ gear interlocking device 盘车联锁装置

~ of the crankshaft 曲轴的车削

~ wheel 转向轮，转轮，转轴手轮

turnout ['tə:naut] n. 装备，设备，产出，产量，到会者，聚集的人，罢工者，服装，装束 ‖ *Syn*. apparatus 器械，设备，仪器；appliance 用具，器具；arrangement 布置；assembly 组装部件；device 装置，设备；equipment 装备，设备，器材，装置；facility 设备，工具；furniture 设备，家具；gear 设备，装备；installation 设备,装置；machine 机器，

机械，机构；machinery 机械(总称)，机器；mechanism 机器，机械装置，机构；plant 设备；provision 装备，供应品；unit 装置，设备

turnover ['tə:nˌəuvə] n. 翻覆，翻折，流通量，营业额，周转，人员更替数，新雇人员比率；a. 可翻转的

turns [tə:n] n. (turn 的复数) 转动，旋转，转变方向，轮流，时机，倾向，(一)回；v. (turn 的第三人称单数) (使)转动，(使)变质，(使)变为，翻转，扭转，超过，车(成)
~ ratio 匝数比，变比，匝比 ‖ **Syn**. ratio of winding 匝数比，线圈比，绕组比

turntable ['tə:nˌteibl] n. 转车，转盘，转台
~ base 转台支座

turpentine ['tə:pəntain] n. 松节油，松脂；v. 涂松节油，采松脂

turret ['tʌrit] n. 小塔，塔楼，炮塔
~ lathe 六角车床
~ milling machine 转塔铣床
~ mooring 转塔系泊
~ mount 炮塔座

turtle ['tə:tl] n. 龟，海龟；v. 翻没，倾覆，捕海龟，捕鳖

TV (television) 电视，电视机
~ and radio set 电视机和收音机
~ broadcast aerial 电视广播天线

tweak [twi:k] n. 捏，拧，扭，苦恼；v. 调节，调整

tween [twi:n] prep. (=between) 在两者之间，在…中间

tweendeck ['twi:nˌdek] n. 甲板间，双层甲板
~ bunker 甲板间燃料舱
~ cargo space 甲板间货舱
~ frame 甲板间肋骨
~ portside 左舷双层甲板
~ ship 双层甲板船
~ space 甲板间舱，甲板间处所

tweendecker ['twi:nˌdekə] n. 多层甲板船，双层甲板船

twin [twin] n. 双胞胎中一人，孪生子；v. (使)成对, (使)偶合，孪生；a. 一对的，相似的，双重的，双联的，双胞胎的
~ bank engine 双排式发动机
~ cabins 双舱
~ cantilevers 双悬臂
~ coil 双线圈
~ crane 双吊起重机
~ engines 双发动机
~ propellers 双螺旋桨，双推进器
~ pulley block 双(联)滑轮组
~ shafting 双轴系

twin-duct 双管道的，双管的
~ ventilation system 双风道系统

twin-input 双输入的
~ single-output gear 双输入单输出齿轮

twin-screw 双螺杆的
~ drive 双螺杆驱动

twine [twain] n. 合股线，细绳，麻线，搓；v. 搓，织，编饰，(使)缠绕

twist [twist] n. 螺旋状，扭曲，盘旋，曲折，手法；v. 拧，绞，搓，捻，扭曲，扭动，扭弯，使转动，缠绕，呈螺旋形，编织
~ drill 麻花钻，螺旋钻
~ drill with cylinder shaft for high speed steel 高速钢直柄钻头
~ drill with morse taper for high speed steel 高速钢锥柄钻头

~ flat drill 麻花平钻

~ gimlet 手摇钻

~ switch 扭转开关

twisted ['twistid] v. (twist 的过去式和过去分词) 拧，绞，搓，捻，扭曲，扭动，扭弯，使转动，缠绕，呈螺旋形，编织；a. 扭曲的，反常的，变态的

~ pair telephone cable for ship 船用双绞线电话电缆

twisting ['twistiŋ] n. 翘曲，扭曲；v. (twist 的 ing 形式) 拧，绞，搓，捻，扭曲，扭动，扭弯，使转动，缠绕，呈螺旋形，编织；a. 缠绕的，曲折的，转动的

~ force 圆周力，切向力

twistlock ['twistlɔk] n. 扭锁

two [tu:] n. 二，两个，一对，两个东西，两点钟，第二个；a. 两个的；num. 二，两个，第二

~ independent power supply 双独立电源

~ part bearing 分轴承，对开式轴承

two-beaked 双喙的

~ anvil 砧，砧子

two-circuit 双回路的，双路的

~ feeding 双路供电 ‖ *Syn*. duplicate supply 双路供电，重复供应

~ method 双回路法

~ parallel 双回路并联

~ radial system 双回路径向系统

~ transformer 双回路变压器 ‖ *Syn*. double column transformer (DblClmnTrans) 双绕组变压器；two-winding transformer 双绕组变压器，双线圈变压器

~ trunk system with one side power supply 单侧供电的双路干线系统

~ tuner 双路调谐器

~ winding 双绕组

two-feeder 双馈电线的，双馈的

~ supply 双馈供电

two-frequency 双频率的，双频的

~ oscillation 双频振荡

~ signal 双频信号

~ system 双频系统

two-input 双输入的，两输入的

~ circuit 双输入电路

~ module 双输入模块

~ servo 双输入伺服系统

~ switch 双输入开关

~ two-output system 双输入双输出系统

two-phase 两相位的，两相的

~ induction motor 两相感应电动机

~ motor 两相电动机

~ short-circuit current 两相短路电流

two-pin 双销的

~ connector 双销连接器

~ plug 双头插头

~ reversible plug 双销可逆插头

~ socket 双销插座

~ system 双销系统

two-pole 两极的，双极的

~ machine 两极电机

~ motor 两极电动机

~ receptacle with grounding contact 具有接地触头的两极插座

~ structure 双极结构

~ switch 双极开关

~ system 双极系统

two-port 双端口的，双口的

~ network 两端口网络，双端口网络

two-position 双位置的，双位的，两路的

~ action 双位置动作

~ attack 两路夹击灭火
~ four-way valve 双位四通阀
~ regulation 双位调节
~ relay 双位置继电器
~ three-way directional control 双位三向方向控制
~ three-way valve 双位三通阀
~ two-way valve 双位双向阀

two-ram 双柱塞的
~ hydraulic steering gear 双柱塞液压操舵装置，双柱塞液压舵机

two-stage 双级的，二级的，两阶段的
~ air compressor 二级空气压缩机
~ design supercharging 二级设计增压
~ design 两阶段设计
~ supercharging 二级增压

two-state 双状态的，双态的
~ circuit 双态电路
~ control 双态控制
~ device 双态器件
~ modulation 双态调制
~ source 双态源
~ system 双态系统

two-step 两步的，二步的
~ action control 两位控制作用
~ charge 两步充电

two-stroke 二冲程的
~ cycle marine diesel engine 二冲程循环船用柴油机
~ cycle 二冲程循环
~ engine 二冲程发动机
~ marine diesel engine 二冲程船用柴油机
~ oil 二冲程油

two-time 二次的，两次的
~ adjustment 二次调整
~ compensation 二次补偿

two-way 双通的，双路的，双向的，两路的，两向的
~ choice 双向选择
~ configuration 双向配置
~ fuse plug 双向熔断器插头
~ fuse socket 双线保险丝插座，双熔丝插座
~ pallet 双向托盘
~ slab 双向板
~ valve 双向阀

two-winding 双绕组的，双线圈的
~ motor 双绕组电动机
~ transformer ballast 双绕组变压式镇流器，双线圈变压器式镇流器
~ transformer 双绕组变压器，双线圈变压器 ‖ *Syn*. double column transformer (DblClmnTrans) 双绕组变压器；two-circuit transformer 双回路变压器

two-wire 双线的，两线的
~ cable 双线电缆
~ monitor 双线监控器
~ operation 双线操作
~ system 双线制
~ transmission 双线传输，双线输电

type [taip] *n*. 类型，类，门，典型，标志，特质，代表，象征，预兆，模范，字体，活字，铅字；*v*. 打字，测定类型，代表，预示

typhoon [tai'fu:n] *n*. 台风

typical ['tipikəl] *a*. 典型的，象征性的，代表性的，特有的
~ cabin 典型舱室
~ example 典型实例
~ example of automatic control system 自动控制系统典型实例

~ fault 典型错误

~ insulating flange joint 标准绝缘法兰接头

~ form 代表式，典型式

typically ['tipikəli] *ad.* 代表性地，作为特色地

U

U-shaped U 形的

~ bow U 形弓

U-slot U 形槽

~ piston U 型槽活塞

UDC (upper dead center) 上死点，上止点 ‖ *Syn*. top dead center (TDC) 上死点，上止点

UFL (upper flammable limit) 易燃上限

ULCC (ultra large crude carrier) 超大型油船

ullage ['ʌlidʒ] *n.* 不足量，瓶空，罐空，损耗，漏损量，空余量

~ board 膨胀余位测板

~ foot (油舱)测深尺

~ hole 膨胀余位测孔

~ port 油位测定孔

~ scale 量油尺，液面计

~ table 测油尺，液舱容积表，罐表

ultimate ['ʌltimit] *n.* 最终，最大极限，最大量，基本原理，基本事实；*a.* 极限的，最佳的，最后的，最远距离的，根本的，最大的，首要的

~ bearing capacity 极限承载量，极限承载力，极限载荷能力

~ bearing strength 弯曲极限强度

ultimately ['ʌltimətli] *ad.* 根本，最后，最终，基本上

ultra ['ʌltrə] *n.* 过激论者，急进论者；*a.* 过激的，极端的

~ filter 超滤器

~ high vacuum measurement 超高真空计量

~ large crude carrier (ULCC) 超大型油船

~ thin laminate 超薄型层压板

ultrasonic [,ʌltrə'sɔnik] *n.* 超声波；*a.* 超声的，超音速的

~ cleaning 超声波清洗，超声波消磁

~ grinder 超声波磨床

~ grinding technique 超声研磨技术

~ inspection 超声波探伤，超声波检查

~ instrument 超声仪器

~ levelmeter 超声波水准仪

~ sensor 超声波传感器

~ test 超声波检测

~ transducer 超声换能器

~ wave fire detector 超声波火灾探测器

~ welding machine 超声波焊接机

ultraviolet [,ʌltrə'vaiəlit] *n.* 紫外光，紫外线辐射；*a.* 紫外线的，紫外的，产生紫外线的

~ flame detector 紫外线火焰检测器

umbrella [ʌm'brelə] *n.* 伞，雨伞，庇护，保护物

UMS (unattended machinery space, unmanned machinery space) 无人机舱，自动机舱 ‖ *Syn*. unattended engine room 无人机舱，自动机舱；unmanned engine room 无人机舱，自动机舱

unaccompanied [,ʌnə'kʌmpənid] *a.* 无人陪伴的，无人伴随的，无伴侣的

~ baggage 非随身携带的行李

unadjustable [,ʌnəd'ʒʌstəbl] *a.* 不可调节的

~ speed electric drive 不可调速电力传

动，不可调速电传动

unambiguous [ˌʌnæmˈbigjuəs] *a.* 清楚的，不含糊的，明确的

unattended [ˌʌnəˈtendid] *a.* 无人看管的，无人照顾的，无人陪伴的，无人出席的，未被注意的
~ engine room 无人机舱，自动机舱 ‖ *Syn.* unattended machinery space (UMS) 无人机舱，自动机舱；unmanned engine room 无人机舱，自动机舱；unmanned machinery space (UMS) 无人机舱，自动机舱
~ equipment 自动设备

unauthorized [ˈʌnˈɔːθəraizd] *a.* 未经授权的，未经许可的，未经批准的

unavailability [ˈʌnəveiləˈbiliti] *n.* 无效，没有利用率

unavailable [ˈʌnəˈveiləbl] *a.* 难以获得的，不可获得的，无法接近的，不在手头的

unavoidable [ˌʌnəˈvɔidəbl] *a.* 不能避免的，不可避免的，不能取消的

unbalance [ˈʌnˈbæləns] *n.* 失衡，失去平衡，紊乱；*v.* 使能避免，使失去平衡，破坏平衡，使心情紊乱 ‖ *Syn.* imbalance 不平衡，不均衡，失调
~ protection 不平衡保护
~ response 不平衡反应
~ rudder 不平衡舵

unbalanced [ˈʌnˈbælənst] *v.* (unbalance 的过去式和过去分词) 使能避免，使失去平衡，破坏平衡，使心情紊乱；*a.* 不均衡的，错乱的，不稳定的，收支不平衡的
~ load 失衡负载，不平衡负载

unbroken [ˈʌnˈbrəukən] *a.* 未破损的，完整的，继续的

unburned [ʌnˈbəːnd] *a.* 未燃的 ‖ *Syn.* unburnt 未燃的

unburnedness [ˈʌnˈbəːndnis] *n.* 未燃尽度

unburnt [ʌnˈbəːnt] *a.* 未燃的 ‖ *Syn.* unburned 未燃的

uncertain [ʌnˈsəːtn] *a.* 无常的，不确定的，不可预测的，靠不住的

uncertainty [ʌnˈsəːtnti] *n.* 无常，不确定，不可靠，半信半疑

uncertified [ʌnsəˈːtifaid] *a.* 未经认证的，无证明书的

unchanged [ˈʌnˈtʃeindʒd] *a.* 未改变的，无变化的

unclad [ˈʌnˈklæd] *v.* (unclothe 的过去式和过去分词) 除去遮盖物，使脱去衣服，剥光；*a.* 赤裸裸的，没穿衣服的
~ laminate surface 叠压板面，层压板面

unclear [ˈʌnˈkliə] *a.* 不清楚的，不明白的，不肯定的

UNCLOS (United Nations Convention on the Law of the Sea) 联合国海洋法公约

unclothe [ˈʌnˈkləuð] *v.* 除去遮盖物，使脱去衣服，剥光

unconfined [ˈʌnkənˈfaind] *a.* 无限制的，无约束的，无拘束
~ compressive strength 无侧限抗压强度，非封闭抗压强度

uncontrol [ˈʌnkənˈtrəul] *n.* 缺少控制

uncontrollable [ˌʌnkənˈtrəuləb(ə)l] *a.* 无法控制的，控制不住的，无法统治的

uncover [ʌnˈkʌvə] *v.* 揭开盖子，揭露，显现，暴露，脱帽致敬

undeliverable [ˈʌndiˈlivərəbl] *a.* 无法投递的，无法送达的

under [ˈʌndə] *a.* 下面的，从属的，下级的，

过少的；ad. 在下面,附属地,下等地；prep. 在…之下,在…之内,在…过程中,以…为动力,在…领导下,低于,少于,小于,假借

~ control 在控制之下

~ frequency protection 低频保护装置

~ normal service load 在正常工况负荷下

~ pressure 在压力下

~ the control of 在…的控制之下

~ the pressure of 在…的压力下

~ the protection of 在…的保护之下

~ the supervision of 在…的监督之下

~ unit test (UUT) 被测部件,被测单元

~ valuation 低估

~ voltage 欠压

~ voltage lock out (UVLO) 欠电压锁定,低压关断

~ voltage tripping test 低压脱扣试验

~ water ecosystem 水下生态系统

~ water environment protecting 水下环境保护

~ way 进行中,在行进

undercharge [ˌʌndə'tʃɑːdʒ] n. 不足量的填充,充电不足,低的索价；v. 不足量地填充,充电不足,索价低于常价

undercoat ['ʌndəkəut] n. 底漆,内涂层,绒毛,(穿在外衣里的)上衣

undercurrent ['ʌndəkʌrənt] n. 潜流,暗流,潜在倾向,电流不足

~ relay 欠电流继电器

~ release 低电流释放

~ tripping 欠流跳闸

underdamp ['ʌndə'dæmp] n. 不完全衰减,不完全减震

underfeed [ˌʌndə'fiːd] v. 不充分供料,未喂饱；a. 由下部加添燃料的

undergo [ˌʌndə'gəu] v. 经历,经验,遭受,承受

underground ['ʌndəgraund] n. 地铁,地道；v. 置于地下；a. 地下的,地面下的,不公开的,秘密的；ad. 在地下,秘密地

~ cable 地下电缆

~ cable box 地下电缆接线盒

underload ['ʌndələud] v. 使装载不足,欠载

~ switch 欠载断路器,轻载开关,小型开关

undermine [ˌʌndə'main] v. 逐渐损坏,侵蚀…基础,削弱

underneath [ˌʌndə'niːθ] n. 下部,底部；a. 下面的,较低的；ad. 在下面,在底下,在下面,在下层；prep. 在下面,在…之下,在…下面,在…领导下,在…控制下

underside ['ʌndəsaid] n. 下面,内面,下侧,下腹

undersign [ˌʌndə'sain] v. 在…下面签名,签名于末尾

undersize ['ʌndəsaiz] a. 较一般为小的,不够大的

undersquare ['ʌndəskweə] n. 下耳戳

~ engine 长行程发动机

understable [ˌʌndə'steibl] a. 欠稳定的

undertake [ˌʌndə'teik] v. 承担,担任,许诺,保证,采取

undervoltage ['ʌndəvəultidʒ] n. 欠电压,欠压

~ device 低压器件,低压装置

~ protection 欠压保护

~ relay 欠压继电器

~ test 欠压试验

~ trip 欠压跳闸，欠压解扣

~ trip coil 欠压脱扣线圈

underwater ['ʌndə'wɔ:tə] *n.* 水面下的水；*a.* 在水下的，在水中的；*ad.* 在水下，在水线以下

~ explosion shock test 水下爆炸冲击试验

~ fittings (船体)水下附件

~ navigation 水下航行

~ operation ship 水下作业船

~ photography 水下摄影

~ plasma cutting machine 水下等离子切割机

~ probing 水下探测

~ robot 水下机器人

~ ship 潜水船，潜艇

~ vehicle 水下航行器

underway ['ʌndə'wei] *a.* 起步的，进行中的，航行中的

~ replenishment 海上补给，航行补给 ‖ *Syn.* replenishing-at-sea 海上补给，航行补给；replenishment at sea 海上补给，航行补给

~ watch 航行值班

undesirable ['ʌndi'zaiərəbl] *n.* 不受欢迎的人，不良分子；*a.* 不合需要的，不受欢迎的，令人不快的，不良的 ‖ *Ant.* desirable 引人注意者；令人想要的，值得要的，合意的，悦人心意的

~ change 不良变化

~ effect 不良影响

undissolved [ʌndi'zɔlvd] *a.* 不溶解的，未溶解的

undue ['ʌn'dju:] *a.* 不适当的，过度的，过分的，未到期的

unduly ['ʌn'dju:li] *ad.* 过分地，过度地，不适当地

uneconomical ['ʌn,i:kə'nɔmikəl] *a.* 不经济的，不节约的，浪费的

UNEP (United Nations Environment Programme) 联合国环境规划署

unequal [ʌn'i:kwəl] *n.* 与他人不同等的人；*a.* 不平等的，不同的，不平衡的，不规则的，不对称的，不胜任的

~ heating 不均匀加热

~ impulse 不等脉冲

uneven [ʌn'i:vən] *a.* 不平坦的，不平均的，不均匀的，奇数的

~ cylinder liner wear 气缸套磨损不均匀

~ wear 不均匀磨损

unevenly [ʌn'i:vnli] *ad.* 不平坦地，不均衡地

unexplosive [ʌniksp'ləusiv] *a.* 非爆炸性的，不爆炸的

unextinguished [ʌniks'tiŋwiʃt] *a.* 未熄灭的，未扑灭的，未消灭的

unfamiliar [,ʌnfə'miljə] *a.* 不熟悉的,不熟知的

unfit [ʌn'fit] *v.* 使不相宜，使不合格；*a.* 不适宜的，不适当的，不合格的，不相称的，不健康的，不强健的

unfitness [ʌn'fitnəs] *n.* 不适当，不胜任

unforeseeable [,ʌnfɔ:'si:əbl] *a.* 不能预见的，预料不到的

~ event 不能预料的事件

unforeseen [,ʌnfɔ:'si:n] *a.* 未预见到的，无法预料的，意外的，偶然的

UNGA (United Nations General Assembly) 联合国大会

unidimensional ['ju:nidi'menʃənl] *a.* 线性

的，一维的，一度的，一次元的，直线型的

unidirectional [ju:nidi'rekʃənəl] a. 单向的，单向性的

~ action 单向行动

~ control 单向控制

~ current 单向电流

~ rotation 单向旋转

~ switch 单向开关

unification [ˌju:nifi'keiʃən] n. 统一，合一，一致

uniflow ['ju:nifləu] a. 单向流动的，单流的

~ scavenging 单流扫气

~ scavenging type engine 单流扫气式发动机

uniform ['ju:nifɔ:m] n. 制服，军服；v. 使规格一律，使均一，使穿制服；a. 统一的，一律的，一致的，均质的，相同的，始终如一的，均衡的 ‖ **Ant**. non-uniform 不均匀的，不统一的，不同的

~ field 均匀场，均强场

~ mean 一致平均

~ pitch 等螺距

~ quality 同样性质

uniformity [ˌju:ni'fɔ:miti] n. 同样，一式，一致，均匀

uniformly ['ju:nifɔ:mli] ad. 一致地，相同地

~ distributed load 均匀分布载荷，等分布荷重

unimportant ['ʌnim'pɔ:tənt] a. 不重要的，次要的，琐细的

uninterrupted ['ʌnintə'rʌptid] a. 不停的，连续的，未受干扰的，不间断的

~ duty 不间断工作方式，不间断工作制

~ power supply (UPS) 不间断电源

union ['ju:niən] n. 联管街，联轴节，联合，合并，结合，并集，联盟，协会；a. 工会的

~ piece 联结零件，连接零件

~ pipe 联接管，管接头

~ purchase system 双杆吊货系统，联杆吊货法

~ purchase pulley 双杆吊货滑轮装置

~ screw 管接头对动螺纹

unique [ju:'ni:k] a. 唯一的，仅有的，独特的，不平常的，特别的

uniquely [ju:'ni:kli] ad. 独特地，唯一地

unit ['ju:nit] n. 装置，设备，部件，个体，小组，(计量)单位，部队单位，个位，最小正整数 ‖ **Syn**. apparatus 器械，设备，仪器；appliance 用具，器具；arrangement 布置；assembly 组装部件；device 装置，设备；equipment 装备，设备，器材，装置；facility 设备，工具；furniture 设备，家具；gear 设备，装备；installation 设备，装置；machine 机器，机械，机构；machinery 机械(总称)，机器；mechanism 机器，机械装置，机构；plant 设备；provision 装备，供应品

~ cargo 单位货物

~ clarifier 单层澄清器

~ store 零件库

~ testing 单元测试法，单元测试，部件测试

unite [ju(:)'nait] v. 联合，团结，结合，合并，黏结，统一，并有，兼备，混合，化合

united [ju'naitid] v. (unite 的过去式和过去分词) 联合，团结，结合，合并，黏结，

统一，并有，兼备，混合，化合；*a.* 联合的，团结的，一致的，共同形成的

~ Nations Committee of Experts on the Transport of Dangerous Goods 联合国危险货物运输专家委员会

~ Nations Convention on the Law of the Sea (UNCLOS) 联合国海洋法公约

~ Nations Environment Programme (UNEP) 联合国环境规划署

~ Nations General Assembly (UNGA) 联合国大会

~ States (US) 美国

~ States Coast Guard (USCG) 美国海岸警卫队

universal [ˌjuːniˈvəːsəl] *n.* 一般概念，一般性，共有特质；*a.* 普遍的，全体的，通用的，宇宙的，世界的 ‖ *Syn.* common 公共的，普通的；commonplace 平凡的；general 一般的，普通的；ordinary 平常的，平凡的，普通的；pervasive 普遍的；popular 大众的，通俗的，普遍的；usual 平常的，通常的，惯例的；widespread 分布广泛的，普遍的

~ grinding machine 万能磨床

~ joint 万向接头

~ milling machine 万能铣床

~ motor 交直流两用机，通用电动机

~ parts 通用零部件

~ selector 万能转换开关，通配选择符

~ switch 万能开关

universally [ˌjuːniˈvəːsəli] *ad.* 普遍地，全体地，到处

unjustifiable [ʌnˈdʒʌstifaiəbl] *a.* 不能分辩的，不合道理的，无法辩护的

unknown [ˌʌnˈnəun] *n.* 未知数，无名者；*a.* 未知的，不出名的，从未发生的，从不存在的

~ quantity 难预测的人，难预料的事

unlay [ˈʌnˈlei] *v.* 解散，拆开，松一松

unleaded [ʌnˈledid] *a.* 无铅的，不含铅的

~ gasoline 无铅汽油

~ petrol 无铅汽油

unlevel [ʌnˈlevl] *a.* 不平坦的，非水平的

~ luffing 非水平变幅

unlit [ʌnˈlit] *a.* 未点燃的，无灯光的

unload [ʌnˈləud] *n.* 卸货，退子弹；*v.* 卸货，去除负担，拆掉，倾销，退子弹

unloader [ˈʌnˈləudə] *n.* 卸料器，卸载机，卸车工，减荷器

unloading [ˈʌnˈləudiŋ] *n.* 卸载；*v.* (unload 的 ing 形式) 卸货，去除负担，拆掉，倾销，退子弹

~ cylinder 卸载油缸

~ discharge of goods 卸货

~ device 卸料装置

~ gear 卸载(传动)装置，卸荷装置

~ valve 卸荷阀，卸载阀

unlock [ˌʌnˈlɔk] *v.* 开锁，开启，揭开，表露，解开，被释放

unman [ʌnˈmæn] *v.* 使怯懦，使泄气，使失去男子气概

unmanned [ʌnˈmænd] *v.* (unman 的过去式和过去分词) 使怯懦，使泄气，使失去男子汉气概；*a.* 无人驾驶的，无人的

~ engine room 无人机舱，自动机舱 ‖ *Syn.* unmanned machinery space (UMS) 无人机舱，自动机舱；unattended engine room 无人机舱，自动机舱；unattended machinery space (UMS) 无人机舱，自动机舱

unnail [ˌʌnˈneil] *v.* 拔除钉子

unnecessarily [ʌn'nesisərili] ad. 不必要地，未必

unnecessary [ʌn'nesisəri] a. 不必要的，多余的，无用的

unobtainable ['ʌnəb'teinəbl] a. 难获得的，无法得到的，不能得到的

unplug ['ʌn'plʌg] v. 拔去插头，拔去塞子，去掉障碍物

unprepared ['ʌnpri'pɛəd] a. 无准备的，即席的，尚未准备好的

unprofessional ['ʌnprə'feʃənl] a. 非专业化的，外行的，违反职业道德标准的

unready ['ʌn'redi] a. 没有准备的，未准备好的，迟钝的

unreasonable [ʌn'ri:znəbl] a. 不讲道理的，不合理的，过度的，不切实际的

unreel ['ʌn'ri:l] v. 回卷，退绕，解开

unreliable ['ʌnri'laiəbl] a. 不可靠的，靠不住的，不能信任的

unrepair ['ʌnri'peə(r)] n. 失修，塌毁，破损，荒废

unrestricted ['ʌnris'triktid] a. 不受限制的，自由的

unroll ['ʌn'rəul] v. 解开，打开，展开，铺开，展现，显示

unsafe [ʌn'seif] a. 危险的，不安全的，不安稳的 ‖ *Syn.* dangerous 危险的；hazardous 危险的，冒险的；perilous 危险的，冒险的

~ temperature 不安全温度

unsafety ['ʌn'seifti] n. 不安全，不安全状态，危险

unsatisfactory ['ʌnsætis'fæktəri] a. 不能令人满意的，不能解决问题的，不符合要求的，不满足的

unsaturated ['ʌn'sætʃəreitid] a. 没有饱和的，不饱和的

~ polyester 不饱和聚酯

unscrew ['ʌn'skru:] v. 旋出螺丝，旋开，松开

unseal ['ʌn'si:l] v. 开启，拆封，打开，拆开

unseaworthiness [ʌn'si:wə:ðinis] n. 不适航性

unseaworthy ['ʌn'si:,wə:ði] a. 经不住海上风浪的，不适于航海的

unsecured ['ʌnsi'kjuəd] a. 不稳当的，不安全的，未固定的，未扣紧的

unseen ['ʌn'si:n] n. 即席翻译；a. 未见过的，看不见的，未经预习的

unsheltered [ʌn'ʃeltəd] a. 未遮盖的，无居所的

~ anchorage 开敞锚地

~ area 无遮蔽区，非阴影区，非防护区

unshroud [ˌʌn'ʃraud] v. 移去遮蔽物，除去面纱，暴露，展示

unshrouded [ʌn'ʃraudid] v. (unshroud 的过去式和过去分词) 移去遮蔽物,除去面纱，暴露，展示；a. 被包围的

~ impeller 开式叶轮，无罩叶轮，无盖板叶轮

unsinkable ['ʌn'siŋkəbl] a. 不会下沉的，不会沉底的

~ lifeboat 不沉救生艇

unstable ['ʌn'steibl] a. 不稳固的，不坚定的，易变的，动摇的，多变的，易于分解的，衰变的

~ protection 不稳定保护

unsteady ['ʌn'stedi] a. 不稳定的，不安定的，颤动的，摇晃的；v. 使不稳定，动摇

~ degree of revolution 转速不稳定度

~ flow 非定常流，非稳定流

unstop ['ʌn'stɔp] v. 拔开塞子，除去障碍

unstow [ʌn'stəu] v. 卸空

unsuccessful ['ʌnsək'sesfl] a. 不成功的，失败的

unsuitability [ʌn'sju:tə'bilәti] n. 不相称，不适合

unsuitable ['ʌn'sju:təbl] a. 不适合的，不相称的

unsupported ['ʌnsə'pɔ:tid] a. 无支持的，无支撑的

~ adhesive film 无支撑胶膜

~ back span 空顶距

unsymmetrical ['ʌnsi'metrikəl] a. 非对称的，不匀称的，不对称的

untie ['ʌn'tai] v. 解开，解放，解决，松开，解开

unto ['ʌntu] prep. 到，向，直到

untrue ['ʌn'tru:] a. 不合标准的，不真实的，不忠实的

unusable [ˌʌn'ju:zəb(ə)l] a. 不能用的

unused [ˌʌn'ju:zd] a. 不习惯的，不用的，不使用的，从未用过的，积累的

unusual [ʌn'ju:ʒuəl] a. 不平常的，与众不同的，不寻常的，不普通的

unusually [ʌn'ju:ʒuəli] ad. 显著地，异乎寻常地，罕有地

unvented [ʌn'ventid] a. 未放气的

unwieldy [ʌn'wi:ldi] a. 笨拙的，不实用的，难处理的，难使用的，笨重的

up [ʌp] n. 朝上的斜坡，上升，向上的运动，向上的倾向；v. 增加，提升，起床；a. 朝上的，提高的，被抬起的，被举起的，向上移动的，方向朝上的，较高的，站立的，直立的，结束了的，完了的，熟知的，内行的，能运行的，开向，驶往，起床的；ad. 向上风，朝上地，在上方地，在表面以上地，可见地，靠近地，完全地，彻底地；prep. 朝高处，朝上游，与…相反

~ stroke 上行冲程

~ to date 最新的，现代的，最近的

~ with 拿起，举起，拥护，起来

update [ʌp'deit] n. 现代化，更新；v. 使现代化，修正，校正，更新

upflow ['ʌpfləu] v. 向上流

upgrade ['ʌpgreid] n. 升级，上升，上坡；v. 使升级，提升，改良品种；ad. 往上 ‖ *Syn*. enhance 提高，增加；heighten 提高，升高；improve 提高，增进；increase 增加，加大；lift 升高，提高；raise 升起，提高；hoist 升起，吊起

uphold [ʌp'həuld] v. 支持，维持，支撑，赞成

upholstery [ʌp'həulstəri] n. 室内装饰，家具装饰业

upkeep ['ʌpki:p] n. 维持，保养，保养费

upload ['ʌpˌləud] n. 向上(作用的)负载，上传的数据；v. 上传，上载

upper ['ʌpə] n. 鞋帮，靴面，兴奋剂，令人兴奋的经历；a. 上面的，上部的，位置较高的，内地的，远离大海的

~ and lower 上下

~ berth 上铺

~ boundary 上边界

~ bunk 上层铺位，上铺

~ casing 上套管

~ center crankshaft bearing 曲轴主轴承上中轴瓦

~ cutoff frequency 上限截止频率

~ cylinder half 上半汽缸

~ dead center (UDC) 上死点，上止点 ‖ *Syn*. top dead center (TDC) 上死点，上止点

~ deck 上甲板

~ end bearing 上端轴承

~ flammable limit (UFL) 易燃上限

~ header 上集管箱，上联箱，上集管

~ heating value 高热值

~ holder block 上压块

~ lever 水平支撑

~ level problem 上层问题

~ limit 上限

~ mid plate 上中间板

~ range limit 测量上限

~ tank 上水箱，上箱

~ temperature limit 温度上限

~ tweendeck 上部甲板间

uppermost ['ʌpəməust] *a*. 至上的，最高的，最重要的；*ad*. 在最上，最初，首先

~ continuous deck 最上层连续甲板

upright ['ʌp'rait] *n*. 垂直，竖立，直立的东西；*a*. 垂直的，竖式的，正直的，诚实的，合乎正道的；*ad*. 垂直地，笔直地，竖立着

~ position 垂直位置，垂直状态

~ pump 立式泵

~ shaft 立轴

~ tubular boiler 立式火管锅炉

UPS (uninterrupted power supply) 不间断电源

upset [ʌp'set] *n*. 翻倒，颠覆，混乱；*v*. 颠覆，推翻，翻倒，扰乱，打乱，打搅，使不适，使心烦

upside ['ʌpsaid] *n*. 上边，上面，上部，上升，优势

upstream ['ʌp'stri:m] *a*. 逆流而上的，向上游的，上游的；*ad*. 向上游，溯流，逆流地

uptake ['ʌpteik] *n*. 举起，上风井，上风烟道，理解，领会

~ casing 烟喉隔层，烟喉外壳

~ header 垂直联箱

~ tube 吸收管

~ valve 吸收阀

~ ventilator 烟道通风筒，烟道通风器

upward ['ʌpwəd] *a*. 向上的，上升的，增长的；*ad*. 向上地，上升地，增长地

upwards ['ʌpwədz] *ad*. 以上，向上

~ of 超过

~ pressure 向上压力

~ stroke 向上冲程

upwell [ʌp'wel] *v*. 上涌

urban ['ə:bən] *a*. 城市的，市内的

~ ferry 城市客运轮渡

urea ['juəriə] *n*. 尿素

urgency ['ə:dʒənsi] *n*. 紧急，紧急的事，强求，催促，坚持

~ signal 紧急信号 ‖ *Syn*. emergency signal 紧急信号；urgent signal 紧急信号

urgent ['ə:dʒənt] *a*. 紧急的，急迫的，催促的，强求的，极力主张的

~ repair 紧急修理

~ signal 紧急信号 ‖ *Syn*. emergency signal 紧急信号；urgency signal 紧急信号

~ telegram 紧急电报

urgently ['ə:dʒəntli] *ad*. 紧急地，急迫地

US (United States) 美国

usable ['ju:zəb(ə)l] *a*. 可用的，合用的，

便于使用的

usage ['ju:sidʒ] n. 使用，用法，习惯，惯例

USCG (United States Coast Guard) 美国海岸警卫队

use [ju:s] n. 使用，利用，用途，效用，使用价值；v. 使用，运用，消耗 ‖ *Syn*. application 应用，运用，施用；utility 效用，有用；utilization 利用

useful ['ju:sful] a. 有用的，实用的，有益的，有帮助的

useless ['ju:slis] a. 无用的，无效的，无益的，无价值的

user ['ju:zə] n. 用户，使用者，使用物
~ guide 用户指南
~ manual 用户手册
~ protocol 用户协议

usual ['ju:ʒuəl] a. 通常的，常有的，常见的，惯例的，平常的，普通的，平时的 ‖ *Syn*. common 公共的，普通的；commonplace 平凡的；general 一般的，普通的；ordinary 平常的，平凡的，普通的；pervasive 普遍的；popular 大众的，通俗的，普遍的；universal 普遍的，通用的；widespread 分布广泛的，普遍的

UTC (Coordinated Universal Time) 协调世界时，世界统一时间，世界标准时间，国际协调时间

utensil [ju(:)'tensl] n. 器皿，器具，用具

utilise ['ju:tilaiz] v. (=utilize) 利用，使用

utility [ju:'tiliti] n. 功用，效用，有用，有益，公用事业；a. 多用途的，各种工作都会做的，能在数个位置作替补的 ‖ *Syn*. application 应用，运用，施用；use 使用，利用，用途，效用；utilization 利用

~ boat 通用小艇
~ circuit 生活用电电路
~ command 使用命令，实用命令
~ control console 使用控制台，操作控制台
~ factor 设备利用系数，利用系数，使用率
~ function 效用函数
~ program 实用程序
~ ratio 利用率

utilization [,ju:tilai'zeiʃən] n. 利用，使用，效用 ‖ *Syn*. application 应用，运用，施用；use 使用，利用，用途，效用；utility 效用，有用
~ factor method 利用系数法
~ rate 利用系数，实用比

utilize ['ju:tilaiz] v. (=utilise) 利用，使用

utmost ['ʌtməust] n. 极限，最大限度，极力；a. 极度的，最大的，最远的

UUT (under unit test) 被测部件，被测单元

UVLO (under voltage lock out) 欠电压锁定，低压关断

V

V-belt V 型带，三角皮带
~ pulley V 型皮带轮，三角皮带轮

V-drive V 型传动

V-engine V 型发动机

V-form V 形的
~ compressor V 形压缩机 ‖ *Syn*. V-type compressor V 形压缩机

V-notch V 型缺口，V 型切口

V-section V 形截面，三角槽断面
~ jack V 形千斤顶

V-shape V 形，V 型，倒三角
  ~ bow V 型弓
  ~ pad V 型垫
  ~ section V 型截面
V-type V 形的，锥形的，三角形的，楔形的
  ~ compressor V 形压缩机 ‖ *Syn*. V-form compressor V 形压缩机
  ~ engine V 形发动机
V-weld V 形焊缝
  ~ with gap 带间隙的 V 形焊缝
  ~ without gap 无缝隙的 V 形焊缝
vacant ['veikənt] *a.* 空的，空白的，空缺的，空闲的，空灵的，头脑空虚的，神情茫然的
vacuum ['vækjuəm] *n.* 真空，空白，封闭状态，真空吸尘器；*v.* 用真空吸尘器清扫；*a.* 真空的，产生真空的，利用真空的，低压气体的
  ~ boiling evaporator 真空沸腾式蒸发器
  ~ boiling type fresh water generator 真空沸腾式造水机，真空沸腾式淡水发生器
  ~ booster 真空助力器
  ~ box 真空箱
  ~ chamber 真空室
  ~ circuit breaker (VCB) 真空断路器
  ~ cleaner 真空吸尘器
  ~ distillation 真空蒸馏
  ~ draw 真空抽吸
  ~ filter 真空过滤机
  ~ filtration 真空过滤
  ~ flash type fresh water generator 真空闪蒸式造水机，真空闪蒸式淡水发生器
  ~ gauge 真空计

  ~ horn 真空喇叭
  ~ manometer 真空压力计 ‖ *Syn*. vacuum pressure gauge 真空压力计
  ~ pressure 真空压力
  ~ protection system 真空保护系统
  ~ pump 真空泵，真空抽气机，蒸汽吸水机
  ~ switch 真空开关
  ~ testing 真空试验
valid ['vælid] *a.* 有效的，有根据的，正当的，正确的 ‖ *Ant*. invalid 残废的，无效的
  ~ certificate 有效证明书
  ~ representation 有效表示
  ~ target 有效部位
validate ['vælideit] *v.* 使有效，使生效，批准，确认，证实，验证 ‖ *Ant*. invalidate 使无效，使作废
validation [væli'deiʃən] *n.* 确认，证实 ‖ *Ant*. invalidation 无效，失效
validity [və'liditi] *n.* 有效，有效性，合法性，正确，正确性
valley ['væli] *n.* 谷，河谷，流域，屋顶排水沟，屋面斜沟
valve [vælv] *n.* 阀，电子管，真空管，活门，栓塞，活栓，瓣膜；*v.* 装阀于，用阀调节
  ~ ablation 气门烧蚀
  ~ body 阀体
  ~ body attachment 阀体连接头
  ~ cage 阀盒
  ~ cap 阀盖
  ~ casing 阀壳，气门盒
  ~ chain 阀盖链
  ~ chamber cover 阀室盖
  ~ chest 阀门室

~ clearance 阀门间隙，阀余隙
~ clearance adjuster 气阀间隙调整器，阀门间隙调节器
~ cock 阀栓
~ cone 阀锥，锥形阀
~ core 阀芯
~ cover 气门套，阀盖，阀套
~ disc 阀盘
~ driving mechanism 阀传动机构
~ duration 气门开启持续时间
~ effect 整流效应，阀效应，单向导电性
~ face 阀面，气门面
~ flap 阀瓣
~ gasket 阀垫片
~ gate 阀门
~ gear 阀动装置
~ grinding compound 磨阀物，凡尔砂，气门研磨剂
~ grinding paste 磨阀膏
~ grinding sand 磨阀砂
~ guard 阀箱，阀门挡板，阀挡板
~ guide 气门导管，阀导承，阀杆导承
~ guide bushing 阀导衬套
~ head 阀头
~ housing 阀套
~ in-head engine 顶阀式发动机，顶置气门发动机
~ inner spring 阀内簧
~ key 阀门键，阀键，阀门扳手
~ lag 活门迟关，阀迟关
~ lash adjusting screw 气门间隙调整螺钉
~ leakage 阀漏失
~ lift 阀门升程
~ lifter 气门挺杆，气门挺柱，阀挺杆 ‖ *Syn*. valve tappet 气门挺杆，气门挺柱，阀挺杆
~ lifter spring 起阀弹簧
~ margin 气门边限
~ mechanism 配气机构，气门机构，阀动装置
~ mechanism casing 配气机构箱
~ mechanism cover 气缸盖罩
~ needle 阀针
~ oil seal 气门油封
~ oil shield 阀防油罩
~ operating mechanism 气门分配机构
~ operation mechanism 阀动机构
~ overlap 气门重叠，气阀重叠，阀重叠，气门叠开角
~ overlap period 气门重叠周期
~ plate 阀板，阀片，配流盘
~ plug 阀塞
~ port 阀口
~ rocker chamber cover 气门摇臂室盖
~ rocker cover 阀摇杆盖
~ rod 阀杆
~ rod guide 阀杆导承
~ rod knuckle 阀杆肘
~ rotator 气门旋转机构，转阀器
~ seat 阀座
~ seat angle 阀座角
~ seat carbon deposit 阀座积碳
~ seat insert 阀座嵌入物
~ seat ring 阀座环
~ seat width 阀座宽度
~ setting table 阀调整记录表
~ shaft bearing 阀轴轴承
~ shaft lever 阀轴杆
~ spindle 阀轴，阀杆
~ spring 阀弹簧

~ spring retainer 气门弹簧座

~ spring collar 阀弹簧座环

~ stem 阀杆

~ throat 阈喉

~ timing 气门正时

~ timing diagram 配气相位图

~ timing sign 气门正时标记

~ to be repacked and refitted 待重新包装和改装的阀门

~ train 气阀机构

~ type arrestor 阀式避雷器

valveless ['vælvles] a. 无阀的

~ engine 无阀发动机

vanadium [və'neidiəm] n. 钒，铅矿

~ content 钒含量

vane [vein] n. 叶片，视准器，照准器，风向标，风环，风信旗，(螺旋桨等的)翼，舵，变化不定的事物

~ compressor 叶片式压缩机

~ pump 叶片泵

~ rotor 叶片转子

~ type oil motor 叶片式油马达

~ wheel 叶轮

vang [væŋ] n. 斜桁支索，张索

vapor ['veipə] (=vapour) n. 水汽，水蒸汽，雾气，气体混合物，郁闷，忧郁病，无实质之物，自夸者; v.(使)蒸发，升华，自夸

~ compression cycle 蒸汽压缩循环

~ compression distillation 蒸汽压缩蒸馏

~ compression distillation plant 蒸汽压缩蒸馏装置

~ compression refrigeration 蒸汽压缩制冷

~ compressor 蒸汽压缩机

~ density 蒸汽密度

~ detection 蒸汽检测

~ emission control system 蒸汽排放控制系统

~ gravitative separation 蒸汽重力分离 ‖ *Syn.* vapor gravity separation 蒸汽重力分离

~ lock system 气锁系统

~ pocket 汽袋

~ pressure 蒸汽压力，蒸汽压

~ scrubber 蒸汽洗涤器，蒸汽清洗装置

~ space 蒸汽域，蒸汽空间

~ trap 除水阀

~ volume load 蒸汽容积

vapor-air 蒸汽空气

~ release valve 蒸汽空气泄放阀

vaporization [,veipərai'zeiʃən] n. 汽化，蒸发

vaporize ['veipəraiz] v. (使)汽化，(使)蒸发

vapour ['veipə] (=vapor) n. 水汽，水蒸气，雾气，气体混合物，郁闷，忧郁病，无实质之物，自夸者; v.(使)蒸发，升华，自夸

var [va:(r)] n. 乏，无功伏安 (无功功率单位)

variability [,vɛəriə'biliti] n. 变化性，易变

variable ['vɛəriəbl] n. 变数，可变物，变量; a. 可变的，不定的，易变的，变量的

~ capacity pump 变量泵 ‖ *Syn.* variable displacement pump 变量泵

~ coefficient 变异系数，变差系数

~ compression ratio (VCR) 可变压缩比

~ cost 变动成本

~ cost ratio 变动成本比率

~ data 可变数据
~ delivery pump 变量输送泵
~ displacement 可变排量，变排量
~ displacement oil motor 变排量油马达
~ displacement system 变排量系统
~ flow 可变流量
~ gain 可变增益
~ gas capacitance sensor 可变气隙式电容传感器，变隙式电容传感器
~ gearing mechanism 传动比调节机构
~ governor gear 可变调速器齿轮
~ inductivity capacitance sensor 变介电常数式电容传感器
~ injection timing (VIT) 可变喷射定时，变更喷油时间装置
~ injection timing mechanism 可变喷油定时机构
~ inlet 可调进气口
~ of winds 风变量
~ order 可变指令
~ parameter 可变参数
~ pitch 可变螺距，可变节距 ‖ *Syn.* controllable pitch 可调螺距，活螺距
~ pitch propeller (VPP) 可调螺距螺旋桨，可变螺距螺旋桨，调距螺旋桨，变距螺旋桨，调距桨 ‖ *Syn.* controllable pitch propeller (CPP) 可调螺距螺旋桨，可变螺距螺旋桨，调距螺旋桨，变距螺旋桨，调距桨，变距桨
~ pressure 可变压力
~ pressure charging system 变压增压系统，可变增压系统
~ resistor 可变电阻器
~ speed 变速
~ speed governor 变速调速器
~ speed governor gear 变速调速器齿轮
~ speed motor 调速电动机，变速电动机 ‖ *Syn*. adjustable speed motor 调速电动机，变速电动机
~ stroke pump 变量泵
~ structure control system 变结构控制系统
~ supercharging system 可变增压系统
~ supply 变动供给
~ transformer 可变比变压器，调压变压器
~ transmission 变速传动
~ working condition 变工况

variably ['vɛəriəbli] *ad.* 易变地，不定地

variant ['vɛəriənt] *n.* 变量，异体；*a.* 相异的，不同的，易变的，另一种形式的

variation [ˌvɛəri'eiʃən] *n.* 变分，变差，磁偏角，变更，变化，变动，变异，变种，变奏，变调
~ analysis 差异分析
~ method 变分法
~ principle 变分原理
~ range 变化区间
~ ratio 变速比，变速范围

variational [ˌvɛəri'eiʃənəl] *a.* 变化的，变化性的，变更的

variegate ['vɛərigeit] *v.* 使成斑驳，使多样化

variegated ['vɛərigeitid] *v.* (variegate 的过去式和过去分词) 使成斑驳，使多样化；*a.* 杂色的，斑驳的，变化多端的
~ lamp 杂色灯

variety [və'raiəti] *n.* 变化，多样性，品种，种类

various ['vɛəriəs] *a.* 各种各样的，多方面的，许多的，各个的，个别的

variously ['vɛərɪəsli] *ad.* 不同地，各种各样地，多方面地

varnish ['va:niʃ] *n.* 清漆，罩光漆，光泽面，假漆，虚饰，外表；*v.* 涂清漆，装饰，粉饰

vary ['vɛəri] *v.* 改变，变更，使多样化，变化，不同，违反
~ in 在…方面变化，在…方面有差异
~ linear model 时变线性模型

varying ['vɛəriŋ] *v.* (vary 的 ing 形式) 改变，变更，使多样化，变化，不同，违反；*a.* 变化的，改变的
~ capacity 变动生产量，变动容量
~ proportions 变化比例
~ speed motor 变速电动机
~ stress 变动应力

vaseline ['væzili:n] *n.* 凡士林

vast [va:st] *n.* 浩瀚，广阔的空间；*a.* 广阔的，巨大的，大量的，巨额的

VCB (vacuum circuit breaker) 真空断路器

VCR (variable compression ratio) 可变压缩比

VDR (voyage data recorder) 航行数据记录仪

vector ['vektə] *n.* 矢量，向量，向量元素，航向，带菌者；*v.* 无线电导引，导航
~ chart 矢量图
~ equation 向量方程，矢量方程

vee [vi:] *n.* V 字形；*a.* V 字形的
~ belt 三角带
~ engine V 形发动机
~ thread V 形螺纹，三角螺纹

veer [viə] *n.* 转向，方向的转变；*v.* (使)转向，(风向)顺(时针)转，放出(锚)

veering ['viəriŋ] *v.* (veer 的 ing 形式) (使)转向，(风向)顺(时针)转，放出(锚)；*a.* 改变的，犹豫的，顺时针方向转向，使船尾转向上风来改变航向
~ wind 顺转风

vehicle ['vi:ikl] *n.* 交通工具，运载工具，车辆，调漆料，媒介物，传达手段
~ deck 车辆甲板
~ ferry 车辆渡船

velocity [vi'lɔsiti] *n.* 速率，速度，周转率，高速，快速
~ error 速度误差
~ error coefficient 速度误差系数
~ error compensator 速度误差补偿器
~ feedback 速度反馈
~ feedback loop 速度反馈回路
~ selector 选速器
~ transducer 速度传感器，速度转换器

vendor ['vendə] *n.* 供应商，卖主，小贩

veneer [və'niə] *n.* 薄板，单板，胶合板，饰面，外表，虚饰；*v.* 镶饰，胶合，虚饰

vent [vent] *n.* 通风孔，排放口，火门，出烟孔，出口，表达，发泄，肛门；*v.* 放出，排出，排放，发泄
~ cock 排气旋塞，放气龙头
~ condenser 排气冷凝器，通风凝结器
~ connection 通气接头，排气接头，排气接管，放气接管
~ cowling 排气管通风帽
~ duct 排气管，通风管道，通风管
~ fan 吸气器，排气器
~ heat loss 通风热损失
~ line 通气管路，出油口
~ mast 通风管桅
~ pipe 排气管
~ screw 放气螺丝

ventilate ['ventileit] v. 通风，换气，开通气孔，提供氧气，公开，公开讨论

ventilating ['ventileitiŋ] n. 通风，通风排气；v. (ventilate 的 ing 形式) 通风，换气，开通气孔，提供氧气，公开，公开讨论；a. 通风的，通风用的
~ arrangement 通风装置
~ fan 通风机，风扇

ventilation [venti'leiʃən] n. 通风，流通空气
~ and air conditioning diagram 通风空调图
~ cowl 通风罩，通风盖帽
~ cycle 通风周期
~ ducting 通风管道
~ hole 通风孔，风眼，通气孔
~ fan 通风风扇
~ fitting 通风配件
~ flue 通风烟道
~ procedure 通风步骤

ventilator ['ventileitə] n. 通风设备，通风机，电扇，空调机
~ trunk 通风管道
~ valve 通风器闸门

venting ['ventiŋ] n. 消除，泄去，排去，通风；v. (vent 的 ing 形式) 放出，排出，排放，发泄
~ system 排气系统
~ valve 通流阀，泄流阀，放气阀

venturi [ven'tuəri] n. 文氏管，文丘里管（一种流体流量测量装置）
~ section 文丘里试验段

verifiable ['verifaiəbl] a. 能作证的，能证实的

verification [ˌverifi'keiʃən] n. 核实，核查，证明，证实，确定，鉴定

~ report 验证报告

verify ['verifai] v. 检验，校验，查证，核实

vernier ['və:niə] n. 游尺，游标，游标尺
~ caliper 游标卡尺 ‖ **Syn.** slide caliper 游标卡尺

versatile ['və:sətail] a. 通用的，多用的，万能的，多才多艺的，多面手的

versatility [ˌvə:sə'tiləti] n. 多功能性

version ['və:ʃən] n. 版本，译文，译本，说法，样式，形式

vertex ['və:teks] n. 顶点，最高点，头顶，天顶

vertical ['və:tikl] n. 垂直线，垂直面，竖杆，垂直位置；a. 垂直的，直立的，顶点的，头顶的
~ acceleration 垂直加速度，法向加速度，法向过载
~ axis propeller 垂直轴螺旋桨
~ band saw 立式带锯机
~ boiler 立式锅炉
~ bollard 垂直系船柱
~ boring mill 立式镗床
~ bow 直立艏，直立型船艏
~ casting 立浇(注)，垂直铸造
~ clearance 竖向净空，垂直间隙
~ component 垂直分量
~ compression 直压，垂直压力
~ compressor 立式压缩机
~ decomposition 垂直分解
~ definition 垂直分解力，垂直清晰度
~ directivity pattern 垂直方向性模式
~ drilling machine 立式钻床
~ driving gear 立式传动齿轮
~ drop 高度差，竖直降落
~ engine 立式发动机

~ extent 垂直范围

~ fire tube boiler 立式火焰管锅炉

~ flow 垂直流

~ hydraulic broaching machine 立式液压拉床，立式液压铰孔机

~ lathe 立式车床

~ load 垂直载荷

~ machining center 立式加工中心

~ milling machine 立式铣床

~ overhead valve 直立气门，直立上置式气门

~ position 竖直位置，Y 轴位置

~ prismatic coefficient 垂直棱柱系数

~ pump 立式泵

~ shaft 立轴

~ smoke tube 垂直烟管

~ triple-tube boiler 立式三管锅炉

~ tube evaporator 立管蒸发器

~ type induction unit 立式感应单元

~ welding position 垂直焊接位置

~ windlass 立式锚机

~ zone 垂直地带

vertically ['və:tikli] *ad.* 垂直地，直立地，陡峭地

very ['veri] *a.* 真正的，真实的，恰好的，绝对的，十足的，特别的；*ad.* 很，甚，极其，非常，完全

~ high frequency (VHF) 甚高频

~ large crude carrier (VLCC) 超大型油轮

~ large scale integration (VLSI) 超大规模集成电路 ‖ *Syn.* very large scale integrated circuit 超大规模集成电路

vessel ['vesl] *n.* 容器，器皿，船，舰，飞船，导管，脉管，血管，管束 ‖ *Syn.* container 容器

~ component vender 船舶零部件供应商

~ draught 船舶吃水

~ engaged in fishing 捕鱼船

~ flooded 进水船舶

~ in distress 遇难船舶

~ listed 在册船舶

~ not under command 失控船舶

~ restricted in her ability to manoeuvre 操纵能力受限船舶

~ traffic service 船舶交通服务

vest [vest] *n.* 汗衫，背心，内衣，防护衣；*v.* (使)穿衣服，授权，授予，赋予，归属

vet [vet] *n.* 老兵；*v.* 检查，审查，修正，诊疗，当兽医

vex [veks] *v.* 使烦恼，使苦恼，使生气，继续讨论，使动荡，使汹涌

VHF (very high frequency) 甚高频

~ radio telephone 甚高频无线电话

via ['vaiə] *prep.* 经过，通过，凭借，取道

vibrate [vai'breit] *v.* (使)振动，(使)摇摆，颤动，犹豫，激动

vibrating [vai'breitiŋ] *n.* 振动，振荡；*v.* (vibrate 的 ing 形式) (使)振动，(使)摇摆，颤动，犹豫，激动

~ reed 振动簧片，振簧

~ wire force transducer 振弦式拉力计，振弦式力传感器

~ wire transducer 振动线转换器，线振式换能器

vibration [vai'breiʃən] *n.* 振动，颤动，摇动，摆动，感应，共鸣，周期现象

~ absorber 减振器，阻尼器，防震材料

~ damper 振动阻尼器，减振器

~ damping 振动阻尼

~ durability test 振动耐久性试验

~ effect 振动效应

~ frequency 振动频率

~ gauge 振动计

~ in the ship's structure 船舶结构振动

~ test 振动测试

vibrograph ['vaibrəɡra:f] *n*. 振动计 ‖ *Syn*. vibrometer 振动计

vibrometer [vai'brɔmitə] *n*. 振动计 ‖ *Syn*. vibrograph 振动计

vice [vais] (=vise) *n*. 老虎钳, 缺陷, 缺点, 恶习, 坏脾气, 堕落; *v*. 钳住, 钳制; *prep*. 代替 ‖ *Syn*. clamp 夹子, 夹钳, 夹住, 夹紧

~ grip 虎钳夹口

~ versa 反之亦然, 反过来也一样

vicinity [vi'siniti] *n*. 附近地区, 邻近, 附近, 接近, 大约程度, 大约数量

victual ['vitl] *n*. 食物, 粮食; *v*. 供应储备食物, 吃, 装贮食物

~ waste 食物残渣

victualler ['vitlə(r)] *n*. 食品供应者, 补给船

video ['vidiəu] *n*. 电视, 录像, 视频; *a*. 视频的, 录像的, 电视的

~ display screen 视频显示屏

~ telephone 电视电话, 可视电话 ‖ *Syn*. viewphone 电视电话, 可视电话; visual telephone 电视电话, 可视电话

view [vju:] *n*. 景色, 风景, 观点, 见解, 意见, 认为, 视野, 观察, 观看, 检查, 核查, 审视, 综览, 目的, 旨在, 期望, 机会; *v*. 观察, 观看, 认为, 看作

viewphone ['vju:fəun] *n*. 电视电话, 可视电话 ‖ *Syn*. video telephone 电视电话, 可视电话; visual telephone 电视电话, 可视电话

viewpoint ['vju:,pɔint] *n*. 观点, 看法

vigia [vi'dʒi:ə] *n*. 疑位浅滩, 疑存暗礁

vigilance ['vidʒiləns] *n*. 警惕, 警戒, 警惕性, 失眠症

~ device 警戒装置

~ system 警戒系统

vigilant ['vidʒilənt] *a*. 警惕的, 警觉的, 警戒的

violent ['vaiələnt] *a*. 猛烈的, 激烈的, 暴力的, 狂暴的, 极端的, 暴力引起的

violently ['vaiələntli] *ad*. 激烈地, 暴力地, 狂暴地, 极端地

virgin ['və:dʒin] *n*. 处女, 童男; *a*. 未使用的, 原始的, 处女的, 纯洁的

virtual ['və:tjuəl] *a*. 虚的, 实质的, 有效的, 事实上的

~ value 有效值 ‖ *Syn*. effective value 有效值, 实际值

virtually ['və:tjuəli] *ad*. 事实上, 实质上, 近乎

viscometer [vis'kɔmitə] *n*. 黏度计 ‖ *Syn*. viscosimeter 黏度计

viscose ['viskəus] *n*. 纤维胶

viscosimeter [,viskə'simitə] *n*. 黏度计 ‖ *Syn*. viscometer 黏度计

viscosity [vi'skɔsiti] *n*. 黏性, 黏质

~ additive 黏度添加剂

~ classification 黏度分级

~ coefficient 黏滞系数

~ improver 增黏剂

~ index 黏度指数

~ index improver 黏度指数改进剂

~ measurement 黏度测量

~ ratio 黏度比

～ regulator 黏度调节器

～ table 黏度表

viscosity-temperature 黏度温度

viscosity-temperature graph 黏度温度曲线图

viscous ['viskəs] *a.* 黏性的，黏滞的，胶黏的

～ damper 黏滞阻尼器

～ damping 黏性阻尼

～ friction 黏滞摩擦

～ impingement filter 黏滞撞击滤尘器

vise [vais] (=vice) *n.* 老虎钳，缺陷，缺点，恶习，坏脾气，堕落；*v.* 钳住，钳制；*prep.* 代替 ‖ ***Syn****.* clamp 夹子，夹钳，夹住，夹紧

visibility [ˌviziˈbiliti] *n.* 可见度，可见性，明显度，能见度，显著

visible ['vizəbl] *n.* 可见物；*a.* 看得见的，明显的，显著的

visibly ['vizib(ə)li] *ad.* 显然，明显地

vision ['viʒən] *n.* 视力，视觉，先见之明，眼力，想象力，幻想，幻影，景象；*v.* 梦见，想象，显示

visual ['viʒuəl] *n.* 画面，图像；*a.* 视觉的，视力的，凭目力的，看得见的，光学的

～ alarm 视觉警报

～ angle 视角

～ display 视觉显示

～ display unit 可视显示单元

～ field 视野，视界

～ flow indicator 目视流量指示器

～ inspection 目视检验

～ inspection for dirt accumulation 积灰的目视检验

～ navigation 目视导航

～ range 视线范围

～ telephone 电视电话，可视电话 ‖ ***Syn****.* video telephone 电视电话，可视电话；viewphone 电视电话，可视电话

VIT (variable injection timing) 可变喷射定时，变更喷油时间装置

vital ['vaitl] *a.* 生死攸关的，重大的，生命的，生机的，至关重要的，所必需的

vitalize ['vaitəlaiz] *v.* 激发，赋予生命，给予生命，使有生气

VLCC (very large crude carrier) 超大型油轮

VLSI (very large scale integration) 超大规模集成电路 ‖ ***Syn****.* very large scale integrated circuit 超大规模集成电路

VOC (volatile organic compounds) 挥发性有机化合物

～ absorption 挥发性有机化合物吸收

～ recovery plant 挥发性有机化合物回收装置

～ recovery system 挥发性有机化合物回收系统 ‖ ***Syn****.* VOC return system 挥发性有机化合物回收系统

voice [vɔis] *n.* 声音，嗓音，发音能力，意见，发言权，语态；*v.* 表达，吐露

～ recognition system 语音识别系统

～ tube 话筒

void [vɔid] *n.* 空间，真空，空旷，空虚，怅惘；*v.* 使无效，离开，撤出，排出，排泄；*a.* 空的，无人的，空闲的，无效的，无用的，没有的

～ space 空隙空间

Voith-Schneider 福伊斯-施耐德

～ propeller 福伊斯-施耐德推进器，平旋推进器，直翼推进器

volatile ['vɔlətail] *n.* 挥发物，有翅的动物；*a.* 挥发性的，可变的，不稳定的，轻快的，爆炸性的，飞行的
~ organic compounds (VOC) 挥发性有机化合物
~ organic compounds absorption 挥发性有机化合物吸收
~ organic compounds recovery plant 挥发性有机化合物回收装置
~ organic compounds recovery system 挥发性有机化合物回收系统 ‖ *Syn.* volatile organic compounds return system 挥发性有机化合物回收系统
~ petroleum 挥发性石油

volatility [,vɔlə'tiləti] *n.* 挥发性

volt [vəult] *n.* 伏特

volt-ampere 伏特安培，伏安
~ characteristic 伏安特性

volt-ampere-hour 伏特安培小时，伏安时
~ reactive 无功伏安时

voltage ['vəultidʒ] *n.* 电压，伏特数
~ across the terminals 端子间电压
~ adjuster 电压调节器
~ amplifier 电压放大器
~ build-up 电压积聚
~ by one phase 一相电压
~ by three phase 三相电压
~ change 电压变化
~ change interval 电压变化间隔
~ class 电压等级
~ comparator 电压比较器
~ control 电压控制
~ control system 电压控制系统
~ current transducer 电压电流传感器，电压电流变换器
~ decouple 电压解耦

~ dependent resistor 压敏电阻
~ deviation 电压偏差
~ dip 电压骤降，电压跌落
~ direction 电压方向
~ distribution 电压分布
~ divider 分压器
~ drop 电压降 ‖ *Syn.* potential drop (PD) 电压降
~ fluctuation 电压波动
~ fluctuation waveform 电压波动波形
~ generator 发动机电动势，旋转电动势，测速发电机，转速(表)传感器
~ grade 电压等级
~ imbalance 电压不平衡 ‖ *Syn.* voltage unbalance 电压不平衡
~ loss 电压损失
~ negative feedback 电压负反馈
~ quality 电压质量
~ rating 额定电压 ‖ *Syn.* nominal voltage 标称电压，额定电压；rated voltage 额定电压
~ reducing starter 降压启动器
~ reference 参考电压，基准电压
~ regulating transformer 调压变压器
~ regulation 电压调节
~ regulation rate 调压率
~ regulator 电压调节器，调压器，稳压器
~ relay 电压继电器
~ setting range 电压设定范围
~ source 电压源
~ source converter (VSC) 电压源换流器
~ source inverter 电压源逆变器
~ spark 电压火花
~ stability 电压稳定性
~ stability factor 电压稳定系数

~ stabilizer 稳压器

~ standard 电压标准

~ surge 电压冲击，冲击性过电压

~ swing 电压摆动

~ transformer 电压互感器，变压器 ‖ ***Syn.*** potential transformer (PT) 电压互感器，变压器，仪表变压器

~ variation 电压变化

voltage-second 伏特秒，伏秒

~ product 伏秒积

voltaic [vɔl'teiik] *a.* 伏特的，电流的

voltmeter ['vəult‚mi:tə(r)] *n.* 伏特计，电压表

~ change-over switch 电压表转换开关

volume ['vɔlju:m] *n.* 体积，容积，卷，册，音量，量，大量，书本，合订本 ‖ ***Syn.*** capability 性能，容量；capacitance (电)容量；capacity 容量，生产量；tankage (桶、槽)容量

~ expansion 体积膨胀

~ expansion coefficient 体积膨胀系数

~ ratio of combustion chamber 燃烧室容积比

volumetric [vɔlju'metrik] *a.* 测定体积的

~ efficiency 容积效率，容积系数，组装效率

volumetry [vɔ'lju:mitri] *n.* 容量分析(法)

volute [və'lju:t] *n.* 涡形，螺旋形，涡形花样，涡螺； *a.* 向上卷的，涡形的，螺旋形的

~ casing 涡线型外壳，蜗壳 ‖ ***Syn.*** volute housing 涡线型外壳，蜗壳

~ chamber 涡室，螺旋室，涡形管

~ pump 涡形管式离心泵，涡囊泵

vortex ['vɔ:teks] *n* 涡流，涡旋，中心，旋风

~ precession flowmeter 旋涡进动流量计

~ pump 涡动泵

~ shedding flowmeter 涡街流量计

voucher ['vautʃə(r)] *n.* 凭证，凭单，证人，保证人，证明者

voyage ['vɔiidʒ] *n.* 航程，航空，旅程，航海记，旅行记； *v.* 航海，航行，驶过，横越，渡过，飞过

~ data recorder (VDR) 航行数据记录仪

~ estimates 航次估算(费用)

~ repair 航修

~ report 航行报告，航次报告

voyager ['vɔiidʒə(r)] *n.* 航行者，航海者，旅客

VPP (variable pitch propeller) 可调螺距螺旋桨，可变距螺旋桨，调距螺旋桨，变距螺旋桨，调距桨，变距桨 ‖ ***Syn.*** CPP (controllable pitch propeller) 可调距螺旋桨，可变距螺旋桨，调距螺旋桨，变距螺旋桨，调距桨，变距桨

VSC (voltage source converter) 电压源换流器

vulnerability [‚vʌlnərə'biləti] *n.* 弱点，脆弱性，易伤性，致命性，攻击

~ of security 安全性漏洞，安全漏洞

vulnerable ['vʌlnərəb(ə)l] *a.* 易受攻击的，易受伤的，易受批评的

#

W-engine W 形发动机

W-plane W 平面

wain [wein] *n.* 北斗七星

waist [weist] *n.* 船腰，腰，腰部，腰身，背心

wake [weik] *n.* 醒，尾迹，痕迹； *v.* 叫醒，激发，醒来，醒着，警觉，振奋

~ current 尾流

~ equalization duct 尾流平衡管

~ factor 伴流系数

~ speed 尾流速度

~ stream 尾流

~ value 伴流值

walkie-talkie ['wɔ:ki'tɔ:ki] *n.* 手提无线电话机

wall [wɔ:l] *n.* 墙，屏障，隔阂；*v.* 分隔，用墙隔开，围以墙，堵塞；*a.* 墙壁的

~ hydrant 墙壁消火栓，墙式消火栓

~ light 壁灯

~ outlet 壁装电源插座

~ panel 墙板，护墙板

~ plug 壁式插头，墙上灯座

~ ventilator 墙壁通风机，墙壁通风器

wand [wɔnd] *n.* 棒，棍，杖

warehouse ['wɛəhaus] *n.* 仓库，货栈，大商店，批发商店；*v.* 贮入仓库

warmer ['wɔ:mə] *n.* 温热装置，使热的人

warn [wɔ:n] *v.* 警告，告诫，通知，预告

warning ['wɔ:niŋ] *n.* 警报，警告，预告，通知，预兆；*v.* (warn 的 ing 形式) 警告，告诫，通知，预告；*a.* 警告的，告诫的，引以为戒的

~ blinker 警告闪光灯

~ board 警告牌，危险标示牌 ‖ *Syn.* warning plate 警告牌

~ facility 报警设施

~ light 警示灯

~ sign 警告标志

~ signal 警报信号

warp [wɔ:p] *n.* 绞船索，牵绳，弯曲，偏差，歪曲，偏见，乖僻；*v.* 曳船，弄歪，变歪，偏离，使翘曲，使不正常，歪曲，使有偏见

warping ['wɔ:piŋ] *n.* 翘面，扭曲，变形；*v.* (warp 的 ing 形式) 曳船，弄歪，变歪，偏离，使翘曲，使不正常，歪曲，使有偏见

~ capstan 卷缆绞盘

~ drum 绞缆筒，卷缆筒，卷索筒，卷绳筒 ‖ *Syn.* gypsyhead 绞缆筒；warping end 绞缆筒，摩擦鼓轮，绞车副卷筒；warping head 绞缆筒，卷缆筒，带缆卷筒

~ winch 绞缆机，牵曳绞车

warrant ['wɔrənt] *n.* 正当理由，根据，证明，凭证，委任状，授权，批准，许可证；*v.* 保证，辩解，担保，批准，使有正当理由

warranty ['wɔrənti] *n.* 正当理由，合理根据，担保，保证，授权

warship ['wɔ:ʃip] *n.* 军舰，战舰，舰艇，舰船

~ anti-explosion 舰船抗爆结构

wash [wɔʃ] *n.* 洗，洗涤，冲洗，洗涤剂，废液，洗的衣服，冲积物，浅水带，洼地；*v.* 洗，洗涤，洗清，弄湿，流过，镀金，粉刷，冲出，冲蚀，搅动，洗澡；*a.* 耐洗的，虚假的

~ deck pipe 洗甲板水管

~ plate 防晃隔舱板，纵向隔板

~ port 排水口

~ room 卫生间，洗漱间，盥洗室 ‖ *Syn.* toilet 洗手间，盥洗室；water closet (WC) 盥洗室，厕所

washer ['wɔʃə] *n.* 垫圈，垫片，衬垫，洗衣人，洗衣机，洗碗机

washing ['wɔʃiŋ] *n.* 洗涤，洗涤物，冲走的东西；*v.* (wash 的 ing 形式) 洗，洗涤，洗清，弄湿，流过，镀金，粉刷，

冲出，冲蚀，搅动，洗澡；a. 洗涤用的，洗涤的

~ machine 洗衣机

~ water 洗涤水

washman ['wɔʃmən] n. 男洗衣工 ‖ laundryman 洗衣工

wastage ['weistidʒ] n. 消耗，损耗，废物，消耗量 ‖ **Syn**. dissipation 损耗，浪费；loss 损失，浪费，损耗；wastage 损耗；wear 穿破，磨损

waste [weist] n. 废物，浪费，损耗，消耗，垃圾，荒地；v. 浪费，消耗，被损耗，使荒芜；a. 废弃的，荒芜的，多余的

~ disposal unit 废物处理装置

~ gas 废气

~ heat 废热

~ heat boiler 废热锅炉

~ heat recovery (WHR) 废热回收，余热回收

~ heat utilization 废热利用

~ Management Plan (WMP) 废物管理计划

~ material 废物

~ water 废水

~ water treatment system 废水处理系统

watch [wɔtʃ] n. 注视，注意，手表，看守，守护，监视，值班人；v. 看，注视，照顾，监视，警戒，守护，看守，守候；a. 手表的，挂表的

~ alarm 值班报警装置

~ keeper 看守人，值更人

~ keeping 值班，值更，警戒

~ keeping cabin 值班室

~ keeping duties 值班责任

~ keeping personnel 值班人员

~ keeping requirements 值班要求

~ your step 注意脚下，小心行事

watchful ['wɔtʃful] a. 警惕的，注意的，警戒的

watchman ['wɔtʃmən] n. 守门人，巡夜者

water ['wɔ:tə] n. 水，雨水，海水，水位，水面，流体；v. 喷淋，供以水，注入水，使湿，加水；a. 水的，水上的，水生的，含水的

~ and dust proof lighting fitting 防水防尘灯具

~ and oil separator 水油分离器

~ ballast 压载水

~ ballast main 压载水总管

~ ballast space 压载水舱

~ ballast tank 压载水舱

~ boiler 开水锅炉，沸水器

~ by-pass inlet neck 旁通进水口

~ circulation 水循环

~ closet (WC) 盥洗室，厕所 ‖ **Syn**. toilet 洗手间，盥洗室；wash room 卫生间，洗漱间，盥洗室

~ cock 水龙头

~ cock body 塞体

~ consumption 水消耗量

~ container 水容器，贮水器

~ container volume 水容器容积

~ contaminant 水污染物

~ contamination 水污染

~ content 含水量

~ cooler 水冷却器

~ cooling 水冷却，水冷法

~ cooling baffle 水冷挡板

~ cooling battery 水冷蓄电池

~ drum 水桶

~ ejector 水力喷射器，水喷射器

~ ejector pump 喷水抽气泵
~ eliminator 挡水板，除水器
~ enter angle 入水角
~ film 水膜
~ filter tank 滤水罐
~ fire extinguishing system 水灭火系统
~ fire main line 消防水总管
~ flow 水流
~ fog 水雾
~ gauge 水位计
~ in oil emulsion 油包水乳状液
~ intake 进水口，水摄入(量)
~ jacket 水套
~ jet 水注，喷水式推进器，喷水口，喷水
~ jet air ejector 射水抽气器，喷水抽气器，喷水空气泵
~ jet air pump 喷水空气泵
~ jet propulsion 喷水推进
~ jet vessel 喷水推进船
~ level 水位
~ level gauge 水位计
~ level indicator 水位指示器
~ level indicator light 水位指示灯
~ level regulator 水位调节器
~ level root valve 水位根阀，水位分支阀
~ level sensor 水位指示传感器
~ line 水线
~ lubricating 水润滑
~ main inlet port 主进水口
~ outlet port 出水口
~ phase 水相
~ pipe 水管
~ plane 水线面，水上飞机
~ plane area 水线面面积
~ plane coefficient (船舶)水线面系数

~ pollution hazard 水污染危害
~ pollution index 水质污染指数
~ pressure 水压
~ pressure tank 水压箱
~ pump 水泵，抽水机
~ pump impeller 水泵叶轮
~ pump pliers 水泵钳
~ pump pulley 水泵皮带轮
~ quality 水质
~ quality monitoring 水质监测
~ regulating valve 水调节阀
~ return 回水
~ return manifold 回水歧管(引擎用以进气和排气)
~ return valve 回水阀
~ ring pump 水环泵
~ seal 水封
~ seal ring 水封圈
~ separator 水分离器
~ shortage 水短缺，缺水
~ spray 洒水，喷水，注水
~ spray system 喷水系统
~ sprinkling system 淋水系统，自动喷水灭火系统
~ supply 水供应，供水
~ supply system 供水系统
~ supply vessel 供水船
~ treatment 水处理，水净化
~ tube 水管
~ tube auxiliary boiler 水管辅助锅炉
~ tube boiler 水管锅炉
~ vapor 水蒸气
~ wall 水冷壁
water-based 水基的，水性的
~ local fire fighting system 水基局部灭火系统

water-cooled 水冷的，水散热的
  ~ compressor 水冷压缩机
  ~ condenser 水冷式冷凝器
  ~ engine 水冷式发动机
  ~ frequency convector 水冷变频器
water-lubricated 水润滑的
  ~ bearing 水润滑轴承
  ~ stern tube 水润滑艉轴管
waterborne ['wɔ:təbɔ:n] a. 水上的，水运的
waterline ['wɔ:təlain] n. (船的)吃水线，水线
waterproof ['wɔ:təpru:f] n. 雨衣，防水衣物，防水布，防水材料；v. 使不透水，做防水处理；a. 防水的，不透水的
  ~ case 防水箱
  ~ hanging bulb socket 防水吊灯座
  ~ layer 防水层
  ~ lamp 防水灯
  ~ socket 防水插座
  ~ switch 防水开关
watertight ['wɔ:tətait] a. 水密的，不漏水的，防渗的，无懈可击的
  ~ box 防渗水箱
  ~ bulkhead 水密舱壁
  ~ compartment 水密室
  ~ door 水密门
  ~ integrity 水密封完整性
  ~ motor 防水电动机
  ~ transverse bulkhead 水密横舱壁
  ~ type 水密型，防水型
waterway ['wɔ:təwei] n. 航道，水道，舷侧排水沟
watt [wɔt] n. 瓦特
wattless ['wɔtlis] a. 无功的，无功率的
  ~ load 无功负荷

wattmeter ['wɔtmi:tə] n. 瓦特计，功率表
wave [weiv] n. 波，波浪，(挥手)示意，致意；v. 波动，飘动，摇动，(挥手)示意，致意
  ~ amplitude 波度，波幅
  ~ band 波段
  ~ bending moment 波浪弯矩
  ~ frequency 波浪频率
  ~ front 波前，波阵面
  ~ height 波高
  ~ length 波长
  ~ making 兴波，造波，波浪形成
  ~ making characteristics 兴波特性
  ~ making interaction 兴波干扰
  ~ making length 兴波长度
  ~ making resistance 兴致阻力
  ~ making resistance coefficient 兴波阻力系数
  ~ pattern 波型，波动图式
  ~ period 波周期
  ~ soldering 波动焊接
  ~ slope 波浪陡度，波面斜度，波倾角，波斜度
  ~ slope capacity 波倾角容量
  ~ suppressor 消波器，防波装置，消波板
  ~ tail 波尾，电波信号的尾部
wave-induced 波浪感生的，波浪诱导的
  ~ bending moment 波浪感生弯矩
  ~ loads 波浪感生载荷，波浪诱导载荷
  ~ load spectrum 波浪载荷谱
  ~ motion 波浪诱导运动
waveform ['weivfɔ:m] n. 波形
wavelength ['weivleŋθ] n. 波长
waviness ['weivinis] n. 波状，波纹形
way [wei] n. 路，路线，路途，习惯，

行业，规模，道路，情形；a. 中途的，途中的；ad. 远远地，大大地，非常 ‖ **Syn**. approach 方法，途径，通路；means 手段，方法；method 方法，办法

~ behind 远远落在后面

~ out 出口，太平门，摆脱困境的办法，活路，生路

WB (way base) 路基

WC (water closet) 盥洗室，厕所 ‖ **Syn**. toilet 洗手间，盥洗室；wash room 卫生间，洗漱间，盥洗室

weak [wi:k] a. 不牢固的，弱的，虚弱的，软弱的，淡的，疲软的，无力的，不耐用的

~ current 弱电

~ current system 弱电系统

wear [wiə] n. 衣服，穿戴，磨损，耐用，经久；v. 穿着，佩戴，留蓄，磨损，销蚀，磨破，磨掉，用完，耗尽，克服，制服，维持，答应，允许，拖延，使船尾向顺风向，使疲惫不堪 ‖ **Syn**. dissipation 损耗，浪费；loss 损失，浪费，损耗；wastage 损耗

~ away 磨损，消逝，衰退，磨减，消磨，虚度

~ down 磨损，损耗，使疲劳，使厌烦，克服

~ extent 磨损量

~ hardness 抗磨硬度，抗磨力

~ limit 磨损极限

~ loss 磨耗减量，磨耗量

~ out 消瘦，穿破，用坏，克服，消磨，疲劳

~ plate 抗磨板，防磨板

~ prevention 防止磨损

~ rate 磨损率

~ ring 磨损环，耐磨环

~ test 磨损试验

wearable ['wɛərəbl] n. 衣服；a. 耐磨的，可穿用的，可佩戴的

wearer ['wɛərə] n. 穿用者，佩戴者

wearing ['wɛəriŋ] v. (wear 的 ing 形式) 穿着，佩戴，留蓄，磨损，销蚀，磨破，磨掉，用完，耗尽，克服，制服，维持，答应，允许，拖延，使船尾向顺风向，使疲惫不堪；a. 穿用的，使疲惫的，磨损的，令人厌倦的

~ ring 耐磨环，止漏环

weather ['weðə] n. 天气，气候，气象，处境；v. (受)侵蚀，(使)风化，经受住，经受风雨；a. 迎风的，露天的

~ deck (船的)露天甲板

weatherproof ['weðəpru:f] v. 使防风雨；a. 防风雨的，不受天气影响的，抗风化的

weathertight ['weðətait] a. 防风雨的，不透风雨的

weave [wi:v] n. 编法，织法，编织，织物；v. 编织，组合，编排，使迂回前进，摇晃

~ through 迂回通过

web [web] n. 网，织物，圈套，卷筒纸，蛛丝，蹼，翼手；v. 使陷入罗网，形成网，环球网(Web)

~ beam 宽板横梁，强横梁

~ frame 宽板肋骨，强肋骨

~ gear 薄片齿轮，无轮辐齿轮

~ member 腹杆

wedge [wedʒ] n. 楔，楔形物；v. 楔入，楔进，楔牢，挤进

~ section 楔形截面

~ section combustion chamber 楔形燃烧室

weft [weft] *n.* 信号旗，求救信号，织物

weigh [wei] *n.* 道路；*v.* 起锚，称重，重压，估量，权衡，斟酌，有影响
~ against 权衡，掂量，与之相当
~ anchor 起锚，起动

weighing ['weiiŋ] *n.* 称重，权衡，权重，悬浮；*v.* (weigh 的 ing 形式) 起锚，称重，重压，估量，权衡，斟酌，有影响
~ cell 称重传感器
~ controller (自动)重量定量器

weight [weit] *n.* 重力，重量，负担，分量，权数，砝码，秤砣，价值，重要(性)，势力，重量单位；*v.* 加重量，加重物，使负重，加重于，使变重，使倾斜
~ belt 配重带，加重带，(潜水等用的)负重腰带
~ governor 荷重调节器，飞重调节器
~ retainer 铅块止滑扣
~ saving 重量减轻，重量节省
~ variation 加权变化
~ vector 权向量

weight-to-power 重量对功率的，重量功率的
~ ratio 重量功率比

weighting ['weitiŋ] *n.* 加权，加重，称量，评价；*v.* (weight 的 ing 形式) 加重量，加重物，使负重，加重于，使变重，使倾斜；*a.* 额外的
~ coefficient 加权系数
~ factor 权重因数
~ method 加权法

weir [wiə] *n.* 坝，堰，鱼梁
~ skimmer 溢流撇油装置，堰式撇油器

weld [weld] *n.* 焊接，焊接点；*v.* 焊接，焊缝，使紧密结合，使成整体
~ assembly 焊接组件
~ bead 焊缝，熔敷焊道，焊珠
~ defect 焊接缺陷
~ flush 焊缝隆起
~ gauge 焊缝量规
~ penetration 焊缝熔深，焊透深度，焊透度，焊穿
~ reinforcement 焊缝补强
~ scantling 焊接尺寸
~ slope 焊缝倾角
~ spatter 焊接飞溅

weldability ['weldə'biliti] *n.* 焊接性 ‖ *Syn.* solderability 软焊性，可焊性

welded ['weldid] *v.* (weld 的过去式和过去分词) 焊接，焊缝，使紧密结合，使成整体；*a.* 焊接的，焊合的
~ connection 焊接连接，焊接头
~ joint 焊接缝，焊接节点
~ pipe 焊接管，焊制管
~ plate girder 焊接板梁
~ structure 焊接结构

welder ['weldə(r)] *n.* 电焊工，焊工
~ certification 焊工证书

welding ['weldiŋ] *n.* 焊接法，定位焊接；*v.* (weld 的 ing 形式) 焊接，焊缝，使紧密结合，使成整体
~ and heat treatment 焊接与热处理
~ cable 电焊电缆，焊接电缆
~ condition 焊接规范 ‖ *Syn.* welding instructions 焊接规范
~ consumable 焊接耗材(包括电焊条、焊丝、焊剂三大类)，焊接材料
~ contactor 电焊接触器
~ current 焊接电流

~ electrode 焊接电极，电焊条，焊条

~ equipment 焊接设备

~ equipment with cutting torch 割炬焊接设备

~ flux 焊剂，焊料

~ inspector 焊接检验员

~ machine 焊机

~ manipulator 焊件支架，焊接机械手

~ mark 熔接痕，焊接标记

~ mask 电焊面罩

~ operator 电焊工，焊接操作机，焊接控制器

~ outfit 焊接配备

~ powder 焊粉

~ procedure 焊接工艺，焊接程序

~ sequence 焊接顺序

~ shrinkage 焊接收缩

~ slag 焊渣

~ wire 焊条，焊丝

well [wel] *n.* 底舱水泵间，储液体容器，泉，源泉，水井；*v.* 涌上，涌出，冒出，流出，溢出；*a.* 适当的，健康的，良好的，恰当的；*ad.* 好，满意地，充分地，彻底地，有理地，适当地，夸奖地

~ casing 套筒

well-connected 精心构思的

well-known 众所周知的，清楚明白的

well-planned 详细规划的，精心计划的

well-proven 充分证明的

wet [wet] *v.* 弄湿，使潮湿；*a.* 湿的，潮湿的，有雨的，多雨的

~ bulb thermometer 湿球温度计

~ cylinder liner 湿气缸套，湿式气缸套 ‖ *Syn.* wet liner 湿衬套，湿式气缸套

~ damage 潮湿损坏

~ saturated gas 湿饱和气

~ sprinkler system 湿式喷水灭火系统

~ suit 紧身潜水衣

~ sump lubrication 湿槽润滑法

whale [weil] *n.* 鲸，鲸鱼，巨大的事物；*v.* 捕鲸，击打，猛击

whaler ['weilə(r)] *n.* 捕鲸人，捕鲸船

whaling ['(h)weiliŋ] *n.* 捕鲸，捕鲸业

~ mother ship 捕鲸母船

~ vessel 捕鲸船

wharf [(h)wɔ:f] *n.* 码头，停泊处；*v.* 靠码头，把货卸在码头上

wharfage ['(h)wɔ:fidʒ] *n.* 码头(总称)

what-if 假设分析，作假定推测

whatever [wɔt'evə] *a.* 无论怎样的，无论哪一种的，什么也；*pron.* 凡是，无论什么

whatsoever [wɔtsəu'evə(r)] *pron.* 任何，无论什么

wheel [wi:l] *n.* 舵轮，轮子，轮状物，方向盘，驾驶盘，旋转，盘旋运动；*v.* 旋转，装轮子，滚动，盘旋，转身

~ barrow 独轮手推车，手推车

~ bearing 轮轴轴承

~ dresser 砂轮修整器

~ house 驾驶室 ‖ *Syn.* bridge 驾驶室

~ house chair 驾驶椅

~ spanner 轮扳手，开阀用扳手

whereabouts ['(h)wɛərə'bauts] *n.* 行踪，下落，所在；*ad.* 在何处，靠近什么地方

whereafter [(h)wɛər'a:ftə] *ad.* 然后，随后

whereby [(h)wɛə'bai] *ad.* 藉此，由此，凭这个 ‖ *Syn.* by which 藉此，由此，凭这个

wherefore ['(h)wεəfɔ:] *n.* 原因，理由；*ad.* 为此；*conj.* 为什么，因此

wheresoever [,weəsəu'evə] *ad.* 在其上；*conj.* 何处，无论何处

whilst [wailst] *conj.* 同时，有时，当…的时候

whirl [(h)wə:l] *n.* 旋转，回旋，昏乱，轮，环，一连串的事；*v.* (使)旋转，急转，急动，急走

whistle [(h)wisl] *n.* 汽笛，汽笛声，口哨，口哨声；*v.* 鸣汽笛，吹口哨

~ and siren control system 号笛控制系统

white [(h)wait] *n.* 白色，空白，白涂料，白种人；*v.* 留出空白处，使变白色，刷白，漂白；*a.* 白色的，纯洁的，无色的，透明的，白种人的

~ cast iron 白口铸铁

~ cotton tape 白色棉纱带

~ enamel paint 白色搪瓷漆

~ Gaussian noise 高斯白噪声

~ metal 白合金

~ metal bearing 白合金轴承

~ metal lining 白合金衬层

~ noise generator 白噪声发生器

~ pollution 白色污染

~ steel turning tool 白钢车刀

whiten ['(h)waitn] *v.* 使白，变白，刷白，漂白

whiteness ['(h)waitnis] *n.* 白，洁白，苍白，清白，纯洁，白色物质

Whittaker-Shannon 维特克-香农

~ sampling theorem 维特克-香农采样定理

WHR (waste heat recovery) 废热回收，余热回收

wide [waid] *a.* 宽的，广阔的，张大的，远离目标的；*ad.* 广阔地，广大地，远离目标地

~ angle 广角，大角度

~ berth 安全距离，安全泊位

widely ['waidli] *ad.* 广泛地，普遍地，广博地，相差大地

widespread ['waidspred] *a.* 普遍的，分布广的，广泛应用，普及的 ‖ *Syn*. common 公共的，普通的；commonplace 平凡的；general 一般的，普通的；ordinary 平常的，平凡的，普通的；pervasive 普遍的；popular 大众的，通俗的，普遍的；universal 普遍的，通用的；usual 平常的，通常的，惯例的

width [widθ] *n.* 宽度，广度，广博 ‖ depth 深度；height 高度；length 长度

winch [wintʃ] *n.* 绞车，绞盘，起货机，摇柄，曲柄；*v.* 用绞车拉，用绞盘吊

~ barrel 绞盘卷筒，绞车卷筒 ‖ *Syn*. capstan barrel 绞盘卷筒，绞盘筒，绞车筒；capstan drum 绞盘卷筒，绞车卷筒；winch drum 绞盘卷筒，绞车卷筒

~ drum clutch shift fork 绞车鼓筒离合器拨叉

~ head 绞车副卷筒

~ house 绞车操作室

winchman ['wintʃmən] *n.* 绞车手，卷扬机操纵工，船舶起货机开关手

wind [waind] *n.* 风，气流，风向，趋势，潮流，气息，呼吸；*v.* 缠绕，上发条，旋紧，弯曲前进，使通风

~ box 风室，风箱

~ brace 抗风支撑

~ break 风障，防风墙

~ calculator 风速计算器

~ force 风力

~ load 风力载荷

~ power 风力

~ pressure 风压

~ shield 减阻帽，遮风屏

~ turbine 风轮机，风力涡轮机

winding ['waindiŋ] *n.* 绕缠，绕组，线圈，卷绕物，绕法，卷法，蜿蜒，迂回；*v.* (wind 的 ing 形式) 缠绕，上发条，旋紧，弯曲前进，使通风；*a.* 弯曲的，旋的，盘绕的，蜿蜒的

~ barrel 绞筒，提升绞筒

~ connection group of the transformer 变压器绕组接线组

~ loss 绕组损耗

windlass ['windləs] *n.* 起锚机，绞盘机，卷扬机，绞车，辘轳；*v.* 用绞盘吊起 ‖ *Syn*. anchor windlass 起锚机

~ and mooring equipment 锚机与泊系装置

~ brake 锚机制动器

window ['windəu] *n.* 窗口，窗，窗户

~ frame 窗框，窗口框架

~ menu 窗口菜单

~ molding 窗口压条

~ type air conditioner 窗式空调器

~ ventilator 通风窗

Windows ['windəus] *n.* 微软视窗操作系统

windsail ['windseil] *n.* 帆布制的通风筒，风车翼片

windscreen ['windskri:n] *n.* 挡风玻璃

windward ['windwəd] *n.* 上风，上风面；*a.* 向风的，迎风的，上风的；*ad.* 向风地，迎风地，上风地

wing ['wiŋ] *n.* 船帆，风向标，翅，翅膀，翼，飞翔，机翼，派别；*v.* 装以翼，飞行，飞过，使飞，空运，增速，侧击

~ nut 蝶形螺母

~ pump 叶轮泵，叶式唧筒

~ shaft 侧轴

~ ship 水翼船

~ tank 翼舱，翼柜，舷顶边舱

wipe [waip] *n.* 凸轮，擦，拭，抹布，吸水纸，一击；*v.* 擦，揩，抹，擦干，揩净，擦掉，揩去，抹掉

~ out 翻倒，封闭，消灭，垮台

wire ['waiə] *n.* 电线，电缆，电报，电信，金属丝，铁丝网；*v.* 装设电线，拍电报，打电报，用铁丝捆绑；*a.* 金属丝制的

~ breakage 断线

~ bristle brush 钢丝刷

~ brush 钢丝刷

~ brush handle 钢丝刷柄

~ brush without handle 无柄钢丝刷

~ clip 线夹，钢丝夹

~ clippers 断线钳

~ connection 线接头

~ cutter 剪钳

~ cutting pliers 剪线钳，克丝钳

~ drawing 抽丝现象，拔丝

~ gauge 线规，线材号数

~ resistor 绕线电阻

~ rope 钢丝绳，钢缆，钢索

~ rope cutter 钢丝绳切割器

~ saw 线锯

~ sling 钢丝吊索，钢丝吊绳

~ solder 焊线

~ spring 钢丝弹簧

~ stripping pliers 剥线钳

wireless ['waiəlis] *n.* 无线电，无线电话系统，用无线电报传送的信息；*v.* 用无线电发送，用无线电联系；*a.* 不无线的，无线电报的

~ communication 无线通信

~ mouse 无线鼠标 ‖ ***Syn***. cordless mouse 无线鼠标

~ operator 无线电报员

~ room 无线电报室

~ set 无线电机

wireman ['waiəmæn] *n.* 线工，电工

wiring ['waiəriŋ] *n.* 配线，接线，连线，架线，电线线路；*v.* (wire 的 ing 形式) 装设电线，拍电报，打电报，用铁丝捆绑

~ diagram 接线图

with [wið] *prep.* 随着，和，跟，关于，和…一致

~ regard to 关于

~ respect to 关于，至于

~ special attention to 特别注意

withdraw [wið'drɔ:] *v.* 收回，撤销，缩回，退出，撤退

withdrawal [wið'drɔ:əl] *n.* 收回，撤退，退回，取消，退隐

withhold [wið'həuld] *v.* 使停止，拒给，保留，抑制，忍住

without [wið'aut] *ad.* 在外，缺少，在屋外；*prep.* 没有，缺少，不，如果没有，要没有；*conj.* 除非，如果不

withstand [wið'stænd] *v.* 反抗，反对，抵抗，顶住，耐得住，禁得起，经得住

~ test 耐受试验，耐压测试

~ voltage 耐受电压，耐压

WMI (Windows Management Instrumentation) Windows 管理规范

WMP (Waste Management Plan) 废物管理计划

wood [wud] *n.* 木头，木材，树木，木制品；*v.* 提供木材，收集木材；*a.* 木制的，疯狂的

wooden ['wudn] *a.* 木制的，木头的，僵硬的，呆板的

~ T-square 木制丁字尺

woodruff ['wudrʌf] *n.* 车叶草

~ key 半圆键，半月销，月牙键

work [wə:k] *n.* 工作，劳动，操作，职业，功，机件，手工，作品；*v.* (使)工作，(使)运转，(使)渐渐移动，起作用，造成，产生，经营，锻制

~ bench 工作台，钳桌

~ breakdown 工作分解，任务分解

~ brittleness 加工脆性

~ condition 工作环境，工作条件，工作状态，工况

~ contract 劳务合同

~ earthing 工作接地 ‖ ***Syn***. work grounding 工作接地

~ function 功函数

~ group 工作组

~ load 工作负载

~ piece 工件，工作物，被加工件，半制品

~ schedule 工作程序表，工作记录，工作进度表

~ sheet for distribution 分配计算表

~ space 工作空间，工作室，字间间隔

~ specification 工作规范

~ spindle 工作主轴

~ station for computer aided design 计算机辅助设计工作站

workability [ˌwəːkə'biliti] *n.* 可加工性，可使用性

workable ['wəːkəbl] *a.* 可工作的，可处理的，可操作的，能运转的
- ~ hatch 工作舱口
- ~ plan 切实可行的计划

workboat ['wəːkbəut] *n.* 施工船，工作艇

workhorse ['wəːkhɔːs] *n.* 重负荷机器，广为应用的设备，做粗工者，驮马

working ['wəːkiŋ] *n.* 工作，工作方式，劳动; *v.* (work 的 ing 形式) (使)工作, (使)运转, (使)渐渐移动, 起作用, 造成, 产生, 经营, 锻制; *a.* 工作的, 运转的, 劳动的, 经营的, 施工用的
- ~ allowance 加工余量
- ~ condition 工作条件
- ~ current 工作电流
- ~ cycle 工作循环
- ~ draft 工作草案
- ~ freeboard 工作干舷
- ~ gauge 工作量规
- ~ grounding 工作接地
- ~ language 工作语言
- ~ liquid 工作液
- ~ load 工作负荷
- ~ medium 工作介质
- ~ or power stroke 工作或动力冲程
- ~ performance 工作性能
- ~ piston 工作活塞
- ~ plan 施工图，工作程序图
- ~ power source 工作电源
- ~ pressure 工作压力
- ~ principle 工作原理
- ~ roller 工作滚轮
- ~ ship 工作船
- ~ speed 工作速度
- ~ stroke 工作行程，工作冲程
- ~ substance 工作物，工质，作用物质
- ~ surface 工作面，加工面
- ~ voltage 工作电压
- ~ volume 工作容积，工作体积
- ~ water level 工作水位
- ~ width 工作宽度，加工宽度

workload ['wəːkləud] *n.* 工作量，作业量

workmanship ['wəːkmənʃip] *n.* 手艺，技艺，作工，技巧

workpiece ['wəːkpiːs] *n.* 工件，加工件

workshop ['wəːkʃɔp] *n.* 车间，工场，作坊，研习会，讨论会
- ~ drawing 车间图纸

workstation ['wəːksteiʃ(ə)n] *n.* 工作站

worm [wəːm] *n.* 蜗杆，螺纹，虫，蠕虫，蚯蚓，小人物; *v.* 螺旋式地卷线，螺旋式地缠(绳)，蠕行，爬行，慢慢前进，曲折行进
- ~ adjustment 蜗杆调节
- ~ and wheel steering gear 蜗杆蜗轮转向机构
- ~ and worm gear 蜗杆蜗轮装置，蜗杆蜗轮机构
- ~ bearing 蜗杆轴承
- ~ brake 蜗杆制动器，蜗杆刹车
- ~ casing 蜗杆罩
- ~ drive 蜗杆传动
- ~ eccentric adjusting sleeve 蜗杆偏心调整套
- ~ gear 蜗轮
- ~ gear drive 蜗轮传动
- ~ geared steering gear 蜗杆式舵机，双蜗杆式舵机
- ~ wheel 蜗轮
- ~ wheel shaft 蜗轮轴

worn [wɔ:n] *v.* (wear 的过去分词) 穿着，佩戴，留蓄，磨损，销蚀，磨破，磨掉，用完，耗尽，克服，制服，维持，答应，允许，拖延，使船尾向顺风向，使疲惫不堪；*a.* 穿旧的，用旧的，穿坏的，用坏的，筋疲力尽的

~ part 磨损部件

~ piston 磨损活塞

worsement ['wə:smənt] *n.* 损坏，破坏 ‖ *Syn*. damage 损坏，损毁，损失，损害；spoilage 损坏

worsen ['wə:sn] *v.* (使)更坏，(使)更糟，恶化，损害

worst [wə:st] *n.* 最坏的事情，最差的情况，最严重的事；*v.* 胜过，击败；*a.* 最坏的，最差的；*ad.* 最坏，最差

worth [wə:θ] *n.* 价值，物价，市价，财产，美德，品格；*a.* 等值的，值钱的，值得的，应得的；*prep.* 相当…价值

worthwhile ['wə:ð'(h)wail] *a.* 值得做的，值得出力的

wound [wu:nd] *n.* 伤口，创伤，负伤，伤害；*v.* ① 伤，(使)伤害，击伤 ② (wind 的过去式和过去分词) 绕，缠，旋紧，上发条

~ rotor 绕线转子

~ rotor induction motor 绕线式转子感应电动机，绕线式电动机

woven ['wəuvən] *n.* 机织织物；*v.* (weave 的过去分词) 编织，组合，编排，(使)迂回前进

~ wire 铁丝网

wrap [ræp] *n.* 外套，围巾，包裹，秘密，约束，限制；*v.* 包装，卷，缠绕，包，覆盖，裹，遮蔽，隐藏，重叠

~ in 裹起来，包入

~ in insulation 用绝缘物包裹

wrapper ['ræpə] *n.* 包装材料，包装纸，书皮

wreck [rek] *n.* 毁灭，失事船，失事飞机，遇难船的残骸，失事，海难；*v.* 破坏，毁坏，拆除，打捞，救助，使遇难，使失事，使下沉

~ diving 沉船潜水，沉船潜

~ hook 救援钩

wrecker ['rekə(r)] *n.* 使船失事的人，肇事者，失事现场清理人

wrench [rentʃ] *n.* 扳钳，扳手，猛扭，痛苦，扭伤，歪曲；*v.* 猛扭，使扭伤，曲解，抢，折磨

wrist [rist] *n.* 腕关节，腕，手腕，腕部

~ compass 手表式指南针

~ pin 活塞销，肘销

~ watch 手表

wrought [rɔ:t] *v.* (work 的过去式和过去分词) (使)工作，(使)运转，(使)渐渐移动，起作用，造成，产生，经营，锻制；*a.* 做成的，形成的，精炼的，锻造的

~ iron 熟铁，锻铁

X

X-cut X 截割

X-ray X 射线

X-weld X 形焊接

XDCR (=transducer) 传感器，换能器，变换器，换流器，变频器

XFMR 变压器，变量器，变换器

XLPE (cross-linked polyethylene) 交联聚乙烯

~ cable 交联聚乙烯电缆

Y

Y-shape Y 形，Y 型
~ cross section Y 形横截面
~ strainer Y 形滤网
~ structure Y 形结构
yacht [jɔt] *n.* 快艇，帆船，游艇
yard [jɑ:d] *n.* 院子，场地，码(等于 3 英尺或 36 英寸或 0.9144 米)，帆桁
~ issue 船厂开工任务发布书
yardarm ['jɑ:dɑ:m] *n.* 桁端，横杆端
yaw [jɔ:] *v.* 偏航，偏离航线
yawl [jɔ:l] *n.* 快艇，小帆船
yearly ['jə:li] *n.* 年刊，年鉴；*a.* 每年的，一年一度的，一年间的；*ad.* 每年，一年一度
yellow ['jeləu] *n.* 黄色，黄种人，黄色颜料，黄色物品；*v.* 变黄，发黄；*a.* 黄色的，黄皮肤，胆怯的
~ brass 黄铜，锌铜合金
~ wax 黄蜡
~ zinc chromate primer paint 黄锌铬酸盐底漆，黄锌底漆
yield [ji:ld] *n.* 生产量，生产物，产额，收益，当量；*v.* 出产，生长，生产，获利，屈服，屈从，放弃，投降
~ coefficient 屈服系数
~ compressive strength 屈服压力强度
~ stress 屈服应力，屈服点
yoke [jəuk] *n.* 横舵柄，轭，轭状物，钳，夹，套，多轨磁头，束缚，支配；*v.* 套上轭，紧密接合，连接
~ pin 轭销
~ ring 轭环，集电环，整流器
~ valve 臂抱式气瓶开关，轭阀

Z

Z-drive Z 型传动，Z 型传动装置
~ propulsion Z 型传动推进
Z-transform Z 变换
Z-type Z 形的
~ transmission Z 形传动
zero ['ziərəu] *n.* 零点，零度，(坐标)起点，瞄准仪，最低点；*v.* 调到零点；*a.* 零的，全无的，没有的，零视度的；*num.* 零
~ adjustment 零位调整，零点调整
~ balance bridge 零点平衡电桥
~ boil-off 零蒸发
~ delivery 零流量
~ drift 零位偏移，零点漂移，起点电容，最小容量
~ drift error 零点漂移误差
~ grade gas 零点气 ‖ *Syn*. air zero gas 零点气
~ graduation 零分划，零位刻度
~ input 零输入
~ input response 零输入响应
~ offset 零点漂移
~ position 零位置
~ position protection 零位保护
~ sequence 零序 ‖ positive sequence 正序；negative sequence 负序
~ sequence current 零序电流
~ sequence impedance 零序阻抗
~ state 零状态，零态
~ state response 零态响应
~ value 零值
~ value insulator 零值绝缘子
~ voltage trip 零电压跳闸

zero-pole 零点极点，零极点

~ frequency compensation 零极点频率补偿

zero-rush 零冲量

~ tappet 无间隙挺杆 ‖ *Syn*. non-clearance tappet 无间隙挺杆

zigzag ['zigzæg] *n*. Z字形，锯齿形，蜿蜒曲折；*v*. 成Z字形，作Z字形行进，曲折前进；*a*. 曲折的，锯齿形的，Z字形的；*ad*. 作Z字形地，弯弯曲曲地

~ riveting 交错铆接

~ route 之字形线路

~ test Z形(操纵)试验

zinc [ziŋk] *n*. 锌；*v*. 镀锌，涂锌

~ alloy 锌合金

~ anode 锌阳极

~ anode to be renewed 待更换锌阳极

~ bar 锌棒

~ coating 锌涂层

~ oxide 氧化锌

~ paint 锌漆

~ plate 锌板

~ plate for boiler 锅炉锌板

~ plate to be renewed 待更换电镀锌板

~ plating 镀锌

~ rich epoxy primer 富锌环氧底漆

~ rod 锌条

~ slab 锌片，锌锭

zip [zip] *n*. 一种程序压缩格式，拉链，精力，活力，尖啸声，无，零；*v*. 给予速度和力量，迅速地做，拉开，拉上，拉开拉链，尖啸而过，飞快移动

~ mode 拉链式

zonal ['zəunl] *a*. 带状的，地区的，区域的，地带的

~ combustion 分区燃烧

zone [zəun] *n*. 地带，地区，区域，范围，时区，环带，圈，晶带；*v*. 环绕，划分成带，分成地带，分成区

~ control 区域控制，分区控制

~ fire alarm control unit 区域火灾报警控制器

~ heater 区域加热器

~ location 区域定位

~ of action 作用区域，作用区，行动地带

~ of contact 接触带

~ reheating air conditioning system 区域供暖空调系统

~ transfer 区域传送，区域转移，区域转换

参 考 文 献

[1] 李品友，等. 轮机英语词汇手册[M]. 北京：人民交通出版社，2005.
[2] 程昕，胡智林，等. 船员适任证书考证必备词汇手册（轮机、电子电气专业）[M]. 大连：大连海事大学出版社，2012.
[3] 郭军武，李燕，等. 轮机英语（操作级）[M]. 大连：大连海事大学出版社，2012.
[4] 党坤，陈坚，张春阳，等. 轮机英语（管理级）[M]. 大连：大连海事大学出版社，2017.
[5] 蒋更红，丁晓梅，赵逾，等. 轮机英语[M]. 大连：大连海事大学出版社，2014.
[6] 王圣莲，王宗瑞. 轮机工程专业英语[M]. 青岛：中国海洋大学出版社，2013.
[7] 赵在理，等. 轮机工程英语[M]. 北京：机械工业出版社，2012.
[8] 党坤，王忠诚，等. 轮机英语阅读与写作[M]. 上海：上海浦江教育出版社，2013.
[9] 党坤，等. 轮机英语听力与会话[M]. 大连：大连海事大学出版社，2016.